Nineteenth-Century Literature Criticism

Guide to Gale Literary Criticism Series

When you need to review criticism of literary works, these are the Gale series to use:

If the author's death date is:	You should turn to:
After Dec. 31, 1959 (or author is still living)	**_CONTEMPORARY LITERARY CRITICISM_** for example: Jorge Luis Borges, Anthony Burgess, William Faulkner, Mary Gordon, Ernest Hemingway, Iris Murdoch
1900 through 1959	**_TWENTIETH-CENTURY LITERARY CRITICISM_** for example: Willa Cather, F. Scott Fitzgerald, Henry James, Mark Twain, Virginia Woolf
1800 through 1899	**_NINETEENTH-CENTURY LITERATURE CRITICISM_** for example: Fyodor Dostoevsky, Nathaniel Hawthorne, George Sand, William Wordsworth
1400 through 1799	**_LITERATURE CRITICISM FROM 1400 TO 1800_** **_(excluding Shakespeare)_** for example: Anne Bradstreet, Daniel Defoe, Alexander Pope, François Rabelais, Jonathan Swift, Phillis Wheatley **_SHAKESPEAREAN CRITICISM_** Shakespeare's plays and poetry
Antiquity through 1399	**_CLASSICAL AND MEDIEVAL LITERATURE CRITICISM_** for example: Dante, Homer, Plato, Sophocles, Vergil, the Beowulf Poet

Gale also publishes related criticism series:

CHILDREN'S LITERATURE REVIEW

This series covers authors of all eras who have written for the preschool through high school audience.

SHORT STORY CRITICISM

This series covers the major short fiction writers of all nationalities and periods of literary history.

POETRY CRITICISM

This series covers poets of all nationalities and periods of literary history.

DRAMA CRITICISM

This series covers dramatists of all nationalities and periods of literary history.

ISSN 0732-1864

Volume 34

Nineteenth-Century Literature Criticism

Excerpts from Criticism of the
Works of Novelists, Poets, Playwrights,
Short Story Writers, Philosophers, and Other
Creative Writers Who Died between 1800
and 1899, from the First Published Critical
Appraisals to Current Evaluations

Paula Kepos

Editor

Tina Grant
Jelena O. Krstović
Joann Prosyniuk
Lawrence J. Trudeau
Sandra L. Williamson

Associate Editors

 **Gale Research Inc.** · DETROIT · LONDON

Contents

Preface   vii

Acknowledgments   xi

Preface

Since its inception in 1981, *Nineteenth-Century Literature Criticism* has been a valuable resource for students and librarians seeking critical commentary on writers of this transitional period in world history. Designated an "Outstanding Reference Source" by the American Library Association with the publication of its first volume, *NCLC* has since been purchased by over 6,000 school, public, and university libraries. The series has covered more than 300 authors representing 22 nationalities and over 15,000 titles. No other reference source has surveyed the critical reaction to nineteenth-century authors and literature as thoroughly as *NCLC*.

Scope of the Series

NCLC is designed to serve as an introduction for students and advanced readers to the authors of the nineteenth century, and to the most significant interpretations of these authors' works. The great poets, novelists, short story writers, dramatists, and philosophers of this period are frequently studied in high school and college literature courses. By organizing and reprinting the enormous amount of commentary written on these authors, *NCLC* helps students develop valuable insight into literary history, promotes a better understanding of the texts, and sparks ideas for papers and assignments. Each entry in *NCLC* presents a comprehensive survey of an author's career or an individual work of literature and provides the user with a multiplicity of interpretations and assessments. Such variety allows students to pursue their own interests; furthermore, it fosters an awareness that literature is dynamic and responsive to many different opinions.

Every fourth volume of *NCLC* is devoted to literary topics that cannot be covered under the author approach used in the rest of the series. Such topics include literary movements, prominent themes in nineteenth-century literature, literary reaction to political and historical events, significant eras in literary history, prominent literary anniversaries, and the literatures of cultures that are often overlooked by English-speaking readers.

NCLC continues the survey of criticism of world literature begun by Gale's *Contemporary Literary Criticism (CLC)* and *Twentieth-Century Literary Criticism (TCLC)*, both of which excerpt and reprint commentary on authors of the twentieth century. For additional information about *TCLC, CLC*, and Gale's other criticism series, users should consult the Guide to Gale Literary Criticism Series preceding the title page in this volume.

Coverage

Each volume of *NCLC* is carefully compiled to present:

- criticism of authors, or literary topics, representing a variety of genres and nationalities
- both major and lesser-known writers and literary works of the period
- 7-10 authors or 4-6 topics per volume
- individual entries that survey critical response to each author's work or each topic in literary history, including early criticism to reflect initial reactions; later criticism to represent any rise or decline in reputation; and current retrospective analyses.

Organization of This Book

An author entry consists of the following elements: author heading, biographical and critical introduction, list of principal works, excerpts of criticism (each preceded by an annotation and followed by a bibliographic citation), and a bibliography of further reading.

- The **author heading** consists of the name under which the author most commonly wrote, followed by birth and death dates. If an author wrote consistently under a pseudonym, the pseudonym will be listed in the author heading and the real name given in parentheses on the first line of the biographical and critical introduction. Also located at the beginning of the introduction to the author entry are any name variations under which an author wrote, including transliterated forms for authors whose languages use nonroman alphabets.

- The **biographical and critical introduction** outlines the author's life and career, as well as the critical issues surrounding his or her work. References are provided to past volumes of *NCLC* and to other biographical and critical reference series published by Gale, including *Short Story Criticism, Poetry Criticism, Children's Literature Review, Contemporary Authors, Dictionary of Literary Biography,* and *Something about the Author.*

• Most *NCLC* entries include **portraits** of the author. Many entries also contain reproductions of materials pertinent to an author's career, including manuscript pages, title pages, dust jackets, letters, and drawings, as well as photographs of important people, places, and events in an author's life.

• The list of **principal works** is chronological by date of first book publication and identifies the genre of each work. In the case of foreign authors with both foreign-language publications and English translations, the title and date of the first English-language edition are given in brackets. Unless otherwise indicated, dramas are dated by first performance, not first publication.

• **Criticism** is arranged chronologically in each author entry to provide a perspective on changes in critical evaluation over the years. All titles of works by the author featured in the entry are printed in boldface type to enable the user to easily locate discussion of particular works. Also for purposes of easier identification, the critic's name and the publication date of the essay are given at the beginning of each piece of criticism. Unsigned criticism is preceded by the title of the journal in which it appeared. Publication information (such as publisher names and book prices) and parenthetical numerical references (such as footnotes or page and line references to specific editions of works) have been deleted at the editors' discretion to provide smoother reading of the text.

• Critical excerpts are prefaced by **annotations** providing the reader with information about both the critic and the criticism that follows. Included are the critic's reputation, individual approach to literary criticism, and particular expertise in an author's works. Also noted are the relative importance of a work of criticism, the scope of the excerpt, and the growth of critical controversy or changes in critical trends regarding an author. In some cases, these annotations cross-reference excerpts by critics who discuss each other's commentary.

• A complete **bibliographic citation** designed to facilitate location of the original essay or book follows each piece of criticism.

• An annotated list of **further reading** appearing at the end of each author entry suggests secondary sources on the author. In some cases it includes essays for which the editors could not obtain reprint rights.

Cumulative Indexes

• Each volume of *NCLC* contains a cumulative **author index** listing all authors who have appeared in the following Gale series: *Contemporary Literary Criticism, Twentieth-Century Literary Criticism, Nineteenth-Century Literature Criticism, Literature Criticism from 1400 to 1800,* and *Classical and Medieval Literature Criticism.* Topic entries devoted to a single author, such as the entry on the textual reconstruction of James Joyce's *Ulysses* in *TCLC* 26, are listed in this index. Also included are cross-references to the Gale series *Poetry Criticism, Drama Criticism, Short Story Criticism, Children's Literature Review, Authors in the News, Contemporary Authors, Contemporary Authors Autobiography Series, Dictionary of Literary Biography, Concise Dictionary of American Literary Biography, Something about the Author, Something about the Author Autobiography Series,* and *Yesterday's Authors of Books for Children.* Useful for locating authors within the various series, this index is particularly valuable for those authors who are identified by a certain period but who, because of their death dates, are placed in another, or for those authors whose careers span two periods. For example, Fyodor Dostoevsky is found in *NCLC,* yet Leo Tolstoy, another major nineteenth-century Russian novelist, is found in *TCLC* because he died after 1899.

• Each *NCLC* volume includes a cumulative **nationality index** which lists all authors who have appeared in *NCLC* volumes, arranged alphabetically under their respective nationalities, as well as Topics volume entries devoted to particular national literatures.

• Each new volume in Gale's Literary Criticism Series includes a cumulative **topic index,** which lists all literary topics treated in *NCLC, TCLC, LC 1400-1800,* and the *CLC* Yearbook.

• Each new volume of *NCLC,* with the exception of the Topics volumes, contains a **title index** listing the titles of all literary works discussed in the volume. The first volume of *NCLC* published each year contains an index listing all titles discussed in the series since its inception. Titles discussed in the Topics volume entries are not included in the *NCLC* cumulative index.

A Note to the Reader

When writing papers, students who quote directly from any volume in Gale's Literary Criticism Series may use the following general forms to footnote reprinted criticism. The first example pertains to material drawn from periodicals, the second to material reprinted from books.

[1] T. S. Eliot, "John Donne," *The Nation and the Athenaeum,* 33 (9 June 1923), 321-32; excerpted and reprinted in *Literature Criticism from 1400 to 1800,* Vol. 10, ed. James E. Person, Jr. (Detroit: Gale Research, 1989), pp. 28-9.

[2] Clara G. Stillman, *Samuel Butler: A Mid-Victorian Modern* (Viking Press, 1932); excerpted and reprinted in *Twentieth-Century Literary Criticism,* Vol. 33, ed. Paula Kepos (Detroit: Gale Research, 1989), pp. 43-5.

Suggestions Are Welcome

In response to suggestions, several features have been added to *NCLC* since the series began, including annotations to excerpted criticism, a cumulative index to authors in all Gale literary criticism series, entries devoted to criticism on a single work by a major author, more extensive illustrations, and a title index listing all literary works discussed in the series since its inception.

Readers who wish to suggest authors or topics to appear in future volumes, or who have other suggestions, are cordially invited to write the editors.

ACKNOWLEDGMENTS

The editors wish to thank the copyright holders of the excerpted criticism included in this volume, the permissions managers of many book and magazine publishing companies for assisting us in securing reprint rights, and Anthony Bogucki for assistance with copyright research. We are also grateful to the staffs of the Detroit Public Library, the Library of Congress, the University of Detroit Library, Wayne State University Purdy/Kresge Library Complex, and the University of Michigan Libraries for making their resources available to us. Following is a list of the copyright holders who have granted us permission to reprint material in this volume of *NCLC*. Every effort has been made to trace copyright, but if omissions have been made, please let us know.

COPYRIGHTED EXCERPTS IN *NCLC*, VOLUME 34, WERE REPRINTED FROM THE FOLLOWING PERIODICALS:

The American-Scandinavian, v. L, September, 1962. Copyright © 1962 by The American-Scandinavian Foundation. Reprinted by permission of *Scandinavian Review.—The British Journal of Aesthetics,* v. 26, Spring, 1986. © Oxford University Press, 1986. Reprinted by permission of the publisher.—*CLIO,* v. 17, Winter, 1988 for "Beyond Humanism: J. A. Symonds and the Replotting of the Renaissance" by Peter Allan Dale. © 1988 by Robert H. Canary and Henry Kozicki. Reprinted by permission of the author.—*Criticism,* v. 25, Spring, 1983 for "Fictions of Authority: Narrative and Viewpoint in Kierkegaard's Writing" by Christopher Norris. Copyright, 1983, Wayne State University Press. Reprinted by permission of the publisher and the author.—*English Fiction in Transition,* v. 5, 1962. Copyright © 1962, Helmut E. Gerber and Helga S. Gerber. Reprinted by permission of the publisher.—*English Studies in Africa,* v. 18, September, 1975 for "John Addington Symonds as a Liberal Historian" by Richard Titlebaum. Reprinted by permission of the publisher and the author.—*The Georgia Review,* v. XXXVI, Fall, 1982. Copyright, 1982, by the University of Georgia. Reprinted by permission of the publisher.—*The German Quarterly,* vol. XXXIX, May, 1966. Copyright © 1966 by the American Association of Teachers of German. Reprinted by permission of the publisher.—*Interpretation: A Journal of Bible & Theology,* V. XXXIX, July, 1985. Copyright 1985 Interpretation. Reprinted by permission of the publisher.—*Journal of European Studies,* v. XIII, 1983 for "The Walpurgis Night: Theme and Variations" by Henry Hatfield. Copyright © 1983 Seminar Press Limited. Reprinted by permission of the author.—*The New Hungarian Quarterly,* v. XXVI, Winter, 1985 for "János Arany and English Literature" by Desző Keresztury. © *The New Hungarian Quarterly,* 1985. Reprinted by permission of the author.—*Southerly,* v. 23, 1963 for "A Danish Poet" by Henry Handel Richardson. Copyright 1963 by the author. Reprinted by permission of the publisher and Curtis Brown (Australia) Pty Ltd., Sydney.—*The Times Literary Supplement,* n. 4009, January 25, 1980. © The Times Supplements Limited 1980. Reproduced from the *The Times Literary Supplement* by permission. n. 2018, October 5, 1940. Copyright by The Times Supplements Limited 1940, renewed 1968. Reproduced from *The Time Literary Supplement* by permission.—*The Victorian Newsletter,* n. 36, Fall, 1969 for "The Italian Renaissance and Some Late Victorians" by Alan P. Johnson. Reprinted by permission of *The Victorian Newsletter* and the author.

COPYRIGHTED EXCERPTS IN *NCLC*, VOLUME 34, WERE REPRINTED FROM THE FOLLOWING BOOKS:

Bilokur, Borys. From "Folkloric Devices in Tjutcev's Poetry," in *The Supernatural in Slavic and Baltic Literature: Essays in Honor of Victor Terras.* Edited by Amy Mandelker and Roberta Reeder. Slavica Publishers, Inc., 1988. Each contribution copyright © by its author. All rights reserved. Reprinted by permission of the publisher and the author.—Binyon, T. J. From "Lermontov, Tyutchev, and Fet," in *Nineteenth-Century Russian Literature: Studies of Ten Russian Writers.* Edited by John Fennell. University of California Press, 1973, Faber & Faber, 1973. © 1973 Faber and Faber Ltd. All rights reserved. Reprinted by permission of the University of California Press. In Canada by Faber & Faber Ltd.—Bretall, Robert. From an introduction to *A Kierkegaard Anthology.* Edited by Robert Bretall. Princeton University Press, 1946. Copyright 1946, renewed 1974 by Princeton University Press. Reprinted by permission of the publisher.—Churchill, Kenneth. From *Italy and English Literature: 1764-1930.* Barnes & Noble Books, 1980. © Kenneth Churchill 1980. All rights reserved. Reprinted by permission of the publisher.—Collins, James. From *The Existentialists: A Critical Study.* Regnery, 1952. Copyright 1952 Henry Regnery Company. Renewed 1980 by James Daniel Collins. All rights reserved. Reprinted by permission of the Literary Estate of James Collins.—Dieckmann, Liselotte. From *Goethe's Faust: A Critical Reading.* Prentice-Hall, 1972. Copyright © 1972 by Prentice-Hall, Inc. All rights reserved. Used by permission of Prentice-Hall/A Division of Simon & Schuster, Englewood Cliffs, NJ.—Diem, Hermann. From *Kierkegaard: An Introduction.* Translated by David Green. John Knox Press, 1986. © M. E. Bratcher 1966. Reprinted by permission of the publisher.—Gregg,

János Arany

1817-1882

Hungarian poet, translator, essayist, and literary critic.

Esteemed as one of Hungary's greatest narrative poets, Arany is best known for his folk epic trilogy, *Toldi* (*Toldi*), *Toldi estéje* (*Toldi's Eve*), and *Toldi szerelme,* and for his *Buda halála* (*The Death of King Buda*), which was intended to be the first installment in another three-part epic. Arany composed the *Toldi* poems in response to the nationalistic fervor of nineteenth-century Europe; believing that a Hun or Magyar epic cycle had been lost over the course of time, he sought to create a national epic similar to Finland's *Kalevala,* a concatenation of poems from that country's oral folklore. Deeply concerned with the moral and political strength of his people, Arany composed ballads and epics focusing on the fortitude and resilience of the Hungarian spirit during times of national disruption. As Watson Kirkconnell has stated, "With Arany, there comes a masterly, restrained, and objective development of national resources, the attempt of a great artist, already saturated in ancient and modern European literature, to give enduring expression to the character and traditions of his own people."

Born in Nagyszalonta, an agricultural town near the border of Hungary and Rumania, Arany was the youngest of ten children in a poor family of noble origin. He completed his early education in his home village and in 1833 was sent to the Collegium in Debrecen. When a lack of funds forced Arany to leave the college one year later, he became an assistant teacher in Kisújszállás. Returning to the Collegium in 1835, he again abandoned his studies within a year to become an actor in a traveling company. Disillusioned by life on the road, he returned to Nagyszalonta and supported himself by serving at various times as a national guardsman, a town notary, and a tutor in a wealthy family.

Arany taught himself several languages in order to read works of literature in their original form. He began reading, writing poems, and translating works into Hungarian in order to master each of the languages. He learned English by reading the works of William Shakespeare, an endeavor that instilled in him an immense respect for the poetic genius of the dramatist and resulted in his critically recognized translations of *A Midsummer Night's Dream, Hamlet,* and *King John.* He later translated the comedies of Aristophanes, for which he received the Karátsonyi prize of the Hungarian Scientific Academy. In 1845 the Kisfaludy Társaság (Kisfaludy Society), the leading Hungarian literary organization, awarded Arany first prize in a contest for his first work, the satirical epic *Az elveszett alkotmány.* However, it was not until he received the same award in 1847 for *Toldi* that he gained widespread recognition as a poet. *Toldi* and its successors were popularly and critically acclaimed, and assured Arany a place with Sándor Petőfi and Mihály Vörösmarty as the leading Hun-

garian authors of the nineteenth century. In 1851, Arany became professor of Hungarian, Greek, and Latin languages and literatures at a college in Nagykőrös, a position he held for nine years until he was elected director of the Kisfaludy Társaság. As head of this influential association, Arany encouraged many promising Hungarian authors by publishing their works. Acceptance of the directorship required that Arany move to Pest, which joined with the adjacent town of Buda in 1872 to form Budapest. While there he edited *Szépirodalmi Figyelő,* Hungary's first journal of literary criticism. Elected to the Hungarian Scientific Academy in 1858, Arany later became its secretary-general. Poor health forced him to resign the post in 1877, and he died in 1882 in Budapest.

While Arany's critical works and translations are considered important by literary scholars, his reputation rests primarily on his work as a poet. Critics admire Arany's creative employment of the ballad, a form of narrative poem that frequently treats such themes as courage, love, and historical events of national interest. Arany composed numerous poems of this type throughout his life, recognizing their special potential to promote national unity during the politically tumultuous period surrounding the

Hungarian War of Independence. As literary historian Béla Németh has asserted, the poems were received enthusiastically by the public: "the nation celebrated in them its greatness and its moral superiority to its oppressors. . . . The readers were firmly reassured about the national character, the national feeling, the national will; all that mattered was to end foreign oppression."

Arany's acknowledged masterpiece is his trilogy, *Toldi, Toldi estéje,* and *Toldi szerelme,* a series of poems concerning the quasi-historical figure Miklós Toldi. *Toldi* relates the adventures of the hero as a young man; *Toldi estéje* concerns his death; and *Toldi szerelme,* the last of the three to be composed, recounts an unsuccessful love affair earlier in his life. Each portion of the *Toldi* trilogy reveals what Arany considered the passionate and proud temper of the Hungarian people, especially when confronted with situations of national or personal honor. Based upon a sixteenth-century chronicle by Péter Ilosvai Selymes, *Toldi* introduces the hero as a youth of exceptional physical strength who undergoes a series of adventures that eventually bring him to the royal court at Pest. He overpowers a previously undefeated foreign knight in a tournament, thereby winning the trophy and restoring his country's honor. Toldi is then knighted by King Louis. *Toldi estéje* tells of Toldi's later life, when, living in a ramshackle house, forgotten by the public, and out of favor with King Louis, he is once more called to defend the honor of his country in a tournament. Afterward, victorious but weakened, Toldi is visited by the king, whom he counsels on the importance of promoting Hungarian strength and unity. After this speech, the elderly knight dies. *Toldi szerelme* is the story of Miklós in the prime of his life. In this poem, Toldi disguises himself as one of his friends and competes in a tournament in order to win the hand of the beautiful Piroska Rozgonyi in marriage. When Piroska marries the friend, Toldi belatedly realizes his own love for Piroska and ultimately kills her husband.

Arany's skillful evocation of the nuances of the Hungarian language earned him widespread praise from literary critics. The *Toldi* poems are also extolled for their complex and detailed character development, reflecting Arany's awareness of the human spirit and the Hungarian national consciousness. Joseph Reményi, a leading Arany scholar, has stated that Toldi " . . . seems a composite portrayal of the strength and weakness of the Hungarian psyche. He is honest and belligerent, dependable and impetuous, loyal and proud, yet inclined to follow his sanguine instincts rather than his judgment founded on facts. . . . [Arany] perceived in Toldi universal human virtues and imperfections, the nobility and tyranny of ambition, but also traits which stem from his Hungarian destiny."

Arany intended to follow *Toldi* with another epic trilogy, this one based on Hun and Magyar mythology. *Buda halála,* the first poem in the series, was the only section to be completed. In this tragic poem, King Buda, the leader of the Huns, divides his kingdom with his younger brother, Attila. Quickly becoming much more powerful than his older brother, Attila is overcome by greed and murders Buda in order to have the throne all to himself. The usurper is ultimately killed as a result of his treason, attesting

to Arany's belief that people must live according to common sense and mental discipline or disaster will result. A tightly constructed tragic lyric, *Buda halála* won the Nádasdy prize of the Hungarian Academy in 1864. The poem was not highly regarded by the public, which did not understand the message Arany wished to convey. Feeling betrayed by and alienated from his people, Arany did not attempt to complete the trilogy. The work was critically well received, however, and scholars such as Frederick Riedl continue to regard Arany as one of "the most striking incarnations of the Hungarian spirit."

PRINCIPAL WORKS

Az elveszett alkotmany   (poetry)   1845
Toldi   (poetry)   1847
   [*Toldi,* 1914]
Murány ostroma   (poetry)   1848
Katalin   (poetry)   1850
Nagyidai czigányok   (poetry)   1852
"Agnes asszony"   (poetry)   1853
"V. László"   (poetry)   1853
Toldi estéje   (poetry)   1854
   [*Toldi's Eve,* 1914]
Kisebb költeményei. 2 vols.   (poetry)   1856
"A walesi bárdok"   (poetry)   1857
   ["The Bards of Wales," 1955]
"Széchenyi emlékezete"   (poetry)   1860
Buda halála   (poetry)   1864
   [**The Death of King Buda,* 1936]
A Szent-Iván éji álom [translator]   (drama)   1864
Hamlet, dán királyfi [translator]   (drama)   1867
János király [translator]   (drama)   1867
Összes költeményei. 6 vols.   (poetry)   1867
Prózai dolgozatai   (essays)   1879
Toldi szerelme   (poetry)   1879
Aristophanes vigjátékai. 3 vols. [translator]   (drama)   1880
Összes költeményei. Prózai dolgozatai. Shakespere forditásai. 6 vols.   (poetry, prose, and drama)   1882-85
Összes munkái. 8 vols.   (poetry and criticism)   1883-85
†*Hátrahagyott iratai és levelezése.* 4 vols.   1888-89   (poetry, prose, and letters)   1888-89
Arany János-Petőfi Sándor levelezése   (letters)   1894
Toldi; Toldi's Eve; Ballads; Selected Lyrics   (poetry)   1914
Összes művei. 15 vols.   (poetry, criticism, prose, and drama)   1951-75
Epics of the Hungarian Plain   (poetry)   1976
Költői művei. 3 vols.   (poetry)   1981

*The sixth canto of this work was published as *The Legend of the Wondrous Hunt* in 1881.

†This work contains the poetry collection *Őszikék.*

Emil Reich   (essay date 1898)

[*Reich was a Hungarian-born English educator and*

man of letters. In the following excerpt, he discusses the influence of the peasant and noble classes upon Arany's poetry, claiming that "theirs is a spirit charming in its rural breeziness and compact humour; fascinating in its naïveté and coyness; but somewhat out of tune with the modern or bourgeois sentiment."]

Outside Hungary, the name of John Arany is seldom heard; and western readers will be astonished to hear that Arany is considered by many of the best known Magyar critics the greatest of the Hungarian poets. Petőfi has never quite pleased the professors of æsthetics and poetry in the various universities and "*academies*" of Hungary; and there being no Magyar Saint Beuves or August Schlegels, to guide, with tact sustained by learning, and learning eased by tact, the tastes and literary opinions of the professorial minds in Hungary, it is not rare to hear and read of Arany as the greatest poetic genius of the Magyars. We hasten to add, that we readily bow to the greatness and charm, and still more to the merits of Arany. He is a great poet indeed. Nearly every one of his numerous ballads, epics and smaller poems is replete with the glamour of true poetry. In point of language he is, no doubt, the most idiomatic and richest of all Hungarian writers. Yet, with all these gifts and excellencies, he is not equal to Petőfi. Reaching, as he did, an age nearly three times as protracted as that of Petőfi, he could yet not, through any stretch of time or effort, attain to powers which have been bestowed upon very few poets. Petőfi ranks with the world's greatest poets; Arany ranks only with the great poets of Hungary. To the strictly Magyar Jingo, as well as to the Magyar professor, Arany may appear greater even than Petőfi; we hope to show that his genius is of a nature at once different from and smaller than that of the incomparable Alexander.

The reader will, we trust, permit us to premise a short remark which, especially for English readers, seems indispensable for a right appreciation of Arany. In England there has long ceased to be a peasantry proper; at any rate, there has for now over 400 years been no such peasantry in England, as may still be seen on the continent generally, and in Hungary in particular. The type "peasant" is at once the arch-type of narrow-mindedness, sordidness, *naïveté*, and spontaneous poetry. He is conservative in the extreme and slow, yet frequently the source of great upheavals and revolutions. His speech is concrete and "*terre-à-terre*," yet at the same time full of quaint metaphors and conceits. His thoughts are all on the line of synthesis; and analysis is as strange to him as generalization. He loves Nature; but he is too much at one with it, part of it, to feel poetically the gulf between Nature and Man. Honour and respect for himself and his ancient customs are as the life-atmosphere of his existence; and thus in the social architecture of the continental state to him is allotted the staying force of the pillars, beams and rafters of the building. This, the general picture of the continental peasant, has to be touched up here and there when meant to represent the Hungarian peasant proper. For, luckily for Hungarian poets, the Magyar peasant, while fully as conservative and old-fashioned as his Austrian or German brother, is considerably less sordid, more frank, and altogether more "gentlemanly." Yet he is a peasant, a part both of Hunga-

ry's civic and natural complexion. Now it is this Hungarian peasant, and his social complement, the rural nobleman, who are the centre of Arany's poetry. We say "complement," for it is at present well understood by all close students of continental nobility, that the latter is, in essence and sociological drift, if not in appearance, one and the same phenomenon as the peasantry. Both classes form the conservative or static forces of continental states, and both are necessary conditions for the existence of a *bourgeois* proper. Without them, or without one of them, the medium or *bourgeois* element is altogether wanting, or, as in England, of a complexion totally at variance with the continental middle class. Now in Hungary, and more especially still, in the Hungary of Arany's youth and first manhood (1840-1870), there was no numerous *bourgeois* proper; and Arany, singing in tones and images flowing from and meant for the two other classes only, is for that very reason *toto coelo* different from most of the German and French and also from English poets. Modern western literature, in Austria and Germany exclusively; in France almost, and in England largely so, is *bourgeois* poetry; poetry written by and for the middle and central classes of the community; or at any rate expressive of sentiments and mental states growing in the atmosphere of *bourgeois* life. The poems of Arany, on the other hand, were growing in the fields and farms of the peasant, and in the manors of the landed nobility; even more in the former than in the latter. Theirs is a spirit charming in its rural breeziness and compact humour; fascinating in its *naïveté* and coyness; but somewhat out of tune with the modern or *bourgeois* sentiment. The more the middle or *bourgeois* class develops in Hungary, the less the fame of Arany will continue unimpaired. His works will be unable to satisfy the poetic needs of a class which he did not know, and with which he had but scant sympathy. His very *naïveté*, his greatest poetic charm, will be found wanting. *Naïveté*, like all other tempers of the heart or mind, has its geography, its *locus*. It does not grow anywhere or everywhere. It requires a peculiar borderland situated where two social classes meet. In that borderland it grows willingly. Such lands are of course to be found only where classes do meet socially. In England, for instance, classes carefully avoid meeting intimately in a social manner; although they do so frequently in a manner political, commercial and religious. Hence, *naïveté* is scarcely to be found, either in English life or in English poetry. By a parity of reasoning, American poetry, based on a life with practically no classes whatever, can boast still fewer of the blossoms of naïve types or naïve style. Arany's world, it is true, is one where the two classes, the nobleman and the peasant, do meet intimately, and thus the flowers of *naïveté* are plentiful. It is a *naïveté* shy of display and timid; a *naïveté* in deeds more than in words; and finally, a *naïveté* of men rather than of women. It has, when enjoyed in Arany's own exquisite Magyar, a favour so pure and hearty, so thoroughly true and poetic as to endear everything it touches. Yet it is the *naïveté* of the peasant, not of the *bourgeois*. It is poor in types, and restricted in emotions. It does not respond to the psychical atmosphere of the ever growing *bourgeois* class in Hungary, and accordingly the numerous readers of that class look for their reading somewhere else. The peasant and the rural nobleman are both captivating types for poets; they do not, however, represent more than a minor aspect of that broad humanity which has so far found its noblest expression in tales, dramas and poems grafted on events or sentiments of individuals outside the clans and septs of peasants and noblemen. The Germans, who have the excellent term of *"bürgerliches Drama"* (*bourgeois* drama), have felt that profound change coming over western literature very keenly; and the greatness of their literature is owing to that circumstance in no small degree. As in Hungary, nearly all great writers were, first magnates, and then noblemen (even Petőfi was a nobleman, although he set no value on that fact), so in Germany all the great writers have been without an exception, *"Bürger"* (*bourgeois*) proper. Now it is the peculiar greatness of Petőfi that many of his poems appeal to the sentiments and mental attitudes of that specifically modern public, the *bourgeois* readers, with a force and sympathy as strong as is the charm of many others to the "common people" or peasants of Hungary. It is said of Pico de Mirandola that while he excited the awe and admiration of the most learned and thoughtful men at the end of the fifteenth century Rome and Florence, the maidens and young men of the beautiful city on the Arno were singing with delight his exquisite lovesongs. Such is Petőfi; such is not Arany. He cannot properly be enjoyed except in his own Magyar, and by readers intimately acquainted with the two classes he belongs to. Not even when he selects, as he sometimes does, foreign subjects, as in his **"The Bards of Wales,"** does he become less "clannish." Of the strongest of all feelings of young humanity, of Love, he has none but epic expression; he never wrote a love-song proper. The women in his epics are mere phantasms, angels or fiends; and his men are peasants or heroes, or both. The point on which he excels every other Hungarian poet, and on which will repose his lasting fame, is his language. It has the raciness of the peasant's talk with the moderation of refined style. In other countries writers introduced new elements of poetic speech by means of using words or phrases taken or imitated from one of the dialects of their province or county. Even in Shakespeare there are traces of the then Warwickshire dialect, and probably still more of Warwickshire folk-lore. German writers have legitimated innumerable provincialisms. Hungarian, on the other hand, has no dialects, or none to speak of. The writer who wants to find new linguistic affluents can turn only to the stock used by the peasants in the vast plain of Hungary. Arany, replete as he was with all the wealth of the language used by the peasants, knew how to ennoble and purify the language of the farmers and shepherds of the *puszta,* and to impart to it much of that Greek simplicity and beauty of which, as a scholar, he was so competent a student. As the French language is not rich in words but in idioms, so Hungarian is not rich in words but in word-formations. Especially the verb admits of a variety of forms and terminations enveloping every shade of thought or movement with the glibness of water. It is in such linguistic feats that Arany shows his genius; and since language in Hungary has an importance tenfold more significant than in countries composed of less polyglot peoples, it is quite natural that in the literary appreciation of Arany at the hands of Magyar critics the political element has played a very considerable part. This is, as we stated above, his great merit. Language in all modern countries has at first been the make of the peasant classes. In them there is that mysterious and instinctive power which has produced the splendid series of Romance and Teutonic languages which, by literary craft, have come to be formed into the diction of Dante, Cervantes, Molière, Shakespeare, and Goethe. Arany, in focussing this power with the strength of a mind at once *logopoeic* and richly stored with knowledge, did an inestimable service to the cause of Magyar Literature and Magyar Nationality. In that respect he occupies in Hungarian Literature a place undoubtedly higher than that of any other Magyar writer. In matter, he could not fully unite the strictly Magyar with the broader European element; in poetic language, on the other hand, he did achieve that union; and it is in that achievement of his that we must look for his specific genius and merit.

Unlike as was Arany's personality to that of Petőfi: the former modest and retiring, the latter self-assertive and dashing; their careers too were equally different from each other. Arany's life (1817—Oct. 22nd, 1882), was one of quiet work first as a teacher, and later on (1860), as president of the Kisfaludy Society, and since 1864, as Secretary of the Academy of Science. The latter part of his life was distressed by persistent ill-health. In character Arany belonged to the select few, who have never stooped to any baseness whatever and never lost sight of the ideals of their youth. He was the intimate friend of Petőfi, who at once recognized his greatness, and the tolerant patron of the younger generation of writers. The nation mourned his death as a national calamity.

Arany is, almost exclusively, a poet of epic songs, epics proper and ballads. Of the former his most finished works are the Toldi Trilogy, consisting of **Toldi** (the name of the hero, published in 1847); **Toldi szerelme** (**The love of Toldi,** published in 1879); and **Toldi estéje** (**The eve of Toldi,** published previously in 1854). These three epics, written in rhymed six-feet stanzas of eight lines each, tell the life-story of an historic Magyar peasant-hero of the fourteenth century, in the times of King Louis, justly called the "Great." He is of herculean strength, of violent temper, but goodhearted, simple, a loving son, and a loyal friend and subject. His struggle against his wicked brother; his love for Piroska, whom, in a passage at arms, he foolishly wins for another wooer; his despair at seeing the idol of his heart the wife of another; finally, his declining years when he finds himself out of accord with the changed times, and retires home to be put into the grave he had dug for himself. Such is, in the main, the contents of the three epics, into which the wizard language of Arany has infused the charms of real poetry. It would be idle to compare Arany's art with that of Goethe's *"Hermann und Dorothea."* Goethe's hero too is rather a peasant farmer than a *bourgeois.* Yet all the other figures of Goethe's masterpiece are endowed with life so intensely *bourgeois,* as to secure admiration for the work in all times to come. Arany's hero; his dear old mother; his brother; his love, etc., scarcely leave the boundaries of peasant-world; and while his epic will thus for ever charm the youth of Hungary, it may in future cease to be an object of lasting admiration on the part of the more mature classes of the nation.

The same great qualities of linguistic *verve* and intense poetic sentiment are to be found in the other epical poems of Arany. In the ***Death of Buda*** (*Buda halála,* 1864), he sings the legendary story of Attila's murder of his own brother Buda (Bleda). In this exquisite epic Attila (or Etele, as Arany calls him), is pictured as a hero of the magnificent type, and nothing could be more removed from the poet's "Etele," than the conventional or historic Attila. Tragical energy and incomparable language render this poem one of intense charm. It was intended for one of three great epics narrating the cycle of Hun legends; of the other two we have only fragments. The romantic story of Wesselényi and Mary Szécsi was made into a charming epic by Arany, under the title *The capture of Murány* (*Murány ostroma,* 1849). In *The Gypsies of Nagy Ida* (*A nagyidai czigányok,* 1852), Arany gave vent, in form of a satirical burlesque, to his profound sorrow over his country's decadence, after the suppression of the liberal movement in 1848-1849. His ballads are generally considered to represent the best specimens of Magyar ballad-writing. It must certainly be conceded that few ballad-writers, whether in or outside Hungary, have so completely hit the true ballad-tone, or internal ring of thought and word adapted to subjects so utterly out of keeping with our modern sentiment. It may be doubted whether Chopin himself in his ballad in F major has so felicitously intuned the lay of olden romance as has Arany in his mostly sombre ballads, such as "Duel at midnight" ("Éjféli párbaj"), "Knight Pázmán" ("Pázmán lovag"), "Marfeast" ("Ünneprontók"). As in the best English or German ballads, events are, as a rule, only indicated, not described, and hurry on to their fatal termination with terrible speed. All is action and fierce movement.

In addition to his activity as a creative poet, Arany also did much for the introduction of foreign and classical literature into Hungary by way of translations. His most successful work in that line were the translations of several dramas of Shakespeare (*Hamlet, Midsummer Night's Dream, King John*), and more especially still his most exquisite (—*pace* all the German philologists!—) translation of the comedies of Aristophanes. (pp. 194-206)

> *Emil Reich, "Arany, Hungary's Greatest Epic Poet," in his* Hungarian Literature: An Historical & Critical Survey, *Jarrold & Sons, 1898, pp. 194-206.*

Frederick Riedl (essay date 1906)

[*In the excerpt below, Riedl summarizes the plots of the* Toldi *trilogy and several of Arany's ballads. He also discusses their themes and the stylistic influences on the works.*]

Arany's work had its roots in the Hungarian popular poetry, and reflects the life and thoughts of the people. His writings, and those of Petőfi, may, in fact, be regarded as a glorification of the popular ballads and tales. Petőfi took the character of his songs and his lyric style, while Arany owed to them his rich language and epic style. Petőfi possessed a thoroughly lyrical nature; he was always swayed by his feelings and could look on nothing in a calm, dispas-

sionate manner. Arany, on the other hand, concealed his feelings and appeared tranquil even when deeply moved. He observed the world accurately on the whole, but he saw all things in a somewhat gloomy light. The chief features of his poetry are its realism and its pondering over the past. It is remarkable that so much objectivity and sobriety should be blended with such strong and deep feeling.

To gain a glimpse of his inmost soul we should turn to his poem called "Epilogue", written towards the end of his life while looking back over his past career. He had struggled for perfection in poetry and had often felt defeated. "The secret blight," he said, "which mars my efforts is my eternal doubt, and the results I have achieved burn me like the blood of Nessos."

Arany wrote two great epics. The hero of one is a man of the Middle Ages, the mighty Nicholas Toldi. The other deals with the Hun kings, Attila and Buda. Each poem consists of three parts, but only the Toldi trilogy was completed.

The first part of *Toldi* is only concerned with a few days in the hero's life. The subject was taken from an old sixteenth-century rhymed chronicle, but Arany greatly improved it, giving the events their psychological basis, and linking the fragmentary incidents of the chronicle by an inner thread of motive. In the old narrative of Ilosvay the hero is a peasant lad of immense strength. Arany's hero is the younger son of a country family of some standing, a noble-minded youth, but brought up to work almost like a peasant on the family estate. Through his trials and sufferings, he is ennobled and made a true knight. There are two brothers, George and Nicholas Toldi. The elder, George, who lives at the Court of Louis the Great, keeps his younger brother on the estate in order that he shall always remain a farmer; otherwise he does not treat him harshly. George comes with his retinue to visit his mother, and in a masterly scene the two brothers are brought face to face, and passionate words pass. George scoffs at his brother until the youth maddened by insults, seizes the mill-stone on which he has been sitting in a remote corner of the courtyard and flings it among his brother's servants, unfortunately killing one of them.

Nicholas then leaves the house, feeling that he must atone for this action by noble deeds. After several days' wandering he arrives at Pest, where, at a tournament, he defeats a Bohemian knight who has been victor in many combats during the previous days. Louis the Great knights him for winning back the country's trophy, while the elder brother is punished for certain misdeeds.

The struggles of a noble nature, the pardonable fault, and the final triumph of the youth, are symbolical of the poet's own life, for he had to endure many a hardship before success was attained.

Toldi was the first epic, in which subject, language and characters were all popular. It made a great stir in the literary world and was awarded the Kisfaludy Society's prize. Every one admired the simplicity of the means by which Arany produced his remarkable poetical effects. There was none of the elaborate grandeur of the old classical epics; there was no artificial rhetoric and no invocation of the Muse.

The language of *Toldi* far excels the flat and lustreless diction of most contemporary scholars and poets. It was as though Arany had discovered an idiom previously unknown. He was profoundly versed in his mother tongue. When we read his writings we seem to hear the rippling of the hidden sources of the Hungarian language. His native tongue, like every other language, was full of old and hackneyed figurative expressions, to which he gave new life and colour.

The second part of *Toldi,* which came third in order of publication, appearing only towards the end of the poet's life, shows us Nicholas Toldi as a man in the prime of life. We read of his chivalric adventures, of his one great love, and of his inward conflicts, more strenuous even than his feats of arms.

His love for Piroska is the chief subject of this part of the poem. The hand of the fair Piroska is offered as the prize at a tournament, and Toldi, out of thoughtless good nature, consents to aid a companion in arms by fighting in his place, with visor down, and carrying his friend's shield and colours. In this manner, contrary to all the rules of chivalry, he wins Piroska for Lorincz Tar. From this deed springs the great tragedy of Toldi's life, for too late he learns to love the lady and to repent the deceit which made her the wife of another. Toldi's misery, the death of Tar and of Piroska follow in dramatic succession.

Arany wove into his poem the campaign of King Louis the Great against Naples (1347-1350), a classical example of the campaigns of the Middle Ages, full of incident and romance. Joan, the beautiful but immoral queen of Naples, had had her young husband, Prince Andrew, the brother of Louis the Great, murdered. Louis marched into Italy to avenge his brother's death, and occupied Naples, and Nicholas Toldi, in order to forget his own love-sorrow, accompanied the King.

The third part of the trilogy is *Toldi's Eve,* or old age. Nicholas Toldi lives in retirement in his decaying house and weedy garden. His king, Louis, who is an Angevin, feels resentment against him because he despises the polish and specious splendour of his Court. Toldi is out of favour and forgotten, and his only companion is his faithful old squire and servant, Bencze. In the opening scene old Bencze is helping his master to dig his own grave. Suddenly, a visitor arrives at the house, a thing which rarely happens now. It is a herald, who has come to tell the old hero that an insolent Italian knight has defeated all the Hungarian champions at the tournaments, has taken possession of the country's shield, and scoffs at Hungarian valour, boasting that he will carry the trophy home. That is enough for Toldi. The old lion becomes young again, as if by enchantment, and is eager for the fray. He sets out, disguised in the habit of a monk. The lists are surrounded by a vast concourse of people, all of them in terrible suspense since no new champion appears against the Italian. But all at once the heralds give a signal as a gigantic old monk arrives on horseback. He is a curious apparition, and his squire still more so. The squire's horse is as old and

as gaunt as his rider's weapons are rusty, and his garments are old-fashioned and shabby. When the people see his rusty weapons they mock him and ask him if he sells them as old iron. The boys tease the old horse, which soon comes to a standstill, and on turning round the poor squire finds that they are holding on to its tail. When the old monk hears the laughter, he turns round and shakes his huge lance at the crowd, whirling it above his head as though it were a lath, so that mockery gives place to awe.

Some whisper that this apparition can be nothing but the ghost of Toldi. The unknown monk conquers the Italian in a masterly fought combat, and then suddenly disappears with his squire by some by-way, and makes for an old house of his in the town. His skill in fighting had made it evident to all the knights and to the crowd, that the monk was no other than Toldi. They stream to his house to bring him in triumph to the king, who is willing to be reconciled with the old hero. But the excitement proves fatal to the old man, who is one of those who "die of their own temperament."

In the king's ante-room some pages sing an ironical song about some old adventure of Toldi. Excited and indignant, the hero whirls round his mace and kills one of the singers. The king is grievously offended, and when Toldi leaves the Court, sends soldiers after him to take him prisoner. The messengers, however, find that he is dying, and the king, much shaken by the news, hastens to Toldi's house.

The aged monarch and aged hero are face to face. Toldi knows that to the ambitious but luxury-loving king his advice was often "a bitter medicine given in a rough wooden spoon," but even now he counsels him to love the nation but not to weaken it by too much planing and polishing. He dies reminding the king of his sacred trust, the future of a people; and soon the plain and strong iron coffin of the hero rests in the grave dug with his own hands. Toldi feels that he is out of place in a world filled with new thoughts and sentiments, and so the last, venerable oak of a vanished forest falls.

Toldi's Eve is a "humorous" epic in the best sense of the word. It possesses the kind of humour which is akin to pathos and tears. Over the whole poem there broods something of the smiling melancholy of autumn, of slow universal decay, in the strength of the hero as in the season, and although we cannot help smiling at the old squire, and even at Toldi himself sometimes, yet we honour and love them.

An important feature of Arany's work is his creation of typically Hungarian characters. If the true Hungarian type were ever lost, it could be revived with the aid of Arany's poems. He touched the very depths of the Hungarian character in creating Nicholas Toldi. Just as the sculptor of the Laocoon selected a powerfully built figure in order to exhibit pain in all its intensity, Arany chose a man of gigantic strength as a means of depicting the convulsions of passion. Every impulse awoke a more powerful response in Toldi than in other men. Toldi is eminently fiery and impulsive and his great physical strength adds to the force of those characteristics. Yet withal he has the most delicate sense of honour and the kindest heart. When roused to fury, he grasps a millstone and hurls it at his tormentors. When living for a time in a monastery, he threatens the prior and his fellow monks because they mock him.

His gaiety, like his wrath, is unrestrained. Even when he is an old man the same features may be still discerned, although they are toned down by age. The old hero who, at the Court of Louis, chastises the pages, reminds us of the young Toldi who punished his brother's squires. A man who is easily roused and is moreover of a full-blooded habit, is very likely to suffer from over-excitement, and to die of a fit of passion. The knight Toldi who seeks to forget his bitter grief in revelry, recalls the young lad whom we saw drinking in the inn on the eve of his first combat. How natural it is that Toldi could not appreciate the Italian culture of the Court, and the dawning of the Renaissance. He, who had been brought up as a farmer, was not likely as a soldier to educate himself and take to ultra-refined Italian habits, especially as in his early years he had fought against the Italians, so that to his naïve soldier's mind it seemed impossible to make friends with a former foe. The polished surroundings of the king tamed the lion from time to time, but the last stab goaded him to wildness again. However, like the lion, he can be noble as well as formidable. He is one of those in whom proneness to anger is linked with great sensitiveness. How tender and faithful he is to his king, to his mother, to the lady he loves, and to his old servant. In the soil of his nature everything grows to great proportions, like one of our plants in a tropical region. What is a small rose-bush with us becomes there a huge tree.

Toldi is a perfect knight. His strong Christian feeling, his loyalty to his king, his respect for women, his kindness towards the oppressed and the defenceless, in short, all that made up the duty of a knight in the Middle Ages, had not been learnt from masters of chivalry, but was native in him. Wherever there is trouble, an instinct prompts him to help. When he sees a widow, weeping at her murdered husband's tomb, he promises to avenge her. When a wild bull tears along the street, Toldi steps forth calmly to meet him as though merely performing an ordinary duty. He pursues a knight who has carried off a lady to the innermost recesses of his castle. On meeting a carriage which has fallen into a ditch, he puts his shoulder under the wheel and lifts it up.

He is always ready to risk his life for his king, even after they have quarrelled. Altogether he is one of those who do everything with their whole soul. Toldi the soldier belongs body and soul to his duty. Toldi the lover is penetrated to the centre of his being by the bittersweet feeling of his love.

Every man possesses the qualities which belong to him as the member of a particular nation, as an individual and as a unit of humanity in general. In Toldi, not only the national and the individual interest us, we are attracted by the universal human element in him. We are not merely touched by his loyalty, and love and filial affection; his career may be regarded as a symbol of human life in general. Paul Gyulai referring to Toldi, asked,

Which of use has not experienced in youth that same restless desire to achieve something, driving him from the family circle out into the wide world? Who does not remember a mother who watched him with an anxious heart, and felt an uplifting sense of triumph at his first success? Who has not, on the threshold of manhood, been guilty of some indiscretion which has caused suffering to others, all unintended it may be, so that a hidden wound pains him even when he is otherwise happy? And when we are old, and our hopes have become remembrances, and the burning flame of desire has died out in ashes; when death has torn our loved ones from our side and we begin to feel out of place in a world which either has forgotten us or mocks us in the pride of its new ideas, do we not all resemble in some respects the aged Toldi?

But what perhaps attracts us most in this noble-minded giant is his highly sensitive conscience. Every fault finds its merciless judge in his own soul. In the first part of the epic the young Toldi unintentionally commits a crime, and then goes straight to the king at Buda, to receive either punishment or pardon. He cannot rest while there is a stain upon his character. In the second part, when Toldi breaks the rules of chivalry by fighting under another's colours and winning the hand of a lady for his friend, and when too late his own passion awakes and gives him infinite pain, it is still the pangs of an uneasy conscience from which he suffers most. Alike in his ballads and in his *Toldi* conscience is king and judge.

Piroska, the most charming of Arany's characters, and drawn with most love on the poet's part, is thoroughly Hungarian. A German poet, in depicting the heroine of so sad a love story, would have made her sentimental, but Arany paints her as a woman of deep feeling, strong and never sentimental.

Arany's work is characterised by its realism. The poet never lost sight of reality even in the highest soarings of his imagination. Whatever he described is so exactly depicted even in its details that we almost fancy he actually saw what he described. Here is one instance among many. Toldi listens sorrowfully to the news brought by his faithful servant. Another poet might have merely said that Toldi's eyes were full of tears, but Arany tells us that "A warm, heavy tear trembled in his eye, and as he, ashamed of his weakness, tried to wipe it away unnoticed with the palm of his hand, it trickled down his little finger."

Another characteristic is his way of presenting a mental phenomenon by means of its effects upon the body. He describes the impotent wrath of George Toldi, for example, as follows:

> All the blood rushed to his head, so that he could only see indistinctly, although it was broad daylight. The statues seemed to dance around him as he nearly fell in his giddiness. Then a cold wave seemed to run down his body. How cold he was; and yet how the beads of perspiration stood out upon his forehead. Then slowly his face became ashy pale, as if there were not so much blood left in him as would furnish one sip for a gnat.

That description offers a concise physiology of anger.

The Hun kings form the subject of another trilogy. ***Buda's Death*** is the title of the first part. In this, Arany combined the fragments from various old chronicles into one great whole and described the combat between the two brothers, Attila and Buda. What the Arthurian legends were for Tennyson, an inexhaustible fount of inspiration, the Hun and Magyar chronicles were for Arany.

According to those chronicles, the Huns were the ancestors of the Hungarians, so that when the Hungarians entered Europe in the tenth century and occupied their country, they were really taking possession of their Hun inheritance, and Arany accepted this theory of the relationship between Huns and Hungarians. After Attila's death, say the chroniclers, his two sons Csaba and Aladár struggled for the crown, the Goths siding with Aladár and the Huns with Csaba.

In the Hungarian traditions the historical Bléda, who appears in the *Nibelungen-Lied,* under the name of Bloedelin, is called Buda. This King divided his kingdom into two parts and gave one to his younger brother Attila. The folly of this policy soon became apparent, for the energetic, chivalrous and able Attila rapidly acquired power and fame, while Buda became the mere shadow of a king.

These differences were accentuated by their respective queens, for Ildikó, the wife of Attila, offended Buda's wife, Gyöngyvér. Their quarrel poisoned the relations between the two brothers, until the sword was invoked to settle the matter. Attila attacked the town which the king had built and which had been named Buda after him, and slew his brother, thus gaining the throne for himself.

The second part of the trilogy is called ***Ildikó,*** and the third, of which there are but a few fragments, is ***Prince Csaba.*** The background of this epic is one of the greatest events in history.

The crisis in the war between the Huns and the Germanic races was the battle of Châlons. Had the result of that battle been different, it might have altered the course of European history. Eastern races instead of western would probably have been the masters of Europe.

The whole plan of Arany's epic, had he completed it, would have been as follows: Attila kills his brother, but he himself is soon murdered by his wife, the German Ildikó (Krimhield). In the battle between his two sons, Csaba conquers Aladár, but later on he is compelled to leave Europe and return to the original home of the Huns in Asia.

The Huns leave behind them the Székely race, however, as a kind of guard over the country. At the end of the poem Arany intended to cast a glance into the future, when the Hungarians should return and enter into possession of the legacy of the Huns, the present kingdom of Hungary.

Arany created a great variety of poetic atmospheres in his epic poems. In the first part of *Toldi* we are wrapt in the golden sunshine of the broad, wheat-growing Lowlands. Everything is boldly drawn and clearly outlined. The second, *Toldi's Love,* is full of the mystic silver moonlight of romance, and the subjective feelings of the poet are revealed. The third, *Toldi's Eve,* is bathed in the melancholy light of an autumn sunset.

The whole tone is different in ***Buda's Death.*** The poem has a kind of antique *patina* over it; its style is concise, and archaic, as though written by a contemporary of Attila, and yet by one who possessed the culture of the nineteenth century. Arany's epics do not differ in style only, but also in the drawing of the characters. Arany made an innovation in the epic by his introduction of minute psychological analysis. He not only gives us the deeds of his heroes and their motives, but he points out clearly what feelings and what passions have led them to act as they do. He shows what these feelings are, how they shape themselves, and what elements are mingled in the soul of the hero.

Arany's poetry reached its highest perfection, perhaps, in his ballads. A famous critic called Arany the Shakespeare of the ballad. Here, too, the poet's work was based upon the popular poetry and tales, and he took as his models both the Scottish and the Transylvanian ballads. The dialogue form prevails in the popular ballad, it is not the poet who tells the story, but the characters themselves, and thus the poem is invested with a dramatic interest. A dim, mystic light pervades everything, and the action is strongly tragic. In each of Arany's ballads some great crime is portrayed, with an equally great punishment resulting from the working of the offender's own mind or conscience.

This led Arany to the frequent description of madness. His ballads show many examples of insanity, all accurately drawn in their physiological and psychological aspects.

Arany's ballads answer to the definition of a ballad as a tragedy told in song. (pp. 227-39)

The origin of some of the ballads may be explained by the circumstances of his life. After the war for freedom, the grief of the patriot was added to his natural melancholy. While that state of mind prevailed he had not perseverance enough to write a long poem, yet he was full of inspiration, and being thus urged in the direction of epic poetry, he composed his short epics, the ballads.

Arany's ballads are amongst the masterpieces of Hungarian poetry. Their subjects were all taken from Hungarian history, with one exception, **"The Bards of Wales";** and curiously enough, although the subject is English, it had a distinctly Hungarian significance. It was inspired by an incident characteristic of the time of absolutism (1849-1860), called after the hated Austrian minister, *The Bach era.* Despotism made a bid for popularity and desired laurels which only a poet can bind into a wreath. Its instruments wished for an ode in praise of the absolute monarch. They secretly approached the chief Hungarian poets, promising them large sums of money, as well as favour, but all declined the task. They went to Arany, who was a professor in a country town, but he rejected their offer with scorn. This attitude of the Hungarian poets is idealised in **"The Bards of Wales."** The subject of the poem is briefly as follows:

King Edward visits Wales after it has been subjugated by

means of terrible bloodshed. Here the owner of Montgomery Castle entertained him in princely fashion, but no bard is found willing to extol the tyrant in the banqueting-hall. Moved to wrath the King gives orders that every bard who refused a song in his praise shall be executed. Five hundred bards lose their lives. But the King, on arriving home, is tormented by visions, and is unable to sleep. The death songs of the martyr bards resound in his ears until he is at last driven to madness.

The most dramatic of Arany's ballads is his **"Call to the Ordeal."**

"The Captive Stork," though not a ballad, is also an allegory belonging to the same period. (pp. 240-42)

Arany and Petőfi stood side by side in life, and together they stand in the history of Hungarian poetry as the most striking incarnations of the Hungarian spirit. The world of Hungarian sentiment and character is revealed in their works, but purified in the sacred fire of poetry. The sun of the nation's literature, which dawned so brightly in 1825, when Vörösmarty's *Zalán's Flight* appeared, attained its zenith in them. (p. 243)

> Frederick Riedl, "John Arany," in his A History of Hungarian Literature, *1906. Reprint by Gale Research Company, 1968, pp. 217-47.*

Alexander Hevesi (essay date 1930)

[*In the excerpt below, Hevesi surveys Arany's major epic poems, asserting that the poet was "a perfect master of epics and ballads," whose impact on Hungarian literature is unparalleled.*]

John Arany was the most cultured poet of the Golden Age of Hungarian literature, the best scholar of the Hungarian language and the greatest translator from various foreign languages. He was a perfect master of epics and ballads; besides this, he was a lyric poet who never wrote a love song, though in his epics he proved himself a master in showing how love can destroy the human soul. His life period from 1817 to 1882 was that of those reserved, absorbed and highly intellectual poets and writers who, like Flaubert, Leconte de Lisle, C. F. Meyer and, one may also mention, Richard Wagner, became prominent after the first epoch of the Romantic revival with its great rebels and great trumpeters. These poets were the heirs of an antiquity extremely rich in colour and form, of a picturesque and ecstatic Middle Ages of wonderful impetus, of a bright Renaissance, and of a present life, well organised, smooth and varied, with which to feed and fertilise their retrospective scholarly nostalgia. For them John Arany is a genuine spiritual brother, and he was born to a great inheritance, able to reap the ripe fruit of a wonderful civilisation. But as in Hungary this civilisation had not developed in the same degree as in other countries, there devolved on Arany the heavy task of creating unaided that valuable material from which he was to build up his own work. While his Western contemporaries could take with both hands all that they required from that common memory of bygone times, Arany was, so to speak, compelled to invent even his own material. And thus the Hungarian poet,

who was born to be the custodian of a great past, had to become the re-creator and re-inventor of an ancient tradition which was in his day half dead and half forgotten. It is not that in Hungary there was not the same exciting and varied succession of Western spiritual currents but, through unfavourable political circumstances, they had never received full development. Hungary, too, had her tender and heroic legends of the Middle Ages and her bright Renaissance, writing, for instance, in striking Latin, a baroque poetry; but it was just those efforts which were most sincere and true to the past that never became a real living tradition. The vivid colours faded away and could not easily be traced in the crude elaborations of the old minstrels and the poor rhymes of early poetasters.

When John Arany appeared as a literary figure in the early forties of the 19th century, he could only find two important and significant realities which were to be accepted and adopted as a foundation for an epic poet who kept close to life itself, and these were the Hungarian soil and the Hungarian peasant. Everything else, past tradition, culture, due expression in language, had to be visualised and completed from the scanty remains of an ancient life which had become faint in the memory.

For this task Arany was predestined by his origin. He was the child of simple peasants, though the whitewashed walls of their humble cottage had preserved the seal of an ancient patent of nobility. The two chief features of the national consciousness, that is, the bright and blood-stained recollection of bygone centuries and the vast reservoir of the mother soil from the remote past which had faded away, and on the other hand the infinite possibilities of a wonderful development are both to be found in the genius of the taciturn and earnest peasant boy. John Arany gazed long at the Magyar plain called the Puszta, at the Fata Morgana or mirage, in Hungarian called Delibab, which means the "puppets of mid-day," mirrored on sultry summer afternoons in a mid-heaven phantasy of dream cities. He gazed at the lakes and forests, herds of cattle and flocks of sheep on the pastures till the whole history of Hungary was a vision completely outlined before him.

His first great work is about a hero of the Middle Ages, the valiant Nicholas Toldy, taken from an old 16th century rhymed chronicle of little or no literary value. Out of this story Arany created a masterpiece equal to Mistral's great Provençal poem *Mireio,* couched in similar powerful and idiomatic language. This epic made him famous throughout the whole country overnight. The hero is the younger son of a family of poor gentry, a lad of herculean proportions, who, from his remote world of futile dreams and meaningless trials of his strength, emerges at the brilliant Court of King Louis the Angevin, who in Hungary is justly known as Louis the Great. And here, after many sufferings and trials, young Toldy is valued as a true knight, and thus finds his due place in the noble hierarchy of that bright Hungary of the end of the Middle Ages, representing in his forceful personality both the past and the future of his country. He is the very literary synthesis of the Romantic revival, when Hungarian poets were absorbed in melancholy brooding on bygone times, and of the great democratic outburst which was the principal interest and achievement of the seventies.

John Arany, who especially at first, like his great friend Alexander Petőfi, was regarded as a poet of peasant or popular life, was really no more a folk poet than Petőfi. Soon after he had published his *Toldy,* he translated *King John,* and his version can, without exaggeration, be called a marvel among translations. I have never come across any translation from Shakespeare, either in German, French or Italian, that has so perfectly rendered the melody of the original.

Nor can Arany be regarded as a folk poet in the third part of *Toldy,* which he wrote soon after the first. This work, which is called *Toldy's Evening* or *Old Age,* is not only a great piece of literature but a very peculiar manifestation of a remarkable poetical genius. In the first part of the work, the rural Hercules made his way from his humble village to the Court. In the third he has grown old and is humiliated and disillusioned, but the aged stalwart has still to undergo sufferings and trials. He is living in a tumbledown house waiting for death when he is recalled to Court. There he appears as a gigantic old monk on horseback and in a great combat vanquishes the foreign knight who had defeated all the champions of Hungary and boasted that he would carry home the prize of the tourney. This simple hero of the Middle Ages is a stranger at the brilliant Court. He does not understand the new generation and they do not understand him. In spite of his heroic achievements his day is really over, and he goes home to be laid in the grave which he had dug for himself.

Thus at the age of 30 or so, Arany wrote an epic poem of old age, unforgettable in its portrayal of the stage of decay in life and nature, and nothing is more curious than a comparison of the initial stanzas of the two parts. The first is a vivid picture of the summer heat:

> The burning sun had scorched the barren
> ground,
> On which a flight of famished locusts found
> Their pasturage; no grass in all the lea,
> No spot of green in all the field we see.
> Within a hay-stack's shadow ten or more
> Field labourers are sound asleep and snore,
> Although but empty or half laden were
> The wagons which to load had been their care.

The second is the autumn of life and nature:

> All nature's face assumed a greyer hue,
> The dry leaves fell, to hoar-frost turned the dew;
> Shorter each day the journey of the sun,
> And longer sleeps he when his course is done.
> On the horizon's furthest rim he rests;
> "Come with me," to the old folks he suggests.
> In answer many an old man shakes his head.
> Yet one by one they go at last to bed.

Arany kept on working with a wise and steady optimism for literature till the war of independence ended in the suppression of liberty. This date was the turning point in his life. The national disaster seemed to reshape and remodel this noble spirit; his character, which had been calm and harmonious, was touched with the venom of doubt, of idle brooding and mistrust. With bleeding heart he wrote an epic poem of scathing satire in which he pilloried the leaders of the Hungarian Revolution with his eyes fixed on the unhappy nation which had been cast down from the summit of its rapid and brilliant development into the depths of glorious, but hopeless, ruin.

Yet, in that oppressive, gloomy and ghostly atmosphere of the fifties, when Hungary was ruled and ground down by Austrian officials, when the prisons were too narrow to make room for the many thousands whose only crime was their patriotism—in the years of this dreadful terror, both physical and mental—John Arany created a poetry of a new kind to give, in a veiled form, expression to the inmost feelings of his people; or, to be more exact, he renewed and remodelled a kind of poetry which had long been forgotten, namely, the Scottish ballad which, with its abrupt mysterious and suggestive style, was admirably adapted to render all the feelings hidden in the hearts of the conquered and oppressed. Arany put some symbolic events of Hungarian history into ballads, and thus he voiced the despair and hope of the country. In only one of these ballads he takes his subject from English history. It is entitled **"The Bards of Wales,"** but the English story is only an opportunity to present Hungarian conditions in disguise. The Austrian Minister, hated in Hungary, tried secretly to approach the foremost Hungarian poets and writers to induce them by money and favours to sing in praise of the absolute Monarch. They all refused, at their head Arany, who was at that time working as a classical schoolmaster in a country town. It was this that gave rise to the ballad, in which conquered Wales stands for Hungary.

In Montgomery Castle the feast is spread for King Edward, but not a single bard is to be found who will sing the praise of his country's tyrant. Five hundred bards die the martyr's death, but not one, to save his life, will say "Long live King Edward." But when, after the slaughter, the King wishes to sleep, the bards whom he has killed fill his ears with "curses dread to hear" and, rising above the noise of the fife and drums, above

> all the trumpets' blare,
> Five hundred voices sing aloud the martyr's glo-
> rious air.

The dawn of a new era is approaching. The nation is reconciled with its King. The Compromise of 1867 (the Ausgleich) is concluded with Austria. Arany's ambition to work awakes again. He completes *Toldy* and publishes the second part of it, *Toldy's Love,* a fine epic poem with a certain distinct resemblance to Ariosto. By this love epic Arany takes rank with the greatest word painters in world literature. With his vigorous imagination, he presents marvellous pictures of the early Renaissance.

After this he starts his great trilogy of the Huns, the first part of which he calls *Buda's Death.* The object of this work and its achievement may almost be called superhuman. He wished to fill the gap in the prehistoric conscience of the nation by creating for it the mythology which it lacked. And he created it on tragic lines, as Hebbel did in his great trilogy of the Nibelungs.

Meanwhile years passed and Arany, who, as we have seen, already felt himself an old man at thirty, when he at last really reached old age suddenly became a lyric poet, and indeed an altogether unique and wonderful phenomenon in the history of literature. In his earlier years he had suppressed the lyric streams which would naturally have burst from him and did not allow them to overflow, except in the flaming and high-coloured stanzas in the second part of his *Toldy.* During his last years, this scholar and poet, the most cultured of Hungarian writers, the author of translations of Shakespeare and Aristophanes which are like genuine creations and influenced literature in the highest degree—this delicate and reserved man of a rare nobility and integrity, after living many years in the capital, suddenly found again in himself the genuine peasant that was slumbering in his breast and haunting his spirit; he suddenly felt homesick for the fields and meadows where he had once lived and dreamed, and wrote a series of old-age lyrics, among which are masterpieces of feeling and form.

Arany, like Mistral, is unknown in Europe save to a limited circle of scholars, but there never was a poet so well versed in European culture and tradition and certainly never one who has done so much for Hungarian literature. He, as much as any of our poets, is restricted to his native language, and there is no imaginable translation which could give an adequate idea of the perfection of his style. He is the master and teacher of generations still unborn. (pp. 94-8)

> *Alexander Hevesi, "Two Great Hungarian Poets," in* The Slavonic Review, *Vol. IX, No. 25, June, 1930, pp. 94-106.*

Watson Kirkconnell (essay date 1936)

[*Kirkconnell was a Canadian educator who wrote widely on European literature. In the following excerpt, he examines the inspiration for and influences on the* Death of King Buda, *concluding that Arany's poetry reflects the character and traditions of the Hungarian people.*]

Arany is possibly the ripest scholar and greatest artist among all of the Magyar poets, and the stamp of his scholarship and art is manifest on all of his published work: the epic-trilogy dealing with Toldi, the Hun-cycle trilogy (of which *The Death of King Buda* is the first part), his numerous ballads and lyrics, and his translations of Shakespeare's *Hamlet, King John,* and *Midsummer Night's Dream.*

His so-called "Hun-cycle" epic trilogy was planned with great care. The first part, *The Death of King Buda,* was to deal with the fratricidal rivalry between Attila and his ill-fated elder brother Buda. The second, *Ildikó,* dealing with the great campaigns by which Attila became known to Europe as "the Scourge of God," was to culminate in a lurid prophecy that because of Buda's death the whole Hunnish empire would pass away. The third epic, *Prince Csaba,* was to include Ildikó-Kriemhild's revenge on the Nibelungs, her murder of Attila, the subsequent wars in which her son Aladár was defeated by his brother Csaba, and the departure of Csaba from Europe, together with a prophecy that his descendant Arpád, leader of the Magyars, would return four centuries later to enter into the

European inheritance of Attila. *The Death of King Buda,* a 2752-verse poem of genuine power, was published in 1864 and was forthwith awarded the Nádasdy prize of the Academy. The two remaining parts of the trilogy exist only as posthumous fragments.

The primary source from which these epics are drawn is the medieval chronicle-legends of the Magyar people. What the Arthurian cycle of legends was to Tennyson, these Hungarian chronicles were to Arany. Accepting their general tradition that the Huns of the fifth century A.D. were the ancestors of the invading Magyars of the ninth century, he sought to quarry out from the chronicles such materials as might erect a great epic of Hungarian destiny. The elements of historicity in the chronicles are almost as hard to verify as those in Arthurian romance. For over a century, Hungarian linguists, explorers, and men of letters have made this a matter of the most highly specialized research and controversy; and on such Enchanted Ground a non-Magyar will scarcely dare to tread. *Hypotheses non fingam.*

In form and treatment, *The Death of King Buda* is in the Vergilian tradition. On *a priori* grounds, one might have expected something analogous to that integration of Finnish folk-legends by which Elias Lönnrot organized the *Kalevala* into a quasi-epic. Arany's poem, on the contrary, is modelled in many respects after the *Aeneid.* Not only is it duly written in twelve parts, but the sixth canto, like the sixth book of the *Aeneid,* divides the two main phases of the action by a romantic interlude of dreamlike quality. Moreover, Arany's chief type of poetic ornament is the epic simile, often developed at great length as in the similes of the gathering noon-day storm, of the herd of horses in the squall, and of the foraging ants, all in Canto XI. The list of grim portents in that same canto is reminiscent in detail of the close of Vergil's First *Georgic.* Supernatural machinery in the classical tradition is also introduced, but the Turanian war-god Hadur is used instead of any deity of the Graeco-Roman Pantheon. The supernatural Sword which he bestows on King Attila will at once remind the English reader of the sword Excalibur, so mysteriously presented to King Arthur in Malory and in Tennyson. In still other respects, the poem challenges comparison with the Icelandic Eddas and *Volsungasaga* and the *Nibelungenlied* of medieval Germany; but the work of the Magyar poet remains distinctively his own.

Foremost among the characteristics of the Magyar trilogy is Arany's deliberate attempt to secure realism in setting and character. There are here none of those myths of Teutonic deities which dominate the Old Norse versions and their romantic opera derivative in Wagner's *Der Ring des Nibelungen;* neither is there much hint, in terminology and conception, of those anachronisms of chivalry that are so prominent in the final recension of the *Nibelungenlied.* In the opening canto of *The Death of King Buda,* the Huns are dwelling in tents on the plains of Hungary. Their manner of life is pagan and barbaric. When King Buda and his younger brother Attila make a solemn compact together, it is sealed by a primitive blood-oath and by the typically Hunnish sacrifice of a white horse for augury. The subsequent debauch of the household is primitive and realistic.

Again, in Canto III, when Attila wishes to send a letter to his wife, he carves his message in runes on a piece of rosewood; and in Canto VIII the beaters in the hunt use wooden tomtoms and the *tárogató* or Hungarian horn. The arrival of Ildikó at the camp of Buda in Canto V and the description of Attila's palace-tent in Canto X are both definitely Asiatic in colour rather than European. When the hunt on Mount Mátra is followed by a mighty feast, a Hunnish minstrel, singing to his lute, tells a legend of how twin-brothers, the ancestors of the Huns and the Magyars, first wandered from Asia into Europe in pursuit of a "wonder-hind." Incidentally, one may suspect that many a Magyar reader finds the epic's supreme interest in this romantic legend, with its tradition of Hun-Magyar origins and its thrilling episode of the rape of one hundred and two beautiful girls by Hunor and Magyar and their five-score knights. These girls, like the Sabine maidens of Roman legend, soon grow reconciled to their audacious husbands and become the proud mothers of the Hunnish and Magyar clans.

The epic's supernatural apparatus, as already mentioned, is Asiatic rather than European. In Canto VIII, Hadur, the supreme God, who is about to send Attila a dream of destiny and a sacred Sword as a pledge, is described almost as if he were a sort of glorified Hunnish chieftain; while in the midst of the hunt, when Buda is attacked by a furious buffalo bull, Attila, in a moment of "second sight," sees the bull transformed into Ahriman, the Devil of Zoroastrianism. Such are some of the devices by which Arany sought to make his poetry consistently national, giving it throughout a tone that Magyars might feel to be in harmony with their own traditions. His very style, which in other poems is suffused with the whole range of romantic atmosphere, takes on in his Hun-cycle work a concise archaism of quality that is as obvious and as successful as is Thackeray's assumed Addisonian style in *Henry Esmond.*

A further outstanding characteristic of Arany's work is its interest in psychology. In Icelandic saga and German folk-epic, action is everything. Arany betrays a modern interest in the inner springs of action. The plot of **The Death of King Buda** has already been indicated. King Buda, the weak elder brother, decides to share his throne with the younger and more martial Attila. The latter is affectionate and loyal towards Buda, and many forces must be brought into play before the final catastrophe of fratricide becomes possible. The characters of the two brothers are deeply involved. Buda is pusillanimous and lacking in decision; Attila is an energetic and chivalrous man of action. Buda's very ineffectuality makes him moody and fearful as to his brother's loyalty; Attila's warm heart, under provocation, is capable of terrific anger. Buda shows himself timid in army manoeuvres and incompetent in hunting; Attila is so formidable as a warrior and so popular with the army that he has trained that it is to him and not to Buda that envoys come from the Byzantine emperor, asking for friendship and assistance.

Other characters enter into the tragic motivation, especially Dietrich of Bern, Gyöngyvér the wife of Buda, and Ildikó (Hildiko, Hilda, or Kriemhild) the wife of Attila.

Dietrich, unlike the noble and temperate warrior of the *Thidrekssaga* and the *Nibelungenlied,* appears as a palsied, grey-haired old man, cunning as a fox, who gratifies a deep-hidden Teutonic hostility against the Huns by sowing suspicion of each brother in the other's breast. Buda believes Dietrich unreservedly, for the latter's insinuations have an affinity with the poisonous doubts of his own brooding mind. On the other hand, when Dietrich seeks to caution Attila against Buda, Attila rejects his suggestions with righteous anger, but his confidence is nevertheless shaken. More potent still as a disruptive force is the bitter enmity between the two wives, strongly reminiscent of the quarrel between Brunhild and Kriemhild in the *Nibelungenlied.* Gyöngyvér, who is the elder of the two, is the aggressor, made furious by the sight of Attila's growing glory while her husband fades into insignificance. Her hatred is intensified by the fact that she is barren while her younger rival is the happy mother of a handsome boy. The quarrel breaks into open flame when Gyöngyvér's pet falcon is slain by Ildikó's bird in the course of the hunt. Ildikó meets the fury of the older woman with all the arrogance of youthful beauty and the contempt of a primitive mother for her barren rival. The breach between the two is fierce and irreparable, and it is all that Buda and Attila can do to restrain their wives from open violence. In Canto X, it is the termagant upbraidings of Gyöngyvér that stir Buda up to fatal defiance of Attila and to the ultimatum that results in his doom. Gyöngyvér is a tragic figure, linked to the failing fortunes of a *roi fainéant* and hastening on their common destruction by passions that she is unable to control. Our sympathies tend, however, to be with young Ildikó (Kriemhild) who in spite of her earlier grief over the death of Siegfried and her implacable desire for revenge on his murderers has yet found real happiness with her husband Attila.

Still another marked characteristic of Arany is his preoccupation with moral responsibility. The central theme of the whole Hun-trilogy is the fatal fault of Attila in slaying his brother. Hadur, the almighty Lord of Hosts, had presented him with the Sword in accordance with a decree that he should be "master of the Earth, if master of himself." Instead of this, he sullies the holy weapon with the incontinent crime of fratricide. It is true that the provocation is great, but the crime remains. It is noteworthy that the pressure of circumstances, as so often in Shakespearean drama, is brought to bear on the one serious flaw in an otherwise noble character. Attila, a hero of truly epic stature, is unable to bear injustice with a temperate spirit. His anger, like that "baleful wrath of Achilles, the son of Peleus" that in Homer "hurled forth many stout souls of heroes to Hades," is disastrous in its consequences and unchains a tempest of discord that destroys his empire. This haunting sense of the grave consequences of human acts, found alike in Arany's ballads and in his epics, is a close link with some of the greatest masters of literature. Arany has been called "the Shakespeare of the ballad," but the same dramatic concentration of motive and feeling is to be found in his epic verse.

Such are some of the qualities of style and treatment that give distinction to Arany's work. He himself had a theory that in the tenth century (just before missionary Christianity stamped out all pagan poetry among them) a great folk-epic was taking form among the Magyars; and incomplete as his own Hun-trilogy remains, its powerful first part goes a long way towards giving them in its place a great literary epic that is truly national. Before his time, the chief Hungarian poets, influenced by the general currents of European literature, had been derivatively Neo-Classical like Bessenyei and Virág and derivatively Romantic like Kölcsey and Vörösmarty. With Arany, there comes a masterly, restrained, and objective development of national resources, the attempt of a great artist, already saturated in ancient and modern European literature, to give enduring expression to the character and traditions of his own people. As an epic poet, he may not stand with Homer, Vergil or Milton; but among epic poets of the second rank—Statius, Claudian, Boiardo, or Tasso—he must be recognized as occupying a place of honourable achievement. This intrinsic poetic worth, coupled with the peculiarly Magyar orientation of his work, makes unusually important the interpretation of his poetry to nations other than his own. (pp. ix-xvi)

> *Watson Kirkconnell, in a preface to* The Death of King Buda: A Hungarian Epic Poem *by János Arany, translated by Watson Kirkconnell and Lulu Putnik Payerle, Benjamin Franklin Bibliophile Society, 1936, pp. ix-xviii.*

Joseph Reményi   (essay date 1952)

[*Widely regarded as the literary spokesman for America's Hungarian community during the first half of the twentieth century, Reményi produced numerous translations and critical essays that have been instrumental in introducing modern Hungarian literature to American readers. In the following excerpt from an essay originally published in 1952, he praises Arany as a quintessentially Hungarian poet who revitalized his country's literature through the use of its "mythological and chivalric past."*]

Arany was as much at home in antique cultures, in Hungarian mythology, or in the chivalric age of the Hungarian past as in nineteenth-century Hungarian atmosphere. He could give familiar and unfamiliar facts or fancy a magic air, and while he rarely adorned his writings with classical allusions, unless the theme required them, he seemed to weave Hungarian destiny into a harmonious whole with universal destiny. In reading his lyric and epic poems, his ballads, essays, and critical comments or his Aristophanes, Shakespeare, Goethe, and Gogol translations, it is at once apparent that he possessed disciplined imagination, erudition, and the mastery of words. Without injecting into his work a pronounced didactic purpose, as creator and critic he proved a supreme teacher of his nation.

The focal point of his art is his Hungarianism. He was not a chauvinist but truly a Magyar poet, as Vergil was a Roman poet. One cannot appraise him properly without taking into consideration Carl Jung's "collective unconscious" applied to poetically expressed historical and ethnic problems. This is especially true in regard to his magnificent epic works. But in his contemporary topics, too, one is aware of a poet who saw his duty in serving humani-

ty within the framework of the Hungarian ethos. Some of his poems written after the War of Independence in 1848-49, when the allied armies of Austria and Russia overpowered Hungary, are such that only the wounded Hungarian spirit can thoroughly appreciate them. For example, a poem like **"Leteszem a lantot" ("I Lay the Lute Down")** of which this is the last stanza:

> I lay the poet's lute down. Dull as lead
> It irks the hand. And who still asks for song?
> Who can rejoice in flowers that are dead,
> Who seeks their mouldering fragrance to prolong?
> If man destroy the tree, the bloom it bore
> In shrivelling beauty perishes anon.
> Youth of my soul, returning nevermore,
> Ah, whither, tell me, whither hast thou gone?

Not merely a disappointed youth sings thus, not merely "youth that found the world so fair" and was cheated out of its trust, but *Hungarian* youth, abandoned by hope, deserted by its own future. To be sure, the cultural immobility of his socially retarded environment could have had a deadening influence upon Arany, but this did not happen; it rather stirred him to songs in which despair was routed by the courage of imagination or tempered by resignation. Like the hero in Hungarian parables, Arany could conquer the seemingly unconquerable. The effect of ancient chants, historical or local romances and fables, helped to deliver a personality which, despite the stress of political and cultural insecurity, remained a free and reliable agent of his creative power. The use of formal diction in his poetry as well as the use of folkish idiom reveal him as a stanch defender of words sanctioned either by tradition or by verbal intuition.

Inherently diffident, Arany tried to conceal his identity in many of his poetic works; he succumbed to that "private sensibility" which R. P. Blackmur, the American critic [in his *Double Agent,* 1936], observes in certain modern poets. His act derived from the belief that the poet should not occupy his time with trivia; what sets the poet on the right path is the acknowledgment of the difficulties of his task, the ability to reconcile the flight into fantasy or feeling with a close check on reality. Arany was a major poet and critic who would not permit his spirit to deviate from the goal of artistic expression. (pp. 106-07)

While Arany's works mirror some influence of Homer, Vergil, the *Nibelungenlied,* Transylvanian and Scottish folk ballads, it is generally conceded that his originality is beyond dispute, and that as a bard of ballads he has no rival in Hungarian literature. His precursors in this genre, such as Ferenc Kölcsey and Károly Kisfaludy, reminiscent of their German models, or Mihály Vörösmarty and János Garay, whose ballads were closer to their Hungarian roots, lacked Arany's genius as a ballad poet, although they were able creators, and Vörösmarty, especially through his romantic imagination, is a superb representative of the Hungarian creative spirit. No doubt, Arany's epic writings take precedence over his other poetic works, but it would be wrong to consider his lyric and elegiac poems inferior. In order to form an adequate idea of Arany one is perhaps right in saying that in his pure lyrics, conditioned by diffidence, one missed the vitality of his epic poetry, but they too evidence an infallible sense of composition and linguistic acuteness. In his correspondence with Hungarian poets and writers, such as Sándor Petőfi, Ferenc Toldy, Mihály Tompa, József Lévay, Pál Gyulai, Antal Csengery, various themes are sounded which he later used in his writings. He was a master of his craft, who provided aesthetic and moral leadership in an age when in the Hungarian world of letters the trend of patriotic clichés and journalistic dexterity was beginning to replace creative conscientiousness. With reference to his interest in the past it should be said that by recognizing the precarious position of the Hungarian nation in the pattern of European civilization—the Eastern and Western contradictions—he had to create a symbol of the past in order to give the present an accent of historical, psychological, and cultural continuity. He was afraid that, separated completely from its mythological and historical soil, the Magyar nation would not have sufficient perseverance to face the future with fortitude. Since the eighteenth century there have been several European—mostly German—scholars with a Cassandra-like disposition who sang a dirge over the grave of Hungary.

"Arany is the greatest artist of the Hungarian language." His works appeared in eight volumes; then four more volumes were added, containing his letters and other material. There is also a six-volume edition of his poetry exclusively, and there are several one-volume editions. His ballads were illustrated by Hungarian artists, such as Mihály Zichy, György Buday, and others. Despite the radical change in the political and social structure of Hungary, Arany's reputation is as secure as it was when he reached the peak of his creative and critical activities. There is an attitude of deference in Hungary regarding Arany, although his works offer a striking contrast between the taste and horizon of nineteenth-century Hungarian literature and the literary principles of today. In Hungary, as in other countries, all sorts of prognostications are made as to the character and essence of the literature of the future, but it seems obvious that as Dante's relationship to Scholasticism does not make of him a literary "displaced" person in twentieth-century Italy, Arany's position too is unchanged in twentieth-century Hungary. Of course, something unforeseen may happen, yet it seems improbable that those in political power will ever try to prohibit the enjoyment and appreciation of this poet.

Of his epic works the Toldi trilogy represents him in the fullness of his poetic genius. Like so many of his compatriots, he was conscious of the fact that Hungary was living on the outer edge of Western civilization; and the feeling of national uneasiness, which is common to all Hungarians, was also one of his noticeable attributes. But he was unwilling to yield to national pessimism. To counteract the challenge of defeatism it seemed imperative to reabsorb into his poetic works the spirit of the mythological and chivalric past. He found delight and support in the vaguely known data of Hungarian mythology and history, and he was convinced that there must have been a Hun and Magyar epic cycle which was destroyed by the indifference of time.

For his epopoeia, *Toldi,* he borrowed the raw material

from Péter Ilosvai Selymes, a sixteenth-century Hungarian chronicler, but in manner, form, style, and outlook the work brought a new experience to Hungarian literature. In **Toldi, Toldi szerelme (Toldi's Love)** and **Toldi estéje (Toldi's Eve)**—while originally written in a different chronological order, but united through the central character—Arany is shown as a national poet with a positive attitude toward the meaning of the Hungarian spirit. The first part is naïve and realistic, the second romantic, the third tragic. In this epos Arany evidences an unusual power of characterization. The first and second parts consist of twelve cantos, the third of six cantos, each part written in double rhymes. The hero, Miklós Toldi, who lived in County Bihar and was a contemporary of Nagy Lajos (Louis the Great), the fourteenth-century Hungarian Anjou ruler, seems a composite portrayal of the strength and weakness of the Hungarian psyche. He is honest and belligerent, dependable and impetuous, loyal and proud, yet inclined to follow his sanguine instincts rather than his judgment founded on facts. His relationship to his heartless brother, György, who is a courtier, his legendary prowess proved in combat with the Czech knight in a tournament, his love for Piroska Rozgonyi, his behavior that explains the king's confidence in him, but also makes the king's resentment plausible, show Miklós Toldi as a man who reaps the benefits and suffers the consequences of his emotions and actions. As if the poet would be saying: so much Hungarian land lies fallow that could be made productive; how much better could the Hungarian psyche be developed, if only it knew self-control. However, the final picture of Miklós Toldi is sympathetic; it is the picture of a valiant individual, a knight of worthy impulses. The standard by which Arany judges his hero—and he transmits the validity of this standard to the reader—is moral; he perceives in Toldi universal human virtues and imperfections, the nobility and tyranny of ambition, but also traits which stem from his Hungarian destiny.

In the first part of the epos there are splendid descriptions of the Puszta (Hungarian prairie). Arany's power of character delineation is shown in his penetrating insight into human nature, and his ability to share this insight with the reader. In the second part, the characterization of Piroska Rozgonyi, a woman of deep feelings, is very well done, and the portrayal of her husband, Lőrinc Tar, a rather half-witted person, who is slain by Miklós Toldi. In the third part we meet Toldi in his aging years. The epic ends with his death. He is buried by his faithful servant, Bence. There are lively dialogues in this section, a mingling of sorrow and humor, graphic descriptions of mass movements and battles; the third part presents the accounting of a man's life whose achievements and failures, whose inability to avoid pitfalls and ability to sustain our admiration for him, are made interesting and symbolically significant because of Arany's psychological authenticity and sense of the poetically concrete. Besides the characters already mentioned, one cannot forget Piroska's distinguished father, Miklós Toldi's generous and affectionate but strict mother, the complex character of the king and his haughty mother, Elizabeth, the Hungarian noblemen and princes of the Church, the Czech and Italian knights, and minor characters such as Zách, Örzse, Mária, Anikó. These characters—hot-blooded or calm, noble or ignoble—are presented under changing conditions, but they are always recognizable as well-drawn human beings and remain memorable personifications of an imaginatively and ethically reconstructed epoch of Hungarian history.

Watson Kirkconnell, the Canadian scholar and poet, is right in declaring [in his *Magyar Muse,* 1933] that the Toldi trilogy is Arany's "masterpiece." One also agrees with his estimate of *Buda halála (The Death of Buda)* as a masterpiece, despite the fact that it is an unfinished work. Arany's plan was to write a trilogy with a Hun and Magyar mythological background; it is regrettable that only the first part was written. In 1864 he was awarded the Nádasdy prize of the Hungarian Academy for *Buda halála.* In the twelve cantos of *Buda halála* he again proved himself a major epic poet. Arany's vision was to recreate—perhaps with the Finnish *Kalevala* in mind—an epic of Hungarian myth. It was to be the mirror of a past that could only be poetically realized. It is the story of King Buda, the leader of the Huns, and his younger brother, Attila, and the story of their struggle for power, in which Attila proves superior. The *Death of King Buda* "brings to life a theme from the ancient chronicle-cycles and treats its saga-elements with poetic imagination, while at the same time it reflects the more recent Hungarian character and folk-customs, transposed into ancient times." "The work is a true mirror of ancient Hungarian life and character as they appear in Magyar legends, and is a proof of the maturity of modern Hungarian poetry." One of the most charming and moving parts is the minstrel tale of Hunor and Magyar, the progenitors of the Hun and Magyar people, told in the sixth canto. It begins thus:

> The bird flies on from bough to bough.
> The song is pass'd from lip to lip;
> Green grass grows o'er old heroes now,
> But song revives their fellowship.
> Forth to the hunt they ride again,
> The brave sons that fair Enéh bore,
> Hunor and Magyar, champions twain,
> Ménrót's twin sons in days of yore.

The Canadian translator adhered to the four-lined stanzas of the original but altered the rhyming pattern. It seems that he solved his versifying problem, and the a-b-a-b rhyming scheme he employed instead of Arany's closed iambic couplets does not detract from the quality of the epos, which is crowded with character portraits and emotional and descriptive scenes. Arany's linguistic virtuosity, the value he places on psychological and verbal archaisms, his hauntingly imaginative response to folk tales show that he had not only an awareness of the literary and moral horizon of his work, but also that he found an artistic answer to the problem he was interested in as a Hungarian and as a poet.

The influence of Vergil's *Aeneid* is perceptible "in his epic similes and by dividing the two main phases of the action by a romantic interlude of dream-like quality." Consistent with epic traditions, there are supernatural elements in his work. The spiritual and poetic tools Arany used for the unraveling of the Hun and Magyar myth and historical past are at the same time intricate and simple. The masculine characters, such as Buda, Attila, Dietrich, or the feminine characters, such as Ildikó and Gyöngyvér, the meaning of the "Sacred Sword," the significance of Hadúr, the Almighty Lord of the Huns and Magyars, Buda's sharing his kingdom with Attila, Dietrich's counsels, the hunt, Attila's going to war, the death of King Buda, and other scenes of the plot are vividly and convincingly communicated to the reader. The action is swift; in parts its development is dramatic, only rarely overlabored. As source material Arany used Ammianus Marcellinus' *Rerum Gestarum Libri XXXI,* Jordanes' *origine actibusque De Getarum,* Priscus Rhetor's *Excerpta de legationibus,* the *Nibelungenlied,* Amédée Thierry's *Histoire d'Attila,* Simon Kézai's medieval Hungarian chronicles written in Latin, and a few Hungarian works written in the nineteenth century. However, it would be a mistake to say that Arany leaned too heavily on these sources. He was first of all a poet. "The ants of love run mad in every vein"; in this simple metaphor Arany expresses Ildikó's feeling of desire, when at night she thinks that she hears Attila returning to her. Metaphors, such as the one just quoted, delightful imagery, breathtaking scenes, compensate the reader for the occasional monotony of the metric form. As in his Toldi trilogy, in *Buda halála* too Arany is interested in the motivation of action, besides the poetic quality of expression.

That Arany was primarily a poet is, of course, seen in his other epic works and in his lyric poems. His ballads have the quality of dramatically exciting, versified tales based on actual or assumed events; they reveal the skill of the born ballad poet. **"Ejféli párbaj" ("Midnight Duel"), "V. László" ("Ladislaus the Fifth"), "Bor vitéz" ("Hero Bor"), "Szondi két apródja" ("The Two Pages of Szondi"), "A walesi bárdok" ("The Bards of Wales"), "Agnes asszony" ("Mistress Agnes")** and his other ballads are adaptations of known or not sufficiently substantiated historical topics in which sometimes mystery and magic enhance the intensity of narration; much, however, owes its existence to Arany's resourceful imagination. While one senses an echo of the Romantic Revival, it seems justified to say that essentially it was not the Romantic Revival that influenced Arany and led to the production of his perfect ballads, but his genius for this type of poetic expression. Several ballads of Bürger and Uhland, Longfellow and Swinburne, "stories in song" are, in a limited sense, conscious emulations of the folk ballad; this is true in the case of Arany too, except that the Hungarian poet's spirit and manner seem to blend more naturally with the combined elements of the folk and the literary ballad.

Arany's ballads and romances often have allegorical significance; for instance **"The Bards of Wales,"** while "nominally a theme from British history, really represents a repudiation by Magyar poets of overtures for support made during the eighteen-fifties by Austrian tyrants." Arany himself was approached by the authorities to write a eulogy to the Austrian emperor, which he refused to do. When we read in the first stanza of **"The Bards of Wales"** that

> Edward the king, the English king
> Bestrides his tawny steed,
> "For I will see if Wales" said he,
> "Accepts my rule indeed,"

it is the Hungarian poet speaking in opposition to the absolutistic intentions and policies of the Austrian oppressor. But Arany's genius was not solely confined to ballads and romances; he wrote a number of ironic or folkish narrative poems of exceptional artistic quality. *Murány ostroma (The Siege of Murany), A Nagyidai cigányok (The Gypsies of Nagyida),* "Csaladi kör" ("Family Circle"), *Boland Istók (Foolish Steve), Katalin (Catherine),* "Jóka ördöge" ("The Devil of Jóka"), "A rab gólya" ("The Captive Stork"), evidence not only Arany's predilection for the narrative type of poetry, but his comic sense for which, as some of these poems indicate, he was singularly well equipped. His **"Vojtina ars poetikájából" ("The Ars Poetica of Vojtina")** is a satirical argument for poetic idealism. One does not observe in any of his poems a loose usage of words. He knew that as a poet his task was to sing, as a Hungarian his task was to register and express his anxiety about the fate of the nation, and as man to seek justice. His intellectual lyrics are represented by such odes as **"Széchenyi emlékezete" ("In Memory of Széchenyi")** or **"Dante"** of which the last stanza reads thus:

> Can Deity this spirit then enfold?—
> Divinity, the undivided one.—
> Or can the moral eye indeed behold
> The spiritual essence known of none?
> The years by thousands pass and disappear,
> Yet while one dream our dim earth has endow'd
> Let it instruct the faithless to revere
> The Godhead hidden in the pillar'd cloud.

It would be interesting to compare William Butler Yeats' poems written in old age, his irritations caused by the passingness of life, with János Arany's *Őszikék (Meadow Saffron)*. "In these poems Arany is sagacious like a poetic Nestor and resigned to the inevitable like a highly sensitive individual drawn by the shadow of death" [Joseph Reményi, in his Hungarian Literature, 1946]. Here and there he points to the futility of being, yet the following lines he liked to quote from Horace's ode to Apollo:

> Frui paratis, et valido mihi
> Latoe, dones, et, precor, integra
>   Cum mente; nec turpem senectam
>   Degere, nec cithara carentem.

It is to the credit of Pál Gyulai that some of the "old-age" poems appeared at all; he insisted, despite Arany's constant refusal, upon their publication in *Budapesti Szemle (Budapest Review)* which Gyulai edited. Later all the poems were published in book form. Arany's reticence in *Őszikék* is also observable in his early lyric poetry.

The Hungarian poet's intellectual honesty and factual knowledge plus his aesthetic sensitivity found an excellent vehicle in his expository writings. His essay on Miklós Zrinyi, the seventeenth-century Hungarian epic poet, and Torquato Tasso, the Italian Renaissance poet, his portraits of Hungarian writers and poets, such as István Gyöngyösi, Lőrinc Orczy, József Gvadányi, Dávid Szabó, Gedeon Ráday, his interpretation of József Katona's *Bánk bán (Banus Bank)*, the first true Hungarian tragic play, his appraisal of the Hungarian naïve epos and of Hungarian prosody in general, link Arany with the best scholars and writers of similar vein of the Western world. Among his

poetic disciples Károly Szász, József Kiss, Andor Kozma, Miklós Bárd, and Gyula Rudnyánszky must be mentioned. According to János Horváth, the literary historian, "influenced by Arany, Hungarian national taste has matured and historical awareness has deepened"; and according to Gyula Farkas, another literary historian, "the true Hungarian metric form was defined by János Arany with decisive finality." His translations of the comedies of Aristophanes, of Shakespeare's *King John, Hamlet,* and *Midsummer Night's Dream,* Goethe's "Ballade vom vertriebenen und zurückkehrenden Grafen" and Gogol's *The Cloak*—and other translations—prove the rich poetic and communicative nature of the Hungarian language, when used by a master. Although conditioned by his Hungarian cosmogony, János Arany gave validity to the profound truth that man, when his ideas and emotions are expressed with artistry, finds the consciousness of his universality in any language. (pp. 109-16)

> *Joseph Reményi, "János Arany, Poet and Critic (1813-1871)," in his* Hungarian Writers and Literature: Modern Novelists, Critics, and Poets, *edited by August J. Molnar, Rutgers University Press, 1964, pp. 106-116.*

Béla G. Németh   **(essay date 1982)**

[*In the following excerpt, Németh traces Arany's literary career. Special attention is given to the poet's "subjective" verse, with its reflections on the events of Arany's own life and times.*]

When, after his venture with the strolling players [as a young man], Arany resolved to take a job in public administration, the most permanent element in his life began to show itself a certain ambivalent attitude compounded by uncertainty. He became an exemplary office worker; he dispatched the affairs of his community with considerable expertise and goodwill. But, although he had made up his mind to be "just like anybody else, an ordinary man", although he settled down in the manner of any village clerk and threw himself into his notarial duties, his nights were devoted to reading. He read political papers and a great deal of literature, but only the classics, ending with Goethe and Schiller, obtaining them from one of his former headmasters. He learned English by reading Shakespeare, French by reading Molière; he read Virgil in Latin and Homer in Greek. He not only read, he wrote poems and made translations. All this was done spontaneously for himself, for an "ordinary man" would be given no literary commissions. At the time he was still unfamiliar with the contemporary authors in his own country and abroad. The only exception was Byron. This proud, rebellious and homeless noble, this archetype of the Romantic spirit, made a lifelong impression on the conscientious, exemplary clerk who had retreated to the traditional world and was by now the ideal head of a family. But the ordered life and the personality of a poet, the role provided and the role desired, no longer coincided. His final decision was exactly the opposite of what he had originally intended, as he was later to write in **"Looking Back" ("Visszatekintés").**

Much as I crave independence,
Still my chains I gladly wear
Lest at last my bold resistance
Make my lot the worse to bear:
Like the wild beast of the saying,
Which the ropes though never tore,
Yet in struggling and in swaying
Got itself entangled more.

While his lower-class liberal political views, fostered by his newspaper reading, won him a number of sympathizers in his village, his ideas and dreams as an artist, stemming from his reading of the classics, and his "writer's personality" tended to set him apart. Later, in maturity, he regarded the happenings in the world, the titled office-bearers in public life, from his own private viewpoint. He felt himself above them; he saw through them; and while he stood in fear of them he also despised them. His first work, *Lost Constitution (Elveszett alkotmány,* 1845), was born out of such sentiments. He had not originally intended to write a literary work. He had planned to amuse himself with an ironic picture in a series of grotesquely Baroque scenes of the same lies told in their demagogic election campaigns by the liberals and the conservatives. As the rhetoric of both parties was very similar to the bombastic Romantic epics of the time written in hexameters he parodied that genre deliberately or otherwise. The work has no plot as such: it is more a series of election episodes centred on the leaders of the two parties. The long poem, headed by a didactic allegory on mutual understanding and the great role to be played by the "small and simple people" who work for the community, was entered in the competition for a satirical work organized by Kisfaludy Society. He won the competition, and the leading body in literature consequently recognized in him a writer of importance. Although he was then thirty, he had still developed no individual style. Familiarity with the Romantics had taught him what to reject but not what he wanted.

It was Petőfi's poetry that liberated Arany and gave him a sense of direction. It proved to him that he could indeed give open expression to the vision of that true and simple world which he had created for himself. Within six months he had written his narrative poem *Toldi* (1847) and hardly any other work of Hungarian literature has enjoyed a greater success. Briefly, the story runs as follows: Miklós Toldi, the younger son of a noble family but brought up to work almost as a peasant on the family estate, lived in a village with his widowed mother. His brother György, an effete courtier at the court of King Louis the Great returning home on a visit, taunted Miklós and even allowed his soldiers to insult him. In a moment of anger Miklós accidentally killed one of the soldiers and was forced to flee. He finally managed to enter the royal court in disguise and unrecognized, and there he defeated the hitherto unbeaten foreign knight, thus redeeming the reputation of his country. The king pardoned him and took him into his service.

Toldi contains all the elements which Romanticism had introduced into Central Eastern Europe. The subject was historical, recalling the days of national glory. The hero was a historical character from the Middle Ages, whose memory had been preserved and enshrined in folk legend. He had lived, it is true, on the periphery of great historical events, but had been in touch with some of the central figures in these events. His character and his deeds had caught the popular imagination. He lifted millstones, fought with wolves, he broke bulls with his bare hands. He fell in with robbers, and untrained, defeated the professional foreign fighter. He is the strong man of folk imagination, the hero who avenges the outraged feelings of the people. And whatever the folk legends and the desires of liberal-democratic Romantics failed to supply was supplied by the poet. Toldi is not only a strong man. He is the natural, simple soul, untainted by the vices of civilized society, by the false world of his superiors. He is unselfish but self-respecting and is conscious of himself as a man. He wishes to fulfil his natural destiny as dictated by the demands of his own nature, but is hindered by the depravity of the world and the unjust disposition of society. The poem tells the story of a brave, simple, true man of the people who overcomes all obstacles and gains his due becoming the ideal hero and the man who is master of himself in the process.

The work also answers the special needs of Hungarian Romanticism. Toldi is the embodiment of national solidarity. He is of noble origin, yet lives among the people. The nation is presented as it once was, according to the Romantics, and as it should be again: a family community, governed by the rules of justice and nature. *Toldi* is essentially a lyric work, as Arany himself later pointed out. It presents no Utopia, it illustrates no thesis, it is an inner reality, a vision.

As on autumn nights a shepherd's glowing fire
Shines across the *puszta's* vast empire,
So Toldy's face looms large in imagination,
Wellnigh from a depth of nine-ten generations.

—begins the poem. It is a dream, the dream of a man feeling himself in the grip of a world alienated from all that is human, who in his loneliness envisioned a world of his own: a true world, a democracy of his own. It is the vision of one who was both a man of the people and an intellectual; who rising, left the peasant world, but still preserved the feeling, the desires and the imagination of that world. It is a Herderian, a "patriarchal" vision. His belief in its reality infuses Toldi with an idyllic sense of joy, running bright through the poem. Although he was no adherent of Petőfi's "style-democratism", this sense of joy gave Arany's complex style a flavour of populist directness and natural simplicity. Petőfi became attracted to him, aroused by his faith in a democratic future which made them friends and allies, although their views were never identical.

The success of *Toldi* placed Arany among the leading writers of the time. He now had the opportunity to gain insight into public and literary life, and this led to *Toldi's Eve (Toldi estéje,* 1847-48). This new work describes how little Toldi's desires were satisfied at the court of the king, and how little this world understood him. Here the poet shows no great sympathy for Toldi. He even treats him with a certain ironic humour. He is well aware that the road which the world takes leads to the court and its ways.

But he is fearful that this will not end the alienation by mankind. The road which history had taken had led to capitalist development, and not to a patriarchal democracy based on family trust; such a society promised little for the world he aspired to see. The sheer poetry of the second work is even more evident than the first work. Although Toldi is treated with a loving humour, this humour is outweighed by the elegiac tone of the whole. *Toldi's Eve* is an elegy in the form of an epic, one of the most beautiful elegies in Hungarian literature.

Towards the end of his life Arany wrote the middle part of the trilogy, *Toldi's Love* (*Toldi szerelme*, 1879). It dealt with the adventures of the hero in his full manhood, the deeds that led to maturity, and his disappointment in love. The self-irony is unmistakable; the treatment suggests that compared to *Toldi* the poem is not much more than the trifling of an elderly man.

Arany whole-heartedly espoused the cause of the revolution and the struggle for freedom; he even took up arms. But his confidence and certainty had ebbed away. The collapse of the revolution confirmed that something had been lost forever.

After 1849, Arany turned to lyrical poetry, something which he had no desire to do believing his gift lay in epic poetry. In the period immediately following the revolution, he tried to write a national epic poem. His lyric poetry was a kind of by-product in achieving this. But, in the final attempt of this kind, his epic poem *The Death of Buda (Buda halála)*, the "means" were more modern in tone; the lyrical aspects of his work had become more modern than the epic.

These lyrics were born out of the conflict between the ideal and the reality in the years following the revolution, heightened by the subjugation of the nation.

By that time Arany was the man of the widest knowledge in literature and philosophy in the country. His lyrics reflect the various currents of European thought around the middle of the century. The disintegration of the "whole", doubts concerning "cognition", the relativity of truth, the lack of "universal" historical objects, scepticism concerning the equation of "development" and progress, the conflict between "moral" responsibility and material determinism, the immorality of "power" and the defencelessness of labour, the fragmentation of the "traditional" community, the disaccord between the individual and the community, between individual man and social man, and his increasing loneliness and alienation—all these were the subjects of Arany's poems.

> Indifferent the world, the living,
> A ballroom crowded to extreme:
> It brings abundant tears to eyes
> If friend a friend should recognize.
>
> The people seen as through a curtain,
> I do not know a face for certain . . .
> Oh, what a crowd! And I alone,
> Although their ways are all my own.
>   **("In the Garden"—"Kertben")**

and again, in **"Thoughts"** (**"Gondolatok"**):

> Gain and effort fall miles apart,
> And cheating, made a perfect art,
> Sits high, enthroned in every heart.

or again, in **"In the Garden"**:

> . . . Man, a selfish,
> Gluttonous lump of flesh and hide,
> Like a hungry caterpillar;
> Gains his advantage and takes a bite.

For ten years of his life, he lived in this state of doubt and aimlessness, overwhelmed by a sense of futility. And he suffered the usual outcome of such feelings: the wish for death, the longing for an existence unencumbered by consciousness, the attraction of the refuge offered by an irrational freedom.

> My soul, sailor of the ocean,
> Fears to pull in newer harbours . . .
> Let's away then, off with cautions,
> Rock, my ship, on currents streaming,
> Rushing I shall have no notions
> What is *death,* and what's out *dreaming.*
>   **("My Hope"—"Reménvem")**

He wrote at the beginning of that decade. At the end of it he wrote:

> Every moment but frightens me,
> And what comes next a burden be;
> My steps tread on the serpent's head,
> Today I hate, tomorrow dread.
>   **("The Eternal Jew"—"Az örök zsidó")**

He referred to himself as Hamlet, choosing the hero of doubt, the Prince of Denmark, as the symbol of a disillusioned generation. It is perhaps for this reason that he was able to make one of the best European translations of *Hamlet* (1865).

Yet all this is not Romantic lyricism. Nor can it be compared to the disillusioned, self-analytic lyric poetry of the Positivist period. It lies somewhere between the two, perhaps a little closer to the latter. Arany was not indifferent to the need to resolve these contradictions and achieve a single, integral, moral and assured image of the world. Nor did he lose touch with reality or delude himself with illusions; while not succumbing to complete and final disillusionment. His lyric poetry is of confrontation, the poems have two poles. One is constant: a desire for the ideal. The other fluctuates: he takes an episode from daily, contemporary life in which to clothe his thoughts: he quietly grafts the trees in his garden; he looks out from his room at the misty tedium of the autumn; he says goodnight to his small son, and ponders on the child's future. His poetry is highly subjective; his work is empirically analytical, soberly reflective and intellectual in character.

The language and the whole style of his lyric poems were something he deliberately created. Not for him was the style derived from folk or populist poetry—straightforward, unambiguous, natural. His aim was preciseness, the preciseness of the Classics. He deliberately went to the literary language of ancient writers and primitive folk poetry and saying, chose the words and phrases most loaded with possible meanings and associations. The language, the fruit of his intensive reading and research, makes him consequently, one of the most "difficult" of Hungarian poets. He makes use of every possible stratagem and device offered by language, cunningly devised to enhance one another; words, sounds, phrase-structure, embodying a thousand carefully controlled nuances, allusions and combinations; at once concrete and tangible, and yet universal. True to the tradition of Herderian Romanticism, he believed that such a use of language is the most effective in folk poetry and the "primitive" epic. It is for this reason that he considered the ideal to be folk poetry.

There is a musical principle in his constructions. The work unfolds through gradual progression in time, achieving complexity through variation. The poet forces a fragmentary and contradictory world into the unity of a harmonious work. And it is all done with a touch of irony, a breath of melancholy, suggesting that he neither denied the need for unity, nor its possibility.

As a result the beauty of his poems is seldom revealed at first reading. They do not sweep the reader away or overwhelm him with a flow of words and dramatic appeal, offering instant experience. He is far from the great spontaneous spates of declamation and rhetoric of Hugo and his followers. The poems of Arany are rarely suitable for declamation. They were conceived in meditation and are for meditation.

Hardly any trace is to be found in Arany of the hard complete disillusionment of Baudelaire and his like who represented the new and "sensational" element in Western poetry of that time. His work is much more akin to the gentler disillusionment seen in the lyric poetry born *"zwischen Himmel und Erde"* in the grip of the real and the ideal, the *"poetischer Realismus",* halfway between a harmony created by free will and stark unharmonious reality. His nostalgic, stocky humour and his cult of remembrance recalls Keller, his kinship with nature and immediacy of his descriptions Storm; his detached discipline of form and his retreat behind a wall of objectivity, Meyer. And also Tennyson, but the Tennyson who, on occasion, dared to be unharmonious.

Often, however, he managed to achieve a balance between the ideal and the real by references to and associations with styles alien to the experience and to the logic of the work itself such as Romanticism, Biedermeier, the cult of sentiment, didacticism, and in consequence he only managed to produce some twenty faultless poems during this period in an original style completely his own. **"Years, You Years to Come"—"Evek, ti még jövendő évek"; "I Put down the Lute"—"Letészem a lantot"; "Autumn"—"Ősszel"; "In the Garden"—"Kertben"; "Looking Back"—"Visszatekintés"; "Dante"; "A Drop of Balm"—"Balzsamcsepp"; "On the Slope"—"A lejtőn"; "A Beautiful Autumn"—"Kies Ősz"; "Oh, do not Look at Me"—"Oh! ne nézz rám"; "To my Son"—"Fiamnak"; "Morning and Evening"—"Reg és Est"; "The Eternal Jew"—"Az örök zsidó",** etc.

The importance of Arany's lyrics of this period was made clear in the second half of the twentieth century, in the light of the lyric poetry written by Babits and Attila

József, at a time when attention was focussed on the position of the individual. But it was accepted in Arany's time that the lyric poem took second place to the epic. Such was the strength of this view that Arany himself, after his earlier lyrics which he simply regarded as the outcome of the compelling circumstances of the moment, considered the epic his chosen field. He prepared himself for his role and mission as an epic poet by the study of critical and analytical works on the theory of poetry and of modern and ancient authors, and by unceasing meditation. He believed that the task of the poet was to create and revive in a contemporary context the common and single-minded national consciousness, feeling and character that had been lost. And the most effective way of doing this was to treat some historical subject in an epic manner. The present had no ideal heroes to appeal to the nation as a whole and would raise questions, especially that of "pauperism", to which the poet could not give an answer or offer a solution. On the other hand, to ignore such questions would only widen the gap and increase the uncertainty. Such thinking came perilously close to that somewhat reactionary aspect of Romanticism which combined the national-popular element in the doctrine of Herder with the philosophy of history enunciated by Savigny, leading to pseudo-historical ideas and the idealization of the peasant as an idyllic figure.

The extent to which his work suffered from this attitude can be seen in the fragments he wrote on contemporary subjects, especially in *The Village Fool (A falu bolondja,* 1851), in which the talented son of a peasant drifts away and, in assuming a series of undignified, laughable roles, becomes the village fool.

Fortunately, Arany also incorporated into the work a typically "un-Romantic" element. He held the view that although the national character is best preserved in the common people, it may become primitive because of their intellectual isolation, therefore, it should be impregnated with values originating in the superior culture of the day. He saw his age as Virgilian: it was not destined to create anything new in culture or art; its main task, therefore, was precisely that work of impregnation. This is a typical "educational" postulate of the age of Comte and Herbart.

This twofold theory is the basis of the epic poem *The Death of Buda (Buda halála,* 1863). It is the first part of a trilogy, but can in fact stand on its own as an independent work. It deals with the struggle for the throne between the great Hun king, Attila, and his brother Buda. Arany forced the material of a magnificent psychological novel into a form which was archaic and obsolete, bringing his power of artistic discipline and his vast fund of knowledge to bear on its composition. This work is imbued with all the delicate perception found in the analytic novel to the development of a tragic situation which from its first conception develops inexorably, through the minutest reactions of mind and heart, moving inevitably to its tragic climax.

In this work he warns that catastrophe cannot be avoided unless we submit to the dictates of common sense and the laws of nature through mental discipline and self-knowledge.

The Death of Buda is a tragedy of role and personality. King Buda, in a moment of impetuous generosity, divides his power between himself and his younger brother, Attila. They both accept roles which are inconsistent with their personal characters, the one of them is too weak, the other too strong to share power. It leads to their deaths. Buda dies first at the hand of Attila, and as the other parts of the trilogy were intended to illustrate, Attila then meets his death as a result of his crime. Apart from the warning implicit in the work, this wonderfully concentrated work contains another motif or rather another overtone. It may have been deliberately intended by Arany, or it may have emerged from the devices of style employed—the tragic note, balladistic tone, the short, melancholy summing up. It is the rolling of history, of destiny. Not the mysterious, mythical history, the "destiny" of Romanticism but the horrible cogwheel system of the Positivist era, coldly exposed with critical detachment. The question of the system is clear; the process by which the cogwheels shred all who fall between them is equally explicit, but its object remains concealed. This aspect of the work is no more than an undertone, yet it reveals how few illusions Arany had retained concerning the historical development of his time.

The Death of Buda was the climax of Arany's ten years' search for an epic role; it was his intention that the work should take the same place in public estimation as *Toldi.* But in vain. Apart from *Toldi,* Arany, desiring fame as an epic poet, is still best known for his famous ballads. These ballads were in fact earlier than the search for an epic role. He began to write them in 1853, five years after the failure of the War of Independence, a time when the Hungarians opposed a passive resistance to Habsburg domination. Arany was attracted to the group headed by Kemény and Csengery, the leaders of the movement for passive resistance; he made friends with them and accepted some of their views. In particular, he was concerned to preserve national unity and promote the moral strength of the nation, and it was with this aim in view that he composed his ballads. Their subject-matter is generally taken from sad and difficult periods in national history, especially from the fourteenth and fifteenth centuries, the periods of Anjou and Hunyadi, and from the period of Turkish occupation.

"László V" (1853) deals with the unhappy son of Albert Habsburg, his conflict with the nation, his breach of faith and his atonement. "Mátyás's Mother" ("Mátyás anyja", 1854) is about the imprisonment in Prague of the young Matthias Corvinus and his mother's struggle to secure his release; "Klára Zách" (1855) about the criminal participation of the wife of Charles Anjou in the rape of a noble's daughter, and "The Two Pages of Szondi" ("Szondi két apródja", 1856) about the loyalty of a castellan's pages. Arany's subjects included tales from common life. In "Mistress Agnes" ("Ágnes asszony", 1853), for instance, he deals with a peasant woman who, with her lover, killed her husband, and went mad as the consequence of her crime.

When Arany wrote, the ballad was an outmoded genre, only to be found in the village and market-place. Arany raised it again to the rank of literature, and in this type of poem one might rank him next to Goethe. They were excellent means of arousing the national consciousness and a national determination to survive. But they were at the same time objective projections of his ambivalent attitude, his suffocating mood and his moral strength. This is clearly shown by the **"Bards of Wales" ("A walesi bárdok")**. The Emperor Franz Joseph only visited Hungary for the first time five years after the 1848 Revolution had been crushed. The authorities requested writers to produce poems of welcome. Arany replied with the ballad of the Welsh bards who went to the scaffold for refusing to pay homage to the conquering English king, Edward I, a story based on legend.

Arany's ballads were greeted with unbelievable enthusiasm. The nation celebrated in them its greatness and its moral superiority to its oppressors, and its right to the tragic assumption of a better future founded upon this "superiority" and "greatness". It neither could nor would listen to the poet struggling painfully with uncertainty and doubt, which echoes through the ballads as it vibrated in the lyrics. It clung to the illusion that national sentiment and will were omnipotent, an attitude by no means rare during the more tragic periods in the history of small nations. Arany's ballads were read as the counterparts of Jókai's romantic novels: the readers were firmly reassured about the national character, the national feeling, the national will; all that mattered was to end foreign oppression.

The range of Arany's art was extremely wide, but especially reveals the psychological associations of the Hungarian sentence, which it would never be possible to reproduce in translation. A single line often contains implicit references to different experiences, judgements, approaches, feelings and distances. Many writers of ballads followed in his footsteps. The ballad is at once the easiest and the most difficult of genres. His imitators chose the easier aspects, and Arany himself, either because of the appearance of a host of imitators or perhaps because the ballad could not replace the great epic of his aspirations, gave up writing them.

His ballads were welcomed with passionate enthusiasm while *The Death of Buda* with obligatory enthusiasm and total incomprehension. The public expected and believed that it had been given in these ballads an overall image of the world, a faith in life justified by simple sentiments of nationalism and a knowledge of the national will. In *The Death of Buda* they were in fact given a poem which embodied Arany's inner struggle with the strict teachings of self-knowledge and self-control, self-discipline, and the ethical discipline of feelings and will, in a form which was too difficult for, and too alien from, the period. The result was that *The Death of Buda* did not bring the poet close to the nation, nor did it enable him to fulfil what he believed to be his mandate, or resolve his doubts and uncertainties.

After the reception accorded to *The Death of Buda* and his four long years of failure as the editor of a literary review, he could not but become aware of his loneliness and his alienation from the people. "You don't want me as a *praeceptor*—very well, you don't want me," was the way he summed up his situation in a mood of bitterness. His alienation from the world became unmistakably clear to him in 1867, when a certain amount of independence was restored to Hungary, and the part liberal, part capitalist and part feudal world of the Dual Monarchy was established, with its mob of lesser nobles and junkers which, while maintaining the privileges of the landed class, introduced into Hungary the selfish, corrupt, jostling society and class characteristics of the bourgeois establishment. Arany did not even begin to work on the other parts of his trilogy. He turned to silence. He buried himself in his work as the General Secretary of the Hungarian Academy of Sciences and threw himself into the translation of the complete works of Aristophanes. *"Seul le silence est grand,"* he too could have written on the next ten years of his life.

But it was with a painful, wise resignation, rather than in bitterness, that he ended; he left with an elegy. A few years before his death, after retirement, he spoke again. It was not that he now had more leisure, but that he was no longer a public official.

The lyric poetry of his later years wonderfully reflects the autumn light of an old man's life. The style is far more even, more contained and consistent than that of his first lyrical period. He was, however, too old and too tired for the great disillusionment peculiar to the second half of the century, as exemplified first by Baudelaire and then by Nietzsche. In some of his poems, however, we hear the note which accompanied him throughout his career—the tragic sense of misgiving, of a mistaken life, an existence missed. But his work did not lead to any final confrontation. It remained mostly on the level of objective recollection, a summing-up, a farewell. Most often he recalled his childhood not directly, but in the form of wonderful "peasant" ballads akin to the doomed and concentrated mystery of Storm's *Schimmelreiter* and to Hardy's descriptions of village life (**"Corn-husking"**—**"Tengerihántás"**, 1877; **"Red Rébék"**—**"Vörös Rébék,"** 1877; **"Ordeal of the Bier"**—**"Tetemrehívás,"** 1877). He bade farewell to his unfulfilled dreams in poems characterized by nostalgia and melancholy, lightened by humour, but elegiac in the deeper sense. He came a step nearer to *"poetischer Realismus"* but a gentler, more "poetic" version. These melodious poems are more concerned with emotion, with gentle memories, than with argument and the inner drama of conflict. There is even a touch of Impressionism in his enjoyment of colour, his love of word-play and soft music. What is most authentic of the man is the dignity with which he registers objectively, undramatically, with a proud, sour reserve, without a smile or tear, that he did what he was able to do, and must accept what is still left for him. His poetry is infused with the most profound of his qualities, his firm, humane, moral sense. Most beautiful of these poems are **"In the Market"** (**"Vásárban"**); **"Under the Oaks"** (**"A tölgyek alatt"**); **"Naturam furca expellas"**; **"I Have No Need of the Hoarfrost"** (**"Nem kell dér"**); **"This Life"** (**"Ez az élet"**); **"Until the Very End"** (**"Mindvégig"**); **"Dreary Hour"** (**"Meddő órán"**); **"Once More This Time"** (**"Még ez egyszer"**), etc.

It was undoubtedly his role to sum up and to crown all that had gone before. Not only populism, even though he himself claimed throughout his life to be a "populist" or "popular-national" poet. But, while Petőfi—the true populist poet—had a strong aversion, like the other members of young Europe, towards Goethe, Arany regarded him as the king and final word on his kind of populism. Arany absorbed, summed up and then developed further whatever Hungarian literature had until then created or adopted. His work, consequently, was also closely related to Classicism which it continued and transmitted. (pp. 234-45)

Béla G. Németh, "János Arany," in A History of Hungarian Literature, *by István Nemeskürty and others, edited by Tibor Klaniczay, translated by István Farkas and others, Corvina Kiadó, 1982, pp. 233-45.*

Dezső Keresztury   (essay date 1985)

[*Keresztury is a Hungarian literary historian. In the excerpt below, he examines the thematic and stylistic influences such English authors as Spenser, Byron, and Shakespeare had on Arany's poetry.*]

János Arany (1817-1882) was one of the greatest of Hungarian poets. . . . In the Hungarian national consciousness he is coupled with Petőfi, and for many, he is the best loved and most often quoted Hungarian classical poet. Indeed, to many he is what Goethe is to the Germans, or Blake, Byron, and perhaps even Shakespeare, are to the English. In comparing him with Goethe, I do not wish to compare two noncomparable œuvres (such comparisons point to differences as much as to similarities), I am only thinking of their roles as national poets.

But to stay with Goethe as an example: both Goethe and Arany drew from the fount of folk poetry and classical tradition. Both reshaped their nations' language and literature by crowning the revolutionary achievements of their youth through the revival of their national (and European) past and by pointing the way to future development. Both were self-taught, speculative, inventive, creative spirits. Both wished to create order in the intellectual storms around and within them, to find, in Arany's words, "the inner form which almost corresponds to the subject." But the differences are equally striking. The composer Zoltán Kodály and the poet Gyula Illyés used almost identical words to define him: "Arany is the Hungarian people." (p. 67)

His colossal and profound knowledge came from literary sources. There is evidence that the most important elements of his satiric epic, *Az elveszett alkotmány* (*Constitution Lost*, 1845), his first relentlessly realistic portrayal of society, came from the classics and contemporary papers, and that he did not write his greatest epic, the *Toldi* trilogy, in one breath; although he spent decades collecting source material to ensure the "authenticity" for the Hun-Magyar epic which he intended to be his *chef d'œuvre,* he could not find enough building blocks for the second part in Péter Ilosvai Selymes's narrative poem of 1574. When he edited journals in the 1860s in Pest, he daily visited the editorial offices of *Pesti Napló,* the most prestigious daily of the time, where he read the leading European papers.

Arany was also well informed on contemporary foreign literatures. He was interested in the English language from his earliest years. In this he was obviously partly influenced by the anglophilia fashionable in Central Europe during the first half of the nineteenth century, which played a definitive role in the unfolding of the Hungarian Reform Age. From the beginning, Arany was especially influenced by English literature, from Shakespeare to Byron and Dickens.

The influence of contemporary English writers who were considered classics in their own lifetimes can be traced through Arany's entire career, serving him either as examples to emulate or to shun. Though English works such as *Paradise Lost* or the *Songs of Ossian* spread through Central Europe first through Latin and then German, Arany soon tried to read these and all other works that he felt were of importance, in the original. Nevertheless, the only tangible effect *Paradise Lost* had on him was that his first work, which immediately brought him a prize, was given the title of **Constitution Lost.** So it remained for the works of Shakespeare to exercise the most profound influence on Arany's entire œuvre.

Arany learned English for Shakespeare's sake and, as Kossuth did in prison, from the works themselves. At first he was probably swept along by the whirlwind which in the age of Romanticism arose in Northern and Central Europe around Shakespeare. Here, Shakespeare strongly influenced the birth of national consciousness, the development of a national theatre and drama; indeed, in Hungary, as elsewhere, he became a national bard.

This is one reason why, when Arany had decided to become a wandering player, his teacher in Debrecen exhorted him: "Shakespeare, and nothing but Shakespeare, *domine!*" Later, a friend gave him an English grammar. "And I studied it," the poet recalled when writing about the beginnings of his love affair with the English language, "I laughed at the bizarre pronunciation of the written words, I worked on Hamlet's monologues . . . until I wanted to compare the German Shakespeare with the original. The task was difficult but inspiring; a fair at Debrecen brought me cheap editions of *King John* and *Richard II* . . . and before I knew it, *King John* spoke to me in Hungarian iambic pentameter."

From then on, Shakespeare would not let go of him. The Bard stood at the cradle of his early plays (which he subsequently burned); traces are left on Arany's ballads—perhaps that is why he was called "the Shakespeare of the ballad" by the man who edited them; Arany began to translate into English József Katona's *Bánk bán,* written in 1818, though not produced until 1833, the "tragedy of the Hungarian nation," because "it's so Shakespearean;" Shakespeare also provided a touching note to Arany's old age, namely that, having learned the language only with his eyes, Arany could not comprehend it when spoken, and could not have his beloved English texts read to him (though he had set its rules of pronunciation into verse as an exercise), and, first and foremost, Shakespeare was the recurrent object of the efforts which led to the publication of the first Hungarian *Complete Works,* under Arany's guidance.

For decades, Arany turned time and again to those plays he had once attempted to translate and which he was later to finish for the collected works: *A Midsummer Night's Dream, King John* and *Hamlet.* Of the rest of his drafts of Shakespeare translations he kept only the Queen Mab speech from *Romeo and Juliet.* He had planned to translate *The Merry Wives of Windsor* for the National Theatre, but was outstripped by a more facile translator. He was looking for allies to help realize his great ambition, which during the 1840s was very much in the air. The actor Gábor Egressy, who was also a first-rate organizer, had suggested that Arany, Petőfi and Vörösmarty, the three poets most suited, should undertake the complete Shakespeare. Petőfi contributed *Coriolanus,* Vörösmarty *Julius Caesar* and *King Lear,* and had begun *Romeo and Juliet.* When Arany moved to Pest in 1860, a former colleague, who had also been a teacher and who came into a handsome inheritance, commissioned the Kisfaludy Society, of which Arany was the president, to undertake the project. With great care and expertise, Arany first defined the principles of translation, still valid today, recruited the translators, corrected the finished products and undertook the editing. He defended Shakespeare's roughnesses, and insisted that the translation be made true to form, should reflect the nature of spoken speech and be easy to deliver on stage. With his own translations, he furnished a powerful poetic example for his demands. To this day, dozens of lines from his *Hamlet* translation live on as idioms in the Hungarian language.

In his early career, besides Shakespeare, Arany also owned a volume of Byron, later obtaining an annotated edition. Throughout his life, Arany wrestled with the charismatic poet's presence. Indeed, Arany's relationship with Byron caused him much more agitation than his relationship with Shakespeare. Byronism, which swept over Europe and caught the fevered imagination of many figures in the Hungarian Reform Age, from the aristocratic reform politician Széchenyi to the plebeian revolutionary poet Petőfi, would have also disturbed Arany's peace of mind, had he not met with it only in his full maturity, by which time he had learned, like so many of his contemporaries, to make his mind the "tyrant of his heart."

Even so, the English poet who had such an unsettling and shocking effect on people, inducing them to flight, was present at the birth of all of those Arany works in which the poet wished to show the perverseness of his age through a distorting mirror. The motto of **Constitution Lost,** for example, was taken from Byron: "Oh, thou world! Thou art indeed a melancholy jest." Byron offered the best example for the freedom with which Arany and his contemporaries were to attack their age through the use of satire and irony, raising satire to the level of great poetry, turning the illusions of the times into the subject of poetry, and everyday language into the vehicle of lyrical expression. Byron also provided an example for the brave mixing of genres considered mutually exclusive till then, for the use of new styles, attitudes and modes of representation. Arany's *Constitution Lost,* a work hardened into shape after a sudden eruption of volcanic passion and insight, is not a traditional mock heroic, but "just a meek humorous-satiric-allegoric-comic something," to use its author's description. A similar, though much more incisive mixture of styles characterizes Arany's *A nagyidai cigányok* (*The Gypsies of Nagyida,* 1850), a satiric narrative poem which is a bitter reaction to the failure of the 1848-49 War of Independence. This comic epic, too, owes much to the example set by Byron.

One of Arany's greatest narrative poetry projects, *Bolond Istók,* which he spent long years to prepare and which was left to us only in fragments, also owes its inception to a bitter, intensely personal Byronic view. The title (*bolond:* fool; *Istók:* one of the familiar forms of *István* or Stephen) points to the poet's painfully personal and communal theme: the failure of a talented man to find his true place and role in life. As with Byron, this too is characterized by a strange dual consciousness. The dramatic scenes in the Alföld, the Great Plain, described with such seeming objectivity, could be taken for a naturalistic handling of the subject. The child who is brought into a world of the utmost human misery causes his mother's shame and his grandmother's death. His drunkard godmother gives him a girl's name and leaves him by the roadside, where Gypsies find him and barter him to a childless farmer couple. Istók could be taken as a version of the type of hero whom we meet in romantic novels such as Dickens', which Arany liked so much. But Arany had no intention of writing a sentimental novel dedicated to misery. From the outset, the figure of the hero is bathed not only in the bright light of emotion, but also in that of the painful self-irony which Arany used to describe himself. Of this grimace, it would be difficult to tell how much is owed to this great satirist's propensity for distortion and to his depressing, stormy indignation with life. But it also owed something to the complex and virtuoso art of Byron, whom Arany mentions in *Bolond Istók* with unconcealed admiration.

When in 1867 Arany considered the work he had begun in 1850, he wrote: "In the unconstrained form of the work I found an apt vehicle for the expression of both my subjective experiences and feelings and the humour inherent in the way people felt." After the failure of the War of Independence, such feeling had shaken the poet's soul to its core. But Arany left the poem unfinished. The new tone and form fell on unresponsive ears; what is more, the eruption of universal pain seemed to destroy everything in and around it.

The second canto of the planned epic, perhaps his richest narrative masterpiece, was written in 1872 with the resigned wisdom of a man remembering his past, a man who called the English poet he still thought so highly of a shipwrecked genius.

Byron's art also had a fruitful effect on Arany's euphoric states of mind. Arany had left off his translations of *Parasina* and *Sardanapal,* perhaps because he could not find an appropriate solution to the greatest difficulty in translation: "The English language is made up mainly of one-syllable words . . . while we conjugate even our one-syllable words until they become four or five syllables long." So Arany translated poems which he found a challenge and which stood as substitutes for his own work. It is interesting to note that in the volume of his collected poems, Arany included translations from Moore and Burns along with his own. In this volume he also published the only translation of Byron he ever completed, a canto from *Don Juan,* which he entitled "The Greek Minstrel." He set the date "1848" right under the title though the translation had been made in 1845, and sent it to his friend István Szilágyi, who had it published in 1856, after smoothing over some of the rough spots. In the 1856 edition of Arany's shorter pieces, he could not very well include his dangerous revolutionary poems. "The New Greek Minstrel" was meant as a substitute.

Today we know that in this translation the poet saw not only the chance to sing a patriotic lament but also a liberating example for the expression of complex feeling, a vehicle for expressing his own objectified personal moods and his world of past experience. In the generally accepted image of Arany, the Byronic inspiration seems out of place; even for those contemporaries who understood him, the Byronic influence produced "puzzling" works.

Out of all the unfinished Byronic, romantic narratives produced by Arany, there is only one finished piece, a lyrical narrative, *Katalin,* from the autumn of 1850. All at once, the poet known for his naive, Homerian popular realism, presented his readers with a wildly romantic subject and the forms of expression which he himself had inveighed against not long ago with words like sentimental and affected. He took the story from a collection of gothic horror stories meant for romantic readers and poets. But he raised its old-fashioned, ineffective style and taste to the level of true art, demonstrating that he could handle it on a higher plane than the hacks of cheap sensationalism.

Arany's choice may have also been influenced by the fact that in 1850, just after the trauma following defeat in the War of Independence, he needed a subject through which he could give his imagination free rein without having "the skeleton of reality" leering at him. However, his choice must have been more influenced by a desire to reject the popularism of those who imitated Petőfi, and whose works were becoming all form with little content. Arany used the iambic octameter, which was unusual at the time. "I formed *Katalin* in imitation of Byron's stories, more as an exercise in form than with any poetic intention in mind . . . because I read somewhere in Byron that he complains about the eight-syllable form and finds it difficult to move in. [. . .] I have never seen here a longer poem of this type, done in rhyme and rhythm." Arany also spoke about his greatest mistake: "wanting to make it Byronic, I piled image on top of image."

Once again, as his own severest critic, Arany deceived his followers a little. For if we accept the fact that the romantic story merely served as a vehicle to show off his poetic facility, we must also admit that the stream of images gushes like some geyser breaking through the dam of restraint, as if the poet had found his way back to a road he had once taken and enjoyed. These images floating in a strange, dreamlike light possess a different poetic and linguistic quality than the calm, naive realism of *Toldi.* The whole is imbued with a symbolic meaning, making the images the vehicles of some sort of visionary fancy. They are called upon to make tangible and accessible to the reader what is taking place both within the characters and the soul of the poet himself, struggling with the demons of his fate. *Katalin,* just as so many of Byron's works, surprises us not only with its transitory, inspired lyricism and fragile dream-like quality, but also with the calculating consciousness with which the Hungarian poet handles his subject and mode of expression.

These Byronic experiments were also significant because in them the poet developed the devices he was to use in his second great ballad period, which went well beyond naive simplicity. Among these were the suggestive gaps, for example, with which the most important aspects of the emotion-filled story are presented, so that everything that has been omitted must be supplied by the reader's imagination. It was here that he developed a plastic compression which fuses body and soul, action and atmosphere into an organic whole and is so characteristic of Arany's mature works. Alongside the hatred of tyranny and sympathy towards human pain and suffering, is to be found poetic justice, which attacks the sensitive nerve fibers of the human conscience. There are chimeras who drive the guilty into insanity—the phantoms of the soul which shape our lives. There is also the complex formation of the ballad: parallel structure, variations on inner rhythm here flashing like lightning, there fading in a sigh, recurring motifs which change their colours and meaning, and of course, Ossianic backdrops.

This is, in fact, the third area of influence that English poetry exerted on Arany.

His plan for a large-scale Hun-Magyar trilogy, which was only partly realized, was meant to offer a measure of comfort to a nation trampled into the dust after 1849. It was intended to present the people with the glory of an idealized historical past that had no basis in fact. The entire epic was to represent the Magyar Conquest of the ninth century A.D. as a continuation of Attila's legacy, the once powerful Hun empire which had disintegrated centuries before. (The historical facts are that in the centuries before the Conquest, the Magyars were, like the Huns, a warring and nomadic people, but there was never any ethnic or blood relationship between them.)

However, as he looked around him, Arany found support for his Hungarian utopia. In this, too, he had affinities with contemporary artists both at home and abroad. It was at this time that they were beginning to shape (or were already rounding out) their own special national conceptions; here Herder's theory of organic growth, which also prophesied the decline of the Hungarians and other small nations, played a major role. Those who were shaping the reawakening (or awakening) sense of national purpose were looking for vestiges of ancient and folk poetry free of the contamination of civilization, and which were ethnic and authentic. Once found, it was collected and published; if only a fragment was found, it was completed; where nothing existed, it was forged so as to satisfy expectations; the more they did this, the greater influence they had, even if the source was already proven to be a fake.

This is why, even alongside Homer, Ossian could retain at least a symbolic prestige. Herder's important essay, which presented the poet of the sunny southern disposition and the one of northern gloom as equals, exercised a legend-creating force for a whole century.

The deep influence of this parallelism affected Arany at the initial stage of the crisis in his career, a period of pain and torment. By nature and inclination he was the last Hungarian Homer, the descendant of the popular blind Greek bard, but he felt that his circumstances made him into a Hungarian Ossian, without a people he could "rouse with his song."

In **"Ősszel" ("Autumn")**, one of his most beautiful "elegiac-odes," composed in 1850, Arany offered a personal version of the Herderian parallel. Even the tone signals a change: Arany does not draw his subject from the peasant life of the revolutionized present, and does not wish to write according to "folk schemes," as he had done not long ago, with Petőfi, but to turn to the classics: "What is there left to do? Perhaps to read . . . / Stay, Homer, with your bright skies, / Stay here now . . . Come Ossian / With your misty, dim-lit song." (Prose translation.)

Ossian influenced only Arany's feeling about being a poet; more specifically, it helped him express this feeling. This was especially true of this phase of his career, which he himself described as "the time . . . not suited for longer poetic things . . . in the period of the defeat following 1849, which settled with lead weight especially on the soul of the poet . . . Thus I became, despite my inclination, direction and working techniques, a subjective poet, tearing my tormented soul into various lyrical sighs. When after these convulsions my peace of mind began to return, I turned to the ballad." His sights were set higher than in the naive ballads of his first period.

Of **"Roz gonyiné" ("Mrs Rozgonyi")**, a traditional ballad which though in a Hungarian folk song tone, treated a historical subject, Arany wrote to his editor: "You will find it hard to believe that this simple, naive thing is the result of studying foreign authors, and that its predecessor is in those Scottish ballads which are a thousand times more *ballads* than the *ach* and *oh* histories later made of them by the Germans." Arany made subject, form and environment Hungarian, and emphasized that he did so "in imitation only of the *thrust* of the ballad." In order to make his models known, on March 13, 1853, soon after his own ballad appeared, he published his translation of the Scottish folk ballad, "Sir Patrick Spens" in *Szépirodalmi lapok.*

This translation furnishes a clear indication of the features that Arany considered as constituting the thrust of a Scottish folk ballad. Besides the Ossianic tone, he was especially impressed by the peculiar mode of versification which relied on gaps in the narrative. These old ballads seemed archaic and folk-like, arty and naive, lyrical and objective, all at the same time. The manner of the whole, coloured with the many types of speech, the conjuring forth of images through the dialogue, offered good narrative, drama and poetry simultaneously. Arany could especially identify with the sympathetic descriptions of scenes rather than their emotional explication. He considered a poem good only if the inner form held the subject and the mode of expression together.

In Scottish folk ballads, Arany had found something he had been searching for in order to advance as a poet. By referring to the clean source of Hungarian folk poetry which he had faithfully followed, he wished to prove that his choice was apt. In the thrust of these Scottish ballads, he found affinities with Hungarian folk poetry, even though the Scottish ballads were popularized by that other European trend which was so close to Ossianism, if not actually merged in it. Indeed, *Reliques of Ancient English Poetry,* collected by Thomas Percy, was here and there suspiciously similar to the cycle of poetry collected, translated and forged by Macpherson. Arany, whose new enthusiasm for Ossian I had already mentioned, familiarized himself with the ballads he subsequently took as his models from an anthology entitled *British Classical Authors,* which was published by L. Herrig in 1852, and of which "Ancient English Popular Ballads" constituted only one chapter. (pp. 68-75)

In his essays related to English literature, Arany was most interested in two subjects—the similarity in the way Hungarian literature developed and the cause of folk poetry collecting. However, he put the journals in his charge at the service of one more important cause.

Arany and his colleagues knew that while Hungarian poetry stood on a par with the best in the world, Hungarian literature lagged far behind in the drama and especially in the novel, the leading literary form of the age. These forms were finding the road to development in ways that Arany and those who professed the same principles, disapproved. Following French examples, in the drama such development favoured playing for effect, while in the novel, it went after adventurous-romantic or naturalistic trends. This explains the efforts of Arany and others to make the great Greek dramatists and especially Shakespeare the touchstones and the examples to emulate. Apart from Arany's devotion to Shakespeare, he also translated Sophocles and, with exemplary speed, though mainly for his own pleasure, he translated all of Aristophanes.

Arany, however, never wrote a novel and, since his early attempts at translating English novels were not successful, he translated none. Even when his work as editor forced him to translate short stories (from German), he chose Gogol's "The Overcoat", that masterpiece of realism which has had such a profound effect on all of European literature. This work was probably the touchstone for Arany's own idealized realism.

Arany knew where the novel was headed, writing in 1863, that "prose narrative has shed its fustian trappings. Instead of objectifying hair-raising adventures, fantastic surprises and theories, it seems to be on the best road to the representation of psychological states and of life—especially life in Hungary—as action. Why deny it, there is yet much that is superficial, timid in approach and without the proper depth of execution—a sure hand is yet lacking—but we can expect the direction itself to lead our narrative literature in the right direction."

Thus, through Arany's influence, the contemporary English novel came into prominence. He had read Dickens in English as a young man and later admired Dickens' social criticism and talent for organizing literary life. In Thackeray, Trollope, George Eliot, in Goldsmith and Sterne, too, he appreciated their complex authentic depiction of reality, the touch of the poet in them, and the humour and irony with which they confronted the hopelessness of man's condition.

One of the most personal and, at the same time, clearly social goals of Arany's great poems was to triumph over—or at least mitigate through the harmony of poetry—the insistent disharmony of life. It was, among other things, for such a resolution through harmony that Arany took as his guide English literature, and within it, certain English novelists, the more so as they furnished such fine examples for the depiction of special, real—Hungarian—themes. (pp. 76-7)

Dezső Keresztury, "János Arany and English Literature," in The New Hungarian Quarterly, *Vol. XXVI, No. 100, Winter, 1985, pp. 67-77.*

FURTHER READING

Cushing, G. F. Introduction to his *Hungarian Prose and Verse,* pp. xi-xxxv. London: Athlone Press, 1956.
　　Discusses some common themes in the Hungarian poetry of the politically unstable mid-nineteenth century, deciding that Arany "typified the mood of the time."

Czigány, Lóránt. "Post-Revolutionary Disillusionment." In his *The Oxford History of Hungarian Literature from the Earliest Times to the Present,* pp. 198-216. Oxford: Clarendon Press, 1984.
　　Traces Arany's career, with special attention given to the inspiration for, and thematic concerns of, the poet's ballads and epics.

Kerékgyártó, Elemér. "Toldi in Life and Legend." *The Hungarian Quarterly* VII, No. 2 (Autumn 1941): 355-65.
　　Suggests possible historical and mythological models for the Toldi of Arany's epic trilogy.

Kirkconnell, Watson. Introduction to his *The Magyar Muse: An Anthology of Hungarian Poetry, 1400-1932,* pp. 15-26. Winnipeg, Manitoba: Canadian Hungarian News, 1933.
　　Outlines the history of Hungarian literature from medieval times until the early twentieth century. In a brief passage, Kirkconnell deems Arany "Hungary's greatest master of the epic and the ballad."

———. "The Tapestry of Hungarian Literature." In his *World Literatures,* pp. 134-53. Pittsburgh: University of Pittsburgh Press, 1956.
　　Traces the history of, and influences upon, Hungarian literature from the tenth century until the early twentieth century, with commentary on Arany's *Buda halála.*

Reményi, Joseph. *Hungarian Literature.* Washington, D.C.: American Hungarian Federation, 1946, 48 p.

Concise overview of Hungarian literary history. Provides a brief discussion of Arany's achievements.

Tezla, Albert. "Authors from 1450 to 1945: Arany János." In his *Hungarian Authors: A Bibliographical Handbook,* pp. 36-52. Cambridge, Mass.: Belknap Press of Harvard University Press, 1970.
    Provides a brief biographical sketch of Arany and lists first editions of his works and major bibliographical, biographical, and critical studies of the author.

Pierre Jean de Béranger

1780-1857

French lyricist, poet, and autobiographer.

Béranger was the most popular French poet of the early nineteenth century. He wrote satirical light verse and new lyrics for traditional melodies, often on the subjects of democracy and the French Revolution.

Born in Paris, Béranger was neglected by his parents and grew up in his grandfather's care. He was greatly impressed by the French Revolution of 1789, and its ideals of liberty, equality, and fraternity are hallmarks of his later work. After serving for a short time as a printer's apprentice, he encountered a club of songwriters in a Paris tavern, and decided to pursue lyric writing as a profession. In 1804, he sent some of his work to Lucien Bonaparte, Napoleon's brother, and in this way established a patronage entitling him to a small annuity. Before any were published, his lyrics circulated throughout France in the form of handwritten copies. "Le roi d'Yvetot" (1913; "The King of Yvetot"), a ballad about a king whose "only work was pleasure," was widely recognized as a lighthearted jab at Napoleon, who at the time was leading France into battle with Russia, Prussia, Austria, and Great Britain. In 1815, Béranger published his first collection of lyrics, *Chansons morales et autres.* The Bourbon monarchy, restored to power after Napoleon's defeat in 1815, found Béranger's lyrics objectionable for their occasional bawdiness and irreverent attitude toward the Church. Charged with religious and moral outrage, he was sentenced to two separate prison terms, the first for three months after the publication of *Chansons* in 1821 and the second for nine months after the publication of *Chansons inédites* in 1828. Béranger retained the public's sympathy, however, and such prominent literary figures as Victor Hugo, Alexandre Dumas, and Charles Sainte-Beuve visited him in prison. Béranger wrote his most blatantly political songs to support the movement to drive the Bourbons out of France in 1830; Albert Thibaudet wrote, "No product of the mind contributed more than Béranger's songs to the destruction of the government of the Bourbons." Béranger was elected to political office in 1848, but declined to serve, preferring to continue as a songwriter. When he died in 1857, the government of Napoleon III, responding to overwhelming public sentiment, staged a magnificent funeral in his honor.

Béranger's nostalgia for the France of the Revolution underlies much of his verse, and his songs primarily address national concerns, including eulogies for war heroes, satires of the numerous regimes that ruled France during his lifetime, and celebrations of the peasantry. Wistful and sincere in emotion and simple in style, his songs appealed to all classes of French people, and in 1858 an *Atlantic Monthly* profile reported that France was "carrying him to the very borders of legend, and evidently preparing to canonize him one of the Saints in the calendar of the fu-

ture." Since his death, critics have acknowledged that Béranger's celebrity exceeded his talents, and as a consequence his work has received little attention. In France he is remembered as an important champion of republicanism.

PRINCIPAL WORKS

Chansons morales et autres (lyrics and poetry) 1815
Chansons (lyrics and poetry) 1821
Chansons nouvelles (lyrics and poetry) 1825
Chansons inédites (lyrics and poetry) 1828
Chansons nouvelles et dernières (lyrics and poetry) 1833
Oeuvres complètes. 4 vols. (lyrics and poetry) 1834
Songs of Béranger (lyrics and poetry) 1837
Lyrical Poems (lyrics and poetry) 1847
One Hundred Songs (lyrics and poetry) 1847

Béranger: Two Hundred of His Lyrical Poems (lyrics and poetry) 1850
Ma biographie (autobiography) 1857
  [*Memoirs of Béranger,* 1858]
Oeuvres posthumes, oeuvres complètes (lyrics and poetry) 1857
Correspondance de Béranger. 4 vols. (letters) 1860

The London Magazine (essay date 1828)

[*In the following essay, the critic views Béranger as a poet whose work has appeal for the general population and for the scholar as well.*]

Napoleon had been, a second time, expelled from the imperial throne; the allied armies were encamped in the middle of Paris; the Bourbons, protected by foreign bayonets, had returned to their capital, and marked their restoration by the bloody re-action of proscriptions and death. Ancient abuses were re-appearing; and pretensions the most odious or contemptible were loudly held out by the anti-national party, which had then possession of the two chambers. France was afflicted, even to consternation; but, restrained by the presence of an army of occupation, and by the sight of the scaffolds which, on every side, were prepared for patriotism, she repressed her complaints, and concealed even her sadness.

It was at this period—in these days of mourning and of dread, that an obscure citizen, formerly a 'reader' in a printing-office, who—as he says himself—in his song entitled **'Le vilain,'** owes to no distinction of nobility the De which precedes his name,—in a word, that De Beranger, then about thirty-five years old, seized his lyre and sang the reverses and misfortunes of his country. Up to that time, his songs had been only light and gay: they now became bold and severe. The poet abandoned the criticism of individual faults and follies, and became the interpreter of the griefs of his fellow-citizens—the organ of all national sentiments—the avenger of the public wrongs. It was no longer, as formerly, in the burning verses of **'La bacchante,'** or, as in the couplets of **'La grand'mère,'** voluptuousness which formed his inspiration. It was no longer against 'Les sénateurs muets de l'empire,' and *'les roitelets* de la fabrique de Napoléon,' that he aimed his humorous shafts. He had now become the apostle of liberty. Poor,—living only by a trifling clerk's place in the University,—he preferred poverty to the baseness of concealing the sentiments which burned within him. Excited, touched, made indignant by the sight of the evils suffered by his country, he poured tears and consolations upon the wounds of the victims—he showered satire and contumely upon the head of the oppressors. In **'Le vieux drapeau,'** he sang with enthusiasm the old triumphs of France—in **'Plus de politique,'** he bewailed her recent reverses—in the pieces entitled **'Louis XI,' 'Les révérend pères,'** '—**Halte là!—le chant de victoire des Ottomans,'** he brought the most overwhelming accusations against tyranny, fanaticism, arbitrary power—the shameful corruptions, the anti-social leagues, in a word all the atrocities which the policy of kings has brought into use to enslave their people. What a cry of profound indignation, mingled with contempt,

against the barbarous indifference of the kings of Christendom with regard to Greece, is there not in this chorus of victory, repeated, even six times, by the Ottoman barbarians!

> Exterminons une race invincible:
> Les rois Chrétiens ne la vengeront pas!

Sometimes De Beranger goes beyond the age in which he lives—as for instance, when he ridicules with so much wit, in **'La prisonnière et le chevalier,'** the boasted gallantry of the knights of old—when, in a piece truly lyrical, he presents to us the image of Louis XI., like a pale phantom, seeking a smile in the spectacle of the happiness of the villagers, and finding only fear:—

> Quand sur nos bords, on rit, on chante, ou aime,
> Louis se retient prisonnier,
> Il craint les grands, et le peuple, et Dieu même,
> Il craint surtout son héritier!

—or when, in **'Octavie,'** he recalls to that beauty whom ambition condemned to receive the caresses of Tiberius how tyranny withers and destroys all to which it comes near:—

> . . . . . sous la pourpre, on sent ton esclavage,
> Et, tu le sais, l'esclavage enlaidit.

—What knowledge of the human heart is there not in this threat, made to a woman! What vigour of pencil in the former quotation, in which four verses are sufficient for the poet's purpose—and the soul of the tyrant Louis XI stands unveiled before us!

All the best affections, every generous sentiment, respect for the laws of humanity—toleration, philosophy, veneration for a Supreme Being—the most sublime feelings of the soul, and the warmest pity for misfortune—all are conspicuous in the writings of De Beranger—and especially in **'Le Dieu des bonnes gens,' 'Les enfans de la France,' 'Le cinq Mai,'** and **'La bonne vieille.'** Sentiment, in its best sense—remembrances and hopes—the delicate niceties of feeling—and sublime love of country—make of this last piece a perfect composition, of which it has been said with truth, that there is no model in either ancient or modern literature. After the example of Tibullus, Parny had interrupted the transports of a happy passion to bewail the death of its object. Beranger, not less touching than the lover of Eleonora, addresses, as it were, his last wishes to his mistress. Still young and pretty, he makes her a kind and good old woman, who laments her friend:—

> Lorsque les yeux chercheront sous vos rides,
> Les traits charmans qui m'auront inspirés,
> Des doux récits les jeunes gens avides
> Diront: quel fut cet amant tant pleuré?
>   . . . . .
> On vous dira: savait-il être aimable?
> Et sans rougir vous direz: Je l'aimai.
> D'un trait méchant se montra-t-il coupable?
> Avec orgueil, vous répondrez: Jamais.

This mode of bringing oneself upon the stage is both ingenious and dramatic. It has, in this instance, enabled the poet to paint, without offence to modesty, his soul pure, and frank,—as he had already, in another song (**'Ma vocation'**) drawn the picture of his person—*laid, chétif, souff 'rant et rampant sous la chaine du plus modique em-*

ploi—without making a parade of vain candour. Beranger acts from impulse, from inspiration, above all from sentiment. Every time he speaks of himself, we are not content with forgiving him—we love him the more; and that because he talks of himself as he would talk of others—without false modesty, without timid periphrasis, without fear of exposing his weaknesses. There is not, however, any one of his songs which has himself for its sole subject: in all, even in that one in which he may be considered the most egotistical, we ever see him hastening to get beyond the narrow circle of personal things, and to bring back his ideas, as in the two last stanzas of **'La bonne vieille,'** upon the misfortunes of his country, and the hopes of immortality.

Beranger, like La Fontaine, pleases every class of readers. The million see in his songs only that which is on the surface; while men of elevated understanding and delicate taste find in them a thousand things unperceived by the multitude. His epigrammatic turns, his powers of satire, his criticisms of the old annals—his recollections of a man great by his fortune, his reverses, and even by the despotism which caused his ruin,—his sympathy with the people—the war he wages with all sorts of abuses—the destruction which he predicts to the Jesuits—in a word, all that he has, so to speak, of *tangible,* has caused the popularity of his songs. All France has sung, and sings still, **'Le Marquis de Carabas'**—a portrait full of spirit, and infinitely like, of the men of the *ancien régime,* and of their pretensions at once ridiculous and obsolete;—**'La vivandière,'** a creation new, and fit to eternize, from generation to generation, the memory and the glory of the French arms—**'Les missionnaires,'** a picture, full of piquancy, gaiety, and sense, of the propensities, the projects, and the habits of the sons of Loyola; **'Le cinq Mai,'** a noble tribute of sympathy to the man who joined two crowns, who gave the law to twenty nations, and who perished on a rock, forsaken. All these pieces, and a hundred others, are known by heart, repeated, and admired by the people. But others, such as **'Lafayette en Amérique,'** where republican ideas are happily mingled in the narrative of one of the finest events of modern times—**'Les esclaves gaulois,'** addressed to Manuel, after his infamous expulsion from the Chamber of Deputies, in which, under the veil of allegory, the poet reproaches his fellow-citizens with their cowardly submission to an oppressive government, and **'La sainte alliance des peuples'**—(of which we shall cite a stanza or two)—will never be thoroughly understood but by thinking minds, which can penetrate beyond the surfaces of things:—

> Oui, libre enfin, que le monde respire;
> Sur le passé jettez un voile épais.
> Semez vos chants aux accords de ma lyre,
> L'encens des arts doit briller pour la paix.
> L'espoir riant, au sein de l'abondance,
> Accueillera les doux fruits de l'hymen:
> Peuples, formez une sainte alliance,
> Et donnons nous la main!

De Beranger has opened in France a new branch of poetry. He is the real creator of the national-philosophical song, of which Rouget de Lisle, and M. J. Chenier, in the two master-pieces, the Marseillais hymn, and the *Chant du dé-*

part, had scarcely done more than reveal the existence. Without a rival in this first style, he is also without a superior in those which have been adorned by Parny and Collé, by Parnard and Desangiers.—"The elegant composition, the polished verses of Horace," says M. Tissot, in his essay on the poetry of Beranger,—"the brilliant descriptions of Propertius, the tender supplications of Tibullus, inspire us with very little interest for the fair ones whose chains they bore: no one envies the lovers of Pyrrha, of Cynthia, or of Nemesis. But the Lisette of Beranger, simple, tender, feeling, yet, at the same time, arch and mischievous, possesses a singular charm; we believe in the happiness of her poet. And then, how he speaks to her of love!—Now it is in the tone of Parny, proposing to Eleonora to come and dwell in the fields—now it is that of Voltaire in the Epistle des *Tu* et des *Vous;* and now one would say it was Chaulieu become more feeling, mingling the gaiety of an enlivened guest with political recollections, and afterwards humbly stooping the neck to the yoke presented by his mistress."

This last expression recalls to our memory the song entitled **'Ma république'**—a song full of grace and of originality, which contains, in a light shape, allusions to the greatest events of the age. . . . (pp. 173-76)

It has been said that Panard used to get drunk, and fall asleep at table: that wine and sleep gave him inspiration, and that if he were suddenly awakened, and asked for a song, he would pour forth lavishly the most charming verses, the offspring of the moment. Wine is not thus the mover of Beranger's genius. He declares, in his song entitled **'Les petits coups,'** that

> Il suffit d'un doigt de vin
> Pour réconforter l'espérance.

When Beranger sings the pleasures of the table, it is not in the *abandon* of drunkenness; it is far less from a taste for debauch than from the necessity to rescue himself from the sad and saddening thoughts with which the misfortunes of his country surround and torment him. Let us listen to his convivial philosophy, depicted in this strophe, which is comparable to all that Horace and Anacreon have done, the most elegant and delightful:—

> Du sommeil de la liberté
> Les rêves sont pénibles:
> Devenons insensibles
> Pour conserver notre gaîté.
> Quand tout succombe,
> Faible Colombe,
> Ma muse aussi sur des roses retombe,
> Lassé d'imiter l'aigle altier
> Elle reprend son doux métier:
> Bacchus m'appelle, et je rentre au quartier,
> Adieu donc, pauvre gloire!
> Deshéritons l'histoire;
> Venez, amours et versez nous à boire.

In all the songs of De Beranger, we recognise a man who feels what he writes—who understands what he is speaking of, and who speaks of it in a way to make it understood by every one. In some of his songs, passages have been pointed out which are not exempt from indelicacy. This is a blemish which we do not seek to excuse, because, before him, Molière and La Fontaine have given sad examples of the same fault. But it is very rare—and, excepting the song of **'La bacchante,'** which caused De Beranger to be accused before the tribunal of Correctional police, we could scarcely cite more than two or three, in which there is any real offence against propriety.

The songs of Beranger do not all deserve the title of *odes* which Benjamin Constant has given them. In several of them, there are faults of style, incorrect rhymes, inversions, and sometimes constraint of language. But these faults are not of a nature to become contagious—while the numberless beauties we find in Beranger may tend to produce them in others, and to fertilize the genius of his successors. No one has possessed, to the same extent with himself, that admirable art of creating a frame-work—a scene, a reality, and a reason—for his subject—of inventing an action, and rendering it in a dramatic manner. Thus, through all the careless gaiety which breaks out in the light and frivolous song, **'Les gueux,'** and in that entitled **'Le nouveau Diogène,'** we can trace that contemplative spirit, which while it makes us laugh at others, finds means of giving a lesson to those who really listen.

If Beranger had chosen to support men in power, he would, as well as several Academicians and others whom we could name, have obtained places, honours, and pensions. His first attempts at poetry procured him, in 1806, the protection of Lucien Buonaparte—the Lorenzo de Medicis of the family: but he would accept nothing from him—and sang the praises of his protector only after he had fallen into disgrace with Napoleon. During the hundred days, he was offered the lucrative office of Censor, which he refused. Deprived of his place of 1200 francs a year, in the Council of Public Instruction, M. Laffitte offered him one under him, with a large salary; but he refused this also, preferring, like the wolf in the fable, to be poor and lean, and to keep his neck free from the mark of the collar. Before the loss of his place, he wrote, as he has said, to amuse himself—now he writes for bread—and he lives free, independent, loved, esteemed, admired by all France, except the Jesuits and the Ultras. (pp. 177-78)

"Characters of Contemporary Foreign Authors and Statesmen: De Beranger," in The London Magazine, *n.s. Vol. 22, No. IV, September, 1828, pp. 173-78.*

Walter Bagehot   (essay date 1857)

[*Bagehot is regarded as one of the most versatile and influential authors of mid-Victorian England. In addition to literary criticism, he wrote several pioneering works in the fields of politics, sociology, and economics. As editor of the* London Economist, *he was instrumental in shaping the financial policy of his generation. Despite their diverse subject matter, Bagehot's works are unified by his emphasis on factual information and his interest in the personalities of literary figures, politicians, and economists. His works are also noted for their humorous tone, reflecting Bagehot's belief that "the knack in style is to write like a human being." Many modern commentators contend that it is partially because of the "readable" quality of his prose that Bagehot's writings, which were primarily composed as journalistic pieces, are still*

enjoyed today. In the following review of Oeuvres complètes, *Bagehot celebrates Béranger's poetry as an illumination of the French national character and compares his philosophy to that of Horace.*]

The invention of books has at least one great advantage. It has half-abolished one of the worst consequences of the diversity of languages. Literature enables nations to understand one another. Oral intercourse hardly does this. In English a distinguished foreigner says not what he thinks, but what he can. There is a certain intimate essence of national meaning which is as untranslatable as good poetry. Dry thoughts are cosmopolitan; but the delicate associations of language which express character, the traits of speech which mark the man, differ in every tongue, have not even cumbrous circumlocutions that are equivalent in another. National character is a deep thing—a shy thing; you cannot exhibit much of it to people who have a difficulty in understanding your language; you are in strange society, and you feel you will not be understood. 'Let an English gentleman,' writes Mr. Thackeray,

> who has dwelt two, four, or ten years in Paris, say at the end of any given period how much he knows of French society, how many French houses he has entered, and how many French friends he has made. Intimacy there is none; we see but the outsides of the people. Year by year we live in France, and grow grey and see no more. We play *écarté* with Monsieur de Trêfle every night; but what do we know of the heart of the man—of the inward ways, thoughts, and customs of Trêfle? We dance with Countess Flic-flac Tuesdays and Thursdays ever since the peace; and how far are we advanced in her acquaintance since we first twirled her round a room? We know her velvet gown and her diamonds; we know her smiles and her simpers and her rouge, but the real, rougeless, *intime* Flicflac we know not.

Even if our words did not stutter, as they do stutter on our tongue, she would not tell us what she is. Literature has half mended this. Books are exportable; the essence of national character lies flat on a printed page. Men of genius with the impulses of solitude produce works of art, whose words can be read and re-read and partially taken in by foreigners to whom they could never be uttered, the very thought of whose unsympathising faces would freeze them on the surface of the mind. Alexander Smith has accused poetical reviewers of beginning as far as possible from their subject. It may seem to some, though it is not so really, that we are exemplifying this saying in commencing as we have commenced an article on Béranger.

There are two kinds of poetry, which one may call poems of this world, and poems not of this world. We see a certain society on the earth held together by certain relations, performing certain acts, exhibiting certain phenomena, calling forth certain emotions. The millions of human beings who compose it have their various thoughts, feelings, and desires. They hate, act, and live. The social bond presses them closely together; and from their proximity new sentiments arise which are half superficial and do not touch the inmost soul, but which nevertheless are unspeakably important in the actual constitution of human nature, and work out their effects for good and for evil on the characters of those who are subjected to their influence. These sentiments of the world, as one may speak, differ from the more primitive impulses and emotions of our inner nature as the superficial phenomena of the material universe from what we fancy is its real essence. Passing hues, transient changes have their course before our eyes; a multiplex diorama is for ever displayed; underneath it all we fancy—such is the inevitable constitution of our thinking faculty—a primitive immovable essence, which is modified into all the ever-changing phenomena we see, which is the grey granite whereon they lie, the primary substance whose *débris* they all are. Just so from the original and primitive emotions of man, society—the evolving capacity of combined action—brings out desires which seem new, in a sense are new, which have no existence out of the society itself, are coloured by its customs at the moment, change with the fashions of the age. Such a principle is what we may call social gaiety: the love of combined amusement which all men feel and variously express, and which is to the higher faculties of the soul what a gay running stream is to the everlasting mountain, a light, altering element which beautifies while it modifies. Poetry does not shrink from expressing such feelings; on the contrary, their renovating cheerfulness blends appropriately with her inspiriting delight. Each age and each form of the stimulating imagination has a fashion of its own. Sir Walter sings in his modernised chivalry,

> Waken, lords and ladies gay,
> On the mountain dawns the day;
> All the jolly chase is here,
> With hawk and horse and hunting-spear.
> Hounds are in their couples yelling,
> Hawks are whistling, horns are knelling,
> Merrily, merrily, mingle they;
> Waken, lords and ladies gay.

> Louder, louder chant the lay,
> Waken, lords and ladies gay;
> Tell them youth and mirth and glee
> Run a course as well as we.
> Time, stern huntsman, who can balk?
> Stanch as hound and fleet as hawk;
> Think of this, and rise with day,
> Gentle lords and ladies gay.

The poet of the people, *'vilain et très vilain,'* sings with the pauper Bohemian,

> Voir c'est avoir. Allons courir!
> Vie errante
> Est chose enivrante.
> Voir c'est avoir. Allons courir!
> Car tout voir c'est tout conquérir.

> Nous n'avons donc exempts d'orgueil,
> De lois vaines,
> De lourdes chaines;
> Nous n'avons donc exempts d'orgueil,
> Ni berceau, ni toit, ni cercueil;

> Mais croyez-en notre gaîté,
> Noble ou prêtre,
> Valet ou maître;
> Mais, croyez-en notre gaîté,
> Le bonheur est la liberté.

> Oui, croyez-en notre gaîté,
> Noble ou prêtre,
> Valet ou maître;
> Oui, croyez-en notre gaîé,
> Le bonheur est la liberté.

The forms of these poems of social amusement are, in truth, as various as the social amusement itself. The variety of the world, singularly various as it everywhere is, is nowhere so various as in that. Men have more ways of amusing themselves than of doing anything else they do. But the essence—the characteristic—of these poems everywhere is, that they express more or less well the lighter desires of human nature;—those that have least of unspeakable depth, partake most of what is perishable and earthly, and least of the immortal soul. The objects of these desires are social accidents; excellent, perhaps, essential, possibly—so is human nature made—in one form and variety or another, to the well-being of the soul, yet in themselves transitory, fleeting, and in other moods contemptible. The old saying was, that to endure solitude a man must either be a beast or a god. It is in the lighter play of social action, in that which is neither animal nor divine, which in its half-way character is so natural to man, that these poems of society, which we have called poems of amusement, have their place.

This species does not, however, exhaust the whole class. Society gives rise to another sort of poems, differing from this one as contemplation differs from desire. Society may be thought of as an object. The varied scene of men,—their hopes, fears, anxieties, maxims, actions,—presents a sight more interesting to man than any other which has ever existed, or which can exist; and it may be viewed in all moods of mind, and with the change of inward emotion as the external object seems to change: not that it really does so, but that some sentiments are more favourable to clear-sightedness than others are; and some bring before us one aspect of the subject, and fix our attention upon it, others a different one, and bind our minds to that likewise. Among the most remarkable of these varied views is the world's view of itself. The world, such as it is, has made up its mind what it is. Childishly deceivable by charlatans on every other subject,—imposed on by pedantry, by new and unfounded science, by ancient and unfounded reputation, a prey to pomposity, overrun with recondite fools, ignorant of all else,—society knows itself. The world knows a man of the world. A certain tradition pervades it; a *disciplina* of the market-place teaches what the collective society of men has ever been, and what, so long as the nature of man is the same, it cannot and will not cease to be. Literature, the written expression of human nature in every variety, takes up this variety likewise. Ancient literature exhibits it from obvious causes in a more simple manner than modern literature can. Those who are brought up in times like the present, necessarily hear a different set of opinions, fall in with other words, are under the shadow of a higher creed. In consequence, they cannot have the simple *naïveté* of the old world; they cannot speak with easy equanimity of the fugitiveness of life, the necessity of death, of goodness as a mean, of sin as an extreme. The theory of the universe has ceased to be an open question. Still the spirit of Horace is alive, and as potent as that of any man. His tone is that of prime ministers; his easy philosophy is that of courts and parliaments; you may hear his words where no other foreign words are ever heard. He is but the extreme and perfect type of a whole class of writers, some of whom exist in every literary age, and who give an expression to what we may call the poetry of equanimity, that is, the world's view of itself; its self-satisfaction, its conviction that you must bear what comes, not hope for much, think *some* evil, never be excited, admire little, and then you will be at peace. This creed does not sound attractive in description. Nothing, it has been said, is so easy as to be 'religious on paper:' on the other hand, it is rather difficult to be worldly in speculation; the mind of man, when its daily maxims are put before it, revolts from anything so stupid, so mean, so poor. It requires a consummate art to reconcile men in print to that moderate and insidious philosophy which creeps into all hearts, colours all speech, influences all action. We may not stiffen common sense into a creed; our very ambition forbids:—

> It hears a voice within us tell
> Calm's not life's crown, though calm is well:
> 'Tis all perhaps which man acquires;
> But 'tis not what our youth desires.

Still a great artist may succeed in making 'calm' interesting. Equanimity has its place in literature; the poetry of equipoise is possible. Poems of society have, thus, two divisions: that which we mentioned first, the expression of the feelings which are called out by the accidents of society; next, the harmonised expression of that philosophy of indifference with which the world regards the fortunes of individuals and its own. (pp. 233-38)

'Though France herself denies,' says a recent writer, 'yet all other nations with one voice proclaim her inferiority to her rivals in poetry and romance, and in all the other elevated fields of fiction. A French Dante, or Michael Angelo, or Cervantes, or Murillo, or Goethe, or Shakespeare, or Milton, we at once perceive to be a mere anomaly; a supposition which may, indeed, be proposed in terms, but which in reality is inconceivable and impossible.' In metaphysics, the reason seems to be that the French character is incapable of being mastered by an unseen idea, without being so tyrannised over by it as to be incapable of artistic development. Such a character as Robespierre's may explain what we mean. His entire nature was taken up, and absorbed in certain ideas; he had almost a vanity in them; he was of them, and they were of him. But they appear in his mind, in his speeches, in his life, in their driest and barest form; they have no motion, life, or roundness. We are obliged to use many metaphors remotely and with difficulty to indicate the procedure of the imagination. In one of these metaphors we figure an idea of imagination as a living thing, a kind of growing plant, with a peculiar form, and ever preserving its identity, but absorbing from the earth and air all kindred, suitable, and, so to say, annexable materials. In a mind such as Robespierre's, in the type of the fanatic mind, there is no such thing. The ideas seem a kind of dry hard capsules, never growing, never enlarging, never uniting. Development is denied them; they cannot expand, or ripen, or mellow. Dogma is a dry hard husk; poetry has the soft down of the real fruit. Ideas seize on the fanatic mind just as they do on the poetical; they

have the same imperious ruling power. The difference is, that in the one the impelling force is immutable, iron, tyrannical; in the other the rule is expansive, growing, free, taking up from all around it moment by moment whatever is fit, as in the political world a great constitution arises through centuries, with a shape that does not vary, but with movement for its essence and the fluctuation of elements for its vitality. A thin poor mind like Robespierre's seems pressed and hampered by the bony fingers of a skeleton hand; a poet's is expanded and warmed at the same time that it is impelled by a pure life-blood of imagination. The French, as we have said, are hardly capable of this. When great remote ideas seize upon them at all, they become fanatics. The wild, chimerical revolutionary, mad Frenchman has the stiffest of human minds. He is under the law of his creed; he has not attained to the higher freedom of the impelling imagination. The prosing rhetoric of the French tragedy shows the same defect in another form. The ideas which should have become living realities, remain as lean abstractions. The characters are speaking officials, jets of attenuated oratory. But exactly on this very account the French mind has a genius for the poetry of society. Unable to remove itself into the higher region of imagined forms, it has the quickest detective insight into the exact relation of surrounding superficial phenomena. There are two ways of putting it: either, being fascinated by the present, they cannot rise to what is not present; or, being by defect of nature unable to rise to what is not present, they are concentrated and absorbed in that which is so. Of course there ought not to be, but there *is,* a world of *bonbons,* of *salons,* of *esprit.* Living in the present they have the poetry of the present. The English genius is just the opposite. Our cumbrous intellect has no call to light artificialities. We do not excel in punctuated detail or nicely-squared elaboration. It puts us out of patience that others should. A respectable Englishman murmured in the *Café de Paris,* 'I wish I had a hunch of mutton.' He could not bear the secondary niceties with which he was surrounded. Our art has the same principle. We excel in strong noble imagination, in solid stuff. Shakespeare is tough work; he has the play of the rising energy, the buoyant freedom of the unbounded mind; but no writer is so destitute of the simplifying dexterities of the manipulating intellect.

It is dangerous for a foreigner to give an opinion on minutiæ of style, especially on points affecting the characteristic excellencies of national style. The French language is always neat; all French styles somehow seem good. But Béranger appears to have a peculiar neatness. He tells us that all his songs are the production of a painful effort. If so, the reader should be most grateful; *he* suffers no pain. The delicate elaboration of the writer has given a singular currency to the words. Difficult writing is rarely easy reading. It can never be so when the labour is spent in piecing together elements not joined by an insensible touch of imagination. The highest praise is due to a writer whose ideas are more delicately connected by unconscious genius than other men's are, and yet who spends labour and toil in giving the production a yet cunninger finish, a still smoother connection. The characteristic aloofness of the Gothic mind, its tendency to devote itself to what is not present, is represented in composition by a want of care in the pettinesses of style. A certain clumsiness pervades all tongues of German origin. Instead of the language having been sharpened and improved by the constant keenness of attentive minds, it has been habitually used obtusely and crudely. Light loquacious Gaul has for ages been the contrast. If you take up a pen just used by a good writer, for a moment you seem to write rather well. A language long employed by a delicate and critical society is a treasure of dextrous felicities. It is not, according to the fine expression of Mr. Emerson, 'fossil poetry;' it is crystallised *esprit.*

A French critic has praised Béranger for having retained the *refrain,* or burden, *'la rime de l'air,'* as he calls it. Perhaps music is more necessary as an accompaniment to the poetry of society than it is to any other poetry. Without a sensuous reminder, we might forget that it was poetry; especially in a sparkling, glittering, attenuated language, we might be absorbed as in the defined elegances of prose. In half trivial compositions we easily forget the little central fancy. The music prevents this: it gives oneness to the parts, pieces together the shavings of the intellect, makes audible the flow of imagination. (pp. 242-45)

A certain intellectuality . . . pervades Béranger's love-songs. You seem to feel, to see, not merely the emotion, but the mind, in the background viewing that emotion. You are conscious of a considerateness qualifying and contrasting with the effervescing champagne of the feelings described. Desire is rarefied; sense half becomes an idea. You may trace a similar metamorphosis in the poetry of passion itself. If we contrast such a poem as Shelley's *Epipsychidion* with the natural language of common passion, we see how curiously the intellect can take its share in the dizziness of sense. In the same way, in the lightest poems of Béranger we feel that it may be infused, may interpenetrate the most buoyant effervescence.

Nothing is more odd than to contrast the luxurious and voluptuous nature of much of Béranger's poetry with the circumstances of his life. He never in all his productive time had more than 80*l.* a year; the smallest party of pleasure made him live, he tells us himself, most ascetically for a week; so far from leading the life of a Sybarite, his youth was one of anxiety and privation. A more worldly poet has probably never written, but no poet has shown in life so philosophic an estimate of this world's goods. His origin is very unaristocratic. He was born in August, 1780, at the house of his grandfather, a poor old tailor. Of his mother we hear nothing. His father was a speculative sanguine man, who never succeeded. His principal education was given him by an aunt, who taught him to read and to write, and perhaps generally incited his mind. His school-teaching tells of the philosophy of the revolutionary time. By way of primary school for the town of Péronne, a patriotic member of the National Assembly had founded an *institut d'enfants.* 'It offered,' we are told, 'at once the image of a club and that of a camp; the boys wore a military uniform; at every public event they named deputations, delivered orations, voted addresses: letters were written to the citizen Robespierre and the citizen Tallien.' Naturally amid so great affairs there was no time for mere grammar; they did not teach *Latin.* Nor did Béranger ever acquire

any knowledge of that language; and he may be said to be destitute of what is in the usual sense called culture. Accordingly it has in these days been made a matter of wonder by critics, whom we may think pedantic, that one so destitute should be able to produce such works. But a far keener judge has pronounced the contrary. Goethe, who certainly did not undervalue the most elaborate and artful cultivation, at once pronounced Béranger to have 'a nature most happily endowed, firmly grounded in himself, purely developed from himself, and quite in harmony with himself.' In fact, as these words mean, Béranger, by happiness of nature or self-attention, has that *centrality* of mind which is the really valuable result of colleges and teaching. He puts things together; he refers things to a principle; rather, they group themselves in his intelligence insensibly round a principle. There is nothing *distrait* in his genius; the man has attained to be himself; a cool oneness, a poised personality, pervades him. 'The unlearned,' it has been said, 'judge at random.' Béranger is not unlearned in this sense. There is no one who judges more simply, smoothly, and uniformly. His ideas refer to an exact measure. He has mastered what comes before him. And though doubtless unacquainted with foreign and incongruous literature, he has mastered his own literature, which was shaped by kindred persons, and has been the expression of analogous natures; and this has helped him in expressing himself.

In the same way, his poor youth and boyhood have given a reality to his productions. He seems to have had this in mind in praising the 'practical education which I have received.' He was bred a printer; and the highest post he attained was a clerkship at the university, worth, as has been said, 80*l.* per annum. Accordingly he has everywhere a sympathy with the common people, an unsought familiarity with them and their life. Sybarite poetry commonly wants this. The aristocratic nature is superficial; it relates to a life protected from simple wants, depending on luxurious artifices. 'Mamma,' said the simple-minded nobleman, 'when poor people have no bread, why do not they eat buns? they are much better.' An over-perfumed softness pervades the poetry of society. You see this in the songs of Moore, the best of the sort we have; all is beautiful, soft, half-sincere. There is a little falsetto in the tone, everything reminds you of the drawing-room and the *pianoforte;* and not only so—for all poetry of society must in a measure do this—but it seems fit for no other scene. Naturalness is the last word of praise that would be suitable. In the scented air we forget that there is a *pavé* and a multitude. Perhaps France is of all countries which have ever existed the one in which we might seek an exception from this luxurious limitation. A certain *égalité* may pervade its art as its society. There is no such difference as with us between the shoeblack and the gentleman. A certain refinement is very common; an extreme refinement possibly rare. Béranger was able to write his poems in poverty: they are popular with the poor.

A success even greater than what we have described as having been achieved by Béranger in the first class of the poems of society—that of amusement—has been attained by him in the second class, expressive of epicurean speculation. Perhaps it is one of his characteristics that the two are for ever running one into another. There is animation in his thinking, there is meaning in his gaiety. It requires no elaborate explanation to make evident the connection between scepticism and luxuriousness. Every one thinks of the Sadducee as in cool halls and soft robes; no one supposes that the Sybarite believes. Pain not only purifies the mind, but deepens the nature. A simple happy life is animal; it is pleasant, and it perishes. All writers who have devoted themselves to the explanation of this world's view of itself are necessarily in a certain measure Sadducees. The world is a Sadducee itself; it cannot be anything else without recognising a higher creed, a more binding law, a more solemn reality—without ceasing to be the world. Equanimity is incredulous; impartiality does not care; an indifferent politeness is sceptical. Though not a single speculative opinion is expressed, we may feel this in **'Roger Bontemps':**—

Roger Bontemps.

Aux gens atrabilaires
Pour exemple donné,
En un temps de misères
Roger Bontemps est né,
Vivre obscur à sa guise,
Narguer les mécontents;
Eh gai! c'est la devise
Du gros Roger Bontemps.

Du chapeau de son père
Coiffé dans les grands jours,
De roses ou de lierre
Le rajeunir toujours;
Mettre un manteau du bure,
Vieil ami de vingt ans;
Eh gai! c'est la parure
Du gros Roger Bontemps.

Posséder dans sa hutte
Une table, un vieux lit,
Des cartes, une flûte,
Un broc que Dieu remplit,
Un portrait de maîtresse,
Un coffre et rien dedans;
Eh gai! c'est la richesse
Du gros Roger Bontemps.

Aux enfans de la ville
Montrer de petits jeux;
Etre un faiser habile
De contes graveleux;
Ne parler que de danse
Et d'almanachs chantants;
Eh gai! c'est la science
Du gros Roger Bontemps.

Faute de vin d'élite,
Sabler ceux du canton;
Préférer Marguerite
Aux dames du grand ton;
De joie et de tendresse
Remplir tous ses instants;
Eh gai! c'est la sagesse
Du gros Roger Bontemps.

Dire au ciel: Je me fie,
Mon père, à ta bonté;
De ma philosophie
Pardonne la gaîté;

Que ma saison dernière
Soit encore un printemps;
Eh gai! c'est la prière
Du gros Roger Bontemps.

Vous, pauvres pleins d'envie,
Vous, riches désireux,
Vous, dont le char dévie
Après un cours heureux;
Vous, qui perdrez peut-être
Des titres éclatants,
Eh gai! prenez pour maître
Le gros Roger Bontemps.

At the same time, in Béranger the scepticism is not extreme. The skeleton is not paraded. That the world is a passing show, a painted scene, is admitted; you seem to know that it is all acting and rouge and illusion; still the pleasantness of the acting is dwelt on, the rouge is never rubbed off, the dream runs lightly and easily. No nightmare haunts you, you have no uneasy sense that you are about to awaken. Persons who require a sense of reality may complain; pain is perhaps necessary to sharpen their nerves, a tough effort to harden their consciousness: but if you pass by this objection of the threshold, if you admit the possibility of a superficial and fleeting world, you will not find a better one than Béranger's world. Suppose all the world were a *restaurant,* his is a good *restaurant;* admit that life is an effervescing champagne, his is the best for the moment.

In several respects Béranger contrasts with Horace, the poet whom in general he most resembles. The song of **'Roger Bontemps'** suggests one of the most obvious differences. It is essentially democratic. As we have said before, Béranger is the poet of the people; he himself says, *Le peuple c'est ma muse.* Throughout Horace's writings, however much he may speak, and speak justly, of the simplicity of his tastes, you are always conscious that his position is exceptional. Everybody cannot be the friend of Mæcenas; every cheerful man of the world cannot see the springs of the great world. The intellect of most self-indulgent men must satisfy itself with small indulgences. Without a hard ascent you can rarely see a great view. Horace had the almost unequalled felicity of watching the characters and thoughts and tendencies of the governors of the world; the nicest manipulation of the most ingenious statesmen; the inner tastes and predilections which are the origin of the most important transactions; and yet had the ease and pleasantness of common and effortless life. So rare a fortune cannot be a general model; the gospel of Epicureanism must not ask a close imitation of one who had such very special advantages. Béranger gives the acceptors of that creed a commoner type. Out of nothing but the most ordinary advantages—the garret, the almost empty purse, the not over-attired *grisette*—he has given them a model of the sparkling and quick existence for which their fancy is longing. You cannot imagine commoner materials. In another respect Horace and Béranger are remarkably contrasted. Béranger, sceptical and indifferent as he is, has a faith in, and zeal for, liberty. It seems odd that he should care for that sort of thing; but he does care for it. Horace probably had a little personal shame attaching to such ideas. No regimental officer of our own time can have 'joined' in a state of more crass ignorance than did the stout little student from Athens in all probability the army of Brutus; the legionaries must have taken the measure of him, as the sergeants of our living friends. Anyhow he was not partial to such reflections; zeal for political institutions is quite as foreign to him as any other zeal. A certain hope in the future is characteristic of Béranger—

> Qui découvrit un nouveau monde?
> Un fou qu'on raillait en tout lieu.

Modern faith colours even bystanding scepticism. Though probably with no very accurate ideas of the nature of liberty, Béranger believes that it is a great good, and that France will have it.

The point in which Béranger most resembles Horace is that which is the most essential in the characters of them both—their geniality. This is the very essence of the poems of society; it springs in the verses of amusement, it harmonises with acquiescing sympathy the poems of indifference. And yet few qualities in writing are so rare. A certain malevolence enters into literary ink; the point of the pen pricks. Pope is the very best example of this. With every desire to imitate Horace, he cannot touch any of his subjects, or any kindred subjects, without infusing a bitter ingredient. It is not given to the children of men to be philosophers without envy. Lookers-on can hardly bear the spectacle of the great world. If you watch the carriages rolling down to the House of Lords, you will try to depreciate the House of Lords. Idleness is cynical. Both Béranger and Horace are exceptions to this. Both enjoy the roll of the wheels; both love the glitter of the carriages; neither is angry at the sun. Each knows that he is as happy as he can be—that he is all that he can be in his contemplative philosophy. In his means of expression, for the purpose in hand, the Frenchman has the advantage. The Latin language is clumsy. Light pleasure was an exotic in the Roman world; the terms in which you strive to describe it, suit rather the shrill camp and the droning law-court. In English, as we hinted just now, we have this too. Business is in our words; a too heavy sense clogs our literature: even in a writer so apt as Pope at the *finesse* of words, you feel the solid Gothic roots impede him. It is difficult not to be cumbrous. The horse may be fleet and light, but the wheels are ponderous and the road goes heavily. Béranger certainly has not this difficulty; nobody ever denied that a Frenchman could be light, that the French language was adapted for levity.

When we ascribed an absence of bitterness and malevolence to Béranger, we were far from meaning that he is not a satirist. Every light writer in a measure must be so. Mirth is the imagery of society; and mirth must make fun of somebody. The nineteenth century has not had many shrewder critics than its easy natured poet. Its intense dullness particularly strikes him. He dreads the dreariness of the Academy; pomposity bores him; formalism tires him; he thinks, and may well think, it dreary to have

> Pour grands hommes des journalistes,
> Pour amusement l'Opéra.

But skilful as is the mirth, its spirit is genial and good-natured. 'You have been making fun of me, Sydney, for twenty years,' said a friend to the late Canon of St. Paul's, 'and I do not think you have said a single thing I should have wished you not to say.' So far as its essential features are concerned, the nineteenth century may say the same of its musical satirist. Perhaps, however, the Bourbons might a little object. Clever people have always a *little* malice against the stupid.

There is no more striking example of the degree in which the gospel of good works has penetrated our modern society, than that Béranger has talked of 'utilising his talent.' The epicurean poet considers that he has been a political missionary. Well may others be condemned to the penal servitude of industry, if the lightest and idlest of skilful men boasts of being subjected to it. If Béranger thinks it necessary to think he has been useful, others may well think so too; let us accept the heavy doctrine of hard labour; there is no other way to heave the rubbish of this world. The mode in which Béranger is anxious to prove that he made his genius of use is by diffusing a taste for liberty, and expressing an enthusiasm for it; and also, as we suppose, in quizzing those rulers of France who have not shared either the taste or the enthusiasm. Although, however, such may be the idea of the poet himself, posterity will scarcely confirm it. Political satire is the most ephemeral kind of literature. The circumstances to which it applies are local and temporary; the persons to whom it applies die. A very few months will make unintelligible what was at first strikingly plain. Béranger has illustrated this by an admission. There was a delay in publishing the last volume of his poems, many of which relate to the years or months immediately preceding the Revolution of 1830; the delay was not long, as the volume appeared in the first month of 1833, yet he says that many of the songs relate to the passing occurrences of a period *'déjà loin de nous.'* On so shifting a scene as that of French political life, the jests of each act are forgotten with the act itself; the eager interest of each moment withdraws the mind from thinking of or dwelling on anything past. And in all countries administration is ephemeral; what relates to it is transitory. Satires on its detail are like the jests of a public office; the clerks change, oblivion covers their peculiarities; the point of the joke is forgotten. There are some considerable exceptions to the saying that foreign literary opinion is a 'contemporary posterity'; but in relation to satires on transitory transactions it is exactly expressive. No Englishman will now care for many of Béranger's songs which were once in the mouths of all his countrymen, which coloured the manners of revolutions, perhaps influenced their course. The fame of a poet may have a reference to politics; but it will be only to the wider species, to those social questions which never die, the elements of that active human nature which is the same age after age. Béranger can hardly hope for this. Even the songs which relate to liberty can hardly hope for this immortality. They have the vagueness which has made French aspirations for freedom futile. So far as they express distinct feeling, their tendency is rather anti-aristocratic than in favour of simple real liberty. And an objection to mere rank, though a potent, is neither a very agreeable nor a very poetical sentiment. Moreover, when the love of liberty is to be imaginatively expressed, it requires to an Englishman's ear a sound bigger and more trumpet-tongued than the voice of Béranger.

On a deeper view, however, an attentive student will discover a great deal that is most instructive in the political career of the not very business-like poet. His life has been contemporaneous with the course of a great change; and throughout it the view which he has taken of the current events is that which sensible men took at the time, and which a sensible posterity (and these events will from their size attract attention enough to insure their being viewed sensibly) is likely to take. Béranger was present at the taking of the Bastille, but he was then only nine years old; the accuracy of opinion which we are claiming for him did not commence so early. His mature judgment begins with the career of Napoleon; and no one of the thousands who have written on that subject has viewed it perhaps more justly. He had no love for the despotism of the Empire, was alive to the harshness of its administration, did not care too much for its glory, must have felt more than once the social exhaustion. At the same time, no man was penetrated more profoundly, no literary man half so profoundly, with the popular admiration for the genius of the Empire. (pp. 249-58)

Although we are very far from thinking that Béranger's claims on posterity are founded on his having utilised his talent in favour of liberty, it is very natural that he should think or half-think himself that it is so. His power over the multitude must have given him great pleasure; it is something to be able to write mottoes for a revolution; to write words for people to use, and hear people use those words. The same sort of pleasure which Horace derived from his nearness to the centre of great action, Béranger has derived from the power which his thorough sympathy with his countrymen has given him over them. A political satire may be ephemeral from the rapid oblivion of its circumstances; but it is not unnatural that the author, inevitably proud of its effect, may consider it of higher worth than mere verses of society.

This shrewd sense gives a solidity to the verses of Béranger which the social and amusing sort of poetry commonly wants; but nothing can redeem it from the reproach of wanting *back* thought. This is inevitable in such literature; as it professes to delineate for us the light essence of a fugitive world, it cannot be expected to dwell on those deep and eternal principles on which that world is based. It ignores them as light talk ignores them. The most opposite thing to the poetry of society is the poetry of inspiration. There exists, of course, a kind of imagination which detects the secrets of the universe—which fills us sometimes with dread, sometimes with hope—which awakens the soul, which makes pure the feelings, which explains nature, reveals what is above nature, chastens 'the deep heart of man.' Our senses teach us what the world is; our intuitions where it is. We see the blue and gold of the world, its lively amusements, its gorgeous if superficial splendour, its currents of men; we feel its light spirits, we enjoy its happiness; we enjoy it, and we are puzzled. What is the object of all this? Why do we do all this? What is the universe *for?* Such a book as Béranger suggests this difficulty in its strongest form. It embodies the essence of all that

pleasure-loving, pleasure-giving, unaccountable world in which men spend their lives,—which they are compelled to live in, but which the moment you get out of it seems so odd that you can hardly believe it is real. On this account, as we were saying before, there is no book the impression of which varies so much in different moods of mind. Sometimes no reading is so pleasant; at others you half-despise the idea of it and half-hate; it seems to sum up and make clear the littleness of your own nature. Few can bear the theory of their amusements; it is essential to the pride of man to believe that he is industrious. We are irritated at literary laughter, and wroth at printed mirth. We turn angrily away to that higher poetry which gives the outline within which all these light colours are painted. From the capital of levity, and its self-amusing crowds; from the elastic *vaudeville* and the grinning actors; from *chansons* and *cafés* we turn away to the solemn nature, to the blue over-arching sky: the one remains, the many pass; no number of seasons impairs the bloom of those hues, they are as soft to-morrow as to-day. The immeasurable depth folds us in. 'Eternity,' as the original thinker said, 'is everlasting.' We breathe a deep breath. And perhaps we have higher moments. We comprehend the 'unintelligible world;' we see into 'the life of things;' we fancy we know whence we come and whither we go; words we have repeated for years have a meaning for the first time; texts of old Scripture seem to apply to *us* . . . . And—and—Mr. Thackeray would say, You come back into the town, and order dinner at a *restaurant,* and read Béranger once more. (pp. 263-64)

We may conclude as we began. In all his works, in lyrics of levity, of politics, of worldly reflection,—Béranger, if he had not a single object, has attained a uniform result. He has given us an idea of the essential French character, such as we fancy it must be, but can never for ourselves hope to see that it is. We understand the nice tact, the quick intelligence, the gay precision; the essence of the drama we know—the spirit of what we have seen. We know his feeling:

> J'aime qu'un Russe soit Russe,
> Et qu'un Anglais soit Anglais;
> Si l'on est Prussien en Prusse,
> En France soyons Français.

He has acted accordingly: he has delineated to us the essential Frenchman. (pp. 266-67)

> *Walter Bagehot, "Béranger (1857)," in his* Literary Studies, Vol. II, *1911. Reprint by E. P. Dutton & Co., 1927, pp. 233-67.*

The Atlantic Monthly   (essay date 1858)

[*In the following essay, the critic observes that Béranger's lyrics are inspired by patriotism, belief in equality, and opposition to religious hypocrisy.*]

Béranger is certainly the most popular poet there has ever been in France; there was convincing proof of it at the time of and after his death. He had not printed anything since 1833, the epoch when he published the last collection of his poems; when he died, then, on the 16th of July, 1857, he had been silent twenty-four years. He had, it is true, appeared for a moment in the National Assembly, after the Revolution of February, 1848; but it was only to withdraw again almost immediately and to resign his seat. In spite of this long silence and this retirement, in which he seemed a little forgotten, no sooner did the news of his last illness spread and it was known that his life was in danger, than the interest, or we should rather say the anxiety, of the public was awakened. In the ranks of the people, in the most humble classes of society, everybody began inquiring about him and asking day by day for news; his house was besieged by visitors; and as the danger increased, the crowd gathered, restless, as if listening for his last sigh. The government, in charging itself with his obsequies and declaring that his funeral should be celebrated at the cost of the State, may have been taking a wise precaution to prevent all pretext for disturbance; but it responded also to a public and popular sentiment. At sight of the honors paid to this simple poet, with as much distinction as if he had been a Marshal of France,—at sight of that extraordinary military pomp, (and in France military pomp is the great sign of respectability, and has its place whenever it is desired to bestow special honor,) no one among the laboring population was surprised, and it seemed to all that Béranger received only what was his due.

And since that time there has been in the French journals nothing but a succession of hymns to the memory of Béranger, hymns scarcely interrupted by now and then some cooler and soberer judgments. People have vied with each other in making known his good deeds done in secret, his gifts,—we will not call them alms,—for when he gave, he did not wish that it should have the character of alms, but of a generous, brotherly help. Numbers of his private letters have been printed; and one of his disciples has published recollections of his conversations, under the title of *Mémoires de Béranger.* The same disciple, once a simple artisan, a shoemaker, we believe, M. Savinien Lapointe, has also composed *Le petit évangile de la jeunesse de Béranger.* M. de Lamartine, in one of the numbers of his *Cours familier de littérature,* has devoted two hundred pages to an account of Béranger and a commentary on him, and has recalled curious conversations which he had with him in the most critical political circumstances of the Revolution of 1848. In short, there has been a rivalry in developing and amplifying the memory of the national songster, treating him as Socrates was once treated,— bringing up all his apophthegms, reproducing the dialogues in which he figured,—going even farther,— carrying him to the very borders of legend, and evidently preparing to canonize in him one of the Saints in the calendar of the future.

What is there solid in all this? How much is legitimate, and how much excessive? Béranger himself seems to have wished to reduce things to their right proportions, having left behind him ready for publication two volumes: one being a collection of his last poems and songs; the other an extended notice, detailing the decisive circumstances of his poetic and political life, and entitled *My Biography.*

The collection of his last songs, let us say it frankly, has not answered expectation. In reading them, we feel that the poet has grown old, that he is weary. He complains continually that he has no longer any voice,—that the tree is dead,—that even the echo of the woods answers only in prose,—that the source of song is dried up; and says, prettily,—

> If Time still make the clock run on,
> He makes it strike no longer.

And unhappily he is right. We find here and there pretty designs, short felicitous passages, smiling bits of nature; but obscurity, stiffness of expression, and the dragging in of Fancy by the hair continually mar the reading and take away all its charm. Even the pieces most highly lauded in advance, and which celebrate some of the most inspiring moments in the life of Napoleon,—such as his Baptism, his Horoscope cast by a Gypsy, and others,—have neither sparkle nor splendor. The prophet is not intoxicated, and wants enthusiasm. On the theme of Napoleon, Victor Hugo has done incomparably better; and as to the songs, properly so called, of this last collection, there are at this moment in France numerous song-writers (Pierre Dupont and Nadaud, for instance) who have the ease, the spirit, and the brilliancy of youth, and who would be able easily to triumph over this forced and difficult elevation of the Remains of Béranger, if one chose to institute a comparison. We may well say that youth is youth; to write verses, and especially songs, when one is old, is to wish still to dance, still to mount a curvetting horse; one gains no honor by the experiment. Anacreon, we know, succeeded; but in French, with rhyme and refrain, (that double butterfly-chase,) it seems to be more difficult.

But in prose, in the Autobiography, the entire Béranger, the Béranger of the best period, the man of wit, freshness, and sense, is found again; and it is pleasant to follow him in the story of his life, till now imperfectly known. He was born at Paris, on the 19th of August, 1780; and he glories in being a Parisian by birth, saying, that "Paris had not to wait for the great Revolution of 1789 to be the city of liberty and equality, the city where misfortune receives, perhaps, the most sympathy." He came into the world in the house of a tailor, his good old grandfather, in the Rue Montorgueil,—one of the noisiest of the Parisian streets, famous for its *restaurants* and the number of oysters consumed in them. "Seeing me born," he says, "in one of the dirtiest and noisiest streets, who would have thought that I should love the woods, fields, flowers, and birds so much?" It is true that Béranger loved them,—but he loved them always, as his poems show, like a Parisian and child of the Rue Montorgueil. A pretty enclosure, as many flowers and hedges as there are in the Closerie des Lilas, a little garden, a courtyard surrounded by apple-trees, a path winding beside wheat-fields,—these were enough for him. His Muse, we feel, has never journeyed, never soared, never beheld its first horizon in the Alps, the ocean, or the illimitable prairie. Lamartine, born in the country, amid all the wealth of the old rural and patriarchal life, had a right to oppose him, to put his own first instincts as poet in contrast with his, and to say to him, "I was born among shepherds; but you, you were born among citizens, among proletaries." Béranger loved the country as people love it on a Sunday at Paris, in walks just without the suburbs. How different from Burns, that other poet of the people, with whom he has sometimes been compared! But, on the other hand, Béranger loved the dweller in the city, the mechanic, the *ouvrier,* industrious, intellectual, full of enthusiasm and also of imprudence, passionate, with the heart of a soldier, and with free, adventurous ideas. He loved him even in his faults, aided him in his poverty, consoled him with his songs. Before all things he loved the street, and the street returned his love.

His father was a careless, dissipated man, who had tried many employments, and who strove to rise from the ranks of the people without having the means. His mother was a pretty woman, a dressmaker, and thorough *grisette,* whom his father married for her beauty, and who left her husband six months after their marriage and never gave a thought to her child. The little Béranger, born with difficulty and only with the aid of instruments, put out to nurse in the neighborhood of Auxerre, and forgotten for three years, was the object of no motherly cares. He may be said never to have had a mother. His Muse always showed traces of this privation of a mother's smile. The sentiment of home, of family, is not merely absent from his poems,—it is sometimes shocked by them.

Returning to his grandparents in Paris, and afterwards sent to a school in the Faubourg Saint-Antoine, where, on the 14th of July, 1789, he saw the Bastille taken, he pursued his primary studies very irregularly. He never learned Latin, a circumstance which always prejudiced him. Later in life, he sometimes blushed at not knowing it, and yet mentioned the fact so often as almost to make one believe he was proud of it. The truth is, that this want of classical training must have been felt more painfully by Béranger than it would have been by almost any other person; for Béranger was a studied poet, full of combinations, of allusion and artifice, even in his pleasantry,—a delicate poet, moreover, of the school of Boileau and Horace.

The *pension* in the Faubourg Saint-Antoine, even, was too much for the narrow means of his father. He was taken away and sent to Péronne, in Picardy, to an aunt who kept an inn in one of the suburbs, at the sign of the Royal Sword. It was while he was with this excellent person, who had a mind superior to her condition, that he began to form himself by the reading of good French authors. His intelligence was not less aroused by the spectacle of the events which were passing under his eyes. The Terror, the invasion by the armies of the Coalition, the roar of cannon, which could be heard at this frontier town, inspired him with a patriotism which was always predominant in him, and which at all decisive crises revived so strongly as even to silence and eclipse for the moment other cherished sentiments which were only less dear.

"This love of country," said he, emphatically, "was the great, I should say the only, passion of my life." It was this love which was his best inspiration as poet,—love of country, and with it of equality. Out of devotion to these great objects of his worship, he will even consent that the statue of Liberty be sometimes veiled, when there is a necessity for it. That France should be great and glorious, that she should not cease to be democratic, and to advance toward a democracy more and more equitable and favorable to all,—such were the aspirations and the programme of Béranger. He goes so far as to say that in his childhood he

had an aversion, almost a hatred, for Voltaire, on account of the insult to patriotism in his famous poem of *La pucelle;* and that afterwards, even while acknowledging all his admirable qualities and the services he rendered to the cause of humanity, he could acquire only a very faint taste for his writings. This is a striking singularity, if Béranger does not exaggerate it a little; it is almost an ingratitude,— for Voltaire is one of his nearest and most direct masters.

There is, indeed, a third passion which disputes with those for country and equality the heart of Béranger, and which he shares fully with Voltaire,—the hatred, namely, we will not say of Christianity, but of religious hypocrisy, of Jesuitic Tartuffery. What Voltaire did in innumerable pamphlets, *facetiœ,* and philosophic diatribes, Béranger did in songs. He gave a refrain, and with it popular currency to the anti-clerical attacks and mockeries of Voltaire; he set them to his violin and made them sing with the horsehair of his bow. Béranger was in this respect only the minstrel of Voltaire.

Bold songs against hypocrites, the Reverend Fathers and the Tartuffes, so much in favor under the Restoration, and some which carry the attack yet higher, and which sparkle with the very spirit of buffoonery, like **"Le bâtard du pape"**; beautiful patriotic songs, like **"Le vieux drapeau"**; and beautiful songs of humanity and equality, like **"Le vieux vagabond"**;—these are the three chief branches which unite and intertwine to make the poetic crown of Béranger in his best days, and they had their root in passions which with him were profound and living,—hatred of superstition, love of country, love of humanity and equality.

His aunt at Péronne was superstitious, and during thunder-storms had recourse to all kinds of expedients, such as signs of the cross, holy-water, and the like. One day the lightning struck near the house and knocked down young Béranger, who was standing on the door-step. He was insensible for some time, and they thought him killed. His first words, on recovering consciousness, were, "Well, what good did your holy-water do?"

At Péronne he finished his very irregular course of study at a kind of primary school founded by a philanthropic citizen. During the Directory, attempts were made all over France to get up free institutions for the young, on plans more or less reasonable or absurd, by men who had fed upon Rousseau's *Émile* and invented variations upon his system. On leaving school, Béranger was placed with a printer in the city, where he became a journeyman printer and compositor, which has occasioned his being often compared to Franklin,—a comparison of which he is not unworthy, in his love for the progress of the human race, and the piquant and ingenious turn he knew how to give to good sense. From this first employment as printer Béranger acquired and retained great nicety in language and grammar. He insisted on it, in his counsels to the young, more than seems natural in a poet of the people. He even exaggerated its importance somewhat, and might seem a purist.

Béranger's father reappeared suddenly during the Directory and reclaimed his son, whom he carried to Paris. The father had formed connections in Brittany with the royalists. He had become steward of the household of the Countess of Bourmont, mother of the famous Bourmont who was afterwards Marshal of France and Minister of War. Bourmont himself, then young, was living in Paris, in order the better to conspire for the restoration of the Bourbons. The elder Béranger was neck-deep in these intrigues, and was even prosecuted after the discovery of one of the numerous conspiracies of the day, but acquitted for want of proof. He was the banker and money-broker of the party,—a wretched banker enough! The narrative of the son enables us to see what a miserable business the father was engaged in. This near view of political intriguers, of royalists driven to all manner of expedients and standing at bay, of adventurers who did not shrink from the use of any means, not even the infernal-machine, did not dispose the young man already imbued with republican sentiments to change them, and this initiation into the secrets of the party was not likely to inspire him with much respect for the future Restoration. He had too early seen men and things behind the scenes. His father, in consequence of his swindling transactions, made a bankruptcy, which reduced the son to poverty and filled him with grief and shame.

He was now twenty years old; he had courage and hope, and he already wrote verses on all sorts of subjects,— serious, religious, epic, and tragic. One day, when he was in especial distress, he made up a little packet of his best verses and sent them to Lucien Bonaparte, with a letter, in which he set forth his unhappy situation. Lucien loved literature, and piqued himself on being author and poet. He was pleased with the attempts of the young man, and made him a present of the salary of a thousand or twelve hundred francs to which he was entitled as member of the Institute. It was Béranger's first step out of the poverty in which he had been plunged for several years, and he was indebted for the benefit to a Bonaparte, and to the most republican Bonaparte of the family. He was always especially grateful for it to Lucien, and somewhat to the Bonapartes in general.

Receiving a small appointment in the bureau of the University through the intervention of the Academician Arnault, a friend of Lucien Bonaparte, Béranger lived gayly during the last six years of the Empire. He managed to escape the conscription, and never shouldered a musket. He reserved himself to sing of military glory at a later day, but had no desire to share in it as soldier. He was elected into a singing club called *The Cellar,* all of whose members were songwriters and good fellows, presided over by Désaugiers, the lord of misrule and of jolly minstrels. Béranger, after his admission to the *Caveau,* at first contended with Désaugiers in his own style, but already a ground of seriousness and thought showed through his gayety. He wrote at this time his celebrated song of the **"Roi d'Yvetot,"** in which, while he caricatured the little playking, the king in the cotton nightcap, he seemed to be slyly satirizing the great conquering Emperor himself.

The Empire fell, and Béranger hesitated for some time to take part against the Bourbons. It was not till after the battle of Waterloo and the return of Louis XVIII. under con-voy of the allied armies, that he began to feel the passion of patriotism blaze up anew within him and dictate stinging songs which soon became darts of steel. Meanwhile he wrote pretty songs, in which a slight sentiment of melancholy mingled with and heightened the intoxication of wine and pleasure. **"La bonne vieille"** is his *chef-d'œuvre* in this style. He arranged the design of these little pieces carefully, sketching his subjects beforehand, and herein belongs to the French school, that old classic school which left nothing to chance. He composed his couplets slowly, even those which seem the most easy. Commonly the song came to him through the refrain;—he caught the butterfly by the wings;—when he had seized the refrain, he finished at intervals, and put in the nicer shadings at leisure. He wrote hardly ten songs a year at the time of his greatest fecundity. It has since been remarked that they smell of the lamp here and there; but at first no one had eyes except for the rose, the vine, and the laurel.

The Bourbons, brought back for the second time in 1815, committed all manner of blunders: they insulted the remains of the old *grande armée;* they shot Marshal Ney and many others; a horrible royalist reaction ensanguined the South of France. The Jesuit party insinuated itself at Court, and assumed to govern as in the high times of the confessors of Louis XIV. It was hoped to conquer the spirit of the Revolution, and to drive modern France back to the days before 1789; hence thousands of hateful things impossible to be realized, and thousands of ridiculous ones. Towards 1820 the liberal opposition organized itself in the Chambers and in the press. The Muse of Béranger came to its assistance under the mask of gay raillery. He was the angry bee that stung flying, and whose stings are not harmless; nay, he would fain have made them mortal to the enemy. He hated even Louis XVIII., a king who was esteemed tolerably wise, and more intelligent than his party. "I stick my pins," said Béranger, "into the calves of Louis XVIII." One must have seen the fat king in smallclothes, his legs as big as posts and round as pin-cushions, to appreciate all the point of the epigram.

Béranger had been very intimate since 1815 with the Deputy Manuel, a man of sense and courage, but very hostile to the Bourbons, and who, for words spoken from the Tribune, was expelled from the Chamber of Deputies and declared incapable of reëlection. Though intimate with many influential members of the opposition, such as Laffitte the banker, and General Sebastiani, it was only with Manuel that Béranger perfectly agreed. It is by his side, in the same tomb, that he now reposes in Père la Chaise, and after the death of Manuel he always slept on the mattress upon which his friend had breathed his last. Manuel and Béranger were ultra-inimical to the Restoration. They believed that it was irreconcilable with the modern spirit of France, with the common sense of the new form of society, and they accordingly did their best to goad and irritate it, never giving it any quarter. At certain times, other opposition deputies, such as General Foy, would have advised a more prudent course, which would not have rendered the Bourbons impossible by attacking them so fiercely as to push them to extremes. However this might have been, poetry is always more at home in excess than in moderation. Béranger was all the more a poet at this period, that he was more impassioned. The Bourbons and the Jesuits, his two most violent antipathies, served him well, and made him write his best and most spirited songs. Hence his great success. The people, who never perceive nice shades of opinion, but love and hate absolutely, at once adopted Béranger as the singer of its loves and hatreds, the avenger of the old army, of national glory and freedom, and the inaugurator or prophet of the future. The spirit prisoned in these little couplets, these tiny bodies, is of amazing force, and has, one might almost say, a devilish audacity. In larger compositions, breath would doubtless have failed the poet,—the greater space would have been an injury to him. Even in songs he has a constrained air sometimes, but this constraint gave him more force. He produces the impression of superiority to his class.

Béranger had given up his little post at the University before declaring open war against the government. He was before long indicted, and in 1822 condemned to several months' imprisonment, for having scandalized the throne and the altar. His popularity became at once boundless; he was sensible of it, and enjoyed it. "They are going to indict your songs," said some one to him. "So much the better!" he replied,—"that will gilt-edge them." He thought so well of this *gilding,* that in 1828, during the ministry of M. Martignac, a very moderate man and of a conciliatory semi-liberalism, he found means to get indicted again and to undergo a new condemnation, by attacks which some even of his friends then thought untimely. Once again Béranger was impassioned; he declared his enemies incurable and incorrigible; and soon came the ordinances of July, 1830, and the Revolution in their train, to prove him right.

In 1830, at the moment when the Revolution took place, the popularity of Béranger was at its height. His opinion was much deferred to in the course taken during and after "the three great days." The intimate friend of most of the chiefs of the opposition who were now in power, of great influence with the young, and trusted by the people, it was essential that he should not oppose the plan of making the Duke of Orleans King. Béranger, in his Biography, speaks modestly of his part in these movements. In his conversations he attributed a great deal to himself. He loved to describe himself in the midst of the people who surrounded the Hôtel of M. Laffitte, going and coming, listening to each, consulted by all, and continually sent for by Laffitte, who was confined to his armchair by a swollen foot. Seeing the hesitation prolonged, he whispered in Laffitte's ear that it was time to decide, for, if they did not take the Duke of Orleans for King pretty soon, the Revolution was in danger of turning out an *émeute.* He gave this advice simply as a patriot, for he was not of the Orleans party. When he came out, his younger friends, the republicans, reproached him; but he replied, "It is not a king I want, but only a plank to get over the stream." He set the first example of disrespect for the plank he thought so useful; indeed, the comparison itself is rather a contemptuous one.

He afterwards behaved, however, with great sense and wisdom. He declined all offices and honors, considering his part as political songster at an end. In 1833 he published a collection in which were remarked some songs of a higher order, less partisan, and in which he foreshadowed a broader and more peaceful democracy. After this he was silent, and as he was continually visited and consulted, he resolved upon leaving Paris for some years, in order to escape this annoyance. He went first to the neighborhood of Tours, and then to Fontainebleau; but the free, conversational life of Paris was too dear to him, and he returned to live in seclusion, though always much visited by his troops of friends, and much sought after. In leaving Paris during the first years of Louis Philippe's reign, and *closing,* as he called it, *his consulting office,* his chief aim was to escape the questions, solicitations, and confidences of opposite parties, in all of which he continued to have many friends who would gladly have brought him over to their way of thinking. He did not wish to be any longer what he had been so much,—a consulting politician; but he did not cease to be a practical philosopher with a crowd of disciples, and a consulting democrat. Chateaubriand, Lamennais, Lamartine,—the chiefs of parties at first totally opposed to his own,—came to seek his friendship, and loved to repose and refresh themselves in his conversation. He enjoyed, a little mischievously, seeing one of them (Chateaubriand) lay aside his royalism, another (Lamennais) abjure his Catholicism, and the third (Lamartine) forget his former aristocracy, in visiting him. He looked upon this, and justly, as a homage paid to the manners and spirit of the age, of which he was the humble but inflexible representative.

When the Revolution of 1848 burst unexpectedly, he was not charmed with it,—nay, it made him even a little sad. Less a republican than a patriot, he saw immense danger for France, as he knew her, in the establishment of the pure republican form. He was of opinion that it was necessary to wear out the monarchy little by little,—that with time and patience it would fall of itself; but he had to do with an impatient people, and he lamented it. "We had a ladder to go down by," said he, "and here we are jumping out of the window!" It was the same sentiment of patriotism, mingled with a certain almost mystical enthusiasm for the great personality of Napoleon, nourished and augmented with growing years, which made him accept the events of 1851-2 and the new Empire.

The religion of Béranger, which was so anti-Catholic, and which seems even to have dispensed with Christianity, reduced itself to a vague Deism, which in principle had too much the air of a pleasantry. His *Dieu des bonnes gens,* which he opposed to the God of the congregation and the preachers, could not be taken seriously by any one. Nevertheless, the poet, as he grew older, grew more and more attached to this symbol of a Deity, indulgent before all else, but very real and living, and in whom the poor and the suffering could put their trust. What passed in the days preceding his death has been much discussed, and many stories are told about it. He received, in fact, some visits from the curate of the parish of Saint Elizabeth, in which he lived. This curate had formerly officiated at Passy,—a little village near Paris, where Béranger had resided,—and was already acquainted with the poet. The conversations at these visits, according to the testimony of those best in-

formed, amounted to very little; and the last time the curate came, just as he was going out, Béranger, already
dying, said to him, "Your profession gives you the right
to bless me; I also bless you;—pray for me, and for all the
unfortunate!" The priest and the old man exchanged blessings,—the benedictions of two honest men, and nothing
more.

Béranger had one rare quality, and it was fundamental
with him,—obligingness, readiness to perform kind offices, humanity carried to the extent of Charity. He loved
to busy himself for others. To some one who said that time
lay heavy on his hands, he answered, "Then you have
never occupied yourself about other people?" "Take more
thought of others than of yourself" was his maxim. And
he did so occupy himself,—not out of curiosity, but to aid,
to succor with advice and with deeds. His time belonged
to everybody,—to the humblest, the poorest, the first
stranger who addressed him and told him his sorrows. Out
of a very small income (at most, four or five thousand
francs a year) he found means to give much. He loved,
above all, to assist poor artisans, men of the people, who
appealed to him; and he did it always without wounding
the fibre of manhood in them. He loved everything that
wore a blouse. He had, even stronger than the love of liberty, the love of equality, the great passion of the French.

He spent the last years of his life with an old friend of his
youth by the name of Madame Judith. This worthy person
died a few months before him, and he accompanied her
remains to the church. He was seventy-seven years old
when he died.

Estimating and comparing chiefly literary and poetic merits, some persons in France have been astonished that the
obsequies of Béranger should have been so magnificently
celebrated, while, but a few months before, the coffin of
another poet, M. Alfred de Musset, had been followed by
a mere handful of mourners; yet M. de Musset was capable of tones and flights which in inspiration and ardor surpassed the habitual range of Béranger. Without attempting here to institute a comparison, there is one thing essential to be remarked: in Béranger there was not only a poet,
but a man, and the man in him was more considerable
than the poet,—the reverse of what is the case with so
many others. People went to see him, after having heard
his songs sung, to tell him how much they had been applauded and enjoyed,—and, after the first compliments,
found that the poet was a man of sense, a good talker on
all subjects, interested in politics, a wonderful reasoner,
with great knowledge of men, and characterizing them
delicately with a few fine and happy touches. They became
sincerely attached to him; they came again, and delighted
to draw out in talk that wisdom armed with epigram, that
experience full of agreeable counsels. His passions had
been the talent of the poet; his good sense gave authority
to the man. Even by those least willing to accept popular
idols, Béranger will always be ranked as one of the subtil-
est wits of the French school, and as something more than
this,—as one of the acutest servants of free human
thought. (pp. 469-76)

"Béranger," in The Atlantic Monthly, *Vol. I,
No. IV, February, 1858, pp. 469-76.*

Maximilian J. Rudwin   (essay date 1924)

*[In the following excerpt, Rudwin analyzes Béranger's
attitude toward the devil in his songs "La descente aux
enfers," "Le bon diable," "La mort du diable," and
"L'ange exile."]*

The man who first said a good word for the Devil in the
nineteenth century did not belong to the Romantic school.
A greater révolté than the Romantics, Jean Pierre de Béranger (1780-1857) had to be attracted to the great Rebel.
But in contradistinction to his Romantic contemporaries,
our song-writer, who was nurtured in the teachings of the
eighteenth century, continued the Classical tradition in his
dealings with the Devil. He treated Satan in a humorous
vein and used him mainly as a medium for satire. The sati-
rists have at all times employed the prosecuting attorney
at the celestial court extensively in their sarcasms, whether on politics, religion or domestic affairs; and, as was the
case of William Hogarth, this practice often recoiled on
their own heads.

It is known that Béranger believed neither in the Devil nor
in Hell. As a matter of fact, his belief in a benevolent Deity
may also be called into question. He remained an unbeliever to the end of his days. Upon reading Chateaubriand's
Génie du Christianisme (1802), he made in his twenties a
grand but fruitless effort to become orthodox in his faith.
The exertions on the part of his sister, a nun, to convert
him to Catholicism during the last years of his life, proved
just as unsuccessful. Certain it is that he did not believe
in a Devil external to man and in a Hell as a geographical
unit. In a very characteristic fragment, entitled **"Enfer et
diable,"** and written between 1847 and 1851, our author
teaches the important if not orthodox lesson that every
human being is his own devil and the maker of his own
hell:

> Sachez que chacun est son Diable
> Que chacun se fait son Enfer.

[Know that everyone is his own devil and that everyone
makes his own hell.]

The Persian poet has expressed the same idea in the following couplet:

> I sent my soul into the invisible.
> Some letter of the after-life to spell.
> By and by my soul returned and answered.
> "I, myself, am heaven and hell."

"Vous n'avez pas des idées justes de notre enfer," complains LeSage's Asmodeus. In [**"La descente aux enfers"**]
impiously named after the *Descensus Christi ad Inferos*
(3rd cent.), we find Béranger's vindication of the Devil
and Hell. Our ballad-maker descends to the domain of the
Devil on a broomstick in company with a modern witch,
a young and beautiful woman. As the imps of Hell lack
no appreciation of beauty, they come in swarms to kiss her
naked feet. The netherworld, according to our author, is
not what the lying priests have always described it to be.
They used the fear of Hell as a means of driving men into
the Church. The underworld resembles more a voluptuous
Turkish harem than a vaporous Turkish bath. The court
of the King-Devil cannot be surpassed in luxury by that

of any earthly ruler. Our visitor to the infernal regions found no traces of kettles or flames and heard there no howling or gnashing of teeth. On the other hand, he found the floor strewn with oyster shells and empty bottles. The souls who are fortunate enough to go to Hell, eat and drink and make merry. Nothing is less frightful than the sight of Satan. The infernal monarch is a devil of a good fellow *chez lui*. He issues his severest decrees to the clinking of glasses and the playing of reed-pipes. His infernal majesty is a very genial host and entertains his guests royally. The spiritus infernali is surrounded at the banquet table by a crowd of red-faced drinkers, for whom he keeps pouring bourgogne and champaign. There is not much decorum in the halls of Hell. Ixion is sleeping on the shoulder of Tantalus who is dead drunk, and Epicurus is making love to Ninon de Lenclos. After reading this poem, one is inclined to exclaim with St. Paul: "O death, where is thy sting? O grave, where is thy victory?" The author himself draws a lesson from his words:

> Si, d'après ce qu'on rapporte.
> On bâille au céleste lieu,
> Que le diable nous emporte,
> Et nous rendrons grâce à Dieu.

Béranger's "bon Dieu" is not much different from his "bon Diable." In ["**Le bon Dieu**"] we find the conception of a God, who, in a similar way, eats and drinks, sleeps and swears. This indulgent, even negligent God suffers his arch-enemy the Devil to play havoc with his world and laughs when he hears that our kings claim to represent him on this earth. The monarch of the Heavens amuses himself in his gay moments by passing in review the proceedings of popes and princes in this world—qu'on prétend que je gouverne; and each of his reflections ends in the exclamation:

> Si c'est par moi qu'ils règnent de la sorte.
> Je veux bien que le diable m'emporte.

The Byronic Devil is nearer the truth when he exclaims in *The Vision of Judgment* (1822): "I've kings enough below, God knows!"

["**La mort du diable**"] is a satirical song directed against the Jesuits. Béranger was always poking fun at the priests. Even the Pontiff in the Vatican was not spared by his bold and boisterous satire. In Voltairean fashion he laughed Old Mother Church to scorn. For mere humor, this poem is almost unrivalled. It figured prominently among the poems selected as a basis for Béranger's indictment. The piece was denounced by the priests as irreligious and blasphemous, and its author was declared an enemy to religion. To this day, Béranger is believed by the Catholics to have been diabolically disposed. The archbishop of Paris and the other bishops hurled their anathemas in pastoral letters against our poet.

In "**La mort du diable**," Béranger gives the old legend of the death of the Devil a new and novel turn. He is not concerned with the demise of the high and mighty personage but with the events following it. The song is a satirical attack against Satan's supposed successors. The monks and priests wail when the news of the Devil's death reaches them. The reason is not that they loved Lucifer so well.

What worries these good men is the fact that they have lost with his death their means of a livelihood. The Devil being dead, what man will now pay them to be delivered from his clutches? But Ignatius Loyola, the founder of the order of the Jesuits, bids them to stop their wailing. He himself now intends to succeed to the power of the prince of this world; and in order to be delivered from him, men will now pray and pay more than ever before. The reader would like to hear the poem in Béranger's own words. It is not so easy to give in a few excerpts an idea of the delicious humor and irony which this poem contains. We shall give it then in full first in the original and then in the first English translation.

> Du miracle que je retrace
> Dans ce récit des plus succincts
> Rendez gloire au grand saint Ignace,
> Patron de tous nos petits saints.
> Par un tour qui serait infâme
> Si les saints pouvaient avoir tort.
> Au diable il a fait rendre l'âme.
> Le Diable est mort, le diable est mort.
>
> Satan, l'ayant surpris à table.
> Lui dit: Trinquons, ou sois honni.
> L'autre accepte, mais verse au diable,
> Dans son vin, un poison béni.
> Satan boit, et, pris de colique.
> Il jure, il grimace, il se tord;
> Il crève comme un hérétique.
> Le Diable est mort, le diable est mort.
>
> Il est mort! disent tous les moines;
> On n'achètera plus *d'agnus*.
> Il est mort! disent les chanoines;
> On ne paiera plus *d'oremus*.
> Au conclave on se désespère:
> Adieu puissance et coffre-fort!
> Le Diable est mort, le diable est mort.
>
> L'Amour sert bien moins que la crainte;
> Elle nous comblait de ses dons.
> L'intolérance est presque éteinte;
> Qui rallumera ses brandons?
> A notre joug si l'homme échappe.
> La Vérité luira d'abord:
> Dieu sera plus grand que le pape.
> Le Diable est mort, le diable est mort.
>
> Ignace accourt: Que l'on me donne,
> Leur dit-il, sa place et ses droits.
> Il n'épouvantait plus personne;
> Je ferai trembler jusqu'aux rois.
> Vols, massacres, guerres ou pestes.
> M'enrichiront du sud au nord.
> Dieu ne vivra que de mes restes.
> Le Diable est mort, le diable est mort.
>
> Tous de s'écrier: Ah! brave homme!
> Nous te bénissons dans ton fiel.
> Soudain son ordre, appui de Rome.
> Voit sa robe effrayer le ciel.
> Un choeur d'anges, l'âme contrite.
> Dit: Des humains plaignons le sort;
> De l'enfer saint Ignace hérite.
> Le Diable est mort, le diable est mort.
>
> [I sing today a lay of lays,
> A glorious miracle you'll see,

Give the great saint Ignatius praise,
Of little saints the glory he.
A dirty trick—if saints can trick,
And if the truth may all be said,
Has done the business for Old Nick,
The Devil's dead—the Devil's dead!

Old Nick went out one day to dine,
And pledg'd the saint to drink his health,
Aye, said the saint—and in the wine
Some holy poison dropp'd by stealth;
Gripes seiz'd the Devil—cruel-sick—
He swears—he storms—and hangs his head,
Then bursts, as bursts a heretic—
The Devil's dead—the Devil's dead!

Alas! He's dead—the friars said,
The Devil an Agnus shall we sell:
Alas! the canons cried—he's dead—
Not one *oremus* shall we tell.
The conclave is in deep despair,
Power and the iron chest are fled,
O we have lost our father dear,
The Devil's dead—the Devil's dead!

Love is not half so strong as fear,
For fear was constant with her gifts.
Who now her blazing torch uplifts?
If man from us should once be free,
What light may beam upon his head;
God greater than the Pope shall be—
The Devil's dead—the Devil's dead!

Ignatius came—"Let me but take
His place—his right—and see; in brief—
He has made men for ages quake.
I'll make kings tremble like a leaf!
With plagues, thefts, massacres, I'll ban
Both north and south—where'er I tread;
Leave ruins both for God and man—
The Devil's dead—the Devil's dead!"

"Come, blessed one," they uttered, "come,
We hallow thy most saintly gall"—
And now his Order—sent from Rome—
O'ershadows, darkens, curses all.
I heard a choir of angels tell
Their sympathies for man, they said,
"Ignatius is the heir of Hell,
The Devil's dead—the Devil's dead!"]

Béranger, however, could also speak of Satan seriously. In [**"L'ange exilé"**] addressed to a young woman, in whom our author believes to have discovered an angel exiled from Heaven, the legend of the fall of the angels is treated seriously. Among the legions of Lucifer was an angel who repented of his sin. The Lord brought him up from Hell to pass a period of probation on earth. This exiled celestial moves among men with his divine lyre to charm away their sorrows and to comfort them in their afflictions. As soon as he redeems himself in the eyes of God, he will be recalled to Heaven.

According to another version of the legend, the angels who were not hurled into the bottom of Hell but banished to our earth had maintained a neutral position in the rivalry between the Lord and Lucifer. It is not so generally known that during the war in Heaven the angels were not wholly divided into two opposing camps. There were many spirits who, untouched by partisan passions, remained aloof from the conflict and refused to don the uniform. They demanded their right of keeping out of a war which they did not bring about and in which they had no interest whatever. When the Lord defeated his enemy and cast him and his legionaries into the abyss, he did not hurl also the neutral angels into Hell, but, in order to give them another opportunity to choose between him and his rival, cast them down to the earth to which the scene of the battle had been transferred. From these angels, who married mortal maidens (cf. Gen. vi., 1), there has developed a race which has always shown a striking contrast to the human family. It has furnished humanity with its prophets and poets, with its reformers and revolutionaries. All great men at all times and in all places have belonged to this mysterious race which does not proceed from father to son, like other races, but appears here and there, at recurring intervals, in the families of mankind. The descendants of this union between the sons of God and the daughters of men have always stood in the first ranks of those who seek peace and abhor murder. They have proven valiant warriors in the eternal conflict between the Good and the Evil for the mastery of the world. They have long ago redeemed themselves, but they will not return to Heaven until they have also redeemed all men. (pp. 170-77)

> *Maximilian J. Rudwin, "Béranger's 'Bon Dieu' and 'Bon Diable',"* in The Open Court, *Vol. XXXVIII, No. 3, March, 1924, pp. 170-77.*

Georges J. Joyaux   (essay date 1953)

[*In the following excerpt, Joyaux chronicles the reaction to Béranger's work in the United States as it was revealed in the literary press.*]

In a study of *French Thought in American Magazines: 1800-1848,* made by the author of this paper, 4462 references to French literary, political, and other ideas were collected. A large number of these items—reviews, notices, articles, and the like—concerned French poetry, and a chapter was therefore devoted to American attitudes toward French poets and poetry during this period. An examination of the evidence thus obtained showed that American magazines kept in close touch with the poetic achievements of contemporary France, displaying particular interest in the rising Romantic school. It was equally clear, from the nature and extent of the periodical references, that American critics and reviewers had little sympathy for the products of the Romantic movement. Of all the French poets mentioned in American magazines during the period 1800-1848—practically the whole gallery of French poetry, classic, neoclassic and romantic—Béranger's name appeared most often. Altogether, there were 55 references to him, either in essays on French poetry, in reviews of his literary productions, or in translations from some of his songs. Lamartine, the runner-up, appeared only 48 times. Furthermore, there is qualitative as well as quantitative proof of Béranger's favorable reception in American magazines, for the praise he received is duplicated in the case of no other French literary figure—poet, novelist, dramatist, or critic.

The first American periodical reference to Béranger, a reprint in French of one of his songs, appeared in a French magazine published in America, *L'abeille américaine,* in 1818: **"Si j'étais petit oiseau."** This song, extracted from Béranger's first collection (1815) reappeared later in translation in another magazine. In 1821 Béranger published an enlarged edition of his songs. . . . [On] December 8, 1821, "he appeared before the Royal Court which condemned him to three months in jail, and to pay a fine of 500 fr." From that time on his fame was established, "this condemnation bringing upon him the aureole of a martyr" [*Dictionnaire de Biographie Française,* (V, 1459)]. Two years later, another of Béranger's songs, this time in translation, was published in *The Minerva.* The same year there appeared the first extended complimentary reference to the French song writer. The *New Monthly Magazine and Literary Journal* started in October, 1823, a series of articles intended to familiarize American audiences with living French poets—a series that ended, however, with the third installment after treating Béranger, Lamartine and Delavigne. The opening paragraph of the first article indicated the high esteem in which Béranger was held in America during the whole period. The author declared him to be " . . . one of those geniuses who are rare in the poetical literature of every nation, but most rare in that of France." The essay also included a short biographical notice of the songwriter, drawn largely from Béranger's own songs, from which the author quoted in the original. Béranger's low birth, his constant struggle for survival, his refusal to be "patronaged," received particular emphasis. The author of the essay believed that Béranger had no peer in France, nor indeed in any other country, past or present. Horace, he believed, perhaps came closest to equalling the art of the Frenchman, though he judged the Roman to be lacking in some of the necessary elements of character and genius. There was no doubt in the author's mind that Béranger's "songs" were worthy of a better name, and he did not hesitate to refer to them as "odes." After an exhaustive eulogy of Béranger's talents,—"which fitted him for the very walks of poetry," though Béranger chose mere song to display them—the writer concluded by reproducing, in the original, one of Béranger's most popular pieces, **"Le vieux drapeau."**

In 1825, the *Museum of Foreign Literature and Science* reproduced from the *London Magazine* an article on French literature entirely devoted to a laudatory review of Béranger's **New Songs** (1825). The essay, dated April, 1825, opened with the words, "This work may take its station at no remote distance from the imperishable models of our literature." The rest of the article carried out this theme: in the opinion of the author, the **New Songs** "may bear a comparison with the works of the greatest poet France ever produced. I mean Jean de La Fontaine." The same remarks concerning Béranger's low origins, his gentle character, his complete devotion to the "people," were made in this essay, as in the preceding one:

> He has from his earliest youth been exposed to the most fearful anxieties and sufferings—he was extremely poor. . . . As soon as the manual labour by which he gained his daily subsistence was over, he sat down and wrote a song. This was his way of fixing things in his memory, of writing his Journal.

In a word, Béranger was assumed to be both the French counterpart of the American self-made man, and a lover of the people whose feelings he transcribed in his songs. These factors greatly helped in making him a favorite in America, as opposed to Lamartine and Delavigne, "his noble rivals . . . who deliberately seat themselves to their desks and say Lord Byron and Greece are in fashion." The critic's conclusion was clear and definite: "All I contend is, that De Béranger is the first of living French poets; the one whose works have the greatest chance of seeing the 20th century." Next in line, he ranked Lamartine and Delavigne. If his prophecy was correct in respect to Delavigne, who like Béranger is considered today a very minor figure in French literary history, he was greatly mistaken in his judgment of Lamartine, recognized today as one of the great lyricists of the Romantic movement.

In [June] 1827, the *American Quarterly Review* published a 28-page essay on contemporary French literature. The review of two literary histories of France afforded an occasion for the reviewer to "introduce to our readers in a very compendious and cursory manner, the French writers of the present period." Among the array of names—many of which have since been completely forgotten—Béranger was granted two pages, the reviewer considering him as "unquestionably . . . the poet the most original and philosophical, and one of those most richly endowed with poetic genius." As to his songs, he said, they are of "the most sublime and pathetic strains, worthy of the lyre of Pindar or the lute of Anacreon." Yet at the same time the critic pointed out that Béranger's success lay chiefly in his popularity with the crowd, rather than with the literary elite: "Béranger is the more popular writer. . . . For ourselves we confess our partiality to Lamartine." The few lines he later devoted to Lamartine may explain why Lamartine never received the popular acclaim of Béranger, and may also explain the latter's success. "He appears, indeed, a being rather of some intellectual sphere, than belonging to this world of corporeal substance."

Béranger's *Chansons inédites* appeared in 1828. Because of their attacks on Charles X, the throne and the altar, they brought their author another nine months in jail and a much heavier fine, 10,000 fr. The following year, this new edition was very favorably reviewed in two important American periodicals. The May issue of the *Museum of Foreign Literature and Science* reprinted an article from the *London Weekly Magazine,* which said:

> According to our theory . . . , the authors of the regeneration of French poetry, which has now commenced, are the song writers of France. . . . The song writer has moved at will through the regions of poetry, protected from interference by its insignificance. In composing a simple ditty . . . , he has sometimes produced a sublime ode, and his ingenuous strains have sunk deep into the hearts and imaginations of the people, imbuing them with true spirit of poetry, and sapping in silence their ancient prejudices, which would have stood unmoved before the attack of an open enemy.

The other essay, published in the July issue of the *North American Review,* was more openly dedicated to the genius of Béranger, "the most popular living poet of France." His success, the reviewer felt, was primarily due to his singing the woes and glory of his fatherland, at a time when France was particularly in need of a *troubadour.* In order for Béranger to attain the position in the top rank of French poets, the reviewer felt, "It was requisite that his songs should be French in spirit, that their subject should be France, 'la belle France,' and that that subject be treated with . . . devotion and exclusiveness of feeling. . . . " However, the critic at the same time was aware of some of the defects of Béranger's earlier songs—"licentiousness, indecency"—and he warned his readers against the moral danger they presented:

> (Though) a selection from the songs of Béranger would be, both as very difficult poetry, and as models of beautiful writing, a most agreeable acquisition to the young and inexperienced . . . , (yet), it is only to the more mature and stable, those whose heads are not turned by the mere sound of a French rhyme . . . , that we should be willing to commit this collection, unexpurgated.

However, the writer concluded that to those more mature readers, "No injury can be apprehended from the grossness, the licentiousness and the frivolity that pervade [Béranger's] earlier works." In their turn, "from this dross they will be able to extract much of the precious metal, the smelting of which could with no propriety be confided to younger hands."

The Revolution of 1830 which ended the Bourbon régime naturally brought about an increase in the popularity of Béranger. Charles X and the throne had been, from the very beginning, one of Béranger's main targets; he gave voice, in his songs, to the silent hatred which the French people at large had held for the Restoration; thus, when success came, Béranger was immediately hailed as a prime mover in the victory of the people over the forces of oppression. Louis XVIII, and to a still greater extent Charles X, had been viewed unfavorably in America: their attempt to restore absolutism, their devotion to Catholicism—which had favored the Jesuit revival of the 1820's—added to the Americans' traditional dislike for kings, both explain this country's favorable reaction to the overthrow of the monarchy. It is necessary to add, however, that they did not approve of the Revolution in itself, fearful as they were of its future developments. At any rate, and as a result of it, Béranger's fame in America received another boost: of the total number of references to Béranger, 34 appeared in the decade 1830-1840.

In 1831 a contributor to the *Southern Review* discussed Béranger's Songs (editions of 1826 and 1828), with the avowed intention of "calling the attention of the literary public to a writer infinitely more deserving of their notice than the herd of English poetasters whom we republish if we do not read." In this article there also appeared some slight reference to the licentiousness of some of Béranger's earlier writings. Though the reviewer expressed his regret that, "for the sake of decency . . . , [these] were not consigned to an early grave and a brief epitaph," it was clear that this alleged licentiousness did not cause the turmoil aroused by the novels of Victor Hugo, Balzac, and above all of George Sand.

The same year, the November issue of the same magazine contained an informative and critical essay on Casimir Delavigne, the neo-classical poet and dramatist, occasioned by a review of a new edition of his poems and his dramas. In this long essay—26 pages—the writer made clear that he ranked Delavigne below Béranger as a poet, attacking the former on two grounds: the stateliness and gravity of his poetry, and his tendency to side with the ruling power, whether it be Napoleon or the King. The opposite qualities, the reviewer felt, were associated with Béranger, and in a large measure, they were at the very basis of the latter's success in America as they were, indeed, in France. Béranger's poetry was written for the people, and in a language borrowed from the people; furthermore, he persistently fought the Bourbons, the enemies of the people, never abating in his admiration for the Emperor, the people's favorite.

Béranger's role in the Revolution of July 1830 was the main topic of an article appearing in the September issue, 1833, of the *Knickerbocker Magazine* [see excerpt above]. In the second paragraph the author of the essay commented on those characteristics of the French which Béranger so skillfully and artistically represented in his songs: "Their gay, happy temperament, ever suggesting a ready escape into the bright worlds of fancy and imagination, from the dull reality of life . . . have made its inhabitants [France's] particularly susceptible to the influence of the spirit of song." Béranger himself received fulsome praises from the writer: "There is much, very much in the character of Béranger to admire; with a reputation such as but few authors have ever lived to experience, he is one of the least assuming of men." Among those qualities singled out for praise were his modesty, his independence, and his refusal to serve interests other than the people's, qualities eminently appealing to American readers. In conclusion, the author asserted that Béranger's songs "may be said to have exerted a far greater influence than any other engine brought to bear upon the mass of the people, in exciting the late revolution of that country." The article ended with the reproduction in English of six of Béranger's songs.

The same year, the *Museum of Foreign Literature and Science* reprinted, from English magazines, two essays on Béranger and his influence. Both were pervaded with the same sentimental admiration for the French songwriter. In the second, particularly, the author took occasion to compare songwriting in France to that in England, a comparison weighted heavily in favor of Béranger. He concluded his essay, "No wonder that a writer of Béranger's powers should possess, not merely popularity, but a degree of literary rank and eminence which we in this country find it difficult to understand as enjoyed by any songwriter whatever."

Yet, among the chorus of praise for Béranger in American journals, there were a few voices raised in dissent. As early as 1828, as has been indicated, a few critics expressed a preference for Lamartine, relegating Béranger to the second flight of genius. Thus the editor of *The Select Journal of Foreign Periodical Literature,* in the issue of October, 1833, declared in introducing a review reprinted from *Tait's Edinburgh Magazine:* "It is worthwhile to know something of his character [Béranger's], his style and genius. But his immorality and licentiousness are such that the knowledge would be dearly purchased by familiarity with his works." Commenting on the high rank which the British reviewer attributed to the French writer, the editor of the *Journal* further added, "In assigning to Béranger the rank which he does, he seems to us to have mistaken a very happy knack at versification, and power of ridicule and sarcasm, for poetical genius." In the light of Béranger's tempestuous career, this statement shrewdly placed a finger on the problem his poetry presented to the critic; on the one hand his undeniable artistry and cleverness in the choice of rhythms—illustrated at its best in his refrains—and on the other his witty and biting satire of the royalty, the nobility and the clergy.

Two years later the March issue of the *American Quarterly Review* contained a 20-page review of Lamartine's *Harmonies poétiques et religieuses.* Though willing to grant Béranger a major role in the regeneration of French poetry, the author of the essay prefers not to refer to him as a poet. Much more worthy of the name, the writer feels, is the author of the *Harmonies,* who "has enriched incalculably the French language, founding a new school of poetry more agreeable to nature and to a cultivated taste." Naturally the reviewer refused to concur with those who, in comparing the two men, the poet and the chansonnier, "have awarded the palm of superiority . . . to the gay chansonnier, on account of the greater fancied utility of his publications." At the same time the reviewer showed himself well aware of the differences in these writer's audiences; while Béranger is the poet of the people, by whom he is easily and completely understood, Lamartine's poetry appeals only to a restricted number, "for the home of his muse is in the magnificence of woods and rivers and mountains where she communes with ideal beings, and revels in a world of her own creation." In concluding the article, the author expressed the hope that Lamartine's works may become better known in America, confident that "they will be highly appreciated when known."

Let us not conclude, however, that 1835 marks a turning point in America's estimate of Béranger. Unsympathetic criticism of him was the exception, not the rule, in American magazines. Indeed, in 1837, a translation of two of Béranger's best-known pieces, **"The Grave of Manuel"** and **"My Coat,"** published in the April issue of the *New Yorker,* was introduced with these words: "The distinguishing characteristics of Anacreon, Tyrtæus, and Horace have combined to form a Béranger, who has exercised a greater dominion over the hearts and minds of his countrymen than any other poet of ancient or modern times."

In the following years, the body of references to Béranger consists chiefly of translation from his songs, thus keeping an interest in him alive among American readers. In 1844, the *Columbian Lady's and Gentleman's Magazine* published "Some Things of Béranger by Park Benjamin," in which for the first time, mention was made of the need for

a complete and accurate translation of Béranger's songs. Referring to a collection of Béranger's pieces, which had appeared the same year in Philadelphia, the editor of the magazine declared, ". . . The pieces should . . . , for the most part, be entitled: 'Lines suggested by such and such a song of Béranger.' " The article itself was composed of several songs in translation, which the author offered to his readers as better than those contained in the collection referred to. The author's opinion of Béranger was clearly stated in his opening apostrophe, addressed to the French song writer:

> Dear, delightful Béranger! Art thou not heart and soul a Frenchman? Art thou not, as we know thee by thy songs, the embodiment of good humor? There is mirth even in thy sadness, joy in thy sarcasm. What tenderness is there even in thy strength—how soothing and pleasant a tone pervades thy very strains of triumph and of war! Other poets we may admire, but thee we love. . . . I have my favorites, but I am persuaded that Jean Pierre de Béranger is my favorite of favorites. He seems to me the darling child of Nature. She has dowered him with her choicest treasures.

A similar adoration is reflected in a reprint from the *Glasgow Citizen* appearing in the December 28, 1844, issue of *Littell's Living Age.* The author of the essay, who sees in Béranger "the first of the French lyrical poets," feels that he "has well been named the Burns of France." The main part of the article is an endless praise of the *chansonnier,* pointing out among other things his sway over the popular mind: "There is no doubt that his Chansons had an immense influence in producing the Revolution of 1830, although he does not view the existing government with approbation and has refused everything in the shape of boon or favor at its hands."

Toward the end of the period considered, it is evident that Béranger's fame did not decline in America. In the last two years, 1847-1848, there appeared ten references to the "gay chansonnier," seven of these being translations from his songs. The *Eclectic Magazine of Foreign Literature, Science and Arts* published in March, 1847, and in June, 1848, two laudatory items on Béranger, reprinted respectively from *The People's Journal* and *Howitt's Journal.* In the latter year the *Literary World* for March published the last reference to Béranger. Besides the usual praises of the *Chansonnier,* hailed as "the greatest lyric poet of the age," Béranger was defended against those accusations of licentiousness which at times had been levelled at him: "[He] has been called, but most unjustly, the poet of licentiousness."

Towards the end of the period 1800-1848, there occurred a considerable improvement in the quality of American criticism, an improvement responsible for the rehabilitation in the late 1840's of some of the French romantics, such as Victor Hugo, George Sand and Balzac. Lamartine, who on the whole was persistently ranked below Béranger, was similarly reevaluated; soon it was realized, at least by the critics themselves, that his poetry, though less popular, was nevertheless far more elevated and worthy of a better rank than the one it had been assigned to so far.

Yet this reclassification was not accomplished at the expense of Béranger's own writings. He did not suffer from the newer criticism, undoubtedly on account of his sentimental hold on his readers.

The quotations given in the preceeding pages furnish strong evidence of the extent of Béranger's fame in America. The reasons which explain it have been pointed out in the many references to the *chansonnier* and to other French poets. The very reasons for the cool reception given to Lamartine, recognized today as a far greater lyricist, were behind the favor enjoyed by the songwriter. The cornerstone of Béranger's success was his ability to express, in the people's own words, the moral and spiritual sufferings of the country. This closeness to the people, the fight he led on its side for its emancipation, the facility with which one could read and also memorize his pieces, explain as well his success in America.

Another element which accounted in great measure for Béranger's warm reception in the United States is to be found in his attitude towards Napoleon. In *French Thought in American Magazines: 1800-1848,* it was shown that after Waterloo, and more especially after Napoleon's death, in 1821, there occurred in America a great reversal of attitude regarding the French Emperor. Americans hated him while he held France in chains and the world in terror, but pitied him after he was defeated and exiled. The conditions were now reversed; Napoleon was no longer the menace, but the butt of bitter attacks from all sides, even from those who had been his best friends and warmest admirers during his lifetime. This situation, naturally, found a response in the hearts of Americans, and soon they began to express their compassion, affection and at times admiration for the underdog. By celebrating the achievements of *le petit caporal,* whose legend he helped to keep alive, Béranger could be sure of at least some prospects of popular success. (pp. 269-77)

> *Georges J. Joyaux, "The Reception of Pierre-Jean de Béranger in America: 1818-1848," in* The French Review, *Vol. XXVI, No. 4, February, 1953, pp. 268-77.*

FURTHER READING

Black, Frank Gees. "Hugo and the Death of Béranger." *The Romantic Review* LIV, No. 2 (April 1963): 121-27.

> Presents historical data in order to characterize the "differences of temperament and circumstance" between Béranger and François-Victor Hugo.

Forster, Joseph. "Béranger." In his *Some French and Spanish Men of Genius,* pp. 183-209. London: Ellis and Elvey, 1891.

> Favorable character sketch.

"Béranger: His Genius and Influence." *The Knickerbocker* II, No. 3 (September 1833): 171-87.

> Discusses Béranger's career, depicting him as an honorable and brilliant songwriter.

Price, Joseph. "Pierre Jean de Béranger: The Poet of the People." *The New-Yorker* III, No. 3 (8 April 1837): 33.

> Profile of Béranger that describes him as "decidedly the most popular man in France, and one of the most accomplished and elegant of its scholars."

Roberts, John G. "Béranger's Neglected Poem to Manuel." *Modern Language Notes* LIV, No. 1 (January 1939): 32-5.

> Presents and discusses Béranger's song "A Manuel," a tribute to his friend Antoine Manuel and an expression of patriotic sentiment.

Thibaudet, Albert. "Courier and Béranger." In his *French Literature from 1795 to Our Era,* translated by Charles Lam Markmann, pp. 79-86. New York: Funk & Wagnalls, 1967.

> Brief passage about Béranger as part of a general study. Thibaudet writes, "A mixture of limited rationalism, simple politics, ordinary common sense, and preaching, prosaic literature was given by Béranger exactly and fortunately the form that suited it, the popular song."

Johann Wolfgang von Goethe

1749-1832

German poet, novelist, dramatist, short story and novella writer, essayist, critic, biographer, autobiographer, and librettist.

The following entry presents criticism of Goethe's drama *Faust,* consisting of *Faust. Die Erster Teil* (*Faust. Part One,* 1808) and *Faust II* (1832). For discussion of Goethe's complete career, see *NCLC,* Volume 4; for discussion of Goethe's novel *Die Leiden des jungen Werthers* (*The Sufferings of Young Werther*), see *NCLC,* Vol. 22.

Faust is considered a literary masterpiece and Goethe's finest work. Written in verse, the drama relates the adventures of a despondent academic whose pursuit of fulfillment through knowledge and worldly experience is assisted by the devil Mephistopheles. While the legend of Faust has been traced to early Christian writings and became a popular literary focus during the Renaissance, most critics consider Goethe's adaptation its most comprehensive and innovative treatment.

Faust was composed over a period of sixty years. Goethe began recording his ideas for an adaptation of the Faust legend in 1770, while studying law at the University of Strausberg. During the next five years, while he practiced law in Frankfurt and enjoyed great success as a poet and novelist, he began to work on the manuscript of *Faust,* producing a first draft, which later became known as the *Urfaust.* This early version of the drama, which was not published in Goethe's lifetime, reflects the passion and spiritual turmoil characteristic of the literature of the *Sturm und Drang* (storm and stress) movement introduced by Goethe and other young German dramatists. In 1775 Goethe was invited to Weimar to serve as privy councillor to Karl August, the Duke of Saxe Weimar; he remained in this capacity for eleven years, finding little time for literary pursuits. In 1786, however, he embarked on a two-year excursion in Italy, initiating a period generally regarded as a turning point in his career. His creative vigor was renewed by his exposure to Classical art, to the principles of which he became committed, and he recommenced work on the *Faust* manuscript as well as several other projects. Returning to Weimar in 1788, Goethe resumed some of his administrative duties but focused on his poetry, scientific studies, and *Faust.* In 1790 he published *Faust: Ein Fragment,* a work that he would later revise as *Faust. Part One.*

In 1794 Goethe became acquainted with Friedrich Schiller, a professor in the neighboring village of Jena who shared Goethe's interest in Classical art and poetry. The two established a close personal and working relationship, exchanging criticism of each other's works in progress and collaborating on a volume of poetry. Encouraged by Schiller's enthusiasm for the Faust project, Goethe resumed work on *Faust* in 1797, completing the first part in 1806— one year after Schiller's death—and publishing it in 1808.

Although *Faust. Part One* was an immediate critical success, Goethe did not direct his attention to its conclusion for another seventeen years, during which time he continued to produce poetry and novels, earning international acclaim as one of the century's most important writers. He completed *Faust II* in January of 1832, giving the manuscript to his literary executor for inclusion in the thirty volumes of his collected works to be published after his death. He died ten weeks later.

Faust is prefaced by three sections: "Dedication" and "Prelude in the Theater" introduce the Faust legend and Goethe's particular adaptation of it, while "Prologue in Heaven" presents God and Mephistopheles discussing Faust's outlook on life. Mephistopheles suggests that he can tempt Faust—a fundamentally vital man who is continually questing for fulfillment through spiritual and intellectual challenges—into staid satisfaction. God allows him to carry out his plan. The dramatic action of *Faust. Part One* begins when the title character is introduced in his study as an academician who has lost enthusiasm for life. Unable to satisfy his intellectual aspirations through practical science, alchemy, or religion, Faust is disgusted with his chronic discontent and contemplates suicide. Mephistopheles appears in Faust's study and proposes that he can help Faust achieve fulfillment by providing a wide range of experience through which Faust may acquire knowledge and happiness. Disbelieving the claim, Faust accepts the suggestion and agrees to surrender his soul to Mephistopheles should he ever express happiness and wish for the moment to linger. The two then venture forth to test their agreement. An opportunity arises when Faust sees a young woman he desires, and Mephistopheles arranges for him to meet her. Margarete, a simple and uneducated girl, often referred to by the diminutive name "Gretchen," responds to Faust's overtures and falls in love with him. He convinces her to administer a sleeping potion to her mother and free herself to meet with him and consummate their love. The consequences of their passion comprise what critics refer to as the Gretchen tragedy. After her mother dies from an overdose of the sleeping draught, Gretchen's brother learns of her affair with Faust, and, in defending her honor, is killed by Mephistopheles and Faust. Faust flees with Mephistopheles, leaving Gretchen alone to discover that the liaison has resulted in pregnancy. Mephistopheles, in an effort to keep Faust's mind off the recent developments, takes him to witness "Walpurgisnacht," a grotesque and licentious celebration among a convocation of witches. The ritual disturbs Faust, and he succumbs to its hypnotic influence. When he recovers, he learns of Gretchen's fate and demands that Mephistopheles help him find her. Driven mad by her unfortunate circumstances, Gretchen has murdered her child and is imprisoned pending execution. Faust meets with her in the prison and tries to convince her to escape with him, but she refuses, preferring to face God's judgment. At her death Mephistopheles observes that "she is judged," while a voice from above pronounces that she "is saved." The first part of the drama concludes as Gretchen ascends to heaven calling Faust's name.

Faust II opens in an emperor's court where Faust and Mephistopheles are posing as magicians at a court celebration. Mephistopheles, at the request of the emperor, conjures forth Paris and Helen, historical figures of the Trojan war. Faust, entranced by Helen's beauty, reaches out to touch her. He is instantly struck down by an unseen force and remains motionless as Mephistopheles carries him back to his study. Mephistopheles then wanders into the laboratory of Wagner, Faust's former colleague. Wagner is in the middle of an experiment in which he is attempting to create a "homunculus," a humanlike creature reduced in size and endowed with supernatural powers. Mephistopheles assists in the experiment and gives life to the homunculus, who, after discerning Faust's plight, enters the study and reads the mind of the unconscious Faust. Faust's dreams indicate that he desires Helen of Troy. The homunculus returns to Mephistopheles, suggesting that they transport Faust to the realm of Classical myth, where the Walpurgisnacht celebration of the ancients is taking place and where Faust may recover in Helen's presence.

During this "Classical Walpurgis Night" scene, similar to that of the witches in *Faust. Part One,* Faust regains consciousness, finds Helen, and becomes romantically involved with her. Faust and Helen live together, producing a child, Euphorion, who dies tragically when he tries to fly. Helen is eventually called back to the realm of Classical myth, and Faust is borne up into the heavens where

he is afforded a panoramic view of Earth. From this experience he conceives an idea to build a network of dikes along a shoreline that will control the sea and create a new expanse of land over which he may rule. Mephistopheles helps Faust to realize this goal, and Faust becomes a great overseer and lord of the area. As the drama concludes, Faust's life draws to a close. He utters the words that he wagered he would not, expressing satisfaction with life and bidding the moment to linger. Mephistopheles immediately lays claim to Faust's soul. Nevertheless, as Faust dies, he is lifted up into heaven and redeemed.

The vast scope and unique textual history of *Faust* have challenged conventional critical methods. Most commentary debates the unity of the drama, examines it as a reflection of Goethe's intellectual development, or discusses issues specific to its several subplots. The nature of Faust's pact with Mephistopheles, for example, has prompted several analyses of the drama's first and final scenes in an effort to determine whether or not Faust loses the wager and whether or not he deserves salvation. Most critics agree that Faust's redemption is not an anomaly in the drama. Some commentators suggest that a close study of the language of the pact, specifically its verb tense and mood, indicates that Faust actually wins the wager on a technicality of semantics. A more widely accepted interpretation maintains that Goethe intended Faust's salvation to result from his well-intentioned strivings on Earth; his goals become less self-serving during the course of his adventures and, in the words of Harry Steinhauer, "it is because of his conversion that Faust is saved." However, some critics contend that Faust loses the wager and should, accordingly, be damned. In this context, Erich Heller has found that Faust's redemption reflects Goethe's failure to comply with the literary principles of tragedy. The so-called Gretchen tragedy is another subplot prompting critical debate. Detailed character analyses, examinations of Gretchen's function in the drama, and speculations on the identity of the woman in Goethe's life after whom he modelled the character of Gretchen are lines of inquiry frequently pursued. Henry Hatfield has claimed that Gretchen operates as the tragic hero of *Faust,* stating that "it is *her* tragedy." Ronald Peacock, however, has studied ways in which Gretchen provides a simple and essentially realistic love interest, while also functioning as a force morally opposed to Mephistopheles; she is, therefore, "the symbolical instrument of Faust's redemption."

Since the publication of the second part of the drama, critics have noted distinct stylistic, tonal, and thematic inconsistencies between parts one and two that bring into question the overall sense and continuity of *Faust.* No critical consensus has been reached regarding the work's unity, which remains perhaps the most frequently debated issue relating to the drama. Among the many readings of *Faust,* two interpretations prevail. One view holds that *Faust* achieves unity through either poetic or thematic devices, the development of which may be traced through both parts of the drama. Ulrich K. Goldsmith, for example, has examined the unifying effect of such motifs as the Gretchen tragedy established in part one, finding recurring instances in part two in which Gretchen's spirit indirectly influences Faust's decisions and, eventually, his fate. Similarly, such critics as Stuart Atkins and Alexander Gillies have shown ways in which religious themes or elements of romance and tragedy have been consistently rendered throughout *Faust.* The other view, upheld in the criticism of Ronald Gray and others, maintains that *Faust* lacks a constant purpose; however, such critics maintain, this apparent shortcoming is an inevitable consequence of Goethe's emphasis on other aspects of the drama. More uniform plot construction and characterization between the two parts, they stress, would diminish the effect of the drama as a reflection of Faust's views. Gray argues that continuity should not be demanded of *Faust,* observing that Faust himself "expects no pattern or logical sequence in his life . . . he expects only an aimless succession of pleasure and pain which will change and change about as best they may."

Faust is also studied as a reflection of Goethe's intellectual development as a literary artist and philosopher. Gustav Mueller has asserted that "*Faust* as a whole perfectly embodies the principles of Goethe's thinking: It is an organic growth through polarities or contrasts, an evolution rounded out in a circle and a spiral ascent from simple to complex, integrated forms." Thomas Davidson and others have detected in *Faust* the influence of the Italian and Teutonic philosophical traditions, with their divergent emphases of morality on the one hand, and intellectualism on the other. These critics contend that Goethe's integration of the two philosophical strains in *Faust* indicates his commitment to both moral and intellectual freedom as integral aspects of the human condition. Similarly, many critics have noted ways in which Faust's experiences, specifically his abortive attempts to achieve happiness and knowledge, reflect Goethe's espousal or rejection of such philosophies as idealism, realism, and rationalism. Others, however, have questioned the usefulness of such philosophic approaches to *Faust.* While acknowledging the pervasiveness of Goethe's philosophic convictions, Harold Jantz has found that "the application of conventional philosophic methods to the criticism of the work has led to some strange misapprehensions, and has sometimes mantled it in deepest obscurity." He maintains that "*Faust* is poetry, *Faust* is symbol, and the poetic symbolic approach can be the only primary one," arguing that any insights into Goethe's philosophy must be acquired through literary interpretation rather than formal philosophic analysis.

Eudo C. Mason has praised the complexity of *Faust,* which gives rise to a variety of interpretations. Philosophical and literary intricacies, however, have presented various obstacles to the drama's practical application in the theater. Although seldom performed on stage, *Faust* remains a popular literary study, and, in Mason's words, an "outstanding literary work of the modern world."

Johann Christoph Friedrich von Schiller   (letter date 1797)

[*Schiller was a dramatist, critic, poet, and principal fig-*

ure in the German classicist movement who earned international acclaim for his historical dramas as well as his essays on dramaturgy and aesthetics. Schiller was also a close friend of Goethe and encouraged him to pursue his interest in the Faust legend. Many critics regard his persistence as instrumental to Goethe's completion of the first part of Faust. *In the following excerpt, Schiller expresses his concerns for the successful resolution of the drama.*]

I have now again read **Faust,** and my head grows dizzy in thinking on the solution. This is, however, quite natural, for the matter depends on a particular point of view, and so long as one has not that, even a subject less rich than this would embarrass the understanding. What concerns me is, that, from his character, Faust seems to require a totality of material, if in the end the idea is to appear completely carried out, and for a mass that boils up to such a height I know of no poetic rope that will hold it together. Well, you will know how to get out of the difficulty.

For example, it would be necessary, according to my view, that Faust be conducted into practical life, and whatever part you select for him out of this mass, it seems to me that, from its nature, it will require a too great circumstantiality and breadth.

In regard to the treatment, I think the great difficulty is easy to get through with between sport and earnest. Understanding and Reason seem to me in this subject to wrestle together for life. In the present fragmentary form of **Faust,** this is strongly felt, but expectation is referred to the developed whole. The Devil, through his materialism, pleads for the understanding, and Faust for the heart. Occasionally, however, they seem to change parts, and the Devil takes Reason under his protection against Faust.

One difficulty I find therein, that the Devil through his character, which is material, annuls his existence, which is ideal. As he stands there, it is only Reason that can comprehend him and give him value.

I am very curious to see how the popular fable will fasten itself to the philosophical part of the whole. (pp. 270-71)

> *Johann Christoph Friedrich von Schiller, in a letter to Johann Wolfgang von Goethe on June 26, 1797, in* Correspondence between Schiller and Goethe from 1794 to 1805, *translated by George H. Calvert, Wiley and Putnam, 1845, pp. 270-71.*

Friedrich Schelling   (essay date 1809)

[*A German philosopher, Schelling was one of the most prominent representatives of Idealism in nineteenth-century thought. His numerous writings include* Ideas towards a Philosophy of Nature *(1797) and* System of Transcendental Idealism *(1800). In the following excerpt, originally part of a lecture on the philosophy of art delivered between 1799 and 1804, published in 1809, and reprinted in his* Collected Works *(1859), Schelling offers a brief discussion of the* Fragment of 1790, *praising Goethe's technique and speculating on the story's conclusion.*]

[It] is without doubt most appropriate to mention the greatest German poem, Goethe's *Faust.* But it is difficult to offer a sufficiently convincing judgment concerning the spirit of the whole based on what we possess of it thus far. So my claim that this poem is by intention far more Aristophanic than tragic may seem striking, in face of the usual view.

Therefore I shall content myself with offering a very general view of this poem, so far as I think I understand it.

Not only is there a sense of fate in the plot; here the "In-Itself" of the universe and of nature confronts as an insurmountable necessity the knowledge of the individual as an individual. The subject as subject cannot enjoy the infinite as infinite, which is nonetheless a necessary inclination of the subject. Here, therefore, is an eternal contradiction. At the same time, the power of fate, which here stands in opposition to and in conflict with the subject, is more ideal, as also holds no less true for the plot. A suspended harmony could here be established in two directions, and the conflict could seek a twofold solution. The point of departure is the insatiable thirst to behold and, as subject, to enjoy the inner essence of things; and its initial direction is to satisfy ecstatically this insatiable desire beyond the aims and limits of reason, as expressed in this passage from *Faust:*

> Go, spurn intelligence and science,
> Man's lodestar and supreme reliance,
> Be furthered by the liar-in-chief
> In works of fraud and make-believe,
> And I shall have you dead to rights.

The other way out for the mind's unsatisfied striving is that of plunging into the world, to experience earth's sorrow and happiness. In this direction as well the result is decisive; here, too, it is eternally impossible for the finite to participate in the infinite; which is expressed in these words:

> Fate has endowed him with a forward-driving
> Impetuousness that reaches past all sights,
> And which, precipitately striving,
> Would overleap the earth's delights.
> Through dissipation I will drag him,
> Through shallow insignificance,
> I'll have him sticking, writhing, flagging,
> And for his parched incontinence
> Have food and drink suspended at lip level;
> In vain will he be yearning for relief.

In Goethe's *Faust* both these tendencies are represented or, rather, immediately united, so that the one proceeds directly from the other.

For dramatic reasons greater weight had to be placed on the second tendency, the encounter of such a mind with the world. So far as we can tell from the *Fragment,* we clearly recognize that *Faust* is intended to advance in this direction to the heights of tragedy.

Yet the cheerful quality of the whole, even in the first draft, the truth of its misguided striving, the authenticity of a demand for the highest life, already allows us to expect that the conflict will be resolved at a higher level and

that Faust will attain fulfillment by being raised up to higher spheres.

In this regard, strange as it may seem, this poem has a significance which is truly comparable to Dante, though it is more of a comedy and divine more in a poetic sense than Dante's *Divine Comedy.*

The wild life into which Faust throws himself becomes by a necessary consequence a Hell for him. His initial purification from the pangs of knowledge and false imagination, in accord with the playful intention of the work as a whole, will have to consist in an initiation into the basic principles of devilry, as the appropriate basis for an enlightened perspective on the world—just as his fulfillment will consist in rising above himself, by which he may perceive and learn to enjoy what is essential.

Even so little concerning the nature of this poem, which in part must be intuited more than known, shows how completely original it is in every aspect, a work comparable only to itself and completely self-contained. The kind of fate [it demonstrates] is unique and would deserve to be called a new discovery, were it not to an extent already present in the German temper and thus represented in its essential form in the mythological person of Faust.

Through this singular conflict, which begins in knowledge, the poem has assumed an epistemological aspect, so that if any poem may be called philosophical, then Goethe's *Faust* above all deserves this distinction. A magnificent spirit, which here unites the power of this exceptional poet with the profundity of a philosopher, has opened in this poem an eternally fresh source of knowledge, which would itself suffice to renew science (*Wissenschaft*) in our time and to infuse into it the freshness of a new life. Whoever seeks to penetrate the true sanctuary of nature, let him be nourished by these tones from a higher world and let him drink in its power in early youth, a power which emanates from this poem, as if in dense rays of light, and which thus moves the inner heart of the world. (pp. 437-39)

Friedrich Schelling, "On 'Faust' as Tragicomedy," in Faust: A Tragedy *by Johann Wolfgang von Goethe, edited by Cyrus Hamlin, translated by Walter Arndt, W. W. Norton & Company, Inc., 1976, pp. 437-39.*

Madame de Staël   (essay date 1810)

[*A French critic and novelist, Madame de Staël is credited with bringing the influence of German Romanticism to French literary and political thought, particularly through* D'Allemagne (1810), *an extensive French commentary on German culture. In the following excerpt from that work, she examines Goethe's interpretation of the Faust legend, focusing on his characterization of Mephistopheles and Faust.*]

Among the pieces written for the performance of puppets, there is one entitled "Dr. Faustus, or Fatal Science," which has always had great success in Germany. Lessing took up this subject before Goethe. This wondrous history is a tradition very generally known. Several English authors have written the life of this same Dr. Faustus, and some of them have even attributed to him the art of printing—his profound knowledge did not preserve him from being weary of life, and in order to escape from it, he tried to enter into a compact with the devil, who concludes the whole by carrying him off. From these slender materials Goethe has furnished the astonishing work, of which I will now try to give some idea.

Certainly, we must not expect to find in it either taste, or measure, or the art that selects and terminates; but if the imagination could figure to itself an intellectual chaos, such as the material chaos has often been painted, the *Faustus* of Goethe should have been composed at that epoch. It cannot be exceeded in boldness of conception, and the recollection of this production is always attended with a sensation of giddiness. The Devil is the hero of the piece; the author has not conceived him like a hideous phantom, such as he is usually represented to children; he has made him, if we may so express ourselves, the evil Being *par excellence,* before whom all others are only novices, scarcely worthy to be the servants of Mephistopheles (this is the name of the dæmon who has made himself the friend of Faustus). Goethe wished to display in this character, at once real and fanciful, the bitterest pleasantry that contempt can inspire, and at the same time an audacious gaiety that amuses. There is an infernal irony in the discourses of Mephistopheles, which extends itself to the whole creation, and criticizes the universe like a bad book of which the Devil has made himself the censor.

Mephistopheles makes sport with genius itself, as with the most ridiculous of all absurdities, when it leads men to take a serious interest in any thing, that exists in the world, and above all when it gives them confidence in their own individual strength. It is singular that, supreme wickedness and divine wisdom coincide in this respect; that they equally recognize the vanity and weakness of all earthly things: but the one proclaims this truth only to disgust men with what is good, the other only to elevate them above what is evil.

If the play of *Faustus* contained only a lively and philosophical pleasantry, an analogous spirit may be found in many of Voltaire's writings; but we perceive in this piece an imagination of a very different nature. It is not only that it displays to us the moral world, such as it is, annihilated, but that Hell itself is substituted in the room of it. There is a potency of sorcery, a poetry belonging to the principle of evil, a delirium of wickedness, a distraction of thought, which make us shudder, laugh, and cry, in a breath. It seems as if the government of the world were, for a moment, entrusted to the hands of the Dæmon. You tremble because he is pitiless, you laugh because he humbles the satisfaction of self-love, you weep, because human nature, thus contemplated from the depths of hell, inspires a painful compassion.

Milton has drawn his Satan larger than man; Michael Angelo and Dante have given him the hideous figure of the brute combined with the human shape. The Mephistopheles of Goethe is a civilized Devil. He handles with dexterity that ridicule, so trifling in appearance, which is nevertheless often found to consist with a profundity of malice;

he treats all sensibility as silliness or affectation; his figure is ugly, low, and crooked; he is awkward without timidity, disdainful without pride; he affects something of tenderness with the women, because it is only in their company that he needs to deceive, in order to seduce; and what he understands by seduction, is to minister to the passions of others; for he cannot even imitate love. This is the only dissimulation that is impossible to him.

The character of Mephistopheles supposes an inexhaustible knowledge of social life, of nature, and of the marvellous. This play of *Faustus,* is the night-mare of the imagination, but it is a night-mare that redoubles its strength. It discovers the diabolical revelation of incredulity,—of that incredulity which attaches itself to everything that can ever exist of good in this world; and perhaps this might be a dangerous revelation, if the circumstances produced by the perfidious intentions of Mephistopheles did not inspire a horror of his arrogant language, and make known the wickedness which it covers.

In the character of Faustus, all the weaknesses of humanity are concentrated: desire of knowledge, and fatigue of labour; wish of success and satiety of pleasure. It presents a perfect model of the changeful and versatile being whose sentiments are yet more ephemeral than the short existence of which he complains. Faustus has more ambition than strength; and this inward agitation produces his revolt against nature, and makes him have recourse to all manner of sorceries, in order to escape from the hard but necessary conditions imposed upon mortality. (pp. 440-42)

　　　　　Madame de Staël, "Faustus," in Faust: A Tragedy by Johann Wolfgang von Goethe, *edited by Walter Arndt, translated by Cyrus Hamlin, W. W. Norton & Company, Inc., 1976, pp. 440-42.*

Johann Wolfgang von Goethe and Johann Peter Eckermann (conversation date 1829)

[*Eckermann was Goethe's companion and secretary between 1823 and 1832. In 1837 he published* Gespräche mit Goethe in den letzen Jahren seines Lebens (Conversations with Goethe, *1850*), *a transcription of his discussions with the writer. The work is prized as an important source of information on Goethe's ideas in his later years. In the following passages from that book, the two men discuss the plot, characterization, and staging of* Faust.]

Sunday, December 6, 1829.

To-day after dinner, Goethe read me the first scene of the second act of *Faust.* The effect was great. We are once more transported into Faust's study, where Mephistopheles finds all as he had left it. He takes from the hook Faust's old study-gown, and a thousand moths and insects flutter out from it. By the directions of Mephistopheles as to where these are to settle down, the locality is brought very clearly before our eyes. He puts on the gown, intending to play the master once more, while Faust lies behind a curtain in a state of paralysis. He pulls the bell, which gives such an awful tone among the old solitary convent-halls that the doors spring open and the walls tremble. The servant rushes in, and finds in Faust's seat Mephistopheles, whom he does not recognize but for whom he has respect. In answer to inquiries he gives news of Wagner, who has now become a celebrated man, and is hoping for the return of his master—he is, we hear, at this moment very busy in his laboratory, trying to make a Homunculus. The servant retires, and the Bachelor enters—the same whom we knew some years before as a shy young student when Mephistopheles (in Faust's gown) made game of him. He is now a man, and so full of conceit that even Mephistopheles can do nothing with him, but moves his chair farther and farther and at last addresses the pit.

Goethe read the scene to the end. I was pleased with his youthful productive strength, and with the closeness of the whole. "As the conception," said Goethe, "is so old—for I have had it in my mind for fifty years—the materials have accumulated to such a degree that the difficulty is to separate and reject. The invention of the second part is really as old as I say; but it may be an advantage that I have not written it down till now when my knowledge of the world is so much clearer. I am like one who in his youth has a great deal of small silver and copper money; which in the course of his life he constantly changes for the better, so that at last the property of his youth stands before him in pieces of pure gold."

We spoke about the character of the Bachelor. "Is he not meant," said I, "to represent a certain class of ideal philosophers?"

"No," said Goethe, "the arrogance peculiar to youth, of which we had such striking examples after our war for freedom, is personified in him. Indeed, everyone believes in his youth that the world really began with him, and that all merely exists for his sake.

"Thus, in the East, there was a man who every morning collected his people about him, and would not go to work till he had commanded the sun to rise. But he was wise enough not to command till the sun of its own accord was on the point of appearing."

Goethe remained awhile absorbed in silent thought; then he began as follows:

"When old, we think of worldly matters otherwise than when young. Thus I cannot but think that the dæmons, to tease and make sport with men, have placed among them single figures so alluring that everyone strives after them, and so great that nobody reaches them. Thus they set up Raphael with whom thought and act were equally perfect; some distinguished followers have approached him, but none have equalled him. Thus, too, they set up Mozart as something unattainable in music; and thus Shakespeare in poetry. I know what you can say against this thought; but I only mean natural character, the great innate qualities. Thus, too, Napoleon is unattainable. That the Russians were so moderate as not to go to Constantinople is indeed very great; but we find a similar trait in Napoleon, he had the moderation not to go to Rome."

Much was associated with this copious theme; I thought in silence that the dæmons had intended something of the

kind with Goethe—he is a form too alluring not to be striven after, and too great to be reached.

Wednesday, December 16, 1829.

To-day, after dinner, Goethe read me the second scene of the second act of *Faust,* where Mephistopheles visits Wagner, who is on the point of making a human being by chemical means. The work succeeds; the Homunculus appears in the phial, as a shining being, and is at once active. He repels Wagner's questions upon incomprehensible subjects; reasoning is not his business; he wishes to *act,* and begins with our hero, Faust, who, in his paralysed condition, needs a higher aid. As a being to whom the present is perfectly clear and transparent, the Homunculus sees into the soul of the sleeping Faust; who, enraptured by a lovely dream, beholds Leda visited by swans, while she is bathing in a pleasant spot. The Homunculus, by describing this dream, brings a most charming picture before our eyes. Mephistopheles sees nothing of it, and the Homunculus taunts him with his northern nature.

"Generally," said Goethe, "you will perceive that Mephistopheles appears to disadvantage beside the Homunculus; who is like him in clearness of intellect, and so much superior in his tendency to the beautiful and to a useful activity. He styles him cousin; for such spiritual beings as this Homunculus, not yet saddened and limited by a thorough assumption of humanity, were classed with the dæmons, and thus there is a sort of relationship between the two."

"Certainly," said I, "Mephistopheles here appears a subordinate; yet I cannot help thinking he has had a secret influence on the production of the Homunculus. We have known him in this way before; and, indeed, in the *Helena* he always appears as secretly working. Thus he again elevates himself with regard to the whole, and in his lofty repose he can well afford to put up with a little in particulars."

"Your feeling of the position is very correct," said Goethe; "indeed, I have doubted whether I ought not to put some verses into the mouth of Mephistopheles when he goes to Wagner and when the Homunculus is still in a state of formation, so that his co-operation may be expressed."

"It would do no harm," said I. "Yet this is intimated by the words with which Mephistopheles closes the scene:

> 'Am Ende hängen wir doch ab
> Von Creaturen die wir machten.' "

> We are dependent, after all,
> On creatures that we make.

"True," said Goethe, "that would be almost enough for the attentive; but I will think about some additional verses."

"But those concluding words are very great, and will not easily be penetrated to their full extent."

"I think," said Goethe, "I have given them a bone to pick. A father who has six sons is a lost man, let him do what he may. Kings and ministers, too, who have raised many persons to high places, may have something to think about from their own experience."

Faust's dream about Leda again came into my head, and I regarded this as a most important feature.

"It is wonderful to me," said I, "how the several parts of such a work bear upon, perfect, and sustain one another! By this dream of Leda, *Helena* gains its proper foundation. There we have a constant allusion to swans and the child of a swan; but here we have the act itself, and when we come afterwards to *Helena,* with the sensible impression of such a situation, how much more clear and perfect does all appear!"

Goethe said I was right.

"You will see," said he, "that in these earlier acts the chords of the classic and romantic are constantly struck; so that, as on a rising ground, where both forms of poetry are brought out and in some sort balance one another, we may ascend to *Helena.*

"The French," continued Goethe, "now begin to think aright on these matters. Classic and romantic, say they, are equally good: the only point is to use these forms with judgment, and to be capable of excellence—you can be absurd in both, and then one is as worthless as the other. This, I think, is rational enough, and may content us for a while."

Sunday, December 20, 1829.

Dined with Goethe. We spoke of the Chancellor; and I asked whether he brought any news of Manzoni, on his return from Italy.

"He wrote to me about him," said Goethe. "The Chancellor paid Manzoni a visit; he lives on his estate near Milan, and is (I am sorry to say) always ill."

"It is odd," said I, "that persons of distinguished talents, especially poets, have so often weak constitutions."

"Their extraordinary achievements," said Goethe, "presuppose a very delicate organization, which makes them susceptible to unusual emotions and capable of hearing celestial voices. Such an organization, in conflict with the world and the elements, is easily disturbed and injured; he who does not, like Voltaire, combine with great sensibility an equally uncommon toughness, is liable to constant illness. Schiller was always ill. When I first knew him, I thought he could not live a month; but he too had a certain toughness; he kept going for many years, and would have done so longer if he had lived in a healthier way."

We spoke of the theatre, and how far a certain performance had been successful. (pp. 332-36)

We pursued this subject, talking of the chief actors of the Weimar stage, and their performance in several parts.

Meanwhile, **Faust** came once more into my head, and I talked of the way to render the Homunculus clear on the stage. "If we do not see the little man himself," said I, "we must see the light in the bottle, and his important words must be uttered in a way that would surpass the capacity of a child."

"Wagner," said Goethe, "must not let the bottle go out of his hands, and the voice must sound as if it came from the bottle. It would be a part for a ventriloquist such as I have heard. A man of that kind would solve the difficulty."

We then talked of the Grand Carnival, and the possibility of representing it upon the stage. "It would be a little more than the market-place at Naples," said I.

"It would require a very large theatre," said Goethe, "and is hardly to be imagined."

"I hope to see it some day," was my answer. "I look forward especially to the elephant, led by Prudence, and surmounted by Victory, with Hope and Fear in chains on each side. This is an allegory that could not easily be surpassed."

"The elephant would not be the first on the stage," said Goethe. "At Paris there is one, which forms an entire character. He belongs to a popular party, and takes the crown from one king and places it on another, which must indeed have an imposing effect. Then, when he is called at the end of the piece, he appears quite alone, makes his bow, and retires. So you see we might reckon on an elephant for our carnival. But the whole scene is much too large, and requires an uncommon kind of manager."

"Still, it is so brilliant and effective that a stage will scarcely allow it to escape. Then how it builds itself up, and becomes more and more striking! First, there are the beautiful gardeners, male and female; who decorate the stage, and at the same time form a mass, so that the various objects as they increase in importance are never without spectators and a background. Then, after the elephants, there is the team of dragons, coming from the background, through the air, and soaring overhead. Then the appearance of the great Pan; and how at last all seems afire, until put out by the wet clouds that roll to the spot. With all this carried out as you have conceived, the public will, in its amazement, confess that it has not senses and intellect enough to appreciate such spectacular riches."

"Pray, no more about the public," said Goethe; "I wish to hear nothing about it. The chief point is, that the piece is written; the world may now do with it as it pleases and use it as far as it can."

We then talked of the Boy Lenker.

"That Faust is concealed under the mask of Plutus, and Mephistopheles under that of Avarice, you will have already perceived. But who is the Boy Lenker?"

I hesitated, and could not answer.

"It is Euphorion," said Goethe.

"But how can he appear in the carnival here, when he is not born till the third act?"

"Euphorion," replied Goethe, "is not a human, but an allegorical being. In him is personified poetry; which is bound to neither time, place, nor person. The same spirit who afterwards chooses to be Euphorion appears here as the Boy Lenker, and is so far like a spectre that he can be present everywhere and at all times."

Sunday, December 27, 1829.

To-day, after dinner, Goethe read me the scene of the paper-money.

"You recollect," said he, "that at the imperial assembly the end of the song is that there is a want of money and that Mephistopheles promises to provide some. This theme continues through the masquerade; when Mephistopheles contrives that the Emperor, while in the mask of the great Pan, shall sign a paper, which, thus endowed with a money-value, is multiplied a thousandfold and circulated. Now, in this scene the affair is discussed before the Emperor, who does not know what he has done. The treasurer hands over the bank-notes, and makes everything clear. The Emperor is at first enraged; but afterwards, on a closer inspection of his profit, makes splendid presents of paper-money to those around him. As he retires, he drops some thousand crowns; the fat court-fool picks these up, and goes off at once to turn his paper into land."

While Goethe read this fine scene, I was pleased with the happy notion of deducing the paper-money from Mephistopheles, and thus so strikingly bringing in and immortalizing one of the main interests of the present day.

Scarcely had the scene been read and discussed, when Goethe's son came down and seated himself with us at the table. He told us of Cooper's last novel; which he had read, and which he now described in his graphic manner. We made no allusion to the scene we had just read; but he began of his own accord to tell a great deal about Prussian treasury-bills, and to say that they were paid for above their value. While young Goethe went on talking in this way, I looked at the father with a smile, which he returned; and thus we gave each other to understand how very apropos was the subject of the scene.

Wednesday, December 30, 1829.

To-day, after dinner, Goethe read me the next scene.

"Now they have got money at the imperial court," said he, "they want to be amused. The Emperor wishes to see Paris and Helen; and through magical art they are to appear in person. However, since Mephistopheles has nothing to do with Greek antiquity, and has no power over such personages, this task is assigned to Faust, who succeeds in it perfectly. The scene showing the means Faust must adopt to render the apparition possible is not complete yet. . . ." (pp. 336-39)

> *Johann Wolfgang von Goethe and Johann Peter Eckermann, in a conversation on December 6, 1829, in* Conversations with Goethe *by Johann Peter Eckermann, edited by J. K. Moorhead, translated by John Oxenford, 1930. Reprint by Everyman's Library, 1946, pp. 332-39.*

Denton J. Snider   (essay date 1886)

[*Snider was an American scholar, philosopher, and poet who closely followed the precepts of the German philosopher Georg Wilhelm Friedrich Hegel and contributed greatly to the dissemination of his dialectical philosophy in the United States. In the following excerpt from an* overview of the second part of *Faust, Snider praises Goethe as a master stylist.*]

In the Second Part of ***Faust,*** Mythology becomes universal, both in its form and in its meaning. The poem contains not a single Mythology of one time or of one people, or a single mythus thereof, but has the emphatic tendency to weave into its texture all Mythologies, of the most different times and peoples. But it employs not Mythology alone: it has also symbol, allegory, personification, even down to the riddle, yet each springs up in its own place and takes its part in the grand poetical cosmos. Besides these multitudinous forms transmitted to him, the poet frequently constructs a Mythology of his own, at first hand from Nature, going back to the original mythical fountain of the world, and making it pour forth again its primal treasures. The first myth-making faculty of the primitive race and the last flower of human culture bloom here, side by side, or rather they grow together into one colossal new product, the oldest and newest mythical gifts of man united into a world-embracing poem.

The chief Mythologies of this poem are the Greek and Teutonic, or Classic and Romantic. These have had and still have the main influence upon the hearts and imaginations of men; they indicate also great epochs in the World's History; they still represent phases of individual development, and remain its best poetic expression. ***Faust*** is primarily the bearer of the Teutonic mythus, upon which the Classic mythus is to be engrafted, the process of which takes place in this poem as it took place in history, and as it takes place to a greater or less extent in the culture of every individual. A reconstruction of the world's development we have here in a new mythical form, though its materials be old; the mythus of all culture it is, which unites the streams of the great Mythologies into its own mighty mythical river, and thus rises to the proportions of the World's Mythus.

But in these heathen elements of the poem we must not forget the Christian Mythology, which is here too, and is everywhere, playing into the work. The legends of the Church take their place in the poet's Whole, which winds up in the supreme religious mythus, that of the future state. Then the Devil, whose mythical origin is directly deduced from Christianity in the poem itself, is always present, and runs through the entire action with his problem. By means of these Biblical influences a Semitic thread is woven through the poem, in indissoluble intimacy with its dominant Aryan elements.

The Second Part opens with the fairy Mythology drawn out of Shakespeare, but modeled anew and with a fresh significance. From some old hint the poet constructs a new order of mythus, or a mythologem, such as Homunculus of Romantic, and Euphorion of Classic, fable. Allegory undisguised steps in, as seen in the Boy Charioteer; then the poem speaks in abstract personification, as in Hope, Fear, Prudence; symbols cunningly constructed and bearing deep meanings move through the picture, as we observe in that wonderful Elephant of the Masquerade. Again the verse flows into plain narrative, showing its sense on the surface, or under the most transparent covering; often it breaks into an apothegm or proverb, or turns to abstract reflection. Even Philosophy with its most abstruse forms is present, as we can observe in the scene of the Mothers; Religion, too, is on hand, with its legends and festivals and symbols, as we have already noticed. What a broad sympathy, what a universal culture is demanded of the reader of this poem! Too great, have been the demands on this and on the poet's own generation; the result is, his work has not been understood.

And now we must fully comprehend the relation of the poet to the mythus which he unfolds. Goethe is no longer the myth-maker in the primitive sense; he has not the naive faith of early peoples who recount in mythical form supernatural wonders. He does not believe, and he would not have his readers believe, in the literal raising of treasures out of the earth, in the literal transmutation of the base into the precious metals. The ancient story of Helen he tells again; but not with the immediate faith of old Homer; we feel that he has another meaning, that there is an element of intention, of conscious mythologizing which belongs to a new spiritual time. Hence there is a loss of instinctive utterance, of beautiful poetic childhood; but manhood, too, must have its mythus, and Goethe is its best spokesman. Accordingly there is a gain more than compensating for the loss; indeed the old mythus cannot mean much to us, till it be transfigured into its modern form.

For instance, treasures are raised out of the earth by the plow, by the various methods of agriculture. The baser metals are transmuted into gold in mining and manufacture; the iron and copper flow into a golden stream by Industry. Thus the old magic and alchemy are transformed into the Mythus of Industry, of which they are indeed the early half-articulate harbingers. We must always feel this second intention in the mythical work of Goethe; the first intention of the simple legend has long since passed away. In this second sense Goethe believed in the mythus, and we believe in it, for it is the great reality before our eyes. The interpreter whose only function is to help the reader do without an interpreter, has, for his brief duty, the task of pointing out the second intention above noticed, as it unfolds out of the old mythus into the new.

The attitudes of the mind toward the mythus, as toward religion, are, in the main, three: 1st. The time of unquestioning credence, when the miraculous element finds no mental obstacle. 2nd. The time of doubt and denial, when miracle, legend and religion are regarded as false, or largely as mere superstition. 3rd. The time of return to faith, not to the primal unconscious one, but now to a conscious one, which sees the truth of the early belief, yet sees too, its imperfect form, which caused the denial. Goethe in this Second Part of *Faust,* essentially takes this third standpoint, rescuing for the cultured world the mythus, and restoring the same to a new faith, which again becomes fresh in our hearts. He asks us no longer to accept the literal word, but to probe to the inner spirit; in fact he rebuilds the mythus in accord with this spirit, and wins it back from its long banishment amid the realms of darkness.

To illustrate our meaning still further, let us take one of the few mythical lines of American poetry; it is written by Emerson upon the fight at Concord, in which the embattled farmers stood,

> And fired the shot heard round the world.

This line is not a mere image or poetic figure, but a little national mythus, in which lies embosomed the meaning of the American Revolution to the world. Yet Emerson did not believe, nor expect us to believe, that there was any gun whose report could be heard over the globe. The particular fact of that shot is a lie, not credited by any American, however great his patriotism; but the universal fact of it is truth, profoundly believed by every American, and, indeed, by every thinking man. It is clear that, unless we reach down to this universal fact, we lose the poetry, and the line becomes not only prose but a falsehood. The poet is consciously mythologizing right out of the heart of his time; no Greek or Teutonic fable is this, but the most modern, the very mythus of gunpowder, which is here made universal, the bearer of an idea, so that its report is heard round the world. An ideal report is this certainly, yet the truth and the sole truth of the matter; the rest is a lie. But it is easy to comprehend a single line of this kind, we know; what if we have thousands of lines and a whole mythical system, which seems all false and unintelligible, till we behold the truth of it under its disguise?

In some such way we are to study Goethe's mythical procedure, for we may be sure that he is not simply narrating a pretty story to amuse his reader. If the poet has nothing better to do than that, let his book be burnt, for it cannot mean anything to an earnest man. Far otherwise is its lesson, as we gather it; the poem preaches the deed and not amusement; its object is to fill, not to kill time; and a part of its own heroic deed is to read it. But why should the poet then hide his meaning under such a veil, why does he not speak out plainly? Reader, he does not hide it, it hides itself, if it be hidden to thee; whether it be hidden or not, depends upon the vigor of thy eye-sight. All things spiritual have a material time-garment, which may hide them to some, but in reality is that which reveals them. The mythus takes this little story or occurrence, a mere shell of Time, hollow, even false, and fills it with an eternal thing; it transfigures the appearance, the lie, into truth. Moreover it corrects our material age by pointing to a Beyond, and by excluding from its poetic sanctuary the denier of spirit.

The connection between the First and Second Parts of the poem is specially maintained in the two leading characters, the natural and the supernatural, Faust and Mephisto, representing the two great strands which are wound together into the one work. The mythus of the old Faust-books and puppet-plays is continued in the Second Part, and adhered to even more rigidly than in the First Part. For the mythus has to be given to the poet by his people, he cannot make it, though he be the first to unfold it into its full significance.

The wonderful doings of Faust at the court of the German Emperor, as they are transmitted in legend, are the grand frame-work of this entire Second Part. That is, Faust passes from the individual, domestic and social sphere, in which he has been detained hitherto, into the State, a higher institution, passes from a lesser into "the greater world." This political setting will hold all of Faust's activity till the last scenes, when the religious world enters, and the State with its Present yields to the Church with its Future.

These miraculous doings of Faust in full may be divided into four chief actions: the making of money, the bringing of Helen, the winning of a battle, and the final fight with the Devil. The Teutonic, Greek and Christian mythologies have severally their places in these four grand actions, which become, in Goethe's hands, vast mythical reservoirs into which he pours the development of the race, and the culture of the individual. They must all be read with that second intention, to which allusion has been made; the outer letter of the legend must be illuminated with the inner spirit, before it can be truly seen.

For instance, the magic making of gold and raising of treasures, become, by a poetic transmutation more magical than alchemy, the making of money in the modern sense, the creation of wealth through material Industry; the bringing of Helen becomes the long training of the man for his highest performance, or the Culture of the Individual; the winning of the victory for the State shows the trained individual Faust applying the new material resources of Industry and the spiritual results of culture, first to the saving of the State, and then to its regeneration; the battle with the Devil, lost by the Protestant Faust of the legend, is won by the new Faust of Goethe, whereby we may see that his career is at bottom in harmony with the religious movement of man. These four grand actions, all-embracing in their sweep, indicate likewise the four main divisions in the organism of the poem.

Thus the miracles of Faust are made to shadow forth the miracles of our modern civilization; yesterday's magic is to-day's reality, and it may be to-morrow's ruins. Wonderful is the sympathy of the poet who could see and feel in this wild hocus-pocus of his Teutonic ancestors an honest attempt to utter something deep in themselves, something dark, which was struggling to be born into the light of the sun. Often frantic, often stupid, and always chaotic are these throes of the popular heart seeking utterance, hardly more than a cry or short forced pulsations of voice; but the poet touches the dark word, and it bursts into sunrise illuminating a world. This Faust magic, so beloved of the people, was a genuine thing to them, nay, to all time; it was not to be cast aside as mad fancy, or pure superstition, but was to be set forth in a great poem, which truly brings to speech the inarticulate fable. Magic is not now the wonder, but magic realized in the world before our eyes, in railroad, telegraph, telephone, all of which are legends more miraculous than any yet told in folklore.

The poet's work is, therefore, not the making, but the unfolding of the mythus into its true poetic flower. The poet may be truly said to interpret the mythus to his own age; unless he has this power, he can have little to say. Not merely to tell the story over again, as some former time told it—what is the use of that? Not an imitation his work must be, not a simple repetition or transference; with the gift of story-telling there must be the gift of interpretation, of working the significance of his own time into the legend,

or rather of developing the legend into his own time, out of its earlier germ. His is the gift of poetic vision, which sees truth in fabulous forms, and reveals it anew, still in fabulous forms, which hold not the old but the new spirit. All this poem may be called a vast interpretation of the Faust mythus, yet in a mythical form still; as the perfect flower is but the dark seed or germ unfolded to completeness in the light of Heaven.

This Second Part is not specially remarkable for imagery, or for those flowers which the reader expects to pluck as he dallies along its avenues and sideways. He must work into the conception, if he would find the true image, which is the whole work given in one colossal cast of the imagination. Too often with our poets the theme is utterly prosaic, though it be strown with many pretty posies; these do not grow as native flowers out the soil of the subject-matter, but are exotics with a sickly growth in an artificial environment; or possibly parasites clinging to a dead or even rotten trunk. Goethe is a grand builder, and his material is the pure marble, out of which he constructs his entire temple; he puts no plaster facings on it with an external marble glitter. Herein he is more Greek than Romantic, more Homer than Shakespeare, the latter of whom swathes his grand poetic conceptions in countless layers of images, one often heaped on top of the other.

Nor can it command a dramatic interest in the ordinary sense of the word, though it be a drama. It has no knot, strictly; it rests on no dramatic complications which are all loosened at once by a solution. It is rather a development and not an envelopment; it takes as its dramatic form the unfolding of man, and of the devil also, the drama of the spiritual growth of the race. It has thus the last and deepest of all forms, so comprehensive that the name of drama hardly applies to it longer. All other dramas seem beside it certain small eddies more or less profound, in the Time-stream; this is the river itself in its everlasting sweep onward. It has well been called a drama of ideas; instead of characters we behold ideas acting and enduring; persons in it become what they were on the old stage, a speaking mask, through which the idea is voiced. Often we are in doubt whether the person be a living reality or some spectral phantasm; but we need not be in doubt concerning the idea uttered by him, which truly is all there is of him, or indeed of anybody or anything.

The difference between the First and Second Parts is great, but the profounder and more important fact is their harmony. They must be felt as one, the outflow of the same poetic soul, though at many diverse periods of life. The true discipline of the study of *Faust* is not attained till this harmony be attained in thought and feeling. The two Parts show great diversities: the First is more impulsive, the Second more reflective; the First has more joy in a sensuous fullness of expression, the Second is more sober and of stricter form; the First has more passion, the Second more thought; or, as the poet himself declares, the one is more subjective, the other more objective. The First Part moves in a limited even narrow sphere—old Teutonic life, with scarcely a hint of antiquity or of the great world stage; the Second moves at once to court, to the European current, into which the classic world pours with a broad full stream, and we behold a multifarious image of the History of Europe. The First shows a descent from guilt to guilt; the Second shows the return, the grand palingenesis, chiefly through the Renascence. There are many other points of distinction, which the reader will make for himself, but the greater fact is their unity, the fact toward which the earnest student must always strive. Too exclusive devotion to the First Part in its special diversities and peculiarities may beget an indifference to the Second Part. When we hear a man praising the First Part, at the expense of the Second Part, we may be assured that he has not reached and felt the heart-beat of the First Part which he is praising, for it is one with the heart-beat of the Second Part. Again we must affirm the profoundest fact of both is their unity. We may be caught in the fervor, the brilliancy, the deviltry of the First Part, or some other special phase; then we may find the Second Part unenjoyable, with its calmness, its movement out of deviltry, its sententious form of utterance. Broaden yourself till you can take in both, else you will truly possess neither, for both have their deep primitive fountain in the same poetic soul.

We see in this poem the idea of Development raised to the supreme literary form, which becomes one with the movement of mankind. This idea was caught by Goethe distinctly from his study of Nature, out of which he transported it into Literature. But it has been the driving-wheel of all Occidental civilization in contrast with Oriental fixity. Its first expression is in the Greek Theogony, in which, time after time, a system of higher Gods supplants a system of lower Gods, so that in oldest Hellas Theology was a progressive science, which it has hardly been since. But its completest spiritual expression is found in German Philosophy from Leibnitz to Hegel, to the last of whom, verily the last German Philosopher, this idea was the all-in-all, the soul of his dialectic, and the world was simply the unfolding of the idea into reality. Hegel is indeed in many ways the philosophic counterpart of Goethe. It is true Goethe disclaimed being a philosopher, and declared that he had "no philosophical organ;" still, as W. Von Humboldt told him, and as Schiller intimates, he was a philosopher, only his manner of philosophizing was different from the ordinary way, and the abstract metaphysical method was repugnant to him. Who can read his books and not see that he is a great thinker and is occupying himself with the profoundest problems of thought? Metaphysical cobwebs, spun for the sake of spinning, or to catch some wandering insect he took no delight in, nor does any earnest healthy human soul. He is the poet of culture by virtue of his thought; he is no Burns singing native wood melodies like the bird on the branch, which sound so delightful to the ear of the passing traveler; but one gets tired of bird-music, however sweet, and in fact one has not the time to listen to it long. Far different is the Faust strain of Goethe, it is the choral anthem of the Universe, to whose music your life must be set, if you wish to live harmoniously. His poetry is not, let it be repeated, to amuse your vacant hour, or to rest your tired moments; you must give to him your best hour, if you will understand him; he rejects the off-scourings of your busy day, he will have your highest moment, and not once but many times. Your supreme vocation for the time being must be to understand him. The reason why he refuses to open his treasures

to so many people, is, that they bring as their sacrifice to his altar, the offals of their intelligence. If you devote to Mammon the best of your labors, no true God or no true man is going to accept the remaining refuse of your life, he will keep out of your company.

In this sense of a continuous unfolding, the poem is to be read and construed. We must see the genesis of part out of part, the subtle transition must be closely watched in all its connecting threads. An interpretation has this business in the main; it is altogether the most difficult matter for the reader, and for the interpreter, which, if he does not get, he cannot reach the heart of the book. Philological, historical, mythologic difficulties are small in comparison; indeed they can be carried along unexplained often with little detriment, if one is borne deeply in the thought of the poem. But if the thought be not gained or be lost, what have you gotten? Here is the grand mistake of most editors and commentators. They seem to take for granted that the thought of the poem and its structure are plain to every reader, while this little mythologic allusion or that little grammatical solecism is unintelligible. Often it may remain unintelligible without much loss; but the thought and structure must be seized, if we wish to possess the work.

The conception of *Faust,* Goethe writes in 1832, goes back more than sixty years; in this first conception was included much of what is found in the Second Part at present. Particularly the elaboration of the "Helena" occupied him in this early period, and it must have been a constituent element of the first written plan or scheme. Such a plan of the continuation of Faust we find by the conversations of Eckermann, Goethe intended to insert in his autobiography for the year 1775.

But Margaret supplanted Helen in the First Part; one grand stage of Faust's development had in consequence to be carried over into a new realm. The idea of a Second Part must have already dawned on Goethe in 1797, when he wrote the Prologue in Heaven; Schiller speaks of it in the "Correspondence," as a matter determined. The two women of the poem, the German and the Greek, Nature and Culture, could not be well brought together; they are centers of the two different Parts, and probably first compelled the division of the poem.

In 1824, Goethe aged 75 years, was giving what he thought to be the final revision of his works—well might he think so! when he took in hand again his autobiography (*Dichtung und Wahrheit*). Three parts of this work had appeared in the years 1811-14; the fourth part with which he had formerly been unable to proceed, was taken in hand, and the attempt was made to bring it to completion. It contained the events of the year 1775, and in it the plan of the continuation of Faust, as conceived at that time, was to be inserted. So much we learn from the faithful Eckermann.

But Eckermann, who was his literary assistant and counselor, urged him to lay hold of the plan, and to complete it poetically. To this sympathy and encouragement of Eckermann we owe the Second Part, as Goethe has himself declared. Of course all the fuel was there, only the lighted shaving was wanted to kindle it. This was Eckermann's gift, he could stir the old conception "of more than sixty years," could rouse the aged man to one final concentrated act of will running through seven years, till the work was done; then the hand fell and the old bard was dead, with his long swan-song ended.

Thus the Second Part in the circumstances of its composition differs from the First Part in two important regards. First, the Second Part is one great outflow, belonging to one period, whereas the First Part is scattered through forty years, is the product of very different periods, has more inequality, has greater leaps in it, and in certain points is more difficult to understand. There is an evenness and symmetry in the Second Part, while the First Part has ruggedness, irregularity, more changes in style.

The second fact is that the Second Part was written in Goethe's old age, after life had given him all its experience, and had put into his hands nearly every literary form, and had calmed his passion into wisdom. In a sense, there is more variety than in the First Part, but this variety is mastered, it has no tendency to become independent. Nearly every kind of marble on the earth goes into the temple, but it is all hewn and fitted into its place, and is made to express one note in the grand harmony, being dominated fully by one idea, one ultimate form. All colors are here, still they belong to the Whole, and are subdued to its central thought.

It is not a product of senile weakness, as has been often charged, but of senile vigor, and just for this reason has a peculiar flavor among all written books. Yes, there is old age here, but an old age which has resumed and digested a long life, indeed, an old age which takes up and lives the life of mankind in its own life. No youth, no man of middle age could do this; the work is the purest crystallization of turbulent youth, studious and active middle age; the old man's imagination becomes a poetical universe. The sympathetic reader will feel the advantages of Age in this book as in old wines; doubtless, too, with certain disadvantages thereof.

The poetic process of Goethe is essentially the same in the Second Part as in all his works. He does not necessarily begin with the idea and incorporate it with an image; he rather begins with the image, and expands and fills it with an idea. Neither side is wanting; it were no true poetry if image or idea should be absent. He looks at an object, becomes one with it, sinks wholly into it, till he lives in an unconscious condition with its inmost nature, till he sees and feels its growth, germ, development, till its idea dawns upon his soul, not as an abstract thought, but as the very picture of the object. This condition is what he often calls his "dumpfheit," or period of poetic hibernation; moreover he speaks of himself as a sort of somnambulist, doing many wonderful feats unconsciously, which he would not dare attempt when awake. This power he has, of becoming one with Nature and feeling her secretest throb, then uttering the same in song; so he tells what the bird is singing, what the animal is doing, what Nature is saying. In like manner he treats the historic event, he sinks into it, lives with it, till he hears its voice, what it says and means, which is the voice of the future. The affair of the Diamond

Necklace in which he saw a sign and heard a voice, is an example; it was a symbol in his use of the word.

In this sense he says that "everything that happens is a symbol." It has an outer phenomenal side, which, however, is but the expression of the soul of the event, its idea. The poet seizes the image of the event and makes it transparent with the idea, not always with intention perhaps, but because he cannot do otherwise. He says somewhere "all our knowledge is symbolical;" this is to know a thing truly, to see its idea in the event or fact. "Alles Vergaengliche ist nur ein Gleichniss," declares the same thing; what is phenomenal and transitory is only a likeness in which is imaged the eternal. Reading his **Wilhelm Meister's Apprenticeship** in his old age, he finds it "symbolical," and in his sense it is.

Two opposite errors are here possible: We must not consider **Faust** as an image merely, a series of events or pictures; it is also an idea. But it is not some abstract idea merely, illustrated by a story or legend; the legend is the very form and speech of the idea, and the idea has its truest reality in the legend. The intuitive and the intellectual standpoints are united in the supreme poetic act; our thought may separate them for a moment for definition, but must never leave them separated. The highest appreciation of **Faust** unites image and idea into one poetic flash, and thus approaches the original creative act of the poet.

Everywhere, even in his scientific writings Goethe sees forms, and fills them; in the sky among the clouds, forms, forms; on the earth below, in its deep caverns, forms, forms; in the kingdom of flowers, forms, forms; in the animate world, forms, forms. He seems to have stood in more intimate relation to this formative energy of Nature, than any other recorded man; he turned to it, was happy only in contemplating it. But not only did he contemplate it; he sank into it with feeling and instinct, was absorbed into the object, became one with its soul, slept with it in unconscious hibernation, yet wandered about as a poetical somnambulist, when he began to sing. A sort of insensible sense was his state of poetic activity.

He is the greatest poet of these late centuries, not because he has used the most images or the most beautiful images, but because he makes his image tell its deepest truth, makes it speak the profoundest and best idea to men. A sensuous indulgence in images, which float before the mind as shows, is not his poetic method; many a lesser poet surpasses him in brilliancy, color, vividness. But he makes his event or fable or other image tell its last story, speak its truest word; verily he appreciates appearances better than other writers, since he sees so much more in them. To the humblest trope he gives great honor, making it reflect its true soul or thought, and transforming it into a bearer of profound wisdom.

If the Second Part takes up and utilizes every species of poetic form, as parable, myth, symbol, even the riddle, in like manner it embraces almost every kind of meter, ancient and modern. Rhyme and rhythm, long and short verses, with every variety of harmonious intonation, play through the musical phantasmagory, yet under law always. In this respect the Second Part has often been compared to a symphony with its ranks of instruments, wood, metal, string; each has its place, its peculiar tone-color, its solo, when it sinks back into the harmonious blending of the whole. Flute, violin, and horn, in many shades we hear; still it is one harmony, and organic. It may be said that the metrical work of the Second Part is of itself a most prodigious effort, by the greatest master of versification: in this respect alone it must remain a mine for all future poets. Herein it differs from the other Greatest Poets; Homer and Dante have but one measure, Shakespeare mainly one, with delicate lyrical snatches here and there.

Faust, too, has in the main but one measure, the free doggerel, whose lines vary from two to six feet, with consecutive, alternate, or remoter rhymes. This measure is very pliable in the hands of the poet, it drops at times almost into prose, and then rises into a rapturous flight; a light, easy garment at all times, borrowed, it is said, mainly from genial old Hans Sachs, the shoemaker and poet of Nuremberg. In the Second Part the metrical treatment is rather more strict than in the First Part, more of a classic reserve, and often breaking into gnomic terseness, a style much cultivated by Goethe in his later years. Then comes the infinite movement of his lyric forms, the rainbow playing over the waters, till even the doggerel passes into the purest sculpturesque serenity of the Classic Iambs of Sophocles, with rhythmic measures of the Greek chorus. To hear all this music is indeed a great training. It is a Wagnerian strain which overwhelms at first and which can be conquered only by time and much effort.

Herein Goethe has shown the true way of metrical procedure, his *Faust* resumes all meters to a degree, it is the very bloom of the measured speech of the world, and just therein is original in the supreme sense. Goethe does not have to fling himself out of the traces of Time to be original; the great lines of culture he keeps within while advancing them; the Universe is large enough for his originality. Never odd, he is still original in being the most human of humanity; every man may see in him nothing bizarre but rather his own true self. Hence Goethe never, with one or two possible exceptions in youth, quit the principle of measured speech for poetry, a principle laid down by old Homer at the beginning of Literature; his respect for it increases with age, in the Second Part of *Faust* its sway is absolute. Whitman is perhaps the most notable instance of the opposite tendency; maddened by the narrow and senseless restraints of English verse, and wearied to death by its eternal Iambic shuffle, he seizes the edifice which holds him a prisoner, like another Sampson, and tears it asunder in a fit of mighty wrath, and reaches liberty, but just therein destroys himself. He takes no free old measures, makes no free new measures, but substantially throws away all measured speech, and thereby abandons the first architectonic principle of poetry, without which it can never rise up a beautiful structure out of prose. There must be proportion, measurement, symmetry, which always make harmony possible; there must be a recurrence of the beat after a fixed interval, which must be felt to be coming, else there is a jar in the strain. Whitman has been called the Poet of Democracy with its measureless ocean; but we protest, freedom is not lawlessness in politics or poetics; more freedom we must have, but with

it a more profound law; America is not outside of the World's History but inside of it, a resumption of it all, and its final perfect bloom, or to be such. Originality without oddity is the true originality, and the great man does not destroy the old, but transfigures it into the new.

This metrical treatment is a true image of Faust in all his career, especially his political; he fights for the ancient realm of the Emperor, and saves it from revolution; but at the same time out of the unrestrained sea he raises a new land, with new inhabitants, free men upon a free soil, which comes not by destroying but by preserving the old; from this new point he transforms all the world into freedom, not by destruction, but by reconstruction. In a similar spirit the poet has preserved the old meters, but out of them made a new music, and built a new harmony, which has not destroyed but really preserved and rejuvenated the measured speech of men. In this fact we see Goethe himself as the universal man of our time, the man who takes in the past, and foreshadows the future; the most conservative of men, called an aristocrat often, with much truth, yet the most progressive, nay, most radical of men, so devoted to humanity that he will not let one of its acquired treasures be lost, nor permit it to be cramped from free development by its most sacred institutions.

The grand episode of Helen which, first and last, is more than half of the entire Second Part, is thrown into the world-movement of the poem, especially into its institutional movement. This is distinctively the Hellenic portion in all phases from the first origin in Homer to its final extinction. It gives what is called the Renascence or New Birth of Time, which occurs at given periods in the History of Culture. It arises when the shackles of custom and convention begin to cramp the human spirit, it opens a world of intellectual freedom, followed often by political regeneration. It comes from a new study and spiritual taking-up of ancient fresh sources of inspiration, chiefly from those of Hellas. There was a Roman Renascence in the time of Augustus, in which Greece gave a sort of spiritual glory to a declining political world. There was a medieval Renascence, slight, but it gave Dante. There was the great Renascence, properly so-called, that gave us Luther in the North, Michael Angelo and Raphael in the South, culminating in the mighty poetic voice of the Renascence, William Shakespeare. Then there was the recent German Renascence, begetting modern German Literature, in which Goethe is the central figure. This process of the Time-Spirit, the renovation of the decadent soul through a new culture, is imaged in the total "Helena," not merely in the Third Act. Faust, of course, has to go through this regenerating process before he can transfer it to his country and to his age.

The grand significance of a Renascence in the development of the race is here imaged. The Poet himself participated in it, nay, he studied and took up into his own culture all previous Renascences. Besides going to the fountain head, ancient Homer and the Greek Poets, he worked into the Roman Renascence with deepest sympathy, the least of them all, because it gave no practical regeneration to the Roman World. Ovid and Horace, wild Martial, and even little Propertius, mostly Greek transfusions into

Latin, wrought upon Goethe prodigeously, he imitated them and became more original than his Originals. The Italian Renascence, chiefly through its Art, its best manifestation, makes an epoch in his life through his visit to Italy. The German Renascence of the 16th century furnished him his grandest theme, this Faust, who is a product of it, and through whom the twin German Renascences of the 16th and 19th centuries are joined together poetically, being cognate in so many points.

Here again Goethe's whole activity is a resumption and new unfolding of the world's activity in this line; his works are a commentary and fresh edition of all the Renascences from the Roman down; this is again his true originality, to be as great as the world and as broad as humanity, as old as the Past, as new as the Present. A commentary on Time is his works, giving an image thereof; the part of Helen is, as it were, this image, and this double image, the process of the new Birth unfolding all the while, yet mirroring itself in this process, even to making new pictures of former pictures of itself. The Culture of the Individual it shows, yet this culture is also shadowed forth as the movement and soul of a period. The "Helena," placed in the institutional frame-work of a German State, is German in outer form and speech, yet it tells the tale for the future, and in its way prophesies the American Renascence, also to spring of the ancient Greek fountain head, and outlines in a general way all succeeding Renascences. Not simply Art and Literature does Helen influence, she goes into the practical world, and transforms it; her goal is not merely humanism, but humanity.

It was long thought that this Second Part of *Faust* could not be put upon the stage, being quite unpresentable to the outer eye. The poet never saw it on the boards, yet he must have thought that some day it might be produced, as he has arranged the scenes for stage-effect, and given numerous stage-directions. He saw it as a drama, it moved before his inner vision as a grand world-action, quite beyond the possibilities of the theatrical arrangements of the time. But here too, he was a prophet, and wrote for the future. Our own age has witnessed repeated representations of it, with great, even popular effect in Germany. Many important points are brought out in the scenic interpretation otherwise hidden; the newest and best commentary on it has been the acting of it. The report goes that many enjoy it in the representation, who cannot read it beyond the first scenes.

Here again it prophesies the new Drama, the Drama of Ideas, and a new histrionic Art. Doubtless the operatic innovations of Wagner paved the way; indeed, there are many cognate points between Wagner's *Trilogy* and Goethe's *Faust,* in their demands upon the theater and upon the audience, as well as in their significance. Even Shakespeare felt the limits of the old stage, and chafed against them; his best play in many respects, *Tempest,* is quite unrepresentable in the old fashion. It too is a Drama of Ideas, moving upon an inner stage, that of the Imagination; when those Ideas, Caliban, Ariel, even Prospero, are placed upon the outer boards, there seems some vast loss. Yet the new theatrical art may yet recover the loss; indeed the tendency is leading thither. The presentation of Wagner's op-

eras has left Germany on a tour round the world; we may expect Goethe's *Faust,* the whole of it, to follow in the wake.

But the acting of *Faust* can never supplant the reading of it; indeed, it cannot be well understood on the stage, till after a thorough reading; it is like *Hamlet,* a good theatrical presentation is a sort of commentary to help the reader, rather than the spectator. A great play is one which cannot have its resources exhausted in a mere visual scenic production; thus they are only suggested, and provoke the spectator to read it, if he has not read it. No wonder Shakespeare's plays were printed surreptitiously in his own time, they drove the public naturally to read them. Some actors, with professional narrowness would have us believe that the only way of understanding Shakespeare is by seeing him acted. Not so; it is but a side and that too, the external side of him; it is but a commentary, very valuable, but not the most valuable; hundreds read him to one who sees him. There are drawbacks to a scenic presentation, it may be poor or perverted, it may give a false idea, and always runs the danger of emphasizing too strongly the sensuous visual element in Shakespeare.

It would indeed require an ideal combination in a theater to produce *Faust.* A manager who would direct all his histrionic forces, nay, his mechanical effects to bring out the Whole; an actor who would become truly a mask for the idea, a mask of flesh and blood, imaging and uttering only the spirit within, abjuring all outer sensational appeals; in fine, the idea must act and speak always, a supersensible world dropping for a moment into the senses. Such a theater will yet be, indeed, in supreme Art always has been; but it is now to become our permanent and conscious possession. Goethe, who was Manager, Poet, and even Actor in one, was well aware of the difficulty with the modern stage: in his "Prelude on the Stage" he has introduced the three characters speaking; there the Manager and Actor seem quite intractable to the idea of the Poet, they scorn his Whole, and turn to the immediate reward of sensuous effects; but the Poet persists, and writes his drama anyhow, appealing prophetically to the Future.

The drama of *Faust,* the drama of the soul, must chiefly appeal to the single human soul reading and studying it. For the reader can go backward, forward, fast or slow, can stop and think, or even wait for a little growth over night. After all the stage is really the inner one, not bound to Space or Time, and chiefly not bound to these few hours' representation in a given spot. The dramatic form cannot be dropped, for this is inherent; but the drama has gone inside and is playing there; you have a theater and company all to yourself. In fact it is your own play, the play of your life, or you must make it such. (pp. vii-xxxv)

Denton J. Snider, in a introduction to his Goethe's Faust, Second Part: A Commentary on the Literary Bibles of the Occident, *Ticknor & Co., 1886, pp. vii-xl.*

A. R. Hohlfeld (essay date 1901)

[*Below, Hohlfeld traces the development of the dramatic conflict in* Faust, *asserting that Goethe's "plan and pur-*

pose" for the drama is to depict Faust's ultimate redemption as reflecting the central conflict of interests between God and Mephistopheles.]

Being a giant among works of poetry, Goethe's *Faust* suffers the fate of almost all things gigantic, be they the work of nature or of human genius. Many men of note have admitted that the first impression which they received from the reading of *Faust* did not entirely come up to their expectations. But have we not all heard of similar comments on St. Peter's in Rome, on Beethoven's symphonies, on Raphael's Sistine Madonna, on Mont Blanc, or on Niagara? There are objects that transcend our powers of immediate comprehension and require a more gradual process of familiarization. Besides, it is a well-established fact that we generally approach such objects of universal admiration with unduly exaggerated expectations. As the best music demands repeated hearings before it admits us to an intimate appreciation of its subtlest charms, so also must the greatest works of literature be read again and again, and more in a reverential than in a purely critical spirit, before they reveal to us their innermost beauty and meaning. But whereas a work of average, or even more than average, significance may hardly sustain our interest at a second or third perusal, the truly great work will become the more attractive the more we grow familiar with it. Thus it is with Goethe's *Faust.*

In this statement the great majority of the serious-minded readers of *Faust* will probably concur, even if with certain individual modifications and reservations, if we are willing to confine what has been said to the First Part. If, however, you are not prepared to admit the same, or nearly the same, for the Second Part, those who are the most ardent students of *Faust* will tell you it is because you have not read it often enough. This much is true, many critics of sound taste and judgment, especially in more recent years, have claimed that the long-maligned Second Part of Goethe's *Faust* has gradually acquired for them a charm and significance not only equaling but even surpassing that of the First Part, which all admire. As for myself, I have not exactly reached this point yet, and hardly know whether I am traveling on any very direct road leading to it; but so much is sure: careful and repeated reading has filled me with a growing admiration, not to say a growing sense of awe, of the gigantic sweep and vast scope of the poet's *plan* and *purpose* in the Second Part, even though, in my present estimation, the artistic *execution* of this plan is often unsatisfactory, perhaps must needs be unsatisfactory, since the very design seems to transcend the boundaries of dramatic art, if not of all art. (pp. 295-96)

On account of [the] disrupted mode of composition and publication [of *Faust*], as well as on account of the unmistakable differences in tone and spirit which characterize different portions of the work, it has been commonly assumed that the drama as a whole, however sublime in thought and sentiment, however fascinating and powerful in its individual scenes, lacks unity of plan and purpose. Great stress, in this connection, has again and again been laid on a few evident incongruities that are found in the narration of some events and in the delineation of one or two of the characters. These, however, affect only details, without touching any vital point in the poet's unity of purpose. On the other hand, it should be well understood that if I am inclined to claim for *Faust* unity of plan, I do not claim for it unity of action in the technical sense in which the term is applied to the drama. There can be no doubt that Goethe's *Faust* neither is nor was meant to be a regular drama, but rather a vast epic built on dramatic lines.

Instead of one action or conflict, which is gradually intensified, reaches a climax, and then speeds on to its final catastrophe, instead of one such action, as in an ordinary drama, we have in *Faust* a succession of apparently disconnected episodes, of which at least two (the Gretchen tragedy in the First Part, and the Helena episode in the Second Part) attain to the scope and importance of well-nigh complete dramas within the drama. With the exception of Faust and Mephistopheles, the persons figuring in one episode rarely reappear in another, and certainly Faust and Mephistopheles are the only characters that figure in the entire drama from beginning to end. It might thus appear as if the individuality of Faust alone was forming the connecting link between the various episodes, between which there would thus exist not an artistically organic connection, but merely a personal or biographical bond.

Such, however, is not the case. All of the episodes are organic parts of one consistent theme; they are not loosely connected through the figure of Faust, but form consecutive stages in the development of a higher action or conflict, which is not, and cannot be, directly represented on the stage, but which embraces all the various episodes in one supreme unity of purpose. This real unity of the drama is found in the conflict between God and Mephistopheles for the possession of Faust's soul. That is to say, the question which the drama tries to solve, and to which everything in it is made subordinate, is the question whether the forces that we consider antagonistic to the divine side of human nature are strong enough so to ensnare a soul so richly endowed as that of Faust as to make it hopelessly forget its divine calling and idealistic cravings. This conflict is clearly outlined in the Prologue in Heaven, where, when the Lord speaks of Faust as his "servant," Mephistopheles sneeringly replies:

> Forsooth! he serves you after strange devices:
> No earthly meat or drink the fool suffices:
> His spirit's ferment far aspireth;
> Half conscious of his frenzied, crazed unrest,
> The fairest stars from heaven he requireth,
> From earth the highest raptures and the best,
> And all the Near and Far that he desireth
> Fails to subdue the tumult of his breast.

THE LORD

> Though still confused his service unto Me,
> I soon shall lead him to a clearer morning.
> Sees not the gardener, even while buds his tree,
> Both flower and fruit the future years adorning?

MEPHISTOPHELES

> What will you bet? There's still a chance to gain him,
> If unto me full leave you give,
> Gently upon *my* road to train him!

THE LORD

> As long as he on earth shall live,
> I make no prohibition;
> While Man's desires and aspirations stir,
> He cannot help but err.

When, thereupon, Mephistopheles expresses his confidence in his ultimate victory, he is interrupted by the following words:

THE LORD

> Enough! What thou hast asked is granted.
> Turn off this spirit from his fountain head;
> To trap him, let thy snares be planted,
> And him, with thee, be downward led;
> Then stand abashed, when thou art forced to
>   say,
> A good man, through obscurest aspiration,
> Has still an instinct of the one true way.

In other words, Mephistopheles is promised not to be interfered with in his plans for Faust's spiritual ruin, while, at the same time, we receive the indirect assurance that Faust, though he will not be preserved from error and sin, will ultimately remain victorious.

Thus we have in Faust an essentially dramatic conflict, only with this marked difference from the ordinary drama, that the conflict is a spiritual one, and that, hence, the two antagonistic powers cannot be directly represented as *dramatis personae*. It is true, the antidivine principle appears personified in the figure of Mephistopheles, one of the most marvelous creations of a poet's imagination, utterly fanciful and yet strikingly realistic, as interesting and fascinating as he is repellent and terrible. The divine element, however, the poet was unable to represent similarly. It appears confined to Faust's own soul, as the voice of his conscience, his better self.

After the character of the struggle that is to ensue has thus been indicated, the drama proper begins. The first scenes, answering the purpose of what we call the "exposition" of a drama, acquaint us with Faust's character, his past life, his present mood and surroundings. Here Faust appears as the very counterpart of Mephistopheles. The latter proves himself a mocking, unimpassioned spirit, of no mean intellectuality, it is true, but without a trace of idealism, a cold pessimist of low aims and unclean motives. Faust, on the other hand, is the heaven-daring Promethean idealist who is not willing to admit the reality of the intellectual limitations inherent in man's nature. He yearns for communion with the spirit world, for insight into the most secret fountains and subtlest processes of nature and of human life. His thirst for truth and experience are not to be quenched by the knowledge which he has been able to gather and the inadequacy of which he keenly feels. Neither creed and dogma on the one hand nor the results of philosophy and science on the other have satisfied him. He desires to fathom the universe, to know and to experience all things.

But, in considering this state of turmoil in Faust's soul, we must not overlook the fact that his error and waywardness are only relative. His striving after light and truth is indeed service of the deity, for it cannot be found or served except in light and truth. His error rather consists in the fact that in his ideal flights he not only forgets the serious limitations to which human nature is subject, but also neglects and scorns the manifold duties and pleasures resulting from our daily intercourse with our fellow men— duties and pleasures which must, and in a large measure can, console us for so many yearnings that are doomed to remain unfulfilled. Thus Faust appears indeed as we found him depicted in the Prologue in Heaven, a "servant of God," but one whose service is as yet confused and without clearness of vision, and who, therefore, has not yet found that supreme peace of soul that to Goethe means salvation.

In its last analysis, the conflict between Faust and Mephistopheles is a strictly human one. Both Faustian and Mephistophelian tendencies we all find in our own natures. Like Faust, we can say of ourselves:

> Two souls, alas! reside within this breast,
> And each withdraws from and repels its brother.
> One with tenacious organs holds in love
> And clinging lust the world in its embraces;
> The other strongly sweeps, this dust above,
> Into the high ancestral spaces.

Be it humiliating for our race or not, the fact remains that all men partake more or less of that coarser, disenchanted, coldly materialistic, frivolous nature that is the sphere of Mephistopheles. We are not planned as beings of angelic purity. But it should be our constant endeavor to ennoble and purify the coarser elements within us by means of our higher instincts. This is rarely accomplished without a struggle, and this struggle, as has been shown above, is the principal theme of Goethe's *Faust.*

Let us then proceed to a brief review of the development of this dramatic conflict.

Mephistopheles, we must imagine, has been hovering around Faust like the hawk that is circling around the prey which it has spied in the fields. At last, when the opportunity seems favorable, he gains access to Faust's company, succeeds in interesting him in *his* way of looking at life, so diametrically opposed to that of Faust, and finally, when he finds his victim in an opportune mood of utter despair, ready to do anything that would seem to promise escape from the unbearable discontent gnawing at his soul, he proposes a pact, a written agreement signed with blood, through which Faust's soul is eventually to come into his possession.

I say "eventually," and thereby indicate the profound change which Goethe has introduced in this feature of the old legend. All other treatments of the Faust legend, it is true, contained a pact between Faust and the devil; but in all of them, and so also in Marlowe's *Doctor Faustus,* the pact was of such a nature that it required Mephistopheles to serve Faust in all of his desires for a fixed number of years, generally twenty-four, after the expiration of which period Faust's soul was to be the devil's. Such a mechanical device, permitting of no dramatic conflict and suspense, and making the ruin of a human soul dependent on the lapse of a fixed number of years, could not satisfy Goethe, nor indeed any truly modern poet.

The old pact was the natural result of a mediaeval view of life, according to which every effort of man to get beyond the limits of traditionally sanctioned knowledge was a crime. According to it, every independent searcher after truth was a heretic and magician, and every heretic and magician in a league with the spirit of evil, speeding along the road to everlasting ruin. The eighteenth century, however, was preeminently characterized by the spirit of free inquiry. No longer was it held to be a sin, but rather man's highest aim and object in life, to search for the truth and to remove false traditions standing in the way of its light. To such an age Faust, tormented by his unsatisfied yearnings for profounder knowledge, could no longer be presented as an object lesson of timid moralizing, by means of which men should be impressed with the awful fate awaiting him who might dare to move away from the traditional standards of knowledge, no matter how worn and void of truth they might happen to be. By such an age Faust's striving could no longer be considered as in itself sinful, but rather as the brightest light of the divine fire burning in man's soul. Irrevocably to commit him to the spirit of evil as punishment for this superhuman striving would have been nothing short of condemning the very spirit of progress and investigation that is the keynote of modern culture and civilization. Faust's error that was to bring suffering and wrong-doing into his life, as into that of others, was not his striving as such, but his *excessive* striving, that tried to disregard all limitations of human existence.

An illustration of Faust in his study by Eugene Delacroix.

From such a point of view the pact between Faust and Mephistopheles could not remain the same as in the legend; in fact, in Goethe's conception it has become almost the very opposite. In the old legend, it was Faust's striving that condemned him; in Goethe's *Faust,* the ultimate salvation of Faust is made dependent on his not ceasing to strive. If Mephistopheles succeeds, by the pleasures and activities which he is able to furnish, so to captivate Faust as to make him satisfied—i.e., so to suppress his better nature that he will cease to strive after the highest things attainable to man—then, but not until then, is he to belong to Mephistopheles. No individual error will condemn Faust, nor, indeed, will any individual act save him; but everything will depend upon the spirit underlying his actions. Such is the Goethean form of the pact between the two.

FAUST

When on an idler's bed I stretch myself in quiet,
There let at once my record end!
Canst thou with lying flattery rule me,
Until, self-pleased, myself I see—
Canst thou with rich enjoyment fool me,
Let that day be the last for me!
The bet I offer.

MEPHISTOPHELES

Done!

FAUST

And heartily.
When thus I hail the moment flying:
"Ah, still delay, thou art so fair!"
Then bind me in thy bonds undying,
My final ruin then declare!
Then let the death-bell chime the token,
Then art thou from thy service free!
The clock may stop, the hand be broken,
Then Time be finished unto me.

Now the conflict between Mephistopheles and Faust's better self commences. Henceforth it is not only Mephistopheles' office to do Faust's bidding, but it is moreover incumbent upon him to choose those allurements through which he hopes to enslave his prospective victim. The various spheres of experience through which Faust now passes form the central portion of the entire drama, and allow us to distinguish five distinct stages: (1) The sphere of coarse revelry, represented by the drinking scene in Auerbach's *Keller;* (2) the sphere of womanly love, represented by the tragedy of Gretchen; (3) the sphere of restless but as yet rather purposeless activity in the circles of worldly power and social distinction, represented by the scene at the emperor's court in the first act in the Second Part; (4) the sphere of historical and aesthetic pursuits, represented by the Classical Walpurgis Night and the Helena drama; (5) the sphere of practical usefulness, based on ethical and unselfish motives, represented by Faust's noble effort to wrest land from the sea and to make it the abode of a free and happy people. After that follow the concluding scenes of the Second Part that depict the struggle of devilish and angelic hosts for Faust's soul, and its final entrance into heaven.

Even this brief enumeration of the five principal stages of the action—one might well call them the five acts of a vast dramatic composition—establishes, or at least suggests, one important fact. The spheres in which we encounter Faust and Mephistopheles represent an ascending scale, if judged from the standpoint of their intrinsic value to human life. The first stage, the scene in Auerbach's *Keller,* exhibits a wanton waste of human energy; while the last scene, by the seashore, represents one of the highest aims of human life: unceasing, well-defined activity aiming to produce, within the limits of what is feasible, the greatest possible good to multitudes of others. From this it further follows that, while at first the influence of Mephistopheles over Faust is increasing and leads the latter deeper and deeper into sin, with the beginning of the Second Part, however, Mephistopheles' influence commences to wane. He still must do Faust's bidding, but the latter more and more assumes the leadership, and suggests the aims of their joint activity.

Let us now examine somewhat more in detail the five principal stages, or episodes, of the drama, and, in so doing, we shall especially try to determine in what spirit Faust enters upon each of these typical spheres of experience and in what spirit he again emerges from each of them. After the pact has been made, Mephistopheles, in answer to Faust's question, "Now, whither shall we go?" replies: "As best it pleases thee. The little world, and then the great, we'll see." This programme is strictly carried out. The first two episodes—the student's scene in the wine vault, as well as the entire Gretchen drama—constitute the experiences in the narrower world of personal relations; the last three—the scenes at court, the Helena drama, and the active life at the seashore—constitute the experiences of the broader world of activity in government, art and science, and cultural labor. Mephistopheles of course begins at the bottom round of the ladder. He would fain win Faust at the lowest price, with the least outlay of exertion on his part. He, therefore, first tries to lure him into a life of vulgar and soulless revelry. But it is characteristic that during the entire scene in Auerbach's *Keller* Faust remains a passive spectator. He speaks only twice, first, on joining the company, "Fair greeting, gentlemen!" and not very much later, "To leave them is my inclination." The first attempt of Mephistopheles has been a flat failure. Far from satisfying Faust, he has not even succeeded in interesting him.

His next scheme is more deeply laid. Faust's sensual nature, that has been utterly neglected in his previous life, is skillfully aroused by Mephistopheles in the scene in the witch's kitchen, so that when he first meets pure and lovely Gretchen, he, as Mephistopheles himself says,

> talks like Jack Rake,
> Who every flower for himself would take,
> And fancies there are no favors more,
> Nor honors, save for him, in store.

He brutally says:

> And if that image of delight
> Rest not within mine arms to-night,
> At midnight is our contract broken.

Mephistopheles has a good chance for success this time. But his purpose is again to be foiled. According to plan, Faust is henceforth to lead the life of a libertine, whom he will drag through dust and mire from one victim to another.

The Gretchen tragedy is undoubtedly not only the most powerful part of the Faust drama, but to the great majority of readers it even is the real center of interest, that which **Faust** first suggests and stands for. The exquisite delicacy of some if its opening scenes, as well as the terrible pathos of its final catastrophe, of which an English critic has said that its tragic intensity has never been paralleled and can never be exceeded, make it a complete drama in itself, the interest in which has induced the poet to develop it far beyond the proportions which it should have as only one of the episodes of the larger drama. The chief point of interest from our present point of view is the consummate skill with which the poet makes Gretchen's purity and loveliness transform Faust's libertinism into truly impassioned love, much to Mephistopheles' dismay, who again sees his prey slipping from his hand. This change of sentiment on the part of Faust does not save Gretchen, but, in a sense, it does save Faust, at least from immediate ruin. When Faust's true love for Gretchen awakens, he flees from her, for he feels and knows that, with all his love for her and hers for him, he is utterly unable to procure her that happiness which she deserves. The chasm between the two is too great to be bridged over, even by love. Faust says of himself:

> I am the fugitive, all houseless roaming,
> The monster without aim or rest,
> That like a cataract, down rocks and gorges
>   foaming,
> Leaps, maddened, into the abyss's breast!
> And sidewards she, with young, unwakened
>   senses,
> Within her cabin on the Alpine field.

But Mephistopheles, who, in his blind eagerness, cannot give up his game as lost, succeeds again in lulling Faust's conscience to rest. Faust returns to Gretchen, and an awful vista of sin engendering sin opens before our eyes. Gretchen, all confidence and love, falls. Her mother dies from the effects of the sleeping draught administered to her. Gretchen's brother attacks his sister's lover, and, in the ensuing combat, is killed. Faust must flee to escape the hands of justice, while Gretchen, crazed with the awful consciousness of her sin, drowns her child and is cast into prison. These awful results of his first wrong plunge Faust deeper and deeper into sin, but at the same time reawaken his conscience and the determination to right his wrong as much as possible, even though it be at the risk of life and liberty. Thus a spiritual disposition is engendered in Faust, which is far from the one which Mephistopheles desired to produce, in fact a state of soul that must needs help a man, in whom all good has not died out, to regain "the right road," from which he has strayed. Mephistopheles has again failed. Faust comes out of this awful experience heavily laden with guilt, but unquestionably a better man than when he first saw Gretchen.

Here ends the First Part, and even from this brief outline it must be apparent that the drama could not possibly end here, where most readers drop it. We are in the midst of a conflict, not at its end. If it were the real ending, only one of two issues is possible. Either Faust has won. But this, despite all of his repentance, is not to be thought of while he is still in the very midst of the awful consequences of his wrongdoings. Or Mephistopheles has won. Then "the Lord" has lost, and the spirit of the drama would be pessimism too terrible to think out to its last consequences. It needs no proof that Goethe, the serene optimist, could never have considered such a solution. As a matter of fact, the division between Parts I and II is merely accidental and outward, not essential or organic. Only the second act of the vast five-act drama has closed; the third act begins with the Second Part.

In tracing the hero's career through the Second Part, I shall endeavor to give a brief running account of the principal events themselves, for I cannot presuppose for it the same general acquaintance with the story of the plot as everybody possesses for the First Part. On the other hand, the Second Part, about twice as long as the First, teems with such a mass of detail that only the most significant elements can be referred to.

In the opening scene we find Ariel and his elfs ministering to Faust, who lies in unconscious sleep; in other words, the good and gentle influences of life gradually heal Faust's broken spirit. Then the third great episode of the drama begins. Faust is introduced to the emperor's court. In various scenes we find him engaged in a life of busy activity. He is no longer solely seeking selfish enjoyment. He is exerting himself. But there is a lack of purpose and conviction in all of his doing. According to a distinction dear to Goethe, Faust appears now *geschäftig,* and not *thätig*— i.e., busy but not truly active. He resembles a man who delights in using his powers and testing his strength, but who is not sufficiently clarified in his purposes to devote his energies to the service of high and worthy ideals. In fact, Faust still allows Mephistopheles to conduct matters pretty much as he pleases, and Mephistopheles sees to it that the activities in which they engage shall ultimately result in harm, or, at least, be of no value.

The scenes of court life, relating to government and to pleasure, are varied and full of life, but only one fact is of special significance for the further development of the plot. The emperor has heard of, and during some carnival festivities has himself experienced, Faust's magic skill. As a supreme test he therefore asks that Faust conjure up, for the court's entertainment, the shades of Paris and of Helen. Mephistopheles, when asked by Faust for assistance, must admit that, as the devil of northern cloudlands, he possesses no power over the sunny forms of southern climes. The beautiful cannot be the sphere of the spirit of evil and meanness, for Goethe firmly believed in the ennobling and uplifting influences of the beautiful. Thus Faust is forced to act for himself, independently, and he undertakes the enterprise, even though at the risk of losing his life in it.

Here, I believe, lies the turning point in the drama considered as a whole. So far Mephistopheles has suggested what has been undertaken; this time the suggestion comes from a neutral source, the emperor; henceforth it will be Faust

himself who will set up his own goal for his activity. Thus far Mephistopheles has accomplished everything, inviting Faust merely to passive enjoyment; this time, however, Faust acts without Mephistopheles; soon we shall see Mephistopheles forced to employ his energies in pursuance of Faust's self-chosen aims.

Paris and Helen appear as shades, and are admired and criticized by the court in a soulless manner. Only Faust is really struck with the sublimity of Helen's beauty, so much, in fact, that during the next, the fourth, episode the effort to win her becomes the controlling influence of his life—i.e., he enters the sign of the aesthetic ideal. For his search for Helen, and his final wooing and wedding of her, we must not interpret as a return to the sphere of sexual love, as portrayed in the Gretchen tragedy. Helen, in our drama, is not so much the ideally beautiful Grecian as rather the Grecian ideal of beauty in art and life, and thus, in a measure, an incarnation of some of the highest human achievements of the past. In search of it and in communion with it, Faust is therefore actuated by a truly lofty and noble aim in life, although not yet by the loftiest and noblest.

Two of the most famous and, in many respects, most beautiful portions of the Second Part are devoted to the portrayal of the sphere into which we have now entered— namely, the so-called Classical Walpurgis Night, and the Helena drama proper.

The Classical Walpurgis Night has been developed as an elaborate Grecian counterpart of the mythical Walpurgis Night festival on top of the Brocken mountain, as it is portrayed in the First Part. The invention as a whole is Goethe's, while the various elements of it have been freely taken from old Grecian fables and myths. The understanding and appreciation of the whole requires a fairly extensive familiarity with even minor and remote details of Grecian folklore so that for most readers an intelligent study of at least this portion of the Second Part is impossible without a running commentary. The scene has been developed to its present proportions largely for its own sake and interest, but its organic relation to what precedes and follows is distinct. Faust, haunted by the picture of Helen, is bent upon finding means for winning her back from Hades, and information as to the most efficacious mode of procedure might be gathered at this annual spirit-reunion on the plain of Pharsalus, in Thessaly. For here, where in 48 B.C. the famous battle between Caesar and Pompey was fought, the memory of this epoch-making event is renewed annually (so Goethe will have us believe) by a gathering of spirits in the neighborhood of the battlefield during the night following the anniversary of the battle. It certainly is a superstition of the folklore of many peoples that great and decisive battles, as, e.g., the battle of Marathon between the Athenians and Persians, and the battle of the Romans and Germans against the Huns on the Catalaunian Plain, were each year fought over and over again by spirits in the air. Since thus on the Pharsalian battlefield all of the principal characters of Greek legend are going to assemble, Faust hopes to be able to find among them some news of Helen. And, indeed, after a series of inquiries and varied adventures, the famous sorceress, Manto, ultimately shows Faust the entrance to the lower world beneath Mount Olympus, where he is to plead with Persephone for Helen's return to the upper regions. A noble scene, which was to depict Faust's experience in Hades, and thus was to form the connecting link between the Classical Walpurgis Night and the Helena drama proper, the poet unfortunately never wrote. At any rate, Faust's suit must be supposed to have been successful, for in the third act Helen appears in the world of man.

The scene shifts to Sparta, to a place in front of the palace of Menelaus. Helen herself, surrounded by her retinue of Spartan women, imagines that she is just returning home from Troy, sent ahead by her husband to make all necessary preparations for an elaborate sacrifice. Mephistopheles appears, disguised in the ugly shape of one of the Graiae or Phorcyads, the three sisters dwelling in utter darkness and possessing only one eye and one tooth in common, who in the Greek imagination were the acme of everything horrible and repulsive. This form he, the lover of everything ugly, has borrowed from the Phorcyads during the Classical Walpurgis Night, while his victim, Faust, hardly his victim any longer, has been in search of the sublime beauty of Helen. Mephistopheles pretends to be an old stewardess at Menelaus's palace, and tells Helen that she herself is to be the victim to be slain at the sacrifice, for which her enraged husband has ordered her to prepare. But he promises her easy delivery from certain death if she will but place herself under the protection of his master, who, during Menelaus's absence, has acquired power and land in the mountain districts to the north. Helen, thoroughly frightened, gives her consent, and, by magic, she is transported to Faust's stronghold, which is represented as a Gothic castle of the Middle Ages. Faust greets her with profound respect and admiration, offers his protection, and wins her love. The offspring of this union of Faust and Helen is a supernatural child, Euphorion, who, driven by his ethereal nature, tries by all means to rise above the level of his surroundings, climbing and flying upwards, but suddenly falling dead at his parents' feet. In the figure of Euphorion Goethe offered a delicate tribute to the memory of Lord Byron, whose premature death at Missolonghi had occurred but shortly before the time when the Helena drama was elaborated, and whose poetic genius Goethe greatly admired. Euphorion, dying, entreats Helen not to leave him alone in the realm of darkness. She, irresistibly drawn on by her son's prayer, vanishes, leaving Faust again alone.

This time Faust has enjoyed true happiness, the recollection of which is free from the sting of remorse. But even it, being only temporary, did not furnish a lasting and never-failing source of satisfaction.

But before we, like Faust, leave the sphere of the aesthetic ideal, I should like to call attention to one more feature of this portion of the drama, which evidently is symbolic and largely even allegorical in its nature, and severely taxes the imagination of even the most willing and best-prepared reader.

Aside from the personal compliment to Byron, the figure of Euphorion, more broadly interpreted, would seem to represent modern romanticism in general. As Euphorion

is the offspring of the Helen of the ancients and of Faust, who, in these scenes, appears as one of those baronial knights of the Middle Ages, who actually established themselves in various parts of Greece in connection with the fourth crusade of 1202, so was modern romanticism, in some measure, the result of a fusion of the spirit of ancient and Renaissance art with the spirit of the romantic literature of the Middle Ages. Thus understood, the poet's plan seems to have been to place before us a kaleidoscopic vision of the whole development of the art and culture of the past, from the days of the glory of Greek art down to the poet's own time.

Such a plan is probably too bold and vast for artistic treatment, especially for treatment in dramatic form. To admit, therefore, that from an artistic standpoint, Goethe's treatment of it is hardly quite satisfactory is no serious reproach on his poetic genius. Like Faust himself, he seems to have attempted the impossible. But the attempt itself should not be ascribed to a wanton desire of doing something perhaps never attempted before; for it is a necessary and logical part of the whole plan. If Faust is to exhaust all the experiences of man, the question had to be answered whether there was not, perhaps, something in the achievements of the past that could have granted the longed-for satisfaction. The poet's answer to this quest is a negative one. The past, no matter how beautiful, cannot be the fulfillment of the needs and desires of the present. It can and should furnish stimulants and materials toward the mastery of the problems of the present, but it cannot itself offer their solution.

And so we follow Faust to the last sphere of his experience. Carried back from Greece to Germany on a magic cloud, Faust passes over plains, rivers, and seas. When Mephistopheles asks whether, in all they have seen, there was nothing that evoked in Faust the desire to devote his energies to it, the latter, remembering the sight of the waves of the sea lashing a waste and desolate shore, exclaims:

FAUST

The sea sweeps on, in thousand quarters flowing,
Itself unfruitful, barrenness bestowing;
It breaks and swells, and rolls, and overwhelms
The desert stretch of desolated realms.
There endless waves hold sway, in strength
    erected
And then withdrawn—and nothing is effected.
If aught could drive me to despair, 'twere, truly,
The aimless force of elements unruly.
Then dared my mind its dreams to over-soar:
Here would I fight—subdue this fierce uproar!
And possible 'tis!—Howe'er the tides may fill,
They gently foam around the steadfast hill;
A moderate height resists and drives asunder,
A moderate depth allures and leads them on,
So, swiftly, plans within my mind were drawn:
Let that high joy be mine for evermore,
To shut the lordly Ocean from the shore,
The watery waste to limit and to bar,
And push it back upon itself afar!
From step to step I settled how to fight it:
Such is my wish: dare thou to expedite it!

Mephistopheles is willing, for the terms of the pact demand that he should be. As a reward for valuable assistance which they render the emperor in his war against a powerful rival, Faust receives the desolate and undesirable seashore as a fief. Here he spends the rest of his life, building dikes, digging canals, constructing harbors, sending out his ships over all the seas. Constantly he fights against the renewed encroachments of the water, and thereby turns a useless, uninhabited stretch of land into a cultivated district, a fit abode for free and labor-loving men to live and prosper in. He has at last discovered the blessing that dwells in strenuous exertion and unceasing labor, provided it be prompted by noble motives and directed toward worthy ends. He no longer labors for himself alone; he works for the benefit of others, and therein seeks and finds his own joy and prosperity. He creates values where before him there were none; he carries the stir of human labor and the voices of human joy and human sorrow into places filled before by the monotonous roar of the unfeeling elements. The over-exalted dreamer and reckless and regardless egotist has changed at last into a culture hero, who has experienced the saving grace of strenuous devotion to duty in the service of mankind.

Finally, in this unceasing but serene activity in the interests of human culture and progress, in his watchful care not only for the welfare of his fellow-men, but even of coming generations, Faust seems to have found that continued peace of soul for which he has been yearning so long, and which nothing else had been able to furnish him. It is true, he is blind, bowed down by care and extreme old age; but he is none the less eagerly bent on performing the duties of each day. Thus he much reminds us of the poet himself, who penned the last lines of the drama as an octogenarian, and was not willing to pause or rest until this supreme work of his life should be completed.

In this spirit Faust exclaims:

> Yea, to this thought I cling, with virtue rife,
> Wisdom's last fruit, profoundly true:
> Freedom alone he earns as well as life,
> Who day by day must conquer them anew.

His ideal striving has not left him to the last. For even now it is not so much the pleasure at what he has already achieved, as rather the anticipation of what he still hopes to accomplish in the future, that makes him say:

> Then to the moment might I say:
> Linger awhile, thou art so fair.

With such words on his lips and such thoughts in his soul, he dies, clear in his conception of his relation to the world, sure of his purpose, pure in his motives, a redeemed man.

He professes no creed, but his convictions are borne by the loftiest principles. But, even though in anticipation of still greater bliss in the future, he has spoken the fatal word to the fleeting moment: "Linger awhile, thou art so fair." So, technically, mechanically, Mephistopheles might claim, and does claim, to have won his wager. But the angelic hosts that come to carry Faust's soul into eternity convince him, despite his impotent rage, that he is deceived. Nothing that *he* has given Faust causes the latter to speak

the important words. Faust has won the wager. He is saved.

In the last act of the drama one more point might demand some elucidation. Mephistopheles to the last remains in Faust's company, who even uses him for the consummation of his high purposes. To a mediaeval mind this fact alone would even to the last condemn Faust as ensnared in sin. This, however, is far from Goethe's much profounder conception of the relation between the two. Even though Mephistopheles represents the coarser, more vulgar tendencies of human nature, he still represents energy. This force is not to be thrown aside, not to be destroyed; it is to be subdued, to be forced to do the bidding of the higher spiritual nature. That, according to Goethe, is the true solution of the conflict each man is waging. When, at the end of his career, Faust, though unintentionally, causes the death of the good old couple, Philemon and Baucis, and the destruction of their property, I believe the poet does not only wish to emphasize the fact that the individual must not stand in the way of the common progress and benefit, but rather to show that the subjugation of our lower impulses is never completely accomplished. Even with the wisest and best of men their coarser instincts will occasionally escape the control of their higher nature. Again, it is not the individual act that condemns or saves, but rather the spirit from which the deed flows, that adds to our credit or guilt. Of this the chorus of angels assure us as they carry Faust's immortal part aloft:

> The noble spirit now is free,
> And saved from evil scheming:
> Whoe'er aspires unweariedly
> Is not beyond redeeming.

(pp. 297-314)

A. R. Hohlfeld, in his Fifty Years with Goethe: 1901-1951, *The University of Wisconsin Press, 1953, 400 p.*

Georg Lukács (essay date 1940)

[*Lukács, a Hungarian literary critic and philosopher, is acknowledged as one of the leading proponents of Marxist thought. In the following excerpt from an essay originally published in 1940, he interprets the "Gretchen tragedy" from a Marxist perspective.*]

The *Urfaust* and the *Fragment of 1790* are . . . dominated by the Gretchen tragedy. And however the proportions change in the later, completed version, it is this tragedy which preponderates in the popular imagination. In the broad, mass effect of *Faust,* the Gretchen tragedy, along with the tragedy of immediate knowledge and that of the pact with the devil, is dominant even today. In large measure this is justified. For the immediate poetic impression of the "little world", in which what pertains to the species forms only a backdrop and determines only the peculiar form of typical characterization and the direction of the plot, is inevitably bound to be stronger than the impression made by the rigorously objectified philosophic and poetic profundity of the "great world" in part two.

Whatever the clarity or vagueness with which the youthful Goethe envisaged the outline of the entire poem, there is no doubt that, even then, he was most affected poetically by the tragedy of Gretchen. And this is understandable. For this was something young Goethe could adequately enlarge on. Indeed, it was a central theme not only of his own early writings, but of all German literature of this epoch.

In *Dichtung und Wahrheit,* Goethe mentions that the friend of his youth, Heinrich Leopold Wagner, plagiarized him by making use of what he had related concerning the Gretchen tragedy. Now, to what extent can this really be considered plagiarism? Wagner presents the tragic fate of a girl seduced in accordance with the spirit of the age: as a glaring example of class oppression of the bourgeoisie and petty bourgeoisie by the nobility. A large number of similar dramas were written during the period, of which the most outstanding from among the young generation are those by Reinhold Lenz. The handling of this example of class oppression at that time reached its apex in Lessing's *Emilia Galotti* and Schiller's *Kabale und Liebe.*

The popularity of this theme is by no means accidental. It also plays a considerable role in the English and French literature of the Enlightenment from Richardson to the *Figaro* of Beaumarchais. In the class conflict between nobility and bourgeoisie, individual cases of flagrant injustice were necessarily bound to be placed in the foreground, so long as the oppressed class was not yet sufficiently developed. One need only think of Voltaire's great campaigns on behalf of justice of which Lessing's *Rehabilitations* [*Rettungen*] and the appearance of young Lavater constitute feeble analogies in Germany. The seduction of bourgeois girls by aristocrats and the resultant tragedies understandably form an important part of this still insufficiently developed revolt against feudal domination. And it is obvious that all these tendencies were bound to appear even more in the foreground in Germany, where the bourgeoisie was weaker, than in France.

From the social standpoints, then, the tragedy of the bourgeois maiden seduced is only one of many abuses perpetrated by degenerate feudalism. From the standpoint of poetic creation, however, this theme has advantages such that it became, not by chance, the principal dramatic theme of the German Enlightenment. Above all, in a palpable and terse manner, it concentrates, in a typical individual case which is easy to relive imaginatively, the most repugnant features of the oppression, features apt to rouse spontaneously to indignation the whole bourgeoisie (even its least developed elements). In doing so, this theme provides just the possibility of differentiating, with social exactness and vividness, the typical necessity involved; the possibility of indicating poetically the most varied forms in which it manifests itself (e.g. the court in Lessing and Schiller, the officer life in Lenz and Wagner, the tutors in Lenz, etc.). It is precisely this theme, moreover, which presents, with the greatest efficacy, the antithesis of the first importance: that of the two moralities—the moral depravity, the moral nihilism of the nobility and the wholesome moral sensibility of the bourgeoisie. Finally, the weakness of the bourgeois, their impotence in the face of the nobility can be presented in a perfectly truthful manner in this theme; yet it is able to give expression successfully to their passive and authentic heroism which is neither violent nor affected. So it is not by chance that, even in the politically most passionate dramatist of "Storm and Stress", in the young Schiller, the sale of soldiers by the princes forms only an episode in the central love tragedy.

The poetry of Goethe's youth also forms part of this current, but, right from the beginning, Goethe has a unique position and unique formulation of the problem. He presents something broader and deeper than do his contemporaries: he gives a critique of the love relationship in bourgeois society in general. Engels describes in detail how the social earthquake which gave the bourgeoisie its leading economic position also brought forth the modern forms of love and marriage, but, at the same time—with the same socio-economic necessity—made their realization in life very rare exceptions. It is this internal contradiction of bourgeois society that forms the point of departure for the creative work of young Goethe. And it does so, in accordance with his whole tendency, from the standpoint of the full development of the personality, which also belongs to that complex of problems that the emergence of capitalism and the ripening of the bourgeois revolutions put on the agenda; problems of which, however, the economic and social structure of this same bourgeois society also prevents even an approximate solution. The love tragedies of young Goethe present, in deeply experienced individual destinies, different combinations of both these groups of social contradictions. The problem of the class conflict as it bears on sexual relations, a problem brought to the fore by his contemporaries, remains an important factor for him also, but, nonetheless, only one factor of this totality.

The rare realization of the unity of individual love and marriage among the ruling classes of bourgeois society—Engels never tires of repeating that this problem is quite different from the plebeian strata and especially for the proletariat—has economic and social foundations. But this realization occurs in individual cases only through crises and tragedy. The conflicting social tendencies fight out their battles in the emotional life, the thought, and the social activity of men. The most primitive form of these contradictions is that between emerging passionate love and the economic and social well-being of the individual. Stated crudely, it is the problem of whether love and marriage are or are not advantageous to his "career"—where the "career" may be of the most varied kinds, from the brutal material pursuit of success to the inner unfolding of the personality, from the most base and narrow egoism to really tragic conflicts.

This is the way in which young Goethe poses the problem in *Götz* and *Clavigo.* With Clavigo, the problem seems more plain and simple; in Weislingen it is complicated by his concomitant love for Adelheid. But we must not overlook the fact that his love for Adelheid is closely bound up with the question of his "career": whether Weislingen will rally to the opposition of the knights, Götz and Sickingen, or whether he will seek recognition at court. In both cases—although Goethe carefully balances out the real causes—all his sympathy is on the side of the girls sacrificed. Weislingen and Clavigo are depicted as weaklings, as wavering characters who fail disgracefully when it comes to proving their human worth. With Goethe, this sort of characterization is a judgment on himself, but one that is one-sided and simplified. This simplification manifests itself also in the fact that the victims, surrounded with all his sympathy, appear pale and bloodless in their poetic depiction. In the poetic reality of *Götz,* Adelheid not only triumphs over Marie; as a poetic figure, she is also more vital, fuller, more convincing, more exciting.

The reason for this is precisely the poet's judgment on himself. Goethe proceeds here mainly on the basis of blame without considering the problem in its most complex and psychologically deepest aspects. But this is how he experienced it in his own being. We know how Goethe conceived the development of man's potentialities. This development is impossible without love. The ascetic is an incomplete human being. The passion of individual love, precisely because it is both the most elementary, the most natural of all passions, and also, in its present individualized form, the finest fruit of culture, represents the most genuine fulfilment of the human personality, so long as its development is regarded as a "microcosm", as an end in itself. It can attain to this fulfilment only when the passion of love becomes a sweeping current into which flow, in their supreme perfection, the noblest spiritual and moral strivings of the individual; when the power of love, which unifies the personality, effectually raises everything in man to the highest level attainable.

Goethe's lyric love poetry often expresses this world-feeling in a poetically perfect form. His poem, **"The Metamorphosis of Plants,"** shows most clearly how closely bound up this feeling is with his world-view—especially his philosophy of nature. This is not a didactic philosophical poem. If Goethe expounds poetically the evolution of the plant world in the form of an explication to Christiane Vulpius, she herself is not a constructed and fictitious listener of an abstract exposition. The law of the growth and nature of love grows, in the intellectual as well as in the poetic sense, directly and organically out of Goethe's poetic and intellectual explication of natural phenomena. This is why Goethe can end his poem thus:

> Oh, think also how, from the seed of our acquaintanceship,
> sweet habit has gradually grown within us,
> how friendship has powerfully issued from our hearts,
> and how at last Amor engendered blossom and fruit.
> Think how multifarious the forms—now this one, now that,
> silently evolving—Nature has lent to our feelings!
> Rejoice also in the present day! Holy love
> aspires to the noblest fruit of like-mindedness,
> a like view of things, so that, in harmonious contemplation,
> the pair may unite and discover the higher world.

> [O gedenke denn auch, wie aus dem Keim der Bekanntschaft
> Nach und nach in uns holde Gewohnheit entspross,

> Freundschaft sich mit Macht aus unserm Innern enthüllte,
> Und wie Amor zuletzt Blüten und Früchte gezeugt.
> Denke, wie mannigfach bald die, bald jene Gestalten,
> Still entfaltend, Natur unsern Gefühlen geliehn!
> Freue dich auch des heutigen Tags! Die heilige Liebe
> Strebt zu der höchsten Frucht Gleicher Gesinnungen auf,
> Gleicher Ansicht der Dinge, damit in harmonischem Anschaun
> Sich verbinde das Paar, finde die höhere Welt.]

This ideal of a harmonious love which promotes the highest harmonious development of the personality grew out of the ground of bourgeois society. But the realization of this ideal is obstructed by the development of the very social reality that engendered it. And this is directly due not only to economic and social factors, such as the economic drawbacks of a marital union, nor only to external differences in class and internal differences in culture which are difficult to bridge: the immanent logic of personality development also sets limits to the realization of this ideal in bourgeois society.

From this point of view, the impossibility of a real equality of man and woman in bourgeois society appears in the most varied forms, from the most brutal to the most spiritual. Without love, the self-perfection of the personality is impossible, or at least very incomplete. But in a society divided into classes, this self-perfection, to which the deep spiritual and sensual comradeship between man and woman belongs, necessitates a solitary development whereby the man imposes on himself an unfettered and unattached existence without family, without wife and children. This is true at least at the beginning of his quest, at the stage of (inevitable) erring, until he finds the course of action proper to him—mastery in his command of the given realities of the world and of his own potentialities.

In a society divided into classes, therefore, a premature union, even one founded on the deepest and most genuine love, can become the starting-point of irresolvable tragic conflicts. If it endures, the young man involved in the union will be the victim; if, under the pressure of his fettered possibilities for development, he breaks away, then the girl must be sacrificed.

These are the contours of young Goethe's tragedies of love. Because of his deep human decency and ever alert sense of responsibility, swift renunciation became the recurring leitmotif of his youth. Precisely because he became aware of this conflict at a very early age, the inevitable parting already cast its shadow on his intense, most enriching, and happiest love. At the age of eighteen, at the height of his intense passion for Käthe Schönkopf, Goethe writes to his friend, Behrisch: "I often say to myself: if she were yours now, could anyone but death contest your claim to her or deprive you of her embrace? Imagine what I feel, everything I think about—and when I come to the end, I pray God not to give her to me."

Here we have the archetype of all young Goethe's subsequent love tragedies, from Friederike Brion to Lili

Schönemann, in which material factors in general could play no role. In his drama, *Stella,* Goethe presents the whole complicated inner dialectic of these feelings. He has Cecilia, forsaken by Fernando, say: "He always loved me, always! But he needed more than my love. I had to share in his wishes. . . . I pity the man who clings to a girl. . . . I consider him a prisoner. Even they are always saying it is so. He is drawn from his own world into ours, one with which he has basically nothing in common. He deceives himself from a time, but woe to us when he opens his eyes!"

The various forms of (unconscious) deception and self-deception, which result from such situations as a matter of course, are also presented with great finesse in this drama. If Goethe had succeeded in making his male heroes convincing expressions of all the motifs which led in his own case to these conflicts; if he had not limited himself in his characterization of Fernando merely to the psychology of love, hesitancy, and infidelity, then he would have written in *Stella* one of the greatest love tragedies of the age.

Egmont and the poem, **"Before Justice"** **["Vor Gericht"]** (1776-77), show another aspect, no less tragic, of the same conflict. Whereas the girls of the upper strata of the bourgeoisie can only be innocent wilting victims of the love tragedy, the plebeian girls have the courage to accept love with all its uncertainty, insecurity, all its social and psychological consequences. They have the courage to defy proudly the prejudices of bourgeois society and find in love itself—for all its transitoriness—in loving and being loved, their self-consciousness and their moral support. To her mother's groans of alarm that she has become a depraved creature, Klärchen proudly answers: "Depraved? Egmont's beloved depraved?" And in the poem cited above, Goethe has his unwed mother say:

> I will not tell you by whom I had it,
> this child in my womb.—
> "Shame!" you spit out: "a whore!"—
> But I'm an honest woman.
>
> [Von wem ich es habe, das sag' ich euch nicht,
> Das Kind in meinem Leib.—
> Pfui! speit ihr aus: die Hure da!—
> Bin doch ein ehrlich Weib.]

The tragedy of Gretchen is the most typical of all these dramas. We have already pointed out that in Faust, as in Gretchen, Goethe gives expression not only to the passion of love itself, but also to all its stages of development, from its frivolous and half-conscious beginnings to the deepest tragedy. All the great tendencies of evolution are concentrated in the person of Faust. When, turning to life, he approaches Gretchen, the sad burden weighs on him of the scarcely surmounted tragedy of immediate knowledge and his pact with the devil. And, at the height his ecstasy with Gretchen, enraptured by the charm of her person and her nearness, there is at work in him the invincible aspiration: to go further, higher! Faust knows, even if he does not wish to admit it to himself, that he cannot long stay in the "little world" of Gretchen. But his urge to take leave of it has nothing more in common with the external social goals of success of a Weislingen or Clavigo or with the purely subjective unrest of Fernando. With him, it is actually a question of a restless urge to perfection.

Hence, his love for Gretchen is also tragic for Faust himself. The tragic intensification manifests itself most clearly in the fact that the opposed forces which produce the conflict no longer assume the form of distinctly different characters as in Goethe's other youthful dramas. It is from within rather that Faust's upward striving and his relationship with Gretchen mutually reinforce and at the same time destroy each other. The scene that we have already examined, which forms a turning-point in the destiny of Faust's love, shows this irresolvable tragic connection. Faust flees Gretchen in order to save her; flight and solitude give a new and unexpected uplift to his spirit, to his world-view. But it is precisely his love for Gretchen which bears him aloft, so that his flight is rendered futile—not, of course, without the assistance of Mephistopheles, too. Thus the highest and most spiritualized stage of Faust's love becomes fateful for the destiny of Gretchen. That Faust is fully aware of his destiny mitigates nothing; his awareness is only a subjective consciousness of the irresolvable character of the situation. Even at the height of natural-philosophical fervour Faust's *Weltanschauung* is unable to answer Mephistopheles' cynicism: it is unable to resolve the moral dilemma:

> What heavenly joy exists within her arms!
> Let me warm myself on her bosom!
> Don't I always feel her distress?
> Am I not a fugitive roaming homeless,
> a monster without aim or rest,
> that, like a waterfall, rushes down from rock to
>   rock
> eager to plunge raging into the abyss? . . .
> What must come, let it come quickly!
> Let her destiny crash down upon me,
> and let us perish together!
>
> [Was ist die Himmelsfreud' in ihren Armen?
> Lass mich an ihrer Brust erwarmen!
> Fühl' ich nicht immer ihre Not?
> Bin ich der Flüchtling nicht, der Unbehauste?
> Der Unmensch ohne Zweck und Ruh'
> Der wie ein Wassersturz von Fels zu Felsen
>   brauste
> Begierig wütend nach dem Abgrund zu? . . .
> Was muss geschehn, mag's gleich geschehn!
> Mag ihr Geschick auf mich zusammenstürzen
> Und sie mit mir zugrunde gehn!]

We find the same high level of typicality in Gretchen. She is neither a heroine, like Klärchen, nor an anaemic sacrificial lamb, like the two Marias. (Even as regards social class, she stands between two extremes). All the spiritual and moral prejudices and weaknesses of a girl from the lower middle class are present in her. But, at the same time, her feelings are absolute and intact, her devotion is unconditional, and she possesses courage, selflessness, and clarity of feeling with respect to persons and even ideas.

It is true that objectively the—very complex—factor which leads to separation manifests itself just here. It is important that, after the peripeteia in "Forest and Cave", Faust also seeks an ideological *rapport* with Gretchen. And if, in his discourse on God since become famous, he goes a long way in adapting his (and Goethe's) wholly immanent pantheism to the religious mentality of Gretchen, this is not the mere mimicry of a lover who wishes to bring about at any price a psychological and spiritual union, but rather a tendency, often manifest in Goethe himself, to make his Spinozism unpolemical, to show a far-reaching tolerance in the presence of sincere faith if only it is faith in something and not nihilistic indifference. This is why Gretchen's words

> All this sounds very fine and good;
> much the same as the pastor tells it,
> although in slightly different words.
>
> [Das ist alles recht schön und gut;
> Ungefähr sagt das der Pfarrer auch,
> Nur mit ein bisschen andern Worten.]

have a double meaning. At the moment of ecstasy, the two of them achieve a psychological and spiritual *rapport* on the subjective level; objectively, however, and without their being aware of it, the abyss which will separate them is already opening up here. Whence the complicated dialectic involving, on the one hand, deep sincerity and mutual self-revelation, and one the other, deception and self-deception which, in a society divided into classes, are characteristic of love, even in its most exalted form. Accordingly, Cecilia says in *Stella:* "We believe the men! If, in moments of passion, they deceive themselves, why should *we* not be deceived?" And at the height of the tragic involvement, when Gretchen is already in prison, Faust says: "And her crime was an error of goodness!"

But the fact that Gretchen does not understand Faust's philosophy, or else misinterprets it on her lower level of culture, also has two aspects in which the justification and the tragedy of her situation find expression. When she reproaches him with the words: "You are not a Christian," this is intellectually, no doubt, the uncomprehending reproach of a petty bourgeois girl; but, from a human and moral standpoint, it refers to the decisive tragic point in the highest development of Faust's personality: to his indissoluble liaison with Mephistopheles. And Faust can only confront it with embarrassed and evasive excuses, for he is aware, and has just admitted to himself in the scene, "Forest and Cave", that Mephistopheles has become indispensable to him. The impossibility here of breaking through the barrier of unintended tragic insincerity lies, then, not in the intellectual difference between Faust and Gretchen, nor in the inability of Gretchen to understand Faust completely, but rather in the involvement of the Mephistophelian in even the highest human aspirations.

This is why—despite the depth of Faust's love, his pity and compassion—Mephistopheles is in very large measure (relatively) right when, confronted with the highest ideological and moral uplift of Faust's love, he merely points cynically to the consequences of the bed and rejoices in it. Both the function and the limitations of Mephistopheles clearly manifest themselves here. The essence of Gretchen is inaccessible to him; nor does he understand the core of Faust's real inner conflicts—but the course of this tragedy is nonetheless paved all along with the stones of his "wisdom". Because Gretchen is inaccessible to Mephisto, her love is also completely unproblematical. And her tragedy

unfolds with the same necessity from this straight and narrow character of her undoubting and unreflecting love as does the tragedy of Faust from the fact that he is torn between his desire to immerse himself in his life-work and the ecstatic happiness of his love.

The greatness of Goethe's typification consists, therefore, not only in the general truthfulness to life of all the elements of this evolution up to its tragic climax, but also in the fact that its unfolding, the antagonistic mixture of high and low motifs, always remains deeply typical. The result is that the entire history of the love, from its—half fortuitous—origins to its—inevitably tragic—break-up is expressed here in all its important stages of development. This is why Gretchen, like the other heroines of "Storm and Stress", has to be a girl from the lower social strata who is seduced and whose seduction leads to her downfall. But Goethe's depiction of this downfall, which contains all the social motifs of "Storm and Stress", goes deeper. Not only is the development which leads to this downfall more complete, but it is also more abundant in dramatic contradictions. For "Storm and Stress" there were only two possibilities: either frivolous, casual seduction and abandonment after the satisfaction of lust, or true love which remains constant as love, but proves unavailing against the irresistible might of class stratification. The Gretchen tragedy unites both series of motifs on Goethe's own higher level. Faust loves Gretchen right to the end. But—as his passion increases—he is nonetheless inwardly untrue to her, because the elements of his development which transcend her gain strength along with the strengthening of his passion for her and its fulfilment. And Gretchen not only sacrifices for her love her honour and existence, her mother and brother, but—in the prison scene—despite all her passionate attraction to Faust, who appears unexpectedly at the moment of her greatest need as lover and rescuer, she also senses the end of his love:

> Your love for me, where
> has it gone?
> Who has taken it from me?
>
> . . . . .
>
> It's as if I had to force myself on you,
> as if you were pushing me from you.
> And yet it is you, with look so kind, so good.
>
> [Wo ist dein Lieben
> Geblieben?
> Wer brachte mich drum?
>
> . . . . .
>
> Mir ist's, als müsst' ich mich zu dir zwingen,
> Als stiessest du mich von dir zürück;
> Und doch bist du's, und blickst so gut, so
>   fromm.]

Into the tragic fluctuations of this omnipotent passion with its irreconcilable abysses; into this psychological-spiritual development of love enters Mephistopheles. Tearing it apart he presses for a decision on the terrestrial, practical rescue of Gretchen. At this point, Gretchen makes her final decision: she will not be rescued by a Faust to whom Mephistopheles is indispensable. This is why the voice from above can proclaim: "She is saved!"

This—transcendent—salvation of Gretchen, which was appended to the version of 1808 and does not exist in the *Urfaust,* forms just as much a part of the "phenomenological" foundation of the complete work as does the subsequent transcendent salvation and perfection of Faust. In both cases, it is obviously not a question of any religious belief of Goethe in the hereafter, but of the poetic synthesis of his recognition that any human perfection—whether for Faust's type or that of Gretchen—was impossible in the socio-historical reality known to him, along with his unshakable faith in a future development of mankind which would one day resolve these problems in a manner also not known to him. But since Goethe's horizon was defined by bourgeois society, he could not create even a utopian picture of this future. (*Wilhelm Meister's Travels* presents the last stage of Faust's development more broadly and concretely but does not touch on the problem of his "redemption".) Thus, Goethe's faith in the future had to remain simple faith which, as such, cannot of itself be productive of any concrete artistic reality. This explains his choice of the Catholic heaven as a concluding image—an arbitrary choice if considered from an intellectual and philosophico-historical standpoint.

Goethe himself felt that in giving expression to simple faith he would have faced the great danger of artistic vagueness. In a conversation with Eckermann, he expresses the opinion that he would have easily fallen victim to this danger "if I had not given my poetic intentions a salutary and limiting form of consistency by means of sharply defined Christian ecclesiastical figures and conceptions." And Goethe always exercised an unlimited inner freedom in his choice of such mythical embodiments of his poetic tendencies: he treated *all* myth with the greatest spiritual sovereignty. On one occasion he wrote to Jacobi: "As for myself, considering the multifarious tendencies of my nature, I cannot make do with one way of thinking. As poet and artist I am a polytheist; a pantheist, however, as scientist, and one as decidedly as the other." Once these assumptions are accepted, the Christian heaven results naturally enough from the general tone of the sixteenth century, and its Catholic character follows from the greater palpability of this mythology.

All this is only formal, however, yet there are still two factors for which the Catholic mythology could serve as a material means of expression to present themes which are entirely extraneous to it. These are the internal movement, which is always important in *Faust,* and its poetically perceptible expression. The hierarchical character of the Catholic heaven provides Goethe with a structured stage for this internal movement. In a general sense, it already exists in Dante. In his poem, however, only the poet moves upward in the hierarchical structure; otherwise—apart from a few exceptions, such as when the souls take leave of Purgatory—every soul is assigned a definite place. This hierarchy, then, is only a context within which Dante moves: in which he changes inwardly and, outwardly, moves from place to place. In Goethe, both appear much more dynamic—insofar as the brevity of the scene allows for it. A further growth and continuing development is clearly implied in the case of Faust. In Goethe, the souls

redeemed move about freely in heaven. The Mater Gloriosa says to Gretchen:

> Come, thou, rise to higher spheres!
> If he senses thee, he will follow.
>
> [Komm, hebe dich zu höhern Sphären!
> Wenn er dich ahnet, folgt er nach.]

Hence, Goethe's heaven is Catholic only in an aesthetic and formal sense; in content it evinces the extension of Goethe's conception of an eternal perfection of the human race. It is a symbol for a unity that Goethe could not represent concretely—the unity formed by the genuine fulfilment and the boundless progress of man:

> Everything transient
> is but a semblance;
> the unattainable
> here is enacted;
> The indescribable
> here is accomplished . . .
>
> [Alles Vergängliche
> Ist nur ein Gleichnis;
> Das Unzulängliche
> Hier wird's Ereignis;
> Das Unbeschreibliche
> Hier ist es getan . . .]

Goethe deals in the same way with the Catholic notion of grace as coming from on high and transforms it imperceptibly into its opposite by giving it a terrestrial and immanent character. Let us recall the verse, already cited, that Goethe called the key to the whole work. It continues as follows:

> And if a love from on high
> intercedes in his favour,
> the blessed host will come to meet him
> with a most heartfelt welcome.
>
> [Und hat an ihm die Liebe gar
> Von oben teilgenommen,
> Begegnet ihm die selige Schar
> Mit herzlichem Willkommen.]

The love still seems symbolically ambiguous here, although this milieu, which is Catholic in appearance, does echo with something resembling grace. But even this echo cancels itself out. It is not by chance that the concluding verses just cited, which are only apparently Christian and imply an essentially pantheistic dialectic of evolution, end on an entirely earthly note:

> The Eternal Feminine
> Draws us upward.
>
> [Das Ewig-Weibliche
> Zieht uns hinan.]

It is also not by chance that the entire poem ends with the love union of Faust and Gretchen; a utopian perspective, but one that is earthly in content. The few remarks preceding the conclusion make its meaning clear as expressed in the fine and delicate style typical of Goethe. Gretchen perceives the ascent and purification of Faust and turns to the Queen of Heaven with the entreaty: "Grant it to me to instruct him"; an entreaty followed by Mary's answer, cited above, and the closing verses. For Faust, then, heaven is the culmination of his development projected into the hereafter, a development of which the crowning highpoint is his reunion with Gretchen. All the rest is only milieu, mediation, decoration. Gretchen is the spirit of perfection in Faust's striving, just as Klärchen was the spirit of freedom for Egmont as he went to his death.

Now what is it that Faust learns from Gretchen, this Faust who already became the instructor of the "blessed boys" during his ascent?

Here we encounter an extremely important variation and development, in Goethe's old age, of his conception of human perfection. It involves the struggle of two tendencies for supremacy, and it follows from the nature of the case that, with Goethe, it can only be a question of another form of equilibrium between these two tendencies and not a strict choice involving the complete acceptance of one and the complete rejection of the other.

The first tendency is the maximum development of the various capacities of man, their perfection to the point of mastery. With Goethe, who conceives every activity as practical, as a consciously intensified interaction with objective reality, this means, at the same time, a broad and deep understanding of reality. The second tendency is that of the inner human harmony in the development of these capacities. Mastery in the practical sphere should not—in conformity to the internal tendency of the capitalist division of labour—make of men brilliant monsters of specialization. The growth of the discrete and dominant capacities should be accompanied rather by a harmonious growth of the *whole* man.

On the basis of this conception of Goethe, the deep impression that Hamann made on his youthful development becomes comprehensible. Goethe formulates this influence thus: "Everything that man attempts to accomplish, whether it is realized by deed, word, or some other way, must arise out of a unity of all his powers; everything partial is objectionable. A splendid maxim, but difficult to follow. . . . In speaking, man must, for the moment, become one-sided; there is no communication, no instruction without separation."

In the reality in which he lived, Goethe knew that these two tendencies were contradictory and even irreconcilable, although only their synthesis can make men really harmonious and whole. During the happiest period of his maturity, he projected their union (in *Wilhelm Meister's Apprenticeship*) in the form of a social utopia. But the social experiences of the later decades, the experience of capitalism, of which, in its role as developer of the forces of production, he approved without any sentimental reserve, and his dawning insight into its social contradictions led him to adopt an attitude of resignation in this matter. *Wilhelm Meister's Travels* and the second part of *Faust* definitely renounce his turbulent youthful demands for harmony and the utopian dreams of his mature manhood. But Goethe's renunciation was, as it were, only "Realpolitik", only practical, only an expression of what was not a renunciation in principle of his earlier hopes. This ideal continued to remain the central theme of his perspective on the future. He knew, however, that, for contemporary reality, this ideal was only just an ideal.

Nonetheless, the more Goethe became resigned and approved the practical development of the discrete human capacities which—precisely in and through their discreteness—promote the domination of the forces of nature and thereby the continuous development of the human race, the more energetically he sought everywhere in reality the real tendencies and actualities in which human harmony and perfection have been realized, even if only on the basis of an objective renunciation of another sort.

A democratic and plebeian side of Goethe's world-view is revealed here. He says: "the least man can be complete if he moves within the limits of his capabilities and aptitudes, but even *good qualities* are obscured, counteracted, and destroyed if that indispensable harmony required is lacking. This misfortune will manifest itself even more often in the modern age. . . . " This assertion contains an important rejection of any spiritual aristocracy, not to mention the cult of genius. The element which could compensate for the rupture of human harmony caused by the one-sided and monstrous development of the discrete capacities of man. Goethe did not discover in those men who find inner fulfilment in aesthetic consciousness. Rather he sought the realization of his ideal, which is engendered by life, and therefore, guaranteed by life, in certain men of a predominantly plebeian type whose conditions of existence no doubt denied them the highest spiritual development but whose innate ability permitted their capabilities to grow in spontaneous harmony.

Goethe was far from seeing this as a Rousseauian ideal and wanting to reduce evolution to this level. His love and respect for such figures, his understanding of their (relatively) human superiority over the products of capitalism which surpass them in talent and intellect, derive precisely from the fact that he saw in them a real guarantee for the human possibility and attainability of the harmony of which he dreamed; harmony at the highest level of the development of all human capabilities.

It is not by chance, then, that Goethe found this form of human perfection more often in the plebeian ranks than in the dominant social classes, and more often among women than among men. The imperishable charm of Goethe's female characters—whether Iphigenia or Philine, Klärchen or Ottilie, Natalie or Dorothea—rests precisely on this human perfection which, if compared to that of the important men, is extensively limited but intensively harmonious. Here, too, Goethe was no Rousseauian, although on this score he did learn a great deal from Rousseau's social criticism. Not for a moment did he think of reducing Egmont to the intellectual level of Klärchen or Faust to that of Gretchen. Even the romantic longing for this sort of more primitive perfection is entirely lacking in him, and hence, in his heroes also.

But he did see in these female figures an essential aspect of human perfection in general, perfection in which a series of qualities, especially moral ones, would manifest themselves on a higher and more exemplary level than in those men who conquer objective reality with the greatest show of virtuosity, talent, and erudition. And he dreamed that at later stages of mankind's development the highest intellectual attainments, the inner and outer unfolding of individual talents would, without foregoing any of these gains, reach the inner completeness, the moral and aesthetic harmony of such women.

This contrast occupied Goethe all his life. In *Tasso,* the solution still has here and there a courtly and aesthetic flavour. [*Wilhelm Meisters Lehrjahre*] signifies a resolute break with all social externalities (from a social standpoint, every marriage in this work is a misalliance). He presents here the utopia of a small circle of people who achieve an intensive human harmony at a high spiritual level and whose example is meant—à la Fourier—to have propaganda effect.

Only later, when he gained a clearer insight into the capitalist society developing before his eyes, did he arrive at the sharp contrast between "the little" and "the great world". This cleavage between the two worlds, which was always basic to Goethe's view of the erotic and its poetic expression, was bound to open up more widely given his unconditional devotion to current "demands of the day", which he neither ignored nor combatted, because he was in no respect a Romantic. However, as this contrast grew in emphasis, so, at the same time, did the necessity of resolving it in a conceptual-utopian, poetic-transcendent form. Hence, the Catholic heaven at the conclusion is the human harmony and perfection which grew out of the "little world" united with the boundless perfection of the "great world" and the perpetual development of the personality founded on mutual assistance and "instruction"; a progress that has no need of Mephistophelian forces. All this, Faust must "learn" in heaven from Gretchen.

The course leading to this perfection was the course of practical activity followed by Faust. This is why, as already mentioned, Goethe did not depict Faust's subsequent remorse, but rather the healing of his tragic wounds through a new relation to nature, to life, to action. And this means of surmounting the tragedy does not signify any forgetfulness or frivolous abandonment of the victim, but precisely the courageous recognition of the irresolvable character of such conflicts in this world, in contemporary society, along with the persistent demand for a solution which would really overcome them for all mankind. When Helen disappears, her robe becomes for Faust a magic cloud which swiftly carries him "above everything base" [*über alles gemein*]; and after alighting on a lonely rocky peak, he sees this robe gradually dissolve into cloudy images, first Juno, Leda, and Helen, then a final figure:

> Deceives me a charming image,
> semblance of youth's first supreme good, now
> long-forgone?
> Earliest treasures deep within my heart well up:
> So light and lively, it suggests to me Aurora's
> love,
> the first, swiftly felt, scarcely comprehended
> glance
> that, had I held it fast, all treasure had outshone.
> Like beauty of the soul ascends this gracious
> form,

dissolving not, but rising into the ether,
bearing with her the best of my inner being.

> [Tauscht mich ein entzückend Bild,
> Als jugenderstes, längstentbehrtes höchstes
> Gut?
> Des tiefsten Herzens frühste Schätze quellen
> auf:
> Aurorens Liebe, leichten Schwung bezeichnet's
> mir,
> Den schnellempfundnen, ersten, kaum verstand-
> nen Blick,
> Der, festgehalten, überglanzte jeden Schatz.
> Wie Seelenschönheit steigert sich die holde
> Form,
> Löst sich nicht auf, erhebt sich in den Äther hin
> Und zieht das Beste meines Innern mit sich
> fort.]

With this image, the image of Gretchen-Aurora (dawn), in his soul, Faust now rejects the temptation of Mephistopheles which would give him "the kingdoms of the world and all their splendours" and decides to follow the course of personal renunciation and devotion exclusively to the cause of practical activity. Viewed from an external and psychological standpoint, this is the point at which he is furthest removed from Gretchen's "little world" and its intensive harmony. From the standpoint of Goethe's philosophy of history, however, it is just here that he enters upon the right course. It is just here that the battlefield appears on which the Mephistophelian force is opposed by Faust with the highest consciousness and the greatest energy, although, for the time, in a manner which is also tragic and futile. But this tragedy also points the way beyond the purely tragic. In succumbing, Faust saves the innermost nucleus of the human personality and opens the way to a transcendent and utopian salvation of the human race.

"The Eternal-Feminine leads us on": not for nothing is this the last word, not only of the poem, but also of the poet, Goethe. It is his last avowal of the possibility of a perfection of man *on earth,* a perfection of man as a physical and spiritual personality, a perfection founded on his mastery of the external world and the elevation of his own nature to spirituality, to culture and harmony, without a denial of its natural character.

Since Plato's *Symposium* and Dante's Beatrice love has never carried such weight in the world-view of a genius. But the love of Plato and Dante is essentially other-worldly and ascetic. Goethe, the contemporary and champion of those tendencies which became the "three sources of Marxism", is essentially entirely immanent, entirely this-worldly. The aesthetically Catholic form of the conclusion can mislead only reactionary romantics or shallow liberals. (pp. 217-34)

> *Georg Lukács, in his* Goethe and His Age,
> *translated by Robert Anchor, 1968. Reprint by
> Grosset & Dunlap, 1969, 258 p.*

Gustav E. Mueller   (essay date 1948)

[*Mueller is a Swiss philosopher, poet, playwright, and critic. Here, he analyzes* Faust *in terms of its thematic similarities to the philosophy of German Idealism as represented in the works of G. W. F. Hegel.*]

Faust, the servant of the Lord, begins his story with the passionate exclamation: "Alas, theology!" Thus also begins the story of that historical epoch which has no name, because it was pleased to call itself continuously "modern". It would be fitting to call this period between Renaissance and World-War "Faustian."

The Renaissance throws itself with a mystic ecstasy to the bosom of nature. It is born out of the spirit of late "Medieval" mysticism, which gradually has toned down the *unio mystica* with God until it became *unio erotica* with nature. *Deus sive Natura.* Pagan naturalism is reborn with an infinite zest and with a passionate vengeance. What keeps these flying sparks of the Renaissance together, is their common anti-Christian pantheism, their anti-metaphysical metaphysics.

How is this union with nature to be established? Through adventure and discovery? Through massing of riches by a new economy of boundless profits? By the release of natural energies in the new national state-absolutism? In Art?

Philosophy developed in two contradictory directions: either the union with nature was to be established by my very own experience—real is what I can sense and so verify; or the union with nature was to be found in the identity of my logical and constructive *ratio* with the mathematico-logical order of the object of science.

Both these "schools" reached their terminals in the blind alleys of seventeenth century rationalism and eighteenth century empiricism and psychologism. Our Faust tries both ways and finds both wanting.

Goethe further does in his literary creation what idealism from Leibniz to Kant and Hegel has thought. Young Leibniz, sixteen years old, on a walk through the park of Leipzig, had the same bright Idea and made it the program of his life work: the "modern" scientism must be limited and must be harmonized and reconciled with the classical and the scholastic Christian metaphysics of "substantial forms" of life. Kant means the same thing when he writes in the preface to his *Critique of Pure Reason,* that he had to destroy the metaphysical claims of empirico-rational sciences to make room for faith: this is the meaning of the title. Hegel's dialectic completes the process and reestablishes human value-problems to their central and metaphysical place in philosophy.

Goethe's *Faust* is the literary culmination of this movement, usually referred to as German idealism. The sequence of Leibniz, Kant, Schelling, Fichte, Schleiermacher, and Hegel corresponds to the sequence of Bach, Haydn, Haendel, Mozart, and Beethoven in music, and Lessing, Winckelmann, Herder, Schiller, and Goethe in literature. (pp. 125-26)

The *Faust* as a whole perfectly embodies the principles of Goethe's thinking: It is an organic growth through polarities or contrasts, an evolution rounded out in a circle and a spiral ascent from simple to complex, integrated forms. The first scenes in heaven and the two wagers correspond to the end and the salvation. The *Urpolarität* of good and

evil appear as background poles of the tragedy. The magic scenes in the beginning alienating Faust from natural and ethical reality and preparing the Gretchen tragedy correspond to the magic scenes after the Helena tragedy leading Faust back from the land of ideas to participation in practical-earthly business. The Gretchen tragedy in the center of the first part corresponds to the Helena tragedy in the center and second part; the romantic Walpurgic Night, the way away from Gretchen, corresponds to the classic Walpurgic Night, the way to Helena. The end of the first part, the complete subjectivity and isolation, corresponds to the beginning of the second part, the complete externality and objectivity of Faust's social experience. The first part as a whole projects an inner feeling into the world, the second part as a whole draws the world into the subject, whereby the latter is made a member of universal forms and ideas of reality, culminating in the beloved community of all life, the *communio sanctorum.* The verse of the first part is musical, immediately felt, warm and bursting with vital energy; the verse of the second part is visionary, saturated, condensed, soft and clear, even flowing in ever-changing measures and rhythms. (p. 141)

But this beauty as synthesis of the living-organic process of intuition, with the perfect structure of form, still leaves the most important question unanswered. What is the philosophical content, what is the worldview of *Faust?* To answer this question we must understand the relation of God, Faust, and Mephisto.

The prologue in Heaven views the world-theater from God's vantage point. The angels, like the "mothers" of the second part, are principles of cosmic order, unfailing intelligences administering their assigned spheres of activity: The first stanza represents cosmic order in a Ptolemaic astronomical image; the second, mundane order in a Copernican image; the third, the organic order of "night and day."

> Thy heralds, Lord, in adoration,
> Praise the mild movement of thy day.

They do not comprehend God, the absolute, unbroken unity of all being, they only serve him. Into this timeless harmony breaks Mephisto, "As once again, O Lord, Thou drawest near" with this temporal, momentary, transient word. He also is real in God's creation. And he finds this creation in general and man in particular as incomprehensible and irrational "as on the primal day."

Why has God given to man a ray of his light, reason, by which he nevertheless cannot live and which he only misuses?

> A little better he might live, hadst Thou not
>   given
> To him the reflex of the light of heaven.
> He calls it Reason, using it, at least,
> To be more animal than any beast,
> And by your Grace's leave, he seems to me
> Like some long-legged Grasshopper to be,
> Which ever flies and flying springs
> And in the grass the same old ditty sings.

The Lord does not defend his creation, wherein he assigns to the doubting Mephisto his place, but gives him permission to try, whether man, Faust, would be satisfied with anything more or less than what he is.

> Draw Thou this spirit from his source astray
> And, canst thou comprehend him,
> Lead Him with thee on thy downward way,
> And stand abashed when thou art forced to say:
> A true man, though obscure his impulse, yet
> Is ever conscious of the one right way.

Heaven closes after revelation and promise is given. The universal harmony of laws and order, presiding over the tumult and chaos of finite life and becoming, the absolute being as one and other, as unity and disruption, is beyond the grasp of the devil; but the Lord admonishes his "true sons" to philosophy:

> Enjoy the rich, the everliving beauty!
> Creative power, that works eternal schemes,
> Clasp you in bonds of love, relaxing never,
> And what in wavering apparition gleams
> Fix in its place with thoughts that stand forever.

The devil is left sitting in his purposeless darkness, yet he "Can't afford to break with Him," which would throw him into his absolute, unthinkable Nothing.

The next scenes acquaint us with Faust's double nature. He is teacher, but wisdom cannot be taught. He is a metaphysician who wants to detect the "inmost force which holds the world and guides its course", and he has an idea of the universe wherein all things are harmoniously interconnected:

> To build the Whole how each part weaves,
> One in the other works and lives.

But this idea of the absolute being is *only* in idea. He resents to only think it and not to be it. From thought, from contemplative life, he turns to life of action:

> Courage I feel forth to the world to fare,
> The woes of earth, the bliss of earth to bear,
> With storms to battle I would dare
> And in the crash of shipwreck not despair.

But this longing for active life also fails, because human action is modest and conditioned. Faust despairs, not only because he is torn between unreconcilable desires of leading at once the life of a thinker, a man of action and of enjoyment, but also because in none of these modes can he escape his finitude. Disgusted with life and spirit alike, solitary, oppressed by "dead tradition," unable to break his existential isolation, he takes refuge in suicide. This shall prove to himself that he is at least absolute master of existence, that he is superman and in this freedom to toss everything away, equal to a god. The toll of Easter bells and the chorus of angels singing of resurrection and of an apostolic life keeps him back and reminds him of his innocence as a child. Christian religion to the modern man is here a sentimental reminiscence. The walk on Easter morning shows his relation to his fellowmen. They treat him with respect and gratitude, but he is tormented by his insufficiency and by the superficiality of living a life of general opinions: "O happy man who could succeed out of this sea of error to break free!" He calls on Eros, longing for infinity. Instead, out of the gray dawn of the many-colored world the spirit of night and of negation draws near, dog-shaped. The great experiment begins.

What Faust had tried in suicide, the devil now offers as a possibility of life, to find the absolute in the finite. He fails because he fails to draw Faust from his original double nature. Faust experiences the violation of enduring, moral world-orders as guilt of conscience, the only enduring result binding him to the world he wanted to overcome in smashing it to pieces. Failing in this he tries the other extreme, to live in ideas. This is his own temptation, Mephisto can only grant the means. Faust demands Helena.

> MEPHISTO: I've no concern with heathen Lords and Ladies They have their own peculiar Hades. Still—there are means.
>
> FAUST: Then speak and lose no time.
>
> MEPHISTO: I'm loath to unveil a mystery so sublime. In solitude are throned the Goddesses, No space around them, place and time, still less; Only to speak of them embarrasses, They are The Mothers.
>
> FAUST (terrified): Mothers!
>
> MEPHISTO: Hast thou Dread?
>
> FAUST: The Mothers! Mothers! a strange word is said.
>
> MEPHISTO: It is so. Goddesses unknown to ye The Mortals—named by us unwittingly. Delve in the deepest depths must thou to reach them: 'Tis thine own fault that we for help beseech them.
>
> FAUST: Where is the way?
>
> MEPHISTO: No way! To the Unreachable Not to be reached. Out to the Unbeseechable Never to be besought. Art thou prepared?

And later:

> Formation, transformation,
> The eternal mind's eternal creation
> Forms of all creatures—there are floating free.

After having surrendered the key of libido to Faust, Mephisto's active role ends. We have seen how Faust, again compelled by his double nature, must give up Helena and also absolute power and be satisfied with his purely human existence, which he had cursed in the beginning and so opened the way to the devil. As the devil has said of man—He again sits in his grass, after a short flight, and sings his old ditty.

From Faust's, from the human point of view, there was progress from step to step, and the devil, accordingly, has regressed; in the beginning he has all initiative. In the middle he is a partner, at the end Faust does not even recognize him any more and calls him "manager". Mephistopheles has to be content to manage the inseparable "war, business, and piracy" and their "mighty men," who furnished the realistic background for Faust's idealistic Utopia, and to protect Faust from communistic revolution.

From the devil's point of view there was no progress, but only an empty circle and a meaningless flight:

> Past and pure Naught, complete monotony!
> What good for us, this endless creating?
> What is created then annihilating?
> "And now it's past!" Why read a page so twist-
>   ed?
> 'Tis just the same as if it ne'er existed,
> The Void forever I would much prefer.

The blind Faust flatters himself with future happiness; his will to live is based on self-deception; his actuality is not less miserable than in the beginning. He reigns over

> Lemurs, ye shambling creatures
> Of sinews, ligament and bone
> Patched shreds of semi-natures,

who have

> . . . forgotten why the call
> Was made for our assistance.

On those half-starved, regimented labor battalions who serve their mechanical "jobs" in a vast industrial empire, the direction and meaning of which they don't know, on them deluded Faust pins his hope of a free human community.

From God's point of view, Faust is saved:

> The noble spirit now is free,
> And saved from evil scheming:
> Whoe'er aspires unweariedly
> Is not beyond redeeming.

And

> All cursed with error
> Truth be their healing!
> Glad self-retrieval
> Free them from Evil,
> In the unfolding breast
> Blessed, to rest!

Faust is a temporal creature, he lives his concrete time, renewing the past in his active reminiscence, living with the "silvery phantoms of the world before," trusting the duration of time which carries him along in faithful constancy, renewing him as refreshing presence, reaching out in anticipating the future.

For Mephistopheles "time masters him." Time from his point of view is pure negativity, the past is no more, the future never yet, and the now an illusory dividing line between the two other nothings.

For God time is eternal presence, always fulfilling and remaking life as temporality, its empty, abstract Mephistophelian "clock," by which the devil thinks he can measure Faust's life-time, and Faust's struggling and existential time are moments in the eternal spectacle of divine destination.

Faust's subtitle is "a tragedy". The attempt of the Renaissance man to find the absolute in a given self and in a given world has failed. But a return to the unbroken scholastic philosophy, where God is immediately and doubtlessly given to man in historical tradition and where the world is a direct and continuous ladder to God is impossible to the Faustian soul.

Faust finally accepts his limitation and his problematic finitude on a faith, which is liable to fail. The absolute is present through its own negations, the limited values of life, which can never hold it and represent it adequately, but neither is the absolute to be found outside and apart from them. It lives through their limitation and thus proves itself to be their salvation.

Both Dante's *Divine Comedy* and Goethe's **Faust** present a unity of opposites, a dialectical structure of life. But Dante sees and shows this dialectic from the point of view of the eternal totality and unity itself, whereas Goethe places us in the midst of the dialectical movement as such. Instead of Dante's limpid serenity and quiet transparency, we find ourselves in the thick of real and temporal process whose outcome is at any moment doubtful and ambiguous for all participants concerned. Life is its own hell and its own purgatory at the same moment. Aesthetic love animates and guides both poems, the love that draws Dante through hell and purgatory to paradise and is revealed as the ground of them all, the love that drives Faust to his delights and to his despairs:

> The wild desires no longer win us,
> The deeds of passion cease to chain;
> The love of Man revives within us,
> The love of God revives again.

Aesthetic love is the symbolic unity of the soul and body in all human and cosmic dimensions of the poem. Beatrice and Margaret are one.

But since in Dante the poles of the dialectic and the struggle of contradictions within these poles are kept apart and all phases of this life are looked at from the outside, the divine comedy preserves the quiet and contemplative tone of sublime seriousness throughout, while the dominant style of **Faust** is irony. Its irony is the balance of the holy-profane, the serious-humourous, the tragic-comic elements.

Every elevation is punched by a Mephistophelian antithesis. Mephistopheles, the spirit of contradiction, ironizes his own negativity, especially in the scenes with the student in the first and in the second part, or to mention another instance, when he makes fun of his own abstract scientism:

> By that I know the learned lord you are!
> What you don't touch is lying leagues afar;
> What you don't grasp is wholly lost to you;
> What you don't reckon, think you, can't be true;
> What you don't weight, it has no weight, alas!
> What you don't coin, you're sure it will not pass.

Every project undertaken ends in the contrary of what was meant. The devil is constantly disappointed no less than Faust.

The poem itself proclaims irony as style principle, when Faust teaches Helena to play with rhymes. The art medium is artistically limiting its own seriousness, the whole sphere of aesthetic reality is shown by art to be a limited kind of reality,—this is the meaning of Helena and her garment left to Faust. This aesthetic irony is analogous to the logical limitation of the sphere of cognition within the dialectic of philosophical thinking.

It is for this reason that Hegel has declared irony to be the central style principle of "modern art" and Faust to represent an "absolute philosophical tragedy."

So far we have attempted to interpret *Faust* out of itself and out of the aesthetic categories of its poet, as they become operative in the play.

We can now understand it also as analogy to philosophy—Goethe's *Faust* is in literature what Hegel's system is in philosophy. One cannot express the philosophy of *Faust* without developing Hegel's dialectic. This is of course, not a matter of "influence"—Goethe was not influenced by the study of Hegel's works, but it is an exemplary demonstration of a deep organic kinship gladly recognized by both men. It is fundamentally the same world-view evolving in the different media of logic and poetic imagination.

Both Goethe and Hegel are intuitive thinkers. They both are anti-abstract, anti-rationalistic, but also anti-subjective thinkers. Hegel says that to think without thinking something is like swimming without going into water, and Goethe says that he has always avoided thinking about thinking.

"All we can be aware of and all we can talk about are manifestations of the idea," is Goethe's statement of a common principle. Hegel says that nothing can be thought that is not a living reality, his "concept" is the dialectical unity of a form and a content which are inseparable, but not therefore one. They are one only in their polarity. And Goethe says that he is glad that he has ideas which he can see with his eyes.

What is thought, then, is a living and moving, a concrete shape of universal life. The thinker is to say "what is," he is to translate the movement of a meaningful reality into a self-comprehension, a self-understanding, the poet is to shape and to present this same content in his images to the imagination. Emerson calls Goethe the writer of the world, pointing to this epic-objective quality, this plastic-philosophical roundness of Goethe's expression. The same thing could be said of Hegel.

Behind and beyond all particular efforts of presentation lies the whole as the truth of all particularities. "You always comprehend particular experiences as organs of the whole reality," Schiller writes to Goethe—he could have written it to Hegel also. But this whole is not something in itself, besides its self-manifestations—it exists in its movements, it persists through the movements, even destroying them. "Whatever once was, there burns and brightens free In splendour—for 't would fain eternal be," says Faust in this Hegelian manner.

Both Goethe and Hegel are all-absorbing universalists, who do not ask, What can I get from reality? But rather, what can I find in reality? And the universe is the only one thing concrete enough to let them lose themselves in it. But in losing yourself you shall find yourself; personality is established through participating in the widening circles and spheres of existential experience. "The highest good

of moral creatures is personality," says Goethe, and Hegel: "In the Christian world the subject is not a mere accident of the deity, but an infinite end in himself—in this divine world the creation of true individuals is all that matters: the state may demand its sacrifice to save the whole, but in relation to God and in God's realm it is an end in and for itself."

This universalism of both men includes those limiting standpoints which would deny it. There are other monads with different modes of life, which are unwilling or unable to share with you. They must be understood in their difference whether they agree to that or not. "No one has a right, if he does not know how to solve such contradiction with *Geist* (spirit) in understanding the other, even if he is not understood in turn," says Goethe, and Hegel: "A true refutation must enter the force of the adversary and must put itself within its limitation; to criticize from the outside, just to maintain one's right where the other is not, does not further anything."

Goethe is lyrical as Hegel is existential. Goethe writes nothing of importance that is not a confession, and externalization of an internal movement. Hegel writes nothing of importance that is not filled with his own feeling and his own participation—his world-soul is his Faust. He is just as scornful of a mere antiquarian, ungenuine, unexistential curiosity, an irresponsible, abstract, nonparticipating knowledge, as Faust is of Wagner. To such, "The *Geist* of times is a book with seven seals."

Both Goethe's *Faust* and Hegel's philosophy celebrate the primacy of contemplative reason—action and activism are immature and provisional evaluations within the totality of life; they are and express negation, limitation, subjectivity, and impatience; they are necessary and ingredient moments of the whole life:

> Man's active nature, flagging, seeks too soon the
>   level;
> Whence, willingly, the comrade him I gave,
> Who works, excites, and must create, as Devil.

But seen in the eternal presence of the whole as whole, all such tension and "oughts" are mediated and at rest in being:

> Thou fortunate vision,
> Of all thou wast 'ware,
> Whatever it might be,
> Yet still it was fair.

says Lynkeus at the end of Faust; and Hegel in his preface to the *Phenomenology of Mind,* speaks of the life of reason as the "Bacchanalian revel wherein no member is not drunk, but which is at the same time transparent serenity" in being.

Both for Goethe and Hegel there is no direct, immediate, romantic identification with the absolute. "To reach the infinite, reach out in all dimensions of the finite," says Goethe, and Hegel: the absolute is grasped only in and through negations of itself, in the determinate and limited manifestations of its dialectic. For this reason they are anti-romantic; Hegel calls the romantic immediacy an "insanity" that tramples our common humanity underfoot, and Goethe calls romanticism "illness." They are both classical in their respect for essential measures and for the value of limitations.

There is also a close analogy between Faust's relation to the Christian religion and Hegel's philosophy of the Christian religion. For *Faust I,* it appears as a sentimental reminiscence and a tradition still hanging around.

> Feeling is all in all:
> The Name is sound and smoke.

In Hegel's early reflections on Christianity he hopes to replace Christianity with a national and ethical culture on a philosophical basis.

At the end of *Faust II,* the destruction of Christian culture is the symbol of a deluded humanity. The Christian Cura (a central theological concept in St. Augustin) comes to make Faust blind in order to lead him back to a truly human existence. The same change takes place in Hegel's work: In his philosophy of Religion, the Christian dogma is defended as an accurate religious expression of the fundamental metaphysical truth of the dialectical life of the absolute. The Trinity is the Christian revelation of the absolute truth that God is both transcendent and immanent, present in time and history and at the same time transcending them and taking them back into his eternal being.

For both Hegel and Goethe Christianity is a symbol of a human-divine reality. Both think Christianity within their own world of truth as one of its major manifestations. Thus the Christian symbol is used as frame in Faust, and Hegel liked to express his philosophy to the layman in Christian terms.

Both decline to treat Christianity as an irrelevant superstition, and both decline to accept it as the one and only access to the absolute.

A last analogy may further prove their similarity. Goethe knew that his Faust is a symbol of a historical epoch, "We are the last ones, my dear Eckermann." Hegel knew his philosophy as a harmony and reconciliation of the mind with itself, which would not necessarily mean a harmony and reconciliation of historical life. He wants at least to save the spirit of his culture, before night would fall. "Our shape of life grows old. And it is in the gray of dust that the owl of Minerva ventures its flight." Both visioned the future with misgivings. God will destroy this world to bring about a new order, says Goethe: barbarian masses will rise, says Hegel.

They were aware of their differences. It was Hegel's whole business to be aware of the limitations of his own logical medium. His idea is self-transcending. The poet accompanied the sending of a drinking glass as a present to Hegel with the note: "The Urphenomenon recommends itself to the Absolute." Which jest is interpreted in the Theory of Colours—We must confess the limitations of perception. The philosopher shall take them up in his region.

But they were more aware of their solidarity—We have already quoted Hegel's complete approval of the Faustian philosophy. Goethe writes after Hegel's death and a short time before his own: "A sequence of consistent moments is always a modification of eternity itself, and it was given you to be always yourself in all transitions and thus to satisfy my way of thinking as well as Hegel's." And to Varnhagen about the same time: "The foundation of this theory lay beyond my horizon, but where his doing reached me and where it influenced my efforts, I was always truly and spiritually furthered."

For Hegel the history of philosophy was the adventure of the mind to discover itself within its worlds. There is only one philosophy, but that one philosophy unfolds itself in the contradictory movements of its self-formulation. To know what you are you must know what you were, and to know what you were you must also know what you are. Likewise Goethe: "Who cannot give account of three thousand years must live in darkness, inexperienced from day to day." "History of man is man himself, and we may equally contend that the history of knowledge is one with knowledge itself . . . For merely looking at a thing does not further . . . but if we look into the world attentively we already are theorizing. To do this with consciousness, with self-knowledge, with freedom, and, to use a dangerous word, with irony, such a skill is necessary if we want to avoid abstraction, which we fear, and to gain a living result, which we desire."

Hence our analogy of *Faust* with Hegel's philosophy necessarily implies further comparisons with some other prominent philosophies of the past, without which our understanding of *Faust* would still be "abstract."

Goethe's enthusiasm for the "ancient" Greeks is well known. The center of *Faust II* lies in Greece, significantly the Greece of Homer and the pre-Socratic cosmology.

In our interpretation we emphasized the symbolism of the four elements: the solid earth, the fluid water, the gaseous air, the energetic fire. As the Milesians, Goethe also does not separate their physical appearance from their qualitative, expressive function, which establishes an affective continuum with the life of man. There is nothing that is dead in nature, what we call so is an abstract and purely external approach, a lack of understanding for the cosmic life appearing to us in sense-qualities. "I followed Hylozoism and always left its profound meaning untouched in its dignity and sanctity; it made me unreceptive, even intolerant against a way of thinking, which believes in a dead matter." When Hegel says that there is not one proposition of Heraclitus that is not absorbed in his logic, Goethe might have said with equal truth that there is not one image of Heraclitus that is not absorbed in his *Faust.*

Goethe's world is a Heraclitean eternal flux, a fluid ever new becoming, a harmony formed of contrasts, a dynamism and relativism wherein the "way up and the way down are one and the same," because there are no absolute "ups" or "downs" in this living sea of creation:

> Descend then! I could also say: Ascend!
> 'Twere all the same.

And:

> Like heavenly forces rising and descending
> Their golden urns reciprocally lending,

With wings that winnow blessing
From Heaven to Earth I see them pressing,
Filling the All with harmony unceasing.

Or:

In the tides of Life, in Actions storm,
A fluctuant wave,
A shuttle free,
Birth and the Grave,
An eternal sea,
A weaving, flowing
Life, all-glowing,
Thus at Time's humming look 'tis my hand pre-
pares
The garment of Life which the Deity wears.

Also Heraclitus' aristocratism, the disdain of the many is present:

The few, who thereof something really learned
Unwisely frank, with hearts that spurned con-
cealing
And to the mob laid bare their thought and feel-
ing
Have evermore been crucified and burned.

Faust II corrects this aristocratic individualism through social idealism. Heraclitos' "fire" burns in the first act of the second part:

They haste to quench the fire, but none
The swiftly kindling flames can shun,
That flash and dart on other heads
'Til wide the conflagration spreads:
Wrapped in the element, in turn
The masking groups take fire and burn.

The great "Pan" burns because he does not heed the Heraclitean counsel to "limit his draught of joy, in season," because Heraclitus demands a courageous stand in the flux of life, "as if battling for our city walls."

This leads to Plato. His dialectic preserves the flux as the "other of the One." His Eros is the One and the Other as a living and creative movement, reminiscent of the ideas seen in heaven or before birth and longing to see their counterpart in this life. Almost literally he reappears in **Faust:**

The Day before me and the Night behind,
Above me heaven unfurled, the floor of waves
beneath me—
A glorious dream!

And:

Two souls, alas! reside within my breast,
And each withdraws from, and repels its brother
One with tenacious organ holds in love
And clinging lust the world in its embraces;
The other strongly sweeps this dust above,
Into the high ancestral spaces.

Faust's Platonism lies in this essential dualism of his nature. He knows himself, as Plato achieved self-knowledge in fulfilling the demand and in answering Socrates query: What am I?

Aristotle is present in Faust with his "Entelechy," that is the individual, unique substance, the unrepeatable organic form of this individuality, which is indestructible or immortal;

The traces cannot, of mine earthly being;
In aeons perish—

Goethe, in his conversations with Eckermann, makes himself the connection here with the Leibnizian Monad.

Life is dynamic and fluid, it appears in qualitative polarities visible in the elements, it has a dual and dialectical structure and it is absolutely individuated. In those propositions we may summarize the essential analogies of the **Faust** with his great Greek ancestors.

We have already placed the **Faust** within the movement of "modern" philosophy. But there is one thinker who is particularly influential: Spinoza. This philosophical recluse, absorbed in rational demonstrations of his universal system, seems to be utterly contrary to the expansive artist of life, Goethe. Their incompatibility seems enhanced by the contemptuous remarks of the champion of pure reason against the sensuous consciousness of art. In the summary of the first book of his *Ethics* he refers to the beautiful as human idiosyncrasy, as a finite illusion. He says the beautiful is on the same level as stinking. It is a tickling of nerves, at best agreeable because useful for healthy recreation, as taste for wholesome food is biologically useful. Art keeps man in fetters of an inadequate, merely sensuous image-making, and prevents him by its flattery to rise above the level of subjective, private perspectives to the eternal realm of substantial reality and its universal and necessary truth.

Yet Goethe loved Spinoza. His mentor, Herder, aroused his interest and presented him with a Latin edition. He first read him together with Frau von Stein, and from then on Spinoza became a constant companion. But also Lessing, Herder, Schelling, Schleiermacher received Spinoza enthusiastically, all of them founders and leaders of aesthetic idealism.

This paradox is instructive. In an essay, dictated by Goethe to Frau von Stein, one can watch the transformation of Spinoza's system into a Goethean aesthetics. It shows how a poet may misread a philosopher. But that such a misinterpretation is possible also shows the deep rooted affinity between the philosophical and the artistic art of living.

We follow Goethe's essay:

Spinoza's substance is "being" identical with "perfection." It explains itself, as it cannot be explained by anything else. It is the only being completely intelligible.

Goethe reads: "the infinite substance, or complete existence, cannot be thought by us." "One cannot say that the infinite has parts. All limited existences are in the infinite."

"Each existing thing has an existence in itself, and so also the harmony (*Uebereinstimmung*) according to which it exists." "The measuring of a thing is a coarse action, which cannot be applied to organisms except in a very imperfect manner."

Evidently, what Goethe had in mind was not Spinoza's system, but something entirely different. He thinks of an organism or of a work of art, which is an indivisible organic whole, and each part expresses the nature of that whole as an organ or a member. It cannot be understood mechanically or mathematically, it is not rational at all. "A vitally existing thing can be measured by nothing that lies outside of itself." What for Spinoza is true only of his substance, for Goethe becomes true for a finite existence—the work of art must have an inner form, felt as harmony (*Uebereinstimmung*); there must be nothing in it which could not be derived from this inner unity of the work.

Spinoza says that a true "idea" must be the same as its "ideato," in other words, the logical system is identical with the system of objects. This principle of rationalism, Goethe reads as follows: "Souls which have an inner force to expand, begin to order, to facilitate knowledge, begin to arrange and to conjoin to reach enjoyment." Only a limited shape continuously offers this possibility of enjoyment. Thus rationalism is transformed into aesthetic idealism—an inner content of mind comes to rest and fulfillment in external embodiment. Beauty is not deeper or stronger than its embodiment, there is no more beauty in nature than the spectator or artist actualizes.

Spinoza distinguishes levels of knowledge as confused when oriented in mere appearing finite "modi," as clear and rational when oriented in the attributes of geometrical space and logical order, as adequate and philosophical when oriented in the substance which is identical with system.

Goethe derives from this the main categories of style: "If the soul becomes aware of relations in a germinal state, so to speak, so that their unfolded harmony could not be apprehended or felt completely, such an impression we call great."

"We call the object beautiful, if it is limited to such an extent that we can easily comprehend it, and if its relation to our nature is such that we like to comprehend it."

If "extension" is a worthy attribute of the divine nature, then it is also worthy as a medium of the fine arts. Herder's *God* here complements Goethe's essay, in that Herder transforms space into a symbolic medium for the expression of the movements of the soul, analogous to time in music.

The last fourth of Goethe's Spinoza essay deals with ethical questions. Goethe feels the kinship in his aesthetic with Spinoza's contemplative attitude.

Spinoza's God does not work for external purposes, which would show that he is in need of something that he lacks. Man is to imitate God. He is not to weep and laugh but to understand.

The life of understanding is the blessed life, because it is united in truth with eternal being that is blessed in itself, beyond the never ending search of pragmatic sciences and the relativity of empirical ends and the dogmatism of practical either/or purposes.

Goethe agrees in rejecting external teleology, as if God had created the oak so that man might have a cork for his bottle.

He also agrees in criticising narrow, selfish, private dogmatisms of practical parties: "They will hold that circle as the safest and the most certain, which is the most comfortable for them to think, and it is most noticeable that they look down and pity others, who are not so easily satisfied and who strive to visit and get acquainted with more relations concerning human and divine things; they let them know whenever there is an opportunity, with a spiteful modesty, that they have found a truth and a certainty far above all rational proof and demonstration. . . . For one who wants to know more there is little consolation in that he must constantly hear, that he must become more and more simple minded, that he must have only one point in mind, that he must not mind manyfold complexities, only then in such a state of mind is he to find happiness."

But while Goethe finds Spinoza's contemplative attitude congenial, he must on the other hand save tears and smiles, the primal affections of his art.

And so the understanding of affections is transformed into an aesthetic understanding.

What greater degree of poise can there be than when passions and deeds of the soul are embodied in the symbols of art. This too is dispassionate contemplation. In such symbols all can share and all can be united in joy.

For Spinoza the good life is a satisfaction of the soul, serenity of a cloudless contemplation, self-realization of our rational nature through that "adequate knowledge, which grasps the same and essential nature in the part and simultaneously in the whole." Negatively, the good life is the emancipation from passion by recognizing their mechanical causes and their finite character.

When Goethe came to Weimar he was determined to "still his wild desires", and Spinoza supported his will "to live with the world in peace."

But here also Spinoza is completely transformed. Goethe knew from his own experience that the best aid against the passions in his soul and against anger and limitations from the neighbor, was to write them off, to give them artistic objectivity, to behold them in an ideal mirror, to de-realize and universalize them in delectable images.

His Spinoza essay concludes, therefore, with observations on narrow-minded prejudices, which are wants, and on the "grace of nature which furnishes men with such self-satisfaction in their straits." This is the artistic delight in the portrayal of all sorts of life, which in *Faust* appears for the first time, after his Spinoza studies, in the scene of the Easter walk, where Faust contemplates a vividly portrayed "sea of errors," the common life of the common people.

The best aid against the tyranny of passions is their knowledge as art. The more diversified and the more numerous they are presented to a beholder, the less can he become ensnared by any single one of them. While Spinoza links them with external causes and presents them as if they were connected in themselves: "It seems only," says the

Mephistopheles (seated) advises the Freshman on his course of study.

Spinoza essay, "that states and things are produced through one another, but this is not so; rather one living nature (*Wesen*) presents an occasion for an other one to realize itself in a definite manner." This seeming connection among themselves is an accurate aesthetic idea of what the work of art does, and so is the occasion of a definitely determined mood of the beholder, occasioned by the contemplation of his own objectified state of mind. Thus we become free and experience that joy and delight which Spinoza calls the intellectual love of God and which Goethe has transformed into the aesthetic love of the soul of man in his derealized appearance.

Goethe's Spinozism is a misunderstanding. Hegel compresses this transformation into his lapidary word; The Substance is also Subject. Goethe is reported as saying that he has never tried to read Spinoza systematically, that he only "looked into" him. He does not bother about the logical cogency of axioms, propositions, proofs and demonstrations. For him, Spinoza's system is a work of art. Reality is best known through the "adequate intuition" of art and philosophy, hence, a disguised aesthetics.

This aesthetic reading of Spinoza was indirectly justified and prepared by Kant. His theory of experience reduced Spinoza's metaphysical Substance and Cause to categories of scientific object-thinking, to principles of logical formulation of given perceptions.

But his *Critique of Judgment* restores Spinoza's terms of Wholeness, Intellectual Intuition, Joy, disinterested interest, harmonious interplay of all faculties, derealization of all finite contents and purposes; they recur as ideals of aesthetic and organic-symbolic contemplation.

It is this book that won Goethe's approval of Kant. Hegel praises it as transition to his dialectical idealism. His own aesthetics firmly establishes the aesthetic world view as a constituent but limited aspect of the absolute.

In Goethe's *Faust* his so-called Spinozism is the *cantus firmus* in the vocal oratorium and celebration of the divine-human mystery; it imparts to the whole dialectical structure the meditative energy, that makes Faust a philosophical poem.

After the Easter Walk, the scene in "Cave and Forests" shows Faust in this mood of a grateful self-limitation and self-realization through the corresponding "attributes" of divine life: "the kingdom of nature with power to feel and to enjoy it" and "the ranks of living creatures . . . my brothers"; and the inner life where "in my breast the deep mysterious miracles unfold."

In the transition to the second part, substantial and self-affirmative nature is known through her modi, her deeds and suffering, while the "sun" of the absolute is the background of its immense and innumerable manifestations.

And Lynkeus at the end sings the praise of the world as divine spectacle.

After the breakdown of the Goethe-Hegel synthesis, of natural science, cultural and religious values and especially after the triumph of naturalisms, nationalisms, and pragmatisms coupled with the mass regimentation of our machine civilization, aesthetic idealism is remembered with gratitude. (pp. 142-63)

> *Gustav E. Mueller, "Goethe's Faust and German Idealism," in his* Philosophy of Literature, *Philosophical Library, 1948, pp. 125-163.*

D. J. Enright   (essay date 1949)

[*Enright is an English critic and poet best known for his conversational style and sardonic treatment of cultural pretensions in literature and criticism. In the excerpt below, he considers the importance of the "Prologue in Heaven" as an outline of the play's central concern: Faust's attempt to define morality and live in accordance with a moral code.*]

The Prelude on the Stage, with which [*Faust*] opens, is an unimportant exercise but [*The Prologue in Heaven*], on the other hand, is of prime importance. It is the beginning of the play proper, it suggests the middle, and it states the end. In three lovely songs, the Archangels describe with attractive conciseness the glories of the created world: in tone they bear some resemblance to several of Rilke's specifically religious poems (notably "The Girls' Prayers to Mary" and "Annunciation"):

> And tempests bluster in a wager, from sea to land, from land to sea, raging, forging an encoiling chain of deepest energy. There flames electric desolation with thundering strokes along the way. But, Lord, your messengers must honor the easy motion of your day.

The rhythm is one refreshingly unlike the Miltonic march-on-velvet which in the past has been predominantly popular with poets essaying a similar subject: it is a steady, confident praise of creation with, always implicit, a hint of personal humility, an awareness of "not unto us the glory." This is a point well worth making, right at the start, not only because of the chance it gives me to refer to Rilke (whose prestige is so high at the moment), but also because the first speech of Mephistopheles, which occurs directly after the Archangels' impressive paean, is such a striking and significant contrast. But (by the way) do not look for this contrast in any of the available English translations. For when Mephistopheles begins to speak, the translators at once seem to heave a sigh of relief as they drop the highfalutin' tone they used for the Archangels and fill Mephistopheles' mouth with all manner of "good lack!" and "marry" as if he were some kind of fifth-rate Shakespearean rustic. There is nothing of this in the original; certainly Mephistopheles does not speak in the elevated measures of the Archangels, but neither is he so devilishly jocular.

His speech begins in a familiar, equal-to-equal manner, but it becomes a moving indictment, not so much of mankind as of their creator; it is a reply to the Archangels—*they* mention only the awe-inspiring wonders of Nature, but Mephisto (the abbreviation will save paper) deplores the fact that he cannot regard mankind in the same rosy light. *He* is concerned with the debit side of creation:

> I have nothing to say about suns and worlds; I

only see how men torment themselves. This little god of earth remains true to type, as strange as on the first day. He'd have managed a little better if you had not allowed him a glimmer of divine light—he calls it Reason and uses it only to be beastlier than any beast. He seems to me, if your grace will permit, like one of those long-legged grasshoppers, always flying and springing into the air and then singing their old song in the grass. If only he would stay there in the grass! But no, he must bury his nose in every kind of mess.

"Singing their old song in the grass" is an ironic retort to the first line of the *Prologue,* "The sun makes music in its ancient fashion." "Die Sonne tönt nach alter Weise."

The Lord answers Mephisto's criticism of his ability as creator by drawing his attention to Faust, "my servant," whom Mephisto depicts as a typical romantic hero:

Indeed! he serves you in an odd manner. The fool's food and drink are not of this world. An inner fermentation drives him on, half-conscious of his madness—from Heaven he demands its loveliest stars and from the earth its highest joys, and neither near nor far can appease his agitated breast—.

But the Lord replies

Though at present his service is confused, soon I shall lead him into clarity. For the gardener knows, when the young tree shows green, that blossom and fruit will grace the future years—,

and this is a statement of his policy toward mankind in general. Mephisto, however, remains unconvinced, reasoning that since man is a hybrid creature, between the angel and the ape, he cannot lead the pure singleminded life as it is conceived in Heaven—and he must therefore endure a painful perverted form of animal existence. Furthermore, Mephisto wagers that he will be able to turn Faust into the path of absolute evil if the Lord will give him a free hand. With the famous line, "Es irrt der Mensch, so lang' er strebt" ("as long as he strives, man must err"), the Lord grants him permission to do his worst without divine intervention:

Enough, it is in your hands! Divert this spirit from its fountainhead and, if you can grasp it, lure it along your downward path; and stand in shame when you are forced to confess: a good man, in his dim urgency, is still conscious of the right way—.

One observes that this is spoken less in the manner of a wager than in the terms of a statement. The action of the whole play is summed up in this passage as in a kind of précis: Faust *will* be "lured along the downward path"; he *will* be "still conscious of the right way." The predetermined character of the play, thus announced at its very inception—and strengthened by the Lord's explicit and confident reference to Mephisto as a spur to slothful man, a "creator" of a kind, even—may at first seem rather discouraging to modern readers, may seem perhaps as blasphemous, in a different way, as it would have appeared to the right-minded Lutherans who edited Faust-books

with the intention of scaring their readers out of the unholy zeal for improper knowledge. (pp. 9-14)

With Goethe we have a gradual change of attitude toward Faust (a change, that is, in his conception of the philosophical significance of this pregnant character) which occurs over a period of almost sixty years. It will be well to mention here that the *Urfaust* (which Goethe wrote about 1773, though it was not published till 1887) is an unambiguous tragedy in which both Faust and Gretchen are doomed to hell, while the *Faust: Ein Fragment* (published in 1790) is essentially the *Urfaust* with the tragic catastrophe omitted, and with a changing but as yet uncrystallized conception of Faust and a more significant kind of Mephistopheles, an emissary (vaguely) of the divine powers. In the definitive play, *Faust, Erster Teil* (published in 1808), of course, Gretchen is received into Heaven as a penitent, Faust is preserved for his adventures in the Second Part, and the character of Mephistopheles takes a definite shape.

The point I must make, as emphatically as possible, is that the play under examination in this [essay] is the First Part of *Faust* as it stood after Goethe had made his final alterations, and any reference to earlier versions or conceptions of individual characters is to be made only for the light it will throw on this final version. The theme was one with which Goethe lived the greater part of his creative life, and the kind of significance it had for him varied in the way I have indicated; the sad thing is that critics have spent so much time and labor in the study of the earlier versions that when they come to the culminating First Part their approach is vitiated, they deplore that such and such should have been omitted, or added, or altered; and the fact that Goethe's literary use of the legend should have changed seems to them sufficient proof of artistic (or philosophical) uncertainty. But Goethe's creative life was abnormally long, and it is very reasonable to expect his philosophical opinions to remain consistent throughout, or the works of art in which they play some part to form a consistent whole. After all, the changing mind of Goethe is more interesting, and more valuable, than the consistency of thought displayed in the work of, say, Schiller. The First Part must be judged as a work in its own right; if it is, I think the various anomalies of character and the vacillating intentions which have troubled the commentators, and which they point to as relics of an earlier conception of the play, will very quickly disappear. If the reader confines himself to the printed word on the page in front of him then he will find no valid reason for surprise or dissatisfaction when Faust finally eludes the trap-door into Hell—no, the only possible reason is one not found in the printed word, for it resides in an almost obsessional memory of the *Urfaust,* of Marlowe's tragedy, of the *Volksbuch,* or a proleptic knowledge of the Second Part. I really think that the person who comes to *Faust* with no scholarly preconceptions will have the best chance of comprehending what the play is about—which suggests that the neglect experienced by the work during recent years may finally prove to have done it a considerable service.

To return to the *Prologue in Heaven:* it ends with Mephisto, alone, making a little joke:

I like to see the Ancient from time to time, and I'm careful not to offend him. It is really handsome of so great a gentleman to chat so humanly with the Devil himself.

The misapprehension under which he labors is already fairly clear: he does not agree with the Lord's description of him as one "who tempts and excites and must, as devil, create," as, that is, an instrument of divine influence, since with the traditional conceit of the Devil he prefers to regard himself as the biblical serpent of Eden, as an individual master-force—as a king in Hell rather than a servant of Heaven.

The one clear fact that emerges from the *Prologue* is this: the drama is to turn on the question of whether man is a successful creation, whether the Lord's experiment in crossing the angelic with the animal has produced a form of life which is a useful advance on the emptiness of Chaos. Will Faust (as a representative man) under temptation and, more than that, during the enactment of evil, still retain his divine acknowledgment of the distinction between good and evil? The issue at stake is *not* whether Faust can resist evil desires—obviously he cannot—but whether he can be brought into absolute and genuine unconsciousness of the moral distinction. We must give due significance to those words of the Lord which I have already quoted,

> A good man, in his dim urgency, is still conscious of the right way.

The aspect of the drama as a *testing* of the Lord's fitness as a creator has not been sufficiently noted, perhaps because whereas commentators are ready enough to expound the wager which Mephisto makes with Faust (the "bargain," that is) they have generally ignored this dispute between Mephisto and the Lord which results in what is the primal wager, usually on the flimsy grounds that the *Prologue* is a "later interpolation" (that is, it was not in the *Urfaust* or the *Fragment* and therefore cannot be of any real significance). Mephisto is perhaps not exactly the Devil, but rather the devil's advocate who resides in every human breast, and his quarrel is not with man, whom he pities as one might pity a badly brought-up child, but with the parent of mankind. One might describe this as the Prometheus theme inverted, for the indignation of this Prometheus is shown to be ill-timed and inapposite and far from disinterested. And, if I may be allowed to re-state them, the terms of the wager which is to decide this momentous question are not the simple "heads or tails" of morality on the one hand and immorality on the other: it is evidence of *non-morality* which will lose the Lord his case, and it is up to Mephisto, as the dissenting party, to gather such evidence. The structure and tone of the *Prologue in Heaven*, with the powerful impression it conveys of the invulnerability of Heaven, prepares us for the final victory of the Lord and his vindication as creator. But I do not think that such foreknowledge should detract from the play's interest: it is not a detective novel of the kind whose interest lies solely in the criminal's attempt to evade the law, for the whole point of *Faust* lies in the way in which the moral faculty survives and operates in various kinds of experience and under conditions where one might expect it to suffer annihilation. The Devil may think he

calls the tune, but Nature "is a great organ on which our Lord God plays, and the Devil blows the bellows." Nor is the question quite as simple as this, because Mephisto's powerful cunning and the poor showing Faust makes in their arguments cause the reader's impression of divine omnipotence to fade somewhat. The reader who desires an element of suspense in his drama will not be disappointed after all: this is theodicy come alive. (pp. 15-21)

> *D. J. Enright, in his* Commentary on Goethe's Faust, *New Directions, 1949, 158 p.*

Harold Jantz   (essay date 1951)

[*In the following excerpt, Jantz examines the structure, characterization, and symbolism in* Faust, *arguing that these elements of the drama accurately reflect the literary and philosophic ideals of the Renaissance as well as those of Goethe's own time.*]

It would be possible to multiply the connections of *Faust* to the Renaissance many times over, but it is not necessary. The chief question posed . . . is whether the values and principles, the personalities and actions of the drama, in their larger interrelations and sequences, resemble those of the Renaissance more than they do those of Goethe's own age. The answer seems to be, yes, they do. The drama is not subjective and not of the eighteenth century with some decorative Renaissance coloring; it is largely objective, of the Renaissance with some intentional anachronisms and with the personal coloring and blending which accompanied the act of poetic creation. Viewed in its own proper time in which the poet placed it, its seeming discontinuities and contradictions resolve of themselves, and the total work exhibits lines of unity previously unobserved. In its own intellectual atmosphere it lives and breathes, has dimensionality and resonance and coherence. By contrast, it seems to be out of its element in the eighteenth century, for Goethe took into his *Faust* phases of Renaissance conviction and imagination with which his own epoch for the most part was not concerned.

In this particular work Goethe was, in the fullness of his creative originality, an "old-fashioned" artist who clung to the old exalted values of the Renaissance and of a freshly revived antiquity, rejecting the prevailing standards of the Enlightenment, Revolution, and romanticism, as well as the basic assumptions of the philosophies of his day. In technique, too, the protean variety of German, Italian, and Neo-Latin forms in the poem points intentionally and meaningfully to the past (and to the future), as does the vast dramaturgy of Renaissance and Baroque spectacle contrasting with scenes of sensitive intimacy, as does also the unchecked creative boldness of its language which is unparalleled since the days of Shakespeare. That Goethe himself thought of his language and expression as Renaissance in character is indicated by his suggested improvement of the French translations that continued to appear during his old age: Soret reported that Goethe thought *Faust* should be translated into the French of the time of Marot; that means, into Renaissance French, before the drastic pruning of the language. Two years later he repeated the same thought to Cousin. This too, like so much in old Goethe, points back unmistakably to mental associations he had formed in his youth, as a passage in his autobiography tells us: "When in my youthful years my attention was more and more directed to the German quality of the sixteenth century, I soon extended my inclination also to the French of that glorious epoch. Montaigne, Amyot, Rabelais, Marot were my friends and aroused my sympathy and admiration."

For such a long time has the intellectual atmosphere of the eighteenth century, particularly of the Storm and Stress, been studied and taken for granted as the natural environment of the Goethean Faust, that the suggestion of another possibility may be a bit disconcerting. However, the new evidences and demonstrated hypotheses are not necessarily in direct opposition to traditional attitudes, for there are many points of agreement, and both will have to be kept in mind.

Anyone who wishes to estimate the relative scope of the old and the new hypotheses, can make a fairly crucial test if he asks himself the following two questions: What eighteenth-century work aside from Goethe's *Faust* is comparable to Pico's, for instance, for giving an all-over, *structural* outline of the character, place, and destiny of the "Faustian" man? (The factor of structure is decisive and, of course, precludes any anthology of scattered parallels in word and thought, however compendious, and also any incidental or peripheral phases of the work.) Secondly, what actual personalities of the eighteenth century have as many centrally "Faustian" traits about them as have, for instance, Leonardo, Michelangelo, Paracelsus, Dee, Bruno, or Kepler? In answer, Herder's name is almost certain to come up, but not if the characterizations of Herder by Goethe himself, by other contemporaries, and by the modern biographers are kept in mind. The reader may also find it surprising as well as amusing to read what Herder himself had to say about Goethe's *Faust.*

However, the drama goes beyond either Goethe's or Faust's proper period. There is in it from the beginning a tendency toward breaking the temporal shackles; with the sundering of them the action extends backward and forward to conquer all the time of which man's mind is the master. And this again is characteristic of the Renaissance: the three faces of time are virtually a symbol of the fifteenth and sixteenth centuries. Though in a larger sense *Faust* is a timeless drama, as far beyond the limitations of its own period setting as it is beyond Goethe's age or our own, it can properly be called a drama of the Renaissance because that epoch is its point of departure and furnishes its fundamental premises, from which alone its problem, action, and solution can be truly understood. It is naturally not a historical drama, nor does it exhibit any of the traits of that genre except for a few minor details.

The protagonist is a Renaissance man not so much in the sense that he is a specific or a representative personage of that era as in the sense that he stands as the most vital and eloquent symbol of its distinctive and central drive: the will to all-inclusive synthesis—not the medieval synthesis of the *Summa* which subsumes everything to a pre-formed system and method, but a synthesis which allows everything to come together freely, find its own level and natu-

ral integration, and gradually emerge out of a seeming confusion into a living, dynamic interrelation of forces and influences. This has a far greater claim to agreement with truth and reality than has the violent procrusteanism of any philosophic system.

Perhaps one of the chief causes of misunderstanding is the tendency to consider *Faust* as a philosophic poem rather than as a symbolic poem. It is a philosophic poem only in the original sense of the word philosophy: love of wisdom. In the stricter sense, however, philosophy distinguishes and divides, symbol identifies and unites. The application of conventional philosophic methods to the criticism of the work has led to some strange misapprehensions, and has sometimes mantled it in deepest obscurity. *Faust* is poetry, *Faust* is symbol, and the poetic symbolic approach can be the only primary one. Though Goethe went to great effort to come to a sympathetic understanding of the systematic and idealistic philosophers of his own day, their way of thought was alien to his own and their way of expression distasteful. Those concepts which he ostensibly took from them, on closer inspection usually turn out to be reformulations of thoughts which he already knew from the older authors he loved. His natural affinities were always for the unsystematic philosophers and especially for those thinkers who believed that all phenomena are symbols, that is, genuine realities in full harmonious relation to the greater and deeper realities which they reveal and conceal.

From the time of Luden's long conversation with Goethe on *Faust,* in 1806, to the present, there have been fervent admirers of the work who have given up the hope of finding the unity within it and have resigned themselves to enjoying its separate beauties and fragmentary greatnesses. There have been others in recent times who have attempted to give a specious unity to it by forcing it into the patterns of their latest philosophical fads, not infrequently doing violence thereby to the express poetic intention of the author. Perhaps they have been led to this subjective and willful course because the philosophies of Goethe's own day cannot be brought into any significant over-all correspondence to the work.

Not nearly as reprehensible as the willfully subjective, often negativistic perversion of the meaning of *Faust,* and yet grave, is the long-standing, particularistic tendency toward seeing Faust the man as a specifically German phenomenon. On the contrary, Faust is throughout and in essentials a European, and only at times and in accidentals a German, even as he is in essentials a Renaissance man, the master of three thousand years, and only in that larger sense a projection of Goethe and his age. (pp. 124-28)

Nothing which has been said about the work and its author, however, should be construed as implying that Goethe's ways of thinking, feeling, reacting, creating were exclusively or even primarily those of the Renaissance. Though he felt at home in that period, he did not confine himself to its fundamental premises, underlying attitude and outlook, nor did he advocate that they be restored to primacy for his own times or for the future. We know that he wrote not only the masterpiece which was based on these premises but that he also, for example, had the breadth and flexibility of genius to write another master-piece, a contemporary one, out of his own times and for his own times, namely his *Wilhelm Meister.*

Though a contemporary novel is on a different artistic plane from a symbolic representative drama, and cannot in certain ultimates be compared with it, we can, neverthe-less, observe that *Wilhelm Meister* is also in two parts, was begun in youth and finished in old age, that it also breaks through the limits of its own time into a great pan-oramic vista of the future, and likewise rises above its art form to a higher literary level. But how different are its basic assumptions, its accepted standards and points of view!

Omitting here, of necessity, all discussion of its many re-semblances to *Faust,* from the obvious to the very subtle ones, omitting also the discussion of its startlingly ad-vanced exploration of the subconscious and the other X-factors of human existence, let us, for the sake of compari-son, state briefly what standards and criteria are assumed and accepted for the life and development of Wilhelm and his associates.

The characters in the novel are thoroughly "modern" peo-ple of the period around 1800. They only rarely step out of the framework of reference of their times; the problems they find in their environment and in themselves, the mea-sures they take to solve them are in true correspondence to the age in which they live, move, and have their being.

Wilhelm is the social personality of his day who is educat-ed in society and for society. He quickly acquires the wid-est possible variety of social relations; all the things he most wishes to do have to be done in cooperation with oth-ers; and every significant new stage in his career represents an advance in human understanding and social insight, until we finally see him and his associates developing even beyond their enlightened social-minded aristocracy to the initiation of a great experiment in industrial democracy on American soil, with themselves as equals among other workers—this a vision (or better, an insight) of Goethe's to which no other eminent man of letters was to attain for some time to come.

The complex of basic assumptions and motivations then is something like this: being a useful member of society is the highest ideal; achieving some work which receives so-cial recognition is the highest glory; helping to reform or to establish a society in which a harmonious mutual ad-justment is possible, in a carefully balanced reciprocity be-tween the individual and the group, that is the ultimate ex-alted effort in which a human being can engage. These are, of course, simply the accepted standards and attitudes of the novel, not its ideological framework, theme, or any-thing of the kind; the work has far greater dimensions.

If we measure *Faust* against these criteria, we can observe an almost total discrepancy. Only the ending is in essential harmony, when old Faust is prepared to lay down his aris-tocratic rule, since his new land has by that time devel-oped to the point where it can be taken over and main-tained by "a free people on a free soil," of whom he would like to be one. There is then an entirely different way, from very different assumptions, toward much the same end.

This similarity of final vision and achievement, together with what God plainly says about Faust in the "Prologue" and what the angelic messengers say after his death, shows us that Goethe emphatically approved of Faust's way through life; his many other statements, in letters and con-versations, especially to Eckermann, exclude the possibili-ty of any other interpretation. Since, therefore, the record is completely clear that Goethe commended the life, pur-pose, and achievement of both Faust and Wilhelm Mei-ster, and since the one will not conform to the basic criteria of the other, we are obliged to ask the question: what are the fundamental premises according to which the life and destiny of Faust are intelligible? (pp. 129-31)

To speak in Renaissance symbolic language: man occupies a middle position in the cosmos, comprising within him-self the whole range of creation from mass and matter, through plant life and animal sensation, on to the highest cognizance of spirit and intellect, aspiring even toward communion with the Godhead. He thus has an advantage even over the angels: he is the only one of God's creatures who is able to comprehend within himself, in epitome, the totality of creation.

Man in his unique middle position contains in abstract all the parts and forces of the whole of creation; he even has a due portion of that primordial chaos out of which cos-mos and light were born through the seed-power of the di-vine Logos. He thus owns potentially everything necessary for making himself into a microcosm which can be brought to ever more perfect harmonic correspondence to the macrocosm. Man, with his free choice, can, of course, also sink down to any level on the way toward disintegrat-ed chaos; he can also stop far short of perfection on the way up and attain to only fragmentary correlation and in-complete harmony.

Within the framework of this philosophy the chief duty of man is to develop himself into as full and perfect a micro-cosm as his natural endowments and powers will permit. Far from being the egoistic aim it may at first seem to be, it is in its Renaissance cosmic setting the most noble and godly action that man can undertake. The doctrine of har-monic correspondence between microcosm and macro-cosm implies clearly that man can be effective in this world only to the extent that he has brought himself into harmony with the world, only to the extent that he makes the laws of the universe the principles of his own action. This is old Stoic doctrine, which was developed by Kepler and others, was borrowed by Kant as well as by Goethe, and naturally makes allowance for human imperfection and shortcomings.

Only like can truly know like and be effective in it; thus the more perfect a cosmic replica man can make of him-self, the greater will be his understanding of the universe, and the abler will he be to perform the task befitting his middle position between the spiritual and the material. That task is to aid creation on its way upward to God, to spiritualize the material, to give higher integration to lower forms, even to convert a portion of chaos into or-dered cosmos. In other words, the Renaissance believed that God intended man to participate in the creative pro-cess, on the human level; to the extent that man did so, he was fulfilling his highest destiny and aiding in the elevation and redemption of the world. The history of the word "creation" as applied to human achievement is an indication of the strength and spread of this heterodox conviction.

In the Renaissance the emphasis was on the *individual in* society rather than on the *member of* society. Not that the social obligations of man were repudiated, but that they were assumed to be dependent on even higher obligations. If man fulfilled his divine destiny, the result would be an improvement of the world, and that would include his fellow men. For man to make human betterment his sole purpose would be a reprehensible limitation of his duties which are equally owing to the rest of creation and to God. Social improvement, therefore, cannot be the purpose, but it will be one end result of the right human effort of a good man who has performed for God his ennobling duty toward himself and the world.

It is thus Faust's duty to expand his understanding by the full range of experiences attainable to man, and not to desist from his studies in the great university of the world until he has such a practical and well-rounded comprehension of the laws of life and the cosmos that he feels a spontaneous inner urge to participate in the act of creation on its own terms. (This basis for action is quite unlike the theoretical constructionism of an idealist visionary, whose efforts to foist his artificial social pattern on human reality can lead only to the misery and degradation of mankind.) Faust's last great work is the rescue of one disintegrated, formless, fruitless corner of chaos, turning it into an integrated, formed, fruitful realm of cosmos. Significantly, he concentrated on the work itself, with creative activity his primary purpose, and only near the conclusion did he realize what a glorious future result would come from his microcosmic effort. His previous wanderings through space and time and his stations along the way are, from the Renaissance view, not at all the rootless, purposeless drifting of a self-indulgent tourist, they are the creative, productive fulfillment of his human destiny and God's purpose.

In the "Prologue" the Lord had announced what He expected of Faust; His norms, be it noted, are not social, but far greater and more encompassing. Faust fulfills his mission in the only way a mortal can fulfill such an overwhelming mission. After him man will have higher potentialities, he will have greater strength and confidence to penetrate ever deeper into chaos, to separate and mold it into cosmos, to integrate it into ever higher forms. One end-product or even by-product of a great and good man having lived, searched, and created in this world is that the boundaries of light and vision are thereby extended for the rest of humanity, even if human betterment was not a prime motive force within him.

The Greeks would have called him a "hero" and established him like Heracles or Asclepius among that group of demi-gods, or translated him to a star (a poetic idea of which Goethe was fond). The Renaissance would have granted him unreserved honor with full ceremonial accompaniment, and even recorded his errors and falls with awed respect and the properly humble "how much the more to me."

Goethe decided in conclusion to stage for Faust a full-scale celestial apotheosis, or rather ascension, in an appropriate Renaissance-Baroque manner. Since he thereby indicated that Faust's course on earth had been achieved in accordance with God's will, it might be a bit presumptuous for anyone to lay claim to a judgment better informed than Goethe's and a justice more wisely administered than God's. The poet wanted to give us this other view of life, he felt we needed it, and by this time, looking back over the total results of a century of socially oriented endeavor, we should know whether we do need it and how much we need it.

It is evident from *Wilhelm Meister* that Goethe was not a reactionary who turned back to Renaissance ways and attitudes in denial of his own age and its tendencies. And yet, with astonishing prevision he saw the other side of the developing new century, saw that even its laudable social ideals might suffer the baneful results of their one-sidedness and insufficiency. The conversations with Eckermann are full of this, and there is also the famous letter to Zelter of June 6, 1825, with his devastating prognosis of the nineteenth century.

With unerring intuition Goethe saw that the new age needed what it had already thoughtlessly pushed aside. And so he felt impelled again and again throughout his life to take up a work begun in early youth, even though in his maturity, when the new attitudes predominated in him, he experienced considerable difficulty in recovering once more a conscious understanding of the basic Renaissance assumptions on which he had planned and begun it. By old age he was not only completely clear about it again, he saw it with far wider and deeper perspective. He discerned the threads which ran to it from remotest time, and helped spin the threads which reach from it to his own time and into the future.

To offset the ideal of the skilled and competent specialist perfectly integrated into the social pattern of his day, and withal a fine well-rounded human being, Goethe realized that the world needed the vision of the man who makes it his primary life work to encompass the totality of human experience and insight, to transcend all the barriers of space and time that hem him in as an individual, who perhaps even neglects the demands that his fellow men feel they may reasonably make of him, in order to progress to that great creative synthesizing act which will raise his world to a higher level of integration, and mankind to a higher level of understanding. The world needs such men for its own salvation, since the end product of perfect social integration is complacency, intolerance, stagnation, and a stultifying mediocrity.

Perhaps Goethe never consciously considered just why *Faust* and *Wilhelm Meister,* these two so very different works, should become the occupation of a lifetime. Obviously both were deeply important to him; he had two very different attitudes toward life which he felt it important to express. But we must not forget that he devoted much more attention and loving care to *Faust* than he did to *Wilhelm Meister,* he began it sooner, stayed with it longer, spoke of it more often and more warmly, and left the second part sealed as his last literary testament to the future. The contemporary novel was important to him, but the symbolic representative drama was more important.

Two equally wrong claims can be made, and have been made concerning **Faust:** one, that it is a sure and sufficient guide for modern man; two, that it has nothing to offer our times except a warning example against everything "Faustian." The drama is a poetic masterpiece, not an ethical-philosophical treatise. We should turn to it not to learn precepts for life but to learn life. And life is in it in symbolic, truthful statement, life in all its achievement, in all its frustration, in all its glory, in all its grimness, not as the idealist poet would like it to be, but as the objective poet knows it is. The Philemon and Baucis episode, for example, ought not to have happened, but in the reality for which it is a symbol, it always has happened, in every colonial project in the history of man, even in the most humane and enlightened. It is the poet's duty neither to suppress that side of reality nor to excuse it but only to present it in valid symbol.

In the midst of the world as it is, the poet placed the man with the unquenchable expansive drive, the restless urge to explore all the world's values in every direction, who dared to venture beyond the limits set to mortal man and to bring back with him from beyond what he needed and desired for this life. Like the several Renaissance men we have observed, he mastered the world creatively before he was able to master himself. Through his own fault as well as through the treachery of circumstances he repeatedly fell into error and sin, yet for all that, he developed into a personality of all-encompassing, overwhelming greatness, according to the potentialities with which the poet had endowed him.

Far from being a subjective writer who used the large framework of **Faust** for a vast series of greatly varied and highly colorful personal portraits and scenes in masquerade, Goethe was in the unrolling of this drama the creator of an integrated work, of a full and self-sufficient entity. A true creator must be like God, evolving a vast and complex universe, remaining warm and sympathetic, it is true, but aloof and divinely impersonal, not concealing the faults of his hero, not ameliorating or artificially diverting the terror, the tragedy, and the guilt, allowing the hilarious, the witty, the trivial to enter, as in life, sometimes at incongruous moments, all in the interest of a higher truth than mere surface consistency, letting his figures and events run their own course according to their own bents and conflicts, in brief, giving his creation its own proper life in its own atmosphere.

What may always remain something of a mystery is Goethe's uncanny ability to penetrate to the vital center of the Renaissance. Perhaps with his poetic intuition Goethe created with a deeper truth and accuracy than he knew; perhaps with his great empathic powers delicately controlling the sum of his knowledge, he could view and represent the age of Faust more authentically than any one for the next century and longer. Whatever the case may be, the picture of the Renaissance that has developed out of the far-ranging studies of recent decades corresponds in a remarkable way to the great lines and masses as well as to the details on the canvas of the master. (pp. 131-37)

Harold Jantz, in his Goethe's Faust as a Renaissance Man: Parallels and Prototypes, *Princeton University Press, 1951, 198 p.*

Erich Heller   (essay date 1952)

[*Heller was a Czechoslovakian-born educator and critic. Below, he suggests that the contradictory nature of Faust's quest for both emotional and intellectual fulfillment demonstrates Goethe's unwillingness to accept the despair that lies at the heart of tragedy. As a result, Heller claims, despite its other achievements,* Faust *fails as an effective tragedy.*]

Any criticism of Goethe requires the utmost tact. Not only is the man so immense—and nothing is more difficult in criticism than to keep alive at every moment that sense of proportion which the very difference in level between creativeness and critical judgment demands; criticism is, alas, an unaristocratic habit, easily tempted into a false intimacy, in praise and negation alike—but also so much of the perennial discussion about Goethe is so massively wrongheaded, and so passionate, that it has filled the atmosphere around him with an abundance of electrical charges, making it all too easy to produce short circuits. I am saying this because I wish to speak of a limitation in Goethe's range of awareness and of a defect in his sensibility, and because I believe, paradoxically enough, that this limitation lies in the very boundlessness of his genius, and the defect in the inexhaustible richness of his sensitivity. It would be preposterous to derive the standards for an assessment of Goethe's achievements from anywhere else but the great classics of European civilization. Yet it would be futile to seek a place for him in a pattern determined by Homer, or Sophocles, or Virgil, or Dante, or Shakespeare. His range is too wide, and his gifts too universal ever to find full realization in one type of work alone, and his genius too diffused ever to concentrate on a single exemplary, classical achievement; and while in scope he is too vast ever to represent the character of an age, the mode of his imagination, its susceptibilities and idiosyncrasies, partake, at the same time, too definitely of the unresolved problems of the late eighteenth century for him easily to be acknowledged as being for all times and all places. With regard to Goethe's position within his own nation, it is very revealing that it could be said with some justice—as it was said immediately after the Second World War by Karl Jaspers—'that we came face to face with experiences in which we had no inclination to read Goethe, but took up Shakespeare, or the Bible, or Aeschylus, if it was possible to read at all'.

What was the nature of the experience in the face of which Goethe offered no help? It was the very kind of experience before which Goethe himself always proved helpless: the exposure to the manifestations of evil and sin. 'The mere attempt to write tragedy might be my undoing,' he once said, and it was the truth—at least for the greatest part of his life. Among his dramas there are three dramatic poems which, more than any other dramas he wrote, established his fame: **Iphigenie, Tasso, Faust.** All of them are potential tragedies, indeed so much so that one may feel that the tragic conclusion could only be avoided at the price of complete artistic conclusiveness. They show a moving and yet unsatisfactory reluctance of mind and imagination to accept the rule of the road leading to the very centre of human destiny. This is not to imply that in that very centre there dwells, inescapably, tragedy. But once a man is compelled to penetrate to that central point in all seriousness, then there is only one region left that stretches, for the European, beyond tragedy. Beyond Hamlet and the rest that is silence, there stands only Prospero:

> And my ending is despair,
> Unless I be reliev'd by prayer,
> Which pierces so that it assaults
> Mercy itself, and frees all faults.

> (pp. 39-41)

Under such auspices what was to become of a dramatic plot in which a man enters into a contract with the Devil, signing away, on certain conditions, the fate of his soul? What was to become of *Faust?* One may well ask. It took Goethe, all in all, sixty years to decide, or rather to decide that he would not quite decide. Certain things, however, the play decided for him. For instance, that it would, being Goethe's, become a lyrical masterpiece. There is no greater and no more varied lyrical poetry to be found within the German language. And more: *Faust* became a pageant of the human spirit on its voyage throughout the ages. An extraordinary wealth of mythological creatures, Teutonic, Greek, Christian, populate the scene, all testifying to their creator's inexhaustible imaginative power. And still more: the hero of the play was to become the representative of a whole epoch of history, its lust for knowledge, for power over nature, its intellectual and emotional instability, its terrible failure in love, humility and patience. And still more: the first part of the play, dominated by what is usually called the Gretchen tragedy, was to bring out most movingly the undoing, by the Faustian manoeuvres, of what was left in the world of simplicity of heart, devotion of love and innocence of feeling. This part of what is, after all, called the tragedy of Faust, developed by its own momentum into a poetic and dramatic achievement so immaculate that it will, I think, for ever hold its place by the side of what is great in the literature of the world—and this precisely because in its design it is not, in the traditional sense, tragic but lyrical. It is what might have become of the play *Hamlet* if Ophelia and not the Prince of Denmark were to be its protagonist. In other words, Goethe may have succeeded in creating a new genre: sentimental tragedy, or the tragedy of human *feelings:* Werther, Gretchen, Ottilie. What he could not write was the tragedy of the human *spirit.* It is here that the tragedy of Faust fails and becomes illegitimately ambiguous, because there is for Goethe in the last analysis no specifically *human* spirit. It is fundamentally at one with the spirit of nature. Hence it is He, the Spirit of Nature, or the Spirit of Earth, not God or the Devil, who holds in his hands the final decision over Faust's bliss or damnation. Had He, when He appeared to Faust in the first scene of the play, not rejected him, neither God in Heaven nor the Devil in Hell would have had a chance. And one of the only two scenes in which Faust really regrets that he has committed himself to his satanic company is the great monologue *Wald und Höhle:*

> Erhabner Geist, du gabst mir, gabst mir
> alles . . .

> Oh thou great Spirit, thou has given me all . . .

when it appears that this Spirit did not crush him after all.

There are in this vast display of demons great and small only two that affect Faust demonically; certainly not God, who is a jovial old gentleman, enlightened and rather commonplace in some of his utterances ('Ein guter Mensch, in seinem dunklen Drange, Ist sich des rechten Weges wohl bewusst', which really means not more than that a good man will not altogether go astray; a conviction not so difficult to hold that it would need a divinity to persuade one), and certainly not Mephistopheles, a Voltairean spirit, with whom Faust is from the very beginning on terms of great familiarity. Goethe himself, in a conversation with Eckermann (March 2nd, 1831), has denied him all demonic properties: 'He is altogether too negative,' he said, and has explicitly stated in the play itself that he is of lesser rank than the Spirit of Earth. But the two which teach Faust what a real demon is are the Earth Spirit and the Mothers, the innermost spirits of nature and life. They represent the demonic element in Goethe's genius. It is in union with this element that Faust seeks his happiness from beginning to end, or *almost* to the very end, and not in the realization of a specifically human spirit. And Faust has been in contact with those demons before Mephistopheles enters the scene. This contact means black magic, and Faust is a magician when the curtain rises. It is this that reduces the *dramatic* stature of Mephistopheles to all but nil, and not the rather naïve consideration that Goethe has forestalled all dramatic tension in this respect by making, in the Prologue, the Lord himself, a sure winner, as it were, party to the wager. All that Mephistopheles can do for Faust is to give him a hand in a job of which he already knows the essential tricks of the trade. And throughout the play the Devil performs hardly any magical feats with which one would not willingly credit the magician himself who had already succeeded in establishing contact with the very spirit of life.

All this would be rather irrelevant if it were not at the centre of the essential ambiguity of *Faust*—the most striking outcome of Goethe's avoidance of tragedy. What does Faust *really* expect of Mephistopheles? Still more magic? No; but contentment, rest, peace; to be able to say to the moment: 'Verweile doch, du bist so schön'. [Stay, thou art so fair.] In other words, life is good. True, this is preceded by Faust's contemptuous identification of such a state with self-complacency. But it is the words themselves, not what leads up to them, which become the condition of the wager. And their poetic truth gives the lie to the preamble. They are made of the same stuff as 'Es sei, wie es wolle, Es war doch so schön!' And this the devil is to provide? The very same devil whom Faust, a few scenes later, when he has found temporary peace in the company of the Spirit of Nature, knows to be the spirit responsible for

> So tauml' ich von Begierde zu Genuss
> Und im Genuss verschmacht' ich nach Begierde

> Thus I tumble from desire to fulfilment
> And in fulfilment I crave for more desire

for ever destroying that very peace which communion with the Spirit of Nature gives him. With the Devil defined as the spirit of negation and unrest, this becomes indeed a very strange condition meaning in fact that the Devil is to have Faust if Faust ever escapes the Devil.

What, on the other hand, is the condition of the wager between the Lord and Mephistopheles?

> Zieh diesen Geist von seinem Urquell ab
>
> Drag this spirit away from the very source of his life

The Lord, that is, challenges Mephistopheles to alienate Faust from the springs of life, to uproot him. If he succeeds, Faust will be his. This sounds more like 'Deprive him of all peace, if indeed you can' than 'Make him contented with the moment'. And in the end, when Faust, anticipating this peace and contentment, blinded by anxiety, deluded into the belief that the great work of colonization has begun while, in actual fact, the busy noise is merely the sound of shovels digging his own grave, utters the fatal words, in the face of a vision so totally unconvincing in its meagre guilt-burdened town-and-country-planning bliss that one cannot but agree with Mephistopheles that it is the emptiest moment of his life, then the Devil is cheated of his apparently well-deserved prey by the feeble trick of a future tense ['Im Vorgefühl von solchem hohen Glück'], and by the intervention of divine grace called down upon him by the only human love Faust ever received and experienced.

How is this? Faust has indeed promised that he would content himself, even anticipated the enjoyment of peace ['Geniess' ich jetzt . . .'] in his vision of the contented future. He has satisfied the Devil who has never been found wanting in the shrewd judgment of any situation, and is, having faithfully renounced his programme of eternal striving, carried into Heaven in reward for his determination to strive eternally:

> Wer immer strebend sich bemüht,
> Den können wir erlösen.
>
> It is the struggling, striving man
> Whom we are free to save.

What is at the root of such confusion, which has indeed defeated four generations of interpreters of *Faust,* and, if we are to trust Eckermann's report, Goethe's own faculties as a commentator? It would be tempting to relegate it to the place where many an impenetrable mystery is stored, were it not for the persistent suspicion that we are faced here not so much with a genuine poetic paradox as with a plain contradiction. It is the inevitable contradiction of the undedicated mind and heart. In Faust's world there are no real loyalties to be realized and no real commitments to be broken. Both his eternal striving and his desire for peace are merely the extreme stations of his mind and heart in their never-ending voyage of self-exploration. His 'tragedy' is that he is incapable of tragedy. For tragedy presupposes the belief in an external order of things which is indeed incomplete without the conformity of the human soul, but would be still more defective without the soul's freedom to violate it. Yet Faust's dilemma is different. His 'two souls' are merely the one soul divided in itself because it knows of no independent external reality to which it is related as a free agent. Faust is in every essential respect Goethe's *alter ego,* the embodiment of that part of his self which remained unprotected by his apparently fondest trust and belief: that he belonged to Nature as her most precious possession. Faust, outside this zone of safety, is therefore torn between the belief in a world to which, strive as he may, he has no access whatever, and the belief in himself as the creator of his own world. Thus the spiritual extremes of his existence are not guilt and atonement, but despair and titanism. It is a situation unresolvable in tragedy.

Nature is fundamentally innocent, and Goethe's genius is in communion with Nature. Hence there can be, for Goethe, no catharsis, only metamorphosis. It is never with the spirit of a transcendent God or with the spirit of Man that Goethe's potentially tragic heroes are reunited after their dramatic crises. When the crisis is over, they are at one again with the spirit of Nature. They are not purified in a tragic sense, not raised above their guilt through atonement, but enter, as it were, a biologically, not morally, new phase of life, healed by oblivion and restored to strength through the sleep of the just. This is what happens to Orestes, and what happens to Faust at the beginning of Part II. Both put down their cup of Lethe and burst into magnificent praises of Nature. But such, clearly, could not have been the conclusion of Faust. He had to be saved or damned, for Heaven and Hell had become involved by virtue of the legendary pattern. But it is *only* by virtue of the legendary pattern that they have become involved at all. For the world of Faust is only just Christian enough to have room for purgatory. It is a purgatory suspended between two half unreal spheres. Hence 'Mephistopheles must only half win his wager', and Faust be 'only half guilty', as Goethe himself put it in a letter which looks forward to the play's 'most serene conclusion' when 'the old Lord may exercise his privilege of mercy'.

What is Faust's sin? Restlessness of spirit. What is Faust's salvation? Restlessness of spirit. The confusion lies in a perpetual criss-crossing of restless strivings of different qualities: the striving for peace, and the striving for sensation; or, to put it differently, and in terms of the quality of the contentment sought, the striving for that peace that passeth all understanding, and the striving for a state of calm, an 'enough' which is merely a state of emotional exhaustion. What the heavenly powers mean by that striving which carries its own salvation must surely be different from the striving the goal of which Faust hopes to achieve with the help of black magic and the Devil. Yet these two kinds of striving perpetually get into each other's way throughout the poem, and the entanglement is at its worst in the crucial last scene of Faust's life when his desire for doing good and for the realization of his humanity within its decreed limits is inextricably bound up with the delusion and madness of titanism. Of these two strivings the one desires the attainment of the superman, the alchemist heightening of all human faculties, whereas the other aims at renunciation and resignation to the simple state of man. The first is the native element of Goethe's genius, the second the longing of Goethe's moral existence.

Könnt' ich Magie von meinem Pfad entfernen,
Die Zaubersprüche ganz und gar verlernen,
Stünd ich, Natur, vor dir ein Mann allein,
Da wär's der Mühe wert, ein Mensch zu sein.

Could I forget my sorcery, and ban my magic,
    stand,
stripped of it utterly, oh Nature, face to face with
    thee,
it would be worth while then to be a man.

This outcry of Faust's, towards the end of the play when he is visited by *Sorge*—and this is the second place where Faust is prepared to renounce the Devil—reveals perhaps Goethe's deepest secret. To cut the umbilical cord joining him with Nature and her magic power, not to remain what he once called 'a magic oyster over which there pass mysterious waves', to be face to face with Nature and escape the fate of Proteus—this only would be human happiness. Over and over again he sought deliverance from his genius in work, in the practical jobs of everyday life, through Wilhelm Meister's, through Faust's solution, and so desperately that as a man of fifty he confessed to Schiller (January 6th, 1798) that he owed it to him if he had learned to 'look at the manysidedness of my own inner being with more justice. . . . *You* have made me a poet again which I had all but ceased to be.' Such was the nature of his genius and the character of his age that the spirit could only live at the expense of life, and life only at the expense of the spirit. Thus the meaning of creative genius as well as the meaning of doing the sober work of the day, inwardness as well as action, had to remain puzzles to each other, anonymous, undefined strangers. They never met in a common dedication and could not be at peace with each other because they knew no will other than their own. And at such distance from 'la sua volontate è nostra pace' neither divine comedy nor human tragedy can be written.

It was impossible for Goethe to accept this situation, and impossible, by the very nature of things, to solve it. Hence his perpetual oscillation between the precarious magic of the inner communion with the deep where the Earth Spirit dwells, and the moral determination to reconcile himself to the cruder demands made on human existence by society, with the emphasis of approval shifting to and fro between the two: Egmont and Oranien, Tasso and Antonio, Prometheus and *Grenzen der Menschheit,* elective affinities and legal bonds. Was harmony ever to be achieved? The answer may be found in the ambiguity of *Faust.* (pp. 55-63)

> *Erich Heller, "Goethe and the Avoidance of Tragedy," in his* The Disinherited Mind: Essays in Modern German Literature and Thought, *1952. Reprint by Farrar, Straus and Cudahy, 1957, pp. 37-63.*

Harry Steinhauer   (essay date 1956)

[*In the following excerpt, Steinhauer examines ways in which Faust earns salvation, even though he seems to violate the pact into which he entered with Mephistopheles, and should apparently forfeit his soul.*]

Faust's pact with the devil surely presents the most baffling of all the problems raised by Goethe's poem. We are here at the very heart of the myth which the action of the drama illustrates. Goethe has used the wager between God and Mephistopheles and the pact between Faust and the Devil to symbolize the issues which are at stake in Faust's career on earth. In the background we see God waiting patiently for the moment when His trust in Faust will be vindicated. On this vital theme of wager and pact, if anywhere, we have a right to expect unequivocal clarity: on the terms of the pact, on the positions taken by the contracting parties, and on the outcome of the conflict between them. Yet, if we are to believe the critics and commentators, Goethe has hung a veil of confusion over this whole area, so that we are prevented from catching even a glimpse of his intentions. For the last fifty years critical opinion has been sharply divided on the fundamental question as to which of the two protagonists emerges victorious. Some hold with Faust; others either side with Mephistopheles or believe that the duel ends in a draw, and that Faust is saved only by an act of grace, which is bestowed on him as by a deus ex machina.

Even those who grant Faust salvation through his own works are puzzled by the pact itself. Faust vows that he will never express satisfaction with the present moment. He agrees that his soul will be forfeit to Mephistopheles if he utters the phrase "Verweile doch, du bist so schön." At the end of his career, in one of the crucial passages in the drama, he says these very words which he had declared to be taboo, he bids the fair moment linger awhile. Yet he escapes the devil's clutches. From all the hard and able thinking that has gone into the interpretation of this key dilemma, nothing more convincing has emerged than the casuistic explanation that Faust does not really say "Verweile doch." As he surveys the potential future of his vast irrigation scheme, he sees a vision of glorious achievement at some distant time. "If this vision *were* reality," he says, "I *could* bid the moment stay." Because Faust has prudently expressed himself in the conditional mode, he has saved himself from the devil's claws. Even more astonishing than the explanation itself is the fact that Erich Trunz, the very able editor of the newest Goethe edition, has chosen it as the most convincing of all those in stock.

In all this bustle of explaining no one has cared to defend the position that, in making Faust repeat the very words he had vowed not to utter, Goethe knew what he was about. Actually the problem raised by the pact and wager is not a difficult one to solve if one sticks to Goethe's text and takes stock of the conditions under which this unique poem came into being. For whatever views one may hold on the value of the biographical method in literary criticism, in the case of so avowedly a subjective artist as Goethe it is essential to make use of this approach. True, even in Goethe one must beware of equating the work of art with the life of the poet; but there is a much more organic connection between Goethe and Faust, Werther, and Wilhelm Meister than there is between the more objective artists and their heroes. This connection may help us to understand what would otherwise baffle us.

We know that Goethe took sixty years to write his *Faust* and that in those sixty years his attitude to life and his system of values radically changed. If the poem *Faust* was to reflect Goethe's innermost convictions about life, it was bound to show a dichotomy in *Weltanschauung.* For Goethe incorporated in the final version of the poem parts which he had composed in his early twenties. The finished work then should reflect both the world of [*The Sorrows of Young Werther*] and that of the [*Wilhelm Meisters Wanderjahre*].

Our first question therefore is: How did Goethe see his hero when he first began work on *Faust?* The answer is, of course, given by the *Urfaust* and by those scenes in the completed Part I which fill out the lacunae left by the early fragments. Now the opening scenes of the *Urfaust* are essentially a satire on the *Aufklärung,* with the hero representing the Rousseauism of the *Sturm und Drang,* while the "villain" of the piece is an *Aufklärer.* It is the same situation that we find in *Werther,* where the role of rationalist "villain" is assigned to Albert.

It requires no profound insight to identify the early Faust as a *Sturm und Drang* titan. But who is the villainous *Aufklärer?* Not Mephistopheles; for the Mephistopheles of the *Urfaust* is not as yet a philosophical devil; he has no *Weltanschauung.* The villain is Wagner; in this pedantic schoolmaster Goethe has concentrated all the qualities of mind which he, as a champion of Rousseauistic feeling, abhorred. Wagner is the Albert of the *Urfaust.* What irritates Werther about Albert is his sweet reasonableness, his perpetual contentment and equanimity of soul, his readiness to make fine distinctions in the interests of truth. "Now you know" writes Werther to his friend Wilhelm in the letter of 12 August, "I like the man very much, except for his 'and yet.' For doesn't it go without saying that every general proposition has its exceptions? But the fellow is so just! When he believes he has said something too hasty, too general or half-true, he cannot cease limiting, modifying, adding and subtracting until in the end there is nothing left of the matter." And in the same letter Werther reports how he flared up at Albert's moderation with the challenge: If effort is strength, why should hypertension be its opposite? ("Wenn Anstrengung Stärke ist, warum soll die Überspannung das Gegenteil sein?"). The contrast between *Aufklärung* and *Sturm und Drang* could not be more pungently formulated than it is in this one sentence. To an apostle of passion like Werther, an Albert can be only a fool or a knave, a blundering, pedantic spoilsport or a frustrating devil. Goethe-Werther decided to depict him as a fool—that is, as a caricature composed of smugness, self-satisfaction, and obtuseness. It is the same with Wagner; he too is a caricature, composed of traits which, to anyone but an ardent Rousseauist, would appear to be eminently desirable and perfectly suited to a life in society.

It has not been generally recognized how minutely Goethe has worked out this contrast between the two antagonistic points of view, both in the *Urfaust* and in the last version of the poem.

Wagner first appears in Faust's study because he believes he has heard Faust declaiming from some Greek tragedy. He has come to listen in the hope that he may learn something new about the art of oratory, which is so useful in persuading and controlling people. It is no accident that the young Goethe chose oratory as the theme by which he could best illustrate the difference in outlook between Faust and Wagner, that is, between the *Sturm und Drang* and the *Aufklärung.* In the 1740's a vigorous controversy was waged in France over the nature of the actor's art, crystallizing in a dispute between the playwright Rémond de Saint-Albine and the actor Riccoboni. Diderot, who showed a keen interest in dramatic theory—witness his *Entretiens sur le Fils naturel* (1757) and *De la Poésie dramatique* (1758)—took up the question in his correspondence with Mme Riccoboni in 1758. In 1769 there appeared a brochure entitled *Garrick ou les acteurs anglais;* it was signed Antonio Sticoti and purported to be a translation from the English. Diderot replied to this pamphlet in Grimm's *Correspondence* (1 October and 15 November 1770). These articles were the kernel of the *Paradoxe sur le comédien* (published posthumously in 1830), which goes over the same ground that is presented, in compressed form, in the opening scene of the *Urfaust.*

The subject, then, was timely. It had been in the air for a generation when Goethe began to write the *Urfaust.* And we may assume with confidence that cultivated Germans knew about these matters. Lessing's writings support this assumption. However, there are more vital factors than mere fashion concerned in this controversy. Oratory, rhetoric, the art of persuasion is a characteristic product of rational ages and rational cultures. It is an art that flourished in Greece and Rome and which we associate with France of the Classical Age. Richard Müller-Freienfels argues that the spirit of oratory, combining the didactic with the histrionic, pervades all French and Italian art, even their lyric poetry: "One might characterize the special brand of German feeling as 'musical' in contrast to the 'rhetorical' type of the Romance peoples. The Latin (like the Greek of later antiquity) expresses his feelings best in oratory, through the word, the concept, supported by vigorous gesture. For him the rational factor is paramount even in the emotional sphere. The German, on the other hand, best expresses his emotions without words, not graphically but vaguely, with infinite overtones, in short: musically." One recalls Settembrini in the *Zauberberg,* the "organ grinder," apostle of *ratio,* the word, the well rounded period. In the *Betrachtungen eines Unpolitischen* much is made of the antithesis between Western rationalism, legalism, rhetoric, the cult of the word, the insistence on strict adherence to the letter of a contract—and Germanic *Innerlichkeit,* which is profoundly emotional, not vocal, and acts according to the spirit. It is a view which is succinctly stated in an aphorism by Schiller: When the soul *speaks,* it is, alas, no longer the *soul* that speaks ("*Spricht* die Seele, so spricht, ach, schon die *Seele* nicht mehr").

So it is here. Wagner values the social art of eloquence; Faust rejects it with contempt. "Unless you feel it, unless it comes from your soul and compels the hearts of all your audience with the joy of primitive power, you will never succeed. Sit there for ever, gluing together little bits, brewing a stew from the leavings of others, and blow up a paltry flicker from your little heap of ashes! You may win the admiration of children and monkeys, if that's what you're after; but you will never convert hearts to your heart unless it comes from your own heart."

Wagner fails to see the point of Faust's remark and insists on the importance of form in this, as in every, art. To this Faust again replies that form does not matter; it is the spirit that counts (Es trägt Verstand und rechter Sinn/Mit wenig Kunst sich selber vor; / Und wenn's Euch Ernst ist, was zu sagen, / Ist's nötig, Worten nachzujagen?). And so, from a narrow discussion of artistic techniques, they shift into the deeper waters of history and philosophy. Wagner is revealed as a typical eighteenth-century rationalist-optimist, a believer in progress and perfectibility, proud of man's achievements in knowledge and control of nature. The disillusioned Faust can only meet this cheerful and (to him) smug contentment with sarcasm, bitterness, and searing contempt. For when he considers what he would like to know—what holds the world together at its core ("was die Welt im Innersten zusammen hält")—Wagner's pride in our present accomplishments appears petty indeed.

Clearly Wagner's goals seem puerile beside the lofty aspirations which Faust expresses in the opening speeches of this scene. But if we can only forget that Wagner is presented to us as the caricature of an *Aufklärer,* as seen by an ardent champion of Rousseauism, it will become evident that he stands for a serious attitude toward life which derives from a long and respectable tradition in European thought, stretching from Socrates to Bernard Shaw—a tradition, moreover, which Goethe will not ridicule, nor even reject, all his life.

The argument between Faust and Wagner is continued in the scene before the city gate. Again Goethe contrasts Faust's romantic unhappiness with Wagner's optimistic rationalism. Though this scene was composed at a time when Goethe had long outgrown the philosophical position that dominates his writings of the *Sturm und Drang* period and hence the **Urfaust,** it recaptures completely the mood of the earlier day. Here too, if we penetrate behind Wagner's pedantic manner to the attitude he represents, we shall find that he talks good bourgeois common sense, if not very lofty idealism. One must admire the minute consistency with which Goethe has worked out the dialogue between the two men so as to reveal the philosophical position taken by each: Faust, the worshipper of nature, the admirer of the simple pleasures of the common folk, lavish in his disparagement of his own deficiencies; Wagner the intellectual aristocrat, scorning the vulgar mob, showing as a rationalist only a perfunctory interest in nature (that "vegetable world" to which Baudelaire refused to lend his enthusiasm), naïvely and frankly avid for fame, as an ancient Greek or a man of the Renaissance would have been. Even such a trifle as the difference in attitude to domestic animals is not forgotten.

With Wagner's disappearance from the scene, the role of rationalist villain is taken over by Mephistopheles—not in the **Urfaust** or **Fragment,** but in the post-Italian portions of Part I. When Mephistopheles first appears before Faust, he characterizes himself as the spirit of nihilism—I am the spirit of constant negation ("Ich bin der Geist, der stets verneint"). That is indeed his ultimate rôle; but for the

present this definition fits only partly. Throughout Part I Mephistopheles represents the negative principle in the same sense as Albert does in *Werther,* inasmuch as all reason (Schopenhauer's *principium individuationis,* Nietzsche's Apollonian principle) is "critical," stressing the idea of intellect as a controlling force, what Irving Babbitt called the *frein vital* as opposed to the *élan vital,* which underlies the romantic ideal of expansion to the infinite. To the ecstatic *Stürmer und Dränger* all criticism as such is the diabolical principle, because it thwarts the creative impulse—Thus you oppose your cold devil's fist to the beneficent creative power that is eternally stirring within us ("So setzest du der ewig regen, / Der heilsam schaffenden Gewalt / Die kalte Teufelsfaust entgegen"—lines 1379-81). So Goethe-Werther saw the *Aufklärer* Albert and all the prudent, circumspect folk who irritate Werther beyond the breaking point. To the mature Goethe, however, criticism in itself is no longer diabolical; on the contrary, it is a salutary force in life because it saves man from the pitfalls of extremism. Criticism becomes diabolical only when it breaks the barriers set up by good sense and good taste. Then it is really destructive of life. And this nihilism is the proper sphere in which Mephistopheles moves.

A close study of the text shows that Goethe has mixed the two conceptions of Mephistopheles: the earlier one which sees him as an *Aufklärer,* and the later which defines him as the spirit of absolute negation. It is the later Mephistopheles who takes darkness as his symbol and whom Faust describes as the son of chaos. But during the discussion which culminates in the pact (and indeed throughout most of Part I) Mephistopheles faithfully plays the rôle of *Aufklärer* in succession to Wagner. It is in this rôle that Mephistopheles and his troop of spirits deplore Faust's blasphemous cursing of all existence and urge him to rebuild the world anew by coming to terms with the "reality principle," which Faust has hitherto defied.

But is it not completely perverse to find the nihilist Mephistopheles sponsoring a constructive philosophy of life, while Faust, the apostle of creativity, appears in the rôle of the nihilist? The situation does indeed seem paradoxical until we realize that nihilism is an essential part of Faust's pattern of behavior.

Mephistopheles has described that pattern in a homely but very apt and important image in the "Prologue in Heaven":

> The little god of the world remains true to type and is as weird today as he was at creation. His life would be on a slightly higher level if You hadn't given him the light of the heavenly luminary. He calls it Reason and uses it solely to be more beastly than any beast. He seems to me, with Your Grace's permission, like one of those long-legged grasshoppers, which is constantly on the wing and leaps as it flies and the next moment sings its old song in the grass again. If only he were content to lie in the grass! In every filth he must bury his nose. . . .

The point of Mephistopheles' contention is that man would have been better off without the gift of reason at all; for then he might at least have lived in a state of animal naturalness. But, having been endowed with the heavenly light, he abuses it and so sinks below the level of the healthy animal to that of the beast. To illustrate his point Mephistopheles compares man to a grasshopper, who falls *because* he tries to leap too high and then, having fallen (or been disillusioned), grovels in the mire in total abandonment. While Mephistopheles uses this image to characterize mankind in general, his figure fits titanic man and Faust especially. For Mephistopheles evidently sees Faust as an exemplar of the whole human species. And so he goes on to describe Faust's character in terms of this grasshopper existence: boundless striving to attain an unrealizable, superterrestrial ideal, followed by inevitable frustration and disillusionment and ending in despair and bestiality. This is the pattern of conduct which Faust reveals in the opening scenes, during the promenade with Wagner before the city gate, in the pact scene, and later in the Gretchen tragedy. It is the pattern of romantic morality, which Irving Babbitt has described as a sharp cleavage between nobility of intention and sordidness in execution. It is that extremism which Pascal condemns in one of the *Pensées:* "Man is neither angel nor beast. It is his misfortune that when he wants to become an angel, he becomes a beast." Except that where Pascal confines his strictures to the moral sphere, Mephistopheles refers to a general philosophical attitude. In the same vein Montaigne writes: "Between ourselves, these are things I have always noted to be in singular accord: supercelestial opinions and subterranean morals."

If we bear in mind this image of Faust as a grasshopper, an extremist, an apostle of an all-or-nothing philosophy (like Ibsen's Brand), we shall be able to grasp the implications of the argument that develops between him and Mephistopheles in the pact scene. This argument we must now examine. But it is well to remember that, when two people enter into an agreement, each has a vested interest which he seeks to safeguard and will act to protect. We must not forget, moreover, that one of the contracting parties is the Devil, who is not above taking advantage of his opponent's innocence.

What, then, do the two opponents want? Faust's position is clear enough. For this dynamic extremist salvation (or the good life) lies in eternal striving for the unattainable, while contentment with life leads to stagnation, which for him is tantamount to damnation. This position is very adequately stated in the formula "Verweile doch."

What Mephistopheles expects to gain from the transaction is not so obvious. He wants Faust to be damned, of course. But how is Faust to act in order to be damned? We know Mephisto's views on man as a grasshopper. The road which, in Faust's opinion, leads to salvation (that is, the road of titanic idealism), is for Mephistopheles the sure way to damnation. Hence, since he wants Faust to be damned, it is in his interest that Faust should go through life as a romantic extremist, as Spengler's "Faustian man." Therefore he would heartily agree with Faust in the latter's determination not to become contented with life. In other words Mephistopheles, the Devil, is delighted to hear Faust vow that he will never say "Verweile doch." This fits in perfectly with his plan to lead Faust to damnation. Hence, though the two men are enemies, they can agree on a formula, because behind the formula lies a way of life to which the two antagonists apply a radically different valuation. This is a paradox which is fateful for the outcome of the pact.

Let us now look at the actual pact and the argument that leads up to it. Throughout the negotiations we see Mephistopheles in the rôle of a tempter, whose task is made easy for him by the fact that, in his opinion, Faust is already on the road to ruin. All that Mephistopheles need do is to confirm Faust in his present course and fervently hope that he will keep to it. It is in this spirit that he says to Faust: I can satisfy your craving for the impossible and unattainable ("Ich gebe dir, was noch kein Mensch gesehen," etc.). Faust replies contemptuously: "How can a petty philistine like you, an *Aufklärer,* an Albert, understand the lofty aspirations that move a noble romantic idealist like me?" And he suggests a series of physical impossibilities as a symbol of the extreme idealism which alone could satisfy him. Mephistopheles remarks coolly: "Such a catalogue of unattainables does not dismay me at all. But" he adds devilishly, "couldn't I interest you in something more reasonable, something that we can enjoy in peace and contentment?" Faust's reaction recalls that of Madame de Rénal in one of her religious moments when the "devil" Sorel tries to reason with her [In Stendhal's *Le Rouge et le Noir*]—"Julian felt that the slightest reasoning irritated her, rather than calmed her; she saw in it the language of the devil." So it is with Faust: the word "Ruhe" which Mephistopheles has used—"Doch, guter Freund, die Zeit kommt auch heran, / Wo wir was Guts in Ruhe schmausen mögen"—is the red rag of irritation to him. *He,* the noble aspiring idealist, is to be ensnared by sordid goals of satisfaction, enjoyment, contentment? And so he makes the famous speech: If ever I lie down in contentment on my bed of ease ("Werd' ich beruhigt je mich auf ein Faulbett legen") and goes on to utter the fateful formula "Verweile doch." And he adds: "This is no act of criminal presumption on my part. As soon as I cease developing I am a slave; whether to you or to someone else, what does it matter?" . . .

In other words: Don't imagine, you philistine, that the way of idealism is a struggle for me, entailing unnatural effort. It is my chosen way of life, my path to salvation, the only attitude that makes life tolerable for a man who has the divine spark in his soul. Hence there is no danger that I will ever forsake this view of life, pact or no pact. His position is like that of Kafka's hunger artist, who cannot understand why the philistine public regards his fasting as a triumph of spiritual power, when it is to him a perfectly natural routine of living.

Mephistopheles the *Aufklärer,* the legalist, the Western *Zivilisationsliterat,* insists on a written agreement, duly signed and sworn. To this Faust scornfully replies in much the same terms as Thomas Mann used against the Allied Powers in his *Friedrich und die Große Koalition* and in the *Betrachtungen eines Unpolitischen.* What value is there in treaties and agreements, Faust asks, when the spirit which they are to embody is lacking? And conversely: what sense is there in adhering to treaties, when the spirit that engendered them is no longer there? "Does not the world rage on with all its torrential power? And shall a promise restrain me?" However, he continues, in this instance there is no danger that I shall ever break the agreement; for it is the very meaning of life to me that I keep it.

Faust then tells Mephistopheles what he expects from the transaction: nothing less than the totality of experience (the ideal of the *Sturm und Drang*), not a mere sipping and nibbling here and there, as Mephistopheles has just suggested, least of all a chasing after vulgar pleasure: "And what is allotted to all mankind, I want to enjoy in my innermost soul, grasping with my mind the heights and depths of experience, loading men's weal and woe upon my breast, thus extending my Self to embrace their Selves, and in the end foundering with them. . . ." "Your program," Mephistopheles replies, "might be suitable for a god, but what limited mortal could ever achieve it?" One may wonder whether the Devil is not risking a good deal in talking such good sense so frankly to Faust. But he knows his opponent. There is no more likelihood of Faust being deflected from his extremist course than there is that Werther will ever be converted to Albert's commonsense philosophy of life. "Allein ich will!" is Faust's answer; and this highly irrational reply convinces Mephistopheles that Faust's mind is set beyond recall. He can now safely play with his victim, tell him some of the facts of life without running the slightest risk that Faust will listen to him.

What you want, Mephistopheles therefore says, exists only in the mind of a poet, who can invent super-heroes, combining in their person all the choice traits that men admire ("Assoziiert euch mit einem Poeten," etc.). But the sarcasm is lost on Faust. "If I cannot attain such lofty heights" he says earnestly, "what am I?" "You are," Mephistopheles replies, "a human being with human limitations, which you can never overcome, try as you will." But Faust can only repeat his basic position, which is summed up in the last line of his next speech: "I am no nearer to the Infinite."

After Faust has left his study, Mephistopheles gives a masterly summing up of Faust's character in the speech: "Verachte nur Vernunft und Wissenschaft." He repeats, from his own point of view, what Faust has told him: that there is really no need of a pact between them, since what is involved here is a conflict between two philosophies of life. Just as Faust felt certain that he would never deviate from his way of life, so Mephistopheles hopes that Faust may never do so. "There is no need to lead you astray; you are doing my work for me. So just keep on despising reason, allow yourself to be beguiled by the deceptive spirit of magic and you will ultimately become my victim."

There is one further factor that must be considered in Faust's relationship with Mephistopheles, and this seems the proper place to do so. I refer to the motifs of anxiety and magic.

Ernst Trautmann, Konrad Burdach, Max Kommerell, Paul Stöcklein, and others have shown how the motif of *Sorge* frames the whole Faust poem, occupying strategic positions at the opening and close of the work. Following Kommerell, I would emphasize that the theme of magic is inextricably linked with that of anxiety in a rhythm of ebb and flow.

The early scenes of the drama show a Faust who is driven to the point of despair by the many disillusionments which life has brought him. The principal agent in the crippling of the faculties that further life is anxiety or *Sorge*. In the opening scene of the poem *Sorge* is used as a general term for a complex of destructive forces that beset the human mind, ranging all the way from specific material cares— "Sie mag als Haus und Hof, als Weib und Kind, erscheinen"—to that most subtle form of spiritual unhappiness which Max Brod, in a happy phrase, has called "edles Unglück" or metaphysical suffering, and which results from the compromises we make with the reality principle when we "come to terms with life." Most agonizing of all: even our noblest flights of fancy, those rare moments in which we seem capable of rising into the ethereal realms of pure Platonic ideas, are withered by the poisonous breath of *Sorge*. For the faculty of imagination, as Goethe sees it, is a mixed blessing: on the one hand it gives birth to life-furthering hope; but it also breeds life-destroying care. Elsewhere, Stöcklein points out, Goethe expresses the same thought in mythological terms: the two daughters of Epimetheus are Elpore Thrasaia (bold hope) and Epimeleia (care). That same imagination, Goethe says, which can magnify the tiny germs of our ideas into grandiose dreams and fabulous Utopias, can also blow up our petty, prosaic frustrations into frightful nightmares. In this way *Sorge* commingles with the elemental forces in life to undermine the human entelechy. In the language of Freud: the death instinct turns against the life force in man and paralyzes him.

This is Faust's state of mind at the opening of the poem. He tries various avenues of escape: communion with the World Spirit, then with the Earth Spirit; but is rejected by both. In his despair he attempts suicide, but is deflected from his course by the memories of his carefree youth. But Faust is not the person to go through life on the memories of a former paradise of innocence. His black moods will recur. Salvation, or what looks like it, is offered him by Mephistopheles through the instrumentality of magic. Now magic is essentially a forcing of nature, an attempt to transcend the bounds of the natural. By putting magic at Faust's disposal, Mephistopheles is to free him from the anxiety to which normal man falls heir as he attempts to wrestle with the problems of life.

The Gretchen episode suggests that a good man—ein guter Mensch—does not escape *Sorge* even with the aid of magic; for there remains remorse, which Faust feels throughout the later course of that love affair. And at the end of his career, after the fateful episode of Philemon and Baucis, Faust realizes that this recourse to magic was an unmitigated evil because it made him the slave of forces which were unnatural, which no more belonged to his legitimate sphere of being than the World or Earth Spirits did. Ultimately it becomes necessary for Faust to renounce magic. But will he be able to do so?

Every student of Goethe knows of the change in general outlook which the poet underwent after his *Sturm und Drang* days; and there is general agreement as to the character of that new attitude toward life. Within five years of his arrival at Weimar, Goethe writes **"Grenzen der Menschheit,"** which forms a convenient "before and after" piece when set alongside the earlier poem **"Prometheus."** I do not like the word "renunciation" which Gundolf and others use to describe the later attitude, because renunciation is altogether too negative a concept for Goethe, although it must be granted that some of the late works (such as *Die Wahlverwandtschaften*) are the products of this temporary negative mood. Renunciation does not describe adequately the spirit underlying the poems **"Selige Sehnsucht"** or **"Lied des Lynkeus,"** which may be regarded as typical of the late Goethe. The former of these poems anticipates Nietzsche's Dionysian principle, at least insofar as it represents a joyful acceptance of life, an *amor fati*—although there is a strong element of the Apollonian or intellectual and serene in Goethe's position; and this Apollonian element is revealed even more in the Lynkeus song. Speaking very broadly, one might say that the later Goethe championed the view of life which he had ridiculed in his youth. I hasten to add that Goethe did not become an *Aufklärer* à la Friedrich Nicolai or Heine's Dr. Saul Ascher. What I mean is: when we consider the strident irrationalism of his *Sturm und Drang* period, we may say that he gradually moved in a direction which, for want of a better word, might be described as "realistic." Certainly in resuming his work on *Faust,* he must have realized that the ideological position held by Mephistopheles was now more sympathetic to him than that represented by the early Faust. Indeed Schiller pointed this out to him in a letter of 26 June 1797, in which he remarked of the (as yet) fragmentary poem: "Through his realism the Devil is in the right before the tribunal of the understanding and Faust before that of the heart. But at times they seem to trade rôles and the Devil protects reason against Faust." Here Schiller put his finger on the dilemma which faced Goethe: while we may be on Faust's side with our emotions, feeling that he is a high-minded man despite his dubious conduct, our intellect compels us to form the judgment that Mephistopheles is in the right, not merely from the lowly point of view of practical common sense, but from that of genuine wisdom (Vernunft).

What could Goethe do? He could turn on Faust and pronounce him a failure, as some recent interpreters think he actually did. It is beyond the scope of this paper to argue this point; I prefer to cast my lot with those who believe that Goethe presents us with a Faust who is saved and who deserves to be saved. This view bases itself on the assumption that the Faust of Part II is an altered Faust. Konrad Burdach formulates concisely when he writes that Faust's redemption, as Goethe indicates in the highest poetical symbolism, results from a transformation, indeed a reversal, of his nature. However, a good deal of opposition has arisen to this interpretation of the course of events. The opponents see no change of heart in Faust; his conduct at the end of his career on earth shows no moral improvement whatever. The Exhibit A which all the accusers brandish in our faces is the "Philemon and Baucis" episode. This shocking deed, they claim, reveals Faust in a much sorrier light than the Gretchen tragedy. Well, does it? Faust's treatment of the old couple is, of course, a crime; but surely it is a crime with a difference. The Gret-

chen tragedy was the direct consequence of Faust's selfish titanism. Faust's conduct toward Gretchen was steeped in hypocrisy, as the clear-headed Mephistopheles was quick to point out in the "Forest and Cavern" Scene, and which justified the Devil's conception of Faust as the supreme grasshopper. . . . The crime against the old couple, on the other hand, occurs as part of an unselfish, humanitarian enterprise. It is one stain on a field of white. While Faust admits his selfish motive in wanting the property of the tenants, he at least feels ashamed of his greed: "Und wie ich's sage, schäm' ich mich." It might be argued, moreover, on Faust's behalf that he has some justification for finding the idyllic existence of the old people intolerable. For their naïve religion, their refusal to cooperate in the social project that Faust has undertaken, is static and reactionary. What Faust has yet to learn is perhaps the hardest lesson of all for the responsible ruler: that no mission in life, however noble, sanctions a disregard of human rights. Faust does learn that lesson before his death, as we see from his last speech, in which he dreams of a vast settlement with millions of people living, not in security, but an active and free life—"Eröffn' ich Räume vielen Millionen, / Nicht sicher zwar, doch tätigfrei zu wohnen."

However, to the objection that Faust commits crimes to the very end of his life, Goethe has given an answer in the "Prologue in Heaven": Man errs as long as he lives. Error does not bother Goethe as much as the frame of mind (Gesinnung) which produces it. Where there is good will or consciousness of the right way, there salvation is possible. We may regard this good will as the secular equivalent of theological faith, and find support for Goethe's position in Luther's saying: Good deeds do not make a good man, but a good man does good deeds. And does not Kant begin his *Second Critique* by emphasizing the all-importance of the proper frame of mind for ethical conduct? In short, Faust is saved because he finds the right way, rather than because he does the right things.

What then is the right way? The very first scene in Part II tells us in the famous image of the rainbow: Life is the colored reflection of the sun ("Am farb'gen Abglanz haben wir das Leben"). No longer to insist on looking right into the sun, but to be satisfied, truly satisfied, with its reflected light; or, to use once more Mephisto's homely figure: no longer to act the grasshopper "whose vaulting ambition o'erleaps itself"—this is the new direction for Faust. Several well-known aphorisms by Goethe deserve to be recalled at this point: "There is nothing sadder to behold than a direct striving for the unconditional in this completely conditioned world." "No one is more a slave than he who thinks he is free but is not." "A man need only declare himself to be free and from that moment on he feels himself to be bound. If he dares to call himself bound, he feels free." "He who early learns restraint, attains freedom with comfort; he who submits to it late, gains but a bitter freedom."

But if Faust had developed no further than to recognize the importance of self-limitation and renunciation in life, Goethe would hardly have granted him salvation. The other feature in Faust's new program is activity—though of a special kind. Not just activity, that dynamism that

Ernst Robert Curtius excoriated in his book *Deutscher Geist in Gefahr.* Nor is it the exploratory, trial-and-error activity that W. H. Auden attributes to Faust when he writes in an essay on Kafka:

> In these quests, the faith in religious authority is lacking, and what is sought is an individual and immediate certainty, without faith, that the subject is "in the truth." This can only be acquired by exploring *all* the possibilities of one's nature, good *and* evil, for it is only when a man knows them all, that he can be perfectly certain which is the right one; as long as there is a single possibility untried, he cannot *know* that it should be rejected, he can only *believe* it should.
>
> The hero of such a quest must be willing and daring enough to try everything, however shocking; he must surrender completely to whatever the immediate moment suggests; he must at all costs avoid making an irrevocable choice. The artistic difficulty in writing a quest of this kind is that, as the possibilities are infinite, the quest can never end, and any ending—for a book must end sometime—is arbitrary. The ending of ***Faust*** is artistically unsatisfying because the reader is not convinced that Faust is saved, nor indeed is Goethe, for the angels sing of Faust—"Joyfully we receive this man in his pupa state"—i.e. his development is still incomplete.

That this is a misunderstanding of Goethe's intention seems to me obvious. Goethe wants neither blind activity nor boundless activity (even when it is directed toward a goal, as in the opening scene of ***Faust***) nor smug satisfaction. What he recommends is a constant striving within the bounds of the possible; an ideal most clearly formulated in the well-known couplet: "Would you stride into the Infinite? Go within the Finite in all directions. . . . " There is, for Goethe, a way of attaining the unattainable: horizontally rather than vertically, by working at many possible, limited things rather than by attempting the one impossibility. Wilhelm Meister ends his long search as a surgeon, Faust as a social engineer, whereas Werther commits suicide and the early Faust nearly does so. The practical, limited, prosaic careers of Wilhelm Meister and the mature Faust symbolize the goal of striving within the limits of the Finite.

In tracing the evolution from medieval to modern times, G. K. Chesterton has supplied the finest formula for Goethe's mature ideal. In his study of Chaucer he writes:

> Up to a certain time life was conceived as a Dance, and after that time life was conceived as a Race. Medieval morality was full of the idea that one thing must balance another, that each stood on one side or the other of something that was in the middle and something that remained in the middle. . . . Now since that break in history [i.e., the Renaissance] the Dance has turned into a Race. That is, the dancers lose their balance and only recover it by running towards some object, or alleged object; not an object within their circle or their possession, but an object which they do not yet possess. It is a flying object; a disappearing object; and, as some hold, a disappointing object. . . . One is rhythmic and recurrent movement, because there is a known centre; while the other is precipitate or progressive movement, because there is an unknown goal. The latter has produced all that we call Progress; the former produced what the medievals meant by Order; but it was the lively order of a dance.

Faust's development approximates to what Chesterton has described here as the course of our whole Western culture, but in reverse: Faust has moved from the race to the dance. His progress in this direction has been slow (Goethe subscribed to the Neptunist hypothesis in evolution): from the first formulation of his new way of life in the image of the rainbow to his final realization of it in practice, a long life has passed. It is the Philemon and Baucis episode which reveals to him the fatal hindrance to salvation: the fact that he still maintains a link with magic through his association with Mephistopheles. Faust draws the right conclusion: he must renounce magic. He does so in the scene which is emotionally the most moving in the whole poem: the scene in which he confronts *Sorge.*

Faust knows that the renunciation of magic will again bring him face to face with the full force of anxiety from which he had fled years ago. But he now recognizes that there is no way around this difficulty. He is ready to go right through it and finds that one can conquer anxiety without the help of magic, or at least conquer it sufficiently to live successfully. He has arrived at a true acceptance of life, has achieved the ability to withstand frustration.

Konrad Burdach and others have pointed out the close parallel between this and the first *Sorge* scene, even to some of the formulations used by Goethe. For us the important fact is that Faust himself recognizes the connection between anxiety and magic. For it is only now, when the four sisters visit him, that he gives utterance to the wish that he might dispense with magic for ever and face life with his natural powers alone: "I have not yet fought my way into the open. If I could remove magic from my path, forget altogether the incantations; if I could stand before you, Nature, a man alone—then it would be worthwhile to be a human being."

When Care asks him if he has never known her, Faust gives an answer that, at first sight, seems irrelevant, but is really very much to the point. It is the speech: "I have but raced through the world," in which he again states his new attitude toward life and adds that anyone who has found the right path need fear none of the frustrations and anxieties that are likely to beset him on the way to his goal: "To the able man this world is not mute. What need has he to roam in eternity? He perceives what is palpable. Let him then stroll through life in this way. When ghosts haunt him, let him pursue his way, let him find his torment and his joy in moving forward, he that is unsatisfied at every moment. . . . "

The opening and closing lines of this passage must be combined; together they yield Faust's ideal: constant striving, but within limits. And if we look back to the opening scene of Part II, we shall find the same combination of opposites there. For the speech which ends with Faust's new vision of the rainbow as the symbol of successful living also contains the couplet:

> Du regst und rührst ein kräftiges Beschließen,
> Zum höchsten Dasein immerfort zu streben.

(You [i.e., the rainbow] stir and move a vigorous resolve in me to strive constantly toward the highest existence.) With this ideal as a guide it is possible to overcome *Sorge.*

But Goethe had learned through bitter experience that life is anything but a serene Olympian existence. He passed this insight on to Faust, by the dramatic device of letting Care blind him. Though she can blind him, she can no longer cripple him, as she did during their first encounter. The added frustration of blindness merely spurs him on to greater efforts. A wonderful parallel this to the myth of Jacob wrestling with the Angel. Jacob escapes with a dislocated hip; he limps but is not paralyzed. And so it is with Faust.

With this symbolic conquest of anxiety Faust triumphs over life. Since Goethe has taken pains to review, in Faust's last speech, what Faust stands for, it is worth while to summarize his credo here. It is practical activity that now commands Faust's attention, not "what holds the world together at its core." The activity is not for his selfish ends; it provides opportunity for others to be active. There must be freedom (the word is used four times in this one passage), but a freedom that is fought for. Faust dreams of making life comfortable for the millions; but he does not wish to supply them with a stagnating security; hence danger will be ever present, to be overcome by courage and enterprise. Such an ideal, says Faust, could make one content with life.

As an artist Goethe had an obligation to round out the fable of the pact, which forms the framework of the whole action. Many voices have been raised to suggest that this task was beyond him and that he failed to solve the problem of what to do with Mephistopheles' claim on Faust's soul. It seems to me, on the contrary, that Goethe's handling of this problem is masterly. The contention of this study has been that the later Faust has been converted to the general point of view which Mephistopheles represented in the early scenes of the poem and to which the Lord, in the "Prologue in Heaven," gave His consent as the right one. It is because of this conversion that Faust is saved. It is therefore most fitting that, at the dramatic moment before Faust's death, Goethe should put into his mouth the words "Verweile doch," which symbolize the attitude that brings salvation. To condemn Faust for saying them is as sensible as to punish a man who once vowed to commit some outrageous deed and has now gone back on his oath and refuses to carry out his intention. The logic of the situation demands that Faust should forswear himself. He has been doing so, both in word and deed, from the opening of Part II.

A parallel situation in the last act of Bernard Shaw's *Back to Methuselah* throws a clear light on what is involved here. Strephon and the maiden have vowed eternal loyalty to an emotional state which is, in essence, very much like that of the *Sturm und Drang* Faust. And now the more mature maiden wishes to emulate the ancients and devote herself to the life of the intellect alone.

STREPHON. But your vow. Have you forgotten that? We all swore together in the temple: the temple of love. *You* were more earnest than any of us.

THE MAIDEN. [with a grim smile]. Never to let our hearts grow cold! Never to become as the ancients! Never to let the sacred lamp be extinguished! Never to change or forget! To be remembered for ever as the first company of true lovers faithful to this vow so often made and broken by past generations. Ha! Ha! Oh dear!

STREPHON. Well, you need not laugh. It is a beautiful and holy compact; and I will keep it whilst I live. Are you going to break it?

THE MAIDEN. Dear child: it has broken itself. The change has come in spite of my childish vow.

Does this mean that we are back in the old argument between Faust and Mephistopheles as to whether agreements should be kept to the letter or only in spirit? Not at all; for there is another factor involved here. Faust has been converted to the view which both God and the Devil agree to be the right one. That conversion Faust formally announces, first in the image of the rainbow, and now by repeating the formula "Verweile doch." All three now agree that Faust has become a "good man." What is there to condemn him for: because he has seen the error of his ways? The fact is that, in the relations between Faust and Mephistopheles, the usual associations with the words "pact," "wager," "agreement" are misleading. The issue between the two protagonists is a philosophical one: Which way of life brings salvation? In this conflict of opinion Mephistopheles was right and Faust wrong. As long as Faust persisted in his error, he was courting damnation. Once he recognized his error, he was on the road to salvation. And as soon as he was able to throw off the trappings that went with his erroneous past [i.e., magic], he had earned his salvation.

Mephistopheles himself would have been compelled to concede all this. Why then doesn't he admit that he has lost the wager? Why does he feel cheated at losing Faust's soul? Goethe has given a clear answer to this question in Mephistopheles' speech: "No pleasure brings him satisfaction, no happiness is adequate for him. Thus he continues to whore after transient forms. The last, wretched, empty moment—the poor fellow would like to hold fast to it. . . ." Mephistopheles is obviously not aware of the change in attitude that has occurred in Faust. He still thinks of his protégé as the romantic titan, whose aim in life is to squeeze the utmost from the present moment. Apparently he has failed to hear with his mental ear the real significance of Faust's statement "Verweile doch." He sees in Faust's last words only blind striving of the *Sturm und Drang* kind, whereas, for Faust, activity now means something quite different.

We are now in a position to grasp the full import of the argument between God and Mephistopheles in the "Prologue in Heaven." What secret information did the Lord possess that made Him so confident of the final outcome of the wager in favor of Faust? The answer is: the Lord foresaw the change that would take place in Faust: that he would, sooner or later, abandon his extremism, his grasshopper existence, and face life again with the power of accepting frustration. This turn of events, we must assume, Mephistopheles could not foresee, any more than Faust himself. Mephistopheles proceeded on the assumption that a *Weltanschauung* is a function of temperament. Once a romantic, always a romantic, he reasoned. Faust was doomed to remain the grasshopper all his life and would therefore deserve damnation.

Two problems in this area still remain to be solved. Earlier in this study I spoke slightingly of those who base Faust's salvation on his use of the conditional mode. But the question persists: why does Faust say the fateful words so indirectly? That Goethe placed some special emphasis on this conditional is proved by the fact that the manuscript originally had the exact formula that Faust had vowed not to utter: "I shall say to the moment—Stay awhile, thou art so fair." Why did Goethe change *werde* to *würde?* It is clear from what has been said here, as well as from other sources, that Goethe did not want to leave the impression that Faust had become a perfect man. For this reason, as W. H. Auden points out, he had the angels stress Faust's chrysalis state and point out that it is his striving, rather than his actual achievement, that wins him salvation. And the very last speech in the poem emphasizes this same theme: that life on this earth can only achieve success symbolically rather than actually. To Eckermann (6 June 1831) Goethe remarked that, although Faust showed a steady moral improvement to the end, he still needed the aid of Grace to obtain salvation. That same feeling of human imperfection is expressed here by the use of the conditional mode. Faust accepts the philosophy of "Verweile doch" in principle and even puts it into practice; but he feels that he is not yet ready to enjoy the fruits of this insight because he is not worthy of them. "*If* I were to live long enough in the light of my new outlook on life without sliding back into the hubris of magic, I *could* say that I have lived a successful life. I have not come that far yet; but my ultimate formula for salvation *would be:* Verweile doch." This, it seems to me, is implied in the conditional statement. So that, whether Faust speaks the fateful words in the indicative or conditional is irrelevant to the central fact that he is saved *because* he says them—that is, because he accepts the attitude to life that they imply.

The second problem concerns the character of Mephistopheles. Is it not rather disturbing that God and Mephistopheles should be on the same side in their theological and ethical views? Should not the Devil deny God's code of values? The answer is that Goethe's devil is not the Satan of Milton or the Lucifer of Gnosticism. He is, as he himself says, the spirit of negation, whose business it is to destroy accepted values rather than to set up new ones. He recognizes God's standards and busies himself with the task of preventing men from living by them.

Apart from *Hamlet* there is no other work in world literature that has aroused so many interpretations as Goethe's *Faust.* No single interpretation has solved all the problems the poem raises and I am not vain enough to think that mine has. I do believe, however, that I have given a possible reading, one which is consistent with Goethe's general views on life, both in his youth and maturity; a reading which uses the facts of Goethe's mental development to resolve the difficulties raised by the pact and wager. This interpretation absolves Goethe from the charge made by Korff that he "deliberately surrounded the wager and Faust's end on earth with a peculiar obscurity." That there is a lack of clarity in the matter is painfully obvious from the record of Goethe criticism. But I cannot see that the obscurity can be blamed on Goethe. It arises primarily from the fact that Goethe swapped horses in the midstream of life, changed his basic attitude to life. This fact is generally known and has often enough been applied to *Faust* as well. But the implications which it has for the outcome of the wager have not been seen. To establish this connection has been the aim of this study. (pp. 180-200)

Harry Steinhauer, "Faust's Pact with the Devil," in PMLA, *Vol. LXXI, No. 1, March, 1956, pp. 180-200.*

Stuart Atkins (essay date 1958)

[*Atkins is an American educator and critic specializing in German poetry and drama. Below, he discusses the epilogue of* Faust *as a recapitulation of the complex themes developed in the play, praising Goethe's "highly complex poetic vision."*]

The episode of Faust's interment has been the counterpart of Prologue in Heaven, although it is not an epilogue to the Tragedy of Faust but an integral part of its dramatic action. The heaven of medieval and Baroque morality play has been economically reintroduced as the burst of light diagonally above Mephistopheles' hell-mouth, and as in a morality the symbols of good and evil have stood for the last time in sharp contrast. Yet Faust's view of man and man's world is not dualistic and theological, but monistic and humanistic; his sense of the oneness of God and Nature, of the divine and the human, is the expression of a fundamentally anti-transcendental naturalism, unobtrusively present in Prologue in Heaven, whose first clear spokesmen in *Faust* were the Poet and the Player of Prelude on the Stage. Although Interment effectively insists that Faust has defeated Mephistopheles and, simultaneously, serves to complete the cosmic framework which permitted *Faust* to be a drama of symbolic supernaturalism, its ambiguous morality-play machinery can leave uncertain—especially in the theater—whether the dying Faust believes he is about to enjoy salvation and heavenly bliss or remains a humanistic naturalist until he finally loses all consciousness. The scene Mountain Gorges: Forest, Rocks, and Hermitage, serves both to clarify this final point and, returning us once more to the realm of finite human beings in which *Faust* opened (Dedication, Prelude on the Stage), to recapitulate in the form of a dramatic epilogue all the salient features—the symbolic characters, themes, ideas, and motifs—of the complex tragedy now terminating.

The first and last scenes of *Faust* in which its protagonist is an active participant both take place at night, but even as the opening scene in Faust's study was preceded by a sunlit Prologue in Heaven, so is his interment followed by the radiant daylight of Faust's last vision. The setting of Mountain Gorges, however, is no Old Testament heaven, but a Catholicized Arcadia, for *Faust* has not been a Christian mystery play, a drama of religious edification, and Faust has not been a Christian whose good works could earn him immediate admission to the company of Saints. The placing of this epilogue to the tragedy of a humanistic naturalist in a milieu familiar from Catholic legend, painting, and drama is thus ironic, if not startling, and after the anti-clerical and anti-transcendental tones repeatedly heard in *Faust*—tones that cast subsequent light on the omission of conventional Christian elements in the not irreligious, but still only superficially traditional, Prologue in Heaven—it is evident that Catholicizing symbolism is here introduced solely in the interest of artistic economy. Anchorites, then, are still creatures of this world, however near to God their solitary devotions may succeed in bringing them, while the Church Fathers, Blessed Boys, Penitents, and Virgin Mother who utter, or share in the utterance of, over four-fifths of the lines comprising this scene, have all known mortal existence. Although its religious symbolism may thus seem to make Mountain Gorges tantamount to an Epilogue in Heaven, by virtue of its predominantly temporal components it is rather an Epilogue on Earth, a companion piece to Dedication, Prelude on the Stage, Pleasant Landscape, and the opening soliloquy of High Mountains, a scene whose desolate landscape it shares, and the counterpart of Margarete's visions of the afterlife in Cathedral and Prison. Like Prison, moreover, it too recalls Piranesi, though not a dungeon from *The Prisons,* but a wild landscape from *The Views of Rome.*

Whereas Faust's rock-bound Arcadia was a "universal" symbol to which special and even highly individual significance was attached, the rocky hermitage of Mountain Gorges is one which, at least in terms of the symbolism of *Faust,* is totally significant—that is, it represents all the realms of experience in which Faust has moved in the course of the tragedy. Into the classical paradise of Shaded Grove are introduced the still tame beasts of the Judaeo-Christian Garden of Eden—the mute and friendly lions of the Anchorites' opening chorus—and that "natural" wildness of landscape which no Arcadia could properly possess and which to varying degrees characterized the realm of impersonal Nature whenever Faust sought refuge in it (Forest and Cave, Pleasant Landscape, High Mountains). The human or once-human figures who appear may at first sight seem mostly new, but when they speak it quickly becomes clear that they are metamorphoses of Faust and other dramatic characters from his past experiences, a fact emphasized not only by what they say, but also by the metrical and verbal echoes of earlier moments in the Tragedy of Faust which mark their speech. For this heaven-like world remains from beginning to end the projection of a Faust who can no longer experience anything new, who may only draw upon memories of what he has done, has felt, has thought, and has imagined.

Although he proclaims the final Faustian insight that love

is essence of God-Life, the Pater Ecstaticus is a self-tormented mystic who vacillates between earth and heaven, between a physical reality that he depreciates as transitory and a quintessential Love that he fervently prays may become his through physical suffering. His is the religious equivalent of Faust's sentimental confusion of love and self-destruction at the end of Forest and Cave, and like Faust then, the Ecstatic Father is one as yet incapable of selfless devotion—hence the emphatic repetition of "me" at the end of four successive lines in his brief speech, and hence also the motif of levitation, which recalls Euphorion's unsuccessful attempt to free himself of earthbound man's necessary limitations. More stable and less egocentric by far is the Pater Profundus, whose first two stanzas incidentally picture the larger landscape of which this mountain scene is but a part. Speaking in the verse form of the Archangels' descriptive hymn at the opening of Prologue in Heaven, he discerns, much as they did, in the workings of the physical world the evidence of God-Love's universal presence, which is represented by the same four elements that represented the cosmos at the end of both Faust's Classical Walpurgisnight and his *Helen.* Unlike the Archangels, however, but like the Faust of Pleasant Landscape and High Mountains, he delights equally in the great and small phenomena of Nature. Yet he, too, has not achieved the release from self he ardently desires and, the religious counterpart of the would-be intellectual superman who on Easter Eve felt hopelessly crushed by his inability to transcend the limits of finite-sensual knowledge, regards himself as the helpless prisoner of his merely-finite senses, so that his "Tormented by dull senses' confines" is the harsh antithesis of the Lord's benedictory "Encompass you in love's propitious bonds."

More important than these two Church Fathers, who have represented both universal forms of religious experience and critical moments in Faust's religious-intellectual development, is the Pater Seraphicus, whose first speech marks an abrupt transition from contemplative and descriptive elements, largely lyrical and retrospective, to an immediate present and to dramatic action. The "median elevation" to which the stage direction assigns him indicates that he, like Faust from Pleasant Landscape on, is content to know of God only what has meaning for life on this earth—hence the Calderonian redondillas, the verse of idyllic realism in the Philemon and Baucis scene, that distinguish his speech and that of the Blessed Boys while they remain with him. Completely unconcerned with self, like Faust in his best moments, he marks the approach of the "morning cloudlet" which conceals a chorus of boys who died at birth. This bodiless "band of youthful spirits"—whose method of transportation recalls the cloud from which Faust emerged after his classical Walpurgis Night and which symbolized his recognition that Helen and Margarete, "Aurora's love," were one person—are a last memory of the child Faust never saw. Counterparts of Homunculus by virtue of their insubstantiality and power of levitation, they share with him the fact that their voice must be projected ventriloquistically, although at the moment they are content to enjoy pure—or mere—"being." Invited by the kindly Seraphic Father to see the world through his eyes, they receive a lesson in seeing which is the counterpart of the lesson in talking in rhyme that Faust gave Helen in his second great dream. But the sight of a majestic and gloomy landscape is so overpowering that they immediately beg to be released and are sent on their way to higher, less substantial spheres where they can grow as they draw strength from "God's presence." Although it will transpire in the course of the scene that this advice does not represent highest wisdom, it does reveal that, for Faust, God is, as in Prologue in Heaven, the supreme symbol of growth and development (*Werden*), and it projects into a spirit-world the same forces and patterns that Faust made basic to his triumphant vision of life in the Galatea scene of Classical Walpurgisnight.

Accepting the Seraphic Father's words of dismissal as a promise that they shall see God—"Godly this teaching, / Be now at ease; / Whom you respect, / Him your eye sees"—the Blessed Boys move off to the highest peaks of the stage set. If the incongruity of disembodied spirits holding hands and dancing in a circle to express their joys is a variation on the motif of the still vial-confined Homunculus' power to smell the freshness of marine vegetation, the dance motif itself, like its rhythms, recalls the opening of the pastoral dance passage of the Euphorion episode. As the Blessed Boys sing "Whom you respect, / Him your eye sees," the Angels who bore away "the immortal part of Faust" in the preceding scene make a significantly timed entrance. For it is Faust, not God, whom they are to see and respect. Hovering high above the earth, these Angels—the only never-mortal figures of Mountain Gorges—announce that "a noble spirit" has been saved from evil, that is, from the annihilation for which Mephistopheles has always stood. Whereas Prologue in Heaven merely promised that Faust would ultimately find man's proper path and achieve clarity of insight as he followed the path of error which is life, Faust allows himself a last aerial translation and potential heavenly salvation. For the Angels' "Whoever strives with all his heart, / For him there is redemption," is not the fulfillment of any promise, but rather the symbolic expression of Faust's conviction that his resolution of Pleasant Landscape, "Ever to strive toward life's most perfect forms," is the best possible general formulation of the moral imperative which consciousness of man's divine dignity must predicate. This resolution was, as Faust ultimately recognized, inspired by the example of Margarete's heroic selflessness, and now he again acknowledges his profound debt to her by having the Angels immediately add,

> And if a love from up on high
> Has given him assistance,
> The blessed creatures of the sky
> Must welcome his appearance.

That the Angels' "love from up on high" is a specific reference to Margarete becomes clear from the Younger Angels' immediate revelation that the roses which contributed so much to Mephistopheles' final defeat and humiliation came from the fair hands of "Penitents whose love is saintly"—the only non-recapitulatory detail of the first angelic sub-chorus. That Faust's translation to heavenly choirs is only a symbolic-secular apotheosis—the nontragic counterpart of Margarete's last moments—is next made clear by the More Perfect Angels, who express his full awareness of the all-too-human weaknesses that

would long exclude him, though not perhaps eternally, from any strictly Catholic heaven. "It somewhat stirs our ire / This earth to carry, / For were it cleansed by fire, / 'Twould still be sorry." If their pharisaical tone is a nice reminder of Faust's unshakable anti-transcendentalism, even more so is their insistence that only the active intervention of God—"Eternal Love only"—could separate a vigorous human spirit from the elements that it has tenaciously attached to itself. And if Faust's body and soul are still one, constitute a "Union of two natures / Still joined as one only," he is clinging tenaciously to that contradictory finiteness which is human identity—hence the echo of his Easter Walk observation, then the expression of helpless frustration, "Two souls, alas, do dwell within my breast . . ."

Still another echo from Outside the City Gates, this time of Faust's paean to spring, follows as the Younger Angels propose that Faust be placed "for a start— / And continuing betterment—" in the company of the Blessed Boys, who are now individual cloudlets basking "in the new spring" of new life in a new world. The prospect of constant achievement of something more and more like perfection which Faust here suggests is, for the purely human plane of being, a counterpart of the progression from lower to higher forms of life that Homunculus was promised if he wed the sea, and it is therefore with the reintroduction of the supreme symbol of man's innate power of metamorphosis, of growth and development, that the Blessed Boys take custody of Faust's body. "Gladly we welcome / This chrysalid entity, / Pledge that we'll come / To have angels' identity. / Break the cocoon that / Covers his person! / His is already the beauty and greatness / Of life itself sacred." In the Hermes chorus of Shaded Grove the chrysalis symbolized man's divinely natural impulse to achieve freedom and autonomy and so live fully even at the necessary price of self-destruction so quickly paid by Euphorion, Hermes' mortal counterpart. In Faust's vision of an afterlife, therefore, his very imperfection, the fact he has lived a full life, endows him with attributes that beings who can hardly be said to have lived at all must perforce acknowledge as highest values, and the divine worth of mortal man remains for him inextricably one with man's inevitable shortcomings and weaknesses.

Faust's thoughts now turn from himself to Margarete, imagined as one of a constellation of women the central star of which is the resplendent Queen of Heaven herself. These figures are neo-Catholic counterparts of Galatea and her attendants, to whose fleeting passage this ascension of Virgo as described by the Doctor Marianus closely corresponds. As Galatea was the classical symbol of the mystery of divinely human perfection—"Earnest, and of godlike air, / Deservedly immortal, yes, / But like mortal women fair / In her tempting gracefulness"—so is the "Highest Mistress of the World" the symbol of that cosmic mystery which is man's power of selfless, "sacred love" and which the Doctor Marianus begs may be visibly revealed to him "in the blueness / Of heaven's outstretched panoply." Yet Faust's Mater Gloriosa also shares attributes of Margarete and Helen; like the former she is "pure in the best sense," like both she is to be revered in her motherhood, and like the latter she is "coequal of the gods" (Faust's exact words to Chiron) and, as in Faust's *Helen,* an "elected queen." For if this Virgin Mother is endowed with divinity, it is because she is endowed with finest human qualities; and if she can also inspire courage and assuage passion, it is because she embodies values and insights the necessary corollary of which is the responsibility to act upon them.

Even before the Mater Gloriosa has appeared the Doctor Marianus directs his attention to the penitent women kneeling before her—that they are first seen as "delicate clouds" is again a reminder of the wisp of cloud that in High Mountains represented "Aurora's love"—and declares,

> You have never been traduced,
> Yet yours is the privilege here
> That those easily seduced
> Trustingly to you draw near.
>
> Hard indeed it is to save
> Those by weakness jaded,
> Yet how can desire's slave
> Burst his bonds unaided?
> Feet will slip when slopes are smooth,
> Girls forget what matters,
> When they see a friendly look,
> Hear a speech that flatters!

These rather worldly observations from one who but a moment earlier was transported by a vision of heavenly perfection are the explanation of why Faust the intransigent anti-transcendentalist allows himself the use of Catholic symbolism. For mariolatry is here simultaneously awareness of an ideal of perfection and acknowledgment that such perfection is beyond mortal strength, is a special form of Faust's more general insight that error and aspiration are necessarily inseparable, while the belief that divine forgiveness of sin is always possible represents a special form of his realization in Pleasant Landscape that no man can be said to live so long as he remains paralyzed by a sense of guilt hopelessly unatonable.

When the Mater Gloriosa floats into view with the Chorus of Penitent Women, three of these join in a prayer asking her forgiveness for one of their number. Each is a prototype of Margarete, and as each recalls the good works that have gained her grace, some important aspect of Margarete's life or character is in turn recalled. Mary Magdalene's willing humility is thus a reminder of the humble services Margarete gladly performed for her infant sister; the Samaritan Woman's allusions to Jacob's well recall both the idyllic and patriarchal motifs which Faust chose to associate with her way of life, and the moment of her first clear consciousness of guilt (the scene At the Well); while Mary of Egypt's exclusion from church and her repentant flight to the wilderness are reminders of the ostracism which finally drove Margarete to flee her home with her newborn child and of her awareness that she could not live a life of exile. If the three Penitents insist that Margarete "Knew not that she might be sinning," this is less a statement of fact than an expression of Faust's awareness that the greater guilt by far was always his. And if they describe her as one "Who but once forgot herself," it is because Faust recognizes in purgatorial atonement, in pen-

ance achieved after death, a valid symbol of the truth that no single error, whatever it may be, can seriously diminish the worth of a good human being.

That Faust does not regard the three Penitents' intercession as anything but an expression of his profound sense of Margarete's fundamental goodness becomes clearer when she herself now adds her prayer to theirs. For although it echoes her outpouring of grief to the Mater Dolorosa of the scene By the Ramparts, there is not the least evidence of contrition in her declaration that she wants divine pardon as a sign of approval of the happiness which Faust's return already affords her. Margarete is thus a symbol here of joyous and selfless devotion, of love so great that it is worthy of transcending death, rather than the individual who once embodied these virtues, and so the tragic form which her life finally assumed can at last be forgotten as she becomes simply a special manifestation of God-Love, that force awareness of whose existence may in some measure compensate men for life's tragic failures and life's destruction. Indeed, implicit in any concept of tragedy is the subjective feeling that no failure may be complete, that there is always some triumph of the spirit, and this Faust here projects as Margarete's sense of happiness.

The concrete symbol of human worth is still man developing and growing, however, and this man is Faust, who is now brought to the foreground as the Blessed Boys, joining the Mater Gloriosa and her penitents, announce that he still grows apace and can, as one who has lived and

Gretchen awaits Faust's return.

learned, become their valuable teacher. For even this heaven would be only a meaningless utopian dream if its creatures could not in some way acquire knowledge of actual finite existence. Aware that he has himself learned much from the example of Margarete's selfless love and basic integrity of character, Faust now lets her beg permission to instruct him in this new and brighter world. The feeling of rejuvenation he enjoys—his reappearance as the young man who lived the first great stage of his symbolic journey through life under the star of Margarete—is both a reminder of earliest happiness and an expression of the view, which he came to share with the Player of Prelude on the Stage, that true youthfulness is to be ever young in spirit. But his feeling of release "from every earthly fetter" is, like his sense of being blinded by overwhelming radiance, also the warning that death and final release are now imminent. The text of his last dream-play becomes suddenly laconic as the Mater Gloriosa answers Margarete's prayer by completing its third quatrain: "Arise and come to spheres celestial! / If he divines you're there, he'll follow too."

When profane love has thus been unconditionally recognized as the supreme finite symbol of God-Love, the Queen of Heaven and her attendants rise out of sight. Faust's dream ascension, the counterpart of Margarete's earthly apotheosis, is completed as the Doctor Marianus falls prostrate in prayer and calls upon all whose hearts are softened by repentance—"Alle reuig Zarten"—to avail themselves gratefully of the power of metamorphosis that enables men to realize their innate compulsion to follow what they are obscurely aware is their proper course.

> Let each better impulse be
> Ready for thy service;
> Maiden, Mother, Goddess, Queen,
> Keep thy mercy for us!

And so, as the several persons of Margarete-Galatea-Helen are now subsumed in the one person of Mary Mother of God, all the voices that have been heard during the scene join, as once did those of the Triumph of Galatea, in a final chorus proclaiming the ultimate mystery.

> Things without permanence
> Are symbols only;
> What man can not achieve
> Here is seen acted;
> What's indescribable
> Here may be fact;
> For womanhood's essence
> Serves as our guide.

In the higher worlds of myth and of poetry, and there only, can the idea of perfection implicit in man's awareness of the finite and transitory find nearly adequate expression, and there only can Dedication's things that have ceased to be become "realities" and visible event (*Ereignis*). Not God the Father, God the Son, or God the Holy Ghost, but a human-divine embodiment of "Das Ewig-Weibliche" is, even in the moment of mystic feelings which is Faust's final relinquishment of identity, the supreme and most comprehensive symbol of all those things which men regard as evidence that life is neither Mephistopheles' "void eternal" nor the romantic's vague aspir-

ing, but is, rather, directed striving with meaning certainly intuitable if not certainly knowable. Love as physical and spiritual escape from self, as passively confident faith and actively heroic devotion, as the never entirely unselfish impulse to realize great visions and as disinterested kindness and mercy—this is "Das Ewig-Weibliche," the ideal of eternity and perfection mystically embodied by the frailty which proverbially is woman.

Mountain Gorges, the epilogue on earth which so unqualified an affirmation of secular experience as *Faust* almost demanded, has ended with all the tragedy's highest moments once more recalled. For all its surface diversity, *Faust* has proved to be always concerned with central aspects of human experience and has, in the course of its often seemingly associative unfolding, demonstrated that in art, as in the love affair which the Player of Prelude on the Stage offered as a symbol of the poet's right and duty to use life and life's chance associations as the model of what he creates, unity may be one with most multifarious complexity. If the vision of life offered in *Faust* has been complex, it still remains an imperfect symbol of life's fullness—"Alles Vergängliche / Ist nur ein Gleichnis," or, as Faust declared in Forest and Cave, "That nothing perfect ever can be man's, / That now I feel." But since life itself is compounded of evident causes and apparent chance, of elements more and less meaningful, the very imperfection of *Faust* makes it a faithful symbol of that totality of experience which is each individual's human lot—"Das Unzulängliche, / Hier wird's Ereignis"—and it may be rightly claimed that all its scenes and even its most peripheral elements have contributed to making more nearly perfect the poet's naturalistic vision of transcendence never to be known apart from immanence. The very ambivalence of the symbols of Mountain Gorges is thus a last insistence that neither religion nor art, Goethe's "secular gospel," can unambiguously express the essence of life, and so the very process by which Catholic symbols are made catholic, in the sense of universal, to describe the Indescribable contributes fully as much to the leaving of a final impression of incommensurability on all planes of experience as does the direct poetic statement of Faust's dying visions.

The original premises of *Faust,* the inseparability of art and life, of good and evil, of the human and the divine, of the physical and the spiritual—these ambivalences have been poetically stated as the Tragedy of Faust the representative man whose final translation to a "new" sphere has left him still finite, real, imperfect, moving unnamed but with consciousness of his finite identity into the unknown of God Unknowable. If Margarete could be granted an apotheosis, it was ultimately a sentimental and hence secular one representing an instance of pathetic fallacy justifiable artistically by its function as the climax of Faust's experience of sentimental irresponsibility. Faust himself, however, can be granted no apotheosis; for if he were merged with God Unknowable, he would cease to be Faust and man, would lose the power of growth and metamorphosis without which there could be no knowledge of God-Love and God-Life.

Since *Faust* is a self-contained poetic statement, it may, I think, be properly doubted whether its complex totality can be further illuminated by any recapitulation beyond that which Goethe himself provided in its final scenes. Individual readers will undoubtedly recall other elements of the text which seem to them no less important than those Goethe chose to emphasize in his recapitulations, but when the complexity of the work of art rivals that of life itself it is inevitable that the relative importance of its constituent parts will vary even for the same reader according to the circumstances of his contact with it. This is, indeed, surely the most important reason why *Faust* has suffered such completely contradictory interpretations, and often even self-contradictory ones, for the structural complexity which contributes so greatly to its effective mirroring of life's totality also prevents the function of some of its parts, and even the literal meaning of what it says at certain points, from being transparently obvious and immediately understandable. In consequence, for instance, critics who know perfectly well that Faust's classical Walpurgis Night is a phantasmagoria easily forget its dramatic premise and unconsciously begin to treat Helen or Phorkyas or Euphorion as autonomous *dramatis personae,* with the result that the most important scenes of *Faust* imperceptibly cease to be parts of the Tragedy of Faust and become simply masque-like passages of allegorical-didactic poetry interspersed with disparate dramatic and lyric moments. Or, to offer one more example, the first episode of the Lemures, which helps to prepare symbolically for the quickness with which Faust's death follows upon his renunciation of magic, is often read as evidence that Faust's brave new world was created, not by ruthless exploitation of human labor, but by the use of supernatural creatures—an inevitable misunderstanding if the stage direction "Mephistopheles, preceding in the role of overseer," is taken to mean that one who a few minutes earlier was clearly Faust's first executive officer should suddenly be the head of a gang of manual laborers. It is to obviate such confusion, which is actually legion, that this interpretative reading of *Faust* has been written. Much meaning can be read into *Faust,* and there is unquestionably far more meaning to it than I have been able to indicate, but I am convinced that satisfactory and satisfying insights into what it "means" are most likely to be the corollary of an understanding of what it actually says and of a recognition that it sustains its dramatic form uninterruptedly from beginning to end.

For *Faust* is, as its full title insists, basically a tragedy. Heroic tragedy in the great tradition of Aeschylus, Sophocles, Euripides, Shakespeare, and Calderón, the drama of man destroyed by the larger force than himself which is life and yet enjoying triumph in inevitable defeat, *Faust* is perhaps the last great poem of its kind in the world's literature to satisfy the Aristotelian demand that tragedy inspire not only pity but also fear and admiration (awe). That it should have been conceived when it was, is even more extraordinary than the grand but not unique scale of its execution, inasmuch as Goethe wrote it in an age whose rationalists, under the influence of ethical deism and naturalistic philosophy, had long since degraded tragedy to a form of psychological *drame à thèse* in which tragic guilt was simply willful or, more and more often, unwitting violation of a conventional code of morality; and whose romanticists, under the spell of idealistic phi-

losophies and transcendental impulses, either had no sense of tragic necessity or else envisioned its resolution on some "higher" plane. Like that of Oedipus or Hamlet, Faust's moral and tragic guilt is but the concomitant of finite efforts to live in an imperfect world nobly and heroically; no natural moral law of compensation metes out justice to him, no providence intervenes to reward or punish him. It may be inevitable and necessary that the most harmonious human life know some dissonance and failure, but only when these are magnified by art and represented as counterbalanced by courage and a sense of clear purpose is high tragedy achieved.

Faust, then, represents such an achievement and is in the last analysis the expression of a profoundly tragic view of life. Yet, like all great tragedy, it is at the same time an expression of man's uncrushable feeling that life is always somehow still worth living, and it satisfies in very great measure his need to believe that helpless pessimism is not the final answer to the riddle of existence—hence the high esteem in which it has been held by readers of many different kinds. The elegiac tones of Dedication; the terrible despair of Faust in the first scenes of the Tragedy; his deliberate seduction of Margarete and the suffering it leads to; the many pictures of human stupidity, folly, selfishness, self-deception, and self-degradation; the political and social corruption represented by the Emperor's court; the traits of sadistic cruelty to which Faust gives vent in Before Menelaus' Palace; the only partially concealed horrors of the war by which Faust restores a worthless prince to his throne; the ruthlessness with which he creates his new dominion and destroys the idyllic world of his neighbors; and, above all, Mephistopheles' iterated expressions of cynical pessimism—all these things and many more make very plain that Goethe had few illusions about how difficult it is for man to attain to anything approximating a good life. And although, again and again in *Faust,* life's dissonances are momentarily resolved with the aid of satire and humor—at greatest length in the high comedy of Classical Walpurgisnight—the ultimate resolution is always on the plane of tragic irony, however strongly tinged this may be, as in the Euphorion episode or in Mountain Gorges, with comic pathos.

The dignity of man, to which Margarete, the neo-mythological mystery of Homunculus, Helen, Euphorion, Philemon and Baucis, Faust himself, and the three thousand years of Western civilization recalled by *Faust* all bear witness, is thus no expression of mere optimism, and Goethe's well-considered naturalistic humanism is far removed from that blind arrogance which inspired Swinburne to proclaim, "Glory to man in the highest, / For man is the measure of things." As Faust is no paragon of virtue, so is *Faust,* however extraordinary it may be as a poetic achievement, the imperfect work of an imperfect man well aware of these facts. But for all his profound insight into human frailty, and because he understood men as only the greatest poets of all time have been able to understand them, Goethe still felt compelled to testify with *Faust* that he recognized in man's imperfect striving for natural truths a universally shared pattern of religious experience. And as long as it can be felt that the value attached to aspiration in *Faust* is rightly a positive one, so long also must *Faust* remain one of the greatest secular poetic statements of how man searches for the meaning of life and of God.

But *Faust* is not a great drama because it expresses Goethean wisdom, a view of life which many men have shared before and since Goethe's time. It is great because it communicates a poet's highly complex vision with an exemplary effectiveness, with an artistic economy unrivaled by any other tragedy or tragic cycle of comparable scope. For all its poetic prodigality, the multiplicity of subordinate dramatic actions and the broad variety of motifs demanded by its theme of symbolic totality, the clarity of the large design of *Faust* is effectively insured by the familiarity of the Faust legend, itself but a special form of the universal myth of the magus, from which all the salient features of its plot ultimately derive. The almost systematic exploitation of already established literary forms permits an economy of dramatic statement, occasionally bordering upon the elliptical, which neither purely naturalistic nor purely experimental writing can ever achieve. Yet artistic convention never becomes a substitute for poetic statement; every symbol is defined within the text itself, and all but the most familiar of the classical and historical allusions in which it abounds are, like the literary devices to which symbolic significance is attached, given their value by the contexts in which they stand. Although every theatrical device, from those of the most primitive to those of the most sophisticated stage, that can externalize dramatic action seems to be exploited at some point in *Faust,* careful attention to psychological verisimilitude in the delineation of all important characters endows the tragedy as a whole with biographical concreteness, with human interest in the best sense of that often misused phrase.

The first great work of Western literature since Shakespearean tragedy to speak not, like French classical tragedy or the eighteenth century's bourgeois genres, for one social class; to speak not, like the morality play or its more sophisticated counterparts, the *drame à thèse* and "philosophical" tragedy, for one religious or philosophic system—*Faust* is a dramatic action set forth, despite the theatrical machinery for which its text gives full license, almost exclusively through the spoken word, so that with a few sound effects actors in any costume can, on a bare stage, project the many settings which it seems to demand. Long though it be as a drama, *Faust* is a remarkably close-knit text which, thanks to a structural economy made possible as much by the full exploitation of parallelistic variation as by the artistic shorthand of continuous use of standard literary conventions, communicates a highly complex poetic vision without ever giving the effect of skeletal bareness. As André Gide wrote of *Faust* in his journal under the date June 26, 1940, "Everything in it is saturated with life. Thought is never presented in it in an abstract form, just as sentiment is never separated from thought, so that what is most individual is still heavy with meaning and, so to speak, exemplary." With its symbols and motifs, its themes and its characters, its forms and its actions, all reciprocally strengthening their separate contributions to the total poetic statement, *Faust* must communicate to him who temporarily suspends disbelief that unique aesthetic experience which only the greatest works of the world's literature have the power to convey. (pp. 263-77)

> *Stuart Atkins, in his* Goethe's Faust: A Literary Analysis, *Cambridge, Mass.: Harvard University Press, 1958, 290 p.*

Ulrich K. Goldsmith   (essay date 1966)

[*In the following excerpt from an essay that originally appeared in the* German Quarterly *in 1966, Goldsmith suggests that* Faust *achieves unity from its adherence to poetic principles.*]

It took precisely one hundred years after Goethe's death before the first serious and comprehensive attempt was made to interpret Goethe's *Faust, a Tragedy* (in two parts) as a coherent whole rather than a collection of fragments which earlier commentators thought the poet put together haphazardly. In 1932 Heinrich Rickert's book was published under the title *Goethe's Faust: its dramatic unity.* However, the author was a philosopher. He and others since have tried to see the unity of the poem in a philosophical or theological idea. This idea simplified would be of man on a quest, falling into error, and finally redeemed. Aside from ignoring Goethe's warning that he had not strung the life of Faust "on the thin and meagre thread of a single idea running through the whole," the idea of quest, error, and redemption implies two things: 1) the notion of the moral perfectibility of man, 2) the classical idea of tragedy, according to which the hero endangers his perfection and mars his progress through error or guilt, but is purified through repentance and transfigured as he loses his life.

Neither of these two concepts, however, fits the Faust drama: (1) A close reading of both parts will show that Faust *learns* and matures a great deal in the course of the several episodes from his life in the small and in the great world, but insight and knowledge, gained through multifarious experience, do not make one a better or more perfect man (morally speaking). Quite deliberately Goethe shows Faust in his old age, "about one hundred years old," as a very powerful, covetous, and ill-tempered landlord, on whose shoulders falls the responsibility for the death and accidental cremation of Philemon and Baucis, old cottagers who refused to let themselves be expropriated by him. Further support for the insufficiency or irrelevance of merit in Faust's earthly career can be found in the last scene of *Faust II,* the epilogue, in which "the immortal part" of Faust ascends into an otherworldly realm where he has to continue to learn before he can enter the presence of divinity, but where it is emphasized that "love from above" or, to be specific, the sacrificial love of "a penitent soul, once called Gretchen," must intercede for him. So, if Faust is to be thought of as having achieved some kind of acceptability (not moral perfection—because he himself never repents!) it is not attained during his earthly life. Faust's unorthodox salvation is a very ambiguous matter. It comes within his grasp at the feet of the Virgin not only regardless of his merit, but also without any expressly expiatory effort on his part. A peculiarly ironic light is shed on the hero's ceaseless striving: the chorus of angels grants that one who strives *can* be saved:

> He whose striving never ceases
> Can be redeemed by us.
> And if eventually Love
> Has from on high participated
> There comes to greet him joyfully
> The company of heaven.

However, what redeems the great man, whom the Earth Spirit once mockingly called "Superman," is the love of the sweetheart of his youth, i.e., both the love she bears him and his own unforgotten love for her.

(2) It is easy to see why Faust's tragedy is not a tragedy in the classical sense. As has just been said, Faust never repents. By that I do not mean that he does not *regret* anything—indeed, he feels bitter remorse and shameful guilt at the end of Part I when he realizes that he has caused or helped to cause the deaths of Margarete, her baby, her mother, and her brother, just as he later regrets and resents the Philemon and Baucis disaster (both times he tries to blame the thing on Mephistopheles, incidentally!). Yet, he recovers from guilt and the consequent moral paralysis in a manner different from all methods of expiation in the religious sense; especially, he does not pay with his own life for his crimes. In fact, his very crimes and mistakes, providing the means of new insights and enlightenment, spur him on to explore further the possibilities of human existence at the risk of getting involved in new errors. We are informed of the creative function of evil in the Prologue in Heaven, where the Lord, far from scorning this fallen angel as the adversary, refers to him as the rogue who has a gadfly-like function in His scheme of things and must "goad and tease / And toil to serve creation, though a devil." Faust is freed from the burden of guilt and remorse through no formal religious means of grace, such as confession and absolution. Rather he regains his mental balance after the Gretchen tragedy through the healing processes of nature which conclude with the balm or boon of forgetting (symbolized by a reference to the river Lethe) and, after the death of the old cottagers, through a re-examination of his existential position, which results in a renewed resolve to pursue fruitful action.

The recognition that the Faust poem cannot be forced into the categories of perfectibility and classical tragedy does not mean that it has no unity. Rather its unity is assured by other factors. Two of them are to be found in the treatment of Faust and Margarete. The first is this ability of Faust to proceed undaunted by failure and error through an escalated series of experiences. The other is the role of Margarete, which secretly extends beyond her death through the whole poem to the very end of the Epilogue of Part II. Some people see a problem here; they ask: how can, in a Christian framework, which Goethe's *Faust* ostensibly possesses, the redemption of the hero be effected by his former beloved rather than by the Christian Redeemer? The answer is twofold: (a) the drama is not, strictly speaking, Christian, just as its author must not be given that label; (b) Goethe was writing poetry and was not concerned with religious dogma. He would, I am sure, have insisted that the poet is free to use traditional religious symbols and ideas for artistic purposes and to transform their meanings in the process.

In order to see the origin of such a detached attitude we must pause to consider for a moment the significance which the Christian faith had for Goethe and how it impinged on his portrayal of Gretchen. She is the only one among the multitude of characters in the drama whose very essence can be described as that of a faithful member of the Church, and when she is faced with Faust, who is not, her troubles begin. During the catechisation scene in Martha's Garden, as she listens to Faust's exuberant pantheistic Credo, Margarete remarks very perceptively:

> All that is very well and good
> Our pastor almost says the same,
> Only in somewhat different words . . .

and further on, more bluntly: "You lack Christianity." Margarete is right about Faust's religion and her anxiety about his soul is justified. From the Christian standpoint she would be right if she extended this appraisal to the whole poem and its author. This is not the place for a thorough discussion of Goethe's religion; suffice it to say that Goethe habitually veiled his innermost convictions, that he could be mordantly critical of the Church, that he did not accept the Christian revelation; that, on the other hand, in his old age he assigned the Christian religion to the highest rank among all formal religions and called it "an ultimate stage which mankind was able and bound to reach." Goethe never committed himself to any closed set of doctrines. With ironic detachment he rejected all denominational claims to exclusive validity; finally, among his "Maxims and Reflections" we find this aphorism: "As natural scientists we are Pantheists, as poets Polytheists, ethically: Monotheists." One year before his death he said in a letter to his friend Boisserée that he belonged to the sect of the Hypsistarians (they existed at the end of the 3rd century, worshipped God under the name of "hypsistos" which means "Highest," and under the visible sign of light and fire; the Hypsistarians knew no minor gods or mediators).

So, while Goethe was detached from all organized religion, he had the deepest respect for Christianity. This is evident in the treatment of the character of Margarete. Her whole earthly existence—her upbringing, her daily routine, her faith, her sinning, her final decision to surrender to God's judgment—are unambiguously placed within the Catholic Christian frame of reference. It is important to realize, however, that the presentation of her earthly fate, the so-called "Gretchen-Tragedy," comprises only one-sixth of the total work, which consists of 12,111 lines. In the sphere of the Mater Gloriosa toward the end of the Epilogue, through the special significance attached to her intercession, her stature has been heightened far beyond that of an ordinary "saved" Christian soul in heaven. What was a very human Gretchen now assumes the role of a mediator who has died a sacrificial death. But (and this emphasizes the unity the Gretchen figure lends to Parts I and II) there is a hint of this aspect of her death even in the first part, in the powerful prose scene entitled "Desolate Day in Open Country," which was contained in Goethe's earliest draft of *Faust* and was never subjected to revision: Her youthful lover senses the vicarious meaning of her ruin when she is in prison as a child-murderess. He curses Mephistopheles for having kept the news of her plight from him. He is enraged at his companion's icily cynical remark "She is not the first" and then exclaims: "Misery and woe . . . o that more than one poor being should be whelmed in this swamp of wretchedness; that one first victim could not atone for the guilt of all others by its agony of suffering . . . The anguish of this one soul strikes me to the very heart, while you grin coolly at the fate of thousands."

This is only one example of many subtle interrelations that exist between the various parts of the poem. They follow their own laws, which are neither philosophical nor theological, but poetic.

A third important unifying factor can be seen in the figure of Mephistopheles, whose presence is felt in varying degrees from the very first scene to the last but one. It is fairly obvious, however, that he cannot simply be identified with the devil of Christian theology or folklore. He has, it is true, many of the outstanding characteristics of the Evil One, but frequently they are mixed with others or they alternate with quite undevilish qualities. It has been suggested that Mephisto and Faust must be understood as two sides or two aspects of one person—a very attractive and helpful suggestion, but for my taste a little too philosophical. The drama's own poetic law requires that we consider him a separate entity who comes as the agent of a force outside Faust's personality. Since this force is, according to the Prologue, not absolute evil, but rather roguishness, it is plausible that Mephisto turns out to be an enlightened gentleman who carries his wickedness becomingly and wittily much of the time. There are occasions when Mephistopheles appears more attractive, more interesting, yes: even wiser and more perspicacious than Faust. This applies to his conduct in the pact scene and in the scene in which he advises the freshman. In at least one instance Faust apparently shocks the devil himself by his lustful impatience: just after seeing Gretchen for the first time he gives Mephisto the order to go and win her for him. Mephisto says he knows her "for a thing of innocence . . . and over her the devil has no power." Unimpressed, Faust says rather crudely, "But, none the less, she must be turned fourteen," whereupon the devil expostulates:

> You speak like John the Libertine
> Who thinks he has a right to every flower,
> Knowing no favor and no honor
> Beyond his reach, to pluck it and devour . . .

In this case, you may object and say that Mephistopheles is only pretending to be on the side of virtue and that this is part of his technique to whet Faust's appetite, and that, anyway, he must have brought about the apparent chance meeting; for how is it that he knows all about her? Very well, then this would be another ambiguity and we should acknowledge ambiguity to be one of the poetic laws.

If we go to the second part, however, especially to Act III, the Helena-Act, we find such a different kind of Mephistopheles that you might very well be inclined to wonder what has become of unity and consistency. He has had to assume a classical disguise; to be suitable it had to be an embodiment of ugliness (rather than evil), so he gives up his very name and sex in order to become one of the Phorkyads, women of horrible aspect, possessing only one eye and one tooth among them. The greatest surprise comes at the conclusion of the Faust-Helena encounter, which was brought about with her help. Phorkyas speaks to Faust about a priceless gift which will allow him to soar aloft as long as he holds on to it. There is no suggestion of the diabolical in the following words:

> What things remain from all you had, hold fast.
> The robe, release it not! Already demons
> Begin to pluck it by the hems, in zeal
> To drag it to the shadow-realm. Hold fast!
> True, this is not the Goddess you have lost,
> But god-like is it. Take the priceless gift
> To serve the flight in which you soar aloft;
> 'Twill bear you swiftly up above all dross,
> On through the ether, if you can endure,
> We meet again, very far from here.

This is spoken as Helena follows Euphorion, the offspring of her union with Faust, into death and returns to Hades. The preceding stage direction reads: "She embraces Faust, her bodily form vanishes, her robe and veil are left in his arms." The veil symbolizes poetry. In his great poem, entitled "Dedication" ("Zueignung"), which opened the first volume of the first edition of Goethe's collected writings in 1787, truth is allegorically represented as an attractive female figure whose form has evolved out of the morning mist. She hovers above the poet and offers him as a gift:

> Woven from misty fragrance of the morn and
>   sunlight
> The veil of poetry from the hand of truth
> (Der Dichtung Schleier aus der Hand der
>   Wahrheit)

The veil will, so she promises, transform the noon's sultriness into a cool evening breeze if he will but throw it into the air. In our passage from the Helena-Act the transformation cloud-into-veil is reversed. After Phorkyas has spoken the line "We meet again, far, very far from here" the garments of Helena "dissolve into clouds; enveloping Faust they lift him on high and bear him from the scene."

The Phorkyad's preoccupation with poetry is not ended quite; she now gathers up "Euphorion's robe, mantle, and lyre, from the ground" (he was a poet) and "steps forward to the proscenium, holds up the spoils, and speaks." Note now that she changes her tone abruptly to what can quite readily be identified as Mephistophelian cynicism:

> This find I call a happy ending!
> What if the flame is done, past mending,
> It's not a world to weep about.
> Enough is left for poet's consecration,
> To stir up envy in their guilds devout;
> And if I can't provide the inspiration,
> At least I'll lend the wardrobe out.

(If we changed the word "poet's" to "graduates'" we would have an amusing motto for a college president's commencement address.)

At this point we can look again, more closely, at what was said before about Faust's early love for Margarete as playing an essential role in his eventual salvation. I mentioned that he never forgets her. We know nowadays that the unconscious mind does not forget. Goethe knew it too and he knew also the implication that the lapse of time has no meaning for the unconscious. Consider now what happens to Faust and the cloud which was Helena's robe and veil and is now his means of air travel. It transports him very far (as Phorkyas predicted), namely back from Greece to some "mighty summit of jagged rocks," presumably in the Alps. "The cloud parts and Faust steps forth." Receding, the cloud then resumes "a giant and yet a god-like woman-form" in whom Faust means to recognize Juno, Leda, or Helen. But then he discovers a wreath of mist still clinging to him "with a gentle cheer and cool caress." As it, too, gradually lifts itself up Faust says:

> . . .—Am I bewitched by pictured form,
> A glimpse of tender youth's high bliss I long had lost?
> The earliest treasures of the heart come welling up:
> Aurora's love, that means for me light-soaring wings,
> The first, so swiftly felt, scarce comprehended glance,
> Which, claimed and held, all other treasure could outshine.
> Now like the soul's pure beauty mounts the lovely form,
> Nor suffers change, but floats to ether far on high,
> And all that's best within my soul it bears away.

This witchery, this recollection of the earliest love, has been accomplished in poetry, with the help of poetry. It is in the nature of poetry, too, to be unconcerned with the lapse of time. Goethe said of Poetry that it was "bound neither by time, nor by place, nor by any person." A maxim, I wish to add, which Goethe took quite literally as his justification for confronting Helen of Troy with Faust, the Renaissance man, and for equating their offspring with Lord Byron, thus roughly spanning 3000 years and audaciously insisting that poetry brings all this easily within the confines of the unity of time. This may sound like a tongue-in-cheek statement; actually, its audacity has a deeper significance. For Goethe the reality of poetry transcends the reality of the phenomenal world, and his dramaturgy in *Faust II* rejects tenets according to which the action must "imitate" this reality. He could have said with Giuseppe Verdi: "It may be a fine thing to imitate reality, but to invent reality is much better." The reality which Goethe invented was the meeting of a flesh-and-blood Faust with a live, flesh-and-blood Helena. When the poet had written the first part of the third act (previous to the writing of Acts I and II!) and remarked to Schiller: "My Helena has really stepped on stage" ("Meine Helena ist wirklich aufgetreten"), I believe he felt that he had created precisely that kind of reality. Further elaboration of this intricate problem is called for.

Fascinating encounters between figures from different ages had, of course, long since been acceptable artistic devices, but the poets would designate one of the conferees as the ghost of a dead person or would locate the meeting in some otherworldly place, such as Hades, Purgatory, or Paradise, arrangements which would not lack credibility in ages when the reality of such places was scarcely doubted. In order to transcend Time (and Death), Space (and Life) had to be transcended too. When Dante meets Adam in the xxivth canto of the *Paradiso* the poet spans 6500 years. In Christopher Marlowe's *Dr. Faustus* the *ghost* of Helena appears to Faust, an episode which Marlowe found in the Faust chapbook. When Goethe in Act I of *Faust II* has Faust conjure up the shade of Helena in the course of his command performance before the Emperor and his court, he echoes the old motif, but in Act III he does something new: he has Faust meet the "real" Helena, in the Here-and-Now. The "Here" are "rich fantastic buildings" of a medieval castle just north of Sparta, the "Now," for Helena, is immediately after her return from ruined Troy. For Faust it is the time of the Crusades. It has been very difficult for the critics to accept this fusion of different time and place elements as "reality" within the poem. What Goethe did with Faust and Helena is, indeed, a highly complex matter, and it took him more than thirty years to complete the five acts of the second part. The framework within which he had to place them was the medieval pact between Man and Devil, a subject matter which was resuscitated during the waning of the age of Enlightenment. However, Goethe's Faust, as he delivers himself into the hands of his roguishly diabolical guide, disavows any interest in the Hereafter because no data as to its nature were available to man. Still, he is bent on exploring all the aspects and dimensions of life on this earth. In the "Classical Walpurgis Night" (Part II, Act II) we find him in search of the past, precisely: the mythological past of ancient Greece. The re-experiencing of classical antiquity had been one of the chief intellectual concerns of the second half of the 18th century (Lessing, Winckelmann, the Romanticists). The medieval trick of conjuring up the ghost of Helen of Troy in Faust's study or at the Emperor's court satisfied neither Goethe nor his contemporaries. They stood at the threshold of an age which wanted to know and experience history as it really was ("wie es wirklich gewesen ist"). So when Goethe *has* Faust produce the ghost of Helena before the Emperor, the show ends disastrously because Faust tries to seize her as if she were a physical reality. A second attempt to obtain Helena occurs at the end of the second act when the prophetess Manto guides Faust into Hades. Orpheus-like, he is expected to bring Helena back from the dead. Goethe had long planned to show Faust in Hades, moving the Queen of the Underworld to tears through his eloquent plea for Helena's release. Apart from a few discarded lines of this speech the scene was never written. Instead, we move directly into the third act: Helena appears on stage at the precise "historical" moment of her return from Troy. The fact that Goethe dispensed with the Orcus-scene is not accidental and hardly due to poetic impotence. It was deliberate and perhaps necessary. The aim of the scene had been to induce Persephone to permit Helena to "re-enter reality" ("wieder in die Wirklichkeit zu treten"). Goethe found it could be more effectively realized, I submit, if he removed the scene from the spectator's view and left it underground, so to speak, all the more startlingly then to present us with the accomplished fact of Helena's appearance on her native soil. This is the Helen, then, who comes to Faust and is "grasped" by him. Thus, if only for a moment, Faust experiences antiquity. However, it is an "impossible" undertaking—characterized thus by Manto herself—and had to end tragically. The symbolical meaning of the encounter may well be defined as a reliving on the part of Faust of that great part of the Western cultural heritage which is ancient Greece and which is gone forever, but it had to be represented as a momentary union between two people of flesh and blood.

If this interpretation of Goethe's artistic intent is correct, it should, moreover, be clear that the Helena act is not to be understood as a "dream play" of Faust's creative imagination. The attempt to explain it—or explain it away—in this manner is due to the persistent desire of interpreters to establish overt causal connections between the various parts of **Faust II** or, if they are absent, to find some substitute. Also, they seem to be unwilling to impute to Goethe what is taken for granted in the work of such 20th century writers as Pirandello, Cocteau, and Max Frisch: the discarding of empirical space and time as criteria of poetic "reality" within a work of art.

The transformation of the cynical Mephisto into Phorkyas and of the sinister and contriving Phorkyas into one who speaks with authority about the god-likeness of poetry and encourages Faust to grasp it so as to rise about all common things can now be seen as a plausible suppression, on the part of Goethe, of the devilish side of Mephistopheles in favor of the all-absorbing task of the Faust-Helena episode.

The Germans like to form compound words with the prefix *Ur-,* meaning "original" or "basic," so the Gretchen tragedy has been referred to as Faust's "Ur-erlebnis" or "basic human experience." The Helena-Act, by contrast, represents a "Bildungserlebnis" or "experience of an element of our culture." These two educational experiences of Faust are steps in a sequence which becomes progressively more subtle, but neither its aim nor its effect is that of a gradual moral perfection. The second of these two serves Faust not to become a better man, but to understand himself better and to grasp, in particular, the meaning of the "Urerlebnis" in all its depth—and unmarred by remorse. What happens here is part of the process which the Lord indicated when he said that he would lead this darkly striving man into clarity.

I have previously touched upon some of the ambiguous aspects of the figure of Mephistopheles. As far as the dramatic structure is concerned he has, however, a very clear function: He is the antagonist and not just a side-kick of Faust, not simply the servant, like Don Quijote's Sancho Panza or Don Juan's Catalinón, but rather a "high contracting party," as it were. He and Faust are grimly locked in a continuous struggle from the moment of the poodle's first appearance until the death of the 100-year-old dictator. Their association is an essential structural factor contributing to the unity of the drama. Mephistopheles is ever-present: he takes the professor out of his study, persuades him to go pub-crawling and witch-visiting, he makes assignations for him, he takes him hither and thither by various private means of transportation (magic cloaks, fire-breathing horses, pretty clouds, or instanta-

neous removal from this planet with the help of a magic key). When he is not at his side he is lurking in the bushes or waiting at the gate. Faust never quite knows what Mephisto might be up to when he is not looking. Just after the pact, Mephisto enacts a beautiful take-off of the professor and fills the mind of a delighted freshman with naughty advice. In Act I of Part II he rides in the back seat of Faust's carriage during the carnival and causes an uproar among the equally delighted, but outwardly scandalized, women through a lewd pantomime. When Faust has an accident and faints at the Emperor's Court Mephisto picks him up, takes him home, and puts him to bed. Then he not only watches over his sleep, but he helps Wagner produce Homunculus, the little airborne test-tube man who can read and interpret Faust's dreams while he dreams them.

I will not go into all the details of the pacts or wagers which were concluded between these two parties and, earlier, between the Lord and Mephistopheles. So much has been written about them! Let me stress only a few points concerning these agreements which furnish the framework and ground rules for the entire action of the drama: 1) The Mephisto-Faust deal is not forgotten in the course of the 2nd part; nor does the actual piece of paper get lost which Faust has had to sign in his own blood. Mephisto carries it on him and produces it when Faust has breathed his last. 2) We do not know the exact wording of the document Faust has signed. Mephisto did not compose it during the scene in Faust's study; he seems to have had a form ready. After all, one may expect the devil to carry the tools of his trade with him. The only hint we have of some of the small print on the form comes when, after the opening gambit, Faust wants Mephisto to state his conditions more clearly and the latter says:

> Well, here on earth I'll be obligated to serve you
> Will tirelessly comply with your least wish or
>   whim, while
> You shall undertake to do the same for me
> If and when we meet again in the beyond.

This is the conventional traditional gist of a Pact with the Devil. Faust is not interested in Mephisto's terms, for he has a low opinion of his services, and he turns the pact into a wager, betting that Mephisto will never be able to satisfy Faust with anything he can offer. 3) They shake hands after Faust has reformulated the agreement, the gist now being that Faust agrees to be carried off by the devil if and when he should discover a moment in his life with the devil that he could call "beautiful" or "fair" and whose passing he would deplore. In Philip Wayne's translation it reads:

> If to the fleeting hour I say
> 'Remain, so fair thou art, remain!'
> Then bind me with your fatal chain,
> For I will perish in that day.

There is no evidence that Mephisto changes the time-honored form so as to include this new-fangled condition; nor does Faust check on the text, contemptuous as he is of written agreements . . . surely, a strange way to conduct such important business! But, regardless of what the paper may say, Mephisto remembers Faust's wording when the blind old man is dead. 4) Faust dies after he has formulated his wish-dream of draining a swamp and setting a free and active race on the new-gained land, and, in anticipation of such an achievement, has exclaimed:

> Then to the fleeting hour I could say
> 'Remain, so fair thou art, remain!'

5) Thus it happens that as he savors such prospects of self-glorification, Faust discovers a moment worth living for. Note now the ambiguity of what follows:

Mephisto is greatly surprised:

> This wretched, empty moment at the last
> He sought, poor wretch, to grasp and hold it
> fast.

and he admits that Faust really never fell victim to the devil's temptations:

> Me he did sturdily withstand:
> Time wins, with Greybeard stretch'd out on the
> sand.

Yet, since the letter of the agreement has been fulfilled, he claims to have won his wager with Faust, and we almost sympathize with him, though the powers that be insist that the spirit of that agreement as well as the spirit of the Lord's pronouncements in the "Prologue in heaven" take precedence over the literal terms of the Faust-Mephisto agreement. The point is that Mephisto had received the Lord's permission to try to lead Faust gently down *his* path and the promise that the Lord would not interfere—a dubious promise!—because He was confident that a good man like Faust (He calls him His "servant") would in his innermost being remain ever mindful of the "right" path and, surely, the Lord would never be suspected of unfounded confidence.

So the cards are stacked against Mephistopheles: the Lord uses the rogue for his own creative purposes, and omniscient and omnipresent as He is, He has long since predicted the happy ending. We are left to marvel that the clever jester cannot see through this divine joke, and wish that he might at least have risen to the impish equanimity of Robert Frost, who wrote:

> Forgive, O Lord, my little jokes on Thee.
> And I'll forgive Thy great big one on me.

6) In any case the pact and wager framework makes it clear that, contrary to the Faust of earlier versions, Goethe's hero does not sell his soul or services to the devil and, even if he had tried to, the Lord would not have allowed him to do what is clearly not within the competence of a mortal, i.e., to dispose of his immortal soul. We know, however, that Faust had no intention to try since he declared expressly that the afterlife, if it existed, held no interest for him.

Having considered the unity of *Faust I* and *II,* first in the characters of the three chief *dramatis personae* and then in the contractual framework, and having realized that the drama follows its own (poetic) laws which cannot be grasped with ready-made concepts imposed from without, we will ask next: what manner of man is this Faust that he apparently commands so much attention even today.

He is evidently more than the historical figure of a 16th century quack doctor. Some see in him a representative man of the Renaissance, others see him as an 18th century man, others again say that he is a bit of both of these and modern man of the technical age to boot. I would say that he is all of these things but that the emphasis shifts and varies in the course of his long career. In his pre-pact days, especially in the opening monologue, we have a 16th century man in his "Gothic vault" who, like Vesalius or Paracelsus, rejects dry academic schooling and wants to learn from nature the secrets of life. At the same time his ardour is that of a pre-romanticist strongman or "Kraftgenie," who immediately after his hour of depression during which he signed the pact with the devil aspires to experience, in all its depth and breadth, what it means to be human:

> My heart, from learning's tyranny set free,
> Shall no more shun distress, but take its share
> Of all the hazards of humanity . . .

His ambition to expand his ego and explore all potential human experience and to ignore Mephisto's attempts at debasing him in a succession of cheap sensual delights finds fulfillment when he falls in love with Margarete. In his apostrophe to the Earth Spirit in "Forest and Cavern," he testifies to having thus found "deep secret wonders" revealed in his own heart.

In the 2nd part Faust is maturer, conscious of man's limitations, and willing to be satisfied with beholding the "colored reflection" of life instead of the

> . . .vision clear,
> How secret elements cohere,
> And what the universe engirds . . .

which he demanded in the opening monologue. We have already pondered over Faust's most classical stage during the Helena experience.

It is after this that Faust assumes some distinctly modern attitudes. His interest in science is revived, without the youthful emotionalism that aimed at penetrating the heart of the Universe. He is now interested in curbing the uncontrolled forces of Nature, "the useless strength of the unruly elements" that "saddened him to desperation" as he watched the ceaseless surge of the waves of the sea, not unlike the Lisbon earthquake that enraged Voltaire. But just as modern technology offers the means to exert vast powers over men and nations, so Goethe shows Faust keen on taming nature in order to become an owner of land and a ruler of men. The ambiguous light in which Faust the ruler is shown seems to reflect Emerson's statement that technical invention is a human calamity, or the saying of the Chinese sage that technicians have rotted the hearts of men. But Goethe was not a defeatist, and technological projects, like the draining of the Zuider Sea and the building of the Panama Canal, fascinated him as much as did pure research and had his approval. Himself an active experimental scientist as well as a statesman and administrator, he watched the early stages of the industrial revolution and knew the implications. No wonder that we find the old Faust involved in dreams of technological and social progress. The Faust of the opening monologue came into being about twenty-four years before the invention of the steam engine and seventeen before the outbreak of the French Revolution. The fifth act of *Faust II* was written several years after Napoleon was exiled to Elba and about concurrently with the building of the first railroad in England.

I should like to dwell briefly on the significance of Faust's last, vast undertaking on earth. Following the Helena experience, when we find him in the jagged mountains, the devil tries to tempt Faust with the riches of the world. This time Faust knows quite unequivocally what he wants and speaks with authority when he says to the antagonist:

> How can you know what man desires?
> Your bitter mind, where envy breeds,
> What can it know of human needs?

Then he proceeds to outline his plan to harness the forces of nature, which will give him power and possibly benefit mankind. Mephisto has to comply, although the goal will be reached by a rather devious route and by means that are not very savory: the two of them have to help the Emperor win a war in order to gain a strip of seashore on which to base their colonialist operations. These in turn are successful and lucrative as Mephisto uses slave labor and engages in world-spanning piracy; his motto is: Might is Right ("Man hat Gewalt, so hat man Recht"). It is in this whirl of unscrupulous activity that Faust daydreams of completing here "the masterpiece of human ingenuity" ("Des Menschengeistes Meisterstück"); then the Philemon and Baucis catastrophe occurs and Faust is pulled up sharply as he regrets his ill-tempered rashness. In the ensuing self-examination, heralded by the appearance of the four allegorical ghost-like figures of Need, Guilt, Distress, and Care (only Care wins access to Faust's presence), Faust arrives at this bold conclusion:

> I have not fought my way to freedom yet.
> Could I but clear my path of magic,
> Could I unlearn all spells and incantations
> To face you, Nature, as one man of men,
> It would be worth it to be human then.

Faust has almost come full circle: he wishes to be a mere man among men, but just as his restless curiosity did not allow him to be content for long on that Easter Sunday, so now he is not able to break the spell for long and after he has been blinded by the breath of Care he gives new orders to Mephistopheles. But at least he has realized finally what it would mean to be free and what it would mean to be a man among men, and that these are things worth living for. Even though he does not achieve the freedom he finds desirable, it is in connection with this insight about himself that he has the final vision of a free people on free soil. This is a goal which would make him wish for the fleeting hour to remain.

Goethe's treatment of Faust is ironical. He is not a satirist, the difference being that the satirist distorts while the ironist portrays what pertains to man on this earth "by leaving it as it is—namely, open. That means: he points at the inscrutability, perplexity, ambiguity, and perhaps also at the temporary nature and instability of the human condition."

In conclusion, I should like to focus on what might be called the representative stature of Faust. Aware of the danger of generalizations, I would say that he represents some essential aspects of European and, by extension—so as to include us Americans—of Western man. André Siegfried, the famous geographer and member of the French Academy, in his last lecture before his death, addressing a Franco-German audience in Ludwigsburg, said that a European considers man to be the measure of all things (after Protagoras the agnostic) and believes that he who helps himself will have the assistance of God ("Hilf dir selbst, so hilft dir Gott!" as the German proverb says). This implies a peculiarly Occidental skepticism: Man says there is a Providence but acts as though it did not exist. The very structure of the Faust poem is informed by this attitude. There is a double action: the tragedy proper and, like a belt around it, a mystery play, earthly and celestial, in time and in eternity. Only at one point does the outer frame intrude upon the earthly scene (the "Voice from above" at the end of Part I). As far as Faust is concerned he proceeds on his own strength, tacitly assuming that God, whose existence he never denies, will neither help nor hinder him. The Lord in the Prologue expressly withdraws his hand and yet expects Faust to arrive in the realm of clarity eventually. For Goethe man is a citizen of two worlds, but civilization in the Here-and-Now depends on his acting as though he alone were responsible and the Beyond did not exist. (pp. 55-72)

> *Ulrich K. Goldsmith, "Ambiguities in Goethe's 'Faust'," in his* Studies in Comparison, *Hazel E. Barnes, William M. Calder III, Hugo Schmidt, eds., Peter Lang, 1989, pp. 55-74.*

Liselotte Dieckmann   (essay date 1972)

[*Dieckmann is a German-born American educator and critic whose studies focus on the nature and history of various symbols in German literature. In the following excerpt, she analyzes symbolism, myth, and point of view in* Faust.]

An author who wants to present a man's life on earth might choose to do this by "realistic" means such as we find in most nineteenth-century novels. This was not at all Goethe's intent. Instead, he wrote a highly imaginative work, making full use of the fantastic possibilities of the subject matter. He tied his fantastic material to reality, however, by making the real as well as the imaginary material symbolic. Almost as in a medieval work, the reader has to be alert simultaneously to the immediate literal significance and to the larger symbolic reference of every passage. In the following [essay] I give some examples of this symbolistic technique.

Goethe's symbolism in *Faust,* though taken from nature like that of most other poets of his time, has a distinguishing character. In the first place, the nature images are almost always dynamic, that is, nature is shown in motion and flux. It is neither static nor picturesque. Almost every image and symbol can be shown to express some sort of motion, change, or development. In the second place, Goethe was very specially attracted to water in all forms.

Its ever-changing quality, its perpetual motion, the fact that it is a life-giving force—all combined to make it his favorite source of images and symbols. Thus Thales can say to the ocean:

> Everything out of water began!
> Everything does the water sustain!
> Ocean, grant us your ceaseless reign!
> Were there no clouds by you outspread,
> Were no rich brooklets by you fed,
> Nor rivers down their courses sped,
> Nor streams brimmed full bed after bed,
> Where would our world be, or mountain, or
>   plain?
> It is you who the freshness of life still maintain.

Goethe is particularly aware of the natural cycle of water. As it evaporates over the ocean, moves in clouds back to the land, falls as rain, collects to form springs and rivers, and flows back to the ocean, water affords an ideal image of the neo-Platonic world-soul, which similarly emanates into matter and then returns to itself. When Goethe, for instance, uses the waterfall as an image of man's life, he is fully aware of its "falling" quality within this cycle.

Another favorite source of imagery for Goethe is the neo-Platonic analogy between the sun and God (or mind, truth, etc.), and the changes from light to darkness and from darkness to light which reflect the condition of man. The dualism in Faust's own life . . . is expressed in this imagery. Goethe connects it symbolically with dualism of body and mind and uses it as a central image linking physical and spiritual life. Two striking examples of this symbolism may be seen in the first and last scenes in which Faust appears on stage. Both of these scenes are entitled "Night." The first is preceded by the angelic scene mentioned above, which is bathed in light; the last is followed by a light scene in which Faust's immortal part is carried upward. Thus the beginning and the end of Faust's life are set off on stage to symbolize his dark corporeal position on earth in sharp contrast to the scenes of brightness. This symbolism pervades the entire work. Even the devil understands it when he says to Faust: "Your lives alone by day and night are dated."

The work as a whole is written in clusters, or, to use one of Goethe's own terms, "tapestries" of symbols. Gold is such a complex symbol. It is a negative symbol because it is a destructive force. Whenever Faust needs gold, Mephistopheles has to procure it, whether as a present for Margaret or as the hidden treasure on whose presumed existence the Emperor bases his paper money. Gold is also connected with the volcanic eruption that disturbs the serenity of the Classical Walpurgisnight, just as it is seen in the veins of the Hartz Mountain in the first Walpurgisnight. It causes strife, war, and destruction wherever it is wanted, and falls therefore naturally under the dominion of Mephistopheles. In the Masquerade scene, when Faust disguised as Plutus displays gold, it turns into flames, expressing the court's greed and the illusory quality of possessions in general.

Another symbolic arrangement is that which Goethe himself called "mirror reflection." Faust is reflected in a number of figures such as the Boy-Charioteer, Homunculus,

Euphorion, Lynceus, each of them indicating and elucidating one facet of Faust's character. The mirror image of a woman that Faust sees in the Witches' Kitchen appears in the play as Gretchen, Helen, Galatea, Mary. The women themselves are in turn reflected in cloud formations. (See the beginning of Act IV.) Such reflections occur also for objects and events. The sun is reflected in the rainbow; water reflects life. Goethe has placed a large number of such "mirrors" in the work, bewildering us perhaps by their multiplicity, but orienting us unerringly toward the themes, characters, and events which they reflect.

The symbolistic treatment of the work makes it possible for the author to use as symbols both "real" and "mythological" characters and events. The Margaret scenes are a good example of this mixture since Goethe made a special effort to make her appear "real." Not only is she fully human, but in the events of her life preceding her encounter with Faust, time, place and causality are clearly indicated. We are in a "neighbor's garden," the time is evening, and the reason for her visit to the neighbor is that she has found in her room a little treasure chest of unknown origin which has no place in her regular, well-ordered life.

The chest, however, introduces Margaret to a new dimension of existence: It is on the instigation and with the help of the devil that Faust has put the chest in her room. And though her neatly ordered mind senses a mystery, her life has no defense against "demonic" forces. Thus a "mythological mode" is superimposed on her "realistic" existence and the union of the two modes of perception and presentation produces her bewilderment and ultimately her tragedy.

Myth, of which in *Faust* the demonic is part, is the creative poetic force that holds the work together. For *Faust* is not only a myth in its entirety; it is composed of myths and these are only partly of Goethe's own creation. They come from many worlds—classical, Germanic, Christian, neo-Platonic—and are intermingled freely with "real" characters. Thus Homunculus, whose origins lie in the neo-Platonic mysticism of the Renaissance, represents on a mythological level a modern view of evolution, and the marriage between the "real" Faust and the "mythological" Helen becomes a myth of art. All characters in the play are in fact equally real, regardless of their mythological features, since reality is measured only in terms of poetic reality. Hence, the monsters of the Classical Walpurgisnight appear more substantial and significant than the "real" characters at the Emperor's court who have to act out a masquerade in order to feel that they exist. The one standard applicable to all characters is that of poetic effectiveness.

Among the many myths on which the play draws, there is one which is disturbingly often taken to be part of the philosophical meaning of the work, though actually it is part of the mythological structure. This is the world of Christianity, which appears from beginning to end. Literally the Lord is present in the Prologue in Heaven, just as the Queen of Heaven is present in the last scene. There are moreover Christian scenes and references throughout.

The mere existence of a devil is of course a sign of the presence of a Christian world.

This Christian world is treated, in agreement with the general polar rhythm of the work, in two entirely different ways—positive and negative. Negatively, the Christian world is not mythological: The many direct quotations from the Bible used by Goethe himself as marginal notes or spoken by the main characters are intended to be blasphemy. Particularly frequent are references to the Trinity, which, in each case, is blasphemously represented to be worldly, illusory, or devilish. Plutus-Faust's words to the Boy-Charioteer are likewise blasphemous—"Beloved Son, in thee I am well pleased"—signaling at the very least a moment of outrageous hubris. Positively, on the other hand, Christian doctrines are treated as myth—though myths with universal appeal: The idea of a human Mother of God or the resurrection of Christ from the grave may move an unbeliever as much as a believer. Their hopeful promise is in fact the point for which Goethe uses them.

To be sure, these Christian scenes are not arbitrarily chosen. They are a natural and important part of the Faust legend, and, given Goethe's inclination to keep his hero in his original sixteenth-century environment, he must include the religion in which Faust was raised and from which he broke away. But within the frame of Goethe's work, they have no Christian meaning. The author does not aim, as the chapbook does, at Christian propaganda. The Christian imagery is simply a mythical setting for the hero's life and thought.

The case is only apparently different for the neo-Platonism that pervades the work. To be sure, Goethe longed in his youth to commune through nature with a world-soul. Even in his later years he kept a vision, however sober and restrained, of an all-pervasive life force, and continued to visualize this force as an animating world-spirit. But this was always less a philosophical than a mythical view. In fact, the neo-Platonic myth is the central myth of the work: The soul enters the body, suffers from the burden of the body, and happily returns to its source after death.

Intricately related to this body of neo-Platonic myth, but expanded by Goethe into a rich and separate mythology, is the world of magic, involving the innumerable spirits and demons who surround Faust throughout his life. The figures of the first Walpurgisnight and of the Witches' Kitchen are by and large of Goethe's invention. Those of the second Walpurgisnight he took from ancient, rarely quoted sources, but transformed them into creatures of his own. The grand irony of the second or Classical Walpurgisnight is that, while its characters are taken from antiquity (although certainly not from classical Greek literature), they are reshaped to transmit Goethe's very modern "myth" of evolution. All of these figures mingle easily in the poem with historical personages, who, in turn, receive a mythological coloring from their context, and all of them must be considered, ultimately, to be projections of Faust's own inner drives and subconscious forces.

Mythology is the pervasive mode of *Faust,* and as with all mythology, its truth is suspended between reality and fantasy.

Goethe's effort to present life as flux finds expression in the fact that nothing in the play is static; scenes, characters, natural events are presented on the stage in constant motion. Sometimes this motion is described, as when Faust tells us of the sunrise at the beginning of Part II: first the gradual change, occurring before the sun appears, from plain light to varying colors, then the coursing of the sunlight from peaks to valley, where it finally hits Faust's eyes directly. Similar techniques are used to describe movements of characters and events on the stage wherever they are too complex to be visually presented to the audience. Sometimes the motion is incorporated in stage directions:

> (Girl players, young and pretty, join the crowd: confidential talk is heard. Fishers and bird-catchers, with nets, rods and snares, come forward.)

And sometimes there are passages in which the motion of the characters is seen against a background that seems to fly by:

> Tree after tree, with what mad haste
> They rush past us as we go,
> See the boulders bending low,
> And the rocks of long-nosed sort
> How they snore and how they snort.

Even the beauty of woman has to be seen in motion to become an object of love. Chiron, the centaur who carried Helen of Troy on his back when she was a child, states that beauty which rests in itself is rigid, but that it becomes irresistible when it starts to move and overflow with joy and the love of life.

In the chapbook Faust has a strong desire to eliminate both time and space. He flies to the stars and, in thus overcoming the limitations of space, simultaneously overcomes time, at least for the nonduration of his flight. Goethe's hero, who is allowed a much longer life span, knows this desire too. But it does not have for him the urgency it has for the older Faustus, and although he wishes in vain that he could fly toward the sun, most of his desires are easily fulfilled.

What matters in Goethe's work is not the fulfillment of the hero's a-temporal and a-spacious wishes, but rather the creation of a poetic reality in which time and space have no realistic function except to represent dimensions of the mind and imagination. The overcoming of space is taken care of by the existence of a magic carpet which carries Faust and Mephistopheles wherever they want to go. In some instances there is even no carpet, and we suddenly find the strange couple in a place far away from that of the previous scenes. From the point of view of stage requirements, the overcoming of space is not really a problem. Goethe shows some of Shakespeare's sovereign disregard for changes in locale, and vastly enlarges on it. But he carries his delight in toying with space very far. When Faust leaves Greece, Helen's clothes transformed into a cloud carry him to the high Alps, and as he watches the disappearance of this cloud in the East, he sees simultaneously far in the Northwest the North Sea lapping the coast of the Netherlands. Neither Greece nor the Netherlands are literally named in this scene, but they are clearly suggested. As Mephistopheles joins Faust—using seven league boots—they step down in no time to the foothills where the battle of Act IV will take place.

Time is as easily overcome on stage as place, and Goethe uses every possible device at his disposal to indicate the timelessness of the events of Faust's life. We are dealing here, however, with a more complex problem. On the one hand, Faust, though at first rejuvenated, is subject to the laws of maturing and aging. We are never told his age nor how much time he spends in this action or that, until we learn, in Act V, that he is one hundred years old and that time, even for him, will "stand still." On the other hand, within the span of his long life, time operates in interesting ways to accomplish mythical events. Thus Helen of Troy, coming back to Greece after the Trojan War, walks immediately into Faust's medieval castle. She and her maidens travel from Sparta to the northern Peloponnesus in the time span of a few minutes, yet centuries pass of which we are unaware. Similarly, her son grows from childhood to adulthood within moments—and with his growth several further historical centuries are disposed of. Another reversal of time takes place in the case of Homunculus; having destroyed his vial at the feet of Galatea, he will start life at the beginning of time.

Even more complex is the treatment of causation and motivation. Cause-effect relationships in this mythical world are as loosely handled as psychological motivation. Sometimes they are supplied, but just as often as not the perplexed reader or listener asks in vain why certain events occur. We are never told why Faust should appear at the Emperor's court, or why Menelaos, although not coming on stage, should twice be heard. The reader is expected to take at face value so many astonishing things—such as spirits, monsters, and witches—that the absence of causality becomes as acceptable as the fluidity of time and space. Where causality is needed for the understanding of the meaning, however, Goethe provides it. In the purely human realm of Gretchen, causality is strictly adhered to, as it is again in the fifth act, in the story of Philemon and Baucis.

Psychological motivation is a somewhat different problem because it so greatly affects the believability of the hero. Goethe offers us a good deal of it, as when Faust despairs of the insufficiency of scholarship. But even here much of the motivation for action or suffering goes beyond directly determinable psychological sources. We must keep in mind that the work is more world oriented than mind oriented, and that its myths depict the external world rather than the human mind. Its purpose is often not to explore the depth of Faust's mind, but to place him in such a relation to the given world that he may view it without despair. The moments in Faust's life when his subconscious *is* suddenly revealed therefore stand out. Such moments occur with his reawakened childhood memory during Easter night, with the shudder that seizes him when Mephistopheles mentions the Mothers, with his sudden vision of Gretchen and the red band around her neck while he is dancing with a witch. Mostly, however, Goethe does not conceive Faust as a man burdened by memories.

Often psychological motivation is less significant than symbolic value. Faust's claustrophobic reaction in his study is a good example of the dual interpretation required in such scenes. While he certainly feels hemmed in and almost strangled by his environment, his response is also intended to convey to us a statement about the limitations of scholarship in general. Similarly, at the beginning of Act IV, when we find him in the Alps, we must be aware that the vastness of the view not only corresponds to Faust's desire for large views—in contrast to his former life in his study—but is at the same time a symbolic image of the growth of his mind. There are other scenes requiring dual interpretation. The beginning of Part II with its health-restoring magic is such a moment. After a night's sleep Faust's guilt feelings disappear. This is the naked psychological fact. But what we see on stage are the songs and actions of spirits whose words dispel the guilt feelings. The magic of the Witches' Kitchen with its awakening of sexual desires is likewise a psychological moment transformed into a symbolic scene. Even Faust's dreams are art works rather than memories. As a revelation of his subconscious they are, I believe, useless because they are too obvious, too complete, too formed into consistent images and stories. They resemble daydreams in which the mind *creates* a story rather than chaotic night dreams, rising from the subconscious.

As was noted earlier, man's inner drives manifest themselves in the poem as demonic powers. Goethe follows here the method of ancient myth, one of whose characteristic features it is to transform human forces into mythological characters and stories. Though the reader should recognize Goethe's intention to externalize internal events, he should not interpret these mythological features necessarily as allegories of the mind. Sometimes they represent Faust's own dark forces, but more often they are representations of universal energies surpassing the individual's narrow range.

If myth is the warp of the poem, irony is its woof. Faust's higher and lower soul—his spiritual striving, which is, for better or worse, coupled with his sensuous desires—clearly calls for a dualistic treatment. Mephistopheles is therefore provided to serve as the representative of man's physical nature, of the beast in man. In addition he makes a witty, ironic, cynical companion. The Lord likes him because he is a rogue. In contrast to Faust's humorlessness—a smiling Faust being completely unthinkable—the devil provides the play with laughter. Just as man on earth—like it or not—is tied to his body, so Faust is bound to his laughing, irreverent companion.

This is a blessing from a reader's or spectator's point of view. Without it, nothing would be more tedious than Faust's eternal yearning for idealistic solutions he never finds. But for every one of them Mephistopheles supplies the right ironic puncture. He deflates Faust as often as Faust begins to soar; and while this hurts the hero's finer feelings, he cannot escape the realization that Mephistopheles is partly right. So we have the alternately painful and ridiculous spectacle of a man whose appealing romantic yearnings are constantly dissolved in his companion's acid remarks. Mephistopheles' down to earth realism is actually closer to our own thinking than the ever-deluded dreams of Faust. The devil calls things by their true name, exposing the real motives behind the sham actions. No weakness or frailty escapes him, and he thus becomes, paradoxically, the only truly honest character in the work. Since he is not subjected to emotions, he can laugh where others suffer. But even his laughter is not offensive, because of its fundamental honesty and truth. Nothing and no one in the entire poem, including Helen of Troy, escapes being commented on mockingly by Mephistopheles, and often by other characters. Except for the angels, who have only one viewpoint, and Mephistopheles, who maintains the opposite point of view, no character in the play stands on solid ground. The function of the devil is precisely to prevent anyone's doing so. There is doubt, mockery, foul play in every phase of the work as soon as Mephistopheles appears on the stage.

Each time Faust realizes the truth of Mephistopheles' irony he gets angry. The closer the devil's irony hits home, the angrier he becomes. For him the ironic mode of his companion is disgusting and, although true, ultimately unacceptable. There is not a single passage in the whole work where Faust returns irony with irony. He can order the devil around, but he cannot rise above him to the point where the ironic stance would pass from Mephistopheles to himself. In this respect the protagonist never grows, and the function of the two characters and their interrelationship remains the same throughout the work.

Other characters in the work are mocked at with the same intent of revealing their weaknesses. The student who later appears as Baccalaureus is a prime victim of Mephistopheles' deflating irony. The philosopher Anaxagoras in the Classical Walpurgisnight, whose "volcanistic" theory of the origin of life Goethe despised, is made ridiculous when he sees the moon coming down to destroy the earth, an event on which Thales drily comments:

> What things the good man saw and heard:
> Myself I know not what occurred.
> Nor of such feelings was aware.
> Let us confess, there's madness in the air:
> Yet Luna yonder seems to hold
> Her course as calmly as of old.

At times, particularly in Part II, Goethe's irony turns even against the devil. We see him made fun of in the Classical Walpurgisnight by the ancient monsters who are older and wiser than he. At the end of the play we see him lose his bet, in a particularly ludicrous scene. The play thus takes back much of Faust's own seriousness through the author's ironic mode. Even the Lord in the Prologue in Heaven is spoken of mockingly by the devil.

The irony so pervasively present in the play is not its only deflating device. Satire—not frequently used by Goethe—is just as prevalent. From Faust's serious vows of eternal love for Margaret to the events at the Emperor's court, there stretches a line of satire which could hardly be more devastating to human institutions and beliefs. The court scenes in which the devil is allowed full play are an especially grand occasion for biting satire. Nor does the scope of Goethe's satire stop there. It hits the Christian religion and its institutions just as hard as the worldly institutions.

The church with a capacious maw is blest:

> Whole countries she has stowed away,
> Yet had no surfeit to this day;
> The church alone, dear ladies, can digest
> Ill-gotten goods with real zest.

Thus a duality of viewpoint is always present and we would be quite wrong to take sides. The rhythm of the play demands an alternation of high aspirations and devilish irony, each negating the other. Faust is not upbraided by a moralist, but laughed at by a wit whose realistic outlook on human nature is sharper and more penetrating than his own. Thus the danger of moralism is avoided without the loss of moral judgments. The reader must realize, however, that there exists a difference between a serious censure of evil deeds and the ironic posture that Mephistopheles takes. The devil cannot possibly wish to improve Faust's moral position. So, though the devil's irony lays bare Faust's weaknesses, these weaknesses are not condemned either by him or by the author. The serious reader may condemn them; the play does not. Irony thus adds a dimension to the dialectics of good and evil: It does not pass judgment, but holds a pointing finger up and smiles. (pp. 15-26)

> *Liselotte Dieckmann, in her* Goethe's Faust: A Critical Reading, *Prentice-Hall, Inc., 1972, 96 p.*

Henry Hatfield   (essay date 1983)

[*An American educator and critic, Hatfield is the author of numerous books on German literature and has served as editor of* The Germanic Review. *In the excerpt below, he assesses the Walpurgis Night scenes as powerful depictions of evil in* Faust.]

It is a striking but not really paradoxical development that the Walpurgis Night became a literary motif or theme in the eighteenth century, a period when superstitions about witchcraft radically declined. [The critic adds in a footnote that "Walpurgis Night is the term generally applied to a great convention of witches and devils taking place in remote, usually wooded mountainous areas where they hope to be safe from detection. . . . The Brocken, also known as the Blocksberg, the highest elevation in the Harz Mountains in East Germany, is probably the most famous meeting place for the unholy tribe; it was there that Goethe's Faust repaired in search of adventure, wishing to experience the lowest as well as the highest possibilities of mankind."] This of course was the work of the Enlightenment, whose founding fathers long preceded the century of Voltaire and Lessing—men like Johann Wier and Friedrich von Spee, as well as such later figures as Defoe and Michelet. When, late in the century, the countervailing movement, Romanticism, took up the Walpurgis theme, it was a literary rather than a visceral phenomenon. Goethe, whose *Walpurgisnacht* in ***Faust*** was the model for all the important literary "Sabbaths" known to me, was equally outstanding as an *Aufklärer,* a pre-Romantic, and a Romantic even though he gave unconditional allegiance to none of these schools of thought. No significant creator of a Walpurgis Night believed in its myth, but the most outstanding, writing *as if* they believed, wrung symbolic truth from the ancient fiction. (p. 56)

[Goethe] never literally believed in the legends treated here. He saw their potential as symbols, however; thus witches, attractive or ugly, were admirable expressions of sexuality; the Brocken itself an apt mountainous setting for a whole parliament of evil, a hell—or rather semi-hell—transposed upward. As for the devils, Mephistopheles himself points out that men are rid of the Evil One; evil persons remain. If Goethe did not have enlightened, rational objections to the grotesque medieval creations, he often had aesthetic ones. After his first Italian journey (1786-88), his taste was formed primarily on Raphael, Palladio, Graeco-Roman statues, and in literature, on Homer above all others. Obviously, he was a poet of great "negative capability" and, even in his years of extreme classicism, around 1800, could capture the exuberance of witches as they flew up to their rendezvous on Walpurgis Night or the outspoken eroticism of a naked sorceress. Yet Winckelmann's aesthetics, as well as enlightened philosophy, modified and moderated his view of witchery. Some elements of the witch tradition, however, were too crude for him. As we shall see, Goethe dropped a powerful, truly infernal song from his portrayal; similarly, he cut the dominating figure of Satan as the all-powerful black goat.

Although one of the most "Gothic" scenes in *Faust,* "Witch's Kitchen", contains in miniature virtually all the elements of a full-fledged Walpurgis Night; although in it we have both sensual beauty and grotesque literary and political satire, comic touches (some of them sadistic), and references to old superstitions, it is in the "Walpurgis Night" proper that the drama of *Faust I* reaches a climax. Faust there descends to the lowest of his many experiences but turns away from it, however belatedly. The action of the Walpurgis Night follows immediately upon the terrifying scene "Cathedral", which presents Gretchen in the very depths of despair. She swoons—as Barker Fairley put it [in his *Goethe's Faust,* 1953], the poem itself swoons—and we move from Gothic darkness to the ultimate blackness of the Witches' Sabbath. There is no reason to reduce it to a mere erotic dream plus nightmare of Faust's.

The scene shows Mephisto's effort to keep the protagonist away from Gretchen. Faust weakly complies, almost to the end. Further, the devil obviously hopes to win the wager for Faust's soul, seducing him from activity by tempting him to join in wild orgies and by displaying startling, infernal spectacles. Or one can explain Faust's behaviour in terms of his resolve to experience intensely the highest and the lowest and to "appease glowing passions". By showing us Faust at his worst, Goethe has really forced him to change course and to try at least to return to his deserted love. Otherwise the Lord's designation of him as "a good man" would be proved false—which would be unthinkable. Note that the peripety is linked to the recognition: seeing or thinking he sees Gretchen he becomes a different person, no longer interested in phantoms.

As one might expect, the scene has been purged of much that is ugly and shocking in the accounts of the Witches' Sabbaths in Praetorius or the *Hammer of Witches.* The dreadful fear of betrayal and punishment—the spectre that haunted the witches' gatherings—has gone. Only a writer sceptical about witchery could humanize these conventions, managing to avoid debunking on the one hand and superstitious credulity on the other. Passages of satire on contemporary figures have nothing to do with the story of Faust, but they remind the reader that he is being presented with a fictive and highly composite scene.

Steering a middle course, Goethe depicts the fat, vulgar witch Baubo but deletes the powerful infernal chant intoned by Satan and an adoring chorus. Baubo, gross and bawdy, specializes in obscene jokes and masturbation. In Goethe these details are not mentioned but the point is made indirectly: she rides on a sow, which is her symbol; Baubo is the mother figure of witchery and has a large following of lesser creatures. The suppressed chant celebrates sex and gold in an extraordinarily crude manner. Like a modern guru combining oversimplified Marx with oversimplified Freud, Satan presents the two entities as *the* pillars of all life. Or, in the words of the chant, they reveal the trace of eternal life and deepest nature. Satan, as Goethe implies, has degraded nature by putting it into this context. As one who, following Spinoza, equated nature with God, the poet was apparently incensed by this Satanic interpretation. Hence, at least in part, the savage language of these verses, which might well have shocked the frequenters of Joyce's Nighttown.

Turning back to the text, we find Faust and Mephisto climbing the Brocken, that citadel of the dark forces. They are seen near the villages of Schierke and Elend—villainy and misery—names which cast light on Goethe's attitude towards the whole milieu. Perhaps a contrast between the misery of the poor and the voluptuous doings on the mountain top is also intended. Faust senses the approach of spring; his companion feels wintry. Not only is he cold personally; devils as such are often conceived of as cold. Doubtless this helps them to bear the climate down below. Very gradually the tone shifts from an almost Dionysiac exuberance to the uncanny. Within the suddenly transparent mountain one sees gleaming gold—Mammon. A few lines later Lord Mammon is cited, almost identical with the metal but quite possibly the important devil mentioned in *Paradise Lost.* John Gearey [in his *Goethe's "Faust"— The Making of Part I,* 1981] points out the virtuosity of Goethe's treatment here: "The demands made upon poetry by 'Walpurgis Night' as it moves from night in the real world to the glow of the satanic realm are met to a degree where the scene seems to acquire a life of its own, like a dream. . . . "

For the first time we hear a chorus of witches in a brief song; it ends with typical coarseness: "The witch she farts, the goat he stinks". One can tone down the vulgarity of the "Sabbath" but not expunge it completely. And after all, rebellious women on a rampage hardly converse like elegant ladies in Proust or Henry James, yet for over a century or somewhat more the verbs in the offending line were cut, as was, more understandably, the conversation between Mephisto and the Old Witch. Generally, though, Goethe tends to rehabilitate "witches": they are vulgar but pathetic rather than evil.

Some voices lament that they cannot rise from the ground; despite all efforts, they remain sterile. Like the Half-Witch, they cannot keep the pace, suggesting writers who never produce. The reference to persons who cannot rise at this point is a sexual as well as a literary one. Imperceptibly, the summit has been reached; the wanderers from below meet the descending cloud of witches. The whole top of the Brocken, shown here as a plateau, is covered with witches, devils, and other questionable persons. Music is heard; a hundred bonfires have been lit. People dance, chatter, cook, drink, make love; as would be expected, many are naked.

The Huckster Witch shows her wares; she has no dagger or goblet that has not played a part in some vicious crime. When she mentions jewelry which has figured in the seduction of a lovable woman, or swords which served to stab opponents in the back, the reference to Faust's misdeeds is obvious. Apparently he is too self-centred to catch it, but if this encounter mirrors what he is trying to forget, as I think it does, then in his unconscious he has not forgotten the seduction of Gretchen or the murder of her brother. Whatever his offences, he is by no means a beast. He has a conscience which functions intermittently but does function. In an excellent note, Erich Trunz points out that the magical effect of the scene arises from the reciprocity of the inner and the outer world; the objective concretion of the myth symbolizes the internal sphere: the witch mirrors Faust's sexuality, and so on.

From here on, Faust encounters a series of more or less witchlike persons. Lilith, "Adam's first woman", but ultimately of Babylonian and Assyrian origin, is notorious for leading young men astray and killing small children; surely there may be a link here to Gretchen's half-crazed infanticide. As a seductress and vampire, Lilith leads up to the Young Witch. Erich Neumann notes, in his devoutly Jungian *The Great Mother,* the young beautiful seductress is often linked to the old, frighteningly ugly hag; just that happens here. Dancing with the Young Witch, Faust tells her of his "lovely" dream—sexual but still more or less within the limits of taste. He has climbed upon an apple tree and plucked two "lovely" apples—the symbol refers both to breasts and to the primal sin in Eden. Mephisto's comments on his partner are hard, not soft "porn"; they refer with graphic coarseness to the Old Witch's genitals; she does not resent the obscenity but matches it. Sex plus the diabolic is ugliness.

The poem shows Faust's shock when a red mouse jumps out of the Young Witch's mouth; in folklore mice are closely linked with witches, who often appear as red mice. Then a pale, fair young girl in chains reminds him of Gretchen; Mephisto identifies the apparition with Medusa. Probably Faust has projected his loved image on the phantom; Mephisto is simply lying.

With some reason, critics have felt that Goethe fails us here. Whereas Faust shows real sympathy for his lost love, he gives no indication that he will do anything about the situation, though this soon transpires. Before this occurs, however, Mephisto easily diverts Faust's attention to the pleasantries of the scene "Walpurgis Night's Dream". Faust has indeed responded, however briefly, to Gretchen's plight. His love for her seems to be based on memories of partly physical attraction and ensuing sexual love; this is far more honest than his rhetorical flights before the

seduction. This was no "platonic" love but something elemental and irresistible. Goethe may have felt that "a good man struggling in his darkness" might learn much in a Witches' Sabbath, but hardly find salvation there.

In Goethe's rendering, authentic evil appears only sporadically, yet his "Walpurgis Night" retains its power; we sense moral truth all the more sharply, perhaps, when there is no question of literal belief in the overt action. At least a few scholars have urged that Faust has been exposed to all the evil he can put up with; out of revulsion as well as feeling for Gretchen, he reverses the course of his life; as has appeared, "Walpurgis Night" contains the peripety of *Faust Part I.* Very true, but there is more to it. His rejection of witchcraft prefigures his renunciation of all magic, which is the peripety of *Faust II,* indeed of the poem as a whole, though that lay many years ahead in his career, as in Goethe's. Similarly, as Faust came to feel that witchcraft is evil and inconsequential in the long run, the poem implies, in the final defeat of Mephisto, that *all* evil is stupid. (pp. 57-61)

[The Classical] Walpurgis Night (written some thirty years after its predecessor) fits into the grand strategy of *Faust* more neatly than into the dark tradition of witchcraft. Restored to strength after the breakdown caused by his last heart-rending encounter with the doomed Gretchen, the somewhat chastened Faust will pursue worthier, less egocentric goals. In line with Goethe's conviction that the Greeks are the highest conceivable models of nobility and beauty, he must return to classical Greece. In the Second Part, the poet remarked, the reader enters a "loftier, broader, brighter world", than in the First.

Why then bring in the Witches' Sabbath motif? Goethe favoured a technique in which a theme or image would be brought back on a higher level; he tended to use the spiral as a metaphor for this type of structure. The reader notes that ugliness, guilt-ridden sex, witches, and the devil Mephistopheles recur but are marginal, and in Mephisto's case usually ridiculous.

Further, Goethe had come to realize that ancient Greece had, after all, a dark, superstitious, even vulgar aspect. Formerly, as in his *Iphigenia in Tauris,* he had seen Greece almost entirely through Winckelmann's eyes: his Greeks were noble; their art like their whole culture embodied chaste simplicity and serene grandeur. But Goethe's first encounter with Winckelmann had taken place some sixty years before. Goethe perceived an instinctual, more or less Dionysian side to Hellenic life which Winckelmann largely ignored or simply failed to see. Goethe did not try to refute his master in matters of art; he complemented him.

Finally, if Faust's adventures in Greece were limited to a pure, harmonious, even paradisiacal sphere, the element of conflict, essential for genuine drama, would be lacking. The magical, uncanny element does much to save the Hellenic sections of *Faust II* from being too close to the epic.

Goethe keeps much of the characteristic machinery of the Witches' Sabbath but the intent is now quite different. The tone and settings are frankly fantastic; there is no attempt to convince readers that what they see is "real". Quite often, characters speak ironically of themselves or of each other. We are presented with a supra-historical spectacle, reaching from the days of the Trojan War to Goethe's partial anticipation of the theory of evolution. Although grotesque figures abound, the thrust is toward beauty, toward life. In the first Walpurgis Night, Faust was escaping from reality, above all from his commitment to Gretchen; now he is moving circuitously back toward reality.

Faust seeks for Helen of Troy, as the avatar of the Greek spirit, even more as a gloriously beautiful woman. Twice Faust had "seen" the begetting of Helena—the famous encounter of Leda and the Swan. This union becomes a symbol of aesthetic, healthy sexual love.

The Classical Walpurgis Night begins in a properly eerie way. Faust and his companions arrive by a magical flight at the Pharsalian fields in Thessaly, in north-eastern Greece where Julius Caesar defeated Pompey in 48 B.C. Goethe invented the notion that the ghosts of certain lesser classical figures gathered here annually—a parallel to the yearly legendary celebration of the original Walpurgis Night. Appropriately, the opening is dark, for the battle illustrates the futility of war and specifically the end of Roman freedom. Thus the anniversary is a weird one—a *Schauderfest.* Yet while the "old" Walpurgis Night went from exuberance to gloom, the classical reversed the development, ending in a celebration of life. It has been noted that the Classical Walpurgis Night is not meant to distract Faust but to concentrate his powers.

Several details remind the reader of the earlier celebration. Glowing watch fires recall the bonfires that glowed at the summit of the Brocken. As a Northerner, Mephistopheles feels lost among strange, mocking spirits. Where before he could dance with witches unafraid, now he is surrounded and bewildered not only by witches but by more dangerous spirits. From the Harz to Hellas, he remarks, all these spooks are cousins. As Barker Fairley remarked, the passage shows the intimate bond between Puritanism and sin.

Before sinking into invisibility for the rest of the Classical Walpurgis Night, Mephisto himself undergoes a temporary metamorphosis. Goethe wished to use him as Faust's factotum in Act III, or "The Helena" as he liked to call it—more precisely to use him as the mistress of Helen's household. This of course entailed putting Mephisto into flowing classical robes, and yet preserving his negative character and ugly appearance. Among the most repulsive women in ancient mythology were the Phorkyades or Graeae, three weird hags who had only one eye and one tooth among them. He persuades them to lend him the appearance of one of them, and is now ready for his future role, disguised as a Greek woman. Ugly as Mephisto and his new acquaintances are, the thrust of this long series of scenes is away from the grotesque and toward the classic. (pp. 61-3)

In the meantime, the action becomes less and less Walpurgian. Faust's stature grows as he nears Helen; he is becoming a full-fledged hero. The language soars, and the act ends in a crashing climax fusing poetry, music, and spectacle. But that is another story. The Classical Walpurgis Night has led Faust to the gates of Helen's world. Like his earlier adventures, it will be not forgotten but transcended. (p. 63)

Henry Hatfield, "The Walpurgis Night: Theme and Variations," in Journal of European Studies, *Vol. 13, 1983, pp. 56-74.*

John R. Williams   (essay date 1987)

[*In the excerpt below, Williams examines the textual history of* Faust.]

Faust, if only because of its sporadic and protracted composition, can be said to reflect only erratically the literary and intellectual fashions and movements of the age of Goethe. Certainly, **Faust I** is unthinkable without the German Enlightenment, or *Aufklärung,* without the eighteenth-century tradition of domestic drama; and yet it is scarcely a typical product of the Age of Reason. The early draft form of the **Urfaust** bears clear traces of the preromantic *Sturm und Drang* (Storm and Stress) movement; but while **Faust I** is undoubtedly in many respects a romantic work, and while its final completion overlaps with early German Romanticism, it is not a product of the German Romantic movement as such, towards which Goethe preserved a distant and not uncritical stance. Nor does **Faust I,** on the other hand, reflect, except in very broad terms, the Weimar Classicism against which its final phase of composition was set. Paradoxically, for all the classical features of the second part, it was here that Romanticism left its mark in style, form and structure, in the theatrical irony and extravagance, in the lyricism, and in the often fantastic treatment of the subject. The operatic *Gesamtkunstwerk* of **Faust II** was not without influence on the later music dramas of Richard Wagner; and indeed much of the second part is devoted to the notion of a synthesis of the classical and the romantic, the ancient and the modern. Yet for all its eccentric 'modernity', **Faust II** is equally indebted to the traditions of Baroque theatre and spectacle, of the morality play and the *theatrum mundi.* Above all, however, its allegorical and thematic reference identifies it firmly as a product of its own age, the early nineteenth century.

It is not possible to say when Goethe first set pen to paper on the subject of Faust; but, since he mentions his early work on the play in the same breath as **Götz von Berlichingen** and his novel **Werther,** we can assume from this and from references in correspondence that a first fragmentary draft was written down at various intervals between 1769 and 1775. This 'Frankfurt manuscript' was taken by Goethe to Weimar in 1775, and we are told that he read from it to different audiences over the next few years. It is to this that we owe any knowledge of the early form of the work; for, on completing **Faust I** in 1806, Goethe evidently destroyed his earlier manuscripts, without realizing or remembering that a lady of the Weimar court, Luise von Göchhausen, had borrowed it and copied it some time during the late 1770s. This copy, rediscovered among the Göchhausen papers by the Goethe scholar and editor Erich Schmidt in 1887, was published by him in the same year under the title *Goethes Faust in ursprünglicher Gestalt nach der Göchhausenschen Abschrift (Goethe's Faust in its*

Original Form after the Göchhausen Copy). It became known as the ***Urfaust.***

The ***Urfaust*** version is not a complete play in itself, and was never thought of as such by Goethe; it represents only the state of composition at the time it was copied down—though this has not prevented its frequent and successful performance on the stage. Very broadly, it comprises the Gretchen tragedy of the final version of ***Faust I,*** with some variations and transpositions, but without the 'Wald und Höhle' and 'Walpurgisnacht' episodes, preceded by Faust's opening monologue, the first scene with Wagner, a version of the student scene and a version of 'Auerbachs Keller' which is in prose, except for the songs and the first eight lines. The action leaves many questions unanswered; not only the exact circumstances of Valentin's death, and of Faust's adventures between that and the prison scene, but also the crucial details of Faust's introduction to Mephistopheles, and of the nature of the pact between them, are missing. Moreover, Goethe has already in the ***Urfaust*** introduced a motif that has muddied the critical waters ever since. The parting words of the Erdgeist in the ***Urfaust,*** 'You are the equal of the spirit that you grasp, not mine!', can reasonably be taken as a reference to Mephistopheles, even as an undertaking by the Erdgeist that it will send to Faust a spirit that he can comprehend. And there is a clear suggestion in the later ***Urfaust*** prose scene, which corresponds to the 'Trüber Tag. Feld' scene of ***Faust I,*** that Mephisto was sent to Faust by an 'infinite . . . great, glorious spirit'. We shall return to the so-called 'Erdgeist controversy' in due course. Otherwise, while the ***Urfaust*** is theatrically perfectly viable, and while the Gretchen tragedy arguably works even more compellingly than in its final version of ***Faust I,*** where it is interrupted and retarded by several interpolated scenes, this prototype version of Part One is still bedevilled by the problem that the university scenes and the love action, the so-called 'Gelehrtentragödie' and the 'Gretchentragödie' ('scholar's tragedy' and 'Gretchen tragedy') are, largely because the former section is so sketchy and episodic, only loosely connected.

The ***Urfaust*** was the product of the 1770s in Germany, and it reflects as much as anything else the interests and enthusiasms stimulated by Herder and the nascent *Sturm und Drang* reaction against the more mechanistic aspects of mid-eighteenth-century rationalism on the one hand and against the slavish neo-classicism of the Leipzig school on the other. We must guard against over-crude distinctions here; the *Sturm und Drang* is unthinkable without the *Aufklärung* (Enlightenment), and indeed many literary historians will question the very term 'Storm and Stress', which was fortuitously and sensationally applied to certain short-lived aspects of late Enlightenment German literature in the 1770s. And Goethe's Faust drama, even in this initial form, is itself a product of the Enlightenment, of the literary, religious and intellectual emancipation of the middle-class intelligentsia in Germany, with its attendant literary forms—specifically, that of domestic drama.

Nevertheless, the inherent titanism of the figure and theme of Faust, the fascination of the genius or hero beyond the common run of humanity, the arrogant and amoral self-assertion of an intellectual giant, the defiant Prometheanism and the mythical symbolism of the Faust material—these are the elements of the Faust legend that appealed to the young Goethe, rather than the theological and intellectual allegory that, as far as we can judge, Lessing had intended to work into his Faust drama. The creative and literary models of the young Goethe were worlds away from the canonical Gallic neo-classicism advocated, indeed prescribed, by Gottsched and his school, and far enough, too, from Lessing's own reworking of Aristotelian poetics in his theoretical and dramatic works. The colossal impact of Shakespeare on the younger generation of this decade is attested in Goethe's euphoric ***Rede zum Schäkespears Tag*** (***Speech for Shakespeare's Anniversary***) of 1771, in Herder's Shakespeare essay, and in J. M. R. Lenz's dramaturgy; and it is exemplified equally extravagantly in Goethe's ***Götz von Berlichingen***—which overlaps with the beginnings of the ***Urfaust.*** And while Gerstenberg, Wieland, Eschenburg and Lessing himself had played a major part in the introduction of Shakespeare to the educated German public, it was Herder and the *Sturm und Drang* that championed an informal, anti-classical, 'open' form of drama on what they perceived to be the Shakespearian model: a contemptuous disregard for the dramatic unities; a vision of Shakespearian drama as unvarnished nature, and of Shakespeare as the 'interpreter of nature in all her tongues', as 'only and always the servant of nature'; and an exuberant response to the poetic appeal of Shakespeare's apparently chaotic universe, which was fused into an organic whole by the creative power of the poet. Whatever violence it may have done to Shakespeare's aesthetic, this was the model that informed Goethe's early plays and fragments.

It was also Herder who stimulated in Goethe a cultural enthusiasm for German history, turning his attention towards the fifteenth and sixteenth centuries, to figures like Dürer, Maximilian I, Luther and Hans Sachs, to the robust language of the vernacular Bible, to the idiom of *Knittelvers,* to the national past of an Empire that was even then tottering on its foundations, and was only a generation away from final extinction in Goethe's youth. It was this enthusiastic and, to be sure, chauvinistic perception of the religious, artistic and literary vigour of the German Renaissance and Reformation that Goethe held up as a mirror to his own age; and it produced, among other things, his ***Götz von Berlichingen***—a Shakespearian chronicle drama based on a somewhat fanciful historicism and on the heavily partisan autobiography of the embittered and disillusioned Gottfried von Berlichingen—and his poetic and symbolic treatment of the shadowy figure who haunted the cultural fringes of early sixteenth-century Germany, Faust.

Herder was also responsible for another major influence on the style and content, perhaps also on the structure, of the ***Urfaust.*** The *Sturm und Drang* assertion of nature against sophistication, of creative originality and freshness against academic and derivative formalism, had found its most vivid formulation in Herder's essay 'Über Oßian und die Lieder alter Völker' ('On Ossian and the Songs of Ancient Peoples') which opened the *Sturm und Drang* manifesto, *Von deutscher Art und Kunst (On German Character and Art)*. This rhapsodic treatise affected contemporary aesthetic values and perceptions and, above all through Goethe, infused the folksong idiom into German poetry of the time. As in his judgement of Shakespeare, it is the 'spirit of nature' that is for Herder the overriding characteristic of the poetry of unsophisticated peoples, of the bards and minstrels, of the sagas and epics, of Homer and Ossian—that is, of poetry before 'art came and extinguished nature'. Uncritical, unsystematic and indeed plain wrong as many of these assumptions were, the effect was radical; and Goethe, encouraged by Herder to pillage the Alsatian countryside for folksongs from the mouths of ancient peasants, also transformed the material he found into the seemingly artless songs that are part of German literature: **'Heidenröslein'** and **'Der König in Thule'** are two outstanding examples, one of which was actually incorporated into the **Urfaust.** The story of Faust and Gretchen shows, among other literary influences, the traces of the *Sturm und Drang* perception of the folk-ballad tradition—in its frank treatment of a classic story, in the 'Sprünge und Würfe', the gaps and leaps in the action, that Herder had recognized as a salient characteristic of popular poetry, the 'aerugo' or patina, the weathering effect of oral transmission. It has, indeed, been suggested that Goethe changed the name of the traditional Johann Faust to Heinrich because 'Heinrich and Margarete' are names redolent of the ballad tradition. For all the metaphysical and theological dimensions of the Faust legend, it was a combination of the lyrical idiom of folksong, the robust vulgarity of the stage tradition and the popular appeal of the chapbook narratives that Goethe was at pains to preserve in his original drafts—in short, what he vividly termed the 'woodcut-like' character of the sixteenth-century fable.

A further major factor that attracted Goethe to the Faust legend was his interest in what he called, in *Dichtung und Wahrheit,* 'mystischkabbalistische Chemie'—an early enthusiasm which, he tells us, he was careful to conceal from Herder's sarcastic attention. Goethe's lifelong preoccupation with alchemy and astrology, with the mystical and hermetic traditions of the Middle Ages and the Renaissance, is generally believed to have been stimulated by his close relationship with a pietistic friend of his mother, Susanna von Klettenberg, during the period of convalescence in Frankfurt from the illness that had cut short his studies at Leipzig. Together with this sympathetic companion, who, as Goethe put it in his retrospective autobiographical account, had 'inoculated him with the disease' of cabbalistic science, he explored the hermetic and neo-Platonist writings: Welling's *Opus mago-cabbalisticum,* Basilius Valentinus, Paracelsus, the *Aurea Catena Homeri,* and Gottfried Arnold's *Unparteiische Kirchen- und Ketzerhistorie.* Even the physician treating his illness, according to Goethe, dabbled in herbal medicines and alchemical preparations, which he (illegally) dispensed himself and administered to receptive or interested patients, along with 'certain mystical chemical and alchemical books'.

It is likely that Goethe's interest in Paracelsus, Agrippa and other hermetic writings predates this convalescent period of 1768-9; and, while it was probably during this peri-od that he actually practised experiments in the field of alchemy and proto-chemistry, his interest in and knowledge of alchemy, astrology, neo-Platonism and hermetic mysticism extended through his whole life and, in one way or another, informed much of his creative and theoretical writing—to some degree, at least, Goethe was not unlike Newton. Just how far he ever believed in any literal sense in the truth or efficacy of such theory or practice is difficult to say; what is certain is that, well after his early interest in that tradition as an 'imaginatively serious phenomenon', he retained a strong sense of the symbolism and poetic resonance of alchemy and astrology, and that his use of such material is informed and authoritative, whether he is drawing on it to convey the 'authenticity' of visions and magical incantations, whether he is using it for overtly satirical or sarcastic purposes, or whether he is exploiting it for allegorical and symbolic reference in his **Märchen (Fairy Tale),** or in the figure of Homunculus in **Faust II.**

One further literary tradition should be mentioned in connection with the **Urfaust:** that of domestic tragedy, or *bürgerliches Trauerspiel.* This relatively new tragic genre, the literary precipitation of the growing economic power and assertion of the middle classes in the eighteenth century, had found its way into Germany from England and France under the influence of Lillo, Diderot and Mercier; and it was Lessing who, struggling to establish a native theatrical tradition in defiance of the prescriptive neo-classicism of Gottsched's Leipzig school, had devised in his *Hamburgische Dramaturgie* the theoretical framework for domestic realism in the drama.

It is by no means clear how far Goethe in his **Urfaust** was writing consciously or unconsciously within the tradition of *bürgerliches Trauerspiel.* For all the homely domesticity of parts of the Gretchen tragedy, there is not a great deal of common ground, apart from the basic story of the seduction of a simple girl by a 'gentleman', and of the ensuing pregnancy, abandonment and infanticide, between Goethe's treatment of the theme and the social drama of his contemporaries. Certainly, Lessing's criterion of characters who are 'of the same stuff' as the audience—'mit uns von gleichem Schrot und Korne'—can scarcely be applied to Faust, let alone to Mephistopheles. And we see little enough of Gretchen's family in the **Urfaust**—though Valentin's rigid sense of family honour and respectability is consistent enough with a line of domestic autocrats from Lessing's Odoardo Galotti or Wagner's Meister Humbrecht to Schiller's musician Miller. We know Gretchen's petty-bourgeois milieu largely by hearsay from her own account, from Faust's sentimentalized perceptions, or—most briefly, but vividly—from the censorious gossip of Lieschen at the well. Nevertheless, the milieu and its ethos are there; and it is precisely the homely idyll of this circumscribed domestic world that attracts Faust's restless and destructive temperament and creates the collision of divergent social, psychological, intellectual and sexual assumptions. . . . But if this is domestic drama, it is domestic drama with a supernatural dimension; and the **Urfaust** remains a hybrid and fragmentary work, the two distinct elements of 'Gelehrtentragödie' and 'Gretchentragödie' being juxtaposed, and only to a certain extent integrated.

The second major phase of work on *Faust* overlaps with a momentous experience in Goethe's life, his Italian journey of 1786-8. He had entered into a contract with his publisher Göschen for an edition of his works; and this was no doubt why, even on his apparently precipitate departure from Karlsbad for Rome (in fact, a plan long since devised and cherished), he took with him to Italy a number of uncompleted projects, among which was the 'Frankfurt manuscript' of *Faust,* or at least a form of it. It is not possible to establish how much, or exactly which, new material Goethe wrote in Italy, and how much was written after his return to Weimar in 1788. It is often assumed, largely on formal grounds, that the scenes 'Hexenküche' and 'Wald und Höhle', or parts of them, were completed in Italy; but this is inconclusive, since Goethe made every effort to think himself back some fifteen years in order to integrate the new material into the *Urfaust* version—as he put it in a letter from Italy in 1788, if he 'smoked the paper', no one should be able to distinguish the new material from the old.

The *Fragment* drops the atmospheric little scene 'Land Strasse' ('Country Road') that prefaced the Gretchen tragedy in the *Urfaust,* and, sadly, removes some of the more robust vulgarities of the student scene. 'Auerbachs Keller' is recast in verse; more significantly, Faust now, in contrast to the earlier version, takes virtually no part in the pranks, standing silently by as Mephisto performs them in his stead. The new 'Hexenküche' ('Witch's Kitchen') scene is written in to help to bridge the *Urfaust* gap between the university scenes and the Gretchen tragedy; it also appears to contain, as we shall show in the commentary below, some allusive references to the contemporary political situation in France. The most significant additions in the *Fragment* are: the hundred lines of dialogue between Faust and Mephisto; a further twenty-two lines of dialogue after the student scene; and the hybrid 'Wald und Höhle' ('Forest and Cavern') scene, which incorporates Faust's violent tirade of self-hatred that had, in the *Urfaust,* been placed after the Valentin scene. The Faust-Mephisto dialogue still tells us nothing of the means by which Mephistopheles was introduced to Faust, nor of the nature of the pact between them.

Otherwise, the most striking feature of the *Fragment* is that it breaks off abruptly at the end of the cathedral scene—in spite of the fact that Valentin's first monologue, and the last three scenes 'Trüber Tag. Feld' ('Dreary Day: Field'), 'Nacht. Offen Feld' ('Night: Open Country') and 'Kerker' ('Dungeon') had already been written in the *Urfaust.* It seems that Goethe felt there was a gap in the action at this point that needed to be filled; it was the gap into which he later wrote the 'Walpurgisnacht'. The *Fragment* was published in volume 7 of Goethe's works, the *Schriften,* by Göschen in 1790.

It was largely at Schiller's prompting that Goethe resumed work on the third and final phase of *Faust I.* As early as 1794, Schiller had begged Goethe to let him see the unpublished material relating to the *Fragment,* which he described as a 'torso of Hercules'. It was not until June 1797, however, that Goethe felt inclined to resume serious work on *Faust,* and he made a revealing remark in a letter

to Schiller of 22 June that year. Their common interest in the ballad form, he said, had brought him back to this 'hazy and misty path'—'diesen Dunst- und Nebelweg'. It seems it was the impetus of their collaboration on the ballad, one of Goethe's early *Sturm und Drang* enthusiasms, that led him back to his Faust material; but this remark also betrays the effort of will and imagination required, now even more than some ten years previously, to think himself back into the alien, unclassical material of the Faust legend. 'Dunst und Nebel', a phrase suggestive of what now seemed to him the immature and confused time of his initial preoccupation with the theme, are indeed the very words he uses in the dedicatory poem 'Zueignung', also written in 1797, with which *Faust* opens, and in which he describes his ambivalent feelings at resuming work on the popular and romantic subject of Faust: blurred memories and figures from earlier times rise around him 'out of haze and mist.'

Schiller had also, as he so often did, urged Goethe to impose on the episodic and heterogeneous material of his earlier drafts the conceptual unity of an overall symbolic idea. For all its poetic individuality, Schiller wrote, the drama required a symbolic dimension; the demands of the theme were both poetic and philosophical, and, whether he liked it or not, the nature of the subject would impose on Goethe a philosophical treatment—his imagination 'would have to adapt itself to the service of a conceptual idea'. With characteristic critical acumen, Schiller diagnosed the inherent problems of the *Urfaust* and *Fragment* versions: the problem of unity, the imbalance between the tragedy of Faust and the tragedy of Gretchen, the tension between the representative and the individual status of the central figure, and the lack of a clear, indeed of any, metaphysical or symbolic superstructure for the disparate experiences of Faust. And while Goethe may have chafed under Schiller's insistence that he should submit his poetic imagination to a conceptual framework; while he may subsequently have declared that there is no single 'idea'—such as the issue of Faust's salvation—that informs 'the whole and each particular scene'; while he may have protested that, unlike Schiller, who was one of those 'who work too much from the idea', he himself had never striven for abstraction, or sought to hang his works 'on the meagre thread of a single consistent idea'—nevertheless, it seems that Goethe was not unresponsive to Schiller's strictures and observations. It was no doubt in part due to Schiller's advice that in 1797 Goethe wrote, apart from the opening dedicatory poem, the two scenes 'Prelude in the Theatre' and 'Prologue in Heaven' that encapsulate the dramatic action of *Faust* within a wider framework.

It was over the next three or four years that Goethe went on to complete *Faust I;* and we can assume that he had by now some idea of contriving Faust's ultimate salvation, even if the final stages of the process were not to be fully formulated until some twenty-five years later. Above all, what he referred to as the 'great gap' ('große Lücke') of the pact and wager scene was filled out in a way which, in conjunction with the issues raised in the 'Prologue in Heaven', leaves open the possibility, if it does not suggest the probability, of Faust's redemption. Also added was the first 'Studierzimmer' ('Study') scene, detailing the introduction of Mephistopheles, and, as a prelude to this, the 'suicide' scene and the 'Easter Walk', or 'Vor dem Tor', scene. A further odd, and not entirely happy, change in the construction of *Faust I* was the transposition of the 'Wald und Höhle' scene to an earlier stage in the Gretchen episode—as it seems, to the time *before* her seduction by Faust, rather than after, as in the *Fragment.* The problems and implications of this shift are discussed in the commentary below. The Valentin scene (the brief monologue of the *Urfaust* had disappeared from the *Fragment*) was now re-introduced, but before the cathedral scene, not after it as it had been in the *Urfaust;* and it was extended to include Valentin's death and his denunciation of Gretchen. No doubt the dramatic sequence was thereby improved, since Valentin's curse, and his death, lend added force to the awesome and claustrophobic scene in the cathedral, where Gretchen's guilt and remorse overwhelm her; moreover, this crisis is also now directly followed by the nightmarish 'Walpurgisnacht'—a powerful transition exploited by many producers of the play.

The 'Walpurgisnacht' was a further important addition to the dramatic and theatrical dimensions of the work; the same cannot be said of the feeble satirical intermezzo, 'Walpurgisnachtstraum', or 'The Golden Wedding of Oberon and Titania'. There is, however, some evidence, to which we shall return later, that Goethe originally planned a rather different form and function for the 'Walpurgisnacht', which was to have been integrated more closely with the fate of Gretchen. The remaining principal alteration undertaken in the final writing of *Faust I* was the versification and revision of the final 'Kerker' scene. This scene was recast in verse, as Goethe wrote to Schiller, in order to mitigate the direct effect of such harrowing material. But if the final version is any less harrowing than the *Urfaust* scene, this is due not so much to the change from prose to verse as such but rather to the consequential changes and extensions in the text—the revised version is less starkly economical in expression than the *Urfaust* scene. Presumably for the same reason—in order to introduce a note of reconciliation into the stark human tragedy of Gretchen—Goethe added the theatrical assurance of her salvation in the voice from above, answering Mephisto's 'Sie ist gerichtet!' with: 'Ist gerettet!'.

For all his intensive work on *Faust I* between 1797 and 1801, it was another five years before Goethe brought himself to a final revision—ironically enough, after Schiller's death. Political disruption in Germany, the Napoleonic invasion and occupation of most of the German territories, further delayed its publication until 1808, when it appeared as Volume 8 of the Cotta edition of the Collected Works (*Goethes Werke*). A further interesting feature of Goethe's work on *Faust* around 1800 is a poem entitled 'Abschied' ('Farewell'), which, also written in four stanzas of *ottava rima,* was evidently intended to serve as an epilogue balancing the formally identical poem 'Zueignung'. Whereas the prefatory poem had described Goethe's mixed feelings at resuming work on the intractable subject of Faust, the valedictory 'Abschied' expresses his unequivocal break with the literary and emotional confusions of his youthful masterpiece. Goethe looks back from the present vantagepoint of his high classicism, from present

clarity, to the narrow and barbarous circle of magic and superstition, to the obscure German past that had been the creative context for *Faust I.* It is clear from this poem and from Goethe's correspondence that, for all the care he took to fuse the new material of this third phase of composition with the earlier versions, he felt profoundly out of sympathy with what he frequently refers to as 'this barbaric composition', 'the nordic phantoms', 'nordic barbarism', 'this witches' product'. What is remarkable is not so much that Goethe left certain loose ends untied in his final version of *Faust I*—the Erdgeist question, the 'Walpurgisnacht' and its odd sequel, or the whole question of Faust's salvation—but rather that he should have brought it to any kind of completion.

The poem 'Abschied' does not, however, as is often assumed on the evidence of its first stanza, mark Goethe's intention at the time of breaking completely with the subject of Faust—though it was to lie dormant for some twenty years after 1806, and it was indeed fortuitous enough that the second part was eventually completed. In fact, this 'epilogue' might even have been conceived as a prologue to the projected second part, for in the following stanzas he talks, not of abandoning the subject, but only of turning his back on the 'emotional confusion', on the 'narrow circle of barbarities and magic', and of redirecting his vision in place and time away from the violent political convulsions of the present day: eastwards towards Greece, and backwards to the ancient world. This is not only in general terms an expression of Goethe's philhellene high classicism of the decade 1795-1805; it can also be taken as a specific reference to the dramatic fragment also written in 1800, entitled 'Helen in the Middle Ages' (*Helena im Mittelalter. Satyr-Drama. Episode zu Faust*). These 269 lines of dialogue between Helen, her chorus and Phorcyas correspond to the opening section of the third act of *Faust II,* which was rewritten in 1825-6 when Goethe once again resumed work on *Faust.*

It is extraordinary to us, now, how patronizingly and dismissively Goethe treated, or at least appeared to treat, the work that has come to be regarded as his undisputed masterpiece; and it is odd to recall that at the time he seemed to regard *Faust I* as no more important, even as less important, than his preoccupation with classical aesthetics or his scientific research into optics. This is not to suggest that he failed to take *Faust I* seriously; after all, he did finally complete the project, if only with a considerable effort, and he took great pains to organize the 'barbarous' material and to give the work, which by its very nature tended towards a chaotic linear formlessness, an overall theatrical, theological and metaphysical framework. Critics who detect in the 'Hexenküche' or the 'Walpurgisnacht' sections an ironical or disdainful dimension absent from the *Urfaust* version may well be correct; but they are judging with the hindsight allowed by the discovery of the Göchhausen manuscript.

Nor can it be conclusively argued that Goethe, in giving the final version of *Faust I* a quasi-Christian framework, was thereby wholly ironizing or demystifying the religious assumptions that, for him, were largely responsible for the diabolistic trappings of the traditional legend. It is of course true that Goethe was no orthodox Christian believer; it is true that for all his earlier and later admiration for the Reformer, he deplored Luther's vision of a world infested by devils; it is true that the 'old heathen', above all in his commitment to pagan classical culture and civilization, regarded Christianity with more or less baleful mistrust and suspicion—especially in its more extreme manifestations among the younger generation of German Romantics; and it is true that he described the Middle Ages in a letter to Iken as a period of 'monkish barbarism', and in *Faust II* as a 'benighted age of chivalry and clericalism.' But Goethe knew and acknowledged—indeed, this recognition underlies the very fabric of *Faust II*—that he was, willy-nilly, the product of a Western, Germanic and Christian tradition. And for all his nostalgic Hellenism, he acknowledged that ancient Greece was an ideal—an imperishable ideal, but an irrecoverable one. Even at his Hellenic perihelion, as it were, at the time of his greatest attachment to classicism and his furthest alienation from Christian and Germanic traditions, precisely at the time of writing the 'Prologue in Heaven' and the 'große Lücke' scenes of *Faust I,* he still retained a sufficient empathy with Christian systems to use them, in however heterodox and symbolic a manner, for the metaphysical superstructure of *Faust.* No one without such an imaginative and empathetic understanding could have written the scene in which Faust, for all his lack of true faith, is held back from suicide by the traditional sounds and associations of Easter, the scene in which Faust seeks revelation from his translation of St John's Gospel, Faust's 'catechism' to Gretchen, or the passages that reveal Gretchen's anguished religiosity.

Goethe was to return to Christian models, too, for the final scenes of the drama because, as he put it, he needed to give a firm delineation to his poetic intentions if he was not to lose himself in vague spiritual abstractions. He does not appear to have believed in the literal truth of his Christian theological material any more than he believed in the occult or hermetic systems, or indeed in the classical myth, that he drew on his *Faust;* he exploited all these systems for his own purposes, and more especially Christianity, because it provided a richly resonant and above all a familiar corpus of iconography and doctrine.

The history of the composition of *Faust II* is not nearly as tortuous or as protracted as that of the first part. Apart from the fragment *Helena im Mittelalter,* there is some evidence that Goethe thought out, and might also have written down, some sections of the last act relating to Faust's salvation in or around 1800; but between 1806 and 1824 he did virtually nothing further on the subject, except to dictate in 1816 a scenario which evidently represents his original conception of the second part. This is a rather bizarre romance in which the broad lines of Acts I-III are in part discernible, together with one or two motifs from Act IV. While the setting is the Germany of Maximilian I, Helen is magically conjured from Hades within the fairy-tale, medieval context of a castle whose owner is crusading in Palestine. The son of Faust and Helen strays beyond the limits of the enchanted castle, and is killed by 'a consecrated sword'. After the disappearance of Helen and her son, monks attack the castle, but with the help of

Mephistopheles and his three henchmen Raufebold, Habebald and Haltefest, Faust avenges his son's death and wins great estates.

It is not until 1825, however, that any serious attempt to resume work is recorded; and once again, the external stimulus was Goethe's preparation of his works for publication by Cotta in the Complete Works, the *Vollständige Ausgabe letzter Hand.* No doubt Eckermann's persistent urgings for a second part were also a factor. In 1825 Goethe worked on some sections of Act V, but this was soon abandoned in favour of Act III; the death of Byron at Missolonghi in May 1824 may well have been the stimulus to modify the Helen episode of the 1816 scenario, and to use the 1800 Helen fragment as the starting point for an episode which, as he later wrote to his friends, spans 3,000 years of history from the fall of Troy to the Greek Wars of Liberation. Completed by June 1826, what was to be the third act of *Faust II* was published separately in 1827 in volume 4 of the *Ausgabe letzter Hand* as 'Helena. Klassisch-romantische Phantasmagorie. Zwischenspiel zu *Faust'* ('Helen: Classical-Romantic Phantasmagoria: Interlude to *Faust'*).

From May 1827 Goethe began to work systematically on what he now designated his 'Hauptgeschäft', his 'principal task'—the completion of *Faust II.* Much of the first act (up to line 6036) was completed by January 1828, and these scenes were published that Easter, appended to the text of *Faust I* in volume 12 of the *Ausgabe letzter Hand;* this was the last section of the drama of which Goethe actually saw the publication. By the first weeks of 1830 Act I was complete, and Act II was also written during that year—substantially by June, but with later additions in December. The beginning of Act V (the Philemon and Baucis episode) was ready by May 1831; this was grafted on to the earlier material dating from 1825, and possibly also from 1800. Act IV was written in the first half of 1831, and the whole manuscript was ready by 22 July. It was sealed, though it was reopened, and some alterations were made, in January 1832. *Faust. Der Tragödie zweiter Teil* was published posthumously in 1832 in volume 41 of the *Ausgabe letzter Hand.*

It was no small thing, as Goethe remarked, to complete in his eighty-second year a work conceived in his twentieth. Naturally enough, he saw his whole Faust drama as a single entity, and insisted on more than one occasion that he had carried the second part within him as an 'inner fable' for many years; indeed, we have seen that, even at the point of breaking with the past 'barbarities' of *Faust I,* he was already planning, and even executing in some detail, the classical episodes of the second part. He was, on the other hand, fully aware that *Faust I* and *Faust II* did not constitute a closely unified work in any conventional dramatic or even thematic sense; and he stressed not only the distance between the Faust of the 'old, rude folk tale' and his recasting of the figure in *Faust I* but also the further extension and elaboration of Faust's character in the second part. The first part, said Goethe, had represented a man who, confined and ill at ease within his earthly limitations, considered the highest knowledge and the finest possessions inadequate to satisfy his aspirations, who therefore remained dissatisfied and discontented in all areas of his experience. In the second part, on the other hand, he had aimed to elevate his material beyond this previous 'wretched sphere of experience', and to show such a man in 'higher regions', to lead him through 'more worthy circumstances'.

Such views and intentions may well have been coloured by Goethe's somewhat patronizing retrospective opinion of his youthful work; but time and again he stressed the differences between the two parts in conception and intention. The second part, he wrote, could not and should not have been as fragmentary as the first; it engaged the mind more than the first part, and was designed for the rational reader; the story was more conceptual, wherever the imagination of the poet might lead it. The second part dealt with the 'splendid, real and fantastic' errors of a man, experienced in a 'nobler, worthier, higher' sense than in the 'common' first part. The first part dealt with the specific; the second tended towards the 'generic'. The first part was 'almost entirely subjective'; it concerned a constricted, more passionate individual; the second part was more objective, revealing a 'higher, wider, brighter, less passionate world'.

Whatever Goethe might have meant precisely by these categories, it is clear that he himself regarded the two parts as very different, though by no means separate, parts of a whole. This is not to deny any overall unity or continuity between the two parts, whether structural or formal, dramatic or thematic. Quite clearly, there are echoes and cross-references between them; the figures of Faust and Mephistopheles are common to both parts; the human action is encapsulated within the framework of the 'Prologue in Heaven', even within the 'Prelude in the Theatre', and within the terms of the pact and wager between Faust and Mephisto. The second part represents Faust's experiences in the 'wide world' after the 'narrow world' of Part One. . . . But the unity or continuity of the whole, however it is defined, does not alter the fact that the two parts are very different in kind, in structure and characterization, in literary idiom and style, in scope and treatment.

To be sure, *Faust I* itself was scarcely a conventional dramatic structure; the *theatrum mundi* framework, the episodic and open construction, the huge variety of language and verse forms, the supernatural elements, the mixture of farce and pathos, the loose ends and the drastic plunges and leaps of the dramatic line, the interpolation of ephemeral and satirical allusions—all this had distinguished Part One from any single contemporary dramatic tradition, in particular from *tragédie classique* on the one hand and *bürgerliches Trauerspiel* on the other. Indeed, only a very liberal conception even of Shakespearian drama could be given as the model for *Faust I.* Nevertheless, the first part, at least in the Gretchen tragedy, can be said to have remained fundamentally within the Aristotelian canon of the theatre, if not in any formal or structural sense, then at least in the sense that it demands, and relies upon, an empathetic emotional response from its audience or reading public. *Faust II,* on the other hand, demands and relies on a very different reaction; as Goethe suggested, the mind and the intellect, indeed the learning and the education,

of the reader are engaged, rather than his emotions. The action is abstract, literary and allegorical rather than sensuous, dramatic and mimetic.

The characterization of the main figures changes accordingly. As Goethe also intimated, the Faust of the first part is a passionate, subjective individual who moves in what Goethe calls the 'Halbdunkel' ('twilight') of a relatively realistic environment. To be sure, the Faust of the first part is a dual personality, both renegade intellectual and young lover; of course he has, over and above his specific human individuality, a representative function. The action is both naturalistic and symbolic; if Faust is not Everyman, he stands in some measure for human curiosity and aspirations, however exceptional his situation and his opportunities. The Faust of the second part, however, while not entirely purged of human individuality, is far removed from the psychologically differentiated and motivated personality of the first part; he is no longer an individual in a dramatic context but an emblematic figure whose epic experiences are not those of any single person but rather those of modern Western man, just as the whole action of *Faust II* is an allegorical representation of certain areas of Western European history and culture within the scope of Goethe's knowledge and experience. The Faust of Part One had been a recognizable human and emotional figure—that is, within all the limits and qualifications of dramatic and aesthetic reality; Gretchen, even more so, had responded in terms of normal dramatic psychology. There is little of that in the Faust or the Helen of Part Two. Faust appears in a series of roles, each determined by the symbolic or allegorical context in which he moves: as Plutus, as court financier and necromancer, as a travelling philhellene, as a crusading knight, as the military arm of the Empire, as trader, civil engineer and colonist—in short, as a composite historical figure. Helen, similarly, is a composite, symbolic and emblematic figure playing out an extended and complex allegory of the reception of classical culture by the modern Western imagination.

The same principle applies to many other characters. Frau Marthe, Valentin, the peasants and the townsfolk of Part One belong to dramatic naturalism; the Student, too, and even Wagner, for all his function as representative of academic traditions, are situated within a relatively realistic context. The same is scarcely true of the Baccalaureus or of Wagner in Part Two, where their representative function dominates; and the figures of Homunculus and Euphorion, of Chiron and Proteus, of the Emperor and his court, have their symbolic functions within the historical and cultural allegories of *Faust II.* Mephistopheles, certainly, was hardly a character of conventional dramatic psychology even in the first part; his reactions and his behaviour are determined not by any human motivation but by his cosmic or dramatic function as tempter or clown, adversary or companion of Faust, and his protean role goes far beyond the normal pattern of human or even diabolic behaviour. But in *Faust II* Mephistopheles also appears in a far wider range of guises and masks adapted to the allegorical context: as court jester, as Zoilo-Thersites, as Avaritia, as Cagliostro, as Sheherazade, as Old Iniquity, as Phorcyas, as Faust's 'military adviser', as his bailiff and agent, and finally once more in burlesque as the Satan of traditional superstition. He also appears as stage prompter, as *répétiteur* and manipulator of the action. His function as tempter and negator is preserved, as are his roles as mock sermonizer and moralist, as humorist and wit, as jester and cynical commentator; but the scope and variety of these roles are vastly broadened, consistent with the shift of the drama on to a wider 'generic' and symbolic level.

Eckermann suggested—and Goethe evidently concurred in the notion—that the various episodes of *Faust II* formed self-contained worlds of their own, which were not connected by any dramatic causality, but were linked only as the separate adventures and experiences of the central figure; this, Eckermann added, was similar to the structure of the *Odyssey* or *Gil Blas*. The allusion to an epic structure is interesting; for Goethe and Schiller had, at the time of the final composition of Part One, discussed and corresponded on the subject of epic and dramatic poetry in some detail. The dramatic action, they suggest in their collaborative essay on epic and dramatic poetry, is a tightly knit sequence of events that proceeds precipitately towards its conclusion; the broader and more deliberate progress of the epic dwells on the significance of separate episodes, developing them and elaborating them in a way the drama cannot. Drama tends towards naturalism, the mimetic imitation of reality, while the interest of epic is in its broader, more detached narrative perspective depicting an individual's active involvement in wider affairs.

Now, while it is clear that, as well as the relentless causality of dramatic action, the first part of *Faust* includes episodes of epic breadth, reiteration and 'retardation'—for example, in the 'Vor dem Tor', 'Wald und Höhle' and 'Walpurgisnacht' scenes—it is equally clear that in the second part the epic dimension, as Goethe and Schiller understood it, dominates, and even supersedes, the dramatic. It is true that *Faust II,* unlike *Faust I,* is divided into five 'acts'. On the other hand, these five acts have little enough discernible causality in dramatic terms, except on the most tenuous level: for example, that the inflation engineered by Faust and Mephisto in Act I precipitates the bankruptcy and rebellion that allow Faust to intervene and save the Empire in Act IV; or that Faust's intervention in Act IV leads to his enfeoffment with the coastal territories that he develops in Act V—a dramatic link that Goethe did not even think necessary to present on stage. If the dramatic structure of *Faust II* is sporadic and fortuitous, however, the broad epic structure, based, as I hope to demonstrate below, on the historical allegory informing the action of the second part, is altogether more consistent and satisfactory.

If Part One was influenced in its form and structure more than anything else by the 'open' form of Shakespearian drama, or at least by the *Sturm und Drang* perception of it, Part Two in many respects manifests the theatricality of the symbolic drama of the Spanish Baroque, the operatic spectacles and transformations, the mannerism and allegory of Calderón. While remaining essentially theatrical, *Faust II* stretches the scope and resources of the stage to the limit—and perhaps beyond. Neither development of character nor continuity of dramatic action constitute

the principal unity of the second part; perspectives of time and place shift constantly, and the *Gesamtkunstwerk* draws on a whole range of available forms of entertainment and spectacle: on the *trionfo* and allegorical review, on pageant, masque, music, choreography and the visual arts.

As I have tried to show, the **Urfaust** was the product of Goethe's youthful enthusiasms and cultural stimuli. In the **Fragment** and **Faust I,** he built on and extended this basic material, he overlaid it with a philosophical or theological framework, but without obscuring it. Historically speaking, **Faust I** remains essentially a product of the eighteenth century, of the Germany of Gottsched and Lessing and Frederick the Great, of Europe before the French Revolution, before the Napoleonic invasion of Germany, before the formal demise of the German Empire and before the Romantic movement in German literature. Even if the later stages of its composition overlap with some of these events, it scarcely reflects them, except for some of the political and satirical references in the 'Hexenküche' and the 'Walpurgisnachtstraum'. Indeed, in many ways **Faust I** predates Goethe's own classicism, even if its completion is almost synchronous with the decade of Weimar Classicism; Goethe himself testified how alien the theme and its treatment had been to him during that decade.

Faust II, on the other hand, is essentially a product of the nineteenth century. It was written after the French Revolution, and, with the exception of the opening of Act III, which is a monument to Goethe's philhellene classicism, after the dissolution of the Holy Roman Empire, after the defeat of Napoleon and the Restoration in France and Germany. It was written on the eve of the Industrial Revolution; it even covers the period of the 1830 July Revolution in France—and Goethe, at the age of 80, watched with great alarm that political upheaval, the shock-waves of which even reached Weimar, though in very attenuated form. **Faust II** was also written after the main impulse of German romanticism had spent itself, and well after Goethe had seen the high-minded but precarious classicism carefully and energetically nurtured by himself and Schiller run into the sand. **Faust II** was written by a man of great age, by a mind which, while still capable of 'renewed puberty' and of exquisite, seemingly artless lyrical poetry, tended naturally towards sceptical detachment and ironic scrutiny, towards a playfully serious complexity of vision and expression.

The complexity of **Faust II** lies not so much, or not only, in the mass of scholarly or recondite allusion that the reader is challenged to recognize and discover in the text, as Goethe plays a part-whimsical, part-serious game of literary hide-and-seek. It also consists in the extraordinary process of reflection and layering that Goethe employs, whereby primary levels of meaning both conceal and reveal secondary or tertiary levels. Thus behind the court of a composite, but by no means idealized, Renaissance Emperor, behind the intrigues and feuds, the hedonism and irresponsibility of a regime on the verge of collapse, we perceive the economic and political state of late eighteenth-century Europe, in particular of pre-revolutionary France. Behind the mischief-making of Mephistopheles, we perceive the charlatanry of a Cagliostro, who was himself for Goethe the very symbol and symptom of corruption and decadence in a frivolous French court. Behind the masquerade of a Roman or Florentine carnival, we perceive a comment on trade, money, wealth and credit in a pre-industrial society.

Behind the arrogant ravings of a young graduate lies a caricature of the solipsistic absolutism of German idealist philosophy; behind Homunculus, the product of Wagner's crazed alchemist's dream, lies a not unhealthy scepticism towards uncontrolled scientific experiment, as well as towards romantic Frankenstein fantasies. At the same time, by Goethe's own testimony, Homunculus incorporates some of his most personal beliefs in human personality or 'entelechy', its existence before physical birth and its survival beyond physical death, as well as his biological credo of morphological evolution, metamorphosis and growth.

Behind the Battle of Pharsalus that marked the end of the Roman Republic, and the Battle of Pydna 120 years earlier that had signalled the end of Hellenic power in the eastern Mediterranean and the rise of that same Republic, we perceive the primal mythical battle that also took place in Thessaly, the struggle of Gods and Titans; and forward in time, all the historical recurrences of that original struggle which, as Erichtho predicts, will repeat itself into eternity. Gods and Titans, Greeks and Trojans, Greeks and Romans, republicans and monarchists, Guelphs and Ghibellines, aristocrats and sansculottes—the allegories of the 'Klassische Walpurgisnacht' extend from the mythical past to the modern age, to the French Revolution and even to the July Revolution of 1830.

Behind the obstinate bickering of two cranky savants, Thales and Anaxagoras, behind the conflicting claims of neptunist and vulcanist theories, lie not only Goethe's own keen and informed geological and anatomical studies but also his own gradualist political thinking. Behind the third act of *Faust II* lie 3,000 years of European history. Behind the fantastic encounter between the Greek heroine and the Germanic crusader is an allegory of the reception of the classical heritage by the modern Western world up to and including Weimar Classicism; the historical fate of the classical sites under successive occupations up to the Greek Wars of Liberation; Goethe's own lifelong preoccupation with Hellenic art and literature; and the synthetic reconciliation of classical and romantic, Hellenic and Germanic, pagan and Christian traditions. Above all, there is the recognition that the classical ideal is an irretrievable but infinitely precious heritage in modern Western culture.

Behind the collapse of empire and the insurgence of a rival emperor in Act IV is the Napoleonic occupation of the German territories of the Holy Roman Empire, and the formal demise of that Empire in 1806. Behind the dubiously engineered defeat of the rival emperor and the restoration of imperial offices we perceive not only the 'Golden Bull' of 1356 by which Charles IV established the constitution of the German Empire but also, in the restoration of a fatally weakened imperial authority, an allegory of the restoration of feudal monarchy in Europe after 1815 in an intricate and precarious system of 'balanced' powers.

Behind Faust's reclamation schemes of Act V, his commercial ventures and his dreams of settlement, we perceive not only a reference to the devastating North Sea floods of 1824-5, and no doubt to other historical precedents, but also more generally the development of modern civil and industrial technology, of world trade and perhaps even of colonialism; the ruthless exploitation of labour and machinery; the destruction of traditional social patterns in the Philemon and Baucis episode; and the utopianism—whether proto-Marxist, capitalist, philanthropic or doctrinaire—of early nineteenth-century social visionaries.

Faust II is, in the phrase of G. C. L. Schuchard, a poetic and symbolic representation of modern man and modern life. But over and above this extended historical allegory, it is also the continuation—and here the continuity of Goethe's *Faust* must be stressed—of the existential progress of a deeply flawed human individual, of his struggle to fulfil himself by effort and experience. It is the charting of the spiritual development of a man who finally renounces metaphysical speculation and the temptation of miraculous powers in order to affirm the value of limited but constant practical striving for a realizable vision. While Faust dies without achieving more than a provisional glimpse of that vision, his life, which has from the beginning evidently been guided by a providential 'Urquell', is granted the final affirmation of a grace beyond human judgement that does not take issue with a moral balance-sheet of debit and credit. Goethe's Faust, relentlessly and indeed ruthlessly pursuing his destiny through the two parts of the drama, is an eccentric and, for all his ambivalence, ultimately positive representative of Goethe's age, much as the Dr Johannes Faust of the narrative legend had been an eccentric, if negative, representative of his age.

Goethe himself was more than aware of the posthumous exegetical problems *Faust II* would present. From many references he made to correspondents, we can detect a cautious delight in his anticipation of future efforts to crack the code, to tease out the clues to the secrets he had smuggled into the work. As he wrote to J. H. Meyer, for every problem that is solved, a new problem presents itself, and yet, he hoped, it would give pleasure to anyone alive to the implications of subtle signs and gestures; indeed, such a person, he suggested, might well find in the work more than he had put there. Critics have not been slow to take up this challenge, and *Faust II* criticism is beset by the suspicion of finding in it more than Goethe intended; but that is the licence of the scholar that he himself anticipated. And in almost his last words on what it pleased him to call 'these very serious jests', Goethe feared a worse fate for his work than critical dismemberment. In such 'absurd and confused times', he feared, his long and honest endeavours with this 'strange edifice' would be poorly rewarded; he imagined that it would perhaps founder and be driven on to the shore, would lie there like a wreck in fragments and, for the time being at least, would be engulfed by the sands of time. . . . (pp. 24-45)

John R. Williams, in his Goethe's Faust, Allen
& Unwin, 1987, 248 p.

Elizabeth Starr   (essay date 1989)

[*In the following excerpt, Starr examines ambiguities in the plot and characterization of* Faust, *contending that they provide a structural metaphor for Faust's efforts to distinguish between illusion and reality.*]

Illusions have been associated with Faust from the figure's inception. They complicate our readings of the myth in all of its manifestations. In the case of Goethe's *Faust,* generations of readers have navigated the play's multiple styles, plots, and realities, weighing events as they unfold for their actuality. My own approach focuses on *Faust's* structural as well as magical deceptions. I read the play removed from the intellectual and cultural traditions that surround it, and unburdened by prior treatments. Yet encouraged by recent interest in deconstruction and self-reflexivity, I find my efforts to make sense of the play's ambiguities reflected in Faust's own drive to understand the universe. His struggle for clarity in the face of illusion both thematizes and invites interpretive involvement.

Encountering *Faust* as a whole, the reader may note the play's uneven structure and its depiction of a journey into ever more baffling dimensions. Goethe seems to toy with levels of literary reality already in the "Dedication," by conjuring "wavering shapes" that eventually assume a questionable substantiality. This ambiguity is further suggested by the "Prelude on Stage," which relativizes the scenes that follow by exposing the play's intentionally deceptive theatricality. Faust's opening monologue in "Night," for example, acquires in juxtaposition with the self-referential "Prelude" an irony that might suggest reading it as purposely comic lamentations. This may be one reason why conservative teachers and editors presenting *Faust* to the uninitiated often delete the "Prelude" entirely.

Yet the reinstatement of chunks of text usually seen as superfluous calls attention to the textual asymmetry that permits omissions in the first place. Goethe's three prefatory texts, the "Dedication," the "Prelude," and the "Prologue in Heaven," precede *Der Tragödie erster Teil* proper, yet are not matched by any postlude or epilogue at the close of *Part II*: the ostensible frames of the text are not closed. It seems as if Goethe himself were uncertain—or deliberately ambivalent—about the status of the three frames, placing them simultaneously outside *Der Tragödie erster Teil* but within *Faust: Eine Tragödie.* This equivocation, though perhaps minor, suggests an instability in *Faust,* as if the text were about to unravel or dissolve. The reader is left with the unsettling impression that *Faust's* boundaries cannot be definitively fixed.

The reader may also feel as perplexed by the play's thematic ambiguities as by its unstable structure. At the very beginning of "Night," the action moves with a minimum of exposition to the play's pivotal conflict, central both to Faust's characterization and to the entire motion of the plot: Faust's desire to learn "what, deep within it, holds the world together." The play frustrates the reader's attempt to discover the answer it gives to its own question, however, by supplying an overabundance of seemingly contradictory solutions. Faust himself generates excess in translating the "Logos" of the New Testament with four

ambiguously interlocking terms: "Word," "Mind," "Power," and "Deed." In addition to the hero's early attempts to define the nature of creation, Mephisto advances darkness, the sirens invoke "Eros," and Pater Profundis calls on love, as competing definitions. Whose answer is final? The Lord, whose word might carry most weight, remains absent. The quest for ultimate reality, so clearly set up at *Faust's* start, remains open and unstable at the end.

Even on the ostensibly straightforward level of the plot, the resolution waivers: does Faust win or lose his bet with Mephisto at the end? Of his last speech before his death, one could argue that Faust has both uttered the fatal words stipulated in the wager with Mephisto and only referred to them obliquely. This built-in ambivalence permits both Faust and Mephisto to win and lose simultaneously, Mephisto easily seen as winning by the letter and Faust in spirit. Whether we read Mephisto as "really" winning or "really" losing the contest, however, the incontrovertible result is Faust's ascension through the mountain gorges to—we imagine—heaven. Despite the seemingly deliberate ambivalence of the climax, the text proceeds in disregard of this problem to its predetermined end.

Faust's most far-reaching instability is evident in its hazy border between illusion and reality. Though Faust himself seems relatively untroubled by "life's crazy labyrinth," the reader may not feel so fortunate. In fluctuations that undermine conventional expectations of textual consistency, *Faust's* multiple realities—theatre, heaven, spirit world, Germany, court, Walpurgis Night, and Greece, to name a few—are juxtaposed in a dynamic that continually threatens to puncture itself and blow itself out of existence.

The intrusion of unexpected realities begins to emerge, however, as essential to the very existence of the plot, as early as the end of the first scene in Faust's study. Practically speaking, Faust's journey is already over: rebuffed by the Earth Spirit, he has determined that not until death can he achieve the knowledge he craves, an intuition borne out by both the Lord's proclamation in the "Prologue" and the play's mystical conclusion. In addition, he already defines himself, without Mephisto's having to lift a finger, as the dust-eating worm of the devil's vengeful desires. Yet the deus ex machina of a heavenly chorus descends to dissuade Faust from his festive suicide and propel the plot forward, simply, perhaps, for the sheer fun of the next ten thousand or so lines.

The reader may be inclined to read on for Mephisto's sake alone: demon, artist, and clown in one, he captures the imagination from his first irreverent appearance on the stage of heaven, poking fun at both "the small god of the world" and the reigning "Old Man." The latter, recognizing humankind's propensities to confusion and sloth, capitalizes on Mephisto's talents as entertainer by sending him to earth as an attractive and stimulating companion, hardly a tempter. As expert magician, Mephisto moves easily on all the planes posited in *Part I,* and appears throughout *Faust* in myriad shapes and transformations, suggesting both the ease with which realities can shift, and his own central role as the shifter. His slipperiness only accentuates the difficulty of separating levels of reality, however. Thus although the text provides us with what appear to be real and unreal characters, opposing Gretchen and Wagner to witches and spirits, their separateness must already be called into question by a character capable of transgressing the boundaries and pulling other characters after him.

To complicate the matter, Mephisto's empty but always entertaining illusions, such as drilling wine spouts into tables in Auerbach's Cellar, are continually pitted against equally wavering images representing the fullness of divine reality. Mephisto's strategy is to make things appear to be what they are not, his motto reading: "False image and word, change scene and perception!" The Lord, by contrast, reminds the archangels of the eternal form behind appearances, positing all of creation as an illusion behind which deeper reality lurks: what is "real" vis-à-vis Mephisto's magic becomes "unreal" when held up to the light of the Lord's eternal ideas. We observe that although some of *Faust*'s illusions dissolve as quickly as they appear, like Mephisto's grape arbors, others possess an unexpected solidity and potential for growth, suggesting different principles at work behind the illusions.

The difficulty of defining and separating illusion from reality seems to escalate throughout *Part II,* where the blending of real and unreal becomes a leitmotif of the text. One of the first scenes at court may be representative. Faust saves the emperor and his collapsing realm by masterminding an illusion of fabulous wealth: reams of paper money backed, in theory, by as yet unmined resources. Not only does an illusion fostered by mere slips of paper approved by an unwitting ruler evoke the very real effect of an empire-wide spending spree, but it also elicits differing readings from Faust and Mephisto: a literal one from the latter, a much more figurative one from the former, idealizing the riches present in spirit behind the printed bills and represented by them. The bills, in their simultaneously concrete and phony existence, can be seen to operate as a metaphor for texts in general and their multiple levels of interpretation. Like Faust's money, a printed text is a tangible object that can be used and enjoyed, as well as the oblique representation of meanings other than itself—at once concrete and illusionary, real and unreal.

Part II documents the coincidence of contradictory realities in an ever more literary context. Just a few scenes after the carnival of paper money, Faust finds he cannot step into the apparition of Helena he has conjured for the king's amusement. When he attempts to do so, the vision not only dissolves, but explodes with a bang; Faust's matter and Helena's anti-matter cannot mix. Yet once the action moves to Greece, the obstacles to the union of reality and unreality are removed, this odd couple even engendering a son, Euphorion, without blowing themselves to pieces. What change has occurred to permit Faust's union with Helena? Greece, like Faust's money, can be seen to offer a concrete illusion, this time expanded so that a new reality is suggested, reminiscent of the theatrical universe of the "Prelude" in its ability to incorporate contradictory viewpoints. The very nature of this quasi-literary region seems to be that the real and unreal exist simultaneously,

different facets of reality coming into focus by turns, depending on the multiple perspectives of both reader and characters, and on how the kaleidoscope is held to the light.

The scenes in Greece involving Homunculus, Wagner's artificially created man, thematize *Faust*'s coincidence of real and unreal. Homunculus is moved by the goal of leaving his bottle and "coming into being" (7830-31). He apparently succeeds in the finale of the "Classical Walpurgis Night," yet we cannot be sure which definition of reality the kaleidoscope has cast up to us. Amidst general celebration, Homunculus—"seduced" by Proteus—emerges from his glass and dissolves into fire. It remains uncertain, however, whether he has been destroyed in the explosion, like the apparition of Helena before him; whether he has transcended his artificiality and indeed moved into the reality he craved; whether he has simply come out of his glass and undergone no real change at all—or all of the above. This last may be safely possible in a region as ambiguous as Homunculus himself: a stylized Greek world of myth, literature, theatrical disguises, and, as the name "Proteus" suggests, simultaneous possibilities.

Conflicting yet concurrent realities may offer a metaphor for the nature of literary creation, presented in *Faust* as a reflection of the creation of the universe. The poet is the first to voice this view in the "Prelude": "Who secures Olympus and unites the gods? The power of man, revealed through the poet!" Literary creation, a "revelation" of human artistic powers transmitted through the body of the artist, advances itself as the force capable of integrating the text's contradictions—of holding it all together. When Faust searches for the essence of creation, and the text answers with a range of irreconcilable answers, such overabundance both offers a metaphor for the creative principle at the text's (the world's) core, and calls for a mind that can assimilate the concurrent perspectives.

The creative mind which *Faust* depicts and demands is, however, not so much that of a poet as that of a reader—in this case Faust, in a double role as stand-in for the reader himself grappling with the play's ambiguities. Over the course of the play, Faust develops into an ever more able interpreter; his striving, like the reader's, is a search for the Rosetta stone that will unlock the world's text. Early on, the Earth Spirit rejects Faust with the words, "You are like that spirit which you comprehend." Though Faust is not yet able to grasp the Earth Spirit in "Night," the situation changes by "Wood and Hollow," in part thanks to Mephisto, whose deceptions even Faust must now recognize as indispensable spurs both to his striving and to his growing subtlety as a reader, mastering and outgrowing each reality, each chapter, in turn.

In the "Prelude," the director knows a successful play must offer a broad palette of amusements so as to appeal to the widest possible audience despite unequal levels of sophistication. The Helena-conjuring scene in the first act of *Part II* dramatizes this principle as well as highlights the qualitative differences between Faust's readings and those of others around him. Mephisto, totally unmoved by Helena, is the stony ground on which no seed takes root, as in the biblical parable; the lords and ladies, by contrast, respond to the apparition's sexual titillation. Faust alone reads Helena in a manner that expands on his reading of the paper money, daringly interpreting her literally: "I take my stand! These are realities." These multiple readings, ranging from the meaningless to the stimulating to the profoundly real, are all teased from the experience of one artistic creation, the conjuring trick. Yet Faust's reading is the one that eventually proves most fruitful, opening the way to his union with Helena in Greece.

The play's invitation to extravagantly multiple readings is modeled not only in individual scenes such as this one, but also in the opposing viewpoints Faust and Mephisto offer throughout, from their attitudes toward nature, love, money, and pranks, to their readings of Faust's final words. Although Faust's viewpoints may be the ones covertly subscribed to by the text, we also know that his actions this side of heaven are "confused." His predetermined position as the Lord's favorite aside, Faust demonstrates his superiority to Mephisto again not so much in his sorcery as in his ability to read—illusions, events, mysteries, the universe—at a level several grades above Mephisto. Who is the one left empty-handed at the end?

The plot of *Faust* may be summed up as the education of one exemplary man to ever fuller readings of the universe around him, in search of the most profound experiences possible, reflecting the reader's position opposite the text itself. Yet Goethe teases the reader—far more than the unwitting Faust—by first promising insight and then withholding it coyly until after the death that closes the play; the Lord's assurances that Faust's readings will ultimately attain clarity do not extend to us.

But if the Lord denies us a frontal view of his clarity, the text nevertheless provides suggestive sideways glimpses. One clue to the nature of the fullest readings possible is to be found in Faust's journey to the Mothers. Their domain, exclusively female, suggests the classical Muses, and foreshadows the eternal feminine mentioned at the close of *Part II.* Within their realm, reality continually changes and shifts, first as insubstantial as a bubble, then fixed at its core, in a manner reminiscent of the Lord's divine ideas: "Formation and transformation, eternal Mind's eternal dialogue." It is under their tutelage that Faust conjures a Helena that develops from an empty illusion into one full of growth and possibility. The Mothers thus depict a universe both profoundly real and profoundly illusory, for which literary creation offers the best metaphor this side of death (the reader being barred from following Faust to the other side).

Faust's metaphors for the operation and nature of literary creation—themselves metaphors for the larger but inexpressible creation of the universe—are carried through to the final scene of *Part II,* "The Mountain Gorges." The boundary-transgressing properties of a mountain setting have already been suggested by *Part I*'s Walpurgis Night orgy on the Blocksberg, depicting a space where the spirit world coincides with the prosaic German. The location of the gorges is implied in "Laboratory" as well, where Homunculus mentions them in his list of upcoming Greek landmarks at the classical Walpurgis Night. Set in this explicitly literary landscape, the unstably reacting elements

of a transformed Christian tradition, Greek choruses, simultaneously real and allegorical mountains, and at least one previously "real" character, Gretchen, reappearing in the new role of a penitent, offer themselves as reflections of an underlying unity only suggestible in literature.

Exactly what this all-inclusive reality might be, or where the eternal feminine is "pulling us," I cannot hope to say, nor do I believe that *Faust* provides definitive answers—or at least not the ones we might have been led to expect. Rather, the text offers a long metaphor of possibilities. The entire play has been concerned with Faust's search for ultimate reality in the face of competing and contradictory universes; here, the final speech of the Chorus Mysticus suggests that the clarity the Lord promises Faust at the start can be grasped within the world of the text only by embracing the simultaneous yet shifting possibilities of literary art. *Faust*'s final statement is that truth and the kaleidoscope of colorful reflections in "eternal yet changing" form are inseparable.

The unstable form of the text, rife with the ambivalences outlined earlier, proves an apt structural metaphor for the theme of mutable literary reality which *Faust* develops, the final speech of the Chorus Mysticus acting as a black hole into which the rest of the text, in all its colorful liveliness, is drawn. Although *Faust*'s structural frames appear to remain open, any postlude or epilogue would prove superfluous to the workings of the creative principle's oscilating realities, as would any definitive pronouncement that the play is about "love" or "striving" or "redemption."

But if underlying all of *Faust*'s wavering shapes nothing more tangible can be discerned than the abstract idea of creation, it almost seems as if Faust's passion for all-encompassing experience has been miserably co-opted; no more life pulses in this eternal idea than if Wagner himself had devised the schema. *Faust*'s structure seems to posit a reality at its center around which the kaleidoscope turns, but when taken apart it reveals neither beads nor little shards of colored glass; the play's best trick is that so many patterns were cast by an empty cylinder. If a unifying idea is, when all is said and done, absent, we may be no closer to comprehending the contradictory realities of the play's surfaces than we were at the start, looping back to Faust's opening monologue and repeating that "there's nothing we can know."

If nothing else, however, *Faust* suggests that the trip itself is its own reward, offering along the way entertaining metaphors for its own labyrinthian workings. The entire surface and action of the play becomes a metaphor for literature as a whole, a construct playful, self-contradictory, and self-reflexive, and a space where the ineffable content of experience is presented to the reader as simultaneously real and unreal. Goethe's withholding of a final message, despite dozens of set-ups and promises, throws the reader back to the level of the textual surfaces themselves, where an appreciation of the play's mesh of reality and illusion, in continual transformation, generates pleasure if not precision.

The spiralling motion of my reflections—moving from curiosity about the ambiguities of *Faust*'s structure to frustration with its conflated realities to a new appreciation of the play of its linguistic surfaces—may even offer one more analogy to what seems to me to be the play's point: that it is precisely in its shifting surfaces that *Faust*'s contradictory realities are agreeably and meaningfully conjoined. Struck by the rainbow upon awakening rejuvenated at the start of *Part II*, Faust himself attests to this intrinsic quality of both literary illusion and the pleasure its readers take from it: "Ponder on it, and you will grasp it more completely—we draw our life from colorful reflections" (*Ihm sinne nach, und du begreifst genauer: Am farbigen Abglanz haben wir das Leben*). (pp. 133-41)

> Elizabeth Starr, "Illusion and Reality in Goethe's 'Faust': A Reader's Reflections," in Faust Through Four Centuries: Retrospect and Analysis, *edited by Peter Boerner and Sidney Johnson, Max Niemeyer Verlag, 1989, pp. 133-42.*

Rocco Montano (essay date 1990)

[*In the excerpt below, Montano proposes that the conclusion of* Faust, *in which Faust is redeemed, undermines standard interpretations of the play as a Classical or Romantic tragedy.*]

In act 1 of *Faust. Part Two,* Faust, complying with a promise he made to the Emperor, asks Mephistopheles that he be granted the power of fetching from the kingdom of the dead Helen of Troy, along with Paris. For Mephistopheles, Faust's promise was the result of "mad unwisdom." What Faust now asks is beyond all conceivable power. Yet, since Faust insists, Mephistopheles explains to him that to win back Helen from the past one must go the realm of the Mothers; merely thinking of this place makes Mephistopheles himself shudder.

Faust, therefore, will make this perilous journey alone; he must go where the Mothers "dwell in solitude sublime . . . beyond the world of place and time." Somehow this evokes the expedition, described in Plato's *Phaedrus,* to the plain beyond the boundaries of the world, where time and space no longer exist, a place that is a "colorless, formless and intangible, truly existing essence . . . visible only to the mind, the pilot of the soul." But we may soon recognize that Faust is not to rise to what Plato calls "the plain of truth" that is placed "above the heaven," in the "upper region." Faust has long since abandoned the upward path of true knowledge. At the very beginning, Mephistopheles explained to him that his way had to be in the opposite direction: "knowledge and fair reason you'll despise, The highest powers by which poor mortals rise."

Along with the suggestion from the *Phaedrus* and with Plutarch's description of the kingdom of the Mothers (which Goethe himself mentioned to Eckermann) another passage from Plato must have echoed in the poet's mind. This is the reference, in the *Timaeus,* to something that may be called "the mother and receptacle of all things" and that is itself "invisible and formless, all-embracing." Mephistopheles speaks to Faust of "waste and solitude,"

of the "eternal void afar" where there is no substance and everything changes no less than in Plato's "receptacle": everything is "Formation, transformation." Certainly, in Goethe's configuration, the journey is not an ascent: it is "to the deep," to the "deep of deeps . . . where the Mothers stand . . . in infinite space eternal and alone." In fact, the end of the journey cannot be "the plain of truth" as in *Phaedrus,* but "the eternal void," the nonbeing. Mephistopheles himself, though the symbol of Negation, would lose his identity where Good and Being do not exist and there is "Nothing." He is not going to the realm of the Mothers.

Faust's assertion that "in . . . Nothing may the All be found," we see the idea that Nothingness and Being may converge at an unthinkable distance. The kingdom of the Mothers represents the ultimate source of reality. The prize, however, of Faust's appalling adventure, what he gains from his plunge into the abyss of being, is nothing else than the object of a typical romantic dream, of the longing, that is, for the ideal Greek fatherland of Beauty and Harmony that typified the whole era of romanticism. For the reader this causes a sense of futility, one that is intensified by the gossip accompanying the apparition of Helen and Paris at the court of the Emperor.

Unlike Dante as he journeys through hell, Faust's self-determined immersion in the lake of total Absence and unceasing Transformation leaves him unchanged. Dante portrays himself as being constantly affected by the atmosphere of darkness through which he journeys and by each torment that he experiences. The pilgrim, Dante, the protagonist of the infernal adventure, becomes absorbed in the same deception and delusion in which Francesca, the personification of courtly love, has lost herself. He is clearly contaminated by the sin of curiosity for which Ulysses has lost his life and his soul. The situation is quite different with Faust's venture. Despite his bloody pact with the devil, Faust remains substantially unchanged, as a man, through both parts of the play. Complicity with the devil does not destroy Faust's basically good inclinations. Faust can only remain dear to a woman as saintly as Margareta because his soul has not really fallen prey to evil. Goethe's romantic mind could not conceive of a totally evil being but of a rebel who, either from ambition or an instinctive need to revolt, finds himself passing beyond the accepted limits, charting a course of defiance and murder. There could indeed be defiance and even murder; but such a protagonist could not lose those characteristics that make him a hero. If the Faust of Marlowe and of the original were recalled to life by a poet in the romantic period, this was because the romantic sensibility saw in Faust the noble rebel, the man who, while yielding to Satan, still retains his nobility or even gains in beauty and worthiness because of his chosen course.

The story, as one can easily perceive, goes back to Milton's Satan, the symbol of perverse beauty. Faust had to be the new hero, at once noble and destructive, allied with the forces of evil and yet still carrying the flame. It might be suggested that perhaps he is even closer to God than all church-worshippers and righteous moralists. As a matter of fact, he is even expected to be saved, though by a rather strange Christian god. No real corruption must exist. There must be a noble sinner, not too different from Schiller's Robbers. Goethe himself had long since, in his ***Wilhelm Meister's Apprenticeship,*** sought to delineate the figure of an ambivalent, indefinite, or characterless hero finally achieving, through error and generous, if not virtuous deeds, some kind of sublimation. The old values of goodness and reasonableness could no longer possess great appeal. And in ***Wilhelm Meister,*** too, we are asked to witness that all errors, all paths, all experiences in their aimlessness are only accidents: dispersion is a viable way of reaching redemption. Life is planned by someone unknown to us; it is comprised of wickedness and heroism, of intermingled sensuality and idealism. No choice really exists. In the book of destiny every error, every downfall, becomes functional. The hero must be ambiguous, characterless. He is like nature, humanity being expected to be the toy of an unending series of unfathomable accidents. The half-Catholic, half-Protestant Abbott of the tower sets down the axiom that no judgment is possible; destiny is unlike those human teachers who know only one set of rules. Like Goethe, the Abbott believes only in the all-consuming force of nature, for which cruelty and benevolence have equal values. Transcending the old, humanistic standards and system of values there is now the romantic exaltation of the instincts and the irrational. "I trusted my nature and followed my impulses," Rousseau's Héloïse had already proclaimed. Rousseau himself had been a "lonely wanderer," as he describes himself in his last work. From Rousseau, streams had proceeded in the double direction of Kant and the *Sturm und Drang* to converge in Goethe himself.

Everyone knows that Goethe made every possible effort to reconcile the *Sturm und Drang*'s rebellion against rules, faith in genius and instinct, with classical control. From Kant he derived a strong, decisive trust in reason. One may even say that he even corrected Kant's subjectivism, for while in Kant it is established that "the understanding does not derive its laws (*a priori*) from nature, but prescribes them to nature," to Goethe it was fidelity to the "ultimate phenomenon" (*Urphänomen),* that perhaps more profoundly constituted the only rule. Yet fidelity to the object and to nature did not contradict the *Sturm und Drang*'s appeal to instinct and the rejection of established principles. The hero whom the poet portrayed in ***Wilhelm Meister's Apprenticeship*** was a hero receptive to all kinds of experiences and finally led to acknowledge the sacredness of all reality. The work was a kind of repository of all romantic myths: the Hamletic hero overcome by melancholy; the world of imagination and theatrical fiction contrasted with reality; the Furies and the dreams of Beauty and primeval innocence, incest and purified love, neoclassical art and medieval Germany; the dream of a language transcending all national dialects; and the nostalgia for a life detached from all terrestrial burdens. Everything will eventually be redeemed, as we know. "God"—Luther had already read in Saint Matthew— "makes his sun rise on the evil and the good."

Faust's entire journey, we should not forget, takes place under the aegis of the spirit "that endlessly denies" the Prince of Darkness. To make us realize, from the begin-

Goethe in January 1832, two months before his death.

ning, how vast is Faust's distance from what is right, the poet has shown him, before his first meeting with Mephistopheles, evoking the most impassioned longings of his soul. We have heard him pronouncing the noblest sentiments against Wagner's sterile bookish wisdom. He has recalled the sounds "of early years" calling him to life, the "sound of boding fullness," the "sweet celestial strain"; he has walked among the crowd at night and proclaimed, "Here I am man, and claim man's element." We are left, then, with little doubt that the journey with the devil will be a downward one. Goethe has by no means obscured the value of the knowledge that Faust rejects. We know that it is not just medieval science or Wagner's "unearthing worms," nor his father's murderous physics that Faust leaves behind. We see clearly that Mephistopheles appears to him, now in the garb of a traveling scholar, at the moment when he has once again committed himself to magic. Faust has initiated his confrontation with the snares of a devious theology that is no longer content with the accepted traditional reading, "In the beginning was the Word," but which instead manipulates the Scriptures through tortured exegesis. Well beyond medieval logic and the perilous recipes of magic and alchemy, Faust has indeed already spurned "fair reason" and "the pastures far above."

It is such a refusal that is the starting point of the "venture."

And then, to demonstrate how devious is the course that Faust is actually charting, there is the story of Margareta; her pure desires that Mephistopheles cannot comprehend, her "sacred worth" of innocence, the "solace that she brings," together with her profound feeling that, despite all his profession of belief, Faust has "not Christ within." He is clearly on the other side, despite the sorrow that he eventually feels for Margareta's ruin. Her firm decision to atone for her misdeeds and to pay for Faust's lapse tells us something about both her goodness and the wickedness of those who have destroyed her.

Despite all we are shown about Faust's course of destruction, however, **Faust. Part One** can still be seen as a tragedy on the order of a medieval legend, or of Marlowe's *Doctor Faustus*—a tragedy, that is, of the sinner who has fallen irreversibly into the deathtrap of the devil. When, on the last fatal morning, Faust says, "Would I had never been born" and Mephistopheles calls him imperiously, "hither with me," we sense that Faust is enchained, perhaps irremediably. And yet we cannot say that Faust's soul has been genuinely destroyed. We feel that the man who abandons Margareta may still be capable of wishes that are not completely evil. We may pity him; we may see something of ourselves in the tragic course he has pursued, has set for himself. In many ways this is the essential tragedy that Goethe has written, that of a worthy character entrapped by evil machinations.

To comprehend the nature of Goethe's accomplishment one must first consider classical tragedy, and then the second great flourishing of world drama, the Elizabethan theater. It may be recalled that Greek tragedy had its origins in sacred rite. It consisted of the reenactment of some intervention on the part of gods to strike down people even in their happiest moments. The representation was intended to remind the audience that nobody is safe, that life is subject to unforeseeable and inevitable strokes from above. The common belief at the time was that those humans who experienced such disaster were guilty of some kind of transgression, of *hubris* or excess, and that this was eventually punished by Zeus. That was the fate of mortals: "The hand of Zeus"—we read in *Agamemnon* by Aeschylus—"has cast / The proud man from high place." Even if it was an ancestor who had caused the original transgression, punishment could still destroy the fortune of a living descendant. The examples of great families in which this had happened became the subject of tragic representations. It was always the striking hand of God. In the same *Agamemnon,* the Chorus, the interpreter of popular feelings, says:

> When man has once transgressed
> and his wealth and pride
> spurned the high shrine of Justice, nevermore
> may his sin hope to hide.

The cause of Agamemnon's death on his victorious return from Troy was traced to Atreus's murder of the children of his brother, Thyestes. Atreus, one remembers, was Agamemnon's father. We should observe, however, that such reconstructions of memorable downfalls were part of popular belief. Those with a more elevated understanding of the essence of life—and Aeschylus, as well as Sophocles, was certainly among them—knew that the cause of Agamemnon's death, and others such as Oedipus and Prometheus, were the result of some mysterious will of Zeus that was only linked superficially to some personal or ancestral flaw. In *Agamemnon* the death of the victorious king is clearly shown to be the consequence of his wife's, Clytemnestra's, furious love for Aegisthus. Oedipus is not punished for any fault of his own—he is described in the play *Oedipus Rex* as being the "best of men," "the most pious." Nor does his ancestors' offense against the gods contribute to his misfortune. It is simply the obscure will of Zeus that has determined his ruin.

Aristotle saw at the basis of tragedy some accidental error and the turn of some unforeseeable *peripeteia.* In reality, ancient drama offered a reminder to people that mortals are inevitably exposed to the unfathomable will of the gods. Witnessing a dramatic presentation of a famous downfall supposedly made people aware of an inescapable condition shared by all. The recognition of the unknowable ways of the gods was the real subject matter of the representation. There was no escape. In the case of Elizabethan tragedy, and of Shakespeare's in particular, we have Christian tragedy. This drama portrays sorrowful circumstances and ruinous downfalls that are beyond explanation. The mind of the spectator finds itself confronted with every conceivable cruel turn of events. But the attention of both poet and audience are focused on what is good and worthy and on what is wicked in human conduct. Death and misfortune may always come. The Christian world has but deepened the awareness of the uncertainty of life. "We are not the first / who with best meaning have incurred the worst," says Cordelia. Yet what matters now is the awareness that life possesses both good and evil, both of them viewed by God. Implicitly there is the presupposition that goodness, even if undermined in the events of the world, will yet be acknowledged in another life. There is, then, a "meaning" in life: it is not just subjected to fatality and the whims of some god. Superseding wordly misfortune is the appeal to a divine justice that certainly operates—but perhaps not in this life. What critics have said about "tragic justice" or what is called "medieval metaphysics" is pure fabrication: no one—certainly not Shakespeare—can expect that there is redress of chastisement in this life, but all are hopeful of a reward for the good in the hereafter. There is pain, evil in the world, but there is an opening, another dimension: the demise of the good is accompanied by resignation and trust. The cruel deeds of others serve as a mirror for those capable of learning about the meaning of life. Tragedy—Christian tragedy—sensitizes one to the fact that beyond humanity's errors and the accidents of life, there is at least finality in this world, and that the next world validates goodness in mortal life.

In the case of **Faust. Part One** we are still in the presence of some acts of blindness that presumably will meet with punishment in another life. Faust, running towards new errors, new acts of defiance, may offer a lesson for the soul similar to the one that can be drawn from Shakespeare's Christian drama. Certainly this was not Goethe's purpose in planning his work, but as it stands the first part of the dramatic poem may be read in this way, as a tale of defiance and damnation, comparable to that of Ulysses in Dante's *Inferno*.

But it is known that the true motivation of the work was quite different. The basic idea was to show a hero who, having escaped from the stranglehold of morality and authority, having set for himself a course toward the unreachable and the forbidden, would still be saved. The protagonist's resounding, proud words—"to bear my human fate as fate's surmounter"; "to rise to the sphere of pure activity"; "to prove in man the stature of God"; "risk more than death, yea, dare my dissolution"; "let come what will"—were intended to be the utterances of an indomitable hero. Certainly they struck most sympathetic chords in the romantic generation. First of all, Goethe could not ignore the promise made in the *Prologue in Heaven* that Faust would be saved.

Surely, we cannot expect to find in *Faust* definitive statements in favor of revolt and denial. Goethe, as is well known, endeavored throughout the work to find a balance between the opposing weights of ancient wisdom with its established principles and the appeal of unlimited defiance. The final result is a peculiar ambivalence: the joyous ring of Easter bells and the blissful tone of the Mass alternate with the slander directed against the church, which "can swallow gold and lands and such / and never feel that she had had too much." Faust simultaneously symbolizes both progress / humanitarianism and murderous destruction; Bauci tells us that in Faust's utilitarianism, which is called progress, the tail of the devil is involved. The city that should be built, as Mephistopheles suggests, through Faust's efforts, is also intended to be the city where Mephistopheles will be at home, adored by everybody.

Romanticism and classicism remain complementary in the poet's mind. To the first Walpurgisnacht (*Faust I*) corresponds the classical Walpurgisnacht (*Faust II*) and of it Mephistopheles says, "I see myself at home"; "Absurdity reigns here as in the North . . . Here is still your universal masquerade." The ideal love of Helen's beauty in *Part Two* is as fleeting and delusive as the earthly love in *Part One*. Everything is negative and positive at the same time. Homunculus, the subman, will be the expedient in the search for Helen. Like Wilhelm's, Faust's destiny will be consummated through his errors. Reconciliation, in fact, is at the root of Goethe's philosophy. But here, in *Faust*—a poem, we should not forget, conceived in the middle of the romantic revolution—the poet is bound to prove that denial and destruction, the very road to hell, are eventually the path to salvation. At least, those who sin grievously are also human; they, too, deserve admiration and can be accepted by God. But this belief, as Goethe certainly realized, is not easily reconciled with the Christian conception of God. The many years that elapsed before he finished the work; the fact that he never decided to publish it; the long dragging through the chatters of Nymphs, Monsters, Sirens, Ancient Philosophers, Nereids, Lamiae and Tritons and Phorkiades: these all reflect the difficulties that faced him. And the truth is that he did not succeed at all in solving the problem.

True, eventually Faust is assumed to enter paradise. But many of the episodes that should lead to that conclusion do not seem to function towards that effect: at least their functionality escapes us. For thousands of lines the protagonist and even his companion seem to be out of sight. At a certain point Faust and Helen have entered a cave and there a child is born and is already leaping, climbing the cliffs. He is warned by both Faust and Helen in paired rhymed verses, "to curb, ah curb, at parents' desire, Over-impetuous projects of fire." There are new songs; but then "hope of sweet restraint is banished." "Euphorion leaps higher . . . Victor-like, in armour gleaming." He appears, in fact, not like a child, but "an armed youth." Death is already decreed for him and he soon "casts himself in the air," as the stage direction tells us.

Three thousand lines are devoted to the Walpurgis Night, Helen's episode and the birth and death of Euphorion, almost two-thirds of the whole drama enacted in *Part One*, including the prelude and the *Prologue in Heaven*. And it might be added that the long lyrical dialogues do not blend easily in our mind with the drama of Faust's soul. Even the relevance of the meeting with Helen and the birth and the disappearance of Euphorion to Faust's ruin seems very tenuous. Perhaps the greatest significance of these episodes is an allegorical one depicting the rediscovery of Hellenic aesthetics in the romantic age. Lynceus appears as the genius, both poetical and philosophical, of Germany and the new literature. One may even suspect that he is Goethe himself, the great observer and the greatest spirit of the new poetry. They jointly seem to address a fervent paean to Helen's timeless beauty and, of course, Lynceus-Goethe is now enchained by Faust.

Contrary to interpretations dating back as far as Goethe's own time, everything in the episode seems to suggest that Euphorion, the offspring of the nuptials between the fire of the northern hemisphere and the spirit of Hellas, may be Hölderlin: the philosopher-poet, a spirit too detached from the soil and driven by impossible dreams, always close to the brink, "through the clouds sweeping," and finally doomed to self-destruction. This is, at any rate, more a meeting of poetical worlds than a struggle for salvation and perdition. What is relevant here for the drama of Faust's soul is the fact that, not unlike the adventure with Margareta, the union with Helen is doomed to disappointment and tragedy. Like Margareta's child, Euphorion, born from the union of minds, precipitates from his too-daring flights. New temptations then arise, no longer linked to poetical dreams of Arcadia and timeless beauty, but related to this world, to power and glory, to Germany. Mephistopheles, once again reversing Scripture, suggests that Faust should seek the glory of the Kingdom of the World; he therefore proposes to Faust that a large city with narrow, contaminated streets and the "ceaseless flow of human ants" is the proper place for a devil's kingdom. But Faust has other aspirations. He speaks of a battle against the sea to draw it back from submerged land. Activity is everything to him; and there is no greater deed than "to hold the lordly ocean from the shore." Mephistopheles must cooperate in this new daring adventure.

Again, despite the poet's avowed desire to achieve a fusion of romanticism and classicism, one does not feel a sense of tight, harmonious composition in the episodes that follow: the battle between the Emperor and his rebel lords and the repugnant pact between the Emperor and the Archbishop are somewhat digressive. With act 5, however, the drama takes on again its intense, tragic rhythms. Faust is now concerned with the reclamation of the land and with the considerable task of building the dikes that will keep the ocean from flooding the plain once again. It seems that finally the man who has encountered so many temptations and deceptive dreams is now engaged in a humanitarian, progressive undertaking that perhaps will also bring about his personal redemption. But progress does not necessarily mean promotion of the good. As a matter of fact, this seemingly humanitarian project also involves "sacrifice of human blood."

Ships loaded with every variety of merchandise are landing where once there was only marshland, and we soon learn that the *Three Mighty Fellows,* the cursors, are the ones who have secured the rich cargo and who have helped the Emperor to win his battle. Baucis and Philemon will *accidentally* be devoured by the fire, while Mephistopheles is on the scene. Lynceus, the poet, expresses from his tower his happiness in looking at the things of the world and sings with equal fervor about the fire in which the two old people and a stranger are engulfed. As soon as Faust rejoices for the "boundless space" that he can "overlook clear," Mephistopheles and his Three Fellows appear. We know the source of that happiness. Care soon takes possession of Faust's soul. By blinding him, it takes away from him the empty joy of looking at the boundless vista for which he has labored so arduously.

In reality, as Mephistopheles comments, Faust has worked only for hell. Neptune will destroy the dikes. Ruin is the only end and Faust dies still proclaiming that he merits paradise for his awesome work; those who break new paths, he claims, deserve redemption. But Mephistopheles has declared, "Gone to sheer Nothing"; a little before this, Care has said that Faust was preparing "his soul for Hell." And the fact is that in his long, stormy career Faust does not reach even a delusive moment in which he may pronounce the conditions of his wager: "Remain, so fair thou art, remain!" Even from a completely earthly and ephemeral viewpoint, his "storming through life" has led to complete vanity. Mephistopheles is completely realistic in his evaluation: "sheer Nothing." As expected, he has kept no promises.

This could have been the conclusion of the drama, telling us that there is no peace, no salvation in endless, vain conquests involving power and lust. But Goethe could not ignore his romantic wager that Faust, the new hero, would be saved. When the poet published *Faust. Part One* the answer conformed with Christian tragedy: one might think that the association with Mephistopheles and the series of wrongdoings must inevitably end with the hero's doom. But Goethe never renounced his intentions of bringing the drama to the promised conclusion. For some

decades he was presumably at pains to find a way. Ultimately, perhaps, he felt that the solution was self-evident, that simply on the basis of his unquenchable thirst for knowledge, his perennial dissatisfaction, and his endless striving, Faust deserved to ascend to paradise. He finds himself in agreement with the romantic assumption that defiance, toil, and reaching beyond added up to genuine sanctity.

The considerable difficulty lay in the fact that the God we meet in the prologue is the Christian, or even the Catholic God and it is impossible to assume that such a God will save the Faust we follow until his death. Through the sortilege of his great art, Goethe has given a great many people the impression that eventually, despite his troublesome career—or because of it—Faust is allowed into heaven, but salvation for such a protagonist must necessarily constitute a parody of Christian paradise—a paradise to which one rises without penance or without faith, through disbelief and defiance. True, in the last act of the drama, we have a large number of characters who superficially may remind us of the Catholic hereafter. There is a chorus of Angels, a Pater Ecstaticus, a Pater Profundus, a Pater Seraphicus, and, later, in what one may call the masquerade, a chorus of Boys, of Younger Angels, a Doctor Marianus, a Magna Peccatrix, a Mater Dolorosa, a Mater Gloriosa. But one is likely to ask oneself what kind of "mothers" these figures are. The Virgin Mary, implored by Saint Bernard, wins for Dante access to the ultimate vision of God. But Dante is vouchsafed this supreme gift only at the end of a long path of self-recognition and atonement. All the impediments, all worldly interests and passions first had to be overcome. A pilgrim's faith and understanding of love, his hope and an act of absolute humility gain for Dante access to sanctity.

We find nothing of the kind in the last act of *Faust. Part Two.* And even if we think of the justice of God, which, as Luther wanted to interpret Saint Paul, saves us regardless of any merit or discovery of the truth on our part, we would still be infinitely distant from Goethe's idea of heaven as a paradise for lovers and aspiring sorcerers, which a person such as Faust can enter by following to the end a path of earthly, bloody conquests, romantic dreams, and moral blindness. Nothing in Faust's ascent to heaven can be reconciled with any Christian idea of the hereafter. Nothing in the drama can warrant an assumption such as Faust's. We can easily understand how the author of *Faust* may have felt that after long toil and daring exploits, acts of defiance and sorrow, after a life encompassing all possible human experiences, his hero deserved to be saved. What we have, however, is a paradise made to order and a process of salvation surely in conformity with romantic expectations, but totally at odds with all Christian thinking, certainly in open conflict with the image of God presented in the prologue.

The fact is that we do not have here the Renaissance Christian tragedy that might present the doom of a hero subjected to the "slings and arrows of outrageous fortune" or to malice from some human antagonist. It is not the spectacle of people bringing on their own physical or spiritual ruin contemplated with a religious consciousness of the unpredictable ways of God. But neither do we have a consistent dramatic conclusion of a struggle for a great soul redeemed by suffering. The ending of the work does not show any greatness; instead, it seems like a fabrication. The hero is not subjected to our compassion, nor is he really saved and raised to sublime heights. Goethe has created one of the most imposing works of world literature, but we do not have the genuine romantic tragedy that one might have expected. Ultimately tragedy is avoided, but Faust's entrance into heaven nevertheless is quite dubious. As we have said **Faust. Part One** may constitute a tragedy in the line of Shakespeare or Marlowe, even if this was not Goethe's intention. With the second part, however, one has mostly a feeling of ambiguity. It is difficult to identify a romantic conception of tragedy on the basis of Goethe's dramatic poem. (pp. 134-44)

> Rocco Montano, "Faust and Romantic Trage-dy," in Aesthetics and the Literature of Ideas: Essays in Honor of A. Owen Aldridge, edited by François Jost and Melvin J. Friedman, University of Delaware Press, 1990, pp. 134-44.

FURTHER READING

Andrews, William Page. *Goethe's Key to "Faust": A Scientific Basis for Religion and Morality and for a Solution of the Enigma of Evil.* 1913. Reprint. Port Washington, N.Y.: Kennikat Press, 1968, 79 p.
   Excerpts Goethe's miscellaneous writings for the purpose of elucidating some of the more complex ideas developed in *Faust.*

Bennett, Benjamin. *Goethe's Theory of Poetry: "Faust" and the Regeneration of Language.* Ithaca, N.Y.: Cornell University Press, 1986, 352 p.
   Proposes to deduce Goethe's theory of poetry by examining *Faust* in the context of "antipoetry," the "verbal strategem that defeats the ironic process."

Boerner, Peter and Johnson, Sidney, eds. *Faust through Four Centuries: Retrospect and Analysis.* Tübingen: Max Niemeyer Verlag, 1989, 272 p.
   Collects critical analyses of the Faust legend and its several literary renditions, including that of Goethe.

Brown, Jane K. *Goethe's "Faust": The German Tragedy.* Ithaca, N.Y.: Cornell University Press, 1986, 263 p.
   Interprets *Faust* "in the context of European romanticism and in terms of the many texts that Goethe's play exploits and responds to."

Burke, Kenneth. "Goethe's *Faust. Part I*" and "*Faust II*— The Ideas behind the Imagery." In his *Language as Symbolic Action: Essays in Life, Literature, and Method,* pp. 139-62, 163-85. Berkeley and Los Angeles: University of California Press, 1966.
   Discusses Faust's *streben,* or striving, and Gretchen's role as a sacrificial victim as well as other symbolic themes in *Faust I.* The second essay examines the structure and language of *Faust II.*

Cottrell, Alan P. *Goethe's "Faust": Seven Essays.* Chapel Hill: The University of North Carolina Press, 1976, 143 p.
   Includes such essays as "The Theme of Sacrifice and the Questions of Faust's Redemption," "Chalice and Skull: A Goethean Answer to Faust's Cognitional Dilemma," and "Faust's Blindness and the Inner Light: Some Questions for the Future."

Davidson, Thomas. *The Philosophy of Goethe's "Faust."* 1906. Reprint. New York: Haskell House, 1969, 158 p.
   Reprints six lectures delivered by Davidson on such issues as Faust's motive for entering into the pact with Mephistopheles, the nature of his relationship with Gretchen, and his salvation at the play's conclusion.

Delp, W. E. "The Earth Spirit in *Faust.*" *Modern Language Review* XXXVII, No. 2 (April 1942): 193-97.
   Surveys critical reaction to Faust's invocation of the *Erdgeist,* or Earth Spirit, in part one of the drama and suggests an unconventional interpretation of the *Erdgeist* as representative of the "ugliness in life."

"Goethe's Posthumous Works.—No. 1. *Faust.*" *The Dublin University Magazine* II, No. X (October 1833): 361-85.
   Early critical assessment of *Faust* stating: "Goethe's works altogether court a *second,* and even a *third* reading; . . . whilst, at the same time, every new perusal will afford a new source of delight."

Earle, M. "A *Faust* Problem: What Was the Homunculus?" *Poet-Lore* XIII, No. 2 (April, May, June 1901): 269-75.
   Examines various critical interpretations of the "homunculus," the test-tube creature who assists Faust in the second part of the drama.

Fairley, Barker. *Goethe's "Faust": Six Essays.* 1953. Reprint. Oxford: Oxford at the Clarendon Press, 1965, 132 p.
   Influential study of *Faust* offering discussions of structure, characterization, and themes as unifying elements of the drama.

Faust, Albert B. "On the Origin of the Gretchen-Theme in *Faust.*" *Modern Philology* XX, No. 2 (November 1920): 181-88.
   Examines several theories concerning the identity of the woman on whom Goethe modeled the character of Gretchen, concluding that "the key to the origin of the Gretchen theme is found in a study of the social conditions of Goethe's time."

Flax, Neil M. "The Presence of the Sign in Goethe's *Faust.*" *PMLA,* 98, No. 2 (March 1983): 183-203.
   Semiotic analysis in which the critic challenges conventional interpretations of symbolism in *Faust,* suggesting that the drama "not only shares the perplexities of Romantic aesthetics in general; it also reveals how these perplexities are historically embedded in a theory of signs."

Geary, John. *Goethe's "Faust": The Making of Part I.* New Haven, Conn.: Yale University Press, 1981, 228 p.
   Traces the development of Goethe's philosophical convictions through the first part of *Faust.*

Gillies, Alexander. *Goethe's "Faust": An Interpretation.* Oxford: Basil Blackwell, 1957, 225 p.
   General commentary on the sequence of events in *Faust,* intended to prepare the reader for the "immense and often confusing mass" of *Faust* criticism.

Gray, Ronald. *"Faust Part I"* and *"Faust Part II."* In his *Goethe: A Critical Introduction,* pp. 126-59, 160-85. London: Cambridge at the University Press, 1967.

Finds *Faust* a paradoxical and disjointed work, whose faults are representative of the philosophy advanced therein.

Haile, H. G. *Invitation to Goethe's "Faust."* University, Ala.: University of Alabama Press, 1978, 190 p.

Examines each major section of *Faust* as it reflects Goethe's creative and intellectual development.

Hatfield, Henry. *"Faust I: The Little World"* and *"Faust II: The Great World."* In his *Goethe: A Critical Introduction,* pp. 132-76, 177-221. Cambridge, Mass.: Harvard University Press, 1964.

Provides overviews of *Faust I* and *Faust II,* commenting on their literary predecessors, unifying themes, and trends in *Faust* criticism.

Heller, Otto. *Faust and Faustus: A Study of Goethe's Relation to Marlowe.* 1931. Reprint. New York: Cooper Square Publishers, 1972, 174 p.

Contends that Goethe's adaptation of the Faust legend was directly influenced by Christopher Marlowe's *Tragical History of Dr. Faustus* (1604), citing as evidence similarities in structure and language.

Jacob, Cary F. "The *Faust* Attitude toward Women." *The Sewanee Review* XXVI, No. 4 (October 1918): 417-33.

Studies Goethe's representation of women in the characters of Gretchen and Helena and examines their role in the salvation of Faust.

Jantz, Harold. "Patterns and Structures in *Faust:* A Preliminary Inquiry." *Modern Language Notes* 83, No. 3 (April 1968): 359-89.

Challenges conventional criticisms of the play's structure and philosophical content, proposing that *Faust* be studied as a complete and closely-knit text the emphasis of which is symbolic rather than philosophic.

Kaufmann, M. "Goethe's *Faust* and Modern Thought." *The Scottish Review* XVIII (July 1891): 143-74.

Considers "the claims of the *Faust,* not so much as a German classic, but as a dramatic representation of nineteenth century thought, and as a world poem, facing the problem of life and offering a modern solution to it."

Keller, William J. "Goethe's *Faust,* Part I, as a Source of Part II." *Modern Language Notes* XXXIII, No. 6 (June 1918): 342-52.

Detects parallels in plot and imagery in *Faust I* and *Faust II,* suggesting that Goethe based several passages in *Faust II* on areas in *Faust I* that he found inadequately expressed and in need of enhancement.

Lamport, F. J. "Synchrony and Diachrony in *Faust.*" *Oxford German Studies* 15 (1984): 118-31.

Discusses the structure of *Faust,* focusing on "time within the poem, the relation of the poem to the lifetime of its author, and the time relation between the poem and us."

Mason, Eudo C. *Goethe's "Faust": Its Genesis and Purport.*

Berkeley and Los Angeles: University of California Press, 1967, 423 p.

Seeks to "elucidate the visionary conception or 'inner fairy tale' that shapes itself in Goethe's *Faust*" through an examination of the relationship between the *Urfaust, Faust I,* and *Faust II.*

Peacock, Ronald. "*Faust Part One.*" In his *Goethe's Major Plays,* pp. 149-202. Manchester, England: Manchester University Press, 1959.

Examines ways in which Goethe incorporated elements of several literary forms in *Faust I,* citing the drama as one of Goethe's most complex and resourceful works.

Stawell, F. Melian and Dickinson, G. Lowes. *Goethe & Faust: An Interpretation.* London: G. Bell and Sons, 1928, 291 p.

Offers an introductory overview of each section of *Faust,* which the critics characterize as Goethe's "greatest and most representative work."

Thurnau, H. C. "Faust and the Good Life." *Philological Quarterly* XII, No. 3 (1933): 269-79.

Calls attention to "Goethe's recognition in *Faust* of self-surrender and self-control as fundamental virtues, to the embodiment of these virtues in his two outstanding creations, Gretchen and Helena, and to the influence of these *personalities* upon the character of Faust."

Ugrinsky, Alexej, ed. *Goethe in the Twentieth Century.* New York: Greenwood Press, 1987, 197 p.

Collects essays presented at a forum occasioned by the 150th anniversary of Goethe's death. Included in this collection are "Federico García Lorca's Debt to Goethe's *Faust,*" by Elizabeth Bohning and Judy B. McInnes; "Goethe, Jung: Homunculus and Faust," by John Fitzell; "The Influence of Goethe's *Faust* on Hans Henny Jahnn," by Thomas Freeman; and other studies.

Vickery, John B. and Sellery, J'nan, eds. *Goethe's "Faust, Part One": Essays in Criticism.* Belmont, Calif.: Wadsworth Publishing, 1969, 183 p.

Contains several important essays on *Faust I* by such noted Goethe scholars as Barker Fairley, Stuart Atkins, and Eudo C. Mason.

Wicksteed, Philip H. " 'Magic'—A Contribution to the Study of Goethe's *Faust.*" *The Hibbert Journal* X, No. 4 (1911): 754-64.

Discusses ways in which the magic practiced by Mephistopheles and Faust impedes Faust's search for intellectual and spiritual contentment.

Willoughby, L. A. "Goethe's *Faust:* A Morphological Approach." In *Goethe: Poet and Thinker,* edited by Elizabeth M. Wilkinson and L. A. Willoughby, 1962, pp. 95-117.

Studies the elements and structure of language in *Faust* as a means of understanding the central themes of the drama.

Yuill, W. E. " 'My Father Was a Good Man, Not Too Bright.' On Translating Goethe's *Faust. Erster Teil.*" *German Life and Letters* XLI, No. 4 (July 1988): 402-12.

Assesses the strengths and weaknesses of several popular English translations of *Faust I.*

Jens Peter Jacobsen

1847-1885

Danish novelist, short story writer, and poet.

Jacobsen is considered one of the most seminal Scandinavian novelists of the late nineteenth century. An enthusiastic proponent of the scientific theories of Charles Darwin, he is often linked with the Naturalist writers, who sought in their fiction to demonstrate the workings of heredity and environment in human society. However, critics note that the social commentary in Jacobsen's work is often overshadowed by his luxuriantly descriptive style, his effete and often masochistic eroticism, and his perceptive depictions of individual psychology. His synthesis of these various elements is regarded as an important contribution to the development of modern literature, and commentators have found the seeds of numerous literary styles in his work.

Jacobsen was born in 1847 in Thisted, a small village on Denmark's Jutland peninsula. His parents were uneducated merchants, but their financial success enabled Jacobsen to aspire to higher education. He attended the provincial school in Thisted, where he demonstrated a particular interest in botany. Apart from the sciences, he did not distinguish himself academically, and it was not until 1867, after four years of preparation and a failed attempt to pass his entrance exams, that he was admitted to the University of Copenhagen. One factor that protracted Jacobsen's studies was the increasing amount of time he had begun to devote to literary interests. In Copenhagen he met Georg Brandes and several other participants in the fledgling Modern Breakthrough movement, a group whose members rejected the Romantic idealism and aestheticism that had dominated European literature through the first half of the nineteenth century, seeking instead to realistically depict social problems in literature. Despite Brandes's discouraging reception of his early poetry, Jacobsen continued to write, and his literary endeavors gradually thrived alongside his scientific studies. In 1872, having published several widely debated articles on Darwinian theory, Jacobsen translated Darwin's *On the Origin of Species* (1859) into Danish, and, in 1874, he followed with *The Descent of Man* (1871). During this period he also published a novella, *Mogens.* Its favorable reception encouraged him to begin work on a historical novel, *Fru Marie Grubbe, (Marie Grubbe),* based on the life of a notorious seventeenth-century noblewoman who left her wealthy husband to marry an uneducated merchant and later lived with a peasant boatman. In 1872 he was diagnosed with tuberculosis and given two years to live. He continued work on *Marie Grubbe,* which was published to wide acclaim in 1876, rendering its author a nationally known figure. He had begun work on his second novel, *Niels Lyhne,* in 1874, but the increasing severity of his illness protracted his always laborious composition process, and the novel was not completed until 1880. During the final years of his

life, Jacobsen produced only a few short stories. He died in 1885.

Marie Grubbe, Jacobsen's first novel, chronicles the protagonist's life from adolescence to old age, demonstrating how her three romantic liaisons progressively enhance her self-knowledge and sexual satisfaction although they diminish her social and economic status. To explain Grubbe's seemingly self-destructive behavior, Jacobsen depicts the social and psychological factors involved in her decision, and his characterization has been commended in particular for its psychological verisimilitude. Jacobsen presented his portrait of Marie Grubbe in a vivid, lush, and historically accurate setting. This backdrop and the detailed style in which it is delineated have been widely praised; however, some reviewers criticized Jacobsen's style as precious. *Marie Grubbe,* wrote Paul Rosenfeld, "smells overly of lavender."

As he explained in an 1878 letter to Brandes, Jacobsen intended that *Niels Lyhne* depict the spiritual quandary of the generation preceding his. Reared in the intellectual ethos of Romanticism, the members of this generation had been taught to view the universe as divinely ordered and essentially benevolent. However, mid-nineteenth-century scientific discoveries, including those of Darwin, increasingly challenged such presuppositions and led to dramatic personal and social upheavals as belief systems and mores were reassessed and, in some cases, rejected. In *Niels Lyhne* Jacobsen sought to describe the emotional impact of this transition. Jacobsen's blueprint for the novel notwithstanding, critics have observed that *Niels Lyhne* is less a social than an individual study. This may have resulted from Jacobsen's deteriorating physical condition, which prevented him from remaining in Copenhagen while he was writing, and thus removed him from the contemporaries who might have contributed material to help him realize his initial intentions. Isolated, weakened, and depressed in Thisted, he focused instead on a hero whose state of mind resembled his own. His protagonist is a young man who aspires to greatness—personal, poetic, and romantic—but whose pervasive impotence prevents him from realizing any of his grandiose ambitions. In *Marie Grubbe* Jacobsen was concerned equally with character and setting; in *Niels Lyhne,* he focused on his protagonist to the almost completion exclusion of contextual detail, and critics have observed that the novel's sparse historical information derives more from Jacobsen's own era than from the previous generation. Yet many deem it the better work, praising Jacobsen's delineation of its yearning but weak title character, while disagreeing to some extent in their interpretations of its meaning. Some hold that Niels Lyhne's sorrows accumulate because he inhabits the Naturalists' indifferent universe; others assert that he engenders his own unhappiness when he fails to defeat his self-acknowledged weaknesses, a psychological test which typically determines the outcome of Romantic novels. Most critics concur that the novel's exhaustive depiction of the dynamics (and stasis) of an individual psyche, its uninhibited discussion of sexuality, and its demonstration of irresolvable anguish mark the novel as an early example of what later came to be known as Decadent literature. Stylistically, critics feel that the later work extends *Marie Grubbe*'s lavish, luxuriant detail into the excess typical of Decadent fiction, using minute observations to emphasize his psychological portraiture. Judged by some as overly subtle and oppressively languorous, this style is used to reveal a central consciousness whose atheism, confused and sometimes masochistic sensuality, and ineffectiveness—all characteristic of the Decadent hero—offended many contemporary readers.

Jacobsen's short fiction is also highly regarded. *Mogens* follows a young man through a passionate but callow affair and into the sexual fulfillment and emotional maturity he achieves in a subsequent relationship. Although its narrative is considered underdeveloped and disjointed, *Mogens* is also regarded as the promising debut of an innovative and already sophisticated stylist. Respected and, according to Niels Lyhne Jensen, often imitated, "Pesten i Bergamo" ("Plague in Bergamo") depicts the variously ineffectual reactions of Bergamo's medieval peasants to a pestilence. "Fru Fønss" ("Mrs. Fønss"), Jacobsen's last work of fiction, presents a widowed mother who becomes estranged from her children when she remarries. On her deathbed she writes a letter, commonly read as Jacobsen's own farewell, expressing her love for them and for life. As Jensen points out, Jacobsen's affinity for brief, imagistic scenes is well suited to stories and sketches because they do not require the narrative coherence necessary in longer works of fiction.

Praised in particular for demonstrating the spiritual and intellectual temper of a transitional era, Jacobsen is universally acknowledged as one of the authors who engendered the modern era in Scandinavian literature. Both his alienated protagonists and his detailed and sensual prose were widely imitated in the decades following his death, and his works prefigured the treatment of psychological and existential questions which became prevalent in fiction during the twentieth century.

PRINCIPAL WORKS

Fru Marie Grubbe: Interieurer fra det syttende Aarhundrede (novel) 1876
  [*Marie Grubbe: Interiors from the Seventeenth Century,* 1914]
Niels Lyhne (novel) 1880
  [*Siren Voices,* 1896; also translated as *Niels Lyhne,* 1919]
Mogens og andre Noveller (novella and short stories) 1882
  [*Mogens, and Other Stories,* 1921]
Digte og Udkest (poems) 1896
  [*Poems by J. P. Jacobsen,* 1920]
Samlede Vaerker. 5 vols. (collected works) 1924-29

Francis Hackett (essay date 1918)

[*In the following excerpt from a review of* Marie Grubbe, *Hackett commends both Jacobsen's painterly historical detail and his realistic characterizations.*]

At first sight **Marie Grubbe** (pronounced Groob-eh) bears close resemblance to most historic novels. [Translator Hanna Astrup] Larsen's able and sympathetic introduction quotes a letter from the author to Edvard Brandes, written from Copenhagen in 1873, "Just think, I get up every morning at eleven and go to the Royal Library, where I read old documents and letters and lies and descriptions of murder, adultery, corn rates, whoremongery, market prices, gardening, the siege of Copenhagen, divorce proceedings, christenings, estate registers, genealogies, and funeral sermons. All this is to become a wonderful novel to be called **Mistress Marie Grubbe, Interiors from the Seventeenth Century.** You remember, she is the one who is mentioned in Holberg's Epistles and in *The Goose Girl,* by Andersen, and who was first married to U. F. Gyldenlöve and afterwards to a ferryman." Except for the lively words "adultery" and "whoremongery" and the promising words "corn rates" and "market prices," there is an ominous sound about this memorandum. It makes one feel that Mr. Jens Peter Jacobsen might reproduce When Knighthood Went to Seed. But there is salvage in the fact that Ulrik Frederik Gyldenløve was once viceroy of Norway, and that his wife did actually go from her exalted station to the more mobile but less distinguished position of ferryman's wife. The "wonderful" novel, in truth, belies neither the threat nor the promise of its author's letter. It is at once historical in the stiff sense and in the free sense, portraying a true human being but not quite as if she were living on the next floor.

It must be said at once that Jens Peter Jacobsen had an admirable idea of the uses of his rich material. It was his object to weave it into something much more decorative than an ordinary novel can afford to be, something at the same time quite different from the sentimental conventionality of looking patronizingly backward. In this his success may be acknowledged, especially in so capable a translation. What he has created is, in one aspect, a tapestry of the Danish seventeenth century, with the marked events of the epoch picked out in definite figures, and the background peculiarly finished and glowing. Thus we have, in the first hundred pages of a book only 250 pages long, the farmhouse of Erik Grubbe with its sun-heated garden, gilly flowers and honeysuckle, its clattering yard and racing greyhounds, its lord and its pastor getting quarrelsomely drunk by candlelight while the child Marie is made to suffer by Erik Grubbe's housekeeper-mistress. We have, in quick succession, the town life of the young girl at her aunt's, with the siege of Copenhagen enveloping its pieties and formalities; and we have the siege itself, first driving the townsmen to frenzy against pro-Swedes and pacifists, and then settling down to the business of victory. The love-making and death of a great military hero—with a death-bed repentance of the most delectable description—precede the raising of the siege, and with it comes the rebound of Marie's ascetic maidenliness when her accession to grown-up clothes coincides with peace ("How fascinating the eager parley about whether this silk chamelot was too thick to show the lines of her figure or that Turkish green too crude for her complexion!") So far the story has the growth and undergrowth of a fine tapestry, its flatness and its decorum, its drama cleverly disjointed at the sideboard and brought forward in treasurable detail. The humanity does not begin to glow in Marie Grubbe until the worthless Ulrik Frederik puts away his first wife and weds Marie Grubbe and leaves her in a passionate loneliness when he goes to the wars in Spain.

The ripening of Marie's temperament never destroys the decorative quality of the novel, but it introduces a reality that is quite unaffectedly modern. When Ulrik comes back tanned and thickened and drunken, Marie's flaming resentment is human; and the scene in her garret in the Norway castle, when he strives to bully her back to him, is like male and female since the first apple fermented. The note of reality is preserved especially in Sti Høgh, the man in whom the mouse of introspection has gnawed through the strands of faith. Marie is deceived when Sti Høgh lays out two rude Germans (Germans were rude in the seventeenth century); but Marie is undeceived after their year of liaison in Paris. Except for the moonlight of Nürnberg there is no ray of beauty for her from her thirtieth to her forty-

sixth year. Then she falls in love with the young coachman of her new prosaic, miserly husband and, at forty-six, the full vigor of her temperament asserts itself. Up to that time she has known viceroys and gallants and high-browed sceptics and curmudgeons and bullies, but never a lover. "She had grown fuller of form and paler, and there was a slow languor in all her movements. Her eyes were generally quite empty of expression, but sometimes they would grow strangely bright, and she had fallen into the habit of setting her lips in a meaningless smile." But Sören's beauty, seen on the night of the fire, arouses in her a need which finds manifestation, and her capture of Sören is one of the most spirited pages in literature.

She is driven out, like the wife in *In the Shadow of the Glen,* but she goes with complete acceptance of the fate that at last she could invite with open arms. Sören is rather bewildered. Still, he loves her. And, as he shows in beating her, he treats her as an absolute equal. The scene in the tavern with the public executioner is unforgettable, as also that beautifully imagined scene in which she ferries the bloated and degenerate Sti Høgh across the stream, and talks to him in the idiom of a peasant addressing superiority.

The last half of this novel has less self-conscious style, fewer jewels of the Walter Pater variety. I must say I prefer it. But I know few novels of any civilization, Danish or otherwise, which selects so perfectly the episodes that confirm an epoch. The epoch was fascinating to Jacobsen for many reasons. His eye is ravenous for color, and he has the excuse of remoteness to justify his epicurean, hypersensitive pictorial art. But better than the epoch is Marie Grubbe. She looks out of her time wistfully and burningly, with eternal gaze.

Without knowledge of the original I should not dare to call **Marie Grubbe** a masterpiece. In its translation it appears too staccato, too stilted, to be termed great. But whatever the artificiality that comes from trimming one's work excessively, there is in this tale a very haunting beauty and a personality that can scarcely be forgotten. I could imagine a strange and moving play made from **Marie Grubbe,** one that showed faithfully the apparent descent of this ardent and unsatisfied woman, a descent that was really an evolution—one by which, at the sacrifice of externals, a heart was courageously appeased. (pp. 237-38)

> *Francis Hackett, "Marie Grubbe," in* The New Republic, *Vol. XV, No. 190, June 22, 1918, pp. 237-38.*

Paul Rosenfeld (essay date 1925)

[*Rosenfeld was a respected American music and literary critic. In the following essay, he admires the pensive lyricism of Jacobsen's novels, and the ethereal sensitivity of their characters, asserting that* Marie Grubbe *and* Niels Lyhne *contributed to the larger European resurgence of the Romantic novel.*]

Jacobsen is the seraph of Danish literature. Even in translation his prose sings with frail unearthly fervor. Across scenes of desire and of death, of yearning and of catastrophe, the tender melodiousness spreads a soft and golden tone. The world lies mellow in these novels like light caught on surfaces of highly waxed old wood. *Marie Grubbe,* "interiors" from out the courtly life of the seventeenth century, is the work of a Vermeer in words, and pearly as one of the canvases of the magic Dutchman. And the semi-biographical *Niels Lyhne* is a poem of late summer afternoon and sunset, suffused deeply with the very breath of the hour. Images may lift the prose into wild romantic flight; the soul may speak to Niels in savage trumpet blasts; and sprays of blossoming roses build castles and vaulted choirs with their fat bloom. But vibrancy and power are both absent from the tone. The springtide when it comes flooding the valley where the anæmic northern woman Niels' mother lies dying is honeyed and hurtless, soft and idyllic and caressing only; a drift of naïve bright flowers, a sparkle of gliding waters, a rain of soft delicious lights and scents. And the vignettes of the damp, dreary northern fall, and of the wet and endless Baltic winter, are suffused equally with the wistfulness and delicacy of sunset hue.

It lies, the wistfulness, in the tales themselves not less than in the carrying form. They, too, have a "dying fall"; bring dreamy and rich tenderness awash together; sing with the bowing of the heart before the helplessness of the feminine soul. *Marie Grubbe* figures the destiny of the passive creature through the person of a patrician woman of the court of Frederick the Third, dainty and over-tense, filled with infinite capacity for passion and pain; and submitted helplessly to the men to whom she gives herself; first the handsome faithless bastard; then the courtier weak and sensitive like herself; last the groom who takes her far from the life she has known into poverty, and loves her and beats her because he loves her, and then is brought back to her cabin broken and dying. Through a protagonist of a different sex and through the atmosphere of a different century, *Niels Lyhne* achieves much the same effect. For the exquisite reconstructions of the scenery and spirit of the past there are substituted tiny impressionistic paintings of the Danish countryside and of Copenhagen before the war of 1864. But the narrative sings the same painful wonder over the destiny of the inactive inaggressive being. The hero is the weary end of an ancient line, a half poet of sensuous ineffectual cast. And all the characters in the novel, Niels' mother like himself, Begum, Mrs. Boye, Fennimore, Gerda, are dreamers, dainty and lacking in power of the will. The mother passes her girlhood in perpetual daydream, tries to find a reality in marriage, and sinks disappointed into her fantasies. Only during the months when death is close upon her does she taste of the living beauty for which she pined all her days. Niels, apparently gifted for creation, possessed of the capacity for feeling from which poetry is supposed to flow, welling in exquisite and poignant emotions, never achieves anything durable. Some inward fatigue weighs upon him. He cannot successfully leave his dreams. Loves and a marriage come to Niels. But life slips through his fingers. His friends die or become estranged from him. After the death of his young wife and child he loses interest in living; and in the end perishes in the Schleswig war rich in ecstasy and suffering, and poor of some miracle which should have happened and filled his hands, and never came.

Jacobsen was faced with imminent death while working on these romances. Restless years in Copenhagen filled with inconclusive love affairs and much dissipation had eaten heavily into his small store of health; and he returned to his mother in the country under sentence from the doctors, and condemned to a bare régime. And in the dreamy beauty of his tales, he expressed the feeling of his own end which could not ever have been far from him those last years: *vita somnium breve;* existence full of rich and painful things, and yet unsubstantial as mist; destiny carrying him upon its silent rushing stream into known gray lands far from the comforting and familiar objects to which he would have clung. But it is not only the sign of an individual state of being which this impeccable hand set down. The resignation, the softness and dreamy melancholy of these tales is characteristic of nineteenth century Denmark after the defeat at the hands of Prussia; and characteristic at the same time of a condition which transcended by far the confines of the small Scandinavian state. Want of some inner faith in life, some power of momentum, was in the cultivated individuals the world through; and left them static and directionless in a luxurious atmosphere. And sometimes, it is the whole north of many centuries that speaks in this wistful music. Unfriendly nature has ever tended to produce folk rich in inner development, in imagination and the power of feeling, and still curiously incapable of laying aggressive hand upon the moment. The blood rushes up, and then hesitates near the surface; an immediate response and clearing does not come. Devastating northern longing: the yearning of the human being, cast into bitter climes, for the warmth, the ease and carelessness of the south and the sun, sucks life away. And yet, no south and tropic heat can bring relaxation. In Africa, fulfillment remains as distant as in Scotland and Brandenburg and Denmark. There is no giving in; and yearning, always.

These novels are part of general European literature, too, through the influence exerted by them. They have played a rôle in the development of the novel in countries other than their own; in Germany, particularly. For just as Jacobsen the lyric poet has come to stand in something of the relation of a forerunner to Stefan Georg, to Rainer Marie Rilke and Hugo von Hofmannsthal, to the entire group of German poets moving toward ever more refined means of expression, so Jacobsen the romancer has contributed to the defeat of the naturalistic school of novel-writing in Teutonic lands. With *Marie Grubbe,* with *Mogens* and in particular with *Niels Lyhne,* he helped exorcise Zola, and bring about a recrudescence of the analytical novel. For just and poetic translations are the rule in Germany; and *Niels Lyhne,* little diminished in the process of adaptation, appeared in German at the moment when its particular impulse was most living. It was the moment when the reaction against the complete preoccupation with the composition of society and complete neglect of the psychology of the individual, of which Zola and his followers all over the Continent had been so guilty, had begun to gather head in artistic circles. The century, it will be remembered, had begun with transcendentalism, and seen flourish a novel that mirrored and analyzed almost exclusively the self. Indeed, for the novelists of the romantic school, the world itself was but an emanation of the ego. But with the rise of industrialism and the ascendancy of its accompaniment, positivism, the novel had swerved into the study of the forces and conditions of nature and society to which the individual is subjected. The self ceased to interest exclusively, and diminished in importance for the novelist. In Balzac, the two worlds, the subjective and the objective, are still fairly well balanced. But with the arrival of naturalism, the psychology of the individual was degraded to minor importance. In the novels of Zola the characters are not very much more than types—prostitutes, laborers, peasants, artists, priests and others. The world is conceived as having an existence entirely independent of the visions of the characters. Indeed, it is almost conceived as having an existence entirely independent of the vision of the novelist himself. To be sure, Zola had defined the naturalistic novel as "nature viewed through a temperament." In truth, however, his ideal was the scientific document, the abstract and passionless narration of "facts." Had he been able, he would have created fictions approximating the deadly reports of social investigators. Luckily for the novel, Zola oftentimes failed of his goal. He was too much the rhapsode, the symphonist. The tediousness of complete impersonality has been attained only by his unique disciple, Pierre Hamp. Still, his theories, his pseudo-scientific attitude, continued to weigh upon the form. Before the visions of the novelists all over Europe there continued to float the *ignis fatuus* of the "experimental" romance, the scientific work.

Toward 1885, the individualistic reaction set in. The self was once more become the center, the principal matter, the object of analysis. The new psychological novel was born; Bourget introduced Stendhal anew to France; Maeterlinck translated Novalis; in Germany, folk ceased laughing at the romantic school. And if the pendulum did not swing back all the way to the ground of the romanticists, if novelists did not again conceive the world as an emanation of the ego, nevertheless, Zola's conception of a world independent of the vision of his characters, was entirely abandoned. The study of the external world as the mirror and revealer of the self, came into being. Henceforward, landscapes, inanimate nature, the objective world, were to be represented only because of what the characters felt toward them and because of the strata of their selves revealed in the transference.

And Jacobsen in *Niels Lyhne* gave the young German novelists of the nineties a perfectly realized example of a "subjective" novel. Of his two chief works, *Marie Grubbe* is perhaps the less "subjective"; it is more dramatic, and full of a color which is more of the century than of the heroine. Indeed, at moments it seems slightly derivative from the "interiors" of the Dutch painters. But *Niels Lyhne* pictures primarily the states of an individual soul, and with profound psychological insight records the development of a sensibility. It concerns itself almost exclusively with the inner life of its hero, with his feelings and fantasies and moods. The novelist lingers with greatest love over the moments of intense lyricism, when the soul of his man becomes an ecstatically vibrating organ. And though the drama stands clear, the lyrical states embody the story no less than the scenes of action. Moreover, the world of Niels is exclusively his own idea. The very quality of the hero and his mother come to us through the landscapes and descriptive pieces.

And throughout the post-naturalistic epoch of German prose, one feels the influence of this finely shaded painting of elusive mood. It is in Schnitzler, in Mann, in Voigt-Diedrichs. If their prose has remained less diapred and melodious, and their novel-writing more documentary, they nevertheless follow on many paths trampled by Jacobsen. The dreamy young Viennese of Schnitzler, responsive to scarcely another interest than love; Tonio Kröger and Hanno Buddenbrook of Mann, what are they but younger brethren of Niels Lyhne? More recently, another figure has joined the cohort of brothers. It is that of Malte Laurids Brigge, of Rilke; Niels Lyhne once again; but become more sinisterly enervate and neurotic.

Possibly, for us, *Marie Grubbe* will prove more lastingly attractive. We have had the benefit of the form of *Niels Lyhne,* and the stuff of the earlier book is a little more solid. Jacobsen was a dying man when he wrote the history of the nineteenth century dreamer, *Frühgereift und zart und traurig;* and his illness seems in one or two instances to have dimmed his artistic vision. The book smells a trifle overmuch of lavender. The latter chapters, which deal with the maturity of the hero, are somewhat thinner than the earlier ones recounting his boyhood and adolescence. Unable to live himself out because of his consuming malady, Jacobsen was doubtlessly unwilling to face the maturity of his character with the same intensity with which he faced his youth; and less richly stocked with material for the painting of the man's years. Very little is said of the wedlock of Niels and his girl-wife. And although the picture of Niels' encounter with his young aunt in the darkened, rose-scented room; of his farewell to Erik; and of Fennimore's revery in the warm chamber while she waits for her lover stand clear in one's memory as beautifully achieved things, the novelist has expended the treasures of his lyricism most lavishly on the scenes of death which are too frequent, and nearly cloying. The novel is overful of premature deaths. Practically each one of the principal characters meets an untimely end. Niels' father and mother die in early middle life. Edele, Erik, Gerda, Niels himself, perish in their youth. It is a little as though Jacobsen, aware of his own swiftly approaching extinction, and overcome by the pathos of his existence, had unconsciously desired to insist upon, and bring forcibly home to his readers, the sadness of a lot like his own.

And still, there is little to choose between the two little masterpieces. One shuts both books with the satisfaction which comes from having encountered beautifully accomplished work. With somewhat less of appetite, less of volume and flow than his contemporaries in France and Russia had, Jacobsen nevertheless achieved almost perfectly what he set out to do, and produced rich things with unforgetable suave and singing surfaces. We return to them. For they were made with the wisdom of the violet and the pine: and both plants are content to remain themselves. (pp. 289-300)

Paul Rosenfeld, "Jens Peter Jacobsen," in his Men Seen: Twenty-Four Modern Authors, *The Dial Press, 1925, pp. 289-300.*

Alrik Gustafson   (essay date 1940)

[*Gustafson was an American critic who wrote extensively on Scandinavian literature. In the following excerpt, he explains that the characters in* Niels Lyhne *represent the varied responses of mid-nineteenth-century youth, reared during the Romantic period, to the scientific spirit of their era. Although he considers the novel's style overly mannered in places, and Niels Lyhne's religious feeling sketchily and unrealistically developed, Gustafson praises Jacobsen's delineation of the hereditary and environmental influences that ultimately paralyze Niels's romantic and creative endeavors, and lauds the work as the first Scandinavian psychological novel.*]

Jacobsen's second novel *Niels Lyhne* deals with contemporary Danish life—not with the '70's and '80's, Jacobsen's own generation strictly speaking, but with the transitional period which led immediately up to these two decades and which reflected many of the essential problems of these decades. *Niels Lyhne* is primarily a study in decadent psychology. Niels, the hero of the novel, goes through all of the successive phases of a progressive disillusionment, a disillusionment which finally brings him to "the death—the difficult death." An incurable romantic dreamer by temperament, and yet harboring a skeptical hereditary strain in direct opposition to his romantic dream world, Niels came to find that the realities of life serve but to shatter his inner dream world at every point. And so he finally dies—bravely? . . . yes, so we are told. Yet how sadly hopeless his last days were, days without form or direction, a poignantly meaningless succession of hours: "He had lost faith in himself, lost his belief in the power of human beings to bear the life they had to live. Existence had sprung a leak, and its contents were seeping out through all the cracks without plan or purpose." The reader of the novel may be permitted to judge for himself with what degree of buoyancy or vigor Niels at last came to formulate the final solitary postulate in his ultimate strangely decadent stoic profession of faith: "To bear life as it is! to bear life as it is and allow life to shape itself according to its own laws."

If *Niels Lyhne* is, in the first place, a study in the decadent psychology of a particular individual, whose every mood is dissected and whose final tragic destiny is pursued relentlessly to its hopeless end, the novel is also to be looked upon more broadly as symptomatic of a generation. Niels is the transition type of the mid-nineteenth century—a youth nurtured early in an unreal world of Romantic literature, but a youth who comes by degrees face to face with the sterner materials of an actual world. He comes thus, in the last analysis, to represent the tragic merging in a single personality of romanticism and realism—

wandering between two worlds,
The one dead, the other powerless to be born.

The novel in this sense becomes a penetrating analysis in fictional form of certain developmental phases in nineteenth century European culture, particularly as they find expression in the artistic and intellectual life of Scandinavia in the middle and late nineteenth century. The two worlds which make their impacts upon Niels, the world of romance and the world of reality, are illustrated in the pages of the novel in a great variety of ways. Most significant, perhaps, in the impressionable, formative period of Niels's childhood and early youth, were the extreme romantic tastes of his mother, who was constantly dreaming about

> . . . snowy Alpine peaks above blue-black mountain lakes, and sparkling rivers between vine-clad banks, and long lines of mountains with ruins peeping out of the woods, and then lofty halls with marble gods . . .

(pp. 89-90)

But this dream world of Romanticism, into which Niels had been introduced by his mother was already crumbling under the weight of its own extravagant superstructure long before the middle of the nineteenth century. And what remained of the crumbling edifice was shattered almost beyond recognition by the new spirit of science and the frontal attack of the empirical sister philosophies of utilitarianism and positivism. Men had come to see that there is a tremendous disparity between the fairest dreams of romance and the cold facts of reality; and many of them went on to conclude, as Jacobsen puts it, "that even the fairest dreams and the deepest longings do not add an inch to the stature of the human soul." And so they turned their backs on romanticism and hailed a new order of realism.

Those who were strong could make such a shift with impunity, and suffer no ill effects. Not so with the more sensitive, those who were more emotionally impressionable; and among these was Niels Lyhne. Gladly as Niels ultimately welcomed, on the theoretical side, the new intellectual freedom afforded by a world of reality, his emotional roots, and all that these implied in terms of his unconscious and subconscious character, were too deeply implanted in the world of romance to be summarily torn up with no attendant strain upon the delicately balanced fibres of his spiritual organism. And so he became—not consciously it must be stressed (for a conscious artistic "program" of decadence had not as yet been formulated), and yet very really—an inevitable victim of that kind of spiritual *malaise* which came by the end of the century to be called decadence. If one objects, on purely literary historical grounds, to calling Niels a decadent, he is in any case a transition figure of the mid-nineteenth century which was being swept rapidly toward decadence in the more strictly historical *fin de siècle* sense of the term. (p. 92)

Those who have read both *Marie Grubbe* and *Niels Lyhne* in the original will feel a distinct difference in stylistic tone; and this difference will be felt even more sharply by those readers who have also gone through the pages of *Mogens,* the short story which was composed before Jacobsen first became stricken by disease. There is a certain youthful effusiveness, a kind of hearty exuberance just short of vigor in the description of nature in both *Mogens* and *Marie Grubbe* that is almost totally lacking in *Niels Lyhne.* Marvelously beautiful as are some of the descriptive passages in *Niels Lyhne,* theirs is the beauty of decay: a note of nervous artificiality infuses them. One might dip into the pages of *Niels Lyhne* and find almost anywhere such passages as these:

> . . . The sitting-room was flooded with sunshine, and a blossoming oleander made the air heavy with its sweet fragrance. There was no sound except a muffled splash from the flowerstand whenever the goldfish moved in their glass dish. . . .
>
> One evening she [Niels's mother] was sitting alone in the summer parlor, gazing out through the wide-open doors. The trees of the garden hid the gold and crimson of the sunset, but in one spot the trunks parted to reveal a bit of fiery sky, from which a sunburst of long, deep golden rays shot out, waking green tints and bronze-brown reflections in the dark leafy masses.
>
> High above the restless tree-tops, the clouds drifted dark against a smoke-red sky, and as they hurried on, they left behind them little loosened tufts, tiny little strips of cloud which the sunlight steeped in a wine-colored glow.

It is clear from such passages that the subtly beautiful disintegration of decadence is at work on Jacobsen's style, a style which in earlier years, despite its disturbing involutions, its artificial mannerisms, and its laboured precision of word choice, managed somehow to retain a certain spontaneity, a certain undeniable vigor of its own—a vigor as of the fine breath of springtime, pulsing though never violent, strong and yet not muscular. The style of *Niels Lyhne,* on the other hand, is a style fitted to late summer and early autumn moods—a style enervatingly heavy in both its movement and its imagery, a style thoroughly in keeping with the weary ennui which Niels always came to feel after some tentative excursion into the world of action and passion outside his own brooding inner self. It must have been particularly *Niels Lyhne* that the Swedish poet and critic Ola Hansson had in mind when he spoke of Jacobsen's style as reminding one of a "hot-house or a garden of roses."

In November 1878 Jacobsen, who because of the precarious condition of his health had fled temporarily to Montreux in the south of France, penned a long letter to Georg Brandes in which he indicates what he is trying to do in *Niels Lyhne.* This letter reveals clearly that Jacobsen's central purpose in *Niels Lyhne* was to make a careful, objective study in a transitional decadent generation—a generation of youth which sought various ways out of a common dilemma, with no single individual of this generation finding a wholly satisfactory solution of his immediate personal problem. The novel itself reveals how carefully Jacobsen had analyzed the various types representative of this generation of youth and the way in which each attempted to work his way out of the hopelessly entangled web of mood and idea and circumstance which surrounded him. Those who—according to Jacobsen's letter to Brandes—"struck out against the old but did not respect the new which they themselves accepted" are represented in the novel by Dr. Hjerrild, a young medical man, completely disillusioned, a thoroughgoing skeptic, who scoffed freely in one of the important passages in the novel at Niels's idealistic atheism. Those who—as described in the

letter—finally succumbed to "the siren voices of tradition and childhood memories on the one hand and the thundering condemnation of society on the other" are to be found represented in the novel in such a character as Fru Boye, who talked with a certain daring charm of the necessity of freedom in art and poetry, and even for that matter in love, but who finally found established society too strong for her.

Fru Boye and Dr. Hjerrild are but two of the typical representatives of a generation of transition which *Niels Lyhne* concerns itself with. Others are also sketched by Jacobsen in these pages, some in greater, some in less detail. It is, of course, in Niels himself that we find by far the most exhaustive and penetrating analysis of a representative of this generation of transition. Idealistic in intent, yet often weak in character, Niels goes through his short experience of life a constant victim of his own ineptness and his own illusions. Both heredity and an early environment had dealt unkindly with him; and ultimately, in young manhood, he comes to succumb to an inevitable, almost sordid fate—without, however, either yielding, as had Fru Boye, to a society which he despised, or giving himself up to the kind of worldly cynicism represented in Dr. Hjerrild. For the former of these he was too sensitive, for the latter he was perhaps too weak. (pp. 93-5)

At various times in his short, tragic experience of life Niels becomes deeply preoccupied with religious considerations. Sincere as Jacobsen doubtless was in his effort to present the religious theme in his novel, it must, I think, be the judgment of posterity that the specifically religious element in *Niels Lyhne* is hardly convincing. There is something forced and wooden for the most part in the way in which the religious material is introduced, so forced and wooden that even the sympathetic reader who preserves any vestige of critical balance tends to be disturbed, if not definitely skeptical for a moment, both as to Jacobsen's knowledge of human psychology and his ability to motivate with intelligence and critical taste certain of the narrative episodes in his novel. We are expected, for example, to accept without protest the assumption that Niels as a boy of twelve, because of a single experience in which his prayer had not been answered, arrives at the theoretical conclusion that there is no God. Hardy's grotesquely pathetic little Father Time goes even farther, we remember, not without a shudder; but Father Time is one of those melancholy prodigies in the English novelist which even Hardy enthusiasts would rather pass over in silence. About the only thing we can be thankful for is that Hardy *did kill* his gruesome little creation at a tender age. What he should have done with Father Time had the child continued to drag out an unbearable existence is beyond at least the average human imagination.

The boyhood atheism in Jacobsen's Niels seems questionable enough in itself; but we might feel, at least, that it was fitted less artificially into the general narrative pattern of the novel were we kept even occasionally aware of Niels's religious position in the years which immediately follow. But not so. We do not come upon the religious theme again until quite late in the novel, when Niels has reached the estate of manhood—and then in an episode which seems rather forcibly foisted upon the reader for purposes expository rather than narrative. It is in this passage that Niels defines his position as an idealistic atheist to his friend Dr. Hjerrild, whose practical-minded skepticism cannot but smile in not entirely gentle irony at the adolescent vehemence with which Niels insists upon his melancholy paradox: "There is no God, and man is his prophet." Near the very end of the novel, it is true, the religious element seems more convincingly motivated than it had been before; but perhaps our impression is more favorable at this point largely because we sense in the later developments of the novel the close autobiographical parallel in Jacobsen's treatment of the religious theme. We know that Jacobsen himself was soon to face "the death—the difficult death"; and we know that he was steeling himself to face death, as Niels did finally, without the comforting solace of a traditional religion. Though our consciousness of this parallel may tend to soften the severity of our judgment of Jacobsen's treatment of the religious theme in the last chapters of *Niels Lyhne,* we can hardly count Jacobsen among the novelists who deal adequately with the religious theme. Jacobsen's *Niels Lyhne* lacks almost entirely the profundity of religious analysis which we come upon in Sigrid Undset's *Kristin Lavransdatter;* and even Selma Lagerlöf's *Jerusalem* goes far beyond *Niels Lyhne* in its understanding of religious psychology. It may be that Jacobsen's characters hardly lend themselves to convincing religious portraiture . . . it may be that Jacobsen himself was temperamentally incapable of creating a convincing religious problem in fiction . . . it may be—and this seems most reasonable—that Jacobsen, a scientist, was too close to the essentially materialistic science of his century. . . . Whatever the reason, it would seem apparent that Jacobsen is superficial in his religious analysis in *Niels Lyhne*—superficial at least in comparison with the maturity of his art and critical judgment as reflected in almost any other important aspect of his novel. (pp. 96-7)

If Jacobsen's touch is uncertain in his handling of the religious problem in *Niels Lyhne,* he is by contrast firm and convincing in his treatment of those other phases of Niels's inner development which affected his character and gradually combined to result in an attitude of disillusioned hopelessness which finally led him to a form of exit from this world just short of suicide. It is in Jacobsen's penetrating analysis of the double influence on Niels's character of heredity and environment, and the way in which these two influences ultimately come to affect the will, that the novel achieves its real intellectual distinction and its permanent critical significance.

As a scientist Jacobsen was by training highly conscious of the determining influence of heredity upon human character. It is therefore natural for him to sketch in the opening chapters of *Niels Lyhne* the family history of Niels's parents, though he does not go to the length of providing the reader with such an elaborate genealogical machinery as is to be found in Zola's Rougon-Macquart novels. Especially important are the detailed references to heredity which Jacobsen introduces so skillfully in the two opening chapters of *Niels Lyhne.* The first chapter is given over almost entirely to an analysis of the temperament and character of the parents of Niels as they had been determined

by the earlier history of their families. The opening paragraphs strike the note which is maintained throughout the chapter—

> She [Niels's mother] had the black, luminous eyes of the Blid family with delicate, straight eyebrows; she had their boldly shaped nose, their strong chin, and full lips. The curious line of mingled pain and sensuousness about the corners of her mouth was likewise an inheritance from them, and so were the restless movements of her head; but her cheek was pale; her hair was soft as silk, and was wound smoothly around her head.

> Not so the Blids; their coloring was of roses and bronze. Their hair was rough and curly, heavy as a mane, and their full, deep, resonant voices bore out the tales told of their forefathers, whose noisy hunting-parties, solemn morning prayers, and thousand and one amorous adventures were matters of family tradition.

The Blids had lived solidly, at times even lustily; but "beauty never stirred any raptures in them, and they were never visited by vague longings or day-dreams." But Bartholine, daughter of the Blids and future mother of Niels, differed markedly from the usual Blid formula— "She had no interest in the affairs of the fields and the stables, no taste for the dairy and the kitchen—none whatever." Poetry, in consequence, became her passion— romantic poetry, we recall, in which "grief was black, and joy was red," and in which fantastically heroic men found inspiration for triumphantly heroic labors in passionately devoted women.

And as Bartholine read such poetry she dreamed— dreamed, and prayed, that *she* might one day meet and be loved by a prince among men. A suitor did finally come to her—almost, it seemed, as in her beloved poems. (pp. 98-9)

Bartholine's suitor, the young Lyhne, was, it is to be noted, "the *last* scion" of what had once been a strong, vigorous family; but the family had just about exhausted its early vigor after "three generations . . . among the most distinguished people in the county." We are told further that in the young Lyhne's person, was to be observed all of the physical traits of his family—

> but more faintly, and, in the same manner, the family intelligence seemed to have grown weary in him. None of the mental problems or finer artistic enjoyments that he encountered stirred him to any zeal or desire whatsoever. He had simply striven with them in a painstaking effort which was never brightened by joy in feeling his own powers unfold or pride in finding them adequate. Mere satisfaction in a task accomplished was the only reward that came to him.

During his courtship with Bartholine, however, the young Lyhne managed somehow, and not without a certain sincerity of feeling, to overcome the natural lethargy which he normally had toward the world of beauty which was supposed to be found in nature and in books. And Bartholine was entranced, beyond herself with joy—here, in the flesh, *was* her hero of romance!

Bartholine was happy; for her love enabled her to dissolve the twenty-four hours into a string of romantic episodes. It was romance when she went down the road to meet him; their meeting was romance, and so was their parting. It was romance when she stood on the hilltop in the light of the setting sun and waved him one last farewell before going up to her quiet little chamber, wistfully happy to give herself up to thoughts of him; and when she included his name in her evening prayer, that was romance, too.

The period of courtship was short, full, intense: for Bartholine it was breath-takingly perfect; and for young Lyhne of Lønborggaard it provided a genuine, though momentary, glow of young, romantic enthusiasm. And the first year of married life continued in the same exaggerated lyric vein,—

> But when their wedded life had lost its newness, Lyhne could no longer conceal from himself that he wearied of always seeking new expressions for his love. He was tired of donning the plumage of romance and eternally spreading his wings to fly through all the heavens of sentiment and all the abysses of thought. He longed to settle peacefully on his own quiet perch and drowse, with his tired head under the soft, feathery shelter of a wing. He had never conceived of love as an ever-wakeful, restless flame, casting its strong, flickering light into every nook and corner of existence, making everything seem fantastically large and strange. Love to him was more like the quiet glow of embers on their bed of ashes, spreading a gentle warmth, while the faint dusk wraps all distant things in forgetfulness and makes the near seem nearer and more intimate.
>
> He was tired, worn out. He could not stand all this romance. He longed for the firm support of the commonplace under his feet, as a fish suffocating in hot air languishes for the clear, fresh coolness of the waves. It must end sometime, when it had run its course. Bartholine was no longer inexperienced either in life or books. She knew them as well as he. He had given her all he had—and now he was expected to go on giving. . . .

Bartholine, indeed, gradually came to feel some half-formed misgivings that her "hero" was not all that she had dreamed him to be; but her own romantic yearnings were insatiable, and so her husband's apparently growing indifference to an artificial world of romance "only made her pursue romance the more ardently, and she tried to bring back the old state of things by lavishing on him a still greater wealth of sentiment and a still greater rapture, but she met so little response that she almost felt as if she were stilted and unnatural." When she finally came to see clearly that her husband could not maintain the almost tropical romantic luxuriance with which her own dream-world had invested him, she became bitterly disappointed in him and withdrew into herself to grieve over her disillusionment.

And the opening chapter of **Niels Lyhne** is brought to a conclusion with a short paragraph containing the single laconic announcement: "Such was the state of things between man and wife when Bartholine brought forth her first child. It was a boy, and they called him Niels."

The second chapter continues, and with even greater emphasis, to develop the implications of hereditary influence upon character—now upon Niels, the delicately sensitive child of such a strangely assorted mating as was that of Bartholine and young Lyhne of Lønborggaard. And in addition to the emphasis which this chapter places upon the influence of heredity, we find preliminary evidences in these pages of that other influence—environment—which is to play a profoundly tragic part in the formation of the character of Niels. The child, we find, combines in his temperament both his mother's dangerously romantic ecstasy, and his father's curious compound of practicality and "strange, vegetative trance." At first the child drew mother and father together again, but only momentarily—only over his cradle; for as Niels began to grow the parents again drew apart, inevitably, struggling "unconsciously for mastery over his young soul from the moment the first gleam of intelligence in him gave them something to work on."

Bartholine, of course, tried to influence her child through his imagination. She never tired of telling Niels stories of high romance, tales in which magnificent heroes, often sorely tried, managed always somehow to extricate themselves from what seemed to be inextricable predicaments. Niels, as a child of Bartholine's, was not lacking in imaginative sensibility; and so he would often follow his mother's words with an emotional abandon which went far to alleviate the bitterness which Bartholine had felt earlier on the occasion of the gradual defection of her husband from these same worlds of romance. But her joy in Niels was not unmixed. Intensely as the boy would enter into the stories of his mother's romantic dream-world, he would oftentimes, in the very midst of some impossibly heroic narrative, feel half-consciously that this world of story was a conjured one—not one that really existed, or even could exist.

> . . .Often his mother would tell him stories and describe the woeful plight of the hero, until Niels could not see any way out of all this trouble, and could not understand how the misery closing like an impenetrable wall tighter and tighter around him and the hero could be overcome. Then it happened more than eleven times that he would suddenly press his cheek against his mother's and whisper, with eyes full of tears and lips trembling, "But it isn't *really* true?" And when he had received the comforting answer he wanted, he would heave a deep sigh of relief and settle down contentedly to listen to the end.
>
> His mother did not quite like this defection.

It is clear from this passage, and from the paragraphs in the novel which immediately follow, that the boy's half-formed consciousness of the discrepancy between the actual world and the world of romance was not primarily a sign of a saner, healthier, more balanced view of existence which might later in life enable him to break the subtly decadent appeal that romance exercised over his boyhood imagination. Niels's boyhood skepticism—it is important to note—was motivated more by fear than by insight. The romances terrified the boy, even while they fascinated him. But life, as he viewed it afar off, terrified him even more. He half suspected, with the vague premonitory clairvoyance of the child, that life itself might be evil—and that, unlike the heroes of his mother's romantic tales, who always somehow triumphed over insuperable odds, he might not have the power to cope successfully with life. (pp. 100-03)

Thus it was that a curiously defective mixed heredity and a hopelessly dual and contradictory childhood training combined to make a pathetically confused battlefield of the delicately sensitive mind and soul of the young Niels. The dangerous ecstasy of his mother's temperament gave battle in Niels's very blood to the vegetative earthiness of his father's essentially heavy, placid nature; and neither could attain the mastery, for neither contained sufficient vigor to give any substantial centrality to Niels's boyhood character. And this struggle in the blood was intensified, as the boy grew up, by two modes of training diametrically opposed, each appealing to the boy by turns, and the two in combination certainly portending final disaster for Niels.

As the novel proceeds, less specific attention is given to the element of family inheritance; but the emphasis already placed upon heredity in the first two chapters lingers on in the reader's memory—tending to explain by a kind of echo-like implication much that follows in Niels's life, and lending a deeply rooted, organic inevitability to the final tragedy of Niels.

It is with the problem of the will that Jacobsen becomes primarily concerned in his analysis of the character of Niels in the remainder of the novel. Jacobsen saw—as did his French contemporary Paul Bourget in the *Essais de psychologie contemporaine* (1883)—that the central, or at least the ultimate, problem in the psychology of decadence is the problem of the will. The genuine decadent is a completely disillusioned man, a man, therefore, in whom will, as an instrument of morality, tends to become increasingly less active—until, theoretically at least, it ceases to exist at all as a stabilizing influence in life or art. In the character of Niels, Jacobsen analyzes this process of individual decadence, the gradual disintegration of a human will. Not that Niels becomes a deliberate doctrinaire decadent, such as Huysmans has created in the character of des Esseintes in *À rebours* (1884). Niels retains some of his early idealisms even to the end; but by nature and by his early childhood training he is fundamentally unstable in character, and this instability became more pronounced in his youth and early manhood, ultimately culminating in a series of personal disasters that destroy almost every vestige of any power of will that he may have had earlier in life.

Despite Niels's tentative childhood skepticisms over against the world of romance to which his mother introduced him, a skepticism that grew even more pronounced in his youth, he never could quite shake off, even when he had grown to manhood, the early fascination that this world of romance had held for him. It is not difficult to see that the emotional abandon with which Niels threw

himself into certain experiences of his later life, particularly his series of distinctly dubious *affaires du coeur,* found their psychological, if not physiological, origins largely in the sensuous emotional chaos growing out of his early interest in literary romances. In later life he merely transfers his romantic sensibilities to a new object—women in the flesh. The half-hesitant hysterical intensity of his emotional responses to at least two of these women, Fru Boye and Fennimore, is of a piece with his childhood passion for romantic tales. He was fascinated by these women, and yet half-fearful of plunging boldly into the full warm stream of passion. He "was afraid in his inmost heart," we are told in connection with the Fru Boye affair, "of this mighty thing called passion." Fru Boye he never actually possessed, except in the spasmodic morbidities of an imagined world. Fennimore he did possess, though only after she had become another man's wife. In both cases, however, ultimate frustration was his fate; and in both cases frustration led to disillusionment, disillusionment to a brooding melancholy, and brooding melancholy to mental and emotional lassitude—a slow but steady disintegration of the will.

It might be said that Niels's will, like Hamlet's, was "sicklied o'er with the pale cast of thought." He lived timidly, always in a world of reflection, and shrank instinctively from deliberate vigorous action. . . .

It is in such a weak, hesitant state of mind that Niels often found himself in the days of his maturity—especially in his relations with women and in his abortive efforts to become a poet. He found himself in such a condition in the very midst of his strange bit of love-making with Fru Boye, whom he might easily have possessed had he been a man of action. Instead, with characteristic indecision, he merely surrounded her in his imagination with a passionately sentimental halo; and when finally she announced to Niels her decision to capitulate to a critical society by "marrying into respectability," Niels could but brood and reflect—and with what characteristic inability to pass any vigorous judgment! (pp. 104-07)

Niels's feeble efforts to become a poet—no more happy than his adventures with women—serve further to illustrate that "lame reflectiveness" in his character. In fact here, even more than in his *affaires du coeur,* do we come upon evidences of a weak indecision—an indecision which proved to be completely fatal to any successful creative efforts. From the days of his childhood Niels had dreamed of one day becoming a poet. Characteristically, however, in those later days of youth and early manhood when the creative urge tends to be most vigorous, Niels revealed a temperamental indecision which made impossible on his part any vigorous creative activity as a poet. He was intelligent enough in these years to recognize the faults of the older Romantic poetry, its bombast, its love of facile paradox, its superficial primitivism; but he was not strong enough to create anything more significant, more virile— he could not bring himself to break fresh ground in other directions. (p. 108)

Niels's creative instinct, it is interesting to note, was most active during the emotional upsurge in the first stages of his strange love affair with Fru Boye. After that—except

for a weak, wholly tentative rekindling of his poetic enthusiasms which happened to be associated with his mother's
death days—Niels's creative energies steadily diminished,
until they finally ceased to exist at all long before Niels
himself found some kind of peace in physical death. The
scrupulously exacting ideal of art which he had talked of
to his mother as she lay dying was obviously beyond his
power of execution, though he insisted on this occasion,
with characteristic emotional accompaniments, upon
making eternal vows to realize it. "Dearest, dearest!" he
cries out to his dying mother, in a flood of hysterically heroic sentiment,

> I *shall* be one of those who fight for the greatest,
> and I promise you that I shall not fail, that I
> shall always be faithful to myself and my gift.
> Nothing but the best shall be good enough. No
> compromise, Mother! When I weigh what I have
> done and feel that it isn't sterling, or when I hear
> that it has a crack or a flaw—into the oven it
> goes! Every single work must be my best! . . .

Such a rigid ideal of a perfected art requires the severest
discipline of will to realize—the very quality of character
most obviously lacking in Niels. He had poetic sensitivity,
imaginative insight, and a rare gift of language; but he was
timid in moments of actual creative activity, too critical
of his own work—and so in the end everything went "into
the oven." His poetic flights were fragmentary, incomplete, infused so deeply with the disintegrating breath of
decadence that they had not sufficient vitality to take the
final, perfect form of which he dreamed. To Niels had not
been given the rare creative gift of a Baudelaire, who alone
among decadent poets seemed able to express profoundly
decadent themes in a strong and perfectly moulded classical art form.

Niels's mother died soon after her son's vows had been
given. Immediately thereafter Fru Boye broke with Niels.
Meantime he read much, and wrote a little—nothing,
however, that satisfied his own fastidious spirit. It was
Fennimore's engagement, and subsequent marriage, to
Niels's friend Erik that became the last, and fatal, blow to
Niels's waning desire to become a poet. He could not even
at this time, however, totally forget his early dreams of a
poetic career. They haunted him oftentimes, like subtly
leering, strangely reproachful spirits; but they could not
lash him into action. They merely served to feed his already "lame reflectiveness" with more materials productive of self-irritation, self-disgust, and an ever more enervating weariness.

> That unexpected engagement had been a hard
> blow to Niels. It had a benumbing effect on him.
> He grew more bitter and less confiding, and had
> no longer so much enthusiasm to pit against
> Hjerrild's pessimism. Though he still pursued
> his studies, their plan was less and less definite,
> while his purpose of some time completing them
> and beginning his real life-work flickered uncer-
> tainly. He lived much among people, but very
> little with them. They interested him, but he did
> not in the least care to have them be interested
> in him; for he felt the force that should have
> driven him to do his part with the others or
> against them slowly ebbing out of him. He could

wait, he told himself, even if he had to wait till
it was too late. Whoever has faith is in no
hurry—that was his excuse to himself. For he
believed that, when he came down to the bedrock of his own nature, he did have faith strong
enough to move mountains—the trouble was
that he never managed to set his shoulder to
them. Once in a while, the impulse to create wel-
led up in him, and he longed to see a part of himself freed in work that should be his very own.
For days he would be excited with the happy, titanic effort of carting the clay for his Adam, but
he never formed it in his own image. The will
power necessary to persistent self-concentration
was not in him. Weeks would pass before he
could make up his mind to abandon the work,
but he did abandon it, asking himself, in a fit of
irritation, why he could continue. What more
had he to gain? He had tasted the rapture of conception; there remained the toil of rearing, cher-
ishing, nourishing, carrying to perfection—
Why? For whom? He was no pelican, he told
himself. But argue as he might, he was dissatisfied with himself and felt that he had not fulfilled
his own expectations; nor did it avail him to carp
at these expectations and ask whether they were
well founded. He had reached the point where
he had to choose, for when first youth is past—
early or late in accordance with each person's individuality—then, early or late, dawns the day
when Resignation comes to us as a temptress,
luring us to forego the impossible and be content. And Resignation has much in her favor; for
how often have not the idealistic aspirations of
youth been beaten back, its enthusiasms been
shamed, its hopes laid waste!—The ideals, the
fair and beautiful, have lost nothing of their radiance, but they no longer walk here among us as
in the early days of our youth. The broad, firmly
planted stairway of worldly wisdom has conveyed them back, step by step, to that heaven
whence our simpler faith once brought them
down; and there they sit, radiant but distant,
smiling but weary, in divine quiescence, while
the incense of a slothful adoration rises, puff on
puff, in festive convolutions.

Niels Lyhne was tired. These repeated runnings
to a leap that was never leaped had wearied him.
Everything seemed to him hollow and worthless,
distorted and confused, and, oh, so petty! He
preferred to stop his ears and stop his mouth and
to immerse himself in studies that had nothing
to do with the busy everyday world, but were
like an ocean apart, where he could wander
peacefully in silent forests of seaweed among curious animals.

He was tired, and the root of his weariness
sprang from his baffled hope of love; thence it
had spread, quickly and surely, through his
whole being, to all his faculties and all his
thoughts. . . .

Thus with a kind of infinitely oppressive weariness,
brought on by personal disillusionment and indecision,
and intensified by the vacillation and enervating spirit of
his generation, Niels Lyhne finally resigns himself to the
emptily quiet waters of poetic sterility.

Niels was but one of the weak, indecisive, over-reflective children of an uncertain, weakly groping period of transition moving on vaguely toward what seemed to be a more vigorous modern world. He had little strength of his own, and only had he been carried on the sturdy shoulders of a literary movement which had something of the outward strength and confidence of a *fait accompli* might he actually have opened his creative vein. He rejects the methods and themes of Romantic poetry as outworn, inadequate, unreal, and therefore not worthy of his own talents; but he has not sufficient strength of will to shape the products of a new, living, and vigorous literary realism. He remains, in consequence, unproductive, sterile—a poet not meanly endowed by nature, but one who never brought the creative process to fruition. Heredity had given to him poetic sensibilities, together with a character that was essentially weak; and the environment of his youth—falling in an unstable period of intellectual and aesthetic transition—had provided that further element of instability in his life which made the final fate of Niels, as artist and as man, inevitable. The skillful manner in which Jacobsen traces this intricate interplay of forces that work upon Niels's will and finally effect the complete decay of his creative powers remains one of the few permanent achievements in the analysis of decadent literary psychology. If *Niels Lyhne* had no other qualities as a novel, it would remain a classic on the strength of this distinction alone.

We have seen, however, that Jacobsen's novel can claim distinctions other than that which concerns itself narrowly with the particular psychological problem of the disintegration of the individual will. *Niels Lyhne* is a memorable novel because of a remarkably subtle and beautifully modulated style . . . because of its penetrating analysis of certain general cultural phases of mid-nineteenth century life . . . because of its incisive study of particular influences, hereditary and environmental, upon the developing taste and intelligence of Niels. To these another—finally—must be added. *Niels Lyhne* is the first Scandinavian novel which gives an adequate treatment to those treacherous subconscious and unconscious levels of human consciousness which have come so to preoccupy many a novelist of our later day. To the present-day reader, who has been exposed to a James Joyce and Marcel Proust, a Dorothy Richardson and a Virginia Woolf, Jacobsen's occasional ventures in the pages of *Niels Lyhne* into the field of the subconscious and the unconscious may seem so incidental and fragmentary as to be of no real importance. The impression, however, is hardly a fair one; for, in the first place, it must be remembered that Jacobsen was something of a pioneer in the fictional emphasis upon the unconscious and subconscious phases of human psychology, and, in the second place, his actual accomplishments in the portrayal of such psychological phenomena are certainly neither mean nor accidental.

It is too much, of course, to expect to find in *Niels Lyhne* a thoroughgoing stream-of-consciousness novel in the manner of *Ulysses* or *Remembrance of Things Past,* or even *The Waves.* Niels is not being subjected more or less constantly by the author to any either elaborate or simple psychoanalytic treatment in which a host of more or less wayward impulses are noted or explained. Having been

composed in the late 1870's, *Niels Lyhne* illustrates in substance most of the traditional practices in the technique of the novel as it was written during these years in Denmark and on the Continent. The discerning reader of Jacobsen's novel, however, will take note of some passages, not so infrequent, which strike a new note—if not in the broad processes of narrative technique, at least in the immediate manner of conceiving human character under the stress of particular circumstances. Space will permit me to deal with only one of these passages in any detail, though such passages might readily be multiplied. The passage in question—of central importance in the conduct of the novel because it deals penetratingly with the psychology of one of Niels's loves—should be quoted in some detail:

> They [Fennimore and Niels] scoured the forest from end to end, eager to find all its treasures and marvels. They had divided it between them as children do; the part on one side of the road was Fennimore's property, and that on the other side was Niels's, and they would compare their realms and quarrel about which was the more glorious. Everything there had names—clefts and hillocks, paths and stiles, ditches and pools; and when they found a particularly magnificent tree, they gave that too a name. In this way they took complete possession and created a little world of their own which no one else knew and no one else was at home in, and yet they had no secret which all the world might not have heard.

> As yet they had not.

> But love was in their hearts, and was not there, as the crystals are present in a saturated solution, and yet are not present, not until a splinter or the merest particle of the right matter is thrown into the solution, releasing the slumbering atoms as if by magic, and they rush to meet one another, joining and riveting themselves together according to unsearchable laws, and in the same instant there is crystal—crystal.

> So it was a trifle that made them feel they loved.

> There is nothing to tell. It was a day like all other days, when they were alone together in the sitting-room, as they had been a hundred times before; their conversation was about things of no moment, and that which happened was outwardly as common and as every-day-like as possible. It was nothing except that Niels stood looking out of the window, and Fennimore came over to him and looked out too. That was all, but it was enough, for in a flash like lightning, the past and present and future were transformed for Niels Lyhne by the consciousness that he loved the woman standing by his side, not as anything bright and sweet and happy and beautiful that would lift him to ecstasy or rapture—such was not the nature of his love—but he loved her as something he could no more do without than the breath of life itself, and he reached out, as a drowning man clutches, and pressed her hand to his heart.

> She understood him. With almost a scream, in a voice full of terror and agony, she cried out to

him an answer and confession: "Oh, *yes, Niels!*"
and snatched away her hand in the same instant.
A moment she stood, pale and shrinking, then
sank down with one knee in an upholstered
chair, hiding her face against the harsh velvet of
the back, and sobbed aloud.

That latter-day form of the stream-of-consciousness technique—which drops all exposition and allows the odd
fragments of consciousness to take more or less exact form
in equally odd fragments of words, phrases, or sentences—
is not here attained; nor for that matter is it attempted.
But the passage—in its emphasis upon the dramatic, unconscious *precipitation* of emotional experience into forms
beyond our control, and yet forms of a most significant
kind—reflects a conception of human psychology which,
when more universally grasped and more consistently applied by later novelists, was to issue into that literary technique in fiction which we now refer to as the stream-of-
consciousness technique.

At least two things would seem to be of particular interest
in the passage quoted: first, the novelist's explicit recognition of the supreme importance of accidental, quite unconscious, even unidentifiable detail, physical or psychic, or
both, which precipitated the instantaneous emotional recognition on the part of Fennimore and Niels; and secondly, the completeness of that recognition—a completeness
which suggests the fundamentally organic nature of the
psychic experience and the relation which the whole has
to certain deep-seated laws of nature, primarily psychic in
kind, and yet inextricably intertwined with and dependent
upon the laws which govern physical phenomena. It is
such a passage as this that gives significant content to a
slightly cryptic statement by Jacobsen in his letter to
Georg Brandes on the origins and composition of *Niels
Lyhne:* "The emphasis throughout is placed particularly
upon the psychological and also upon the physiological."
As a scientist Jacobsen felt profoundly the intimate relation between the mind and the body, the mental and the
material; and everywhere in his novels does he keep this
relationship in mind. The paragraphs from *Niels Lyhne*
which I have quoted should sufficiently demonstrate Jacobsen's consciousness of the intimate relation existing between the physical and the mental. If more evidence is
needed, I refer the reader to the pages immediately following the quoted passage, pages in which the physical phases
of the love of Fennimore and Niels are given what for Jacobsen is almost brutally sensual expression.

Upon reading these pages we can understand perhaps even
today why it was that they—conceived with a severely
naturalistic objectivity, and containing no expression of either praise or blame for the actions described—stirred up
a fury of criticism among such critics in Denmark as felt
it their duty to guard "the moral contents of literature."
The novel was roundly condemned for its immoral tendencies by a critic in *Fædrelandet;* and many smaller organs of opinion took up the hue and cry from this very influential journal. The liberal Danish critics, such as Georg
Brandes, were not of course disturbed by the moral questions involved. They praised the novel as a matter of
course, though there seems to be some evidence to prove
that they were not entirely satisfied with it—at least not

as satisfied as they had been with *Marie Grubbe* four years
earlier. It is interesting to note, incidentally, that the most
enthusiastic contemporary praise for *Niels Lyhne* came
from two famous Norwegians, Henrik Ibsen and Alexander Kielland. Ibsen, who seems to have been tremendously
impressed by the novel, is reported to have said: "*Niels
Lyhne* is the best book in our century." And Kielland had
written to Hegel: "That book, it seems to me, is the greatest that has appeared in my time. There is an infinity of
things one can learn from it and admire in it."

It was natural that the novel should arouse both shocked
condemnation and extreme praise at the time of its appearance. Its daring treatment of certain phases of the psychology of sex and its apparently sympathetic attitude toward
literary and aesthetic decadence (a sympathy which Jacobsen himself denied vigorously) would hardly fail to invite indignant attacks upon the novel; and attacks on the
part of the shocked "moral guardians" of society would
naturally arouse the liberal critics of the day to a spirited
defense. *Niels Lyhne,* however, is not to be finally evaluated in terms either of contemporary condemnation or contemporary praise. Today it neither shocks us as it did one
class of an earlier generation, nor does it strike us as being
the best book in the century. Present day criticism is ready
to admit, however, that *Niels Lyhne* is a notable novel—
perhaps the greatest among the group of novels written in
the last two decades of the nineteenth century which occupy themselves with the problem of decadence. *Dorian
Gray* is by comparison merely clever, *À rebours* by comparison but a kind of fictional *tour de force,* and Herman
Bang's *Generations without Hope* a decadent novel too
heavily burdened with a massive weight of naturalistic detail. Garborg's *Trætte Mænd* ("Weary Men"), with its
grim Carlylean irony, is in some senses a more powerful
decadent novel than *Niels Lyhne;* but it does not hold together with the finely balanced unity of tone and theme
that is attained by Jacobsen in his profoundly subtle characterization of a decadent spirit. (pp. 109-16)

> *Alrik Gustafson, "Toward Decadence," in his*
> Six Scandinavian Novelists, *The American-
> Scandinavian Foundation–Princeton Universi-
> ty Press, 1940, pp. 73-122.*

Boris Kidel   (essay date 1946)

[*Kidel was a Russian-born English journalist and critic.
In the following essay, he chronicles Jacobsen's intellectual development and literary production, noting his autobiographical characterizations, the meticulous detail
in his novels, critical reception of his works, and his substantial influence on German literature.*]

The problems that Jacobsen raises in his novels have a particular significance at the present time, because the events
of the past ten years have blocked for millions of young
people the escape into professions and jobs, and their
whole personal life has contracted itself around the dream
of their minds. In the frame-work of community living,
the radius of personal experience has almost shrunk into
non-existence. This involuntary abstention from living has
created among the young an atmosphere of day-dreaming

and Niels Lyhne's problems—the problems of a poet 'manqué'—reveal a striking resemblance to the deadlock in the lives of a whole generation.

The Danish writer Jens Peter Jacobsen, himself in a constant struggle between the exigencies of Reality and the presuppositions of his imagination, was aware of the problems and sufferings confronting the artist, who though driven by a daemoniacal urge to create is stunned by the helplessness of his vision. Instinctively the young writer turns away from Reality, because this formless pile of mass-experience reeks of every-day problems and quarrels, of the daily habits, all of which are common property; the young man surrenders to the beautiful path traced by his imagination unwilling to acknowledge that his dreams roam in a shadow world devoid of all contact with the grey street below his window. But Jacobsen, though deeply entangled in this eternal conflict, believed that the novelist had to achieve some synchronisation between the flight of his imagination and the relatively slow pace of every-day existence. He was fully conscious of his own failings and so the 'leitmotif' in his works constantly hums the theme of self-accusation. He accepted the immoral aspect of wishful thinking, and convinced of the absence of a supernatural power capable of interfering between human beings and their actions, he saw a supreme value in the doctrine of evolution.

Jacobsen's dilemma becomes very clear in a letter to Edvard Brandes that he wrote in 1872. He said:

> I am beginning to discover that I was born really to do nothing. I sit every day 3-4 hours at a stretch on a bridge and smoke the most incredible number of cigarettes, then I let the ash fall into the water and it spits s-s-s-s- as rings form in the water. This is great fun.

In another letter, the writer compares himself to a sailing boat on a calm sea and adds that it would be better to use oars instead of waiting for the breeze.

Jens Peter Jacobsen was born on the 7th of April 1847 in the little Danish town of Thisted, which lies sheltered in a quiet bay of North-Western Jutland. He was the eldest son of a family which was descended from old peasant and sailor stock. His consumptive father, a wealthy merchant, exercised little influence on his eldest son. The relationship between mother and son, on the other hand, had the quiescent colours of complete tenderness; we can almost see this old woman, who adored poetry in her youth, nursing her grown-up son when he returns ill from Copenhagen.

Jacobsen left Thisted at sixteen and went to a Copenhagen private school; here he neither distinguished himself by particular intelligence or hard work. Labelled as a crank by his school-friends, he devoted his whole time to the study of botany. In 1868, he became a student at Copenhagen University. This young man from the provinces was reserved in his manner, even slightly gauche, and always spoke quietly with an ironic tone in his voice, hiding his true convictions. He was tall and narrow-chested and the long fair hair often fell over his forehead.

In the course of his studies, Jacobsen discovered Darwin for Denmark and was the first to translate *The Origin of Species* and *The Descent of Man.* At about the same time, while still a student, he made the first attempts to explore the vague poetic plans, which were sweeping hazily through his mind. The first step into literature was an endeavour to fuse a romantic-epic style with Nordic Sagas and mediaeval subjects; dissatisfied, Jacobsen turned to lyrical poetry, but lacking spontaneity, these verses were carefully arranged mosaics, devoid of rhythm and compression.

He was fortunate to live in one of those periods when intellectual problems vibrate with earnest intensity through the whole youth of a country. Georg Brandes was just beginning his famous lectures on the main trends of European literature in the nineteenth century, and as the acknowledged leader of all literary life, he introduced to Denmark the contemporary French and German authors. Under Brandes' guidance, Jacobsen published his first long short story, *Mogens,* in 1872.

Mogens, the hero of this story, is 'a painter without hands', his eyes see the universe through a veil of poetry, every day of his life is a delicate romantic song, but he floats like a wisp of cloud through his youth, seeing and feeling but never making the effort to explore and control the multitude of beauty rising before him. There is no doubt that Jacobsen projected his own personality, in a magnified form, into Mogens; the great Danish writer shunned all contact with reality, or rather he preferred to evade all situations that could lead to disappointment, and could not be lived within the boundaries of his dreamworld. Like Mogens, Jacobsen derived all his happiness from lying in the fields, listening to the twittering of the birds and watching the trees waver in the wind.

Mogens, which had an enthusiastic reception in Danish literary circles, already possessed all the basic features of Jacobsen's style. Scene after scene is treated against the background of a yearning atmosphere; a languorous clearness and burning colours pervade this short story, which is a mosaic-like collection of throbbing impressions of human beings and nature.

In the autumn of 1872, Jacobsen contracted consumption after wading barefoot through a swampy moss. In spite of his illness, he began an extensive study of the seventeenth century for his historical novel *Marie Grubbe.*

Sir Edmund Gosse says in his introduction to the English translation of *Niels Lyhne:*

> In my own journal of a visit to Denmark in 1874, I find under the date May 24, this entry:
>
> 'Georg Brandes told me today that the only young man who shows anything like first-rate promise now is a certain J. P. Jacobsen who is only twenty-three. (He was really twenty-seven, but looked so youthful that Dr. Brandes must have under-estimated his age.) He is a botanist and a Darwinian, but he has begun a historical romance, of which Brandes has seen the early chapters. But, he added dropping his voice suddenly into an almost querulous tone, "he is the only one, and now—*han döer*—he is dying." This Jacobsen is hopelessly ill, with consumption at Thisted, and will probably die without

having produced anything finished enough for publication.'

Jacobsen lived for another eleven years and continued writing *Marie Grubbe.* His moods quivered from sublime serenity to darkest self-torture, then irritated by the effects of his illness and nauseated by the painful slowness of the execution of his work, he left Denmark and travelled to Italy. In the long northern winter nights, Italy had seemed a soft alluring paradise, but on arriving in the South, Jacobsen's expectations were unfulfilled; the dust, the heavy sun, 'the silly lemon trees', Capri, Florence, everything was shabby and banal in comparison to the extravagant mental pictures.

In autumn, Jacobsen returned to Denmark and settled down in Thisted with his mother. The tiring struggle with words that refused to fill the blank page began anew; every chapter of *Marie Grubbe* had to be won against the heavy odds of failing health and a lethargic temperament.

Already in 1875, Jacobsen was planning *Niels Lyhne,* although the historical novel was still unfinished. The contemporary theme of the novel that Jacobsen was sketching in his mind overshadowed *Marie Grubbe* so that its final chapters have a sharp fragmentary style, which hints that the writer had lost interest in Marie's fate. In December 1876 the young author published his first novel and at once it was recognised as the greatest historical novel in the Danish language.

The state of his health was deteriorating; in the autumn of 1877, he went to Montreux with the intention of publishing *Niels Lyhne* in February of next year. But soon after his arrival, Jacobsen realised the futility of his exaggerated hopes to write a novel in five months and he admitted to Edvard Brandes that he was progressing very slowly with his book. Time was circling faster and faster around the dying writer, the pincers of consumption closed tighter and the next years of his life—no longer peaceful dreams in green meadows—became a restless journey across Europe. His travels were not the feverish search for a 'beyond', a dream country somewhere in the South; his journeys breathe the poignancy of the realisation that he would always arrive in *Cythère* and that dreams no longer offered a shadow from the beating sun of Reality.

Throughout 1879, Jacobsen was so ill that he could hardly write a letter and the manuscript had to be laid aside. *Niels Lyhne* was finally completed in Thisted in December 1880 and again new plans gripped the writer but his power of creation had worn itself out. The last four years of his life were spent with his mother in Thisted, only occasionally visiting the capital. His last published work was a collection of almost perfect short stories. Georg Brandes has written of those last years how Jacobsen was growing weaker each day. He was slowly being broken, the house was crumbling piece by piece, stone by stone. It was painful to listen to his cough and his gauntness was a terrifying sight.

Jacobsen died his difficult death in Thisted on April 30th, 1885.

The brooding indecision, which pervades Ibsen's plays, rules over the lives of Jacobsen's men and women, and the Danish writer analyses the torpid unawareness of raw truth from all possible angles. Niels, Eric, Fennimore, they all stand in the wings, anxiously fingering their sensations and their thoughts, but when the foot-lights glare, then their hopes and certainties uncoil under the stab of Reality.

The novel *Niels Lyhne* consists of a number of incidents that shape the life of a man whose poetic perception is coupled to the sagging weight of dilettantism. The roots of this Wertherian tragedy are deeply embedded in Niels's childhood; even when fairy-tales have been stripped of their magic, the boy continues to poeticise his life by letting his imagination swoon in stories that he himself invents. Niels, failing in his intentions all through his life, finally as an atheist betrays his life-long belief by falling on his knees and imploring God for the life of his dying son.

Jacobsen achieves his effects by draining each situation of all its descriptive possibilities, he draws out a wealth of vibrating impressions from each fleeting scene, so that the reader's mind never finds the opportunity to create a personal image of the writer's pictures. Every dull country flower, every straggling shadow, every ray of light is dismembered by the author, then recreated and transformed into a phenomenon of beauty. The mind is numbed and drugged by his descriptions, which glorify the air as it hums through the tree-tops, which delight in the musty smell of a room that has been shut up for the summer. The Danish writer draws and paints with his words, but he skilfully evades the slope leading to barren lyrical prose, because his eyes have the tempering glance of an ironic analyst.

The development of a plot or of a situation in the poetical novel tends to be slow as this medium is closely akin to the diary technique, but Jacobsen—perhaps the greatest exponent of the poetical novel—swerves his writings aside from static contemplation. There is a continuous development in the characters of Niels, Marie and all the others that cross the narrative; we watch the years slide by, and with each winter the bitter disappointment in the hearts of Jacobsen's men and women grows riper. Jacobsen, the painter, explores the dullest detail in a room, he observes faces and clothes, but when dealing with characters of human beings he stands aside. Fennimore, Bartholine, Eric, they all reveal their inner selves by their unconscious actions, by their conversations and by their mannerisms.

Jacobsen's two major works show a distinct orientation towards tragedy; failure and disappointment are the recurrent sign-posts on the road along which his heroes are travelling. In their youth, their hearts are filled with soaring dreams and ambitions which—they imagine—will suddenly fade into Reality, they poeticise inexperienced love, they lie in the sun and dream of the novels and pictures that will startle the world. But when the tremulous note of youth has turned into the tired cacophonous warble of middle-age, then these men and women swing their day-dreams back to their past yearning to relive bygone days.

This refusal to accept the rules of Reality is the centre of the lives of these people; this non-recognition implies failure and disappointment in all the varied experiences that confront the human being. Yet Jacobsen does not over-stress the tragic aspect of this inert blindness that goes on hoping despite the realisation that miracles never happen. The Danish writer blends his sympathy for Niels and Eric with an exquisite irony which is very similar to Gogol's 'laughter across tears'. Niels swaying perilously on his skates when Fennimore shouts to him that she will never see him again, Fru Boye's final meeting with Niels, all these are highly dramatic incidents which would flavour of the ridiculous if they were not toned down by irony.

Jacobsen is not the inspired, impulsive writer dealing with factors unknown to his experience, he is not attempting to give a new interpretation to a particular aspect of man's life, not pretending to cast a beam of light on an unexplored turning; his work is a skilful elaboration of his own life, of the incidents that chiselled his personal attitude to the world. He projects his own individuality into Niels, Eric and even into Marie Grubbe. On this magnified scale, Jacobsen's personal experiences become synonymous with the problems of all humanity.

While the other great modern poetical novels—such as Hoelderlin's *Hyperion* and Novalis's *Ofterdingen*—are purely deductive works, poeticising the vague realities of day-dreams, Jacobsen's genius is supported by his own wordly experience, and this experience transcending its narrow borders, develops our glimmering understanding of the thousands of impressions, feelings and still-born thoughts that come and go and are forgotten. Jacobsen elaborates on the flashes of realisation or illumination that are consciously registered by the mind, while Proust translates the sensations and thoughts that flicker in the depth of the unconscious.

Niels's first encounter with the set of young artists in Copenhagen, and the sudden awakening on hearing his innermost thoughts spoken out aloud by others is a picture whose outlines are immediately recognised by the reader. The writer, however, clarifies the impression cast by our own experiences, he elucidates the hovering recollection by exploring the thought behind the laughter, the careless gesture, the deep shadows, which only an artist's eyes can perceive.

Though Jacobsen's central figures are the products of his self-analysis, the subsidiary characters are no mere half-finished sketches. A whole world with all its mysterious whims and peculiarities throbs in Fennimore, Fru Boye and Edele; they are conceived by a mind that has an intuitive grasp of psychology, by a mind that has the gift of distinguishing the seemingly inconsequential impulses and gestures, pointing towards the centre of the heart. The scene of Fennimore's immediate reaction to the news of her husband's death is unforgettable, because with a few strokes, Jacobsen penetrates into the secret recesses of the woman's mind and thus grafts her to the reader's consciousness.

The personal character of Jacobsen's writing is not so apparent in his earlier work *Marie Grubbe.* Though essentially a historical novel, it is a timeless work of art, attempting to depict the life of an average woman. Stylistically, it lacks *Niels Lyhne*'s enchanting lightness, but continuity and characterisation are firmer than in the later novel. Against the background of the 17th century, Jacobsen weaves the life story of Marie Grubbe, who though constantly betrayed by the stretching images of her dreams, never turns her head back to retrieve the past. The stuttering rhythm of this heroic blindness is brilliantly fused with the even melody of events outside in the world. The eyes of a Brueghel see the Danish-Swedish war, and again other scenes are—as Hans Bethge, one of Jacobsen's German biographers points out—reminiscent of Rembrandt and other painters of the Dutch School. The novelist intoxicates the imagination when he describes the dark colours of the room, where old Grubbe and the priest are snoring drunkenly, while drops of the spilt beer are trickling from the table and uneasy shadows are cast by the burnt down candles.

It is impossible to overrate Jacobsen's influence on German literature and particularly on Rilke. In a letter to Franz Xaver Kappus, Rilke wrote in 1903 from Viarregio:

> If I am to say from whom I learnt anything about the essence of aesthetic creation, its depth and its eternity, then there are only two names I can name: that of Jacobsen, the great, great poet, and that of Auguste Rodin. . . .

The Dane was Rilke's supreme literary inspiration and *Malte Laurids Brigge* as well as the early short stories bear the stamp of the poet's admiration for *Niels Lyhne* and *Marie Grubbe.*

Prof. Butler, in her recent work on Rilke, attributes to Jacobsen the poet's conception that each human being should strive for his or her own personal death. However, her analytical evidence for the contention that the Danish writer was the source for Rilke's glorification of death as the beginning of life is flimsy and debatable. It is rather more likely that a scene like Ulrick Christian's death in *Marie Grubbe* contributed to the growth of the germ already existent in Rilke's mind. The austere rigidity of Marie's course through life, her steadfast loyalty to herself cannot have failed to impress Rilke, but it can be deduced from his letters that the centre of his admiration was Jacobsen's style and not the strange deaths occurring in the historical novel. The characters in *Niels Lyhne* disregard the inevitable and when Death suddenly lurches into their homes, they are taken unawares, so that when Fennimore hears of her husband's death, she hurls herself against the door struggling with the key to refuse admission to the unexpected.

The experience of reading certain passages from Jacobsen's works evokes the same aesthetic bewilderment as does the first hearing of a Mozart Andante. The mind surrenders to a dream—to the dream of a vision that seems already to have been perceived in some previous existence. The rainbow of words endow the writer's searching soul analysis with a translucent depth. With piercing sincerity, Jacobsen restates the age-old truth that Reality pays no heed to the supplications of our dreams: the novelist has drawn the veil from the abyss that gapes so dangerously near the heights of our fantasy.

The modern novel seldom outlives its author, but Jacobsen's bewitching mastery over words and his comprehension of the inconsequential curves of human behaviour have given him a place at the side of Flaubert, Henry James and Tolstoy. Apart from the fact that existing English translations do little justice to Jacobsen's genius, a new rendering of his novels would perhaps help to free the cornered minds of the war generation who are dreaming of the life they cannot lead. (pp. 123-30)

> *Boris Kidel, "Jens Peter Jacobsen," in* The New Spirit, *edited by E. W. Martin, Dennis Dobson Ltd., 1946, pp. 123-30.*

Børge Gedsø Madsen   (essay date 1962)

[*Madsen is an American educator and critic specializing in Scandinavian literature. In the following essay, he reviews Jacobsen's critical reception. Madsen disagrees with scholars who contend that Jacobsen is best understood as a morbid and unbelieving scientist, asserting that, despite his obvious personal identification with the enervated dreamers who populate his works, Jacobsen also affirmed the possibility of happiness in both his literature and his life.*]

The recent re-issuing of the English translations of J. P. Jacobsen's novels *Niels Lyhne* and *Marie Grubbe* by The American-Scandinavian Foundation is a heartening indication that Anglo-American interest in Jacobsen is at least stable and possibly may even be growing. For many years J. P. Jacobsen has enjoyed a high reputation in Germany, and lately he is also coming into his own in France where his very similarity to such writers as Flaubert and the Goncourt brothers actually militated against his acceptance for a while. For a long time French critics felt that what Jacobsen had accomplished in the psychological novel had already been done, and done better, by French psychological novelists. This Gallic self-suffiency is gradually yielding, however, to a deeper understanding of the finer points of Jacobsen's art, as is testified, for instance, by a recent French doctoral dissertation on Jacobsen and a detailed, appreciative review of *Niels Lyhne* by Jacques de Lacretelle. In the United States and Great Britain Jacobsen is valued highly by a small group of *literati* and college professors teaching Scandinavian literature, but in these countries he is still not nearly as well known as he deserves to be. It would be most gratifying if the reprinting of the two books could gain new American and English readers for J. P. Jacobsen, one of the most complex and original writers of nineteenth-century Danish literature. And readers already familiar with *Niels Lyhne* and *Marie Grubbe* might have their interest sufficiently re-kindled to feel tempted to acquaint themselves with Jacobsen's excellent short stories and the best of his lyric poetry. To readers proficient in the Danish language Jacobsen's letters, which give a delightfully informal portrait of the man, may be strongly recommended. Warm, humorous and self-ironical, they are completely free from the stylistic artificiality which occasionally mars the prose of his fictional works. Besides, the letters contain a great number of inci-sive critical observations on the art of writing which are very helpful for a full understanding of Jacobsen's literary objectives.

In histories of Scandinavian literature J. P. Jacobsen has been characterized traditionally as a literary naturalist imbued with the spirit of scientific positivism and philosophic materialism. Critics have stressed his training in natural history, his studies of Darwin and translations of Darwin's two major works, and his prize-winning essay on freshwater algæ. Great importance has been attached to the young Jacobsen's hesitation between the career of a natural scientist and that of a poet. Jacobsen's main works have been analyzed thoroughly from this point of view: the Darwinian inspiration of *Mogens* (1872) has been pointed out; the naturalistic elements in *Marie Grubbe* (1876) and *Niels Lyhne* (1880) have been isolated and neatly classified; and much has been written about Jacobsen's noble atheism, his dignified insistence that men have the strength and moral courage to lead their lives in accordance with the laws of nature.

Undoubtedly the emphasis on J. P. Jacobsen's naturalism and atheistic positivism is valid and necessary, but his positivistic philosophy of life contains only part of the truth about him, and perhaps not the most interesting part. Re-

A portrait of Jacobsen.

cent Jacobsen scholarship in Scandinavia has amply demonstrated what some of the older Jacobsen scholars had already begun to suspect, namely the indisputable fact that J. P. Jacobsen's talent is essentially lyric, and that his attitude towards human life is a profound feeling of compassion, a patent departure from doctrinaire naturalism which insists on objectivity and impassivity. As a result of this realization, an increasing stress is being placed on the importance of Jacobsen's poetry for a complete understanding of the writer and the man. Even Jacobsen's novels, it may well be argued, are more lyric in composition than genuinely epic in structure. From a conventionally formalistic point of view, both *Marie Grubbe* and *Niels Lyhne* might seem to be poorly constructed (Strindberg felt that structurally *Niels Lyhne* falls apart), with vague and psychologically unconvincing transitions between the various stages in the lives of Marie and Niels. A critical reader might enquire: Exactly *how* does the sensitive, proud Marie Grubbe become so debased and demoralized that she is able to content herself with the coarse, vulgar Søren? Precisely *when* does Niels Lyhne become an atheist? The books seem to supply no satisfactory answers to these legitimate questions. But if the two novels are read as a series of lyric or lyric-dramatic *situations,* these objections become unimportant. The characters then seem to be true to life in each given situation, and Jacobsen's famous "pearl-embroidery" style with its intricately modulated rhythms commands the attention which it so richly deserves. As characteristic examples of this kind of writing might be mentioned the opening pages of *Marie Grubbe* describing the erotic day dreams of the young girl Marie, and in *Niels Lyhne* the boy Niels confronted with his aunt Edele, dressed disturbingly in exotic Gypsy costume, and later Niels in the suggestive rocking-chair episode with Mrs. Boye. The lingering sensuality of these scenes is rendered in a remarkably poetic way by Jacobsen's sensitive style.

Thematically, also, there exists a close connection between Jacobsen's poetry and his fiction. In his illuminating essay on J. P. Jacobsen in Volume IV of *Illustreret dansk Litteraturhistorie* Vilhelm Andersen pointed out that the leading motif of the cycle of youthful poems "Hervert Sperring" (1868) recurs in *Mogens, Marie Grubbe,* and *Niels Lyhne.* Stated briefly this motif deals with the conflict between the world of dreams and the world of reality, a conflict in which the introspective Jacobsen himself was deeply immersed. In "Hervert Sperring" a poetically talented youth is introduced to the world of poetry by his mother. After this he feels dissatisfied with the world of reality and escapes to the world of fantasy and dreams. He becomes a captive of his dreams which take on an increasingly sensual nature. He meets a young woman of spiritual beauty and wins her love. Gradually, however, Hervert's confidence in his own ability to hold her affection is weakened, and he leaves her. When he returns, she belongs to another. Despairingly, he plunges into sensual pleasures in order to forget and is brought to the verge of madness. The dangerous, forbidden dreams of the past reappear and destroy him.

The conflict from "Hervert Sperring" is resolved optimistically in *Mogens,* the only one of Jacobsen's works that ends happily. After the loss of Camilla, Mogens is in danger of suffering the fate of Hervert. But with the aid of Thora he establishes a normal human relationship, overcomes his fear of sexuality and "adjusts" successfully to reality. In *Marie Grubbe,* on the other hand, Marie's youthful dreams of love, happiness, and beauty are destroyed cruelly by reality. She is disillusioned in her love for Ulrik Christian, Ulrik Frederik, and Sti Høg because of the weakness of these men and has to settle for the more purely physical gratifications involved in her relationship with Søren. At the end of the novel, however, she is not defeated by reality, she is resigned to it. She is happier with Søren than she had been with any of her more aristocratic companions. And when Jacobsen towards the end confronts the old Marie with the debauched, burned-out daydreamer Sti Høg, the disillusioned Marie is clearly represented as the superior person of the two. But the note of sadness which pervades *Marie Grubbe* stems from the fact that if Marie in the process of adjusting to reality is not defeated, she is cheapened and coarsened, degraded and animalized. The romantic sensitivity and hopefulness of youth has yielded to the dumb resignation of old age. In the pessimistic *Niels Lyhne,* finally, Niels Lyhne, daydreamer and impotent poet, is defeated by reality. His failure to make a forceful impression on life is illustrated by his abortive attempts at literary creativity and his inability to hold the affection of the three women in his life: Mrs. Boye (the Lady), Fennimore (the Woman), and Gerda (the Child). The most decisive defeat in Niels Lyhne's life, the most graphic illustration of his failure to cope with reality, is his inability to adhere to his atheistic convictions in a moment of crisis. When his child is dying, the freethinking Niels breaks down and prays to God for help, to no avail. After this philosophic defeat, as he considers it, he is a broken man, a mere automaton. His joining the Danish army in the Dano-Prussian war of 1864 is no act of patriotism but an escape, a flight from a reality which has proved too much for him. He is dead spiritually long before he is hit by the Prussian bullet. It is true that at the very end Niels retrieves some measure of his lost dignity by dying "standing" and "in armor," but this final scene does not greatly modify the impression of defeat and failure which the novel produces. The story of Niels' human fallibility as it is described by Jacobsen, critically and sympathetically at the same time, ends on a note of melancholy resignation which is very typical of much of Jacobsen's work.

The conflict between the world of dreams and the world of reality is a very common motif in the Danish novel which has received incisive treatment by, among others, Hans Egede Schack, Johannes Jørgensen, Harald Kidde, Johannes V. Jensen, and Jacob Paludan. But in Jacobsen this conflict was intimately personal, and that gives to his analysis of it a peculiar intensity, especially in *Niels Lyhne* where Niels is partially modeled on the author himself. The passivity inherent in excessive indulgence in daydreaming was felt by Jacobsen to be a very real personal danger, and to a certain extent the portraits of Niels and also of the tutor Bigum in *Niels Lyhne* are self-criticisms, self-judgments on the part of the poet, as is Harald Kidde's portrayal of Tue Tavsen in the novel *Aage og Else* (1902-03). In the great scene in *Niels Lyhne* where Bigum confesses his "impossible passion" for Edele Lyhne, Edele—functioning as Jacobsen's mouthpiece at this point—pronounces a severe judgment on the kind of person who, refusing to face reality, insists immaturely on having his dream at all cost. Says Edele:

> Your love does not offend me, Herr Bigum, but I condemn it. You have done what so many of us do. We close our eyes to our real life, we will not hear the 'No' it pronounces in the face of our wishes, we would forget the deep gulf it reveals to us—the gulf that lies between our longing and its object. We must have our dreams. But life has nothing to do with dreams; not a single obstacle can be dreamed away from reality, and in the end we lie wailing beside the gulf, which has not changed, but is just as it always was. It is we ourselves who have changed; for those dreams have excited our thoughts and worked up our longing to the highest possible pitch. But the gulf has grown no narrower, and our whole being is consumed with the desire to reach the other side. But no, always no—nothing else. If only we had bethought ourselves in time! But now it is too late; we are unhappy.

Although the note of self-criticism in this passage is unmistakable, at other points in *Niels Lyhne* the judgment on the dreamer is attenuated by a touch of sympathy, because Jacobsen is so deeply involved personally in his situation. To be sure Niels Lyhne's mother Bartholine, another poetry-struck daydreamer, is also criticised for her addiction to ineffectual romantic dreams, but the judgment on her is tempered with understanding of her plight, as Jacobsen describes it in a couple of lines in which the personal accent is evident: " . . . and she dreamed a thousand dreams of those sunny places and was consumed with longing for her true, rich self, forgetting, what it is so easy to forget, that even the fairest dreams, even the deepest longings, add not a single inch to the stature of the human soul." "What it is so easy to forget" gives Jacobsen away, it is a *mot d'auteur*. J. P. Jacobsen's attitude towards the dreamer is, in other words, ambivalent, partly critical, partly sympathetic.

Aside from embodying Jacobsen's main motif, the conflict between dreams and reality, the celebrated scene between Bigum and Edele Lyhne is characteristic of his work in still another respect. Like so many other Jacobsen characters, Bigum in this scene is *powerless* to change his fate; he is doomed inexorably to suffering and humiliation. Yet, though his pain is very real, he seems at the same time to feel a perverse half-pleasure in debasing himself before Edele. Descriptions of this kind of ambivalent emotions: pleasure derived from pain and a general feeling of impotence occur with striking frequency in Jacobsen's works, from the first to the last. The whole progressive debasement of Marie Grubbe is a case in point. She demeans herself with Søren, flouts everything she used to believe in, but this degradation is not without its emotional compensations. Jacobsen writes: "In this self-abasement there was a strange voluptuous pleasure, which was in part gross sensuality, but in part akin to whatever is counted noblest and best in woman's nature. For such was the manner in which the clay had been mixed out of which she was

fashioned . . . ." The masochistic nature of the young Marie's Griseldis fantasies at the beginning of *Marie Grubbe* is an expression of an identical emotional state. Very similarly, Fennimore in *Niels Lyhne* derives a strange pleasure from debasing herself after the shattering of her romantic dreams about love in the disillusioning marriage with Erik Refstrup. Jacobsen describes her frame of mind in these words:

> . . .for a woman who has been hurled on to the pavement from the purple bed of her dreams almost finds it in her heart to hate any one who would spread a carpet over the stones. In her first bitterness she is determined to feel the hardness in all its intensity; not satisfied with going her way on foot, she drags herself along on her knees, choosing just those places where the road is steepest and the stones are sharpest. She desires neither hand nor help, nor will she raise her head, however heavy it may grow: she will bend her face to the very dust and taste it with her tongue.

The fanatic, self-torturing flagellants in **"The Plague at Bergamo"** come to mind as another illustration of the pleasure-in-pain motif, and many other examples of this sort of emotional ambivalence in Jacobsen's work could be listed. Sometimes Jacobsen does not stress actual physical pain but is content to emphasize the powerlessness inherent in a particular situation, the impossibility of gratification of an ardent desire, as for instance in the famous, oft-quoted lines:

> Lad længes, lad grædes med Evigheds-Savn,
> Der er kun en Stofhob, en Daad og et Navn.
>
> (Though you may yearn, though you may weep with eternal longing There is only a heap of matter, a deed, and a name.)

In his provocative doctoral dissertation *J. P. Jacobsen: Digteren og Mennesket* (1953) the Danish Jacobsen scholar Frederik Nielsen attempts to account for Jacobsen's preoccupation with the pleasure-in-pain motif by arguing that temperamentally J. P. Jacobsen was "algolagnic," a fancy word for masochistic. At first blush Frederik Nielsen's theory may seem farfetched, even fantastic, but he adduces so much evidence in support of his thesis that it is difficult not to agree with him, at least partly. Thus it would seem that Nielsen's findings tend to underscore, to some degree, the "decadence" which other scholars have detected in Jacobsen's work.

Although many algolagnic and decadent features may in fact be pointed out in Jacobsen's works, these elements in his books should not be stressed to the exclusion of all others. They are counterbalanced by Jacobsen's sense of humor and his unceasing craving for health and harmony, both physical and emotional. In his eagerness to prove his thesis about Jacobsen's algolagnia, Frederik Nielsen occasionally goes overboard. After the completion of *Niels Lyhne,* Jacobsen had planned to write another novel, a more cheerful book "with a little genuine wildness whistling in all the corners." He describes the plan of this work in a letter to Edvard Brandes of February 25, 1881. Frederik Nielsen quotes from this letter and surmises that the projected novel, if it had been written, would have become like *Marie Grubbe* and *Niels Lyhne* "prose-lyrical descriptions of algolagnic dreams, feelings, and situations." But Frederik Nielsen forces the argument here; he omits lines from this letter which contradict his theory. In English translation the entire passage in question from Jacobsen's letter reads as follows: "The next one must be something bright and light and sumptuous, full of the joy of life and humor, extensive festively comic passages now and then, and a little genuine wildness whistling in all the corners." "Bright and light and sumptuous" and "full of the joy of life"—that hardly sounds like algolagnic dreams, feelings, and situations!

In connection with this whole discussion of the morbid, "algolagnic" elements in Jacobsen's work, it might also be well to recall the significant line in *Niels Lyhne* where Jacobsen speaking directly in his own person, not through a character, expresses his belief in health and the "greatness" of health: "And it is on the healthy in you that you must live; it is the healthy which becomes the great." This may sound like a platitude but, as Vilhelm Andersen has observed, only in the mouth of the healthy, not in the mouth of the sick. Although Jacobsen's life from 1873—the year which saw the outbreak of his grave illness, tuberculosis—to his death in 1885 was made miserable by poor health and consequent despondency, he did not become embittered and warped in his outlook on life. Despite his own misery and loneliness, Jacobsen did not cease to believe in the possibility of human happiness, and part of his greatness lies in this. The novella *To Verdener* (*Two Worlds*), by many regarded as Jacobsen's central work, calmly juxtaposes the world of suffering and the world of joy in two characters, the hopelessly sick woman and the newly married bride. Desperately the invalid seeks to rid herself of her illness by casting it as an evil spell on the more fortunate woman. She is indeed cured, but only to be consumed by a feeling of burning remorse which can only be stilled in death. For her no journey from the world of pain to the world of joy is ever possible. Like the author she is an outcast, forever doomed to remain outside the pale of human happiness. But though Jacobsen identifies himself partly with the invalid and all his sympathy and restrained pity go out to her, he is sufficiently sane, harmonious, and detached to recognize the existence of happiness in the joy of the young bride. A little sadly, but with a determined desire to be just, he salutes her rapture in a nostalgic "toast of dreams" (en Drømmeskaal). And finally **"Fru Fønss,"** Jacobsen's last completed work, his so-called farewell to the world, expresses his conviction that life does not consist merely of suffering and misery, as Mrs. Fønss exclaims: "I never resigned; because happiness did not come to me, I never believed that life was only shabbiness and duty; I knew that happy people existed." Jacobsen, too, knew that happiness exists; but in his own works, it must be admitted, he has dwelled more upon the dark side of existence than on the bright. Life and joy are by him constantly viewed in the shadow of death and pain. Because of his great powers of empathy and his wise tolerance, however, Jacobsen's work will always remain profoundly humane, profoundly moving. With the exception of Herman Bang, Danish literature has no more compassionate interpreter of the human condition than the naturalist J. P. Jacobsen. (pp. 272-79)

Børge Gedsø Madsen, "J. P. Jacobsen Reconsidered," in The American-Scandinavian Review, *Vol. L, No. 3, September, 1962, pp. 272-79.*

Henry Handel Richardson   (essay date 1963)

[*Henry Handel Richardson was the pseudonym of Ethel Florence Lindesay Richardson Robertson, an acclaimed Anglo-Australian novelist and critic considered among the foremost exponents of the Naturalist school. In the following excerpt, she commends Jacobsen's subtle perceptions and depictions and appraises his works, concentrating on* Niels Lyhne.]

In the literary revival that took place in Denmark a quarter of a century ago, two writers stand out prominently among the rest: Holger Drachmann and Jens Peter Jacobsen. Drachmann, versatile, many-sided, intensely prolific, wasting the strength of his genius in numberless places, always impetuous and hot headed, not seldom unchastened and unrestrained; Jacobsen, reticent and self-reliant, the follower of a conscious ideal, the true literary aristocrat, impatient of all whose motives were not as disinterested as his own, who, dying in his prime, left his country two slender octavo volumes as his life-work and his legacy. It is the latter writer, the author of *Niels Lyhne* and *Fru Marie Grubbe,* who is the subject of the present sketch.

Into the seventies he came, bringing to the bald and lifeless prose that had resulted from the revolt against Romanticism, warmth and light and colour. The luxuriant beauty of his style is unapproached in modern Scandinavian literature. No other Northern writer has had his mastery over language. Yet it was no instantaneous growth, this style of his; the germs of it were in the air. He himself confesses that he owed much to Andersen, and one has only to turn to Björnson's early work, to see that he is also in Björnson's debt. Upon all that was fanciful, and coloured, and picturesque, in the styles of such writers, Jacobsen seized and made it his own. He condensed, refined, enlarged. He selected with the patience and devotion of a Flaubert—not a superfluous word in a phrase, each word laden with significance. And his sentences swing along, sometimes half a line long, sometimes half a page, but always full of music, and often of a strange exotic beauty. It is not, however, alone the rich originality of his language that carries us away. What more even than the verbal beauties of these pliant, sinuous phrases, gives colour to his pages, is the wealth of imagery they contain. There is hardly a thought—and few modern books are more thickly studded with fine, stimulating thoughts—but Jacobsen throws it into plastic form. To him it rises up and becomes part of the great world of light and colour at which he never ceased to marvel, and he brings it home to us in a kind of picture-writing that stamps it indelibly upon the mind. Does he wish to paint the triumphant progress of a great artist? His "career on earth is like a Bacchic procession, that sweeps triumphantly through all lands and scatters golden seed on every side—a genius on every panther." Or the merciless fleetness of time? Time stands, like a fisher, "out there in Eternity, immersed to the waist, hauling in the hours so that they glide past—twelve white and twelve black—incessantly, incessantly." Is it the shattered ideals of our youth?

> Our ideals, our bright, beautiful ideals . . . wander no longer on earth in our midst, as in the early days of our youth. They have been led back, step by step, up the broad-based stairs of worldly wisdom, to the heaven from which our simple faith once drew them down; and there they sit, radiant, but afar off, smiling, but weary, in divine inaction, while the incense of an inert and fitful adoration ascends in solemn clouds to their throne.

But Jacobsen is not alone the master of a unique style; he is the finest, most spiritual poet that the North has produced. No other Scandinavian writer approaches him in delicacy of poetic insight, in intensity of vision, and in the orginality of temperament across which he viewed his corner of life. With the first piece of imaginative literature he published, he was recognised as a new force in Danish letters, and hardly ten years later Dr Brandes could write, "We have all learnt from Jacobsen." There is not a book published today in Scandinavia that does not show traces of his influence, and to the younger generation in Germany he has long been master and friend. This influence is significant for one who, as a boy, wrote, "Wealth of words is no sign of wealth of thought," and whose collected works cover barely a thousand pages.

An interesting figure is this young author, this pale consumptive poet, whose life was cut off in its prime. His best years were those immediately succeeding 1870, when he began to take part in the literary life of Copenhagen, and when a presentiment of his true calling was gradually ousting his beloved science from its place. By day the student among his books, by night he was usually to be found in the cafés of the capital, where the chief literary coteries had their meeting-places. Here he would sit for hours, always by preference the listener, except sometimes late in the night, when wine or a sympathetic hearer unsealed his lips. He hid his sensitiveness and rich inner life under a veil of reserve which was rarely raised, and the quiet irony, now pungent, now gently humorous, that grew upon him as he grew in assurance, was only another form of self-defence. Warm in his patriotism, his feelings for his country culminated in his love for Copenhagen. He yearned for it with an intense homesickness, when necessity forced him to a "living grave" in Thisted, his little Juttish birthplace. Even among the beauties of Italy, the old longings overcome him, and he yearns for Copenhagen as his goal. Never was he more content than in his small room, in the heart of the city, where, among his books and hyacinths, he spent his days. Riches he never knew, and the means for the necessary journeys to the South were not always forthcoming. But his needs were as few as his life was uneventful. Against his illness he held out as long as possible, making light of it, and striving to deceive himself and others. Not until he learned that the lung he believed sound was as far gone as the other, did he give up hope. He died in the spring of 1885, having just completed his thirty-eighth year.

As a lad of sixteen he had left his home in Copenhagen, where he studied in preparation for the university. At this time science was the ruling passion of his life, and, to the neglect of the classics, he lay from morning until night, fishing algae in the town-moat. He was one of the first of the younger generation in Denmark to come under Darwin's influence; he wrote several essays on the Darwinian theory, and translated the *Origin of Species,* and the *Descent of Man.* Besides this he gained the university's gold medal with an essay on the *Desmidiaceae,* and sketched out the early chapters of a history of Denmark's plant life. But literature was not neglected. In 1867, turned twenty, he set about making poetry in earnest, and, in the handful of verse he has left, there is more than one lyric of a delicate and haunting charm. But he belonged essentially to an age that has found its vehicle of expression in prose, and this he was not slow to discover. In 1872 he published a story called *Mogens,* which created a stir in the literary circles of Copenhagen; it was recognised at once that a new talent had arisen in their midst. The surprise was that Jacobsen should be the author; the solitary student of science was the last person to whom one would have looked for the pre-Raphaelite delight in detail, the wonderful mood-painting of this story, with its breath of keen, fresh life, and rich, expressive language. Few young writers have made their first plunge into literature as mentally ripe as Jacobsen; in his later work the finesses grew finer, and the peculiarities more marked, but, in his most characteristic traits, he is here once and for all himself. *Mogens* is a delightfully fresh little story, full of sunlight and forest breezes, and told with a restrained and delicate humour unsurpassable of its kind. It bubbles over with the joy of living, and could only have been written by one who had his life and strength before him, who felt "strong as only he can feel, who still bears all his songs unsung in his breast."

There is much of this spirit and vitality in Jacobsen's historical novel, *Fru Marie Grubbe,* which was written between 1873 and 1876. The beautiful and high-spirited Marie Grubbe who, from being the favourite of an admiring Court, sinks through all grades of society until she becomes the beggar by the roadside, was a real personage of the seventeenth century, of whose life some record has been preserved. In his *Epistles,* Holberg mentions a meeting he had with Marie Grubbe, then over sixty years of age; and more than one story-teller tried his skill on her attractive history. Among others, Andersen has a story called "Hoönse-Grethe's Familie," in which the old woman of the henyard is no other than Marie Grubbe. But it was only by means of the psychological novel that the story of her life could be made credible. For Marie Grubbe is what Goethe calls a "problematical nature," and spends her life in a vain search after an ideal. A romantic, high-souled girl, she passes from disillusion to disillusion, ultimately to find, amidst poverty and labour, as the wife of a poor ferryman, more true happiness than she has ever known before. It says much for Jacobsen's art that he could make her story not only probable, but also sympathetic to us. Marie's fate, as he describes it, is inevitable. Her character is worked out with infinite care; we realise that her desire to drink life in, in long draughts, to bear great suffering and taste great joy, her keen and ill-repressed vitality, must all inevitably make for unhappiness. Even in the sordid commonness of her later lot, we cannot but respect this strong nature, which has had the courage to live its own life, and is haunted by no weak regrets.

In the matter of style, *Fru Marie Grubbe* is an acknowledged masterpiece. Jacobsen has caught the tone and reflected the spirit of the age of which he wrote, in a way which, in itself, is enough to set the book in the very front rank. No labour was too arduous for him, no ideal too high, and the result is an almost unequalled revival of the speech of a bygone day. But what makes *Marie Grubbe* unique as a historical novel is the vivid pictures it gives of the Danes and the Denmark of two and a half centuries ago. "Interiors from the Seventeenth Century" was the secondary title originally appended by the author, and these brilliant scenes that pass before our eyes like the coloured symmetries of a kaleidoscope, these finely wrought interiors, have more than the name in common with the delicate work of the old Dutch schools of art. They live before us in their finest, most intimate details. Town and country, palace and hut, the scene is rapidly shifted. And the men and women who cross the stage are the true children of their time; they are not modern figures clad in the garb, and merely speaking the phrases of a bygone day; they live the life of the seventeenth century, and respond involuntarily to its sympathies and ideas. It is qualities such as these that make *Fru Marie Grubbe* the finest historical novel in the Danish tongue.

In 1882 Jacobsen gathered into one volume, the half dozen short stories he had written at intervals since *Mogens.* Of this somewhat unequal collection, the last, **"Fru Fönss"**, shows us Jacobsen at his best. Nowhere may the exquisite delicacy of his work be better studied than in the first few pages of this story. And he has written nothing more impressive, in its noble simplicity, than the letter of farewell with which it closes. It is more than a mother's farewell to her children; virtually the last thing Jacobsen was to write, it is the farewell of a dying man to the great, fragrant, coloured world he loved so well—the cry of melancholy that has been wrung from many a strong, sensitive heart, at our century's end, by the tragedy of what Maupassant has called "l'Eternel Oubli".

> When people love, Tage and Ellinor, my little Ellinor, the one who loves best must always humble himself, and so I come to you once more, as I shall come to you in thought every hour of the day, as long as I am able to do so. He who has to die, my children, is very poor—I am very poor, for the whole of this beautiful world, which for so many years has been my rich and blessed home, is about to be taken from me; my chair will stand empty, the door will be closed upon me, and I shall never set foot here again. Therefore I look at everything with the entreaty in my eyes that it will remember me; for this reason I come to you and implore you to love me with all the love you once gave me; for, remember this, to live in memory is the only share in the human world that from now on will be mine. Only to live in memory, nothing, nothing more. . . .

But all that is best and ripest in Jacobsen's work is to be found in *Niels Lyhne* (1880); in this, his second and last novel, the whole of his genius first came to light. *Niels Lyhne* is one of those quiet, unobtrusive books which, making no immediate bid for popular favour or success, slowly and surely win a place for themselves in the abiding literature of their time. Jacobsen's novel is already a classic in Scandinavia, and Germany, quick in appreciation, has long regarded it as a landmark in modern literature.

Jacobsen tells us what, in his eyes, was one of the chief merits of his book. "Something that I value very highly about it," he writes, "is that the people, the characters in it, are Danish through and through." This fact gives the novel a peculiarly vital interest, but it does not aid a foreign appreciation of it. Its very "Danishness" makes us ready, on first acquaintance, to class it as morbid and unhealthy. The mournful, elegiac atmosphere that pervades it is something unfamiliar to us; the passionate, yet futile dreaming of the figures that move across its pages is irritating to us more practical. There is something dreamy and indecisive about the spiritual atmosphere of Denmark; with all their clearheadedness, something passive and shadowy about its people. They lack a strongly marked individuality—only the exceptions are "underlined words". And it is truly so in the book before us; faithful types are these many men and women with their rich spiritual lives, their vast dreams which grow with the years—dreams which a small inner voice whispers to them that they will never realise—their passive resignation to the inevitable when life becomes too much for them. "We must not run away," says his friend's wife to Niels Lyhne, "anything rather than that"; and Niels yielded, "and resolutely gave up thinking about it, as he gave up thinking of so many things he could have wished otherwise." And after his own "fall", his desertion of the ideal cause for which he has striven, there is no attempt at a compromise with himself. Life has been harsh enough to him, but a Niels Lyhne of a sterner, sturdier race might have struck boldly out once more.

There is a scene in this book where Niels, after having come unshaken through some of the severest trials that can befall a man, is vanquished by the sight of a little child's suffering, and, falling upon his knees, raises his hands to the God he has hitherto denied. This was the nucleus around which the book arose. For, as Jacobsen explained in a letter to Dr Brandes, his original plan was to write a book about "half-hearted freethinkers, those who found the burden too heavy for them in the hour of trouble." It was to play in "the generation that was as old as we are now, when we were born," writes its author in 1878; "for that generation had its freethinkers, too, although their ideas were somewhat vague, and their freethinking was romantically confused." The first title chosen was "Niels Lyhne, the Story of a Youthful Generation", but not many letters later Jacobsen writes that the secondary title is to fall away, as Niels has become the all-important figure. It is not difficult to perceive the discord that runs through *Niels Lyhne.* The author's first idea was to trace the history of a little band that was in advance of the religious ideas of its day; the book was to be the story of a group, not of an individual. But Jacobsen was for the most part an exile from Copenhagen, where it would alone have been possible to collect material, and make the necessary studies. It is, therefore, not surprising that in the four years of composition, the *milieu,* the ideas, and the aspirations of the day of which ***Niels Lyhne*** treats, are more and more faintly indicated, until at length there is nothing to remind us that we are not reading of our own day. And in all this Jacobsen was abetted by the fact that he had made his hero a poet. For, after all, the religious interest of the book is of the slightest. Niels shakes off his faith, as a child, when a passionate appeal to heaven has been denied him, and takes his stand with those who "spend their strength in kicking against the pricks"; but we hear no more of his religious life, until one evening, many years later, when, under the rational, practical onslaughts of a friend, he bursts into an inspired defence of atheism. The book's unsurpassable worth lies in the picture it gives of the growth and development of a poetic, introspective nature, of the people, events, and ideas that leave their mark upon it, of the intellectual currents that bear it away; and there is small doubt that, as Jacobsen warmed to his work, he gave always more of himself and his own spiritual life.

"A poet who is not a poet," is the author's description of his hero. And this is another link in the tragedy of Niels Lyhne's life. Circumstances have marked him out for a poet, but the conditions of his life have ill-fitted him for the task. Child of a commonplace, practical father, and a dreamy, romantic mother, the two sides of his nature are always at war; even as a child the land of fancy, in which he is so much at home, is nothing to him but a consciously fictitious refuge, to which he can fly when reality becomes too exacting or too dull. Pupil of a poor, proud, imaginary genius, who unconsciously helps to destroy his faith in God and man; sensitive and lonely, disappointed in his hopes of love, always thrown back upon himself, and finding no stay in his art—that is how we know Niels, Niels with his dreamy indecision and paralysing discretion, his plans too vast to be realized, his self-communings and his self-despair. There is little external incident in Niels Lyhne's life; it is for the most part his "sentimental education" that is unfolded before us—an analysis of the temporary relations in which he stands to various women. Of the secondary characters in the book, two play a more important part than the rest. Erik Refstrup, the friend of his childhood and youth, is one of those bold, intrepid natures for which people of Niels' temperament feel an intense admiration. Erik eventually becomes a painter, and his art seems to him an untold mine of wealth, but Niels knows better, seeing, with a fatal clearness, that "no matter where Erik dived into the ocean of beauty, he always brought the same pearl to light." Between the two friends comes Fennimore, sweet, tragic Fennimore, the most delicately drawn of all this gallery of women's portraits. Loved by Niels and won by Erik, this provincial Consul's daughter first steps towards us, fresh with all the breezes of her North Sea home, and yet already lightly touched with the fateful breath of passion which helps to bring about the tragedy of her marriage, undermines her relations with Niels, and impels her to a violent repentance when she learns of Erik's death.

An exceeding delicacy of feeling stamps all Jacobsen's work, and gives it a colour peculiarly its own. His nerves and senses are alive in an extraordinary degree to what the ordinary onlooker neither hears nor sees. For him, a crumpled heap of roseleaves has a thousand different tints, the changing expressions of a girl's eyes, the movements of a girl's hands are filled with poetical significance. And this mental sensitiveness is still more noticeable when he comes to treat of the human heart. The great passions are not wanting in his books, but where he excels is in defining the secret stirrings that give them birth, in describing the finest shades of our varying feelings, the almost imperceptible movements of our soul. Finally this subtleness of perception enables him to do what had not been done before him, namely to translate into words, to give definite expression to certain moods and states of mind, which had previously not found expression in literature. Vague, elusive emotions, shadowy, rapidly fleeting moods that belong to the half-unconscious side of our life, and are dim even to ourselves, Jacobsen seizes and draws to the light of day.

His early scientific interest in nature soon passed into the love and admiration of the poet, and everywhere the glories of the visible world make a passionate appeal to him. Other Danish writers have stood in a wider, more comprehensive relation to nature, none in a more intimate one than he. And his feelings for nature culminate in his love of flowers. "No one in Denmark," says his greatest critic, "has loved and understood and sung flowers as he." All were his cherished personal friends; if he had a preference, it was perhaps for hyacinths and cherry-blossom. In ***Niels Lyhne,*** he returns again and again, to the masses of delicate blossom that arch in countless forms against a cloudless sky, grow rose-red in the setting sun, and become "a great rose-castle, a rose-cathedral"; and little "flower-pieces", such as the following, seem to resemble delicate miniatures, traced on the finest ivory:—

> Meanwhile the gorgeous festival of spring was being celebrated around her; it was rung in by the white bells of the snowdrop, and joyfully greeted by the veined chalice of the crocus. Hundreds of little mountain streams rushed headlong down into the valley to announce that spring had come, but they were all too late, for on every green bank past which they hastened, stood primroses in yellow and violets in blue, and nodded, "We know it, we know it, we knew it before you!" Willows hoisted yellow streamers, and curly ferns and velvety moss hung green festoons on the naked walls of the vineyards. . . . High above these flowers of earth, and borne on the trunks of hoary cherry-trees, countless flower-islands swayed in the soft breeze; the light foamed on their white coasts, and the butterflies spotted them with red and blue, when they brought tidings from the flower-continent below.

The unity of Jacobsen's books is to be sought exclusively in the mental growth of the chief character; other figures are introduced only as long as they are necessary to the development of this character, and then let go, often without a parting word. All technical considerations were of small importance in their author's eyes; as long as the internal unity of his books satisfied him, he was regardless of their outward form. His method of work is peculiar to himself, and he follows his hero from early childhood to the end. But the reflections that are thrown upon his mirror—to use Stendhal's image of a novel being a mirror borne by a man who journeys along a great highway—are few, for he dwells only on those moments of a life which are of the supremest psychological importance.

His talent was essentially a lyric one, and he lacked dramatic feeling; there is hardly a dramatic situation in either of these novels. Nor is there any artistic crescendo, any intensifying of emotion, as the books approach their end. Our interest in *Marie Grubbe* slackens perceptibly towards the close, and, powerful though the last chapter of *Niels Lyhne* be, we have been made to feel only too plainly that the fire in Niels' soul has burnt itself out. There is a melancholy air of reality about the last pages of both books, with their subsiding emotions and unexciting deaths; the great climaxes of life have come and gone when the blood was hot and the senses were keen; custom and eventless monotony have done their work. In a faithful chronicle of her life, Marie Grubbe, dulled and blunted with life and years, must necessarily be of less interest to us than in the heyday of her hopes and aspirations, and Niels Lyhne, his shield down and its device effaced, a less vital figure than when, in all the enthusiasm of untried ardour, he rapturously defends his faith. Both these books are sad books, but it is wrong to stamp them as pessimistic; there is no pessimism here, but the pessimism which weak minds draw from outward defeat. And both Niels and Marie are, in the best sense, victors; both live and die for an idea, both have strength to fight to the end. And though Niels dies, his cause does not die with him; there are other fighters coming, and, with those who have already gone, they will in time help to form a "line of spiritual ancestors on whom their descendants will look back with pride"; though he be weak and fail, the mighty cause of Truth lives—of that he is confident, "for its beautiful countenance remains as radiantly beautiful as ever, as full of majesty and undying light, no matter how much dust is whirled against its white forehead, or how thick the poisonous vapours gather round its head."

Niels Lyhne might be called a book of unrealised ideals. Hardly one of the many people that cross its pages attains his heart's desire. All these men and women aim too high; they are none of them satisfied with the lot that has fallen to them, they will have no tree but the sky, all have a touch of divine discontent. And they beat their wings and break them against the unyielding barriers of life, which hem them in as the idea of Fate hemmed in ancient tragedy. Too late Niels learns that the only thing to do is "to bear life as it is, and let it take shape according to the laws that govern life." For most of them the lesson is too hard, and their hearts break in learning it: Edele Lyhne, who has set her love on the great artist to whom she is but one of the admiring throng; Bigum, schoolmaster and genius, who hugs himself with the thought that mankind will never know what it has lost in him—"His genius should not be thorn-crowned by an inappreciative world, but just as little should it wear the contaminating purple of the world's approval"; Erik, who looks for a world in his thin streak

of art; Niels' mother, who sits by her hearth in the north of Jutland, and dreams of the beauties of the unknown world, and who, when she stands in the midst of it all and finds the reality lag behind the dream, still does not lose heart, for "she hoped on the other side of the grave to find herself face to face with all the splendour, and one in spirit with that ideal beauty, which here on earth had filled her with dim hopes and longings. . . . And she dreamed many a melancholy dream of how in memory she would look back on what earth had given her, look back on it hereafter from the land of immortality, where all the beauty of the earth, for all time, would be on the other side of the sea." And lastly Niels, dreamer and poet, who goes through life seeking an ideal love, an ideal friendship, which shall fill the aching void of his soul, and who learns only on his deathbed, "the great melancholy truth, that a soul is always alone."

Jacobsen is a mental aristocrat; his books are for the few, not the many—in this respect of apartness he resembles Walter Pater. Like Pater, too, he worked slowly, and with the severest self-criticism; he had no more sympathy for those who, in these self-conscious days, played the naïvely irresponsible with regard to their art, than for those who did not believe, as earnestly as he, that "every new book must be produced by a struggle with oneself to get the utmost out of oneself."

When he began to write, the great wave of Naturalism that arose in France had just reached Denmark, and the young author naturally adopted the new and captivating principles as his artistic creed. Flaubert was the object of his especial admiration; and all through his work, there is the realist's stern determination to face life as it is. But he wore Naturalism only as an outer garment; by temperament, he was more akin to the little group of psychologists, whose headstone of the corner is Henri Beyle, and again, there is more than one trait in his work which directly connects him with the old Romantic School: he has all Tieck's contempt for the utilitarian—never, in his books, is there question of the practical or material—and his heroes are the dreamers, the poets, whose conflicts are not those of this world. What, perhaps, gives his work its most characteristic stamp is a rare poetic imagination, an imagination which transfigures all its touches. He wrote almost wholly in prose, but it is as a poet that one thinks of him and knows him; with poets alone is it possible to compare him.

Niels Lyhne has been called the Bible of young Scandinavia. And, if we wish to grasp the peculiar, indefinable essence of the Northern mind, it is to this book we shall turn rather than to many that have won a wider European fame. But *Niels Lyhne* is not merely an enduring monument, raised to his country by the greatest modern Danish writer; its issues are wider. It is one of those books which are of infinite suggestiveness, which seem to open up vistas before and behind, to give the idea of loftiness and space. There is a touch of the "melancholy of eternity" upon it. It embodies, in a peculiar degree, the hopes and struggles, the dreams and disillusions of our century's end. (pp. 40-51)

Henry Handel Richardson, "A Danish Poet,"
in Southerly, *Vol. 23, No. 1, 1963, pp. 40-51.*

Robert Raphael   (essay date 1975)

[*Raphael is an American educator and critic who specializes in Scandinavian studies. In the following excerpt he contends that, despite Jacobsen's penchant for close observation and detailed description, his Naturalism differs from that practiced by many of his contemporaries, and, citing his works' stylized eroticism, allies him instead with the Decadents, principally Algernon Swinburne.*]

[In Georg Brandes] existed the ground for a novel literary orientation that in great part was to characterize the 1870s and 1880s. It was an orientation that eschewed metaphysical experience or reflection. Guided by the boundless scientific optimism of the age, this new literature made it a point to scrutinize the morass of society's problems with the rigor and objectivity of the laboratory. Progress, or perhaps a kind of redemption, might be achieved by having to face the revelations obtained through the author's dispassionate, microscopic observation. Social man, it was believed, found himself imprisoned by heredity, and milieu. The author's mission, and that of the reader, was to face the fact and try to improve man's lot by altering social conditions. If, however, society was beyond help, then one might, as Ibsen intimated in his social plays, simply blow it up. Thus derived the hope, and the optimism—such as it was—that moved the hand of the naturalist.

Jens Peter Jacobsen, however, was not, in any true sense of the term, a naturalist. If he shared his colleagues' enthusiasm for objective observation—he did, after all, begin as a botanist—it was with an entirely different purpose in mind. Man, subject to outside conditions beyond his control, was also the prisoner of his instincts, the unguarded victim of all its hellish urgings and half-hidden drives. The individual personality, not society, was a morass. Darwin, Swinburne, and Walter Pater became for Jacobsen what Darwin, Brandes, and Zola were for a time for Ibsen and Strindberg. He, like the naturalists, shunned any kind of metaphysics but for a different reason and with a different purpose. Because if, in Pater's words, "the whole scope of observation is dwarfed to the narrow chamber of the individual mind . . . each mind keeping as a solitary prisoner its own dream of a world," then, Pater concludes, living must remain "one desperate effort to see and touch; we shall hardly have time to make theories about the things we see and touch"; a deep-seated esthetically valid self-realization, therefore, must be the end in view, not the scrutiny of society or its betterment. With a keen, microscopic eye of his own, Jacobsen was bent on bringing to light not the problems of social man but the terrors and the glory of the individual psyche.

Furthermore, although he was a Darwinist *par excellence,* having literally transmitted Darwin's thinking into Scandinavia by his own translations in the early 1870s, Jacobsen did not keep in step with any of the other literary Darwinists of his time. While they were bringing up social problems for debate, Jacobsen remained intent on the per-

fection of a literary style he called his "pearl embroidery." Jacobsen's whole artistic orientation became, therefore, far more akin to the opulence of Pater or Swinburne than it was to any of his naturalist contemporaries and their objective dissections of society.

J. P. Jacobsen was born in the small town of Thisted in the northwest corner of Denmark's Jutland peninsula, where he spent nearly twenty-two of his thirty-eight years, passing away there on April 30, 1885. In boyhood, his dominant interests were botany and literature. As early as his ninth year, inspired by reading Danish poets, Jacobsen began writing short verses. By the time he entered Copenhagen's university, in 1867, he could not decide, as he phrased it, "between the lyre or the microscope." Nor was it always a simple thing for him during his young adulthood to keep a proper balance between the compelling sadomasochism which fed his fantasies on the one hand, and the pristine gaze of the cool scientist on the other. In fact, his growing maturity both as a poet and as a naturalist led him in time to achieve a fruitful union of erotic insights, keenness of observation, and literary inventiveness. All of that came with age. By 1868, Jacobsen's literary activity had reached, in the dramatic poem **"Gurresange",** those contrasts of shade and light and the exquisite texture that were to become the wings of his lasting fame. Arnold Schönberg set the German translation to music in 1910. In that same period, Jacobsen the scientist made his debut with the first translations into a Scandinavian language of Darwin's *On the Origin of the Species* (1871-1873) and *The Descent of Man* (1874). Although Darwin had already been a topic of debate in Denmark, it was Jacobsen's translations which made Darwin generally known throughout the Nordic countries, and which caused the English scientist's thinking to become a part of the new spirit of "breakthrough" in Scandinavia's literature. Fluent in English since boyhood, Jacobsen, the ruthless naturalist and the atheist who had been influenced by Strauss and Feuerbach, was very susceptible to Darwin's theories about man's evolution and biological fate.

In the novella **Mogens,** which was composed during the spring of 1872, Jacobsen not only made his debut in literary prose, but he also revealed that he was a contributor to the spirit of "breakthrough" which was thriving around him. For in **Mogens,** nature and human action are both viewed with a hard objectivity and magnified detail such as had not existed in the romantic prose of an earlier day. With his sharp scientific gaze intensified by Darwin, but softened by his sure poetic instincts, Jacobsen makes of **Mogens** a portrait of man and nature as a wholesome totality, wherein human feeling and action are sound—perhaps because they need not rely upon a heaven which is empty. In the end, **Mogens** seemed to blast like a hurricane against the reaction and conservatism that prevailed in Danish letters. The work's atheism and its naturalism, its very fresh and inventive style and its high level of esthetic communication, left no doubt that Jacobsen was fulfilling the challenge of Georg Brandes that the modern artist be a new kind of aristocrat. Jacobsen's cultural contemporaries were well aware of that fact. What they, however, could not surmise was that in depicting preconscious and even subconscious thought in what seemed apparently irrational deed, Jacobsen was placing himself as an artist under the kind of extreme pressure that can only produce novel, often unique, orientations. It was what Carlyle and Baudelaire had done before him, and what Proust, Thomas Mann, and Kafka were to do after him.

With the appearance of the novel *Marie Grubbe* late in 1876, readers no doubt surmised from its subtitle, "A Lady of the Seventeenth Century," as some believe still, that Jacobsen's major aim was to depict veraciously the times and the existence of history's Marie Grubbe, at least from her fourteenth year in 1657 until her death in 1718. The store of detail vividly culled from Danish history, together with the bounty of elegant vignettes and earthy color recalled from everyday life in Denmark's baroque age, gives ample cause for this belief to appear a fact. Despite the novel's historical authenticity and richness, Jacobsen's object is not an elaborate recreation of seventeenth-century Denmark.

This novel is essentially about the personality and development of Marie Grubbe alone, thus much of the author's detailed historical background ultimately bears little, if any, relevance to the profound changes within her, viewed—as they always are—from the author's unique and innovative perspective. Yet the antique settings and picturesque dialogue may be seen as germane, if only because these elements provided him with a unifying scrim, a strategic artistic leverage that allowed him to maintain firm stylistic control of all his esthetic data. During 1873, the writer scrupulously gathered as much historical detail as possible from documents and letters of the period in Copenhagen's Royal Library. In this endeavor Jacobsen's strategy was hardly different from that of European contemporaries who successfully exploited the materials of history with the same artistic intent. Gustave Flaubert, in his novel *Salammbô* of 1862, used ancient Carthage as a means of gaining stylistic control of, and unity in, his material precisely in the way Richard Wagner did when he used nearly every facet of sixteenth-century Nuremberg in order to manipulate and clarify the artistic environment of his *Die Meistersinger,* which premiered in 1868.

Using the external authority of history, Jacobsen had a solid platform of fact on which he could juxtapose and control all of the major data relating to the historical Marie Grubbe and her age with such success that he achieved exactly what he was after from the beginning: a unique and unifying vision of Marie's existence and psyche as it resided in his artist's eye. Moving within his historic frame, Jacobsen was free to bore into layers of personality that had scarcely been revealed with such unrelenting light before; he was, in fact, now able to turn himself into his main characters whenever and however he chose. This technique had, of course, been fruitfully employed a generation before by Flaubert, who, using his observations of the French provincial middle class, transformed himself into Emma Bovary. Jacobsen, indeed, could have said about his *Marie Grubbe* what the French writer, in that legendary statement, proposed about his own book: "Madame Bovary c'est moi." Emma and Marie are certainly akin in many essential ways. Both are youthful victims of powerful illusions regarding romantic love,

illusions that were largely shaped by their adolescent reading. But, whereas Emma is ostensibly ruined by her books, Marie, in the end, proves to be not nearly so blind. Marie learns relatively soon about the sham of society's mores, its ideas of status, and its precarious system of social roles, and she grows to scorn them. At the same time, she also learns to spurn all notions about eroticism but her own, gradually becoming strengthened to confront—just as Jacobsen did—the innermost abyss of her personality. Unlike Emma Bovary, who perceives these things too late and remains powerless to react or change, Marie Grubbe is able to survive her final years of poverty and obscurity by regarding the world and herself without flinching. Her surroundings have ceased to be relevant in any way. That is why she can accept death, as she informs Holberg in the novel's last pages, without fear or the consolation of belief in a hereafter. Marie may be said to face the same kind of "difficult death" that Niels Lyhne was to do, and for nearly the same reason.

Jacobsen was perhaps the most creative Darwinist in the Europe of his day. This clearly distinguishes him from Flaubert, whose most renowned work appeared two years before *On the Origin of the Species* was published in 1859. As a scientist, the Danish author was in a position to understand Darwin's significance as few other Europeans, among them Zola and Swinburne, could. Like them, Jacobsen found himself quickly responding to the English scientist's shattering effect on traditional ideas concerning God, the universe, and man's fate. Finding his own insights confirmed in Darwin, Jacobsen rejected once and for all the long sacrosanct teleological view of the origins and destiny of man. The Dane came to see that the final goal of human evolution was *not* the perfect adaptation of the organism to its environment, an adaptation that would reveal the perfection of God's plan, to say nothing of the perfectibility of man himself. Instead, Jacobsen understood what only a bare handful of intellectuals, by 1872, were able to: the venerated teleological concept of existence simply did not correspond to fact; evolution and the human predicament were not purposive at all. Far from being naturally perfectible, man was but the helpless victim of heredity and milieu, depending as every other creature on laws of natural selection. If man achieved any advance over his condition, it was strictly by random chance.

It is no surprise, therefore, that Marie Grubbe herself may be regarded as the genuine offspring of the author's Darwinism; the novel was begun the same year he was translating *On the Origin of the Species.* When one speaks of *Marie Grubbe* as Scandinavia's first naturalistic novel, therefore, it is because one notices the way in which the author shows the life of the protagonist evolving almost inevitably out of inborn propensities which are lucidly revealed in the novel's first episode. Developing through conflict with—and perceptions about—her milieu, Marie, in the last pages of the work, may even be looked on as a Darwinist in her own right. Certainly her atheism and Darwinism are implied when she proclaims to Ludvig Holberg (who was a major figure of the Enlightenment, supporting its confident, teleological views of God and His universe) lack of belief in an after life and asserts her strong belief in self.

All this evidence, however, does not make **Marie Grubbe** a naturalistic work. If it were that, Jacobsen could never have permitted himself the apparent luxury of what he termed the "pearl embroidery" of his distinctive style. This style had come into being in the exquisite images and phrases of the **"Gurresange"** before any real contact with Darwin. It was a style that no naturalist ever could devise. In the novella **Mogens** Jacobsen developed it further, to a point where the whole of nature, rather than being portrayed naturalistically, is perceived as a purely esthetic experience from first to last. No naturalist, Jacobsen should rather be regarded as a stylist, a term which applies to those European artists who now are seen to have created under the headings impressionism, estheticism, or decadence. In its salient aspects, Jacobsen's art may therefore be viewed as being far more in tune with that of such writers as Wilde, Hofmannsthal, or D'Annunzio, members of the generation that followed his, than he was with contemporaries such as Zola or Ibsen. But by the 1870s, the chief stylists of Jacobsen's time had already emerged clearly into sight. They were England's Walter Pater and, above all, Algernon Swinburne. Indeed, it scarcely astonishes us to learn that by 1870, Jacobsen, whose command of English was excellent, ordered his publisher to get copies of everything Swinburne had in print. Jacobsen devoured all of it with unceasing fascination. Swinburne can be seen as an interest that preceded, and survived, the author's active preoccupation with Darwin, and with good cause.

The content, but more particularly the style, of Swinburne's *Atalanta in Calydon* (1865) and the famous *Poems and Ballads* (1866) confirmed by resplendent example what Jacobsen had already begun to surmise: Art could be more than a tool with which one fashioned profound and disturbing vistas of the personality, it might also provide a usefully complete and wholly self-justifying end in itself. The terrors of personality and existence could be squarely confronted when perceived from the distance of a lovely esthetic surface; perceived, that is, *with style.*

Using unending beauty of esthetic surface, Jacobsen provided himself with an observation tower from which he was able to survey in the peculiarly impersonal manner of the stylist the often highly disturbing emotions of Marie Grubbe. Like Swinburne, who was an admitted sadomasochist, Jacobsen reveals, from the outset, the horrors of Marie's intensely eroticized personality, which parallels his own. In the sexual fantasies with which the novel opens, eroticism is seen as something that is scarcely separable from psychic and physical torment. Jacobsen's vision of eroticism as a series of sadistic violation and masochistic self-violation was shared by not just a few of his contemporaries besides Swinburne, among them Baudelaire, Huysmans, Wagner, and Strindberg. This vision was to culminate in the gorgeous textures and frightening content of Oscar Wilde's play *Salome* in 1893, a work whose lurid depictions had already been prefigured in 1876 in Gustave Moreau's painting based on the same theme, and by Wagner's *Parsifal* of 1882.

Through the acute lens of his sustained and exquisite style, Jacobsen probes the abyss of Marie's erotic life, delving first into her fantasy of self-violation in the role of Grisel-da, and, pursuing her sexual daydream further, the author details a second violation that would end in self-destruction were the dreamer not to awaken from her reverie, as she, of course, must. "Stripped by a black and shaggy hand . . ."—it is clear that the owner of the hand is Bertel of the turnpike house to whom Marie is strongly attracted—the fourteen-year-old girl imagines herself in the role of Brynhild, a character from the romantic legends of her reading. Tossed into the dust by sadistic "Bertel," who grasps her by strands of long black hair, Marie's ankles are tied to the long tail of a snorting black stallion. At this moment, Marie's free association breaks off, and none too soon.

These astonishing episodes are detailed by Jacobsen by means of an uncanny use of the interior monologue technique that appears as modern and effective as Molly Bloom's soliloquy at the close of Joyce's *Ulysses*. This technique had, of course, already been employed with some subtlety by Laurence Sterne in his novel of 1759, *Tristram Shandy*. The principles of eighteenth-century empirical psychology and mental association, however, were later exploited by romantic poets to produce a *de facto* kind of stream-of-consciousness, or interior monologue, in works by authors such as Novalis, Lamartine, de Vigny, Leopardi, and Wordsworth. Even the apprenticeship novels of Charles Dickens written in the first person may, from a certain point of view, be described as a stream-of-consciousness approach. Certainly Dujardin who, in his *Les lauriers sont coupés* of 1887, wrote a novel in the form of the interior monologue, cannot be said to have achieved, in the retrospect of today, Jacobsen's merit as the progenitor of this technique in its modern form, even if Joyce in his *A Portrait of the Artist* of 1916 deliberately borrowed the technique from the Frenchman.

After the author brilliantly lights up the erotic crannies of Marie's psyche through her daydreaming in the novel's initial episode, he does not spare us its consequences. Jacobsen's microscopic eye pursues Marie's erotic frustrations and masochistic gratifications into adult life and old age, and reveals how his protagonist learns to regard and accept unflinchingly the experiences and drives of her personality that cannot simply be wished away. In the end, unlike Emma Bovary, Marie Grubbe learns to fashion a durable inner life that provides her with solace even in her old age.

The position of Jacobsen's cultural niche in the nineteenth century is clear. Although he enlists both heredity and milieu as major factors in the lives of Marie Grubbe, and Niels Lyhne, his Darwinism does not make of him a naturalist in the manner of Zola or Hauptmann or the Strindberg of *Miss Julie* or anyone else. Moreover, other important writers who were never in the cause of naturalism, not least among them Thomas Mann, were sometimes at pains to detail the effects of environment and heredity. In Jacobsen's case, Darwinism and all that it implied for his age was only a part of the means. The artistic end was style, those esthetic arabesques and excesses, that "pearl embroidery" whose excruciating limits were finally achieved a decade or two after him, first in Huysman's *À rebours* and the poetry of Mallarmé, and ultimately in the stylistic floods we associate with *art nouveau* and the *fin de siècle*. Jacobsen belongs in the society of "the melancholy company," those decadents and esthetes spoken of at length by Marie Grubbe's onetime lover, the voluptuary Sti Høg, who is none other than the author's own representative and spokesman. Sti Høg, just as the artist Jacobsen himself, burns with that "hard, gemlike flame" described by Walter Pater in his depiction of the beautiful experience. For through the consistently sensuous, esthetic flow created by a beautiful style, Jacobsen knew, the terrors of the mind and experience could be faced and endured as never before. (pp. vi-xviii)

> *Robert Raphael, in an introduction to* Marie Grubbe: A Lady of the Seventeenth Century *by J. P. Jacobsen, translated by Hanna Astrup Larsen, second edition, The American-Scandinavian Foundation and Twayne Publishers, 1975, pp. v-xviii.*

Niels Lyhne Jensen   (essay date 1980)

[*Jensen is a Danish educator and critic who specializes in Scandinavian literature. In the following excerpt, he asserts that Jacobsen's suggestive vignettes find their ideal form in his shorter works, summarizing and appraising* Mogens, Two Worlds, *"The Plague in Bergamo," and "There Should Have Been Roses."*]

Besides his novels Jacobsen wrote over the years some short works in prose which are traditionally referred to as novellas. The term is not well chosen, as only one of these pieces conforms to the classical novella type. They range from one short novel to mythlike tales and a lyrical fantasia.

Though they are not many, the novellas suggest that the short form suits Jacobsen's talent better than the novel. His penchant for the tableau or interior—on which the individual chapters of the novels tend to focus—here comes into its own as does his preference for the evocation of moods. Besides, the short form suited his easygoing temperament, and during the last years of ill health short pieces in prose were about all he was able to muster. (p. 106)

The first published work by Jacobsen is the long novella or short novel ***Mogens.*** It appeared in the magazine *Nyt dansk Maanedsskrift* (*New Danish Monthly*), edited by Vilhelm Møller, a close friend of Jacobsen's and known as a critic and translator of Turgenev. Without any declared editorial program the magazine still became the organ of the writers of the "Modern Breakthrough," carrying, among other things, Georg Brandes's essay on Renan, samples of his translations from John Stuart Mill, Drachmann's early poems with revolutionary themes, his correspondences from England, and Jacobsen's articles introducing Darwinism. (p. 108)

Mogens is about the career of a young man from his first experience of love to his happy marriage and integration as a person. In between it describes a crisis of erotic debauchery and despair caused by the death of Mogens's first love and rooted in his immature and traumatic attitude to woman. In a sense the story conforms to the tripar-

tite pattern of the "Bildungsroman": from innocence to a crisis of love and faith to final harmony. ***Mogens,*** however, differs from this development in some significant respects.

The main character of the story is a young man of twenty when he is first introduced to the readers. Though he stems from the educated, well-to-do class of higher civil servants and landowners, which is also Niels Lyhne's background, he is singularly devoid of the cultural veneer of this social set. In company he is gauche and coarsely sincere. In the opening scene of the first chapter Mogens catches sight of a girl's head among the foliage in the woods, and as if prompted by instinct runs toward it. This encounter is the beginning of a love affair with young Camilla, the daughter of a retired civil servant, resulting in a respectable engagement. This idyllic development is cruelly broken off when Camilla dies in a fire in the family townhouse. Mogens, when rushing to her rescue, is only in time to watch her perish in the blaze. When clear of the burning house he runs off on a lunatic chase till he is found in the woods, suffering from a bout of nerve fever. After his recovery he tries to forget his smarting loss by dissolute living in the company of pedlars, horse-dealers, and their women. He brings this phase of his existence to an end when he brutally breaks off an affair with a woman of easy virtue. Tasting the dregs of his excesses he is the victim of the somber disillusion and desolation expressed in the following reflection:

> Everything was very sad, all of life empty behind him, dark before him. But such was life. Those who were happy were also blind. Through misfortune he had learned to see. Everything was full of injustice and lies, the entire earth was a huge rotting lie. Faith, friendship, mercy, a lie it was, a lie was each and everything. But that which was called love, it was the hollowest of all hollow things. It was lust, flaming lust, glimmering lust, smoldering lust, but lust and nothing else.

Mogens is roused from his melancholy stupor when during a lonely nightly stroll he is moved to tears by a woman singing from a house of her longings and dreams. As he gets to know her, he regains a positive attitude to life and humanity. When he marries the girl he seems set for happiness, but because of a sexual trauma, related to the death of his first fiancée, and the period of wild living following after, he wants the marriage to be platonic, darkly seeing sensual passion as impure and destructive. Thanks to the girl's healthy instincts and sexual initiative their union is fully consummated, leaving both partners as persons spiritually and physically fulfilled.

To an even greater extent than ***Niels Lyhne*** this story lacks the attention to environment that makes it possible to interpret the characters in terms of their origins, social standing, and psychological makeup. Mogens is the only figure of which we get more than the flimsiest impression, and even he is full of contradictions and vagueness. We are supposed to believe that this young man of twenty still entertains schoolboyish dreams of going to sea, and that the son of a county sheriff shows his reaction against conventional literary culture by absorbing himself in folktales and chapbooks. Also, the rough manner which is his main characteristic at the beginning of the story vanishes without a trace when he enters society after the crisis though the lapse of time in the story is a matter of months.

Due to the above-mentioned characteristics the figure of Mogens has been interpreted in conflicting ways. He has been regarded as a child of nature, a Darwinian version of the Rousseauean innocent who responds to instinctive urges when he runs toward the girl in the opening scene. Vilhelm Andersen [in *Illustreret dansk Litleraturhistorie IV*] sees his behavior as an instance of sexual selection, mistaking the Darwinian concept for the Goethean idea of elective affinity. It is as ill-founded when Mogens's realist view of nature, expressed in a central scene in the story, is claimed to represent a scientific view of Nature. "I can take joy in every leaf, every twig, every beam of light, every shadow. There isn't a hill so barren, nor a turf-pit so square, nor a road so monotonous that I can't for a moment fall in love with it."

Mogens seems certainly a rebel against convention through his contempt of literary culture and salon conversation, but it does not, as it has been believed, make him a spokesman for Brandes's radical teachings in the famous lectures on *Main Currents*. Jacobsen probably knew very little of their contents when he wrote his story.

It has also been attempted to see Mogens as representing "the superfluous man," the weak-willed type of dreamer one associates with Turgenev's Rudin, but the characterization hardly fits. Mogens does not strike the reader as unfit for life, and the problem of dream-reality, so central to *Niels Lyhne,* does not offer itself to Mogens and cannot be said to determine his development.

Allowing for the fact that Jacobsen has not succeeded in making his hero a homogeneous character, Mogens's career may be understood as the traumatic development into a mature personality of a young man ridden with fear of erotic passion and inhibited in his relationship with women by the guilt he feels at his own erotic fantasies. The crisis caused by Camilla's death in the blaze may be seen as having a psychological counterpart in Mogens's burning possession of her in his erotic daydreams. Also here she ultimately perishes in the flames, that is, as a virgin idol she ceases to be. The frenzied chase cross-country after the fire is an escape; the bouts of irrational aggression that punctuate it are both attempts at suppressing the memory of the catastrophe and expressions of his disgust with his foul deadly desire (as for instance when he absurdly attacks a dark heap of dirt rising from the snow). The trauma of his relationship with Camilla explains his cynical attitude to his amours during his period of debauchery as well as his wish for his marriage to be platonic, which her death in a fire-accident does not.

Contrary to the fabrications of literary historians *Mogens* never to Jacobsen's contemporaries and associates seemed a turning-point in Danish literature or a clarion-call of the new Realist movement. Georg Brandes, for one, considered it trivial while regarding *Marie Grubbe* as Jacobsen's true breakthrough and contribution to the new literary school.

Too much may have been read into the story, but it still holds good that *Mogens* represents a view of life distinct from the one found in the fiction current at the time of its appearance. Its view of man may be dualist, but Mogens does not strive to establish a harmonious idealist world view. He is triumphant in his struggle to come to terms with the animal forces within himself, but the saving principle is to him not spirit, but Nature.

The novelty of the novella's descriptive style has not been disputed by any one. Jacobsen has learned from Turgenev, from whose "Three Encounters" Jacobsen literally transposes the intense lyrical scene where Mogens listens to a woman singing unseen behind curtains. Jacobsen also derives from Turgenev the evocative lyrical quality of his descriptions of nature and the adoption of a central perspective for descriptions of scenery presenting them as observed from the point of view of a protagonist present in the landscape.

Both elements are manifestly present in the famous opening passage describing the woods. The playful animation in the description of the trees when it speaks of "joyous maple-trees with gayly indented leaves" is clearly inspired by Hans Christian Andersen. The sense of material richness in the description of the lichen turning into brocade with the rain and the penchant for arabesque patterns reflected in the comparison of the oak-tree branches to "grossly misdrawn old Gothic arabesques" are both unmistakeable characteristics of Jacobsen's own manner. That is also true of the keen observation of the minutest detail as when he points to the "withered leaves that lay on the grass and rolled themselves up with sudden little jerks as if they were shrinking from the sunbeams." This keenness of vision is displayed in the bold impressionism of the description of the oncoming rainstorm:

> Suddenly a small dark spot appeared upon the light-gray mold, another, three, four, many, still more, the entire molehill suddenly was quite dark gray. The air was filled with nothing but long dark streaks, the leaves nodded and swayed and there rose a murmur that turned into a hissing—rain was pouring down.

The phenomenological apperception of the passage serves not only the impressionist technique, but it also says something about the passive lethargy of the person placed as an observer in the landscape.

Jacobsen's experimenting with descriptive techniques, new to Danish literature at the time, is nowhere more in evidence than in the passage where he describes the colors of the room in Camilla's townhouse:

> Within the room all forms and colors had come to life. Whatever was flat extended, whatever was bent curved, whatever was inclined slid, and whatever was broken refracted the more. All kind of green tones mingled on the flower-table, from the softest dark-green to the sharpest yellow-green. Reddish-brown tones flooded in flames across the surface of the mahogany table, and gold gleamed and sparkled from the knick-knacks, from the frames and moldings, but on the carpet all the colors broke and clashed mingled in a joyous shimmering confusion.

In this passage the colors, in keeping with the effect of Impressionist painting, are abstracted, so to speak, from the objects of which they are attributes, as well as activated through the verbs of motion describing them. Jacobsen writes as if striving to overcome Lessing's distinction between literature as presenting events in time and pictorial art objects in space.

If *Mogens* may still succeed in captivating readers today it is thanks to the originality of its descriptive art and by the vigor of its youthful affirmation of life and happiness. In this respect it stands apart in Jacobsen's work, only linking up with the very last story he was to complete and publish. (pp. 108-13)

Two Worlds dates from the time after the period of illness and dejection during Jacobsen's stay in Italy in 1879.

The story is set in Austria in a village situated on the banks of the river Salzach. The central character is a poor woman suffering from a wasting disease. Despairing in medical treatment she accepts the advice of a one-eyed man she meets at a country fair. She must cure herself by black magic. She is to throw a bundle prepared from edelweiss, rue, blighted corn, and a splinter from a dead man's coffin at a woman passing through running water. Shortly after she has performed her sinister rite, she exults in a remarkable recovery. Gradually, however, her sense of well-being gives way to remorse. A nightmarish vision of the woman to whom she believes to have passed her malady haunts her. Eventually her sick conscience gets the better of her, and she drowns herself in the river at the very spot where she cast her bundle. As the water closes over her head, a boat passes on the river carrying the very young woman against whom the fatal witchcraft was practiced. She is unharmed, jubilant in her feeling of youth and fulfilled love.

The theme here is the problem of freedom and guilt which also entered Mogens's and Henning's stories as well as the Fennimore episode in *Niels Lyhne.* The woman cannot take the consequences of her deed. Her Christian upbringing gets the better of her. The confrontation with Christianity is evident, both from the marks of the cross the woman makes in the mud of the river bank before drowning herself and from the fragment of spirited conversation heard from the boat as it passes on the river the first time: "Happiness is decidedly a pagan idea. You cannot find the word in the New Testament."

Jacobsen here adumbrates ideas that Nietzsche, though he did not like the word happiness, was to explore in *Beyond Good and Evil* and *The Genealogy of Morals,* not to mention Henrik Pontoppidan in *Lykke-Per* and "The Great Spook."

There is still in *Two Worlds* a tragic compassion and pessimistic view of fate: some seem born to suffering, poverty, and unhappiness. These features are clearly suggested in the stirring opening passage of the story:

> The Salzach is no cheerful river, and there is a village on its eastern shore that is very dreary, very poor, and strangely quiet.

> Like a miserable gang of sickly beggars whom

the water has stopped as they cannot pay the ferry-levy, the houses are huddled on the edge of the river bank, poking with their rotting crutches in the filmy stream. From the back of the balconies their black lack-lustre window-panes scowl out from under the overhanging eaves in spiteful sorrow at the more fortunate houses over there, which detached, or in pairs and clusters, are spread on the green plain, stretching into the golden haze of the distance. But there is no light surrounding the poor houses. Only cowering darkness and silence, burdened by the sound of the river, sluggishly, endlessly oozing by on its course, so spent, so strangely absent-minded.

One finds here the pity mixed with disapproval afforded the sick, superstitious woman who cannot bear life as it is and allow it to shape itself according to its own laws. The passage marks a movement away from analytical realism through the symbolically charged picture of the village. That is also true of the fact that none of the characters in the story is named, but referred to in general terms: the ailing woman, the young woman, the one-eyed old man. *Two Worlds* by its softly cadenced prose and intense lyrical mood seems the quintessence of Jacobsen's prose art, pointing the way to the writers in Scandinavia who in the 1880s and 1890s—Ola Hansson being an obvious example—attempted to break away from orthodox Realism.

The development away from Realism and a contemporary setting is also recognizable in the tale "**The Plague in Bergamo.**" It dates from 1881-82, but has affinity to titles listed by Jacobsen in 1874. The theme of flagellation, which is central to the story, was . . . the subject for an essay written by Jacobsen when still at school in 1867. Jacobsen also dwells on self-torment in the unfinished dramatic soliloquy "**Faustina**" (1870). The plague story may have been on his mind when in 1879 he made enquiries with an English bookseller for a copy of W. M. Cooper's *Flagellation and the Flagellants* (1870). Jacobsen's main source of inspiration is, however, the description of the plague in Florence in 1348 to be found in Giovanni Boccaccio's *Il Decameron* (1350), from which several significant details can be seen to be derived.

Jacobsen's story concentrates on an incident during the plague in the old city of Bergamo in Northern Italy. As Old Bergamo gets isolated from the surrounding country because of the contagious disease, the inhabitants first work together in piety and charity to avert its worst consequences. But as all is no avail, the mood changes. As the burghers throw themselves into endless orgies of drinking, sexual license, and black magic, mere anarchy is let loose upon the city. All charity and mutual aid are forgotten. The dead are left to rot under the blazing summer sky and the sick are abandoned or even stoned away from the houses. As the pestilence waxes in the unrelenting summer heat, a procession of flagellants approaches the city one day. When the stigmatized fraternity enters the city gate with crosses and banners of fire, they are received with scorn and hostility by the drunken crowd. After a while the curiosity of the revelers is roused and they follow the fanatics as they move into the long-deserted cathedral of the town. Here the flagellants continue scourging themselves in the nave, incited to a frenzy of anger and hatred as the boozers perform an obscene parody of the Mass before the high altar. At the very height of the outrage a monk among the fanatics gets up to deliver a hell-fire sermon working up to the conclusion that Christ, when mocked on the cross by the pitiless crowd, tore Himself loose and worked no atonement. His final sentence—No Christ died for us on the Cross!—strikes the stupefied carousers with terror, but their growling threats and abject appeal—Crucify him!—make no impression on the flagellants as they move out of the church and, descending into the plain, are soon lost out of sight.

The gripping story gives expression to the author's obsession with death and reflects his tragic and passionate rejection of religious atonement and the afterlife. It explores three ways, equally vain, of coming to terms with death. One is the ordered social ritual piety, Apollonian in character, to which the inhabitants of Bergamo turn in the first instance. The other two, an orgy of sensual excess, and its opposite, insane mortification of the flesh, are both Dionysian in their ecstasy and transcendence of all bounds. Their point of contact is realized by the revelers: " . . . it was a small spot of madness within their brains that understood this mania."

Jacobsen's insight here brings Nietzsche's "The Birth of Tragedy" to mind, where he describes the Dionysian celebration in these words: " . . . this phenomenon that pain produces enjoyment, that jubilation will draw dolorous notes from the breast. From the highest joy sounds the cry of terror or the nostalgic lament over an irrevocable loss."

The author's attitude to all three responses to the pestilence is entirely negative. His apparent sympathy with the burghers who, when first struck by the plague, turn to good works and cooperation, while piously appointing the Holy Virgin Podesta of the City, is revealed as deadly irony when the passage relating this is followed by the shattering comment: "But none of this helped. There was nothing that could help."

The carousing and promiscuity to which the desperate Bergamasquians resort are described with undisguised revulsion. If Jacobsen in the description of the well-meaning attempts of the citizens to alleviate their plight dismisses the conventional Christian worship of his bourgeois contemporaries, his remark about the orgiastic phase, that it was led by two gray-headed philosophers who had worked blasphemy into a system, seems a ferocious swipe against the enthusiasm for the supposed life-cult of the Renaissance and pagan antiquity entertained by the anti-clerical radicals who were otherwise his comrades-in-arms.

The flagellants are no ordinary Christian ascetics. Their worship takes the form of an ecstatic self-humiliation: "That they were less than dogs before His feet, that they were the lowest vermin eating the dust before his feet." Furthermore, they are united in a fanatic belief that they, with the rest of the world, are doomed. The monk's brimstone-and-sulphur sermon stresses this point: it holds up no hope of salvation for the elect. Its vision of a merciless Godhead is akin to the one found in Niels Lyhne's prayer at his child's deathbed, and the flagellants' hopeless faith has something in common with the passionate atheism Niels clings to in death. Even though the fanatics' uncanny creed may have some affinity to the author's somber view of life, their fanaticism is nevertheless described with definite disgust: "In the midst of the nave the holy ones stopped and groaned their agony. Their hearts boiled within them in hatred and lust for vengeance."

Jacobsen's analysis of their religious fervor and its motivation once again brings Nietzsche to mind. The words just quoted are like an echo of his words in *The Genealogy of Morals* concerning the pious: "cellar beasts full of revenge and hatred."

The animal image, which occurs so often in Jacobsen's descriptions of human passion and sensual excess, is particularly conspicuous in **"The Plague in Bergamo."** When the flagellants approach the city in silence, the tread of their bare feet is ominously like that of a herd of animals. Their wild eyes and foaming mouths during the self-scourging in the cathedral make them like the dogs they wish to be in the eyes of the Lord. Finally, when the monk looks at the threatening crowd after his sermon, he sees "distorted faces with dark holes for mouths, in which the teeth showed like the rowed teeth of predatory animals."

Here Jacobsen takes further the insight into mass psychology he displays in the crowd scene in the fourth chapter of *Marie Grubbe*. It is a paradox that Jacobsen, whose fiction is largely devoted to the loneliness and isolation of the individual soul, should show his profoundest and most original insight when dealing with the reactions of a human mob.

The storyteller mostly views the scene from an exalted vantage point and at an ironic distance. In **"The Plague in Bergamo"** there is, indeed, none of the compassion with human suffering which is otherwise characteristic of Jacobsen's work. On the contrary, this tale of woe seems to be told with an undertone of nihilistic glee—born out of despair—as it strips the human condition of all hope, meaning, and dignity. It is a superb artifact, but its perfection and poise are attained at a price, the humanity that generally informs Jacobsen's art.

Jacobsen's attention to the cadence and musicality of his prose is nowhere more pronounced than in **"The Plague in Bergamo."** It is organized with a sovereign sense of variation in tempo and register.

The opening passage employs a restrained lingering tone with its spare, factual account of the outbreak of the pestilence, only tautened with a note of the terror to come in the effective dosage line about the isolation of Old Bergamo: "And they could not flee as those of the new city had done."

With the description of the disintegration of all standards in the second phase of the effect of the plague, the restlessness and panic are underlined by an expansive polysyndetic syntax and dramatic exclamations, reminiscent of the rhetoric in the clergyman's fulminations at Ulrick Christian's deathbed in *Marie Grubbe:*

> And when the people realized this, and grew
> firm in the belief that heaven could not (or would

not) help them, they did not merely lay their hands in their laps saying that whatever had come, would come, no, it was as though sin had issued from a secret stealthy disease and had grown into an open raging plague which went hand in hand with the physical disease in order to kill the soul as the other leveled the body. So unbelievable were their deeds! so horrible their inveteracies!"

As the story gathers momentum with the advent of the flagellants, the pace of the prose is intensified by a change from the preterite to the present tense. At the same time the narrative fleetingly adopts the viewpoint of the onlookers:

> Brown, gray, black are the colors of their clothes, but all carry a red mark on their breasts. A cross, as they near. For they draw continually nearer. They press upwards towards the old City along the steep wall-flanked path. A throng of white faces, they carry their scourges in their hands. A rain of fire is painted on their banners. And the black crosses swing from side to side in the crowd.

Similarly, at the end of the monk's sermon the culmination of the story is signified by a change from reported to direct speech:

> And these below looked up at him who hung there weak and suffering. They looked at the plaque at His head, where it was written: King of the Jews, and they mocked Him and called up to Him: "You, if you really are the Son of God, climb down from your cross." The only begotten Son of God was seized with anger, and saw that these folk were not really worthy of salvation, and he tore His feet away from the nail that held them, and he balled His fists over the nailheads and drew them from the wood, so that the arm of the cross bent like a bow, and He jumped to the ground and snatched up His garment, so that the dice rolled down on the slope of Golgotha, and He lashed out with it in the rage of a king and ascended into heaven. And the cross remained empty and the magnificent work of redemption was not completed. There is no intermediary between us and God; no Jesus died on the cross for us; no Jesus died on the cross for us!

It is a mark of Jacobsen's brilliant grasp of his narrative art that after the tremendous coup of this final line he is still able to give a stirring subtlety to what follows, when he lets the crowd repeat the demand of the mob at Pilate's trial of Christ: "Crucify Him."

"The Plague in Bergamo" is one of the most memorable examples of poetic prose in Scandinavian literature, ranking with the lyrical rhetoric in *Fear and Trembling* and Hans Christian Andersen's powerful nature hymn in "The Wind's Tale." It seems the unavoidable inspiration for the "Miserere" chapter in Johannes V. Jensen's novel *The Fall of a King* (1900) and might well have been in the mind of Martin A. Hansen when he wrote his gripping tale about the pestilence in a Danish village, "Sacrifice" (1947). It is also a fair guess that Ingmar Bergman used

Jacobsen's story for the flagellants incident in *The Seventh Seal* (1956), unless he draws on Strindberg's *Folkungasagan* (1899), Act IV, where the flagellants' appearance with a symbolic Plague Maid is obviously inspired by Jacobsen's story.

Another and bizarre example of Jacobsen's experimenting with other modes of fiction than Realism is the piece of lyrical reverie **"There Should Have Been Roses"** or **"From the Sketchbook."** It dates from the period after his third trip abroad in 1879, as the Italian setting suggests. The fantasy is anticipated, however, in one of Marie Grubbe's waking dreams described at the beginning of Chapter XVI. It appeared in *Novellas and Sketches* and is the most important entry under the second category.

"There Should Have Been Roses," where fictional reality fades into dream and fantasy burgeons fantasy in an elusive sequence, is hard to summarize. The plane of factual reality restricts itself to a place a few miles from Rome (in an early draft on the Via Salaria or near the palazzo of the Colonnas) where the road after crossing a river by a bridge ascends from the Campagna to pass a wall of a villa garden before losing itself behind a cluster of houses. A wanderer briefly passes on his way to the city, leaving the unseen observer, in whose consciousness and silent dramatic soliloquy all is contained, to reflect on the ambivalent mood of weary alienation and wayward yearning that besets the wanderer in the endless plain. As a better alternative he settles in a sheltered nook to observe the garden wall opposite with its wrought-iron balcony, adorning it in his imagination with languid yellow roses or hardy fresh ones as the choice may be! His fancy makes him dream up a decaying villa behind the craggy wall where in the past the inhabitants presumably cursed the enclosing garden and in frustrated yearning and passion looked into the distance of the Campagna from the latticed balcony curving out from the protecting wall. At this point the dreamer rearranges the scene to make it fit for the performance of a *proverbe*. With a widening of the road a battered tufa fountain is introduced with a dolphin squirting a lame jet from its one unstopped nostril. The imaginary *proverbe* is a dialogue between a page on the balcony, dressed in yellow, and a blue one sitting on the fountain. The two parts are imagined to be taken by actresses, both idealized Pre-Raphaelite beauties. The innocent page in blue is to be performed by a blonde with a past, the experienced one in yellow by a dark-haired beauty who has no story at all. The pages' conversation about the mysteriousness of women and the unattainable attention of the adored one, rapt in dreams where the admirer has no place, is interrupted when a lizard creeps along the balcony railing. As the observer attempts to stone away the intruder, his fantasy is gone! But only for a short while. Suddenly fancy takes over again and reality is lost sight of for good as the pages reappear to continue their quarrel about love. The blue page speaks of his longing to realize the dream of love; the yellow one praises the eternal freedom of the dream against the ephemerality of fulfilled desire. You are happy! they protest to each other as they part, disappearing in a flutter of the rose petals there should have been on the garden wall!

As will be clear from the summary there is in the sketch a recurrent double movement: reality is constantly left behind as the observer rearranges and populates the empty scene before his eyes, but his fantasies all return to the divided mood prevailing when fancy took leave of the real world: the unrest and isolation that beset the wanderer in the endless plain. What is and what might have been point to one end, which is always present. Frustration and disillusion invade the dreams, and fancy is not in full control, as the intrusion of the lizard suggests. The malaise of the human condition, from which there is no escape, is pointedly reflected in a series of objective correlatives: the opposition of the languid yellow roses and the fresh hardy ones, the dolphin with its abortive spray, the balcony curving out from the monotonous line of the wall while remaining a barrier to life and longing.

The existential theme of the sketch is intimately related to its subtle exploration of the nature of fictional reality. All that happens here does not really happen. The roses are never really there, even in fiction, for they are never decided on! In the dreamt-up *proverbe* nothing is what it seems: women take the part of men, and the actresses are imagined to be the very opposite of what they impersonate. In keeping with this the period of the setting is to be vague and uncertain. The involutions of the make-believe here represent the boldest arabesque pattern Jacobsen produced! Finally the very dramatic soliloquy that contains it all seems revealed as a fiction. The past conditional verbal tense of the title, **"There Should Have Been Roses,"** suggests that the immediacy of the unidentified observer's voice is a contrivance to present a memory. That in itself makes the whole thing evanescent, for we recall events, not fantasies.

Apart from one notable recent example [Finn Stein Larsen, *Prosaens Monstre*] critics on Jacobsen have not paid much attention to this work. Almost the only early critic to give it special attention was Hermann Hesse, who, when quite young, contributed an essay on Jacobsen where he makes the following comment:

> There is little meaning and thought in it, but neither do we seek for that, for in our dreams we have seen equally magnificent sequences of images in which there were as little meaning and coherence, and which still came from our inmost self and in a strange way filled us with the fragrance of their beauty.
>
> Also in these powerful dream images Jacobsen has something of the consistency and honesty of the Realist, though we do not demand any other proof than the silent acclaim of our feeling. In addition, these creations are of such a distinctly novel kind that no ordinary evaluation through comparison with similar works is possible.
>
> For the moderns now writing Jacobsen is a valuable example of the completely modern writer who through a particularly strict Realist training has returned to the traditional high sphere of the imaginative writer.

Hesse's words offer evidence of Jacobsen's importance to the writers in the German-speaking countries who worked to overcome Realism. Hesse is right in stressing the novelty and originality of the piece, but he fails to appreciate its intellectual rigor. For all its spontaneity it is written with conscious art, and rather than an aesthetic extravagance it is a penetrating analysis of the epistemological predicament of the creator of fictions, as well as a statement of the central existential themes of Jacobsen's work. (pp. 115-25)

The last work Jacobsen managed to complete, **"Mrs Fönss"** was written after 1879 and finished in 1882 to appear in *Noveller og Skitser,* published in that year. This story represents a return to a contemporary Realist setting as well as being an advocacy of the ideas of the "Modern Breakthrough." Its theme is a woman's choice between her duty toward her children, on one hand, and her self-realization and personal happiness on the other. It seems inescapable to point out that it was written at the time when Henrik Ibsen's *A Doll's House* was the principal talking-point in all intellectual circles in Denmark.

Mrs. Fönss is a forty-year-old widow of the Copenhagen bourgeoisie who travels in the south of France with her teenage son and daughter in an attempt to make the girl recover from an unhappy love affair. While staying at Avignon with another Danish family Mrs. Fönss meets the man she loved in her youth and whom she has not forgotten through her long years of a pleasant marriage of convenience. Their renewed acquaintance leads to a proposal, which Mrs. Fönss happily accepts. As she informs her children of her decision to marry again, they react with unexpected disapproval, vehemently reminding her of her duty to them. The passion of their appeal to conventional norms Jacobsen perceptively shows as rooted in an Oedipal attachment, as is clear from the son's outburst:

> Have you any idea of the things you make me think of? My mother loved by a strange man, my mother desired, held in the arms of another and holding him in hers. Nice thoughts for a son, worse than the worst insult—but it is impossible! must be impossible! must be! Are the prayers of a son to be as powerless as that?

One will also notice here a motif recurrent in Jacobsen's work: the idea of the compelling prayer, the fanatic desire to change what cannot be changed. Mrs. Fönss remains unshaken in her resolve, and mother and children part. After five years of happy married life with her husband in Spain Mrs. Fönss is stricken by a fatal illness. Her farewell letter to her estranged children protesting her love for them and affirming her joy in life and acceptance of the finality of death is the moving ending to the story.

Mrs. Fönss's farewell letter is perhaps the most famous passage in Jacobsen's work for the sentimental reason that it has been interpreted as the moribund writer's last message to his friends and readers. That is, however, a consideration entirely extraneous to our reading of the story. In terms of the structure of the novella the letter seems stuck on as the theme is felt to be fully developed with Mrs. Fönss's courageous choice. To Jacobsen the ending may have seemed justified by his conviction, expressed in a letter to Edvard Brandes in 1880, that there is no other ending possible to a work of literature than death. It is also conceivable that Jacobsen uses the ending of death to show that Mrs. Fönss's liberation as a person must also involve her renunciation of religious faith.

Mrs. Fönss is the most positive human figure in all Jacobsen's work, an idealizing but convincing portrayal of a woman. She is harmonious, gentle, warm, dignified, and courageous. She embodies Jacobsen's ideal of living according to one's nature. Her story confirms for once Jacobsen's claim after the reception of *Niels Lyhne* that he was not himself a pessimist.

As often with Jacobsen the story contains a tableau which is at one time its artistic culmination and its center of meaning. It is the description of Mrs. Fönss on the eve of her new life. She is in the reading-room of her hotel, trying to overcome the dreamlike state her idleness has occasioned:

> The white papers there on the table, the portfolios with their large letters, the empty plush-chairs, the regular squares of the carpet, and even the folds of the rep curtains—all this looked dull under the strong light.
>
> She was still dreaming, and dreaming she stood and listened to the long-drawn singing of the gas-flames.
>
> The heat was such as to make one almost dizzy.
>
> To support herself she slowly reached out for a large bronze vase which stood on a bracket fixed in the wall and grasped the flower-decorated edge.
>
> It was comfortable to stand thus and the bronze was gratefully cool to the touch of her hand. But as she stood thus, there came another feeling also. She bean to feel a contentment in her limbs, in her body, because of the plastically beautiful position which she had assumed. She was conscious of how becoming it was to her, of the beauty which was hers at the moment, and even of the physical sense of harmony. All this gathered in a feeling of triumph and streamed through her like a strange festive exultation.
>
> She felt herself so strong at this hour, and life lay before her like a great radiant day, no longer like a day declining toward the calm, melancholy hours of dusk. It seemed to her like an open wide-awake space of time, with hot pulses throbbing every second, with joyous light, with energy and swiftness and an infinity without and within. And she was thrilled with the fullness of life, and longed for it with the feverish eagerness with which a traveler sets out on a journey.
>
> (pp. 126-29)

Mrs. Fönss's dreaming is a triumphant realization of her feminine power, a shedding of the inauthentic life of her past and the beginning of her liberation as a person. Through this tableau, which is done with Jacobsen's utmost painterlike care, he attempts to combine her spiritual experience with his own adoring visualization of her. In the detailed picture the angular shapes of the inanimate surroundings provide a contrast to the plastic vitality of her female form to reflect the process at work in her soul.

She is said to be conscious of the grace of her languid pose in a way normally only an onlooker (in this case the author) can be. That may be said to reveal his involvement with his creation, but is it not true that self-conscious gracefulness is a way of describing the posing of women in the aesthetic painting of Jacobsen's day? His affinity with the Pre-Raphaelite movement is nowhere more pronounced than in this picture of Mrs. Fönss. William Holman Hunt's painting, *Isabella and the Pot of Basil* (1867), where she clutches the brim of the pot supported by a console, is a more striking confirmation of the said correspondence in manner and mood than one could hope for.

Jacobsen's minor prose works do not, perhaps, reveal new facets of his talent as a writer to readers of his two novels. Yet, in his two best stories, **"Two Worlds"** and **"The Plague in Bergamo,"** he develops his particular mode of lyrical fiction to its highest and most powerful refinement. **"There Should Have Been Roses"** provides an unequaled example of the boldness and originality of his artistic vision. No experiment in the fiction after his day could have surprised him.

As was to be expected there is no great variety in themes. Love and death, dream and reality remain, from the very first completed story to the last fragment, the constant concern of this writer. His obsession with death and disillusionment gives a somber note to all he wrote, but the positive ending of his first published novella and the resigned and moving affirmation of life and self-realization in **"Mrs. Fönss"** goes to show the kind of positive world-view toward which he was struggling. (pp. 129-30)

> *Niels Lyhne Jensen, in his* Jens Peter Jacobsen, *Twayne Publishers, 1980, 187 p.*

FURTHER READING

Baer, Lydia. "Rilke and Jens Peter Jacobsen." *PMLA* LIV, Nos. 3,4 (September 1939; December 1939): 900-32, 1133-80.
> Traces Rainer Marie Rilke's identification with, creative use and translation of, and eventual progression beyond Jacobsen.

Ingwerson, Niels. "Problematic Protagonists: *Marie Grubbe* and *Niels Lyhne*." In *The Hero in Scandinavian Literature: From Peer Gynt to the Present,* edited by John M. Weinstock and Robert T. Rovinsky, pp. 41-61. Austin: University of Texas Press, 1972.
> Asserts that, although the endings of *Niels Lyhne* and *Marie Grubbe* can be seen as Naturalistic, both novels also utilize the psychological quest structure common in Romantic literature.

Madsen, Børge Gedsø. "Georg Brandes' Criticism of *Niels Lyhne*." *Scandinavian Studies* 38, No. 2 (May 1966): 124-30.
> Concurs with Brandes's charge that *Niels Lyhne* is both historically inaccurate and vague, but concludes that the novel is nonetheless a perceptive character study.

Nielson, Marion Louis. "Jens Peter Jacobsen, 1847-1947."
Western Review 12, No. 2 (Winter 1948): 91-5.
    Provides a brief, chronological review of Jacobsen's
    work, and praises him for pioneering the modern psy-
    chological novel in Scandinavia.

Søren Kierkegaard

1813-1855

(Full name Søren Aabye Kierkegaard) Danish philosopher and theologian.

Kierkegaard was a prolific and imaginative writer who profoundly influenced modern philosophical and religious thought. Noted figures such as writers Henrik Ibsen, Franz Kafka, and Albert Camus, Existentialist philosophers Jean-Paul Sartre, Martin Heidegger, and Karl Jaspers, and religious thinkers Paul Tillich and Karl Barth are all indebted to Kierkegaard. His works, esteemed as trenchant studies in religious reform, social criticism, psychology, and communication, display Kierkegaard's skill as a unique stylist with an ability to tailor form to the specific intent of a composition, whether a scholarly treatise or an impassioned anti-intellectual discourse. Kierkegaard opposed the tradition of Western philosophy as represented by the complex idealistic philosophical system of G. W. F. Hegel, whose goal was the identification of universal truths. He insisted instead that the individual must acknowledge the importance of faith and the limitations of reason—the governing faculty in Hegel's philosophy—and accept personal responsibility for determinations of truth and appropriate courses of action, an idea that came to be seen as a central component of the philosophy of Existentialism in the twentieth century. For Kierkegaard, human individuality is most fully expressed in religious experience, specifically in Christianity. In fact, William Barrett described Kierkegaard's mission as the concern with "what it means concretely for the individual to be a Christian," maintaining that "Kierkegaard stated the question of Christianity so nakedly, made it turn so decisively about the individual and his quest for his own eternal happiness, that all religious writers after him seem by comparison to be symbolical, institutional, or metaphorical."

Kierkegaard was born in Copenhagen just two months after his parents married. His father, a wealthy retired wool merchant and widower with six children, wed Kierkegaard's mother, a former servant of the family. Frail, slightly disfigured, and evincing great intellectual promise, Kierkegaard was the favorite child of his father. By most accounts his mother was distant and impersonal. The children were raised in a staid environment dominated by their father, who read theological and philosophical works; he practiced a stern method of education and a devout brand of Lutheran Christianity. Kierkegaard spent most of his rather solitary childhood indoors and the solemnity of his life was exacerbated by the precipitous deaths of five of his siblings. His father, whom he revered, entertained him with narratives of imaginary peoples, lands, and sights, and the young boy was further exposed to culture and learning by local intellectuals who gathered at his father's house for discussions. Kierkegaard graduated with honors from a local school and in 1830 matriculated at the theological seminary of the University of Copen-

hagen with plans to become a Lutheran minister. His mother died in 1834, and the following year Kierkegaard began a period of prodigality and frivolous neglect of his studies that lasted about six months. Some scholars attribute this phase to disillusionment with his father's austerity, which Kierkegaard suspected was a manifestation of guilt from a boyhood blasphemy and from the seduction of Kierkegaard's mother. His father died in 1838. After ten years of studies, including courses in philosophy that sparked his opposition to Hegel's philosophy, Kierkegaard passed the theological examination with distinction, but he decided against entering the ministry. Upon completing his dissertation *Om Begrebet Ironi med stadigt Hensyn til Socrates (On the Concept of Irony, with Special Reference to Socrates)* in 1841, he received the Master of Arts degree.

That same year Kierkegaard ended his thirteen-month engagement to eighteen-year-old Regine Olsen, whom he had met in 1837. Although the reason for the breakup of their relationship is unknown, commentators speculate variously that Kierkegaard had consecrated himself solely to God, that he enjoyed the concept of ideal love more than the experience of actual love, or that he did not want to subject another person to his deep pensiveness and melancholy. Regardless, Kierkegaard's relationship with Olsen left a lasting impression that is evident from references and letters to her in his *Papirer (Journals)*. He never sought employment, living on an inheritance from his father that dwindled steadily but enabled him to subsidize the publication of his works.

Kierkegaard never married and for the remainder of his life led a reclusive existence that was interrupted by two turbulent incidents. In a letter published in 1846 under the pseudonym Frater Taciturnus, he attacked the popular political journal the *Corsaren (Corsair)* for what he perceived to be unscrupulous incitive tactics. The editors of the journal retorted with several caricatures, one of which depicted Kierkegaard as a spindly, homely hunchback and another that portrayed him as a star in the middle of an otherwise empty universe; this incident brought him the status of a notorious and mocked eccentric. Beginning in 1854 and continuing into the next year, Kierkegaard—incensed by what he perceived to be an unmerited tribute to a particular church official as "a witness to the truth"—published nine issues of "Øjeblikket" ("The Moment"), a series of pamphlets in which he derided ecclesiastical compromise with the state and worldly interests and disdained the hypocritical complacency of Christians. These tracts, which were republished in 1855 as *Hvad Christus dömmer om officiel Christendom (Kierkegaard's Attack upon "Christendom")*, received public scorn. Soon after this affair Kierkegaard suffered a paralyzing stroke. During the several weeks that he lingered bedridden, he continued his protest by refusing to receive the sacrament of communion from a clergyman. He died in the fall of 1855.

Kierkegaard reacted strongly against systematic philosophy, particularly Hegel's abstract, conceptual thought, and considered himself not a philosopher but a religious thinker. As Paul Ricoeur has noted, however, he was greatly influenced by Hegel's concepts, vocabulary, and manner: "It is not just a biographical trait or a fortuitous encounter but a constitutive structure of Kierkegaard's thought that it is not thinkable apart from Hegel." In polemics with Hegel that reached their height in *Philosophiske Smuler (Philosophical Fragments; or, A Fragment of Philosophy)*, Kierkegaard—under the pseudonym Johannes Climacus—spurned his predecessor's glorification of reason and claimed that life cannot be circumscribed by an Idealist system of pure thought: "In relation to their systems most systematizers are like a man who builds an enormous castle and lives in a shack close by; they do not live in their own enormous systematic buildings." Kierkegaard acknowledged the usefulness of reason and such disciplines as the natural sciences, mathematics, and logic, but dismissed claims that these delineate actual existence in its entirety. He also repudiated Hegel's claims to objectivity, declaring that a human is not pure thought or intellect but a being whose consciousness is conditioned by historical and hereditary limits. The examining consciousness can never fully achieve detached, impartial reflection: "Life can never really be understood in time simply because at no particular moment can I find the necessary resting place from which to understand it—backwards." Claiming to reject reflective, theoretical philosophical systems and conceptual, universal truth, Kierkegaard emphasized the concrete example and the individual case. He advocated the discovery of subjective truths and personal validation through choice: "The choice itself is decisive for the content of the personality, through the choice the personality immerses itself in the thing chosen, and when it does not choose it withers away in consumption." In *Begrebet Angest (The Concept of Dread)*, writing under the pseudonym Virgilius Haufniensis, Kierkegaard explained that each person determines his or her essence through choice. Upon recognizing that the possibility of choice exists, the individual can view it as a gift or an overwhelming burden. The latter view is a predominant characteristic of existential anxiety, alternately termed dread.

Propounding perhaps the most salient feature of his thought, Kierkegaard delineated modes of living that comprise the three possible orientations within life: the aesthetic, the ethical, and the religious. Although the modes are neither mutually exclusive nor necessarily permanent, one predominates during any given period. Each mode has merit but, for Kierkegaard, the religious orientation is supreme. Attributed to the pseudonym Victor Eremita, Kierkegaard's acclaimed *Enten/Eller (Either/Or: A Fragment of Life)*, presents a choice, as suggested in the title, between two modes, the aesthetic and the ethical. The aesthetic sphere is limited to a continual search for new, stimulating experiences. Characterized by emotional detachment, the aesthetic individual recognizes others only as variables in this unending quest. Eventually, when the potential for novel experiences is exhausted, the aesthetic person suffers from boredom; ultimately, if the individual continues in this mode despite recognizing the impossibility of resolution, boredom will become despair. Kierkegaard considered Don Juan, with his innumerable loves and infidelities, the archetype of the aesthetic persona. In contrast, the ethical sphere is identified with marriage and responsibility, and is consistent with reflection and self-appraisal—behavior that is inimical to the aesthetic way of life. The change to the ethical orientation from the aesthetic involves an intellectual conversion. The ethical person, whose being is validated by a sense of duty, identifies a rational system of universal rules as the basis for action. Kierkegaard argued that the foundation of this life is invariably arbitrary and subjective because no objective criterion exists for determining rationality.

Written under the pseudonym Hilarius Bogbinder, *Stadier paa Livets Vej (Stages on Life's Way)* introduces the religious sphere; although similar to the ethical sphere, it is the only source of lasting spiritual peace. For Kierkegaard the transition to the religious sphere is accomplished through a "leap of faith"—perhaps the best known of his doctrines—that consists of staking one's whole being and future upon belief in God, a transcendent and essentially unknowable entity. Impetus for action arises from faith in God, who is recognized by Kierkegaard as the sole legitimate basis for the resolution of moral questions. Instead of reason, intensity of feeling provides the foundation for both choice and truth. In the pseudonymous *Frygt og Baeven (Fear and Trembling: A Dialectical Lyric by Johannes de Silentio)*, he cites the biblical story of Abraham and Isaac, in which Abraham prepares to kill his only son,

Isaac, at the behest of God, as the model for the "teleological suspension of the ethical"—meaning the subordination of rational, ethical criteria to faith. In this sense, admitted Kierkegaard, Christianity is "irrational."

As a social critic and religious reformer, Kierkegaard protested mass taste and mass opinion, and identified a pervading malaise, which he described in *En literair Anmeldelse, To Tidsaldre (Two Ages: The Age of Revolution and the Present Age, A Literary Review)*: "Our age is essentially one of understanding and reflection, without passion, momentarily bursting into enthusiasm, and shrewdly relapsing into repose." In contrast, he advocated individuality and commitment: "The thing is to find a truth which is true *for me,* to find *the idea for which I can live and die.*" These themes, as well as reverence for sincerity, converged in Kierkegaard's assault on Christian hypocrisy in *Attack upon "Christendom".* He deprecated those who falsely claim to live up to the severe demands of Christianity and perceived incongruity in the fact that an increasingly secular society considers Christianity a birthright rather than a distinction that must be arduously earned at every moment: "One thing I will not do, not for anything in the world. I will not by suppression, or by performing tricks, try to produce the impression that the ordinary Christianity in the land and the Christianity of the New Testament are alike." Hence, Kierkegaard disdained the contemporary institution of the established church with its rituals and dogmas, insisting instead upon a personal relationship with God based on the essence of Christianity. He also accentuated the anguish and isolation the individual experiences once God's infinite distance from base humanity becomes manifest.

Kierkegaard's writings, as George Steiner noted, comprise two different forms: "The more 'literary' texts alternate with devotional, homiletic works of an uncompromisingly pastoral, pietistic character." Kierkegaard asserted that despite the duality of his technique, which was evident as early as 1843 in the artistic *Either/Or* and the didactic *Opbyggelige Taler (Edifying Discourses),* and which continued until late in his career, his concern as a writer was always religious. The artistic, literary works employ a variety of techniques to communicate indirectly rather than proselytize. Kierkegaard's pseudonyms, for example, have significance in relation to particular texts, such as the repetition apparent in the name Constantine Constantius, the pseudonymous author of a work entitled *Repetition.* Perhaps more importantly, the pen names permitted Kierkegaard to suggest various possibilities and present conflicting viewpoints without appearing to endorse any particular stance, in accordance with his statement that "in all eternity it is impossible for me to compel a person to accept an opinion, a conviction, a belief. But one thing I can do: I can compel him to take notice." Complex narrative structures facilitate Kierkegaard's design by motivating readers to make interpretations in order to orient themselves within the text. For example, *Either/Or* contains two secondary texts, each of which has a tertiary text, resulting in five intertwined texts, each attributed to authors other than Kierkegaard. The artistic works often present dialectic between personified states of mind or intellectual positions, resembling the Socratic method employed in the dialogues of Plato. Kierkegaard followed the Socratic procedure of *maieuesis,* or "midwifery," which strives through a dialectical posing of questions and answers to bring forth the truth that exists within the participating parties. Hence, as Naomi Lebowitz observed, the artistic works invite the reader to make a personal evaluation: "The purpose of Kierkegaard's literature is to stimulate the reader to make his own movements of faith."

Other related and often complicating strategies of Kierkegaard's artistic, literary works include the employment of fables, fairy tales, and aphorisms; an insistence on subjectivity and personal expression; the deliberate and frequent use of paradox; and a conscientious avoidance of didacticism. The literary works, according to Jean-Paul Sartre, "constitute, by their very negation of any effort to know them, a reference back to the foundations of such an effort. Kierkegaard made use of irony, humour, myth and nonsignifying sentences in order to communicate indirectly with us." Referring to Kierkegaard's exploration of communication and literary theory, Steiner stated: "No psycho- or sociolinguist, no satirist in the vein of Kraus and Orwell, has provided sharper insights into the frozen, cliché-ridden routines of common communication." In contrast, Kierkegaard's literary reviews, polemics in the press, and admonitory works present a straightforward prose style that resembles edifying discourse or a Christian sermon. His experimentation with vehicles and modes of expression has been compared to the writing styles employed by the German philosopher and intellectual revolutionizer Friedrich Nietzsche. Indeed, Jaspers wrote of Kierkegaard and Nietzsche: "They were creative in language to the degree that their works belong to the peaks of the literatures of their countries; and they knew it. They were creative in the thrilling way which made them among the most widely read authors, even though the content was of the same weight and their genuine comprehension of the same difficulty as that of any of the great philosophers."

During his lifetime, Kierkegaard's compatriots recognized him as a capable author, citing his wit and stylistic flair. However, they dismissed him as a philosopher, and his writings, which resisted categorization in established literary genres and opposed contemporary intellectual and religious thought, had little impact outside Denmark for nearly seventy years. Two decades after Kierkegaard's death, Danish literary critic Georg Brandes became the first significant figure to acknowledge the importance of his work. This recognition encouraged the translation of Kierkegaard's writings into German, and his entire corpus was translated by the beginning of World War I. A twentieth-century revival of his thought was spurred between the wars by the German philosophers Jaspers and Heidegger and, soon after, by the French Existentialists Sartre and Camus.

Many scholars find Kierkegaard's criticisms of Hegel to be ad hominem attacks that inadvertently highlight flaws in Kierkegaard's own works. Although Kierkegaard claimed that Hegel failed to justify the hegemony accorded to reason, Kierkegaard himself glorified irrationality and individual freedom without sufficient justification;

he denied the existence of absolutes yet posited freedom as a single ultimate value. Kierkegaard disparaged reason, averring that it cannot lead to faith; yet through the didacticism of his religious works he attempted to provide reasons to become a Christian. Some commentators defend Kierkegaard against the charge of inconsistency by contending that his works provide psychological motivation rather than logical argumentation. Kierkegaard also perceived Hegel's writings to be over-intellectualized and abstract, yet George E. and George B. Arbaugh have noted that his own writing—which evinces an Hegelian propensity for long, convoluted sentences—is sometimes nearly indecipherable: "Kierkegaard is often discouragingly difficult. At times he is so dialectical that even his abstruse and dialectical arch-enemy Hegel would have had difficulty in following his train of thought." T. W. Adorno similarly insists that "verbosity is the danger of all Kierkegaard's writings. It is the verbosity of an interminable monologue which, so to speak, does not tolerate any protest and continually repeats itself, without any real articulation. This loquaciousness is intensified in his religious writings to the point of being painful." Kierkegaard's apologists have argued that the density and complexity of the works are indicative of the effort and patience required for true learning, original thought, and personal growth.

Critics often attack the religious element of Kierkegaard's thought as totalitarian because he maintains that one must subordinate reason and intellect to faith. According to Kierkegaard, God must not be questioned or doubted and Christianity should dominate all aspects of life. Insistence on the separation and distance of the individual from God contributes to the seeming bleakness of Kierkegaard's theology and contrasts with the comforting assertion of many modern scholastics that God dwells within each person. Some scholars find his requirements for Christianity too stringent, asserting that even Kierkegaard fell short of the mark he had set. They add that his criticism of the Church is unconstructive as well as unrealistic in its condemnation of social aspects of an institution that is likely to remain an integral part of society. Other commentators evaluate his works from a psychological or biographical perspective and find Kierkegaard's retreat to radical Christianity directly related to his experiences as a social misfit. According to this view, a self-righteous brand of Christianity gave Kierkegaard a sense of superiority over those who dismissed him as a crank or ridiculed his physical deformities. Others have asserted that Kierkegaard's insular, austere upbringing determined the severity and melancholy of his Christianity.

Those who find Kierkegaard's philosophy excessively introverted, such as Marxist critics, object that he ignored the social component of existence, the relationship of the individual to society. However, supporters of Kierkegaard aver that the individual is the fundamental unit of society and must be the focus of any social reform. Modern critics have contested Kierkegaard's emphasis on the individual and religion; according to Paul Bové, many find "Kierkegaard's theocentrism and attention to the self incompatible with formalist, structuralist, post-structuralist, or neo-Marxian methodologies which, in various ways, deconstruct or demythologize the ideologies of religion and self-

hood." Other recent criticism credits Kierkegaard with insights that anticipate Freud's work in psychology. Robert Solomon attested that "Kierkegaard's analyses of 'dread' and other passions are among the most perceptive essays in psychology in the nineteenth century."

Kierkegaard's life and works evince a complexity that tends to distract from the concern with authenticity that he held to be the central and enduring focus of his life: "I want honesty. . . . I am not a Christian severity as opposed to a Christian leniency. . . . I am—a human honesty." Kierkegaard's visionary thought and insistence on individual integrity rendered him an outcast in his time and has made him, Hermann Diem attested, a wellspring for our own age: "Kierkegaard was of no significance for the intellectual history of the nineteenth century. All the problems of our century, in contrast, have gathered around his work, meeting there as at a focal point; we see our problems better in Kierkegaard than almost anywhere else."

PRINCIPAL WORKS

Om Begrebet Ironi med stadigt Hensyn til Socrates (treatise) 1841
 [*On the Concept of Irony, with Special Reference to Socrates,* 1966]
Enten/Eller. 2 vols. [as Victor Eremita] (treatise) 1843
 [*Either/Or: A Fragment of Life.* 2 vols., 1944]
Frygt og Baeven [as Johannes de Silentio] (treatise) 1843
 [*Fear and Trembling: A Dialectical Lyric by Johannes de Silentio,* 1939]
Gjentagelsen: Et Forsøg i den experimenterende Psychologi [as Constantine Constantius] (essay) 1843
 [*Repetition: An Essay in Experimental Psychology,* 1941]
Opbyggelige Taler (essays) 1843-44
 [*Edifying Discourses,* 1943-46]
Begrebet Angest [as Virgilius Haufniensis] (treatise) 1844
 [*The Concept of Dread,* 1944]
Philosophiske Smuler [as Johannes Climacus] (essay) 1844
 [*Philosophical Fragments; or, A Fragment of Philosophy,* 1936]
Stadier paa Livets Vej [as Hilarius Bogbinder] (treatise) 1845
 [*Stages on Life's Way,* 1940]
Tre Taler ved taenkte Leiligheder (essays) 1845
 [*Thoughts on Crucial Situations in Human Life: Three Discourses on Imagined Occasions,* 1941]
Afsluttende uvidenskabelig Efterskrift [as Johannes Climacus] (essay) 1846
 [*Concluding Unscientific Postscript to the Philosophical Fragments,* 1941]
En literair Anmeldelse. To Tidsaldre (criticism) 1846
 [*Two Ages: The Age of Revolution and the Present Age, a Literary Review,* 1978]
† "Bogen om Adler" (criticism) 1846-47
 [*On Authority and Revelation: The Book on Adler,* 1955]
Kjerlighedens Gjerninger (essays) 1847
 [*Works of Love,* 1946]

Opbyggelige Taler i forskjellig Aand (essays) 1847
  [*Edifying Discourses in a Different Vein,* 1938]
Krisen og en Krise i en Skuespillerindes Liv [as Inter et
  Inter] (essays) 1848
  [*The Crisis and The Crisis in the Life of an Actress,* 1967]
Christelige Taler (essays) 1849
  [*Christian Discourses,* 1939]
Sygdommen til Døden [as Anti-Climacus] (essay)
  1849
  [*The Sickness unto Death,* 1941]
Tre Taler ved Altergangen om Fredagen (essays) 1849
  [*Three Discourses at the Communion on Fridays,* 1939]
Tvende ethisk-religieuse Smaa-Afhandlinger [as H. H.
  Moreover] (treatises) 1849
  [*Two Minor Ethico-Religious Treatises,* 1940]
Indøvelse i Christendom [as Anti-Climacus] (essay)
  1850
  [*Training in Christianity,* 1941]
Om min Forfatter-Virksomhed (criticism) 1851
  [*On My Work as an Author,* published in *The Point of
  View for My Work as an Author*]
Til Selvprøvelse (essay) 1851
  [*For Self-Examination,* 1940]
‡ *Hvad Christus dömmer om officiel Christendom* (criti-
  cism) 1855
  [*Kierkegaard's Attack upon "Christendom", 1854-1855,*
  1944]
§ *Synspunktet for min Forfatter-Virksomhed* (criticism)
  1859
  [*The Point of View for My Work as an Author: A Report
  to History,* 1939]
Papirer. 20 vols. (collected journals, memoirs, note-
  books, and letters) 1909-48
  [*Sören Kierkegaard's Journals and Papers.* 7 vols., 1967-
  78]
Samlede Vaerker. 20 vols. (collected works) 1962-64
Kierkegaard's Writings, 26 vols. (collected works)
  1985-88

The Present Age, a partial translation of *En literair Anmeldelse, To
Tidsaldre,* was published in 1940.

†Written in 1846-47; published in *Papirer,* vol. 7.

‡Originally published in 1854-55 as nine pamphlets entitled
"Øjeblikket" ("The Moment").

§Written in 1848.

Andrew Hamilton   (essay date 1852)

[*In the following excerpt from his* Sixteen Months in the
Danish Isles *(1852), Hamilton offers a contemporary
perspective of Kierkegaard and observes that "there is no
Danish writer more in earnest than he, yet there is no one
in whose way stands more things to prevent his becoming
popular."*]

There is a man whom it is impossible to omit in any account of Denmark, but whose place it might be more difficult to fix; I mean Søren Kierkegaard. But as his works

have, at all events for the most part, a religious tendency,
he may find a place among the theologians. He is a philosophical Christian writer, evermore dwelling, one might
almost say harping, on the theme of the human heart.
There is no Danish writer more in earnest than he, yet
there is no one in whose way stand more things to prevent
his becoming popular. He writes at times with an unearthly beauty, but too often with an exaggerated display of
logic that disgusts the public. All very well, if he were not
a popular author, but it is for this he intends himself.

I have received the highest delight from some of his books.
But no one of them could I read with pleasure all through.
His **Works of Love** has, I suppose, been the most popular,
or, perhaps, his **Either/Or,** a very singular book. A little
thing published during my stay, gave me much pleasure,
Sickness unto Death.

Kierkegaard's habits of life are singular enough to lend a
(perhaps false) interest to his proceedings. He goes into no
company, and sees nobody in his own house, which answers all the ends of an invisible dwelling; I could never
learn that anyone had been inside of it. Yet his one great
study is human nature; no one knows more people than
he. The fact is *he walks about town all day,* and generally
in some person's company; only in the evening does he
write and read. When walking, he is very communicative,
and at the same time manages to draw everything out of
his companion that is likely to be profitable to himself.

I do not know him. I saw him almost daily in the streets,
and when he was alone I often felt much inclined to accost
him, but never put it into execution. I was told his 'talk'
was very fine. Could I have enjoyed it, without the feeling
that I was myself being mercilessly pumped and sifted, I
should have liked very much.

> *Andrew Hamilton, in an excerpt in* The
> Laughter Is on My Side: An Imaginative In-
> troduction to Kierkegaard, *edited by Roger
> Poole and Henrik Stangerup, Princeton Uni-
> versity Press, 1989.*

Georg Lukács   (essay date 1909)

[*Lukács, a Hungarian literary critic and philosopher, is
acknowledged as one of the leading proponents of Marxist theory. His development of Marxist ideology was part
of a broader system of thought which sought to further
the values of rationalism (peace and progress), humanism (Socialist politics), and traditionalism (Realist literature) over the counter-values of irrationalism (war), to-
talitarianism (reactionary politics), and modernism
(post-Realist literature). In major works such as* Studies
in European Realism *(1950) and* The Historical Novel
*(1955), Lukács explicated his belief that art is wasteful
and harmful if not made creatively consonant with history and human needs. In the following essay, which was
written in 1909 and first published the following year,
he presents Kierkegaard's relationship with Regine
Olsen as evidence that the philosopher ordered his life
according to an exacting ideal that is incompatible with
the inherent ambiguity and uncertainty of life.*]

What is the life-value of a gesture? Or, to put it another

way, what is the value of form in life, the life-creating, life-enhancing value of form? A gesture is nothing more than a movement which clearly expresses something unambiguous. Form is the only way of expressing the absolute in life; a gesture is the only thing which is perfect within itself, the only reality which is more than mere possibility. The gesture alone expresses life: but is it possible to express life? Is not this the tragedy of any living art, that it seeks to build a crystal palace out of air, to forge realities from the insubstantial possibilities of the soul, to construct, through the meetings and partings of souls, a bridge of forms between men? Can the gesture exist at all, and has the concept of form any meaning seen from the perspective of life?

Kierkegaard once said that reality has nothing to do with possibilities; yet he built his whole life upon a gesture. Everything he wrote, every one of his struggles and adventures, is in some way the backdrop to that gesture; perhaps he only wrote and did these things to make his gesture stand out more clearly against the chaotic multiplicity of life. Why did he do it? How could he do it—he of all men, who saw more clearly than any other the thousand aspects, the thousand-fold variability of every motive—he who so clearly saw how everything passes gradually into its opposite, and how, if we look really close, we see an unbridgeable abyss gaping between two barely perceptible nuances? Why did he do this? Perhaps because the gesture is one of the most powerful life-necessities; perhaps because a man who wants to be "honest" (one of Kierkegaard's most frequently used words) must force life to yield up its single meaning, must grasp that ever-changing Proteus, so firmly that, once he has revealed the magic words, he can no longer move. Perhaps the gesture—to use Kierkegaard's dialectic—is the paradox, the point at which reality and possibility intersect, matter and air, the finite and the infinite, life and form. Or, more accurately still and even closer to Kierkegaard's terminology: the gesture is the leap by which the soul passes from one into the other, the leap by which it leaves the always relative facts of reality to reach the eternal certainty of forms. In a word, the gesture is that unique leap by which the absolute is transformed, in life, into the possible. The gesture is the great paradox of life, for only in its rigid permanence is there room for every evanescent moment of life, and only within it does every such moment become true reality.

Whoever does more than merely play with life needs the gesture so that his life may become more real for him than a game that can be played by an infinite choice of moves.

But can there really be a gesture vis-à-vis life? Is it not self-delusion—however splendidly heroic—to believe that the essence of the gesture lies in an action, a turning towards something or a turning away: rigid as stone and yet containing everything immutably within itself?

In September 1840 it happened that Sören Aaby Kierkegaard, Master of Arts, became engaged to Regine Olsen, State Councillor Olsen's eighteen-year-old daughter. Barely a year afterwards he broke off the engagement. He left for Berlin, and when he returned to Copenhagen he lived there as a noted eccentric; his peculiar ways made him a constant target for the humorous papers, and al-

though his writings, published under a variety of pen-names, found some admirers because they were so full of wit, they were hated by the majority because of their "immoral" and "frivolous" contents. His later works made still more open enemies for him—namely, all the leaders of the ruling Protestant Church: and during the hard fight he fought against them—contending that the society of our time is not a Christian one and indeed makes it practically impossible for anyone to remain a Christian—he died.

A few years previously Regine Olsen had married one of her earlier admirers.

What had happened? The number of explanations is infinite, and every newly published text, every letter, every diary entry of Kierkegaard's has made it easier to explain the event and at the same time harder to understand or appreciate what it meant in Sören Kierkegaard's and Regine Olsen's life.

Kassner, writing about Kierkegaard in unforgettable and unsurpassable terms, rejects every explanation. "Kierkegaard," he writes, "made a poem of his relationship with Regine Olsen, and when a Kierkegaard makes a poem of his life he does so not in order to conceal the truth but in order to be able to reveal it."

There is no explanation, for what is there is more than an explanation, it is a gesture. Kierkegaard said: I am a melancholic; he said: I was a whole eternity too old for her; he said: my sin was that I tried to sweep her along with myself into the great stream; he said: if my life were not a great penitence, if it were not the *vita ante acta,* then. . . .

And he left Regine Olsen and said he did not love her, had never really loved her, he was a man whose fickle spirit demanded new people and new relationships at every moment. A large part of his writings proclaims this loudly, and the way he spoke and the way he lived emphasized this one thing in order to confirm Regine Olsen's belief in it.

. . . And Regine married one of her old admirers and Sören Kierkegaard wrote in his diary: "Today I saw a beautiful girl; she does not interest me. No married man can be more faithful to his wife than I am to Regine."

The gesture: to make unambiguous the inexplicable, which happened for many reasons and whose consequences spread wide. To withdraw in such a way that nothing but sorrow may come of it, nothing but tragedy—once it was clear that their encounter had to be tragic—nothing but total collapse, perhaps, just so long as there was no uncertainty about it, no dissolving of reality into possibilities. If what seemed to mean life itself to Regine Olsen had to be lost to her, then it had to lose *all* meaning in her life; if he who loved Regine Olsen had to leave her, then he who left her had to be a scoundrel and a seducer, so that every path back to life might remain open to her. And since Sören Kierkegaard's penitence was to leave life, that penitence had to be made the greater by the sinner's mask, chivalrously assumed, which disguised his real sin.

Regine's marriage to another man was necessary for Kierkegaard. "She has grasped the point very well," he wrote, "she understands that she must get married." He needed her marriage so that nothing uncertain, nothing vague should remain about the relationship, no further possibility, only this one thing: the seducer and the jilted girl. But the girl consoles herself and finds the way back to life. Under the seducer's mask stands the ascetic who, out of asceticism, voluntarily froze in his gesture.

The transformation of the girl follows in a straight line from her beginning. Behind the fixedly smiling mask of the seducer frowns, as fixedly, the real face of the ascetic. The gesture is pure and expresses everything. "Kierkegaard made a poem of his life."

The only essential difference between one life and another is the question whether a life is absolute or merely relative; whether the mutually exclusive opposites within the life are separated from one another sharply and definitively or not. The difference is whether the life-problems of a particular life arise in the form of an either/or, or whether "as well as" is the proper formula when the split appears. Kierkegaard was always saying: I want to be honest, and this honesty could not mean anything less than the duty—in the purest sense of the word—to live out his life in accordance with poetic principles; the duty to decide, the duty to go to the very end of every chosen road at every crossroads.

But when a man looks about him, he does not see roads and crossroads, nor any sharply distinct choices anywhere; everything flows, everything is transmuted into something else. Only when we turn away our gaze and look again much later do we find that one thing has become another—and perhaps not even then. But the deep meaning of Kierkegaard's philosophy is that he places fixed points beneath the incessantly changing nuances of life, and draws absolute quality distinctions within the melting chaos of nuances. And, having found certain things to be different, he presents them as being so unambiguously and profoundly different that what separates them can never again be blurred by any possible nuance or transition. Thus Kierkegaard's honesty entails the paradox that whatever has not already grown into a new unity which cancels out all former differences, must remain divided forever. Among the things you have found to be different you must choose one, you must not seek "middle ways" or "higher unities" which might resolve the "merely apparent" contradictions. And so there is no system anywhere, for it is not possible to *live* a system; the system is always a vast palace, while its creator can only withdraw into a modest corner. There is never any room for life in a logical system of thought; seen in this way, the starting point for such a system is always arbitrary and, from the perspective of life, only relative—a mere possibility. There is no system in life. In life there is only the separate and individual, the concrete. To exist is to be different. And only the concrete, the individual phenomenon is the unambiguous, the absolute which is without nuance. Truth is only subjective—perhaps; but subjectivity is quite certainly truth; the individual thing is the only thing that is; the individual is the real man.

And so there are some major, typical cycles of possibilities

in life, or stages to use Kierkegaard's language: the aesthetic, the ethical, the religious stage. Each is distinct from the other with a sharpness that allows of no nuances, and the connection between each is the miracle, the leap, the sudden metamorphosis of the entire being of a man.

This, then, was Kierkegaard's honesty: to see everything as being sharply distinct from everything else, system from life, human being from human being, stage from stage: to see the absolute in life, without any petty compromises.

But is it not a compromise to see life as being without compromises? Is not such nailing down of absoluteness, rather, an evasion of the duty to look at *everything?* Is not a stage a "higher unity", too? Is not the denial of a life-system itself a system—and very much so? Is not the leap merely a sudden transition? Is there not, after all, a rigorous distinction hidden behind every compromise, hidden behind its most vehement denial? Can one be honest in face of life, and yet stylize life's events in literary form?

The inner honesty of Kierkegaard's gesture of separation could only be assured if everything he did was done for Regine Olsen's sake. The letters and diary entries are full of it: had they remained together, not even Regine's bubbling laughter would have broken the sombre silence of his terrible melancholy; the laughter would have been silenced, the lightness would have fallen wearily to the stony ground below. No one would have benefited from such a sacrifice. And so it was his duty (whatever it may have cost him from the point of view of human happiness, of human existence) to save Regine Olsen's life.

But the question is whether Regine's life was the only thing he saved. Was not the very thing which, as he believed, made it necessary for them to part, essential to his own life? Did he not give up the struggle against his melancholy (a struggle which might have been successful) because he loved it more dearly, perhaps, than anything else, and could not conceive of life without it? "My sorrow is my castle," he once wrote, and elsewhere he said (I quote only a few examples to stand for many more): "In my great melancholy I still loved life, for I loved my melancholy." And writing about Regine and himself: ". . . she would have been ruined and presumably she would have wrecked me, too, for I should constantly have had to strain myself trying to raise her up. I was too heavy for her, she too light for me, but either way there is most certainly a risk of overstrain."

There are beings to whom—in order that they may become great—anything even faintly resembling happiness and sunshine must always be forbidden. Karoline [Schelling] once wrote of Friedrich Schlegel: "Some thrive under oppression, and Friedrich is one of them—if he were to enjoy the full glory of success even once, it would destroy what is finest in him." Robert Browning rewrote Friedrich Schlegel's tragedy in the sad history of Chiappino, who was strong and noble, delicate and capable of deep feeling so long as he remained in the shadows and his life meant only wretchedness and fruitless longing; when misfortune raised him higher than he had ever hoped in his wildest dreams or most foolish rantings, he became empty, and his cynical words could barely disguise the pain he felt at becoming conscious of that emptiness—the emptiness which came with "good fortune". (Browning called this disaster "a soul's tragedy".)

Perhaps Kierkegaard knew this, or perhaps he sensed it. Perhaps his violently active creative instinct, released by the pain he felt immediately after the break with Regine, had already claimed in advance this only possible release. Perhaps something inside him knew that happiness—if it was attainable—would have made him lame and sterile for the rest of his life. Perhaps he was afraid that happiness might not be unattainable, that Regine's lightness might after all have redeemed his great melancholy and that both might have been happy. But what would have become of him without his melancholy? Kierkegaard is the sentimental Socrates. "Loving is the only thing I'm an expert in," he said. But Socrates wanted only to recognize, to understand human beings who loved, and therefore the central problem in Kierkegaard's life was no problem for Socrates. "Loving is the only thing I'm an expert in," said Kierkegaard,

> just give me an object for my love, only an object. But here I stand like an archer whose bow is stretched to the uttermost limit and who is asked to shoot at a target five paces ahead of him. This I cannot do, says the archer, but put the target two or three hundred paces further away and you will see!

Remember Keats' prayer to nature:

> A theme! a theme! great nature! give a theme;
> Let me begin my dream.

To love! Whom can I love in such a way that the object of my love will not stand in the way of my love? Who is strong enough, who can contain everything within himself so that his love will become absolute and stronger than anything else? Who stands so high above all others that whoever loves him will never address a demand to him, never be proved right against him—so that the love with which he is loved will be an absolute one?

To love: to try never to be proved right. That is how Kierkegaard described love. For the cause of the eternal relativity of all human relationships, of their fluctuations and, therefore, of their pettiness, is that it is now the one who is right, and now the other; now the one who is better, nobler, more beautiful, and now the other. There can be constancy and clarity only if the lovers are qualitatively different from one another, if one is so much higher than the other that the question of right and wrong (in the broadest sense) can never be posed, even as a question.

Such was the ideal of love of the ascetic medieval knights, but it was never to be as romantic again. Kierkegaard's psychological insight robbed him of the naïve belief (naïve for a Kierkegaard) that the beloved woman whom the troubadours renounced in order to be able to love her in their own fashion—or even the dream image of such a woman, who can never and nowhere be real—might be different enough from reality for their love to become absolute. This, I believe, was the root of Kierkegaard's religiosity. God can be loved thus, and no one else but God. He once wrote that God is a demand of man, and man clings

to this demand to escape from the wretchedness of his condition, to be able to bear his life. Yes, but Kierkegaard's God is enthroned so high above everything human, is separated from everything human by such absolute depths—how could he help a man to bear his human life? I think he could, and for that very reason. Kierkegaard needed life to be absolute, to be so firm that it tolerated no challenge; his love needed the possibility of embracing the whole, without any reservation whatsoever. He needed a love without problems, a love in which it was not now the one, now the other that was better, not now the one, now the other that was right. My love is sure and unquestionable only if I am never in the right: and God alone can give me this assurance. "You love a man," he wrote, "and you want always to be proved wrong against him, but, alas, he has been unfaithful to you, and however much this may pain you, you are still in the right against him and wrong to love him so deeply." The soul turns to God because it cannot subsist without love, and God gives the lover everything his heart desires. "Never shall tormenting doubts pull me away from him, never shall the thought appeal me that I might prove right against him: before God I am always in the wrong."

Kierkegaard was a troubadour and a Platonist, and he was both these things romantically and sentimentally. In the deepest recesses of his soul burned sacrificial flames for the ideal of a woman, but the self-same flames fed the stake upon which the self-same woman was burned. When man stood face to face with the world for the first time, everything that surrounded him belonged to him, and yet each separate thing always vanished before his eyes and every step led him past each separate thing. He would have starved to death, tragically, absurdly, in the midst of all the world's riches, had woman not been there from the start—woman who knew from the start how to grasp things, who knew the uses and the immediate significance

An 1847 painting of Regine Olsen.

of things. Thus it was that woman—within the meaning of Kierkegaard's parable—saved man for life, but only in order to hold him down, to chain him to the finiteness of life. The real woman, the mother, is the most absolute opposite of any yearning for infinity. Socrates married Xanthippe and was happy with her only because he regarded marriage as an obstacle on the way to the Ideal and was glad to be able to overcome the difficulties of marriage: much in the way that [the German mystic Heinrich] Suso's God says: "You have always found recalcitrance in all things; and that is the sign of my chosen ones, whom I want to have for myself."

Kierkegaard did not take up this struggle; perhaps he evaded it, perhaps he no longer needed it. Who knows? The world of human communion, the ethical world whose typical form is marriage, stands between the two worlds of Kierkegaard's soul: the world of pure poetry and the world of pure faith. And if the foundation of the ethical life, "duty", appears firm and secure compared with the "possibilities" of the poet's life, its eternal evaluations are yet, at the same time, eternal fluctuations compared with the absolute certainties of the religious. But the substance of those certainties is air, and the substance of the poet's possibilities is likewise air. Where is the dividing line between the two?

But perhaps this is not the question to ask here. Regine Olsen was for Kierkegaard no more than a step on the way that leads to the icy temple of nothing-but-the-love-of-God. Committing a sin against her merely deepened his relationship to God; loving her with suffering, causing her to suffer, helped to intensify his ecstasies and to fix the single goal of his path. Everything that would have stood between them if they had really belonged to each other only gave wing to his flight. "I thank you for never having understood me," he wrote in a letter to her which he never sent, "for it taught me everything. I thank you for being so passionately unjust towards me, for that determined my life."

Even abandoned by him, Regine could only be a step towards his goal. In his dreams he transformed her into an unattainable ideal: but the step that she represented was his surest way to the heights. In the woman-glorifying poetry of the Provençal troubadours, great faithlessness was the basis for great faithfulness; a woman had to belong to another in order to become the ideal, in order to be loved with real love. But Kierkegaard's faithfulness was even greater than the troubadours', and for that very reason even more faithless: even the deeply beloved woman was only a means, only a way towards the great, the only absolute love, the love of God.

Whatever Kierkegaard did, and for whatever reason, it was done only to save Regine Olsen for life. However many inner meanings the gesture of rejection may have had, outwardly—in Regine Olsen's eyes—it had to be univocal. Kierkegaard sensed that for Regine there was only one danger, that of uncertainty. And because, for her, no life could grow out of her love of him, he wanted with all his strength—sacrificing his good name—that she should feel nothing but hate for him. He wanted Regine to consider him a scoundrel, he wanted her whole family to hate him as a common seducer; for if Regine hated him, she was saved.

Yet the break came too suddenly, even though long and violent scenes had helped to prepare the way. Regine suddenly had to see Kierkegaard as different from the man she had previously known; she had to re-evaluate every word and every silence of every minute they had spent together if she was to feel that the new was indeed connected with the old—if she was to see Kierkegaard as a whole man; and from that moment onwards she had to see whatever he might do in that new light. Kierkegaard did everything to make this easier for her, to channel the current of her newly formed images in a single direction—the direction he wanted, the only one he saw as leading to the right goal for Regine: the direction of hate against himself.

This is the background to Kierkegaard's erotic writings—especially the "Diary of a Seducer"—and it is this that gives them their radiance, received from life itself. An incorporeal sensuality and a plodding, programmatic ruthlessness are the predominant features of these writings. The erotic life, the beautiful life, life culminating in pleasure, occurs in them as a world-view—and as no more than that; a way of living which Kierkegaard sensed as a possibility within himself, but which not even his subtle reasoning and analysis could render corporeal. He is, as it were, the seducer *in abstracto,* needing only the possibility of seduction, only a situation which he creates and then enjoys to the full; the seducer who does not really need women even as objects of pleasure. He is the platonic idea of the seducer, who is so deeply a seducer and nothing else that really he is not even that; a man so remote, so far above all other humans that his appeal can scarcely reach them any longer, or if it does, then only as an incomprehensible, elemental irruption into their lives: the absolute seducer who appears to every woman as the eternal stranger, yet who (Kierkegaard was incapable of noticing this aspect), just because he is so infinitely remote, barely avoids appearing comic to any woman who, for whatever reason, is not destroyed when he looms up on the horizon of her life.

We have already said that the role of the seducer was Kierkegaard's gesture for Regine Olsen's sake. But the possibility of being a seducer was already latent in him, and a gesture always reacts back upon the soul that makes it. In life there is no purely empty comedy: that is perhaps the saddest ambiguity of human relationships. One can play only at what is there: one cannot play at anything without it somehow becoming part and parcel of one's life; and although it may be kept carefully separate from the game, life trembles at such play.

Regine, of course, could only see the gesture, and the effect of the gesture forced her to re-evaluate everything in her life so that it became the exact opposite of what it had been before. At least, that was what Kierkegaard wanted, and on this he staked everything. But something that has been lived in corporeal reality can, at most, only be poisoned by the realization that it was a mere game; a reality can never be completely and unchallengeably re-evaluated; only one's view of that reality and the values one attaches to that view can change. What had passed between Regine and Kierkegaard was life, was living reality, and it could only be shaken and irretrievably confounded in retrospect, as the result of a forced re-evaluation of motives. For if the present forced Regine to see Kierkegaard differently, then this way of seeing him was sensual reality only for the present; the reality of the past spoke in a different voice, and could not be silenced by the feebler voice of her new knowledge.

Soon after the actual break Kierkegaard wrote to Bösen, his only dependable friend, that if Regine knew with what anxious care he had arranged everything and carried it through once he had decided that the break had to come, she would by that very fact recognize his love for her. When, after Kierkegaard's death, Regine read his posthumous writings, she wrote to Dr. Lund, his relative: "These pages put our relationship in a new light, a light in which I too saw it sometimes, but my modesty forbade me to think that it was the true light; and yet my unshakable faith in him made me see it like that again and again."

Kierkegaard himself felt something of this uncertainty. He felt that his gesture remained a mere possibility in Regine's eyes, just as Regine's gesture had in his own eyes. The gesture was in no way sufficient to create solid reality between them. If there was a way in which he could find true reality, it was the way to Regine: but to travel that way, however cautiously, would have been to destroy everything that he had accomplished so far. He had to remain frozen in his outwardly rigid, inwardly uncertain posture because, for all he knew, everything in her life might really be settled and certain, after all. Perhaps, if he had made a move towards her, he would have encountered living reality? But only perhaps. Ten years after the breaking off of the engagement he still did not dare to meet her. Perhaps her marriage was only a mask. Perhaps she loved him as before, and a meeting would have cancelled out all that had happened.

But it is impossible even to maintain the rigid certainty of one's gesture—if indeed it ever is a real certainty at all. One cannot, however much one may want to, continually disguise so deep a melancholy as a game, nor can one ever definitively conceal such passionate love under an appearance of faithlessness. Yes, the gesture reacts back upon the soul, but the soul in turn reacts upon the gesture which seeks to hide it, it shines forth from that gesture and neither of the two, neither gesture nor soul, is capable of remaining hard and pure and separate from the other throughout a lifetime. The only way of somehow achieving the outwardly preserved purity of the gesture is to make sure that, whenever the other person momentarily abandons his stance, this is always misunderstood. In this way accidental movements, meaningless words carelessly spoken, acquire life-determining significance; and the reflex produced by the gesture is in turn strong enough to force the impulse back into the same self-chosen stance. When they parted, Regine asked Kierkegaard almost childishly, in the midst of tearful pleas and questions, whether he would still think of her from time to time, and this question became the *leitmotif* of Kierkegaard's whole life. And when she became engaged, she sent him greetings expecting a sign of approval, but by doing so she set off

quite another train of thought in his uncomprehending mind. When he could no longer bear the weight of the mask and thought that the time had come for mutual explanations, Regine, by agreement with her husband, returned his letter unopened, making a gesture of certainty to make sure that everything should remain uncertain for ever more—since in any case, for her it had always been so—and to make sure that, once Kierkegaard was dead, she herself should grieve over the uncertainty she had created by refusing to hear his explanation. Whether they met or did not meet, the pattern was always the same: a hasty impulse leading out of the gesture, then a hasty return to the gesture—and the other's failure to understand both.

Where psychology begins, monumentality ends: perfect clarity is only a modest expression of a striving for monumentality. Where psychology begins, there are no more deeds but only motives for deeds; and whatever requires explanation, whatever can bear explanation, has already ceased to be solid and clear. Even if something still remains under the pile of debris, the flood of explanations will inexorably wash it away. For there is nothing less solid in the world than explanations and all that rests upon them. Whatever exists for a reason may have been its opposite for another reason—or, under slightly changed circumstances, for the same reason. Even when the reasons remain the same—but they never do—they cannot be constant; something that seemed to sweep the whole world away at a moment of great passion becomes minutely small when the storm is over, and something that was once negligible becomes gigantic in the light of later knowledge.

Life dominated by motives is a continual alternation of the kingdoms of Lilliput and Brobdingnag; and the most insubstantial, the most abysmal of all kingdoms is that of the soul's reason, the kingdom of psychology. Once psychology has entered into a life, then it is all up with unambiguous honesty and monumentality. When psychology rules, then there are no gestures any more that can comprise life and all its situations within them. The gesture is unambiguous only for as long as the psychology remains conventional.

Here poetry and life part company and become tragically, definitively distinct. The psychology of poetry is always unambiguous, for it is always an *ad hoc* psychology; even if it appears to ramify in several directions, its multiplicity is always unambiguous; it merely gives more intricate form to the balance of the final unity. In life, nothing is unambiguous; in life, there is no *ad hoc* psychology. In life, not only those motives play a role which have been accepted for the sake of the final unity, and not every note that has once been struck must necessarily be silenced in the end. In life, psychology cannot be conventional, in poetry it always is—however subtle and complex the convention. In life, only a hopelessly limited mind can believe in the unambiguous; in poetry, only a completely failed work can be ambiguous in this sense.

That is why, of all possible lives, the poet's life is the most profoundly unpoetic, the most profoundly lacking in profile and gesture. (Keats was the first to recognize this.) That which gives life to life becomes conscious in the poet;

a real poet cannot have a limited mind about life, nor can he entertain any illusions about his own life. For a poet, therefore, all life is merely raw material; only his hands, doing spontaneous violence to living matter, can knead the unambiguous from the chaos of reality, create symbols from incorporeal phenomena, give form (i.e. limitation and significance) to the thousandfold ramifications, the deliquescent mass of reality. That is why a poet's own life can never serve as the raw material to which he will give form.

Kierkegaard's heroism was that he wanted to create forms from life. His honesty was that he saw a crossroads and walked to the end of the road he had chosen. His tragedy was that he wanted to live what cannot be lived. "I am struggling in vain," he wrote, "I am losing the ground under my feet. My life will, after all, have been a poet's life and no more." A poet's life is null and worthless because it is never absolute, never a thing in itself and for itself, because it is always there only *in relation to something,* and this relation is meaningless and yet it completely absorbs the life—for a moment at least; but then life is made up of nothing but such moments.

Against this necessity, the life of Kierkegaard—whose mind was never limited—waged its royally limited struggle. It might be said that life cunningly gave him all that it could give and all that he could ask for. Yet life's every gift was mere deception; it could never, after all, give him reality, but only lure him deeper and deeper, with every appearance of victory and success—like Napoleon in Russia—into the all-devouring desert.

This much his heroism did achieve, in life as in death. He lived in such a way that every moment of his life became rounded into the grand gesture, appearing statuesquely sure, carried through to the end; and he died in such a way that death came at the right time, just when he wanted it and as he wanted it. Yet we have seen how unsure his surest gesture was when seen from close by; and even if death overtook him at the climax of his most real, most profound struggle, even if it came as he wanted it to come, so that, dying, he could be the blood-witness of his own struggle, yet he could not be its real blood-witness. For, despite everything, his death pointed at several possibilities. In life, everything points at more than one possibility, and only *post facto* realities can exclude a few possibilities (never all of them, so that only one central reality is left). But even those open the way to a million new ones.

He was fighting the Christianity of his time when death overtook him. He stood in the midst of violent struggle; he had nothing more to seek in life outside that struggle, and he could scarcely have been fighting any harder. (Some incidental factors, too, made his death fateful. Kierkegaard had lived off his capital all his life, regarding interest as usury in the way religious men did in the Middle Ages; when he died, his fortune was just running out.) When he collapsed in the street and they took him to hospital, he said he wanted to die because the cause he stood for needed his death.

And so he died. But his death left every question open: Where would the path which broke off suddenly at his grave have led to if he had gone on living? Where was he going when he met his death? The inner necessity of death is only in an infinite series of possible explanations; and if his death did not come in answer to an inner call, like an actor taking his cue, then we cannot regard the end of his path as an end and we must try to imagine the further meanderings of that path. Then even Kierkegaard's death acquires a thousand meanings, becomes accidental and not really the work of destiny. And then his purest and most unambiguous gesture of his life—vain effort!—was not a gesture after all. (pp. 28-41)

> Georg Lukács, *"The Foundering of Form Against Life: Sören Kierkegaard and Regine Olsen," in his* Soul and Form, *translated by Anna Bostock, Merlin Press, 1974, pp. 28-41.*

Karl Jaspers   (lecture date 1935)

[*One of the great figures of twentieth-century Existentialism, the German philosopher and psychologist Jaspers posited that Being can be apprehended only by transcending the intellect. His writings include* Philosophie *(1932;* Philosophy, *1967-71),* Der philosophische Glaube *(1948;* The Perennial Scope of Philosophy, *1949), and* Einfuhrung in die Philosophie *(1950;* Way to Wisdom: An Introduction to Philosophy, *1951). In the following excerpt from* Reason and Existenz, *Jaspers identifies fundamental similarities in the life and thought of Kierkegaard and Nietzsche. These two are the most significant influences on contemporary philosophy, he declares, because through their work "we have become aware that for us there is no longer any self-evident foundation. There is no longer any secure background for our thought." Jaspers's commentary on Kierkegaard and Nietzsche was originally presented in a lecture at the University of Groningen, Holland, in 1935.*]

The contemporary philosophical situation is determined by the fact that two philosophers, Kierkegaard and Nietzsche, who did not count in their times and, for a long time, remained without influence in the history of philosophy, have continually grown in significance. Philosophers after Hegel have increasingly returned to face them, and they stand today unquestioned as the authentically great thinkers of their age. Both their influence and the opposition to them prove it. Why then can these philosophers no longer be ignored, in our time?

In the situation of philosophizing, as well as in the real life of men, Kierkegaard and Nietzsche appear as the expression of destinies, destinies which nobody noticed then, with the exception of some ephemeral and immediately forgotten presentiments, but which they themselves already comprehended.

As to what this destiny really is, the question remains open even today. It is not answered by any comparison of the two thinkers, but it is clarified and made more urgent. This comparison is all the more important since there could have been no influence of one upon the other, and because their very differences make their common features so much more impressive. Their affinity is so compelling, from the whole course of their lives down to the individual details of their thought, that their nature seems to have been elicited by the necessities of the spiritual situation of their times. With them a shock occurred to Western philosophizing whose final meaning can not yet be underestimated.

Common to both of them is a type of thought and humanity which was indissolubly connected with a moment of this epoch, and so understood by them. We shall, therefore, discuss their affinity: first, in their thought; second, in their actual thinking Existenz; and third, in the way in which they understood themselves.

Their thinking created a new atmosphere. They passed beyond all of the limits then regarded as obvious. It is as if they no longer shrank back from anything in thought. Everything permanent was as if consumed in a dizzying suction: with Kierkegaard by an otherworldly Christianity which is like Nothingness and shows itself only in negation (the absurd, martyrdom) and in negative resolution; with Nietzsche, a vacuum out of which, with despairing violence, a new reality was to be born (the eternal return, and the corresponding dogmatics of Nietzsche).

Both questioned reason from the depths of Existenz. Never on such a high level of thought had there been such a thorough-going and radical opposition to mere reason. This questioning is never simply hostility to reason; rather both sought to appropriate limitlessly all modes of rationality. It was no philosophy of feeling, for both pushed unremittingly toward the concept for expression. It is certainly not dogmatic scepticism; rather their whole thought strove toward the genuine truth.

In a magnificent way, penetrating a whole life with the earnestness of philosophizing, they brought forth not some doctrines, not any basic position, not some picture of the world, but rather a new total intellectual attitude for men. This attitude was in the medium of infinite reflection, a reflection which is conscious of being unable to attain any real ground by itself. No single thing characterizes their nature; no fixed doctrine or requirement is to be drawn out of them as something independent and permanent.

Out of the consciousness of their truth, both suspect truth in the naive form of scientific knowledge. They do not doubt the methodological correctness of scientific insight. But Kierkegaard was astonished at the learned professors; they live for the most part with science and die with the idea that it will continue, and would like to live longer that they might, in a line of direct progress, always understand more and more. They do not experience the maturity of that critical point where everything turns upside down, where one understands more and more that there is something which one cannot understand. Kierkegaard thought the most frightful way to live was to bewitch the whole world through one's discoveries and cleverness—to explain the whole of nature and not understand oneself. Nietzsche is inexhaustible in destructive analyses of types of scholars, who have no genuine sense of their own activity, who can not be themselves, and who, with their ultimately futile knowledge, aspire to grasp Being itself.

The questioning of every self-enclosed rationality which tries to make the whole truth communicable made both

radical opponents of the "system," that is, the form which philosophy had had for centuries and which had achieved its final polish in German idealism. The system is for them a detour from reality and is, therefore, lies and deception. Kierkegaard granted that empirical existence could be a system for God, but never for an existing spirit; system corresponds with what is closed and settled, but existence is precisely the contrary. The philosopher of systems is, as a man, like someone who builds a castle, but lives next door in a shanty. Such a fantastical being does not himself live within what he thinks; but the thought of a man must be the house in which he lives or it will become perverted. The basic question of philosophy, what it itself is, and what science is, is posed in a new and unavoidable form. Nietzsche wanted to doubt better than Descartes, and saw in Hegel's miscarried attempt to make reason evolve nothing but Gothic heaven-storming. The will-to-system is for him a lack of honesty.

What authentic knowing is, was expressed by both in the same way. It is, for them, nothing but interpretation. They also understood their own thought as interpretation.

Interpretation, however, reaches no end. Existence, for Nietzsche, is capable of infinite interpretation. What has happened and what was done, is for Kierkegaard always capable of being understood in a new way. As it is interpreted anew, it becomes a new reality which yet is hidden; temporal life can therefore never be correctly understood by men; no man can absolutely penetrate through his own consciousness.

Both apply the image of interpretation to knowledge of Being, but in such a fashion that Being is as if deciphered in the interpretation of the interpretation. Nietzsche wanted to uncover the basic text, *homo natura,* from its overpaintings and read it in its reality. Kierkegaard gave his own writings no other meaning than that they should read again the original text of individual, human existential relations.

With this basic idea is connected the fact that both, the most open and candid of thinkers, had a misleading aptitude for concealment and masks. For them masks necessarily belong to the truth. Indirect communication becomes for them the sole way of communicating genuine truth; indirect communication, as expression, is appropriate to the ambiguity of genuine truth in temporal existence, in which process it must be grasped through sources in every Existenz.

Both, in their thinking, push toward that basis which would be Being itself in man. In opposition to the philosophy which from Parmenides through Descartes to Hegel said, Thought is Being, Kierkegaard asserted the proposition, as you believe, so are you: Faith is Being. Nietzsche saw the Will to Power. But Faith and Will to Power are mere *signa,* which do not directly connote what is meant but are themselves capable of endless explication.

With both there is a decisive drive toward honesty. This word for them both is the expression of the ultimate virtue to which they subject themselves. It remains for them the minimum of the absolute which is still possible although everything else becomes involved in a bewildering questioning. It becomes for them also the dizzying demand for a veracity which, however, brings even itself into question, and which is the opposite of that violence which would like to grasp the truth in a literal and barbaric certitude.

One can question whether in general anything is said in such thought. In fact, both Kierkegaard and Nietzsche were aware that the comprehension of their thought was not possible to the man who only thinks. It is important who it is that understands.

They turn to the individuals who must bring with them and bring forth from themselves what can only be said indirectly. The epigram of Lichtenberg applies to Kierkegaard, and he himself cites it: such works are like mirrors; if an ape peeks in, no apostle will look out. Nietzsche says one must have earned for oneself the distinction necessary to understand him. He held it impossible to teach the truth where the mode of thought is base. Both seek the reader who belongs to them.

Such thinking is grounded in the Existenz of Kierkegaard and Nietzsche insofar as it belonged to their age in a distinctive way. That no single idea, no system, no requirement is decisive for them follows from the fact that neither thinker expressed his epoch at its peak, that they constructed no world, nor any image of a passing world. They did not feel themselves to be a positive expression of their times; they rather expressed what it was negatively through their very being: an age absolutely rejected by them and seen through in its ruin. Their problem appeared to be to experience this epoch to the end in their own natures, to be it completely in order to overcome it. This happened at first involuntarily, but then consciously through the fact that they were not representatives of their epoch, but needling and scandalous *exceptions*. Let us look at this a little closer.

Both had become aware of their *problem* by the end of their youth, even if unclearly. A decision which gripped the entire man, which sometimes was silent and no longer conscious, but which would return to force itself upon them, pushed them into a radical loneliness. Although without position, marriage, without any effective role in existence, they nevertheless appear as the great realists, who had an authentic feeling for the depths of reality.

They touched this reality in their fundamental experience of their epoch as ruins; looking back over centuries, back to the beginnings in Greek antiquity, they felt the end of this whole history. At the crucial point, they called attention to this moment, without wanting to survey the meaning and course of history as a whole.

Men have tried to understand this epoch in economic, technological, historico-political, and sociological terms. Kierkegaard and Nietzsche, on the other hand, thought they saw a change in the very substance of man.

Kierkegaard looked upon the whole of Christianity as it is today as upon an enormous deception in which God is held to be a fool. Such Christianity has nothing to do with that of the New Testament. There are only two ways: either to maintain the deception through tricks and conceal the real conditions, and then everything comes to nothing; or honestly to confess the misery that in truth, today, not one single individual is born who can pass for a Christian in the sense of the New Testament. Not one of us is a Christian, but rather we live in a pious softening of Christianity. The confession will show if there is anything true left in this honesty, if it has the approval of Providence. If not, then everything must again be broken so that in this horror individuals can arise again who can support the Christianity of the New Testament.

Nietzsche expressed the historical situation of the epoch in one phrase: God is dead.

Thus, common to both, is an historical judgment on the very substance of their times. They saw before them Nothingness; both knew the substance of what had been lost, but neither willed Nothingness. If Kierkegaard presupposed the truth, or the possibility of the truth of Christianity, and Nietzsche, on the other hand, found in atheism not simply a loss but rather the greatest opportunity—still, what is common to both is a will toward the substance of Being, toward the nobility and value of man. They had no political program for reform, no program at all; they directed their attention to no single detail, but rather wanted to effect something through their thought which they foresaw in no clear detail. For Nietzsche, this indeterminateness was his "larger politics" at long range; for Kierkegaard, it was becoming Christian in the new way of indifference to all worldly being. Both in their relation to their epoch were possessed by the question of what will become of man.

They are modernity itself in a somersaulting form. They ran it to the ground, and overcame it by living it through to the end. We can see how both experienced the distress of the epoch, not passively, but suicidally through totally doing what most only half did: first of all, in their endless reflection; and then, in opposition to this, in their drive toward the basic; and finally, in the way in which, as they sank into the bottomless, they grasped hold upon the Transcendent.

(i) *unlimited reflection.* The age of reflection has, since Fichte, been characterized as reasoning without restraint, as the dissolving of all authority, as the surrender of content which gives to thinking its measure, purpose, and meaning, so that from now on, without hindrance and as an indifferent play of the intellect, it can fill the world with noise and dust.

Kierkegaard and Nietzsche did not oppose reflection in order to annihilate it, but rather in order to overcome it by limitlessly engaging in it and mastering it. Man cannot sink back into an unreflective immediacy without losing himself; but he can go this way to the end, not destroying reflection, but rather coming to the basis in himself in the medium of reflection.

Their "infinite reflection" has, therefore, a twofold character. It can lead to a complete ruin just as well as it can become the condition of authentic Existenz. Both express this, perhaps Kierkegaard is the clearer of the two:

Reflection cannot exhaust or stop itself. It is faithless, since it hinders every decision. It is never finished and, in the end, can become "dialectical twaddle"; in this respect, he called it the poison of reflection. But that it is possible, indeed necessary, lies grounded in the endless ambiguity of all existence and action for us: anything can mean something else for reflection. This situation makes possible on one side a sophistry of existence, enables the Existenz-less esthete to profit, who merely wants to savor everything as an interesting novelty. Even if he should take the most decisive step, still he always holds before himself the possibility of reinterpreting everything, so that, in one blow, it is all changed. But on the other hand, this situation can be truly grasped by the knowledge that insofar as we are honest we live in a "sea of reflection where no one can call to another, where all buoys are dialectical."

Without infinite reflection we should fall into the quiet of the settled and established which, as something permanent in the world, would become absolute; that is, we should become superstitious. An atmosphere of bondage arises with such a settlement. Infinite reflection, therefore, is, precisely through its endlessly active dialectic, the condition of freedom. It breaks out of every prison of the finite. Only in its medium is there any possibility of an infinite passion arising out of immediate feeling which, because it is unquestioning, is still unfree. In infinite passion the immediate feeling, which is held fast and genuinely true throughout the questioning, is grasped as free.

But in order to prevent this freedom from becoming nothing through vacuous reflection, in order for it to fulfill itself, infinite reflection must strand itself. Then, for the first time, does it issue out of something real, or exhaust itself in the decision of faith and resolution. As untrue as the arbitrary and forced arrest of reflection is, so true is that basis by which reflection is mastered in the encounter of Existenz. Here Existenz is given to itself for the first time, so that it becomes master of infinite reflection through totally surrendering to it.

Reflection, which can just as well dissolve into nothing as become the condition of Existenz, is described as such and in the same way by both Kierkegaard and Nietzsche. Out of it, they have imparted an almost immeasurable wealth of thought in their works. This thinking, according to its own meaning, is possibility: it can indicate and prepare the way for the shipwreck, but cannot accomplish it.

Thus, in their thinking about the possibilities of man, both thinkers were aware of what they themselves were not in their thought. The awareness of possibilities, in analogy to poetry, is not a false, but rather a questioning and awakening reflection. Possibility is the form in which I permit myself to know about what I am not yet, and a preparation for being it.

Kierkegaard called his method most frequently, "an experimental psychology"; Nietzsche called his thought, "seductive."

Thus they left what they themselves were and what they ultimately thought concealed to the point of unrecognizability and, in its appearance, sunk into the incomprehensible. Kierkegaard's pseudonym writes: "The something which I am . . . is precisely a nothing." It gave him a high satisfaction to hold his "Existenz at that critical zero . . .

between something and nothing, a mere perhaps." And Nietzsche willingly called himself a "philosopher of the dangerous perhaps."

Reflection is for both pre-eminently self-reflection. For them, the way to truth is through understanding oneself. But they both experienced how one's own substance can disappear this way, how the free, creative self-understanding can be replaced by a slavish rotation about one's own empirical existence. Kierkegaard knew the horror "of everything disappearing before a sick brooding over the tale of one's own miserable self." He sought for the way "between this devouring of oneself in observations as though one were the only man who had ever been, and the sorry comfort of a universal human shipwreck." He knew the "unhappy relativity in everything, the unending question about what I am." Nietzsche expressed it:

> Among a hundred mirrors
> before yourself false . . .
> strangled in your own net
> Self-knower!
> Self-executioner!
> crammed between two nothings,
> a question mark . . .

(ii) *drive toward the basic.* The age which could no longer find its way amidst the multiplicity of its reflections and rationalizing words pushed out of reflection toward bases. Kierkegaard and Nietzsche here too seem to be forerunners. Later generations sought the basic in general in articulateness, in the esthetic charm of the immediately striking, in a general simplification, in unreflective experience, in the existence of the things closest to us. To them, Kierkegaard and Nietzsche seem useful; for both lived consciously with a passionate love for the sources of human communicability.

They were creative in language to the degree that their works belong to the peaks of the literatures of their countries; and they knew it. They were creative in the thrilling way which made them among the most widely read authors, even though the content was of the same weight and their genuine comprehension of the same difficulty as that of any of the great philosophers. But both also knew the tendency of the verbal to become autonomous, and they despised the literary world.

Both were moved by music to the point of intoxication; but both warned of its seduction, and along with Plato and Augustine belonged to those who suspected it existentially.

Everywhere they created formulas of striking simplicity. But both were full of concern before that simplicity which, in order to give some deceptive support to the weak and mediocre, offered flat, spiritless simplifications in place of the genuine simplicity which was the result of the most complicated personal development, which, like Being itself, never had a single rational meaning. They warned, as no thinker before had, against taking their words too simply, words which seemed to stand there apodictically.

In fact, they went by the most radical way to the basic, but in such a fashion that the dialectical movement never stopped. Their seriousness was absorbed neither into an illusion of the dogmatic fixedness of some supposed basis, nor into the purposes of language, esthetic charm, and simplicity.

(iii) *arrest in Transcendence.* Both pursued a path which, for them, could not end short of a transcendental stop, for their reflections were not, like the usual reflections of modernity, stopped by the obvious limits of vital needs and interests. They, for whom it was a question of all or nothing, dared limitlessness. But this they could do only because from the very beginning onwards they were rooted in what was at the same time hidden from them: both, in their youth, spoke of an *unknown God*. Kierkegaard, even when twenty-five years old, wrote: "In spite of the fact that I am very far from understanding myself, I have . . . revered the unknown God." And Nietzsche at twenty years of age created his first unforgettable poem, "To the Unknown God":

> I would know Thee, Unknown,
> Thou who grips deep in my soul,
> wandering through my life like a storm,
> Thou inconceivable, my kin!
> I would know Thee, even serve Thee.

Never in their limitless reflection could they remain within the finite, conceivable, and therefore trivial; but just as little could they hold to reflection itself. Precisely because he had been thoroughly penetrated by reflection, Kierkegaard thought: "The religious understanding of myself has deserted me; I feel like an insect with which children are playing, so pitilessly does existence handle me." In his terrible loneliness, understood by and really bound to absolutely no one, he called to God: "God in heaven, if there were not some most inward center in a man where all this could be forgotten, who could hold out?"

Nietzsche was always conscious of moving on the sea of the infinite, of having given up land once and for all. He knew that, perhaps, neither Dante nor Spinoza knew his loneliness; somehow, they had God for company. But Nietzsche, empty in his loneliness, without men and without the ancient God, envisaged Zarathustra and meditated upon the eternal return, thoughts which left him as horrified as happy. He lived continually like someone mortally wounded. He suffered his problems. His thought is a self-arousal: "If I only had the courage to think all that I know." But, in this limitless reflecting, a deeply satisfying content was revealed which was in fact transcendent.

Thus both leaped toward Transcendence, but to a form of transcendence where practically no one could follow. Kierkegaard leaped to a Christianity which was conceived as an absurd paradox, as decision for utter world negation and martyrdom. Nietzsche leaped to the eternal return and supermen.

Thus the ideas, which were for Nietzsche himself the very deepest, can look empty to us; Kierkegaard's faith can look like a sinister alienation. If one takes the symbols of Nietzsche's religion literally, there is no longer any transcendental content in their will toward immanence: aside from the eternal cycle of things, there is the will to power, the affirmation of Being, the pleasure which "wills deep, deep eternity." Only with circumspection and by taking

pains does a more essential content emerge. With Kierkegaard, who revivified the profound formulas of theology, it can seem like the peculiar art of perhaps a nonbeliever, forcing himself to believe.

The similarity of their thought is ever so much more striking precisely because of their apparent differences: the Christian belief of the one, and the atheism emphasized by the other. In an epoch of reflection, where what had really passed away seemed still to endure, but which actually lived in an absence of faith—rejecting faith and forcing oneself to believe belong together. The godless can appear to be a believer; the believer can appear as godless; both stand in the same dialectic.

What they brought forth in their existential thinking would not have been possible without a complete possession of tradition. Both were brought up with a classical education. Both were nurtured in Christian piety. Their tendencies are unthinkable without Christian origins. If they passionately opposed the stream of this tradition in the form which it had come to assume through the centuries, they also found an historical and, for them, indestructible arrest in these origins. They bound themselves to a basis which fulfilled their own belief: Kierkegaard to a Christianity of the New Testament as he understood it, and Nietzsche to a pre-Socratic Hellenism.

But nowhere is there any final stop for them, neither in finitude, nor in an explicitly grasped basis, nor in a determinately grasped Transcendence, nor in an historical tradition. It is as though their very being, experiencing the abandonment of the age to the end, shattered and, in the shattering itself, manifested a truth which otherwise would never have come to expression. If they won an unheard-of mastery over their own selves, they also were condemned to a worldless loneliness; they were as though pushed out.

They were exceptions in every sense. Physically, their development was in retard of their character. Their faces disconcert one because of their relative unobtrusiveness. They do not impress one as types of human greatness. It is as if they both lacked something in sheer vitality. Or as though they were eternally young spirits, wandering through the world, without reality because without any real connection with the world.

Those who knew them felt attracted in an enigmatic way by their presence, as though elevated for a moment to a higher mode of being; but no one really loved them.

In the circumstances of their lives, one finds astonishing and alien features. They have been called simply insane. They would be in fact objects for a psychiatric analysis, if that were not to the prejudice of the singular height of their thought and the nobility of their natures. Indeed, then they would first come to light. But any typical diagnosis or classification would certainly fail.

They cannot be classed under any earlier type (poet, philosopher, prophet, savior, genius). With them, a new form of human reality appears in history. They are, so to speak, representative destinies, sacrifices whose way out of the world leads to experiences for others. They are by the total staking of their whole natures like modern martyrs, which, however, they precisely denied being. Through their character as exceptions, they solved their problem.

Both are irreplaceable, as having dared to be shipwrecked. We orient ourselves by them. Through them we have intimations of something we could never have perceived without such sacrifices, of something that seems essential which even today we cannot adequately grasp. It is as if the Truth itself spoke, bringing an unrest into the depths of our consciousness of being.

Even in the external circumstances of their lives we find astonishing similarities. Both came to a sudden end in their forties. Shortly before, without knowledge of their approaching end, they both made public and passionate attacks: Kierkegaard on church Christianity and on dishonesty, Nietzsche on Christendom itself.

Both made literary reputations in their first publications; but then their new books followed unceasingly, and they had to print what they wrote at their own expense.

They also both had the fate of finding a response which however was without understanding. They were merely sensations in an age when nothing opposed them. The beauty and sparkle of language, the literary and poetic qualities, the aggressiveness of their matter all misled readers from their genuine intentions. Both, toward the end, were almost idolized by those with whom they had the least in common. The age that wanted to surpass itself could, so to speak, wear itself out in ideas casually selected out of them.

The modern world has nourished itself on them precisely in its negligence. Out of their reflection, instead of remaining in the seriousness of endless reflection, it made an instrument for sophistry in irresponsible talk. Their words, like their whole lives, were savored for their great esthetic charm. They dissolved what remained of connections among men, not to lead to the bases of true seriousness, but in order to prepare a free path for caprice. Thus their influence became utterly destructive, contrary to the meaning of their thought and being.

Their problem became clearer to them from their youth onward through a continually accompanying reflection. Both of them, at the end and in retrospect, gave us an indication of how they understood themselves through a total interpretation of their work. This interpretation remained convincing to the extent that we, today, in fact understand them as they wished to be understood. All their thought takes on a new sense beyond what is immediately comprehensible in it. This picture itself is inseparable from their work, for the fashion in which they understood themselves is not an accidental addition, but an essential feature of their total thought.

One of the motives in common for the comprehensive expression of their self-understanding is the will not to be mistaken for someone else. This was, they said, one of their deepest concerns, and out of it not only were they always seeking new forms of communication, but also they directly announced the total meaning as it appeared to them at the end. They always worked by all possible means to prepare a correct understanding of their work through the ambiguity of what they said.

They both had a clear perception of their epoch, seeing what was going on before them down to the smallest detail with a certitude that was overmastering: it was the end of a mode of life that had hung together for centuries. But they also perceived that no one else saw it, that they had an awareness of their epoch which no one else yet had, but which presently others, and finally all, would have. Thus they necessarily passed into an unprecedented intensity of *self-consciousness.* Their Existenz was in a very special state of affairs. It was not just a simple spiritual superiority which they must have noticed—Kierkegaard over everybody who encountered him, Nietzsche over most—but rather something monstrous which they made themselves into: unique, solitary world-historical destinies.

But this well-grounded self-consciousness, momentarily expressed and then suppressed again, is always with Kierkegaard moderated through the humility of his Christian attitude and, with both, is tempered by the psychological knowledge of their human failure. The astonishing thing with them again is that the precise mode of their failure is itself the condition of their distinctive greatness. For this greatness is not absolute greatness, but something that uniquely belongs to the situation of the epoch.

It is noteworthy how they both came to the same metaphors for this side of their natures. Nietzsche compared himself to the "scratchings which an unknown power makes on paper, in order to test a new pen." The positive value of his illness is his standing problem. Kierkegaard thought he indeed "would be erased by God's mighty hand, extinguished as an unsuccessful experiment." He felt like a sardine squashed against the sides of a can. The idea came to him that, "in every generation there are two or three who are sacrificed for the others, who discover in frightful suffering what others shall profit by." He felt like an "interjection in speaking, without influence upon the sentence," like a "letter which is printed upside down in the line." He compared himself with the paper notes in the financial crises of 1813, the year in which he was born. "There is something in me which might have been great, but due to the unfavorable market, I'm only worth a little."

Both were conscious of being exceptions. Kierkegaard developed a theory of the exception, through which he understood himself: he loved the universal, the human in men, but as something other, something denied to him. Nietzsche knew himself to be an exception, spoke "in favor of the exception, so long as it never becomes the rule." He required of philosophers "that they take care of the rule, since he is the exception."

Thus the last thing either wished was to become exemplary. Kierkegaard looked upon himself as "a sort of trial man." "In the human sense no one can imitate me. . . . I am a man as he could become in a crisis, an experimental rabbit, so to speak, for existence." Nietzsche turned away those who would follow him: "Follow not me, but you!"

This exceptionality, which was as excruciating to them as it was the unique requirement of their problem, they characterized—and here again they agree—as pure mentality, as though they were deprived of any authentic life. Kierkegaard said that he was "in almost every physical respect deprived of the conditions for being a whole man." He had never lived except as mind. He had never been a man: at very most, child and youth. He lacked "the animal side of humanity." His melancholy carried him almost to the "edge of imbecility" and was "something that he could conceal as long as he was independent, but made him useless for any service where he could not himself determine everything." Nietzsche experienced his own pure mentality as "through excess of light, through his radiance, condemned to be, not to love." He expressed it convulsively in the "Nightsong" of Zarathustra: "Light I am; ah! would that I were Night! . . . I live in my own light. . . . "

A terrible loneliness, bound up with their exceptionality, was common to both. Kierkegaard knew that he could have no friends. Nietzsche suffered his own growing loneliness in full consciousness to the limit where he felt he could endure it no longer. Again, the same image comes to both: Nietzsche compared himself to a fir tree on the heights overlooking an abyss: "Lonely! Who dares to be a guest here? Perhaps a bird of prey, gloating in the hair of the branches. . . . " And Kierkegaard: "Like a lonely fir tree, egoistically isolated, looking toward something higher, I stand there, throwing no shadow, only the wood dove building its nest in my branches."

In great contrast to the abandonment, failure, and contingency of their existence was the growing consciousness in the course of their lives of the meaning, sense, and necessity of all that happened to them.

Kierkegaard called it Providence. He recognized the divine in it: "That everything that happens, is said, goes on, and so forth, is portentous: the factual continually changes itself to mean something far higher." The factual for him is not something to abstract oneself from, but rather something to be penetrated until God himself gives the meaning. Even what he himself did became clear only later. It was "the extra which I do not owe to myself but to Providence. It shows itself continually in such a fashion that even what I do out of the greatest possible conviction, afterwards I understand far better."

Nietzsche called it chance. And he was concerned to use chance. For him "sublime chance" ruled existence. "The man of highest spirituality and power feels himself grown for every chance, but also inside a snowfall of contingencies." But this contingency increasingly took on for Nietzsche a remarkable meaning: "What you call chance—you yourself are that which befalls and astonishes you." Throughout his life, he found intimations of how chance events which were of the greatest importance to him carried a secret meaning, and in the end he wrote: "There is no more chance."

At the limits of life's possibilities came not any heavy seriousness, but rather a complete lightness as the expression of their knowledge, and both used the image of the dance. In the last decade of his life Nietzsche, in ever-changing forms, used the dance as a metaphor for his thought, where it is original. And Kierkegaard said, "I have trained myself . . . always to be able to dance in the service of thought. . . . My life begins as soon as a difficulty shows up. Then dancing is easy. The thought of death is a nimble dancer. Everybody is too serious for me." Nietzsche saw his archenemy in the "spirit of seriousness"—in morals, science, purposefulness, etc. But to conquer seriousness meant not to reject it for the thoughtlessness of arbitrary caprice, but rather to pass through the most serious to an authentic soaring, the triumph of which is the free dance.

The knowledge that they were exceptions prevented either from stepping forth as prophets. To be sure, they seem like those prophets who speak to us out of inaccessible depths but who speak in a contemporary way. Kierkegaard compared himself to a bird which foretells rain: "When in a generation, a thunderstorm begins to threaten, individuals like me appear." They are prophets who must conceal themselves as prophets. They were aware of their problem in a continual return from the extremities of their demands to a rejection of any idea which would make them models or ways of life. Kierkegaard repeated innumerable times that he was not an authority, or a prophet, apostle, or reformer, nor did he have the authority of position. His problem was to awaken men. He had a certain police talent, to be a spy in the service of the divinity. He uncovered, but he did not assert what should be done. Nietzsche wanted to "awaken the highest suspicion against himself," explaining that "to the humanity of a teacher belongs the duty of warning his students against himself." What he wanted he let Zarathustra say who left his disciples with: "Go away from me, and turn yourselves against me." And, even in *Ecce Homo,* Nietzsche says: "And finally, there is nothing in me of the founder of a religion. . . . I want no believers. . . . I have a terrible anxiety that some day, they will speak reverently of me. I will not be a saint, rather a Punch. Maybe I am Punch."

There is in both a confusing polarity between the appearance of an absolute and definite demand and, at the same time, shyness, withdrawal, the appearance of not betting anything. The Seductive, the Perhaps, the Possible is the manner of their discourse; an unreadiness to be a leader was their own attitude. But both lived in secret longing to bring salvation if they could, and if it could be done in human honesty. Accordingly, both toward the end of their lives became daring, desperate, and then, in utter calm, rose to public attack. From then on, the reticence of merely envisaging possibilities was given up for a will to act. Both made a similar attack: Kierkegaard attacked the Christianity of the church; Nietzsche attacked Christendom as such. Both acted with sudden force and merciless resolution. Both attacks were purely negative actions: deeds from truthfulness, not for the construction of a world.

The significance of Kierkegaard and Nietzsche first becomes clear through what followed in consequence. The effect of both is immeasurably great, even greater in general thinking than in technical philosophy, but it is always ambiguous. What Kierkegaard really meant is clear neither in theology, nor in philosophy. Modern Protestant theology in Germany, when it is genuine, seems to stand under either a direct or indirect influence of Kierkegaard.

A profile drawing.

But Kierkegaard with regard to practical consequences of his thought wrote in May, 1855, a pamphlet with the motto, "But at midnight there is a cry" (Matthew 25:6), where he says: "By ceasing to take part in the official worship of God as it now is . . . thou hast one guilt less, . . . thou dost not participate in treating God as a fool, calling it the Christianity of the New Testament, which it is not."

In modern philosophy several decisive themes have been developed through Kierkegaard. The most essential basic categories of contemporary philosophizing, at least in Germany, go back to Kierkegaard—Kierkegaard whose whole thought however appeared to dissolve all previous systematic philosophy, to reject speculation, and who, when he recognized philosophy, said at most: "Philosophy can pay attention to but cannot nourish us."

It might be that theology, like philosophy, when it follows Kierkegaard is masking something essential in order to use his ideas and formulas for its own totally different purposes.

It might be that within theology there is an unbelief which employs the refined Kierkegaardian intellectual techniques of dialectical paradox to set forth a kind of creed which can be understood, and which believes itself the genuine Christian faith.

It might be that philosophizing in the fashion of Kierkegaard secretly nourishes itself on the substance of Christianity, which it ignores in words.

The significance of Nietzsche is no clearer. His effect in Germany was like that of no other philosopher. But it seems as though every attitude, every world-view, every conviction claims him as authority. It might be that none of us really knows what this thought includes and does.

The problem, therefore, for everyone who allows Kierkegaard and Nietzsche to influence him, is to become honest about how he really comes to terms with them, what they are to him, what he can make out of them.

Their common effect, to enchant and then to disillusion, to seize and then leave one standing unsatisfied as though one's hands and heart were left empty—such is only a clear expression of their own intention: that everything depends upon what their reader by his own inner action makes out of their communication, where there is no specific content as in the special sciences, works of art, philosophical systems, or some accepted prophecy. They deny every satisfaction.

In fact, they are exceptions and not models for followers. Whenever anyone has tried to imitate Kierkegaard or Nietzsche, if only in style, he has become ridiculous. What they did themselves at moments approaches the limit where the sublime passes into the ridiculous. What they did was only possible once. To be sure, everything great is unique, and can never be repeated identically. But there is something essentially different in our relation to this uniqueness: and this whether we live through them, and, by making them our own, revive them, or see them through the distance of an orientation which changes us but makes them more remote.

They abandon us without giving us any final goals and without posing any definite problems. Through them, each one can only become what he himself is. What their consequences are is not yet decided even today. The question is: how those of us shall live who are not exceptions but who are seeking our inner way in the light of these exceptions.

We are in that cultural situation where the application of this knowledge already contains the kernel of dishonesty. It is as though through them we were forced out of a certain thoughtlessness, which without them would have remained even in the study of great philosophers. We can no longer tranquilly proceed in the continuity of a traditional, intellectual education. For through Kierkegaard and Nietzsche a mode of existential experience has become effective, whose consequences on all sides have not yet come to light. They posed a question which is not yet clear but which one can feel; this question is still open. Through them we have become aware that for us there is no longer any self-evident foundation. There is no longer any secure background for our thought.

For the individual working with them, there are two equally great dangers: really to encounter them and not to take them seriously at all. Unavoidably, one's attitude toward them is ambivalent. Neither constructed a world, and both seemed to have destroyed everything; yet both were positive spirits. We must achieve a distinctively new relation to the creative thinker if we are really to approach them otherwise than we would any great man.

With respect to our epoch and the thought of Kierkegaard and Nietzsche, if we pose the question, what now? then Kierkegaard points in the direction of an absurd Christianity before which the world sinks away, and Nietzsche points to the distance, the indeterminate, which does not appear to be a substance out of which we can live. Nobody has accepted their answers; they are not ours. It is for us to see what will become of us through ourselves as we look upon them. This is, however, in no way to sketch out or establish anything in advance.

Thus we would err if we thought we could deduce what must now happen from a world-historical survey of the development of the human spirit. We do not stand outside like a god who can survey the whole at a glance. For us, the present cannot be replaced by some supposed world history out of which our situation and problems would emerge. And this lecture has no intention of surveying the whole, but rather of making the present situation perceptible by reflecting upon the past. Nobody knows where man and his thinking are going. Since existence, man, and his world are not at an end, a completed philosophy is as little possible as an anticipation of the whole. We men have plans with finite ends, but something else always comes out which no one willed. In the same way, philosophizing is an act which works upon the inwardness of man, but whose final meaning he cannot know. Thus the contemporary problem is not to be deduced from some a priori whole; rather it is to be brought to consciousness out of a basis which is now experienced and out of a content still unclearly willed. Philosophy as thought is always a consciousness of Being which is complete for this moment, but which knows it has no final permanence in its form of expression. (pp. 23-48)

> *Karl Jaspers, "The Origin of the Contemporary Philosophic Situation: The Historical Meaning of Kierkegaard and Nietzsche," in his* Reason and Existenz: Five Lectures, *translated by William Earle, The Noonday Press, 1955, pp. 19-50.*

T. W. Adorno   (essay date 1939)

[*A German-born philosopher, literary and cultural critic, musicologist, and sociologist, Adorno greatly influenced the intellectual foundations of revolutionary thought in postwar Europe. He is closely associated with the Frankfurt Institute for Social Research, a center for Marxist studies, and aided development of the Institute's "Critical Theory." Critical Theory is an approach to the analysis and criticism of philosophies and ideologies intended to allow movement toward an objective and creative view of society untainted by false theories and inherited assumptions. In* Minima Moralia *(1951) and* Dialektik der Aufklärung *(1947;* Dialectic of Enlightenment, *1972), Adorno stated that the arrogant denial of our oneness with nature is the original sin of our society. In the following excerpt, he identifies the related weakness and strength of Kierkegaard's religious doctrine of love as, respectively, the glorification of love displaced to the realm of the abstract and of love uncontaminated by ulterior motives and other mundane flaws.*]

The observations presented in this study are intended to be philosophical rather than historical. They attempt to throw some light on a text of Sören Kierkegaard, concerning the position of basic concepts of religious ethics in the present situation. At the same time I should like to go beyond a mere critical analysis of the text. There may also be some historical interest involved in the analysis, since the work to be discussed is one of Kierkegaard's lesser known writings. As far as I know, it is not accessible in English. It is the book *Leben und Walten der Liebe (Works of Love),* published in 1847, a collection of so-called edifying discourses linked to each other by the concept of Christian love.

Kierkegaard's literary production falls into two distinctly separate parts, the philosophical writings and the religious sermons. This rough and schematic division is justified in Kierkegaard's case: justified by himself. Whereas all his philosophical writings were published anonymously—even those with the open theological tendencies of his later period, such as the *Krankheit zum Tode (Sickness unto Death)* and the *Einübung im Christentum (Training in Christianity)*—he published the religious sermons under his own name. This distinction was made most methodically. He alternated between these two methods of publication from the very beginning of his literary career, since *Entweder/Oder (Either/Or).* He was guided in this procedure by the basic idea that one ought to lure man into Truth. That is to say, truth, according to Kierkegaard, is no "result," no objectivity independent of the process of its subjective appropriation, but really consists in the process of subjective appropriation itself. In his philosophical writings, Kierkegaard goes so far as to say that subjectivity is the truth. This sentence is not, of course, to be understood in the sense of philosophical subjectivism, such as Fichte's, of whose language it reminds one. Its intrinsic meaning is that Truth exists in the living process of Faith, theologically speaking, in the imitation of Christ. Kierkegaard's philosophical writings attempt to express this process of existential appropriation through its different stages—which he calls aesthetic, ethical and religious—and to guide the reader by the dialectics of these stages to the theological truth. But he deemed it necessary to contrast as the "corrective" to this process the positive Christianity which one should achieve, though Kierkegaard never pretended to have achieved it himself. This contrast is provided by religious sermons. One may safely assume that Kierkegaard, who did not share philosophy's optimism of being able to produce the Absolute from itself, rebuffed this optimism even where his own philosophy was involved. In other words, he did not believe that a pure movement of thought could possibly lead up to Christianity, but only, in Kierkegaard's language, to the border of Christianity. He regards that Christian standpoint as being based on revelation. Hence, it maintains a transcendence of the movement of thought which does not permit philosophy to reach Christianity by a procedure of gradual transitions. According to this conviction, the Christian, from the very beginning, must face philosophy independently and distinctly. With Kierkegaard philosophy assumes the paradoxical task of regaining the lost position of an *Ancilla theologiae* and, in the last analysis, must abdicate. One may just as easily formulate the relation in the reverse way. The idea of a reason which attains the Absolute not by maintaining itself in complete consistency of thinking, but by sacrificing itself, indicates not so much the expropriation of philosophy by theology as the transplantation of theology into the philosophical realm. Indeed, the Christian, as a stage, fits perfectly into the hierarchy of Kierkegaard's philosophy, and all the categories which Kierkegaard regards as specifically Christian appear within the context of his philosophical deductions. They are, as it were, invested only post festum with the insignia of Christian revelation. This is particularly true of the doctrine of the radically different, of the qualitative jump, and of the paradox. These questions, however, can be settled only in connection with an actual text of Kierkegaard's.

The text to be discussed here has a particular bearing upon these questions. What is introduced here as an exegesis of Christian Love, is revealed, through a more intimate knowledge of Kierkegaard's philosophy, as supplementing his negative theology with a positive one, his criticism with something edifying in the literal sense, his dialectics with simplicity. It is this very aim which makes Kierkegaard's sermons such tiresome and unpleasant reading. At every point, they bear the hallmarks of his trend of thought. Yet at the same time, they deny this strain and affect a sort of preaching naiveté. This naiveté, being produced dialectically and by no means primarily, threatens to slip into loquacious boredom at any moment. Verbosity is the danger of all Kierkegaard's writings. It is the verbosity of an interminable monologue which, so to speak, does not tolerate any protest and continually repeats itself, without any real articulation. This loquaciousness is intensified in his religious writings to the point of being painful. A Hegelian philosopher deliberately talks circumstantially, imagining himself a Socrates conducting his conversations in the streets of Athens. There is reason to suspect that even the pain and the boredom are planned by the cunning theologian, as Kierkegaard repeatedly styled himself. If the philosophical writings wish to "cheat" the reader into truth, the theological ones, in turn, wish to make it as difficult, as uninteresting, as insipid to him as possible. In one passage of the **Works of Love,** Kierkegaard says that he actually intends to warn us against Christianity. It is one of the basic aims of all his writings to rejuvenate Christianity into what it was supposed to have been during St. Paul's times: a scandal to the Jews and a folly to the Greeks. The scandal is Kierkegaard's Christian paradox. The folly to the Greeks, however, is the laborious simplicity which Kierkegaard stubbornly upholds throughout the religious sermons.

A brief summary of the book on Love is pertinent at this point. Kierkegaard speaks of Christian Love for man, but in pointed contrast to natural love. He defines love as Christian, if it is not "immediate" or "natural," or as Kierkegaard puts it, if one loves each man for God's sake and in a "God-relationship." Kierkegaard never concretely states what this love means. He comments upon it only by means of analogy. Negatively, however, his concept of love is distinct enough. He regards love as a matter of pure inwardness. He starts from the Christian command "Thou shalt love." He interprets this command by emphasizing its abstract generality. Speaking exaggeratedly, in Kierkegaard's doctrine of Love the object of love is, in a way, irrelevant. According to Kierkegaard, the differences between individual men and one's attitude towards men are, in the Christian sense, of no importance whatever. The only element of "this man" which is of interest to the Christian is "the human," as revealed in this person. In love, the other person becomes a mere "stumbling block" to subjective inwardness. This has no object in the proper sense, and the substantial quality of love is "object-less." In Kierkegaard's doctrine the "Christian" content of love, its justification in eternity, is determined only by the subjective qualities of the loving one, such as disinterestedness, unlimited confidence, unobtrusiveness, mercifulness, even if one is helpless oneself, self-denial and fidelity. In Kierkegaard's doctrine of love, the individual is important only with respect to the universal human. But the universal consists in the very fact of individualization. Hence love can grasp the universal only in love for the individual, but without yielding to the differences between individuals. In other words, the loving one is supposed to love the individual particularities of each man, but regardless of the differences between men. Any "preference" is excluded with a rigor comparable only to the Kantian Ethics of Duty. Love, for Kierkegaard, is Christian only as a "breaking down" of nature. It is, first of all, a breaking down of one's own immediate inclination which is supposed to be replaced by the God-relationship. Hence the Kierkegaardian love applies to the farthest as well as to the nearest. The concept of the neighbor which Kierkegaard makes the measure of love is, in a certain sense, that of the farthest: whomever one happens to meet is contrasted, in the very abstractness of such a possibility, with the "preference" for the friend or for the beloved one. Kierkegaard's love is a breaking down of nature, moreover, as a breaking down of any individual interest of the lover, however sublimated it may be. The idea of happiness is kept aloof from this love as its worst disfigurement. Kierkegaard even speaks of the happiness of eternity in such gloomy tones that it appears to consist of nothing but the giving away of any real claim to happiness. Finally, this doctrine of love is a breaking down of nature by demanding from the simple lover the same characteristics Kierkegaard's doctrine of Faith demands from the summit of consciousness. The *credo quia absurdum* is translated into the *amo quia absurdum.* Thus Kierkegaard admonishes the loving person to maintain faith in a once beloved person, even if this faith has lost any rational justification. He ought to believe in the person in spite of any psychological experience which is taboo, according to Kierkegaard, as being "secular." Here, the transformation of love into mere inwardness is striking. This Christian love cannot be disappointed, because it is practiced for the sake of God's command to Love. The rigorousness of the love advocated by Kierkegaard partially devaluates the beloved person. There is a line of Goethe: *Wenn ich dich liebe, was geht's dich an*—if I love you, what concern is it of yours? Kierkegaard would certainly have rejected this dictum as "aesthetic": one may say that it is the implicit theme of the "Tagebuch des Verführers" ("Diary of the Seducer"). This "erotic immediacy," however, reproduces itself, as it were, in Kierkegaard's religious doctrine of love. It is of no concern, to the Christian beloved one, whether or not he is loved. He has no power over this love. Incidentally, the reproduction of Kierkegaard's "aesthetic" standpoint in his religious stage, for which this example has been given, recurs throughout his work. It is unnecessary to point out how close this love comes to callousness. Perhaps one may most accurately summarize Kierkegaard's doctrine of love by saying that he demands that love behave towards all men as if they were dead. Indeed, the book culminates in the speech *Wie wir in Liebe Verstorbener gedenken* (How to think with love of those who passed away). There is good reason to regard this speech as one of the most important pieces he ever wrote. I should like to emphasize, even at this point, that the death-like aspect of Kierkegaard's love comprises the best and the worst of his philosophy. The attempt to explain this will be made later.

Theologians will not overlook the close connection of this doctrine of love with the wording of the Gospel and also with certain Christian traditions such as the distinction between Eros and Agape. But nor will they overlook the transformation of these motives, which it is difficult to call anything but demonic. The overstraining of the transcendence of love threatens, at any given moment, to become transformed into the darkest hatred of man. Similarly, the humiliation of the human spirit before God comes close to the naked hybris of the same spirit. By means of its radical inwardness, it is prone to conceive itself as the sole ground of the world. In spite of all the talk of the neighbor, the latter is nothing but the stumbling-block to prove one's own creative omnipotence as one of love. The forces of annihilation are scarcely tamed by this doctrine of love. The relapse into mythology and the lordly demonology of asceticism is enhanced by Kierkegaard's reckless spiritualization of love. He sets out to expel nature with a pitchfork, only to become Nature's prey himself. Let us take Kierkegaard's interpretation of the command "Thou shalt love." In its proper place, this command means the suspension of universal "justice." It "sublates" the concept of moral life as a closed interrelation of guilt and punishment insofar as they are regarded as equivalents which can be exchanged for one another. Christian love takes a stand against the mythological notion of destiny as one of an infinite relationship of guilt. It protests against the justice—an eye for an eye, a tooth for a tooth—in the name of Grace. The Christian "Thou shalt love" puts a stop to the mythical law of atonement. Kierkegaard, too, attacks the principle of "an eye for an eye, a tooth for a tooth." But he hardly ever mentions the idea of grace. He "mythifies" the "Thou shalt love" itself. I have previously stated that it means, in its Christian sense, the barrier against the universal relationship of atonement. Kierkegaard does not understand it as such a barrier. He makes it dialectical in itself. The Hegelian in Kierkegaard dwells on the contradiction of the "Thou shalt" of the command and its content: love cannot be commanded. This very impossibility becomes to him the core of the command. "Thou shalt love" just because the "Shalt" cannot be applied to love. This is the absurd, the wreckage of the finite by the infinite which Kierkegaard hypostatizes. The command to love is commanded because of its impossibility. This, however, amounts to nothing less than the annihilation of love and the installment of sinister domination. The command to love degenerates into a mythical taboo against preference and natural love. The protest of love against law is dropped. Love itself becomes a matter of mere law, even

if it may be cloaked as the law of God. Kierkegaard's super-Christianity tilts over into paganism.

By so doing, Kierkegaard's doctrine of love offers itself to the smuggest sort of criticism. It is one single provocation, folly in reality and scandal. As far as my knowledge of the literature goes, only Christoph Schrempf has dealt with the doctrine of love in detail. As a matter of fact, he honorably stumbles at every stone Kierkegaard throws in his way. He objects to Kierkegaard on the ground that he neglects the preceding internal relationship between two persons, which he regards the necessary condition of love. He further objects in that love cannot be commanded, whereas this very impossibility makes the paradoxical center or perhaps the blind spot in Kierkegaard's doctrine. Opposing Kierkegaard, he defends preference as something beautiful; he attacks the theory of self-denial, maintaining that no lover ever denies himself but just "realizes" himself in love. At this point, I do not wish to judge the truth or falsity of this criticism. The points made by Schrempf are necessary consequences of that demonic "mythification" of Christianity which I have tried to make clear. It is senseless to discuss the theses on the basis of common sense since, according to Kierkegaard, they presuppose the suspension of common sense. But I would go beyond that. In a way, Schrempf's objections are too cursory. Closer examination shows that Kierkegaard's rigorousness which Schrempf naively takes for granted is not quite rigorous. One might almost say: that it is not rigorous enough. Kierkegaard's doctrine of love remains totally abstract. Of course, he repeatedly gives examples such as that of the obedient child. But he always remains on the level of the metaphorical, of illustrations from the treasure of his autobiographical experience, such as the motive of the "poet," or his relation to Regina Olsen. And he never goes into any real, non-symbolical, non-metaphorical case of human love in order to apply his doctrine to it. On the other hand, he always insists on the "practice of real life." His failure to reach this practice by his concepts, and the unyielding abstractness of his doctrine, are symptoms that it is not quite as substantial as it pretends to be. Hence Schrempf's objections bear so little fruit, and it is therefore important critically to analyze the actual presuppositions of Kierkegaard's doctrine. Then I shall try to show the critical elements of Kierkegaard's rigorousness which goes far beyond the limits of that narrowness which it deliberately exhibits.

The main presupposition is the category of the neighbor and the historical changes it has undergone. Let us discuss this more closely. Kierkegaard asks: who is man's neighbor? He answers, according to his idea of absolute inwardness: "The neighbor, strictly speaking, is the reduplication of one's own ego. It is what philosophers would call 'the otherness,' that is, where the selfish element in one's love for oneself is to be revealed. As far as the abstract idea is concerned, the neighbor must not even be here." The abstractness of the neighbor, which has been mentioned earlier, is explicitly acknowledged by Kierkegaard. He even makes it a postulate, as an expression of the equality of men in the eyes of God: "The neighbor is everybody . . . He is your neighbor by being your equal before God, but this equality is due unconditionally to every man, and everybody has it unconditionally." Thus the neighbor is reduced to the general principle of the otherness or of the universal human. Therewith, the individual neighbor, despite Kierkegaard's incessant talk of "that particular individual" (hiin Enkelte, dieser Einzelne) definitely assumes the character of contingency. "When you open the door behind which you have prayed to God and walk out, the first man whom you see is the neighbor whom thou shalt love." The particular reality which I encounter in my neighbor is thus rendered totally accidental. This implies one thing from the very beginning: that I must accept the neighbor whom I happened to meet as something *given* which ought not to be questioned: "To love thy neighbor means to be essentially and unconditionally present to each person according to the particular position in time given to him"—given to him externally, independent of oneself. In other words, Kierkegaard's doctrine of the neighbor presupposes a providence or, as Kierkegaard states, a "governance" which regulates human relationships and gives one a certain person and no other as a neighbor. In one passage, he frankly demands that one should "put oneself in the place where one may be used by governance." This necessarily gives rise to the objection of how one can maintain the concept of the practice of real life as a measuring rod of the love for the neighbor, if one excludes from this practice the specific being of the world? How is practice possible without the acting person's initiative in the very sphere that Kierkegaard takes for granted as a matter of Providence? It is of particular interest to observe how Kierkegaard surreptitiously raises this objection against himself and how he compromises with it. This happens in the discourse on mercifulness. Here he puts the question to himself of how the love to the neighbor is possible, if the loving person is powerless; that is to say, if this love cannot alter reality given by "Providence." The method he makes use of is exceedingly characteristic. For he is struck by the fact that this possibility of powerless love of the neighbor is actually not thought of in the Gospels. Hence he employs a device hardly compatible with his orthodox dogmatism. He modifies, as it were, biblical parables, in order to make them fit present reality. He tells the story of the Samaritan with the alternation that the Samaritan is incapable of saving the unfortunate man. Or he assumes that the sacrifice of the poor widow, which is supposed to be worth more than that of the rich, has been stolen without her being aware of it. Of course he maintains that her behavior is still that of true love. I should like to emphasize the configuration of the motives at hand. Pure inwardness is made the only criterion of action at the very moment at which the world no longer permits an immediate realization of love. Kierkegaard is unaware of the demonic consequence that his insistence on inwardness actually leaves the world to the devil. For what can loving one's neighbor mean, if one can neither help him nor interfere with a setting of the world which makes such help impossible? Kierkegaard's doctrine of impotent mercifulness brings to the fore the deadlock which the concept of the neighbor necessarily meets today. The neighbor no longer exists. In modern society, the relations of men have been "reified" to such an extent that the neighbor cannot behave spontaneously to the neighbor for longer than an instant. Nor does the mere disposition of love suffice to help

the neighbor. Nothing is left to "that particular individual" but to cope with the very presuppositions which Kierkegaard excludes from practice as a product of providence. Kierkegaard denies reification. As a matter of fact the whole personalism of his philosophy aims at this denial, for a thing, "an object is always something dangerous, if one has to move forward. An object, being a fixed point in a finite world, is a barrier and break and therewith a dangerous thing for infinity. For love can become an 'object' to itself only by becoming something finite." In other words, it becomes impossible, if, on the basis of the material presuppositions of their relations, men have become objects, as is the case in our epoch. One could even go further. The form in which the concept of the neighbor is used by Kierkegaard is a reification itself compared with the Gospels. The neighbor of the Gospels implies fishermen and peasants, herdsmen and publicans, people whom one knows and who have their established locus in a life of simple production which can be realized adequately by immediate experience. One cannot imagine the Gospels taking the step from this concrete, unproblematic neighbor to the abstract, universal idea of neighborhood. Kierkegaard has the abstract concept of man of his own period and substitutes it for the Christian neighbor who belongs to a different society. Hence, he deprives both of their sense. The Christian neighbor loses the concreteness which alone made it possible to behave concretely towards him. Modern man is deprived of the last chance of love by moulding love after the pattern of frugal conditions which are not valid any longer. This contradiction is mastered only by Kierkegaard's stubborn maintenance of the "givenness" of social order. The maintenance is socially conformist and ready to lend its arm to oppression and misanthropy. Kierkegaard demands that one should "find the given or chosen object worthy of one's love." Such a demand is not only impossible to fulfill; by its acceptance of the given, it acknowledges the very same reification of man against which Kierkegaard's doctrine of love is directed. It is evident that Kierkegaard here follows the Lutheran doctrine of absolute obedience to the authority of the State. In the face of Kierkegaard's radical theological subjectivism, however, this spiteful orthodoxy leads to absurd inconsistencies and even to insincerity. The presuppositions of this doctrine of the neighbor and, at the same time, of love itself, are untenable.

A doctrine of love which calls itself practical cannot be severed from social insight. Such an insight is denied to Kierkegaard. Instead of any real criticism of inequality in society, he has a fictitious, merely inward doctrine of equality:

> Christianity . . . has deeply and eternally impressed the kinship between man and man. Christianity establishes it by teaching that in Christ each particular individual is equally akin to God and stands in the same relation to God. For Christianity teaches each individual without any difference that he is created by God and redeemed by Christ.

Sometimes Kierkegaard's way of speaking of the equality of men before God assumes the character of involuntary irony: "The times are gone when only the powerful and noble ones were men and the other people slaves and serfs." The irony cannot escape Kierkegaard's attention. He uses it as a medium of his religious paradox. With some haughtiness, he says: "Christianity simply does not enter into such things. It applies eternity and is at once at its goal. It leaves all differences in existence, yet teaches eternal equality." The more liberty and equality are interiorized, the more they are denounced in the external world:

> Externally everything, so to speak, remains as it was before. The man is to be the wife's lord and she is to be subservient to him. Within the inwardness, however, everything is changed, changed by this little question to the wife, if she consulted her conscience whether she wants this man as her lord . . . What Christ said of this realm, that it is not of this world, applies to everything Christian. Foolish people have tried foolishly, in the name of Christianity, to make it secularly manifest that the wife is empowered with the same rights as the man. Christian religion never demanded or wished anything of that sort. It has done everything for the woman, if she is ready to content herself in a Christian way with the Christian. If she does not want that, the mean external position she might obtain in the world is nothing but a poor substitute for what she loses.

Such theorems bring to the fore what was hinted at earlier, namely, that in a certain sense Kierkegaard's religious rigorousness is not seriously meant and that it is better to analyze its presuppositions than sentimentally to criticize it. Kierkegaard raises the objection against himself which is due in a state of universal injustice: "Is it not a fundamental demand that there should be every possible help for the needy and that, if possible, want itself should be abolished?" Kierkegaard dismisses this question all too easily: "Eternity says however: there is only one danger: the danger that mercifulness is not practiced. Even if every want had disappeared, it must not have necessarily disappeared through mercifulness. In such a case, the misery that no mercifulness has been practiced would be a greater misery than any other secular one." The following is symptomatic of the flippancy of a rigorousness which is ready to leave everything in its status quo. Kierkegaard is insatiable in condemning the world, worldliness, and its limited worldly aims. He does not hesitate, however, to qualify his own rigorousness as soon as he speaks, as it were, as a social pedagogue. "Indeed, we do not intend to make an adolescent conceited, and to excite him to condemn the world in a quick, busy way." Kierkegaard's ascetic rigorousness is carried through only abstractly. It is soft-pedaled as soon as it could lead to serious conflicts with the "existing" condemned by Kierkegaard in abstracto. At such a moment, wordliness must not be condemned under any circumstances.

Kierkegaard's doctrine of love keeps itself within the existent. Its content is oppression: the oppression of the drive which is not to be fulfilled and the oppression of the mind which is not allowed to question. Kierkegaard's love is a love that takes away instead of giving. Such he formulates himself: "Then the woman was taken from the man's flank and given to him as company; for love and community first takes something away from man before giving anything." But, at the same time, this oppression of the individual implies a criticism of what could be called, in Hegelian language, bad individuality. The individual, in his self-assertion and isolation, is visualized as something contingent and even as a mere veneer. The thesis underlying the present study, the thesis which I should like to put forward for discussion, may be expressed as follows: Kierkegaard's misanthropy, the paradoxical callousness of his doctrine of love enables him, like few other writers, to perceive decisive character features of the typical individual of modern society. Even if one goes so far as to admit that Kierkegaard's love is actually demonic hatred, one may well imagine certain situations where hatred contains more of love than the latter's immediate manifestations. All Kierkegaard's gloomy motives have good critical sense as soon as they are interpreted in terms of social critique. Many of his positive assertions gain the concrete significance they otherwise lack as soon as one translates them into concepts of a right society.

Before going into further detail, I should like to comment on an objection which might be raised at this point. One might consider that the critical insight for which I give Kierkegaard credit is as abstract from the reality as his doctrine of the neighbor. It is possible, perhaps, to attribute this critical insight to his general idea of worldliness, instead of to a specific coinage of it for the present situation. This however, would oversimplify matters. The abstract generality of his doctrine of the neighbor is not altogether voluntary. It is due to a position of constraint: to the incompatibility of the Christian command to love in its pure form with present society. Kierkegaard's philosophy, however, aims in all its stages—even in the aesthetic one—at the "instant," which is supposed to be the paradoxical unity of the historical and the eternal. It is probably uncertain whether Kierkegaard was ever capable of "filling out" this paradox or whether it merely remained a program. This much, however, is certain: as a critic, he actually grasped the instant, that is to say, his own historical situation. It is highly significant that his polemic chef d'oeuvre bears the title *Der Augenblick (The Instant)*. Kierkegaard was Hegelian enough to have a clean-cut idea of history. He is not satisfied by simply contrasting the eternal with an abstract contemporariness which, at any given moment, is supposedly equally far and near to the eternal. He conceives history to be related to Christianity. His concept of this relation, however, turns the Hegelian idea of the self-realization of the world-spirit upside down. To him the history of Christianity is, roughly speaking, the history of an apostasy from Christianity. He contrasts the conviction of the loss of all human substance to the current conviction of progress, or rather, he conceives progress itself as the history of advancing decay. It is at this point that critics of modern culture such as Karl Kraus followed Kierkegaard most closely. Kierkegaard regards the criticism of progress and civilization: as the criticism of the reification of man. He belongs to the very few thinkers of his epoch (apart from him I know only Edgar Allan Poe and Baudelaire) who were aware of the truly chthonian changes undergone by men, as it were, anthropologically, at the beginning of the modern industrial age: by human behavior and the total setting of human experience. It is this awareness which invests Kierkegaard's critical motives with their genuine earnestness and dignity. His *Works of Love* contains an extraordinary testimony to that awareness. For here Kierkegaard gives an account of a tendency in today's mass society which, during his time, must have been very latent: the substitution of spontaneous thinking by "reflectory" adaptation taking place in connection with modern forms of mass information. Kierkegaard's hatred of the mass, however conservatively it styles itself, contains something of an inkling of the mutilation of men by the very mechanisms of domination which actually change men into a mass. "It is as if the time of thinkers had gone." The following quotation most clearly shows Kierkegaard's realization of the abolition of thinking by information and "conditioned reflexes":

> All communication is supposed to assume the comfortable tone of the easy pamphlet or to be supported by falsehood after falsehood. Indeed, it is as if, in the last instance, every communication ought to be manipulated in such a way as to make it possible to promulgate it in an hour's time at a public meeting. Half an hour is spent in noisy expressions of applause and opposition, and during the other half hour one is so dizzy that one is incapable of collecting one's own thoughts.

Kierkegaard, in speaking of the mass meetings of the 1848 period, seems to have heard those loudspeakers which filled the Berlin Sportspalast one hundred years later.

To return to the social aspect of Kierkegaard's doctrine of love, let me give the following examples. Kierkegaard, to be certain, does not touch on secular injustice and inequality. But the misanthrop Kierkegaard has a very sharp eye for discovering them—the eye of love, one should say. He suspects, for example, that the doctrine of civic equality has an ideological element. He is familiar with the fact that members of different classes who behave towards each other in the name of Christianity as if they were nothing but men, do so, generally, only in order to maintain the fiction of civic equality and thus better to reserve civic inequality. Kierkegaard is full of mockery for what he calls "welfare"—a mockery which easily can be understood as plainly reactionary. But by denouncing the worldly happiness which is aimed at through welfare as something poor compared with eternity, he does not merely mean a postponement ad Kalendas Graecas. He knows something of the wretchedness of that very happiness welfare provides to men. This becomes particularly evident in a demand that Kierkegaard raises again and again: "In order to get into a relation with the Christian, one must first become sober." Of course, the demand of soberness first takes something away: the happiness gained through drunken ecstasy. But does not this happiness only cheat us of another happiness which is absolutely denied to us in the world as it is? Kierkegaard's demand for sobriety is not that of the Philistine. It attacks the shams of mere individuality, the making absolute of accidental "differences," and all the false happiness connected with them. Behind this sobriety lies the profound knowledge that in the last analysis the differences between men are not deci-

sive. For all the features of individualization and specification owe their very existence to the universal injustice which makes this man thus and not otherwise—whereas he could be different.

The significance of "could be different" is the measure of the "taking away" of Kierkegaard's love. The counter-concept that he contrasts to the worldly which he intends taking away is that of possibility. The possibility, according to Kierkegaard, is to be maintained against mere existence. He means by that the paradox Eternal, the Christian *absurdum*. But it is directed at the same time against the typical character I mentioned previously: the character which is no longer capable of the experience of possibility. The theory of possibility is, first of all, directed against knowledge, particularly against empirical knowledge. This, however, is not to be taken as "anti-intellectual." The knowledge against which Kierkegaard struggles is the knowledge of the man who is positive as regards what has taken place since the beginning of the world and what will take place for all the future. It is the knowledge of mere after-construction, the principle of which excludes anything radically new. This is the point attacked by Kierkegaard's criticism of psychology and, as one would call it today, of positivism. To him, psychology is distrust of the possibility. He formulates his attitude towards it as follows: "What is the enticing secret of distrust? It is an abuse of knowledge: by a resolute ergo, that one transforms knowledge into faith. As if this ergo were nothing! As if it ought not to be noticed at all, for everyone has the same knowledge and necessarily draws the same conclusion from it, as if it were eternally certain and settled that pre-existing knowledge necessarily determines the act of inference." Against this knowledge there is possibility which he interprets as hope. Hope is, according to Kierkegaard, the "sense for the possibility." "But the hope that remained did so only with the loving one." "The man who knows mankind, who knows its past and future, has a secret affinity to Evil. To believe nothing at all is the very border where the belief in evil begins. For the good is the object of the belief and therefore whoever believes nothing is ready to believe the bad." Kierkegaard goes even beyond that. Fundamentally (and this reveals an Utopian tendency aided even by his conservatism which denies it) he cannot even imagine that one could breathe for one moment without the consciousness of possibility, that is to say, without hope of the transfiguration of the world. "Truly, anyone who does not wish to understand that man's entire life-time is the time of hope, is in despair." The worldliness that Kierkegaard wants to "remove" is actually the stage of despair. Kierkegaard has introduced the concept of the existential seriousness into philosophy. In the name of hope, he becomes the foe of seriousness itself, of the absorption by practical aims which is not suspended by the thought of what is possible. The following passage could very well be used against Kierkegaard's present successors, the German existential philosophers, particularly against Heidegger. Nothing serves to better differentiate between Kierkegaard and his heirs than his turning against "seriousness."

> Alas, how often reconciliation has failed, because one handled the matter too seriously and

also because one did not learn from God the art (which one must learn from God) of achieving something with deep inner seriousness and yet as easily and playfully as truth permits. Never believe that seriousness is peevishness; never believe that the distorted face which makes you sick is seriousness. No one can know seriousness unless he has learnt from seriousness that one can be too serious.

The seriousness rejected by Kierkegaard is the bourgeois seriousness of business and competition: "They judge that such a man"—that is, one who hopes—"is not serious. Making money, however, is serious. To make a great deal of money, even through the slave-trade, is serious. To promulgate some truth, if one makes ample money by doing so, (since this and not the truth matters): is serious." Kierkegaard's doctrine of hope protests against the seriousness of a mere reproduction of life which mutilates man. It protests against a world which is determined by barter and gives nothing without an equivalent.

Kierkegaard's view of our love for the dead derives from this protest. I have already mentioned that it is both the worst and the best part of his doctrine of love. Perhaps an explanation can now be attempted. The bad side is obvious: love for the dead is the one which most rigidly excludes the reciprocity of love that necessarily takes the beloved one as living himself. Thus it appears to be the reified and fetish love kat'exochen. But, at the same time, it is love absolutely void of any barter, of any "requital," and, therefore, the only unmutilated love permitted by our society. The paradox that the only true love is love for the dead is the perfect expression of our situation. Let me try to interpret the real experience behind Kierkegaard's theology of love for the dead in the words of a secular philosopher of our own time:

> On the death bed, when death is certainty, the rich and the poor are alike in many regards. For with death a man loses his "relationships": he becomes nothing. The proudest kings of France had to have this experience. The enlightened and humane physician who tries to help the lonely dying man in the hour of his last ordeal, not for the sake of economic or technical interest but out of pity—this physician represents the citizen of a future society. His situation is the present image of a true humanity.

What Kierkegaard says of God as the last one who remains with the dying man is in deepest accordance with the "present image" of a true humanity, however little Kierkegaard might have interpreted his idea of the Eternal as such an image.

I should like to conclude with a selection of passages from that sermon **"Wie wir in Liebe Verstorbener gedenken"** (**"How to Think in Love of Those Who Passed Away"**). After the above remarks, they hardly need any interpretation. Kierkegaard calls death the "powerful thinker who does not only think through any sense illusion down to the bottom, but actually thinks to the bottom." This reminds one of that poem of Baudelaire's which invokes Death as *vieux capitaine*. The relation to the dead is characterized as one free of aims:

Truly, if you thoroughly wish to ascertain, how much love is in you or in another person: watch only the behavior to a dead one . . . For the dead man is cunning. He has really drawn himself totally out of any entanglements. He has not the slightest influence which could aid or hinder his opposite neighbor, the loving one . . . That we think lovingly of those who passed away is a deed of truly unselfish love.

Kierkegaard describes mourning as follows: "We must not disturb the dead by wailing and crying. We must treat a dead person as a sleeper whom we do not dare to awaken, because we hope he will awake voluntarily . . . No, we ought to think of him who passed away, we ought to weep softly but weep for a long, long time." Kierkegaard realizes the enigmatic interweaving of death and childhood: "It is true that he does not cause any troubles, as the child sometimes does. He is not the cause of any sleepless nights, at least not by the troubles he causes. For, oddly enough, the good child causes no sleepless nights; the better the dead man was, however, the more sleepless nights he causes." To Kierkegaard's contemplation, even death assumes the expression of paradox. The thesis is:

> Yes, the loving memory must . . . defend itself against reality, lest reality should become too powerful by ever new impressions and blot out the memory. It also has to struggle against time. In brief, it must not allow itself to be induced to forget and must fight for the liberty of maintaining memory in love. . . . Certainly, no one is as helpless as the dead man.

Now the opposite:

> For a dead man is very strong though he does not seem so. It is his strength that does not change. And the dead man is very proud. Did you not notice that the proud man tries to show nothing to him whom he holds in most profound contempt; that he does everything to appear absolutely unchanged as if nothing had happened, just in order the more deeply to let down the one held in contempt?

And, finally, the lofty bridge between Kierkegaard's criticism of seriousness and the love for those who have died:

> If it would not sound so merry (as it can sound only to him who does not know what seriousness is) I should say one could put this inscription over the door of the cemetery: "Here no one is urged" or: "We do not urge anybody." And yet I shall say so and shall firmly stick to what I have said. For I have thought so much about death that I know well: no one can talk seriously about death who is incapable of utilizing the cunning lying in death, the whole deep-thinking roguishness of death—the roguishness to resurrection. The seriousness of death is not the seriousness of the eternal. To the seriousness of death belongs this particular awakening, this deep-thinking jesting overtone. Of course, apart from the thought of eternity, it is often an empty, often cheeky jest, but in connection with the thought of eternity, it is what it ought to be; and then, indeed, something radically different from that insipid seriousness. The latter is least of all

capable of conceiving and maintaining something of the tension and bearing of the thought of death.

The hope that Kierkegaard puts against the "seriousness of the eternal" is nothing but the hope of the reality of redemption. (pp. 413-29)

T. W. Adorno, "On Kierkegaard's Doctrine of Love," in Studies in Philosophy and Social Science, *Vol. VIII, No. 3, 1939, pp. 413-29.*

Robert Bretall   (essay date 1946)

[*An American educator and critic, Bretall edited and wrote several works on philosophy. In the following excerpt, he asserts that Kierkegaard regarded the power of his thought and the brilliance of his writings as "by-products" of his ongoing efforts to fulfill the responsibilities of a true Christian.*]

My whole life is an epigram calculated to make people aware.
—THE JOURNALS (1848)

One hundred years ago in the city of Copenhagen there lived a man—"fantastic," eccentric in many of his ways and ideas, deeply sensitive and morally courageous—whom the English-speaking world is now coming to recognize as one of the most important literary figures of the nineteenth century and one of the greatest, most individual thinkers of all time. These are broad claims and they cannot be wholly substantiated by a book like the present one; a certain amount of evidence may, however, be presented for the benefit of those who would like this evidence collected in one volume rather than distributed over some two dozen. Such is the purpose of this anthology.

Kierkegaard's "time" has come; his position in the history of Western thought is in one sense assured. The past decade has seen the publication in English of all his major works, whereas not a single complete translation existed previously. He has been called "the greatest Protestant Christian of the 19th century" [by H. A. Reinhold in "Søren Kierkegaard" in *The Commonweal* XXXV (10 April 1942)] and "the profoundest interpreter of the psychology of the religious life . . . since St. Augustine" [by Reinhold Niebuhr] (to quote only two appraisals out of many). Although the fourteenth edition of the *Encyclopaedia Britannica* has about 125 words on S.K., it may be assumed that the next edition will have several times as many, while the Communists have recently found him worthy of long and violent denunciation.

The tardy recognition of Kierkegaard's genius is attributable, first to the fact that he wrote in a minor language, and secondly to at least two characteristics of the writings themselves: their individuality of form, whereby they resist being pigeonholed in the established literary genres; and their content, which went strongly against the grain of most philosophical and religious thought at the time, and only later could be recognized for its essential modernity. Time and again history has rewarded those who swim against the current and oppose the thought-patterns of their age, rather than those who, in one way or another,

allow themselves to be borne along on the tide of "contemporary thought"; and Kierkegaard's passionate opposition to the intellectualism and aestheticism of his era is paying him rich dividends today.

Almost totally neglected by his contemporaries—or, when he was not neglected, scorned and treated as a dangerous fanatic—Kierkegaard remained in obscurity until more than two decades after his death, when he was discovered by the Danish critic, Georg Brandes. Himself an agnostic—and confirmed in his agnosticism by S.K.'s uncompromising portrayal of Christianity—Brandes saw in the **Concluding Unscientific Postscript** "not only a new book, but a new *kind* of book"; and through Brandes Kierkegaard's fame began to spread through Germany as well as Scandinavia, the complete works being translated into German around the turn of the century. The way had been prepared by Schopenhauer and Nietzsche, and Kierkegaard added new impetus to the great revolt against Hegelian philosophy—though in point of time he had been one of the very first to react against Hegel's intellectualism and to launch the counter-movement in the direction of temporality, concreteness and the "individual." In America William James was a part of this movement, and in France Henri Bergson; but in Germany the new trend took the name of "existentialism," with Kierkegaard—the Kierkegaard of the **Unscientific Postscript**—as its acknowledged

Kierkegaard at his high desk.

forerunner. It is this Existentialism—developed and elaborated by a number of contemporary philosophers, but especially by Karl Jaspers and Martin Heidegger—which is having so extraordinary a vogue in France at the present time.

To point out all this is perhaps unnecessary, and certainly it is un-Kierkegaardian; for if ever a man discounted popularity on principle, it was S.K. He held that to read a man's works because of the reputation he has acquired is to read them in a way that prevents or at least seriously hinders one from reacting to them independently; and in his own life he carried this principle to fantastic extremes. While he was at work night and day on some of his greatest books, he would not fail to put in an appearance at the theater every evening "for just ten minutes, no more," so that people would go on thinking of him as the desperate dilettante he actually had been in his earlier youth. Later on this inverted pretense was dropped; but the only "authority" he ever coveted was the authority his words might have as they echoed through the consciousness of that "solitary individual" to whom they were all dedicated.

Putting aside, therefore, the opinions of others, we may well ask ourselves what foundation there is for considering Kierkegaard one of the intellectually and spiritually great. One quality of his mind is indeed undeniable—viz. its enormous *range*. . . .[Witness the variety:] (1) a masterly short novel, the well known "Diary of the Seducer," together with the humorous part of another novel, *Repetition;* (2) the "Banquet" scene from *Stages on Life's Way,* which has been hailed as the modern counterpart of Plato's *Symposium;* (3) the subtle, abstruse thinking of the *Philosophical Fragments* (an ironical title, as the reader will discover) and its great successor, the *Unscientific Postscript;* (4) the absorbing and astonishingly modern psychology of "despair" in *The Sickness unto Death* [Bretall adds Kierkegaard's other great psychological work, *The Concept of Dread,* in a footnote]; (5) the analysis of "the public" and the levelling process of modern society—an adumbration of Ortega y Gasset's "mass man"—in *The Present Age;* (6) the various beautiful and moving religious discourses, the tone of which moves constantly from impassioned utterance to the strictest dialectic and back again; and finally (7) the terse and biting satire of S.K.'s final period, in *The Attack upon "Christendom"* and many of the *Journal* passages. Further divisions and subdivisions could be made, but these are enough to show in a general way how many strings S.K. had to his bow. Incredible as it may sound, it is difficult to think of any writer, ancient or modern, who had as many—or who used them any more effectively.

For Kierkegaard does not merely cover all of these different fields; he is penetrating in each of them, with the penetration born of his one overmastering desire to become clear about himself through incessant reflection and self-analysis. It was a way that led through suffering known only to himself, though we can appreciate something of what it cost to become "the exception" and to be "sacrificed" for the edification of mankind. It was a way that led

through conflict and the bitterness of estrangement, but it was also a way that led to peace and joy.

> Humanly speaking, what a painful thing thus to be sacrificed! . . . But on the other hand God knows well . . . how to make it so blessed a thing to be sacrificed, that among the thousands of divers voices which express, each in its own way, the same thing, his also will be heard, and perhaps his especially, which is truly *de profundis,* proclaiming: God is love. . . .

S.K. does not want us to be dazzled by the individual excellences—literary, philosophical, or otherwise—which abound in his works; for they are by-products, existing incidentally to the main design of a life which was identical with what it gave to the world—an unbroken fabric whose unity is the more amazing the more we see of its diversity. If purity of heart, in Kierkegaard's beautiful formula, is "to will one thing," then purity of mind is to think one thing—"not to have many thoughts, but to have one thought" (like Socrates, who "always said the same thing") and that one absolute. Early in life he made the discovery that one must "find a truth which is true *for me*—the idea for which I can live and die." When S.K. wrote these words in his *Journal* he already suspected what his "idea" was, and before long he had become certain. The idea was Christianity; and his one thought was "what it means to be a Christian—in Christendom."

To those who would question this choice of theme—and, having traced the various influences which led S.K. to choose it, perhaps flatter themselves that they had "explained" Kierkegaard and need not trouble themselves about him further—to these gnostics the answer comes in the form of a *tu quoque.* It is impossible to reach an absolute beginning, and there is no such thing as "presuppositionless thought." The man who pretends that his view of life is determined by sheer reason is both tiresome and unperceptive: he fails to grasp the elementary fact that he is not a pure thinker, but an *existing individual.* To one who has chosen Christ, says S.K.:

> the only possible objection would be: but you might possibly have been saved in another way. To that he cannot answer. It is as though one were to say to some one in love, yes, but you might have fallen in love with another girl; to which he would have to answer: there is no answer to that, for I only know that she is my love. The moment a lover can answer that objection he is *eo ipso* not a lover; and if a believer can answer that objection he is *eo ipso* not a believer.

"Existential thinking" begins at a definite point, which others may regard as arbitrary but which is not at all arbitrary for the thinker himself, since it expresses his "ultimate concern" as an existing individual; it is quite simply "the idea for which he would be willing to live and die." And his task is to understand the multiplicity of things from this particular point of view. It is true that Adolf Hitler was an existential thinker, of sorts; so are most of the inmates of insane asylums. To this charge, so frequently brought against existentialism, there is a pragmatic answer—and another answer, which applies to Christianity alone. The pragmatic answer consists simply in pointing out that the false "ultimates" refute themselves in experience: they lead to the disintegration of a personality and not to its unification. The other answer is that Christianity by definition excludes irrationalism: the "choice" here cannot possibly be arbitrary, because it is the choosing of Eternity in time.

Both of these answers are implied in Kierkegaard, yet he would have been loath to use them, for in doing so one steps out of the faith-relationship, which has "objective uncertainty" as its correlate. "The lover who can answer the objection is *eo ipso* not a lover, and the believer who can answer the objection is *eo ipso* not a believer." Knowledge and faith, for Kierkegaard, are polar opposites: knowledge is objectively certain, but it deals only with "the possible," i.e. the hypothetical (cause and effect, condition and conditioned, premise and conclusion); faith is highly uncertain, but only by taking the "leap" and exercising it does one come into contact with actuality—the actuality of one's own being.

> The only reality accessible to any existing individual is his own ethical reality. To every reality outside the individual, even his own *external* reality, his highest valid relation is cognitive; but knowledge is a grasp of the possible and not a realization of the actual; the knowledge of actualities transmutes them into possibilities, and the highest intellectual validity of knowledge is attained in an even balancing of alternative possibilities with an absolutely open mind.

This "even balancing" is what Kierkegaard accomplishes in such works as *Either/Or, Stages on Life's Way, Fear and Trembling,* and *Philosophical Fragments.* In each of these books alternatives are delineated, but no choice is made between them: this is left up to the reader, the "existing individual" for whom alone the choice can have significance. For Kierkegaard to choose on behalf of his readers would be meaningless; this is why he did not want any "disciples." Like Socrates, he employed "indirect communication" when he was dealing in terms of *knowledge;* but in his religious discourses he addresses the reader directly, using every available means to persuade him to become a Christian.

What is it, then, to become a Christian—in Christendom? In *The Point of View for my Work as an Author* S.K. tells us that the whole of his authorship centers about this one question; everything he wrote is relevant to it—even the "Diary of the Seducer"—and he proceeds to show us how. I do not wish to anticipate his explanation here; but briefly, S.K.'s great insight was into the fact that a Christian environment, far from helping one to become a Christian, puts special obstacles in the way, and particularly two—the *aesthetic* obstacle and the *speculative* obstacle.

In the early ages of Christianity, to be a Christian meant to separate oneself from the crowd—to do what was not easy to do, humanly speaking. It meant an effort, it meant sacrifice; it *cost something.* Today, says Kierkegaard, the situation is exactly the opposite: one becomes a Christian by the easiest and most natural of processes. Not only have the sacraments of the Church been formalized to the point where they are little more than social functions (so that

a christening and a cocktail party go hand in hand); but even these formalities are no longer necessary, since it is assumed that "everyone is a Christian" who lives in a "Christian" land. The tragedy that "nowadays all are Christians" is a real one, since the idea of being or becoming a Christian is thereby emptied of the significance it originally had. It is for this reason, and this reason alone, that Kierkegaard attacks "the aesthetic way of life," the way of feeling and enjoyment, the way of "immediacy"; and it is important to realize this. His assault has nothing to do with Puritanism or with any doctrine that pleasure is wrong *per se.* The aesthetic, he said, "has not to be abolished but *dethroned*"; it must cease to be the motivating power of a man's life, and it must be removed from the sanctuary of religion. This again does not mean that one should not take pleasure in worshiping God; it means that the worship must go back to something which is not aesthetic to begin with—not simply "doing the natural thing" in a "Christian" society, or in any way following the path of least resistance. When Christianity is made so attractive that pretty nearly everyone accepts it as a matter of course, then one can be sure it is not true Christianity that is being presented—not the Christianity of Him who made the taking up of one's cross the condition of discipleship.

The second obstacle to becoming a Christian in Christendom is the *speculative* one. Not only may people accept the Gospel (or what they think to be the Gospel) because it is made easy and attractive for them; but they may accept it because it is made to appeal to their intellects as logical or reasonable—i.e. as *sanctioned by human reason.* But "the reasonableness of Christianity" is treason to Christianity because it subjects the self-revelation of the infinite God to finite human standards. Abhorrent to S.K. above all else was the condescending attitude of the Hegelian philosophers of his day, who were continually "going further" than Christianity—i.e. from a supposed higher vantage-point looking down upon such doctrines as the Incarnation and the Atonement and showing that they were indeed true—if one understood them in a certain sense, etc. S.K. felt that one should either give up Christianity altogether—or else accept it as what it claims to be, the ultimate truth about human existence, a truth which man could not have discovered for himself. In order to show that the Hegelians were on the wrong track he brought to the fore the *paradoxical* quality of Christian truth and the fact that, so far from appearing true to the human intellect, it constitutes an "offense" to our intellectual faculty as such. The central notion of the Christian faith—the idea of *God in time*—is purely and simply a contradiction, for God is by definition eternal. The early Christians knew that their faith was not intellectually respectable, and they believed against the understanding; the modern Christian, after hearing the sermon of a Liberal Protestant clergyman or reading a Catholic treatise on "natural theology," is tempted to believe because his understanding assents to what is presented. But to believe because the understanding assents is in reality *not to believe.*

Kierkegaard's treatment of faith *vs.* reason opens up perspectives into the history of philosophy which can hardly be entered here, and I wish merely to suggest that his position is not quite what it may appear to be on the surface.

The advent of Christianity posed a new problem for philosophy, a solution of which was reached in the medieval synthesis of St. Thomas Aquinas: faith and reason were harmonized by carefully delineating their respective spheres. This synthesis was broken up by the centrifugal and individualistic forces of the Renaissance, with the result that reason (in one form or another, patently or disguised) tended to gain the upper hand. This was true of the English Empiricists almost as much as of the great Continental Rationalists Descartes, Spinoza, and Leibnitz; only in the radical skepticism of David Hume does the element of "belief" (very much secularized in form) come to assert itself once more. Kant put an end to the pretensions of the older rationalism, but with his doctrine of the thing-in-itself and the transcendental Ego paved the way for a new and bolder rationalism—that of Hegel. It was against this that S.K. reacted so violently, and for this very reason he sometimes swings to the opposite extreme and appears to be a fideist who would cut himself off completely from the intellect and its claims. Here as elsewhere he was a "corrective," providing the emphasis which was needed at the time; but his considered viewpoint was not fideistic. As we shall see, he himself was capable of the most abstract thinking: in the **Journals** he speaks of using the understanding in order to believe *against* the understanding, and this was precisely his aim. As Lowrie says [in his *A Short Life of Kierkegaard*], he was essentially a "Catholic Christian"—understanding the word "catholic" in its broadest sense as the opposite of sectarianism and one-sidedness of every sort.

But S.K. was also a Protestant, and the whole tenor of his thought points toward a new and distinctively Protestant synthesis, parallel to the medieval Catholic one. In the "philosophical theology" of Paul Tillich we can see the beginnings of such a synthesis, and Tillich's work owes much to Kierkegaard. Without S.K.'s passionate protest against the rationalizing theology of his day, and without his conception of existential thinking, the way to such a synthesis could hardly have been opened.

I am not at all sure, however, that he would appreciate this role. He emphatically did not want to be embalmed and tucked away in "a paragraph of universal history," however important the paragraph might be. His appeal is ever to the living individual, the solitary, concerned individual who, not unmindful of his eternal destiny, seeks an absolute direction for his life amid the relativities of time. To such a one Kierkegaard speaks—indirectly at first, then directly and with mounting eloquence. And such a one can hardly fail to listen. (pp. xvii-xxv)

> *Robert Bretall, in an introduction to* A Kierkegaard Anthology, *edited by Robert Bretall, Princeton University Press, 1946, pp. xvii-xxv.*

Reinhold Niebuhr   (essay date 1951)

[*Niebuhr is considered one of the most important and influential Protestant theologians in twentieth-century America. The author of such works as* The Children of Light and the Children of Darkness *(1944) and* Christian Realism and Political Problems *(1953), he persistently stressed the reality of original sin and emphasized the tragic condition of fallen humanity, opposing the secular and liberal Christian tendency toward discounting sin in favor of economic and political explanations of human misery. Niebuhr saw the problem of modern humanity as one in which an overwhelming sense of confusion and meaninglessness have been brought on by technocracy and the resulting rush for power. In the following excerpt, he criticizes some aspects of Kierkegaard's thought as simplistic or reductive.*]

It is obviously perilous both to the content of the Christian faith and to the interpretation of life to place [extensive] reliance on the coherences and rationalities, the sequences and harmonies, of nature and reason. But the perils in the other direction are vividly displayed in contemporary as well as older Christian existentialism. The primary peril is that the wisdom of the Gospel is emptied of meaning by setting it into contradiction to the wisdom of the world and denying that the coherences and realms of meaning which the cultural disciplines rightfully analyze and establish have any relation to the Gospel.

Kierkegaard's protest against Hegelianism betrays him into a position in which all inquiries into essences, universal forms, are discounted in order to emphasize the existing particular. The existing individual, which is the only particular in history with its own internal history, is made symbolic for particulars, though others have no internal history and therefore no integral individuality, which could be known existentially. They must be known by fitting them into genus and species.

Kierkegaard, furthermore, exploits the inner contradiction within man as free spirit and contingent object too simply as the basis of faith. According to him, the individual, by embracing this contradiction in passionate subjectivity, rather than by evading it, comes truly to himself, chooses himself in his absolute validity. Though the writings of Kierkegaard contain a genuine expression of the Christian faith and are an exposition of the Pauline statement, "That I might know him, no rather that I might be known of him," there are notes in Kierkegaard's thought according to which the self really saves itself by choosing itself in its absolute validity. Sometimes this means that passionate subjectivity becomes the sole test of truth in such a way that a disinterested worship of an idol is preferred to the wrong worship of the true God. This allows for a justified condemnation of a false worship of God, but it also lacks any standard by which the true God could be distinguished from a false one. In other words, a passionate Nazi could meet Kierkegaard's test. There are standards of judgment in Renaissance and liberal universalism which make their ethic preferable to this kind of hazardous subjectivity.

Sometimes Kierkegaard does choose a rigorous universalism to express the ethical life of the self in its absolute validity. In his **Works of Love** Christian love is universal love, expressed as a sense of duty. It is a universalism almost identical with Kant's dictum that we must make our actions the basis of universal law. But there is no grace, no freedom, no release in it. It is full of the sweat of a plodding righteousness, and it hides the fact of the self's continued finiteness.

Both errors, though seemingly contradictory, prove that the problems of life have been solved too simply by embracing the inner contradiction in human existence and not by a genuine commerce of repentance and faith between finite and sinful man and the grace of God. It is a warning that we cannot simply equate the Christian faith with a philosophy which embodies particularity and contradiction rather than one which obscures the particular and the contradictory. (pp. 162-63)

> *Reinhold Niebuhr, "Coherence, Incoherence, and Christian Faith," in* The Journal of Religion, *Vol. XXXI, No. 3, July, 1951, pp. 155-68.*

Aage Henriksen   (essay date 1951)

[*In the following excerpt, Henriksen examines the interpretive difficulty posed by the pseudonymity of Kierkegaard's authorship and enumerates critical approaches to the study of Kierkegaard's works.*]

Within the humanities the relation of parts to totalities has only exceptionally been so clearly or convincingly elucidated that an isolated study of a subject can at the outset be dismissed as valueless. The enquirer's choice of subject, his point of view, must as a rule be regarded as a private matter, which is characteristic of him as a human being more than as a scholar. It is the treatment of the subject, his manner of arguing and combining, his method, which shows his scholarly competence.

Within Kierkegaard-research it is otherwise. Since its beginning there has been disagreement concerning viewpoints as well as methods; most vehement, however, in the case of viewpoints. Søren Kierkgaard himself has most thoroughly prepared the way for this conflict, amongst other things by his book ***The Point of View for my Work as an Author*** which was written in 1848, but published posthumously in 1859. Here he endeavours to show that the individual works of his authorship belong together in an indivisible production, and that his personal life has been subordinate and adjusted to his work as an author in such a way that his life and work appear as a totality, a spiritual complex, whose parts and aspects must not be regarded, and cannot be interpreted, isolatedly, but only as parts of a long spun-out half human, half divine process of reflection, whose organising thought has been to point out, without authority, the Christianity of the New Testament. This attempt by Søren Kierkegaard to create unity in his life work and show the way to future interpreters has produced uncertainty and bewilderment. The disagreement as to what is the proper attitude to assume towards the Kierkegaardian complex, has gone so far that some enquirers have disputed, not only the validity of other enquirers' results, but simply the very existence of a subject concerning which a literature has already grown up. The cause of the confusion now is not only that Søren Kierkegaard's viewpoint for his activity as an author differs considerably from that which his interpreters naturally feel prompted to adopt, but also that Søren Kierkegaard's literary understanding of himself is not constant.

The direct statements concerning his production which he prepared in the 1840s have indeed as their common aim that of uniting and giving perspective, but the unifying ideas change, so that the application of the later excludes the application of the earlier statements.

If, for instance, we try to understand what was Søren Kierkegaard's exact intention in using pseudonyms, we are led to a decisive ambiguity in his self-interpretation. When he began to issue his pseudonymous writings he apparently intended, or it was his intention in principle, to keep his own person entirely outside. When ***Either-Or*** appeared there was, in fact, for some time a doubt as to who had written it, a doubt which Søren Kierkegaard himself sought to strengthen in the article "Who is the Author of ***Either-Or?***", which urges the expediency of the author remaining unknown. Not until February 1846 did he admit in "First and Last Explanation", which is a supplement to ***Unscientific Postscript*** that he was the author of the authors and explain that the essential reason for the pseudonymous machinery was "the production itself, which for the sake of the dialogue, of the psychologically varied difference in the individualities poetically demanded that unconcern in good and evil, in contrition and elation, in despair and arrogance, in suffering and exultation etc. which is only ideally limited by the psychological consequence which no actually existing person within the moral bounds of reality dare permit himself or will want to permit himself." And he alleges that the readers who have summarily identified him with the pseudonyms "really have cheated themselves by getting my personal identity to drag along instead of a poetically-real author's dually reflected light individuality to dance with; paralogistically intruding, have deceived themselves by meaninglessly eliciting my private individuality from the evasive dialectical duality of qualitative contrasts". In ***The Point of View*** we read, however, that the duality in his authorship was from the very outset represented by: ***Either-Or*** and ***Two Edifying Discourses*** and not, as had erroneously been supposed, by the first and second parts of ***Either-Or;*** that "while ***Either-Or*** attracted all the attention and no one heeded ***Two Edifying Discourses,*** these nevertheless meant that it was, precisely, the edifying aspect which was to be brought to the fore, and that the author was a religious author who, therefore, had never himself written anything æsthetic, but used pseudonyms for all the æsthetic works, while the ***Two Edifying Discourses*** were by Magister Kierkegaard"; the pseudonymity is here his incognito for the religious, the duality of the æsthetic and the religious is the sustaining principle of his authorship, and therefore the series of publications, after two years' exclusive religious production, is concluded, "as a testimony and as a precaution, with the small æsthetic article by a pseudonym: Inter et Inter". It is thus emphasised here that the prerequisite for understanding the spirit of his production is the recognition that the contrasts are kept together in one mind. Further Kierkegaard explains in special chapters that he adapted his personal conduct so as to support the effect of the books; when his production was predominantly æsthetic he tried to create the illusion of an idler in the eyes of his readers, later when it was predominantly religious he practised Christian self-denial in all humility.

It appears from this that different functions are assigned to his pseudonymity, and that it is asserted to be carried through with varying degrees of effect. It has two forms, each corresponding to a particular kind of religious tactics; and to make the confusion complete, Kierkegaard calls both kinds indirect communication. In his production up to and including *Unscientific Postscript* indirect communication is contrasted with Hegelian direct communication of objective knowledge, the method being that the narrator, after producing his testimony, destroys himself and leaves the reader deserted with a statement in which qualitative contrasts clash. The reader can only save himself from the dilemma by a personal recognition and solution of the problems. In *The Point of View* the indirect statement is contrasted with the direct preaching, which would lead the hearer to the truth by persuasion. It is interpreted as a method of inveigling him into the truth, by the teacher's pretending to be in the pupil's situation (delusion) and thus achieving personal contact; thereafter he slowly uncovers the truth, so that the learner, absorbed in his interest, with the speed of abandonment, is made to run right into the most decisive precepts of the religion. Hence, in the first case salvation is to come by self-activity, in the second case by imitation, by the current in the works being induced in the reader. In the first instance the pseudonymity is to be taken absolutely, in the second instance as a provisional screen suggesting the author's feeling of estrangement among the æsthetic categories. That one of the very few writings of Søren Kierkegaard which no one attributed to him before he admitted the authorship himself, belongs to the last group, where the unity behind the contrasts was to be divined, is another matter which tells us a good deal of how the *Point of View* came into existence. It was *The Crisis and a Crisis in the Life of an Actress,* the short series of articles from 1848, which was to show that the duality of the æsthetic and the religious was present to the very last; he himself called it pseudonymous, but it was actually anonymous, signed with the mark: Inter et Inter, which presumably can never, or at any rate not in Kierkegaard's sense, be called a pseudonym, that is to say, a poetically real author-individuality.

From this schematic explanation of an ambiguity in his self-interpretations it will be understood that we cannot quite simply adopt Søren Kierkegaard's view of Søren Kierkegaard's production. The opposite procedure of disregarding Søren Kierkegaard's explanations about the importance of the indirect statement for the construction of his work and about the purpose and consequence of the pseudonymity will, however, also entail difficulties and unsatisfactory solutions. Torsten Bohlin, for instance, in his investigation of Søren Kierkegaard's dogmatic views arrives at the result that Kierkegaard, in the books *Philosophical Fragments* and *The Concept of Dread* published with four days' interval, gives two irreconcilable determinations of the concept of sin. It is a matter of surprise to him, an interesting psychological problem that Kierkegaard was able to avoid noticing the contradiction between the two works and the inconsistency in his own thinking. It is undeniable that there is a similarity between Torsten Bohlin pondering on the interesting psychological problem and the contemporary readers of Søren Kierkegaard who "unfamiliar with the courtesies of a distancing ideality, by a mistaken intrusion on my actual personality have garbled their impression of the pseudonymous books, have cheated themselves, really have cheated themselves by getting my personal reality to drag along instead of a poetically real author's dually reflected light ideality to dance with— — —". But if then we follow the author's suggestion "to cite the respective pseudonymous author's name, not mine", then indeed the special problem is solved, but it returns as the problem of the entire production.

It will appear from these examples that whether or not we follow Søren Kierkegaard's directions, we shall have reason to regret both procedures. This is a conclusion drawn on the basis of few observations but which will be confirmed by the succeeding analysis of the main works written about Kierkegaard. A point of view which neither violates the totality nor the separate parts does not seem to have been attained by anybody. The core of the authorship has not been penetrated.

Of the many viewpoints adopted in the course of time three stand out as simple and primary, the remainder being derivatives and combinations of them. The three main points of view group themselves in two pairs of contrasts: opposed to the contention that the study of Søren Kierkegaard should aim at understanding the expression, the literary form, stands the view that the contents of the production, the thoughts and ideas, are the central thing. The group of enquirers who study the contents divide into two formations, one of which maintains that the individual works should be understood as parts of the totality of the production; the other, that it is the history of Søren Kierkegaard's spiritual development which unites the production.

There is no consistent adherence to the formal point of view in Scandinavian research. It has been adopted in Germany by a dialectic school under the direction of the ingenious theologian Hermann Diem. In a treatise entitled "Methode der Kierkegaard Forschung" (the Method of Kierkegaard Research) (*Zwischen den Zeiten* 1928) he sharply maintains the impossibility of arriving at any understanding whatever of Søren Kierkegaard's life work by means of the current comparative and genetic methods. Kierkegaard was an existential dialectician, declares Diem in good agreement with certain statements by Kierkegaard himself; but he had no system, only a method, the dually conceived dialectical method—behind which, it is true, there were certain views. Its application requires two persons, teacher and pupil, in Socratic conversation with each other, the one who has knowledge asking the questions, the one who seeks knowledge giving the answers. When both have their attention directed towards the same subject during the conversation, it is the questioner's mission to release his counterpart from his immediate relation to the subject—which may be philosophy, or the prejudice that man is capable of knowing anything at all—by resolving it into nothing by abstraction. If they succeed in bringing this course to a close, a new inner process, self-activity, will thereby be released in the questioned person. He must now, personally, without the assistance of teacher or knowledge, solve the problems of his existence. It was in order to arrive at this result: that the person questioned, the reader, should be released from all external authorities and learn to think for himself, that Søren Kierkegaard, adopting a pseudonym, attempted to disappear behind his works in Socratic concealment. The work done to demonstrate the personal element in his production is therefore in conflict with Søren Kierkegaard's express wishes and an obstacle to the right understanding of his work. Comparative studies of his teaching and that of the Church, of his and Hegel's doctrines, are likewise at best useless, because Søren Kierkegaard had no doctrine, merely a method. We gain no understanding of or profit from Kierkegaard's books by talking of him, but by entering into conversation with him.

Just as Diem can prove the justice of his opinion by quoting Søren Kierkegaard, notably *Unscientific Postscript,* so also representatives of the view that Kierkegaard's production forms a totality can refer to his self-interpretations, not only to the *Point of View* but to later publications such as *Of My Authorship* and the preface to *Two Discourses at the Communion on Fridays* from 1851. Rudin has done so and thus taken the concept "totality" in a narrower sense, i.e. he has accepted Søren Kierkegaard's contention that his production, with the aid of Providence, has been built up around the one constructive idea of calling attention without authority to the Christianity of the New Testament. The totality view in a wider sense, energetically maintained by Emanuel Hirsch and Valter Lindström among others, covers the conception that the course of the production may have been determined by Kierkegaard's personal history, but it is sustained and pervaded by a religious totality view; this totality view, which can be deduced from the works and described systematically, is the unity behind the multitudinous and varied production, against the background of which apparent inconsistencies in Kierkegaard's thinking, and contradictions between the individual publications, resolve themselves into a harmony.

The third point of view, that which has dominated Scandinavian research and according to which the individual works must be interpreted separately and their peculiarity be explained psychologically, can be scientifically defended by a well-founded distrust of Søren Kierkegaard's retrospective interpretations and the substantiated observation of changes in his views; this is indeed the reason why several theologians, among them Torsten Bohlin, have joined in the psychological study of Søren Kierkegaard. The majority of enquirers, however, have been so strongly and irresistibly drawn towards the obscure and intriguing connection between Kierkegaard's private history and his public works, which already his contemporaries could dimly see, that no argument against a purely personal historical and genetic explanation of his production has been able to deter them from adopting the psychological view. (pp. 7-12)

> *Aage Henriksen, in an introduction to his* Methods and Results of Kierkegaard Studies in Scandinavia: A Historical and Critical Survey, *Ejnar Munksgaard, 1951, pp. 7-15.*

Karl Jaspers (essay date 1951)

[*In the following essay, Jaspers evaluates Kierkegaard's criticism of the church and his "negative resolution" of Christianity. In Jasper's judgment, Kierkegaard's religious thought cleared the way for new beginnings yet refrained from indicating specific solutions or imposing limitations on human exploration. Jasper's study first appeared in his* Rechenschaft und Ausblick *(1951).*]

Kierkegaard died in 1855. As late as 1900 he was still little known outside the Scandinavian countries. True, there had been some selected German translations; in 1896 there had appeared a stout volume entitled *Angriff auf die Christenheit* which contained all the documents of the Kierkegaardian struggle against the Church. A wider circle first became aware of him through other sensational publications. In 1904 Inselverlag published letters and notes on his relationship to his fiancee, in 1905 the *Tagebuch des Verführers,* and in the same year the *Buch des Richters.* This last, translated by Gottsched at Basel, is still an excellent selection from Kierkegaard's diaries which provide us with a remarkable impression of his character. In 1909 began the definitive twelve-volume edition of his works edited by Gottsched and Schrempf, through which one can become thoroughly acquainted with his work. Kierkegaard became a figure of the first rank in the German intellectual world. He was like a discovery.

Still his name scarcely appeared in the area of academic philosophy before 1914. It was still absent from our histories of philosophy. Shortly before the first World War he became an event for certain young men who were studying theology or philosophy. Today his work has been translated into French and English. His significance is growing throughout the West and even in Japan. Dialectical theology and all shades of existentialism have relied heavily on Kierkegaard. The source of their fundamental principles is obvious.

Among young students today the interest in Kierkegaard is as great as it is in Nietzsche. Lectures and seminars on the one are as likely to be filled as those on the other. Still the questions of what the real Kierkegaard was, what he signified historically, and what his present influence is, cannot be answered unequivocally. In the short space of this [essay] I will attempt a few demonstrations.

Kierkegaard is a Christian philosopher, but of a remarkable kind. He does not profess himself a Christian and yet he says that the truth of Christianity is everything to him. Furthermore, his works are of very great interest for the unbeliever. He is a writer, a thinker, and a master of language. No reader of *Either/Or,* his first great work and a sensational success in Copenhagen in 1843, is forced to take note that a Christian has written it.

In the pseudonyms under which Kierkegaard published most of his work, he invented "thinkers" whom he permitted to expound his position: the aesthetic man with his sovereign freedom in taking hold of every possibility of life and of spirit; the ethical man with his well-established moral realization in the husband and the citizen; the religious man who out of his own inner cataclysm hearkens to that call of God at which the aesthetic order will be set aside. Through such development in the figures which represent thinking existence Kierkegaard was able as he said "to read once more, where possible in an interior way, the original text of individuals, of the human existence-relationship, known of old and handed down to our fathers."

The event appears to be simple, fair and gratifying: progress through human possibilities leads by ascent over the stages of the aesthetic, the ethical, the humanly religious to the truth, and this truth is Christianity.

But Kierkegaard's position is in no way so direct. He gives no systematic teaching and asks that the opinions of the pseudonyms not be taken for his own. He shows only the possibilities, so as to leave the decisions to the reader. If the reader wishes to have the decisions made for him by Kierkegaard it is rendered very difficult for him. The reader does not find in the work of Kierkegaard the objective, clearly-defined grounds by which he could hold himself convinced. He may find himself in treacherous quicksand in which he has lost his footing.

Indeed Kierkegaard in retrospect has said of his works that they were all written by him in order as it were to deceive men into Christianity. While he took his stand on the ground of this world (on that which interests the men of this world), he wished to lead mankind there where this ground leaves off and the truth of Christianity shines in its splendor, or perhaps there where the capacity for belief is granted by the grace of God.

Kierkegaard refuses to say that he is a Christian and believes as a Christian, but at the same time he states that Christianity is something so high that he dare not aspire to it as long as his own life is not adequate to it.

We ask: of what sort of Christianity was Kierkegaard thinking?

The belief that God has appeared to the world in the person of Jesus Christ is called Christianity. This belief, moreover, is beyond our understanding. A human being is not God, and God is not a particular human being.

Kierkegaard lived in our own age—an age in which the conception of the God-Man in all its seriousness, literalness, and reality is no longer believed with firm or unquestioned certitude. One seeks to make the conception somehow bearable and comprehensible to his understanding, tries to confirm it by historical research in Scripture, wishes to convince himself through speculative dogmatics.

According to Kierkegaard all of this already involves an abandoning of Christian faith. For the truth of this faith cannot be perceived, cannot be discovered historically, cannot be thought speculatively. It does not like human truth slumber within us as a hidden bud which need only be awakened. It is not like human truth communicated from teacher to scholar, where the scholar learns only incidentally from the teacher what he might well have been able to discover for himself. On the contrary Christian faith develops outside of and in opposition to human truth. It comes to us from elsewhere. God alone gives us the capacity for belief. One statement of Jesus was enough

for His contemporary generation: We have believed that in these years God revealed Himself as a humble servant, lived among us and then died. This statement was enough to make them mindful. In later ages man believes because of this account of the contemporary, as the contemporary believed because of the capacity which he himself received from God. All study, all demonstration, all attempts to make it plausible or practical would be to no purpose.

For the understanding the concept of the God-Man is a paradox. Faith is unreason and therefore is to be attained only through the subjugation of the understanding. Kierkegaard understands that this must be so: if God wants to reveal Himself to man He cannot show Himself directly. For in that case there would be no bond between God and man; man would be as it were crushed and undone. Therefore God must show Himself while at the same time He conceals Himself. He dare not be knowable as God. Therefore He appears in the form of a humble servant in all the humiliation of a crucified criminal.

This God-manifestation is an indirect communication. Even when Christ says that He is the Son of God, it is not a direct assertion because since it stands in contradiction to His humanity it is patently absurd. To understand this assertion, an act of faith is necessary.

Indeed Kierkegaard forbids us to hold as Christian faith what is only human religiosity. Faith in God, the One, the Unchangeable, the Eternal Lover; the totality of human consciousness of guilt; life for an absolute end; the intensification of the soul; all of this is merely human but not yet Christian. No—to believe in the unique, the fearful, all the reality exceeding human understanding, all the appearance of God Himself bursting on human thought—this is possible only in a leap thanks to the bestowal of grace, and not through human skill.

But once one believes, then the believer, gaining eternal salvation, stands in a radically different position toward the world and the world toward him. The world must deny him; in the world he must suffer and be denied in order to take up his cross. The distinguishing mark of a Christian is not only the surrender of the understanding ("to believe against reason is a martyrdom"), but is martyrdom itself, whether in boundless pain or in suffering death for following the faith. This is the indispensable sign of being a Christian. It is the consequence of its radical dissimilarity from the world. Christianity implies an irreparable break with the world.

The further consequence of this belief is the breach through mankind: the breach between those who are Christian believers and those who are not. No one can understand the Christian belief (which is humanly unintelligible) except one who is himself a believer. Therefore this faith operates in a detaching, separating, polemic fashion. Its truth is exclusive. The believer experiences "the grief that he cannot sympathize with all humankind as humankind, but essentially only with Christians."

For the believer things can come to the point that he "must hate father and mother." For his feelings will be akin to hatred if he has attached his salvation to conditions which he knows will not be acceptable to them.

It is in this way that that Christianity which he calls the Christianity of the New Testament appears to Kierkegaard. But what, according to Kierkegaard is the situation of Christianity in our time?

Kierkegaard says: New Testament Christianity has disappeared. Today we are all Christians; that is, no one is a Christian.

This is the task Kierkegaard sets himself: to show the real Christianity without deception in order to make becoming a Christian difficult. With this in mind he had written his works for a decade. But then in the last year of his life he proceeds to public and direct attack on the Church, on the Christendom of our times, in order to make genuine Christianity possible again.

Today, says Kierkegaard, we are all born baptized, confirmed as Christians, and everything is in order. But faith cannot come by innate nature. Mankind remains, as it is born, in untruth. It has no way to reach truth of itself. Only when God grants the capacity for belief does man become entirely different; then for the first time does he walk in truth; a sudden leap brings him there. One becomes a Christian through a complete reversal, the second birth. His preceding state was not properly one of existing at all. At the decisive moment he becomes conscious that he was born as himself. He reaches this consciousness not through baptism, since the child knows nothing of the baptism; nor through confirmation since at fourteen he is not yet mature. The consciousness comes to him only through the real second birth.

The open assault on the Church in Copenhagen (1884-5) was the most unrestrained attack on the Christian Church and the one grounded on the deepest seriousness which the nineteenth century had seen. Pointing to the true Christianity of the New Testament, Kierkegaard wished to unmask the Christendom of his own time. He reached a climax in these most drastic statements:

> By ceasing to take part in the public worship of God as it now is, thereby have you constantly one grave sin the less: thereby you take no part in making a fool of God in what is now given out for New Testament Christianity, but which certainly it is not.

He goes further: the proclaimers of Christianity have a pecuniary interest in people calling themselves Christians and in their not getting to know the truth of Christianity. The state is obliged to reduce all preaching of Christianity to a private matter. "Christ demands that one preach the doctrine for nothing; that one preach in poverty, in lowliness, in complete renunciation, in the most absolute dissimilarity from the world."

What motive brought Kierkegaard to this attack? He did not aim at it from the beginning. For years he seemed prepared to become a clergyman. The attack was an ultimate result. In order to find the answer we must draw some hypotheses from his life.

In his early youth the ground was laid. At twenty-two he writes in his diary that he has felt the almost irresistible force of one pleasure after another. He has tasted the fruit of the tree of knowledge and has known a moment of joy in learning, but the knowledge has left behind no deeper mark on himself.

It was necessary for him "to find the truth which is truth for me, and for which I am willing to live and die." He forms the resolution, "Now will I begin to act inwardly." The young man is conscious of having "crossed the Rubicon" because seriousness has been established.

But the realization grows in the course of years to a succession of negative resolutions. The burden of the No! lays itself on Kierkegaard's life. He broke his engagement, marriage was denied him—a fact which, despite numerous interpretations, was largely incomprehensible to Kierkegaard himself—but he remained true to the separated one in a unique way. He entered on no vocation. Whenever he, who had passed the examinations long before, wished to become a clergyman, something was against it which denied it to him.

Nevertheless his thought and poetry grew directly out of the negative. Each *no* produced an almost drunken ferment of creativity.

Kierkegaard was aware of this. Unhappy in love, he was able like no one else to praise the happiness of love. He who did not dare to risk marriage has perhaps written more deeply about marriage than anyone else in world literature.

It was the same with faith. He who could not undertake to be a true believer was able to write about belief. As his description of love has a greater charm than the descriptions of a married man, so his writings on religion have a greater appeal than those of a professional clergyman. What he says moreover is not untrue; what he describes is simply his happier, his better self. In his relations to the world of religion, he is an unhappy lover, not a believer. He has only that which precedes faith—despair—and in it a burning desire for religion.

But this showed the Thinker Kierkegaard that his world might indeed not be true. As a Christian any purely poetic existence is sin to him: to write instead of *being*, to occupy his imagination with good and evil instead of *being*, to think the faith instead of living the faith.

It is the mark of Kierkegaard's seriousness that he cannot be satisfied with the mere display of writing and thinking, no matter how extraordinary his spiritual production might be. What he wrote originated in an earnestness which nothing he wrote could satisfy. This is why his writings are so touching. They are never shallow or arbitrary.

One thing always remained clear to him: it is important to turn from reflection to action. It was Kierkegaard's destiny and his mystery, that this step could not take place in his own life.

In the ***Journal*** we see the vacillation between willing and not willing, the experimentation in thinking, the preparation, the hesitation. In only two directions was firmness attained:

1) in negative resolutions, in conscious self-

appraisal, in fidelity to that which was denied.

2) in the pursuit of literary production, the
   very variety of his work, the aim of making
   man the individual mindful.

Only the open attack on the Church, an action full of risk
and responsibility, seemed to solve the problem of existence, but this was an action which again as action was
only a negation.

How could Kierkegaard endure such living and such
thinking?

Kierkegaard's personal piety in the background of his dialectical interpretation of Christianity, of his distinction between human and Christian religiosity, is simple and
straightforward, as if there all those refined, tormented
thoughts might be forgotten.

So he writes: "The best proof for the immortality of the
soul, for the existence of God . . . , is, properly speaking,
the mark which a man obtains in childhood: this is absolutely certain, because my father has told it to me."

And again: "From earliest childhood on: that is the main
point."

Entirely without reflection—he repeatedly admitted
it—he lived in secret with God as a child with its father.
He saw, though not altogether unequivocally, the direction in his life.

He always spoke simply of the love of God, the eternal
love which is without end: "While I sleep, you wake; and
when waking I go astray, you shape it that the error has
been better than the right."

On his deathbed he answered the question whether he
could pray in peace: "Yes, I can. I pray first of all that all
may be forgiven me. Then I pray that I may be free from
despair in death . . . . Then I pray that I may know beforehand when the last hour has arrived."

He arranged that his tombstone would carry the verses of
the Danish poet Brorson:

> But a short time
> And it is won;
> Then will the whole struggle
> Be melted into nothingness.
>
> Then may I refresh myself
> In the stream of life,
> And forever, everlastingly
> Speak with Jesus.

But this piety was not the motive of his thought and his
action. In his work it is scarcely visible, except in many
passages of edifying discourse.

What Kierkegaard really intended by his attack on Christendom depends also on the foundation of seriousness
which he layed in his youth, and which, as he swept to
such annihilating negation, remained possible for him
throughout the retreat from life because of an unaffected
childlike piety. But decisive for the attack itself was a quite
definite motive.

He wished no revolution; he did not seek at any time to
found a new church. He wanted to have nothing to do
with either the Socialists or Liberals, or with any of the
politicians or agitators, in the planning of programs for the
change of social conditions. He avoided all communication with them although they regarded him as one of
themselves. In all these movements he saw only the road
to the disastrous destruction of our world.

Did he perhaps wish to fight as a Christian for Christianity? to become a new martyr? He expressly said no: "Although I should by my death become a martyr, it would
not be for Christianity." Christianity stands too high for
him. He does not dare to confess himself a witness to the
truth of Christianity. He does not wish to be mistaken.
What then did he wish? Only honesty.

He declares therefore at the height of his open attack:

> I want honesty. . . . Will our generation honor-
> ably, honestly, openly, frankly, directly rebel
> against Christianity and say to God: We can but
> we will not subject ourselves to this power.—
> Very well, then, I am with them.
>
> If they will admit to God how it really stands
> with us men, that the human race in the course
> of time has taken the liberty of softening and
> softening Christianity until at last we have con-
> trived to make it exactly the opposite of what it
> is in the New Testament—and that now, if the
> thing is possible, we should be so much pleased
> if this might be Christianity. If that is what they
> want, then I am with them.
>
> But one thing I will not do. . . . I will not take
> part in what is known as official Christianity,
> which by suppression and by artifice gives the
> impression of being the Christianity of the New
> Testament.
>
> For this honesty I am ready to take the risk. On
> the other hand I do not say that it is for Chris-
> tianity I take the risk. . . .
>
> Suppose that I were to become a martyr: I would
> not even in that case be a martyr for Christiani-
> ty, but because I wanted honesty.

As an honest man Kierkegaard felt himself needed by
Providence. He is—this one time in his life—completely
convinced that God wills what he is doing with his attack.

Is honesty now for him the ultimate end? Not at all, but
it is the indispensable condition. Therefore he begins his
own activity as discreetly as possible: not a witness to
truth, not a martyr, not a warrior for Christianity; he shall
do nothing else but unmask falsehood.

Why? Kierkegaard sees his age plunging into the nothingness of groundless reflection, of total leveling, of representation in which nothing is represented, of appearance with
no sense of value for a foundation, of the universal godless
"as if." Let the new seriousness not be looked for in disease, famine and war; first let the eternal punishments of
hell be present and mankind will become serious again.

In these hopeless circumstances Kierkegaard sets forth
the challenge. The Church should only acknowledge hon-

The woodcut of a caricature by P.C. Klaestrup that appeared in the March 6, 1846 Corsair.

estly that her action and her weakened teaching is not New Testament Christianity. Let this honesty become a reality, this least minimum, and then man must see. It lies in no man's power to direct the progress of the world. The realization of this honesty he understands as a question to the deity. These changes have taken place. Let it appear whether they have the approbation of providence. If not, all must break asunder, in order that in this dread individuals may again emerge who can endure the Christianity of the New Testament.

This attack on the Church (just as Kierkegaard's interpretation of Christianity) appears to us to be plainly ruinous. Christianity, which must have duration in time, permanency in the world, is bound to the Church. That with it is bound up accommodation, limitation, perversion, the Christian of the first centuries understood. The Church is never brought to perfection. The Christian element in it is the constant question, the measure, the claim, the task—and it is always corrupted in the secular world. It is enjoined to destroy itself because one wishes to destroy the bearer of its worldly surrender—the Church.

Furthermore, if the Christian faith through so cunning a dialectic shall be delivered into absurdity, so Christianity, rightly understood in this way, would be impossible for rational man as long as he is neither insane nor dishonest.

In short, if Kierkegaard's interpretation of Christianity was the true one, then this Christianity had no future. Kierkegaard's work for its defence was in reality a work for its destruction, in still another direction than the deceptions and accommodations destroy it.

Is not the life and thought of Kierkegaard also proven to be absurd? Is the self-exclusion from the world and the community, from every realization in the world, not like a form of suicide rather than a faith, which is only discernible in negations:

> what he believes is for the human reason not only beyond reason but is clearly impossible
>
> the act of believing in principle shows itself only as suffering and martyrdom
>
> every realization—marriage, his vocation,—he meets with negative resolution and turns away.

These signs Kierkegaard himself has expressed: he is no model; he is no authority; he does not show the way; he does not preach.

So one must ask in astonishment: what actually was Kierkegaard? what kind of a man, with what mission, with what accomplishment? We see him above all in his personal reality. What an unfortunate man, to whom everything was denied, except that he was a genius in thinking and in writing, and that he knew the deep satisfaction of creating!

At the age of twenty five he writes of himself, "Like a solitary fir, egoistic, secluded and elevated, I stand, cast no shadow, and only the wood dove builds its nest in my branches." And then, "It surely must be frightful on the day of judgment, when all souls again walk into life, there to stand altogether alone, solitary and unknown of all, of all."

And on his deathbed as Boesen reminds him of how many wonderful things had befallen him in life, "Yes, I am very happy about that, and very sad, because I can share the joy with no one."

He speaks of himself as a kind of trial-man, a guinea pig so to speak for existence, and even in his youth he thinks that perhaps in each generation two or three are sacrificed in order to discover through horrible suffering what will be good for others.

Kierkegaard was conscious of his own fate, of this radical and total deprivation of all humanity and of worldly activity. An entry in his diary, one among countless comparable entries, states:

> Now I completely understand myself to be a solitary man without reference to anyone . . .
>
> with only one comfort: God who is Love,
>
> with longing after only one joy, that I might altogether belong to the Lord Jesus Christ,
>
> with longing after a dead father,
>
> worse than isolated through the death of the

only living man whom I have loved in any final sense . . .

In the course of his negative resolution Kierkegaard has outlined possibilities in his work. There is no radical plan of the manifold forms of the lost aesthetic life. There is no grandiose design for marriage and for human (and according to him not yet Christian) religiousness. His work reveals the basic human situation and lack of proportion with unheard of richness. It would not be possible in this brief space to describe the ideal world which Kierkegaard has unfolded.

However everything remains for him in the form of possibility. It is "thought" by the pseudonym, represented in poetic form. The truth appears to be nowhere. The wealth of form of the aesthetic life is everywhere a lost existence. Moreover, the apparent perfection, the ethically bound, metaphysically grounded marriage, human religion, each has its limits. He dares not be sure of himself.

Therefore we are driven from one to another, we have gained no ground. Christianity demonstrating itself in negative resolutions may be understood as absurd—as untrodden a path as the fruitless ground of Nietzsche, of the eternal return, the dionysiac life and the will to power.

But Kierkegaard does not wish to work for this Christianity, but only for honesty. He constantly repeats that he is not an authority, only a corrective. He calls himself a policeman, a spy in the service of the Almighty.

In point of fact Kierkegaard and Nietzsche will remain ambiguous figures. They are illuminators and at the same time tempters. They are purifying agents for seriousness and admit of being called as witnesses for every fraud. They are masters of honesty and yet they make available methods of thought which allow every truth to slip away. They unsettle in order that each may come to himself, and they destroy in the abyss of nihilism.

Therefore it is not possible to follow them as teachers. But all modern philosophizing would be insufficient if it did not come to know the purgatory of their inward search, even in every corner where one may hide himself or strengthen himself.

I am convinced that neither theology nor philosophy can base itself on Kierkegaard. That foundation of forty years ago was not the establishment of a new basis; it was the awakening from a sleep.

When we assimilate his work—and it will not be destroyed in the process—we must not forget his own words: "I will leave behind a not inconsiderable intellectual capital; and alas I know who will probably be my heir, that figure which is so offensively dreadful to me, the lecturer, the professor. And when the professor comes to read even this, the real consciousness will still not touch him. Even this will be lectured about."

In reality, when we speak of Kierkegaard, we must almost certainly succumb to this danger to which we are exposed. In order to escape its power it is necessary that we do not confine ourselves to the intellectual capital but that we allow ourselves to capture the seriousness as well.

We today, on the universal voyage in the storm, look into the darkness. Some of us are permitted to remain for yet a while as if on a happy island, deliberating on a glimpse of the sun. By reflecting under such conditions, the importance of Kierkegaard and Nietzsche grows. Their names have risen to stars of the first magnitude, before which the many post-Hegelian philosophers of the nineteenth and twentieth centuries fade away.

To discuss the question in the world-historical style which Kierkegaard himself so detested, with Hegel something came to an end, something which remained a unity among all differences for a thousand years, and was a matter of course in his own shattering fundamentals. For more than a hundred years, fixed in matter we have been losing our way, and perhaps constantly accumulate more knowledge. Amid the progress in this new world we see Kierkegaard and Nietzsche as storm birds before a hurricane. They show the unrest, the precipitation, and then the strength and clarity of an instantaneously high flight, and again something like circlings and whirls and rapid falls.

They know themselves as sea beacons; by them orientation is possible, but only while one holds himself at a distance from them. To follow them is forbidden by themselves.

They work in such a way that they bring others to themselves to look for decisions from them, but they do not give the decisions.

For the more an age, losing its historical connections, falls into the slavery of the mass, the stronger becomes the claim made by the individual as individual: to be himself; every man is an individual; here is the last basis on which reality can appear.

At such a time, when living on a stage or within a fiction becomes increasingly dubious, one thing remains worthwhile: honesty.

Kierkegaard's claim, closely corresponding to that of Nietzsche, is to be an individual and to be honest. But this claim is recognized by them first in their entire self-testing. What is the Self? What is honesty? Both have experienced it and thought it out to the utmost.

The claim itself is uncommonly small. It has not yet produced what can perhaps be awakened by it. In the case of Kierkegaard and Nietzsche it stands square in the midst of the spiritual riches of the European tradition. Their claim alone remains indivisible and inexorable, while in them the riches of the European tradition focus to a great drama of introspection and interior development.

Or with Kierkegaard is it more than this? When we let pass all the absurdity of a Christian belief so violently understood by him, and all the seductive variety of possibility, does he not still offer us the eternal truth of human religion with a wonderful purity? This truth sets forth

the immutability of God, the presence of this awesomeness and this rest, so that for Kierkegaard all is determined and does not change

that before God we are always in the wrong; that all our rebellion miscarries in the eternity of His unfathomable depth that God is unending Love, so that even at the most frightful time trust can remain in that Providence which we, despite firm obedience to it, do not understand in its enduring ambiguity

These eternal truths, moreover, in the absence of dogmas point only to the possibility of endless fulfillment. They do not endure; their meaning disappears. So much the more wonderful when, in spite of this they always appear again.

The other truths in Kierkegaard's thought are present on biblical grounds:

the world is wrong and it is not to be set right as such, but rather it must go through time in constant change, constantly failing and trying again,—

therefore the unrest of our soul which in this world finds no final resting place. We are the question capable of eternal happiness, and therefore of absolute seriousness, but we remain without an objective answer guaranteed.

Today when we philosophize in consciousness of the cosmic moment,

when we know that something irrevocable has happened, through which all human history experiences a revolution,—

when we see that no man and no people can make satisfaction for this event by any ethical religious reality, through which disaster might be averted and the elevation of man made possible.—

when we think in this ever poor, growing world to discern something as the end of western philosophy in that form which was a single great continuity from Parmenides to Hegel,—

then will we perceive in this era of considerable transition the primitiveness of thinkers such as Kierkegaard and Nietzsche who, in the possession of the medium of thought burst forth as it were, orient us, but yet do not show the way,—

then will we not look to the professional philosophy of the past century for the foundation and value of the world to come, as productive as this professional work has been in historical knowledge. Rather let Kierkegaard and Nietzsche first rouse us to a recognition of the source of that tradition.

It is clear what is now possible. One who has lost all confidence can see the end in Kierkegaard and Nietzsche. But for a confidence which, though unprovable, is at once a confidence in the Godhead and in the potentiality of man, a beginning is perhaps indicated through these thinkers, along with an end. True they do not show the way, nor the content of truth. But they inspire us to seriousness without illusion.

Today in the time of spiritual and material catastrophe through which we are borne on to the coming world, when philosophy has a vanishing significance, it is especially important that we are not satisfied by them.

Philosophy belongs so much to mankind that it must attain a new form. Let us take their seriousness in the tradition as our own seriousness, and then we need not stand

helpless in nothingness, nor be delivered from a groundless individuality into an empty existence.

We can attain the standard, and the light of philosophy will yet be left burning. Kierkegaard and Nietzsche have opened our eyes. To one who has experienced it, it is as if he had had cataracts on his eyes and they have been pierced. Now the question is what will be seen with the opened eyes, what will be lived, what will be done. (pp. 5-16)

> *Karl Jaspers, "The Importance of Kierkegaard," translated by Erwin W. Geissman, in* Cross Currents, *Vol. II, No. 3, Spring, 1952, pp. 5-16.*

James Collins (essay date 1952)

[*An American critic and educator, Collins wrote several works on philosophy, including* The Mind of Kierkegaard *(1953). In the following excerpt, he examines fundamental currents in Kierkegaard's thought—namely the emphasis on the individual, the rejection of the panlogism exemplified by Hegel's speculative philosophical system, and the insight afforded by Christian faith—that provide the groundwork for much succeeding Existentialist thought.*]

Both in his personal life and in his writings, Sören Kierkegaard (1813-55) supplies the prototype of the existential thinker. His own protest against the academic, social, and religious establishments of his day have set a pattern for the existential criticism of the accepted institutions and philosophies of our time. Kierkegaard called himself a thoroughly polemical nature, meaning thereby not only that he possessed a naturally contentious spirit but also that his positive views could only be developed through sharp contrasts and oppositions. He is best understood when placed in the line of European moralists, men who have criticized their contemporaries in a satirical yet constructive way. Despite their attempts to provide metaphysical underpinnings, the existentialists have retained this fundamentally moral orientation of philosophizing. An examination of Kierkegaard's major protests prefigures the lineaments of the existential outlook.

(a) THE INDIVIDUAL VERSUS THE CROWD. Although Kierkegaard is not usually recognized as a social critic, he has offered some penetrating analyses of the social ills of the nineteenth century. His *Works of Love,* composed at the same time as the *Communist Manifesto,* diagnoses the situation of 1848 in an incisive and radical way. Both Marx and Kierkegaard agree that contemporary industrial society has endangered the dignity of the human person. They point out that man counts for nothing in a society that is governed primarily by impersonal "laws" of production and consumption and by the ends of selfish gain. Both critics see that the primacy of human values must be championed against the reigning bourgeois interests. The sharp divergence between them comes when more concrete proposals are made for reconstructing society along humanistic lines. Marx identifies the "truly human man" with the social group which can integrate itself so closely with the processes of industrial production that the gap is

closed between human desires and material possibilities of social control. Thoroughly socialized man, having no illusions about a transcendent goal, is the Marxian solution to the inhumane conditions of the modern world.

Kierkegaard moves in the opposite direction. He does not believe that we are under any necessity to work out the immanent logic of capitalism or that the remedy is to be found in an exclusively social direction. For it is a utopian hope to think that a humane society can be produced without a direct reformation of individual life. Social change within the state is more profound than political reorganization, but the ultimate success of both social and political revolution depends upon the basic transformation of individual existence. Kierkegaard's observation of his environment reveals that men are ridden by a total forgetfulness of what it means to be an individual. His analysis of this condition both harkens back to the Biblical warning against forgetting the manner of men we are and also foreshadows some characteristic existentialist themes.

Kierkegaard refers to man in industrial society as a cipher man or a fractional man, since as an individual he commands no respect and cannot have significance. This is due to the paramount devotion paid to the ideal of equality. Although equality is one of the abiding human goals, it cannot be pursued in isolation from other objectives, such as freedom and personal responsibility, without sacrificing the members of society to the collectivity. The modern individual is "lost" in the crowd and "at a loss" without the crowd. He finds it uncomfortable to stand out in any unusual way, since issues are decided on the basis of what everybody thinks. Anonymity is the saving virtue, numerical superiority the decisive consideration, and mass opinion the criterion of truth. No one cares to act in a distinctive way, since such conduct would count for nothing except as a sign of queerness. Here is a source of the existentialist antipathy toward the anonymous, featureless standards which prevail in our age.

There is need for a recall of the individual to himself, an awakening to the possibilities of self-determination that slumber within him. This is not a plea for economic or political individualism, since the ascendency of the crowd would also result from an individualistic appeal to unbridled self-seeking. Neither laissez faire nor collectivism can arrest the process of universal leveling, since neither policy is directed to an inward edification of the individual self. Kierkegaard looks for "uncommon men," who will take the first steps toward a renascence of personal integrity. These men are not to be found in a privileged class or nation, since it lies in the power of every member of the crowd to extricate himself and realize his own singular nature. This is an aristocratic ideal, to the extent of acknowledging that the best in a man is left untilled when his character is determined mainly by group pressure and catchwords. It is aristocratic in the Socratic sense of singling out each man from the irresponsible public and requiring him to render personal account for what he believes and acts upon. Yet this demand of self-scrutiny can be placed upon *everyone*—this is the personalist way of supporting, in non-quantitative terms, the movement toward equality.

The famous Kierkegaardian doctrine of the three spheres of existence—the esthetic, the ethical, and the religious—fits into this context. It is a theory about stages in the growth of personality rather than a metaphysical scaffolding, after the manner of Hegel's triad of moments. Kierkegaard's dynamic conception of personality is of seminal importance for existential thought. Certain broad and fixed traits belong permanently to human nature. The common human condition is shared by all men and constitutes the given, necessary factor. But man is the one being endowed with conscious freedom and hence with possibilities for existing at various levels of adequacy. He can propose his own leading principles, organize his life around them, and thus transform the given reality into a freely orientated self. There is no place for philosophy of nature in Kierkegaard and the existentialists, because they are wholly absorbed in a study of the venture of human freedom and its pitfalls.

Kierkegaard's descriptions of various moods and attitudes characteristic of the different spheres of existence have inspired a good many later phenomenological analyses. His studies of boredom, despair, and dread have proved to be specially fertile sources. He draws attention more to the dark and turbulent moments than to the tranquil ones. But this is not a morbid preference made in order to institute a literature of gloom and frustration. The underlying argument (lost sight of by those existentialists who revel in such descriptions for their own sake) is that an internal law of growth impels the individual to venture beyond the cautious shores of esthetic satisfaction. If he resists the natural prompting to cultivate ethical and religious qualities, the result is disorder of soul and paralysis in practical affairs. The darker moods announce the consequences of failing to follow through to the full flowering of personal existence.

Boredom, for instance, is a warning that all the goods of life may turn to ashes in the mouth. When a man concentrates all his energies upon pursuit of momentary pleasures, no matter how refined and subtle, he exposes himself to surfeit and a state of tedium from which his esthetic principles cannot rescue him. Anguished dread is the state of spiritual growing pains of a man who stands poised at the brink of personal exercise of freedom, in the full awareness of its consequences for time and eternity. He is held fast in awful fascination at the stakes. Not this or that object but the entire range of objects of mature choice arouses dread in him. If he should then retreat within himself and shut out all aid from God, he is on the road to despair, the "sickness unto death." Kierkegaard's own interest in these states of soul is primarily religious and ethical, whereas his successors have exploited the psychological and metaphysical aspects of such concrete treatments of the human situation.

Yet even Kierkegaard is not innocent of drawing a speculative conclusion from his own choice of subject. He deplores the rationalist tendency to understate the role of the emotions and reduce will to a function of reason. The rationalist account of man is unbalanced for failing to give due weight to the affective side of our lives. An understanding of the whole man and his attitudes toward reality awaits an appreciation of the great resources of the passions, which are decisive in shaping individual outlooks. Without the passional factor, especially will, there is no way of advancing from the dreamy, esthetic state to the moral and religious phases of existence. It is not voluntarism but an honest attempt to see man steadily and in his actual dynamism which prompts this emphasis upon other powers than reason. The persuasiveness and originality of many existentialist arguments are due to this widening of the anthropological horizon to include all the relevant forces in man.

Will and practical reason are accorded more autonomy by Kant than by Kierkegaard. The latter conceives the ethical stage as standing in need of reinforcement from, and alliance with, either the esthetic or the religious principle. Either the ethically responsive person will imagine himself to be acting in accord with a secular moral law of his own making or, perhaps, one to which he is unconditionally related—and then he relapses into moralizing estheticism; or else he will trace the moral law itself to its source in a personal God—and then he completes the movement of existence to its culmination not in duty but in worship. This is an either/or which has continued to confront the existentialists and to differentiate one variety of existentialism from another.

The capstone of Kierkegaard's view of the individual is man's freely acknowledged bond with God. The entire drive of the dialectic of the stages of existence points at the conclusion that to be an individual in the plenary sense is to orientate one's life toward God. On this reckoning, every description of the human person which neglects or depreciates the tendency to transcendence is out of focus. All existentialists, whether admitting the religious solution or not, make allowance for some sort of movement of transcending or seeking beyond the immanent structure of human nature. Kierkegaard's own interpretation rests upon an examination of man's desire for an eternal happiness, a desire that cannot be satisfied by the finite goods and temporal situations of life. Yet he does not admit the naturalist reproach that the inclination to transcend our world is, in effect, a flight from our historical and concrete responsibilities. The individual in the pregnant sense is one who has faith in God's existence. For Kierkegaard, this means having faith in Christ as the God-Man. God is not found by leaving the world behind in a flight to the beyond but by discerning His presence in the temporal process itself.

Religious faith is the Archimedean lever whereby the "accentuated" individual can move the world. It is his foothold and secret strength for withstanding the pressure of the herd. The man of faith is a nonconformist, as far as human conventions and mass impulses are concerned. He can stand out as an exception, since he has accepted a call from God precisely in his own singular reality. Faith is not susceptible of mass techniques: each man believes in his own heart and on his own responsibility. Yet it is a paradoxical vindication of the ideal of equality among men, since it does not fall within the disposition of fortune or of privilege. Each individual can make the act of faith, provided only that he does so on the basis of his own free-

dom. This is the crucial opportunity for becoming an individual in the highest existential sense.

Ideally, Kierkegaard should have rounded out his teaching on the individual with a complementary study of the community. He does make several fugitive references to a new social mode of being which will correspond with his reconstruction of the person. But characteristically, he leaves the task of further social analysis to future laborers in the field, because of the greater urgency of the problem of the individual. His legacy to the existentialists is the problem of reconciling individual and society. His own religious statements underline the difficulties rather than suggest a way of integrating the two poles. Each individual is related to God as the alone to the Alone. Only in God is there a common intersection of the lines of individual destinies. Kierkegaard speaks about God as entering into every personal union among men as the third party, but he does not expand this hint into a thoroughgoing renovation of the basis for social relations. For all merely human associations seem to present threats to individual integrity and barriers between the individual and God. Above all, the Hegelian notion of a concrete universal tends to divinize the actual social institutions and rob the individual of his free, creaturely approach to a transcendent God.

(b) THE EXISTENT VERSUS THE SPECULATIVE SYSTEM. Kierkegaard's attack upon Hegel has been widely reported as a repudiation of all philosophy and of all reason. This interpretation seems the more plausible, at least regarding philosophy, because Kierkegaard himself looked indulgently upon Hegel's claim to have elaborated the definitive philosophy. Hence he seemed to be faced with the alternative of accepting Hegel or of rejecting not only the Hegelian system but all philosophy along with it. Since he regarded this system as the major theoretical bulwark of the mass mind, Kierkegaard could not compromise on the issue as so formulated, despite the disastrous alternative. Although he saluted the Greek realism of Socrates and Aristotle from a distance, he saw no evidence of its survival in his own day. Since all contemporary philosophies were infected with idealism, a repudiation of absolute idealism seemed to Kierkegaard to entail a repudiation of philosophy itself in any concrete form.

Whatever the ambiguity surrounding his attitude towards philosophy, Kierkegaard's mind is clearly set forth in regard to the rationalism-irrationalism controversy. He accepts neither horn of the dilemma, but the popularity of rationalism among his own contemporaries led him to emphasize its shortcomings just as strongly as those of irrationalism. The Kierkegaardian critique of romanticism and the esthetic outlook is aimed at the latter doctrine, whereas his polemic against the Hegelian system is directed against excessive claims made for reason. Several of the existentialists, in turn, have waged battle on both fronts, despite the widespread charge that they tend to foster an irrational point of view.

Kierkegaard balances his stress on moods, passions, and will with an equally vigorous affirmation of the intelligibility of the real order. Things in the world and events in history are not absurd in themselves and their interrelations. They have a definite intelligible structure, which is not only intrinsically knowable but also actually comprehended by God. This is the meaning of Kierkegaard's neglected statement that existing reality *is* a system for God. It stands open to His vision, although it is only by Him that it can be known comprehensively and systematically. As far as creaturely intelligence is concerned, Kierkegaard distinguishes among abstract thought, existential thought, and pure thought. Abstract or objective thinking is the approach employed by the natural sciences, mathematics, and logic. These are valid disciplines and yield reliable knowledge about the essential aspects of things. But they have two limitations: they do not attain to actual existence and do not involve the personal relationship of the knowing individual to the things known. Disinterestedness and objectivity are the primary notes of abstract thinking. This is the proper way to treat things, as distinguished from personal selves. Even human nature, in so far as man is one natural thing along with others in the world, is accessible in a partial way to the objective method.

In order to gain some insight into existence or the disposition of man's freedom, another avenue is needed. Kierkegaard is more successful in describing what existential thinking is *not* than in specifying its positive features. It is not merely an extension of abstract thought, since it does not labor under the two limitations mentioned above. It does attain somehow by reflection to the existential act, and it does include the relationship of the knower to what he knows. In fact, existential knowledge is constituted precisely by the manner in which the meditative individual relates himself to the aims of existence. Existence is not predicated of things but of persons in their moral dispositions. Existential truth, for Kierkegaard, is a moral and religious state of being rather than a purely cognitive perfection. It rests on the attempt to shape one's conduct in accord with what one knows about the purposes of freedom. At its maximum, it is the true or upright state of being fully committed to search for eternal happiness.

Kierkegaard places strict limitations upon the finite understanding of existence and existential truth. In the natural order, an individual can have reflective, existential knowledge only of his own existence and of other selves only in so far as they bear upon his own freedom. Religiously, the power of Christian charity affords direct acquaintance with the existential conditions of other persons through a sort of empathy. On only one point—a negative one—is Kierkegaard emphatic. The existential situation cannot be transcribed within an idealist system of pure thought. For the latter is based upon dialectical necessities and a presumption of the basic completeness of the historical process, whereas existence has freedom and genuine novelty as its proper medium.

Thus Kierkegaard's opposition is to "pure" thought, or the systematic identification of thought and being, rather than to the "abstract" thought of the sciences. His position is nonidealist rather than irrationalist, although he does not see that systematic explanations can be made on a nonidealist basis. The existentialists have followed him in setting off the type of knowledge which deals with *things* in the world scientifically and objectively from that sort which is adapted to the special task of studying the human *person* and the realm of existence. But they have not found in Kierkegaard sufficient indications about the cognitive aspects of existential reflection or subjective thinking. It is not a form of subjectivism and arbitrary creation of fantasies. But directions are lacking about how to discern the natural cognitive factor in the midst of affective sympathy and religious faith. The philosophical status of existential understanding is left in doubt by Kierkegaard.

For Kierkegaard's philosophical descendants, the value of the philosophical life itself cannot be taken for granted. Having been called in question by the sceptical Dane, philosophizing enters again into the category of problems at issue. The venerable axiom: "First live, then philosophize" takes on new relevance from Kierkegaard's suggestion that philosophy may be antivital rather than in continuous harmony with the ends of human life. Above all, metaphysics has been subjected to critical examination, following Kierkegaard's observation that it does not figure as one of the three stages of existence. The unavoidable question arises as to whether there is any legitimate place for metaphysics in an existentially-centered viewpoint. Most existentialists agree that an affirmative answer cannot be made until the history and the methodology of metaphysics have been subjected to a thorough revision.

Another acute problem raised by Kierkegaard is the relation between metaphysics and ethics. In attacking Hegel's ethical theories, he is careful to trace out the metaphysical roots of the position he opposes. This has left the existentialists with the choice of either tackling ethical matters independently or making their investigation contingent upon a previous settlement of the metaphysical foundations of moral theory. Kierkegaard has made it impossible for these philosophers to undertake ethical studies without first declaring their mind, one way or another, about metaphysics and its bearing upon a philosophy of conduct.

Kierkegaard's actual practice often belies his profession of eschewing metaphysical speculation. His criticism of Hegel is carried out in a thoroughly speculative spirit. In order to have a self-sufficient system, Hegel would have to make a "presuppositionless" start in his thinking. When it is a question of human cognition, Kierkegaard believes that such a beginning can be made only at the price of wiping out the distinction between God and the finite mind. There is an implicit realistic metaphysics of creator and creature behind this objection. Kierkegaard withstood any dialectical merging of these two modes of being. Man is genuinely and radically finite, so that at no time in his development does he discover himself to be a phase in the self-explication of the absolute. Hence he cannot draw upon some creative idea implanted in his mind as its a priori structure, on the strength of which an entire philosophical system can be developed from the internal resources of the central idea. Kierkegaard requires a real rather than a dissimulated dependence of human intelligence upon the data of the physical world gained through the senses. In the existentialist tradition, he tends to counterbalance Husserl's claim to make a presuppositionless beginning.

Apart from this polemical appeal to the senses, however, Kierkegaard fails to specify the exact contribution of sensation to human knowledge. He is satisfied with having drawn a distinction between logical motion, with which alone the Hegelian system is equipped to deal, and the real motion of physical processes which is grasped through the senses. Having used this empirical argument of Hegel's chief foes, Trendelenburg and Schelling, he does not follow up its consequences. The senses might be expected to contribute toward knowledge of physical things in their existential character. But Kierkegaard does not follow this lead, since he has associated existence too exclusively with the exercise of human freedom in the formation of self. For the same reason, he is prevented from applying existence to God. He is the fountainhead of the existential commonplace that God *is,* but does not *exist.* Existence cannot be predicated of the eternal, immutable being, since to exist means to be engaged in becoming, time, freedom, and history. This has given rise to the existentialist quandary of how to relate existential thinking to the divine Being, who is by definition placed beyond the existential order. Man is not only central in existence: he is the only truly existential being.

(c) THE ILLUMINATION OF EXISTENCE BY CHRISTIAN FAITH. Kierkegaard was not unaware of the dangers in this conception of existence, since it would seem to cut off man from both God and the non-human world. His own answer to the problem of man's relationship to God was formulated in terms of faith in the Incarnation. In the person of Christ, God Himself enters into the zone of the existential. The immutable becomes a changing being, the eternal puts on temporal process, the suprahistorical enters into history. This is the paradoxical nature of faith. Rather than mediate these extremes of reality in Hegelian fashion, Kierkegaard spoke of faith as a crucifixion of the understanding. He rejected as a rationalistic compromise the customary apologetics of the Hegelian divines. If their explanations were valid, then there would be no room for faith as a free venture.

Kierkegaard injected the problem of Christianity into the heart of existential discussion. He was highly critical of the actual condition of the Established Danish-Lutheran Church as well as of the very notion of "Christendom." To him, these settlements came dangerously close to sanctioning a comprise between Christian faith and the spirit of worldliness. On the other hand, he maintained that the attitude of faith is indispensable for synthesizing the many aspects of existence. The full meaning of living a life under trial, of suffering and sacrifice, of communication and joy, can only be plumbed with the aid of the Christian teaching. Christian faith, as the supremely existential attitude, is the central standpoint from which to develop the implications of these personal situations. For it provides a way in which to reconcile the immanent tendency to remain loyal to our earthly condition and the equally importunate drive toward transcendence. Both movements are strengthened through the gracious initiative of the transcendent being in becoming present as an existent person in history. Whether the *instant,* the act whereby believers are made contemporaneous with Christ through faith in the Incarnation, cancels out secular history or gives it orientation and significance is part of the ensemble of Kierkegaardian problems.

Most existentialists agree that existence is a historical reality and that some sort of faith is a motive force in human history. There is no unanimity, however, on the relevance of Christian faith for the hermeneutic of existence. Several possibilities are opened by Kierkegaard's own wrestling with the problem of faith. His torments of soul can be taken as an involuntary confession of antagonism between his existential insights and the tenets of Christianity. Atheistic existentialists regard as axiomatic the groundlessness of belief in God and Christ, even though this absurdity must be included among the given elements in the historical condition of Western men. Another interpretation is that Kierkegaard misunderstood the relation between Christianity and a philosophy of existence. Instead of patterning a theory of existence after the deliverances of revelation as an independent standard, it might be better to submit these religious deliverances to philosophical analysis and thus to uncover their underlying secular import. Finally, Kierkegaard's reluctance to speak of himself as "being" a Christian can be construed in a strict way as meaning that the Christian life is one of constant "becoming," in which there is no room for complacent assertions of having realized the Christian requirements. It is then possible to accept literally his designation of Christ as "*the* historical, *the* existential" individual, without making this truth the major premise of existential investigation. The culmination of personal life in communion with God would then be intimated rather than laid down as a first principle. Kierkegaard himself leaves his readers free to make their own reading of existence, since such freedom is the condition of acquiring individual selfhood. (pp. 5-17)

> *James Collins, "Existential Backgrounds: Kierkegaard, Nietzsche, Husserl," in his* The Existentialists: A Critical Study, *1952. Reprint by Greenwood Press, 1977, pp. 3-17.*

William Hubben (essay date 1952)

[*In the following excerpt, Hubben maintains that although Kierkegaard's life seems to necessitate a biographical analysis of his works, such interpretations diminish the universality of his writings and mistakenly attempt to impose psychological models on spiritual messages.*]

The Copenhagen street urchins used to shout after Sören Kierkegaard "Either—Or," the title of his two-volume work. Copenhagen's satirical paper *The Corsair* printed not only the most merciless articles against him but also published a series of cartoons depicting him successively as a magisterial hunchback; a thin-legged star gazer; a clumsy horseman riding Pegasus; a shadow in the center of a chaotic universe; a rooster with a top hat, surrounded by cackling chickens also wearing top hats; and each time vitriolic satire accompanied these cartoons. Copenhagen, the little Paris of the North, relished both the stories and the pictures. Kierkegaard's thin legs and crumpled pants had become proverbial, and there was nobody who opposed this cruel, "negative conspiracy," as Kierkegaard called the campaign against himself. Goldschmidt, the clever editor of *The Corsair,* had refused any apologies or retractions. Yet only six days after Kierkegaard's death in 1855, when Goldschmidt was no longer connected with *The Corsair,* he wrote that Kierkegaard was one of "the greatest minds Denmark has ever produced."

These attacks were in part the reaction of a self-satisfied and uninformed middle class to the presence of a genius of Kierkegaard's proportions. The citizens of Copenhagen were incapable of imagining that such an extraordinary man could ever rise from the quiet and perfectly proper atmosphere of their town. They saw in Kierkegaard a threat to the order which they loved as final; Hans Christian Andersen described this way of life very characteristically in one of his stories when he said, "There was brilliant sunshine and all the church bells called the people together. They were dressed up and with their prayer books under their arms they went to church to listen to the minister."

There was enough gossip current to feed the imagination of these dutiful churchgoers. Vehement church controversies were going on; rumors had it that Kierkegaard had to finance his own publications; and, last but not least, there was also a tragic love affair that had ended in a broken engagement. There could be no doubt that this strange character, Sören Kierkegaard, was beyond the pale. The fate of the unrecognized genius was his to the bitter end. Shortly before he died, he wrote prophetically and with very good reason,

> One thing I have come to know thoroughly: the abysmal lack of character in man. But how sad it is, there was yet some truth in me. And after my death they will all praise me in such a manner that the young people will believe I had been respected and revered in life. This, too, is part of the metamorphosis that truth suffers . . . in reality. The same contemporaries who have acted despicably will use the moment after death to say the contrary of yesterday, and thus everything will be confused.

Outward confusion and prophetic clarity were, indeed, the setting for Kierkegaard's entire life.

Sören Kierkegaard (1813-1855) was the youngest child of a large family. His father, Pedersen Michael Kierkegaard, was fifty-six when Sören was born, and his mother, forty-five. The father was a prosperous merchant, and the atmosphere of the home was one of comfort, strictest devotion to church and religion, and melancholy gloom. Michael Kierkegaard had grown up among the poor peasants of the Jütland heath. There, Moravian preachers had so deeply stirred up the people by a religious revival that even children labored under a sense of sin and wished they had never been born. Week after week thunderous sermons of damnation had been showering upon the peasants to shock them into virtue and frighten them into heaven.

The vocabulary of these dark hours had engraved itself deeply upon the mind of young Michael. It is no wonder that after learning of the "sacred wounds and holy blood," "hell being paved with the foreheads of sinful parsons," and youth "being the children of Satan himself," that one day when he was herding the sheep, Michael cursed this terrible God of wrath who would allow no sunshine and

joy in his young life. This curse spread an even greater darkness over his life; he never forgave himself such blasphemy, and there was scarcely a smile on his face from that moment until his death at the age of eighty-two.

Young Sören was present at the interminable discussions his father held with his neighbors. Father Michael was not only a successful business man but also an intelligent reader of theological books. His stern methods of education kept the children indoors. Sören underwent the first exercises for his fertile imagination in extensive indoor "excursions" in the living room, where father and son marched up and down acting as though they were meeting acquaintances in the street, describing fictitious houses, trees, and people, lowering their voices as if the rattle of passing carriages had drowned them out, or commenting upon the produce of an imagined fruit market. The world of sin and guilt was of such reality to Sören that he wrote later, "I have been from childhood on in the grip of an overpowering melancholy . . . my sole joy being, as far as I can remember, that nobody could discover how unhappy I felt myself to be. . . . I have never really been a man, even less a child or youth."

Several times his father took him to the sermons of the famous Bishop Mynster. There was no doubt that the salvation of his soul was the most important concern in Sören's thinking and conversation, as the purity of his soul became his most serious endeavor in later life. For years his father's memory was fused with God's own image, and the old man's later confession of sexual excesses, the "great earthquake" (1835), not only shocked Sören out of reverence for his earthly father but also disrupted his devotion to his divine father. He was deeply ashamed of his father, whom he thought he must henceforth approach "backward with his face turned away so as not to see his disgrace," just as Noah's sons had approached their drunken and naked father.

The curse of sin seemed to hang over the old man and his family: only the oldest son, Peder Christian, and Sören, the youngest of his children, survived. Michael's wife, Sören's mother, had been his servant before she became his second wife, and she remained a somewhat impersonal, shadowlike figure, about whom Sören remained almost entirely silent.

As a university student Sören devoted himself at first to theology but soon turned to the study of literature and philosophy. He lived the life of a bohemian intellectual, and in the style of his contemporaries extolled man's wit and reasoning power as the most fitting weapons for life. Since he had no financial worries, life did not seem bad, after all, and young Sören did not mind accumulating a rather considerable debt which his father had to pay.

The great change came when he broke his engagement to Regine Olsen, his attractive and lovely fiancée, who "was as light as a bird and as bold as a thought. . . ." He had met her when she was only fifteen, and after a two years' engagement, in 1841, he sent the engagement ring back to the disconsolate Regine with the following words: "In the Orient it means death to receive a silken cord, but in this case to mail the ring is likely to mean death for the send-er." There were many mysteries about this step. Because he had missed the warmth of motherly love, did he need the virgin-mother image of this queen (*regina*), whom he continued to adore? Was celibacy one of the indispensable vows for his unordained ministry, itself a rejection of Luther's abolition of it? Did he consider Regine too lighthearted and happy a woman, incapable of bearing his melancholy? Might it have been that his poetic soul could no longer face reality and join *eros* and *agape* in matrimony? Was marriage too convenient a middle-class solution? The fact that he had loved Regine Olsen from the first day on as a poetic reflection of his memory and a lovely mirage rather than as a real being, may have rendered him incapable of marriage, as one of his analysts suspects, although Sören thought himself erotic to an extraordinary degree. Was a sexual sin of earlier years his "thorn in the flesh," of which he spoke repeatedly? Or was the breaking of his engagement perhaps one of his "acts of vengeance" upon society and himself, of which he liked to write? He whose conscience made him feel always in the wrong before God may have acted wrongly even toward his fiancée. He never ceased to love her, and her subsequent engagement and marriage to Fritz Schlegel caused him severe depression.

We have many answers to these questions, but the psychoanalysts, historians, and students of human nature seem unable to unveil the mystery of Sören Kierkegaard's private life. Even he himself, while taking great pains to let the mystery remain what it was, seemed puzzled, and the safest conclusion may be that the life of the spirit was to him the all-dominating concern to which everything else must be sacrificed. He felt called upon to do the "extraordinary thing" but as a writer and Christian, his inability to follow his heart's longing added to the painful memories of this penitent sinner.

This tragic interlude, which had followed by three years his sudden awakening to God's nearness in an experience of "indescribable joy" (1838), his pin-point existence as a solitary seeker after truth, the many open or veiled confessions in his writings, and the tragedy of having to endure the hostility of the public will always be fertile ground for the exploration of biographers and psychologists. The mystery of his genius may remain impenetrable to others; his destiny was equally inexplicable to himself.

In his diaries he calls himself a Janus whose one face laughs while the other one weeps. As a young man of twenty-five he wrote, "I too have both the tragic and the comic in me: I am witty and the people laugh—but I cry." A year earlier, his diary had spoken of practicing "vengeance upon the world" by acting gaily and consoling others but hiding his own anxiety, hoping that "if I can continue with this to my last day in life, I shall have had my revenge." He experienced, indeed, an oceanic feeling of anxiety which modern depth psychology calls a sense of unrelieved suspense. An entry in his diary, dated 1839, reads, "When I am alone in my kayak like a Greenlander, on the world's immense ocean, as much above the waters as underneath and always in God's hands, then it does occur to me to harpoon a sea monster on some good occasion . . . but I don't have the skill to do so." He was no Captain Ahab to attack Moby Dick, the white whale

representing evil. His spiritual abode was the same melancholy that had haunted his father: "What the English say of their home, I have to say about my sadness; my sadness is my castle."

Recent studies have attempted to make a great deal of Kierkegaard's physical deformity as a hunchback. Rikard Magnussen has devoted two volumes to the mystery of Kierkegaard's appearance, concluding from his findings that his hunchback was that same "thorn in the flesh" of which Kierkegaard speaks so eloquently and which has given rise to so many other speculations. Theodor Haecker, the German Catholic expert on Kierkegaard, based a recent and rather verbose study on these "findings," exploiting them metaphysically as a God-given cross to be borne by the Danish writer. We wonder. Apparently Kierkegaard was of the pycnic type, and the effect of a hunchback upon his mind would lend a piquant touch to his psychological profile. But it is hard to see why his contemporary enemies should have been as discreet about the hunchback as they have been (apart from a suggestive cartoon or two) and why unhappy Regine Olsen continued to love him as ardently as ever after the breaking of the engagement. He was weak and sickly and he is likely to have derived from his physical impairment the same spirit of bravado that distinguished Dostoevsky and Nietzsche. But whatever the truth about the hunchback may be, it seems safe to remain conservative toward any of its psychological and religious interpretations.

An 1842 drawing by P.C. Klaestrup, who also produced some caricatures of Kierkegaard in the journal The Corsair.

The psychological impression which the various drawings of Kierkegaard's face convey range from the physiognomy of a pleasant and thoughtful poet to a withdrawn scholar. P. C. Klaestrup's sketch of the nineteen-year-old Sören is the most startling. Kierkegaard's wide and hypnotic eyes, the serious mouth, and high forehead combine to transmit some of the fervor of his passionate thoughts. We may never know which of these drawings is the most authentic.

There are more mysteries about his "thorn in the flesh." Can we consider his short story dealing with the anguish of a lonely bachelor, who considers it a possibility that he is the father of an illegitimate child, an autobiographical reference to his first and only contact with prostitution? If so, it might make another most interesting parallel to Nietzsche's experience in Cologne. Was the unrelieved self-reproach of the story's sad hero this same "thorn in the flesh"? No Freudian alibis were on hand a century ago, and the almost unbearable burden of Protestant sin theology would have been enough to crush Kierkegaard, the sensitive and overscrupulous seeker after purity of heart. Could it have been that such an incident—if at all true—reconciled him first to the confessions of his father and then to his divine Father? We may never know the truth. The mystery of genius ought rather to prevent our attaching too much importance to the incidents of his life and to the details of his appearance. Any attempt to interpret the mission and message of a genius like Kierkegaard through his biography is bound to remain inadequate. His religious message is universal, and the ways of the spirit are beyond and above the categories of psychology.

It was both the burden and pride of Kierkegaard to be a writer, and the many facets of his strange personality expressed themselves brilliantly in his work. He spoke as a poet and scholar, seducer and moralist; he was joyful and witty but also desperately sad; a passionate fighter and a detached observer of others and himself, he was nothing to the exclusion of anything else. Like the possessed man in the parable of the Gadarene swine, he was "many" during the first phase of his writing, and it is one more of his life's mysteries that these almost unbearable tensions did not explode in the complete disorder of mental derangement.

This uncanny versatility of his genius expressed itself in the scintillating varieties of his style. Each time it is perfectly adapted to the overtones it wishes to convey. When he makes the seducer speak, his vocabulary is glib and persuasive; the faithful husband's words are clear and firm; the somber tone of his melancholy spreads a note of gloom; his religious ecstasies are truly infectious; his elegant humor is of the most facile kind; his vitriolic attacks upon church and clergy rally the reader to intense partisanship; and his sermons speak even to modern man's condition with the pathos of Biblical authority. And finally, when he wants to be nothing but the skeptical critic, he conveys an air of superiority that is convincing because it rises not from doubt but from a newly won and profound faith.

Kierkegaard was conscious of these contradictions within himself, knowing that between his melancholia and his true self there was "a world of fantasy which, in part, I have expressed through my pseudonyms." When publishing his *Papers of One Still Living* (1838), he added the remark that they were "published contrary to his will by S.K.," a note symbolic of his inward conflict. His writings during the first two stages of his life, the aesthetic and the ethical, appeared under suggestive, contradictory, and ultimately mysterious pen names, such as Victor Eremitus, Johannes de Silentio, Constantin Constantius, Johannes Climacus, Anti-Climacus, Frater Taciturnus, Inter and Inter, and Hilarius Bogbinder. The indirect method of conveying his thoughts by shreds of witticisms, anecdotes, and volcanic epigrams expressed itself in this disguise not only to camouflage his real personality—if one can speak of such an ultimate core of his being at all—but also to detach his thoughts from their author's personality; he was giving new laws for universal thinking and living. (pp. 3-12)

William Hubben, "Sören Kierkegaard," in his Four Prophets of Our Destiny: Kierkegaard, Dostoevsky, Nietzsche, Kafka, *Macmillan Publishing Company, 1952, pp. 1-42.*

W. H. Auden   (essay date 1952)

[*Often considered the poetic successor of W. B. Yeats and T. S. Eliot, Auden is also highly regarded for his literary criticism. As a member of a generation of British writers strongly influenced by the ideas of Karl Marx and Sigmund Freud, Auden considered social and psychological commentary important functions of literary criticism. As a committed follower of Christianity, he considered it necessary to view art in the context of moral and theological absolutes. According to Auden, the creation of aesthetic beauty and moral order—qualities that exist only in imperfect form in the world of human history—is intrinsic to the world of art. In the following excerpt from his introduction to* The Living Thoughts of Kierkegaard *(1952), Auden discusses the role of suffering in Kierkegaard's life and enumerates fundamental Existentialist principles established by the philosopher.*]

Though his writings are often brilliantly poetic and often deeply philosophic, Kierkegaard was neither a poet nor a philosopher, but a preacher, an expounder and defender of Christian doctrine and Christian conduct. The near contemporary with whom he may properly be compared is not someone like Dostoevsky or Hegel, but that other great preacher of the nineteenth century, John Henry, later Cardinal, Newman: both men were faced with the problem of preaching to a secularized society which was still officially Christian, and neither was a naïve believer, so that in each case one is conscious when reading their work that they are preaching to two congregations, one outside and one inside the pulpit. Both were tempted by intellectual ambition. Perhaps Newman resisted the temptation more successfully (occasionally, it must be confessed, Kierkegaard carried on like a spiritual prima donna), but then Newman was spared the exceptional situation in which Kierkegaard found himself, the situation of unique tribulation.

Every circumstance combined to make Kierkegaard suffer. His father was obsessed by guilt at the memory of having as a young boy cursed God; his mother was a servant girl whom his father had seduced before marriage; the frail and nervously labile constitution he inherited was further damaged by a fall from a tree. His intellectual precociousness combined with his father's intense religious instruction gave him in childhood the consciousness of an adult. Finally he was fated to live, not in the stimulating surroundings of Oxford or Paris, but in the intellectual province of Copenhagen, without competition or understanding. Like Pascal, whom in more ways than one he resembles, or like Richard III, whom he frequently thought of, he was fated to be an exception and a sufferer, whatever he did. An easygoing or prudent bourgeois he could never become, any more than Pascal could have become Montaigne.

The sufferer by fate is tempted in peculiar ways; if he concentrates on himself, he is tempted to believe that God is not good but malignantly enjoys making the innocent suffer, i.e., he is tempted into demonic defiance; if he starts from the premise that God is good, then he is tempted to believe that he is guilty without knowing what he is guilty of, i.e., he is tempted into demonic despair; if he be a Christian, he can be tempted in yet a third way, because of the paradoxical position of suffering in the Christian faith. This paradox is well expressed by the penitent shade of Forese when he says to Dante:

> "And not once only, while circling this
> road, is our pain renewed:
> I say pain and ought to say solace."

For, while ultimately the Christian message is the good news: "Glory to God in the highest and on earth peace, good-will towards men—" "Come unto me all that travail and are heavy laden and I will refresh you"; it is proximately to man's self-love the worst possible news—"Take up thy cross and follow me."

Thus to be relieved of suffering in one sense is voluntarily to accept suffering in another. As Kafka says: "The joys of this life are not its own but our dread of ascending to a higher life: the torments of this life are not its own but our self-torment because of that dread."

If the two senses of suffering are confused, then the Christian who suffers is tempted to think this a proof that he is nearer to God than those who suffer less.

Kierkegaard's polemic, and all his writings are polemical, moves simultaneously in two directions: outwardly against the bourgeois Protestantism of the Denmark of his time, and inwardly against his suffering. To the former he says, "You imagine that you are all Christians and contented because you have forgotten that each of you is an existing individual. When you remember that, you will be forced to realize that you are pagans and in despair." To himself he says, "As long as your suffering makes you defiant or despairing, as long as you identify your suffering with yourself as an existing individual, and are defiantly or despairingly the exception, you are not a Christian."

. . . . .

However complicated and obscure in its developments it has become, Existentialism starts out from some quite simple observations [by Kierkegaard].

a)   All propositions presuppose the existence of their terms as a ground, i.e., one cannot ask, "Does X exist?" but only, "Has this existing X the character A or the character B?"

b)   The subjective presupposition "I exist" is unique. It is certainly not a proposition to be proven true or false by experiment, yet unlike all other presuppositions it is indubitable and no rival belief is possible. It also appears compulsive to believe that other selves like mine exist: at least the contrary presupposition has never been historically made. To believe that a world of nature exists, i.e., of things which happen of themselves, is not however invariably made. Magicians do not make it. (The Christian expression for this presupposition is the dogma, "In the beginning God created the Heaven and the Earth.")

c)   The absolute certainty with which I hold the belief that I exist is not its only unique characteristic. The awareness of existing is also absolutely private and incommunicable. My feelings, desires, etc., can be objects of my knowledge and hence I can imagine what other people feel. My existence cannot become an object of knowledge; hence while, if I have the necessary histrionic imagination and talent I can act the part of another in such a way that I deceive his best friends, I can never imagine what it would be like to *be* that other person but must always remain myself pretending to be him.

d)   If I take away from my sense of existence all that can become an object of my consciousness, what is left?

(1)   An awareness that my existence is not self-derived. I can legitimately speak of *my* feelings. I cannot properly speak of *my* existence.

(2)   An awareness that I am free to make choices. I cannot observe the act of choice objectively. If I try, I shall not choose. Doctor Johnson's refutation of determinism, to kick the stone and say, "We know we are free and there's an end of it" is correct, because the awareness of freedom is subjective, i.e., objectively undemonstrable.

(3)   An awareness of being *with* time, i.e., experiencing time as an eternal present to which past and future refer, instead of my knowledge of my feelings and of the outer world as moving or changing *in* time.

(4)   A state of anxiety (or dread), pride (in the theological sense), despair or faith. These are not emotions in the way that fear or lust or anger are, for I cannot know them objectively; I can only know them when they have aroused such feelings as the above which are observable. For these states of anxiety or pride, etc.,

are anxiety about existing, pride in existing, etc., and I cannot stand outside them to observe them. Nor can I observe them in others. A gluttonous man may succeed when he is in my presence in concealing his gluttony, but if I could watch him all the time, I should catch him out. But I could watch a man all his life, and I should never know for certain whether or not he was proud, for the actions which we call proud or humble may have quite other causes. Pride is rightly called the root of all sin, because it is invisible to the one who is guilty of it and he can only infer it from results.

These facts of existence are expressed in the Christian doctrines of Man's creation and his fall. Man is created in the image of God; an image because his existence is not self-derived, and a divine image because like God each man is aware of his existence as unique. Man fell through pride, a wish to become God, to derive his existence from himself, and not through sensuality or any of the desires of his "nature."

(pp. 168-72)

W. H. Auden, "Søren Kierkegaard," in his Forewords and Afterwords, *edited by Edward Mendelson, Random House, 1973, pp. 168-81.*

Herbert Marcuse   (essay date 1954)

[*A German-born philosopher, educator, and author, Marcuse was adopted by the New Left in the 1960s as a leader in the movement toward social change. In his* One-Dimensional Man *(1964), Marcuse argued that modern technological society had become self-absorbed and that its workers were anesthetized by the products of their own labor. He argued that only those who felt estranged by this inherently repressive system—students, intellectuals, and minorities—could alter it. In the following excerpt, Marcuse asserts that Kierkegaard and Marx represent contrasting antirationalist trends in the search for human fulfillment. Kierkegaard's system focuses on the individual, Marcuse points out, while Marxism is based on society.*]

[We] have to distinguish [Marxian theory] from the other contemporary forms that were built on 'the negation of philosophy.' The deep surge of conviction that philosophy had come to an end colored the first decades after Hegel's death. The assurance spread that the history of thought had reached a decisive turn and that there was only one medium left in which 'the truth' could be found and put into operation, namely, man's concrete material existence. Philosophical structures had hitherto domiciled 'the truth,' setting it apart from the historical struggle of men, in the form of a complex of abstract, transcendental principles. Now, however, man's emancipation could become man's own work, the goal of his self-conscious practice. The true being, reason, and the free subject could now be transformed into historical realities. Hegel's successors ac-

cordingly exalted the 'negation of philosophy' as 'the realization of God' through the deification of man (Feuerbach), as 'the realization of philosophy' (Feuerbach, Marx), and as the fulfillment of the 'universal essence' of man (Feuerbach, Marx).

Who and what will fulfill the essence of man? Who will realize philosophy? The different answers to these questions exhaust the trends of post-Hegelian philosophy. Two general types may be distinguished. The first, represented by Feuerbach and Kierkegaard, seizes upon the isolated individual; the second, represented by Marx, penetrates to the origins of the individual in the process of social labor and shows how the latter process is the basis of man's liberation.

Hegel had demonstrated that the fullest existence of the individual is consummated in his social life. Critical employment of the dialectical method tended to disclose that individual freedom presupposes a free society, and that the true liberation of the individual therefore requires the liberation of society. Fixation on the individual alone would thus amount to adopting an abstract approach, such as Hegel himself set aside. Feuerbach's materialism and Kierkegaard's existentialism, though they embody many traits of a deep-rooted social theory, do not get beyond earlier philosophical and religious approaches to the problem. The Marxian theory, on the other hand, focuses down as a critical theory of society and breaks with the traditional formulations and trends.

Kierkegaard's individualistic interpretation of 'the negation of philosophy' inevitably developed a fierce opposition to Western rationalism. Rationalism was essentially universalistic . . . , with reason resident in the thinking ego and in the objective mind. The truth was lodged either in the universal 'pure reason,' which was untouched by the circumstances of individual life, or in the universal mind, which could flourish though individuals might suffer and die. Man's material happiness was deserted in both cases, by the introversion of reason as well as by its premature adequation to the world as it is.

Rationalist philosophy, the individualists contended, was not concerned with man's actual needs and longings. Though it claimed to respond to his true interests, it gave no answer to his simple quest for happiness. It could not help him in the concrete decisions he constantly had to make. If, as the rationalists maintained, the real unique existence of the individual (which could never be reduced to a universal) was not the primary subject matter of philosophy, and the truth could not be found in or related to this unique existence, all philosophical efforts were superfluous, nay, dangerous. For they served to divert man from the only realm in which he seeks and needs the truth. Only one criterion, therefore, held for a genuine philosophy, its capacity to save the individual.

According to Kierkegaard, the individual is not the knowing but only the 'ethically existing subjectivity.' The sole reality that matters to him is his own 'ethical existence.' Truth lies not in knowledge, for sense perception and historical knowledge are mere semblance, and 'pure' thought is nothing but a 'phantom.' Knowledge deals only with the possible and is incapable of making anything real or even of grasping reality. Truth lies only in action and can be experienced only through action. The individual's own existence is the sole reality that can actually be comprehended, and the existing individual himself the sole subject or performer of this comprehension. His existence is a thinking existence, but his thought is determined by his individual living, so that all his problems arise and are resolved in his individual activity.

Every individual, in his innermost individuality, is isolated from all others; he is essentially unique. There is no union, no community, no 'universality' to contest his dominion. Truth is forever the outcome of his own decision (*Entscheidung*) and can be realized only in the free acts that spring from this decision. The sole decision open to the individual is that between eternal salvation and eternal damnation.

Kierkegaard's individualism turns into the most emphatic absolutism. There is only one truth, eternal happiness in Christ; and only one proper decision, to live a Christian life. Kierkegaard's work is the last great attempt to restore religion as the ultimate organon for liberating humanity from the destructive impact of an oppressive social order. His philosophy implies throughout a strong critique of his society, denouncing it as one that distorts and shatters human faculties. The remedy was to be found in Christianity, and the fulfillment in the Christian way of life. Kierkegaard knew that in this society such a way of life involved incessant struggle and ultimate humiliation and defeat, and that a Christian existence within current social forms was ever an impossibility. The church had to be separated from the state, for, any dependence on the state would betray Christianity. The true role of the church, freed of any restrictive force, was to denounce prevailing injustice and bondage and to point up the individual's ultimate interest, his salvation.

Salvation could not rely upon external institutions and authorities, nor could it ever be attained by pure thought. Consequently, Kierkegaard now shifts the burden of achieving a life in truth to the concrete individual, the same individual who is the basic concern of Christianity. The *individual* is 'the truth,' not reason or mankind or the state—for the individual is the only reality. 'That which exists is always an individual; the abstract does not exist.'

Kierkegaard returns to the original function of religion, its appeal to the destitute and tormented individual. He thus restores to Christianity its combative and revolutionary force. The appearance of God again assumes the terrifying aspect of a historical event suddenly breaking in upon a society in decay. Eternity takes on a temporal aspect, while the realization of happiness becomes an immediately vital matter of daily life.

Kierkegaard, however, was holding to a content that could no longer take a religious form. Religion was doomed to share the fate of philosophy. The salvation of mankind could not any longer rest in the realm of faith, especially since advancing historical forces were in motion, bearing forward the revolutionary core of religion in a concrete struggle for social liberation. In these circumstances the religious protest was weak and impotent, and religious individualism could even turn against the individual it set out to save. If left to the inner world of the individual, 'the truth' gets separated from the social and political vortex in which it belongs.

Kierkegaard's attack on abstract thought led him to assail certain universal concepts that uphold the essential equality and dignity of man. He holds humanity (*reine Menschheit*) to be a 'negativity,' a mere abstraction from the individual and a leveling of all existential values. The 'totality' of reason, in which Hegel saw the completion of the truth, is also a 'mere abstraction.' We can best see how far from a purely philosophical matter is this focusing of philosophy on the uniqueness of the individual and how much it entails his social and political isolation, when we consider Kierkegaard's attitude to the socialist movement. There is no doubt, he says, that 'the idea of socialism and community (*Gemeinschaft*) cannot save this age.' Socialism is just one among many attempts to degrade individuals by equalizing all so as to 'remove all organic, concrete differentiations and distinctions.' It is a function of resentment on the part of the many against the few who possess and exemplify the higher values; socialism is thus part of the general revolt against extraordinary individuals.

The anti-rationalist attack on universals becomes increasingly important in the subsequent development of European thought. The assault upon the universal reason was easily swung to an attack on the positive social implications of this universal. . . . [The] concept of reason was connected with advanced ideas, like the essential equality of men, the rule of law, the standard of rationality in state and society, and . . . Western rationalism was thus definitely linked with the fundamental institutions of liberalist society. In the ideological field, the struggle against this liberalism began with the attack on rationalism. The position called 'existentialism' played an important part in this attack. First, it denied the dignity and reality of the universal. This led to a rejection of any universally valid rational norms for state and society. Later, it was claimed that no bond joins individuals, states, and nations into a whole of mankind, that the particular existential conditions of each cannot be submitted to the general judgment of reason. Laws, it was held, are not based upon any universal qualities of man in whom a reason resides; they rather express the needs of individual people whose lives they regulate in accordance with their existential requirements. This demotion of reason made it possible to exalt certain particularities (such as the race or the folk) to the rank of the highest values. (pp. 262-67)

Herbert Marcuse, "The Foundations of the Dialectical Theory of Society," in his Reason and Revolution: Hegel and the Rise of Social Theory, *Second edition, The Humanities Press, 1954, pp. 258-322.*

F. J. Billeskov Jansen (essay date 1955)

[*In the following, which was originally published in French in 1955, Jansen extols Kierkegaard's ability to harmonize form and content, and praises his effective employment of a wide variety of styles.*]

Most readers of Kierkegaard's work, preoccupied above all with discovering his thought, fail to realize how much attention the author paid to construction and style. His concern for form is not limited to the general plan of a book or article but manifests itself in every turn of phrase. Each feature of his writing is calculated and premeditated, even the violent outbursts which seem most spontaneous. The all-powerful reflection which played so subtle and complicated a game with the pseudonyms also controlled the variations in form within each work.

Kierkegaard was acquainted with literary forms from his earliest youth. He was born in 1813 and grew up in an age when there flourished in Denmark a veritable cult of the art of writing, both in prose and poetry. Denmark's great literary critic of the time was Johan Ludvig Heiberg (1790-1860), an ardent disciple of Hegel. From his judgments of taste there was no appeal. He served as a model for the young Kierkegaard when, in 1834, he made his literary debut in the critical journal published by Heiberg with a highly ironical article on the intellectual powers of women. Kierkegaard's first book [*From the Papers of One Still Living*], a criticism of a novel by Hans Christian Andersen, was in fact an article grown too long for Heiberg's journal. In that book Kierkegaard adopts with all sincerity the role of the philosopher-aesthetician in his reflections on literary matters. Nevertheless he does not attain in his first work the precision and verve of his master. In his early formative years Kierkegaard wrote in two different styles: the first, designed for the public, is the stilted style which we have just mentioned; the second, for himself alone, is the simple and inspired language of his *Journal.* As early as 1835 this personal style, vivacious and poetic, was fully developed; that is to say, when not preoccupied with writing about literature or the public but with his own future, his vocation, and his whole spiritual life, Kierkegaard was already a master of language, a writer, an artist. About 1841, when preparing his academic dissertation, Kierkegaard decided to make his personal language a literary style. In accordance with university regulations a dissertation had to be written in Latin; in certain cases, however, this requirement could be waived, and Kierkegaard applied for a dispensation before submitting his manuscript to the faculty—not because of any deficiencies in his knowledge of Latin but because he had discovered the power of his mother tongue to express philosophical concepts. *The Concept of Irony* (1841) is indeed written to a great extent in a language rarely found in university dissertations. "They will reproach me for the freedom of my style," Kierkegaard wrote in his *Journal,* but added, "the reader will have to forgive my gaiety, and the fact that I sometimes sing to my work in order to lighten my task." A wealth of poetic images occurs throughout the philosophical discussion, and one is conscious of reading a spoken and not a literary idiom. Familiar expressions and plays on words abound, and the syntax is extremely flexible. In its style even more than in its content *The Concept of Irony* is the work of a master.

The author, however, subsequently wished *Either/Or* (1843) to be considered his first book. It is at any rate the first of Kierkegaard's works in which both his thought and his art are revealed in all their depth and variety. *Either/Or* is an extraordinary book; one might almost say that it is unique of its kind. As a novel it is unlike any other, and yet it does not exist in a vacuum. Just as the ideas in it reflect the reactions of Kierkegaard the philosopher to the current opinions of his age, so the form—or rather the multiplicity of forms—reflects the influence of the shape and character of the contemporary novel.

In Germany and the countries of the north the publication of Goethe's *Wilhelm Meister's Apprenticeship* (1794-1796) was an event of the greatest importance. The German romantics regarded it as the prototype of the modern novel and each strove to create in his own manner a universal novel in which the young hero sets out in search of adventure and the world of his dreams. Twenty-five years after the *Apprenticeship* Goethe published *Wilhelm Meister's Travels* (1821-1829) in which the writer, then advanced in years and wisdom, accepts the world of realities.

In the eyes of Kierkegaard's generation *Wilhelm Meister* appeared as one complete and unified work, the philosophical novel *par excellence* tracing the spiritual evolution of an individual, the history of a man and at the same time of an idea.

In February, 1836, Kierkegaard obtained the latest edition of the works of Goethe. From his *Journals* we learn that he read almost without interruption the six volumes containing *Wilhelm Meister*. He wrote down several passages from it and in March, 1836, tried to summarize what he considered to be most "masterly" in the work. He admired the skill with which the author had developed a providential philosophy in such a way that it exists at first independently of the central character but finally becomes incarnated in Wilhelm himself. "That is what makes this novel more than any other seem a perfect whole. It is indeed a mirror which reflects the whole world, a true microcosm." It is obvious that in Kierkegaard's opinion *Wilhelm Meister* is a novel in which the history of a man and the formulation of a doctrine merge into one. It is in this work that Kierkegaard found the perfect example of the symbolic tale and of the character who is at the same time an idea, a type, and a man who by virtue of his mode of existence represents humanity. Kierkegaard did not make his own novels philosophical biographies in the manner of Goethe, but he created characters symbolizing different outlooks on life, like the "aesthetic" and the "ethical" types who form the two poles in *Either/Or,* and, later, the "religious" type as presented in *Stages on Life's Way* (1845).

It was not solely because of its presentation of symbolic character that Kierkegaard took *Wilhelm Meister* as his model. This vast work was for him, as for all the romantic writers of the day, the prototype of the "universal novel"; that is to say, it offered a framework into which every literary form could be assimilated. The extracts of it which Kierkegaard made indicate that in the course of his reading he paused at certain places where the narrative is interrupted. "The study of 'Hamlet and its Production' should be noted in particular," he writes, and further on he notes that "the 'Confessions of a Beautiful Soul' are full of the most profound observations." Goethe's vast novel contains collections of letters, short stories and tales which the characters read for their own entertainment, and finally a diary, "Leonardo's Tagebuch." It is worth noting that in the edition read by Kierkegaard the novel comprises several parts almost unrelated to the whole which are nowadays omitted in most editions. A group of brief reflections is also to be found at the end of Book II of the *Travels:* "Betrachtungen im Sinne der Wanderer. Kunst, Ethisches, Natur," and at the end of Book III there is a similar series of aphorisms: "Aus Makariens Archiv."

It is easy to discover numerous examples of forms peculiar to Goethe in the two great novels by Kierkegaard. Our intention is not, however, to compile a list of comparisons but to reveal the originality of the Danish writer: this lies in the art with which he combines analysis of human character and literary forms. The first part of *Either/Or* begins with a series of exclamations and paradoxes grouped together under the title "Diapsalmata," a word which, according to Kierkegaard, means in this context "refrains"—that is, variations on the theme of tedium as experienced by the aesthete in the face of the drabness and monotony of existence. There follows an extremely varied collection of literary and dramatic studies, together with eloquent and inspired discourses, and the volume concludes with the "Diary of the Seducer." The second part, containing an exposition of the ethical attitude to life, is composed of only two discourses, written in the form of letters and of considerable length. The contrast between the two parts is intentional. The aesthete has no firm base in life on which to rest: he seeks pleasure from the passing moment and is consequently led to experience only despair. His life, like his philosophy, has no order. It is therefore logical that the way in which such an incoherent conception of life is expressed should itself be chaotic. In the general introduction to *Either/Or* the pseudonymous editor states that the first part contains "a number of attempts to formulate an aesthetic philosophy of life, as this permits of no single coherent exposition."

This contrast in form is pursued even in the minutest stylistic details. The aesthete expresses himself by means of exclamations and incoherent outbursts or else in flights of lyrical and ecstatic eloquence. The language of the man of principles is entirely different. Although there is no lack of fervor, his words are calm and harmonious, his sentences well-balanced, and when using poetic imagery he has recourse not to the turbulent visions of the "Diapsalmata" but to scenes of domestic life reminiscent of the genre pictures of contemporary painting.

In *Stages on Life's Way* Kierkegaard's awareness of the expressive qualities of different styles is even more acute. We shall mention only one of the many examples of this to be found. In the diary entitled "Guilty?/Not Guilty?" Kierkegaard has inserted six short stories each of which is written in a particular style. With unrivaled skill he imitates in turn the Old Testament ("Solomon's Dream" and "Nebuchadnezzar"), Herodotus ("Periander"), Shakespeare's King Lear on the heath ("A Leper's Soliloquy") and the contemporary Danish novel ("A Possibility"). So great is the concern for style in these perfect *pastiches* that a gulf seems to separate the writer of the Diary from the

six tableaux which he presents as his own work; the stylistic virtuosity here has to some extent had an effect contrary to that intended by the novelist.

In his philosophical and theological works Kierkegaard changed his method. The characters in *Repetition* and *Fear and Trembling* (both published on October 16, 1843) are already less autonomous than those in the great novels which we have just discussed, and in later treatises the analysis of human types is used only as a means of illustrating a concept or idea which is the real subject of the book. Just as Kierkegaard's first philosophical work bears the title *The Concept of Irony,* so all his subsequent works are named or could be named after the concept examined in each.

Contrast is one of the stylistic effects for which Kierkegaard had a particular preference. In June, 1844, he published two books on similar subjects but written in contrasting styles. *The Concept of Dread* deals with the fall of man and *Philosophical Fragments* with revelation. The first of these two works is an attempt to examine a theological problem from a psychological standpoint; in it Kierkegaard develops his own point of view while discussing the problem in Schleiermacher and other theologians. It is an exposition in conformity with all the rules: the subject matter is divided into chapters and paragraphs, and quotations and technical terms abound. In order to destroy the theological theories of his age, Kierkegaard borrows the very form used by his adversaries. With an irony which is most pungent in the introduction and epigraph, he makes his book resemble as closely as possible the textbooks of the theological faculty. In the presence of this learned treatise on the fall of Adam, one has the impression of reading Latin—the Latin which Kierkegaard had rejected for his dissertation.

Philosophical Fragments, on the other hand, is a book in the Greek style. Both the basic problem and the method of argumentation are borrowed from Socrates:

> How far does the Truth admit of being learned? With this question let us begin. It was a Socratic question, or became such in consequence of the parallel Socratic question with respect to virtue, since virtue was again determined as insight. . . . In so far as the Truth is conceived as something to be learned, its non-existence is evidently presupposed, so that in proposing to learn it one makes it the object of an inquiry. Here we are confronted with the difficulty to which Socrates calls attention in the *Meno* . . . one cannot seek for what he knows, and it seems equally impossible for him to seek for what he does not know. For what a man knows he cannot seek, since he does not even know for what to seek.

It is as if we were listening to the voice of Socrates, an illusion which is never destroyed. Proceeding in the same manner as the Greek philosopher, the author allows the discussion to develop by stages: "Now we shall take our time, there is in any case no need to hurry—we shall discuss this question as the Greeks would have done."

The discussion, however, is Socratic only in form, for its

content is directed against Socrates. Here Kierkegaard proceeds in exactly the same way as in *The Concept of Dread:* he avails himself of the enemy's weapons in order to combat him. A Platonic dialogue generally begins with a Sophist or young man submitting a postulate which Socrates then disproves, but in the *Philosophical Fragments* it is Socrates himself who propounds the thesis destined to be imperceptibly refuted. This time it is Socrates who believes himself to be in possession of some knowledge; the other, who takes his traditional role. This other, though never named, is Jesus Christ. Kierkegaard adopts and exploits with exceptional skill the Socratic indirect or ironic method of argumentation in order to prove that man does not possess in himself the truth about his own being, as taught by the Greek master, and hence that he can know this only through divine revelation.

To this slim volume Kierkegaard attached the vast *Concluding Unscientific Postscript to the Philosophical Fragments* (1846), six times larger than the small work of which it was made the supplement. Yet another contrast! Here the indirect method is replaced by the direct method, and abstraction by a concrete exposition of historical facts. The problem is no longer how to define revelation, i.e., Christian doctrine, but how "I, Johannes Climacus, now thirty years of age, born in Copenhagen . . . am to become a Christian."

In 1848 Kierkegaard wrote two works in which once again a certain similarity in theme is combined with a contrast in literary method. *The Sickness unto Death,* which appeared in 1849, begins in the Hegelian manner with the vaguest of all abstractions, a metaphysical definition of man, and continues with a series of character studies which together form a brilliant portrait gallery of every type of sinner. Despair is here shown to be an awareness of sin which leads the sinner to salvation. In *Training in Christianity,* the publication of which was postponed until 1850, Kierkegaard intends to rouse the reader by means of shock tactics. In words of the utmost gentleness the writer dwells at some length on the invitation which Jesus Christ addressed to all mankind: "Come hither to me, all ye that labor and are heavy laden, and I will give you rest." Then, when the invitation has been accepted and rest and peace seem close at hand, the interpreter of Christianity cries halt. In brutal tones he announces that the invitation comes from the poorest and most despised of men who lived among beggars and lepers over eighteen hundred years ago, and that this deluded vagabond invites us to become his contemporaries: he demands that we, far from being scandalized at his behavior, should believe that he is God himself.

Thus, at the alluring prospect of a peace beyond comprehension the gates of Paradise seem to open—to release a tiger which springs at the throat of those who have answered the call of Christ without once reflecting upon its significance. *Training in Christianity* heralds the attack upon the Church, but before discussing the controversy which ensued, a third and by no means least important facet of Kierkegaard's work must be examined.

The novels and philosophical-theological works of Kierkegaard were published under various pseudonyms. At the same time, however, from 1843 onwards, he wrote a long series of edifying discourses under his own name. For the majority of readers these discourses appear from a literary point of view to be one homogeneous mass. If, however, they are examined more closely it becomes evident that they belong roughly to three different groups, and Kierkegaard took pains to find a distinctive attribute for each: his discourses are successively "edifying," "Christian," and "godly."

Kierkegaard's edifying discourses resemble the sermons of Bishop Mynster, the fashionable preacher of the day, but the philosopher does not attempt to emulate the eloquence of the pulpit: he speaks in a low voice, the tone of which is gentle, intimate, almost tender.

In 1847, a volume of considerable size and import appeared. It was entitled *Edifying Discourses (of Varied Tenor)* and, one could add, of varied styles. In one very lengthy discourse the author's purpose is to show that "purity of heart is to will one thing." The thesis posited, the argument follows, divided and subdivided into numerous sections, until the conclusion is reached. Here it is by reasoned argument that the writer seeks to capture the mind; but if it is the voice of the philosopher which makes itself heard in this treatise, it is, on the contrary, the "poet" who has composed the three discourses on the lilies of the field and the birds of the air. In one of these discourses Kierkegaard relates both the delightful parable of the lilies bowed low with care and that of the wood-pigeon. The collection ends with seven short essays grouped together under the title "The Gospel of Suffering: Christian Discourses." In the severity of the ideas expressed, these discourses are akin to the *Works of Love: Some Christian Reflections in the Form of Discourses,* written in the same year, and to the *Christian Discourses* which were published the following year. Most of the "Christian" discourses by Kierkegaard have an entirely different character. Both gentle persuasion and skillful argumentation are jettisoned in favor of the striking phrase, the unusual image and the paradox. One section of the 1848 collection is therefore appositely called "Thoughts which Wound from Behind—for Edification."

The "Christian" discourses were written for an elite among the public, but in 1849, Kierkegaard decided to write from that time on for the ordinary reader. He returns to his favorite theme *"The Lilies of the Field"* and *"The Birds of the Air"* in a volume [*Edifying Discourses in a Different Vein*] bearing the subtitle *Three Godly Discourses.* This time he no longer relates stories but attempts to bewitch the reader with the magic of his lyrical prose. Each sentence is given a primitive cadence and certain words are repeated at regular intervals so that our brain finally reproduces unaided the *leitmotivs* of the discourses; when this occurs the missionary writer has achieved his purpose. In three discourses written in the same year Kierkegaard raises before our eyes with the art of a sculptor three figures: the High Priest, that is, Christ (Hebrews 4:15); the Publican (Luke 18:13); and finally the Woman who was a Sinner (Luke 7:47).

The "godly" discourses are the first of Kierkegaard's writings in which he uses a popular style of eloquence. *For*

Self-Examination (1851), consisting of three religious discourses, has the subtitle *Recommended to this Present Time* and has as epigraph the following Biblical text: "Knowing therefore the terror of the Lord, we persuade men" (II Corinthians 5:11). Here for the first time Kierkegaard attempts a popular exposition of his theological ideas, and in so doing he was influenced by the sermons of Luther, whom he greatly revered at this time. The language in this treatise is richer and fresher than in the preceding ones. In a "second series," written in 1851-1852 but not published until after the author's death in 1855, the popular tone is accentuated. *Judge for Yourselves!* contains two discourses of which the first in particular ("**On Becoming Sober,**" based on I Peter 4:7) is written in a style approaching brusqueness. Two months before his death, however, and still engaged in battle, Kierkegaard published a sermon which he had delivered in a church in Copenhagen in May, 1851. The text comes from the Epistle of St. James (1:17): "Every good gift and every perfect gift is from above, and cometh down from the Father of Lights, with whom is no variableness, neither shadow of turning." This epilogue to the religious discourses has no distinctive attribute: Kierkegaard calls it, simply and pathetically, "A Discourse."

Both in *Training in Christianity* (1850) and in *For Self-Examination* (1851) Kierkegaard revealed to his contemporaries the disparity between the religion they practiced and true Christianity as he conceived it. He waited three years for a response—would the Church recognize the gulf which separated it from the Christian ideal? Kierkegaard covered the pages of his journal with feverish notes but published nothing before December 18, 1854. On that date a daily paper in Copenhagen printed an article by him attacking Martensen, Bishop of Zealand, who, at the death of his predecessor Mynster, had called the latter a "witness to the truth." This expression, however, had come to be regarded by Kierkegaard as a synonym for the true Christian, that is, the martyr. A controversy ensued. Until May, 1855, more than twenty polemical articles flowed from Kierkegaard's pen, and, when the space allotted to him in a daily paper proved too limited, he proceeded to issue a pamphlet (May 24) and later a review entitled "**The Instant,**" of which nine editions were published in the course of four months. The tenth edition was ready for printing when, on October 2, Kierkegaard was hospitalized for an illness which caused his death on November 11.

In this supreme struggle which exhausted his physical strength Kierkegaard exploited all the resources of his art. Abandoning the indirect method of the pseudonymous works as well as the persuasive tone of the religious discourses, he deliberately adopted the attitude of aggressor: henceforth his role was that of a reformer. The attack against the official Church was violent, uncompromising, a struggle to the death.

The most striking fact to be noticed from a literary point of view is that Kierkegaard never at any time lost control over his means of expression. As much care is given to style as to the other aspects of his writing, sometimes even more. In *Judge for Yourselves!* Kierkegaard had written

a short tale, the story of a theological graduate in search of a livelihood, but only in "**The Instant**" did the tale receive the final touch which transformed it into a masterpiece of irony: "Seek ye first the kingdom of God." The novelist in Kierkegaard placed himself wholeheartedly at the service of the agitator; it is in fact due to his poetic gifts that Kierkegaard became so great a pamphleteer. The sallies and paradoxes of the "Diapsalmata" are transformed into the most biting invectives; the genre-imagery so dear to the man of principle becomes discordant even in form; in place of the parable we find a legend created out of diverse elements by the outrageous imagination of the polemist: Imagine a witness to the truth ending his life of martyrdom on a gridiron upon which he is gradually roasted by a small fire. Imagine then the community deciding to consecrate the memory of this martyr by holding a feast on the anniversary of his death; on this occasion a fish is to be grilled in each house, the best part of which is to be sent to the parish priest!

Flagrant insults accompanied by proper names, veiled sarcasms, and ironical allusions follow each other in rapid succession in the articles of "**The Instant.**" On his deathbed Kierkegaard refused to receive the sacrament from the hands of a clergyman. Nevertheless his funeral took place in conformity with traditional practice, although before the open grave a violent protest was made by a young nephew of Kierkegaard over the presence and concourse of churchmen. He began to recite passages from "**The Instant**":

> We are all Christians, nothing we say can alter this. Even if a man solemnly declares that he is not a Christian but dies leaving just sufficient to pay for the funeral rites and the reverend parson, all his pronouncements will have been in vain— he is a Christian and will be buried as a Christian, so certain is it that we are all Christians.

Thus Kierkegaard, the "magister" of irony, as he called himself when referring to his academic dissertation and university degree, had the last word at his own funeral. (pp. 11-21)

> *F. J. Billeskov Jansen, "The Literary Art of Kierkegaard," translated by Margaret Grieve, in* A Kierkegaard Critique: An International Selection of Essays Interpreting Kierkegaard *by F. J. Billeskov and others, edited by Howard A. Johnson and Niels Thulstrup, Harper & Brothers, Publishers, 1962, pp. 11-21.*

Paul Ricoeur   (essay date 1963)

[*A French philosopher and critical theorist, Ricoeur strove to blend structural and hermeneutical thought into a critical approach that successfully explains the processes of interpretation and the significance of speech. In the following excerpt, Ricoeur finds that Kierkegaard's understanding of evil as a "position"—meaning a state or condition as opposed to an intelligible or defensible concept—indicates his break with the tradition of speculative philosophy. Ricoeur's commentary first appeared in* Revue de Théologie et de Philosophie 13*

(1963) under the title "Kierkegaard et le mal." It was translated into English by David Pellauer.]

The task of celebrating Kierkegaard, who had no pity for ministers and professors, may call forth derision. Can we talk about Kierkegaard without excluding either him or ourselves? We are here to face this ridicule as honestly and modestly as possible. After all, we must also confront Kierkegaard's sarcasm. It is still the best way of honoring him. In any case, it is better to run this risk than to prove him correct out of good manners or through convention. (p. 313)

[We] shall attempt to listen and to understand by simply putting before ourselves a few texts upon which we shall concentrate as narrow and intense attention as possible. These texts are taken from two writings, **The Concept of Dread,** which dates from 1844, and **The Sickness unto Death,** published five years later, in 1849. I want to extract from these two essays Kierkegaard's thought concerning evil by means of as rigorous an exegesis as possible. It is through this *explication de texte* that we run the biggest risk of excluding ourselves. (pp. 313-14)

Why are we stopping with these two texts and why the question of evil?

Let us consider the question of evil first. There is scarcely any need to emphasize that evil is the critical point for all philosophical thought. If it comprehends evil, this is its greatest success. Yet evil understood is no longer evil. It has stopped being absurd, scandalous, beyond right and reason. Yet if philosophy does not comprehend evil, then it is no longer philosophy—at least if philosophy ought to comprehend everything and set itself up as a system with nothing outside itself. In the great debate between Kierkegaard and the system—which is to say, Hegel—the question of evil represents a touchstone beyond compare. . . . [It] is important to understand how Kierkegaard himself thought in the face of the irrational, the absurd. For he did not proclaim; he thought.

There is another reason for talking about evil. It is not only the touchstone for philosophy, it is also the occasion to take by surprise the quality of Kierkegaard's Christianity; I mean his Christianity of the Cross more than of Easter or of Pentecost. But above all, I want to attempt to show how Kierkegaard speaks and thinks about evil; that is, about what is most opposed to the system.

I shall begin with the following brief comment. Neither of these two books constitutes, in any way, a journal or a confession. You will find no trace in these two writings of the terrible confession his father made to him about that day in his youth when, shepherding his sheep on the Jutland heath, he climbed up on a rock and cursed God. Or anything about the precipitous marriage of the widower father to his servant mistress, or of all the deaths that struck the paternal home, as if in punishment for the earlier blasphemy, or of Søren's melancholy, or of the splinter in his flesh. We would be wasting our time if we took the short way of psychoanalytic biography and if we looked in these complicated and argumentative writings for the direct transposition of an emotional life weighed down by torments and remorse. This direct way, from the life to the

work, is absolutely forbidden to us. Not that a psychoanalysis of Kierkegaard, or at least a fragmentary psychoanalytic approach, is impossible, but rather we must resolutely take the inverse way to him—that is, start with the exegesis of texts and perhaps return from them to the life, for there is more in these texts than the biographical odds and ends we might collect.

Thus, let us turn directly to the texts. These two treatises have in common that they are built upon the basis of two feelings or moods, more precisely, two negative feelings or moods whose object remains indeterminate: dread (or anxiety) and despair. Anxiety about what? Despair about what? Yet it is from these two that we must begin, for if we adopt as our starting point what we already know about evil, we will miss precisely what these two moods can teach us. To begin from known evil is to begin from a purely moral definition of guilt, as the transgressing of a law or as an infraction. On the contrary, the question is to discover a quality and a dimension of "sin" that only these profound emotions, ordinarily linked to melancholy or fear, can announce. Because the determination of evil occurs entirely within the orbit of these two moods, the resulting "concept" of evil is profoundly different in each treatise. The analysis of anxiety leads to a concept of sin as event or upheaval. Anxiety itself is a sort of slipping, of fascination wherein evil is circumscribed, approached from back and front. To the contrary, the **Treatise on Despair**—another name for **The Sickness unto Death**—takes place in the midst of sin, no longer as a leap, but as a state: despair is, if we may put it this way, the evil of evil, the sin of sin.

Let us successively consider these two approaches. To finish, we shall try to understand their conjunction.

The first is deliberately anti-Hegelian: leap, upheaval, event, are opposed to mediation, synthesis, reconciliation. In this way, too, the equivocal mixing of the ethical and the logical is broken off: "In logic this is too much, in ethics too little; it fits nowhere if it has to fit both places" (**The Sickness unto Death**). But who then will speak justly about sin? The metaphysician? He is both too disinterested and too comprehensive. The moralist? He believes too much in man's effort and not enough in his misery. The preacher? Well, perhaps, for he addresses himself to the isolated individual, one to one. But do not let him be a Hegelian minister! The dogmatician too, though he only explains sin by presupposing it: "The concept of sin does not properly belong in any science; only the second ethics"— the one that follows dogmatics and that knows the real and sin without "metaphysical frivolity or psychological concupiscence"—"can deal with its apparition but not with its origin." And yet it is as a psychologist that Kierkegaard is going to speak. To isolate the act's radical leap, the psychologist outlines its possibility, thereby in a way approaching the discontinuity of upheaval through the continuity of a sliding or slippage.

The paradox here is that of a beginning. How does sin come into the world? By a leap that presupposes itself in temptation. This is the "concept of anxiety": a psychology as close as possible to the event, a psychology that clings to the event as an advent, a psychology of the *durée* wherein innocence loses itself, is already lost, where it seesaws, totters, and falls. But we do not know innocence. We only know its loss. Innocence is something that "only comes into existence by the very fact that it is annulled, comes into existence as that which was before it was annulled and now is annulled." Hence I only know innocence as lost. I only know the leap of sin in its transition. This is something that is in between innocence that is lost and a leap that proceeds itself in anxiety.

What can be said about anxiety per se? It is the birth of spirit, of that spirit the Bible calls discerning of good and evil. But spirit is still a kind of dreaming. It is no longer innocence, nor yet good and evil. About what then does spirit dream? About nothing. Nothing at all. This nothing gives birth to anxiety. It is why "dread is freedom's reality as possibility for possibility." Nothing—possibility—freedom . . . One sees that ambiguity—the word is Kierkegaard's—is more enigmatic than the already too ethical "concupiscence." A "sympathetic antipathy and an antipathetic sympathy," the subtle Kierkegaard prefers to say. And he calls this ambiguity dialectical, but psychological, not logical. . . . "Just as the relation of dread to its object, to something which is nothing (language in this instance also is pregnant: it speaks of being in dread of nothing), is altogether ambiguous, so will the transition here from innocence to guilt be correspondingly so dialectical that the explanation is and must be psychological."

Will someone say that it is prohibition that awakens desire? Yet innocence does not understand prohibition. This is an explanation after the fact. We should rather say that prohibition is the *word*—the "enigmatic word"—that crystallizes anxiety. The decree alarms Adam because it awakens in him the possibility of freedom. Nothingness becomes the "possibility of the possibility of being able to do something." This is what Adam loves and what he flees.

We should not say that Kierkegaard delights in the irrational. He analyzes, he dissects, he abounds in words. He is the dialectician of the antidialectic. And this paradoxical dialectic culminates in the representation of human beings as a synthesis of soul and body, united in this third term: spirit—spirit that dreams about nothing, spirit that projects the possible. Spirit is the "hostile power" that constantly disturbs this relation, which, however, only exists through it. On the other hand, it is a "friendly power," which desires to constitute exactly this relation: "What then is man's relation to this ambiguous power? How is spirit related to itself and to its situation? It is related as dread."

Hence psychology comes too soon or too late. It recognizes either the anxiety of before, which leads to the qualitative leap—the anxiety of dreaming, of nothing—or the anxiety of afterward, which augments evil—the anxiety of reflection, about something, become in a way nature insofar as it henceforth has a "body." This is why anxiety permeates sex: not that it comes with it but because it comes to it. The anxiety of dreaming becomes flesh and extends an "inexplicable deep melancholy" over everything. It would be a mistake here to look for some kind of puritani-cal repugnance to sexuality. Before Max Scheler, Kierkegaard understood that anxiety does not come from sex but descends from the spirit into sexuality, from dreaming into the flesh. It is because man is disturbed in spirit that he is ashamed in his flesh. The spirit is uneasy in modesty and frightened over assuming sexual differentiation. Thus sin enters the world, becomes a world, and increases quantitatively.

Yet we do not know better what sin is through subsequent anxiety than through prior anxiety. It remains anxiety, closely circumscribed, yet empty at its center: "No science can explain how. Psychology comes nearest to doing so and explains the last step in the approximation, which is freedom's apparition before itself in the dread of possibility, or in the nothingness of possibility, or in the nothing of dread."

The Sickness unto Death, or *Treatise on Despair,* is also a psychological essay. More precisely, according to its subtitle, it is "A Christian Psychological Exposition for Edification and Awakening." Consequently, this treatise associates psychology, in the sense of *The Concept of Dread,* with edification in the sense of the *Edifying Discourses.* We have spoken already of the difference that separates these two treatises: the first speaks of evil as an event, a leap; the second speaks of it as a state of affairs. The substitution of despair for anxiety expresses this shift: anxiety tends toward . . . , despair resides in. . . . Anxiety "ex-ists"; despair "in-sists." What does this shift signify? It is impossible to understand *The Sickness unto Death* without referring back to an earlier essay, *Fear and Trembling,* which situates the meaning of faith and sin beyond the sphere of the ethical. Sin is not the contrary of virtue but of faith, which is a theological category. Faith is a way of being face to face with God, before God. This liaison is elaborated in *Fear and Trembling,* not by means of an abstract discussion about theological concepts, but by way of an *exegesis.* The new concepts are deciphered by means of the interpretation of a story, the story of Abraham. The *meaning* of the sacrificing of Isaac decides the meaning of the concepts of law and faith. Sacrificing Isaac would be a crime according to the moral law. According to faith, it is an act of obedience. To obey God, Abraham had to suspend the ethical. He had to become the knight of faith who moves forward alone, beyond the security of the universal law, or, as Kierkegaard puts it, of the universal. Hence *Fear and Trembling* opens a new dimension of anxiety, which proceeds from the contradiction between ethics and faith. Abraham is the symbol of this new species of anxiety linked to the theological suspension of the ethical.

The concept of despair belongs to the same nonethical but religious sphere as does Abraham's faith. Despair is the negative version of Abraham's faith. This is why Kierkegaard does not first say what sin is, then what despair is; instead he constructs and discovers sin in despair as its religious signification. From there on, sin is no longer a leap but a stagnant stage, a persisting mode of being.

Second consequence: the question is no longer, How did it enter into the world?—through anxiety; but, How is it possible to escape? Despair is thus comparable to one of the "stages on life's way" that Kierkegaard explores in another work. It is a sickness, a sickness one dies of without dying. It is the sickness "unto death," in the way that injustice, according to Plato, in book 10 of *The Republic,* is a living death and the paradoxical proof of immortality. Despair, according to Kierkegaard, is a greater evil than injustice according to Plato, which still refers to the ethical sphere. Yet because it is more grave, it is closer to recovery.

Now, how can we speak of despair? Structural analysis of *The Sickness unto Death* should bring us closer to our problem: What is Kierkegaard's mode of thinking? How is it possible to do philosophy after Kierkegaard? What is remarkable, is that Kierkegaard constructs the concept of despair. A quick look at the table of contents of this treatise reveals a tangle of titles and subtitles. The plan is even curiously didactic. The first part demonstrates this: "The Sickness Unto Death Is Despair." Its possibility, actuality, universality, and forms are carefully distinguished. Its forms are even elaborated in a rather systematic manner, from the point of view of a "lack of finitude" and a "lack of infinitude," from a "lack of possibility"—which is to say of imagination and dreaming—and a "lack of necessity"—which is to say of submitting to our tasks and general duties in this world. The same balancing is renewed with the appearance of new distinctions. The most subtle one is presented as follows: "Despair viewed under the aspect of consciousness," wherein it knows itself or does not know itself. Therefore, there is a despair over "not willing to be oneself" and over "willing to be oneself."

Then the second part, entitled "Despair Is Sin," elaborates all the characteristics of sin according to the model of despair and leads to the conclusion that "sin is not a negation but a position." I will stop with this conclusion, which I will oppose to the nothingness of anxiety.

But first I want to interrogate the strange structure of this treatise. It is impossible not to be impressed by the heavy and laborious aspect of its construction, which resembles an interminable and awkward dissertation. What does it signify? We are confronted by a sort of grimacing simulacre of Hegelian discourse. Yet this simulacre is at the same time the means of saving its discourse from absurdity. It is didactic because it cannot be dialectic. In other words, it replaces a three-term dialectic by a cut-off dialectic, by an unresolved two-term dialectic. A dialectic without mediation—this is the Kierkegaardian paradox. *Either* too much possibility *or* too much actuality. *Either* too much finitude *or* too much infinitude. *Either* one wants to be oneself *or* one does not want to be oneself. What is more, since each pair of contrary terms offers no resolution, it is not possible to construct the following paradox on the one that precedes it. The chain of paradoxes is itself a broken chain—hence the didactic framework, which is substituted for the immanent structure of a true dialectic. The rupture that threatens this discourse must constantly be conjured away or compensated for by an excess of conceptuality and rhetorical hability. From this, finally, comes the strange contrast that it is the most irrational term—despair—that sets into movement the largest mass of conceptual analyses. (pp. 314-20)

Let us examine this somewhat forbidding construction a bit more closely. The kernel about which the great antinomies of despair are constructed is a definition of the self that *The Concept of Dread* prepared us for when it spoke of spirit as the third term—the spoilsport—in the tranquil relation between soul and body. This definition in its disconcerting abstraction runs as follows: the human self is "a relation which relates itself to its own self, and in relating itself to its own self relates itself to another" (*The Sickness unto Death*). Whether out of derision or loving vexation . . . , this definition bears the mark of the Hegelian dialectic. But as a difference from Hegel, this relation that relates itself to itself is more a problem than an answer, more a task than a structure. For what is given in despair is what Kierkegaard calls the "disrelation." This priority of the disrelation throughout the subsequent analysis rests on the structure's relation as an impossible task: the possibility of despair resides in the possibility of a disrelation—that is, in the fragility of the relation that relates itself to its own self, as the expression "and in relating itself to its own self relates itself to another" signifies. For this relation, to constitute oneself is to unmake oneself.

We can already understand what force this union of mood and analysis can give to the Kierkegaardian rhetoric of pathos. Despair exists—or as I have tried to say, insists—in the figures of disrelation. Consequently, everything will be more complicated than in *The Concept of Dread.* Dread or anxiety was fascinated by the nothingness of pure possibility; despair

> is the disrelationship in a relation which relates itself to itself. But the synthesis is not the disrelationship, it is merely the possibility, or, in the synthesis is latent the possibility of the disrelationship. . . . Whence then comes despair? From the relation wherein the synthesis relates itself to itself, in that God who made man a relationship lets this go as it were out of His hand, that is, in the fact that the relation relates itself to itself.

The latter remark allows us to further our explication of the strange expression about a relation that "in relating itself to its own self relates itself to another." In this abandonment, it is *related* to itself as to *another.* Dereliction is the reflective aspect of this abandonment by God, who lets go of the relation as though it escaped his grasp. Kierkegaard, prior to existentialism, discovered this identity of reflection and dereliction.

From here on, all of Kierkegaard's art consists in applying his psychological subtlety to the numerous possibilities offered by the dissociating of this relation that relates itself to its own self in relating itself to another. Kierkegaard's literary, psychological, philosophical, and theological genius seems to me to lie in this half-abstract, half-concrete way of presenting these artificially constructed possibilities, of making the *opéra fabuleux* of despairing states of the soul correspond to this conceptual game. The reader's astonishment, unease, admiration, and irritation depend on this incessant oscillating between the most pointed imaginary experimentation and the most artificial conceptual dialectic. Here are some examples: Man, we are told, is a synthesis of infinitude and finitude, of possibility and necessity. Despair springs up as soon as the will to become infinite is felt or experienced as a lack of finitude, and vice versa. This interplay between opposed concepts is fed by an extraordinary power to create human types, among whom we recognize the hero of fantastic possibilities, the Don Juan of the aesthetic stage, the seducer of the "Journal of a Seducer," Goethe's Faust, and also the poet of the religious stage, the explorer of the open according to Rilke; in brief, the imagination, the crucible of every process of infinitization. The self is reflection, says Kierkegaard, and imagination is the possibility of all reflection. This is why the loss of a place to stand, the endless distance from oneself, is felt or experienced as a loss, as despair. The abstract paradox becomes a concrete one: the "either/or" of the infinite and the finite is the "either/or" that confronts the seducer and, on his level, the hero who does his duty, depicted through the traits of Judge William. The lack of infinity, the narrowness of a mediocre life, the loss of a horizon, are very concrete possibilities, as anyone will discover who feels his own existence as that of a pebble on the shore or one number lost in the crowd.

Yet it is perhaps the last dialectic that clarifies all the others. The worst despair is "the despair that is unaware of being despair." The ordinary person is desperate, is in despair, but does not know it. Thus it is because despair may be unconscious that it has to be discovered, even constructed. The dialectic of the unconscious and the conscious unfolds inside of despair as if within the heart of an ontic possibility, of a mode of being. Consciousness does not constitute despair. Despair exists, or, as I have said, insists. This is why even consciousness attaches itself to despair. The great despair, despair over oneself, the despair of willing despairingly to be oneself, which Kierkegaard calls defiance, represents the final degree of "the constant heightening of the power of despair." Here, more than anywhere else, this possibility may only be tried out in imagination: "This sort of despair is seldom seen in the world, such figures generally are met only in the works of poets, that is to say, of real poets, who always lend their characters this 'demoniac' ideality (taking this word in the purely Greek sense)" (*The Sickness unto Death*). In real life, this supreme despair can only be approached in the most spiritual despair, the despair that no longer has to do with some earthly loss, the despair of not wanting to be helped.

We may now confront **The Concept of Dread** and **The Sickness unto Death** on the point of sin, so circumscribed by two opposed approaches.

The two treatises agree that sin is not an ethical reality but a religious one. Sin is "before God." But while **The Concept of Dread** remains outside of this determination of sin as "before God," **The Sickness unto Death** stands within its heart. **The Concept of Dread** stays purely psychological; **The Sickness unto Death** "edifies and awakens," according to its subtitle. While anxiety was a movement toward . . . , despair is sin. To say this is no longer psychology: "There here may be introduced, as the most dialectical borderline between despair and sin, what one might call a poetic existence in the direction of the religious . . . " (trans. altered).

This "poetic existence in the direction of the religious" has nothing to do with a mystical effusion. It is, says Kierkegaard, "prodigiously dialectical, and is in an impenetrable dialectical confusion as to how far it is conscious of being sin." Everything that will be said from here on belongs to this reduplication of the dialectic when it passes from psychology to poetic existence in the direction of the religious. First, psychology designates sin through the experience of vertigo as a fall, then it designates it as a lack, consequently as "nothing." For poetic existence, sin is a state, a condition, a mode of being; further, it is a *position*.

Let us consider these new dimensions that could not appear in **The Concept of Dread,** first because this treatise stays purely psychological, next because it approaches sin as a leap.

That sin is a *state* is revealed by despair itself. We cannot say that anxiety *is* sin, we can say that despair *is*. In this way, the concept of sin is definitively transported from the ethical sphere of transgression into the religious sphere of unfaith. We may even say, from the sphere where sin is flesh to the sphere where it is spirit. It is the power of weakness and the weakness of defiance. Hence sin is no longer the contrary of virtue but of faith. It is an ontic human possibility, and not just a moral category according to a Kantian ethics or an intellectual defect comparable to ignorance according to the Socratic concept of evil. In other words, sin is our ordinary mode of being before God. It is existence itself as dereliction.

But we come to the final difference between **The Concept of Dread** and **The Sickness unto Death** when we say that "sin is not a negation but a position." This thesis—which Kierkegaard takes to be the orthodox Christian interpretation of sin—is directed against all speculative philosophy. To comprehend evil philosophically is to reduce it to a pure negation: weakness as a lack of force, sensuality as a lack of spirituality, ignorance as a lack of knowledge, finitude as a lack of totality. Hegel identified comprehension with negation or, better, with the negation of negation. It is here that Kierkegaard opposes his most vigorous protest against philosophy—that is, against Hegelian philosophy. If to comprehend is to overcome, that is, to pass beyond negation, then sin is one negation among others and repentance one mediation among others. In this way, negation and the negation of negation both become purely logical processes.

But, if we only comprehend when we negate negation, what do we *say* and *understand* when we say sin is a position! Here is Kierkegaard's response: "I am merely keeping a steady hold upon the Christian dogma that sin is a position—not, however, as though it could be comprehended, but as a paradox which must be believed" (**The Sickness unto Death**).

"A paradox which must be believed." With these words, Kierkegaard poses the question of a genre of language suitable to poetic existence. It is language that must destroy what it says, a language that contradicts itself. In this way, Kierkegaard transfers the aim of negative theology to anthropology when it attempts to say, through the voice of contradiction, that God is a position—beyond being, beyond determinations. To believe and not understand. Of course, Kierkegaard does not refer to negative theology, or to the Kantian abolition of knowledge in favor of belief, but to Socratic ignorance. (pp. 321-25)

Paul Ricoeur, "Two Encounters with Kierkegaard: Kierkegaard and Evil; Doing Philosophy After Kierkegaard," in Kierkegaard's Truth: The Disclosure of the Self, *edited by Joseph H. Smith, Yale University Press, 1981, pp. 313-42.*

Paul Tillich   (lecture date 1963)

[*A German-born American theologian and philosopher, Tillich was perhaps the best known Protestant theologian in America from the early 1930s until his death in 1965. The author of works on the meaning of Christian faith in the twentieth-century, Tillich proposed that religion is the ultimate concern overriding all human activities, and that only by discerning God can modern people discover the courage to be. In books such as* The Shaking of the Foundation *(1948) and* The Courage to Be *(1952), he was able to integrate existential philosophy with the religious basis of human life, suggesting that religion could be a "unifying" center for existence. In the following excerpt, Tillich examines Kierkegaard's criticism of Hegel, his realms of existence—particularly the religious realm—and his criticism of theology and the Danish Lutheran Church. The essay was transcribed from a lecture given in 1963.*]

Søren Kierkegaard must . . . be dealt with as a contributor to the breakdown of the [Hegelian] universal synthesis, although his greatest influence has been exercised in our time rather than in his own. He made a new start based on a combination of an existentialist philosophy and a pietistic, revivalistic theological criticism of the great synthesis. More specifically, he combined Lutheran pietism of the revivalist type, including the orthodox content of revivalism, with the categories of Schelling's existentialism. Although he denied Schelling's solution, he took over the categories. His criticism, together with that of Marx and Nietzsche, is historically most important. But none of these three became influential in world-historical terms in the nineteenth century. Kierkegaard was largely a forgotten individual in his century. I recall with pride how as students of theology in Halle we came into contact with Kierkegaard's thought through translations made by an isolated individual in Württemberg. In the years 1905-1907 we were grasped by Kierkegaard. It was a very great experience. We could not accept the theological orthodoxy of repristination. We could not accept especially those "positive"—in the special sense of "conservative"—theologians who disregarded the historical-critical school. For this was valid science which was carried on by this school. It cannot be denied if honest research is conducted into the historical foundations of the New Testament.

But on the other hand we had a feeling of moralistic distortion and a mystical emptiness, an emptiness in which the warmth of the mystical presence of the divine was missing, as in the whole Ritschlian school. We were not grasped by this moralism. We did not find in it the depths

of the consciousness of guilt as classical theology had always had. So we were extremely happy when we encountered Kierkegaard. It was this combination of intense piety which went into the depths of human existence and the philosophical greatness which he had received from Hegel that made him so important for us. The real critical point would be the denial that Hegel's idea of reconciliation is a genuine reconciliation. Man is not reconciled by the reconciliation in the philosopher's head. (pp. 162-63)

We could discuss Kierkegaard in connection with the existentialist movement of the twentieth century, because he became effective only in our own century. Nevertheless . . . , I prefer to place him in his own historical place where he represents one of the decisive criticisms of Hegel's great synthesis. We will discuss him fairly thoroughly, and you can take this discussion not only as a treatment of nineteenth-century theological thought, but also of twentieth-century theology, for while he wrote in the nineteenth century, his real influence has been significant in the twentieth century. (p. 163)

Kierkegaard has become the fashion in three respects: (a) Religiously, which is most justified, because his religious writings are as valid today as they were when they were written. (b) As the inspiration for the dialectical theology, called neo-orthodoxy in this country. In Europe it is usually called dialectical, which shows its relation to Hegel, for this term is the main principle of Hegel's thinking. (c) As the inspiration for Heidegger, the philosopher who has given the name existentialism to the whole movement which derives from Kierkegaard.

As in the case of most of the anti-Hegelians, Kierkegaard's criticism is based on the concept of reconciliation. For Hegel the world is reconciled in the mind of the philosopher of religion who has gone through the different forms of man's spiritual life: the subjective spirit (which is the psychological side), the objective spirit (the social-ethical and political side), and the absolute spirit (art, religion, and philosophy). The philosopher lives in all of them. He is deeply in the religious realm; he lives in the aesthetic realm; and on the basis of the religious realm he conceptualizes what is myth and symbol in religion. Out of all this he develops his philosophy of religion. In this way he mirrors in his mind the final synthesis after the whole world process has gone through thesis, antithesis, and synthesis. The divine mind, the absolute mind, comes to its rest on the basis of religion within the mind of the philosopher who achieves his highest power when he becomes a philosopher of religion, conceptualizing the symbols of the religious life. This is for Hegel reconciliation. This reconciliation in the mind of the philosopher was the point attached by all those whom I have mentioned—Schelling, Feuerbach, pietists, and natural scientists. They all said the world is unreconciled. The theologians went back to Immanuel Kant and said the prison of finitude is not pierced, not even by Hegel's great attempt. The reconciliation of the finite and the infinite has not yet happened.

Kierkegaard did the same thing in a particular way. In the system of essences reconciliation might be possible, he argued, but the system of essences is not the reality in which we are living. We are living in the realm of existence, and in the realm of existence reconciliation has not yet happened. Existence is the place of decision between good and evil. Man is in the tragic situation, in the tragic unavoidability of evil. This contradiction in existence means that Hegel is seen as confusing essentialist fulfillment with existential unfulfillment or estrangement. I told you that estrangement or alienation is one of the terms which Hegel created, but which is then turned against him. Nature is estranged spirit for Hegel; the material reality is self-estranged spirit. Now Kierkegaard said that mankind is in this state of estrangement, and Hegel's construction of a continuous series of syntheses in which the negativity of antithesis is overcome in the world process is true only with respect to the essential realm. Symbolically we could perhaps say that it goes on only in the inner life of God. But Kierkegaard emphasized that estrangement is our situation. Only in the inner divine life is there reconciliation, but not in our situation.

Hegel had described the inner divine life in his great logic. The logic is the science of essences in their highest abstraction and their inner dialectical relationship. Then the logicians came along. The man who is very important for the criticism of all essentialism is Trendelenburg. Kierkegaard was dependent on him for his logical criticism of Hegel. His criticism was that the logical process is not a real process; it is not a process in time; it is only a description of logical relations. What Hegel did was to confuse the dialectical process of logic with the actual movement in history. While reconciliation is always a reality in the dialectical process of divine life, it is not a reality in the external process of human existence. So from the logical point of

A profile drawing by Marstrand.

view Hegel was criticized for his fundamental confusion of essence and existence.

Hegel was not able to understand the human situation in terms of anxiety and despair. Kierkegaard could not follow Hegel; all his life he possessed a melancholic disposition. This melancholy of which he often spoke was associated with a curse which his father made against God, and he felt that the reaction to this blasphemy of his father was upon him and never left him free. The point is that such a personality was able to discover things which were not so deeply felt by a character as Hegel, who existed in a bourgeois situation, who felt psychologically more safe and was able to conquer the negative and tragic elements of life which he saw.

One of the main points connected with Kierkegaard's melancholic personal condition and his feeling of unreconciled reality was his experience of the lonely individual. Here again we have an anticipation of present-day existentialism. The individual stands in solitude before God and the process of the world cannot liberate him from the tremendous responsibility by which he lives in the situation. Again and again he said that the last reality is the deciding individual, the individual who in freedom must decide for good or evil. We find nothing of this in Hegel. It is very interesting that Hegel who was so universal in his thinking and all-embracing never developed personal ethics. His ethics are objectivist; he subsumed ethics under philosophy of history and philosophy of law. Ethics of family, ethics of state, of community, of culture, all that is in Hegel, but not ethics which has to do with the personal decision of the individual. This was already an element in Schelling's attack against Hegel, but it was stressed more by Kierkegaard than by anybody else.

What is the reason for this experience of solitude? It is due to human finitude in estrangement. It is not the finitude which is identical with the infinite, but it is separated finitude, finitude standing upon itself in the individual person. As long as the identity principle was decisive, it was possible to overcome the anxiety of finitude, of having to die, by the experience of being united with the infinite. But this answer was not possible for Kierkegaard. So he tried to show why we are in anxiety because of being finite and in despair because of being in separated finitude. The first is his description of anxiety and the second is his description of despair. There are two writings which every theologian must read. Both are comparatively short: ***The Concept of Dread*** and ***The Sickness Unto Death.*** I have always criticized the title of the English translation of ***The Concept of Dread,*** because dread is different from anxiety. Dread has in it the connotation of something sudden, whereas what Kierkegaard describes is an ontological state of man. But now in English the term "anxiety" has generally replaced "dread" to describe this state which Kierkegaard has in mind. ***The Concept of Dread,*** in any case, is a fundamental book on the theory of anxiety. It has been more fully developed by others, so that now there is a vast literature on the subject, including the works of people like Freud, Rollo May, *et al.*

Kierkegaard wrote about two kinds of anxiety. The first is connected with his theory of the fall. He symbolized this with the biblical myth of Adam and Eve, and found profound psychological insight there. This is the anxiety of actualizing one's own freedom, which is a double anxiety: the anxiety of not actualizing it, of being restricted and of not coming into real existence, and the anxiety of actualizing it, with the knowledge of the possibility of losing one's identity. This is not a description of an original historical Adam, but of the Adam in every one of us, as the word "Adam" means. In this double anxiety of actualizing oneself and of being afraid to actualize oneself, every adolescent finds himself with respect to sex, his relation to his parents, to the political tradition in which he lives, etc. It is always the question of actualizing or not actualizing one's potentialities.

Finally the decision is made for actualizing oneself, and this is simultaneously the fall. But after the fall there is another anxiety, because the fall, like every trespassing of limits, produces guilt. The anxiety of guilt at its extreme point is despair. This despair is described in **The Sickness Unto Death.** This sickness unto death is present in all human beings. This condition is described with the help of many Hegelian categories, as the conflict between spirit and matter in man, man having finite spirit, man experiencing the conflict in himself, having the desire to get rid of himself, and of being unable to commit suicide because the guilt consciousness makes it clear that suicide cannot help you to escape the situation in which you are. One thing ought to be kept in mind, and that is that the term "guilt" means both the objective state of *being* guilty for something that is wrong, and the subjective state of *feeling* guilty. To confuse these two states can be very bad, for example, when many psychoanalysts say that we must abolish guilt. That is very ambiguous, for what they really have to overcome is misplaced guilt feeling, which is one of the worst mental diseases. But this can be done only if they manage to bring the patient to the point where he faces up to his real state of being guilty, his true guilt in the objective sense. We must make a clear distinction between guilt and guilt feeling. Guilt feelings may be very misleading. In neurotic and psychotic conditions they are always misplaced. One of the defenses of the neurotic is to insist on misplaced guilt feeling because he cannot face reality and his own real guilt. This real guilt is his estrangement from the ultimate that expresses itself in actual acts directed against his own true being.

There is no escape from the sickness unto death; therefore, something must happen which cannot be mediated in logical terms. You cannot derive it from anything in you; it must come to you; it must be given to you. Here the doctrine of the "leap" appears in Kierkegaard. It has already appeared, in fact, in his description of the fall. Anxiety brings man before a decision, for or against actualizing himself. This decision is a leap; it cannot be logically derived. Sin cannot be derived in any way. If it is derived, then it is not sin any more but necessity. Here we can recall what I said about Schleiermacher for whom sin is the necessary result of the inadequacies of our spiritual life in relation to our physical life. That makes sin a necessity, and thus takes the sharpness of guilt away from sin. Kierkegaard repudiates this notion of sin. For him the fall of

man is a leap of an irrational kind, of a kind which cannot be derived in terms of logical necessity.

But there is the opposite leap, the leap of faith. You cannot derive this either from your situation. You cannot overcome the sickness unto death, the anxiety of estrangement. This can only be done by faith. Faith therefore has the character of a nonrational jump in Kierkegaard. He speaks of the leap from the point of view of the individual. He is so well nourished on Hegelian dialectics that he builds up a dialectic of spheres. Between these spheres there is a leap. That is non-Hegelian. But the spheres themselves follow each other hierarchically, and that is truly Hegelian. There are three steps or spheres. You can also call them stages, but they are not so much stages following each other in time as levels lying above each other in space, and coexisting all the time in ordinary human beings. These levels or stages are the aesthetic, the ethical, and the religious. Man lives within all of them, but the decisive thing is how they are related to each other and which one is predominant for him.

Kierkegaard's description of the aesthetic stage was perhaps the most brilliant thing he did. His "Diary of the Seducer", often abused for other purposes, is the most complete description of the aesthetic stage in its complete actualization. Also his analysis of Mozart's *Don Juan* is a great work of literary criticism, philosophy, and theology all in one. The characteristic of the aesthetic stage is the lack of involvement, detachment from existence. It has nothing to do with aesthetics as such or with the arts. Of course, this attitude of mere detachment and of noninvolvement in the situation can take place in relation to music, literature, and the visual arts; but it can also be found in the theoretical or in the cognitive relation to reality. Cognition can have the merely aesthetic attitude of noninvolved detachment. I am afraid this is seen as the ideal even in many humanities courses in the universities. To be sure, there are elements of mere detachment in every scholarly inquiry; detachment will be necessary when dealing with dates, places, and connections, etc., but as soon as you come to interpretation, detachment will be reduced by existential participation. Otherwise you cannot understand reality; you do not "stand under" the reality.

Hegel was regarded somehow as a symbol of the aesthetic attitude, and so were the romantics. Because of their aesthetic detachment they took all the cultural contents on the basis of a nonexistential attitude, a lack of involvement. When I came to this country and first used the word aestheticism in a lecture, a colleague of mine at Columbia University told me not to use that word in describing Americans. That is a typical European phenomenon. Americans are activists and not aestheticists. Now I do not believe this is true. I think there is quite a lot of this aesthetic detachment even in popular culture. It is present in the buying and selling of cultural goods—I spoke about this on the occasion of *Time* Magazine's fortieth anniversary—in which you often see a nonparticipating, nonexistential attitude. Here Kierkegaard's criticism would be valid. Perhaps on the whole this is not a very great danger among the American intelligentsia. My observation has been that they jump very quickly out of the detached aesthetic attitude—in all lectures and discussions, in philosophy and the arts—to the question, "What shall we do?" This attitude was described by Kierkegaard as the attitude of the ethical stage.

In the ethical stage the attitude of detachment is impossible. Kierkegaard had a concept of the demonic which means self-seclusion. This belongs to the aesthetic stage, not going out of oneself, but using everyone and everything for one's own aesthetic satisfaction. Opposed to this demonic self-seclusion is love. Love opens up and brings one out of self-seclusion, and in doing so conquers the demonic. This character of love leads to the relations of love. Here Kierkegaard accepted Hegel's objective ethics—the ethics of family, of vocation, of state, etc. In the aesthetic stage sex produces isolation; in the ethical stage love overcomes isolation and generates responsibility. The seducer is the symbol of irresponsibility with respect to the other one, for the other one is manipulated only aesthetically. Only through responsibility can the ethical stage be reached.

It is interesting as a biographical fact that Kierkegaard never reached two of the decisive things that he attributed to this stage, that is, family and vocation. He lived from some income as a writer, but he never had an official vocation, either in the church or outside of it. And he had this tragic experience with his fiancée, Regina Olson, whom he loved dearly. But because of the inability to transcend his self-seclusion, his melancholic state, he finally dissolved the relationship, and never really overcame the guilt connected with it.

Then Kierkegaard dealt with the religious stage. The religious stage is beyond both the aesthetic and the ethical and is expressed in relation to that which interests us infinitely or which produces infinite passion. . . . Hegel's critics took [the terms interest and passion] from him and then used them in their criticism of him. Hegel said that without interest and passion nothing great has ever happened in history. This notion was now taken over by Kierkegaard into the religious situation and by Marx into the quasi-religion of the nineteenth-century revolutionary movement.

Religion has within itself two possibilities, identity and contrast. The principle of identity is based on mysticism, the identity of the infinite and the finite; and the principle of distance is based on estrangement, the finitude and the guilt of the human situation. We have discussed this often in these lectures. We saw this especially in the contrast between Spinoza and Kant, Spinoza the representative of the principle of identity and Kant the representative of critical detachment. This duality which permeates all human existence and thought is also present in Kierkegaard's description of the two types of religion. He calls these two types "religiousness A" and "religiousness B," but a more powerful way of expressing the same thing is to use the names of "Socrates" and "Jesus." Both of them have something in common. Both of them are existentialists in their approach to God. Neither is simply a teacher who communicates ideas or contents of knowledge. They are the greatest teachers in human history because they were existential. This means they did not communicate contents, but did something to persons. They did not write anything, but they have produced more disciples than anybody else who has ever written anything. All four Greek schools of philosophy were pupils of Socrates who never wrote a thing, and Christianity is the result of Jesus who never wrote anything.

That alone shows the person-to-person situation, the complete existential involvement of these two types of religiousness. But then there arises the great difference. Religiousness A or the religion of Socrates presupposes that truth is present within every human being. The fundamental truths are in man himself. The dialectical or existential teacher has only to evoke them from man. Socrates does this in two ways. The one is irony. This concept is in the best tradition of Romanticism. . . . This means that every special content of which a person is sure is subjected to radical questioning until its insecurity is revealed. Nothing remains as self-evident. In Plato's dialogues Socrates is the leader of the discussions, and he applies irony to the Sophists who know everything, who are the scholars of their time. The Socratic questioning undercut their scholarly self-consciousness, their belief in their infallibility. Socrates did the same thing with the craftsmen, the businessmen, and the aristocratic people who were his followers. The other way is midwifery. This means that the existential teacher brings to birth what is already inside a person, helps him to find the truth in himself, and does not simply tell him the truth. This presupposes the Platonic idea that man's soul has an eternal relation to all the essences of things. So knowledge is a matter of memory. The famous example given in Plato's dialogue *Meno* is of the slave who is asked about the Pythagorean proposition of the three angles of a triangle, and although he is completely uneducated, he is able to understand it because of the mathematical evidences within him. This is not produced in him by external teaching. This is indeed true of geometry and algebra. Everyone can experience in himself the evidence of such things, but this is not true of certain other things. This then led to the resistance of the empirical school against Socrates and Plato, on the one hand, and leads to the other religious type represented by Jesus, on the other hand.

Both Socrates and Jesus communicate indirectly, as Kierkegaard says, but they do not have textbook knowledge of any kind. By indirect communication Socrates brings to consciousness what is in man. Therefore, he is called a religious teacher. I am in full agreement with that. I think it is ridiculous to say that Socrates is a philosopher and Jesus is religious, or perhaps a religionist, a really blasphemous term. Both of them deal with man in his existential situation from the point of view of the meaning of life and of ultimate concern. They do it existentially. In this sense we can call Socrates the founder of liberal humanism, as one of the quasi-religions. Now, if the difference between Socrates and Jesus is not that of the difference between philosophy and religion—which is absolute nonsense here—then what is the difference? The difference is that the indirect ironical teacher, Socrates, does not transform the totality of the being of the other person. This is done only in religiousness B, by the teacher who is at the same time the Savior, who helps the person whom he teaches in terms of healing and liberating. Here another type of consciousness comes into existence. According to this idea, God is not in man. Man is separated from God by estrangement. Therefore God must come to man from outside, and address him. God comes to man in the Christ.

God is not the paradoxical presence in the individual, but he is present outside of man in the Christ. Nobody can derive the coming of the Christ from the human situation. This is another leap, the leap of God into time through the sending of his Son. This cannot be derived from man, but is given to him. This makes Jesus the teacher into the Savior of men. While Socrates is the great existential teacher, Jesus is both the teacher and the Savior who transforms man.

In this way the religious stage has within itself a tension. Hegel's interpretation of the Christ was in the line of Platonism. In Hegel the eternal essential unity of God and man is represented in a complete way in the Christ, but it is also present in every individual. For Kierkegaard God comes from the outside or from above. Here you see immediately the starting point of Karl Barth. According to him, you cannot start with man, not even in terms of questioning. You must start with God who comes to man. The human situation is not such that you can find in man's predicament the question which may lead to the religious answer. In terms of this conviction Barth criticizes my own systematic theology, which in this sense is un-Kierkegaardian. This idea of God coming to man totally from the outside had great religious power, but I would say that its religious power is disproportional to its philosophical power, to the power of thought. It cannot be carried out in such a way. But that is not the point here. The point is that you see the bridge from Kierkegaard to Barth and neo-orthodoxy in the idea of God coming to man from above and from outside him, with no point of contact in man. When Emil Brunner wanted to say that there must be some point of contact, Barth answered with his passionate "No"—this famous essay in which he defends his idea of the absolute otherness of God outside of man. Now, I do not believe this idea can be maintained, but, in any case, negatively speaking, it had great religious power.

This is connected with a concept of truth that has to do with the metaphor of leap. This truth is quite different from the objective truth in the scientific sense. So Kierkegaard makes the following statement, which gives the gist of all his philosophical and theological authorship: "Truth is the objective uncertainty held fast in the most personal passionate experience. This is the truth, the highest truth attainable for the existing individual." Here he defines faith as well as truth, for this is just the leap of faith. A very important element is what he calls the objective uncertainty. This means that theology is not based on objective certainty. A merely objective certainty, as Hegel wanted to reach, is not adequate to the situation between God and man. This would be possible only if the individual had already entered the system of essences, the essential structure of reality. But he has not; he is outside of it, as God is outside of him. Therefore, objective certainty in religion is impossible; faith remains objectively uncertain. Truth in the realm of the objective scientific approach is

not existential truth. Kierkegaard would not deny the possibility of scientific truth, but this is the truth of detachment. It is not the truth of involvement; it is not existential truth. Existential truth is objective uncertainty and personal, passionate experience or subjective certainty, but a certainty which can never be objectified. It is the certainty of the leap.

This subjective certainty of the leap of faith is always under criticism and attack, and therefore Kierkegaard speaks of holding fast to it in a passionate way. In personal existence there is passionate inner movement, and in the power of this passion we have the only truth which is existentially important for us. This is the most significant thing in the world, the question of "to be or not to be." It is the ultimate concern about man's eternal destiny, the question of the meaning of life. This is, of course, different from the truth we approach in terms of approximative scientific objectivity. If we use the term "subjectivity" in connection with Kierkegaard's idea of existential truth, then please avoid the mistake of equating it with willfullness. This is the connotation the word has today. Therefore, it is so difficult to understand a man like Kierkegaard and practically all classical philosophers. Subject means what it says, something standing upon itself, *sub-jectum,* that which underlies. Man is a *sub-jectum,* one who stands upon himself, and not an *objectum,* an object which is in opposition to a subject looking at it. If man is this, then he becomes a thing. This is the sickness of our time. The protest of subjectivity does not mean the protest of willfulness. It means the protest of freedom, of the creative individual, of personality, of man who is in the tragic situation of having to decide in a state of estrangement, in the human predicament. In these ideas we have almost the whole summary of Kierkegaard's theology.

But then Kierkegaard goes beyond this to the question: What can be done to give content to this situation? With respect to the content we must say that not much can be found of it in Kierkegaard. He was not a constructive theologian, and he could not be, because one can be a constructive theologian only if he is not only existentially interested and passionate, but also has an essentialist vision of the structure of reality. Without this, systematic theology is impossible. So we find very little content in the theological or religious writings of Kierkegaard. We have only a continuous repetition of the term "paradox"—leap is simply another word for paradox, that which cannot be derived, that which is irrational and surprising.

There is, however, one content to which he refers all the time, and this is the appearance of the Christ. Thus the leap which is necessary to overcome the situation of doubt and despair is the leap into the reality of the Christ. He states this in a very unusual, paradoxical, and theologically questionable form. He says that only one thing matters: In the year A.D. 30 God sent the Christ for my salvation. I do not need any more theology; I do not need to know the results of historical criticism. It is enough to know that one thing. Into this I have to leap. Then we must ask: Can we solve the problem which historical criticism has opened up by a theology of the leap? I do not believe it is possible. Philosophically the question is this: In which direction am I to leap? You can leap in all directions, but if you have a direction in mind, you already have some knowledge, so it is not a pure leap anymore. If you are in complete darkness and jump without knowing in what direction you are jumping, then you can land anywhere, maybe even on the place from which you jumped. The danger in this concept is asking someone to jump without showing him the direction. Then we have more than subjectivity and paradox; we have willfulness and arbitrariness; we have complete contingency. But if you already know in which direction to jump, in the direction of Christ, for example, then you must have a reason for this. This reason may be some experience with him, some historical knowledge, some image of him from church tradition, etc., but in any case, you have some content. The mere name alone does not say anything. And if you have these things, you are already in the tradition of theology and the church, and it is not a sheer leap any more. This is a problem which we have to say Kierkegaard left completely unsolved. His statement that you have to leap over two thousand years to the year A.D. 30 is simply unrealistic, because nobody can do that. The intellectual leap, or the emotional-intellectual leap, which you are supposed to make with your whole self, is conditioned by two thousand years of church and cultural history. You cannot do that without using contemporary language, and you use language even though you are silent, for internally you speak whenever you are thinking. When you make such a leap, you are using the language of the 1960's, and so you are dependent on the two preceding millennia. It is an illusion to think we can become contemporary with Christ insofar as the historical Jesus is the Christ. We can be contemporary with the Christ only in the way described by the apostle Paul, that is, insofar as the Christ is the Spirit, for the Spirit is present within and beyond the intervening centuries. But this is something else. Kierkegaard wanted to solve the problem of historical criticism by this concept of contemporaneity. You can do this if you take contemporaneity in the Pauline sense of the divine Spirit present to us, and showing the face of Jesus as the Christ. But you cannot escape historical criticism by becoming contemporaneous with Jesus himself. This is the fundamental criticism which we must make from a theological point of view.

We have still to discuss Kierkegaard's critical attitudes toward theology and the church. One can almost say that when Kierkegaard deals with the church or theology, the image which he presents is more a caricature than a fair description. In particular the ecclesiastical office was an object of criticism. He attacked the fact that the minister becomes an employee like all other employees, with special duties and economic securities. This position of the minister, especially its bourgeois elements, of having a career, getting married, raising children, while at the same time proclaiming the impossible possibility of the Christ is for Kierkegaard involved in a self-contradiction. But Kierkegaard does not indicate how this conflict might be solved. Certainly it is a reality, and for Kierkegaard a reality which contradicts the absoluteness of the essence of Christianity. One cannot take this as an objectively valid criticism, because if one did, then one would have to abolish every church office. If the office is not abolished, it is

inevitable that the laws of sociology will make themselves felt and influence the form of the office and those who hold it.

The same thing is true of his attacks on theology. He attacks theology because it is an objectifying attempt to construct a well-formulated system out of the existential paradox. Here again the inadequacy of the situation of the theologian is marvelously expressed, but in terms of a caricature. On the other hand, the question is whether theology is a necessary service of the church. If it is—and it has always been that as long as Christianity has existed; there is theology in Paul and John—then the question arises: Can the theological task be united with the paradox of the Christian message in a different way? When Kierkegaard speaks about the theologian in his attack on theology, he sarcastically suggests: Since Christ was born, let us establish a chair in theology dealing with the birth of Christ; Christ was crucified, so let us make a full professorship for the crucifixion of Christ; Christ has risen, so let us make an associate professorship, etc. This kind of comical attack on theology makes a great impact on anyone who reads it, whether he is a theologian or not. But if it is taken as more than a reminder, if it is taken as a prescription, it means the abolition of theology.

The truth which we can gain from this kind of criticism of theology is the truth of the inadequacy of the objectifying attitude in existential matters. This refers both to the ministry and to theology. In the ministry there is the objectifying factor, the factor of a sociological structure in analogy with all sociological structures. In theology there is a structure of thought in analogy with all structures of thought. This reminder is, of course, of great importance. The minister and the theologian should be forever reminded of the inadequacy, and not only that but also of the necessity of what they are doing. The impossible possibility, as Reinhold Niebuhr, I believe, following Kierkegaard has expressed it, is incarnated in the position of the minister and the theologian. For something which is a matter of paradox, contrary to all expectation, is brought into a form of existence comparable to any other object in time and space. But this is the whole paradoxical situation of the church in the world. You can also express it by saying that the Christian religion is one of the many sections of human culture, but at the same time stands vertically in relation to everything which is culture. From this you can draw the conclusion that Christianity should be removed from every cultural relationship, but if you try to do that, you will find it impossible. The very words you use in order to do it are dependent on the culture from which you will try to detach Christianity. On the other hand, if you do not see the vertical aspect, if Christianity is merely for a class of human beings who are blasphemously called religionists and becomes merely a part of the whole culture, this may be very useful for undergirding patriotism, but the paradox is lost.

Here we face a conflict which is as real, permanent, and insoluble for us as it was for Kierkegaard. Since in Denmark at Kierkegaard's time there was a sophisticated theology of mediation, the prophetic voice could hardly be heard any more. Kierkegaard became the prophetic voice.

The prophet always speaks from the vertical dimension and does not care about what happens in the horizontal dimension. But then Kierkegaard became a part of the horizontal; he became the father of existentialist philosophy, of neo-orthodox theology, and of much depth psychology. Thus he was taken into culture just as the prophets of Israel who, after they had spoken their paradoxical, prophetic word out of the vertical, became religious reformers, and were responsible, for example, for the concentration of the cult in Jerusalem because of the cultic abuses in other places. So out of the vertical there comes a new horizontal line, that is, a new cultural actualization of the prophetic word. This cannot be avoided. Therefore, there is need for the prophetic word again and again which makes us aware that the situation of every servant of religion is a paradoxical one and is in a sense impossible. Kierkegaard's word was not accepted widely in his time, but when people in the beginning of the twentieth century realized the coming earthquake of this century, Kierkegaard's voice could be heard again. (pp. 163-78)

> *Paul Tillich, "The Breakdown of the Universal Synthesis: Kierkegaard's Existential Theology," in his* Perspectives on 19th and 20th Century Protestant Theology, *edited by Carl E. Braaten, Harper & Row, Publishers, 1967, pp. 162-79.*

Hermann Diem (essay date 1966)

[*In the following excerpt, Diem examines the roles of irony and dialectic in the thought and works of Kierkegaard.*]

We have heard what Kierkegaard said of Socrates, his model: Socrates was the first and only man "to give dialectical validity to the category of the individual." What does "dialectic" mean here? The original and simplest form of dialectic is conversation, dialogue. There must be at least two participants, neither of whom can arrive at the truth by himself. They seek instead to determine the truth by exchanging questions and answers, keeping their attention fixed on a common goal that determines the unity of question and answer. This form of dialectical conversation was Socrates' method, as illustrated by Plato in his first Dialogues. Socrates starts from the assumption that he himself does not know anything he can teach to anyone else, while his partner in the conversation obviously claims to know something. Now this supposed knowledge is tested in dialectic conversation; Socrates presses the attack until it becomes clear that the other man also does not know anything. The conversation ends with the apparently negative result that both admit, "I know that I do not know anything." But this negative result, in which false knowledge is destroyed, conceals a positive gain: the partner in the conversation has now been set free to know himself and to seek the fullness of truth within himself.

Kierkegaard took the original dialogic method of Socrates as his point of departure. In his Master's dissertation, *The Concept of Irony, with Special Reference to Socrates,* he worked out the form of this Socratic dialectic in contrast to that used later by Plato, who preserved only the exter-

nal form of the dialogue without permitting any genuine questioning and answering. The dialectic of dialogue implies an attitude of irony in the questioner, behind which he conceals his own positivity in order to prevent any direct relationship from forming between the two men. In this fashion, the other man is set free to work out his own answers and the ideality of his existence is awakened. Irony is the incognito behind which takes place the total transformation demanded by this ideality. It is a "rule of existence; nothing is therefore more absurd than for a writer to express pleasure in having expressed himself ironically now and then. The man who really possesses irony possesses it as long as the day lasts, bound to a form, because it is infinity within him."

Now, like the Athenian Socrates, Kierkegaard also spent a great deal of his time in Socratic conversation upon the streets and among the societies of Copenhagen. The Danish Socrates, however, did what his Athenian counterpart did not do: he wrote books, an amazing quantity of books. One thing is always true of a book: it is a direct, didactic form of communication which has no control over the attitude of the reader. Kierkegaard, however, succeeded in remaining a Socratic ironist even when writing books. He did so by using a tremendous display of dialectic to transform the entire body of his writings into a single great dialogue with the reader. This explains the remarkable literary form he employed, which created a sensation even in 1843, when he published his first great work: ***Either/Or: a Biographical Fragment, edited by Viktor Eremita.*** The two volumes contain the posthumous papers of two different authors, which the editor claims to have found by accident in the secret compartment of a desk he had bought from an antique dealer. Since he could not determine the names of the authors, he refers simply to "the papers of A." and "the papers of B." The editor says of A.'s papers that they "contained diverse attempts to formulate an aesthetic philosophy of life," adding at once, "Such an attempt can probably not be brought off." Be that as it may, an effort is made with passionate consistency to carry these attempts through to the end. The papers of A. comprise all sorts of aphorisms, lyrical outpourings and reflections, discussions of eroticism, the erotic element in music, tragedy, etc., as well as lectures delivered before the *Symparanekromenoi* Society. The papers conclude with the "Diary of the Seducer," which A. claims not to have written himself, but only in turn to have edited, since the refinement of aesthetic pleasure displayed there has clearly become sinister in its own right. As an epigraph, the editor gives to the "papers of A." a quotation from Young: "Is reason alone baptized? Are the passions pagan?" The "papers of B." comprise letters written to A. by a certain Wilhelm, an assistant judge. They deal with "the aesthetic validity of marriage" and "the balance between the aesthetic and ethical elements in the development of the personality." In these letters, disagreeing with his friend A., he supports the claims of an ethical philosophy of life, closing with an "ultimatum," from which the entire work received its title *Either/Or.* He appends the sermon of another friend, on the subject, "The Edifying Value of the Thought That We Are Always in the Wrong Before God."

All these mystifications in literary form and in piling up

of authors and editors of the documents serve the dialectic of communication. Kierkegaard does not appear before the reader as a teacher, trying to convince him of some philosophy through lecture and demonstration.

Instead, he publishes his books under pseudonyms, behind which his own person disappears. Each of these ever-changing pseudonyms represents a specific philosophy and attitude. They possess an inner consistency, representing a certain progress from an existence based on purely aesthetic principles through that based on ethics and religious ethics, culminating in the specifically Christian existence of the man of faith. The reader cannot directly appropriate the philosophy of the individual pseudonyms for the simple reason that the attitude of one figure is always contradicted ironically by that of the others. The reader can never reach a final conclusion backed by the authority of Kierkegaard himself. Kierkegaard disclaims all responsibility for the statements of his pseudonyms, demanding expressly that such statements should be quoted as coming from the pseudonym and not from himself. Kierkegaard says that he prefers to view himself "as the *reader,* rather than the *author*" of the documents, in order to prevent any possible misunderstanding that would place him in the role of a lecturer. In order to prevent this misunderstanding, for example, he has his pseudonymous Johannes Climacus say in the Foreword to the ***Philosophical Fragments:***

> If anyone should be so polite as to attribute a point of view to me, if he should even stretch his gallantry to the limit and accept this point of view because it is mine, I regret his politeness, for he shows it to one who is unworthy. I also regret his point of view, if indeed he has no other point of view than mine. *My* life I can risk, *my* life in all seriousness I can wager, but not that of another. So much I am able to do; it is all, indeed, that I can do, since I have no erudition to offer. . . . my life is all I have; I will risk it the instant a difficulty appears. Then the dance is easy; for the thought of death is a nimble dancer, my dancer; every human being is too heavy-footed for me; therefore I beseech you, *per deos obsecro,* not to ask me, for I will not dance.

In such statements, the reader must not see irony in the diction alone; he must understand it as the attitude behind which the speaker, like Socrates, conceals himself in order to set the person addressed free to achieve his own existence. The ironic form of expression can conceal everything; it restricts neither speaker nor listener to what is actually said. It can bring the listener to reveal himself; it can tempt him along a false trail in order to make him stumble at the end of this road and thus achieve insight. In any case, however, it must never allow the positivity it conceals to become visible. All this assumes, of course, that such a positivity is present. Irony is justified only when it conceals a strong passion for existence. Otherwise it ceases to be an attitude and becomes a rhetorical device, drifting off into petulance and thoughtlessness. Kierkegaard himself gives advice on how to avoid this danger:

> If one wishes to undergo a healthy discipline, one should refrain for a while from the laughter that arouses the passion of antipathy where dark

powers can so easily overpower one, and exercise instead the faculty of seeing the comic side of the person or thing toward which one feels protective, where sympathy and interest, or even partiality, constitute the active defense against recklessness.

Above all, be it noted, irony automatically ceases to be genuine when it is practiced not by an individual, but by the group. Kierkegaard's battle with the *Corsair* was directed against false, unjustified irony; with the assistance of this satirical paper, Copenhagen had become ironic *en masse,* and irony had been degraded into vulgarity.

> Irony presupposes a very specific kind of intellectual training such as is very rare in this generation; and this chaos of human beings claim to be ironists! Irony is by definition nonsocial; an irony among the majority is by definition not irony.

Kierkegaard therefore had to declare war by himself against this false irony. He had to expose himself as an individual to this vulgarity in order to unmask it. Furthermore, he could not wage this war directly, but only ironically: he could not appear on the scene full of moral indignation, but had to issue a challenge to personal combat. The ironist must never directly reveal the value within him in order thus to win a person to the side of a truth. He must instead use all his talent to prevent any direct relationship with himself in order to bring his hearer to achieve his own existence, even if in the process he exposes himself to the accusation of thoughtlessness, of lack of seriousness, etc.

Kierkegaard's own conduct in this battle with the *Corsair* is a good example of this irony as an attitude. At the height of the dispute, when the paper had employed every means to make him ridiculous, Kierkegaard met Goldschmidt, the paper's editor, on the street. Kierkegaard did not engage in remonstrances, but spoke with him, as though not in the least personally involved, about the theoretical rights of Frater Taciturnus, the pseudonym under which Kierkegaard had issued his challenge. A short time later, Goldschmidt surrendered the editorship of the paper.

In Socratic dialectic, this ironic distance must be preserved not only for the sake of the person addressed, so that he is not persuaded of something but rather challenged to think and act for himself, but also for the sake of the speaker himself. This dialogue Kierkegaard conducts with the reader, using pseudonyms as a dodge, is also a dialogue with himself. His work as a writer also advances his own development. With extraordinary ability, both dialectic and poetic, he has the pseudonyms pace off the boundaries of humanity in order to retrieve faith from the realm of speculative philosophy and aesthetic sensitivity and restore it to real existence. Afterward, Kierkegaard saw in all the works he wrote a consistent plan that had not existed at the outset. Instead, "providence," as he put it, had itself educated him in its march of progress by means of this work. What he writes behind the mask of the pseudonyms are the possibilities of his own life, written in his own lifeblood. It is first of all himself whom he recalls to existence through this work.

A caricature by Marstrand.

Now of course all Copenhagen knew who the author of the pseudonymous works was. It was therefore unavoidable that the readers should lose the distance set between them and Kierkegaard by the pseudonyms, taking an interest in Kierkegaard as a person rather than limiting themselves to the pseudonyms. But this interest could cancel out all the irony of the Socratic dialectic and make it ineffectual. In order to prevent such a development, Kierkegaard snatched at yet another means to increase the indirectness of his communication: if he could not hide his person from the readers behind his work, he would have to disguise his person as much as possible. This meant that he had to take the same ironic attitude in his personal relationship to his environment that he took as a writer toward his readers. (pp. 19-24)

> *Hermann Diem, in his* Kierkegaard: An Introduction, *translated by David Green, John Knox Press, 1966, 124 p.*

George Steiner   (essay date 1980)

[*Steiner is a French-born American critic, poet, and fiction writer. A central concern of his critical thought is whether literature can survive the barbarism of the mod-*

ern world. Though some commentators have found fault with his sometimes exuberant prose style, Steiner is generally regarded as a perceptive and extremely erudite critic. The following excerpt is from a review of works by and about Kierkegaard, including N. Viallaneix's Ecoute, Kierkegaard. *Steiner asserts that Kierkegaard's various and complex works form a "single master text" directed toward a single focus: "immediacy of discourse with God."*]

Kierkegaard was conscious of his own prolixity. There is hardly a day in his adult life on which he does not write either for publication or for private echo. His works are a soliloquy all of which is to be overheard by God and much of which is to reach the ears of other men. The act of writing is an immediate extension, a making audible even more than visible, of an unbroken current of inward discourse. Personal solitude (Montaigne in his tower-room, Kierkegaard at his writing-stand are the master builders of echo chambers of silence), the jealous cultivation of spiritual and physical apartness from the "racket" of common speech, were the source and justification of this solipsistic eloquence. Kierkegaard's pseudonyms, like Montaigne's quotations, enact deliberate fragmentations and dramatizations within a primary monologue. They generate anti-echoes, cracks in the mirror, without which the rhetoric of anxious address would lose something of its dialectical appeal.

The outpouring of Kierkegaard's testimony seems to obey a pendulum motion. The more "literary" texts alternate with devotional, homiletic works of an uncompromisingly pastoral, pietistic character. The ***Eighteen Upbuilding Discourses*** follow on ***Either /Or;*** the ***Stages on Life's Way*** precede the intensely personal ***Concluding Unscientific Postscript*** and the *Corsair* polemics; the texts assembled in ***Practice in Christianity*** come between the drama of ***The Sickness unto Death*** and the idiosyncratic, cunningly wrought ***Point of View for My Work as an Author.*** In actual fact, composition is often simultaneous and overlapping, and there is a sense in which the entirety of Kierkegaard's production is an "inter-leaving" in a single master text. So far as publication goes, however, the alternating rhythm is real enough and seems to prolong that duality between the "aesthetic" and the religious which Kierkegaard had analysed in his early books and which he had, according to his own witness, largely surmounted after 1846. It is only in his last publications, in the great "anti-clerical" tracts, ***This Must Be Said, So Let It Be Said, Christ's Judgment on Official Christianity*** and the *Faedrelandet* articles, that Kierkegaard brings the full virtuosity of his literary style to bear on a wholly "sacred" theme. If ***The Book on Adler,*** which Kierkegaard left unpublished, is simultaneously a masterpiece of psychology and ironic stylization, bridging, as it were, the distance between Pascal and Proust, and by exegetic standards, an indecisive, ambivalent text, it is because even at this late stage the oscillations between artistry and naked witness were unresolved.

Kierkegaard himself would repudiate such dissociation. His personal jottings, self-exhortations, scriptural excerpts and shorthand hermeneutics, the voluminous ***Papirer*** (now available in a seven-volume English-language translation), underlie and cement the formally composed, the published books and essays. They direct the entire complex structure towards a single focus: that of immediacy of discourse with God through the sole medium of communication accessible to man, which is that of Christ and of the Word made audible in Christ. Kierkegaard would urge, he does so incessantly, that the "aesthetic" and "ethical" were categories to be transcended, that we may best, perhaps, visualize them as the initial two days on Abraham's journey to Mount Moriah, days whose tenor of unspeakable anguish and acceptance Kierkegaard transcribes in *Fear and Trembling.* To reach the place and order of the sacrificial on the third day of the journey is to enter upon "the infinite liberation of the religious". In this sphere such concepts as "style" and "genre" are inapplicable; or, in Kierkegaardian terms, human discourse achieves its authentic purpose which is that of immediate response, of pure answerability to, the articulate presence of the divine.

Like the late Tolstoy, Kierkegaard would distance the reader from that in his own work which is "wasteful". In both cases, however, this tactic of self-interdict and self-selection is not only ambiguous—at what level did Tolstoy come to regard *War and Peace* and *Anna Karenina* as mundane distraction, to what extent would Kierkegaard confine the essence of his testimony to his overtly homiletic and Christological works?—but also reductive in the light of its own intent. The aesthetician, the musical and literary critic, the secular psychologist, the political analyst, the virtuoso pamphleteer, are as much a part of the "religious" Kierkegaard as are the pietist of the *Papirer* and the preacher of the five *Discourses at the Communion on Fridays.* One must, therefore, learn to read certain parts of Kierkegaard against their author; and one must learn to do so well past the explicit stages of the pseudonymous and the "masked" in the earlier texts.

To do so at any confident level requires Danish; even within Danish, Kierkegaard's idiom presents taxing problems of interpretation.

Kierkegaard's letters are of a piece with his published discourses and the *Papirer*. . . . [It] is precisely because of their closeness to Kierkegaard's motions of spirit and argument that the letters are invaluable. It is in them that we can follow step by step the strategies of ostentatious solitude which Kierkegaard devised after his flight from Copenhagen in October 1841, strategies which depended on the faithful agency of his confidant, Emil Boesen. It is here that we can trace the deterioration of Kierkegaard's relations with Rasmus Nielsen, a crisis of trust which was further to accentuate his sense of aloneness but which also demonstrates, beyond doubt, Kierkegaard's unwillingness to allow anyone too near to the roots of his thought and style. The epistles to J. L. A. Kolderup-Rosenvinge are small masterpieces of self-mockery and speculative gusto. In copious detail, they construe long walks, few, if any, of which actually took place, but whose peregrine evocation gave to Kierkegaard rare moments of sociability. There are the grimly ambiguous cartels to Bishop Mynster and the playful homilies to nephews and nieces from an eccentric but loving uncle. And the correspondence makes

graphic a rather enigmatic, little discussed point: the fact that Kierkegaard's intimate amanuensis as well as his mortal journalistic foe were Jews.

But it is, no doubt, the tremendous letters to Regine Olsen Schlegel of the autumn of 1849, all of which except one have come down to us in draft form, which dominate the collection. Nothing had diminished the terror of the broken engagement. Now, eight years later, and subject to her husband's mediation, Kierkegaard strove to communicate to the beloved the necessary meaning and consequence of his cruel abandon. "Now, however, tranquility surrounds you, so, with reverence for God, weigh everything carefully." To the husband:

> In this life she belongs to you; in history she will stand by my side; in eternity it cannot distress you that she also loves me who already on the day I became engaged to her was ancient and a thousand years too old to be able truly to love any girl, as I ought to have realized beforehand and as I now realize all too superbly well, now that the matter has long ago aged me another couple of thousand years.

One phrase is scarcely credible in its lofty clairvoyance: "And besides, what more can a girl ask? You make her happy in this life—I shall see to her immortality."

The other volume to have appeared (XIV in the series) contains *Two Ages.*

[*Two Ages* is] Kierkegaard's long review-essay on the novel of the same title published anonymously in October 1845 by Thomasine Gyllembourg-Ehrensvärd. For the modern reader, it is Part Three of this monograph which compels interest. In it, Kierkegaard contrasts the age of the French revolutions of 1789 and 1830, as reflected in the characters of the tale, with that of the mid-1840s. The first is "essentially passionate, and therefore it essentially has form"; the second is essentially dispassionate, flaring up in superficial, short-winded enthusiasm, but prudential and complacently lethargic to the core. The age of revolution is dialectical; the realization of an either/or in the existence of each individual enforces action even where such action sharpens contradiction and insoluble paradox. The present age is one of reflective procrastination, of an ironizing devaluation of commitment. In a revolutionary era, existentiality is manifest in character; now there is only an amorphous public. "The coiled springs of life-relationships which are what they are only because of qualitatively distinguished passion, lose their resilience; the qualitative expression of difference between opposites is no longer the law for the relations of inwardness to each other in the relation" (a difficult but key point developed also in the *Papirer*). (p. 81)

If revolutions generate the heroic, the current age breeds nothing but a levelling *invidia*. There is no organic community, only a public assemblage which is "supposed to include everything" in a patronizing catholicity of tolerance. Such an assemblage is an abstraction which finds its specific embodiment in the phenomenon of the modern newspaper (here, Kierkegaard's analysis bears every mark of the *Corsair* duel). By virtue of its dramatic factitiousness, the press provides illusions of significance. The predictable frequency and ephemerality of the events it reports serves two chief purposes: it excites inconsequentiality, and it levels all human concerns to the democracy of gossip. As a result, "chattering gets ahead of essential speaking" and modern man moves, literally, in an envelope of vacant clamour. Only through some "*suffering act*"—Kierkegaard plays on the oxymoron of active pathos—will "the secret agents" of silence and of God's design break through the numbing blandness of the age.

Though, at moments, contracted almost to a short-hand, this is one of Kierkegaard's major psychological-political contributions. We must look to Tocqueville or to the early chapters in Taine's analysis of the *ancien régime* to find a matching strength and delicacy of political perception. The famous diagnosis of "empty noise", of the differences between mass and community, between "oneness" and authentic individuation in Heidegger's *Sein und Zeit,* simply expands Kierkegaard's contrastive sketch. Its present timeliness is unsettling: "Not only do people write anonymously, but they write anonymously over their signature, yes, even speak anonymously." (pp. 81-82)

Kierkegaard's idiom, particularly in his earlier writings, is steeped in the language of Lessing, Hegel, F. Schlegel and Schleiermacher. Key phrases derive directly from Hegel's *Aesthetic* and, though possibly at second hand, from the *Phenomenology.* The architecture of *Either/Or* makes no sense without reference to Schlegel's *Lucinde* and Schleiermacher's letters in answer. More generally, to think theologically and philosophically in the 1830s and 1840s was to think in terms defined by the vocabulary of Kant and German romantic idealism. It was to think, also in reference to Goethe's *Faust,* to the German ballad and to Heine, on each of which Kierkegaard draws abundantly.

[Will new] generations read him as he would wish to be read? This is the question posed, reiterated, pressed home with rhetorical urgency, in Nelly Viallaneix's two-volume thesis [*Ecoute, Kierkegaard*]. It is not, she argues, the master of pseudonymous irony who matters, not the craftsman of an indirect maieutic discourse more teasing than Socrates'. It is the obsessed witness to the immediacy of God and of God in Christ. It is the severely Lutheran, even at various points Calvinist, expositor of the Gospel and of Pauline doctrine. It is, in essence, the begetter of the *Edifying Discourses* and the Pascalian monologist of the *Papirer* (on which Mme Viallaneix draws more constantly than any previous commentator). To "read" Kierkegaard is, albeit unavoidably, to miss the point. What really counts for this compulsive scribe is the oral message, the speech act in its call to live and singular audition. What counts, to a degree which reduces all else to mundane accident, is the prayer, the confessional truth on man's lips and the immediate mystery of God's reply as this reply is *heard,* as it enters vocally into the heart and soul of mortal beings. It is because Kierkegaard's God is "infinite love and infinite pardon", that there is a guarantee of dialogue, that no cry, no supplication addressed to Him in the verity of pain and need, shall remain unanswered. But this wonder, almost this paradox of active echo, depends intimately on the possibility of "acoustic"

experience, on the transmission of the Logos through the literal reality of *parole.* Without such echoing transmission *(Gjenlyden),* man is doomed to a solitude without meaning. Revelation is *spoken.*

In her initial chapters, Mme Viallaneix expounds Kierkegaard's life-long meditations on speech and silence. She analyses the vital distinction between *Stilhed,* the neutral quiet of a natural scene, and *Taushed,* the silence won by self-discipline, by the purging of noise and distraction from one's own tensed spirit. Only this latter stillness can lead to *Huile,* the utter repose that is in God. Viallaneix follows closely Kierkegaard's critique, already implicit in Pascal, of the atrophy of "normal" human discourse. No psycho or sociolinguist, no satirist in the vein of Kraus and Orwell, has provided sharper insights into the frozen, cliché-ridden routines of common communication. We speak "at", not "to" each other. We exchange tokens of inert information. Systematic philosophy, in the Hegelian manner, is nothing more than an apotheosis of this ossification of speech, of this reduction of the unique wonder of felt and imperative meaning to a great dustheap of abstraction. The systematic philosopher, the bishop in his episcopal get-up, the professor on his podium, the journalist and the town-gossip are ontologically identical. They speak without saying, they say without meaning. By their emphasis on the visual, on the linearity of logic as enshrined in the written and the read word, Plato and Descartes have committed western sensibility to a fatal abstraction. They have eliminated from "rational" discourse the central truth of the human body, of the "embodiment" and "bodying forth" of all authentic communication. In the vacuous eloquence of the established churchman and the politician, this disincarnation finds its most vile, unconsciously parodistic, expression.

It follows that it is the supreme task of human consciousness to learn to *listen,* to learn how to hear again the articulate presentness of God in nature and in Holy Scripture. This task demands the utmost self-sacrificial concentration in a world of mundane noise. The ear must be able to pick up, as it were, and to discriminate accurately the threefold categories of divine utterance. God's speech is concretely and incessantly creative; it speaks the world into being. In Christ's ministry, God's speech is that of salvation; to enter upon direct communication with the words of Christ is the only way for man to hear the truth of his own condition. And there is *la Parole réconciliatrice,* the speech of prayer and predication when these spring from the totality of body and spirit of an individual before God. An "Evangel" is a proclamation, a prayer is a speech-act, a psalm is a text sung. To "read" Kierkegaard rightly is to listen to what he is saying to us with such desperate reiteration, and to make of this listening a face-to-face encounter and exchange. It is to bear witness in and through one's daily life to a summoning, to a vocation in the primary sense of the term. Of this vocation, Kierkegaard's massive, often formally brilliant, writings are only a preliminary, finally superfluous vestige. (It may have been this mechanism of self-relegation and this insistence on the preliminary fragment which drew Wittgenstein to Kierkegaard.) "L'oeuvre entière de Kierkegaard répète".

In which "re-petition" we must hear the root-meaning of prayer, of an "asking again".

This is a learned and passionate treatise, instinct with Kierkegaard's own methods of analysis and exhortation. It reminds us powerfully of the central aim of *imitatio Christi* in Kierkegaard's life and thought. It locates, with more exact coherence than any previous treatment except that of Walter Rehm (so often neglected by Kierkegaardians), the crucial function of music not only in the "aesthetical" and in the "ethical" works, but throughout the theology and homiletics. Viallaneix shows that the phenomenon of musicality was essential to the whole Kierkegaardian dialectic of audition, to his critique of worldly speech, to his extended metaphor of God's "instrumental", indeed "orchestral" ubiquity in the sounds and sense of the empirical world. The data of experience, if rightly heard, are the *Klangfigurer,* the shaping vibrato in the harmony that is God. Thus the Kierkegaardian leap into the "absurd" of faith is a leap out of deafness (*absurdité*). And what takes us nearer the heart of Kierkegaard's meaning than the observation in the *Papirer* for 1854 that Christ's cry, "My God, my God, why hast Thou abandoned me?" is terrible, but that God's hearing of that cry is more terrible still! All this is both arresting and suggestive of a "fundamentalist" Kierkegaard whom existentialist philosophers and "literary" readers have lost sight of. (p. 82)

> George Steiner, "Speaking Essentially with God," in The Times Literary Supplement, No. 4009, January 25, 1980, pp. 81-2.

Edward F. Mooney   (essay date 1981)

[*In the following excerpt, Mooney relates the Kierkegaardian Knight of Faith to the discussion of Abraham in* Fear and Trembling. *Both figures, he notes, emphasize an authenticity "of caring and attachment, of grief, love, and selflessness, of courage, risk, and change of self."*]

Fear and Trembling is by common consent one of Kierkegaard's most important and most trying works. It is perhaps the best known of his texts, and among Kierkegaardian catch-phrases, "the teleological suspension of the ethical" is second in currency only to the infamous "truth is subjectivity." No doubt it has caused many to shudder. The book's "terrible pathos" comes from the wild and disturbing interpretation it gives to the biblical story of Abraham and Isaac. How could God have uttered that terrible command, that Abraham's only son be sacrificed? And how could Abraham have assented? Through his mouthpiece, Johannes de Silentio, Kierkegaard seems to argue that, from a rational, ethical perspective, Abraham, the father of faith, must be judged a murderer—and so much the worse for ethics! Faith overrules the ethical prohibition against killing one's son. Obedience to God requires that all other considerations be fanatically suppressed—or so it seems. Faith is utterly absurd. It collides head-on with ethics and reason.

If this initial reading stood, one might shudder not just for Abraham but for reason, faith, and much else, as well.

Happily, this first reading, though it has become a standard interpretation of Kierkegaard's position in **Fear and Trembling,** does not stand up. It focuses too fixedly and without sensitivity to context on the startling suggestions of irrationality. And it misses altogether a central story that Kierkegaard is at pains to tell.

I am persuaded that an absolute antithesis between faith and reason, or between ethics and faith, is not Kierkegaard's final word in **Fear and Trembling.** The possibility that Abraham is holy in God's eyes, though condemned by all ethics, is just that—not a final position, but a *possibility,* a teasing, ironic suggestion meant to "awaken us from our dogmatic slumbers." The Kierkegaardian notions of "the absurd" and the suspension of the ethical do not proclaim new dogmas but work as relativizing notions, dialectical weapons meant to break up old dogmas, to rattle the easy assumption that God's ways are those of any reasonable, commonsensical, respectable middle-class inhabitant of Danish Christendom. Surely a major burden of **Fear and Trembling** is to carry out a skeptical, ironical, relativizing attack on current assumptions. But this is not all the narrative contains. The bold, perverse Kierkegaardian penchant for paradox creates the unmistakable *impression* of a thorough-going irrationalism. But beneath this impression lies a positive and constructive—dare one say *reasonable?*—exploration of human relationship: of separation and attachment, of love and resignation, of care and its display in grief, joy, and welcome. It is this central, neglected story, that I will follow here, letting the more notorious and debated issues unravel as we go. My strategy will be to let the abstractions, paradoxical or otherwise, fall into the framework provided by the underlying story of care and relationship. In a sense, this is Kierkegaard's—or Silentio's—own strategy. The abstract, philosophical question "Can there be a teleological suspension of the ethical?" is raised only *after* the largely neglected, dramatic section entitled "Preliminary Expectoration." I will focus almost entirely on this early section, leaving the question of the "teleological suspension of ethics" for treatment elsewhere.

In the overall scheme of **Fear and Trembling,** resignation is a transitional stage between lack of faith and faith, between shallow unbelievers and heroic men of faith. Characteristically, Kierkegaard mixes abstraction with dramatic portrayal. Occupying this transitional stage or sphere of existence is "the knight of infinite resignation." Although Silentio gives us several portraits of this knight, one of them is central and developed at length.

> A young swain falls in love with a princess, and the whole content of his life consists in this love, and yet the situation is such that it is impossible for it to be realized, impossible for it to be translated from ideality into reality. The slaves of paltriness, the frogs in life's swamp, will naturally cry out, "Such love is foolishness. The rich brewer's widow is a match fully as good and respectable." Let them croak in the swamp undisturbed. It is not so with the knight of infinite resignation, he does not give up his love, not for the glory of the world.

Though caught up in an unhappy love, the young swain

is not shaken by circumstance or opinion. Someone less noble, less knightly, would be swayed by the mediocre "slaves of paltriness"—mediocre and paltry because utterly blind to any real sense of commitment, integrity, or courage. If love for the princess is unrealistic, it should be given up and forgotten. There will be someone else to love soon enough. But the knight disregards such "reasonable" advice. Even though it cannot be "translated into reality," he nurtures his love. It is "the whole content of his life" (even if only an "ideal content").

The knight of resignation

> will have the power to concentrate the whole content of life and the whole significance of reality in one single wish. If a man lacks this concentration, this intensity, if his soul is from the beginning dispersed in the multifarious, he will never come to the point of making the movement (of resignation).

The swain's life is concentrated in the "single wish" (or commitment) to love his princess, come what may. To give up that love outright would be to lose the defining, stabilizing center of self and world. All would be shattered.

In Silentio's view, if one invests concern over a number of interests without a unifying focus, one's integrity is dispersed and diluted. To be unable to concentrate concern in a single wish (or commitment) implies, for Silentio, that "emotional investments" will be cautious, tentative, matters of prudential calculation. What fails here will be made up for there. This "capitalist's approach" lets gain and loss, lets worth in relationship, be set by "market conditions," by judgments of the public at large. How escape this sad parody of personal rapport?

Silentio believes that interests must be *focused,* and around an appropriate object. The capitalist perhaps does concentrate his life around a single commitment: the desire that his lifetime "personal assets" outweigh his losses. Here one can only make a fundamental judgment of value. Can one *really* base one's integrity on taking relationships as items of quantitative value, their fluctuation in worth attentively observed and manipulated, like shares on the stock exchange? Silentio mocks such would-be "errand runners" of the spiritual. The knight of resignation is no opportunist, no speculator in paying relationships. He takes his love as ultimate.

Another distinguishing feature of the knight of resignation is his courage. This appears strikingly in the "self-sufficiency" of his love (free from dependent need), and in his independence of mind (unswayed by "what others would think" about the "foolishness" of his love). But courage also appears in his refusal to be self-deceived about the absence of any realistic possibility for his love. He is completely candid with himself. He does not run from the pain of losing the princess, or pretend that after all perhaps he didn't love her, or that the impossible can somehow be gotten around.

Thus far I have tried to distinguish the knight of resignation from the common crowd, from the "slaves of paltriness." Unlike the crowd, the knight has commitment, in-

tegrity, and courage. He is further than others along the path from superficiality toward faith. But what accounts for the *title* he earns? Why is he a knight of *resignation?*

Silentio speaks of the "movement of resignation" abstractly as "renouncing the finite," "gaining an eternal consciousness," and "transforming temporal love into an eternal one." For those unfamiliar with Kierkegaard's style (or just suspicious of jargon), it will seem forbidding to talk of "the finite," "eternal love," or "eternal consciousness." To get by the opacity of such terminology, we might remind ourselves of Kierkegaard's—and Silentio's—broadest objectives, for there is more here than a tangle of empty rhetoric.

Kierkegaard's interest is not in physicalistic descriptions of Nature, but in personal, existential perspectives—perspectives that articulate moral, aesthetic, and spiritual meanings that can animate or inform a human life. Terms such as "the eternal" or "the infinite" shape and energize such interpretative outlooks, evaluative positions, centers from which we meet the world in action and understanding.

To get at the makeup of the physical universe, a scientist (and often a philosopher) discounts personal standpoints, so far as possible, but to understand an existential stance, the opposite is required. However widely it may be shared, such a perspective reflects a particular way things seem to an individual at a particular time in that individual's development; and that personally "owned" position will itself be located within the larger historical time of community and culture. The personal, existential specificity of such a perspective is not a defect but of its essence. Thus, insofar as it figures in an existential perspective, a concept like "the eternal" cannot be defined free from a context of practical, personal concern. It will be part of a complex web of imagery and interpretation. And in working to "get inside" that perspective, we should not expect an inappropriate precision. Rather than a knack for inventing definitions and testing their fit, we need sympathetic, imaginative responsiveness to the way meanings open up and resonate within experience.

"Eternal consciousness" suggests an experiential standpoint that lies in polar contrast to the standpoint of "temporal consciousness." What would it be like to be caught up entirely in the hourly whirl of things, imprisoned by the press of time, never gaining a vantage point outside of, and looking over, the frantic temporal flux? For the knight of resignation, to gain an "eternal consciousness" would be to gain access to such a vantage point, to gain some freedom from the constricting push and pull of the many petty things that shape the ordinary flow of time. "Finite" and "infinite" are a similar pair of polar contrasts. To be enmeshed in the finite would be to have attachments only to particular, finite things, never responding to ideals that overarch particulars, or to totalities (such as the world itself) from which particulars separate out or emerge, or to "things" like the soul or God, which Hegel had identified as "infinite objects." For the knight of resignation, then, to make "the movement of infinity" would be to gain some freedom from the push and pull of petty, senseless things, gain some access to totalities, ideals, or "things" like God.

Because the knight's tie to the princess is the unifying focus of his identity, her loss reverberates throughout his experience. It seems that "all is lost," and that he "has no self" (even though from an "objective" position much might seem to remain). Self, relationship, and world are torn asunder, stripped of meaning and reality. However, the swain is no ordinary man. He is a person of exceptional strength and courage, in fact a *knight*. Because of his exceptional resources, the loss of the finite turns out not to be shattering through and through. Something is rescued—though not real rapport with the princess.

The knight renounces the self, relationship, and world constituted by his tie to the princess, and in that movement gains an infinite or eternal self, relationship, and world. In renouncing the princess, or by virtue of that act, the knight discovers (or generates) a new perspective—one that is *not* focused by concern for a single, finite individual. This new perspective places the knight outside the push and pull of petty things; and the "objects" this perspective takes are beyond the finite and temporal, too. This new outlook represents the possibility of surviving the crushing loss of the princess, the possibility of a point of leverage from which the old way of experiencing can be abandoned, and its loss felt as only partial—not the utter loss of point of view itself. This new-found perspective Silentio calls an "eternal consciousness." In it, the knight of infinite resignation finds "peace, rest, and comfort in sorrow."

Hardening oneself to sorrow by renouncing particular intense relationships seems to resemble the stoic reaction to a world of pain and trouble. One seeks immunity from the disturbance of disappointment, anger, and guilt. By withdrawing care, the self shields itself from injury or affliction. By renouncing the finite, its power to provoke passional reaction is defeated. But unlike the stoic who extirpates his love, the knight of resignation transforms it. Its new object is "the eternal being," and a shadow of concern remains as a sorrowful glance at the finite. God, for the knight, is not just an ideal of freedom from attachment and reactive emotion. God is love, a love "totally incommensurate with the finite."

Through resignation, a threefold transfiguration of existence is won. Transfigured first is the tie between the knight and his princess: an earthly, finite love becomes an idealized, eternal love. Then, the object of love is transfigured: a love of the princess becomes a love of God. And finally, the lover himself becomes transfigured: his integrity now is based not on a finite tie to another, but on his "eternal consciousness," on his grasp of a point of leverage on the finite.

The knight of resignation's achievement should not be underrated. He has made an advance on the "slaves of paltriness," the burghers, bishops, or thinkers who take faith to be easily won, something naturally acquired by dint of one's parentage, say, or place of birth. He knows real commitment and real loss. He has moved from the crowd of onlookers and donned the garb of spiritual battle. He knows independence, and does not "find the law for his action in others." Even greater, however, is the knight of faith's achievement.

Resignation, we recall, is but a halfway house, not a destination. The next stage of development is faith. Silentio only partially endorses the moves of resignation, for something is surely wrong with wholesale renunciation of the finite. The knight of faith corrects this defect. The knight of faith renounces the finite, as his predecessor did. But in addition, strange to say, he wins it *back* again. He gains an eternal love, but *temporal* loves are his as well. He is at home in the eternal, but happy also in the midst of the world.

In the last part of this essay, I will consider Abraham, who will be Silentio's central case of the knight of faith. For the moment, we will attend to another knight. In the "Expectoration," Silentio imagines a comic encounter with a knight of faith hardly resembling Abraham at all—or so it seems, for this unassuming gentleman looks for all the world like a tax collector.

> Here he is. Acquaintance made, I am introduced to him. The moment I set eyes on him, I instantly push him from me, I leap backward, I clasp my hands and say half-aloud, "Good Lord, is this the man? Is it really he? Why, he looks like a tax-collector!" However it is the man after all. I draw closer to him, watching his least movements to see whether there might not be visible a little heterogeneous fractional telegraphic message from the infinite, a glance, a smile, a gesture, a note of sadness which betrayed the infinite in its heterogeneity with the finite. No! I examine his figure from tip to toe to see if there might not be a cranny through which the infinite was peeping. No! He is solid through and through.

Being at home in the finite, the knight of faith looks ordinary. There is no betrayal of "the infinite," of a soul withdrawn or distanced. Appearances notwithstanding, Silentio is sure it is a knight of faith he encounters.

> [He] belongs entirely to the world, no Philistine more so. One can discover nothing of that aloof and superior nature whereby one recognizes the knight of the infinite. He takes delight in everything, and whenever one sees him taking part in a particular pleasure, he does it with the persistence which is the mark of the earthly man whose soul is absorbed in such things. . . . [*If*] *one did not know him,* it would be impossible to distinguish him from the rest of the congregation [emphasis added].

His delight in earthly things, his joy, is the token of his having welcomed the finite. But how is this man distinguished from a similarly ordinary man who has never undertaken the difficult movement of resignation?

In a passage that, when set against the pathos of Abraham's trial, can be taken only as comic relief, Silentio provides this knight of faith a delightfully banal test.

> Toward evening he walks home, his gait is as indefatigable as that of the postman. On his way he reflects that his wife has surely a special little warm dish prepared for him, e.g., a calf's head roasted, garnished with vegetables. . . . As it happens, he hasn't four pence to his name, and

yet he firmly believes that his wife has that dainty dish for him. . . . His wife hasn't it—strangely enough, it is quite the same to him.

His delightful anticipation of his meal is the sign of his harmony with the finite. The fact that he cannot be unsettled or disappointed should his dish "be impossible" (as the swain's love was impossible) is the sign that he has renounced his claim to the finite. He cannot be embarrassed or thrown off stride by the world's unfolding this way rather than that. He welcomes, and is ready to welcome, all. He is unperturbed by change, yet he has in no way diminished his care for even the least particularity of his existence. Abstractly, Silentio characterizes his condition in this way:

> this man has made, and every instant is making, movements of infinity. With infinite resignation he has drained the cup of life's profound sadness, he knows the bliss of the infinite, he senses the pain of renouncing everything, the dearest things he possesses in the world, and yet finiteness tastes to him just as good as to one who never knew anything higher. . . . [He] has this sense of security in enjoying it, as though the finite life were the surest thing of all. And yet, the whole earthly form he exhibits is a new creation by virtue of the absurd.

Both the knight of resignation and the knight of faith make "movements of infinity," gain an "eternal consciousness" that inures them to change. It would not hurt the young swain, Silentio reflects, to learn that his beloved has married another. But by the same token, Silentio admits, he would be embarrassed were love to become possible—he has written her off, temporally speaking. However it is precisely in this respect that the swain lacks faith. For in addition to the "movement of infinity," the knight of faith can make the move back into the world, finding the taste of the finite good. Unlike the man of resignation, he would be ready to accept the beloved's return. He has not sealed himself off from the possibility of joy. He knows more than resignation, withdrawal, and grief. In *this* respect, he has advanced.

Silentio is frankly baffled by the knight of faith. The knight of resignation he can understand, but not the man of faith. How can one renounce finite life, yet embrace it in joy? With his flair for the dramatic, he speaks of faith as a capacity for the impossible, as achieving its goal "by virtue of the absurd." The knight of faith gets back the finite because he believes that "with God, all things are possible by virtue of the absurd."

Silentio has no interest in clearing up this tangle of paradox. He relishes it. What a delicious affront to those "reasonable men" who think the path to faith is wide, well-marked, and smoothly paved—no doubt traversable in a day! But although we may now understand at least one reason why Silentio speaks in this way, we do not need to settle for such a thin rationale. I will try now to spell out some specific complexities of faith that lead to Silentio's paradoxical expressions. In so doing, I in no way wish to dilute Silentio's claim that faith is stunningly difficult to achieve. I begin with a contrast between types of concern.

If we have cared for a fine old watch and suddenly it is stolen, we feel not only sorrow but anger. Our care for the watch will be linked, in a typical case, with proprietary rights. With a deepening of care goes a deepening of possessiveness—and a deepened capacity for hurt, should our possession-related rights be violated. One way to cancel this capacity for hurt is to renounce our proprietary claims. If we disown our possessions, we may be saddened if they are lost or taken but we will at least be spared the added pain of knowing that our rights have been violated.

Much of the stoic hardening of the self to disappointment and change can be interpreted as a narrowing of the area of proprietary claim. Thoreau remarks that a man is rich in proportion to that which he is willing to give up. Giving something up, we cannot be hurt by its being taken away. Silentio speaks of the knight of resignation "waiving claim" to the finite, "renouncing the claim to everything," and "infinitely renouncing claim to the love which is the content of his life." Renouncing all claim to the princess, he saves himself from hurt should she marry another, and from hurt coming from the finite generally. But the fact that the swain would find the return of the princess an embarrassment indicates that the price he has paid for diminished hurt is a narrowing of care. He would be embarrassed by her return because in some sense he has ceased to care: "he no longer takes a finite interest in what the princess is doing."

But not all cases of care are tied up with proprietary claims. I may enjoy and warmly anticipate the appearance of a sparrow at my feeder. Yet I would claim no rights over this object of my care. The matter of its life and death is something over which I waive all claims. Of course, I would feel indignant were someone maliciously to injure it. But in the course of things, the sparrow will go its way and I will adjust myself to its goings and comings. A concern that forgoes proprietary claim one could call selfless. It would be a concern entirely distinct from the assertion of rights—unless one wanted to speak of the right of the object cared for to its own independence. My joy at the return of the sparrow need be no less for my lacking proprietary claim over it; and my care need be no less for my lacking bitterness or indignation, should it be lost forever.

This distinction between kinds of concern partially clears up the confusing claim that the knight of faith renounces the finite and yet is simultaneously at home in the finite. The knight of faith can both renounce and enjoy the finite because he sees, or knows in his bones, that renouncing all *claim* to the finite is not renouncing all *care* for it. He is at home and takes delight in the finite (witness the tax-collector) because he cares; yet this is a selfless care, for he has given up all proprietary claim. The knight of resignation, on the other hand, cannot distinguish, or blurs together, these two sorts of concern. The swain's care for the princess is diminished as he renounces claim. Hence it seems impossible to him that one might renounce all claim and yet care.

I would like to use this distinction between renouncing claim and renouncing all care to clarify the respect in which, through faith, one could hope to get the princess back. Then I will try to provide a rationale for Silentio's invocation of "the absurd."

The knight of faith retains an openness to joy and the possibility of love that the knight of resignation sorely lacks. In a way that combines admiration and self-pity, the knight of resignation reflects on the man of faith:

> By my own strength I am able to give up the princess, and I shall not become a grumbler, but shall find joy and repose in my pain; but by my own strength I am not able to get her again, for I am employing all my strength to be resigned. But by faith, says that marvelous knight, by faith, I shall get her by virtue of the absurd.

Having renounced all claim to the princess (but not all care for her), the man of faith is ready to welcome her back. He has the strength, courage, or faith to say, "I shall get her by virtue of the absurd," but he cannot force or coerce her return. By an open readiness to receive her, buttressed by the faith that he will get her back, he can welcome her, if she is given. The knight of resignation, using all his strength for renunciation, lacks faith that love is still possible. He blurs his renunciation. Care as well as claim is renounced, leaving him in no position to receive the princess, were she to be given.

The knight of faith gets the princess back, then, only in the sense that he guarantees that the ultimate obstacle to her return—lack of receptivity—will be absent. He does not by his own strength effect her return, but he provides the condition for her return. The rest is up to God. She will not be returned to his keeping unless he is ready in welcome. He does not believe that the impossible can be gotten around by his efforts, but neither does he believe that what is impossible for him is impossible for God. If he gets the princess (which he has faith that he will), it will be through God—and through his own receptivity to the possibility of her return. In Silentio's view each man gets, spiritually speaking, exactly what he deserves. Therefore he has confidence that once the man of faith has put himself in complete readiness for the princess, she cannot but be given; the knight, having placed himself in the position of selfless love, will reap his reward.

Silentio says that the knight of faith believes he will get the beloved "by virtue of the absurd." One reason for this phrase is polemical. It works to counterbalance an easy rationalistic optimism, the idea that by calculation of benefits and burdens one can arrive at the decision to opt for faith; the idea that reality can be captured without remainder by some essentially simple conceptual scheme, with no dark spots before which reason must confess its ignorance; the idea that faith is an early, childish stage in the grand, inevitable development of human rationality, which is now, from our present exalted position, easily understood. But there are at least two other considerations, apart from this polemical purpose, which underlie Silentio's talk of the absurd.

As someone placed this side of faith and at most a man of resignation, Silentio is unable to make the discriminations open to the man of faith. The knight of faith could *reject* the idea that "by virtue of the absurd" he will get

the princess. To the narrator, the knight *appears* to believe this because, as we have seen above, [the narrator] cannot discriminate giving up claim to the princess from giving up care for her. He thus believes (falsely) that the knight of faith has given up all care (in his renunciation) and yet *has* care (in his faith). An absurdity indeed!

Secondly, there is Silentio's sense that the knight of faith is involved in some sort of logical contradiction. This knight believes that "with God all things are possible"— that is, he has hope that the princess might be returned. Yet, having passed through the stage of resignation, he also has a clear-headed recognition that the princess is lost. Faith does the impossible, says Silentio. It believes both that the princess is lost (a belief that separates the knight of resignation from those not yet resigned) and that she will be returned (a belief that separates the knight of faith from the knight of resignation). One interpretative option is to accept Silentio's characterization, to assume that faith just *can* embrace such absurdity. However, a more helpful reconstruction is possible. What appears to be a contradiction in beliefs can be understood as part of a complex test of care.

Within the context in which Silentio is working—the context of faith—these opposing beliefs do not simply cancel each other out. A surface absurdity remains: love is and is not possible; the princess will and will not be returned.

Et Portrait af Søren Kierkegaard.

A woodcut originally published in a Swedish newspaper in 1876.

But a kind of deep structure can be opened up that eases the offense, for these beliefs function crucially as separate measures of care: care is taken as a person's capacity first, for dread and grief, and then, for delight and joy. Faith must be tested and authenticated in two apparently opposed directions at once. "Absurdly," the knight of faith confronts both tests at once, for grief and joy, dread and delight, are coequal measures of care and faith.

The belief that love is impossible (or that the princess is lost) measures a capacity to acknowledge real loss, without which one's care would be exposed as shallow and weak. The capacity to feel deep loss—to care—is authenticated when the swain *does* face the loss of his princess, rather than flee or evade the fact.

The belief that love is possible (or that the princess will be returned) measures a contrasting dimension of care. Here, care is sounded out in terms of a capacity for joyful welcome of what may be given: a capacity to acknowledge the blessings of existence, appearing wonderously, without warning or rationale. An inability to rejoice spontaneously at what gifts time may bring marks a cramped and guarded care. Denying the possibility of joy (through bitterness, resignation, or "common sense") can deplete and poison care. The capacity to remain open to joy—to care—would be authenticated insofar as the swain, moving beyond resignation, could believe he might get the princess back. This is not a matter of rejoicing when grief is called for, but of remaining open to the possibility that occasions for joy have not been utterly erased, even in the moment of grief.

The "slaves of paltriness" fail the test of care-as-capacity-for-grief by refusing to acknowledge that a person could feel the sort of deep loss felt by the swain. But these shallow unbelievers also fail the test of care-as-capacity-for-joy. Silentio showers contempt on such bland optimism and fear of sorrow, contrasting it to the real hope and joy, resignation and grief, of the knight of faith. His is not

> the lukewarm indolence which thinks, "there is surely no instant need, it is not worth sorrowing before the time," [or] the pitiful hope which says, "One cannot know what is going to happen . . . it might possibly be after all"— these caricatures of faith are part and parcel of life's wretchedness, and the infinite resignation has already consigned them to infinite contempt.

The knight of faith's beliefs, as tokens of his condition, are distinguished by their intensity and depth. Having passed the test of care as grief, he moves beyond resignation toward faith by facing the test of care as joy.

Silentio recognizes that the requirement that one's capacity for joy and grief be authenticated simultaneously may result in the *appearance* of a person capable of neither— the capacity for one, as it were, undermining at that moment the capacity for the other. As he puts it,

> Those . . . who carry the jewel of faith are likely to be delusive, because their outward appearance bears a striking resemblance to that which both the infinite resignation and faith profoundly despise . . . to Philistinism.

But faith accepts this risk—that it be mistaken for Philistinism.

The "absurdity" that entangles the knight of faith—the notion that his capacity for grief and his capacity for joy can be simultaneously tested—exemplifies a more general point concerning "logic" and "emotion." Authenticity may not just permit but may *require* that we acknowledge the simultaneous presence of "contradictory" emotions. Thus one can feel both love and hate toward a demanding master, both disappointment and delight at the failure of a colleague, both anger and happy relief at a snub. Whatever the outcome of a purely logical analysis of these cases (perhaps the air of contradiction is without substance), no one would deny that seemingly incompatible feelings are all too often "illogically" intertwined, and that personal integrity can be quickly undercut by a refusal to acknowledge the full complexity and ambivalence of one's emotions.

It is characteristic not only of specifically religious faith but also of the faith that attends any radical growth or change of self that care be plumbed in both directions. It will be tested both as grief and joy, both as dread of what is about to be painfully lost and as full welcome of the new and uncertain, about to be received. It is characteristic of faith and care that these emotions be mixed and acknowledged as mixed; and that the temptation, in the interest of simplicity or logic, to deny one or another emotion in this tensed ambivalence, be resisted.

I have tried to suggest a rationale for the often wildly obscure characterizations Silentio gives of faith. There is the obvious factor of polemical exaggeration and dramatics. Also, there is the fact that from the standpoint of resignation, the contrast between renunciation of claim and renunciation of care will collapse, resulting in the appearance of absurdity: it will appear that the knight of faith cares, and yet has given up all his care. And without care, how can the knight hope to have the princess returned? Finally, there is the fact that from a logical standpoint, the knight of faith appears to hold contradictory beliefs: for example, that he both will and will not have the princess returned. Silentio says the knight of faith believes that "with God, all things are possible." And one might suppose that this meant that God could both return and not return the princess. But our reconstruction took a different tack. The capacity of faith is not the capacity to believe God capable of two mutually exclusive actions, nor the capacity of a person to believe two incompatible propositions, where "believe" means something like "believe that under objective conditions both might be tested and found true." Rather, faith concerns a capacity for care, and the apparently contradictory beliefs were seen to function as measures of grief and dread, of joy and delight, thus authenticating two crucial and apparently opposed dimensions of care.

Our analytical work now accomplished, we can return to the central drama of *Fear and Trembling,* Abraham's trial. At the risk of repetition, it will be worth gathering our insights. We should now be ready to hear that story in a new and compelling way.

Abraham's world has revolved not around a princess but around Isaac and God. Now he learns that his relationship with Isaac (and God) will be tried. He must visibly and dramatically reenact, as it were, the "movements" of resignation and faith. His willingness to sacrifice Isaac betokens his renunciation of all claim to Isaac. Yet that sacrifice is predicated on his unceasing love, which is a sign that he has not lost care for the finite. And by faith, he believes that he will get Isaac back "by virtue of the absurd."

The task set for the Knight of Faith is this:

> to live happily and joyfully, every instant to see
> the sword hanging over the head of the beloved,
> yet not to find repose in the pain of resignation,
> but joy.

However, Abraham does not just *see* the sword hanging over the beloved. He is asked to wield it. Hence his sense of doom is intense, and his capacity for joy, made obscure. From the standpoint of faith, the pain of renunciation concerns the loss of the proprietary claim. Giving up the claim means giving up the sense that one has rights over the matter of Isaac's life and death. That will be a difficult renunciation. To Silentio, and perhaps even to Abraham, it will seem dangerously close to losing Isaac outright. Yet Abraham has faith that Isaac will not be lost. His willingness to sacrifice Isaac shows in the most dramatic way imaginable his severing of the possessive tie. Yet in that severing, a selfless care is renewed and released. His greatness is "a two-edged sword which slays and saves."

The complexity of Silentio's position on the relationship between ethics and faith demands a fuller treatment than I can offer here. But I should note that although Silentio tries us with the dizzying, dissociative view that Abraham is murderous, he also gives us ample evidence that what we confront is not murder but sacrifice. Even in the "Expectoration," which does not really explore the issue, Silentio says that if someone did not love Isaac as Abraham did, then "every thought of offering Isaac would not be a trial, but a temptation," and that such love is "the presumption apart from which the whole thing becomes a crime." In addition, the purpose of murder, ordinarily, is to get rid of someone. Yet Abraham is ready to welcome Isaac back joyously at every moment of his trial. Never does he relax his love or care.

A ritual such as sacrifice is an outward expression for an inward *act:* in this case, undoing possessiveness. Renunciation of possessiveness is more than the self-pitying sense that one is a passive *observer* or *victim* of pain. Abraham cannot chalk up his loss—if it occurs—to some cosmic necessity or tragic fate. He does not just live through that suffering, as he would had God just snatched his son away.

Silentio believes that this aspect of the story is overlooked by his contemporaries. By remembering only that Isaac was returned, the difficulty of sacrifice is brushed aside. Therefore Silentio resolves to force it into view.

> If I were to talk about him, I would first depict
> the pain of his trial. To that end, I would suck
> all the dread and distress and torture out of a fa-
> ther's sufferings, so that I might describe what

Abraham suffered, while nevertheless he believed.

As we read on, Abraham's joy goes unmentioned. But this emphasis exclusively on pain must be viewed as a polemical corrective, for faith involves not "repose in the pain of resignation" but "living happily and joyfully." Abraham cannot be *that* different from the tax collector. He must take delight in the finite.

What could be meant by Abraham's joy? His unceasing love of Isaac betokens a joy in Isaac's existence, and derivatively, in existence generally. In addition, he does not succumb to hatred or resentment of God or life. The paths of suicide or despair are not his. We must suppose that joy is present inwardly, interwoven with fear and trembling, as a correlate of his capacity to affirm existence through and through, while willingly and without reservation acknowledging the inexpungable facts of parting and loss. But the capacity for joy—however tacit—is buttressed by his belief that Isaac will be returned—not in another life but in this one. This belief is both an expression of his joy and its presupposition. The copresence of dread and joy, grief and delight, is the other side of the paradoxical belief that Isaac both will and will not be lost.

Once, in the prelude to *Fear and Trembling,* Silentio imagined Abraham getting Isaac back, but being so embittered by God's request that he was thereafter unable to care—so in a sense (at least in *that* version of the story) *not* getting back his son. But in the central version, Abraham's unceasing love of both God and Isaac makes Isaac's return both full and fulfilling. Abraham does not effect his son's return, but he ensures that there is no inner obstacle to his son's full welcome—should he be given. He ensures that his care is unbroken.

Silentio has failed to sort renunciation of claim from renunciation of care, and so cannot understand the sense in which Abraham might believe that "with God, all things are possible." For him, the phrase either signals the shabby optimism of a confused and pitiful hope, or shows that "by virtue of the absurd," God can return Isaac to Abraham's care, even though Abraham has severed all care. But stepping back, we see that Abraham merits Isaac's return by maintaining a selfless love, by sustaining his care even through the dreadful threat of its loss in the act of renouncing the proprietary claim, and in the crisis of ambivalence, of joy and grief, that attends all fundamental change. His openness, his receptivity to the possibility of return even as he gives up all rights in the matter, substantiates his faith and makes fitting his reward.

> Here an eternal divine order prevails, here it
> does not rain both upon the just and upon the
> unjust, here the sun does not shine both upon the
> good and upon the evil, here it holds good that
> only he who works gets the bread, only he who
> was in anguish finds repose, only he who de-
> scends into the underworld rescues the beloved,
> only he who draws the knife gets Isaac.

I have tried to give a reading of the first parts of *Fear and Trembling* faithful to the spirit and detail of the text. If I have succeeded, the widespread view of Kierkegaard as an arch irrationalist will seem shallow and naïve beside Kierkegaard's own self-characterization as a needed corrective for the age. Also, I trust we will have gained renewed respect for Kierkegaard's grasp of the subtle fine-structure of care and attachment, of grief, love, and selflessness, of courage, risk, and change of self—venerable philosophical concerns as old as the pursuit of wisdom itself, however frequently we find them cast aside. (pp. 100-14)

> *Edward F. Mooney, "Understanding Abraham: Care, Faith, and the Absurd," in* Kierkegaard's 'Fear and Trembling': Critical Appraisals, *edited by Robert L. Perkins, The University of Alabama Press, 1981, pp. 100-14.*

Sister Marilyn Thomas-Faulkenburg   (essay date 1982)

[*In the following essay, Thomas contends that the labyrinthine, deceptive structure of* Either/Or *is intended to draw readers into the "'fragmentary prodigality'" of the text, to jar them into attention, and to encourage interpretation and self-examination rather than provide solutions.*]

If I attempt to elucidate any aspect of Kierkegaard's narrative technique, I will regret it; if I do not attempt to elucidate any aspect of Kierkegaard's narrative technique, I will regret it; if I make the attempt or do not make the attempt, I will regret both.

Immediately, "dear reader," you detect my lack of originality, my plagiarism, my cheap parody of Kierkegaard's own introduction to "An ecstatic lecture," as it is titled. Such a hasty accusation is easily refuted, however. *Either/Or,* the narrative here considered, bears the signature not of Kierkegaard, whose name never appeared on the title page when the book was published in 1843, but of a certain Victor Eremita. He, however, assumes responsibility only as editor of the work. The authors Victor cites are A and B, so designated because even though B has identified himself in his own letters here published as a judge named William, still the A writer remains totally anonymous. Consequently, it is only logical in the name of consistency and for the sake of convenience that Victor designate both voices by letter names only. If you want to be precise in your accusation, then, you should say that I have plagiarized A, since "An ecstatic lecture" from which I borrowed, probably came from A's pen according to the editor.

But who is A? All we are told by the mysterious editor is that A apparently wrote refrains ("Diapsalmata") to himself ("ad se ipsum"), which he, Victor Eremita, accidentally acquired by spending too much money on a secretary he didn't need. In providing the reader with this background, Victor manages to tell his own story in a book that he claims is not his story. One day when he needed money in a hurry, he relates, the drawer of the secretary containing that money would not open. Consequently, in a moment of impulsive anger, he seized an ax, and in the process of hacking the desk to bits, got snowed under by a flurry of papers he had never seen before nor suspected having in his possession. Only after much careful reading (done in the woods while he was supposedly hunting, the papers being carried in his weapon case) was he able to de-

tect that the writing flowed from the pens of two different authors. But it was not to be quite so simple as all that, because the unsolicited inheritance also contained the diary of a seducer, which apparently was the work neither of A nor B. Later Victor discovered that A apparently stole the diary from a seducer, an act A says he repented but has never regretted. Then, too, there was a sermon among the papers, probably addressed to B as well as to a parish of peasants in Jutland. The B author, however, sent it and a large correspondence of his own to A in an effort to help A see the error of his ways. And A, having scrupulously read the diary of the seducer, observes the error of that man's way in his commentary, a commentary that unwittingly condemns in the seducer's behavior the very philosophy by which he defines his own approach to life. In fact, the seducer's reflections form a logical conclusion to A's philosophy of life (which opinion is mine added to all the others).

So the question remains: Whom did I plagiarize (or at least parody)? Will the true author please stand up? To put the question another way: what is there under the sun that is not repetition or doubling (which necessarily implies variation, since it is not the original and must therefore be a copy somehow)? Victor, as editor, claims responsibility for the preface. But it depends for its existence upon the manuscript which it reflects and pretends to interpret. In the same manner, A's text presupposes and serves as an introduction to the seducer's diary. Finally, B writes his letters on the basis of a supposed body of correspondence from A, which (though not a part of the text of *Either/Or*) is the pretext upon which the text gets written. In the end (if one can be so presumptuous as to suppose there can be one in the world of narrative) the reader must consider the possibility suggested by Victor himself in his introduction. Perhaps, he hints, everything is the work of one man presenting different existential possibilities. Victor is thus creating the possibility of his own creator. He is inventing a Kierkegaard. Thus Kierkegaard is fictionalized by and in the text. In one respect Kierkegaard is now a figment of Victor's imagination, who, in turn, began as a figment of Kierkegaard's imagination. In *The Point of View for My Work as an Author,* Kierkegaard himself wrote: "I regarded myself preferably as a *reader* [Kierkegaard's emphasis] of the books, not as the author." Somehow language allows one to step outside of one's thoughts and look at them from a third-person point of view. Such is precisely one of the functions of irony as a narrative device whereby the possible becomes actual (Victor is the editor) and the actual is transformed into the merely possible (Kierkegaard is Victor's hypothetical author).

Such is the power of the ironic voice that it can transform even boredom (should that be your wish at this point) into "any desired degree of momentum." Since the word *boredom* has crept into this discussion of voice and its function in narrative discourse, allow me to deviate from the main focus of the argument to consider the possibilities for irony in that word. We have just observed, by considering the problems of voice in *Either/Or,* how possibility and actuality can change places (Victor displacing Kierkegaard and Kierkegaard displacing Victor). This power of irony to provide actuality even as it suspends what is constitutive of actuality is illustrated by A, whose argument I paraphrase. Since it is good to begin with a principle, according to A, he begins with the principle that "all men are bores," a principle no one would contradict; for if anyone would choose to refute this principle, he would only prove himself the greater bore by doing so. Once settled on a foundation, A's argument can proceed: as Hegel has impeccably demonstrated, a thesis receives its momentum from its antithesis. Boredom, by being not only repellent but "infinitely forbidding," is thereby a negative principle. Consequently, if it is true that every concept contains its own negation, then a reconciliation or mediation of the two will generate a higher synthesis. According to this dialectic, fullness mediated by emptiness should yield a higher concept. As an instance of fullness one might mention pantheism. And the obvious example of emptiness here is boredom, which is by virtue of the syllogism the hidden side of pantheism. Consequently, one can write a history of the world starting with the principle of boredom. The gods were bored, and so they created man; but man was bored and so they created woman; man and woman were bored together and so children were created. Then they all got together and built a tower, such an idea being as boring as the tower was high. The A author continues to build, resting on the foundation of boredom, a cure for all modern ills. It isn't the boredom itself that provides the solutions, but the energy that the concept generates. Whereas direct statement threatens to dry up as quickly as the ink on the page where it is inscribed, indirect or ironic discourse begins with a principle that may be false in itself for the sake of the truth it may yield.

By alluding to the Tower of Babel (and consequently to the confusion of tongues) Kierkegaard provides an apt symbol for a narrative technique attempting to clarify by means of confusion. Language, a marvelous medium for generating more language, is nevertheless helpless in the face of the absolute. Clement of Alexandria, as Kierkegaard once noted, may have written in allegory to conceal the truth from the heretics of his day, but he need not have made any conscious effort if his purpose was to confuse. It is the very nature of language in its metaphorical multiplicity to obscure, to make equivocal. In the case of A's reflections on boredom, however, it is by affirmation of the negative (boredom) that the affirmative is generated. The A writer gets to his intended goal, i.e., the potential of boredom, by playing off of its negative capability. By placing boredom within the context of pantheism as its obverse side, A is enabled to take it out of the realm of emptiness and place it in the order of fullness. Such is the function of irony to deceive one into or out of logic by means of linguistic play. Irony in specific relation to narrative voice can traverse "a multitude of determinations in the form of possibility," poetically living through them, before ending in nothingness.

"But where," I hear you ask, "are you going in this essay? You begin by doubling back on your source and then attempt to justify that act by accusing the text of doing the same thing, of doubling on itself, reflecting, one voice echoing another, each repetition being a distortion of the original since it is not the original. Finally, however, you fall into your own trap when Victor falls into his, i.e.,

when he suggests the possibility of one voice (Kierkegaard's) behind and controlling all narrative voices within *Either/Or.* So what do you mean by suggesting that Kierkegaard is in the work at the same time that he is not? You are obviously contradicting yourself."

Unworthy though I be to presume to loosen even one knot in Kierkegaard's verbal sandal strap, yet will I venture to place my feet in the prints left by those sandals as my way into the labyrinth of his narrative technique, using the thread of his own comments on irony as a guide. Although I shall no doubt end where I now begin as a chaser of the wind (*Windtreiber*), I consider such a title as the greatest of honors when Kierkegaard designated himself a "windsucker (*Vindsluger*)" in relation to Hegel, whom he called the "windbag (*Windbeutel*)." Consequently, while "a German makes wind—and a Dane swallows it," an American herewith dares to chase a puff of it. Moreover, to speak in terms of the labyrinth metaphor, to end where one has begun is the only possible achievement. To be able to say "I've been here before" is to have found a sense of direction. It is an act of self-recognition, the ultimate goal of Kierkegaard's dialectic.

By immersing oneself in the various points of view from Victor Eremita (the hermit) to A (the aesthete) to B (the moralist) to the seducer and the sermonizing priest, the reader encounters a multitude of possible personalities. Kierkegaard is nowhere in the text because the actuality of the narrative is the presentation of sheer possibility. Actuality is suspended and replaced by an actuality that is no actuality. The ironist, Kierkegaard himself explains, is like a king who disguised himself as a butcher and a butcher who happened to look like a king. People laughed at both of them, but for opposite reasons. They laughed at the butcher because he was not the king but looked like one and at the king because he was not the butcher when he looked like one. So, too, with Kierkegaard. What he might look like in the narrative is not what he is. And what he is in himself no one can tell by the narrative in which, if he appears at all, he appears in disguise. Contrary to the conclusion of Kierkegaard's similitude, however (in which the people laughed at both king and butcher), the reader in relation to *Either/Or* does not quite know for sure at whom he is laughing; perhaps it is himself whether he knows it or not. And that is ironic also.

I suggest that one laughs at oneself because for Kierkegaard the object of irony, of unreliable narrators, and of the distancing thus achieved by these devices, is to point out a way that is not the way. The purpose of irony is not to give one a possession in a satisfying conclusion, but to leave all in a state of possibility so that the reader gains the capability of making actual for himself. Therefore, "dear reader," you are the protagonist sent into the narrative labyrinth of possibilities, where, if you do not produce yourself, you will be poetically produced by another, as Victor, for instance, invents Kierkegaard. To see how irony functions within the text, one need only focus attention on the narrators of *Either/Or,* who themselves become the very thing they most oppose. Only in a text where irony is omnipresent is it possible to observe such visible irony ironically operating.

In the chapter entitled "The First Love," the aesthetic man sets out to write a review of a comedy by Scribe, which he has just seen on stage. But before doing that, A describes the two requirements for any aesthetic production: There must be, he maintains, an occasion and a muse. The occasion he describes as the "web in which the fruit hangs"; it often "plays the master," and "decides the matter." Note these two metaphoric definitions from a man who writes elsewhere that every time he sees one he is "seized by an involuntary fright that its [metaphor's] true purpose is to conceal an obscurity of the thought." The aesthetic man then goes on to say that the writing of this review is "the child of the occasion" on which he saw his sweetheart in the audience attending the same play he had come to see because it called forth memories of her. Before he can get on with his little review, then, A must describe his first love, how he met this woman of his dreams, how this love, in order to be the first, had to "open with a snap" like a flower, the feeling having to "burst its locks with an energy like that of champagne." Having thus verbally saturated his reader with the necessity for an occasion, A concludes:

> Still, it was on the occasion of the occasion for this little critique that I had wished to say something quite general about the occasion, or about the occasion in general. It happens, however, quite fortunately that I have already said what I wished to say; for the more I consider this matter, the more certain I am that there is simply nothing to be said about it in general, because there is no occasion in general. So I have come about as far as I was when I began.

Having thus erased the entire credibility of his previous argument about the necessity of an occasion, the A writer goes on to describe another occasion, which occasioned the forthcoming review (if one still remembers his original intent to write one): one day A was visiting a friend who planned to launch a publication, using an article he himself had written for the occasion. The two of them were spending a pleasant forenoon together, A having read the article and made a few suggestions and changes. Just as A "bent over to take an apricot," he "upset the ink-horn over the entire manuscript." The upshot was that A was commissioned to write an article posthaste or be held accountable for the publisher's loss of his good name if the magazine did not come out on schedule. Alas, A relates, the publication never came out anyway. But even though the review was never published in some hypothetical magazine, here we are reading it in published form. The review itself is of little interest, I think, but the occasion has become the matter rather than the master, the fruit rather than the web in which the fruit supposedly hangs. By his own action—and this is where the irony lies—A counteracts his effort at the same time. "The judge," to quote Kierkegaard from *The Point of View,* "is made manifest by his judgment." Through the ironic web of complexity, the sincere reader is guided to the simple, a goal he would not have reached through immediacy or direct communication because the immediate would either be rejected as insulting or be too apparently obvious to make an impression.

A second and irresistible example of irony as a narrative technique that shocks the reader into attention, that leads to insight through the back door, so to speak, is found in the chapter entitled "The Unhappiest Man" (subtitled "An enthusiastic address before the Symparanekromenoi," translated as "the fellowship of buried lives"). Who is the unhappiest man? This question is raised by an inscription on a tombstone somewhere in England. The answer lies buried somewhere in the terms past, present, and future. Stated briefly, A's argument proceeds as follows: Either one is unhappy because "he constantly hopes something that should be remembered," or "he always remembers that for which he ought to hope." As A notes, this state of affairs "is quite enough to drive a man mad, and yet he does not become so, and this is precisely his misfortune." Ironically, A is that man though he knows it not. In conclusion, all that can be said is that

> Language fails, and thought is confounded; for who is the happiest, except the unhappiest, and who the unhappiest, except the happiest, and what is life but madness, and faith but folly, and hope but the briefest respite, and love but vinegar in the wound.

Now, "dear reader," you could have avoided this whole dialectical web that ends in nothing if you had but heeded A's hint at the outset and sat in quiet contemplation of the title without having gone further into this chapter. For, he writes, "a title can be so richly suggestive of thought, so personally appealing, as to leave you with no desire to read the book." The title, like the narrative in general, defeats its own purpose. To devote one's whole life to the goal of avoiding misunderstanding, Kierkegaard once wrote, "would lead to the greatest misunderstanding" (*The Point of View*). In keeping with this remark, *Either/Or* is devoted to the opposite goal, namely, misunderstanding for the sake of understanding. On the other hand, however, maybe one should heed the inscription over A's own papers: "Diapsalmata—ad se ipsum." To read these papers is to commit an act of intrusion, the crime of breaking and entering.

"It does not take much," I hear you interject, "to say that Kierkegaard was a Master of Irony. His own age recognized him as such. What did he hope to accomplish by it? That's the question we want answered." And I say: Thank you for asking. That question brings me to the heart of my own commentary. To mystify or entertain the reader by using a narrative device which disguises, deceives, suspends actuality, or multiplies it indeterminately was never Kierkegaard's purpose as an author. His purpose was simple (and stated incessantly outside of the pseudonymous works) to show what it means to become a Christian in a culture where Christians were everywhere in name but nowhere in fact. In a way, *Either/Or* is all things to all readers, "a Proteus who incessantly alters the deception" in order to reveal a sense of the true by means of the untrue.

Reading *Either/Or* is like overhearing the confessions of sinners who have nothing to repent; so they confess for each other. I don't see their faces, but I can describe them by what they say. In fact, after a while I begin to recognize traces of my own features in theirs. Because I am eavesdropping, their confessions become all the more compelling until I realize that their voices have penetrated, that they are no longer outside but within myself. I, too, like Victor the editor who felt the presence of the Seducer in his room as he prepared to publish the diary, feel quite strange sometimes when reading this book, as though Kierkegaard were coming to me like a shadow hovering over my shoulder, as if he were fixing his eyes upon me and saying: "So you are writing a paper about this book, swallowing my blood 'in order to obtain blood and life-warmth in paragraphs for a while.'" His voice comes as a personal warning to me that "knowing about" is worthless without "being." While A and B are working out their salvation, therefore, I must work out my own in this "fragmentary prodigality" of texts. Without making that leap of faith beyond the text, however, I must end like A, frightened by every metaphor, aware of some obscurity concealed.

The word salvation is the right one in this context, for Kierkegaard always wrote with a religious intent. And yet, religious truth, he maintained, could not be captured by a text, but only lived. Kierkegaard defined "witness" as the highest form of communication because it transcends the function and ability of words. We inhabit a world of texts, however, and within this world Kierkegaard used a form of discourse he discusses in *The Point of View* as *indirect communication,* which deceives a person for the truth's sake. To use Kierkegaard's metaphor, indirect communication is like "bringing to light by the application of a caustic fluid a text which is hidden under another text." Indirect communication presupposes an illusion from which one must be delivered before truth can be imparted, whereas direct communication is the imparting of "a piece of knowledge" to another who is simply unknowing. He is like "a blank sheet of paper upon which something is written." Therefore, "dear reader," your mind contains the text that must be brought to light by the burning away of other texts that have been superimposed somehow. Merely to collect mental texts indiscriminately, one layer eliminating or augmenting the other, is to flounder in a labyrinth of verbal illusion. To live with a sense of direction, one must choose his or her individual text. For to be without one is like the possibility of gaining the whole world while losing one's soul. Indirect communication is the designation that must be used in a discussion of narrative voice in *Either/Or;* for indirect communication implies a "you shall" emphasis, a drawing out of the receiver (the "dear reader") rather than a pouring in of a text by a communicator (a narrative voice). Since the emphasis is intended to rest on the reader, it is appropriate that the narrative voices vanish as they tend to do.

Kierkegaard's narrative, then, disguises, deceives, misleads, vanishes, posits as it retracts, negates as it affirms and multiplies possibilities that threaten to end in nothing. If I attempt to label this technique as deconstructive, I will regret it. If I do not attempt to label it deconstructive, I will regret that. Whether I call it deconstructive or not, I will regret both. Consequently, I will choose neither/nor with regard to *Either/Or.* (pp. 591-600)

Sister Marilyn Thomas-Faulkenburg, "The Reader as Protagonist in Kierkegaard's Narra-tive Labyrinth," in The Georgia Review, *Vol. XXXVI, No. 3, Fall, 1982, pp. 591-600.*

Christopher Norris   (essay date 1983)

[*An English critic and educator, Norris, whose works attempt to bridge philosophy and literary theory, has written extensively on Deconstruction and literary theory. In the following essay, he maintains that oblique literary strategies employed by Kierkegaard, such as shifting viewpoints and pseudonymous narratives, contribute to his success as a writer. However, these indirect authorial tactics, Norris argues, appear to require deconstructive interpretation, a disintegrative approach that would undermine Kierkegaard's fundamental, didactic intent.*]

What might it mean to "deconstruct" Kierkegaard? From one point of view it would produce a reading not only allowed for but actively *preempted* by much of what Kierkegaard wrote. His entire pseudonymous production—the "aesthetic," that is, as opposed to the "religious" writing—can be seen to deconstruct itself at every turn, remaining always one jump ahead of the *hypocrite lecteur* who thinks to have fathomed its meaning. According to his own retrospective account (in *The Point of View for My Work as an Author*), Kierkegaard was wholly in command of this process from the outset. His "aesthetic" production was a means of ensnaring the reader in fictions and speculative arguments which would ultimately self-deconstruct, so to speak, at the point of transition to a higher, ethical plane of understanding. The reader would thus be brought to comprehend the inherent limitations and self-imposed deceits of a purely aesthetic attitude to life. This "ethical" stage would in turn be transcended by a recognition of its own insufficiency in the face of religious experience. Such is the threefold dialectic of enlightenment as Kierkegaard expressly defines it. From the standpoint thus gained atop all the shifting perspectives of Kierkegaard's authorship, the reader will achieve that inwardness of self-understanding which alone constitutes religious faith.

This is how Kierkegaard defends his duplicitous strategies in a key passage from *The Point of View:*

> Teleological suspension in relation to the communication of truth (i.e. to suppress something for the time being that the truth may become truer) is a plain duty to the truth and is comprised in the responsibility a man has before God for the reflection bestowed upon him.

The uses of deception are justified strictly by the interests of a higher, self-authenticating truth. "Reflection" is a highly ambiguous virtue as Kierkegaard describes it. On the one hand it can lead to those fashionable forms of Romantic irony—the endless relativization of meaning and value—which Kierkegaard attacked in the writers of his age. Such was the "aesthetic" attitude pressed to a dangerous and ethically disabling extreme. On the other hand it provides Kierkegaard with a means of "teleological suspension," a strategy for conducting the reader through and beyond the perils of ungrounded reflection. He defends himself in advance against the criticisms of those who would condemn such tactics in the name of a straightforward truth-telling imperative. Things being what they are in the present age, the choice must fall between absolute silence and the use of "indirect communication." And, given that choice, a timorous silence is scarcely to be regarded as "a higher form of religiousness."

The purposes of edification are therefore served indirectly by the detour which leads through various stages of "aesthetic" reflection. Kierkegaard is at pains to demonstrate that this was all along his guiding purpose, and not just an attitude adopted in the wisdom of hindsight with a view to redeeming his early aberrations. He points to the fact that *both* kinds of production were carried on simultaneously at every stage of his authorship, rather than forming a linear progression which might be equated with the gradual maturing of Kierkegaard's soul. Thus the first ("aesthetic") volume of *Either/Or* was written during the period which also produced the first pair of *Edifying Discourses.* Likewise, toward the end of his authorship, when Kierkegaard's energies were mainly devoted to religious productions, he nevertheless wrote a "little article" (*The Crisis and A Crisis in the Life of an Actress*) which belonged to the "aesthetic" dimension. "The Religious is present from the beginning. Conversely, the aesthetic is present again at the last moment."

This reversal of normal expectation is repeated in what Kierkegaard records of his experience in writing *Either/Or.* The first volume (including the famous "Diary of a Seducer") presents an exploration of the aesthetic outlook in all its manifold guises and disguises. The second portion—with Judge William's "ethical" reflections on the sanctity of marriage—seems to offer itself, in private-confessional terms, as the outcome of the first. Yet in fact, as Kierkegaard reveals, the second volume was the first to be composed, and already bore the marks of his limiting judgement on the "ethical" as an ultimate philosophy of life. The author at this stage, he assures us, was "very far from wishing to summon the course of existence to return comfortingly to the situation of marriage." The implied reference is to Kierkegaard's agonized courtship and final rejection of Regina Olsen, an episode which he saw as confirmation of the need to pass from an ethical to a religious order of existence. So far from implicitly endorsing Judge William's sentiments on marriage, the second volume was written from the viewpoint of an author "who religiously was already in the cloister—a thought which lies concealed in the pseudonym *Victor Eremita.*"

The ethical stage is thereby deprived of the culminating weight and authority which it might appear to claim if one reads *Either/Or* in terms of a straightforward narrative-confessional logic. Its arguments are already subject to the same kind of qualifying irony, or "teleological suspension," which works retroactively to frame and disavow the aesthetic attitude. *Either/Or* became a kind of "poetical catharsis," one which was yet unable to "go further than the ethical." Kierkegaard can therefore return to his work as a *reader* in much the same position as any other, compelled to reenact its dialectical structure in terms which define his (past and present) relationship to it. This attitude becomes quite explicit in the closing pages of *The Point of View.* "That I was without authority I have from

the first moment asserted clearly . . . I regarded myself preferably as a *reader* of the books, not as the *author.*" By adopting this viewpoint Kierkegaard can claim a non-privileged but fully "existential" encounter with his own previous productions.

It should be obvious by now that Kierkegaard carries deconstruction only to the point where its strategies supposedly come up against an undeconstructible bedrock of authenticated truth. His techniques of "indirect communication" have a strictly preludial function, designed as they are to confront the fit reader with the absolute necessity of passing decisively beyond them. Self-consciousness and irony exert such a hold on "the present age" that truth cannot emerge except by exploiting such ambiguous means. "Immediate pathos is of no avail—even if in immediate pathos one were to sacrifice his life. The age has at its disposal too much reflection and shrewdness not to be able to reduce his significance to zero." It is almost as if Kierkegaard treated the claims of authentic, truth-telling discourse as a species of mere bad faith in an age so much given over to "reflection." He repeatedly fends off moral objections voiced in the name of what he calls a "scrupulous and pusillanimous notion of the duty of telling the truth." Only by adopting its own forms of cunning indirection can thought regain the authentic inwardness lost to an age of aesthetic self-reflection.

This is of course the point at which Kierkegaard parts company with the present-day avatars of deconstruction. They would deny what Kierkegaard so strenuously asserts: the existence of a grounding authenticity which can call a halt to the mazy indirections of language and motive. For a rigorous deconstructor like Paul de Man, such beliefs are always delusive [according to his *Allegories of Reading: Figural Language in Rousseau, Nietzsche, Rilke, and Proust*], a product of the "normative pathos" which leads us to assume that language should ideally mean what it says, or say what it means. Kierkegaard's project depends on his adopting this sceptical attitude only up to a point, in order to perplex and finally confound the unbelieving reader. One can certainly find many passages, in *The Point of View* and elsewhere, which match de Man by calling into doubt the normative relations of language, truth and subjectivity. Such are Kierkegaard's remarks on the powerlessness of "immediate pathos" (or appeals to self-authenticating belief) in the face of a "reflective" culture at large. Deconstruction turns on a similar claim: that thought should no longer be beguiled into accepting the delusive "immediacy" of language once the instruments are at its disposal for dismantling the covert metaphysics at work behind all such presumptions. For Kierkegaard, however, this work of demystification is always at the service of a higher, ethical or religious imperative. Deconstruction as practiced by conceptual rhetoricians like de Man would surely have figured for Kierkegaard as a warning example of "aesthetic" reflection lost in the abysmal regressions of its own creating.

To read Kierkegaard in the knowledge of modern deconstructionist criticism is therefore to face very squarely the choices which his authorship seeks to impose on the reader. The internal dialectics of *Either/Or* are reproduced at every stage of Kierkegaard's writing, the design being always to implicate the reader in questions of interpretative choice which simultaneously force an ethical decision. The unreconstructed aesthete (or purist deconstructor) will read ***Either/Or*** as a fascinating instance of textual strategies engaged in a shuttling exchange of "undecidable" priorities. He or she will be impressed by the text's unresolved contradictions of viewpoint, its power to suspend or defer any final, authoritative reading. Its title would in this case be taken to signify the holding-together of two possibilities ("aesthetic" and "ethical"), without the least need or justification for choosing between them. Yet this response would of course be "aesthetic" in so far as it refused the absolute choice of priority envisaged by Kierkegaard's authorial design. The alternative ***Either/Or*** of ethical decision is intended precisely to transcend or discredit any such supposedly facile interpretation. Such a text confronts the "implied reader" with problems of interpretative grasp more momentous than those usually entertained by current narrative theory. Kierkegaard—to put it crudely—will see you damned if you don't comprehend the innermost, self-redeeming aspect of his authorship.

For Kierkegaard, there is always a decisive moment of advance from "indirect communication" to truth directly apprehended and thus no longer subject to the ruses and dangers of reflection. To ignore this moment, or wilfully repress it, is to prove oneself lacking in the "serious" powers of mind prerequisite to higher understanding. Kierkegaard's reader is constantly on trial, required to give evidence of his or her capacity for taking this decisive leap into faith. But Kierkegaard's authorship is equally put to the test, since its very reliance on deceptive techniques might actually mislead and pervert the understanding of a previously well-intentioned reader. Kierkegaard counters this likely objection by making it the *reader's* duty to approach his texts with sufficient "seriousness" of purpose. Otherwise, he admits, understanding can only be perplexed and undone by the effects of "dialectical reduplication" everywhere present in his writing. This is the pivotal point of encounter between truth and its indirect means of reflective presentation. The burden now rests with the reader to prove that Kierkegaard's intentions are not simply lost on his or her capacities of inward self-knowledge.

Kierkegaard is at pains to justify his position on this crucial point. His indirect proceedings have to be defended as absolutely necessary if the reader is to grasp the requisite stages of enlightenment. On the other hand that same dialectical grasp can only come about on condition that the reader is *already* endowed with an adequate depth of understanding. As Kierkegaard explains, it is "the mark of dialectical reduplication" that "the ambiguity is maintained." The unfit reader (one assumes) may seize on this ambiguity and rest content with its fascinating play. The elect reader, on the other hand, will respond as Kierkegaard wishes. "As soon as the requisite seriousness grasps it, it is able to release it, but always in such a way that seriousness itself vouches for the fact of it." Again, one could extrapolate something in the nature of an ethical riposte to the claims of current deconstruction. Harold Bloom has already pointed to what he sees as the "serene linguistic nihilism" manifest among certain of his deconstructing colleagues at Yale. Bloom's way of coping with this threat—his wholesale re-writing of poetic tradition in terms of psychic defence and aggression—is perhaps not an earnest of "seriousness" in Kierkegaard's proper sense. But it does partake of the same desire to *save* the authentic individual—Christian or poet—from the otherwise endless fabrications of "unauthorized" language.

Kierkegaard therefore stands in a highly ambiguous relation to certain current theories of reading and textuality. His authorship presents a double and contradictory challenge to the claims of deconstruction. It anticipates those claims to a remarkable degree, making Kierkegaard appear at times a kind of uncanny elective precursor. But it also—and with far greater "seriousness"—promises the reader a viewpoint which would render deconstruction at best redundant, and at worst a species of mischievous "aesthetic" distraction. The remainder of this essay will examine some of the issues raised by this belated encounter.

The deconstructor might ask, to begin with, why it is that Kierkegaard is so often constrained to fall back on distinctly "aesthetic" parables and metaphors when arguing the case for a higher, nonaesthetic truth. Some striking examples have to do with female sexuality, the image of woman as endlessly seductive, developed in relation to the "Don Juan" theme in ***Either/Or***. Kierkegaard reverts to this metaphor in a passage from ***The Point of View*** purporting to explain the approach to truth by means of indirection or "dialectical reduplication."

> For as a woman's coyness has a reference to the true lover and yields when he appears, but only then, so, too, dialectical reduplication has a reference to true seriousness.

The sexual image retains its hold, not only on Kierkegaard's "aesthetic" imagination but on the very process of argument by means of which that stage is supposedly transcended. ***The Point of View*** was written, after all, from the standpoint of one who claimed to re-read and comprehend the entire dialectical progress inscribed in his works. "That I understand the truth which I deliver to others, of that I am eternally certain." Yet this truth appears still incapable of finding adequate expression without the aid of those "aesthetic" parables and devices which characterize the earlier, pseudonymous writing.

The "question of woman" cannot be confined to that single, decisive episode of courtship and rejection in Kierkegaard's private past. That the episode figures in his writing only by indirect allusion—that it belongs, so to speak, to the *vita ante acta* of his authorship—does not prevent it from obtruding metaphorically into the progress of Kierkegaard's arguments. Woman comes to signify, however obliquely, that aspect of dissimulating metaphor and fiction which alone points the way to truth in an age of universal deceit. One is put in mind of Derrida's remarkable pages on the imagery of womanhood in Nietzsche. There emerges a strange articulation of philosophic themes and sexualized metaphor, such that the idea of Woman becomes textually intertwined with a deconstruction of "truth" and its forms of masculine conceptual mastery. Derrida quotes Nietzsche: "Progress of the idea: it becomes more subtle, insidious, incomprehensible—*it becomes female*. . . ." And he offers the following gloss, drawing on Nietzsche's own metaphorical suggestions:

> all the emblems, all the shafts and allurements that Nietzsche found in woman, her seductive distance, her captivating inaccessibility, the ever-veiled promise of her provocative transcendence . . . these all belong properly to the history of truth by way of the history of an error [*Spurs: Nietzsche's Styles*].

Kierkegaard's uses of "aesthetic" indirection—especially where the detour passes by way of woman—are likewise subject to a certain ambivalence which questions his assumed dialectical mastery.

One could press the parallel further. Kierkegaard constructs an entire dialectics of disguised confessional intent, designed to vindicate his treatment of Regina Olsen by viewing it from the standpoint of a higher, self-achieved religious wisdom. In *Either/Or* the "question of woman" is dealt with successively by two powerful ruses of dialectical cunning. The seductress—ever-changing and tantalizing object of "aesthetic" desire—is mastered by the ethical precepts of Christian marriage, as enounced by Judge William in Volume Two. This provisional ideal is in turn rejected from the "higher" religious plane of understanding which Kierkegaard claims as his own in *The Point of View* (and which, moreover, he finds implicit in Volume Two of *Either/Or*). Woman is thus thematized in retrospect as the dark side of man's self-knowledge, the source of an illusion which blinds him to the need for transcendence, first to the ethical, then to the religious sphere of value. Kierkegaard's writings enable him to perform an act of self-vindication so complete that it reverses the roles of innocent and guilty, sinned-against and sinning. Whatever the feelings of guilt that may have attached to the memory of Regina Olsen, Kierkegaard's strategy is designed to convert them into causes of his own deepening estrangement from commonplace human affection, and hence his attainment of a true religious inwardness. The confessional motives of Kierkegaard's authorship can thus be represented under the guise of a spiritual progress from stage to stage of premeditated self-enlightenment.

Yet this process cannot entirely conceal the marks of that original repression upon which Kierkegaard's edifying narrative depends. The fact of his self-inflicted break with Regina is everywhere present in *The Point of View*, for all that Kierkegaard strives to consign it to a remote prehistory of misdirected youth. At the figurative level, as we have seen, these reminders take the form of a recourse to sexual-aesthetic metaphors in order to communicate religious truth. Derrida points to a similar emergence of disruptive "feminized" imagery in Nietzsche's apparently misogynistic writing. Woman, it seems

> is recognized and affirmed as an affirmative power, a dissimulatress, an artist, a dionysian. And no longer is it man who affirms her. She affirms herself, in and of herself, in man . . . and anti-feminism, which condemned woman only

> so long as she was, so long as she answered to man . . . is in its turn overthrown.

Whatever its provision of sustaining alibis, Kierkegaard's narrative still falls victim to the "dissimulating" power of womanly-aesthetic imagery.

Similar complications surface to vex the idealized projection of his "authorship" in its self-professed form of a religious education-into-truth. The Regina episode is cryptically alluded to as a "factum" which Kierkegaard refuses to elaborate, except by stressing its decisive importance and its complex role in the threshold experience which led to his becoming an author. Kierkegaard expressly denies that this experience was directly religious. "I can only beg the reader not to think of revelations or anything of that sort, for with me everything is dialectical." This disclaimer can be seen as consistent with Kierkegaard's reiterated stress on the element of "reflection" prerequisite to any vouchsafing of religious truth. But it also serves the more devious *narrative* function of presenting the youthful Kierkegaard as one "dialectically" removed from the commonplace sphere of human obligation.

> However much I had lived and experienced in another sense, I had, in a human sense, leapt over the stages of childhood and youth; and this lack, I suppose, must be somehow made up for: instead of having been young, I became a poet, which is a second youth.

The "aesthetic" stage thus becomes the pretext—by a kind of narrative doubling—for Kierkegaard's suspension of ethical judgement as regards his treatment of Regina. As a "second youth" it effectively stands in for what the narrative cannot directly face without threatening to undermine its own self-approving moral stance. The broken engagement is represented as a crisis, but one which both begins and ends (it would seem) within a kind of "aesthetic" parenthesis. Only thus can *The Point of View* maintain its precarious narrative coherence *and* the author's claim to moral self-vindication.

Kierkegaard's text therefore works to exclude the possibility of any guilt which might attach to episodes beyond its dialectical control. For all its decisive significance, the event in question is banished to a realm of "aesthetic" exteriority where it cannot interfere with the author's growth toward spiritual inwardness and knowledge. But the price of this exclusion is a certain persistent ambivalence as to the motives and status of Kierkegaard's self-revelation. *The Point of View* supposedly belongs to the religious and inwardly authenticated portion of Kierkegaard's authorship. It stands alongside such works as the *Edifying Discourses,* where the author speaks (we are to assume) *in propria persona* and without the aid of aesthetic ploys and devices. To read it as a species of fiction would surely represent a perverse disregard of the author's very plain intentions. Yet its handling of the Regina episode—displaced and deployed as it is in the interests of "dialectical" coherence—suggests the presence of an overriding *narrative* concern. *The Point of View* has this much in common with the typical nineteenth-century novel. The quotidian sequence of mere "events" is reordered and adjusted to suit the requirements of a well-formed "plot".

Different viewpoints within the narrative are placed and judged according to the dominant authorial voice. Ideally there should take place a final convergence of interpretative views between "implied author" and "implied reader." The narrative works to ensure this convergence, provided always that the reader proves fit to share its commanding perspective.

Kierkegaard offers precisely such a narrative in *The Point of View.* Yet might it not occur to a different kind of reader—one, say, who questioned Kierkegaard's absolute religious assurance—to detect even here the distinctive signs of fictional representation? Kierkegaard refers to the "duplex" character of the event which signalled his religious awakening. In this lay its power of dialectical development and hence the spur to Kierkegaard's incipient authorship. But not all "duplicities" are capable of thus being channelled into the path of a secure dialectical self-knowledge. *The Point of View* lies open to a reading which would question the supposedly decidable choice between "aesthetic" and "religious" modes of understanding. As a self-professed record of Kierkegaard's motives and intentions, it demands that one read in good faith and accept its full authenticity. But to read it as a *narrative*—and one, moreover, which bears distinct marks of its own very deliberate contriving—is to doubt the very grounds of Kierkegaard's crucial distinction. By devising such a perfect sequence of pretexts for his moral life-history, Kierkegaard risks the collapse of his own founding categories. Fact can no longer be separated from fiction, or "aesthetic" motivation from ethical choice. The system of distinctions becomes strictly undecidable.

Paul de Man has described a similar subversive logic at work in the text of Rousseau's *Confessions.* The danger of confessional narratives is that they tend to build up a self-exonerating case for the accused which leaves him paradoxically with nothing to confess. Excuses generate a logic of their own which finally evades the need for "honest" self-reckoning. "The only thing one has to fear from the excuse is that it will indeed exculpate the confessor, thus making the confession (and the confessional text) redundant as it originates." The narrative form permits any number of face-saving strategies, thus providing Rousseau (or Kierkegaard) with a means of transforming guilt into a pretext for displays of redemptive self-approval. At its most extreme this process can substitute the pleasure of a well-told tale for the ethical imperative which supposedly prompted the confession in the first place. Thus, as de Man reads it, "Rousseau's own text, against its author's interests, prefers being suspected of lie and slander rather than of innocently lacking sense." In Kierkegaard's terms, there must always be a risk that the "aesthetic" will return to recapture and distort the deliverance of authentic truth. De Man describes Rousseau's textual predicament in words which might just as well be applied to Kierkegaard. It is always possible, he writes, "to face up to any experience (to excuse any guilt), because the experience always exists simultaneously as fictional discourse and as empirical event." Furthermore, from the reader's point of view, "it is never possible to decide which one of the two possibilities is the right one."

De Man's reading of Rousseau is detailed and compelling, for all its seeming perversity. The central premise is that texts cannot always effectively *perform* what they manifestly set out to *mean.* There is a frequent disjunction between ethical purposes (like the will to confess) and the business of working them out in narrative-textual form. More specifically, there occurs a shift of priorities, such that the reckoning with private guilt becomes subdued to the need for demonstrable public veracity. To confess, as de Man puts it, "is to overcome guilt and shame in the name of truth: it is an epistemological use of language in which ethical values of good and evil are superseded by values of truth and falsehood. . . . " And these latter "epistemological" values are compromised in turn by the inherent tendency of confessional narratives to construct a self-accusing penitential stance by way of exhibiting the penitent's remarkable candour. Confessions of guilt become self-exonerating, but also seem to be intensified by the very tactics which serve to excuse them. In short, "there can never be enough guilt around to match the text-machine's infinite power to excuse."

Kierkegaard's text is not unaware of this irony lying in wait for its good intentions. At one point the question is explicitly raised as to whether his entire "literary production" might not be viewed as self-deluded and belonging to the "aesthetic" sphere. Kierkegaard's defence is curiously unconvincing. Let the reader indeed imagine, by way of experiment, that all his works were composed from the aesthetic point of view. This hypothesis would soon break down when it met with texts (like *The Point of View*) which claimed an edifying purpose. On the other hand, by adopting the contrary hypothesis—that Kierkegaard's entire authorship, including the "aesthetic" texts, was governed by motives of edification—the reader can see how everything ultimately fits into place. It need scarcely be remarked that this argument rests on a foregone assumption that the reader will accept Kierkegaard's categorical distinctions absolutely at face value. He will accept, that is, the progression from "aesthetic," via "ethical" to "religious" self-knowledge, precisely as described (at the manifest level) in *The Point of View.* Again, it is the fit (or "serious") reader who thus falls in with Kierkegaard's purposes. But if one reads his text *against* its manifest intentions—alerted to its blind-spots of metaphor and narrative indirection—one may come to entertain a very different understanding.

Had de Man's deconstructionist arguments been applied to Kierkegaard rather than Rousseau, his conclusions would be yet more disturbing. Kierkegaard stakes his entire religious project on the assumption that his writings can effectually convince and convert the reader to a state of inward grace commensurate with his own. Rousseau is at least intermittently aware of the pleasure to be had from shocking the reader by ever more scandalous examples of his "honest" self-accounting. The air of a "performance," of frank theatricality, is very much a part of Rousseau's confessional style. For Kierkegaard also, but in a more crucial sense, writing must exert a "performative" force if it is ever to serve the purpose of communicating truth. It must function both to authenticate the author's meaning—his "inward" commitment to stand by his words—

A picture of the square in front of the house where Kierkegaard was born, which is between the building on the right and the neoclassical building.

and to produce a correspondingly inward acceptance on the reader's part. Such performative effects (nowadays the province of "speech-act" philosophy) are omnipresent in normal language, but they assume a critical dimension of faith to an author like Kierkegaard. His writing cannot entertain any doubt as to its own capacity for winning the reader to an answering state of hard-earned inward commitment.

It is precisely this faith which de Man so upsettingly deconstructs. His reading of Rousseau dissociates "the cognition from the act", denying that there can possibly exist any genuine, grounding correspondence between linguistic meaning and performative intent. "If we are right in saying that *'qui s'accuse s'excuse,'* then the relation between confession and excuse is rhetorical prior to being intentional." And again: "any speech act produces an excess of cognition, but it can never hope to know the process of its own production (the only thing worth knowing)." De Man's argument turns, as we have seen, on the element of *undecidability* which often prevents any clear-cut distinction between ethics and epistemology, issues of "right and wrong" on the one hand and questions of "true and false" on the other. And this would be enough to radically suspend the entire existential project of faith upon which Kierkegaard's authority stands or falls.

It is Nietzsche who provides de Man with a model and exemplary practice for the strategy of deconstruction. Nietz-

sche's awareness of the figural dimensions of language, the ways in which rhetoric both asserts and undermines its own performance, is the topic of de Man's most compelling chapters in his book *Allegories of Reading*. Nietzsche deconstructs the claims of philosophy by showing how they rest on an acknowledged basis of metaphor and figural representation. The most rigorous effort to exclude such devices from the text of philosophy always at some point fails to recognize their buried or covert metaphorical working. Nietzsche determined to press this insight to the point where it produced an ultimate *aporia* or "undecidability" with regard to all texts, his own included.

Arguments must always be "rhetorical" in the sense of aiming to persuade one of their truth, even where that truth attempts to pass itself off as purely abstract and conceptual. Yet rhetoric also has another, self-critical aspect, exploited by Nietzsche in his relentless uncovering of the tropes and devices which philosophers refused to acknowledge in their own discourse. Rhetoric in this sense is the ceaseless undoing of rhetorically persuasive effects. De Man makes the point with elegant concision. "Considered as persuasion, rhetoric is performative but when considered as a system of tropes, it deconstructs its own performance." The upshot of a Nietzschian critique of language is to break down the system of decidable oppositions which assign a proper place to ethical judgements on the one hand, and analytic concepts on the other. Nietzsche's "genealogy of morals" negates every system of ethical values—religious and secular alike—by claiming to derive their precepts from the will-to-power predominant in various phases of language and culture. On a world-historical scale, this repeats the undoing of "performative" language by the power of demystification vested in the very tropes which compose it. At the same time it admits that any such critique, however "demystified," must always acknowledge its own *persuasive* (or rhetorical) character. What is so difficult to accept, as de Man writes, is that "this allegory of errors" (or undecidability) is the "very model of philosophical rigour."

Kierkegaard and Nietzsche are often classed together as text-book "existentialists," thinkers who rejected the great systematic philosophies of their time in order to assert the freedom of individual choice and values. Certainly they shared an aversion toward Hegel, expressed by Kierkegaard in a famous image: that of the philosopher who erects a magnificent edifice of theory, while dwelling himself in a wretched hovel beneath its shadow. Nietzsche likewise saw nothing but grandiose delusion in the claims of Hegelian dialectic. But the two had very different reasons for adopting this negative attitude to Hegel. Nietzsche's objections took rise from a thoroughgoing epistemological scepticism, a belief that Hegel's entire dialectical system was founded on nothing more than a series of metaphors, or figural constructions, disguised as genuine concepts. In Hegel the will-to-power within language achieved its most spectacular and self-deluded form. For Kierkegaard, the case was to be argued on ethical, rather than epistemological grounds. The danger of Hegel's all-embracing dialectic was that it left no room for the "authentic" individual, the agent of choice and locus of existential freedom. Subject and object, experience and history, were all taken up into a massive unfolding of absolute reason which no human act had the power to resist or decisively push forward. Dialectics in this guise was a form of "aesthetic" aberration, a means of evading responsible choice by setting up a fine philosophical system which the mind could contemplate at leisure.

Nietzsche is decidedly *not* an "existentialist" in anything like the Kierkegaardian sense. His critique of systematic philosophy goes along with an ethical scepticism more sweeping and corrosive than Kierkegaard could possibly maintain. The Nietzschian "transvaluation of values" is finally a matter—as de Man makes clear—of deconstructing ethics by way of an epistemological reduction. Nietzsche stands to Kierkegaard as a false ally, one whose undermining of conventional ideas is in the service of a radically nihilistic outlook. Such scepticism is the enemy of true Kierkegaardian inwardness. This antagonism is all the more evident when a critic like de Man draws out the full deconstructive implications of Nietzsche's thought. The effect on his reading of Rousseau's *Confessions* is a measure of their power to subvert every last vestige of "authentic", truth-telling language. It scarcely makes sense any longer to speak of Nietzsche as an "existentialist" in the company of Kierkegaard and his latter-day progeny.

Yet to treat this antagonism as a matter of straightforward divergence is to ignore the many complicating factors at

work in Kierkegaard's authorship. These take the form—as I have argued—of "aesthetic" and fictional devices which work to suspend the dialectical progress that Kierkegaard equates with the inward coming-to-truth. The duplicity of language is always in excess of the elaborate strategies which Kierkegaard adopts to explain and justify his authorial conduct. Thus *The Point of View,* by its complex "dialectical" reordering of memories and motives, creates a text which partakes as much of fiction as of spiritual self-revelation. De Man describes this alienating logic of narrative contrivance as it affects the writing of Rousseau's *Confessions.* "This threatens the autobiographical subject not as the loss of something that was once present and that it once possessed, but as a radical estrangement between the meaning and the performance of any text." It is equally impossible to decide just how much in *The Point of View* is dictated by a logic of narrative self-vindication basically at odds with Kierkegaard's idea of existential good faith.

De Man's prime example is the case of "the purloined ribbon," an episode in which (according to the *Confessions*) a servant girl was blamed for a theft which Rousseau had himself committed. The enduring shame which resulted from his silent acquiescence is supposedly the spur and motive of Rousseau's confession. But the incident becomes—as de Man reads it—a pretext for narrative "revelations" far in excess of what mere honesty entailed. The plot is further enhanced by the idea that Rousseau (on his own admission) was prompted to betray the girl partly out of motives of obscure sexual attraction and jealousy. But this doesn't so much acknowledge guilt as generate a further excuse for the excessive display of it. "What Rousseau *really* wanted," de Man suggests, "is neither the ribbon nor Marion, but the public scene of exposure he actually gets." The narrative produces guilt to order and profits in turn from the additional interest thus created.

Kierkegaard is far from wishing to impress by guiltily exhibiting his treatment of Regina. Yet his very reticence on the subject is presented as a form of strategic indirection, a means of bringing the reader to appreciate its crucial significance. Like Rousseau, but more subtly, he *stages* a withholding of vital information the more to guarantee its ultimate effect. What de Man writes of Rousseau could equally apply to Kierkegaard:

> The more there is to expose, the more there is to be ashamed of; the more resistance to exposure, the more satisfying the scene, and, especially, the more satisfying and eloquent the belated revelation, in the later narrative, of the inability to reveal.

The difference between Rousseau and Kierkegaard is one of narrative tactics rather than of demonstrable truth-telling probity. Rousseau "reveals" his self-incriminating secrets, projecting them back into a colourfully fictionalized past. Kierkegaard, on the other hand, constructs an exemplary self-justifying narrative which works both to repress and "dialectically" display its motivating secret.

Kierkegaard thus stands in a highly ambiguous relationship to Nietzsche. The working-out of his standpoint as a religious author necessitates a detour through dangerous regions of thought which bring him close to a Nietzschian position of all-consuming sceptical doubt. This "maieutic" strategy—as Kierkegaard terms it—holds out a means of awakening his reader from a state of unreflective slumber. But there is always a risk that the method will get out of hand, that the "aesthetic" production will re-emerge at a stage where its preliminary services are definitely not required. The uses of reflection may not be so easily held within dialectical bounds.

Take the following passage from Kierkegaard's early (pseudonymous) text *Johannes Climacus or, De Omnibus Dubitandum Est:*

> Reality I cannot express in language, for to indicate it, I must use ideality, which is a contradiction, an untruth. But how is immediacy annulled? By mediacy, which annuls immediacy by presupposing it. What, then, is immediacy? It is reality. What is mediacy? It is the word. How does the word annul actuality? By talking about it . . . Consciousness is opposition and contradiction.

The argument has obvious Hegelian overtones, placing subject and object (language and reality) in a constant dialectic of reciprocal negation. It is also much akin to what Derrida or de Man might have to say about the delusions engendered by naive ontologies of language. Deconstruction sets out to demonstrate that meaning can never coincide with its object in a moment of pure, unimpeded union; that language always intervenes to deflect, defer or differentially complicate the relation between manifest sense and expressive intent. Meaning can be neither straightforwardly referential nor ultimately grounded in the speaker's (or author's) will-to-express. Mediation—or "reflection" in Kierkegaard's terminology—is the inescapable predicament of language, whatever those pretences to the contrary maintained by poets, philosophers or the normal run of commonsense metaphysics.

Kierkegaard, of course, entertains this outlook under cover of a pseudonym ("Johannes Climacus") intended to mark it as a strictly "aesthetic" and hence inauthentic standpoint. But this tactic again begs the question of an author's power to bracket certain portions or aspects of his work simply by issuing a magisterial fiat in the name of authority and truth. Here, as in *The Point of View,* the issue is undecidable since Kierkegaard's intentions are not unambiguously there to be consulted. What necessity compels us to acknowledge just one of his implied narrators (the "religious" or authentic), thus consigning the others to a realm of subordinate fiction? As de Man remarks of Rousseau, "the presence of a fictional narrator is a rhetorical necessity in any discourse that puts the truth or falsehood of its own statement in question". This applies as much to ethical or philosophic texts as to those which openly or implicitly acknowledge their fictional status. It thus becomes impossible to separate Kierkegaard's authentic authorship from the surrogate identities deployed in its unfolding. Such supposedly clear-cut distinctions are the basis for our normal (unexamined) classification of "literary" as opposed to "discursive" or "philosophical" texts. Our readings of the latter are thereby de-

prived—de Man argues—of "elementary refinements that are taken for granted in literary interpretation."

Kierkegaard's writing is peculiarly susceptible to such treatment. It provides all the materials for its own deconstruction in the form of those fictions, "aesthetic" devices and allegories of reading which make up the larger part of its production. Or perhaps, indeed, that production in its entirety? Kierkegaard undoubtedly labours to interpellate a reader who will find herself obliged to choose once and for all between alternative positions. But his text is unable to *impose* that choice—or even to state its necessity—without in the process seeming to render it impossible. The edifying logic of "either"/"or" deconstructs into the always-available option of removing the disjunctive bar and deciding that decision is beyond reach. In a passage from *The Point of View,* Kierkegaard reflects on the ironies of public misrecognition suffered in the course of his authorship. "I held out *Either/Or* to the world in my left hand, and in my right the *Two Edifying Discourses;* but all, or as good as all, grasped with their right what I held in my left." To deconstruct Kierkegaard's text is knowingly and consistently to exploit that ever-present chance of interpretative crossed purposes. At the same time it is only to read Kierkegaard according to a logic of interrogative doubt supplied by the text itself.

Nietzsche's deconstructionist interpreters often cite a passage from his essay-fragment "On Truth and Falsehood in an Ultra-Moral Sense." What is truth? Nietzsche asks, and—unlike jesting Pilate—stays to provide an answer to his own question. Truth is

> a mobile army of metaphors, metonymies, anthropomorphisms, . . . truths are illusions of which one has forgotten that they *are* illusions, . . . coins which have their obverse effaced and now are no longer of account as coins but merely as metal. . . .

The passage nicely exemplifies Nietzsche's epistemological scepticism, his reduction of knowledge and values alike to the status of arbitrary fictions, incidental products of the figurative play within language.

One could set alongside it a strikingly similar reflection from Kierkegaard's *Journals,* written during the final few years of his authorship. Here, if anywhere, Kierkegaard speaks *in propia persona,* with the authentic voice of achieved inwardness. The passage needs quoting at some length:

> What money is in the finite world, concepts are in the world of spirit. It is in them that all transactions take place.
>
> Now when things go on from generation to generation in such a way that everyone takes over the concepts . . . then it happens only too easily that the concepts are gradually changed . . . they become like false coinage—while all the time all transactions happily continue to be carried out in them . . . Yet no one has any desire to undertake the business of revising the concepts.

Up to a point the metaphors work to similar effect. Nietzsche and Kierkegaard each perceive a process of conceptual devaluation at work within the handing-down of knowledge and truth. They both attribute this process to the way in which meanings are mindlessly accredited as tokens of a currency subject to no kind of validating issue or control. But where Kierkegaard treats this as a symptom of latter-day cultural malaise—a measure of spiritual inanition—Nietzsche regards it as inevitable, given that all truths and values are arbitrary constructs from the outset. Kierkegaard is still able to imagine a decisive "revision" of values, taken on by the few elect individuals whom Providence singles out for the task. No such intervention is possible for Nietzsche, since the concepts of truth and falsehood are so closely intertwined that thought must be deluded if it hopes to reestablish them on a proper, authentic basis.

This is to state Kierkegaard's difference with Nietzsche as it would strike a convert or implicitly *believing* reader. But again, his argument seems obliged to pass through a detour of strategic indirection which leaves itself open to further deconstructive reading. Under present conditions the Christian "reviser" cannot assume the self-evident truth vouchsafed to an "apostle." His way must necessarily partake of duplicity and fiction.

> If the apostle's personal character is one of noble and pure simplicity (which is the condition for being the instrument of the Holy Spirit), that of the reviser is his ambiguous knowledge. If the apostle is in a unique and good sense entirely in the power of Providence, the reviser is in the same power in an ambiguous sense.

Again the question presents itself: how can limits be set to the dissimulating power of this "ambiguous" knowledge? What is to vouch for these tactics being ultimately on the side of inwardness and truth? The passage provides an answer in the form of that Providence which everywhere governs Kierkegaard's design and underwrites his authorial good faith even where it suffers the necessary swerve into conscious double-dealing. Yet Providence itself appears unable to distinguish such religiously-motivated tactics from the general run of deceit and delusion. In the place of true "apostles" there nowadays come only "connoisseurs in dishonesty," and they—since they are a part of the "general dishonesty"—are treated alike by Providence as "ambiguous creatures."

Kierkegaard's text thus goes to quite extraordinary lengths to make trial of its own most crucial assumption. By the end of his journal-entry the argument has come round to the point of implicitly endorsing *Nietzsche's,* rather than Kierkegaard's own deployment of the monetary image. Or—what amounts to the same thing—it has effectively denied the possibility of deciding between them. Any restoration of authentic truth achieved by the Christian "reviser" can only appear under the worldly guise of dissimulating "ambiguity." If genuine inwardness exists, its credentials are self-evident only to the true believer, and are not to be vouchsafed by way of communicable argument. Nietzsche's contention—that the coinage of truth is always already a devalued and fraudulent currency—seems to infect the very logic of Kierkegaard's argument.

Deconstruction is indeed the devil's work when applied to an author like Kierkegaard. It seeks to undermine conventions of interpretative tact which authority would have us believe are more than just "conventions," providing as they do the very basis of authoritative utterance. Kierkegaard's commentators may disagree as to the best or most fruitful way of interpreting his work. Where some declare in favour of a largely biographical approach, others argue that the writings are more complex and elusive than any meaning conferred on them by the life. There are likewise differences of opinion as regards the relative importance of Kierkegaard's pseudonymous works, or their place and dialectical function within his authorship as a whole. Nevertheless, there is a powerful normative assumption which unites these otherwise divergent views. The commentators' proper concern is always to *expound* an author's texts in obedience to the deep-lying purposive intent which serves to justify both his work and theirs. Kierkegaard's appeal to "providence"—his faith in an end to the duplicities of language—is thereby reproduced in his interpreters. Deconstruction breaks with this providential ethics of reading. It affirms the irreducibility of writing to any preconceived idea of authorial design. In Kierkegaard it meets perhaps the highest and most resourceful challenge to its powers of textual demystification. (pp. 87-106)

Christopher Norris, "Fictions of Authority: Narrative and Viewpoint in Kierkegaard's Writing," in Criticism, *Vol. 25, No. 2, Spring, 1983, pp. 87-107.*

Janet Forsythe Fishburn   (essay date 1985)

[*An American critic and author, Fishburn writes about the role of the ordained ministry in the contemporary Protestant church. Her studies are informed by the historical and theological analysis of the role of family and church in faith formation. In the following essay, Fishburn documents Kierkegaard's insistence, first voiced in* Fear and Trembling, *that the path to truth is to be found in an interpretation of Scripture arrived at through complete commitment to and practice of its content, as opposed to detached, intellectualized exegesis, which leads only to "tragic resignation."*]

Søren Kierkegaard might be gratified to know that the "knight of faith," so illusively portrayed in *Fear and Trembling,* continues to haunt his readers. If his journal can be trusted, he staked his future as an "author" on "*Fear and Trembling* alone." Although he provided few clues to the origin of the book, there is a journal entry from 1848 in which he confesses his hope for the slim volume published in October 1843, under the pseudonym of Johannes de Silentio: "Oh, when once I am dead—then *Fear and Trembling* alone will give me the name of an immortal author."

During a visit to Berlin in May of 1843, Kierkegaard wrote a letter to his friend, Emil Boesen, describing his intellectual activity while there:

> During the past months (in Copenhagen) I have been pumping up a veritable shower bath, now I have pulled the cord, and the ideas stream

down upon me—healthy, happy, plump, merry, blessed children, easily brought to birth, and yet all of them bearing the birth marks of my personality.

It is thought that the "merry, blessed children, easily brought to birth . . . " led to the October 16, 1843, publication of two books—*Repetition* and *Fear and Trembling.* Kierkegaard translator and interpreter Walter Lowrie claims that the essential introduction to *Fear and Trembling* is a knowledge of Kierkegaard's story, especially "the broken engagement" [*A Short Life of Kierkegaard*].

However, given the content of the book, it can be claimed that the broken engagement was the occasion for Kierkegaard's conclusion that he had been called to be a witness to the truth, as he understood it, in his generation. The ideas that came tumbling out of his dialectical consciousness as the twins, published in 1843, had their genesis in the intellectual and personal issues he pursued during an extended period of study at the University of Copenhagen between 1830 and 1840.

A tragic series of deaths in his immediate family—his mother and a sister in 1834, his father in 1838—occurred between 1830, when he began theological study, and 1840, when he finally wrote the theological examinations required of those seeking ordination in the Danish Lutheran Church. Kierkegaard first met Regine Olsen in 1837, they became engaged in September of 1840, and he ended the engagement thirteen months later in October of 1841.

The "healthy, happy children" of the unhappy man who was destined to be the exception to the social norms of his generation—he sought neither marriage nor ordination—had been taking form throughout a period of protracted spiritual quest initiated by the response of his father to the death of his mother in 1834. A crushing disillusionment with the father who had been both his model for faith and his best friend led the twenty-one year old theology student into an intensely personal investigation of the difference between philosophy and Christianity, Judaism and Christianity. As early as November of 1835 he noted in his journal that it is the doctrine of sin that distinguishes Christianity from philosophy. Three months later the observation took on a more personal meaning with his insight that sin manifest as doubt is inherent in temptation: "Christianity states man's cognition as defective because of sin, which is rectified in Christianity: the philosopher qua man seeks to account for the relationship of God and the world."

Prior to this observation concerning the ironic position of the philosopher who seeks to reveal the truth about God to the world while unaware of his own cognitive defects, Kierkegaard had completed an exegesis of Galatians 3:19-4:8 that had apparently convinced him that there is no justification by the law. In the third chapter of Galatians Paul holds up Abraham as a model for a faith like that of the Gentiles in that neither Abraham nor the Gentiles came to believe in Christ Jesus by way of the Jewish law. However, for Jews born under law, the law acted as a custodian until Christ came "that we might be justified by faith" (Gal. 3:24). Paul summarized the distinction between "Jews" and "Christians" by distinguishing between the two covenants related to Abraham and his two wives and his two sons—a covenant of law and slavery and a covenant of grace and freedom. Christians, like Isaac, "are children of promise . . . not children of the slave but of the free woman" (4:28-31).

Kierkegaard completed his exegesis of Galatians 3 and 4 during the spring of 1835. This was followed by formal study of the Epistle to the Hebrews and a translation of James 1-3 during the fall and winter of 1835-1836. Themes pursued in both his philosophical reading and biblical studies between 1835 and 1839 indicate that he was simultaneously working out the distinction between Judaism and Christianity and the exegetical relationship between the Old and the New Testaments. The intellectual milieu in which he studied was one in which there was a growing sense that the church and the New Testament were under attack by those exponents of Hegel's system who were engaged in biblical scholarship. The quest for the historical Jesus had been intensified with the publication in 1835 of Strauss's *Life of Jesus.* [According to Herbert C. Wolf in his *Kierkegaard and Bultmann: The Quest of the Historical Jesus,* the] faculty at the University of Copenhagen considered the threat to biblical faith to be so serious that in 1840 they offered a prize for the best " . . . philosophical inquiry . . . into the question, if and how far the Christian religion is conditional upon the authority of the books of the New Testament and upon their historical reliability." It would seem that the man destined to be "the exception" as an individual was uniquely qualified by the unusual circumstances of his unhappy family history, as well as his exceptional intellectual and emotional acuteness, to engage the theological issues of his age, since those issues intersected his own spiritual quest.

The personal force behind the intellectual task of distinguishing both "the philosopher" and Judaism from the truth of Christianity came from Kierkegaard's need to come to terms with the vengeful God of his father, Michael Kierkegaard. There was no forgiveness in the story of the father who believed that the deaths of five of his seven children at an early age were God's belated punishment of him for committing the sin against the Holy Spirit. It is thought that Michael Kierkegaard, distraught and broken by the death of his wife and daughter in 1834, confessed to his last living children, Peter and Søren, that the family was cursed. He believed that God had punished him and his family because as a poverty-stricken child on the plains of Jutland he had cursed God. During his student years, Kierkegaard had the distinct impression that he, too, would die very young because God punishes the second and third generations.

Between 1833 and 1837, the years of his preliminary New Testament studies and philosophical reflection, Kierkegaard was also reeling under the impact of learning that his mother had been seduced and impregnated by his father while she was the servant girl to his father's first wife. When the first wife of Michael Kierkegaard died, he married the servant girl who quickly became the mother of all seven Kierkegaard children. When the fifth child died in 1834, the two remaining sons had to feel vulnerable to the possibility that the God of their unfaithful father was indeed a God who punished the sons of the fathers. The relationship of Søren Kierkegaard to all of the "children" of his prolific activity as a writer was that of a man who expected to die young. It was also that of a man who readily identified with the plight of an Isaac about to be sacrificed. This story also suggests that Søren Kierkegaard identified with Paul's presentation of Isaac to the Galatians as the child of promise. For Paul, Isaac was a prefiguring of the grace of God revealed when Christ became the curse for us Gentiles ". . . that we might receive the promise of the Spirit through faith" (Gal. 3:13-14). Søren Kierkegaard was born into a Danish Lutheran tradition that had its "Jews" and "Gentiles." But was he the son of Hagar the slave girl, exiled into the wilderness, or the son of promise given—against all odds—to Abraham and Sarah?

Although Kierkegaard never wrote about exegesis or hermeneutics, the center of his biblical hermeneutic is a principle of imitation through imaginative identification. He read Scripture daily for the purpose of spiritual discernment and guidance in his Christian life. In response to the search for the factually true or historically probable element in the Bible that influenced hermeneutics in his day, he persisted in seeking the truth in Scripture through total immersion by identifying with both the writers of Scripture and their subjects. His approach to exegesis was similar to that of contemporary redaction criticism but included the more traditional practice of his day of seeing Old Testament events and types as prefiguring events and types recorded and revealed in the New Testament.

During this intellectually and personally formative period of clarifying his own religious identity, Kierkegaard learned to see himself through Scripture by identifying with the perspective of the writer J. P. Ruckert, whose commentaries on Ephesians and Philippians were published in 1833 and 1834, recommended an exegetical procedure of identifying with Paul as a way to grasp his intentions. The exegete should stand with Paul to grasp the meaning of a passage.

It seems likely that the exegetical procedure of imitation through imaginative identification gradually freed Kierkegaard from the grasp of his father's Old Testament deterministic theology. There are clues scattered through his books indicating his ability to transcend the debilitating limits of the religious tradition he had inherited from his father. There is a mirror analogy motif repeated in two forms—the first appears in "Quidam's Diary" in *Stages Along Life's Way,* 1845; the second, in the directly religious *For Self-Examination* of 1851. In "Quidam's Diary," Kierkegaard describes "quiet despair" in terms of a father and a son: "A son is like a mirror in which the father beholds himself, and for the son the father too is a mirror in which he beholds himself in time to come." A major theme in *For Self-Examination* is the point that the would-be believer must clarify consciousness in the mirror of self-reflection through meditation on God's work in Scripture. Clues scattered through his journal suggest that, while Kierkegaard wrote as to a "confidant," it was the Bible that provided the basis for his self-examination.

As early as 1837 Kierkegaard had begun to associate the restrictive orthodox theology of his father with Jewish le-

galism. He knew from long association with his father that there was little evidence of joy or peace in the silent despair of his father's melancholy Christianity. The question remained, however, of the relationship of the two testaments. The Old Testament figures with which he identified were useful to his attempts to listen to Scripture. Yet, New Testament writers like Luke urged identification with and imitation of Jesus, not of Abraham. This issue, which was both personal and intellectual, was resolved by seeing the Old Testament as prefiguring the New Testament. In the case of Abraham, with whom he associated his father, a contemporary Christian would not see him as a model for faith; rather it was Jesus who was to be imitated. Abraham, however, was a type (if not a model) for faith; he represented the fulfillment of God's promise of salvation made to the Old Testament Hebrews. Although personally haunted by the story of Abraham and Isaac, Kierkegaard interpreted Abraham in *Fear and Trembling* as being like John the Baptist in Luke's Gospel, a precursor of Jesus rather than just a model or hero of faith.

While the hermeneutical principle of interpretation by imitation developed before meeting Regine in 1837, the resolution of the relationship between the testaments probably followed his father's death in 1838. An intense period of Bible study, which began soon after meeting Regine in May of 1837, culminated in May of 1838 with a religious experience described in the journal as "an indescribable joy." Kierkegaard used the language of Paul to indicate that he had experienced the presence of the Lord as an occasion to "rejoice in the Lord always" (Phil. 4:4).

> May 19. *Half-past ten in the morning.* There is an indescribable joy which enkindles us as inexplicably as the apostle's outburst comes gratuitously: "Rejoice I say unto you, and again I say unto you rejoice."—Not a joy over this or that but the soul's mighty song "with tongue and mouth, from the bottom of the heart." "I rejoice through my joy, in, at, with, over, by, and with my joy"—a heavenly refrain, as it were, suddenly breaks off our other song; a joy which cools and refreshes us like a breath of wind, a wave of air, from the trade wind which blows from the plains of Mamre to the everlasting habitations.

The language of "like a breath of wind . . . which blows from the plains of Mamre to the everlasting habitations" suggests a translation of the biblical sense of the presence and power of God's spirit that is found in the Old Testament but gains in emphasis and prominence in the New Testament. This crescendo of the spirit is especially prominent in the gospel accounts of Luke and the related descriptions of the power of the Spirit in the early church in Acts. It was in the plains of Mamre that Abraham built an altar to praise the Lord for the promise that "thy seed" shall be numbered like "the dust of the earth" (Gen. 13:14-18). It was also on the plains of Mamre that three men brought to Abraham and Sarah the birth announcement of the impossible, a son to be born to them in their old age (Gen. 18:1-15).

This experience surely came as an assurance that Kierkegaard was a child of promise, encouraging him in his hope of marriage and toward the conclusion of his theological studies. During 1838 he continued to refine his scriptural foundations for the distinction between Judaism and Christianity with the insight that Jesus is both redeemer and judge. While the Jewish tradition contained the more general emphasis of the story of the God of Israel in history, the Christian was to identify with Jesus who is contemporary to believers through the influence of the Holy Spirit.

During 1839, as Kierkegaard courted Regine and prepared for his theological examinations, he came to terms with Isaac as a figure for grace. Through an exegesis of Romans 9:7 he drew the conclusion that Isaac—the child of promise—was to Abraham a gift of God's grace. However, he cautioned that such a view was received only through faith. There are notes from his theological studies of the winter of 1839-1840 indicating that, under the influence of Tholuck, Kierkegaard has added to his concept of faith as the imitation of Jesus the crucial qualification that a descent into hell was a necessary prerequisite of faith.

When Kierkegaard began keeping a journal in December of 1833, the first entry was a translation into Latin of a part of the Epistle to the Galatians. The second entry, in March of 1834, was an exegetical study with reference to theological questions. Once again, in the spring of 1843—the year of the writing and publication of *Fear and Trembling*—he returned to an exegesis of Galatians 3:23 as he developed the theme of "constance in expectation." "Now before faith came, we were confined under the law, kept under restraint until faith should be revealed." The theme of constancy in expectation is developed in a short paper about the Lukan description of Simeon, Anna, and Lazarus as witnesses to Christ. This suggests that Kierkegaard continued to resolve the issues surrounding the relationship of Israel/Abraham and Christianity/Jesus under the guidance of the Lukan distinction between Israel and true Israel. Abraham belonged to the time of Israel and was a necessary precursor to the time of Jesus. Just as Abraham prefigured Christian faith, so Isaac prefigured Christian grace. Yet only from the vantage point of the time of the church could an interpreter such as Paul, or Luke, see that the promises had been fulfilled in Jesus. Henceforth Judaism would be a necessary precursor to Christian faith in that Jesus was the reality prefigured in Abraham and Isaac. As in Luke, Jesus represented the fulfillment of God's promise of salvation, offered not just to the "Jews" but to the "Gentiles," meaning all people.

Kierkegaard interpreters have remarked about his obvious identification with both Paul and Jesus in his descriptions of himself as an exception, as "the individual," and as the suffering servant. This observation, related to the possibility that it was immersion in Scripture that shaped both his self-understanding and his lifework, may provide a key to the mysteries of the illusive connection between Kierkegaard and his "children." His preoccupation with the Virgin Mary may well be related to his willingness to identify with her as with "an exception." "Behold I am the handmaid of the Lord; Let it be done unto me according to your word" (Luke 1:38).

Both the Gospel of Luke and the Epistle to the Galatians seem to have been guides to Kierkegaard during his stu-

dent years in his attempts to locate how it was that God would work in him to will and to do his good pleasure through his twisted life (Phil. 2:12-13). Kierkegaard had heavily bracketed Galatians 1:15-18 in a study Bible that could have been used during his student years. Considering the evidence of exegetical work on Galatians in 1833-1835, and again in the spring of 1843 when he was probably working on *Fear and Trembling,* it is conceivable that he interpreted his own ill-fated family and his trip to Berlin following the broken engagement in terms of those words of Paul used about his own ministry. Paul, reminding his readers that he was once a Jewish persecutor of Christians and that the gospel he preaches was not man's gospel, describes the beginning of his ministry as follows:

> But when he who had set me apart before I was born, and had called me through his grace, was pleased to reveal his Son to me, in order that I might preach him among the Gentiles, I did not confer with flesh and blood, nor did I go up to Jerusalem to those who were apostles before me, but I went away into Arabia; and again I returned to Damascus (Gal. 1:15-18).

The passage from Galatians may provide clues to the degree of Kierkegaard's self-consciousness in his unusual ministry as the father of a corpus of books even as it influenced the writing of *Fear and Trembling.* Although the exact truth of the claim is impossible to establish, Kierkegaard wrote from Berlin to his friend Emil Boesen indicating that he was then writing *Fear and Trembling* after completing *Repetition* in "less than a fortnight." If, in fact, the Galatians passage describes his interpretation of his unique vocation just after the traumatic breaking off with Regine, it suggests that he saw his mission as like that of Paul, raised up as a Jew but sent out to Gentiles as well as Jews. It could also mean that he, like Paul, lacked the normative credentials for authority—in his case, ordination. It also suggests that he could not count on his own "flesh and blood"—family or spouse—to comprehend or support him in his unusual vocation.

The question posed in *Fear and Trembling* is whether the writer of the book—and hence the reader who shares the writer's historical context—can acquire faith by imitating Abraham. The answer, conveyed through repeated attempts to grasp the faith that undergirded the near sacrifice of Isaac to the God who had given the son as a token of Abraham's promised immortality, is a resounding no.

As a result of the intellectual labors of his student years, Kierkegaard had already concluded that the resolution to theological issues posed by the current quest for the historical Jesus was located in the attitude with which a reader approached Scripture. The reader, genuinely consumed with fear and trembling concerning the life and death issue of salvation, would come to the Bible with a readiness to acquire faith through an imitation of the Jesus presented through the Gospels. The exegesis of Scripture depended on the same attitude of personal receptivity and presupposed that Jesus is contemporary to faith in any age through the work of Jesus and the immediate influence of the Holy Spirit. The religious experience described as an "indescribable joy" of May 1838, confirmed Kierkegaard's belief that the Spirit of the Christ was immediately available to faith. This is the rare but real "instant" of religious experience in which God comes to those who practice constancy in expectation through immersion in Scripture. It is not the immediacy of religious intuition assumed by the Hegelians as the basis of faith. Rather, it is the immediacy of faith that is given to those who follow the Christ through the descent into the hell of self-knowledge through repentance.

Much more than the events of a failed romance must be taken into account if modern readers are to grasp the importance of *Fear and Trembling* to Kierkegaard and its relationship to his other "children." Although the intellectual issues of hermeneutics and exegetical method can be pursued as objective problems to be resolved without reference to the life of the scholar, this was never so for Kierkegaard. His major study of philosophy of religion was done in relation to developing an exegetical method during the same student years in which he was trying to cope with his suspicions about "the eternal darkness" he experienced in his melancholy father. If the convergence of philosophical issues with his reflection on biblical themes is overlooked, the outcome is a Kierkegaard viewed as a philosophical theologian rather than a biblical theologian engaged in apologetics. If the agony of struggling to comprehend the duplicity of a father who had been his personal model for faith is overlooked, then Kierkegaard's principle for biblical exegesis developed during his troubled student years is not granted the position of importance it deserves in his life and thought. The inspiration for the remarkable double cycle of books published by Kierkegaard came from his own life-long immersion in Scripture. His vocational identity as the suffering servant of the truth as he understood it was forged in extensive and persistent imaginative interaction with Scripture. As he pondered his disappointment in failed relationships with his father, with Regine, with the intellectual establishment, and finally with the church, he turned to Scripture as the mirror in which to clarify his own position.

Kierkegaard interpreters do not agree about his intentions for *Fear and Trembling.* While Lowrie regards it as a guarded communication to Regine Olsen explaining the broken engagement of 1841 to her, Danish scholar Gregor Malantschuk views the book as a reflection about why the engagement had to be broken. The interpretation of Kierkegaard's objective in the book hinges on whether he identifies primarily with Abraham or with Isaac in the various presentations of the story of the near sacrifice of Isaac by Abraham. Lowrie believed that Kierkegaard identified with Abraham and was trying to explain to Regine that she was his Isaac. From this perspective, Kierkegaard appears desperately to wish to resume the relationship in the future.

Malantschuk believes that Kierkegaard identified with Isaac and was trying to tell Regine that it was he who was being sacrificed because of his inability to confide to her the shameful secret of his father's sensuality. [In *Kierkegaard's Thought*] Malantschuk writes that:

> As a "modern" Antigone, Kierkegaard felt bound to his father's memory not to speak directly about it to anyone, but since his concep-

tion of marriage required such a direct revelation, the way to marriage was blocked for him. . . . Sometime later, when Kierkegaard has a more detached view of his relations to his father and Regine and can confide more freely on paper, he attaches primary importance in his journal entries about Abraham and Isaac to what must have taken place between his father and him, and only secondary importance to what occurred between him and Regine.

In May of 1843 when Kierkegaard reports working on *Stages,* he confides to his journal that he can see that the broken engagement was evidence of his lack of faith at the time. "Had I had faith I would have remained with Regine." He noted that although he appeared to be faithless, he had intended to honor her rather than make her his "concubine"; he was alluding to the faithless relationship between his parents. This journal entry from five months before the publication of *Fear and Trembling* reveals his horror of repeating his father's failure to confide in the servant girl who became his second wife: " . . . there are so many marriages that conceal their little tale." As if to excuse himself for beginning a relationship that he could not bring to its proper fruition in marriage, he concludes his lonely soliloquy as follows:

> But if I had had to explain myself then (1841) I would have had to initiate her into terrible things, my relation to my father, his melancholy, the eternal darkness that broods deep within, my going astray, pleasures and excesses which in the eyes of God are not perhaps so terrible, for it was dread that drove me to excess, and where was I to look for something to hold on to when I knew, or suspected, that the one man I revered for his power and strength had wavered.

Although given to dramatic alternations in mood and deep ambivalence about himself and his destiny, these two journal entries from May 1843, suggest that in coming to terms with the broken engagement Kierkegaard was beginning to experience a sense of reassurance that in giving up his wish to marry, he had found his proper vocation as a midwife of ideas through the written word. His life-long quest to become the person God intended revolved around the normal Lutheran expectation that the life of Christian faith is lived out on two frontiers, the calling to marriage and the calling to work in the world. On both counts the unusually strained family history rendered Kierkegaard the solitary individual. Instead of marriage, he lived alone. Instead of a churchly vocation and ordination, the choice of his older brother Peter, he "wrote himself into being."

The joy of giving birth confided in the letter to Boesen in 1843 became a birth announcement to the world three years later when Kierkegaard publicly acknowledged that he had written *Fear and Trembling* under the pseudonym of Johannes de Silentio. In 1849, six years after the publication of *Fear and Trembling,* Kierkegaard confided his hopes for the posterity of one of his favorite children, once again to the journal. "Oh, when once I am dead—then *Fear and Trembling* alone will give me the name of an immortal author. Then it will be read, then too it will be tranlated into foreign tongues; and people will almost shudder at the frightful pathos of the book. . . . " By then he had become increasingly willing to express his position as a Christian and as a theologian under his own name. By then he had also been publicly ridiculed and knew what it meant to suffer for his chosen vocation. The book itself became his Isaac. As the token of his continuing life in the future, it was his child of promise.

From the beginning, Kierkegaard wrote with the intention of awakening his reader to self-consciousness. Although the books are written from various perspectives, they all point to the proclamation of the God who saves from the enslaving prison of destiny those who repent and believe. Although *Fear and Trembling* is written in the form of an indirect religious communication from the poetic perspective, Kierkegaard hopes to awaken the reader to the frightful pathos of self-recognition as one who could not work out his or her own salvation. The shudder he anticipated was the acknowledgement of human limitation to understand or create faith. The book was his confession of inability to live up to the expectations about faith that he had inherited from his father and from the Danish church tradition. Yet, like Augustine's *Confessions,* it was also his praise of thanksgiving to God that he had come to see that each generation must learn faith anew.

As suggested on the title page, Johannes carried a message he did not understand. Unlike Kierkegaard's hero Lessing, who had an "uncommon gift of explaining what he himself had understood," Johannes confesses from the outset that he cannot understand the faith of Abraham. Compared to the Hegelians who want to go beyond Christian faith, Johannes could only imagine faith. Yet he admits that he cannot even get as far as Christian faith as he looks at Abraham as a model for faith. The book is written as preparation for learning. It is the confession of inadequacy that comes before Christian faith can be appreciated.

Fear and Trembling is Kierkegaard's propaedeutic to Christian faith. It is distinguished from its theological twin, *The Sickness Unto Death,* by the omission of any reference to sin as that which stands between the religious seeker and God. Whereas *Fear and Trembling* paves the way for faith by clearing away false expectations, *The Sickness Unto Death* is a therapeutic for Christian faith. It provides healing for those who see their sin. Kierkegaard once considered the possibility of publishing *The Sickness Unto Death* and several discourses on atonement under the title *Thoughts Which Heal Fundamentally, Christian Therapeutic.*

The voice of the "silent Johannes" is like that of John the Baptist paving the way in the Danish desert for the one who is mightier—Jesus who will baptize with the Holy Spirit and with fire. *Fear and Trembling* is pre-Christian. Like John the Baptist in the Gospel of Luke, the religious perspective is that of the time of Israel rather than the time of Jesus. Kierkegaard's estimate of Danish civil religion led him to attempt an awakening from latter day forms of legalistic Judaism or from the complacent secularity of early church Gentiles. He wrote in the hope of initiating a serious spiritual quest in persons not yet aware of the alienating and distorting power of sin that creates a chasm between the human and the divine (Luke 16:26). It was also a way of clearing away his own blighted childhood faith.

As the book unfolds, Johannes tries to lead the reader into an acknowledgement that Christian faith can only be comprehended as it is lived in faithful response to God's command. Up to this point Abraham can serve as a type of faith. Yet, precisely at this point, Johannes also tells the reader that while he can imagine what the movements (acts) of faith might look like as demonstrated in the sketch of the "knight of faith," he is unable to make the movements of faith. Implicitly, Johannes has brought the reader to the border between Judaism and Christianity. The "knight of faith" is only a hero of imagination unable to empower the leap of faith or to sustain a poised faith that does not vacillate continually between leap and fall. The "knight of faith" is of no help to those who would live and "walk by the Spirit" (Gal. 5:25).

Kierkegaard wants the reader with a religious predisposition—one who already knows Bible stories and one who worships regularly—to acknowledge that it is one thing to know stories of faith heroes, but it is quite another to experience genuine faith. Faith is the highest passion, but how is such faith attained? For the receptive reader the book might initiate a quest with a seriousness of intent transcending the trivializing effect of those who would "go beyond faith."

In *The Sickness Unto Death* Kierkegaard again makes the point to the receptive reader that the Christian doctrine of sin cannot be comprehended objectively but must be believed and experienced if the words are to have meaning for the believer. Although demonstrating that faith has personal meaning only in relation to the acknowledgement that sin is its opposite, the Christian category of grace is present only in the accompanying *Christian Discourses.* Kierkegaard employs poetic reflection in *Fear and Trembling;* the dialectical presentation of sin in *The Sickness Unto Death* is intended to lead the reader toward personal appropriation of the grace offered through Jesus Christ, the paradox and pattern. In the *Discourses* the gospel as the teacher is presented in a series of meditations on the power of God's grace to overcome sinful anxiety. Here, finally, is the intended healing therapeutic. The true "highness" of Christianity that distinguishes it from the striving of pagan religions is presented in the recognition that "all that is, is of grace."

The Sickness Unto Death points in the direction of experiencing the need for God's grace through repentance, the condition for individual assimilation of the reality of sin. The anatomy of active and passive despair is pressed toward a description of the sin against the Holy Ghost—a step beyond despairing over the forgiveness of sins. The inability of an individual to believe and experience God's forgiveness is less serious than " . . . the sin of abandoning Christianity as falsehood and a lie. . . . " This denial is "the positive form of offense" against God. All prior forms of despair acknowledge that God the adversary is stronger than all human attempts to flee the judging presence of God. Yet the sin against the Holy Ghost is outright denial of kinship between God and human being. The logical conclusion is that such denial is likewise a denial of Christ as the paradox. Finally, to deny the reality of sin is to deny that Christ existed and that " . . . He is what he claimed to be."

"That man was not a learned exegete, he didn't know Hebrew, if he had known Hebrew, he perhaps would easily have understood the story and Abraham." With this disclosure, Johannes de Silentio begins his poetic and dialectical reflections on the faith of Abraham. The disclaimer precedes four versions of what Abraham may have thought as he prepared to sacrifice Isaac, the child of promise, in obedience to God's command. "The man," described by Johannes, gives up his fruitless attempts at imaginative identification with Scripture, concluding that "No one is so great as Abraham! Who is capable of understanding him?"

In the panegyric that follows, the poet exhausts his lyrical attempts to inspire himself by making a hero of Abraham. Yet this, too, is judged a useless exercise insofar as the poet does not become heroic simply by eulogizing a hero, even if the hero is Abraham, the father of faith. However poetic this attempt may be, it is still a eulogy of someone who is dead. Then follows the well-known distinction between "the knight of infinite resignation" and "the knight of faith."

At this point in the narrative, Johannes takes on the role of an orator presenting a passion so gigantic that it would move the audience to sense the dialectical conflict of faith. Although his stated intention is to appeal to the emotions, he contradicts himself by attempting to explain the contradiction that in his obedience to God's command Abraham is potentially a murderer. Admitting that he cannot think such a paradox, the poet then proceeds to describe the paradox as going further than infinite resignation. Standing in polemic against all orators, pastors, philosophers, and theologians of his generation who claim to "go beyond faith," the poet imagines what an Abraham-like "knight of faith" might look like if encountered in his day. Having given imaginative concretion to the dialectic of faith in which the knight transforms "the leap of life into a walk" by virtue of his belief that with God all things are possible, Johannes confesses that he cannot make the paradoxical second movement of faith. He can only get as far as infinite resignation. He closes the poetic reflection saying he prefers describing Abraham in terms of the pain of his trial, admonishing people about the suffering of faith as compared to the ludicrous, cheap edition of Abraham presented by parson-orators who have no idea what they are saying when they admire Abraham's act as merely heroic.

At this point in the narrative, Johannes the dialectician proceeds to think the faith of Abraham to a standstill by posing a series of three ethical issues related to the faith of Abraham. Once again, reason stands mute before the paradoxical faith of Abraham "which no thought can master." In the process, Johannes, claiming to be no "thinker," returns to his criticism of pastors and theologians. This time he castigates the "pious and kindly exegete" who uses his interpretive skills to reduce the intensity of the demand of discipleship in the New Testament to the drivel of "a tasteful explanation." The exegete disposes of Jesus' absolute demand that those who would come to him must hate father and mother, wife and children, brothers and sisters, even their own life, by mistranslating the verb "to hate." The exegete has also ignored the context for the painful command "to hate" kin if necessary (Luke 14:26). Johannes adds that cheap grace can be defended grammatically, linguistically, and analogically by exegetes who distort the meaning and thus present Christianity as "one of the most pitiable things in the world."

Kierkegaard wrote himself into being as he worked out his own salvation with fear and trembling. He did so even as he wrote for readers in his own time or the future. When he wrote *Fear and Trembling,* he was convinced that the orthodox religion of his age, saturated with influences of rationalism, could lead only to tragic resignation—never to Christian faith. This was the joyless "faith" of self-suppression that he had seen in his father. He was further convinced that the joy of God's love could not be experienced without a descent into the hell of self-knowledge. The "frightful pathos" of *Fear and Trembling* was Kierkegaard's preliminary witness to the truth that the choice for Christian faith is made in the utter loneliness of silence before God.

When Kierkegaard confided his hope that *Fear and Trembling* would insure his future, he expressed the doubt of any anxious parent worried about the future of his "chil-

A profile, dated January 15, 1883, drawn by Kierkegaard's cousin, Christian Kierkegaard.

dren." Yet, even as the book is a propaedeutic and prole-
gomenon to his lifework, it serves the same purpose in his
life. As he responded to the influence of Hegelian idealism
on exegesis and preaching in his day, he was working out
his own approach to a Christian faith that "goes beyond"
reason. The critique of the "pastor-orator" and the "pious
and kindly exegete" in *Fear and Trembling* (1843) reappears in *For Self-Examination* (1851). Here the point was
made directly that Scripture is the source of God's blessing to those who see themselves in the mirror of the word.
An exegesis of James 1:22-27 makes it clear that those who
hear the word but do not live it deceive themselves. Kierkegaard's increased criticism of clergy was motivated by
his observation that oratorical preaching by pastors who
misinterpreted the gospel denied congregations the self-
examination requisite to faith.

It would seem that the claim of Johannes de Silentio that
he was "not a learned exegete" because he did not know
Hebrew is an ironic way of suggesting that he could not
understand Abraham because they lacked a common language. The indirect point being made by the Christian exegete Kierkegaard was that persons in his age cannot understand the faith of Abraham because they have been
born into the Christian tradition and not the Jewish tradition. They cannot work out their own salvation by way of
a prior position, the law of Judaism. Neither can they "go
beyond" Christian faith. According to Paul, Christ is the
common language that illuminates the faith of Abraham.
"And if you are Christ's, then you are Abraham's offspring, heirs according to promise" (Gal. 3:29).

Fear and Trembling is a preliminary "expectoration" that
anticipates the later, very direct *Attack on Christendom.*
In contrasting the "knight of infinite resignation" with the
"knight of faith," Johannes de Silentio suggests that faith
is known only by going through the motions. As Kierkegaard attempted to integrate word with deed in his life, his
capacity to explain "what he himself had understood" influenced his writing. It would seem that "the knight" who
eventually grew strong enough in Christian faith to attack
the religious establishment of his day was himself clothed
in "the whole armor of God," standing over against what
he took to be "the wiles of the devil" (Eph. 6:11). It may
be that Søren Kierkegaard—taken by "the world" to be
a philosopher, a theologian, an aesthete, a poet, and a
madman—was demonstrating what it means to be a faithful exegete who "wields the sword of the Spirit, which is
the word of God" (Eph. 6:17). (pp. 229-45)

> *Janet Forsythe Fishburn, "Søren Kierkegaard,*
> *Exegete," in* Interpretation: A Journal of
> Bible & Theology, *Vol. XXXIX, No. 3, July,*
> *1985, pp. 229-45.*

George Pattison (essay date 1986)

[*In the following excerpt, Pattison examines Kierkegaard's literary reviews of novels written by his contemporaries and determines that the reviews represent a
search in literature for evidence of an immanent ethical
system or unifying "life-view." Pattison asserts that instead of affirmation, Kierkegaard finds a trend toward
moral nihilism in modern literature.*]

Kierkegaard's work as a critic of the arts can be divided
into two quite distinct sets of texts. Indeed, the distinction
between them is so marked that it might at first appear
that we are faced with two quite incompatible views of the
nature and function of art coming from the same pen. It
will, however, be argued here that both groups of writings
can be seen within the horizon of a single fundamental
question concerning the relationship between art and the
existential situation of 'modern man'. The group with
which we shall be particularly concerned is that constituted by the three reviews Kierkegaard wrote of contemporary, or at least topical, novels, namely, Hans Christian
Andersen's *Only a Fiddler,* Friedrich Schlegel's *Lucinde*
and Madame Gyllembourg's *Two Ages.* These reviews
form a unitary body of writing within Kierkegaard's total
authorship, not only in terms of thematic unity but also
in terms of vocabulary. The theme may be summed up as
that of the problematic nature of novelistic literature in
the modern, secular age. The key word which links the
three pieces is 'life-view' (Danish = Livsanskuelse), an expression Kierkegaard uses in a very precise sense.

Before looking at these reviews in more detail I shall first
attempt to clarify their relationship to Kierkegaard's other
critical writings and secondly sketch in something of the
conceptual background to Kierkegaard's use of the term
'life-view'.

Ms. M. Jørgensen, whose monograph *Kierkegaard as Critic* is the most substantial contribution to this subject to
date, divides his critical writings into two groups which
she calls the 'aesthetic' and the 'ethical'. This distinction
corresponds to one of the vital dialectical polarities which
run through Kierkegaard's authorship as a whole. In the
narrower sphere of literary criticism it means that in the
former group Kierkegaard judges the works of art with
which he is concerned solely on internal, aesthetic
grounds, i.e., in the light of the question whether the work
corresponds to its essential 'idea'; in the latter group, on
the other hand, the connection between the work of art
and its ethical or social attitude is placed at the centre of
discussion. This categorization is certainly valid in its own
terms, but it is not the only option available. We can also
see the distinction involved as being between those writings which discuss the *theatre* and those which deal with
novelistic literature. In an earlier article ('Søren Kierkegaard: A Theatre Critic of the Heiberg School' in *British
Journal of Aesthetics* 23) I argued that Kierkegaard's theatrical reviews were based on purely aesthetic principles
involving the conformity of the work to the requirements
of its specific genre, principles which Kierkegaard largely
adapted from the leading Danish critic J. L. Heiberg.
Here, however, we see him attempting to evaluate the artistic significance of the works he discusses in the light of
the ethical values which they reveal. But whichever categorization one uses there is clearly a problem: is Kierkegaard simply playing games (he can, after all, be frequently observed teasing his readers with the most complex literary games) or is there a deeper purpose in this use of two
(apparently) conflicting methods of evaluating art?

In terms of the distinction between 'aesthetic' and 'ethical'
modes of criticism it may be pointed out that this relates

to one of the basic themes running through Kierkegaard's early pseudonymous works, namely, that human beings are confronted by a choice between two radically opposed ways of life which Kierkegaard calls the 'aesthetic' and the 'ethical'. The 'aesthetic' way of life (which in many respects corresponds to what later existentialists would refer to as 'inauthenticity' or 'bad faith') attempts to treat life as if it were an object of aesthetic pleasure whereas the 'ethical' point of view involves facing up to our basic moral responsibilities—to others, to ourselves, to God. The 'aesthetic' reviews (all published under one or other of Kierkegaard's pseudonyms) belong within the overall presentation of the aesthetic way of life and serve as illustrations of the cool, detached, highly self-conscious outlook of such an aesthetic dandy. The 'ethical' reviews (published by Kierkegaard under his own name) contribute to his account of the limitations and weaknesses of a merely aesthetic existence and indicate the direction which he thinks should be taken in preference to it. Seeing the distinction in terms of that between the 'theatre' and the 'novel', on the other hand, enables us to argue for a fundamental coherence in Kierkegaard's writings on aesthetics in the narrow, non-existential, sense. For it can be seen that the principle that a work of art can only be evaluated in the categories appropriate to its particular genre is still operative in his reviews of novels. There may well be purely aesthetic grounds for applying ethical criteria to the novel and not to the theatre, if, for instance, it was argued that the novel makes an implicit claim to represent events in or (at least) imaginable as occurring in the real contemporary world of human society—whereas dramatic art is in its very immediacy the representation of an illusory scene, intrinsically limited to the artificiality of the stage. Kierkegaard does not himself offer this argument (or, indeed, explain his procedure in this matter at all) but it is congruent with his practice and there are some remarks in his early journals which suggest that he may well have had some such view of the novel. These remarks concern Goethe's *Wilhelm Meister,* which Kierkegaard evidently regarded as a model work, and which he saw as incorporating a very clear moral view of the world. It is, he wrote, 'truly the whole world seen in a mirror, a true microcosm'. Was it then specifically the novel which had to live up to this requirement to be a mirror to the whole world, 'a true microcosm?'

Although Kierkegaard took from Hegelianism a ready-made table of genres within which to capture and to categorize the varieties of aesthetic experience, neither Hegel himself nor his Danish admirers had much to say specifically about the novel as a distinct form of art and it was not from Hegelianism that Kierkegaard derived the notion of the 'life-view' which was to play a key part in his writing on the novel. The terms *Weltanschauung* and *Lebensanschauung* had been in common usage in German literature and philosophy for a generation or more, but the idea of the 'world-view' came to acquire a special significance for the Danish poet and philosopher Poul Martin Møller (1794-1838). Kierkegaard's friendship with Møller (who taught philosophy in Copenhagen University when Kierkegaard was a student) was one of the most positive and least acrimonious relationships of his whole life. Unfortunately for posterity Møller's literary remains are exceedingly fragmentary and the exact relationship and degree of mutual influence between the two men is almost impossible to gauge precisely.

Like most of his contemporaries Møller was preoccupied with the question of the resolution of the conflict authoritatively defined by Kant, the conflict namely between reason (or freedom) and nature, noumena and phenomena, spirit and sense—and, of course, the further question as to the possibility of establishing a religious comprehension of Being within the horizon of a transcendent unity. Møller did not see these questions in narrowly philosophical terms but as—to anticipate the vocabulary of his more renowned pupil—an existential issue. The 'world-view' which he commends [in his *Efterladte Skrifter*] as the solution to the Kantian dilemma depends on a personal experience of 'the presence of the super-sensuous in the sensuous, when it becomes the object of an experience of a higher kind'. This 'experience of a higher kind' is not, however, a purely inward mystical event but is only possible when it remains true to the world of empirical experience and to the religious content which belongs to the mainstream of Christian culture.

> The Christian tradition, empirical experience, as well as the higher experience in which the super-sensuous encounters us in a real form at particular times and places, give the discrete points which must have their place in a proper world-view, and the systematic, philosophical exposition only expresses with formal perfection that knowledge which is first present in an immediate way and in an inarticulate form.

Such a world-view was, he believed, not only the basis for an authentic human life but was also the presupposition of all true artistic creation—so that 'he who feels himself in discord with himself and with existence cannot possibly be a genuine poet'.

Møller's thought was, however, rescued from a merely sentimental optimism by his assessment of the contemporary intellectual situation. He regards nihilism—represented in literature by Byron, Shelley, Heine and the 'Young Germany' movement and in philosophy by Schopenhauer—as an almost inevitable destiny overshadowing the modern world. Of the spirit of negation which he sees manifested in such figures he writes: 'it is very possible that negation has still not reached the point which must be reached, so that it can be made apparent that the desolation it brings with it is not the sphere in which the human spirit is at home'. He spoke of 'nineteenth century rational man' seeking the promised land in a wilderness. 'You are right', he wryly comments, 'it is all up for my poetry / Now I overturn Art's despised altar . . . And yet— what is life, if the artists flee, / If only seriousness remains, dwelling beneath a roof of ice?' The question which Møller bequeathed to Kierkegaard, then, was this: to what extent can a positive, religiously cohesive vision of reality achieve authentic aesthetic expression in an age shaped by the spirit of nihilism? And it is this question which lies at the heart of Kierkegaard's literary reviews.

[Kierkegaard] published his first book [*From the Papers of One Still Living*] in 1838 and the title itself may well contain an allusion to Møller who had died earlier that year. It is an extended review of Hans Christian Andersen's novel *Only a Fiddler* and it opens, significantly, with an attack on the negative outlook of the younger generation, an outlook which, Kierkegaard tells us, finds its theoretical expression in Hegel's negative dialectics and its practical outworking in the radical politics of the left. Both in theory and in practice we are, he maintains, witnessing 'an *attentat* on the given reality', an attack which he likens to the desecration by Christian missionaries of the ancient Teutonic woods. But behind the philosophical principle of systematic doubt and the political principle of 'Enlightenment' Kierkegaard detects less creditable motives, such as envy and mistrust.

Turning from the wider cultural scene to the narrower field of literature, Kierkegaard offers a brief survey of some of the leading novelists of contemporary Denmark, referring primarily to Madame Gyllembourg, Carl Bernhard and Steen Steensen Blicher. He singles Madame Gyllembourg out for especial praise. He acknowledges that her work will find a more readily sympathetic reception among the older generation than among the more politically orientated young and he asserts that this is because both she and the older generation have what the young conspicuously lack: 'a life-view' of a certain kind. This life-view is described as, firstly, optimistic, not in the world-historical sense but in the more everyday sense that it is always ready to see a hopeful aspect in events and circumstances at the individual, personal level; it is, secondly, positive in its attitude to people, being ready to see a 'divine spark' glowing under the most trivial forms of personal life; it is, thirdly, acquainted with the sorrows and disappointments to which all flesh is heir but none the less retains its essential optimism, which is thus tempered and mellowed by experience. In short it expresses 'the joy which has triumphed over the world'; it is the outlook of 'the individual who has run the race and kept the faith'.

Having indicated the cultural and literary horizons within which he chooses to operate Kierkegaard now closes on his victim. What, he asks, is Andersen's character as a novelist? Firstly, he declares, Andersen is no lyrical genius, since he lacks the naïve self-confidence of one marked out by 'nature's imprimatur'. He is, on the contrary, more like 'a mere possibility of a personality, caught in a . . . web of accidental moods'. But nor does he qualify as an epic writer: 'Andersen has leapt over his *epos*', says Kierkegaard scathingly. This epic stage which Andersen has not negotiated is defined as 'a deep and serious embracing of the given reality . . . a life-strengthening abiding in it and admiration for it'. This, he concedes, is not entirely Andersen's fault, since the point in his life when this should have occurred was a time when Denmark was caught up in political unrest, mostly of a trivial and not very purposeful kind. There was no great task or cause at hand with which the young novelist could identify himself and so transcend his moody subjectivity. Andersen was thus 'continually pushed back down the funnel of his own personality' so that his poetic powers became 'self-corroding' producing 'a kind of disaffection and bitterness towards the world'. Andersen, in short, lacks what Kierkegaard declares to be 'the *conditio sine qua non* for a nov-

elist of the type to which Andersen belongs', namely, the 'life-view', now defined as 'an unshakeable confidence in oneself, even in the teeth of the empirical manifold'. It may, he adds, either take a purely this-worldly form, as a kind of Stoicism, or it may express 'the true Christian assurance' which Paul describes in Romans 8 'that neither death nor life, no angel, no prince, no power, nothing that exists, nothing still to come, or height or depth, or anything in all creation, can separate us from the love of God in Christ Jesus our Lord'. Not that Andersen's work is totally devoid of a unifying idea, but this idea 'is the idea of the downfall of everything noble, genial, exalted', and this is by no means the same as the idea which undergirds an authentic 'life-view'.

What consequences follow from this lack for Andersen's novels? Without the centre of gravity' which the life-view would provide a novel will take one of two forms. Either it will become a platform for some theory, a type Kierkegaard calls the 'dogmatic, doctrinaire novel' (an example of which he finds in Friedrich Schlegel's *Lucinde*) or else it will be too subjective, with a 'too finite and accidental relation to the author's flesh and blood'. It is this latter type which Andersen, in Kierkegaard's view, represents, so much so that the genesis of his novels 'is not so much to be regarded as a production as an amputation of a part of his self'. This deficiency is reflected in the main character of the novel, a gifted musician, whose destiny is said by Andersen to lie in the alternative: 'he must become a rare artist, or else a piddling wretch'. All, it seems, depends on a kind or unkind fate. 'Genius', says Andersen, 'is an egg which aspires to warmth, to be fructified by good fortune . . . '. Not so, retorts Kierkegaard, real genius itself dictates the agenda and *commands* attention: it is like Athena springing forth fully-armed from the head of Zeus.

Kierkegaard concludes the review with the slightly mollifying remark that at least Andersen retained some sort of aspiration towards subjectivity and poetry and did not get swept away by politics as so many of his generation did. But it was no wonder that when, ten years later, Kierkegaard sent Andersen a presentation copy of the second edition of **Either-Or,** Andersen wrote back, 'I had no idea at all that you entertained friendly thoughts of me'. There was certainly little in **From the Papers of One Still Living** to suggest it.

The discussion of Friedrich Schlegel's *Lucinde* is not presented as a review but is embedded in Kierkegaard's M.A. thesis **On the Concept of Irony.** *Lucinde,* published in 1799, was not a contemporary book, but it became a focus of discussion for Kierkegaard's generation when Karl Gutzkow, one of the literary left in Germany, re-published the young Schleiermacher's *Letters on Friedrich Schlegel's Lucinde* in 1835, and himself declared *Lucinde* to be 'the proclamation of the gospel of the flesh'.

Kierkegaard regarded *Lucinde* as a 'doctrinaire' novel, a novel, that is, which lacks a co-ordinating life-view and reduces literature to propaganda. What then was the idea which *Lucinde* propagated? As the title of Kierkegaard's thesis indicates it was the idea of *irony,* of the free, sovereign transcendence of the creative self. At first glance it might appear that Kierkegaard should welcome this over against the unconfident lack-of-self which he condemned in Andersen, but in fact he sees it as a sign of the same basic malaise, the same failure to establish a life-view rooted and grounded in a positive relation to the given reality. Schlegel's concept of irony, which Kierkegaard like many others regarded as an illegitimate extension of Fichte's concept of the Absolute Ego, is seen as expressing an arbitrary attitude to the world, denying all intrinsic value to things and allowing only those values which the self chooses to assign. But this, says Kierkegaard, leads to 'acosmism' and 'docetism', since it means denying the substantiality of the real world. So little does the 'poetry' which such an ironic consciousness produces articulate a real integration of self and world that it is rather to be seen as an exodus from reality, an attempt to replace the real world with the purely fictitious world of the imagination. '. . . [P]oetry [is] *a kind of reconciliation,* but it is *not the true reconciliation* for it does not reconcile me to the reality in which I live'.

The ironist who actually believes in the world created by his own imagination will thus lose all solidity, his experience will lack continuity and dissolve into a sequence of fragmentary moods. His life is a cowardly life because he constantly evades the religious challenge to the self to become transparent to itself in its 'absolute and eternal validity'. It is a self-deceiving life since, far from the ironist being creatively exalted above his moods and experiences he is actually their creature: ' . . . that which is the remarkable thing about *Lucinde* and the whole tendency which is connected with it is that one, in taking the freedom of the self and its constitutive authority as a point of departure, instead of reaching a still higher spiritual existence only arrives at sensuousness, and so to one's opposite . . . '.

The split between self and world which the Romantic consciousness presupposes cannot, Kierkegaard is saying, be solved in its own terms. The Romantic cult of irony leads to the dissolution of the personality which can only be truly healed by the integration of both poles of being in the power of a greater being which transcends them both. Here again it can be seen that Kierkegaard is following closely views expressed by Møller who had written of Schlegel's doctrine of irony that ' . . . irony is a consequent development of the fruitless struggle to construct a self-enclosed ethical system from the standpoint of the individual. This method must necessarily end with the loss of all content, with moral nihilism.' Schlegel and Andersen both embody aspects of the situation of modern nihilism, when the support of a living religious tradition has been eroded, and ideals such as freedom come to possess an increasingly hollow ring in the face of the technical and political systematization of the encompassing social reality.

We now come to the last and most substantial of the three reviews, once more published by Kierkegaard as an independent book. [The work *Two Ages*] deals with the novel *Two Ages* by Madame Gyllembourg, on whom Kierkegaard had lavished such praise in *From the Papers of One Still Living.* Once more he makes great play of that which he admires in the author: her firm possession of a life-view

which imbues her work with 'a quiet joy over life'. He goes on to spell out the proper relationship between this life-view and literary activity:

> The life-view . . . must have ripened in the author before he produces. His productivity is not a moment in his development, but when this development has ripened, then it brings forth as its fruit a work of inwardness. It is not geniality, not talent, not virtuosity which constitutes the work . . . the possibility of being able to write such works is rather the reward which God has bestowed on the author, as he, twice-matured, won in his life-view something eternal.

Kierkegaard draws a contrast between an *author,* whose work is based on such a life-view, and a *poet.* The poet takes us out of the world into the realm of imagination but an author both knows the pain of life in the world and is none the less able to bear the pain and affirm the goodness of life. The author knows how to persuade us to share her view

> . . . by understanding how to find a milder aspect in which to see suffering, by having the patience which expects good fortune to smile again, by the friendly sympathy of caring people, by the resignation which does not renounce everything but only the highest, and by the contentment that changes the second best into something just as good as the highest . . .

Once again Kierkegaard expresses his opinion that this life-view will be more readily received by the older generation. The young, he says, are carried away by the cult of the new and will accept nothing which is not in accord with 'the requirements of the age'; but, he declares, 'Pandora's box could not contain so many misfortunes and so much misery as what is concealed in the little phrase: "the age requires!"' ' In fact the relationship between the generation of the 1790s and the generation of the 1840s ('the present age') is a key feature of the novel itself. For all its turbulence the period of the revolutionary wars was, the author suggests, more fully alive, more meaningful than the present, by comparison, a more sedate, more superficial, more bourgeois age. The present 'rational, reflecting, unimpassioned' age:

> has no fascinating foreigners, no legation of Frenchmen, who almost lead one to forget that the scene is in Copenhagen, and no mighty upsurge from a world-historical catastrophe. Life in the present age is not disturbed by energetic passion, which is formed precisely by its very energy, yes, even its violence; and [the present age] does not hide a forbidden, secret passion's strength. On the contrary, everything is openly indeterminate and thereby trivial, formless, semi-cultivated, obsequious, and is all this quite openly. Here is no mighty revelation and no deep secret, but all the more superficiality.

The novel gives Kierkegaard a cue to propound his own views of 'the present age', and his essay on this theme [which has been translated separately as *The Present Age*] is the lengthiest and most significant part of the book. It is important both for our understanding of Kierkegaard's views on art and for a proper appreciation of his *Zeitkritik* to realize that the context of this essay is a literary review. In the present age, he tells us, publicity takes the place of action, spectating the place of participation, envy replaces enthusiasm, levelling undermines nobility and greatness, meetings and ballotings destroy authoritative leadership, instead of community we have only the anonymous 'public' manipulated by the daily press and instead of serious talk we have only idle chatter. In a word: it is an age in which human existence is radically depersonalized.

It now becomes clear why Kierkegaard regards it as unlikely that the present generation will be able to grasp the life-view on which not only Mme. Gyllembourg's books depend but also, he believes, all serious novelistic art. For the life-view demands a certain confidence in the concrete social matrices of ethical significance. In the present age, when all forms and conventions are exposed to the corrosive scepticism of ongoing rationalization and to the democratic levelling process, all such concrete, publically recognized embodiments of meaning are deprived of content in a silent revolution which 'lets everything remain, but cunningly takes away its meaning'. For example, the Church essentially embodies the values and doctrines of revealed religion, but in the modern secular age, especially in the Protestant State Churches, it merely functions as an ideological self-justification on the part of the established order, a supplier of undemanding *rites de passage*. This means that the complex of meanings which the Church essentially represents is closed to modern man. The language of religion has been corrupted from within and now means simply nothing at all. Not only with regard to religion, but across the whole range of social life Kierkegaard detects a bankruptcy in language itself. The continuity of meaning which sustained social life is broken and in the post-Enlightenment world the Christian culture which provided the objective basis for Mme. Gyllembourg's and Poul Møller's 'life-view' no longer exists. The only authentic form of religion in this situation is, Kierkegaard argues, a religion of radical interiority ('hidden inwardness') in which authority is no longer exercised by recognizable authority-figures but is concealed behind the incognito of suffering. Not only can faith not be identified in terms of institutional membership but no publicly recognizable form can be given to it at all—not even aesthetic form.

The implications of this do not only concern the relation of art to Christianity in the narrow sense, for what Kierkegaard is saying applies to all attempts to express the content of essential personal subjectivity. There is, he holds, a gap between external forms and human significances which is connected with the whole process of Enlightenment but which has become so wide that it simply cannot be bridged.

Nor can the consequences for art be confined to the novel. For Kierkegaard it was axiomatic that art could be seen as developing through more and more concrete forms, from, for example, the abstract immediacy of lyrical poetry to the concrete objectivity of drama. At the same time he shared the idealist conception that the prime task of art was to create an intuition of harmony and joy by presenting the ideal world in a tangible form. Where the novel was distinctive was that the sense of harmony which it

produced had to be, so to speak, tested against real life. The novelist was essentially 'interested' in the real world in a way other artists were not. The novel was thus the most concrete of all forms of art. But if it is no longer possible in the conditions of modern society to create images of harmony and reconciliation which mesh in with what we know of social reality a limit is set for all art. The novel is the place where the ideal of beauty comes face to face with the reality-principle. The consequences of this meeting will necessarily reverberate through the whole field of aesthetic experience. If the novelist cannot, then no artist can give an 'answer' to the crisis of modernity, and Kierkegaard thus takes issue with all those Romantics and their modern heirs who claim that it is art which will liberate us from the de-personalizing forces of a technologically dominated society. Kierkegaard's claim is that it is in the hidden inwardness of religion that we will find the authentic will to resist nihilism, and in this way it is religion, not art, which becomes the true bearer of the humanistic protest against the 'death of man'.

This clearly throws open a wide-ranging discussion of large and complex questions. The aim of this article has been accomplished if it has been shown how these questions arise in the context of Kierkegaard's work as a literary critic. In conclusion, however, I should like to indicate two areas in which these questions might profitably be pursued. First, although the twentieth century has largely turned its back on the idealist view of art which Kierkegaard presupposes, and has rejected the ideal of beauty as the chief aim of art, Kierkegaard's sense of a double-crisis—in man and in art—has been recognized by many artists and writers as relating to the contradictions and anxieties which they too have sought to express. The implications of his view of this crisis should be seen in the light of the work of such as Strindberg, Kafka and Bergman who have wrestled *artistically* with these questions within a common cultural horizon. Secondly, at the theoretical level, it would be highly challenging to set Kierkegaard's discussion of the threefold relationship between art, religion and nihilism alongside that of Nietzsche. It might well be in this context that it would come to be seen in its fullest significance as a major treatment of the honesty and self-deception, the truth and illusion of art in the conditions of the scientific-technological 'age of reflection'. (pp. 161-70)

George Pattison, "Nihilism and the Novel: Kierkegaard's Literary Reviews," in The British Journal of Aesthetics, *Vol. 26, No. 2, Spring, 1986, pp. 161-71.*

FURTHER READING

Arbaugh, George E., and Arbaugh, George B. *Kierkegaard's Authorship: A Guide to the Writings of Kierkegaard.* Rock Island, Ill.: Augustana College Library, 1967, 431 p.

Chronological review of Kierkegaard's works "not intended to enter in great depth the technical problems of interpretation, but to give a relatively simple and . . . inviting introduction to all the works, so that anyone can discover readily and quickly what to expect and where to read."

Arendt, Hannah. "Tradition and the Modern Age." *Partisan Review* XXI, No. 1 (January / February 1954): 53-75.

Contends that Kierkegaard, along with Marx and Nietzsche, effected a rebellion against patterns of thought that had ruled the West for more than two thousand years: "Their greatness lay in the fact that they perceived their world as one invaded by new problems and perplexities which our tradition of thought was unable to cope with."

Baldwin, Birgit. "Irony, that 'Little, Invisible Personage': A Reading of Kierkegaard's Ghosts." *Modern Language Notes* 104, No. 5 (December 1989): 1124-41.

Refers extensively to Friedrich Schlegel's description of the enduring, "ghostly" effects of irony in a discussion of Kierkegaard's claim that irony has "incredibly long-lasting aftereffects" and an "uncontrollability . . . that swallows everything into itself."

Barrett, William. "Kierkegaard." In his *Irrational Man: A Study in Existential Philosophy,* pp. 149-76. Garden City, N.Y.: Doubleday Anchor Books, 1962.

Explores Kierkegaard's central concern, "what it means concretely for the individual to be a Christian," as it informed and guided his life, thought, and works. Barrett declares that "Kierkegaard stated the question of Christianity so nakedly, made it turn so decisively about the individual and his quest for his own eternal happiness, that all religious writers after him seem by comparison to be symbolical, institutional, or metaphorical—in a word, gnostic."

Blackham, H. J. "Søren Kierkegaard." *Six Existentialist Thinkers,* pp. 1-22. New York: Harper & Row, 1959.

Proclaims Kierkegaard "the boldest and the greatest of existentialist thinkers." Blackham remarks that "what he bequeathed to philosophy was his protest against 'pure' thought and irrelevant knowledge and his recall to the permanent basis of human living in the ethical isolation of the existing individual."

Bové, Paul. "The Penitentiary of Reflection: Søren Kierkegaard and Critical Activity." *Boundary 2* 9, No. 1 (Fall 1980): 233-58.

Examines *Two Ages* and finds that critical activity, according to Kierkegaard, must examine its own origins, assumptions, and effects in order to regulate "its own inevitable participation in maintaining and changing society's institutions" or risk remaining a hollow "wit industry."

Cavell, Stanley. "Kierkegaard's *On Authority and Revelation.*" In his *Must We Mean What We Say?: A Book of Essays,* pp. 163-79. New York: Charles Scribner's Sons, 1969.

Analyzes *On Authority and Revelation* and finds that Kierkegaard defines the authentic author as a person "pulled out of the ranks by a message which he must, on pain of loss of self, communicate; he is silent for a long period, until he finds his way to saying what it is he has to say." Kierkegaard's literary method is observed to be an indication of authenticity.

Croxall, T. H. *Kierkegaard Commentary.* London: James Nisbet & Co., 1956, 263 p.

Claims to be a clarification of Kierkegaard's actual text rather than a book *"about"* Kierkegaard. Working from the Danish text rather than the English translations, Croxall analyzes several pseudonymous texts and elucidates their main themes.

Culjak, Toni Ann. "Dickinson and Kierkegaard: Arrival at Despair." *The American Transcendental Quarterly* 1, No. 2 (June 1987): 145-55.

Associates Emily Dickinson's "proto-existential attitude" with the philosophy of Kierkegaard: "They recognize the existential which is a universal result of the purposeful exploration, definition, and assertion of self."

Geismar, Eduard. *Lectures on the Religious Thought of Søren Kierkegaard: The Stone Foundation Lectures Given at Princeton Theological Seminary in March, 1936.* Minneapolis, Minn.: Augsburg Publishing House, 1937, 97 p.

Discusses the significance of Kierkegaard's teaching for modern religion in a world that "cannot be saved by the so-called Christianity of a worldly Church. Kierkegaard therefore demands a Christianity in which the polemic element is emphasized as strongly as it was in the earliest period of its history."

Goebel, Rolf J. "Kafka and Kierkegaard's *Fear and Trembling:* Critique and Revision." *Journal of the Kafka Society of America* 9, No. 1-2 (June / December 1985): 69-82.

Treats Kafka's interpretation of Kierkegaard's "Abraham concept."

Grene, Marjorie. "Søren Kierkegaard: The Self against the System." In her *Dreadful Freedom: A Critique of Existentialism,* pp. 15-40. Chicago: The University of Chicago Press, 1948.

Claims that Kierkegaard erred fundamentally by denying any concept of human community, though Grene adds that "he is so far right, that the root of morality does lie in the individual."

Grimsley, Ronald. "The Don Juan Theme in Molière and Kierkegaard." *Comparative Literature* VI, No. 4 (Fall 1954): 316-34.

Examines Kierkegaard's criticism of Molière's treatment of the Don Juan legend. Kierkegaard is found to assert that Don Juan's fundamental principle, "the moment is everything," is not the conclusion to the problem of existence but the beginning.

Haecker, Theodor. *Kierkegaard the Cripple,* translated by C. Van O. Bruyn. London: The Harvill Press, 1948, 53 p.

Focuses on Rikard Magnussen's studies of Kierkegaard, which document the author's hunchback. Haecker examines "the significance of [Kierkegaard's] congenital deformity at the turning points in his life (his engagement, his row with *The Corsair*), and its relation to, and possible influence on, his thought."

Harrison, Robert Pogue. "Heresy and the Question of Repetition: Reading Kierkegaard's *Repetition.*" *Textual Analysis: Some Readers Reading,* pp. 281-88, edited by Mary Ann Caws. New York: The Modern Language Association of America, 1986.

Examines the meaning of repetition within Kierkegaard's *Repetition* and determines that it is a "mode of 'suspended' discourse": "repetition is neither an idea nor another existential category but the irreducible difference between expression and the immanence of a meaning that never gets produced in the discursive fabric."

Jones, W. Glyn. "Søren Kierkegaard in English Translation." *Yearbook of Comparative and General Literature* No. 35 (1986): 105-11.
　Discusses the difficulties that confront translators of Kierkegaard's work. Jones notes that "it can thus be safely asserted that Kierkegaard in his entirety is now available in reliable English versions, and that although these cannot possibly recreate every subtlety and nuance of the Danish, they have gone as far as can be reasonably expected."

Kaufmann, Walter. "Kierkegaard." *The Kenyon Review* XVIII, No. 2 (Spring 1956): 182-211.
　States that true appreciation of Kierkegaard is possible through initial opposition to his thought: Kierkegaard intended to provoke and stimulate rather than to evoke uncritical approval.

Lapointe, François H. *Søren Kierkegaard and His Critics: An International Bibliography of Criticism.* Westport, Conn.: Greenwood Press, 1980, 430 p.
　Bibliography of criticism that is "as complete as is technically feasible" and that includes criticism in "major" European languages.

Lebowitz, Naomi. *Kierkegaard: A Life of Allegory.* Baton Rouge: Louisiana State University Press, 1985, 242 p.
　Explores Kierkegaard's "cumulative and recapitulated approach to his central concerns" rather than providing a conventional literary analysis of any of his texts: "This book is about the ways in which [Kierkegaard] imagined and effected, through his literature, a passage from the psychological source of his art, his suffering in the world, to faith."

Levi, Albert William. "A Hundred Years after Kierkegaard: The Three Masks." *The Kenyon Review* XVIII, No. 2 (Spring 1956): 169-82.
　Discusses Don Juan, Socrates, and Don Quixote as literary archetypes for Kierkegaard's aesthetic, ethical, and religious spheres of existence.

Lowrie, Walter. *A Short Life of Kierkegaard.* Princeton, N.J.: Princeton University Press, 1942, 271 p.
　A general biography, intended for the non-specialist.

Mackey, Louis. *Kierkegaard: A Kind of Poet.* Philadelphia: University of Pennsylvania Press, 1971, 327 p.
　Examines a few of Kierkegaard's chief works "with a view not only to what they say but even more to how they say it." Mackey asserts that Kierkegaard disdains the "mechanical clatter of logical symbols, the abstemious oneupmanship of language analysis, or the jejune solemnities of the epoché"; in contrast, he poetically unites dialectic and rhetoric to produce "imaginative and affective comprehension."

Nelson, Benjamin. "Preface to the Torchbook Edition." In *The Point of View for My Work as an Author: A Report to History, and Related Writings,* pp. vii-xviii, by Søren Kierkegaard, translated by Walter Lowrie, edited by Benjamin Nelson. New York: Harper & Row, 1962.
　Insists on the centrality of *The Point of View* to any analysis and understanding of Kierkegaard's works. Nelson

states that Kierkegaard's writings utilize the "psychological warfare" deemed necessary to "dislodge his contemporaries from their havens of self-satisfaction and indifference."

Norris, Christopher. "De Man Unfair to Kierkegaard? An Allegory of (Non-) Reading." *(Dis)continuities: Essays on Paul De Man,* pp. 199-239, edited by Luc Herman, Kris Humbeeck, and Geert Lernout. Postmodern Studies 2, edited by Theo D'haen and Hans Bertens. Amsterdam: Rodopi, 1989.
　Discusses Kierkegaard's attempt to employ romantic irony to achieve a "language of authentic inwardness and truth." Norris states that trends in deconstructionist criticism suggest that "romantic irony cannot in the end measure up to those demands placed upon language and narrative by the need for ethical self-knowledge."

Pederson, Bertel. "Fictionality and Authority: A Point of View for Kierkegaard's Work as an Author." *MLN* 89, No. 6 (December 1974): 938-56.
　Maintains that Kierkegaard, in explanation of his work, paradoxically admits only partial comprehension of the writing process yet sketches the total design of the pseudonymous works. Pederson asserts that this fact underscores the fundamental complexity of authorship.

Percy, Walker. "The Message in the Bottle." *Thought* XXXIV, No. 134 (Autumn 1959): 405-33.
　Asserts that Kierkegaard's understanding of faith as the "Absolute Paradox" is erringly founded on the Hegelian/scientific conception of knowledge. Percy states that the Hegelian/scientist mistakenly values only knowledge *sub specie aeternitatis,* "knowledge which can be arrived at anywhere by anyone at any time," thereby dismissing the nonuniversal knowledge implicit in faith.

Perkins, Robert L. Review of *Two Ages: The Age of Revolution and the Present Age. Thought* LIV, No. 215 (December 1979): 441-43.
　Finds *Two Ages* to be valuable as a work of cultural analysis and states that the work is "eminently important now that we are in a period of questioning our political, economic, and social assumptions."

Perkins, Robert L., ed. *International Kierkegaard Commentary: "The Concept of Anxiety."* Macon, Ga.: Mercer University Press, 1985, 203 p.
　Collection of essays about Kierkegaard's *The Concept of Anxiety.*

Pletsch, Carl. "The Self-Sufficient Text in Nietzsche and Kierkegaard." *Yale French Studies* No. 66 (1984): 160-88.
　Asserts that Kierkegaard's *The Point of View for My Work as an Author* and Nietzsche's *Ecce Homo,* autobiographical literary interpretations of the respective authors' works, usurp the role of the reader through self-sufficient deconstruction of the authors' texts independent of any readership.

Poole, Roger, and Stangerup, Henrik, eds. *The Laughter Is on My Side: An Imaginative Introduction to Kierkegaard.* Princeton, N.J.: Princeton University Press, 1989, 245 p.
　Collection of "some of the best texts of Kierkegaard—not the heavy, 'Hegelianized,' incomprehensible texts, but the early, lighter, witty ones of the 1840s." The work was originally intended for Danish readership, which is described as "resentful" toward Kierkegaard.

Reinhold, H. A. "Søren Kierkegaard." *The Commonweal* XXXV, No. 25 (10 April 1942): 608-11.

> Outlines the religious import of Kierkegaard's thought and states that Kierkegaard "throws a new light on faith and its totalitarian all-pervasiveness of life."

Robinson, Fred Miller. "The Word Became Pork: Kierkegaard, Freud and Joke-Work." *Thalia* IX, No. 1 (Spring / Summer 1986): 31-5.

> Focuses on Kierkegaard's insistence that the workings of the comic be brought to consciousness and on Freud's belief that jokes allow us pleasure in overcoming inhibition about blasphemy and nonsense. Robinson asserts that, once understood, the comic is "a signal of and guidepost to our sympathies as much as our prejudices."

Salvatore, Anne. "Socratic Midwifery: Greene and Kierkegaard." *College Literature* 12, No. 1 (1985): 26-32.

> Perceives a common dialectical method in some works of Kierkegaard and Graham Greene. The authors present " 'oppositional' perspectives" that allow the reader to visualize possibilities, think in terms of alternatives, and rely on one's judgment.

Sartre, Jean-Paul. "Kierkegaard: The Singular Universal." In his *Between Existentialism and Marxism,* pp. 141-69, translated by John Matthews. London: NLB, 1974.

> Discusses Kierkegaard's view of paradox as a fundamental aspect of human experience and as an essential component of Kierkegaard's thought.

Schleifer, Ronald, and Markley, Robert, eds. *Kierkegaard and Literature: Irony, Repetition, and Criticism.* Norman: University of Oklahoma Press, 1984, 224 p.

> Collection of poststructuralist critical essays comprising polemical views of Kierkegaard's own work and Kierkegaardian interpretations of *Piers Plowman, The Plain Dealer, Walden,* and *The Mill on the Floss.*

Shilstone, Frederick. "Byron, Kierkegaard, and the Irony of Rotation." *Colby Library Quarterly* XXV, No. 4 (December 1989): 237-44.

> Maintains that Kierkegaard's romantic, ironic concept of rotation mirrors Byron's ironic concept of *mobilité.* Shilstone notes that Romanticism, of which Byron was perhaps the leading representative, gave rise to modernism as prefigured by Kierkegaard.

Smyth, John Vignaux. "Part 2: Kierkegaard." In his *A Question of Eros: Irony in Sterne, Kierkegaard, and Barthes,* pp. 101-259. Tallahassee: Florida State University Press, 1986.

> Explores Kierkegaard's "theory of irony," focusing on his first book, *The Concept of Irony.*

Solomon, Robert C. "Søren Kierkegaard: Faith and the Subjective Individual." In his *From Rationalism to Existentialism: The Existentialists and Their Nineteenth-Century Backgrounds,* pp. 69-103. New York: Harper & Row, 1972.

> Outlines and analyzes Kierkegaard's philosophy, noting the relation of his thought to the ideas of Kant and Hegel.

Sussman, Henry. "Søren Kierkegaard and the Allure of Paralysis." In his *The Hegelian Aftermath: Readings in Hegel, Kierkegaard, Freud, Proust, and James,* pp. 63-158. Baltimore, Md.: The Johns Hopkins University Press, 1982.

> Argues that Kierkegaard's entire production reflects a paralysis that results from the reduction of a continuous Hegelian dialectical development to a "single dialectical cell governed by the logic of *Either / Or*": "On the thematic level, the notions of fear and trembling, dread, and despair all describe the emotional states accompanying situations of unresolvable duality."

Taylor, Mark C. *Kierkegaard's Pseudonymous Authorship: A Study of Time and the Self.* Princeton, N.J.: Princeton University Press, 1975, 391 p.

> Examines how the pseudonymous writings form a consistent body of work anchored by the role of individual faith.

Thulstrup, Niels, and Thulstrup, Marie Mikulová, eds. *Concepts and Alternatives in Kierkegaard.* Copenhagen, Denmark: C. A. Reitzels Boghandel, 1980, 297 p.

> Thirty-seven essays examine various motifs in Kierkegaard's philosophy including communication, the irrational, paradox, the role of repetition, humanity, and existence.

Unamuno, Miguel. "Ibsen and Kierkegaard." In his *Perplexities and Paradoxes,* pp. 51-7, translated by Stuart Gross. New York: Philosophical Library, 1945.

> Finds that Kierkegaard's impassioned, noble brand of individualism was adopted by Ibsen and espoused in his works. Unamuno refers to Kierkegaard as Ibsen's "spiritual father" and "master."

Ussher, Arland. "Kierkegaard: The Shudder before God." In his *Journey through Dread,* pp. 19-58. London: Darwen Finlayson, 1955.

> Focuses on Kierkegaard's reaction against Hegel's abstract philosophical system, which Kierkegaard faulted as lacking concrete ties to human experience. Ussher finds that Kierkegaard was less theoretical and more passionate than Hegel, yet notes that his philosophy has an abstract, mystical quality.

Watson, Richard. "The Seducer and the Seduced." *The Georgia Review* 39, No. 2 (Summer 1985): 353-66.

> Discusses the psychology of those involved in seduction and argues that Kierkegaard allowed himself to be seduced by the potential reward of his relationship with God; the relationship elicited sacrifices with the promise of reward, but the sacrifices were never reciprocated.

Giuseppe Mazzini

1805-1872

Italian critic and political theorist.

Mazzini was a leading advocate of democracy and Italian unification in the mid-nineteenth century. Heavily influenced by the revolutionary sentiments that swept much of the Western world during the late eighteenth century, he championed the overthrow of monarchies and the establishment of democratic governments throughout Europe. For his native Italy, Mazzini proposed the abolition of the various monarchies that had claimed portions of the peninsula for centuries, the discontinuation of papal rule of certain territories, and the unification of the Italian people as a single, democratic republic. Although Mazzini was only one of a number of important proponents of Italian unification, his extensive writings and fervent advocacy served as a powerful impetus to the growing movement, which culminated in the creation of the modern state of Italy in 1870.

Born in Genoa, Mazzini was the only son of a prominent physician and his wife. Mazzini's father was an official in the short-lived Ligurian republic, which was established in the Genovese region in 1797 and dissolved when the area was annexed by Napoléon in 1805; he remained an observer of European politics and a clandestine reader of suppressed liberal newspapers. Mazzini's mother, also actively interested in European politics, presided over progressive salons which assembled frequently and informally in the family's home. A frail and precocious child, Mazzini was tutored at home in Classical history and literature and began to study law at the University of Genoa when he was fourteen. Although an excellent student, he was more interested in politics and literature than in his legal studies, and he formed a society to smuggle in and discuss banned books. During this period he began to publish reviews and theoretical literary discussions in Italian periodicals.

After passing the bar examination at twenty-one, Mazzini began to perform free legal services for the Genovese poor and continued to publish literary articles, several in Italy's leading literary journal, the *Antologia*. Three years later he was invited to enter the Carbonari, a secret revolutionary society inspired by the French Revolution and dedicated to overthrowing the monarchies that had reassumed power in Europe following Napoléon's final defeat in 1815. The Carbonari had diminished in effectiveness by the time Mazzini joined, and, eager to catalyze genuine change, he began to formulate a doctrine and consolidate a faction to realize his goals. In 1830 the Genovese government arrested him for conspiracy. During the six month imprisonment that followed, he refined the creed that became the foundation of La Giovana Italia (Young Italy), his alternative to the Carbonari.

Exiled from Italy upon his release from prison, Mazzini settled in Marseilles, recruiting members for Young Italy

and smuggling its journal back into Italy. When the French government banished him in 1832, he moved to Geneva, where he founded a pro-republican society, Young Switzerland, and a journal to popularize its views. Broadening his scope, Mazzini next inaugurated Young Europe. In 1837 the French government, concerned by Mazzini's increasingly international agenda, pressured Switzerland to banish him, whereupon he moved to London.

Although he continued to venture onto the Continent and even into Italy under assumed names, Mazzini considered England his home for the next forty years. He was initially destitute, but the literary articles—on such figures as Victor Hugo, Alphonse Lamartine, Thomas Carlyle, Dante, and Hughes de Lamennais—he published in English periodicals supplied him with a meager income. In 1839 he resumed his political work, founding an association to enhance the political awareness of London's working-class Italian immigrants, a school for their children, and a newspaper that addressed the Italian proletariat. The numerous pamphlets and letters he wrote during this time advocating the establishment of democratic republics were sent to prospective converts and confirmed agents throughout Europe and the Americas. "I am everywhere," he wrote, "like the Deity." Between 1847 and 1848, the revolutionary sentiments Mazzini had helped to promote from abroad produced a series of sometimes-violent insurrections throughout Europe and resulted in the establishment of independent republics in Naples, Tuscany, Venice, and Rome. Returning to Italy, Mazzini was elected to the Triumvirate which, in 1849, became the executive branch of the newly-established Republic of Rome. However, France and Austria overthrew the Roman republic within months, and he was forced to return to England in 1850. In London, Mazzini resumed his work as a propagandist, traveling to Italy whenever he saw the opportunity to foment insurrection. Increasingly persuaded that the involvement of the working class was crucial to realizing his goals, he spent the final years of his life attempting to school its members in the liberties due them, and in the civic duties that ensued, in his view, from such liberties. He died in Pisa in 1872.

Devout religious beliefs were the underpinnings and orientation of Mazzini's political creed. Convinced that the papacy had been discredited by its ongoing association with corrupt aristocracies and monarchies, he refused to term himself a Catholic. Yet he retained his belief in the existence of a deity and viewed the democratization of government as part of the divine plan for the moral and spiritual improvement of humanity. As a result, Mazzini rejected the exaltation of individual rights inherent in much revolutionary philosophy, emphasizing instead the duty of each citizen to actively aid in the furtherance of the divine plan.

This decree entails obligations for both individual citizens and the states they comprise. According to Mazzini, citizens must accept as their highest duty the participation in their nations' moral advancement. States must distribute wealth, property, and industry equitably so that all citizens are liberated from the physically debilitating and spiritually enervating concerns of poverty, and are thus enabled to assume their civic responsibilities. Mazzini favored nationalizing church lands, aristocratic estates, and major industries and argued that the state must standardize education, so that young people could be imbued with an orientation toward the moral good in numbers sufficient to facilitate its achievement. He also regarded both literature and music as instruments for upgrading the moral tenor of human life. He favored writers and composers in whose works he could discern this aim, and dismissed those in whose works it seemed irrelevant. Spiritual progress was Mazzini's absolute and all-encompassing goal. This emphasis on individual and collective moral duty distinguished him from those who advocated other forms of republican government. Utilitarianism, he thought, defined progress in exclusively material terms. Similarly, socialism and communism sought material benefits as ends in themselves. He favored democratic republics because he deemed the consensus achieved through universal suffrage most likely to discover and enact the divine plan—which transcended national borders. Although he endorsed all nationalist movements that came to his attention (primarily those in Europe), Mazzini saw universal suffrage and national self-determination as a means rather than an end: once established, democratic nations could then form harmonious international associations to morally improve humanity. This international cooperation was, in Mazzini's view, the most effective means to the most important end.

Mazzini has been dismissed as an impractical absolutist. His detractors maintain that he was far more idealistic than the Italian people on whose behalf he claimed to be waging his campaign for national liberation and unification. They also claim that he was unwilling to compromise with the moderate politicians who advocated a less radical transition from absolute to constitutional monarchy, the form of government under which Italy was eventually unified. Despite these criticisms, Mazzini is credited with providing a necessary spiritual stimulus for the Italian unification campaign. Historians concur that he catalyzed and sustained the movement that, under the subsequent aegis of the diplomats he despised, eventually culminated in Italian unity.

PRINCIPAL WORKS

Dell'amor patrio di Dante (essay) 1826
Filosofia della musica (essay) 1836
Byron e Goethe (essay) 1847
   [*Byron and Goethe* in *Essays: Selected from the Writings, Literary, Political, and Religious of Joseph Mazzini*, 1887]
I doveri dell'uomo (essay) 1860
   [*The Duties of Man*, 1862]
Life and Writings of Joseph Mazzini. 6 vols. (autobiography and essays) 1864-70
Essays by Joseph Mazzini (essays and letter) 1894
Scritti editi ed inediti. 100 vols. (autobiography, letters, essays, and criticism) 1906-43
Mazzini's Letters to an English Family. 3 vols. (letters) 1920-22
Mazzini's Letters (letters) 1930

C. E. Maurice (essay date 1867)

[*In the following excerpt, Maurice cites the personal experiences, historical events, and intellectual influences that shaped Mazzini's political convictions. Maurice also maintains that Mazzini was in fact a pragmatic theorist, and asserts that he was an insightful critic of both drama and epic poetry, despite his disregard for technical analysis.*]

The purely autobiographical element in [*The Life and Writings of Joseph Mazzini*] is, indeed, comparatively small; for Mazzini tells us in his preface that he has often declined writing his life, and that it is now only the public part of it that he gives to the world; as his purposes develop, too, he becomes so absorbed in his work that he almost ceases to have any private life; but, in the earlier part of his book, we have a clear view both of those circumstances which first turned his thoughts to that work, and of others that have given it that peculiar colouring which distinguishes it from similar efforts of other men.

The scene with which the volume opens is a fit preparation for such a book. He is walking with his mother on the Strada Nuova at Genoa, just after the failure of the Piedmontese Insurrection in 1821. The leaders of that insurrection are embarking for Spain; "a tall, black-bearded man, with a severe, energetic countenance, and a glance that I shall never forget," accosts Mazzini's mother, and demands money for the refugees of Italy. "This day," he continues, "was the first in which a confused idea presented itself to my mind, I will not say of country or liberty, but an idea that we Italians could, and therefore ought to, struggle for the liberty of our country." . . . I began collecting names and facts, and studied as best I might the records of that heroic struggle, seeking to fathom the causes of its failure. He makes acquaintance with the Ruffinis and others who like him are grieving over the wrongs of their country. The influences of his parents, too, encourage this direction of his thoughts. But the path to political action appeared for the present to be closed to him, and he began to turn his thoughts to literature, and even to have thoughts of devoting himself to it as a profession. Strange to say, however, this pursuit was the means of leading him back to the work which he had half thought of abandoning for it. A literary war was then raging between the "Romanticists" and "Classicists," the latter desiring to reduce all writings to the pattern of the old classical authors, the former trying to develop a more original and modern type of literature. Both parties seemed to Mazzini to have lost sight of their true mission. With the Classicists, of course, he had no sympathy; but even of the Romanticists he says that they,

> founding their new literature on no other basis than individual fancy, lost themselves in fantastic mediæval legends, unfelt hymns to the Virgin, and unreal metrical despair, or any other whim of the passing hour which might present itself to their minds, intolerant of every tyranny, but ignorant also of the sacredness of the law which governs art as well as every other thing.

Yet in this trifling he sees the possibility of higher things. The Romanticist school represents to him the struggle, however imperfectly understood, for national literary life against the fetters of a worn-out pedantry. Taken up in this spirit, it soon widens into a protest against all hindrances to national life. The Government suppresses the *Indicatore Genoese,* in which his articles appear. A new journal is started at Leghorn on the same principle; that too is suppressed, and for a time Mazzini's literary career is brought to an end. But by this time he has collected round him a number of friends who, like himself, have been only using this literary warfare as a preparation for political action; now they feel that their testimony has done its work. "We had proved to the young men of Italy that our Governments were deliberately adverse to all progress, and that liberty was impossible till they were overthrown."

The next step in his career was perhaps the only possible one to a man who was earnestly bent on the object which he had in view. Association, which he afterwards preached as the duty of nations, he then, as now, held strongly to be the duty of individuals. But besides this, a special longing to obey and follow seems to have possessed him. "Reverence for righteous and true authority, freely recognised and accepted, is the best safeguard against authority false or usurped. I therefore agreed to join the Carbonari."

But, with all this eager reverence for authority, Mazzini was not disposed to be a mere puppet in the hands of men of whose purposes he knew nothing; he desired to be led, but he wished also to see the way on which he was to go. The utter aimlessness of Carbonarism disgusted him; its useless forms excited his contempt. He thus speaks of one of the ceremonies of initiation:—

> My friend——congratulated me on the fact that circumstances had spared me the tremendous ordeals usually undergone; and, seeing me smile at this, he asked me severely what I should have done if I had been required, as others had been, to fire off a pistol in my ear which had previously been loaded before my eyes. I replied that I should have refused, telling the initiators that either there was some valve in the interior of the pistol into which the bullet fell, in which case the affair was a farce unworthy of both of us; or the bullet remained in the stock, and, in that case, it struck me as absurd to call upon a man to fight for his country, and make it his first duty to blow out the few brains that God had vouchsafed him.

His complaints reach the ears of the heads of the Carbonari, and he is threatened; in a moment of indignation he thinks of defying the order; but his friends urge on him that he "was thus unconsciously sacrificing the cause of his country to his own offended individuality," and he submits for a time.

But the suspicions of the Government fall on him; by the trick of a spy he is sufficiently compromised to afford ground for an arrest; and he is shortly afterwards conveyed to the fortress of Savona. Here it was that he first conceived that great work to which he afterwards devoted himself. Not Carbonarism only, but every other organization for revolutionary purposes, had failed for want of an *aim.* They had never looked beyond the immediate object, the throwing off the tyranny which was at that time oppressing them. This seemed to Mazzini the great evil which he had to remedy. The society which he had to found must have a clear object, and must know what that object was. The rights of man had been the formula of the past; the salvation of the individual its object. Whatever worth that cry might have had in former days, it had failed of the object at which it aimed. The duties of man must be the gospel of Young Italy; "God and the People" its watchword.

This feeling was strengthened in Mazzini by his intercourse with Lamennais, which led him to hope that even the priests of the established religion of his country might accept his programme. Thus he appeals to them in one passage:—

> Priests of my country, would you save the Christian Church from inevitable dissolution? Would you cause religion to endure strong in its own beauty and the veneration of mankind? Place

yourselves at the head of the peoples, and lead them on the path of progress, aid them to regain their liberty and independence from the foreigner; the Austrian that enslaves both you and them. Have not you, too, a country, and the hearts of citizens? Do you not love your fellowmen? Emancipate them and yourselves. Remember that a priest led the hosts of the Lombard League to the rebuilding of Milan, destroyed by the German soldiery. Do you in turn guide the hosts of the Italian League to plant the banner of Italian freedom upon our Alps. This land, now trampled under the foot of the Teuton, God created free. Obey the decree of God. Raise the war-cry of Julius II. Your voice has power over the multitude. Use your power to restore to your native land the grandeur of which her oppressors have bereft her, to obtain the full and free exercise of their rights for your fellowmen; to found a new pact of alliance between yourselves and the peoples, between liberty and the Church. Priests of my country, the first among you who, warned by the dangers of the approaching European epoch, shall dare to raise his glance from the Vatican to God, and receive his message and inspiration from Him alone, the first among you who shall consecrate himself the apostle of humanity and hearken to its voice; who, strong in the purity of a stainless conscience, shall go forth among the hesitating and uncertain multitude and utter the word RE-FORM, will save Christianity, reconstitute European unity, extinguish anarchy, and put the seal to a lasting alliance and concord between society and the priesthood. But, if no such voice be raised before the hour of common resurrection has sounded, then God save you from the anger of the peoples, for terrible is the anger of the peoples, and your sole path of salvation is the one we have offered you.

This then was to be the basis of the programme of the new society,—duty instead of right, the society instead of the individual. But it was not merely the absolute excellence of this programme that led Mazzini to adopt it, it was not merely his religious feelings that made him aim at the destruction of selfishness; he looked upon it as a step in the development of the history of his country—of all countries. The great element in the education of his countrymen which seemed to him to have been most neglected, and yet to be the one most requiring attention, was "history." Some had written from the aristocratic point of view, others from the Ghibelline, some without any definite aim at all, none with a clear sense of the *mission* of Italy. With Sismondi he has more sympathy than with most of the others, but even of him he says,

> Sismondi—the only foreign writer upon Italy who deserves the name of an historian— notwithstanding his democratic sympathies, and his long and patient study of his subject, has only given us the history of our factions, and the virtues, vices, and ambitions of our illustrious families; without comprehending or suspecting the work of fusion (recognised, indeed, though but slightly indicated by Romagna) that was silently but uninterruptedly going on in the heart of the country.

This, then, was the second great historical error which must be amended by the new society. They were to preach their duties to Italians, not to teach them to clamour for their individual rights, and these duties were to be done by them as an united nation. How then was this union to be brought about? King-made revolutions had failed; the rivalry of the petty states would not allow an individual chosen from one of them to be put above the others; for an aristocracy united with the people there seemed to be no hope from the history of Italy. The new society, then, must proclaim a republic as its object. But a new question presented itself: If men have duties to each other as citizens of a nation, must not the nations which they form also have duties to each other? If they have duties to each other as children of God, can those duties be limited by geographical boundaries? "From the first moment of its existence," he says, " 'God and Humanity' was adopted as the formula of the association with regard to its external relations, while 'God and the People' was that chosen in its relations to our own country."

The subtle question of how far patriotism is a virtue, how far only a wider form of selfishness, is perhaps more nearly, certainly more practically, solved by Mazzini than by any political writer we remember. "Nationality," in a passage we quote below, he calls "the conscience of the peoples." It does not, in his opinion, narrow the sympathies of mankind, but makes them more genuine and definite. With the vague cosmopolitanism of the leaders of the first French Revolution he has no sympathy: their form of propagandism is opposed to all his creed; for he would call out the voluntary union of the peoples, not set those who sympathised with his doctrines in opposition to the rest. For he sees that this part of the old revolutionary doctrine was essentially connected with their doctrine of the Rights of Man, against which he especially protests. "For us," he says, "the starting-point is country: the object or aim is collective humanity: for those who call themselves cosmopolitans the *aim* may be humanity: but the starting-point is individual man."

Starting, then, from this point of "country," he yet denounces vehemently the mere glorification of national peculiarities. In an article which he wrote whilst still a Carbonaro, **"On Our European Literature,"** he protests most indignantly against this error in literary theories, and he is evidently thinking there of the political and moral question also. In this article he labours to refute the mere physical theory of literature, the theory, that is, which ascribes the formation of special literary tastes to differences of climate; a doctrine which he protests against as appealing to national exclusiveness. "Every attempt," he says, "to open up new paths to literary intelligence, and every exhortation to study the master works of other nations, is opposed and met by dulcet phrases about 'our classic soil' and 'the Italian sky;' phrases too readily accepted as an answer by those whose patriotism is satisfied with words alone."

But the view which the new society was to take of this question of the relations of nations to each other must be summed up in his own words:—

> We believe, therefore, in the Holy Alliance of the Peoples, as being the vastest formula of associa-

tion possible in our epoch; in the liberty and equality of the peoples, without which no true association can exist; in nationality, which is the conscience of the peoples, and which, by assigning to them their part in the work of association, their function in humanity, constitutes their mission upon earth, their individuality, without which neither liberty or equality are possible: in the sacred Fatherland, cradle of nationality; altar and workshop of the individuals of which it is composed.

Such, then, is a brief outline of the programme of the new society of which Mazzini now first conceived the idea. We know that many, if not most, Englishmen are apt to suppose Mazzini as a wild dreamer, and essentially unpractical; yet we think that, if foresight for the future, adaptation of means to ends, and study of facts, constitute practicality, the founder of the New Italy must be allowed some claim to that quality. There is, at the same time, a logical basis to his doctrine of the duties of man which distinguishes him from those who are even now preaching it in a somewhat different form. Bravely and nobly as the Comtists have maintained their high creed, there is something vague and unsatisfactory about their notion of humanity which makes it rather "too fine for working-days." Mazzini's sense of a mission from above, his war-cry of "God and the People," supplies a deficiency which those who most desire to sympathise with the efforts of the Comtists must always feel; a deficiency which may lead some people to the most unjust conclusion that their connexion of morality with politics is a mere adventitious part of their scheme, not, as it evidently is with Mazzini, a necessary foundation for the whole.

Nor is it only in the larger and wider sense that Mazzini's programme is practical. In the more conventional use of the word, as a mere condescension to details, "practicality" is one of its prominent characteristics. The following will at once interest and surprise many Englishmen.

> To the State, since justice is equal for all citizens, belongs the unity of the judicial organization of the country, the code, the appointment of judges of the supreme courts, and the magistrates who direct the administration of justice; the communes will elect local juries and the members of tribunals of arbitration and commerce. The State will determine the amount of the national tribute, and its distribution over the various zones of the territory; the communes, under the direction of the State, will determine all local tributes, and also the method of levying national tribute.

The opportunity of developing his idea was soon to come. No sooner was Mazzini freed from prison, and acquitted by the judges for want of evidence, than he once more plunged into political action. The Italian Revolution of 1831 had just broken out, and he crossed over to France, to rouse his countrymen who were there in exile. Here it was that he discovered one of the great errors against which he afterwards most strongly protested. France was to the Italians of that day what Egypt was to the Jews of the days of Jeremiah; and, though indignant at this almost servile trust in a foreign country, Mazzini was inclined at first to sympathise with the feeling which his friends exaggerated.

But a rude shock was soon given to these hopes. Louis Philippe forbad the expedition which Mazzini and his friends were then organizing to Savoy, seized upon all their arms on which he could lay hands, and threatened them with the terrors of the law if they persisted. Mazzini urged on them to continue the expedition, putting among them as many of the French workmen as possible. But the Frenchmen deserted them on an appeal from their officers, and the expedition was abandoned. A short attempt to raise the standard of liberty and truth in Corsica was frustrated by the selfishness of the Bolognese Government, and Mazzini retired to Marseilles to carry out the ideas which he had conceived in the fortress of Savona.

From this time, therefore, dates Mazzini's position as a leader and initiator. Hitherto he had been but one of a large body of men who were struggling by fits and starts for the liberty of their country. Now, as the founder of the Giovane Italia, he was to be the centre and life of a great organized effort, not merely for the freedom and unity, but for the entire regeneration, of Italy, and, if the opportunity should offer, of Europe. One more attempt, however, he made to reconcile his aspirations, to some extent, with the existing institutions of his country. This was the famous letter to Charles Albert, urging on him to ally himself with the popular movement to work out Italian independence and unity. It ends thus:—"Sire, I have spoken to you the truth. The men of freedom await your answer in your deeds. Whatsoever that answer be, rest assured that posterity will either hail your name as that of the greatest of men, or of the last of Italian tyrants. Take your choice." The king accepted the challenge in full, and the first proof of that acceptance was the banishment of Mazzini. Thus finally free to work out his idea, and endeared to the youth of Italy by his sufferings in their cause, Mazzini began vigorously to preach the doctrines which he saw to be then needful for his countrymen. In the sketch which we gave above of the principles on which the Giovane Italia was founded, we alluded chiefly to those evils which, though specially perceived by Mazzini in Italy, were, as he knew, common to all countries in a transitional state. The adoration of France, which we mentioned first, was however a more peculiarly Italian failing. This he traced to two causes—their materialism and their Machiavellianism. For their "idolatry of material interests" he would substitute his faith in God and his doctrine of duty, for their belief in mere cunning diplomacy, his appeal to the people. The enemies, therefore, of the Giovane Italia in every country were the "Moderate" party—those, that is, who, trusting to diplomatic measures without any definite faith of their own, were ready to accept any programme that occasion offered. This party was now at the head of affairs in France where the head-quarters of the Giovane Italia were laid, and they soon began an active persecution against that society and its founder. Unable to enforce the decree of banishment, which in deference to Charles Albert (who had now entirely thrown off the mask, and was showing the true cruelty of his nature), had been issued against them: unable too in any way either to seize the persons or suppress the writings of the society, the French

Government resorted to the meaner and safer weapon of slander. Story after story was invented of the secret doings of the society; again and again Mazzini compelled his enemies to eat their words, and again and again the calumnies were renewed. As Mazzini justly says, "It is the war of cowards, for it is fought without peril, and beneath the shield of power; it silences defence by violence, and takes advantage even of the disdainful silence of the accused to give force to the calumny."

But, in spite of slanders and persecutions, Young Italy laboured on. A journal was started, called after the society, and in this Mazzini and his friends wrote some of their most stirring appeals to their countrymen. Other societies became absorbed in theirs, and amongst them the remains of the Carbonari. Founded, too, by exiles in a foreign country, the possibilities of an alliance with similar societies in other countries were greater, and a union with the Poles, which has ever been one of the chief objects of the sympathies of Italian republicans, was now first begun. In Italy, too, the cruelties of Charles Albert and the other princes had bound together all lovers of liberty, and many who afterwards joined the Moderate party were now in sympathy with the Giovane Italia. At length they once more prepared for action. An army was raised. Armand Carrel and other French republicans prepared to act simultaneously in France. An accident betrayed their plans. The Governments managed by false reports to excite a dread of their intentions. Many were seized and imprisoned; a few recanted; many were condemned to death, and some executed. Jacopo Ruffini committed suicide.

Roused still more by this partial failure, Mazzini at once urged his friends to march on Savoy. The guidance of the expedition was entrusted to Ramozino, a Polish general, strongly against the wishes of Mazzini; but he gave way as usual, and joined the band as a simple soldier. Ramozino appears to have been half fool, half traitor. A failure in the early part of the expedition decided him to desert it at the first pinch; the Italians, alone and unaided, were defeated, and forced to take refuge in Switzerland. So ended the first attempt at action. "The first period of Young Italy," says Mazzini, "was concluded."

The rest of the historical part of these volumes is devoted to the sufferings of the exiles in Switzerland; Mazzini's escape to England, and sojourn there; the infamous episode of the opening of his letters by Sir James Graham; an interesting notice of Mazzini's education of the poor Italian organ-grinders; and a short account of the sad, though noble, effort of the brothers Bandiera. The better-known portion of his life is left for the remaining three volumes, which are not yet published in English.

Before closing this review, however, we must take some notice of the second of these volumes, to which we have very incidentally alluded, and which contains his critical and literary writings. Perhaps the literary efforts of one whose thoughts on every subject are so deeply tinged by his political feeling may be expected to have little interest for the generality of readers; but we think there are some things in this volume well worthy their study. For the mere critical faculty, indeed, of pulling things to pieces, and finding small holes in great works, Mazzini's genius

is eminently unfitted. "Analysis" is the name with which he always condemns the spirit most opposed to the gospel which he preaches. "Synthesis," construction, are his objects; and the circumstances under which he has fought for them have made him perhaps unduly impatient of the literary form of this analysis, and possibly even of the kind of ability displayed in it. Writings and men he considers more as wholes than in detail, and with reference rather to the greatness of the aim and idea than the special grace or delicacy of the means. The cry of "art for art's sake" he denounces as "a false French doctrine." But, though this state of mind may incapacitate him for giving judgment on those kinds of poetry or prose that rest their claim to our admiration purely on their external artistic excellence; yet at the same time, with the greater epic poets, and still more with the dramatists, it brings him into a sympathy, and therefore gives him an insight into their works, which no merely literary critic could have. Take, for instance, the following passage on Æschylus:—

> One might fancy that his heroes were of Titanic race, and only to be overcome by unyielding, omnipotent, and inexorable fatality. But when he felt the soul of the Greek world, liberty, thrill within him, when he remembered having fought at Salamis against the East, and shed his blood in the cause of the European principle against the inertia and servitude imposed by Asia; he protested against and denied the empire of that fatality which from the height of its mysteries and theogony yet dominated his country.

Or, again, this on Shakespeare:—

> His genius comprehends and sums up the past and present; it does not initiate the future. Necessity, which was the soul of the period, stalks invisibly throughout his dramas, magically introduced, whether by art or instinct I know not. I know that its reflex is seen alike on the brow of Othello and Macbeth; it colours the scepticism of Hamlet and the light irony of Mercutio, and it surrounds with a halo of provisioned woe the figures of his women, sacred to love, innocence and resignation.

Again:—

> In Æschylus the individual is divorced from his will; the decree of fatality goes forth while it yet sleeps in his mother's arms; the curse on the father extends to the children, and the only liberty vouchsafed to man is that of dying more or less nobly. In Shakespeare—and this is a real progress—liberty does exist; the acts of a single day, it may be of an hour, have thrown an entire life under the dominion of necessity, but in that day or that hour the man was free, and arbiter of his own future.

Nor is it solely the idea that he admires: when that is present he can admire all its settings and circumstances, and appreciate the distinction between the beauties of rival poets. Thus:—

> In reading Æschylus, the mind is clouded with an ill-defined melancholy. Even when he sounds a hymn of victory over the barbarians, you yet feel within you a sense of that hidden and myste-

rious sadness which ever reveals itself to minds capable of understanding it, in the smallest words of great and prophetic souls;

and yet more in this on Shakespeare:—

> The individual is everything to him, and in the art of depicting a character with a few master-strokes, Dante, Tacitus, Michael Angelo, are his only rivals. He does not laboriously copy, he casts men whole in a single mould; he does not evoke, he creates. Shakespeare's personages live and move as if they had just come forth from the hands of God with a life that, though manifold, is one; though complex, harmonious.

But though he thus, in most of his reviews, subordinates his criticisms on the surrounding circumstances to those on the idea and aim of the poet, we see evidently that he has educated himself into his contempt of "art for art's sake," and that though, as we said, the critical faculty as it is now generally understood has been denied to him, yet the power of appreciating artistic beauty is strong within him, and it is only by careful repression that he keeps it down at all. That, at least, seems to us the natural explanation of the fact that the following passage was first produced, and then condemned to appear as a foot-note:—

> The comparison often instituted by critics between the three Greek dramatists is just, if regarded from an æsthetic point of view, but not so from the point of view of the conception or idea. Sophocles and Euripides are followers; Æschylus is the father of the art. The external representation of the idea is more masterly in them; their form is more graceful and delicate; they arose at a later period, when Greek civilization was greatly refined, and the already improved position of women caused them to exercise a greater influence on society. Sophocles painted, Æschylus sculptured, his forms of art. The strokes are few, but they are the skeleton of a world. Sophocles is the artist-poet, but Æschylus is the high-priest of art—the sacred art inspired by God Himself in all the majesty of those first revelations which initiate the entire series of its subsequent manifestations. I do not speak of Euripides, because, whatever the beauties of his works, there are in them affectations and adulterations of art that already indicate its decay.

(pp. 54-61)

C. E. Maurice, "Life and Writings of Joseph Mazzini," in MacMillan's Magazine, Vol. XVI, No. 91, May, 1867, pp. 54-61.

William Clarke   (essay date 1887)

[*In the following excerpt, Clarke explains Mazzini's belief that the French Revolution's emphasis on individual rights helped to destroy absolute monarchy, but that freely assumed collective duty would be necessary to create a new order.*]

No portion of Mazzini's teaching is more important than his criticism of the ideas summed up in the French Revolution. Mazzini regarded that event as the close, not the opening, of an epoch—the epoch of individual rights, which, after a period of chaos, was to be succeeded by the epoch of association, of collective life. The Revolution finally conquered for man those rights of the individual contended for by the Protestant Reformation, but it necessarily ends, according to Mazzini, in despotism. "When Napoleon, the most powerful *individual* of that period, arose, and, relying upon force, said *Yield*—the revolution gave way before him, and with the exception of a very few, all these men who had sworn to die, or live free, held their tongues, and giving in, sat upon the benches of the conservative senate, or upon the benches of the Institute. Has, then, this individualism done no good work? Yes; it is powerful to destroy, and it has burnt up shams and lies not a few. But Mazzini contends that it cannot create; the new birth can only proceed from the collective life. With Association goes Duty. The individual has hitherto struggled for his rights; he will now co-operate with his nation in the fulfilment of its mission, with the world in its development of the eternal law of progress. This law is regarded as the unfolding of the Divine will in which, as Mazzini's countryman Dante said, is man's peace. "The absence of a highest form of *Duty,* universally accepted, to which every one can appeal, little by little and imperceptibly accustoms people's minds to submission to accomplished *facts:* success becomes the sign of right, and *what is done* takes the place, in men's worship, of Truth." From this it may be seen that Mazzini is wholly opposed to the doctrine that man acts from mere considerations of self-interest. This doctrine, assumed by most economists and politicians as self-evident, but which is visibly losing its hold under the influence of moral teachers like Ruskin, is condemned by Mazzini as resulting in the despotism of authority when starting from the *collective* point of view, and "in the anarchy of animal propensities" when adopted from the *individual* point of view. In no case can it afford a foundation for any true society. "No, certainly," he writes,

> it was not to attain the ignoble and immoral *every one for himself* that so many great men, holy martyrs of thought, have shed, from epoch to epoch, from century to century, the tears of the soul, the sweat and blood of the body. Beings of devotedness and love, they laboured and suffered for something higher than the individual; for that Humanity which ought to be the object of all our efforts, and to which we are all responsible. Before a generation which scorned or persecuted them, they calmly uttered their prophetic thoughts, with an eye fixed on the horizon of future times; speaking to that *collective* being which ever lives, which ever learns, and in which the divine idea is progressively realised; for that city of the human race, which alone, by the association of all intellects, of all loves, and of all forces, can accomplish the providential design that presided over our creation here below.

Mazzini's lofty idealism, his religious spirit, and his constant insistence on duty rather than on rights, frequently brought him into antagonism with many of the revolutionists of Europe, who, while they applauded his struggle for Italy, were by no means animated by the same motives which controlled him. Foremost among these was the famous Russian anarchist, Bakounine who, from an atheistic standpoint, criticised severely the theological politics of Mazzini. Yet Bakounine, while opposing the thinker, admired the man. "If there is a man," he says in his pamphlet (written in 1871) *La Théologie politique de Mazzini et l'Internationale,* "universally respected in Europe, and who, during forty years of activity, uniquely devoted to the service of a great cause, has really merited this respect, it is Mazzini. He is incontestably one of the noblest and purest individualities of our age." Bakounine, like Mazzini, believed in association, but his conception of solidarity was very different from that of Mazzini. "The human species," says this Russian thinker, "like all other animal species, has inherent principles which are peculiarly its own, and all these principles sum themselves up, or reduce themselves, to a single principle which we call solidarity." This is a frank statement of the naturalistic view of man, who is thus regarded as one term of a series of phenomena, and whose desire for union is nothing more than a superior form of the gregarious instinct. This is very different from Mazzini's spiritual union, "his city of the human race," outside time and space.

Equally decisive was Mazzini's opposition to the older French Communism as preached by Proudhon, Fourier, and Enfantin. These doctrines were based, according to Mazzini, on the old and false notions of the rights and the personal gratification of the desires of the Ego; and if carried into practice, would lead either to despotism or anarchy. His attitude towards our current socialism would probably be somewhat different, for that is historical, and is connected with those democratic forms which he thought essential, and which were ignored by the older French Communists. Many Socialists appear to regard Mazzini as mainly interested in the mere political as distinguished from the social question. But this is hardly borne out by his writings, which contain a powerful diagnosis of the present social conditions. Thus he writes—

> And as it is impossible to dream of the moral and intellectual progress of the people without providing for its physical amelioration—as it is absurd to say *"Instruct yourself,"* to a man who is working for his daily bread from fourteen to sixteen hours a-day, or to tell him to *love* who sees nothing around him but the cold calculations of the speculator and the tyranny of the capitalist legislator—the social question was found inevitably grafted upon the question of political progress. Henceforward they could only be separated by destroying both.

And again in the **"Duties of Man"**—"At the present day—and this is the curse of our actual social economy—capital is the tyrant of labour." His economical ideal is thus defined—"Association—but to be administered with a truly republican fraternity by your own delegates, and from which you should be free to withdraw at your own discretion." There is no fundamental divergence between this teaching and that of the present day advocates of Socialism. But it may be admitted that Mazzini was not a great economist; and that his revolt against the present conditions of labour was rather of the heart than of the head, and that he did not fully perceive how those very conditions force on a class struggle even in republican communities like the United States. But if he did not fully

grasp the economical problem, at least Mazzini did not pretend, like so many, that that problem is to be solved by the preaching of morality. No doubt the problem of society is fundamentally a moral one; but then morality is not a metaphysical entity existing outside the real world. It is the expression of a harmonious condition of the individual and society in the actual world. And the charge brought against present economic arrangements is two-fold:—First, that they violate justice by depriving a portion of society of the full result of its labour; and second, that the physical and social conditions under which that portion lives prevent its members from properly developing their faculties, *i.e.,* prevent them from living a truly moral life. If these charges can be sustained, it is evident that the economic problem cannot possibly be separated from the moral problem. And this was undoubtedly Mazzini's view. His objection to a good deal of the Socialist teaching was, that it regarded the social problem as a *merely* economical question; whereas it is truly a human problem of which the economical question is only one factor, however important that factor may be. He thus states the problem in his essay on **"The War and the Commune"**—"The immediate aim of humanity is the harmonious development of all its faculties and forces towards the discovery and fulfilment of the moral law." The fulfilment of that law obviously involves justice in the economic relations of society; and just as obviously does it involve conditions favourable to the growth of every man's moral nature. For men cannot develop their characters in the air, but only in the real world of family life, of property, and of institutions. (pp. xxi-xxv)

> *William Clarke, in an introduction to* Essays: Selected from the Writings, Literary, Political, and Religious, of Joseph Mazzini, *edited by William Clarke, Walter Scott, 1887, pp. i-xxviii.*

John MacCunn   (essay date 1907)

[*In the following excerpt, MacCunn notes the centrality of religiously-motivated collective duty in Mazzini's concept of democracy.*]

All [Mazzini's] hopes for democracy were staked upon its rescue from materialism and secularism. We have his own words here: "On the day when democracy shall elevate itself to the position of a religious party it will carry away the victory, *not before.*" This was the task to which he dedicated his life, and he held to it with the same unfaltering faith and the same unwavering pertinacity with which he wrought for Italian freedom. He long meditated a book upon religion. It was to be his *magnum opus,* and he often chafed, as the years went on, that it was still left undone. But he might well have spared himself his self-reproaches. For, all his life through, he was writing on religion. Religion and politics were in his mind inseparable. To write on the one was to write on the other. Hence the glowing fervour of his phrase. Hence the sustained elevation of his appeal, coupling as it does even the homeliest duties with the loftiest motives. It is not politics as politics are usually written; it is a kind of oratorio in politics.

Nor had he the slightest doubt as to what above all other things was needed. It was a creed—a creed to be held not only by such as might in reflective hours wish to justify their motives to themselves, but to be as the pillar of fire by night and the pillar of cloud by day to radical reformers in the actual campaigns of politics. In this sense Mazzini believed in the need for dogma. Not Catholic dogma nor yet Protestant—for of both he was severely critical—yet dogma in the sense of a settled body of convictions as to the relation of men and nations to God, to which the spirit of leaders and followers alike might ever return for unfailing inspiration and refreshment. Of the possibility of such a creed he was supremely confident. He was prepared to formulate it himself. He even seemingly looked forward to the coming of a day when a new spiritual power would from a regenerated Rome formulate the new Faith for Italy and the world.

It is not within our scope to examine Mazzini's religious creed, and to test the grounds on which he held it. Philosophers and theologians will probably agree that he underrated the difficulties of construction. He was too rationalistic to lean on authority: he was not rationalistic enough to trust to reason when it took the form of metaphysical analysis, of which he had an impatience bordering on hatred. "We will sweep out all that stuff," was his significant remark about Hegelianism. He was a man of intuitions not of analysis. It was convictions he cared for, not inferences and ratiocinations. He is more akin here to Carlyle than to the philosophers. Be this, however, as it may, the point that concerns us here is that he was absolutely convinced that without a religious faith democracy was foredoomed to failure; and the question of interest is Why?

The answer lies in two convictions, upon both of which Mazzini is explicit to emphasis; the one, that nothing less than an unfaltering sense of duty can nerve and sustain the democratic citizen, the other that this consciousness of duty must stand or fall with a theistic faith. We must glance at these in turn.

There is a popular belief that democracy has much to give; and Mazzini shared it to the full. He was optimist enough to think that democracy carried in it the promise of honest livelihood and carefree home, of sound education and an unobstructed civic life, rich in many and varied forms of free association. But he also believed, if he believed anything, that it had in its hand a greater gift than these—the gift of the obligation to live, and if need be readily to die for one's country. Truly he was no preacher or promiser of smooth things to his generation. It startles us to read of the burdens which, in his own political career, he laid on the consciences of citizens. It was neither by mother's tears, nor friends' remonstrances that he could be for a moment stayed in sending young and ardent spirits upon missions which he knew meant death. It was not callousness—for he had one of the tenderest of hearts—nor was it recklessness, which was far from his conspiring and far-seeing mind. It was the settled conviction that failure and death intrepidly encountered are the really sanest and in the long run the most fruitful tribute to political duty. "Merciful," says Carlyle of him, in a startling conjunction of epithets, "merciful *and fierce*." For his own part, he ha-

bitually took his liberty and his life in his hands. And there was a memorable moment in his career, when in '49 the short-lived Roman Republic lay at the mercy of French bayonets, and when, as one of the triumvirs, he urged the Romans to prove to the world that "republics founded upon Faith and Duty neither yield nor capitulate, but die protesting."

This deification of Duty had as obverse a complete distrust of the democracy of Rights. Mazzini's fear for democracy was not the ordinary fear. The ordinary fear is that it will go too far; Mazzini's is that it will go not far enough, because it may rest fatally contented with the enjoyment of its rights. This is the warning that runs through the hortatory and passionate pages of **"The Duties of Man."** It was not that he undervalued civil and political rights. He knew well that these were fundamental conditions of all else. He was the last man to disparage the struggle for rights. But the pity of it was, and the danger, that the citizen, having got his rights, should fancy that this was all, and blindly think that rights were the end instead of, as in truth they are, only the beginnings of a true citizenship. What is the right of free utterance if a man have no word of sincerity or sense to utter? Or the right to worship God to him who shows no desire, either in churches or out of them, to worship anything? Or the right of property to the hewer of wood and drawer of water who can barely earn a subsistence? Or the right to vote to the citizen who is so corrupt that he sells it, or so indifferent that he uses it either not at all or with a deplorable levity? This is the line of thought that saturates Mazzini. He may not have done full justice to rights: he surely did not when he said that "men will not die for rights." It is not the less true that he knew how to value rights more than many from whose lips the word was never absent. For he saw, as only too many cannot see, that the winning of rights is but one of those half-victories which is a whole defeat, if the lesson be not learnt, that when a people has won its rights, it is then only for the first time in a position to begin effectively to do its duties. For there are two ways of teaching mankind to value their rights. The one is to speak to them of their wrongs, and to wake up within them that fury against injustice which is one of the most indestructible passions of the human heart. Nor is this a way unknown to Mazzini. If the Italy we know is another Italy than that of his youth, it is, in part at least, because Mazzini did not know how to spare a despot, whether in Church or in State. "Merciful and fierce." Yet it was not in this method that he reposed his trust, but in the more excellent way of lodging in the heart and imagination of the citizen an ideal of what he had it in him to achieve if only his just rights were given him. It is not rights, it is duties that is the really fundamental and quickening conception.

As with rights, so with interests. It has been said that Mazzini failed to do justice to Utilitarianism, and the fact need not be denied. His biographer tells us that there is no sign of his having read Mill. If he had, he would doubtless have done more justice to the utilitarian ideal which in so many points is like his own. Even in his handling of Bentham, against whom his attack is levelled, he never seems to realise the width of the gulf that parts the Benthamite, with his splendid devotion to the public good, from the fanatics of natural rights. Yet even his failures here serve all the better to illustrate the point. It was because he was so wholly out of sympathy with utilitarianism that he could not do justice to it, and the reason of his lack of sympathy was the conviction that the utilitarian appeal, resting as it does on hedonism, was inadequate to the sacrifices democracy demands. It was equally impotent, he thought, to evoke the spirit of sacrifice and to justify it. It is in vain, so runs his characteristic sum of the whole matter, to adjure mankind in the name of pleasure to die.

It is not to be denied that this criticism at any rate assails utilitarianism on a weak point. When Bentham said that the word *ought* ought to be expunged from the vocabulary of morals, he was certainly giving a hostage to his enemies. He was confirming their suspicion that the Benthamite appeals to Greatest Happiness were, after all, conditional. For were they not conditional upon the contingency that, by grace of nature or by operation of "the external sanctions," self-interest may come to take the form of benevolence. Even Mill, decisive though his divergence from Bentham is, leaves the call to self-sacrifice appropriate only to the select minority in whom social feeling has found favouring soil and needful nurture. There is, in strict logic, no room even in his gospel for those unconditional, those categorical appeals which, however hard to justify in theory, are the clamant practical necessities of reformers. It is, at any rate, in these appeals that Mazzini reposes all his trust. He has a horror of the utilitarian spirit of calculation and compromise. He thinks it would sap all unselfish and heroic effort. He has scant respect for the hypothetical heroism which will undertake difficult duties only under the guidance of political arithmetic. The one sufficient security lies for him in the clear line of duty absolutely without compromise, paltering, or shadow of turning. He would have *ought* and *can* as inseparably knit in the reformer's creed as in the ethics of Kant.

This is high and heroic doctrine. And we must now go on to add that, in Mazzini's eyes, it is likewise impossible doctrine if it does not rest upon a convinced theism. For Mazzini is not to be numbered among those to whom religious beliefs are more or less probably hypotheses or even needful moral postulates. His belief in God is not, as with Kant, a superstructure built on his belief in Duty. On the contrary, his gospel of Duty depends upon his faith in God. Hence his life-long aspiration and effort to make democracy theistic. For a godless democracy was, in his eyes, a democracy with the sinews of all dutiful and sacrificing effort cut.

This is, of course, a strong asseveration. It is not likely to pass unchallenged. And it will certainly be challenged by some in these latter days more than it was in Mazzini's lifetime, though even then he was to most but as a voice crying in the wilderness. For it cannot be said that, since Mazzini's day, democracy has moved towards theism. The drift has been towards "Darwinism in politics." Hence the growth of the conception that society must now be relegated to its place in the order of Nature as a slowly-evolved organism within which the struggle for existence between individuals and groups is checked and softened only by the exigencies of the larger struggle for existence between na-

tion and nation. No one is likely nowadays to deny that the conception has its measure of truth and its fascinations. Nor is it in the least to be wondered at that there are minds to whom it seems so satisfying that, in view of the experimented effectiveness of biological forces as judged by their existing social products, they are content to banish Divine plan in history and Final Causes in social evolution to that crowded limbo of discarded metaphysical figments to which naturalism and agnosticism are so willing, not to say eager, to consign everything that savours of theism.

Nor is this attitude the monopoly of the thinkers. The popular mind, so often prone to be new-fangled over new categories, has fallen in love with the categories of biology. It sees "struggle for existence" and "survival of the fittest" in the competitions, rivalries and conflicts of individuals, of trades, of parties, of nations, of ideals. It echoes the voices that declare society to be "an organism," and it listens to the tales that tell it how this organism has been evolved by the sheer *vis a tergo* of natural forces. So the leaven works. Will of God and plan of providence give ground before the forces and the methods of evolution. The origin of society becomes more and more: its destiny (if it have a destiny) less and less. Human history becomes but a chapter in an infinitely larger work, and the "heaven" of bygone religions is construed as but the subjective vision of fulfilled desire. Nor is it to be in the least degree wondered at if, to a generation now for some time nurtured on a diet of such ideas, the passionate theism of Mazzini should seem strained, dogmatic, superstitious, antiquated, and superfluous, and not the less so when thrust by the rhetoric of a hundred pages into the secular domain of politics. It therefore becomes of peculiar interest to inquire why Mazzini insisted that democracy, in theory as well as practice, must grapple itself to theism.

The answer to this question is two-fold. For whilst on the one hand Mazzini's theism compels him to regard democracy as part of the Divine plan, on the other his faith in democratic ideals compels him to find their justification in his theism. We may look at these two points in turn.

If we are to understand the first of these, the initial step is to realise what Mazzini meant by democracy. He certainly meant more than the word is usually supposed to mean. As a matter of fact, it means different things to different minds. To some it suggests popular rights, to others social or political equality. To not a few, and among them to thinkers of repute like John Austin and Sir Henry Maine, it means no more than a form of government. There is much familiarity with the thing; there is little agreement upon the definition. Now it is not to Mazzini we must go in search of scientific definitions. And indeed it is the distinctive characteristic of his conception of democracy that it is impossible to compress it into a compact formula. But this at least is evident. It is to him more than a form of government. It is a far larger and a more inspiring fact. This is not because he undervalues democratic government. He is, of course, convinced that, wherever there is genuine democracy, there will also in due season be democratic government. But the two things are not identical. Democratic government is not the whole of democracy. It is but one, and among the later, of its fruits. For when democracy at last makes its way into the political constitution it is only because it has, it may be for long, existed elsewhere. For it does not reside only in polling-booths, committee-rooms and parliaments. It has its birth and growth in the awakening spirit of personal independence, in the increasing sense of human worth, in the enhanced respect of man for man, in the passion for equality, in the deepening recognition of the ties that bind the members of the commonwealth each to each. It is these things that are uppermost in Mazzini's thought when he speaks of democracy. Nor do his words leave us in any doubt upon the matter.

> When all men shall commune together in reverence for the family, and respect for property, through education and the exercise of a political function in the State—the family and property, the fatherland and humanity will become more holy than they are now. When the arms of Christ, even yet stretched out on the cross, shall be loosened to clasp the whole human race in one embrace; when there shall be no more pariahs nor brahmins, nor servants, nor masters, but only men, we shall adore the great name of God with much more faith and love than we do now.

Such is Mazzini's definition of democracy "in its essentials." The inference is obvious. For if democracy be anything like this, if it is "in its essentials" a vast spiritual and social movement to which words like these are in any reasonable sense applicable, it is no longer possible, because it would forthwith become a kind of atheism, to rule it out of the Divine plan and relegate it to the rank of a secular product. To the convinced theist, and especially to the theist with strongly pantheistic leanings, it must needs become what Mazzini said it was, "a page of the world's history written by the finger of God." The language, to be sure, is something more than English politicians are accustomed to from their literary leaders. But just on that account they express, in the glow of their religious passion, the central convictions of Mazzini about democracy. It is thus his theism claims democracy for its own.

We reach a similar result when we approach the matter from the other side. For it quickly becomes evident that Mazzini's faith in democratic ideals lands him in theism no less irresistibly than his theism leads to his consecration of democracy. This is not perhaps at first sight evident. For in his account of the way in which the ideals of reformers find their substance and content, he is by no means far removed from other thinkers who are not specially theistic. Like them he turns to history, and he finds there certain institutions, the family, for example, or property, which bear the stamp of permanence. It is a strong presumption in their favour. He is well aware that it is not the business of the reformer to invent all the elements of civilisation *de novo*. Nor is he ever lacking in a reverent respect for the tradition of the centuries. Yet the verdict of history alone is never final. For he is not at all minded to accept the history of the world as the judgment of the world after the fashion of some philosophers. He had too much radicalism and too deep-seated a respect for the individual conscience. Therefore it is only where the verdict of history is at one with the deliverances of the reformer's

own conscience that he finds the criterion by which all institutions and all reforms of institutions must stand to be judged before they can be built into the reformer's ideal. This is his explicit declaration. But, then, there is a further requirement: the ideal must constrain belief. It is this that matters most of all. For nothing is easier than to have ideals with but little accompanying belief. As a matter of fact mankind, and especially political mankind, hold their ideals with all degrees of belief from the shadowy make-believe of the dreamer right up to the absolute faith of the prophet and the reformer. But it is only this last that can satisfy Mazzini. He was not a theorist writing for theorists. Far less was he a dreamer writing for dreamers. He was a reformer writing for reformers upon matters of life and death. And as such he saw with utmost clearness that every ideal that is to move the world must be held with that complete conviction in which lies the open secret of the constraining influence of ideals over the human heart, will, and conscience. It is never enough that the reformer should simply have an ideal, however well thought out. The authority of even the most imposing ideal would collapse from the moment in which whole-hearted belief began to be sapped by half-hearted doubt. For the mere content of an ideal is one thing: the faith with which it is held as summary or symbol of the things that are worth living for or dying for, is another. And it is because he realised the depths of this distinction that so many of Mazzini's pages are filled, sometimes with sorrowful references to comrades who had miserably fallen away from their early ideals, but oftener with impassioned adjurations to stand fast in the political faith. Never had man learnt more completely that lesson which De Tocqueville saw written in democracy—the lesson that "if men are to be free they must believe."

But if this be so, a question at once emerges: How is this belief to be made secure? How is the reformer, in dark days no less than bright, to assure himself beyond misgiving that he is pursuing substance and not shadow, realities and not illusions, in a word, ends that, outliving all failure, will be certain of achievement at last?

To this question there are manifestly many possible answers. Some reformers will simply trust their empirical forecasts, some their intuitions, some the verdict of history, while others, again, will be content to fall back upon the authority of their party or their leader. But none of these resources, nor all of them united, could satisfy the craving of Mazzini for certitude. Nothing could satisfy him short of the belief that God exists and that the will of God will be done on earth. He says this again and again. Personally he was convinced, for he has told us so in moving words, that it was this religious faith that alone enabled him to hold fast to his own ideals through the years of imprisonment, exile, slander, destitution, disillusionment which diversified his life of "rare joys and many sorrows." He claimed no monopoly of such experiences. In his stern scheme of life they were the inevitable lot of many a reformer. And in that conviction he pled with an unwearied iteration that if democracy is to believe in its ideals it must be theistic. His pleadings are not proofs. They are impassioned declarations of articles of faith. When he appeals to the intuitions of conscience, as he does, it is because he sees in conscience a faculty capable of discerning real and permanent values—values discernible by man only because they already exist in and to the mind of God. When he appeals to the tradition of the centuries, as he does, it is only because he believes the whole course of history to be the unfolding of a Divine plan. It is not philosophy. It is faith. It is dogmatism. But it is a faith and a dogmatism into which he would have every reformer to enter if he is to hold fast to that inexpungable belief without which ideals, no matter how magnificent their content, will neither nerve the will to daring nor sustain it in the presence of difficulty and disaster. No reader of his works would dream of calling him an orthodox believer. But his divergence from orthodox believers lies not in that he is less a believer than they, but rather that he carries his religion into his politics and his politics into religion with a passion of conviction such as the orthodox believer might well envy and imitate.

When a thinker is thus possessed by the religious spirit, we may be sure that it follows him into details. For religion like this is not merely one element among other elements in life. It is not content with a departmental influence. It works as the leaven which penetrates and pervades the whole. It is so, at any rate, in this instance, as we find when we turn from fundamentals to his treatment and estimate of the life of the individual man.

It is the irony of our modern life that, just when the individual man has, by the gospel of democracy, been aroused to the consciousness of his worth, dignity and claims, there is borne in upon him by the teachings of science the message of his extreme finite insignificance. "Be free, independent, self-assertive, and see that you be nor defrauded of your rights and hopes"—so run the oracles of democracy. "Yes," rejoins the voice of science, drawing *its* oracles from the wide evolutionary outlook on Nature and History, "but do not forget that in presence of the vastness of cosmic processes, you are a quite insignificant unit, an ephemeron, "a fly of a summer," or, in less metaphorical phrase, a perishable individual with no discoverable core of personality in you, and but one among many transitory specimens of a species which itself is transitory." One need not further labour the point, which, indeed, has become something of a commonplace.

There can be no doubt that Mazzini, though he had but slender dealings with science, felt the acuteness of this antithesis. We see this in the words he puts into the lips of the individual man as there rises before his mind the overwhelming vastness of humanity. It is not the atomist's "Every man for himself," nor the equalitarian's "I am as good as you"—upstart formulas both!—but the words with which the fisherman of Brittany puts out to sea, "Help me, my God! My boat is so small and the ocean is so wide!"

In face of this problem—a problem, be it said, that presses with a painful acuteness on all secularism which claims to be both democratic and scientific—Mazzini has two resources. One lies in the relation of the individual soul, however insignificant it may seem, to God. This was the side of Protestantism he welcomed. To him as to the men of the English Commonwealth, and also to Carlyle, the direct communion between the human spirit and the divine was the source of that individual strength, that defiant independence that comes of conscious dependence upon the Source of all life. There was no shadow of hesitancy in his teaching here. It was central to his creed that, through consciousness of participation in the very life of God, the individual could not only lift himself out of the nothingness that threatens to engulf him, but, if need be, withstand principalities and powers to the face. The second resource lay in the principle of Association which he made it the business of his life to preach to his generation. An atomistic individualism was his abhorrence. It was the sure path to isolated impotence. For if God had made men equals, as he said a hundred times, the "equality" he had in mind was such as pointed the way to that association and mutual helpfulness which is only possible because the equal units are so diverse. Whence indeed it comes that in social life men can gain so much more than they give, flinging into the common stock their own small modicum of faculty, and drawing forth, through the organised power of association, the force and achievement of many who may have where they themselves are lacking. The perception of this made Mazzini naturally the apostle of Association in many modes; but there were two of these for which he more especially stood sponsor, the Family and the Nation.

Whenever Mazzini approaches the Family his radicalism passes into a profound and reverent conservatism. He regards it as "immortal." He says it is more imperishable even than the nation. And of all the maladies that could befall society the deadliest would be the decay of the home. It is not too much to say that for him (unlike some of the later friends of democracy) the decline of the family would be the path to decadence. This was, of course, in part at any rate, because the family was so substantially justified of history. But it was also because he felt, with a pathetic personal conviction, that in missing this, the individual life, be its other resources what they may, runs the risk of an irretrievable impoverishment. "He who, from some fatality of position has been unable to live the calm life of the family . . . has a shadow of sadness cast over his soul and a void in his heart which nought can fill, as I who write these pages for you know." No political thinker has written of the family with a more discerning sympathy than this exile from home as well as country. Even this, however, was far from the central consideration. For this lies in the larger, more civic conviction that the family carries in it the germ and first principle of the public affections. For it was not the family *sentiment* that was uppermost in his thought. He never hesitated to teach that fathers must part with sons and sons with fathers, be the rent ties of human affection what they may, at the call of the State. He always thought politically, so that the home was to him no mere refuge from public cares and disgusts, but—to use his own characteristic words—the place where "between the mother's kiss and the father's caress the child learns the first lesson of citizenship." Hence, as we might expect, it is the civic responsibility of the parent that is the dominant note. "In the name of all that is most sacred," so runs the adjuration, "never forget that through your children you have in charge the future generations; that towards them as souls confided to your care, towards humanity and before God, you are under the heaviest responsibility known to mankind." The doctrine, to be sure, is not new. The same thing was said by Burke when he declared that no cold relation was a zealous citizen, and branded Rousseau as "a lover of his kind but a hater of his kindred." It is thus, with both writers, that the family points onward to the nation.

Very significant in Mazzini's view of the Nation is his attitude towards two groups of social reformers. The first are the earlier socialists of France who seemed to him to sit all too loose to the national life. Intent on their own industrial problem it was their plan, as it has been the plan of most of the many communistic experiments of the United States, to detach themselves as far as possible from the larger national interests, to erect their own industrial experiments, and to leave the great tides of political life to sweep past their doors unheeded. To such as these Mazzini's antipathy was implacable. Eager to foster all reasonable forms of association, and not least industrial undertakings, it was his conviction that all such combinations are pernicious while they last and foredoomed to ultimate failure if, in a spirit of sectional selfishness, they ask their members to abjure upon the threshold the larger interests of citizenship. This runs throughout. Though he was an apostle of co-operation, though no nation could approximate to his ideal which was not rich in many modes of association, his aversion was intense towards all attempts to purchase a limited success for any form of association at the price of an enfeebled patriotism. He was interested in the economic problems that vex modern democracy, but his interest was always more than economic. It was civic and patriotic.

Similarly with his attitude to the socialists who followed Marx, and who were so possessed by the industrial problem that they were ready to subordinate national patriotism to one great international combination of labour against capitalism. Mazzini was not without his sympathies here. He joined "The International," and characteristically did his best to enlist its members in the political movement. But when he found that they were lukewarm to national causes he grew lukewarm to them, and eventually severed his connection. It is characteristic that he seems to have been more sympathetic with the Chartists than with the Socialists. It was not from any coldness to the cause of labour. There was almost nothing which he was not willing and eager to do for the working men of Italy. And it is a touching fact that in all the misery and poverty of exile, a poverty which drove him to the last straits, he gave the evenings of his laborious days, in times long before the evening school was so much in fashion as it is now, to the teaching and befriending of the Italian waifs and strays who eked out a wretched living on the streets of London. But the thing he could not do was even to seem to justify the policy which, in asserting the claims of labour, however just and however urgent, ignored or even subordinated the prior claims of country. "Love your country," he cries, with his wonted impassioned utterance . . .

> it is your name, your glory, your sign among the nations. Give to it your thoughts, your counsels, your blood. Raise it up great and beautiful as it

> was foretold by our great men. And see that you leave it uncontaminated by any trace of falsehood or of servitude, unprofaned by dismemberment. Let it be one as the thought of God.

It was so that in the way men call the nation he worshipped the God of his fathers. Nor is it simply this apotheosis of the nation that impresses us, not even when we read it in the light of his life-long struggle, sometimes in the garret of the conspirator, sometimes on the stricken field, for the unity of Italy; it is also the depth and fervour of the conviction that the man who, for any reason whatever, severs himself from the national traditions, the national struggles, hopes and triumphs, even from the national humiliations, thereby cuts out of his life the interests which make life most worth living, and with the recklessness of a barbarian rejects the instrument that God has put into the hands of the citizen in order that he may lift himself out of the petty round of private cares, trivialities, and even vices into the larger air of the life of the nation. For in one respect Mazzini saw eye to eye with the political thinkers of Ancient Greece. To him as to them the bane and blight of national life was faction, division, the sacrifice of unity to sectional interests. He had bitter experience of this in his own struggles for Italian unity. Nor was he himself guiltless, in the later years of his life, of fostering by his fanatical passion for an impracticable republic the very malady he strove to remedy. But it can always be pled for him with truth that even his worst failures sprang from his passion for the nation. In hating Cavour and counterworking the Italian monarchy he was but giving effect to his settled opinion that it was only as a republic that the Italian nation could stand strong in organic unity.

And yet if Mazzini thus glorified the nation more than any other writer of modern times, it was not because he stopped short at the nation as a final end or highest unity. Quite the contrary. That development of the spirit of nationality which is content to rest in the view of the international system as essentially a struggle for survival amongst rival nations is far from him. He has been called a fanatic for nationality. Yet he was "an international man" if ever there was one. Only, his internationalism was neither, as in Cobden, the internationalism of Trade, nor, as in Marx, the internationalism of Labour. It was the internationalism in the eyes of which a nation is guilty of "the grand refusal" if it do not stand forward and take its place, to the limits of its power, in international politics. In this, and nothing short of this, lies for him the final justification of national existence. For it is not race or geographical boundaries, nor is it even traditions, language, literature, nor yet intra-national ideals, that really make a nation. It is mission. "Little I care for Rome," he once said, "if a great European initiative is not to issue from it." And his reason follows. "We cannot live without a European life." Hence his hatred of Cobdenism. Hence his vituperative vocabulary for non-intervention: "cowardly desertion of duty," "negation of all belief," "political atheism," "the word of Cain." Hence his exhortations to the United States (in 1854) to play its part in world politics. Hence his own passionate sympathies with Poland and the Balkan States, sympathies which he was always ready, nay greedy, to translate into action. In this sense it was Europe, not Italy alone, that was his country.

It is not only Cobdenites who will refuse to follow him here. All radicals who are prone to see in an "active foreign policy" paralysis of social reform and increased burdens on the poor will look with suspicion on the doctrine. Nor is it to be denied that, as coming from a man who united to a deep distrust of diplomacy the conviction that the existing boundaries of European states needed drastic rectification, Mazzini's doctrine of national mission is heavily freighted with War. He was never averse in his own career to rush to the arbitrament of arms. He was prepared to pay the price, if only war meant mission. But even those who may doubt the wisdom of this preaching of a latter-day crusade must, in ordinary fairness, do justice to the grounds upon which it rested. Partly it was the perception that a great nation cannot even if it would, at any rate in Europe, sit loose to international relations; partly the equalitarian conviction that the citizen who believes all men to have worth in the eye of God, cannot abruptly arrest his practical sympathies at the national frontier. "Say not the language we speak is different. Acts, tears, and martyrdom, are a language common to all men and which all can understand." But chiefly it was the faith, integral to his religious and political creed, that the organised nation, and never so much as when it is a democracy, becomes the most effective of all instruments for working out the providential plan among the nations of the world. Most people think of Mazzini as the apostle of Italian unity. But, on his own avowal, he could never have spent his years for Italy had he not believed in the day when free and unified Italy would stand pre-eminent among the nations as, when need arose, the armed champion of struggling or trampled freedom in all lands. It was not the spirit of the filibuster nor was it any mere passion for national glory and aggrandisement that drove him on. It was the peculiar cast of his political religion, which unhesitatingly laid upon the nation in its service of humanity the same spirit of political duty which from first to last he enjoined upon the individual citizen.

It will hardly be denied that this forcible doctrine raises one of the gravest practical problems with which modern democracy has to deal, and upon which the citizen is bound to come to some decision. The reality of international duties is no mere academic speculation. It is a recognised fact. That same consciousness of the worth and claims of the individual which within the nation has clothed the citizen in civil and political rights and freed the slave, has gone far further afield. It has sent forth the many missions of many churches. It has founded aborigines protection societies and championed the cause of native races. It has begotten the spirit that cannot sit still in presence of the spectacle of what it takes to be wrong, injustice, and atrocity done in other lands. This being so, the question from which there is no escape is, How are these cosmopolitan duties to be carried from the region of conviction and sentiment into the world of actuality and fact? To which of the voices is the citizen of the coming years to listen? Is it to the voice of Cobden, unsparing in its denunciations of war and armaments, eloquent for the bloodless victories of commerce, strong in its confident

plea for peaceful national example? Or is it to the voice of Mazzini which, in the name of the brotherhood of men and the providence of God, pled with passionate democratic conviction for the stern duty of armed intervention for the undoing of despotism and the succour of struggling freedom in all lands?

And yet this issue, grave as it is, is after all subordinate to the larger question, if it indeed be true that democracy must be religious or fail. No one can venture to say that Mazzini has proved that it must. It is not for any man to say what forms democracy may assume in the vicissitudes through which it may have to pass. But one thing at least Mazzini has proved. In life and in writings, and in life perhaps more convincingly than in writings, he has shown that the democratic spirit can, by alliance with religion, achieve results which none of its friends can afford to hold light. One of these is the belief in the reality of distant and still unachieved ends which is at once the strength and the solace of the reformer. Another is that personal faithfulness to political duties which is only too apt to be frittered away through indifference when political power is broken up into minute fragments and portioned out to the multitude in wide democratic franchises. A third is the defiant individual spirit, drawn from conscious dependence upon a Divine support, which nerves the citizen to resist the tyranny alike of despotism and of democracy. And still another is the eye to see steadily behind all the more immediate ends of political struggle, with their preoccupying secularities, the lives and destinies of men who are worth working for because even the least of them is regarded as having in him something of the spirit of God. These are the things which Mazzini valued. For him they were of the essence of democracy. His results, of course, rested upon large religious assumptions. And beyond a doubt there are radicals who would be equally willing to take the results and reject the religion on which they rest. It is for them to show how such a course is possible. If they can, it is safe to say that it will only be by traversing Mazzini's democratic gospel from end to end. (pp. 189-212)

John MacCunn, "The Religious Radicalism of Mazzini," in his Six Radical Thinkers: Bentham, J. S. Mill, Cobden, Carlyle, Mazzini, T. H. Green, *1907. Reprint by Edward Arnold, 1910, pp. 185-214.*

Bolton King   (essay date 1911)

[*In the following excerpt, King summarizes Mazzini's social and political ideas and comments on his concept of the social functions of music and literature.*]

What form of government was best calculated . . . to give full play to liberty, to harmonise it with association, to supply a true national education? No form, Mazzini replied, is right *per se.* He held to the full, though probably not recognising it, the scholastic doctrine of government by grace. "Sovereignty is not in I nor we but God." "There is no sovereignty of right in any one; sovereignty is in the aim." A government was legitimate in proportion as it stood for righteousness.

There is no sovereignty in the individual or society, except in so far as either conforms itself to the divine plan and law. An individual is either the best interpreter of God's law and governs in his name, or he is a usurper to be overthrown. The simple vote of a majority does not constitute sovereignty, if it evidently contradicts the supreme moral precepts or deliberately shuts the road to progress.

The will of the people is sacred, when it interprets and applies the moral law; null and impotent, when it dissociates itself from the law, and only represents caprice.

The theory is of course, as in the days of the schoolmen, a tremendous instrument for reform. No institution, no branch of legislature, no church, no prerogative or prescriptive claim has any rights against the Right. Do they or not make for the country's good? By the answer they must stand or fall. The theory is supremely true, and on occasion of highest social value. Its dangers lie in the possibility of mistaken application, and in its tendency to regard the form rather than the spirit of an institution,—a danger especially present to minds like Mazzini's, which are deficient in powers of accurate analysis. An institution, so runs their reasoning, has failed; therefore it is wrong; therefore it must be swept away. Reform is impossible; therefore let there be root-and-branch revolution. It is strange that Mazzini, with his admiration of English habits and dislike of French, did not see how here his logic approximated to the latter. He did not see how plastic institutions are, how it is often better to save the great expenditure of force, that must go to destroy a rooted institution, how it is sometimes easier to change the spirit than the form. In this his political wisdom went astray, and his long profitless crusade against the monarchy is a melancholy illustration of the error.

Thus, then, there is no essential sovereignty in any form of government. But democracy is the form most likely to interpret God's law aright. We must "reverence the people," not because they are the majority, "but because they concentrate in themselves all the faculties of human nature distributed among the several individuals,—faculties of religion and politics, industry and art." In other words, the collective wisdom of the many is likely to excel the wisdom of the few; a democratic state can use the special knowledge of every citizen, and choose the most capable for its administrators; and its judgment is likely to be more four-sided and better informed than that of a state with restricted citizenship. And just as Humanity is the interpreter of God's law, so a people often has an inspiration that seldom comes to individuals, glimpses of the truth that are granted to the multitude in moments of enthusiasm, an instinct that impels it to give power to its best men. He even, inconsistently with his general position, justifies democracy on *à priori* grounds; it is "a potent, undeniable, European fact," and therefore must be a part of God's providential design.

But it is impossible not to feel that all through Mazzini's thought there runs a certain uneasiness about democracy. He accepted it as an inevitable fact; he recognised that at all events it was superior to any government based on privilege; it fitted in with his theory of Humanity and his own passionate sympathies. But he had an intermittent dread

that democracy, like theocracy and monarchy, might forget the law of God. He feared that the French Revolution had started it on the wrong road; he had had his disappointments in Italy; in later life he felt the peril that materialist socialism might deflect it from spiritual ends. He advocated universal suffrage, not because of any absolute virtue in it, but as "the starting-point of political education," and he gravely feared that, till national education had created a national consensus, it might easily become a tyranny of the majority. He preferred a system of indirect election. Towards the end of his life he was a keen advocate of women's suffrage, but he was anxious that the agitation for it should be equally an agitation for their own moral growth, a crusade against "their perennial vanity, their worship of ridiculous fashions, their lightness of parties and conversation," their husband-hunting. And this mistrust made him turn to a strong authority, elected and deposable by the people, but with very extended powers, and charged not only to execute the popular mandate, but go in advance of it. "The supreme power in a state must not drag behind the stage of civilisation that informs it; it must rather take the lead in carrying it higher, and, by anticipating the social thought, bring the country up to its own level." It is for republics to make republicans, not republicans republics. He earnestly repudiated the Whig-American theory of government. Anxiously as he guarded personal and religious and commercial liberty, he wished to see the functions of government, at all events in education and as a stimulating and suggestive influence, as wide and not as narrow as possible. Distrust of government in itself, the whole system of checks and balances, he condemned as weakening the power of the state to promote progress. It is extremely difficult to disentangle with precision what was his ideal constitution, and it may be doubted whether he had worked it out himself. Though he probably had no very strong liking for parliamentary government, he seems to have accepted it, and to have wished to give it large executive powers. But above it, and apparently distinct from the executive, was to be the real "government," the spiritual authority, whose duty it would be to "point to the national ideal," while parliament and the executive "directed the forces of the country" in the road it indicated. But there must be no suspicion of dictatorship, and perfect trust and mutual inspiration must unite the spiritual and temporal authorities.

At all events the ideal government, whatever its precise form, could, he believed, exist only under a republic. The story of his life has shown how passionately he clung to his republican faith; how for it he gave or wasted his best days, how his untamable desire for it tangled his work for Italian Unity. His condemnation of monarchy was partly a theoretical one. The republic was "the most logical form of democracy," the only corollary of liberty and equality; monarchy was founded on inequality, its dynastic interests were not the nation's, and therefore it could never give a country moral unity. Whether absolutist or constitutional, it was a sham, because in modern life it corresponded to no real belief, no essential principle; and because it was a sham, it was the fruitful parent of dishonesty. Quite late in life he somewhat changed his point of attack, and condemned it as possessing no vitality to lead, and therefore impotent to found a strong government. But his indictment, at least in his early years, was drawn mainly from the actual evidence of corruption and misrule in the monarchies of the first half of the century. It may well have seemed impossible then to reconcile monarchy with any national well-being. He made little or no exception for constitutional monarchies. Louis Philippe's rule was small argument for the principle; and as late as 1862 he condemned constitutional monarchy as "incompatible with progress," everywhere outside England. For England, in later years, he made an exception; and his judgment here shows that he could view the issue more serenely, when he escaped from his prejudices. "The struggle, which occupies English life," he said in 1870, "is not between the nation and the monarchy, but between the people and the aristocracy, the latter being the one element of the past, that retains and communicates its vitality." In Italy the facts were after 1848 much the same as in England; but here he was blinded by party feeling, and he could never see that what was the real issue in the thirties had gone into the background. His fallacy was a nominalist one. In his early days there had been a vital difference between monarchy and republic. Afterwards the classification became unreal; and the true differentiation lay in various species of parliamentary government, in various relations between parliament and the executive. In his own Italy today the republic becomes increasingly a factitious and academic issue, as more vital questions make the true dividing lines in politics.

However mistaken his distinction between republic and monarchy, the republic, as he conceived it, was no mere form of government. "God is my witness," he said, "that I pay no tribute to forms." He had little liking for the republic in the United States, with its weak bond of union, and its system of checks and balances. He refused his blessing to the Third Republic in France. "By the Republic," he told the Roman Assembly in 1849,

> we do not mean a mere form of government, a name, a system imposed by a victorious party on its rivals. We mean a principle, a new step forward in education taken by the people, a programme of education to be carried out, a political institution calculated to produce a moral advance; we mean the system which must develop liberty, equality, association;—liberty, and consequently every peaceful development of ideas, even when they differ in part from our own;—equality, and therefore we cannot allow political castes to be substituted for the old castes that have passed away; association, that is a complete consensus of all the vital forces of the nation, a complete consensus, so far as is possible, of the entire people.

For him the republic meant absolute trust between people and government, choice of the most capable and best for office, a veritable national unity, that destroyed party friction and impelled the undivided forces of the country to social legislation. The republic, and it alone, will be the ideal state, God's kingdom realised on earth,

> where institutions tend primarily to the bettering of the most numerous and poorest class, where the principle of association is best developed, where the road of progress has no end, as

education gradually develops and all elements that make for stagnation and immobility disappear, where, in fine, the whole community, strong, tranquil, happy, peaceful, bound in a solemn concord, stands on earth as in a temple built to virtue and liberty, to progressive civilisation, to the laws that govern the moral world.

There, in the people "that knows no caste or privilege, save of genius and virtue, no proletariat or aristocracy of land or finance," in the people "united by the brotherhood of one sole faith, one sole tradition, one sole thought of love," the people that worships principles more than men, that cherishes its past but looks ever forward to its future, resolute to unlock its destinies,—there stands the city of God, "the similitude of that divine society, where all are equal, and there is one love, one happiness for all." (pp. 275-82)

Mazzini's faith in the republic came largely of his conviction that it was the only effective instrument for social legislation. He was sometimes charged with neglecting social for political reform, with preaching, as Bakounine put it, a "detestable bourgeois patriotism." The charge was true for no time of his life, least for his later years. To him the social question was "the most sacred" as it was "the most hazardous" problem of the age. He was one of the first to insist that the rise of the working classes was the great social phenomenon of the century. Political reform, so he told the Carbonari and the Chartists, had its only sufficiency and justification, when it was the instrument of social reform. This did not quite represent his thought, for he was insistent that questions of political liberty and justice intimately touched man's moral development; but he held with equal earnestness that the social question had its independent and undying importance. "There is no such thing," he wrote, "as a purely political or purely social revolution; every true revolution has its political and social character alike."

All his passionate sympathy went out to the disinherited. Compassion, says one who knew him, shone in his face and vibrated in his voice, when he spoke of the masses and their hardships. He felt intensely for a lot, which in the '40s and '50s he believed was growing steadily worse. Indignantly he spoke of the workman's "poverty-stricken, cribbed, precarious life, closing in infirm and squalid and unassisted old age." "The workman has no freedom of contract," he replied to the old economists,

> he is a slave; he has no alternative but hunger or the pay, however small it be, that his employer offers him. And his pay is a *wage;* a wage often insufficient for his daily needs, almost always unequal to the value of his work. His hands can multiply the employer's capital three fold, four fold, but not so his own pay. Hence his incapacity to save; hence the unrelieved, irreparable misery of commercial crises.

And even without crises, "his life is poisoned by a sense of uncertainty and constant dread; and old age,—brought on prematurely by heavy and often unhealthy work,—awaits him, threatening, implacable." His "destiny is that of accursed races,—to live and suffer, curse and die." "A life of poverty and a deathbed in a hospital,—that is what society in this nineteenth century provides for two-thirds of its members in almost every country, eighteen hundred years and more since a Holy One, that men hail as divine, proclaimed that all are equals and brothers and sons of God."

But he was no pessimist, at all events in later years, when he knew the workman better, and saw that, in spite of all, he was advancing and gave promise of infinite further advance. The day of deliverance was near. The workman's emancipation was inevitable, written in the decrees of Providence. The labour question was the acknowledged problem of the time, its solution "the social faith of all men now who love and know." "The upward movement of the artisan classes in our towns," he wrote towards the end of life, "dates back now for more than a century; slow but tenacious in its progress, advancing from decade to decade by a law of increasing momentum, and in these last twenty years growing, visibly for all, in intensity and expansion, and acquiring, as it goes, real power and self-consciousness." It all was "leading up to a great revolution, an impulse given by Providence, nevermore to recede, till it has reached its end." And he gloried in it. Whatever fears he may have had for the working of democracy, he had none for the labour movement. The rise of the working classes was "as a flowing tide, that the divine breath has stirred"; and he watched it "not with fear, but with the loving reverence, with which one watches a great providential fact."

But just because his faith and love were great, he was not afraid to point "the men of labour" to the heights. It was his familiar precept of the moral aim. "Material improvements," he told them,

> are essential, and we will fight to win them; not because men have no other interest than to be well housed and clothed, but because your moral development is stopped, while you are, as you are to-day, engaged in a continual fight with poverty.

So too in his rather scanty references to political economy, he insists that its teaching must always have reference to a moral ideal. Economics must be "the expression not of the human appetite but of man's industrial mission." Otherwise, they "substitute the problem of humanity's kitchen for the problem of humanity," and teach selfishness for individuals and classes and industrial warfare. It was not only that economic progress must aim consistently at personal morality, at making better husbands, fathers, neighbours, that it must be pure of any spirit of bitterness or revenge or aught that sins against the brotherhood of man. Besides all this, it must not be allowed to maim the working man's powers and duties as a citizen, must never be purchased by the sacrifice of political liberty or manliness. He pointed for his moral to France in 1849 and 1850, when the French artisans sold their political rights to Louis Napoleon for the promise of a labour policy. 'Bread and amusements,' he reminded them, were ever the offer of despots. Outside liberty and strenuous political interest there was no salvation, economic or other. The true man will think not only of his class but of his country, and not of his own country only, but of the sufferings and rights

of men the whole world over. If the working classes forgot their political duties, thought lightly of political reform, connived at an unjust foreign policy, they sacrificed one of their nature's noblest functions, and built their own economic progress on the sand. And he believed that, France notwithstanding, the people always knew this in their hearts. The Chartists, he pointed out, with their bare, imperfect political programme, had more followers than all the French Socialists. "The last of those you call political agitators," he told the latter,

> will always have more influence with the people than all your utopias; because at the root of every political question the people has at least a glimpse of something that appeals to its soul, something that gives it self-consciousness and raises its trampled dignity.

The working men of Italy fought like heroes at Milan and Brescia, in Sicily and at Rome, not for a rise of wages, but for the honour of the Italian name, for the free life of their nation. The working men of Paris fought and won in 1848, not because of a financial crisis or their own poverty, but because the monarchy dragged France's glory and duty in the mud, because it refused French citizens a free press, and free right of meeting and association.

It was from this standpoint that he attacked Socialism. We need not concern ourselves with his strictures on the expired schools of the early French Socialists, or with his very crude criticism of Louis Blanc,—criticism, which he would hardly have made in later life, and which is certainly inconsistent with his own social schemes. We can neglect, too, much of his attack on the economic side of collectivism, which he never really understood. It is more to the point to assume a greater knowledge of modern Socialism than he possessed, and see what is his essential relationship to it. He had not a few ideas in common with the Marxite school. His own industrial ideal contained, though he knew it not, the germs of the socialist community. He looked as earnestly and confidently as they do to the death of capitalism, and built his hopes on the development of association; he recognised with them the inevitable historic evolution of the workers, and that it is the march of the humble, unknown multitude, and not the hero, which determines the world's progress; he hailed the time, when classes would be no more, and all be equals in rights and opportunities, and he believed that this equality could never be reached under a capitalist system.

But in root principles he differed from the strict Marxites almost as essentially as he himself supposed. While with him moral and spiritual phenomena are the fundamental facts, Marx builds his system on material phenomena. For the collectivist, man is chiefly the product of his economic surroundings; for Mazzini, the social and industrial environment is only "the manifestation of the moral and intellectual condition of humanity at a given period, and above all of its faith." For the one, history is the sequence of economic cause and effect, and the growth of mind and morals is the secondary consequence of economic facts; with the other, the economic facts, though not neglected, are subordinated, religion is the master principle of human progress, and religious systems are the milestones that mark the road. The two schools are absolutely antagonistic in their conception of the ideal. Marx and his followers would discover it by the right interpretation of the drift of facts; if indeed we can call it an ideal, what is accepted merely as a necessary tendency, and when right and wrong are judged by the fact, not the fact by right and wrong. Mazzini understood to the full the value of facts as conditioning the ideal, as pointing out how far it was attainable at the moment, nay, as in some degree indicating the ideal itself. But to him right and wrong had no dependance on the existing fact; facts tended to approximate to the ideal, because the ideal was sovereign, and Providence guided them towards it; and it was man's free privilege and bounden duty to help the work of Providence, and be lord of facts. Mazzini did not kick against the pricks of economic evolution; he took modern industrialism as it is, and never wished to thwart the natural tendencies of industrial discovery. But he claimed that man has power to turn them to good or evil,—a good or evil that has reference not to them but to a moral end.

Hence their teaching has differed widely in its practical consequences. Marx deduced from his economic studies a confident and detailed prophecy of economic development. It was a faith, whose assurance and optimism gives it a mighty power to sway men, so long as faith stays unquestioned. But economic dogmas, especially of the prophetic kind, are apt to be shaken by the rough wind of facts; and it has been the fate of Marx' system to be line by line explained away by its commentators. If it still retains its influence,—and, indeed, it is a potent influence,—it is because it has quieted scepticism by shedding much of its founder's doctrine, and because it finds and has more or less always found expression in a political programme, such as Mazzini preached, aiming at high ends of liberty and justice. Mazzini, so confident often in his religious and political horoscopes, here chose a humbler part. He insisted indeed on one broad economic principle,—association, and he pointed to certain reforms of immediate practicability. But he resolutely refused to forecast the economic future. Humanity, he would repeat, goes on its own way, and laughs at the man, who finds "the secret of the world under his pillow." "I think," he wrote, "that our problem is not so much to define the forms of future progress, as to place the individual under such conditions as make it easy for him to understand and fulfil it." He created no great party of the proletariat; it was his as useful function to fertilise the moral soil, to inspire all classes with a deeper sense of social obligation, and thus to ease the road for social progress, whatever particular shape the circumstances of the time might counsel it to take.

The two men differ again radically in their influence on class relations. To Mazzini 'the struggle of classes,' however peaceful and legal in its form, would have been a hateful idea. It is true he sternly rebuked the short-sighted folly of the richer classes, and he would find excuses for wild acts or theories of proletariat protest. But he set his face resolutely against class hatred, against dreams of violence and revenge, against social revolutions which worked hardship to the individual. Hopeless as he was of enlisting the upper classes, at least in Italy, on the side of social reform, he set his hopes on the middle classes; and

from the days of the *Apostolato Popolare* down to the last years of life, he preached insistently that middle and working classes must stand together in the social movement. The whole theory of Duty looked to the harmonising of motives, not to the brute struggle of opposing social forces. The collectivist takes the social discord for granted, and bids the workers trust to themselves alone and win their ends by force, however much force may be disguised behind the vote. Each principle has its time; the socialist mistake has been to elevate to a principle, what is the sad necessity of an uninspired age.

It remains to examine Mazzini's own programme of social reconstruction. He lays down certain economic axioms. First, private property must remain, however much the State should try to equalise fortunes through taxation. Mazzini endorses the familiar argument from expediency,—the necessity of property to stimulate labour and encourage invention. But his apology for it is in the main an *à priori* one. "Property," he says,

> when it is the result of labour, represents the activity of the body, as thought represents the activity of the soul; it is the visible sign of our part in the transformation of the material world, as our ideas and our rights to liberty and inviolability of conscience are the signs of our part in the transformation of the moral world. The man who works and produces has a right to the fruits of his own labour; in this resides the right of property.

There is a flavour of Ricardo and Marx in this, and it is easy to see a socialist application, unintended by the writer. Next, the new social organisation must not be the work of compulsion. He saw that voluntary working-class organisation was an essential preliminary to any lasting social advance; and, as we shall see, his own schemes pivot on voluntary societies for cooperative production. And lastly, schemes of economic change must always aim at increasing productiveness. He knew that there could be no serious improvement in the workman's condition, unless the national production were increased; and he seems to have dimly realised that the two things must mutually react, any rise in the workman's income increasing the demand for commodities and thereby stimulating production, and this increase of production in its turn encouraging a further increase of the workman's pay.

When we come to the particulars of his economic programme, we find fertility and boldness of suggestion, but small attempt to work out the details. He was constitutionally unfitted to be an economist; he lacked the necessary precision of thought and accuracy of analysis. He rather despised economic study, at all events when it came from books. A real knowledge of the economic question is to be found, he says, "in the workshops and the homes of the artisans," rather than in "statistics and documents, which are sometimes erroneous, always incomplete, compiled as they are either by officials, whose tendency is to conceal the evil, or by private individuals, whose tendency is to exaggerate it." He trusted to a knowledge of the workman's thoughts and aspirations, gleaned from close and affectionate intercourse, more than to any inquiry into the outside facts of his life.

His suggestions were many. Among the more common-place were free trade in land, legislation to protect tenants, arbitration between capital and labour, national insurance (apparently to be compulsory), the regulation by the state of "that den of robbers," the Stock Exchange. At one time he wished the state to guarantee work for everybody, but as he does not mention the proposal later than 1849, it may be assumed that he relinquished it. For Italy, he suggested a great scheme of home colonisation on her unreclaimed lands; and it is a curious instance of his want of accurate enquiry, that in his advocacy of it he took no account of the all-important factor of malaria. It is curious, too, that, like many Italians at the opposite pole of thought, he disliked emigration, and would gladly have checked what has proved to be one of the chief sources of Italian development. All these, however, were minor suggestions. His programme rested mainly on two proposals,—a radical reform of taxation, and the gradual supersession of capitalism by voluntary cooperative societies of workmen. His canons of taxation are shortly stated and may be shortly summarised. Economy in collection, free trade, no taxes on food, the smallest possible incidence on industry were his fiscal maxims; and he wished to carry them out by abolishing all indirect taxation and, apparently too, all special taxes on land, and substituting a single tax on income, to be graduated and, it would seem, severely graduated. He also proposed that in all cases of persons dying without heirs within the fourth degree, estates should lapse to the state.

He looked for more radical change to his scheme of cooperative production, a scheme which appears in its main outlines as early as 1833, but which he worked out in more detail in the last ten years of his life. It was a special application of the same principle of Association, which he had carried into other branches of social and political activity. He proposed that a great national capital should be accumulated for the purpose. Church lands, railways, mines, and "some great industrial enterprises," which he never specified, were to be nationalised, whether or not with compensation does not appear. At one time he wished to confiscate in Italy the estates of those who fought against the nationalist cause—a proposal strangely out of harmony with his usual tolerance. The income from these sources, from the rents of reclaimed lands and existing national and communal estates, and from properties which lapsed to the state, would form the "National Fund" or "tax of democracy." At one time he destined part of the fund to education, another part to assist any European democracy struggling for its rights. But its main, and perhaps in his later idea its only purpose was to assist the spread of voluntary societies for cooperative production, industrial and agricultural. Any such society, that could prove its members' honesty and capacity, might claim to have its capital advanced from the Fund. The loans were to be at 1 or 1½ per cent., and were to be made through special banks administered by the Communal Councils. Nothing is said as to the repayment of the loans, but as he contemplated the extension of the societies, till they ultimately covered the whole field of industry, we may assume that the loans were to be repaid and passed on to new societies. The societies were apparently to be left absolutely free as to the management of their business, the sale of

produce, and the disposal of their net income. To assist their credit, they were to have the right to deposit any unsold produce in national magazines, and receive in exchange negotiable notes, which, it seems to follow, would have been legal tender. The societies were also to be admitted on equal terms with private firms to contract for government work; this latter was perhaps the first suggestion of a system, which is now working in Italy with some success.

Such were Mazzini's sketchy but suggestive economic schemes,—schemes which, he believed, would ultimately destroy both poverty and capitalism, without hardship to individuals or danger to liberty, leavening the social morality with the God-given principle of association. He seems to have never asked himself what would be the ultimate destiny of his co-operative scheme; had he done so, he must have seen that, by however different a road, it was bound to end in collectivism. It will be recognized now that his plan was in all essentials identical with latter-day socialism, as put out by its best exponents, and it may be claimed that in the world of ideas Mazzini more than Marx is its father. That his scheme would soon come into working, he had little doubt, at all events in Italy. For in his social plans, as in all else, his own Italy was ever uppermost in mind. He knew, when few others knew it, the patience and common-sense and idealism of the Italian artisan, and he proudly counted on him to let Italy lead the nations in the solution of the labour question. (pp. 283-95)

If Mazzini's busy life could have spared more time for literary study, he would probably have been among the greatest critics of the century; perhaps, even as it is, he may rank among them. He misses in his lack of accurate and detailed study; but he has a rare penetration and originality and gift of embracing synthesis. It was his ambition at one time to found an Italian school of criticism, whose mark should be constructive and sympathetic interpretation. Keenly sensitive though he was to beauty of expression, he detested mere criticism of form and the profitless microscopy, that pries for specks in a writer's life or work. He loved to read a great author reverently, hiding rather than exposing his blemishes, penetrating below uncouthnesses of form and casual lapses to the great informing thoughts, that had their lesson for the world. "At the present day," he wrote in an optimistic moment,

> we neither worship a genius blindly, nor outrage him barbarously; we set ourselves to understand him, and we learn to love him. We regard forms as secondary and perishable phenomena; the idea alone is sacred, as a thing baptised to everlasting life, and we try how we may lift the veil that hides it.

He compared genius to the fabled tree of Teneriffe, whose branches discharged showers of refreshing water. "Genius is like this tree, and the mission of criticism should be to shake the branches. At the present day it more resembles a savage striving to hew down the noble tree to the roots."

In his scheme of life the poet had a part of supreme importance. He regarded literature as a "moral priesthood." Poetry would "save the world in its despite," for it was the poet's prerogative to redeem it from doubt and base ideals, to "reveal duties and create affections," to lift men up above the trivial things of life to the eternal verities. "We have," he cries in the forties, "exiled poetry from life, and enthusiasm and faith have gone with it, and love, as I understand love, and constancy in sacrifice, and the worship of great deeds and great men." His own Italy had little of the throbbing national life, in which alone true poetry could flourish; and everywhere an age of faithlessness robbed the poet of his aliment. The time was for the critic,—the constructive, "philosophic" critic; he was the "literary educator," and he could at all events be precursor of the poet of the future, marking the lines on which a modern democratic poetry should travel, and preparing a public to understand him. "The critic," he says,

> is unrelated to genius; but he stands as a link between great writers and the masses; he explores the conditions and literary needs of the time, and preaches them to the nations, that they may learn to feel them, and desire and demand them; in fine, his prophecies prepare a public for the writer:—a more important matter than some think, for very rarely do writers appear before their time.

As critic, then, Mazzini points out the deficiencies of contemporary literature, and the principles which must take it to a higher stage. True art, he lays down, has two great perils to avoid. First, there is the "atheist formula" of 'art for the sake of art';—a heresy he scourged with pontifical anathemas. His attack was not aimed at perfection of literary form. He loved a correct and classic diction, and never underrated style, so long as style was not an excuse for poverty of thought. His criticism went deeper. The artist may not live his own art-life, divorced from the moving world around and all its manifold activities, "floating bubble-like without support," finding his poor inspiration in his own fancies and caprices. There was no true individuality in that; invented though it was to guard the poet's independence, in reality it made him but a passive mirror of each passing impression. Instead of liberty, it brought anarchy and "wild, arbitrary intellectual display." It robbed art of touch with the great facts of life, all fruitful relationship to the struggling, ever learning, ever advancing race. It sent it wandering lawless, purposeless, like a sick man's dreams. The poet ceased to be a thinker and a teacher, and sank to a mere empty singer. "What I want," he said, "is not the Artist but the man-Artist; the High-Priest of the Ideal, not the worshipper of his own Fetishes." Literature must be "the minister of something greater and more valuable than itself."

He was almost equally condemnatory of realism, especially of realistic presentation of nature. It was a criticism that he brought alike against Monti and Victor Hugo and Wordsworth, that they "depicted but never transfigured nature," and thus their art was "useless." The real is the mantle of the true, but not the true; "high poetry is truth, because you cannot trace out or analyse its source." The poet is a "miner in the moral world"; his function is to hew beneath the symbol, beneath the real, to the idea shut in within; questioning nature alike in her beauties and deformities, to find and teach to men "that fragment of God's truth that must exist there." "One thing I know," he says,

"that the phenomena of nature on their moral side and the inner life of man must be the field of modern literature, that physical nature and man's outer life will have their place only as symbols of the first." And nature's lessons must have a practical reference to man's lot and destiny. Even when nature was rightly used and interpreted, there might be too much of it, and he seems to have always given natural poetry a secondary place. "Poetry," he says, "is not in nature but in man."

This brings us to his conception of true art. It must be essentially human, not realistically so, but usefully, practically, didactically. He did not mean by this that it must confine itself to the obvious, outside facts of life. "In every powerful poetic impression the *vague* claims a full quarter, and the vague, which must not be confounded with the obscure, is the soul's own field." But poetry, however much it may concern itself with the spiritual and unseen, must have direct application to the problems of life. "Art lives of the world's life; the world's law is art's law." The poet must gather "the great voice of the world and God," and so interpret it, that men may listen and profit. He must contemplate man both in his individuality and as a social creature, "in his internal and external life, in his place and with his mission in creation." "Poetry,—great, ceaseless, eternal poetry,—exists only in the development, the evolution of life: only there, in life, understood and felt in its universality, can inexhaustible variety be found."

Thus the poet must find his inspiration, not in his own "incomplete, mutilated conceptions," not in the isolated individual, but in the great collective, democratic movements of the people, voicing their dim thoughts and aspirations, "their latent, slumbering, unconscious life." There can be no great poetry to-day, unless the poet identify himself with "the thought fermenting in the breast of the masses and impelling them to action." Poets are the priesthood of the social and political movement, which is the very blood of a modern people; and there is no place for individualist poetry in a social age. "True and sacred art aims at the perfection of society," and the art of the future will be "principally religious and political." He hated the aimless art, that busies itself with the mere picturesque and sentimental, which idealises ages, whose meaning and moral standard have passed. He applauded Schlegel's thesis that poetry must be "national, that is useful and related to the civil and political situation," no longer heedless of the great movements of to-day, but "standing in the centre and swaying the heart of the social impulse." The poet, who went to fight for Greece and died there, typified "the holy alliance of poetry with the cause of the peoples."

This democratic art must have a practical use by being didactic and prophetic. It is not enough that its heart should beat with the people's life; it must help the progress of the race by pointing to the future. Though it may "grow among the ruins, art is ever coloured by the rising sun." "There can be no true poetry without a presentiment of the future"; it is, as said "the extraordinary man," who is the poet of all time,

> The prophetic soul
> Of the wide world, dreaming on things to come.

"Art either sums up the life of a dying age or heralds one

about to dawn; it is no caprice of this or that individual, but a solemn page of history or a prophecy; most powerful, when as in Dante, and occasionally in Byron, it is both." But there is no gift of prophecy without an ideal, and "literature, like politics, has no secure foundation without its fixed beliefs and principles,"—those beliefs which make the future and to which facts must bow. "The true European writer will be a philosopher, but with the poet's lyre in his hands."

> Nature with her thousand voices cries to the poet, "Soar, thou art King of earth." And if we try to pen him down to realism, and rob him of his independent lordship over facts, the poets of the past will answer from their graves, "We were great, because we created." It is for poetry to take the creations of the philosopher and give them life and colour, to explore the truth that lies below the real and illumine it with the light of genius, to interpret the universal laws that rule over human history.

And the poet must not only lift men to his vision, but send them forth in quest of it. He is not only prophet but apostle. It is not enough that he should stimulate thought; he must "spur men to translate thought into action." "Contemplative" poets, Wordsworth and Coleridge for instance, are "incomplete." "The element of Action is inseparable from poetry. Poetry," he says, "is for me something like the third person of the Trinity, the Holy Spirit, which is action." "In order to be a religious poet," he writes in criticism of Lamartine, "it is not enough, in my eyes at least, to say 'Lord, Lord'; it is necessary to *feel* his holy law, and to make others feel it in such sort, as that they shall constantly and calmly act in obedience to its precepts." Just as religion gives life and power to philosophy, so it is for art to grasp ideas, translate them by images and symbols, and make them passionate beliefs. "Poetry is enthusiasm with wings of fire, the angel of strong thoughts, the power that raises men to sacrifice, consumes them, stirs a tumult of ideas within them, puts in their hands a sword, a pen, a dagger." "Written poetry, like music performed, should be in some sense a prelude to other poetry, which the excited soul of the reader composes silently within itself." It will

> teach the young all that is greatest in self-sacrifice, constancy, silence, the sense of solitude without despair, long years of torture or delusion unrevealed and dumb, faith in the things that are to be, the hourly struggle for that faith, though hope of victory there be none in this life.

And therefore art must be ever brave and full of hope, "teaching man not his weakness but his strength, inspiring him not with faintheartedness but with energy and vigorous will." Its song must be always of steadiness and constancy, and "calmness radiate from the poet's brow, as the spirit of God radiated from the brow of Moses on the wandering Israelites." "The artist is either a priest or a more or less practised mountebank." Woe to him, if he teach spasmodic, evanescent effort, or "revolt and impotent despair, that dies cursing, ere it tries to fight, that says 'All things are evil,' because it finds itself unable to create good." Mazzini has no pity for the poet of pessimism,

"whose sense of moral depression and languor" will, if he pose as a religious poet, make his readers "reject religion and him together."

Poetry, then, the modern poetry of action, being essentially related to politics and social life, the poet's themes are in the stir and passion of contemporary events or in national history. What field for literature like the mighty, moving pageant of the democratic world? To watch God's hand guiding the nations to their destinies, to probe the eager ferment of a modern society, to interpret all the dim, half-conscious yearning of the masses,—what inspiration for the poet here! "Popular poetry has invaded everything, the poetry whose epic is revolution, whose satire is revolt." How strong and living are the giants of the Revolution beside the nerveless men and women of the quietist novel.

> Poetry has fled from old Europe to give life to the young, new, beautiful Europe of the peoples. Like the swallow, it has left a crumbling ruin to seek a purer air and a more verdant world. It has fled from the King's solitary throne to find its abode in the great arena of the peoples, in the ranks of martyrs for the fatherland, on the patriot's scaffold, in the prison of the brave betrayed.

The armies of the Convention, the guerilla-bands of Spain, the German students chanting the songs of Körner on the march to battle, the patriot's anguished passion, the dreams of a liberty to be, the world-mission of European civilisation,—these are the modern poet's themes.

> Think you that poetry, whose birth was ushered by such deeds as these, can die ere it has lived? Would you set up the poor, pale, narrow poetry of individuals, a poetry of forms, a poetry that lives and dies in the small circle of a palace or a chapel or a castle,—would you set up this against the grand *social* poetry, solemn and tranquil and full of hope, which knows none but God in heaven and the people upon earth?

An age of science and industry is no enemy to poetry, for the elements of poetry are eternal. "I tell you, in this Europe there is such life, such poetry in germ, the poetry of ages, of all the generations, that genius itself has not yet dared to attempt to develop it." "Here round you," so he speaks to the poet of the future, "here, before your eyes, there is poetry and movement and a European people waiting for you."

The poet has another field in history. Mazzini prophesied a great future for the historical drama. He was inclined to think that drama would be the accepted form of modern poetry, seeing doubtless that drama is the true communion between poet and people, the natural vehicle of the artist, who has a message to deliver. It would be "a kind of popular pulpit, a chair of the philosophy of humanity"; and he looked forward to the day when the great dramas, such as those of "divine Schiller," would be produced on the stage without mutilations or curtailments to a reverent and patient audience. The function of the historical dramatist, as indeed he thought it was the function of the prose historian, was not so much to make minute research of facts, as to disentangle the lessons hidden under every page of history, to interpret the law of human duty and the mystery of existence. Like every other poet, he must start with a philosophy of life, judging all things by his own law, meting out praise and blame, drawing guidance for the future from the past. The dramatist "may call up the shadows of the past, but like the Witch of Endor, in order to constrain them to reveal the future." His personages must be types, each with its social significance; he must not, as Victor Hugo did, overload them with individual traits, till they lose their message for society, but rather, as Schiller with his Marquis di Posa, so "re-create" them, that they may illustrate some general law of life. Mazzini did not see how pale such characters would be; how difficult it was to reconcile them with biographical accuracy, how likely therefore they were to falsify any induction of historical laws.

His theory of music was a very similar one. Music, like poetry, he thought, was nought without a moral intention, without practical teaching and power to inspire. It should be "the purest and most general and most sympathetic expression of a social faith." He pitilessly criticised the music of the thirties, imitative, exhausted, artificial, clever but without creative power. A faithless and corrupt generation asked for music to amuse it; and music had listened and forgotten its mission. There was melody and good instrumentation, but no soul or thought in it. It was "laughter without peace, weeping without virtue." Operas had no unity, no great passionate note; they were ingenious mosaics, much of them mere noise and extravagance, inferior for all their technique to the chants of the medieval Church, when music had a religious work to do. Rossini had done something; he had broken from the old canons and given liberty to music; but he had the defects of the Romanticist school, he had freed but could not create; he had prepared the way for the music of the future, but it was not his to write it. Mazzini however saw indications that the new music was not far off, and its dawn, he believed, would be in Italy. But Italian melody must wed itself to German harmony. Italian music was "lyrical, impassioned, volcanic, artistic," but without unity or soul. German music knew God, but it was mystical and impersonal, out of touch with everyday human life. It dulled men's impulses to action; it stirred them, but to no useful end, left the soul full of great emotion, but uninspired to perform plain duties. Mazzini was assured that Italy would produce the master, who would unite the strength of both schools, keep the religion of the German school, but point it to practical, human ends. At one time he hoped that perhaps Donizetti might live to do this; afterwards he thought that Meyerbeer was "the precursor spirit of the music of the future." He was always thinking of Opera. When he insists that the music should be in keeping with the subject and its period, when he pleads for the symbolic use of the orchestra, for the wider employment of motives, for the development of the chorus on the model of Greek tragedy, for the large use of recitative, for the entire disuse of cadences and flourishes, he is looking to Opera to be the highest form of music, as he looked to the historical drama to be the highest form of poetry. Apparently he wished to wed them, and looked for the day, when great poets would write librettos for great composers.

Mazzini's criticism of music is for its time so fresh, so full of suggestion and prophecy, that it is matter for regret that his knowledge of it was not more extensive. He knew opera and little beyond it; he had some acquaintance with Beethoven, but he does not seem to have been very strongly attracted by him, or to have made much study of him. He wasted on Donizetti and Meyerbeer the enthusiasm, which should have been reserved for greater men. It is unfortunate that he lived before Wagnerian opera appeared in London. It would be possible to show in detail to what a remarkable extent he anticipated Wagner's theories. Wagner, it is true, rejected the historical drama, because he believed the requirements of art to be incompatible with historical accuracy. But his main doctrines are the same as Mazzini's,—the ethical intention of music, the intimate relationship of art to public life, the belief in the people as the fountain of true art, the value of the folk-song, the reconciliation of harmony and melody, the poet and musician stretching hands to one another and giving 'moral will' to music, by uniting 'word' to 'tone' in Opera. It is permitted to think that, Wagner's nationality notwithstanding, Mazzini would have recognised in him the master of the new music, whose dawn he heralded. (pp. 312-23)

Bolton King, in his The Life of Mazzini, *J. M. Dent & Sons Ltd., 1911, 380 p.*

Ralph Flenley (essay date 1927)

[*In the following excerpt, Flenley assesses Mazzini's contributions to Italian nationalism and examines his concept of the ideal state.*]

Mazzini is in some ways the most attractive and interesting of all the great figures of the nineteenth century. He was not always wise, he did not always face facts, his prophecies were often wrong, his views were not in his own day and have not since been accepted as sound in every particular. Yet whilst it is not possible to estimate exactly his influence on Italian history, he is rightly placed first in the list of the makers of that country in the nineteenth century. Nor was his influence confined to Italy. The fact that he lived much in England, wrote much in our tongue and had many friends there, strengthens the appeal of his career to us. Yet his great qualities—his high idealism, hatred of evil, abounding love of mankind, self-sacrifice, simplicity and purity of character, his passionate faith in and unremitting devotion to a great cause—these belong neither to Italy nor England exclusively, but have a universal appeal. And Mazzini had beyond these, and beyond his high intellectual gifts, a personal magnetism which is difficult if not impossible to convey by the printed word, which his portraits hardly reveal to us, but of which there is no doubt.

Joseph Mazzini was born in Genoa in 1805, the year in which this ancient republic was annexed by Napoleon. His father was a doctor attached to the University of that city. As a boy he saw the triumph of Europe over the great Emperor in 1814 bring not the hoped-for free republic again, but merely a change of masters, for Genoa was handed over to Piedmont to stiffen that kingdom against possible

French aggression. His father, like most Genoese, hated the Piedmontese yoke. He had memories of earlier freedom; then of the French Revolution; then of a rule which, if despotic, had not been petty or illiberal, and which had united much of Italy under one rule. There was all this to set off against the illiberal paternalism of the restored king of Savoy, in which all (save Genoese freedom) was to be as it was before 1789. Was it any wonder that the boy grew to manhood protesting against despotic monarchy?

Mazzini's services to his country and his century were in the realm of ideas and inspiration. Action he longed for, and desperately. But whilst all his attempts at action failed, his voice, pen and example were potent weapons. His ideas were developed and expanded in scores of articles, pamphlets and letters, public and private, over forty years. Whilst it is impossible even to summarise in a few lines his teachings—for he was above all a prophet and teacher—some attempt must be made to explain his faith; for in Mazzini the faith and the man were one.

The task to which Mazzini devoted his life was the making of the Italian nation, "a task," he says, "like the task of God, the creation of a people," to make "an Italy one, free and powerful, independent of all foreign supremacy, and morally worthy of her great mission." The setting was provided by nature—the sea on three sides, the mighty hills which he loved on the fourth; these were the "sublime and indisputable boundaries." The elements or raw materials of which a nation could be made were present also in language and literature, race and tradition. But something more was necessary to fuse these elements into a nation. The basis of Mazzini's belief in nationality, as of his belief in all else, was religion.

Mazzini was essentially a religious man. He refused to call himself a Christian, greatly though he admired the example and teaching of Christ. Still less would he hold to either any Protestant creed or the Papacy, which latter became to him "the basis of every tyrannic authority." "God and the People" was his war-cry, to be inscribed on the banners of the revolutionaries of 1848. Faith in God was necessary, because without it a people could not possess a sense of duty. The Gospel of Rights of the French Revolution of 1789 had been a failure just because it was a Gospel of Rights. The new Italian nation must be founded on a Gospel of Duty or it would not, he argued, be a nation at all. And that implied belief in God.

From his faith in God Mazzini drew a belief in Progress. He took issue with Christianity because in it he found no place for such a belief. "From the idea of God," he says, "I descended to the idea of progress; from the conception of progress to a true conception of life." Progress to Mazzini was part of God's plan for mankind which "slowly, progressively makes men Divine." The "fundamental character" of the moral law for society was "progress unlimited and continuous from age to age; progress in every branch of human activity, in every manifestation of thought, from religion down to industry and the distribution of wealth."

From belief in progress as a Divine law to a belief in nationality was for Mazzini but a step, and a short one. The

An 1849 portrait of Mazzini as Triumvir of the Roman Republic.

individual cannot progress alone, but God has made the nation as the instrument for working out the progress of mankind. "Your country," he said to the Italian working men, "is the token of the mission which God has given you to fulfil in humanity." So the nation is sacred, and sacred too is man's duty towards his country. Here in particular was Mazzini's great service to Italy and to his age. The fervour with which he championed the cause of Italian nationality was due to his lofty conception of the origin and functions of the nation. And the enthusiasm which his words aroused was due not merely to the low estate of divided and subjugated Italy or the eloquence of his appeal, but also in part to the deeply religious spirit which shone through his trumpet-like call. "Love your country," he said to the Italians, "it is your name, your glory, your sign among the nations. Give it your thoughts, your counsel, your blood. Raise it up great and beautiful as it was foretold by our great men. And see that you leave it uncontaminated by any trace of falsehood or of servitude, unprofaned by dismemberment. Let it be one as the thought of God." In 1831 Mazzini, already an exile, wrote a famous letter to the new king of Piedmont in which he said, "Place yourself at the head of the nation, write on your flag, 'Union, Liberty, Independence.' Free Italy from the barbarian, build up the future, be the Napoleon of Italian freedom." From this date, and indeed before, Mazzini not merely wrote but worked for the one cause, often in failure, often mistakenly, but ever with the same burning faith. Yet Mazzini never conceived of the nation as all in all, or an end in itself; he was no narrow or exclusive nationalist. The nation was the instrument for the progress of humanity: through the nation was to be accomplished "the brotherhood of all the peoples of Europe, and through Europe of all humanity." Nations were not merely to abstain from oppression, but were to aid positively in the diffusion of the spirit of freedom.

Mazzini's nation was to be a democracy. His definition of a people as "a fellowship of free and equal men, bound together in a brotherly concord of labour towards a common end," implied that. "Your country should be your Temple, God at the summit, a people of equals at the base," he said to the Italians. Only a democracy could fulfil Mazzini's ideal of the nation state fostering civil, religious and economic freedom, encouraging the open and peaceful association of its citizens for the common good, educating all its members for their duties as citizens. He went further: he wanted a republican democracy. It is to be remembered that when Mazzini formed his political ideas, neither in Italy nor in Europe had monarchy shown itself friendly to his principles of political, civil or religious liberty; in fact monarchy generally was much the reverse. Much less had it been shown as yet that a monarchy may be as democratic as any republic. To him monarchy had had its day, like the Papacy. It was based on a system of inequality and led to stagnation; even constitutional monarchy was "incompatible with progress." So Mazzini became a Republican, for, he argued, "the republic is the most logical form of democracy." What he hoped for from a united democratic Italy—and he hoped everything—could best be fulfilled under a republican flag.

Yet just as he tempered his nationalism by a belief in a common humanity, so he could on occasion modify his republican tenets. Here, of course, he was responding to facts, for not merely was the monarchical idea and sentiment strongly entrenched in Italy, but as time went on it became more and more clear that Italy would be united under the Piedmontese crown. Mazzini was not blind to some at least of the dangers of democratic rule, and the republics of France and the United States met with more criticism than approval from his pen. Yet whilst from time to time he checked his republican propaganda he never abandoned his belief in this form of government. As a concession to popular liberty he would have liked to see Italy decide on its Constitution deliberately and in full freedom when united—an impracticable plan, for unity only came under the Piedmontese monarchy directed by Cavour.

The more immediate applications of Mazzini's belief are obvious enough. Italy must be united, not into a federal state as some men thought best, but completely. And for this Austria must be fought—relentlessly and continuously, until she was driven out of the peninsula and her influence there destroyed. The people of Italy must be educated for their high mission as citizens of a great nation, and that nation stirred to a recognition of its responsible position in the world. Education, social reform and association, on all of which Mazzini has much to say, are to weld the free and united nation together to make the land of his ideals. (pp. 84-9)

Ralph Flenley, "Radicals and Nationalists of 1848-50: Mazzini" in his Makers of Nineteenth-Century Europe, *J. M. Dent and Sons Ltd.*, 1927, pp. 84-96.

Times Literary Supplement   (essay date 1955)

[*The following excerpt evaluates Mazzini's importance in the Italian unification movement.*]

Mazzini was not canonized among the heroes of Italian nationalism until after his death, when no longer dangerous. During his lifetime he was a lonely figure in exile, disliked for his republican and democratic ideas more than he was liked for his nationalism. Perhaps only now that Italy is a republic can his merits be studied dispassionately. When he died in 1872 the world still condemned him as an *enragé,* a tyrannicide, a cloak-and-dagger man. Today if he is still out of favour it is for other reasons. Some people will say he went wrong in not merging his own revolutionary movement into the current of revolutionary socialism later in the century. Others would object that the world has suffered too much from nationalism in latter years, or alternatively that his doctrine contains too much that is collectivist and totalitarian, and puts too much weight on metaphysical sanctions and the *duties* of man. But this at least makes him an interesting and controversial figure. As a man of vision he was remarkable. As an agitator and conspirator he was far more effective than his enemies allowed. As a character he was utterly genuine and honest, what John Morley called "the most morally impressive man" he had ever known. Constantly in books he is given the titles of prophet, apostle, and even martyr: the combination of attributes is uncommon.

A National Edition of his writings, begun in 1906, has now reached its hundredth volume, and there is more to come on what it was thought inadvisable to publish under the monarchy. Though Mazzini used to tear up the letters he received, ten thousand of his own have survived, in sum a fascinating documentation of revolutionary conspiracy. His sources of information on political events are sometimes still obscure, but they were often surprisingly accurate, and they stretched even into the inner councils of Napoleon III. His articles and letters cover a wide field, but they all go to show how little he changed in a lifetime of work and thought. For him, action and thought were closely interrelated: politics, religion, philosophical speculation and literary criticism were fused into a monolithic structure that held closely together and withstood the tests of advancing time.

As a man of great sensibility, his views on poetry and art are always worth hearing—he himself thought that the abandonment of a literary career was the first great sacrifice of his life. But his best literary criticism was never far from political implications. Mazzini's admiration of Byron was that of a whole generation of European liberals, and he could never understand the lukewarm attitude to Byron of Englishmen. His friend Carlyle's *Frederick the Great* was declared to be readable but "unredeemably bad and immoral" because it worshipped force; and the *French Revolution* was inadequate because it was merely an illustrated story of individuals, without lesson or meaning, without "collective life", portraying as the result of hunger and material wants what was really "the greatest event of modern times . . . the accomplishment in politics of what Christianity accomplished in morals by the Reformation." Yet another good example comes into a penetrating discussion of Leopardi:

> one feels that at the very moment in which he was or ought to have been most deeply moved by a thought or feeling visiting him, he could not help hunting for the best epithet. It was so with the love of his country too: he *did* love Italy; but almost delighting, I think, with her own ruins and his own despondency.

Mazzini's use of English was not always quite accurate, but it often showed a surprising sense of *nuances* and melody.

This edition of his writings, open it where you will, reveals itself as a primary source-book of European politics. It also gives a minute account of a unique personality. There is more than a little of Leopardi in Mazzini's deeply affectionate but frustrated character. "Life is a mission; there is no happiness here, nor can be: il n'y a qu'une seule vertu, l'éternel sacrifice de soi-méme." His letters show his loneliness, and how dependent he became on the four English ladies who gave him real sympathy and to whom he put on his most attractive side. Working ten hours a day at his desk in London, he expended his own money and health in keeping up single-handed a thin network of conspiracy all over the world. He himself hinted that his compulsive drive to this sort of action might be a kind of unconscious prophylaxis against "lo spleen." Living on £4 a month, allowing himself one luxury in cigars, taking "bark and vermouth" for his maladies, feeding the tame sparrows in his room, playing a sad aria on his guitar, all this was only one side of the man. There was also the indefatigable collector of money for the cause, who even, we now learn, speculated on the Stock Exchange. There was the ex-carbonaro who gave Gallenga (that future correspondent of *The Times*) a *pugnaletto* to assassinate Charles Albert. There was the conspirator who wrote a highly practical manual on guerrilla warfare, and who had the cold courage to send so many of his friends to their death in petty escapades because "ideas ripen quickly when they are nourished by the blood of martyrs." This mild-mannered friend of Ruskin and Swinburne also had a secret cupboard-room ready for emergencies in the house of Mr. Peter Taylor, a member of Parliament.

Mazzini's basic message to the world was that of nationality, "the ruling principle of the future," as he called it. Typically, he made small account of the difficulties involved. He naively thought that there were exact boundaries for each nation, and that within these limits all could live harmoniously together. It was all too easy. Spain and Portugal would be combined, so would the Scandinavian countries. Holland would be joined with Germany, Constantinople with Greece, Brussels with France. There would be a Confederation of the Alps, and a Danubian Confederation instead of Austria. "All this will set your Britishers in a frantic mood. . . . It would be a volume which Posterity will write, but I, busy about details concerning Italy, cannot." Kossuth, the Hungarian, used to say that Mazzini had invented the Rumanians just to make difficulties for Hungary, but this was a kind of conflict Mazzini could not understand. Nor did his self-evident principles welcome the existence of such anomalies as an Irish or Belgian nation. Only those whose struggles made them worthy of freedom could exist, and among these Italy was the *Messiah* nation called to redeem the world. "Italy is, perhaps, nearer than are other countries to the sacred altar on which God will descend": so he wrote in an essay on recent Italian art, with unconscious irony. But in his own generation he was wise, and albeit such patriotism was in part a myth, it was an effective myth. In the early nineteenth century there was plenty of room for criticism of those

> who travel in Italy merely because it is the fashion, who see nothing except the main roads, the principal hotels, the chief theatres, and perhaps some large parties . . . for whom all that Italy contains of value are paintings . . . the poets for whom Italy is altogether dead, because the corpse of a nation is a beautiful image . . . the locusts of literature, they alight to-day on the plains of Italy; to-morrow they will visit Spain.

As well as a nationalist Mazzini was also a liberal; indeed he thought these two went together, and never foresaw how his first ideal might defeat his second. A nation for him had to liberate itself by its own sacrifices, and he thus blamed those in Piedmont who brought in the despot Napoleon III and so denied the liberal principles which alone could justify the Italian national cause. "Any war wherein Italians should combat in the name of independence, disjoined from that of liberty, would lead to tremendous delusions, and the mere substitution of new masters for old." According to his version, this is in fact what actually happened, as King Victor Emmanuel crushed the spontaneous forces of liberation and made Italy anti-liberal by fathering it on Bonapartism and diplomacy. Constitutional monarchy was another such high-sounding deception, and in practice could be "the most immoral and corrupting government in the world."

From this he went on to say that sovereignty resided, not in any fraction of society, but in the whole, for society was not the sum of individuals but "a moral unity." So he could not stomach the victory of the middle classes with their alternative myth of constitutionalism. Mazzini's ideal republic was one in which middle-class and upper-class privilege was abolished by law, and in which no one lacked the necessities of life. His *Doveri dell' uomo* was dedicated "agli operai Italiani." "The common people will be to the epoch just beginning what the bourgeois has been in the past: spur, vigour, intent. Hence the need to educate them." No doubt Mazzini made a tremendous mistake in thinking that the common people would always act justly, that they would rise against tyranny and then resolve all the problems of national and class selfishness which the *ancien régime* had left over. But his belief that the march of democracy was a providential law, "an *émeute* of the human race . . . and irresistible," this uncriticized assumption was a tremendous force in the *risorgimento;* it was where the idealist dreamer became more practical than all the realist politicians.

Mazzini was essentially an idealist, a theoretician who had an ingenuous and uncritical trust in anything that his general theories asserted to be a rule. Sometimes he seems to have lived by maxims: "on ne fusille pas les idées"; "la vie n'est pas une question de plaisir ou de peine; c'est une question de devoir." But these maxims built up into a comprehensive religion, which may have been an illusion but which was internally consistent and externally a cause of effective action. Mazzini himself was deeply religious, much attracted by Christianity if not by Papal Catholicism, and always had it in mind to write a book on religion. "It is in the name of Religion and godlike things that you must appeal to the necessity of an Italian Revolution," he said. Individualism was not enough, nor materialism. "America is the embodiment, if compared to our own *ideal,* of the philosophy of mere *rights:* the collective thought is forgotten: the *educational* mission of the State overlooked. It is the negative, individualistic, materialistic school." If there are Fascist hints in this attitude, the whole scale of values is far from Fascism. This austere sense of duty was in the service of national liberalism, not national socialism. If Mazzini believed in nationalism, he did not equate it with centralized government, and this champion of the idealized State was even accused of pushing liberalism in practice to the point of anarchy. Even his belief in the Idea, in an absolute pattern of Italy laid up in heaven, was also accompanied by a shrewd awareness of material motives for national unification; for instance, the desirability of a national market as a means of raising the standard of life. There is thus a kernel of practicality and common sense about Mazzini that one might miss on any stereotype interpretation of the man. His revolutionary guerrillas were carefully charged to respect property rights, and once he even threw out the surprising suggestion of buying American aid with the offer of a naval base.

Occasional lapses like this did not prevent Mazzini from censuring Cavour and the moderate liberals in Italy for their "paltry, hateful programme of expediency." This invariable opposition to the moderates was in part a failure of sympathy and understanding. He could not believe that diplomacy could alter the condition of the people, or indeed do anything but sanction the *fait accompli.* He also suspected Cavour—that "pallido fantasma di Machiavelli"—of trying to turn Piedmont into a Prussia in home and foreign politics, and like Ludovico il Moro of bringing another foreign tyrant into Italian affairs as a means of canalizing the *risorgimento* into more conservative channels and destroying Italian liberties in the process. The "Doctrinaire or Juste-Milieu school" was liberal only when this was expedient, not out of principle, and the policy of domestic reform was just to take the edge off revolution and make a genuine reformation more difficult. Hence Mazzini's organization of Young Italy and Young Europe in the early 1830s as a school of propaganda and action based on firm principles of liberty, national independence and unification. These are the years when all Mazzini's ideas were developed, in the forcing-house of conspiracy and revolutionary journalism. What we still do not know is how deeply his ideas succeeded in penetrating the various regions of Italy. Mazzini as a practical and not an ideal force in the *risorgimento* is therefore strangely elusive and uncertain.

Probably at no time did he have much hold on the politically conscious classes of Italy, let alone on the common people whom he so idolized. Yet it is also true that nearly all the future leaders of Italy passed through a Mazzinian phase in their political development. He could kindle enthusiasm as no one else, and he alone could raise political problems to the religous level where they became part of God's providence and generated a feeling of historical inevitability. No mere politician like Cavour could supply the same faith, fervour, doctrine and capacity for self-sacrifice. Mazzini's was the voice which Tazzoli recalled on the scaffold at Belfiore. And Giuseppe Bandi testified to this influence:

> I had an infinite desire to see him, the man who, alone, unarmed, and exiled, made all the tyrants of Europe tremble on their thrones. I longed to hear that voice which for so long had made my heart beat and my eyes water with tears, that voice that kept alive in my soul the belief in the triumph soon of a holy cause, just when everyone else was in despair and resigned to live and die as slaves.

Such a man could inspire people to deeds of heroism that again and again, in spite of all the odds, ignited the spark of revolution.

The year 1848 saw the high tide of Mazzinian insurrection. But recent books have tended to alter the canonical view that after this date he was only an ineffective nuisance. The Milan rising of 1853 was not as futile as his enemies tried to make out. For there was a real danger that Piedmont might become content to leave the rest of Italy alone for a number of generations unless a revolutionary situation could be forced on her. Neither the moderates, nor even Garibaldi, were people to start a revolution, though both would follow when one had begun. Even the Genoese rebellion of 1857 may have been necessary for final victory: it certainly helped to banish the alternative solution of another Murat on the throne of Naples and a federal Italian State.

Historians now prefer to speak of the "unconscious collaboration" between Mazzini and Cavour. It was the fear of Mazzini which enabled Cavour to coerce Europe into accepting his own less violent alternative, and which in particular allowed him to use and exploit Napoleon III while yet remaining more or less independent. In another sense it was the pressure of the radical revolutionaries that forced Cavour himself into unequivocal acceptance of nationalism, and of the means of revolution and universal suffrage which in theory he detested. There were even moments, still not sufficiently clear, when Cavour's government, and later that of Rattazzi and Ricasoli, were in unofficial touch with Mazzini, perhaps hoping to win him over to the monarchical side, or to exploit and then disown him after he had served their turn. Mazzini himself must no doubt have approached these negotiations in equal bad faith. For him, the dynasty of Savoy was little better than the Neapolitan Bourbons, and Piedmontese constitutionalism as barren as that of the July monarchy. All one can say is that Mazzini showed greater willingness to compromise than did either the government or even some other of his radical associates, and for this he was never given due credit. In the last resort he was ready to sink his republicanism so long as the nation was made.

Mazzini's success was a real one, but it turned to dust and ashes in his mouth. The moderates feared him as a social revolutionary, as an arrogant, obstinate visionary who was calling in question their own solution to the problem of Italy. His election to Parliament was therefore repeatedly quashed. His newspapers were suppressed in a country which boasted of its free Press. Cavour not only accused him of receiving an Austrian subsidy, but brought in French police with the promise of a *récompense éclatante* for his capture and execution. The English Home Office also had French agents watching him, but these were the sort of policemen who would report his detailed movements at a time when we know that he was hundreds of miles away.

Much more painful to Mazzini than open persecution was the continual defection of former friends who could neither stand his temperament nor understand his tactics. Garibaldi ended ungenerously by calling him "one of the obstacles to Italian unification." Bertani and Medici tried to reason with him against this fatal confidence in popular initiative and the readiness of Italians for nationhood. Bit by bit he saw the nation formed on a different plan from his own. What finally emerged in 1861 was "only the phantom, the mockery of Italy." The general apathy was puzzling. He could not understand why one of his journals had no sale in his own native Genoa, nor why for years he could find no one at all in Naples who would write to him, nor why he seemed to find more sympathy for the Italian cause in England than in Italy. The people's readiness to act grew less, if anything. They preferred to abide by whatever decision was reached on their behalf by others, so long as they were spared the horrors of revolution and civil war. As a last straw, Mazzini now discovered that nationalism was not after all resolving the problems of Europe as he had hoped, but was creating new animosities; it spelt not the emancipation of peoples but their further enslavement.

> I am sick of everything concerning Italy or Europe; without a good sweeping storm there is no hope: the air is polluted; words have lost their meaning; they are usurped by everyone; every rule of political truthfulness and morality is lost.

This disillusionment was necessary to round off the tragedy of his life.

Mazzini's last years were divided between London and Lugano, estranged from almost everyone. In one of his mysterious visits to Italy he was betrayed for the last time, but now he was less dangerous and suffered no more than imprisonment. He had hoped for "one year before dying of Walham Green or Eastbourne, long silences, a few affectionate words to smooth the way, plenty of sea gulls, and sad dozing." But he could not shake off the habits of a lifetime, and lived still the conspirator in the Fulham

Road, with his invisible ink and swordstick. At this time he seems to have been reading much about medieval mysticism and the anabaptists. He was also fighting a lost war against the socialists, whom he reviled as materialists and unpatriotic, but who knew so much better than he how to move the common people to action. In 1872 this future national hero, disguised as a Dr. Brown, furtively arrived for the last time in Italy, and there he died at Pisa under an assumed name. These hundred volumes are his latest monument. (pp. 33-4)

> *"An Idealist in Action," in* The Times Literary Supplement, *No. 2764, January 21, 1955, pp. 33-4.*

E. E. Y. Hales (essay date 1956)

[*An English critic and educator, Hales specializes in Italian and papal history. In the following excerpt, he describes Mazzini's central religious tenets and the philosophers who influenced them, and concludes that Mazzini's theological divergence from the people he sought to unify rendered his religious doctrine less effective than his personal moral example.*]

No doubt, as Mr. Griffith in a recent essay ["Mazzini Yesterday and Tomorrow"] insists, "[Mazzini] had no affinity with Protestantism in any form . . . his thought was dominated by Catholic collectivism and universalism", but he is also right when he insists that Mazzini's upbringing, all that he had heard and thought about "the Elect" and "Duty" had "mediated" Calvinism to him through the filter of Jansenism. To the early influence of his mother and of a Jansenist tutor must, in fact, be attributed the presenting of Christianity to him in a manner which cannot have been without its influence upon the way he developed his own religious thought. It led him to embrace certain elements of puritanism which met with an answering echo more readily in England than they had encountered from his revolutionary friends of Modena or Reggio. It was observed long ago by Gaetano Salvemini that Mazzini's religious influence was exercised in England rather than in Italy, and, most of all, amongst English women; almost the only Italians, in fact, who embraced it fully were those whom these English women married. Salvemini attributed this to the classical tradition in Italy:

> There is very little romanticism in the tradition of our culture, which is almost entirely classical. Mazzini's mysticism is an outlook which does not seem suited to our mental climate, or at least has not hitherto succeeded in establishing itself in it.

These words were written in the year 1915. Since that date the Mazzinian religion has made headway in Italy. Mussolini, concerned to propagate ideas of duty and mission amongst the Italians, made much of Mazzini; but, more important, a new Mazzinian movement arose in Italy out of the war-time resistance and is now organized in the *Associazione Mazziniana Italiana,* which has published studies of considerable interest. There is also, for example, a Mazzinian review, the *Idealismo Realistico;* a recent article in this journal states: "It is clear enough" that, with the decay of Christianity, "the new religion is that of Giuseppe Mazzini".

It goes without saying that this is an extreme standpoint and that the author arranges a somewhat premature burial for the Church in Italy. But it is useful to notice that Mazzini himself did exactly the same thing. Throughout his life, from his early preaching at Marseilles to his last important writing, which was an attack upon the Vatican Council of 1870, he was announcing that the Papacy was dead and that Christianity was dying. And it was precisely his view of the condition of Catholicism in his day that prompted his invocation of the "new religious synthesis", convincing him that humanity was in the very act of bringing forth from her womb the faith of the future. Since, also, it was his rooted belief that religions always emerge from humanity, his diagnosis of the religious conditions of his times was the necessary foundation of his own faith, and this lends a deep significance to the fact that he proved to be wrong about what was happening to Christianity in his own century. For the nadir of the Papacy was not in the nineteenth but in the eighteenth century. Many other observers, besides Mazzini, thought the Papacy was moribund; but actually it was just entering upon a period when it would grow greatly in spiritual (though not in temporal) influence while Christianity, whether Catholic or Protestant, was also about to enjoy a very notable revival, and to be spread all over the world.

The peculiar *animus* with which Mazzini attacked the Church, which helped to drive him on to construct his own theology, was part of his opposition to the ruling political powers of his day in Italy and of his anger at finding the Church generally supporting them. This led him, in the words of the Principessa di Belgioioso, to characterize Christianity as "a stupid and treacherous superstition, thrown in the eyes of the people to blind them and make them obedient to the clergy who had made themselves the chief instrument of the tyranny of the kings". The Saint-Simonians then convinced him that the people were capable of producing a new religion of their own, while the fate of Lamennais, who had tried to invert Catholic Authority, so that it derived from the People, and had been duly condemned by Pope Gregory XVI for doing so, finally persuaded him that the kind of religion for which he was looking could never be found within Christianity. This view was much strengthened in him by what he chose to call the "resignation" of Silvio Pellico, Manzoni, and a host of other Catholic patriots in Italy who seemed to him (as many Protestants later seemed to him in England) to place the salvation of their own souls before the emancipation of Italy.

On the other hand he sharply criticized the French revolutionaries for being anti-religious, and the secularism of many of the radicals of his own day, such as Guerrazzi, or Fazy, or Louis Blanc disgusted him. Religion, he was sure, was necessary; on this point he was at one with the Pope. But while the Papacy, impressed by the sufferings of Pius VI and Pius VII at the hands of the French Revolution, drew the deduction that, since the spirit of revolution was mostly secularist, it was wisest, for the sake of security for the Church's work for souls, to follow Saint

Paul in supporting what was called legitimate authority, Mazzini drew the deduction that something new was alive in humanity which needed to be consecrated in a new religion. And because, throughout his lifetime, the Church continued generally to support the rulers in Italy (though taking a different line in Ireland, Belgium and Poland) Mazzini hardened in his opinion that it was not only blind to the times but also moribund. He may have been right in the former deduction—it is a matter for argument—but he was proved wrong in the latter.

As we turn to the theology he constructed we should notice, in passing, that he was more successful in his political than in his religious forecasts, and this is not without bearing upon his religious teaching because politics, with him, were only a branch of religion. It seemed to many, just after the First World War, that he had rightly understood his times, for the Treaty of Versailles was supposed to create a Europe of free peoples, and many of these peoples, especially those in central and eastern Europe, were those to whose aspirations he had particularly drawn attention. President Wilson, when he was still a professor of history at Princeton, had lectured on him, and it was said that the President's League of Nations had been foreshadowed by Mazzini's Young Europe. Lloyd George, at Genoa in 1922, had exclaimed "How right he was!". And if it is true that today much of Europe—though perhaps not Italy—looks less Mazzinian than it did in 1919 it is still something notable in politics to have been proved right, a hundred years later, even if what has been foreseen does not last. In religion, however, anyhow as Mazzini conceived it, something deeper and more lasting is to be expected of prophecy, and it is not yet clear that the modern European nations bear more than a superficial resemblance to Mazzini's vision. It would rather appear, in fact, as though they were a long way from being his "sacred peoples". They emerged, as he foresaw they would, from out of the ashes of the Austrian Empire, but their relations with Heaven and with each other were not what he intended. They were not free peoples, unravelling, in harmony, the letters of God's law. It may be said that he had warned of the the danger of a narrow nationalism, and also of the danger of materialism, communism, and other things. But the present nations can hardly rightly be seen as imperfect or blighted Mazzinian peoples if only because the faith which he had intended should bless their birth and bring them to fruition has itself not yet emerged. "Not explicitly", some may say, "but perhaps implicitly". But then Mazzini was quite explicit about it, and even dogmatic.

And what was his dogma?

It had all been defined by the year 1836, before he left Switzerland; his English friends, though they often tried, never succeeded in modifying it.

First there is God, a separate, personal God, distinct from His creation. Mazzini clings to this theism, in the face of the pantheists as well as the materialists, and he reaffirms it, in answer to some vision, on his death-bed at Pisa, in March 1872 (*Si, si, credo in Dio!*). Yet Mazzini's God is a distant figure. He has set His universe in motion, giving it a Law of Progress which it must discern for itself and which will ultimately bring it to its own perfection. He does not interfere much in the painful processes of earth; He lives in heaven, where the virtuous, the *buoni,* will ultimately join Him; what happens to the bad, the *tristi,* is left uncertain. Too much a child of the Enlightenment to believe in hell, Mazzini yet does not relish the idea of meeting people like Louis Philippe in heaven.

God despatches to mankind, to guide her, Men of Genius—Hildebrand, Dante, Luther, Descartes, Newton, Napoleon, or Byron; these men point the way to the revelation of "the next letter of the Law". But, for Himself, God remains shadowy, a very pale reflection of the Christian God about whom Mazzini had been taught as a boy. Once He has given to Humanity the Law of Progress He leaves it to unravel that Law, for the most part unaided.

After God, His fundamental law, namely Progress.

Mazzini first learnt about Progress from Condorcet, whose book on the progress of the human spirit he was wont to read during Mass. But he learnt it again from the Saint-Simonians, in their paper the *Globe,* edited by Pierre Leroux, as well as from Herder, Victor Cousin, Comte, and no doubt others. It was the great discovery of the eighteenth century and the faith of the nineteenth. The idea of the progress of humanity provided the mainspring of his whole system, and had he been more severely logical in his theology he might have become, like his mentor Pierre Leroux, a pantheist, and a believer in reincarnation here on earth. Leroux felt that belief in inevitable progress really invited belief in reincarnation because only by reincarnation could the benefits won by progress be enjoyed by the generations which had gained them. God, and a distinct heaven, seemed to lie outside such a system and only to make the whole picture rather untidy. Mazzini felt the force of the argument and admitted to pantheism "in a certain sense". But he nevertheless clung to God and to heaven, and much that he has to say about Men of Genius and about the efficacy of martyrdom really confuses what he had been taught, as a child, about the Christian saints and what he learnt a little later about progress.

With an assurance which, even in the age of the romantics, was remarkable, Mazzini was ready to show how the law of progress had actually worked in history. So we hear much about the "immobile East" (the successor, in the age of the nineteenth century progressives, to the "civilized East" admired by the eighteenth century) and about the idea of liberty being introduced by the Greeks. Christianity had discerned and added a new letter of the law, namely equality, the equality of all men before God, and the Catholic Church of the middle ages had provided a "synthesis" for mankind which, at its best, recognized the liberty, the equality and the essential unity of mankind. Then, in a curious way, the cycle seems somehow to be repeated, for liberty is reintroduced by Luther and Descartes, and equality by the French Revolution. The synthesis, too, has somehow disappeared, and it is the peculiar mission of the nineteenth century to reassert this necessary idea. For the achievement of the eighteenth century and of the French Revolution has been to provide the apotheosis of the free individual—Napoleon, Byron and Goethe are the trio selected by Mazzini to illustrate his teaching that the individual has now attained to the highest point which he can reach in isolation. But the age of individuality is now over, and in future there will be no "great individuals" because the coming age will be the age of association, and especially of the nations. That is as far into the future as Genius (Mazzini) can penetrate, for the time being. But the probability is that the age of the nations will be followed by that of humanity.

Arbitrary and dogmatic as Mazzini was, the development of nationalism since his day has partly justified him, as the development of socialism has partly justified his Saint-Simonian mentors. The Saint-Simonians were chiefly interested in what we should now call the "planning" aspect of the matter, and in the vital rôle which scientists would play in the new civilization. Mazzini was chiefly interested in the nationalist aspect of it, and in the religious justification with which the belief provided him for preaching the moral unity of Italy and, until Italy should be formed, of Young Italy. The Saint-Simonians, as good Frenchmen whose country had been united for some centuries, were not so interested as was Mazzini in nationalism. Mazzini's tutors in nationalism were Herder and Schlegel, whose country, like Mazzini's, was yet to be born; it was from them that he learnt about the missions of the different peoples and about the peculiar contributions which the fatherlands of the future would bring to the common stock of humanity. What seems, today, strangest about these notions is that it does not seem to have occurred to any of the romantics, and least of all to Mazzini, that the age of the fatherlands would be other than an age of peace. "Cabinets may cheat one another", wrote Herder in his *Ideen,* but "Fatherlands do not move against each other: they lie side by side in peace and, like families, assist one another". The romantics had, however, no reason to envisage any difficulties because they had abolished evil as something extraneous and artificial, introduced, for their own ends, by the corrupt powers ruling societies, and shortly to be removed by their own revolutionary efforts. Humanity would be virtuous as well as free once she had shaken off the shackles of the outmoded priesthoods, aristocracies and princes. The people were good. They could be misled, but not for long—the great task (as Rousseau had explained in the *Contrat Social*) was to prevent their being deceived.

When he came to read Lamennais (who had himself read Rousseau, and had tried to graft him on to Catholicism) Mazzini found, in the Breton priest's *Paroles d'un Croyant* (1834), the doctrine of an emergent humanity, a *peuple* which was pure and good, and which contained hidden within itself the Truth; a *peuple* which was the true interpreter of Christianity and which might be deceived by rulers and aristocracies but could never be finally corrupted. Lamennais "perfected Rousseau". Mazzini had already taken from Rousseau that prophet's famous doctrine of the General Will, the notion that the popular will "by virtue of what it is is always what it ought to be", and the belief that this Will periodically expresses itself by laying down the constitutional principles of the State. From Lamennais he proceeded to take even more mystical notions about the People—the notion, for instance, that the Word of God was planted like a seed in Humanity, which was destined to bring it, through infinite suffering, to fruition.

The *Paroles d'un Croyant* inspired Mazzini's **Faith and the Future,** published in the following year, in which . . . he wrapped his belief about with optimistic aspirations in words which would be echoed by romantic progressivists, on both sides of the Atlantic, in poetry and in prose, throughout the century:

> Forms change and are broken. Religions die out. The human spirit deserts them like the voyager the fire at which he warmed himself during the night. He enlightens his way by other suns; but religion remains . . . it disengages itself from the coating which analysis has pierced; it shines pure and brilliant, a new star in the sky of Humanity. But this again is only one beacon the more; and how many must be lighted by faith that the whole of the path of the future may be illumined? How many stars, unravelled concepts of each epoch, must be raised in the sky of intelligence that Man, complete embodiment of the earthly Word, may say to himself: *I have faith in myself; my destiny is accomplished?*

The effect of Mazzini's writing on religion was to encompass the notion of Italy about with fleecy clouds which seemed to bear it upwards towards celestial heights and helped to give to nationalist impulses a heavenly halo and a place in the scheme of things ordained by the Creator. But, reiterated in every article and essay, and in a large proportion of his ten thousand published letters, his concepts, Progress, Humanity, Association, and the rest, naturally tend to pall, and it is hard to agree with the verdict of Bolton King, who said that the loss, somewhere in the Alps, of the manuscript in which Mazzini brought together his religious ideas is a loss more grievous to mankind than that of the manuscript of any unknown Greek tragedy. It is permissible, today, to sigh rather for the tragedy, if only because we have been left in little doubt about Mazzini's religious beliefs.

Beneath the superstructure of Mazzini's dogmatic theology lay its implications in the ordinary life of the individual—his moral theology.

> Life is a Mission. Virtue is sacrifice. Without these two principles I understand nothing.

> Every fact has two laws permanently superior to it. . . . One is the general law of the epoch . . . the other is the universal law of humanity.

Mazzini thought that the general law of his own epoch was that a man must work for the association of the peoples into Nations; he must subordinate every aspect of his individual life to this purpose. Even the most intimate aspects of his family life should be dominated by this duty. He is much preoccupied with the rôle of women in inspiring and educating the young and he unhesitatingly prefers second-rate Italian poets or dramatists, in whom he can find a call to struggle for the national idea, to Manzoni, or Silvio Pellico, or Leopardi.

Since the new religion would be concerned with collectives, its initiator would be a people rather than a person, a people that for long had lain buried, silent, oppressed, ignored. Not the French people; they had more than fulfilled their mission to humanity by their gift of the Enlightenment and of the French Revolution. The new revelation might come from the struggling, heroic Poles, with their passionate patriotism. It might even come from the divided Germans, now awakening to a sense of Fatherland. But Mazzini did not much like or understand the Germans. There was, however, one supremely gifted people, from amongst whom had already, twice, gone forth the word of unity to the world, but who, for long, had lain dormant, and who had never been united into a nation. Surely the Italians had the opportunity, if they would only take it, not merely to unite their country, but to become the initiator-people of the new religion, so that their capital, Rome, city of the Caesars and city of the Popes, might for a third time give forth the word of unity to the world.

With the doctrine of the Third Rome we reach the point where the Mazzinian religion and Mazzini's practical political purposes for Italy become identified. In his prison-cell at Savona he had dreamt, as he stared out upon the sky and the sea, of an Italy one, united, and free, which had thrown out the Austrians, thrown over the princes and the aristocracies, and made of herself a people who could set the example to the new Europe. Was this practical objective, then, the prime reality in his mind, the reality around which his whole religious synthesis shaped itself, merely to provide his politics with a good moral sanction?

We cannot so easily dismiss his religion to a secondary place, if only because most of his religious-political reading, and the framework of his faith, preceded the vision of the future Italy which he saw at Savona. Moreover his religion determined the kind of Italy that he preached. It was precisely because of his religious notions that he wanted to create an Italy with a sense of mission, and that he so detested the kind of Italy conceived by many of the Carbonari and by the later "Moderates". The notion of a nation with a mission is the most distinctive notion in his teaching and it is also what gives a dangerous edge to it. His "Italy" is a very highly charged concept and his attempts to preserve over against it the personal liberties which centre around the family were ineffective by comparison with his main theme, and it is not for them that he is remembered today.

Amongst the consequences of his idea of a messianic Italy were his teaching on National Education, which will instil patriotic precept into the young, and his determination that Italy shall be a large and centralized state and no mere federation. On this latter point he differs fundamentally from Rousseau, who wanted small city states like Geneva. Such states were no use to Mazzini because they were too weak to fulfil missions. It was for their smallness, and their consequent ineffectiveness *vis-à-vis* Europe, that he criticized the Swiss cantons even though they had preserved their republican liberties for five hundred years. The driving force of Mazzini's message is contained in this insistence upon purpose, what we may call his teleology. The individual and the family exist *for* the nation and the nation exists *for* humanity. And since humanity was, in his system, the interpreter of the will of God, its demands were, naturally enough, compelling. For the Christian concept of a soul responsible to God, its maker, and of a political and social order only ordained to safeguard the life of the free soul, he substituted a religion of humanity in which the soul was ultimately responsible to a law progressively discovered by humanity, whose progress its first duty was to foster, through the nation. All his attempts, alongside this collectivism, to preserve freedom for the soul, represented little more than a clinging to the Christian concepts in which he had been nurtured and which, despite himself, he still tried to preserve.

This antithesis becomes most clear when he treats of the supreme test of any faith, namely martyrdom. It is martyrdom that proves to him that progress and humanity are real, for he feels that martyrdom is man's highest act, yet it seems to him a senseless act unless humanity, in its progress, is going to enjoy the fruits. "Can you say 'in the name of thy own advantage sacrifice thyself! In the name of thy well-being die'?" A provocative question, and one which he was entitled to put to the Benthamites, or even to some of the Carbonari. But the martyrs of the centuries of Christendom could have replied:

> We did not suffer martyrdom primarily to win progress for posterity here on earth. We suffered for love of God, and of His truth, for the salvation of our own souls and in the hope of propitiation for the sins of others.

Martyrdom preoccupies Mazzini because he is certain that Italians will never win their liberty until they have learnt to die for it. And he believes that the revolutions of the Carbonari failed because their ideals were insufficiently lofty; they were only trying to win their personal and local rights. The revolutionaries will achieve nothing until they have learnt to think in terms of duty and mission. And Italy will not be made until she, too, is thought of as an instrument for the service of humanity, as possessed, herself, of a mission. All this is, in an important sense, impressive, because it is so infused with the notions of duty and sacrifice. But it is hard to see why Mazzini should deny the equal efficacy of self-sacrifice for purposes other than that of assisting the (inevitable) progress of mankind on earth; why a man might not die for what he called the "negative" right of individual liberty, for which the Carbonari, at their best, had shown themselves ready to die, or, likewise, for the sake of Christian devotion of the kind that sublimated the spirit of Silvio Pellico.

One is compelled to the conclusion that Mazzini's theology was important only to himself and to one or two converts later on, not as a force in history, or intrinsically, or on the merits of its logic, its profundity, or its appreciation of human nature. "For all his love of Dante he lacked Dante's sense of sin", says Mr. Griffith, and who has ever yet constructed a convincing theology while leaving out sin? When Italians won freedom to write and to argue more freely about such matters after the year 1846 they did not concern themselves with Mazzini's God, or with his Progress, Humanity, Duty, Thought-and-Action and the rest; but they did derive inspiration from what he had said about *Italia, Libertà,* and *Il Popolo* and still more from what he had suffered for them. The glow with which he had lit those words might for him be only a reflection of the light within him, but it was the reflection that men

saw. The light itself escaped them, and has escaped most people since.

> Oh if the few intelligent Italians did but understand! If they could only feel, as I feel it, the hidden movement which pulses in the world. . . . If they but understood that either one must resign oneself to perish, blaspheming, in the void, or one must give oneself up to live or to die for the planting of the new faith, the new Gospel which will arise!. . . .

Italians have neither blasphemed in the void nor have they planted the new faith. They have tried, for better or for worse, with success and with disaster, like the rest of mankind, to make their country; and in doing so, despite a sharp quarrel with Rome, they have mostly retained their traditional faith. But in their hard task they have been much strengthened and sustained by Mazzini, and chiefly by the example of his devotion. That devotion was even more obvious at the end of his life than it was when he withdrew from Switzerland; yet his decisive impact had been made before that date. His influence may have been less widespread than she supposed, but it must have been much what that singular lady said who knew him both at Genoa and at Marseilles, and whose remarkable beauty should not be allowed to obscure the fact that she was also intelligent—the Principessa di Belgioioso:

> Mazzini, as soon as he made his appearance [at Marseilles], sought to make himself an ally of God; but his God was the God of French revolutionaries, not the God whom the people of Italy adore; He was a God without forms of worship, without ministers, without churches, almost without laws . . . there was much talk about Giuseppe Mazzini, and the most widely opposed and exaggerated opinions were held about him . . . I believe that Giuseppe Mazzini's intentions were straight and pure, especially in those early days of what he called his apostolate . . . he succeeded, in the course of a very few years, in transforming the Italian people, and in inspiring them with hate of the foreign domination, and with the love of liberty and of independence, and of the freedom of their country.

> (pp. 199-211)

> *E. E. Y. Hales, in his* Mazzini and the Secret Societies: The Making of a Myth, *Eyre & Spottiswoode, 1956, 226 p.*

Gaetano Salvemini   (essay date 1957)

[*Salvemini, an Italian-born American, was a historian, political writer, and educator known for his analyses of and opposition to fascism. In the following excerpt, originally published in 1905 and revised for American publication in 1957, he discusses what he considers flaws in Mazzini's thought, arguing that his concepts of democracy, nationalism, and moral duty could easily be and had in fact been employed in the service of fascism. However, Salvemini praises Mazzini's devotion to the cause of Italian unification.*]

Among [the religious political and social theories of

Giuseppe Mazzini] are many democratic ideas that belong to our own time, embodied in a Utopian theocratic system resembling those in which medieval scholasticism was so prolific: a fusion of Dante's *De Monarchia* with Rousseau's *Contrat Social* and the doctrines of Saint-Simon, achieved by a nineteenth-century Italian patriot and revolutionary.

It is easy to find weaknesses in such a structure, raised as it is by methods so foreign to our own modes of thought; or to point out the many contradictory statements with which it abounds, and its dubious historical foundations.

To take the law of progress alone—the corner-stone of the whole system—it would be necessary, before accepting the forecast of the future that Mazzini bases upon it, to agree that his statements regarding the different historical periods and their religious character were accurate: which no historian would be prepared to do. We should then have to admit that the succession of events—given that they did in fact occur according to the Mazzinian scheme—represented progress: only to find ourselves faced by the probably insuperable difficulty of defining in what, objectively speaking, progress consists. Finally, even admitting that history has evolved as Mazzini would have us believe, and that its development has represented continual progress, so that we may legitimately maintain, on the evidence of all past centuries, that such progress does exist, it would still remain to be proved that mankind, in the future, might not choose other ways and means of achieving it than those laid down by Mazzini; or even that they might not cease to progress at all.

If, however, from this basic assumption of Mazzini's we turn to examine some of his other assertions, doubts and objections rise at every step. We are entitled to question, for instance, whether universal suffrage has ever been the means through which the will of God has revealed itself to man. Universal suffrage is merely the method by which the party in power can be changed without violence when it has lost the confidence of the majority in the electorate. The revolutionary multitudes inspired by God which Mazzini saw ready to rise on every side were but figments of his own imagination. Mazzini did not know Italy. He had been born into a well-to-do family of Genoa, and had travelled no further than Tuscany, which he visited for a few days, before going into exile. He never made any direct acquaintance with the lower classes in different parts of the peninsula, where the 'people' were indifferent to politics and, indeed, altogether reactionary. In Austria, Germany, Russia and Turkey they were even more inert than in Italy. In Mazzini's time national sentiment prevailed only among the Italian middle-classes.

Traditional religious creeds have never merged into any new revelation. And Mazzini's system, founded as it was on the assumed existence of a revolutionary 'people' inspired by God was at fault on other points. Mazzini saw in Europe nations divided from one another by so-called 'natural' frontiers, traced by God from all eternity in the rivers, mountains and seas. In reality, it is only in exceptional cases that a nation occupies territory endowed with obvious geographical frontiers. England's frontier is the sea. The frontiers of Spain and Italy are the sea and the

mountains. For almost all the rest, natural frontiers do not exist. France has natural frontiers on all sides except towards the East, where, in the Rhineland, French and Germans are divided by no well-defined natural boundary. There is no natural frontier between the Germans and the Poles, between the Poles and the Russians, or between the territory occupied by the Roumanians and that of the Magyars. Indeed, Roumania is split up into two parts by a clear-cut natural boundary, that of the Carpathian Mountains. No natural frontier divides Canada from the U.S.A., or the U.S.A. from Mexico. Even the British nation is no longer confined within its own natural frontiers, for during the last centuries it has sent its people out to settle in all parts of the world.

The doctrine of 'natural frontiers' springs from a scholastic equivocation. The geographers, for the purpose of their studies, classify the surface of the earth into 'natural regions'; though even these vary according to different schools of thought. But in actual fact, human groups, in taking possession of the land, have never concerned themselves with such classifications. National frontiers are a product of human will through history. They are the result of struggles between neighbouring groups, each seeking to expand at the other's expense. 'National' frontiers are historical and artificial. They are the work of man.

And why, one may well ask, should Mazzini associate Denmark, Norway and Sweden in a single unit, and divide Germany into two? Or offer her, as he does in 1858, the right to opt for a tripartite Confederation, and, in 1861, for total unification? And why should Switzerland be afflicted with a confederation, when the law of progress implies political unification for all nations? And how is it that—for all his talk of Humanity—the peoples of the world, outside Europe, are wholly absent from Mazzini's thoughts?

Mazzini overlooked the fact that very few national groups form compact units in themselves. Many of them radiate out from their central nuclei, with the result that there are territories in which offshoots from different nationalities are intermingled. Even the Italian people are not alone in inhabiting the territory south of the Alps: there are Germans in the South Tyrol, and, in Istria, Slavs intermingled with Italians. In Mazzini's time, in most countries, the less civilized national minorities were crushed beneath the civil, military and ecclesiastical bureaucracies, mainly drawn from the predominant nationalities. The subject peoples had not yet reached a clear and active consciousness of their individuality: they were 'nations without history'. But after Mazzini's death, every national group gained a sense of its own identity. His doctrine entitled them to self-determination. Thus, in mixed territories, minorities feel entitled to claim their personal, national and political rights against the privileges of the ruling race. According to Liberal doctrine—if one is to be consistently Liberal—no national group is entitled to stifle the national consciousness of individuals belonging to another nationality in mixed territories, or to violate the personal and political rights of their fellow-citizens. Some kind of compromise must therefore be found in order to grant equal rights to all. Liberal doctrine upholds the rights not only of majorities against the privileges of a minority, but asserts a yet higher justice: the safeguarding of the rights of minorities threatened with the oppression of sectarian majorities. The problem of racial minorities is merely part of a general problem: that of the legal status of all minorities, whether religious, political, social or national. And the problem cannot be solved unless the idea of compulsory unity is abandoned, and the criterion of freedom for all loyally accepted. But most men are led by self-interest and their own passions, rather than by doctrines aimed at establishing justice and peace. As a rule, national majorities in mixed territories claim the right of self-determination for themselves against foreign domination, but deny personal and political rights to their own minorities. And the minorities do the same. The result is that in all mixed territories bitter struggles are carried on in support of 'historical rights' on the one hand, and 'national rights' on the other. This is one of the most dangerous sources of moral and political disorder today.

Mazzini, in his ignorance of the problem, maintained that each nation must keep itself immune from foreign infiltration on the territory assigned to it. This would imply the violent expulsion, extermination or assimilation of all alien groups by the ruling race. Such brutality would be wholly opposed to the humane spirit with which all Mazzini's thought is imbued. But his system would logically lead to it.

Another weak strand in his doctrine concerned international relations. Mazzini gave a purely moral form to what he termed the Association of Humanity. He was preaching national independence to all peoples at a time when many of them were wholly lacking in political consciousness. For this reason he stressed, first and foremost, the necessity of breaking every bond that subordinated nation to nation. He refused to accept any form of legal restriction on the independence of each national unit. He would uphold today the doctrine of unlimited national sovereignty. At the same time he wanted national sovereign states to live in peace under the rule of justice; oblivious of the fact that this would entail putting limits upon national sovereignty and was an inherent contradiction. Mazzini solved the problem by asserting that the peoples, once they were free and equal, would be inspired by God with the spirit of justice; and that therefore there would be no need of any compulsion to keep the peace between them. His Association of Mankind was to be simply a system of moral obligation, freely proclaimed by the best among each people, and freely accepted by the conscience of all.

This was not solving the problem: it was evading the issue by means of an entirely unwarranted assumption. In reality, the peoples of this earth are not divinely inspired with an unmixed sense of justice. They are influenced also by other passions, such as blind egoism, the urge to oppress the weak, and revenge. To make Mazzini's doctrine work, the impossibility of reconciling unlimited national sovereignty with international peace and justice would have to be recognized. But even so, the problem of how to subordinate men's interests, habits, passions and prejudices to such a system would remain. (pp. 85-91)

All the problems raised by Mazzini's teaching lead, sooner or later, to a single problem: what is the place of liberty in this doctrine?

Mazzini never asserts that unanimity for mankind is either possible or desirable: indeed, he considers minority heresies as a 'pledge of future progress', and declares that in the new order of Humanity freedom of thought and freedom for heretical belief will be scrupulously respected, because 'thought must only be confuted or destroyed by thought'. It seems that he wants the 'free and educated individual man' to be 'a prophet of future progress'; a function that will consist in 'protesting, in the name of a new goal beyond the immediate one, against any tendency towards the negation of indefinite progress, and against intolerance'. But the individual, though free to think as he likes and to preach his own heresy, must obey the will of the majority, as legally made known; because 'when the people, the collective body of your brothers, declares that such is its belief, you must bow your head and refrain from any act of rebellion'. 'He who withdraws himself, even for a moment, in his actions, from the general line of thought and the national aim, is acting apart from the vital conditions of Association; and this must not be.'

How, then, can the obligation to obey the people, the interpreter of the divine revelation, be reconciled with the right of free belief in heresy as the herald of new progress? Would not the People, too—imbued, according to Mazzini, with the spirit of the God he has wrested from the Catholic Church and from the monarchies, with their claims to Divine Right—become for this very reason, like the Popes and Kings, an infallible idol with whom none would be permitted to disagree?

Mazzini's theory of liberty in general and of the political liberties in particular, is a 'Jacobin' theory that, with its deified People, might well lead to a totalitarian Theocracy more oppressive than any lay dictatorship.

Freedom, for Mazzini, is not the right of all men to use their own faculties in whatever direction they like, without injury to others: 'True freedom does not consist in the right to choose evil, but in the right to choose from among the different ways that lead to good.' 'Freedom is a means for good, not an end.' Freedom, therefore, is to be known by the choice of means, not the end, which will be indicated by the people's interpretation of the Divine will. These are dangerous maxims, which might well lead to the abolition of all liberty.

But Mazzini, in one of his not rare contradictory statements, also affirms that freedom of choice between good and evil must be respected, because 'without liberty, morality could not exist, since, if there were no freedom of choice between good and evil, between devotion to common progress and the spirit of selfishness, there would be no responsibility'. He declares that it is the individual's duty to vindicate his freedom even against the people's will 'in the essential things of life'. And he constructs around the different aspects of political freedom—personal freedom, freedom of movement, of religious belief, of opinion, of expression in print or by any other pacific means, freedom of association and freedom to trade—a theory that is undeniably liberal.

Yet in vindicating his own freedom against possible transgression by the majority in the case of 'the essential things of life', the individual only has a 'right of protest in such ways as circumstances may suggest': a statement that is, in truth, altogether too elastic, and that does not succeed in masking some uncertainty in the thought. And from the number of freedoms that are to be respected—here the logical consequences of his system may be perceived—freedom of education and academic freedom are explicitly excluded: since it is through education that the younger generation learns what is good and what is bad, and the moral goal for which the individual must strive in co-ordinating his efforts with those of the nation and of humanity.

> This cry of academic freedom arose (and it is still of value) wherever moral education is the monopoly of a despotic government, of a reactionary caste, or of a priesthood naturally hostile towards the dogma of progress. It has been a weapon against tyranny; a watchword of emancipation, imperfect but indispensable. Make use of it wherever you find yourselves treated as slaves. But I speak to you of a time in which religious faith will have written the word Progress upon the doors of the temple, and all institutions will, in a different form, repeat that word.

Then the nature of the problem will be changed: it will be the State's task to lay down regulations that will 'make a national Education universal, compulsory and uniform in its general direction, for without unity of education there is no nation'. One of the faults with which Mazzini charged monarchical institutions was that of appointing 'a professor of materialist views in one university, a Catholic in another, and a follower of Hegel in a third'; and in writing to Daniel Stern, with reference to the Hegelians who were teaching at Naples and the possibility of an imminent republican revolution, he added: 'In due time we shall sweep all that stuff away.'

In the last years of his life this subject became one of his *idées fixes*. On November 26th, 1870, he wrote to Aurelio Saffi: 'Having to prove how the Monarchy is lacking in all branches of moral judgment, I need a work on the Universities and on university studies in general, with observations on the professors, of which a list would be needed with the beliefs that they profess: a Catholic beside Moleschott, a Rosminian beside Vera, etc.' And on January 12th, 1871, he wrote: 'I am anxious to carry out my work on present conditions in the teaching profession and the effect upon it of atheism in the government: the professors teach materialist, Catholic, Hegelian or any other school of ideas.' On November 8th, 1871, he wrote: 'Try to help me in collecting material on the moral situation in the teaching profession today; university professors preaching opposing doctrines, and so on. I want to write on national education, and naturally I have to expose the contrast between what is, and what ought to be.'

In the same way Mazzini's standard of literary criticism can be explained. Once it is accepted that art and literature must have a social and educative function, it is natural that Mazzini, although endowed by nature with good taste and a most sensitive feeling for art, and capable—when

not hindered by his own theories—of admirably acute critical judgment, should measure the value of a work of art simply by its degree of conformity with his own social, political and religious ideals; entirely neglecting its aesthetic form. In Dante he only sees and praises the religious and political ideas, in which he perceives 'the same thought that today is deeply-rooted in our epoch'. He dislikes Petrarch, whose work 'already contained signs of a pagan deviation'; and, probably ignorant of his *Sine titulo,* could not appreciate the poet's great work of anti-scholasticism. He had little admiration for Shakespeare, 'who knew nothing of the laws of humanity: the future has no voice in his pages; there is no enthusiasm for great principles'. On the other hand, he had a lively sympathy for Byron, because he saw in him the effects of the desperation to which individualism leads, and 'because in its melancholy and its enthusiasms his work is moral, social and prophetic'. Mazzini was always reluctant, above all in the last years of his life, to recognize the true greatness of Goethe, because Goethe 'found no place in his works or in his sympathies for humanity', his system being 'wholly one of poetic materialism, opposed to the culture of the ideal'. Schiller he exalted, because 'he had sanity of spirit, faith in God and hope in the destinies of mankind, even when he saw it brought low'; his writings 'are an inspiration to sacrifice and noble deeds'. For Foscolo, with his patriotism and misfortunes, Mazzini had a filial devotion. He preferred the Polish religious and patriotic poets to Lamartine and Victor Hugo; showed only contempt for the irreligious Leopardi; and had little sympathy with Manzoni's attitude of resignation. In short, it is clear that since art must have an educative function and freedom of education is suppressed, artistic freedom, too, must be sacrificed on the altar of associated humanity.

It is little wonder, therefore, that the official philosopher of the Fascist dictatorship, Giovanni Gentile, hailed Mazzini as a fore-runner of Mussolini: to produce which metamorphosis he had only to suppress from Mazzini's teaching the rights that freedom bestows, and to leave untouched the duties of discipline. The exaltation of past national glories, and the promise of glory to come, may be an excellent tonic for reviving the self-respect of a people humiliated by foreign domination or internal disruption. But it is also one that may cause a restless and aggressive foreign policy, a lust for conquest—and, consequently, disillusionment, bitterness and unmerited self-contempt—when a country is ruled by men with no sense of balance, unable to distinguish what is possible from what is impossible. Take away the atmosphere of justice and goodness that colours all Mazzini's thought, and one finds that, just as his ideas of liberty can be brought, if somewhat mutilated, into line with Gentile's, so from the Third Rome of Mazzini it is easy to slip—with some necessary falsification—into the Third Rome of Mussolini: with results that the Italians now know to their cost, although unfortunately the disastrous experience has not, as yet, cured them all from the disease of megalomania, or from their weakness for rhetorical excess. (pp. 92-8)

Generally speaking, the greater part of Mazzini's assertions are arbitrary and impossible to prove; while those that, individually, correspond with real historical facts and tendencies are deduced from dubious principles, form an integral part of a questionable system, and interpret real facts in such a way as to make them, too, appear suspect; they may be true, but not for the reasons adduced by Mazzini.

'He had little aptitude', as Masci rightly observes, 'for scientific thought, for relentless reasoning or the analysis of facts; and his mistaken ideas on the scientific method were made worse by his mistaken application of them.' With his passionate nature, he was unable to subject himself to the effort of logical clarification and organization which the scientific and philosophic method demands; but he was ready to interpose with supreme self-confidence in the discussion of any system of ideas. He qualified every theory with postulates that were not susceptible of, indeed were foreign to, any sort of critical analysis, and he made himself the beginning and end of all rational activity; all of which lessened the force of his attacks on certain moral and political ideals as being materialistic and sterile intellectualism.

In proof of the degree in which Mazzini's reasoning faculty was subordinated to feeling, it is enough to observe him in a moment of crisis: when assailed, in the second half of 1836, by that access of despair and doubt which he has described so vividly.

> When I felt myself alone in the world, except for my poor mother, far away and in distress on my account, I drew back in terror at the abyss before me. Then, in that desert, I was faced by Doubt. Perhaps I was wrong and the world was right. Perhaps the idea that I was following was only a dream . . . That day, when my soul was seared by these misgivings, I felt not only inexpressibly wretched, but like a condemned man conscious of guilt and incapable of expiation . . . How many mothers had already wept because of me! How many more would weep if I were to persist in my attempt to rouse the youth of Italy to action in the struggle for a united nation? And suppose this nation were only an illusion? What right had I to decide upon the future and to cause hundreds, nay, thousands of men to sacrifice themselves and all that they held most dear? . . . My anguish was such that I felt near to madness. Had my state of mind endured I should have lost my reason and taken my own life.

Did Mazzini, in such terrible suffering of mind, think of overcoming doubt with the weapons of reason? No; he turned for help to a woman, Eleanora Ruffini; one of those mothers to whom he had already given most cause to weep. 'Women are my advocates with God. While men, for the most part, cry out against us, desert us or slander us, the women I have known have been my most constant and loving friends.' He writes to Eleanora:

> I know not what I would not give for an hour's talk with you, to tell you all that is in my heart and to ask comfort of you, as a holy blessing . . . I would like to speak to you generally of my ideas, and to hear from you—symbol as you are of constancy and resignation—that they are not illusions: *that the mind has not misled the heart,*

> *but that the heart has prompted and willed them.* Since the publication of my ideas on faith, humanity, and the future, is a cause of trouble and persecution for me and for your dear ones, do you love me less? Am I an egoist? Do I heartlessly betray my duties as a man? Do I fail in my love for you and my own family? If I were to die a martyr to our faith, to the faith of Jacopo, would I be unfeeling, would I commit a crime? Say nothing of this to anyone else; but if you can conscientiously give me a word of comfort, do so; if not, be silent, I beg you. I shall know that I am wrong. I shall know that I am pursuing a phantom, that my religion is all false belief and must be given up; and I will give it up, because I believe in you as in an oracle, as in the most virtuous, religious soul, purified and perfected by sorrow, that exists on earth.

This is a method no true philosopher would choose in building up and consolidating his system of ideas.

And how were his doubts resolved? After reasoning things out, according to all the rules of inductive and deductive logic? Alas, no!

> One day I awoke with a tranquil mind, my intellect clear once more, like one who knows himself saved from great peril. The moment of waking had long been one of deep sadness for me, as the consciousness of having to face my troubles returned; and during those months all the unbearable difficulties with which I would have to contend during the day seemed comprised in this instant. But that morning, nature seemed to smile upon me and the light, like a blessing, to refresh the life in my weary veins. And the first thought that flashed upon my mind was this: that I had been misled by my own egoism, and that I had not rightly understood life. As soon as I could do so, I calmly examined everything, and myself, afresh; and I re-made the whole of my moral philosophy . . . I passed from the idea of God to that of Progress; from that of Progress to a new conception of Life, to faith in a mission, and the logical consequence of Duty as the supreme principle. Having reached that point, I swore to myself that nothing in the world should again make me doubt or forsake it.

God, Progress, Mission, Duty: all these appear only when the crisis has been overcome, when serenity and faith have returned, when Mazzini is able to examine himself in peace; in other words, when, having recovered faith in the legitimacy of his own aspirations, he is in possession of the support he needs in constructing—'with luminous clarity'—his own system, and holds at last the criterion of certainty in his hands. All this happens unexpectedly, after a night of placid sleep, when some beneficent process of recovery has brought refreshment to 'the life in his weary veins'.

Mazzini was above all a man of action. Thought was only of value to him in so far as it could be translated into action, and one form of action in particular. His ideas were not the fruit of an effort to understand things objectively; they were an instrument that served him in modifying things in accordance with the ideal in which his own moral sentiments found satisfaction. He took from the philosophic, political and historical ideas current in his time those elements best suited to his own temperamental needs, and put them in such order as practical necessity required. In so doing, he imagined himself to be a philosopher; but even this was largely due to the atmosphere in which his intellectual development had taken place, in a period when it was the fashion to construct philosophical systems that explained the universe. His own attempt, however, was weak and incomplete.

Yet, given Mazzini's particular moral temperament, this very incompleteness and weakness as a thinker is an essential element in the completeness and strength of the man of action. Confronted by Mazzini's definition of God: 'Creator of all that exists; living, absolute thought, of which our world is a ray and the universe an embodiment', Gentile asks: 'Ray or embodiment? Emanative or pantheistic?' and, seeking to understand what Mazzini could possibly have meant by the statement that 'God and the Law are identical terms, and Humanity is the living Word of God', concluded that Mazzini's ideas were indeterminate, fluctuating and fantastic, and that as a philosopher he was really of little account. This is true enough. But what, after all, is more indeterminate, for those who have a different religious faith, or who are not endowed with that special state of mind in which religion has its roots, than—for example—the Lord's Prayer that a Christian repeats? Who is this Father of ours who is in Heaven? What is his Kingdom? And what the trespasses that we forgive? Nevertheless, not one of us who has learnt this prayer in childhood can think of it without feeling a fervent desire for righteousness, for love, for peace, or without the conviction that its Author, though not a philosopher, was a very wonderful character. It is a prayer that does not present a sequence of ideas, but raises a host of feelings. And it is the same with every religious faith; a more or less logical structure of reasoning arises over a sentimental foundation, and always aspires to the status of philosophy: against which critics of different faiths and of no faith at all aim their shafts. But to the believer, the entirety of these vague, indistinct and undemonstrable sentiments, clothed in a majestic familiar language unchanged by time, remains untouched. In the conception that Mazzini had of God, oscillating always between pantheism and theism, it was precisely this oscillation (as Crespi pointed out) that kept his energy up to a high and constant level; because the apostle-hero could always, and at the same time, draw strength and inspiration from two different conceptions of divinity: from the personal God, Who is Father and Law-giver, demanding duty, conflict and sacrifice from him; and from the God in Whom all creation lives, moves and has its being, present always in the spirit of the individual who obeys, fights and suffers, and giving him the faith and strength he needs for his long and desperate ordeal.

We need not, then, stop to criticize the thinker in Mazzini, thereby making the same mistake that he himself made in regarding himself as a philosopher. Let us rather consider the believer, the apostle, the man of action. In other words, having ascertained the content of his religious faith, let us ask what influence it had. How did it direct his actions and those of his followers? And what practical function did it fulfil in the sphere of history? (pp. 99-105)

In seeking to estimate the effect of Mazzini's religious teaching, we are forced to recognize that even among his closest followers there were very few who fully shared his faith.

According to Mazzini's grandiose plans, the organization entitled *La Giovine Europa* ('Young Europe') was to be a training ground for the 'precursors' and 'apostles' who were to elaborate 'a new philosophy, a new political economy, etc.', in the light of the new faith, and to promote its application to 'all branches of social activity and to the study of language, race and historical origins, so that the mission to be assigned by the new epoch to each of the different peoples may be revealed, and the future order in Europe deduced therefrom'. Together with intellectual renewal, moreover, it was to prepare universal insurrection. But the *Giovine Europa* never succeeded in emerging from its rudimentary state. Its propaganda certainly had a tardy and indirect influence on Swiss constitutional reform in 1848, and served to draw the attention of European democrats to the international character of social and political problems. But apart from these very limited results it had no appreciable effect whatever on the development of nineteenth-century philosophic, scientific or political thought. Scarcely three years after that April day in 1834 when seventeen Germans, Poles and Italians—somewhat audaciously taking upon themselves the representation of their own nations and of the whole world—had met in Berne to found the *Giovine Europa,* Mazzini was forced to admit that it had entirely failed of its purpose. 'It is rumoured abroad', he wrote on August 23rd, 1837,

> that I have deserted the *Giovine Europa.* I have every right to say that the *Giovine Europa* has deserted me. Is there a single one of its signatories who shares my ideas on what it should be? The signatories, I say: so much the worse for them if in signing they misunderstood me or made mental reservations! . . . I have been deceived. I am surrounded today by people who call themselves the *Giovine Europa* and reject all its ideas: by people who only see in it a nominal bond for the purpose of conspiracy, not a band of apostles, a mission, the precursors of a new world. All my ideas and all that I have tried to do are scorned, derided, outraged . . . I stand alone, utterly alone: alone with God, with my memories, with my own faith. And if none shares my faith, am I to blame? Do I abandon, desert, the *Giovine Europa* because your *Giovine Europa* is not mine?

Later attempts to revive the original organization under the guise of a 'European Centre' during the second half of 1846, and a 'Central Committee of European Democracy' in 1850 and 1855 were equally unfortunate. It is curious to observe the ingenuous way in which Mazzini set about forming committees from which he expected conspicuous results. 'I already have a representative coming from Germany, where he is well-known as a professor and writer; and I am now concerned with Switzerland and other countries,' he wrote on August 2nd, 1846. A month later, 'I have won over the German, who is the man I wanted,

Jacoby . . . but I am having difficulties in Switzerland, where Dr. Steiger raises objections.' 'I do not agree with you as to the slight importance of the European meeting, if I succeed. As to having no mandate, that is of no consequence. No one can give us one, because the democratic party has not been constituted . . . What I now need is a Greek, and a Southern Slav from the Austrian Empire' (October 6th, 1846). This habit of Mazzini's of making individual men into an embodiment of their countries has aroused lively criticism.

Among Italians, Mazzini's religious teaching had no success. He realized his own solitary position, which grieved him not only at times when he really was deserted by everyone, but also when he had a considerable number of political adherents. During his imprisonment at Gaeta, in 1870, he wrote:

> I know no one in the world at present with whom I could live for more than three days without becoming ungrateful and filled with silent fury. No one knows how disheartened I have been for years: how only my faith in a future I shall never see gives me strength. If I could have my way, I should live in absolute solitude. I have an irresistible need to avoid men, and to be alone with God and the dead.

On April 11th, 1871, he wrote: 'I keep my residence secret from everyone, because I shrink from contact with the Party, which would take up my time and my strength and turn me into a misanthrope in a week or two.' And in June 1871, 'If I let myself be seen, the Party will fall upon me, which would mean I should have no time to myself and should die of rage like a mad dog in a couple of weeks.'

Nor did the Italians who came after him, with certain exceptions, seem better disposed than were his contemporaries to make an effort to understand, far less to adopt, Mazzini's religious revelation in its entirety. Indeed it would seem undeniable that almost all those Italians who claim to be followers of Mazzini are wholly ignorant of Mazzini himself.

His influence as the apostle of a new religion was felt in England rather than in Italy: among radical circles, and particularly by women. Jessie White-Mario and the Signora Crawford-Saffi, transplanted into Italy as the wives of Italians, were among the very few who wholeheartedly accepted the Mazzinian religion.

There were indications of a revival in Italy of Mazzini's religious ideas at the beginning of the present century in the theories of the modernist movement, which had much in common with his. We owe one of the most able and moving commemorative tributes to Mazzini—a Mazzini perhaps not strictly historical because too much Christianized, but presented with a loving understanding of his intimate religious mysticism—to Gallarati-Scotti. And a little book of prayer and of religious *pensées* published with the approval of the ecclesiastical authorities because it contained nothing not strictly orthodox, was also the work of a modernist: for the ecclesiastical censor allowed a passage, signed by the initials G. M., to escape his notice, unaware of the mistake he was making: a typical case of

those silent, subterranean influences, to which we have already referred. But in Italy such instances are rare.

The cultural tradition of Italy contains few romantic elements and is almost exclusively classic. Mazzini's mysticism does not seem suited to, or at least has not yet succeeded in affecting, Italian mental habits. His religion was too political for those who longed for a new faith, and too mystical for those who simply sought freedom for their country; too full of reasoning for the sentimental, and too sentimental for the rational. Far from turning their thoughts to a new religion for Humanity, the Italians had to think of creating their own national unity. They had to fight with dogged determination against the tradition of divine right in order to release civil life from all control by the Church and to construct a new lay administration unfettered by pontifical authority. Was it possible for them to accept, in Mazzini's teaching, a theory so profoundly theocratic, and having, beneath its superficial differences, so many points of contact with that other, the evil effects of which they were condemned to endure?

One of the accusations made against Mazzini by his adversaries, and also by his friends when they broke with him, was precisely this: that he wanted to create a despotic theocracy. Giovanni Ruffini wrote, on November 17th, 1837: 'Mazzini thinks he is Pope, and infallible.' Luigi Carlo Farini wrote of him in 1853: 'He is pontiff, prince, apostle, priest. When the clericals have gone, he will be thoroughly at home in Rome.' Felice Orsini called him 'the new Mahomet'; Sirtori would have nothing to do with Mazzinian 'Theo-democracy'; Proudhon accused him of 'wishing to be Pope'; and Marx derisively dubbed him 'Theopompus'.

If the theological postulates upon which Mazzini based his moral and political system are discounted, in other words, if we do not accept the theory that the people's opinion—more reliable than that of any other, whether individual or collective, pontifical or princely—must be the true interpretation of the divine revelation, and that the authority set up by popular suffrage is necessarily the 'true, good, sacred authority' recognized by all and cheerfully obeyed by all; if we do not believe that the collective will can never be led astray, as all others are at times, and that in choosing the nation's representatives universal suffrage will work in a way entirely different from that with which experience has made us familiar, then the whole of Mazzinian democracy falls to the ground. And in fact, the Italian middle class, which bore the responsibility of carrying through the national revolution, had few illusions, indeed had no reason to have any, upon the infallibility of the people. Mazzini's national democratic republic, emanating from a deified people, must have seemed to them simply a new theocracy, likely to be even more oppressive than the old, precisely because it was to have a democratic and elective basis: for those elected by a popular majority would regard themselves as chosen by God and as instruments not so much of a political as a religious mission. They would thus impose their will on the minority with all the intolerance of those who are convinced of being in possession of absolute truth. The minority would oppose the majority in the name not only of their own political principles but in that of their religious creed. All would claim the tradition of Humanity as their own, and would be convinced of having consulted it with the requisite purity of thought and devotion that Mazzini laid down so ingenuously as the criterion of truth. Each would deny to his opponent the right to invoke tradition or to claim that he was fitted to consult it. In other words, since unanimity is impossible, there would be no lack of social and political strife in Mazzini's new order, but it would be complicated and embittered by religious discord.

And after all, Mazzini's Holy Alliance of Peoples was to be constituted—however paradoxical the statement may at first sight appear—not so very differently from Metternich's Holy Alliance of sovereigns. The monarchs of the Holy Alliance proclaimed their belief in God, in Progress (defined according to their own consciences and to the historical tradition that suited them so well) and even in collective humanity. Does not the preamble to the Holy Alliance invoke solidarity among the peoples, the unity of the human family, and the duty of all men to obey God's law upon earth? The princes, too, had a religion of duty, of their own duty; they made great sacrifices in their effort to govern their unruly subjects, who appeared ignorant of the universal moral law as conceived by the princes themselves, in the light of their own consciences and their familiar traditions. Moreover the princes felt the necessity of bringing their actions in the temporal sphere into conformity with the dictates of the spiritual authority residing in Rome. And the Pope, too, was held to be inspired by God. Did not the princes sign their decrees—including those imposing the death penalty—with an invocation for divine help? And was not the suppression of free thought a logical consequence of the mission that the princes regarded as theirs, of educating mankind and leading them unhindered along the way of righteousness? It was only necessary to replace the Pope by the Council of Humanity, and the Kings by the Peoples, for Mazzini's system to emerge complete; the only difference being that universal suffrage would take the place of heredity in the field of politics, and, in that of religion, of election by the cardinals' vote.

It was natural, therefore, that Mazzini's ideal of God and the People should seem a dangerous return to obsolete traditions, an incomprehensible rejection of all the most precious achievements of the liberal movement. In this connection, De Sanctis' lack of comprehension with regard to Mazzini is characteristic. De Sanctis, who was unquestionably the most open-minded Italian liberal of the nineteenth century, and one who appreciated Mazzini's moral and literary importance better than any of those belonging to his own party and his own time, failed to understand either Mazzini's democratic or theocratic beliefs: the doctrine was so alien to his spirit that he, who understood everything, simply could not take it in.

If, in addition, it is remembered that Mazzini, absorbed as he always was in political and revolutionary activities, had no leisure in which to dedicate himself to systematic religious propaganda, and that when at last, towards the end of his life, he was able to do so, men's minds were already dominated by the positivist reaction against early nineteenth-century idealism, the scanty success and indeed almost complete sterility of his religious teaching can well be understood. (pp. 114-23)

In 1847 Mazzini evaluated the fruits of his own work as amounting to one-fifth of what his movement had hoped. He could not have made a different estimate after 1870.

To produce even this fifth, other forces that were not in sympathy with his own thought and action had powerfully contributed. In so complex a system of cause and effect as that of the Italian Risorgimento, it would be ingenuous to attribute responsibility to Mazzini for the whole of the results achieved.

Many other writers had played their part with Mazzini in fostering now one, now another, of the elements that go to make up Italian national sentiment. From this point of view, not only Dante, Petrarch and Machiavelli, but Alfieri, Foscolo, Manzoni, indeed, all Italian literature down the centuries, had prepared the minds of Italians for the conquest of unity. But so far as practical action was concerned, it is certain that Mazzini, during his years of exile, was ill-informed on the real conditions of the country in which he was to operate; he was too ready to deceive himself as to the millions of men ready to join in brotherly insurrection—Giovanni Ruffini had good reason to christen him Fantasio in his novel *Lorenzo Benoni*—and too prone to despise the slow, cautious, cool-headed nature of the diplomacy on which, nevertheless, it was necessary to rely in an eminently international problem like that of Italy. He was, moreover, averse to any concession whatever on the ideal of national unity which represented the irreducible minimum of his own aspirations, but which to others must often have seemed remote and fantastic. Thus Mazzini unquestionably lacked many qualities that are indispensable in a leader who passes from the preaching of ideas to their practical application through a great political movement. And if Garibaldi had not been the right arm of the national party, as Mazzini was its soul; if Cavour and his successors, with all the conservative party, had not, in their steady support of the Piedmontese monarchy, intervened again and again—turning the results of the national movement to their own advantage, but at the same time consolidating them and procuring them the reluctant sanction of other governments—it would be very difficult to say whether, or to what extent, Mazzini's national 'apostolate' would have been realized at all.

Nor should the work of his disciples, of the fighting men and the statesmen blind us to what was, in reality, the principal factor in the Italian Risorgimento: the anonymous, collective action of those various groups of liberals who were not pledged to any one leader or party, and who with their good sense, their unheroic but able opportunism, knew when to wait and when to take risks, when to protest and when to be silent, how to *reculer pour mieux sauter* and how to combine their efforts, however diverse, in action that seems to us today, from a distance, so admirably well-balanced and co-ordinated.

Finally, it is undeniable that there had been many others, before Mazzini, who had wished to see an Italy no longer dismembered, no longer forgetful of her ancient glory and a pawn in the game to the ambitions of her neighbours. Recent research, although it has eliminated from the ranks of true prophets of Italian unity and independence Dante, Petrarch and all those lesser writers hailed by our fathers as patriots of the Risorgimento if they so much as introduced the name of Italy into their works, has on the other hand revealed the existence of a rich vein of openly national sentiment in the troubled period of French conquest, from 1796 to 1814. These theories, however, of a united Italy, clothed in republican trappings in the early days of Jacobin conquest, and carefully presented in monarchical guise under the Napoleonic despotism, are confined, as Masi observes, merely to the book or pamphlet, or individual aspirations, of some particular poet or patriot; they are Arcadian laments, classical reminiscences, scholastic exercises, vague projects with no plan of execution, or at the most uncoordinated ventures followed by swift disillusionment. With the fall of the Napoleonic Empire and the Treaty of Vienna, the unity of Italy seemed to vanish for ever into the region of dreams. A few references to it can be found in some obscure Carbonaro literature of the years between 1815 and 1831. But from 1815 to 1860 it was firmly believed by all sensible people that the political unification of Italy, whether in a monarchical or republican form, was—to quote Cesare Balbo's words in 1843—'A puerile idea, held at the most by pettifogging students of rhetoric, common rhymesters and café politicians.'

Giuseppe Mazzini, on the other hand, believed the unification of Italy to be not only possible but necessary. He insisted upon it with single-minded obstinacy, and dedicated his whole life to realizing this ideal, from his early, ardent youth to his grief-stricken old age. He preached it incessantly, in the face of ridicule, disappointment and defeat; communicated his own faith to others simply by virtue of being all the more unshaken in his convictions, the more it seemed that facts were against him; and he doggedly opposed any other solution of the problem, clinging desperately to his own faith even when everything appeared to counsel a more limited and practical outlook. He, and he alone, was responsible for that psychological preparation which, between 1856 and 1860, brought to nothing the manœuvres of those Italian liberals who would have accepted a Murat on the throne of Naples, thereby replacing a divided Italy under Austrian domination by an Italy, still divided, but dominated by France; that psychological preparation from which in 1859 sprang the annexations in Central Italy, in 1860 the expedition of the Thousand, and in 1862 and 1867, Aspromonte and Mentana: from which, in a word, sprang Italian unity. It was Mazzini and Mazzini alone, who imposed upon the Italian liberal-nationalist groups the one dominating idea, to which, through all the vicissitudes of the making of Italy, everything else was to become subordinated. (pp. 155-59)

Gaetano Salvemini, in his Mazzini, *translated by I. M. Rawson, Stanford University Press, 1957, 192 p.*

FURTHER READING

Barr, Stringfellow. *Mazzini: Portrait of an Exile.* New York: Henry Holt and Company, 1935, 308 p.

Traces Mazzini's career from his youth through his exile.

Barricelli, Jean-Pierre. "Romantic Writers and Music: The Case of Mazzini." *Studies in Romanticism* 14, No. 2 (Spring 1975): 95-117.

Discusses Mazzini's theories concerning music in the context of Romanticism and explains how many of his political and literary convictions—the necessity of moral purpose, synthesis, and progress—inform his musical precepts.

Garrison, William Lloyd. *Joseph Mazzini: His Life, Writings, and Political Principles.* New York: Hurd and Houghton, 1872, 366 p.

Praises Mazzini's catholic sensibility, noting his advocacy of universal abolition and suffrage, and contending that he was pragmatic in that he provided the vision necessary to catalyze action.

Griffith, Gwilym O. *Mazzini: Prophet of Modern Europe.* New York: Howard Fertig, 1970, 381 p.

Traces the influences and events that shaped the young Mazzini's principles, which Griffith claims were almost completely formed by 1836, and asserts that his political activity after 1848 was more significant than many critics believe.

Handy, Robert T. "The Influence of Mazzini on the American Social Gospel." *The Journal of Religion* XXIX, No. 2 (April 1949): 114-23.

Demonstrates Mazzini's influence on nineteenth-century American clerical social reformers, noting that his thinking was more relevant in countries more industrialized, more affected by Protestantism, and more idealistic than the Italy of his own era.

Hinkley, Edyth. *Mazzini: The Story of a Great Italian.* 1924. Reprint. Port Washington, N.Y.: Kennikat Press, 1970, 287 p.

Biography in which Hinkley discusses criticism of Mazzini's inability to acknowledge conflicting perspectives, but offers a predominantly favorable view of him, attributing his shortcomings to his purity of character and vision.

Marraro, Howard R. "Mazzini on American Intervention in European Affairs." *The Journal of Modern History* XXI, No. 2 (June 1949): 109-14.

Citing Mazzini's letters to various Americans, elucidates the differences between his ideal state, founded on collective duty, and the United States, based on individual rights. Also explains Mazzini's interest in the American Civil War as a moral example and practical model for Italian nationalism, and recounts his conviction that this war imposed upon the United States a duty to forego isolationism and intervene on behalf of European nationalists.

Rossi, Joseph. *The Image of America in Mazzini's Writings.* Madison: The University of Wisconsin Press, 1954, 188 p.

Chronicles Mazzini's interaction with Italian patriots and antipapal factions in the United States; the American social reformer, Margaret Fuller; American officials in Rome; and Young America, a radical wing of the Democratic party. Also explains his interest in abolition and the American Civil War.

Rudman, Harry W. "The Exile Par Excellence: Mazzini's English Life." In his *Italian Nationalism and English Letters: Figures of the Risorgimento and Victorian Men of Letters,* pp. 25-175. New York: Columbia University Press, 1940.

Describes Mazzini's literary and political projects, friends, and admirers in England; recounts the public attention occasioned by the disclosure that the British Foreign Secretary was intercepting his mail; and details Mazzini's use of this publicity. Rudman concludes by delineating the shifting English perception of Mazzini during and after the Roman uprising of 1849, and discussing English literary representations of him.

Salvatorelli, Luigi. "The Definite Formulation: Mazzinianism." In his *The Risorgimento: Thought and Action,* translated by Mario Domandi, pp. 89-98. New York: Harper & Row, 1970.

Analyzes Mazzinianism as one of several approaches to the Italian nationalist movement, concluding that although Mazzini's political perspective was in many respects less practical than his contemporaries', it was nonetheless the most comprehensive, as his spiritual mandate proved the most broadly effective catalyst of the Italian nationalist movement.

Silone, Ignazio. Introduction to *The Living Thoughts of Mazzini,* by Giuseppe Mazzini, translated by Dr. Arthur Livingstone, pp. 1-32. London: Cassell and Co., 1939.

Describes the formation of what Silone considers Mazzini's fundamentally Romantic theories on literature, religion, government, nationalism, and the divine plan for mankind's moral progress. Silone also observes that, while Mazzini's social and political idealism was irrelevant to Italy's impoverished proletariat, the Marxist reformers who prevailed could not permanently improve this class's standard of living because they did not implement Mazzini's democratic safeguards—a failure that Silone claims conduced "to the Fascist counter-revolution."

Srivastava, Gita. *Mazzini and His Impact on the Indian National Movement.* Allahabad, India: Chugh Publications, 1982, 312 p.

Chronicles the formation of Mazzini's doctrines and his attempts to implement them in Italy and Europe, then assesses his influence on the leaders of the Indian nationalist movement.

John Addington Symonds

1840-1893

English historian, poet, critic, biographer, memoirist, and translator.

A prolific author in many genres, Symonds is best known for his seven-volume cultural history *Renaissance in Italy* and for his *Memoirs* and *Letters.* Considered a significant contribution to Renaissance studies, *Renaissance in Italy* has been praised for its insightful analysis of literary and artistic achievements in this period. Three of its volumes, one subtitled *The Revival of Learning* and the two-part *Italian Literature,* remain among the most comprehensive treatments of their subjects in the English language. Symonds's *Memoirs* and *Letters,* presently regarded as his most enduring legacy, are especially valued for the author's reflections on his life as a practicing homosexual. His incisiveness and candor in relating the struggles of his personal life have enabled psychologists and sociologists to view the works as case studies in homosexuality, and have provided valuable insights into social attitudes in Victorian England.

The son of an eminent physician, Symonds was born in Bristol. His mother died when he was four, leaving her husband to care for Symonds and his two sisters. The elder Symonds, who gained renown as a lecturer at the British Medical School, actively pursued many different fields of knowledge; he indulged his love of literature and philosophy by hosting literary soirées to which he invited such prominent thinkers as Francis Newman, W. E. Gladstone, and Alfred Tennyson. Symonds greatly admired his father and anxiously strove, through constant study, to merit his approval; he was thus notably ahead of his classmates upon entering Harrow in 1854. During his years at Harrow, Symonds first encountered open manifestations of homosexual activity. From an early age he had engaged in clandestine sexual games with older male cousins, and had been enthralled by the sensuality of male figures in Greek art; yet the blatant promiscuity of his schoolfellows shocked and repulsed him. Symonds repressed his physical desires at this time and began writing poetry, both to vent his frustration and to express his conception of ideal love.

Symonds entered Balliol College at Oxford in 1858, thriving academically in its scholarly environment. His lengthy poem *The Escorial* won the Newdigate Prize in 1860 and became the first of Symonds's many published works. Upon completion of his studies Symonds was awarded a fellowship to study at Magdalen College, Oxford, where he won the prestigious Chancellor's Prize for an essay on the Renaissance. Symonds became increasingly distracted during this period, however, by a series of emotionally intense though platonic love affairs with various young men, and he struggled to concentrate on his studies. Writing in his diary in 1861, Symonds lamented: "I have ceased to care about the schools. My ship has sailed into a magic sea

with tempests of its own." While at Magdalen, Symonds's involvement in a bitter love triangle with an Oxford undergraduate and a church choirboy prompted a series of events in which Symonds's letters to the former were exposed. Symonds was verbally reprimanded by school authorities and left Oxford several months later, suffering from nervous exhaustion and early symptoms of consumption. Adding to Symonds's ill health at this time were partial blindness and painful genital inflammations. An ophthalmologist attributed Symonds's eye problems as well as his other disorders to the strain of his self-imposed chastity, and recommended that he either marry or take a mistress. Determined to live a more conventional life, Symonds heeded his physician's advice, marrying Catherine North in 1864.

Although he assumed marital relations with his wife and fathered four children, Symonds continued to struggle with his homosexuality. He sought to escape by throwing himself industriously into the study of literature, traveling extensively while busily contributing literary, historical, and travel essays to such journals as the *Cornhill Maga-zine* and the *Saturday Review*. Symonds finally settled with his family in Clifton, a suburb of Bristol, to be near his ailing father. His attraction to a young student he encountered there prompted Symonds to seek a position at Clifton College as a lecturer on Greek literature; the position was granted him in 1869. He and his family inherited Dr. Symonds's mansion upon his death two years later, and it was there that Symonds began his most significant literary projects. *An Introduction to the Study of Dante,* Symonds's first major work, was published in 1872. Consisting essentially of Symonds's lectures on Dante, this work initiated a series of well-received studies of ancient and Renaissance literature and history. *Studies of the Greek Poets,* published in 1873, presents a collection of Symonds's essays and addresses on Classical subjects; *Sketches in Italy and Greece,* published the following year, comprises numerous articles which had appeared in various periodicals during Symonds's earlier travels. Pleased with the generally favorable reception of his works, Symonds embarked on a lengthy cultural history of the Renaissance period in Italy. The first volume of Symonds's *Renaissance in Italy,* subtitled *The Age of the Despots,* was published in 1875. *The Revival of Learning* and *The Fine Arts,* second and third in the series, were published two years later. The two volumes on Italian literature followed in 1881, and the set was completed in 1886 with the publication of the two-part *Catholic Reaction,* a discussion of the sixteenth-century suppression of Renaissance ideals. Charles Kendall Adams, writing in his *Manual of Historical Literature* (1882), aptly summarized the contemporary critical consensus on *Renaissance in Italy* when he asserted: "As a whole, these works are among the most valuable of the many recent contributions to our knowledge of Italy." Symonds also published four collections of poetry during these years, but none earned him distinction apart from his established reputation as a scholar and critic. Treating various aspects of homosexual love, his verse was considered elegant but obscure and excessively emotive.

By 1880 Symonds's advancing tuberculosis forced him to sell his home and move permanently to a more favorable climate in Davos Platz, Switzerland. Having discontinued sexual relations with his wife by mutual consent after the birth of their fourth child, Symonds no longer repressed his homosexuality and began taking various male lovers. During these later years, he also became increasingly concerned with the plight of the homosexual in society. In 1883, he privately published *A Problem in Greek Ethics,* followed by *A Problem in Modern Ethics* eight years later; each dealt with varying social and historical aspects of the phenomenon Symonds referred to as inversion. England's passage of the Labouchère Amendment in 1885 stiffened the penalty for practicing homosexuality in that country, a decision Symonds, in subsequent years, discreetly lobbied to reverse. Assembling data from various medical and sociological sources to support his pleas for tolerance, Symonds eventually published these materials in *Sexual Inversion,* which he co-authored with Havelock Ellis. Symonds further elucidated his views on the subject in the personal memoirs he began writing during this time; however, these remained unpublished for nearly a century. In the last years of his life, despite failing health, Symonds

completed several other notable works, including acclaimed biographical studies of Walt Whitman and Michelangelo. He died of pneumonia in Rome in 1893.

Symonds's *Renaissance in Italy,* a monumental achievement in its day, has become the author's most enduring analytical work. His history enthusiastically promotes Renaissance Italy as the birthplace of modern Humanism. Adapting the theories of such leading nineteenth-century historians as G. W. F. Hegel, Jacob Burckhardt, and Jules Michelet, Symonds viewed history as a progressive, evolutionary process that was liberating humankind from the oppression of moral and political despotism. *Renaissance in Italy,* modeled on the German *Kulturgeschichte* (cultural history) method, features biographical sketches, anecdotes, family sagas, and commentary on politics and art, offering its readers a broad overview of the subject—one of the first such studies in the English language. Symonds's *Renaissance* is also noted for its emphasis on individuals, for Symonds focused especially on those persons whom he felt best embodied or most effectively influenced the spirit of their age. Evaluating Symonds's *Renaissance in Italy,* critic Kenneth Churchill asserted that "to Symonds it was precisely the stress on individualism and the pagan enjoyment of life which was attractive and vital in the Renaissance and which was the major theme running through all his work." Imbued with Symonds's wide learning and astute perception, his history reached an apogee with the publication of *Italian Literature,* and reviewers praised the author's sound grasp of Renaissance intellectual currents and his skill in analyzing literary works as products of their historical milieu. Many early reviewers, however, objected to Symonds's style, finding *Renaissance in Italy* excessively picturesque, sentimental, and weakened by ornate rhetoric and disruptive digressions. Modern commentators largely concur with this assessment; Wallace Ferguson has described *Renaissance in Italy* as exaggerated and somewhat subjective, adding that Symonds "had not the temperament for cool analysis or careful qualification."

Since the publication of Phyllis Grosskurth's biography of Symonds in 1964, and of his *Letters* and *Memoirs* in 1969 and 1984 respectively, critics have increasingly emphasized Symonds's temperament and homosexual orientation in analyses of his works. Derek Stanford notes that "it was the real or fancied vibration, indicative of homosexual interest, which most stimulated Symonds, leading him to choose . . . a subject for critical exploration." For example, his pioneering studies on the lives of Walt Whitman and Michelangelo, in both of whom he detected homosexual yearnings, are considered among his best and most sympathetic biographical portraits. According to Stanford, these and Symonds's other works implicitly justify any cultural attitude that seems to condone sexual love between men. Although few of Symonds's works are still studied, his life as described in his *Memoirs* and *Letters* continues to attract scholarly attention. Critic Arthur Symons wrote of Symonds that "it was the life in him, the personality, that gave the man his real interest, his real fascination."

PRINCIPAL WORKS

The Escorial   (poetry)   1860

An Introduction to the Study of Dante   (criticism)   1872

Studies of the Greek Poets. 2 vols.   (criticism)   1873-76

Sketches in Italy and Greece   (travel essays)   1874

*Renaissance in Italy. 7 vols.   (history)   1875-86

Many Moods   (poetry)   1878

Shelley   (biography)   1878

The Sonnets of Michelangelo Buonarroti and Tommaso Campanella [translator]   (poetry)   1878

Sketches and Studies in Italy   (travel essays)   1879

Animi Figura   (poetry)   1882

Italian Byways   (travel essays)   1883

A Problem in Greek Ethics   (treatise)   1883

Shakspere's Predecessors in the English Drama   (criticism)   1884

Vagabunduli Libellus   (poetry)   1884

Wine, Women, and Song: Mediaeval Latin Students' Songs [translator]   (poetry)   1884

Ben Jonson   (biography)   1886

Sir Philip Sydney   (biography)   1886

The Life of Benvenuto Cellini [translator]   (autobiography)   1888

Essays, Speculative and Suggestive. 2 vols.   (essays and criticism)   1890

A Problem in Modern Ethics   (treatise)   1891

Our Life in the Swiss Highlands [with Margaret Symonds]   (autobiography)   1892

In the Key of Blue, and Other Prose Essays   (essays)   1893

The Life of Michelangelo Buonarroti. 2 vols.   (biography)   1893

Walt Whitman: A Study   (biography and criticism)   1893

Blank Verse   (essays)   1895

Giovanni Boccaccio as Man and Author   (biography and criticism)   1895

Das Konträre Geschlechtsgefühl [with Havelock Ellis]   (prose)   1896; revised and published in English as *Sexual Inversion,* 1897

Last and First; Being Two Essays: The New Spirit and Arthur Hugh Clough   (essays)   1919

Letters and Papers of John Addington Symonds   (letters, notes, and essays)   1923

Letters of John Addington Symonds. 3 vols.   (letters)   1969

Memoirs of John Addington Symonds   (memoirs)   1984

* This work encompasses the single-volume histories entitled *The Age of the Despots* (1875), *The Revival of Learning* (1877), and *The Fine Arts* (1877), as well as the two-volume studies *Italian Literature* (1881) and *The Catholic Reaction* (1886).

Walter Pater   (review date 1875)

[*A nineteenth-century essayist, novelist, and critic, Pater is regarded as one of the most famous proponents of aestheticism in English literature. Distinguished as the first major English writer to formulate an explicitly aesthetic philosophy of life, he advocated the "love of art for art's sake" as life's greatest offering, a belief which he exemplified in his influential* Studies in the History of the Renaissance *(1873) and elucidated in his novel* Marius the Epicurean *(1885) and other works. In the following review of Symonds's* The Age of the Despots, *originally published in the* Academy *in 1875, Pater offers a favorable overview of the work, finding it marred only by what he describes as Symonds's lack of reserve in tone and scope.*]

This remarkable volume [***Renaissance in Italy; the Age of the Despots***] is the first of three parts of a projected work which in its complete form will present a more comprehensive treatment of its subject than has yet been offered to English readers. The aim of the writer is to weave together the various threads of a very complex period of European life, and to set the art and literature of Italy on that background of general social and historical conditions to which they belong, and apart from which they cannot really be understood, according to the received and well-known belief of most modern writers. Mr. Symonds brings to this task the results of wide, varied, and often curious reading, which he has by no means allowed to overburden his work, and also a familiar knowledge, attested by his former eloquent volume of ***Studies on the Greek Poets,*** of that classical world to which the Renaissance was confessedly in some degree a return.

It is that background of general history, a background upon which the artists and men of letters are moving figures not to be wholly detached from it, that this volume presents. By the "Age of the Despots" in Italian history the writer understands the fourteenth and fifteenth centuries, as the twelfth and the thirteenth are the "Age of the Free Burghs," and the sixteenth and seventeenth the "Age of Foreign Enslavement." The chief phenomenon with which the "Age of the Despots" is occupied is that "free emergence of personal passions, personal aims," which all its peculiar conditions tended to encourage, of personalities all alike so energetic and free, though otherwise so unlike as Francesco Sforza, Savonarola, Machiavelli, and Alexander VI, all "despots" in their way. Benvenuto Cellini and Cesare Borgia are seen to be products of the same general conditions as the "good Duke of Urbino" and Savonarola. Such a book necessarily presents strong lights and shades. The first chapter groups together some wide generalisations on the subject of the work as a whole, on the Renaissance as an "emancipation," which, though perhaps not wholly novel, are very strikingly put, and through the whole of which we feel the breath of an ardent love of liberty. In the next two chapters the writer discusses the age of the earlier despots, the founders of the great princely families, going over ground well traversed indeed, but with a freshness of interest which is the mark of original assimilation, with some parallels and contrasts between Italy and ancient Greece, and led always by the light of modern ideas. One by one all those highly-coloured pieces of humanity are displayed before us, those stories which have made Italian history the fountain-head of tragic motives, all the hard, bright, fiery things, the colour of which M. Taine has in some degree caught in his writings on the philosophy of Italian art, and still more completely Stendhal, in his essay on Italian art and his *Chroniques Italiennes.* You can hardly open Mr. Symonds's volume without lighting on some incident or trait of character in which man's elementary power to be, to think, to do, shows forth emphatically, and the writer has not chosen to soften down these characteristics; there is even noticeable a certain cynicism in his attitude towards his subject, expressed well enough in the words which he quotes from Machiavelli as the motto of his title-page: *Di questi adunque oziosi principi, e di queste vilissime armi, sarà piena la mia istoria.*

That sense of the complex interdependence on each other of all historical conditions is one of the guiding lights of the modern historical method, and Mr. Symonds abundantly shows how thoroughly he has mastered this idea. And yet on the same background, out of the same general conditions, products emerge, the unlikeness of which is the chief thing to be noticed. The spirit of the Renaissance proper, of the Renaissance as a humanistic movement, on which it may be said this volume does not profess to touch, is as unlike the spirit of Alexander VI as it is unlike that of Savonarola. Alexander VI has more in common with Ezzelino da Romano, that fanatical hater of human life in the middle age, than with Tasso or Lionardo. The Renaissance is an assertion of liberty indeed, but of liberty to see and feel those things the seeing and feeling of which generate not the "barbarous ferocity of temper, the savage and coarse tastes" of the Renaissance Popes, but a sympathy with life everywhere, even in its weakest and most frail manifestations. Sympathy, appreciation, a sense of latent claims in things which even ordinary good men pass rudely by—these on the whole are the characteristic traits of its artists, though it may be still true that "æsthetic propriety, rather than strict conceptions of duty, ruled the conduct even of the best;" and at least they never "destroyed pity in their souls." Such softer touches Mr. Symonds gives us in the "good duke Frederic of Urbino," his real courtesy and height of character, though under many difficulties; in his admirable criticisms on the *Cortegiano* of Castiglione; and again in his account of Agnolo Pandolfini's *Treatise on the Family,* the charm of which has by no means evaporated in Mr. Symonds's analysis; above all, in the beautiful description, in the seventh chapter, of the last days of Pietro Boscoli the tyrannicide, a striking instance of "the combination of deeply-rooted and almost infantine piety with antique heroism," coming near as it happened, in his friend Luca della Robbia the younger, to an artist who could understand the æsthetic value of the incidents he has related.

I quote a very different episode as a specimen of Mr. Symonds's style:—

> There is a story told by Infessura which illustrates the temper of the times with singular felicity. On April 18, 1485, a report circulated in Rome that some Lombard workmen had discovered a Roman sarcophagus while digging on the Appian Way. It was a marble tomb, engraved with the inscription, 'Julia, daughter of Claudius,' and inside the coffin lay the body of a most beautiful girl of fifteen years, preserved by pre-

> cious unguents from corruption and the injury of time. The bloom of youth was still upon her cheeks and lips; her eyes and mouth were half open, her long hair floated round her shoulders. She was instantly removed, so goes the legend, to the Capitol; and then began a procession of pilgrims from all the quarters of Rome to gaze upon this saint of the old Pagan world. In the eyes of those enthusiastic worshippers her beauty was beyond imagination or description; she was far fairer than any woman of the modern age could hope to be. At last Innocent VIII feared lest the orthodox faith should suffer by this new cult of a heathen corpse. Julia was buried, secretly and at night by his direction, and naught remained in the Capitol but her empty marble coffin. The tale, as told by Infessura, is repeated in Matarazzo and in Nantiporto with slight variations. One says that the girl's hair was yellow, another that it was of the glossiest black. What foundation for the legend may really have existed need not here be questioned. Let us rather use the mythus as a parable of the ecstatic devotion which prompted the men of that age to discover a form of unimaginable beauty in the tomb of the classic world.

The book then presents a brilliant picture of its subject, of the movements of these energetic personalities, the magnificent restlessness and changefulness of their lives, their immense cynicism. As is the writer's subject so is his style—energetic, flexible, eloquent, full of various illustration, keeping the attention of the reader always on the alert. Yet perhaps the best chapter in the book, the best because the most sympathetic, is one of the quieter ones, that on "The Florentine Historians;" their great studies, their anticipations of the historical spirit of modern times, their noble style, their pious humour of discipleship towards Aristotle, Cicero, Tacitus, not without a certain pedantry becoming enough in the historians of those republics which were after all "products of constructive skill" rather than of a true political evolution—all this is drawn with a clear hand and a high degree of reflectiveness. The chapter on *The Prince* corrects some common mistakes concerning Machiavelli, who is perhaps less of a puzzle than has sometimes been supposed, a patriot devising a desperate means of establishing permanent rule in Florence, designing, in the spirit of a political idealism not more ruthless than that of Plato's *Republic,* to cure a real evil, a fault not unlike that of ancient Athens itself, the constant exaggerated appetite for change in public institutions, bringing with it an incorrigible tendency of all the parts of human life to fly from the centre, a fault, as it happened in both cases, at last become incurable. The chapter on Savonarola is a bold and complete portrait, with an interesting pendent on "Religious Revivals in Mediæval Italy;" and the last chapter on "Charles the Eighth in Italy" has some real light in it, making things lie more intelligibly apart and together in that tangle of events. The imagination in historical composition works most legitimately when it approaches dramatic effects. In this volume there is a high degree of dramatic imagination; here all is objective, and the writer is hardly seen behind his work.

I have noted in the foregoing paragraphs the things which have chiefly impressed and pleased me in reading this book, things which are sure to impress and please hundreds of readers and make it very popular. But there is one thing more which I cannot help noticing before I close. Notwithstanding Mr. Symonds's many good gifts, there is one quality which I think in this book is singularly absent, the quality of reserve, a quality by no means merely negative, and so indispensable to the full effect of all artistic means, whether in art itself, or poetry, or the finer sorts of literature, that in one who possesses gifts for those things its cultivation or acquisition is neither more nor less than loyalty to his subject and his work. I note the absence of this reserve in many turns of expression, in the choice sometimes of detail and metaphor, in the very bulk of the present volume, which yet needs only this one quality, in addition to the writer's other admirable qualities of conception and execution, to make this first part of his work wholly worthy of his design. (pp. 3-12)

> *Walter Pater, "Symonds's 'Renaissance in Italy'," in his* Uncollected Essays, *1903. Reprint by AMS Press, 1978, pp. 1-12.*

Edmund Gosse   (review date 1877)

[*Gosse was a prominent English man of letters during the late nineteenth century. A prolific literary historian, biographer, and critic, he remains most esteemed for a single and atypical work:* Father and Son: A Study of Two Temperaments *(1907), an account of his childhood that is considered among the most distinguished examples of Victorian spiritual autobiography. In the following excerpt from his review of the first three volumes of Symonds's* The Renaissance in Italy, *Gosse notes that Symonds is at his best as a literary critic and dullest as a historian. He finds* The Revival of Learning *the most effective of the three works and observes that* The Age of the Despots *is weakened by the author's unsure grasp of political history, while* The Fine Arts *lacks originality both in thought and execution.*]

There is no word more frequently and at the same time more loosely used in the current criticism of the day than "Renaissance." The movement in philosophy, art, and letters which is traditionally known by that name is in danger of being very seriously misunderstood by many of those who undertake to correct our traditional views upon moral and æsthetic subjects. Nothing is more common than to see this "new birth," this revival in thought and practice, treated as though it were simply the introduction into modern life of an idealised Paganism, a charter for sensuous enjoyment beyond all danger of the pangs of a conscience. That this conception underlies the flowery periods of not a few apostles of culture can hardly be denied, and it is difficult to say which is most surprising—the effrontery of a taught critic who takes upon himself the proclamation of such a doctrine, or the carelessness of an ignorant one who dogmatises on the results of a superficial study. That the element of a revived Paganism was not wanting in the agents of Renaissance thought, nay more, that the unbounded worship of beauty led the artists and poets of that time into excesses that endangered the struc-

ture of society, is a fact which cannot be overlooked; but that must be a very shallow examination of the history of the time which fails to perceive, in the first place, that this tendency to Pagan excess was but one of many great streams of influence; and, in the second, that it brought its own swift punishment. This wider view of the subject especially calls for exposition at the present moment, and Mr. Symonds's calm and unbiassed outline of the main historical facts can scarcely fail to be felt to be opportune. The subject, however, is vast; to exhaust it, the history of modern Europe would have to be rewritten. He has, therefore, confined himself to the most tempting division of the subject, and essayed a study of the Renaissance in Italy. In doing so, he has, of course, been obliged to compress the materials before him into a small space, and to pass briefly over the ground trodden by the great historians, by Sismondi and Michelet, by Burckhardt and Muratori. This gives a certain air of poverty to the strictly historical portions, for which we have to blame not the author, but the limited space at his command. At the same time, we doubt whether Mr. Symonds has as much gift in the exposition of history as in criticism, and especially literary criticism. Of the three volumes before us [*The Age of the Despots, The Revival of Learning,* and *The Fine Arts*], the first deals with the purely political division of the subject, the constitutions of the various despotic and democratic governments, and the writings of men eminent for statecraft and policy. The second volume goes over the same period with exclusive reference to the revival of learning, tracing from Petrarch down to Paolo Giovio the gathering enthusiasm for the classics, the frenzy for the collection of MSS., the cultivation of Greek and Latin literature, and the final decline of learning into pedantry. The third volume, chronologically parallel with the others, deals with the fine arts, tracing architecture, sculpture, and painting from their earliest emancipation from barbarism to their decay after the sack of Rome. To these three volumes the author promises eventually to append a fourth, dealing with the development of Italian literature during the same centuries; and this is certainly needed to make the work complete. In the *Revival of Learning,* especially, the mention of such prominent writers as Poliziano and Sannazzaro is curiously insufficient and one-sided, from the fact that these Italian poets are treated only as the authors of certain more or less clever Latin verses. We believe that Mr. Symonds will produce a very interesting volume on early Italian literature, and fill a gap which has too long remained open. For the present, however, we have to consider only the three volumes before us. Of these, we have no hesitation in saying that the *Revival of Learning* is the best, and the *Age of the Despots* the least important. In the former, a subject of which hardly anything is commonly known is treated with taste and vigour by a scholar evidently possessing a thoroughly adequate knowledge of his subject; in the latter, we will not say that there is any lack of knowledge, but there seems to us certainly an inability to grasp the threads of a tangled skein of politics, so as to unwind them into a narrative clearly intelligible to an uninstructed reader. The purely historical pages, in short, are dull; and it is only when the author arrives at a point where he is permitted to make a literary digression that his style becomes enlivened. There are certain chapters in the *Age of the Despots* that are very well written, and which command attention. Those dealing respectively with the Florentine historians and with the *Principe* of Machiavelli are the best. It is curious, too, to note that when Mr. Symonds is at the height of his confusion, in that chapter on the constitution of the Republics, where the laboured sentences seem to cling to one another, and to follow the narrative seems almost impossible, he wakes into sudden animation at the sight of a book, and gives us an epitome of Pandolfini's *Treatise of the Government of the Family* which is really charming. A similar example is the analysis of the *Cortegiano* of Castiglione, which comes to our rescue at the close of a summary of several groups of despots which is not at all remarkable for the historic gift. In the *Revival of Learning,* on the other hand, there is not a tedious chapter, and Mr. Symonds shows plainly enough that he possesses the peculiar gift of analysing pedantry without being pedantic, and of rendering a literary subject which one would be ready to condemn as hopelessly dry interesting and even diverting. The *Fine Arts,* in conclusion, has neither the merits of the one volume nor the drawbacks of the other. It is not in the least tedious, but it has not the charm of complete novelty or originality. In the presence of so many masterly works on Italian art, it is difficult, without extraordinary genius, to produce a thoroughly novel book on the revival of fine art in Italy. Mr. Symonds, however, has the special advantage of having studied Italian painting and sculpture to an extent very rare in English writers, and in all cases on the spot. He says—

> In this part of my work I feel I owe less to reading than to observation. I am not aware of having mentioned any important building, statue, or picture, which I have not had the opportunity of studying. What I have written in this volume about the monuments of Italian art has always been first noted face to face with the originals, and afterwards corrected, modified, or confirmed in the course of subsequent journeys to Italy. I know that this method of composition, if it has the merit of freshness, entails some inequality of style and disproportion in the distribution of materials.

We do not discover this disproportion of which the author modestly fears the existence, but we are conscious of a certain restlessness of judgment, which arises, no doubt, from the mode in which the materials of the work have been collected. The positive observation of a multitude of objects of art has been pretty fully performed by specialists. It is not easy for a critic to follow in the footsteps of Messrs. Crowe and Cavalcavelle in painting, and Mr. Parkins in sculpture, and to pick up much of mere external fact which has escaped these careful students. But in the theory of artistic production and in the higher criticism there is room for infinite analysis and discovery. It is somewhat to be regretted that Mr. Symonds has not kept more rigidly to his own theme—the illustration of the Renaissance spirit as this was manifested in the arts. But if the author's successes in the line of literary criticism have led us to look for too decided an originality in artistic criticism, there can be no question that he has written a sympathetic trea-

tise on Italian art which every one will read with pleasure. (pp. 351-54)

> *Edmund Gosse, in an originally unsigned essay titled "Renaissance in Italy," in* The Westminster and Foreign Quarterly Review, *n.s. Vol. LII, No. II, October 1, 1877, pp. 351-74.*

The Saturday Review, London   (review date 1881)

[*In the following review, the critic offers a generally positive assessment of* Italian Literature, *praising its readability and Symonds's astute treatment of the subject. However, he questions the validity of many of Symonds's general and philosophical reflections.*]

These two volumes [*Renaissance in Italy: Italian Literature*] complete the work of Mr. Symonds on the Italian Renaissance. In the *Age of the Despots* he discussed the political, in the *Revival of Learning* the scholastic, and in the *Fine Arts* the artistic life of the period. To each of the earlier treatises one volume only was devoted. The literature of the age, in which the character and spirit of the people find their fullest and most varied expression, is discussed more exhaustively. The two volumes give the completest account of the subject yet published in English; and they include, besides what belongs strictly to the period of the Renaissance, introductory chapters of great interest, tracing the earlier growth of the Italian language and literature. Of the whole series they form probably the most practically useful part, and give, in a condensed and attractive form, information which has been gathered from the most multifarious sources, and, what is of great value, the latest results of native Italian criticism and research. The general principles according to which the Renaissance is to be judged and investigated are so clearly fixed that it would be no compliment to the soundness of an author's judgment to say that he had offered an original view of the period; but whatever a wide and intimate acquaintance both with the literature itself and with the labours of other scholars in the same field can produce is here offered to the English reader. Like all that Mr. Symonds writes, these volumes are remarkably pleasant reading; and though there are in them some linguistic singularities, to which we shall presently call attention, the exuberance of style which characterizes some of his earlier writings has here been considerably, and with great advantage, tempered and chastened. It may be added that the practical usefulness of the work has been increased by a copious index to these and the preceding volumes.

The first chapter traces the earlier and less known influences which shaped the beginnings of Italian literature, and, in particular, the influence of French poetry and legends, and of the cosmopolitan Court of the Emperor Frederick II, in Sicily. The persistence throughout the greater part of the Peninsula, as compared with other parts of the Roman Empire, of the old civilization, and the absence of feudalism and of an overpowering aristocratic caste, furnished to Italian literature a ground at once popular and historic to start from; and foreign ideas and examples served only, at this earlier period, to suggest the first steps to the native Italian genius. In Dante, Petrarch, and Boccaccio—the triumvirate of the period which followed—this genius appears in its full originality, strength, and independence, borrowing from sources outside itself no more than is inevitable with all literature, and stamping—whatever it borrows with its own spirit and character. The lifetime of the three leaders of Italian literature marks the first period treated by Mr. Symonds. The next is the period of the scholars, in which the re-discovery of classical, and particularly of Latin, models suspended for a time the cultivation of a native literature. But here it is to be remarked that it was by no means a foreign influence which led the men of that period to ignore or despise the capacities of their own language. In preferring Latin to Italian they were only conscious of preferring a past rich in a great literature, and associated with great historical memories, to a present which, because seen without illusion, is always apt to be unfairly disregarded. It must further be borne in mind that humanism furnished a common ground on which men from all parts of Italy could meet, and embraced numbers of persons to whom the Tuscan language and spirit were, if not foreign, still about as much so as the newly-found classical literature which was drawing all Italy after it. Further, the influence of a new spirit, different from all that the men of that age had hitherto known, opening fresh avenues of thought and action, and tending to emancipate men from the thraldom of a Church which the Italians have always seen at its worst, so engaged the interest and enthusiasm of the intelligent classes that, even had they been able to do their own literature justice, they could not but have neglected it for a season to enjoy the new world which was disclosed to them. After a while, however, when classical literature became familiar to them, and had lost the charm of surprise, the balance was redressed, and the language of the people was once more brought back to honour. The second, or humanistic period, with its exclusive devotion to classical models, thus led the way to the third period, in which the Italian genius, trained and developed afresh by long and intimate study of the models of antiquity, turned again to native sources. The greatest name of this third period, which dates from the latter part of the fifteenth century to the Counter-Reformation, is that of Ariosto.

The subjects discussed in these volumes are so manifold that it is impossible within the limits assigned to us to do more than touch briefly on a very few of them. They appear to us to be treated, for the most part, with excellent judgment. In particular we would call attention to the admirable chapter on the *Orlando Furioso* and the no less interesting chapter on Pietro Aretino. With nearly all that is said on the subject of Ariosto's great poem we can fully concur, or, at all events, with nearly all that is said on the subject of Ariosto himself. We should be inclined, however, to mark more strongly the contrast between the genius of Ariosto and the effect which the *Orlando* produces on the reader. From gifts like those of Ariosto, from his wonderful breadth and power, from his admirable sense of style, from his perfect mastery of the material he handles, something more might be demanded than what he actually gives us. This sense of inadequacy between the poem and the poet strikes us when we read the *Orlando Furioso* consecutively and as a whole. When we dip into it, when

we read it occasionally, canto by canto, few poems can be more charming or impress us with a stronger sense of the high gifts of the writer. But when we sit down to read it through, and at the end try to give ourselves an account of the effect it produces on us, we are forced to admit that the total impression is far below what the first impression had led us to expect. And this is not due to a falling off in the merit of the execution, but rather from the sense that the poet has after all been engaged on a task that is beneath him, or at least that does not offer full scope for his power. The *Orlando,* to say the honest truth, is dull when we attempt to read it as we read other poems; it is fascinating when we read it bit by bit. It seems trivial and frivolous when we reflect that it is the poetical masterwork of so great a man and so great an age. The writer is in earnest with his style and form, but not with his subject. There are plenty of passages in Ariosto full of dignity and tragic power; but they are scattered about here and there in his poem. The ground-tone of it is graceful irony; and this tone, though charming here and there, as the break or enlivenment to a more serious strain, becomes itself tiresome when it is protracted through forty or fifty thousand lines of poetry. Not only does the *Orlando* gain greatly by being read piecemeal, but it must have gained still more by being recited, as was commonly a custom at that period, canto by canto. There is much in it which would be greatly enhanced by skilful and dramatic recitation. It contains few or none of the countless passages in Dante and Shakspeare which have to be taken to heart and dwelt on before they can be truly apprehended. It aims at a momentary effect; and this effect is experienced by a listener more easily than by a reader. We have only to try the experiment with a few stanzas delivered by a good reciter to perceive the force of this contrast. There is little in Ariosto to feed on or to muse on. And yet, so great is his power, that we cannot help demanding from him that which he is unable to give. More than almost any other poet, he makes us quarrel with what is good because it is not better. In his case, as Mr. Symonds truly says, we must bear in mind the influence which at this period painting had on poetry, and which caused it to assume a pictorial and external character, to the neglect of the deeper elements of thought and feeling which are peculiarly its province. There are other reasons also why a great poet could not then find the atmosphere needed for the best poetic work—the absence of any genuine national and political life; the prevailing tendency, so fatal to literature itself, to take nothing seriously but literary or artistic interests; and a moral and social corruption so deep and widespread as to drive every thinking man to be either a cynic or a prophet of retribution.

There are few chapters in Mr. Symonds's work which may not be read with interest and advantage, especially those in which he deals with the purely literary aspect of the age. Many, however, of his general or philosophical reflections seem strangely superficial and unsound. "Nature," says the writer, summarizing the teaching of Valla, "nature can do nothing wrong; and that must be wrong which violates nature. It is man's duty, by interrogation of nature, to discover the laws of his own being and to obey these. In other words, Valla, though in no sense a man of science, proclaims the fundamental principle of science, and inaugu-

Symonds at Oxford, c. 1860.

tion which marks both as something to be imitiated or as something even venial. Such a charge, if it has been ever made, needs no refutation. But there is another question, and that is how far it is desirable, in a work intended for general circulation, to give a minute account of customs and of writings which it is painful to dwell on, so profound is the heartless corruption which they reveal. The question is one of degree, and must be settled in his own way by each individual writer. A great age cannot be excluded from historical criticism because of the turpitude which marks it. In the Renaissance especially we find this union of what is noblest and most attractive with what is vilest and most hateful; and it is impossible to study the one without being forced to consider the other along with it. But it is to be regretted that the iniquities of the period should receive fuller illustration than is required for the purposes of impartial history; and, if the charge referred to above has been made against those who have written on the Renaissance, it is probably because this limit has not always been strictly observed. (pp. 236-37)

> *"Mr. Symonds's Literature of the Renaissance," in* The Saturday Review, *London, Vol. 52, August 20, 1881, pp. 236-37.*

Melville B. Anderson   (review date 1887)

[*In the following excerpt, Anderson reviews Symonds's* The Catholic Reaction, *commending the author's sound treatment of his subject but noting a less enthusiastic presentation of his material than in the earlier volumes of his history.*]

If the somewhat blurred impressions of midsummer are to be trusted, Mr. Symonds exhibits, in [his ***Renaissance in Italy: The Catholic Reaction***], signs of fatigue and of relaxing grasp. While the work is thoroughly done, it is evidently *work*,—not the buoyant and exhilarating mental play which rendered many chapters of the earlier volumes so fascinating. I think this would be plain to any reader who should take pains to compare the chapters on Tasso in the second volume of the book before us, with those on Ariosto in ***Italian Literature.*** Still it must be conceded that Ariosto is a much more stimulating theme than Tasso; indeed, the same thing may be said of the general theme of the present volumes,—reaction at its best is not progress, and the reaction with which we are here dealing is one of the most pitiful and depressing spectacles in human annals. A much more unmistakable sign of lassitude on the author's part lies in the apparent fact that he is not in possession of the comprehensive mastery of this period that he has exhibited in treating of the Renaissance proper. He has evidently written these volumes rather in order to complete his work than from any compulsive impulse such as gives life to the earlier parts, and the result is much more a series of essays than an organized and interdependent whole. Perhaps this want of facile mastery is most evident in the final chapters of Part I., where more than a hundred pages are devoted to what might be called extracts from the police records of the sixteenth century: a dark and bloody series of narratives of the crimes accompanying the lust and license with which the high-born Italians endeavored to console themselves for the loss of polit-

rates a new criterion of ethics." In a note to this passage what Valla means by following nature is explained to be simply obeying sensual appetite. Now, in the first place, there is nothing whatever new in Valla's unabashed assertion of hedonism; it is as old as the human race, and it is daily exemplified by the beasts that perish. And in the next place it is in no sense a criterion of ethics, for all ethical systems worth consideration, even those which make pleasure the end of human action, insist on the subordination of temporary or personal pleasure to the permanent good of the individual or of the world at large. A more barren formula than "Follow Nature" was never invented; we all agree to it, but all differ as to what nature is, and how she is to be followed. But probably Mr. Symonds's remark is to be taken as rather rhetorical than as expressing his real opinion. With the English of the book we must again find fault; "resume" in the sense of "to sum up" as in the French *résumer,* "banality," a "back thought" for an *arrière pensée,* "civility" for civilization, and the like, cannot be regarded as improvements on the plain English to which we are accustomed, or as exemplifications of Cæsar's maxim to avoid an out-of-the-way word as we would a rock. One more remark it is necessary to make. Mr. Symonds protests, and with perfect justice, against the view that an analysis of the literature or manners of the Renaissance implies any desire to hold up the corrup-

ical freedom. Here we have detailed narratives of *bravi* and *banditti*, the pathetic story of the Duchess of Palliano, and the terrible tale of Vittoria Accoramboni, the lovely sinner whose sublime audacity fired the massive imagination of her contemporary, John Webster, and enriched English literature with the tragedy of *The White Devil.* Gloomily interesting and sadly instructive as are these tales of violence and rapine and lust and polite ferocity—and of the inhumanity of man to woman,—one can hardly resist the conclusion that it is attaching disproportionate value to them to devote to them one-fourth of one of these portly tomes. The question forces itself upon us, whether they were not thrown in for filling, by an author too jaded to assimilate all the material at his disposal, and to draw from it those graphic and vigorous generalizations of which he is elsewhere so approved a master. At all events, most readers could well have spared a portion of "these funereal records," for the sake of the twenty pages of illustrative extracts from the practically inaccessible works of Giordano Bruno, of which, Mr. Symonds tells us, he made English versions only to reject them "when I found that this material would overweight my book." It is no disparagement of Mr. Symonds to say that these twenty pages from Bruno would probably have turned out to be the most interesting pages of the entire volume.

Of Giordano Bruno the author seems to speak with more of sympathetic animation than of any other of the representative men—Tasso, Sarpi, Guarini, Palestrina, and others,—to whom the second part is devoted. Bruno was, indeed, the most modern man of the sixteenth century. As, in speaking of him, Mr. Symonds shows to the best advantage, I may best serve the reader by quoting an impressive passage containing a summary statement of the debt of subsequent thinkers to the restless and ill-starred Italian. After showing the breadth of outlook gained by Bruno by his acceptance of the Copernican theory of the universe, our author generalizes as follows:

> Bruno thus obtained *per saltum* a prospect over the whole domain of knowledge subsequently traversed by rationalism in metaphysics, theology, and ethics. In the course of these demonstrations and deductions he anticipated Descartes' position of the identity of mind and being. He supplied Spinoza with the substance of his reasoned pantheism; Leibnitz with his theory of monadism and pre-established harmony. He laid down Hegel's doctrine of contraries, and perceived that thought was a dialectic process. The modern theory of evolution was enunciated by him in pretty plain terms. He had grasped the physical law of conservation of energy. He solved the problem of evil by defining it to be a relative condition of imperfect development. He denied that Paradise or a Golden Age is possible for man, or that, if possible, it can be considered higher in the moral scale than organic struggle toward completion by reconciliation of opposites through pain and labor. He sketched in outline the comparative study of religions, which is now beginning to be recognized as the proper basis for theology. Finally, he had a firm and vital hold upon that supreme speculation of the universe, considered no longer as the battle-ground of dual principles, or as the finite fabric of an almighty designer, but as the self-effectuation of an infinite unity, appearing to our intelligence as spirit and matter—that speculation which in one shape or another controls the course of modern thought.

Macaulay called Francis Bacon the Moses of modern philosophy; but Mr. Symonds, by his adoption of "the hackneyed metaphor of a Pisgah view across the promised land," suggests that Giordano Bruno had a much better claim to that high prophetic leadership. He was a hero and a martyr of science, and the story of his vigorous life and of his consistent death at the stake, "turning stern eyes away from the offered crucifix," is very inspiring. But as a whole this book is the melancholy story of the sterilization, blight, dwindling vitality, and moral and intellectual atrophy suffered by the fine Italian genius in the sixteenth century. The Catholic Reaction, or Counter-Reformation, was the sleep of Italy after her day's work. The causes of this great movement, and the reasons why the Italians were so willing to accept it, are treated very satisfactorily by our author. They may be summarized as follows: (1) The chief political cause is to be found in the servitude to which the states of Italy were reduced by Spain. (2) The original intellectual impulses of the Italians are exhausted; they are fatigued with creation. (3) A critical spirit penetrates every branch of art and letters and benumbs all original effort. (4) The re-awakening of Catholic Christianity colors the moral, social, political, and intellectual activity of the Italians with influences hostile to the earlier Renaissance. (5) The shifting of the centre of trade from the Mediterranean to the Atlantic basin gives the death-blow to the commerce of Venice, Florence, and Genoa; while the progress of the Renaissance in the West and North of Europe develops such amazing mental activity that the Italians can no longer claim superiority, even in the realm of mind and culture. The condition of the Italian mind at this period could not be better described than in the following terse sentences:

> They were suffering from grievous exhaustion, humiliated by the tyranny of foreign despotism, and terrorized by ecclesiastical intolerance. . . . The clear artistic sense of rightness and of beauty yields to doubtful taste. The frank audacity of the Renaissance is superseded by cringing timidity, lumbering dulness, somnolent and stagnant acquiescence in accepted formulæ. At first, the best minds of the nation fret and rebel, and meet with the dungeon or the stake as the reward of contumacy. In the end everybody seems to be indifferent, satisfied with vacuity, enamored of insipidity. The brightest episode in this dreary period is the emergence of modern music with incomparable sweetness and lucidity.

I cannot here pursue Mr. Symonds through the successive chapters of the book. Perhaps the most important ones are the second, third, and fourth, of Part I., devoted respectively to the Council of Trent, the Inquisition and the Index, and the Company of Jesus. The first chapter is an able conspectus of the Spanish hegemony, its causes and results. Of the much slighter chapters on "Social and Domestic Morals," mention has already been made. Let it suffice to say, in conclusion, that, although these volumes show marks of weariness, they are the product of a brilliant, experienced, and highly accomplished writer, and they form, on the whole, a worthy conclusion to one of the most noteworthy of the historical undertakings of our times. (pp. 81-2)

> Melville B. Anderson, "The Death of the Renaissance," in The Dial, Chicago, Vol. VIII, No. 88, August, 1887, pp. 80-2.

Edmund Clarence Stedman   (essay date 1887)

[*An important nineteenth-century American critic and anthologist, Stedman gained wide critical influence as the author of* Victorian Poets *and* Poets of America, *published in 1875 and 1885 respectively. In the following excerpt from a revised edition of the former work, Stedman briefly assesses the strengths and weaknesses of Symonds's writings, noting especially that his poetry, while scholarly and exhibiting Symonds's impeccable taste, lacks distinction.*]

Symonds is fairly typical of the best results of the English university training. He is an exemplar of taste; this, and liberal culture, joined with fine perceptive faculties, endow a writer who has the respect of lovers of the beautiful for his service as a guide to its history and masterpieces. A wealth of language and material sustains his prose explorations in the renaissance, his Grecian and Italian sketches, his charming discourse of the Greek poets and of the Italian and other literatures. He has given us complete and almost ideal translations of the sonnets of Angelo and Campanella. Coming to his original verse, we again see what taste and sympathy can do for a receptive nature; all, in fact, that they can do toward the making of a poet born, not with genius, but with a facile and persistent bent for art. The division between friendship and love is no more absolute, as not of degree but of kind, than that between the connoisseur and the most careless but impassioned poet. Symonds recognizes this in a thoroughbred preface to **Many Moods,** a book covering the verses of fifteen years. He proffers attractive work, good handling of the slow metres, and an Italian modification of the antique feeling. There is some lyrical quality in his **"Spring Songs."** Almost the same remarks apply to a later volume, **New and Old.** Its atmosphere, landscape, and notes of sympathy therewith are so unEnglish that one must possess the author's latinesque training to feel them adequately. We have sequences of polished sonnets in the **Animi Figura** and its interpreter, **Vagabundi Libellus.** These studies of a "beauty-loving and impulsive, but at the same time self-tormenting and conscientious mind" are his most satisfactory efforts in verse; but if their emotions are, as he avows, "imagined," he reasons too curiously for a poet. **"Stella"** has a right to complain of his hero, and it is no wonder she went mad. His poems are suggestive to careful students only, in spite of their exquisite word-painting and the merit of sonnets like those on **"The Thought of Death."** Admiring the finish of them all, we try in vain to recall the one abiding piece or stanza. Here is scholar's work of the first order, the outcome of knowledge and a

sense of beauty. Perhaps the author would have succeeded as well as a painter, sculptor, or architect, for in any direction taste would be his mainstay. Nothing can be happier than his rendering, with comments, of the mediæval Latin Students' Songs, neatly entitled **Wine, Women and Song**; and in the prose **Italian By-Ways** his critical touch is so light and rare that we are thankful for his companionship. (pp. 447-49)

> Edmund Clarence Stedman, "Twelve Years Later: A Supplementary Review," in his Victorian Poets, *revised edition, Houghton Mifflin and Company, 1887, pp. 415-83.*

The Nation, New York   (review date 1890)

[*In the following review of* Essays, Speculative and Suggestive, *the critic examines Symonds's approach to literary criticism, exploring his use of ideas related to evolution, and discussing Symonds's linking of literature and religion.*]

Symonds's [**Essays, Speculative and Suggestive**] differ from the ordinary collections of miscellanies by men of letters. Some of the papers are old, some are new, and they deal with many topics; but they are so arranged as to constitute a continuous and for the most part analytical criticism of the art of expression, principally in literature, but also in architecture, sculpture, painting, and music. They comprise, moreover, the fruits of many years of experience in a wide range of scholarly interests, and sum up the reflections of their author on the whole mass of his intellectual acquirements. It is rarely our fortune to find the abstract principles of the art of expression comprehensively handled by a man of high literary culture, and it is even more seldom that he brings his illustrations so readily and in such variety from his own stores of special study. These characteristics, besides the interesting element of personality more keenly felt than in the author's historical and biographical work, give importance to these essays; and, in addition, they will be found to touch upon nearly all the critical questions which have been raised in our time in the province of literature. In noticing a work so multifarious in its matter, it will be convenient to follow a somewhat different order from that adopted by the author, that we may bring out more clearly the main traits of his thought.

The note which is persistently struck throughout is that of the evolutionist, but this is emphasized more than need be. The larger part of Mr. Symonds's conclusions is consistent with other hypotheses than that form of pantheism which he regards as the logical conclusion of the evolutionist, and which he puts in the forefront of his work as its determining idea. To this we shall recur, only noticing it here by the way for the bearing it has on his conception of the office of the critic, which he discusses at large before proceeding to define the methods of the various arts of expression. The kernel of what he has to say concerning the critic is contained in this quotation from Heraclitus: "It behooves us to follow the common reason of the world; yet, though there is a common reason in the world, the majority live as though they possessed a wisdom peculiar each unto himself alone." This "common reason," which is the result of the repeated and concurring decisions of that "wise man" whom Aristotle pronounced the final judge in matters of taste, this authoritative tradition of the past as to what is best, is the one thing which the critic must know and use to test his own "peculiar wisdom" or personal impression. To adopt Mr. Symonds's nomenclature, classical criticism consults only tradition, romantic criticism only the personal impression; to these he adds scientific criticism, which seeks only to understand how any work of art came to be what it is by virtue of its germ and its environment, but delivers no judgment and formulates no law of excellence. Mr. Symonds unites in his conception of the office of criticism the three methods, and requires an understanding of the genesis of the work, a regard for tradition, and an exercise of originality in the act of judgment, if the critic has anything new and personal to offer.

In his own case the original element, as has been said, is derived from the theory of evolution, and in his first application of it to literature there is nothing novel or specially to be remarked upon. He argues that every national type in art goes through a definite process of growth and decay; the idea first is more attended to, then comes into possession of perfect form, and lastly is subordinated to technique, after which the type breaks up and dissipates through exaggeration and separation of its traits. In support of this he adduces the history of Greek sculpture, of Elizabethan drama, of Gothic architecture, and like defined art movements. It does not seem to us that he sufficiently meets the objection that this evolution of the type is merely derivative, and only reflects the evolution of the social group in which the disintegrating energy is really inherent; and therefore his position, that men of equal genius exist at the successive epochs, but are so fatally submitted to the condition of the type contemporaneous with them that they cannot do otherwise than they do, does not appeal to us, especially as it carries levelling consequences in morals, and leads to a phase of indifferentism in that region. The method, too, by which he accounts for those literatures which have not followed the normal course, including the Roman and our modern literatures, by merely classing them all as "hybrids," is a weak escape. The interesting point, however, is not whether he has pushed the doctrine of necessity in evolution too far in this instance and made a too narrow generalization, but to mark the willingness he exhibits to yield everything on the scientific side with a certain intemperance and unguardedness of mind. As soon as he quits the ground of evolution, however, he writes with more precision, and in the admirable chapters on the provinces of the arts we have a valuable abstract of that "common reason" of criticism with regard to them which he began by praising.

Mr. Symonds provokes discussion again when he enters on the vexed question of the relation of the artist to his work, realism or idealism. The way in which he states his conclusions may excuse a moment's detention on the well-worn theme. He starts from the fact that the artist cannot reproduce nature accurately, as is shown by the inferiority of the drawing to the photograph; there is a defect of skill. A second disturbing element lies in the individuality of the artist, who sees the object already modified by his own ca-

pacity of perception, as is shown by the difference of drawings after the same model by hands of equal craft. These two facts import a personal error into every work of art, and also an inevitable inferiority to nature itself. Such idealism as results from these conditions is involuntary; but there is, in addition, a voluntary idealism which the artist employs, by means of composition, expression, and characterization, and through which he becomes as much superior to reality as without them he is inferior. Mr. Symonds thus looks on idealism as the compensation for the necessary inferiority of art to life so long as only imitation is sought after. He goes, however, much further than this, and holds that what the artist gives of his personality and of his thought and feeling about the whole of life, is of vastly more consequence than even his artistic technique, and declares that style of itself without matter has never enforced immortality. As a most striking example of the failure of style in literature he cites the humanist imitators of Cicero and Petrarch. The contents of the work are to him the essential matter; he parts company with the school of art for art's sake as he has already left the realists, and, in opposition to both, maintains that the most possible of expression should be put into the artist's work, and that the method of idealism should be employed to this end. In this spirit he examines Mr. Pater's dictum, some years ago, that "all art constantly aspires towards the condition of music," and Mr. Arnold's more famous deliverance that literature is a "criticism of life," and comes to a more catholic and rational conclusion.

The distinction which characterizes his treatment of these questions, so vigorously debated by our generation, is that he maintains the balance of the antithesis—in Hegel's definition, which he quotes more than once—that "art is the apparition of the idea in sense," or, in his own words, that it is the middle term between reason and sensation. He describes it as "indissolubly bound up with the spiritual nature of man," but at the same time attends closely to the limitations all art is subject to in consequence of that necessity of "form-giving" which Goethe declared was its essence. In the more confined arts, such as sculpture, these limitations are easily analyzed, but no writer, we believe, has treated so directly the less obvious ones which exist in the languages and modify literatures, as is here done in the very interesting chapters upon national style, to which we can only refer. In all this portion of his work we observe a metaphysical prepossession, a tendency to render the world in terms of mind, an exaltation of the spiritualizing faculty in man, and in general the traits which are not habitually associated with that scientific leaning already noticed as characteristic of the author's thought.

The point of union between the evolutionary and idealistic elements in Mr. Symonds's conclusions is a religious feeling. To express this seems to be one of the main purposes of his present work. The argument is sufficiently suggested by our saying that the denial of the advent of mind by special creation in this world, which Mr. Symonds thinks necessary to a thoroughgoing evolutionist, implies to him the existence of universal mind. The term mind he does not limit to what is known to us as mind "in its human differentia"; he postulates mind below and above man's mind, and asks if "we shall not then be bold enough to say that all form is fundamentally a mode of mind?" Again he says:

> We may surmise that what appears as intelligence in the biological series was formerly the same power existing under another manifestation in the inorganic series, just as heat is a mode of motion. . . . In other words, the common substance of the world would now be thought of in successive moments of its evolution, first as endowed with the capacity of form, next as endowed with the capacity of life and progressive consciousness in addition to form.

And as regards "mind" in the "ascending scale of existences," he adds: "Paradoxical as it may seem, it is not incredible that the globe on which we live is more conscious of itself than we are of ourselves; and the cells that compose our corporeal frame are gifted with a separate consciousness of a simpler kind than ours." This is nearly all the light we have been able to obtain upon Mr. Symonds's conception of "universal mind" as he has unfolded it. He attacks the subject, however, in a somewhat different way in the assertion that "the conceptions of God and Law tend to coalesce in the scientific theory of the universe"; and this statement he afterwards explains by defining Law as "the order of the whole regarded as a process of unerringly unfolded energy," and God as "that same order contemplated by human thought as in its essence mind-determined."

This is the clearest account that we can extract of the matter with the best will to be fair to an idea which the author regards as a substitute for religion, and advances with the zeal of a propagandist. He goes on to remark that the Christ-idea, devotion to humanity, is now separated from the originally metaphysical and Alexandrine, but latterly anthropomorphic and Catholic, conception of divinity, and that it is desirable to reunite the Christ-idea with the older Greek conception of God as "the prime principle of law and order," made vital again by science. He sums up the conclusion of the whole matter by saying,

> What religion has to do, if it remains theistic, is to create an enthusiasm in which the cosmic emotion shall coalesce with the sense of social duty, in which self-abnegating submission to the natural order and self-abnegating service of man shall be regarded as the double function of all human beings in the evolution of the universe.

Of the reality and energy of this "cosmic emotion" he seems to have no doubt, and there are indications that he expects that this new phase of religious awe will be something more than a private and personal matter, and may become the principle of a church. In the discussion of Wordsworth's relation to science he says: "The time might come, indeed may not be distant, when lines like those which I have quoted above from the poem composed at Tintern Abbey should be sung in hours of worship by congregations for whom the 'cosmic emotion' is a reality and a religion"; and elsewhere he prognosticates the same honor for some of Shelley's lyrics.

Such speculation belongs with that kind of philosophy which is commonly called "poetical." Its literary applica-

tion is all that concerns us at present. The author makes use of it in three capital instances. He employs it to rehabilitate the myths of the Greeks, to invigorate the imaginative feeling for landscape, and to supply a basis for "democratic art." The Greeks were superior to us in the directness and fulness of their perception of spirituality in nature. The element of truth in their mythology consists in this perception; for, as Mr. Symonds puts it, the world is all soul, and soul in man communicates with soul in nature, nor does the fact that man is compelled to think of soul as human prevent his "entering into a sub-conscious intercourse with beings which are not human and from recognizing their essential spirituality." Of this intercourse Greek mythology is a record and a revelation; and though it came to be disbelieved when nature was regarded, under Christian influences, as the opposite of spirit, we may now resume the truth which it contained, since science has restored spirituality to nature. All this seems to us a very laborious method of asserting the truth of Greek myths for the imagination, as a form of poetry; and if beyond this, as appears to be the case, the author would affirm their truth for the understanding as a form of knowledge, the method is not laborious enough. The mythopœic genius of Shelley is a modified instance of the Greek habit of nature-interpretation: his poetry shows in what way the use of this faculty can be resumed by a modern mind; but no different truth can be predicated of the ancient myths than of Shelley's conscious symbolism. Mr. Symonds admits this parallelism, but would import a certain reality into Shelley's inventions.

In his essay upon landscape he comes upon ground better fitted for his argument, and, apart from this philosophical theory, his account of the development of the feeling for landscape from Greek to English days is a valuable general view of a most interesting subject. He notices the pantheistic temper of the Roman poets, but it is rather in the renascence of the ancient theory in Bruno and the German transcendentalists that he finds the source of the poetic emotion of Goethe, Wordsworth, and Shelley, which ascribes spirituality to nature and penetrates to it as universal mind in the Virgilian rather than the Greek way. The decadence of this pantheistic sentiment in the later poetry of this century does not escape the author's attention, but he relies upon the influence of science to make this mood of contemplating nature habitual and necessary and to develop new motives. The "religion of the future," he adds, will "supply this branch of art with ideality."

But by all odds the most striking application of this philosophy is made in the essay upon Walt Whitman, in which it is invoked as the ground of "democratic art." This as yet unrealized efflorescence of the masses, and particularly of "America," is made necessary by "the advent of the people." Mr. Symonds, indeed, says frankly that the European nations cannot be expected to give up their past; but in America he sees little objection, apparently, to "beginning over again." The matter of democratic art, he announces, is all things whatsoever, since freedom of topic and treatment has been achieved for us by the victory of the Romantic revolution; but he finds a better basis for this unlimited choice and method in the following declaration: "God the divine is recognized as immanent in nature and in the soul and body of humanity; not external to these things, not conceived of as creator from outside, or as incarnated in any single personage, but as all-pervasive, all-constitutive, everywhere and in all. This is the democratic philosophy." The application of this to Walt Whitman's catalogues of objects—his "engine-driver," "member of a fire brigade," "snag-toothed hostler," "farmer's girl boiling her iron tea-kettle and baking shortcake," and to his Orphic sayings, such as, "Whoever you are! how superb and how divine is your body or any part of it" (we take Mr. Symonds's quotations)—is plain and easy. An immanent divinity, equal and the same in all, clearly permits no discriminations, and justifies a very general interest in all sorts of phenomena. The intoxication of the fixed idea in the brain cannot go further than this grotesque exhibition of itself. Democracy must have a "religion," as well as an art and literature, all its own, and "America" finds its gospel as well as its epic in the *Leaves of Grass!* "Cosmic emotion" and "social duty" may pass as phrases of the literary prayer-book, but a pantheism that ends in making Walt Whitman its hierophant is its own burlesque and caricature.

The metaphysical weakness of these volumes, which has been self-exposed, cannot but obstruct the reader's sense of their many excellences in the department of literary criticism. It is, nevertheless, easy to disengage the really solid and valuable matter, which constitutes four-fifths of the work at least, from the vague and hybrid speculation which impairs it as a whole, and which is mainly of interest as an example of the working of an eclectic and assimilative mind amid the confusions of modern thought. As a critic of literature the author brings no inconsiderable matter of his own wide gathering, for he has been a student of culture all his life, and speaks from a various experience. We have touched upon only a small portion of the ideas with which he brings the reader in contact, and these the most general, since they seemed formative in his mind; but he is at his best in dealing with detail, as in the study of the influence of Ausonius and Catullus on the poetry of the rose, or in the notes upon national style, or in the explanation of the spiritual allegories (not the nature-myths) of the Greek mind. His metaphysical method, too, however unsound in itself and fictive in its results, is seriously pursued, and deserves the regard which sincerity, however misdirected, receives. (pp. 173-75)

"Symonds's Essays," in The Nation, *New York, Vol. LI, No. 1313, August 28, 1890, pp. 173-75.*

William Watson   (review date 1890)

[*Watson was an English poet and critic who maintained that a writer should play an integral part in the social and intellectual life of his or her era and participate in the making of decisions regarding public policy. He did not subscribe to the aesthetic temper of the 1890s, and in fact held that the more imaginative realms of poetry are the province of the second-rate. In the following review of* Essays, Speculative and Suggestive, *Watson examines Symonds's application of evolutionary principles to the development of art and literature, commenting favorably on his prose style.*]

The reader rises from these two volumes [Symonds's *Essays, Speculative and Suggestive*] with the sense of having been in contact with a mind of much versatility and range, which has taken the art and literature of various times and lands for its pasturage, and has developed a power of assimilation not uncommensurate with the large capacities of its appetite. The actual addition which these essays make to the original thought of our time may hardly, on examination, prove to be large; in reading them we never feel the thrill, the excitement, not far removed from a kind of awe, which accompanies a sudden sensation of having broken new spiritual ground, or passed, by some happy adventure of the intellect, into a tract of mind which has hitherto remained inviolate and virgin. The footprints of former travellers are indeed everywhere visible; but in following Mr. Symonds's lead we are still grateful for a guide who can point out features of interest which the intrepid explorers, busied in naming mountains and tracking the sources of rivers, left unrecorded and unobserved.

In the essay with which the first volume opens, Mr. Symonds presents with attractive lucidity his conception of the philosophy of evolution; but, in the paper which comes next, **"On the Application of Evolutionary Principles to Art and Literature,"** we find his use of the word "evolution" somewhat confusing, if not self-contradictory. He sets out with the implied intention of tracing a law of development in artistic and intellectual products identical with that which physical science recognises as operative in the world of material phenomena; but presently we find that he is using the term "evolution" in a sense practically undistinguishable from "growth," or from the passage of an individual organism through successive stages of maturity, decay, and dissolution. Before long, indeed, we become not a little bewildered by the protean character which the word "evolution" assumes in Mr. Symonds's hands. While on one page it seems to mean nothing more than a legitimate tendency in art and literature from the homogeneous to the heterogeneous—an inevitable subdivision involving the exchange of a normal simplicity for a no less normal complexity; on the next it appears rather to denote degeneration from primitive largeness of structure towards a loose mass of dismembered atoms, and at times the word looks like a mere synonym for a process of disintegration and dispersion, ending in exhaustion and extinction. Presently—so fluid and elusive is Mr. Symonds's use of it—the word changes colour and signifies, apparently, the dissipation of an original fund of motive force by means of innumerable minor radiations of the initial energy. And yet, again, we find it employed simply as a compendious phrase for a cycle of crescency, culmination, and decadence. Now, it is in the result of the gradually accumulated modifications of structure incidental to the reproductive process in animal life that what we commonly agree to call Evolution is seen; and similarly we require a survey of, at the very least, a series of generations of artistic or literary creators to enable us to infer the operation of an evolutionary principle in art or literature corresponding to that which is visible in the field of biology or anthropology. And just as, from the sheer necessity of limiting the elasticity of words, we do not commonly speak of the journey of a single human being from the womb to the grave as a manifestation of the evolutionary principle, whereas we *may* speak of the emergence of the typical Englishman from the ferment of ethnic elements which went to his making as such a manifestation, so in like manner we may talk of the progress of English fiction from Smollett and Fielding to Mr. Stevenson or Mr. Shorthouse as an evolution; but it would introduce some confusion of language to speak of the evolution of George Eliot, the author of *Romola,* from George Eliot, the translator of Feuerbach. Yet this latter is, by analogy, quite Mr. Symonds's way of using the word, as applied, for example, to the rise and decline of the Elizabethan drama. From Marlowe to Shirley the Elizabethan drama, in form and on the whole in spirit, is really a single organic growth, and to talk of its evolution *within that period* when we simply mean its passage through volcanic and explosive youth to ripened beauty and strength, and its subsequent descent into fatuous senility, is surely to confound ideas, as well as to institute analogies between classes of mental and of physical phenomena which admit of no real parallel. And if we take a more extended survey—reviewing, say, English poetry from Chaucer to Tennyson—it is permissible to doubt whether any law of succession even remotely allied to the Darwinian development-principle can be discerned; for the history of literature, taking periods as wholes, seems often in great measure like the history of party government, a record of total changes of front, periodic reversals of policy, by which one age becomes an abjuration and angry renunciation of its predecessor, to be itself abjured and angrily renounced in turn. Thus, there is room for doubt as to whether literature—a long series of oscillations as of a pendulum—is in its ultimate elements one whit more progressive than geometry. At any rate, when we reflect upon the rather slight ethical advance which literature has made during the tolerably spacious interval which separates the author of the Book of Job from the author of *La Terre*—two representative writers of their times—it becomes increasingly difficult, in applying the evolution-hypothesis to literature at all, to apply it in the optimistic sense which identifies it with ascent moral and spiritual.

When we pass to the other essays composing these volumes—which deal more with concrete subjects, and less with theory and speculation—we are frequently struck with the admirable order and arrangement of ideas which, individually not always of first-class importance, are made to contribute to an interesting collective result. About Walt Whitman nothing more sane and temperate in the way of appreciation has been written than the paper on **"Democratic Art;"** and it is serviceably illustrated by some excellent quotations from Whitman's vigorous prose, always so very much better than his—well, than what his admirers probably call his poetry. Our author treats Whitman with generous sympathy, though in reality one cannot but think that it is Whitman's specific attitude towards the facts of life—an attitude, on the whole, of immense though somewhat startling reasonableness—rather than his really abortive attempt at an artistic presentation of those facts, which fascinates his enthusiastic

critic, who, moreover, cannot sanction such a violent rupture with tradition as Whitman advocates.

> Why, [says Mr. Symonds], should we seek to break the links which bind us to the best of that past from which we came? Achilles has not ceased to be a fit subject for a poem or statue, because we discern heroism in an engine-driver.

Throughout both of these volumes we come upon numerous passages which are not only exceedingly good in themselves, but are especially salutary at the present moment. Thus:

> From time to time critics arise who attempt to persuade us that it does not so much matter what a poet says as how he says it, and that the highest poetical achievements are those which combine a certain vagueness of meaning with sensuous melody and colour of verbal composition. Yet, if one thing is proved with certainty by the whole of literature down to our own time, it is that the self-preservative instinct of humanity rejects such art as does not contribute to its intellectual nutrition and moral sustenance. It cannot afford to continue long in contact with ideas that run counter to the principles of its own progress. . . . Poetry will not, indeed, live without style or its equivalent. But style alone will never confer enduring cosmopolitan fame upon a poet. He must have placed himself in accord with the permanent emotions, the conservative forces of the race; he must have uttered what contributes to the building up of vital structure in the social organism, in order to gain more than a temporary or a partial hearing.

In his use of words Mr. Symonds habitually combines a scholarly precision with a laudable freedom from pedantry. We have heard his style criticised as unduly ambitious in tone, yet it has surely the merits of an efficient instrument which obediently serves its author's will. It is, however, a style not too rich in animal vigour; and it is without surprises, without those charms which startle and waylay us—those incalculable and beautiful apparitions from some unsuspected ambush of personality. But if Mr. Symonds's prose manner does not often, like one of Mr. Coventry Patmore's domesticated angels, "reward us" with that

> variety
> Which men who change can never know,

neither, on the whole, does it tease us with any worse monotony than the monotony which results from almost invariably sound thought, just apprehension, luminous generalisation, and masterly utterance. Between the aesthetic epicure or exquisite literary voluptuary like Mr. Pater, and the purely intellectual connoisseur of men and books and epochs, like Mr. Leslie Stephen, Mr. Symonds occupies a place perhaps scarcely so well defined as theirs, but not less necessary to be filled; and he fills it worthily, by virtue of the trained judgment and varied erudition which he always has at command. (pp. 166-67)

William Watson, in a review of "Essays Speculative and Suggestive," in The Academy, *Vol.*

XXXVIII, No. 956, August 30, 1890, pp. 166-67.

The Atlantic Monthly   (review date 1893)

[*In the following excerpt, the critic reviews Symonds's* Life of Michelangelo Buonarroti, *comparing it to other notable biographies of the artist while assessing Symonds's strengths and weaknesses as a biographer.*]

Mr. Symonds's **The Life of Michelangelo Buonarroti** is the fourth exhaustive biography of the great master which has been issued in the past thirty years. This is a remarkable fact, not to be paralleled in the case of any other artist, nor, so far as we recall, of any other of the world's great men. Three centuries and more after his death, historians are busying themselves with Michelangelo almost as if his life were of contemporary interest; and in addition to the four biographies we have mentioned, many smaller treatises have been devoted to a discussion of his work. Why is this? That Michelangelo was one of the few supreme men, and therefore that he is of perpetual significance, will hardly account for all the attention he has recently received. The dominant explanation is that it is only within the past generation that materials for an adequate biography have been set free. In 1858, his house, with its archives, was bequeathed to the city of Florence, and in the following year the British Museum bought a large batch of his letters. The celebration, in 1865, of the four hundredth anniversary of his birth further stimulated research; the result being that all the biographies which had been written previous to 1860—we except, of course, the lives by Condivi and Vasari, which appeared during his lifetime—have been permanently superseded.

The earliest biographer to avail himself of this new material was the German, Grimm, whose diffuse volumes still enjoy an exaggerated vogue. Grimm had the advantage of first occupying the field, which always counts for much, and by using Michelangelo's career as a thread on which to string much discursive information about the history of Italy from the time of Pius II to the Council of Trent, and many reflections on the fine arts, from Cimabue to Cornelius, he produced an entertaining book. Thirty years ago the Renaissance was less familiar to English readers than it is now, and they were willing to hear what Grimm chose to tell about it while he was incidentally narrating the life of his hero. We need not now insist that this method does justice neither to Michelangelo nor to the Renaissance. He was not a great political figure; he was only indirectly affected by many of the political events to which Grimm devotes much space. With equal relevance might a biographer of Shakespeare deem it incumbent upon him to write the history of England during the reigns of Elizabeth and James I. Therefore, as we have now books in which we can study the Renaissance in proper historical perspective, it seems likely that Grimm's work, which already shows signs of flagging, will not much longer hold its popularity.

Still, by borrowing from Michelangelo's letters at the British Museum, Grimm was able here and there to reveal many lifelike personal traits, an achievement in which he was surpassed by Gotti, the second of the recent biogra-phers. Gotti had access to the Buonarroti archives, and also to the artist's complete correspondence. He restricted himself to the writing of a life instead of a history, and though his style is dull, marked by that tendency to adjectives and the superlative which Italian writers on art and history have not yet overcome, his biography is still the best. Heath Wilson, a patient and discriminating if not an original student of art, proposed to translate Gotti's book into English; but he soon began to paraphrase and to add, until in the end he produced a work which he could fairly call his own. Paying more attention to Michelangelo's art than to his personality, and investigating with much perserverance the remaining frescoes, statues, and drawings, Heath Wilson's is a valuable contribution to a technical understanding of the subject; but his translations from the Italian, whether of Gotti's text or of Michelangelo's letters, display an ignorance of the rudiments of that language which none but an Englishman, with John Bull's hereditary contempt for foreigners and their speech, would have been willing to display.

These being the most important modern lives of Michelangelo, Mr. John Addington Symonds now publishes a fourth. His qualifications for such a task are well known. His voluminous history of the Italian Renaissance, not less than many detached essays, showed him to be familiar with this period not only in its broader phases, but in most of its less explored crannies. He had treated with equal luminousness subjects so different as the philosophy of Giordano Bruno, the rollicking songs of the Goliardi, and the crimes of the fifteenth-century despots. We have come to look for the careful collation of much material, and the straightforward presentation of it, in whatever he writes. He assimilates readily, and often forgets that he did not originate the views he has absorbed. In a word, he is the type of a scholar of remarkable breadth and insatiate curiosity, who has at the same time a faculty of fluent expression uncommon to most scholars. Richter somewhere says that in literature there are two classes: one, of those who, like a great ship, bring a rich cargo from far-off lands; and the other, of those who, like barges or lighters, unload and distribute that cargo. We have no hesitation in assigning Mr. Symonds to the latter class; many are the rich galleons he has helped to unload.

But this lack of originality would not necessarily preclude Mr. Symonds from being an excellent biographer. Lewes, in the last generation, did, in different fields, work similar to that which Symonds has been doing in our time, and Lewes certainly produced an excellent life of Goethe. Mr. Symonds's defects lie deeper. He is essentially an essayist and critic rather than a narrator; and we hold that whoever would write good history or biography, which is merely history in detail, must have the storyteller's gift. This he has not, and no amount of erudition can compensate for its absence. Despite accumulated details and lucid explanations, he never makes us feel that the men and time he describes are quite alive; at most they are galvanized into a semblance of life.

Having spoken in these general terms in order to show that we have applied the highest tests to Mr. Symonds's new work, we are aware that generalizations are often partial, and that many books which fall below the highest yet merit consideration, and even great esteem, and this we can truly say of his *Life of Michelangelo.* He has not been led into Grimm's error of submerging the artist's career in the flood of public events in which he was only partly concerned; he has more literary skill than Gotti; he is not so technical as Heath Wilson. He has endeavored to bring out Michelangelo's personality in deep relief, without, however, slighting his works, and he has furnished a sufficient but not too extensive account of political happenings; and yet his book has stretched to nearly nine hundred pages, more than twice the length of Gotti's volume of biography. Part of this expansion is due to legitimate causes,—to the insertion of new material, and of copious translations from the letters and from Condivi; but the larger part must be charged to the diffuseness of his style, which, though always lucid, is never terse. He has incorporated what are really essays on the fine arts wherever a pause in the narrative gives an excuse for so doing. His intellectual conscience seems to impose upon him the obligation of expressing an opinion about every minute topic which comes in his way, and this, coupled with incapacity for being emphatic, swells his chapters beyond necessary bounds. We shall always remember four or five pages of Ruskin, whether we agree with them or not; but after a few days, only by a strong effort of memory do opinions which Mr. Symonds expresses at ten times that length emerge from a clinging haze.

Nevertheless, Mr. Symonds has done patiently all that it was in his power to do. You feel respect for the pains he has been at to ferret into the obscure places in Michelangelo's career, and you find carefully set down details gathered from many sources. We are not aware, for instance, that any other biographer has given so precisely the long "tragedy of the tomb" of Julius II.; taking up the various contracts by which Michelangelo was harassed for nearly forty years, describing each plan, and tracing the fate of each fragment of the colossal monument. Equally minute is his description of the Medicean chapel, or of the Sistine frescoes, or of Michelangelo's relations with his fellows. He has swept away, we hope permanently, several of the stock legends; as that Michelangelo worked in morose solitude at the ceiling of the Sistine Chapel, envious of the popularity of genial, easy-going Raphael. He has shown anew the absurdity of the common belief that Michelangelo, at past threescore, was romantically in love with Vittoria Colonna, a widow of five and forty, with an absorbing preference for the cloistered life. Since no vehement love affair could be attributed to the master, early biographers and gossips made the most of this Platonic friendship. It is time that the rather cheap romance they fabricated were discarded. Mr. Symonds has also put the sonnets in their proper light, as it is natural that he who long ago made a special study of them should do. But we are astonished that he should blemish a work of this kind by raking up and trying afresh the vile scandals which, if true, could not be proved now, and ought therefore not to be unearthed. To dignify that archruffian, Pietro Aretino, by translating in full the letter in which he vilifies Michelangelo by innuendoes is to show slight respect for decency and a total lack of historical perspective. If all biographers imitated Mr. Symonds in perpetuating the calumnies

which blackguards have uttered about great men, we should ask to have the writing of biographies made a penal offense.

It is not our purpose to traverse the main points in Mr. Symonds's criticism of Michelangelo's art. He agrees with the verdict reached by contemporaries three and a half centuries ago, that the quality of *terribleness* distinguishes Michelangelo's paintings and statues from all others. He recognizes in part the validity of Ruskin's strictures, but he maintains that to see only "anatomical diagrams" in the Sistine frescoes is to see less than they contain. He separates, somewhat arbitrarily perhaps, the artist's development into several periods, laying less stress than usual on the effect the newly discovered antique statues are supposed to have produced on Michelangelo's style, and he assumes that an unrecorded early visit to Orvieto revealed to him in Signorelli's frescoes a pattern for his own. Mr. Symonds's elaborate word pictures of the sculptures and paintings confirm the opinion we had previously formed as to the futility of attempting to convey by language any adequate notion of the quality of a work of art. A description of the artist's subject may well enough be given, but when the critic digresses into technical dissertations on values, and lights and shades, and modeling,—much more, when he gives rein to his fancy or his sentiment, and tells what impression the work produced on him,—he indulges in loquacity of little profit to any student who has not the given work before his eyes. By restraining this tendency, Mr. Symonds could have lessened the bulk of his book without in the least impairing its worth.

But the first question we ask, and the last, is, What manner of man was this Michelangelo? The mighty products of his genius remain. For well-nigh four centuries they have aroused the wonder of men. One school of æsthetic criticism after another has said its say about them. Every traveler in Rome or Florence has lavished his store of adjectives upon them, and then has turned from the contemplation of the works to speculate upon the character of their maker. His genius we all acknowledge, but what of the man,—what of his daily life, his virtues and defects, his power to cope with the vicissitudes of fortune, his personal, mortal part? All this it is the business of the biographer to answer, if he can, in order that we may learn what sort of an instrument Providence chose for these particular revelations.

Mr. Symonds has endeavored to satisfy this legitimate curiosity, and has not failed to make copious use of well known passages in Condivi and Vasari and in the less known letters. These last, indeed, strike us as the most interesting parts of the book. Their characteristic intensity, their evident sincerity, their vigor of thought even when the language is not terse, make Mr. Symonds's style seem sometimes almost pedestrian by contrast. Certainly, if nothing but the following note remained from Michelangelo's correspondence, we could infer much about his character: "Most blessed father, I have been turned out of the palace to-day by your orders; wherefore I give you notice that from this time forward, if you want me, you must look for me elsewhere than at Rome." Remember that the man who wrote this was then a young sculptor of thirty-

Clifton Hill House, Symonds's boyhood home near Bristol.

one, and that the Pope who received it was Julius II, and you will not be surprised that the writer subsequently modeled the Moses and painted the Last Judgment. On the whole, the more we learn of Michelangelo's character,—his "psychology," as Mr. Symonds is fond of calling it,—the more we are disposed to respect it. The sordidness of his habits, in which he reminds us of Turner, and his ambition to be ranked with the best families of Florence— as if any patent of nobility could have ennobled him— were foibles on the surface. In the depths there were virtues which no mean spirit can harbor: loyal support of his kindred, even when they were ungrateful; candor in an age of overweening despots and truckling courtiers; real religiousness in an age when most men sneered at the religion to which, for prudence' sake, they outwardly conformed; and an unswerving fidelity to the ideals of his art. Mr. Symonds errs, we think, in condescending to refute Lombroso and Parlagreco, two psychologists who have recently classed Michelangelo among the unsane men of genius, alleging as proofs his irritability, his love of solitude, his insensibility to women, his timorousness, and similar evidence. What are the facts? Michelangelo started poor, and though usually ill paid, and though he gave much of his substance to his family and received no compensation at all for very important work, he died passing rich. Do prac-

tical men of affairs, whose sanity is taken for granted, achieve more than that? Michelangelo, consecrating his life to his ideal, renounced luxury, curbed his passions, and shunned whatever might interfere with the freest expression of his genius. Are these to be regarded as indications of lack of mental balance? At twenty-four he executed the Pietà, at twenty-seven the David; at thirty he began work on the tomb of Julius; at thirty-one he drew the cartoon for the Battle of Pisa; at thirty-seven he finished the vault of the Sistine Chapel; at forty he was set to work upon the Church of San Lorenzo; at fifty he was occupied with the Medicean monuments; at fifty-four he superintended the fortifications of Florence; at sixty-six he completed the fresco of the Last Judgment; at seventy-one he was appointed architect of St. Peter's, and worked with unabated vigor till his death in his eighty-ninth year. These are but the foremost of his achievements, any one of which would suffice for the fame of a lesser man, and yet we are bidden to look upon him as morbid, as a neurotic subject! How many average men, who, by their commonplaceness, run no risk of falling under this suspicion, pursue their vocation to the age of eighty-nine? We suspect that Mr. Symonds would have done well to have paid no attention to "psychology" of this kind.

In conclusion, we can assure any one who takes up these volumes that he will find in them all the important facts that have hitherto been published concerning Michelangelo. Of Mr. Symonds's methods, which are those of the essayist rather than of the historian, we have sufficiently indicated the limitations. We feel that the materials are here for a first-rate biography, but the ideal biographer, to do justice to the subject, must possess, besides Mr. Symonds's scholarship, a vigor and grasp and sense of vitality such as characterize Carlyle at his best. (pp. 406-10)

> *"Symonds's Life of Michelangelo," in* The Atlantic Monthly, *Vol. LXXI, No. CCCCXXV, March, 1893, pp. 406-10.*

Frederic Harrison   (essay date 1900)

[*The author of many acclaimed works on historical, political, and literary subjects, Harrison was a central figure in the intellectual and political controversies of his day. He was attracted by the philosophical theories of the French philosopher Auguste Comte, and became England's primary advocate of Positivism, a philosophy maintaining that the proper goal of knowledge is the description, and not the explanation, of experienced phenomena. In the following excerpt, Harrison presents an essentially favorable overview of Symonds's literary canon, focusing on the author's artistic growth over the course of his career.*]

More than six years have come and gone since, amongst April blossoms, an English master in the literature of Italy was laid in his premature grave, within that most pathetic and most sacred spot of Rome where lie so many famous Englishmen. 'They gave us,' wrote his daughter in a beautiful record of the last scene, 'they gave us a little piece of ground close to the spot where Shelley lies buried. In all the world there surely is no place more penetrated with the powers of poetry and natural beauty.' All travellers know how true is this: few spots on earth possess so weird a power over the imagination. It is described by Horatio Brown [in his *John Addington Symonds: A Biography*], . . . the volume from which I have been quoting, 'the grave is within a pace of Trelawny's and a hand-touch of Shelley's *Cor Cordium,* in the embrasure of the ancient city walls.' Fit resting-place for one who of all the men of our generation best knew, loved, and understood the Italian genius in literature!

There are not wanting signs that the reputation of J. Addington Symonds had been growing in his latest years, it has been growing since his too early death. His later work is stronger, richer, and more permanent than his earlier work—excellent as is almost all his prose. Even the learning and brilliancy of the *Renaissance in Italy* do not impress me with the same sense of his powers as his *Benvenuto Cellini,* his *Michelangelo,* his last two volumes of *Essays, Speculative and Suggestive* (1890), and some passages in the posthumous *Autobiography* embodied in the *Life* by H. F. Brown. For grasp of thought, directness, sureness of judgment, the *Essays* of 1890 seem to me the most solid things that Symonds has left. He grew immensely after middle age in force, simplicity, depth of interest and of insight. He pruned his early exuberance; he boldly grasped the great problems of life and thought; he spoke forth his mind with a noble courage and signal frankness. He was lost to us too early: he died at fifty-two, after a life of incessant suffering, constantly on the brink of death, a life maintained, in spite of all trials, with rare tenacity of purpose. And as we look back now we may wonder that his barely twenty years of labour under such cruel obstacles produced so much. For I reckon some forty works of his, great and small, including at least some ten important books of prose in some twenty solid volumes. That is a great achievement for one who was a permanent invalid and was cut off before old age.

The publication of his *Life* by his friend H. F. Brown, embodying his own *Autobiography* and his *Letters,* has now revealed to the public what even his friends only partly understood, how stern a battle for life was waged by Symonds from his childhood. His inherited delicacy of constitution drove him to pass the larger part of his life abroad, and at last compelled him to make his home in an Alpine retreat. The pathetic motto and preface he prefixed to his *Essays* (1890) shows how deeply he felt his compulsory exile—ευρετικον ειναι φασι την ερημιαν— 'solitude,' they say, 'favours the search after truth.'—'The *Essays,*' he declares, 'written in the isolation of this Alpine retreat (Davos-Platz, 1890) express the opinions and surmisings of one who long has watched in solitude, "as from a ruined tower," the world of thought, and circumstance, and action.' And he goes on to speak of his 'prolonged seclusion from populous cities and the society of intellectual equals'—a seclusion which lasted, with some interruptions, for more than fifteen years. And during a large part of his life of active literary production, a period of scarcely more than twenty years, he was continually incapacitated by pain and physical prostration, as we now may learn from his *Autobiography* and *Letters.* They give us a fine picture of intellectual energy overcoming bodily distress. How few of the readers who delighted in his sketches of the columbines and asphodels on the Monte Generoso, and the vision of the Propylæa in moonlight, understood the physical strain on him whose spirit bounded at these sights and who painted them for us with so radiant a brush.

Symonds, I have said, grew and deepened immensely in his later years, and it was only perhaps in the very last decade of his life that he reached the full maturity of his powers. His beautiful style, which was in early years somewhat too luscious, too continuously florid, too redolent of the elaborated and glorified prize-essay, grew stronger, simpler, more direct, in his later pieces, though to the last it had still some savour of the fastidious literary recluse. In the *Catholic Reaction* (1886), in the *Essays* (1890), in the posthumous *Autobiography* (begun in 1889), he grapples with the central problems of modern society and philosophic thought, and has left the somewhat dilettante tourist of the Cornice and Ravenna far, far behind him. As a matter of style, I hold the *Benvenuto Cellini* (of 1888) to be a masterpiece of skilful use of language: so that the inimitable Memoirs of the immortal vagabond read to us now like an original of Smollett. It is far the most popular of Symonds's books, in large part no doubt from the nature of the work, but it is in form the most racy of all his pieces; and the last thing that any one could find in it would be any suggestion of academic euphuism. Had Symonds from the first written with that *verve* and motherwit, his readers doubtless would have been trebled.

It has been an obstacle to the recognition of Symonds's great merits that until well past middle life he was known to the public only by descriptive and critical essays in detached pieces, and these addressed mainly to a scholarly and travelled few, whilst the nervous and learned works of his more glowing autumn came towards the end of his life on a public rather satiated by exquisite analysis of landscape and poems. Even now, it may be said, the larger public are not yet familiar with his exhaustive work on Michelangelo, his latest **Essays,** and his **Autobiography** and **Letters.** In these we see that to a vast knowledge of Italian literature and art, Symonds united a judgment of sound balance, a courageous spirit, and a mind of rare sincerity and acumen.

His work, with all its volume in the whole, is strictly confined within its chosen fields. It concerns Greek poetry, the scenery of Italy and Greece, Italian literature and art, translations of Greek and Italian poetry, volumes of lyrics, critical studies of some English poets, essays in philosophy and the principles of art and style. This in itself is a considerable field, but it includes no other part of ancient or modern literature, no history but that of the Renaissance, no trace of interest in social, political, or scientific problems. In the pathetic preface of 1890, Symonds himself seems fully to recognise how much he was used to survey the world of things from a solitary peak. His work then is essentially, in a peculiar degree for our times, the work of a student looking at things through books, from the point of view of literature, and for a literary end—ου πραξις αλλα γνωσις is his motto. And this gospel is always and of necessity addressed to the few rather than to the mass.

Until Symonds was well past the age of thirty-five—*nel mezzo del cammin*—he was known only by his very graceful pictures of Italy and his most scholarly analysis of Greek poetry. I have long been wont to regard his two series of **The Greek Poets** (1873, 1876) as the classical and authoritative estimate of this magnificent literature. These studies seem to me entirely right, convincing, and illuminating. There is little more to be said on the subject; and there is hardly a point missed or a judgment to be reversed. He can hardly even be said to have over-rated or under-rated any important name. And this is the more remarkable in that Symonds ranges over Greek poetry throughout all the thirteen centuries which separate the *Iliad* from *Hero and Leander;* and he is just as lucidly judicial whether he deals with Hesiod, Empedocles, Æschylus, or Menander.

Symonds was certainly far more widely and profoundly versed in Greek poetry than any Englishman who in our day has analysed it for the general reader. And it is plain that no scholar of his eminence has been master of a style so fascinating and eloquent. He has the art of making the

Greek poets live to our eyes as if we saw in pictures the scenes they sing. A fine example of this power is in the admirable essay on Pindar in the first series, when he describes the festival of Olympia as Pindar saw it. And we who have been trying to get up a thrill over the gate-money 'sports' in the Stadium of Athens may turn to Symonds's description of the Olympic games of old—'a festival in the fullest sense of the word popular, but at the same time consecrated by religion, dignified by patriotic pride, adorned with art.' And he gives us a vivid sketch of the scene in the blaze of summer, with the trains of pilgrims and deputies, ambassadors and athletes, sages, historians, poets, painters, sculptors, wits, and statesmen—all thronging into the temple of Zeus to bow before the chryselephantine masterpiece of Pheidias.

These very fine critical estimates of the Greek poets would no doubt have had a far wider audience had they been from the first more organically arranged, less full of Greek citations and remarks intelligible only to scholars. As it is, they are studies in no order, chronological or analytic; for Theocritus and the Anthologies come in the first series, and Homer and Æschylus in the second. The style, too, if always eloquent and picturesque, is rather too continuously picturesque and eloquent. *Con espressione dolcissima* is a delightful variety in a sonata, but we also crave a *scherzo,* and *adagio* and *prestissimo* passages. Now, Symonds, who continually delights us with fine images and fascinating colour, is too fond of satiating us with images and with colour, till we long for a space of quiet reflection and neutral good sense. And not only are the images too constant, too crowded, and too luscious—though, it must be said, they are never incongruous or commonplace—but some of the very noblest images are apt to falter under their own weight of ornament.

Here is an instance from his "Pindar"—a grand image, perhaps a little too laboriously coloured—

> He who has watched a sunset attended by the passing of a thunderstorm in the outskirts of the Alps, who has seen the distant ranges of the mountains alternately obscured by cloud and blazing with the concentrated brightness of the sinking sun, while drifting scuds of hail and rain, tawny with sunlight, glistening with broken rainbows, clothe peak and precipice and forest in the golden veil of flame-irradiated vapour—who has heard the thunder bellow in the thwarting folds of hills, and watched the lightning, like a snake's tongue, flicker at intervals amid gloom and glory—knows in nature's language what Pindar teaches with the voice of art.

And, not content with this magnificent and very just simile, Symonds goes on to tell us how Pindar 'combines the strong flight of the eagle, the irresistible force of the torrent, the richness of Greek wine, the majestic pageantry of nature in one of her sublimer moods.' This is too much: we feel that, if the metaphors are not getting mixed, they form a draught too rich for us to quaff.

Symonds has, however, an excellent justification to offer for this pompous outburst, that he was anxious to give us a vivid sense of Pindar's own 'tumidity—an overblown exaggeration of phrase,' for 'Pindar uses images like precious stones, setting them together in a mass, without caring to sort them, so long as they produce a gorgeous show.' We all know how dangerous a model the great lyrist may become—

> Pindarum quisquis studet æmulari,
> Iule, ceratis ope Dædalea
> Nititur pinnis, vitreo daturus
> Nomina ponto.

Symonds sought to show us something of Pindar's 'fiery flight, the torrent-fulness, the intoxicating charm' of his odes: and so he himself in his enthusiasm 'fervet, immensusque ruit profundo ore.'

Whenever Symonds is deeply stirred with the nobler types of Greek poetry, this dithyrambic mood comes on him, and he gives full voice to the God within. Here is a splendid symphony called forth by the Trilogy of Æschylus—

> There is, in the *Agamemnon,* an oppressive sense of multitudinous crimes, of sins gathering and swelling to produce a tempest. The air we breathe is loaded with them. No escape is possible. The marshalled thunderclouds roll ever onward, nearer and more near, and far more swiftly than the foot can flee. At last the accumulated storm bursts in the murder of Agamemnon, the majestic and unconscious victim, felled like a steer at the stall; in the murder of Cassandra, who foresees her fate, and goes to meet it with the shrinking of some dumb creature, and with the helplessness of one who knows that doom may not be shunned; in the lightning-flash of Clytemnestra's arrogance, who hitherto has been a glittering hypocrite, but now proclaims herself a fiend incarnate. As the Chorus cries, the rain of blood, that hitherto has fallen drop by drop, descends in torrents on the house of Atreus: but the end is not yet. The whole tragedy becomes yet more sinister when we regard it as the prelude to ensuing tragedies, as the overture to fresh symphonies and similar catastrophes. Wave after wave of passion gathers and breaks in these stupendous scenes; the ninth wave mightier than all, with a crest whereof the spray is blood, falls foaming; over the outspread surf of gore and ruin the curtain drops, to rise upon the self-same theatre of new woes.

This unquestionably powerful picture of the *Agamemnon* opens with a grand trumpet-burst that Ruskin might envy—'an oppressive sense of multitudinous crimes'—'the air we breathe is loaded with them'—'Agamemnon, the majestic and unconscious victim, felled like a steer at the stall'—Cassandra with the shrinking of some dumb creature—Clytemnestra, the glittering hypocrite, the fiend incarnate. Down to this point the passage is a piece of noble English, and a true analysis of the greatest of pure tragedies. But when we come to the rain of blood, the waves with their spray of blood, the 'outspread surf of gore,' we begin to feel exhausted and satiated with horror, and the whole terrific paragraph ends in something perilously near to bathos. I have cited this passage as a characteristic example of Symonds in his splendid powers and his besetting weakness—his mastery of the very heart of Greek poetry, and his proneness to redundancy of ornament; his anxiety to paint the lily and to gild the refined gold of his own pure and very graceful English.

I have always enjoyed the ***Sketches in Italy and Greece*** (1874) and the ***Sketches and Studies in Italy*** (1879) as delightful reminiscences of some of the loveliest scenes on earth. They record the thoughts of one who was at once scholar, historian, poet, and painter—painter, it is true in words, but one who saw Italy and Athens as a painter does, or rather as he should do. The combination is very rare, and, to those who can follow the guidance, very fascinating. The fusion of history and landscape is admirable: the Siena, the Perugia, the Palermo, Syracuse, Rimini, and Ravenna, with their stories of S. Catherine, the Baglioni, the Normans of Hauteville, Nicias and Demosthenes, the Malatesti, and the memories of the Pineta—are pictures that dwell in the thoughts of all who love these immortal spots, and should inspire all who do not know them with the thirst to do so. The Athens is quite an education in itself, and it makes one regret that it is the one sketch that Symonds has given us in Greece proper. To the cultured reader, he is the ideal cicerone for Italy.

The very completeness and variety of the knowledge that Symonds has lavished on these pictures of Italian cities may somewhat limit their popularity, for he appeals at once to such a combination of culture that many readers lose something of his ideas. Passages from Greek, Latin, and Italian abound in them; the history is never sacrificed to the landscape, nor the landscape to the poetry, nor the scholarship to the sunlight, the air, and the scents of flower or the sound of the waves and the torrents. All is there: and in this way they surpass those pictures of Italian scenes that we may read in Ruskin, George Eliot, or Professor Freeman. Freeman has not the poetry and colour of Symonds; George Eliot has not his ease and grace, his fluidity of improvisation; and Ruskin, with all his genius for form and colour, has no such immense and catholic grasp of history as a whole.

But it cannot be denied that these ***Sketches,*** like the ***Greek Poets,*** are too continuously florid, too profusely coloured, without simplicity and repose. The subjects admit of colour, nay, they demand it; they justify enthusiasm, and suggest a luxurious wealth of sensation. But their power and their popularity would have been greater, if their style had more light and shade, if the prosaic foreground and background had been set down in jog-trot prose. The high-blooded barb that Symonds mounts never walks: he curvets, ambles, caracoles, and prances with unfailing elegance, but with somewhat too monotonous a consciousness of his own grace. And there is a rather more serious weakness. These beautiful sketches are *pictures,* descriptions of what can be *seen,* not records of what has been *felt.* Now, it is but a very limited field indeed within which words can describe scenery. The emotions that scenery suggests can be given us in verse or in prose. Byron perhaps could not paint word-pictures like Symonds. But his *emotions* in a thunderstorm in the Alps, or as he gazes on the Silberhorn, his grand outburst in Rome—

> Oh Rome! my country! city of the soul!
> The orphans of the heart must turn to thee,
> Lone mother of dead empires!

strikes the imagination more than a thousand word-pictures. Ruskin's elaborate descriptions of Venice and Florence would not have touched us as they do, had he not made us feel all that Venice and Florence meant to him. This is the secret of Byron, of Goethe, even of *Corinne* and *Transformation.* But this secret Symonds never learned. He paints, he describes, he tells us all he *knows* and what he has *read.* He does not tell us what he has *felt,* so as to make us feel it to our bones. Yet such is the only possible form of reproducing the effect of a scene.

It will, I think, be recognised by all, that no English writer of our time has equalled Symonds in knowledge of the entire range of Italian literature from Guido Cavalcanti to Leopardi, and none certainly has treated it with so copious and brilliant a pen. The seven octavo volumes on the ***Italian Renaissance*** occupied him for eleven years (1875-1886); and besides these there are the two volumes on ***Michelangelo*** (1892), two volumes of ***Benvenuto Cellini*** (1888), a volume on Boccaccio (1895), and the ***Sonnets*** of Michelangelo and Campanella (1878). And we must not forget the early essay on Dante (1872), and translations from Petrarch, Ariosto, Pulci, and many more. This constitutes an immense and permanent contribution to our knowledge, for it not only gives us a survey of Italian literature for its three grand centuries, but it presents such an ample analysis of the works reviewed that every reader can judge for himself how just and subtle are the judgments pronounced by the critic. The studies of Petrarch, Boccaccio, of the Humanists and Poliziano, of Michelangelo, Lionardo, Cellini, Ariosto, and Tasso, are particularly full and instructive. The whole series of estimates is exhaustive. To see how complete it is, one need only compare it with the brief summaries and dry catalogues of such a book as Hallam's *Literature of Europe.* Hallam gives us notes on Italian literature: Symonds gives us biographies and synopses.

This exhaustive treatment brings its own Nemesis. The magic fountain of Symonds's learning and eloquence pours on till it threatens to become a flood. We have almost more than we need or can receive. We welcome all that he has to tell us about the origins of Italian poetry, about Boccaccio and contemporary *Novelle,* about the *Orlando* cycle and the pathetic story of Tasso. And so, all that we learn of Machiavelli, Bruno, Campanella, Sarpi is exactly what we want, told us in exactly the way we enjoy. But our learned guide pours on with almost equal eloquence and detail into all the ramifications of the literature in its pedantry, its decadence, its affectation. And at last the most devoted reader begins to have enough of the copyists of Dante and Boccaccio, of the *Hypnerotomachia* and its brood, of *Laude* and *Ballate,* of *Rispetti* and *Capitoli,* and all the languishments and hermaphroditisms of Guarini, Berni, and Marino. Nearly four thousand pages charged with extracts and references make a great deal to master; and the general reader may complain that they stoop to register so many conceits and so much filth.

In all that he has written on Italian art, Symonds has shown ripe knowledge and consummate judgment. The second volume of his ***Italian Renaissance*** is wholly given to art, but he treats art incidentally in many other vol-

umes, in the works on Michelangelo and Cellini, and in very many essays. His ***Michelangelo Buonarroti*** (1892) is a masterly production, going as it does to the root of the central problems of great art. And his estimate of Cellini is singularly discriminating and sound. His accounts of the origin of Renaissance architecture, of Lionardo, of Luini, of Correggio, and Giorgione are all essentially just and decisive. Indeed, in his elaborate survey of Italian art for three centuries from Nicolas of Pisa to Vasari, though few would venture to maintain that Symonds is always right, he would be a bold man who should try to prove that he was often wrong.

But this is very far from meaning that Symonds has said everything, or has said the last word. The most cursory reader must notice how great is the contrast between the view of Italian art taken by Symonds and that taken by Ruskin. Not that they differ so deeply in judging specific works of art or even particular artists. It is a profound divergence of beliefs on religion, philosophy, and history. That Revival of Paganism which is abomination to Ruskin is the subject of Symonds's commemoration, and even of his modified admiration. The whole subject is far too complex and too radical to be discussed here. For my own part I am not willing to forsake the lessons of either. Both have an intimate knowledge of Italian art and its history—Ruskin as a poet and painter of genius, Symonds as a scholar and historian of great learning and industry. Ruskin has passionate enthusiasm: Symonds has laborious impartiality, a cool judgment, and a catholic taste. Ruskin is an almost mediæval Christian: Symonds is a believer in science and in evolution.

The contrast between the two, which is admirably illustrated by their different modes of regarding Raffaelle at Rome, and Michelangelo's Sistine Chapel, is a fresh form of the old maxim—Both are right in what they affirm and wrong in what they deny. Ruskin's enthusiasm is lavished on the Catholic and chivalric nobleness of the thirteenth century; Symonds's enthusiasm is lavished on the humanity and the naturalism of the fifteenth and sixteenth centuries. We accept the gifts of both ages, and we will not dispense with either. Ruskin denounced Neo-classicism and the Humanism of the Renaissance; Symonds denounced the superstition and inhumanity of Mediævalism. But Ruskin has shown us how unjust was Symonds to Catholicism, precisely as Symonds has shown us how unjust was Ruskin to the Renaissance.

Let us thankfully accept the lessons of both these learned masters of literature and art. To Ruskin, the Renaissance is a mere episode, and a kind of local plague. With Symonds it is the centre of a splendid return to Truth and Beauty. Ruskin's point of view is far the wider: Symonds's point of view is far the more systematic. Ruskin is thinking of the religion and the poetry of all the ages: Symonds is profoundly versed in the literature and art of a particular epoch in a single country. Ruskin knows nothing and wishes to know nothing of the masses of literature and history which Symonds has absorbed. Symonds, on the other hand, despises a creed which teaches such superstitions, and a Church which ends in such corruptions. Spiritually, perhaps, Ruskin's enthusiasms are the more important and the purer: philosophically and historically, Symonds's enthusiasms are the more scientific and the more rational. Both, in their way, are real. Let us correct the one by the other. The Renaissance was an indispensable progress in the evolution of Europe, and yet withal a moral depravation—full of immortal beauty, full also of infernal vileness, like the Sin of Milton, as she guarded Hell-gate.

The Renaissance in Italy (alas! why did he use this Frenchified word in writing in English of an Italian movement, when some of us have been struggling for years past to assert the pure English form of *Renascence?*)—*The Renaissance in Italy* is a very valuable and brilliant contribution to our literature, but it is not a complete book even yet, not an organic book, not a work of art. The volumes on art and on literature are in every way the best; but even in these the want of proportion is very manifest. Cellini, in Symonds, occupies nearly five times the space given to Raffaelle. Barely fifteen pages (admirable in themselves) are devoted to Lionardo, whilst a whole chapter is devoted to the late school of Bologna. It is the same with the literature. Pietro Aretino is treated with the same scrupulous interest as Boccaccio or Ariosto. The *Hermaphroditus* and the *Adone* are commemorated with as much care as the poems of Dante or Petrarch. A history of literature, no doubt, must take note of all popular books, however pedantic or obscene. But we are constantly reminded how very much Symonds is absorbed in purely literary interests rather than in social and truly historic interests.

The Renaissance in Italy, if regarded as a survey of the part given by one nation to the whole movement of the Renascence in Europe over some two centuries and a half, has one very serious *lacuna* and defect. In all these seven volumes there is hardly one word about the *science* of the Renaissance. Now, the revival for the modern world of physical science from the state to which science had been carried by Hippocrates, Aristotle, Archimedes, and Hipparchus in the ancient world was one of the greatest services of the Renaissance—one of the greatest services ever conferred on mankind. And in this work Italy held a foremost part, if she did not absolutely lead the way. In Mathematics, Mechanics, Astronomy, Physics, Botany, Zoology, Medicine, and Surgery the Italians did much to prepare the ground for modern science. Geometry, Algebra, Mechanics, Anatomy, Geography, Jurisprudence, and General Philosophy owe very much to the Italian genius; but of these we find nothing in these seven crowded volumes. Symonds has nothing to tell us of the wonderful tale of the rise of modern Algebra—of Tartaglia and Cardan; nothing of the origins of modern Geometry and Mechanics; nothing of the school of Vesalius at Pavia, of Fallopius and Eustachius and the early Italian anatomists; nothing of Cæsalpinus and the early botanists; nothing of Lilio and the reformed Calendar of Pope Gregory; nothing of Alciati and the revival of Roman law. A whole chapter might have been bestowed on Lionardo as a man of science, and another on Galileo, whose physical discoveries began in the sixteenth century. And a few pages might have been saved for Christopher Columbus. And it is the more melancholy that the great work out of which these names are omitted has room for elaborate disquisitions on the *Rifacimento* of Orlando, and a perfect Newgate Calendar of

Princes and Princesses, Borgias, Cencis, Orsinis, and Accorambonis. Symonds has given us some brilliant analyses of the literature and art of Italy during three centuries of the Renascence. But he has not given us its full meaning and value in science, in philosophy, or in history, for he has somewhat misunderstood both the Middle Ages which created the Renascence and the Revolution which it created in turn, nor has he fully grasped the relations of the Renascence to both.

It is impossible to omit some notice of Symonds's poetry, because he laboured at this art with such courage and perseverance, and has left so much to the world, besides, I am told, whole packets of verses in manuscript. He published some five or six volumes of verse, including his Prize Poem of 1860, and he continued to the last to write poems and translations. But he was not a poet: he knew it—'I have not the inevitable touch of the true poet'—he says very justly in his *Autobiography.* Matthew Arnold told him that he obtained the Newdigate prize not for the style of his *Escorial*—which, in its obvious fluency, is a quite typical prize poem—'but because it showed an intellectual grasp of the subject.' That is exactly the truth about all Symonds's verses. They show a high intellectual grasp of the subject; but they have not the inevitable touch of the true poet.

These poems are very thoughtful, very graceful, very interesting, and often pathetic. They rank very high amongst the minor poetry of his time. They are full of taste, of ingenuity, of subtlety, nay, of beauty. There is hardly a single fault to be found in them, hardly a commonplace stanza, not one false note. And yet, as he said with his noble sincerity, he has scarcely written one great line—one line that we remember, and repeat, and linger over. He frankly recalls how 'Vaughan at Harrow told me the truth when he said that my besetting sin was "fatal facility." ' And at Balliol, he says, Jowett 'chid me for ornaments and mannerisms of style.'

Symonds's poetry is free from mannerisms, but it has that 'fatal facility'—which no fine poetry can have. It is full of ornament—of really graceful ornament; but it sadly wants variety, fire, the incommunicable 'form' of true poetry. The very quantity of it has perhaps marred his reputation, good as most of it is regarded as minor poetry. But does the world want minor poetry at all? The world does not, much less minor poetry mainly on the theme of death, waste, disappointment, and doubt. But to the cultured few who love scholarly verse packed close with the melancholy musings of a strong brain and a brave heart, to Symonds's own friends and contemporaries, these sonnets and lyrics will long continue to have charm and meaning. He said in the touching preface to *Many Moods* (1878), dedicated to his friend, Roden Noel, who has now rejoined him in the great Kingdom, he trusted 'that some moods of thought and feeling, not elsewhere expressed by me in print, may live within the memory of men like you, as part of me!' It was a legitimate hope: and it is not, and it will not be, unfulfilled.

The translations in verse are excellent. From translations in verse we hardly expect original poetry; and it must be doubted if any translation in verse can be at once accurate, literal, and poetic. Symonds was a born translator: his facility, his ingenuity, his scholarly insight, his command of language prompted him to give us a profusion of translation in verse, even in his prose writings. They are most of them as good as literal transcripts of a poem can be made. But they are not quite poetry. In Sappho's hymn to Aphrodite, Symonds's opening lines—

> Star-throned, incorruptible Aphrodite,
> Child of Zeus, wile-weaving, I supplicate thee—

are a most accurate rendering; but they do not give the melodious wail of—

> ποικιλοθρον αθανατ Αφροδιτα
> παι Διοδ δολοπλοκε λισσομαι σε

The Sonnets of Michelangelo and of Campanella (1878) is a most valuable contribution to Italian literature. These most powerful pieces had never been translated into English from the authentic text. They are abrupt, obscure, and subtle, and especially require the help of an expert. And in Symonds they found a consummate expert.

. . . . .

It was not until a few years before his death that Symonds was known as a writer on subjects other than history, literature, and art. But in his fiftieth year he issued in two volumes his *Essays, Speculative and Suggestive* (1890). These, as I have said, are written in a style more nervous and simple than his earlier studies; they deal with larger topics with greater seriousness and power. The essays on 'Evolution,' on its 'Application to Literature and Art,' on 'Principles of Criticism,' on the 'Provinces and Relations of the Arts,' are truly *suggestive,* as he claims them to be: and are wise, ingenious, and fertile. The 'Notes on Style,' on the history of style, national style, personal style, are sound and interesting, if not very novel. And the same is true of what he has written of Expression, of Caricature, and of our Elizabethan and Victorian poetry.

The great value of Symonds's judgments about literature and art arises from his uniform combination of comprehensive learning with judicial temper. He is very rarely indeed betrayed into any form of extravagance either by passionate admiration or passionate disdain. And he hardly ever discusses any subject of which he has not a systematic and exhaustive knowledge. His judgment always has much better control over his emotions than has that of Ruskin; he has a wider and more erudite familiarity with the whole field of modern literature and art than had either Ruskin or Matthew Arnold. Indeed, we may fairly assume that none of his contemporaries have been so profoundly saturated at once with classical poetry, Italian and Elizabethan literature, and modern poetry, English, French, and German. Though Symonds had certainly not the literary charm of Ruskin, or Matthew Arnold, perhaps of one or two others among his contemporaries, he had no admitted superior as a critic in learning or in judgment.

But that which I find most interesting—I venture to think most important—in these later essays, in the *Autobiography and the Letters,* is the frank and courageous handling of the eternal problems of Man and the Universe, Humanity and its Destiny, the relations between the individual and the environment. All these Symonds has treated with a clearness and force that some persons hardly expected from the loving critic of Sappho, Poliziano, and Cellini. For my own part I know few things more penetrating and suggestive in this field than the essays on the 'Philosophy of Evolution' and its applications, the 'Nature Myths', 'Darwin's Thoughts about God,' the 'Limits of Knowledge,' and 'Notes on Theism.' Symonds avows himself an agnostic, rather tending towards pantheism, in the mood of Goethe and of Darwin. As his friend puts it truly enough in the *Biography*—'Essentially he desired the warmth of a personal God, intellectually he could conceive that God under human attributes only, and he found himself driven to say "No" to each human presentment of Him.'

In his *Essays* and in the *Autobiography* Symonds has summed up his final beliefs, and it was right that on his grave-stone they should inscribe his favourite lines of Cleanthes which he was never tired of citing, which he said must be the form of our prayers—

> 'Lead Thou me, God, Law, Reason, Motion, Life!
> All names alike for Thee are vain and hollow.'

But he separated himself from the professed Theists who assert 'that God must be a *Person,* a *righteous Judge,* a *loving Ruler,* a *Father'* (the italics are his—Notes on Theism. *Essays,* ii. p. 291). This is nearly the same as Matthew Arnold's famous phrase—'the stream of tendency by which all things seek to fulfil the law of their being'—or 'the Eternal not ourselves that makes for righteousness.' And Matthew Arnold also could find no probable evidence for the belief that God is a *Person.* The reasoning of Symonds in these later essays is not wholly unlike that which leads Herbert Spencer to his idea of the Unknowable—'the Infinite and Eternal Energy by which all things are created and sustained.' But Symonds's own belief tended rather more to a definite and moral activity of the Energy he could not define, and he was wont to group himself under Darwin rather than Spencer.

He had reflected upon Comte's conception of Humanity as the supreme power of which we can predicate certain knowledge and personal relations; and in many of his later utterances Symonds approximates in general purpose to that conception. His practical religion is always summed up in his favourite motto from Goethe—'im Ganzen, Guten, Schönen, resolut zu leben,' or in the essentially Positivist maxim—τουδ ζωντασ ευ δραν—do thy duty throughout this life. But it seems that the idea of humanity had been early presented to him in its pontifical, not in its rational form. And a man who was forced to watch the busy world of men in solitude from afar was not likely to accept a practical religion of life for others—for family, country, and humanity. It is possible that his eloquent relative who built in the clouds of Oxford metaphysic so imposing a nephelococcygia may have influenced him more than he knew. In any case, he sums up his 'religious evolution' thus (*Biography,* ii. 132): 'Having rejected dogmatic Christianity in all its forms, Broad Church, Anglicanism, the Gospel of Comte, Hegel's superb identification of human thought with essential Being, &c. &c. . . . I came to fraternise with Goethe, Cleanthes, Whitman, Bruno, Darwin.'

They who for years have delighted in those brilliant studies that Symonds poured forth on literature, art, criticism, and history should become familiar with the virile meditations he scattered through the *Autobiography* and *Letters* in the memoir compiled by Horatio Brown. They will see how steadily his power grew to the last both in thought and in form. His earlier form had undoubtedly tended to mannerism—not to euphuism or 'preciosity' indeed—but to an excess of colour and saccharine. As he said of another famous writer on the Renaissance, we feel sometimes in these *Sketches* as if we were lost in a plantation of sugar-cane. But Symonds never was seriously a victim of the Circe of preciosity, she who turns her lovers into swine—of that style which he said 'has a peculiarly disagreeable effect on my nerves—like the presence of a civet cat.' He was luscious, not precious. His early style was vitiated by a fatal proneness to Ruskinese. But at last he became virile and not luscious at all.

And that other defect of his work—its purely literary aspect—he learned at last to develop into a definite social and moral philosophy. He was quite aware of his besetting fault. 'The fault of my education as a preparation for literature was that it was exclusively literary' (*Autobiography,* i. 218). That no doubt is answerable for much of the shortcomings of his *Renaissance,* the exaggeration of mere scandalous pedantry, of frigid conceits, and the entire omission of science. It is significant to read from one of Oxford's most brilliant sons a scathing denunciation of the superficial and mechanical 'cram,' which Oxford still persists in calling its 'education' (*Autobiography,* i. 218).

It is a moving and inspiring tale, is this story of the life of a typical and exemplary man of letters. Immense learning, heroic perseverance, frankness and honesty of temper, with the egoism incidental to all autobiographies and intimate letters, and in this case perhaps emphasised by a life of exile and disease, a long and cruel battle with inherited weakness of constitution, a bright spirit, and intellect alert, unbroken to the last. (pp. 126-48)

> Frederic Harrison, *"John Addington Symonds," in his* Tennyson, Ruskin, Mill and Other Literary Estimates, *The Macmillan Company, 1900, pp. 126-48.*

Lafcadio Hearn   (essay date 1915)

[*Hearn was an American fiction writer and critic. Often devoting his short stories and novellas to supernatural subjects, he is best known for his retellings of Japanese ghost stories. As a critic, Hearn ignored the moralistic conventions of Victorian criticism and emphasized the emotional effects of art rather than its social and ethical functions. In the following excerpt, he contends that Symonds's poetry is generally morbid and pessimistic, and lacks merit for want of emotional or intellectual depth.*]

[John Addington Symonds] must certainly be reckoned as one of the pessimistic poets. Indeed, I judge him to be scarcely less of a pessimist than [James] Thomson, although his pessimism was of a different kind and was due to a very different circumstance. Symonds was the son of a celebrated physician of the city of Bristol, and was born in 1840. Inheriting considerable money, he never knew the struggles and hardships that commonly fall to the lot of literary men; he was educated at the best universities, and became a great scholar; he travelled extensively and successfully cultivated a natural taste for art. Young, rich, accomplished, a real man of learning, and a *dilettante* of no common order, the future seemed to be very bright for him. But unfortunately he had inherited the seeds of consumption. In the prime of his life the disease took such a form that he was able to live only by making his home in the mountains of Switzerland, at a great elevation, where the air was extremely pure. To this mountain home he carried his books—books in all languages, collected at great expense, and representing a small fortune in themselves. The rest of his existence was altogether devoted to study and writing. He was a voluminous writer, and a critic of wide reputation. His greatest work, so far as bulk goes, is his history of the Italian Renaissance; but, although a work of great special value, it does not represent his best efforts. Those were put into such books as his *Studies of the Greek Poets,* and his *Sketches and Studies in Italy and Greece.* We have now to consider only his poetry. I mean his original poetry; for he was an extensive and very successful translator. Some of his translations from the Greek Anthology are really the best of their kind, and great praise must be also given to his charming little book *Wine, Women, and Song,* a translation of the student songs of the Middle Ages. But his own poetry belongs to quite another category. There is not much of it, and the best is contained in a thin book called *Vagabunduli Libellus*—which means the little book of the little wanderer. No more dismal collection of poems than this exists perhaps in English literature. The contents are nearly all sonnets upon his own experiences, and the general tone of this introspective work gives one a very unpleasant feeling. The verse is polished, scholarly, brilliant; but the sentiment is morbid to a degree that even the sickness of the author can scarcely excuse. There are two disagreeable elements, both of them totally different from the honest despair and the amorous passions of Thomson. Here we have a great scholar, a man of wealth and high position, apparently relating to us personal experiences of passion which belong to the extremely unhealthy variety, or again expressing to us the perpetual horror of death which haunts him and fills him with a vastness of despair such as only the intellectual mind can feel. The sonnet called **"Pessimism"** well deserves its name. I may cite it simply as a unique production of this class.

> There is a doubt drearier than any deep
> Thought's plummet ever sounded, that our earth—
> This earth where each man bears the load of birth,
> The load of death, uncertain whether sleep
> Shall round life with oblivion—may be worth
> Less in the scale of being than a heap
> Of mildewed ears the farmer scorns to reap,
> Or garners in his barns with sorry mirth.
> Of every million lives, how many a score
> Are failures from their birth! If this be true
> Of seeds, men, species, why not then of suns?

> Our world perchance is worm-gnawn at the
>   core!
> Or in its dædal frame doth cancer brew
> Venomous juice that blent with life-blood runs.

When a man has these imaginations regarding the universe; when he can seriously compare the bright sun and the beautiful world to rotten apples, and speak of all life as failure, we may expect him to have some extraordinary ideas about the soul. And so he has. Death would be a good thing if the soul also die—but he is afraid that it does not die!

> The curse of this existence, whence it came
> We view not; only this we view, that naught
> Shall free man from self's robe of sentient flame.
> There is no cunningest way to murder thought.
> Stab, poison, strangle; yea, the flesh hath died!
> What further skill yields souls their suicide?

One feels tempted to reply to such a question that the best way to destroy one's soul—I use the word soul in the meaning of the higher life of the human being—is to waste time in the composition of such verses. The indulgence of such morbid fancies on the part of a man in the position of Symonds can not but seem to us infinitely worse than the pessimism of Thomson. The Self, the Ego, is a source of constant trouble to this poet; and his very best piece is upon the puzzle which torments him. At some time or other, as his poems confess, he was fascinated by some beautiful Italian, and the subject of the poem is the pain which he felt at his inability to obtain her inner as well as her outer self. This feeling regarding the mystery of another human life has been scarcely ever expressed in a morbid way by an English poet; but it has been a favourite theme with some French writers of the *decadence,* and the great story-teller Maupassant was haunted by it . . . shortly before he became mad.

At a certain time of life every man makes one important discovery, that no being can ever perfectly know the whole character, the whole thought and the whole feeling of another being. There is no exception to this rule; even the son can not know the whole soul of his father, nor the husband that of his wife. Now to the thinker of the Far East or of India, this mystery gives no trouble at all. The eastern philosophers know perfectly well that the inner life of every being reaches back into the infinite, is a part of the infinite; and that an attempt to measure it would be like an attempt to measure the abysses of space. Only in our own day certain western psychologists of note have been studying the Ego or Self as an infinitely complex fact, and . . . have formulated, in accordance with evolutional science, the hypothesis of what is called Multiple Personality. Each person really represents, by heredity, and according to circumstances, an innumerable multitude of other personalities. But to the old western idea of the singleness of self, this discovery of changing personality, of alternating personality, of unfathomable personality, came like a shock, almost like a terror. It is this terror that is expressed in the best of all the sonnets of Symonds, which is number twenty-two in the collection called **"Stella Maris."** I shall quote only the last four lines:

> Self gives not self; and souls sequestered dwell

> In the dark fortalice of thought and sense,
> Where, though life's prisoners call from cell to
>   cell,
> Each pines alone, and may not issue thence.

To a joyous and healthy mind like that of George Meredith, the infinite mystery of self is a delight, a subject of happy wonder, and a constant assurance of the eternity of all that is good and beautiful in the highest life of the spirit. But to a morbid mind, the first shock of this fact brings only strange suspicions and strange despairs. There is not much chance that the poetry of Symonds will live as a whole. Its unhealthiness is not sufficiently counterbalanced by those qualities of deep thought and emotion which may redeem even pessimistic poetry of the blackest description. But one or two pieces in the collection—such as have been already selected for anthologies—will probably take their place in English literature. (pp. 334-38)

> *Lafcadio Hearn, "Pessimists and Their Kindred," in his* Interpretations of Literature, *Vol. I, edited by John Erskine, Dodd, Mead & Company, Inc., 1915, pp. 321-47.*

Arthur Symons   (essay date 1924)

[*While Symons initially gained notoriety as a member of the English Decadent movement of the 1890s, he eventually established himself as one of the most important critics of the modern era. As a member of the iconoclastic generation of fin de siècle aesthetes that included Aubrey Beardsley and Oscar Wilde, Symons wholeheartedly assumed the role of the world-weary cosmopolite and sensation hunter, composing verses in which he attempted to depict the bohemian world of the modern artist. He was also a gifted linguist whose sensitive translations from Paul Verlaine and Stéphane Mallarmé provided English poets with an introduction to the poetry of the French Symbolists. However, it was as a critic that Symons made his most important contribution to literature. His* Symbolist Movement in Literature *(1899) provided his English contemporaries with an appropriate vocabulary with which to define their new aesthetic—one that communicated their concern with dreamlike states, imagination, and a reality that exists beyond the boundaries of the senses. In the following excerpt, Symons explicates a sampling of Symonds's sonnets, commenting favorably on the intensity of his imagery.*]

There is an intense honesty in many of Symonds's letters. I admire him the more for the "crudity of his expressions"; nor do I wonder that he began to yawn over my immature productions and some of his own he least cared for; and as he yawns remembering those lines of Byron:—

> And that which after all my spirit vexes,
> Is, that I find no spot where man can rest an eye
>   on,
> Without confusion of the sorts and sexes,
> Of beings, stars, and this unriddled wonder,
> The world, which at the worst's a glorious blunder.

So I can imagine him in Venice, in Davos, anywhere, puzzling his soul out over the perplexing facts of our most bewildering universe: in which, indeed, we can, with Byron in Florence, "get drunk with beauty," cry out with him— as Dante and Shakespeare cried—for life, life in its entirety, for the naked contact of humanity, as the only warmth in the world; or, as it were in vision, become lost among throngs of spectral beings as real as those Blake and Shelley believed in—whirled from the actual contact of the world itself somewhere into void space between loneliness and utter darkness.

This sonnet must serve my purpose:—

> Hath Sin then force to ripen and unfold
>   The soul's flower to the light of nourishing
>   day,
>   Disclosing potencies that slumbrous lay
> Clasped in the bud, a mine of anthered gold?
> Nay, listen! In some parable 'tis told
>   How that a serpent, weary of his grey
>   Life 'mid the dust upon the world's highway,
> Devoured a toad sweltering with venom cold!
> Swift through those viperous rings the poison
>   ran;
>   With pain he writhed; his bright scales
>   changed their hue;
>   Swelled round his stiffening neck the mon-
>   strous hide;
> Till with a gradual growth from either side
>   Sprouted keen claw and light-embattled van:
>   Then through clear air aloft a dragon flew.

In **"Stella Maris"** there is something inebriating; it is the only self-expression Symonds fused out of living coal into a consuming fire that smokes and consumes itself; in some of these sonnets passion justifies its intoxication by revealing the mysteries it has come to apprehend, and with an elaborate subtlety which renders mood after mood of the fevers and colds of love, of the terrible satiety that follows Hedonism. These lovers—islanded as it were in Venice, in Venice where godless men and wanton women can act out their brief love tragedy, where, against the walls of the palaces, the stagnant water of the lagoons laps, where a few steps this way or that way will plunge them into darkness—must succeed nobly or else fail ignobly. And, just as the flesh cleaves to the bones, and since there is beauty in evil, so the beauty of woman allures us, a beauty which, on one's peril, we dare not avoid. So, in these sonnets, woman is the lure of souls, the modern Lilith.

> Spare me not thou! I would not have thee hide
>   The furnace of that fierce imperious gaze,
>   Nor pray thee for love's sake to veil the rays
> Streaming from thy white soul, thou deified
> Dream of lust intellectual, carnal pride!
>   What though I swoon on the world's stony
>   ways
>   Desiring thee, though 'wildered in thy maze
> Of loveliness I roam unsatisfied:
> Though thou shouldst be for me incarnate Hell,
>   Damnation palpable, a living flame,
>   Grave of mine honour, murderer of my name;
> Nay, though thy love be thirst insatiable,
>   Want unassuaged and passion without aim;
>   Thine am I, thine, thou irresistible!

This sonnet burns inward and outward with the heat of desire unsatiated, with that carnality which is to the senses so provocative, with that inner hell on which the heart of

love forsaken feeds for ever with that damnation which causes the weeds in a witch's naked hands to turn to livid flames. The next sonnet I quote gives me a more peculiar sense of sin that shudders, of the huddled body which crouches like a wild beast in that adorable and at the same time abject abandonment of a woman, than in any modern sonnet after those of Rossetti.

> And then she rose; and rising, there she knelt;
>   And then she paced the floor with passionate
>   tread;
>   And then she sank with that imperious head
> Bowed on bare knees: her broad arms made
>   a belt
> To clasp them; dark rebellious hair was shed
>   In tempest over fixed ardent eyes which dwelt,
>   Searching my heart's heart; yea, my manhood
>   felt
> From that tense huddled form intensest
>   dread.
> Nerves quaked, veins curdled; thin compulsive
>   flame
>   Thrilled through her crouching flesh to my
>   couched soul
>   Expectant; lingering minutes winged with
>   blame
> Swept over us with voiceless thunder-roll,
>   While the vast silence of the midnight stole,
>   Merging our sin, a shuddering sea of shame!

Inevitably one feels the snare of Meredith's "Modern Love" in the last line, and something of his crudity comes to the surface in such lines as these:—

> Who reads may wonder that so crude a fact—
>   Mere love 'twixt man and maid, lawless,
>   unwed—
>   Should by sheer force of scrupulous thought
>   be led
> To such fine issues. 'Twas a trivial act.
> From the bare natural feast of sense and tact
>   Springs healthy flesh newborn, exhilarated:
>   Why should the heart then starve? Why
>   prowl, unfed,
> Lion-like, through wild waste, cave, cataract?
> Verily, there's the problem.

I find hard logic—cruel and concentrated—even when the writer of these sonnets deals with physical love; logic that lacks passion—that is to say, lacks what is most essential in poetry; and yet with this a curious complexity that can betray—perhaps as unaware of that controlling ardour which weds in "frightful nuptials" the Snake and Dove as those forms of Evil and Good are unaware of their creative or destructive potentialities—an unholy depth of acquaintance with the delicious, hidden, tortuous ways of sensation. (pp. 232-35)

> *Arthur Symons, "A Study of John Addington
> Symonds," in* The Fortnightly Review, *Vol.
> 121, No. DCLXXXVI, February 1, 1924, pp.
> 228-39.*

The Times Literary Supplement (essay date 1940)

[*In the following excerpt, occasioned by the centenary of Symonds's birth, the critic offers a sympathetic and ap-*

*preciative assessment of Symonds's life and literary ac-
complishments, noting that the author's emotional de-
bilities thwarted the full expression of his talents.*]

Anniversaries give opportunities for praising; and John
Addington Symonds, born one hundred years ago to-day,
is a writer who has had too little praise in this century. The
biography by his friend Horatio Brown shook the allegiance of some even of the single-minded admirers of his
work. As they watched, in that revealing book, the thwart-
ing and the side-tracking of that "powerful, ambitious and
determined nature," as they learned that Symonds himself
(honest enough, even in his Oxford days, to despise his
own victorious Newdigate) looked down on his life's
work, saw it as second-rate in quality, and in spirit only
what is now called escapist, a refuge from the reality of a
self which he could not integrate, they found themselves
looking with new and colder eyes not on his writings only
but also on that whole business of aesthetic criticism
which to Symonds had become "the Maya-world of
hasheesh."

This ardent seeker after an absolute truth, baffled in his
course by some sort of weakness of spirit as well as by the
very strength of his sensuous enjoyment of the material
world and by a disease which overdrives the mind while
it enfeebles the body, suffered a spiritual disappointment
which cut at the roots of his art. He was denied the one
greatest gift of believing in his job. He was enormously
keen, exceedingly able, laborious in spite of all his sickness; but he knew all the time that this was not his true
pathway to God.

All the more reason for now insisting not on what he
missed but on what he gave. Certain concessions must be
made. The fertility of his mind and the ebullience of his
temperament made writing too easy to him; and his enviable, his admirable delight in beauty flowered a little on
the gaudy side. He wrote too much and too sumptuously
(though Conington's phrase for his poetry, "shady fluency," is neither just to that nor to his prose); and his physical debility thrust him, as he put it, into "the pretty
style"—the style of a popular writer, not of a dedicated
artist like Pater. Yet a man must be pernickety indeed who
does not find Symonds's *magnum opus,* the **Renaissance
in Italy,** a book to take in gulps. The Tennysonian doctrine of it—that as one way of the fulfilment of God is
worn out another succeeds to carry on the process, and the
final paean on the resuscitated Italy which caused the
writer to bow his head in gratitude to Heaven and swear
that, after all, all things are well—from such visions as
these we of to-day turn with a rueful smile to Fisher's preface to his *History of Europe.* But our sad wisdom cannot
rob Symonds's work of any jot of its interest and value as
a history of art, literature, philosophy, science, politics, religion, of all thought, in a richly coloured country during
a richly coloured age.

                    "J. A. Symonds," in The Times Literary Sup-
                    plement, *No. 2018, October 5, 1940, p. 507.*

J. R. Hale   (essay date 1954)

[*Hale is an English educator and critic specializing in*

*Renaissance studies. In the following excerpt, he pres-
ents an overview of Symonds's life and works, focusing
especially on his treatment of the Renaissance in Italy.
Hale points out that Symonds's approach to his historical works was always colored by his belief that history
is "the biography of man."*]

Symonds was not primarily an historian. He made frequent use of historical material, but almost always as a
means of self-expression. By nature, and by urgent desire,
he was a poet. But a temperament incapable of spontaneity
in verse found an easier relief in prose, and in the description of sites and persons belonging to the past he found,
obliquely, much of the release he craved.

This did not prevent him from writing volume upon volume of poems. They came fluently and were corrected
carefully and he was much concerned about their effect on
reviewers. From a child in the nursery, shouting out lines
from *Marmion* on a rocking horse, he had longed to be accepted as a poet. 'Oh, how deeply, fervently I wish it,' he
wrote in his diary in 1866, 'then I might speak out somewhat of that which is within me.' But as a poet he did not
have the gift of nakedness. Self-analysis and embarrassment put the experience at one remove from directness,
consciousness of the importance of what he was saying
and the desire to give it a form in which it would find a
wide response, removed it further, and what should have
been lyric remained descriptive.

Even frank descriptions were more exact and harmonious
in prose. He watched a sunset from his gondola in Venice:

> The sky was one vast dome of delicately gradu-
> ated greys, dove-breasted, ashen, violet, blurred
> blue, rose-tinted, tawny, all drenched and
> drowned in the prevailing tone of sea-lavender.
> The water, heaving, undulating, swirling, at no
> point stationary, yet without a ripple on its vitre-
> ous pavement, threw back those blended hues,
> making them here and there more flaky and dis-
> tinct in vivid patches of azure or of crimson. Not
> very far away, waiting for a breeze to carry them
> towards Torcello, lay half a dozen fishing boats
> with sails like butterflies atremble on an open
> flower: red, orange, lemon, set by some ineffable
> tact of Nature just in the right place to heighten
> and accentuate the symphony of tender tints.

Even in the course of utilitarian historical narrative, moments occur, when a prose never very firm turns to poetry
and the reader sinks in patches of nerveless prolixity, or
pauses dazzled by a vague but splendid light.

These encroachments of poetry were not a bar to his success. The *Athenæum* paid a tribute to them in 1881 by
complimenting Symonds on using in his ***Italian Literature***
a style worthy of the subject. But he knew how unsafe was
the balance between poetry and prose. 'Like many better
men than myself,' he wrote towards the end of his life, 'I
suppose that I have fallen between two stools in art.' He
knew that this was due to lack of concentration and lack
of self-criticism. He complained that he had never been
trained to think. Neither at Clifton, where he first went to
school, nor at Harrow, nor afterwards at Oxford, was
there the sort of mental training he needed to keep him

from a perennial amateurishness. Dispirited, he decided that he could aim no higher than at being a good *vulgariseur.* 'I shall end with being what the French call a *polygraphe fécond*—a jack-of-all-trades, æsthetical, and a humbug who has gorged and disgorged Hegel.' A *polygraphe* he became—Professor Babington's bibliography contains 457 items—but not because of a faulty education. This helpless fecundity was not so easily to be explained.

Symonds never wrote more sympathetically than when he was describing some writer born for poetry but turned aside, like Jonson, by too much study, or like Boccaccio because of parental disapproval, to become a writer of prose. He quoted Boccaccio's regretful words: 'I doubt not that if my father had been indulgent to my wishes while my mind was pliable in younger years, I should have turned out one of the world's famous poets,' and on his own father's death confessed that though 'it seems unfilial, almost impious, to say so, yet it is true that the independence I now acquired added a decided stimulus to my mental growth. My father had been so revered and so implicitly obeyed by me that his strong personal influence kept me in something like childish subjection.' This was in 1871 when Symonds was thirty-one.

Dr. Symonds was a man of physical and mental strength

disturbing to a somewhat sickly and nervous child. A busy and fashionable doctor, his interests seemed to his son to embrace everything worth knowing. He published articles on medical matters but he dabbled also in Greek and Italian art, and Egyptian antiquities. He made a mathematical study of the laws of musical proportion and published the *Principles of Beauty* which contained diagrams of the perfect female form, based on smooth sweeps for the eye muscles. No moment was allowed to pass without profit. There was always a Greek or Latin author open on his table and each day a few pages would be read, the more striking passages translated. Ethnology he mastered as he grew older, and then the topography of ancient Greece. Nor was history neglected: he was perfectly familiar with the details of the Parliamentary War, and could discuss the campaigns of Wellington to the admiration of his military friends. Wherever his son looked, the father seemed to have been before him—always with confidence, impassive confidence of success.

They toured the Continent together in a series of what Symonds doggedly called pleasure trips. One took them from Brussels to Cologne, Berlin, Dresden, the Saxon Switzerland, Prague, Vienna, Salzburg, Munich and the Rhine, all in less than three weeks. Nothing of interest was omitted. Picture galleries and palaces were studied, battle-

Symonds and his wife, Catherine, on their wedding day, 1864.

fields inspected, they rode out in search of fine scenery, toured hospitals, went to the opera, called on distinguished foreigners, and mastered the topographical, geological and antiquarian features of each district. To secure time for sight-seeing, most of the travelling was done by night, in a swaying, jolting carriage. Even here, while the exhausted son tried to sleep, the father would produce Mills's *Political Economy* and read a chapter, and waiting at railway stations was treated as an opportunity for the reading aloud of Milton or Tennyson.

From such a trip Symonds would return excited by what he had seen but nervous and depressed by what he had felt. The rational capaciousness of his father was something he admired without resentment but he was baffled by its remoteness from his own talents. His mother had died when he was four. The relatives who helped to care for the Symonds family were dour and puritanical. Their disapproval, or Dr. Symonds' measured and tolerant persuasion, repelled, one by one, the excesses and enthusiasms of the child. The sense of being alien and inferior spread from one centre of dismay to another. He was conscious of mental ineffectiveness and at the same time ashamed of his physical appearance. Convinced that he was repulsive he dreamed of the ideal beauty of Greek youth, and when his father pointed out, kindly, the morbid element in this, the picture books were shut and the images transferred to daydreams. He became ashamed of his name, of the social status of his family. The daydreams became more frequent, more intense; at times he became confused as to their reality. Yet if his admiration for his father had caused much of this, it also prevented him from retreating altogether into dreams. His father's habits of inquiry, of patient, thorough analysis, had affected him deeply. The challenge was awful, but the duty of accepting it was clear: 'I vowed to rouse myself, somehow or other, to eminence of some sort.' However confused and depressed he might be he 'thirsted with intolerable thirst for eminence, for recognition as a personality'.

This vague ambition, adopted as a shield, became a mania which had greater scope when he left home for Harrow. There in a highly competitive life dominated by games at which he was not adept, his external self, as he wrote in his autobiography, was 'perpetually snubbed, and crushed, and mortified. Yet the inner self hardened after a dumb, blind fashion. I kept repeating: "Wait, wait. I will, I shall, I must." '

In particular he was saved by his father's doctrine of work; work as an anodyne; not an ambition in itself, but something that made possible the fulfilment of ambition. The misfortune was that his work was writing. The habits formed when he used writing as a cure were too strong to throw off when he wished to produce a piece of writing as an end in itself. Accustomed to finding refuge in headlong fluency, he could not go slowly, critically, without admitting the doubt and mistrust from which he had sought escape in writing. Of this he was fully aware, and recognized that out of many books he had written few good paragraphs, and no great line. But the knowledge was of no avail; the confirmed dram-taker could no longer sip and savour.

He found another advocate of work at Balliol in Jowett, and was soon forced, again, and finally, to take refuge in it. For a while, however, his introspection found other channels. 'I went philandering around music, heraldry, the fine arts, and literary studies ruled by sentiment. I wrote weak poetry, I dreamed in ante-chapels. I mooned in canoes along the banks of the Cherwell, or among yellow water lilies at Godstow.' But the issue of ambition was not to be put aside for long. On a reading party in the Lake District he overheard two of his companions discussing him. They spoke of the languor of his temperament and declared that there was no chance of getting a First. 'I then and there resolved', he noted, 'that I would win the best First of my year.'

This he did; and for the rest of his life, in spite of a comfortable private income, he worked and wrote, pausing only when uncertain of what to write next. And these periods were always periods of misery. 'It often occurs to me to think with horror: what would happen if literature failed me? If I did not care to write?' he observed in 1880. He had by this time a family of three girls and a large house and had identified himself with the fortunes of Davos Platz, then in its infancy as a *Kurort*. But the pace was to increase. He noted with satisfaction the number of works he had in hand at the same time; he pointed out the speed with which he produced them. Cellini's Autobiography he translated in four months, Gozzi's bulky Memoirs in five weeks. In one year, 1886, he saw the sixth and seventh volumes of **Renaissance in Italy** through the press, wrote **Sidney** for one series, **Ben Jonson** for another, brought out a volume of **Selections from Jonson,** edited Sir Thomas Browne, wrote an article on Tasso for the *Encyclopædia Britannica* and translated Cellini. The taskmaster of his Oxford days found this as it should be: 'I congratulate you on having finished your *magnum opus,*' he wrote when Symonds had finished the **Renaissance.** 'Your life, notwithstanding its drawbacks, certainly seems to me a fortunate one. For the happiness of life is work, and you are able to do more than anyone else.'

The remark was not a happy one. It was not simply a feeling of social inferiority or physical repugnance that lay behind Symond's pathological productivity; these were only temporary worries. Nor was it merely a conviction of mental inferiority to his father, though this lasted longer. A more crucial obstacle to his happiness was the homosexual element in his nature. Though the issue could be evaded by fashionable discussions about ideal friendship at Oxford it was forced into the open by four things: scandalous misrepresentation; his wish to marry; a religious temperament that, though unorthodox, insisted on categories of right and wrong; the habit not only of introspection, but of serious self-analysis. These factors did not all operate at once. For some years the old daydreams flowed on in his poems, many of which were altered between the first private publication and the subsequent public editions. The sex of the beloved was frequently changed from male to female, passages were excised which, like the following from the original version of **"The Lotus Garland of Antinous"**, reveal an emotion which had become inhibited at the stage of sentimental *schwärmerei:*

the boy
Gazed on his master, and new depths of joy
Unsensual from his limpid eyes brimmed over
Flooding the full soul of his royal lover;
Who seized the cup and bade the bearer bend
As though his breathing mouth new scent might
   lend
To the ripe vine juice: as he lightly bent
His lilied lips beneath the thyrsus leant,
Their lips met.

And the tragedy of men who love both men and women was expressed in a legend in heroic couplets, later suppressed, of a painter who tired of his mistress and fell in love with a boy; he took him to a feast dressed as a girl, and there the boy met and was murdered by the discarded mistress.

Such a dilemma required a solution. With the aid particularly of Whitman's poems, and later through correspondence with their author, he found one not in rejection but acceptance. For Whitman, the lover of both man and woman was not a freak or an exception, but an ideal.

Fast-anchored eternal O love! O woman I love!
O bride! O wife! more resistless than I can tell,
   the thought of you!
Then separate, as disembodied or another born,
Ethereal, the last athletic reality, my consola-
   tion,
I ascend, I float in the regions of your love, O
   man,
O sharer of my roving life.

The fervour of Symonds' discipleship touchingly revealed the gravity of this sexual problem. To an aesthete, a fastidious dilettante, as he was at Oxford where he first read *Leaves of Grass,* a delicate scholar with aristocratic leanings, Whitman's personality and style presented formidable obstacles. But the reassurance he offered was enough to remove them. Whitman became for Symonds the greatest teacher of the age: he taught him to accept his own nature, and Symonds revered him as a Master, thrilled and sustained by his physical strength, spiritual vitality and courage. 'He is Behemoth,' he cried, 'wallowing in primeval jungles, bathing at fountain heads of mighty rivers, crushing the bamboos and the cane-brakes under him, bellowing and exulting in the torrid air. He is a gigantic elk or buffalo, trampling the grasses of the wilderness, tracking his mate with irresistible energy. . . . He is all nations, cities, languages, religions, arts, creeds, thoughts, emotions. He is the beginning and grit of these things, not their endings, less and dregs. Then he comes to us as lover, consoler, physician, nurse; most tender, fatherly, sustaining those about to die, lifting the children, and stretching out his arms to the young men.'

With Whitman's help he came to a working solution. He could marry, and to woman, as wife and mother and physical complement, all his sexual activity would be confined. To man he could extend an ideal love, a *camaraderie,* pure and intense because it was not forced by duty. In such a life a deep affection for his wife could be combined with a glowing admiration for male beauty. Symonds found a wife who understood the dilemma and approved the solution. Indefatigably patient, she helped him to feel secure in it. Balanced between her and a family on the one hand,

and the Swiss peasants of Davos on the other, with whom he tobogganed and drank and sang, and whose athletic prowess he so much admired, he found in work a cure for the depressions that still came. The arrangement could not be quite perfect: the 'amative' and 'adhesive' sides of his personality (in Whitman's words) could not mature equally. Poems written out of sentimental attachments for men even late in his life, reflect the vague yearning of the years in which he fixed their bounds. In the poems of *In the Key of Blue* (1893) evoked by his gondolier and personal servant Angelo, there is a sickliness which his self-criticism would have noticed in any other connection. This was the strain that was found distasteful, that provoked Swinburne's reference to 'such renascent blossoms of the Italian renascence as the Platonic amorist of blue-breeched gondoliers'. The imperfect balance in his nature had a positive effect in his desire to analyse his problem, and to help others who shared it, he did important pioneer work on the nature of sexual inversion and on the ways in which the laws respecting it should be reformed. He wrote two works, privately printed, on the subject, one in 1873 (printed in 1883), *A Problem in Greek Ethics,* the other printed before 1891, as *A Problem in Modern Ethics.* The latter had a somewhat mysterious opening:

It confronts us on the steppes of Asia, where hordes of nomads drink the milk of mares; in the bivouac of Keltish warriors, lying wrapped in wolves' skins round their camp-fires; upon the sands of Arabia, where the Bedaween raise desert dust in flying squadrons. We discern it among the palm-groves of the South Sea Islands, in the card-houses and temple-gardens of Japan, under Esquimaux snow-huts,

etc.; but the tone of both is calm and dispassionate. In none of Symonds' other writings does he argue with such cogency. He had corresponded with Havelock Ellis since 1885 and contributed a great quantity of the material in *Sexual Inversion* published under their joint names in 1897, but thereafter under Ellis's alone.

In this way the distress that Whitman's teaching and a singularly fortunate marriage had not entirely eased, was helped by work. In 1863 a scandalous attack had been made on Symonds which caused him so much suffering that he had to give up his recently-won fellowship at Magdalen. Writing five years later to console a friend who had suffered a great blow, he said: 'It almost cost me my life; for the nervous troubles which have wasted my last five years, intellectually speaking, date from a sort of brain fever produced by the pressure of one horrible haunting pain.' But there was a cure: 'Time, I believe,' he went on, 'and Work must be the great healers.' And again: 'The only way out to avoid being mad or bad, instead of only sad, is work.'

If work was the palliative for two afflictions, a sense of mental inferiority and sexual ambiguity, the craving for it was the symptom of a third, consumption. Most of his life was spent as an invalid, much of it on the move, searching for a climate that would ease his lung complaint. For this reason he settled permanently at Davos, building a house, Am Hof, and living the active life which his children have described: they refer to the exciting effect of the atmosphere of the Alps, the effect it had in tensing lowland nerves. There was also the consumptive's race against time, the need to emphasize the moments of living by actual achievement. In the grip of the same urgency, his son-in-law, Charles Furse, was to finish canvas after canvas up to the moment of his early death. Symonds himself wrote: 'I live really as one who holds his lease of life from week to week; and this is one cause of my feverish energy in writing.' And the effort had to be ratified by print. Most of what Symonds wrote he kept. If a manuscript were not published it went into a 'desolation box' from which it would emerge when times were more favourable—not necessarily revised. Poems, essays, whole books, came out of this desolation box, to appear many years after they were set aside. Literary quality was sometimes less important than the building of landmarks to remind posterity that he had achieved more than most men, and to enable his father's ghost to trace the course of an active career such as he would have admired. When his father died, Symonds wrote, in 1879: 'I had, so to speak, done nothing; and the sort of thing he liked, has come to me in plenty since, so that if my health does not revive and I am to have no further career, I may still think (and he would have thought) that *pro virile parte* with the strength and parts allotted to me, I have lived.'

The temperament that resulted from these conflicts was not an ideal one for a historian. Symonds realized this, and in his autobiography gave an account of his qualities as a writer which make one regret that his habit of analysis was only strong when applied to himself. 'From nature', he wrote, 'I derived a considerable love of books, an active brain, a fairly extended curiosity, receptivity to ideas above the average, an aptitude for expression, sensibility to external objects in the world of things, and intense emotional susceptibility of a limited and rather superficial kind.' His memory, he regretted, was weak. He could only retain facts with an effort, and when that effort was relaxed, they went. He forgot as speedily as he learned. 'I saturate my mind with rapid reading, devour multitudes of books, and make voluminous notes, feeling sure that I shall obtain a general conception of the subject under consideration. Then I return again and again to the leading documents, check every impression of fact by reiterated comparison of my notes with their sources, verify dates and quotations, force myself to attain accuracy by drudgery.' Worse than this, 'My brain was always impenetrable to abstractions. When I attacked them, I felt a dull resistance, a sense of benumbed and benumbing stupor stealing like a fog over my intellect.' As a result, Symonds' historical works contain few ideas. Inevitably, his treatment of the Renaissance, which is itself an idea, suffered. From his first treatment of it, in a University Prize Essay in 1863, to his last in an article in the *Fortnightly Review* in 1893, there is no significant modification. What he revised was the presentation of facts, not ideas or opinions. His method was to fill simple patterns—such as The Four Periods of Humanism—with a wealth of attractively presented detail. It was not enough, 'But literature is a go-cart for the individual, and I am thankful to get along in it.'

This very comment expresses clear self-knowledge, but an inability to use it. When **Renaissance in Italy** was all over

he wrote: 'the odd thing is that one has so little to say upon subjects which have occupied a life-time. I often find that what I wrote between twenty and twenty-five is no shallower than what I can arrive at now.'

In all his life of self-questioning and alternating moods of exhilaration and depression, Symonds only recognized one major crisis. At Cannes, in 1868, all his doubts came to a head. The question posed was a religious one. How could the individual be sure of himself until he knew what was expected of him by the nature of God? The only conformity Symonds respected was with God's intentions as he understood them. He accepted the code of no church nor of society. His own nature must be tested solely against God's. As long as he believed that this knowledge, or a conviction akin to it, could be found, he lived in uncertainty. His longing to know, and his irrepressible scepticism, preserved a constant agitation. The crisis at Cannes brought something like calm. Not because of an illumination that made him see God, but a conviction that he could not be known. Man's duty was to seek him on earth. As his great friend and biographer, Horatio Brown, expressed it: 'for him all *erscheinungen,* all phenomena, are to be studied, none neglected, humanity is to be sounded to its depths, life to be "drunk to the lees".' Symond's own phrase was 'self-merging into the whole'. That Whitman stood ready as guide on this new trail was a great consolation. With him, and with the help of Marcus Aurelius and Goethe, he would strive to 'live resolutely in the Whole, the Good, the Beautiful',

> To perfect self, and in that self embrace
> The tri-une essence of truth, beauty, good;
> This is fulfilment, this beautitude
> Throned high above base fears and hopes more
>   base.

For those who denied constant activity, whose sympathy did not lavishly embrace all creeds and extremes, who had not felt love for all, both man and woman, Limbo waited, full of the wailing ghosts of the unfulfilled:

> We lived not, for we loved not! Dreams are we!
> Death shuns us, who shunned life! What hell
>   shall rouse
> Blank souls from blurred insensibility?

Symonds threw himself into the problems of his literary friends and those of the peasants of Davos. On his travels he tried to mingle with all classes. He upheld conventional marriage but sympathized with the experiment of Noyes's Oneida community of having their women, like their goods, in common. But this was not enough. To an invalid, isolated during a great part of every year in a remote Alpine valley, the Whole of the present was out of reach. That of the past was not, however. Through study it could be regained. And the period in which men lived most wholly, and for the first time began to live by the creed of truth, beauty and goodness was that of the Renaissance of Italy. The middle ages denied beauty and had not been shown the truth. Symonds revolted from 'those medieval lies regarding sexual sinfulness, those foolish panegyrics of chaste abstinence, those base insinuations of base-minded priests'. Blank souls in limbo! The Renaissance brought release, 'we may say with simple accuracy that the Renaissance wrought for humanity a real resurrection of the body, which since the destruction of the Pagan world had lain swathed up in hair-shirts and cerements within the tomb of the medieval cloister'.

The mood which sent Symonds to the Renaissance was exactly that in which he had set his children to tearing up his family papers. Morning after morning they sat in a circle and ripped up the letters and records of seven generations of non-conformist physicians. 'I could not bear to think,' Symonds noted, 'that my own kith and kin, the men and women who had made me, lived in this haunted chamber, from which "eternity's sunrise", the flooding radiance of Nature's light, seemed ruthlessly excluded.' They seemed much less recognizably Symond's own ancestors than the men of the first generations of emancipation, when 'what seems every day more unattainable in modern life, was enjoyed by the Italians'.

Their life, if it were Whole and strove towards the Beautiful, was not necessarily Good. But violent contrasts of good and evil were characteristic of all growth; self-reliance must come first, and it can come, as Symonds knew, only from stress.

> Whoso framed good, framed evil too; and He
> Knows what the earth's huge heart-throbs
> need for life,
> He counterpoised tranquillity to strife,
> Systolë weighed against diastolë.

Contrast, too, was one of his literary patterns. In mediæval Italy from a 'hurricane of disaster rises the clear idea of national genius'. Time and again the formula recurs, the literary effectiveness supported philosophically by Hegel's thesis, antithesis, synthesis.

The Renaissance drew him too because he saw it as a period of 'highly perfected individuality', of men who were whole. Symonds revolted against the undistinguished. He had loathed the mean architecture of Bristol, he disliked Richardson because he was 'essentially a bourgeois', for a time he had been ashamed of his own middle-class origin; a race of natural aristocrats, unbound by convention, free to become whatever they willed, indifferent to the herd—these were his heroes, and he found the material for them in Renaissance Italy. His interest in history was above all personal; he had identified the middle ages with the negation of personality—his interest in the *Divine Comedy* waned when allegory and symbolism replaced personality—and he wrote freely only when history could be written in terms of great men. His adviser Jowett supported him: 'the true interest of history begins with remarkable men and their actions.' And from the remarkable Italians of the present Symonds felt cut off. He loved them, sought out all degrees, made of a Venetian gondolier an intimate friend. Yet there was a barrier. He wrote from Italy in 1873: 'I am like a statue walking among men,' and as late as 1889 concluded regretfully that: 'It is difficult to *know* Italians.' Life was the barrier. It was easier to know the dead.

Those of the dead with whom he felt most at home were the men of the Renaissance. They were the first free men of Europe—'What the word Renaissance really means is

new birth to Liberty,' he wrote in *The Age of Despots*—and they achieved at a bound a degree of personal liberty scarcely obtained since. They lived at a time when man's prison had been left unguarded owing to the assault of antiquity on his mediæval gaolers, and he walked at liberty until the struggle was decided. As far as Italy was concerned, Symonds felt, the prison of the late sixteenth century was ranker than that of the thirteenth, so much did he hate Spanish domination, but the impulse had come, the check would be momentary:

> Onward for ever flows the tide of Life,
> Still broadening, gathering to itself the rills
> That made dim music in the primal hills,
> And tossing crested waves of joy and strife.

Symonds was not really interested in current affairs. When he thought of them it was as a conservative. But philosophically he believed in the perfectibility of man, in some sort of egalitarian Utopia. He preferred to think of the first stages in this course, when a high degree of free personal development was consistent with aristocratic control.

He did not find Italian studies sympathetic simply because it was there, he felt, that cultural and intellectual freedom had been born. He loved the country for itself; its warmth, the relaxed freedom of many of its social customs, its people and towns. He had no real affection for Spain or France, none for 'the beastly Germans', his affection for Switzerland was tempered by the knowledge that it was also his sanitorium. But he wrote of Italy without reservation, and his travel sketches led tourists to places usually ignored before because of their remoteness, the bad state of their inns, or their predominantly mediæval interest. These sketches, indeed, by drawing attention to towns like Assisi and Orvieto which had been most notable in the thirteenth and fourteenth centuries, helped to balance his Renaissance period, which in *Renaissance in Italy* leaned heavily towards the personalities of the sixteenth.

The Renaissance, then, was a period in which Symonds, detaching himself from the present as best he could, found the whole lives, the vivid contrasts, the self-reliant individuals he admired, the greatest promise given modern man enacted in the country he most loved. And what finally enabled him to write about it was the fact that as the historian of its culture he would be dealing with the sort of history he found easiest, literary history. The standards of cultural history were not yet demanding. He assumed that a literary subject could be treated in a literary way, and without the discipline, which he admitted he lacked, necessary to a technical historian. In talking of the evolving spirit of a people, feeling rather than logic or close control over balanced narrative could be the guide.

Since he wrote the Chancellor's Prize Essay of 1863 he had kept the Renaissance in view as the work that was to occupy and steady his mind. In 1865, when he was reading *Romola,* Villari's *Savonarola,* and Grimm's *Life of Michael Angelo,* he wrote: 'I want to keep my mind on that period of European history.' For a while he wavered between three exclusively literary subjects: Greek poetry, Italian poetry and the Elizabethan drama, but in 1870 finally decided on a general cultural history of the Renaissance in Italy. 'My heart bleeds', he wrote, 'to think of my own incapacity for a great work. I must not think of it; for the very thought paralyses.' Two years later there is the same note: 'it is so dreadfully difficult,' he told his sister. Eighteen-seventy-five, when the first part was finished, was a year of extremes. At one moment he proposed to his publisher a grand project for following the as yet uncompleted *Renaissance in Italy* with two other works, one on *Italy and the Counter-Reformation,* and another on *Italy in the Middle Ages,* and then condensing the whole series into one *Kulturgeschichte* of the Italian people. At another he was crying that in an attempt to be accurate: 'I have ended in dullness; seeking to be comprehensive, I have become diffuse.'

The *Age of the Despots* (1875) was followed, nevertheless, by *The Revival of Learning* and *The Fine Arts,* in 1877. Again he wrote despondently to his sister: 'It is a task probably beyond my intellectual grasp, as it is certainly beyond my strength of body.' He felt too that permanent residence at Davos, where he settled in 1880, put an end to any hopes of exact scholarship: 'The forces which, since my boyhood, had been directly and indirectly moulding me for a particular kind of writing, were once more operative. I had to remain a man of letters.' Nevertheless two more volumes, *Italian Literature,* appeared in the following year, and two more, *The Catholic Reaction,* in 1886, which concluded the work.

Renaissance in Italy took eleven years to complete. It consisted of four volumes containing a detailed history of Latin and Italian literature from the fourteenth to the early sixteenth century and a shorter account of art in the same period. (*The Revival of Learning* and *The Fine Arts,* 1877; and *Italian Literature,* 2 vols., 1881.) They were introduced by *The Age of Despots* (1875), designed, in Symonds's words, 'to lay a solid foundation for aesthetical criticism in a study of the social and moral and political condition of the people'. The work was closed by *The Catholic Reaction* (2 vols., 1886), describing how the culture of the Renaissance foundered under Spanish and inquisitorial rule in the second half of the sixteenth century.

Eleven years was too long for the work to succeed as a whole. The first volume, though too slight and general to give the literary volumes the support they needed, was stimulating, while the last, done when Symonds had become bored with the subject, were strained, repetitious and extravagant. The unity of individual volumes was imperilled by their construction. Symonds called the chapters essays, and some of them had been published separately in the *Westminster,* the *Contemporary* and the *Cornhill;* the narrative stream was dammed into a series of articles. *The Age of the Despots* was based on lectures given at Clifton School, and Symonds realized that he had failed to revise all the rhetoric out of them. And he worked, in any case, too emotionally to be able to subordinate the parts to the whole; the topic of the moment seemed all important. In spite of an initial warning that no causes of the Renaissance must be looked for other than in a 'spontaneous outburst of intelligence' when writing of the despots he could not forbear attributing a great part of this to them, or, when dealing with the humanists, saying that thanks to

them 'the proper starting-point was given to the modern intellect'.

While the length of the work led to contradictions within it, it was unrefreshed at any stage by new ideas: the seven volumes were from this aspect scarcely more than an inflation of the prize essay of 1863. The conception of the Renaissance he had gained at Oxford by reading Gibbon, Roscoe, Hallam and Michelet remained the basis of his thought on the subject for the remaining thirty years of his life; in the Sunday Lecture Society paper, *The Renaissance of Modern Europe,* of 1872, the *Renaissance in Italy,* the long *Encyclopædia Britannica* article 'Renaissance' that he wrote in 1885, in the article which appeared in the year of his death in the *Fortnightly Review* on 'The New Spirit, An Analysis of the Emancipation of the Intellect in the Fourteenth, Fifteenth and Sixteenth Centuries', progress was not forward, but upward, in the form of mounting piles of information and literary criticism.

As Symonds described himself as an historian of culture, it is worth considering his indebtedness to Burckhardt. This has been taken to be great. A parallel has been drawn between *Renaissance in Italy* and *Die Kultur der Renaissance in Italien* in which *The Age of the Despots* is said to balance Burckhardt's section on 'The State as a Work of Art'; chapter one of *The Revival of Learning,* on 'The Men of the Renaissance', Burckhardt's section, 'The Development of the Individual', and *The Fine Arts* and *Italian Literature,* Burckhardt's 'The Discovery of the World and of Man'.

Symonds himself said of the *Kultur der Renaissance* in the preface to *The Age of the Despots:* 'It fell under my notice when I had planned, and in a great measure finished my own work. But it would be difficult for me to exaggerate the profit I have derived from the comparison of my opinions with those of a writer so thorough in his learning and so delicate in his perceptions,' and in the second edition (1880), when two more volumes had been written, he added: 'or the amount I owe to his acute and philosophical handling of the whole subject.' There is no reason to doubt Symonds's statement that *The Age of the Despots* owed little to Burckhardt. The original publication of the *Die Kultur der Renaissance* passed unnoticed in England, and the reviews of Middlemore's translation of 1878 gave no hint that the book would become famous. The *Westminster* admitted briefly that it was a 'most valuable treatise' but otherwise it was ignored or noticed slightingly. The *Athenæum* found it hard to read: 'study should not be so severe as to become wearisome', it remarked before coming to the softer conclusion that it would be quite useful as a reference book to supplement Sismondi and Hallam— 'if an index be added'. Symonds's ideas about the period, besides, were largely formed and the method of their treatment decided on by 1863, before he had read the *Kultur der Renaissance,* and nowhere in his published letters does Burckhardt's name appear as a guide and inspiration— significant in a man so ready to praise those who influenced him. The actual plan for the *Renaissance in Italy* was decided on, and not merely for the first volume, before he had seen Burckhardt's book.

Nor did the alterations in the second edition of *The Age*

of the Despots reflect his influence. The only important change was the insertion of a chapter: 'Italian History', giving a political sketch of progress from communes to despotisms which owes nothing to Burckhardt, and the intention of the chapter, to show that during 'this hurricane of disorder rises the clear ideal of the national genius', was directly counter to the other's anti-Hegelian bias. In the following volume of Symonds's work, ***The Revival of Learning,*** he again acknowledges his indebtedness, though: 'At the same time I have made it my invariable practice . . . to found my own opinions on the study of original sources.' And, in fact, Symonds, although echoing Burckhardt's warning against the exaggeration of the classical element in Italian culture, was unable to take advantage of it. His subject is the revival of classical literature, and nothing shall be more important: 'the culture of the classics had to be reappropriated before the movement of the modern mind could begin'. In ***The Fine Arts*** he noted his debt to Burckhardt's *Cicerone,* but whereas Burckhardt had insisted that the development of painting in the fifteenth century, its growing realism, its delight in the human figure, the accurate illusion of space, was due to artists following not antiquity but nature, Symonds insisted on a more dramatic view. 'The old world and the new shook hands; Christianity and Hellenism kissed each other.' Symonds, in fact, was incapable of following Burckhardt, even if he had wished to. The Swiss writer had a far better grounding in the political and economic history of the period, even if little of this appeared in his book, and could see development on several levels, while Symonds could only see it clearly on the literary one. He exaggerated the nature of his own debt to the other; the parallels between their work that he was flattered to see were not really parallels at all, except where both men were responding to the suggestion of Michelet that the period should be seen as that of the discovery of the world and of man. Symonds, too, saw the Renaissance far more in terms of the sixteenth century than Burckhardt. Of the six names to whom he allotted a chapter each—Savonarola, Machiavelli, Cellini, Aretino, Michelangelo and Ariosto—only the first was a *quattrocento* figure.

The approach of the two men to history was quite different. Symonds was interested in literature and individuals and therefore he wrote *Kulturgeschichte.* Burckhardt wrote it because he was interested in the educative value of finding out the character of a period, and this could only be done through cultural history which gave *primum gradum certitudinis.* Symonds's purpose was to entertain ('you will find the chapters on "The Prince", the Popes, and Savonarola most lively'), Burckhardt's was to help his readers to understand themselves through the effort they made to get in touch with the spirit of another age. Symonds was fascinated by the exceptional, Burckhardt was not looking for the unique but the recurrent, he believed 'das Wiederholende wichtiger als das Einmalige!' Symonds wrote to forget himself, Burckhardt believed that simply burying oneself in the past was worthless; an uncertain personality would see the past uncertainly. The disadvantages of the necessarily subjective *Kulturhistoriker* were grave, and he recognized them, even going so far as to warn the audience of his first lecture on *Griechische Kulturgeschichte* that he could not be certain that his

was the right view; they might by the end of the course come to quite different conclusions. These limitations Symonds never saw. It was because he lacked the deep seriousness of Burckhardt's approach to his subject, his certainty about the object of history and his philosophically justified use of *Kulturgeschichte* that Symonds's use of his material was shallow and that his grasp on the work as a whole was infirm.

This lack of control left him free to shape the work with but slight interference from his judgment. He said firmly at the start of the work, for instance, that 'it must not be imagined that the Renaissance burst suddenly upon the world in the fifteenth century without premonitory symptoms. Far from that; within the middle age itself, over and over again, the reason strove to break loose from its fetters', but his temperamental dislike of the middle ages soon asserted itself, and the Renaissance emerged, as he wrote, as the reverse of all that epoch implied of ignorance, sexual narrowness, and priestly superstition. This dislike of the middle ages was, in part, a dislike of the Catholic Church whose interference with morals he loathed. Forgetting the narrowness of his father's church, he concentrated all his hatred of clerical authority on Rome, especially once man had gained the chance of freedom by breaking with her. Of Spain and priests in sixteenth-century Italy he wrote with special emphasis. 'Dukes and marquises fell down and worshipped the golden image of the Spanish Belial-Moloch—that hideous idol whose face was blackened with soot from burning flesh.' Man had for a time obeyed his own conscience, but now 'over the Dead Sea of social putrefaction floated the sickening oil of Jesuit hypocrisy'. The longer the work went on, the more temperament was left unrestrained. The imagery became at the last almost humorously lurid: Italy 'lay trampled on and dying', Spain 'reared her dragon's head of menacing ambition', Germany 'heaved like a huge ocean in the grip of a tumultuous gyrating cyclone'. Reality had quite gone when the historian could write of music at this crisis that it 'put forth lusty shoots and flourished, yielding a new paradise of harmless joy, which even priests could grudge not to the world, and which lulled tyranny to sleep with silvery numbers'.

It is unfair to judge ***Renaissance in Italy*** by its last two volumes. The tendency to extravagance in prose reflects a love of exaggeration in action noticeable in the whole work. Symonds was neither timid nor particularly frail, but he was fascinated by violence—witness his appendix on 'Blood-madness' to ***The Age of the Despots,*** and he relished striking contrasts. And because he saw these from the point of view of a strict notion of right or wrong, the contrasts appeared more lurid than they would to a matter-of-fact observer. The attitude of the amoral man, who killed his enemy and returned to paint an angel, or slept with his daughter and descended to administer the sacrament without a sense of disturbance was one he did not choose to comprehend. He wrote as if they were conscious of their wickedness, turned from good to evil, normal to abnormal with a sense of grinding contrast. Burckhardt described violence without becoming involved in it: Symonds entered the arena. 'Under the thin mask of human refinement', he reported in the ***Revival of Learning,*** 'leered the untamed savage.' In *The Fine Arts* he dwelt on the contrast of Perugino painting his bland pure saints and paying a bravo to assassinate a rival; when he came to the story of Signorelli, confronted by the slain body of his son, he broke into verse to supplement the prose description of how the impassive artist stripped the body and painted it; in a whole chapter on Cellini's contrasted and violent career he permitted himself the self-contradictory observation that his life was 'the most singular and characteristic episode in the private history of the Italian Renaissance'—the exceptional was the rule. Italian life, he wrote in *Italian Literature,* Vol. 2, 'furnishes a complete justification for even Tourneur's plots', and 'who can say that Webster has exaggerated the bare truth?' This is far from the milder travel sketch **'Vittoria Accoramboni',** where he refers to 'the laboured portrait of Flamineo' and admits that Webster's Italian tragedies are true 'not so much to the actual conditions of Italy, as to the moral impression made by those conditions on a Northern imagination'. It was sad that the historian of the *Renaissance in Italy* should have been debarred by his nature from describing the actual conditions of his subject in the same way.

Symonds was mainly interested in individuals. He published lives of Dante, Shelley, Sidney, Jonson, Michelangelo, Whitman and Boccaccio. Of history he wrote: 'We have learned to look upon it as the biography of man,' and true to this attitude he found that 'the Italian history of the Renaissance resumes itself in the biography of men greater than their race.' Rootless and independent himself, consciously exceptional, he found it natural not to relate his protagonists to a background which would, while it explained, absorb them. While Burckhardt emphasized the individual to understand the mass, Symonds laboured to detach him from the mass. 'The work achieved by Italy for the world in that age was less the work of a nation than that of men of power.' It was as true of artists as of despots and humanists: 'the old custom of speaking about schools and places, instead of signalizing great masters, has led to misconception, by making it appear that local circumstances were more important than the facts justify'. Yet as a result of this preoccupation with the individual there emerged much less than a fully representative portrait gallery. In 1863 he had urged that to understand the Renaissance science and exploration must be considered as well as art, philosophy, religion. But as it was only the last subjects that were relevant to his own nature, the great men of science and exploration were barely mentioned. Columbus and Vespucci are passed over. Galileo is noticed in a few words, while Bruno, his contemporary, receives the full treatment appropriate to one whose philosophy had been an inspiration to Symonds. This personal approach increased the disadvantages of concentrating on great men. Though he believed, for instance, that Raphael was a greater artist than Signorelli, he devoted more space to the latter because of his influence on his special hero, Michelangelo.

This was one of the disadvantages of Symonds's real originality. He knew probably more about the period than anyone living. He had read the works he wrote about and never put down a second-hand opinion. If he subscribed to certain earlier views it was from conviction, not from

Symonds with his father and his sister, Charlotte.

habit. It remained a period of picturesque and dreadful personages. Alexander VI still provoked titillating censure ('the universal conscience of Christianity is revolted by those unnameable delights, orgies of blood and festivals of lust'), liberty was still the cry. But here Symonds differed from earlier views. He did not praise the republican age, Italy's glory and man's freedom depended on the despotisms, in the unrivalled development of character they fostered: 'the facts of the case seem to show that culture and republican independence were not so closely united in Italy as some historians would seek to make us believe'. But neither did he follow his old source of 1863, Roscoe, in admiring the Medici. To Symonds they were tyrants, who, so far from promoting the good, progressive elements in the culture of Florence, encouraged the bad; with his strong belief in the self-sufficient individual, Symonds was not much concerned with patronage.

The amount of information in *Renaissance in Italy* makes it still useful, especially the volumes *Italian Literature,* which remain the fullest literary history of the period obtainable in English. Nor is there any substitute in English for *The Revival of Learning,* Symonds remains a useful authority on the central part of his work. It was when he tried to relate this information to a general conception of the Renaissance that he failed.

His use of the term was deceptive. With regard to the arts, there were firm limits. For architecture he followed the divisions of Burckhardt's *Cicerone;* 1420-1500, the age of experiment; 1500-40, of achievement; 1540-80, of decline. For painting, likewise three divisions: from Cimabue to 1400; from 1400 to 1470, from 1470 to 1550, during which the Renaissance 'may be said to have culminated'. For literature, again three periods: from Dante's vision in 1300 to Boccaccio's death in 1375; from 1375 to Cosimo dei Medici's death in 1448; from 1448-1530, which Symonds called alternatively the 'Golden age of the Renaissance' or 'the true Renaissance'. The crucial dates are, then: 1500-40, in architecture; 1470-1550, in painting; 1448-1530, in literature. From his choice of representative individuals and of the *Orlando Furioso* as the representative poem of the Renaissance we can see that as far as the arts were concerned, the first generation of the sixteenth century was the key one, and this definition of the close of the period at least was aided by the generally waning admiration for late sixteenth-century painters. In what he expressly said, then, Symonds was entirely conventional. But because his work, which called itself **Renaissance,** covered the fourteenth and fifteenth centuries, artists of these centuries, particularly the *quattrocento* (the effect of Burckhardt's work was the same) were associated with the term. And Symonds fostered this association by the use of phrases like 'the dawn of the Renaissance', which could cast the terminological net as far back as the small fry of the thirteenth century.

His limits of the period as a whole were less rigid than those he gave the arts. In the preface to **The Age of the Despots** he wrote: 'Two dates, 1453 and 1527, marking respectively the fall of Constantinople and the sack of Rome, are convenient for fixing in the mind that narrow space of time during which the Renaissance culminated.' But to set limits to a culmination reflects Symonds's need to pin down and deal with the complex and abstract by analysis. So we have three ages of this and four of that, neatly dated; moments of caution—'we have to be on our guard against the tyranny of a metaphor', moments of irresolution—'the so-called Renaissance', alternating with precise dates. He knew that it was an age of transition but could not avoid cutting it into segments. He reserved the full sense of the term for the late fifteenth-early sixteenth centuries, but under cover of the title of the book, and images of dawns, beginnings and first glimmerings, the men and the manners of the previous two centuries came in.

His unease when dealing with the theoretical part of his subject caused him to hazard some very shaky theories. The Renaissance Italians were responsive to beauty because in some districts 'circumstances and climate had been singularly favourable to the production of such glorious human beings as the world had rarely seen'. Rapt in a vision of the country and the time 'when lads with long dark hair and liquid eyes left their loves to listen to a pedant's lectures', Symonds allowed himself to suggest an explanation: 'Surely the physical qualities of a race change with the changes in their thought and feeling.'

Similarly uncritical was the use of Hegelian ideas. He often referred to 'the spirit of the times', 'the half-unconscious striving of the national genius', the *Zeit-geist,* without realizing what nonsense this made of his insistence on the dominant role of the individual. He was capable of remarks that reduced the importance of personality to zero. 'The *Zeit-geist* needed Petrarch. He, or someone like him, was demanded to effect a necessary transition.' The creative talents of the humanists which are lauded in one volume, become less independent when in another he states that humanism 'was imperatively demanded not only by the needs of Europe at large, but more particularly and urgently by the Italians themselves'. His faith in progress clashed with his faith in the individual. From one point of view Italy passed on to the rest of Europe the achievements of her great men, from the other she was simply used for a while by the current of the world spirit which was leading Europe to her goal of freedom. Symonds's judgment slept, too, through another clash—that between his prejudices and his optimism. The former caused him to denounce abuses, the latter persuaded him that everything that happened was for the best. The middle ages had been superstitious and ignorant; during them man was degraded and enslaved—but all was for the best, for they kept man fresh, full of illusion for the blessing of the Renaissance: 'Ennui,' said Symonds feelingly, 'and the fatigue that springs from scepticism, the despair of thwarted effort, were unknown.' Classicism led to the neglect of vernacular literature—but this was for the best, for how otherwise could the European nations have become conscious of their bonds with the classic past? The levelling down of the component parts of Italy under a common despotism in the sixteenth century meant the destruction of her most valued characteristic, but it was for the best, for it was a prelude to her becoming a nation. Symonds did not see that when everything, however veiled, is for the best, because the present is as yet the best, the historian is left with little scope for censure of the past.

As early as 1878 the *Quarterly Review* noticed this weakness: 'We find throughout his work a constant conflict between his moral instincts and his philosophical principles, the result of which is a double point of view that produces an impression of infirmity of judgment.' However conscious of this, Symonds could not escape. Dealing with subjects that stimulated his imagination made it hard to be cool and critical. 'Long after work is over', he noted in the autobiography, 'the little ocean of the soul is agitated by a ground-swell; the pulses beat, the nerves thrill and tingle.' He knew that 'changes of style and purple patches deformed the unity and gravity of a serious historical work. Relief from thoughts which had become intolerable had to be sought in brain-labour. That being so, I did not sufficiently count the cost, or approach my theme in a calm artistic spirit.'

This warning did not reach the public, nor perhaps would they have heeded it. Admiration for Italy, once more a free nation, was intense. Travel was cheap and easy. There were guide books and guided tours. From industrialized England lovers of quiet and beauty came, many of them to settle permanently in Italy, where life had such grace and was so inexpensive. And it was not antiquity that appealed, but the Renaissance, with its morality so different from that of the Victorians, its great men they knew so well how to appreciate. With Pater and Ruskin they studied the art of the *quattrocento,* exercising on painters like Botticelli what Symonds called 'our delight in delicately poised psychological problems of the middle Renaissance'. Socially secure, and delighting in the sun, a host of intelligent Englishmen and women dipped their pens in a haze of aesthetic goodwill, and began, with scant historical equipment, to chronicle the towns, the men and the manners of the Renaissance.

The mood even penetrated a tart article on Campanella in the *Edinburgh Review* in 1879. During the Renaissance 'A strange glamour was over men's eyes. As of old, the earth seemed dædal with many-coloured delights. Sorrow and death were hardly perceived as a jar in the universal spring-song of the intellect and the senses.' There was much tearful gratitude for what Italy had done for modern man. She created him and then herself was slain; 'this nation', said Symonds gravely, 'had to suffer for the general good.' He emphasized that the story he told in **Renaissance in Italy** was a tragedy. He showed Italy at the height of her joy and creative power—then her pathetic ruin 'while the races who had trampled her to death went on rejoicing in the light and culture she had won by centuries of toil'. The Italians accepted the task of re-appropriating the classics which were to free mankind, a task which cost them their own literary independence and political liberty. This was false, but no matter how far from the truth sentiment took him, its appeal disarmed criticism.

The effects of his attitude can be seen nowhere more clearly than in the work of Vernon Lee (Violet Paget). In her *Euphorion* (1884) she paid a tribute to Symonds, praising the specially adapted gifts, his infinite patience and ingenuity 'occasionally amounting almost to genius'. She, too, lauded Italy for sacrificing herself for posterity, and went further than her master. She set herself to judge the period, to be shocked, tolerant, understanding and forgiving, as though its tumultuous generations stood before her like an erring but repentant choirboy: 'Our first feeling is perplexity; our second feeling, anger'—but as evil is a necessary part of the mechanism for producing good, we must forgive. How can we help it 'in looking down from our calm, safe scientific position, on the murder of the Italian Renaissance; great and noble at heart, cut off pitilessly at its prime; denied even an hour to repent and amend; hurried off before the tribunal of posterity, suddenly, unexpectedly, and still bearing its weight of unexpiated, unrecognized guilt'?

Her other master was Pater. She aped the purposeful delicacy of his style, she took her title from a passage in his *The Renaissance. Euphorion* was named after the child of the mystic marriage of Goethe's Faust and Helen—the worn-out middle ages joined with age-old but divinely young antiquity to produce the Renaissance. But this technical description is soon set aside. Renaissance is used to describe anything vague but splendid that happened in Italy between Dante and Michelangelo, and anything that resembled it in the north where 'the Renaissance is dotted about amidst the stagnant Middle Ages'.

The term that had grown up to supplement the Revival of Learning and that Burckhardt had tried to restrain to

Italy, was washed free of restrictions by a flood of subjective writing. Rebirth was a fatally attractive image to an age confident of progress. The objections were few and they were brushed aside. Men wished to see the Renaissance by the light in which Symonds had painted it. They accepted the tyranny of a metaphor that he had feared but served. (pp. 169-96)

> *J. R. Hale, "John Addington Symonds," in his* England and the Italian Renaissance: The Growth of Interest in Its History and Art, *Faber & Faber Limited, 1954, pp. 169-96.*

Robert L. Peters   (essay date 1962)

[*Peters is an American educator and critic who has written extensively on Victorian writers and their works. In the following essay, he examines Symonds's aesthetic beliefs, describing the influence of nineteenth-century humanism and science on his thought and artistry.*]

Few once significant Victorian writers are in such paradoxical decline as John Addington Symonds (1840-1893). While several of his works remain in print, he himself, at least as a representative late Victorian writer, has been almost forgotten. His *Life of Michelangelo Buonarroti* (1892) is on the current lists of two American publishers, the heart of his ambitious seven volume *The Renaissance in Italy* (1875-86) is available in paperback, his translation of Cellini's *Life* (1887) remains a frequently printed translation of that work, his study of Walt Whitman (1893) enjoys a quiet favor with Whitman specialists, and isolated poems, particularly the translations from the Greek and a few from his sonnet cycle, **"Stella Maris"** (1884), which should rank higher than it does among Victorian works of this type, occasionally appear in anthologies. Yet, despite this impressive recounting, modern readers of Symonds are seldom aware of his place among the Victorian writers who have been called "aesthetes." The observation Symonds himself made in the unpublished autobiography that he was in the forefront of the writers of his time, seems to us now somewhat egocentric.

It is Symonds the aesthete, with the strengths and weaknesses the term implies, who concerns me in this paper. What follows should perhaps be regarded as a series of notes preliminary to a fuller examination of Symonds' provocative role. I shall first examine some of Symonds' responses to certain nineteenth century aesthetic and intellectual currents and then briefly consider his classicism as a particular manifestation of the late Victorian mood. I shall hope simply to chart some of the main issues and point up a few of the problems related to British Aestheticism. The poles suggested by the title of the paper, as we shall see, were supplied by Symonds himself.

Despite his self-imposed exile to Switzerland and the several complaints he made about his isolation from stimulating minds and libraries, Symonds managed to keep well abreast of new English artistic and intellectual trends. For one thing, he absorbed a good deal of the English Impressionist manner, characteristic of so much of Whistler's painting and of a large portion of the literature of the eighties and nineties. He admired the verse impressions produced by Oscar Wilde, W. E. Henley, and Arthur Symons. Many of John Addington Symonds' own poems present subtle moods and landscapes transformed by shimmering light or by a soft Whistlerian dusk. Too often these works are damaged by an external narrative line and over-wrought emotional effects. In the Venetian poems, for example, Symonds is overly fond of trite romantic situations. Even his better homosexual works (the "she" of **"Stella Maris"** should be "he," and he has named the friends who inspired specific poems), written as they are out of immediate experience, are apt to dissolve into slight sketches tinged with a *fin de siècle* melancholy. We might call such work "attitude" verse, poetry in which emotion is too often stagey and overdrawn.

Some of Symonds' regard for the fluctuating, nervous impression was stimulated by his reading of Walter Pater. He had scrutinized Pater's essays and adapted the famous principle of intensity, rejecting what he thought was the aesthetic description, but keeping the principle of heightened emotion, of the "hard gemlike flame." He also found helpful Pater's idea of *virtue,* the inspiriting emotion of experiences and works of art. He put this theory to its best use in **Michelangelo** where in straightforward chiselled prose he conveyed some of the specific "effects" of the great artist's works, and in ***Studies of the Greek Poets*** (1873), perhaps the solidest of all his writings. He spoke of "the single effect to be produced" by art and complained of another of his masters, Ruskin, that his "paintbox of delirious words" had the effect of making his readers "exchange style for mere imitation," or of conditioning them to prefer a literal transcriptive art to one in which Nature is "manipulated" and her "inner rhythm" revealed. "What one wants in Art," said Symonds, "is something other than the particulars of life." To capture this "virtue" and to record it with "style" was to record one's central impression. The purer and more refined the subject (Symonds' taste was mainly for Greek and Renaissance art) the more "aesthetic" the response. "Style," he said, "consists in making that necessary modification [of surpassing the literal fact of nature] subserve poetic purposes." While accuracy makes for "honest prose," "modification" serves the "inner and idealising faculty," enabling the poet to render that single and "peculiar chord" of beauty. Symonds' cautionary attitude towards Ruskin, it should be noted, did not prevent him from absorbing some of Ruskin's impressionist style. [In a footnote Peters adds: "Symonds' enthusiasm for Robert Louis Stevenson's writing was also an influence on his prose."]

Symonds was aware also of Victorian experiments in the interrelationships of the arts, and his efforts to explore overlappings were generally intelligent and distinguished. Symonds' knowledge of music and its boundaries was sensitive and informed. He knew more about techniques than either Swinburne or Whistler, drew frequent analogies between music and the other arts, and produced skilful lyrics directly inspired by music. Among the latter are **"A Violin Improvisation"** and the untitled manuscript poem which opens, "I saw a lute hung on a forest tree." Reflecting his reading of Hegel and Pater, he described for his friend Henry Sidgwick (22 Aug 1867) the power he discerned in music, and particularly in Beethoven's work, as a synthe-

sizing art. "A great symphony or an organ voluntary," he wrote, "can alone" perfectly reconcile "the miseries of an agitated existence":

> The truest *Versöhnung* in art I know is to be found in Beethoven's C Minor Symphony. There he first posits all the contradiction of passions, aspirations, and sorrows, then combines them without losing their separate individualities; but so transfiguring them that the termination is triumph; the victory and majesty of the soul are wrought out of its defeats and humiliations. Music alone can do this.

We are reminded of Pater's famous dictum about the arts aspiring to "the condition of music," a dictum Symonds knew well. But when he came to consider Pater's ideal in **"Is Music the Type or Measure of All Art?"** he once again modified Pater's views, arguing for a less abstract idea of music as pure aesthetic rapture. He argued also—and this is his chief contribution to the discussion—that music can never supplant poetry as the leading art form. Although he admitted that music through motion unifies and synthesizes ("Music is at the same time the abstract science of all harmonious motion, and also its concrete expression. . . . ", he extolled poetry's ability to resolve the "abstractions of music and the plastic arts" into "her own province of pure intellectual thought." A vague ideal of a transcendent music, Symonds believed, could never adequately represent the supreme stage of art ("this discrimination of an *Anders-streben . . .* is after all but fanciful." A tenuous balance between the concrete and the abstract, between feeling and mind, was the ideal. Horatio F. Brown, commenting on these ideas, stressed the duality of Symonds' temper: Symonds' "governing qualities," said Brown, were "acute sensibility, and intense intellectual activity; he felt profoundly through his aesthetic sensibility, but his intellectual vigour could not let him rest there; he desired to know as well as to feel." Symonds himself denied that any art of lasting consequence could be exclusively "abstract": "whatever art has touched acquires a concrete sensuous embodiment, and thus ideas presented to the mind in art have lost a portion of their pure thought-essence." While this passage reads like a rather ponderous translation from Hegel, he also expressed the idea more simply: "Art . . . is a middle term between reason and the senses."

If Symonds was less ascetic than Pater, he was more consciously intellectual and scholarly than Wilde. I do not overlook Wilde's considerable power of stating a point and developing it: as an essayist he was brilliant in a way that Symonds, who had difficulty in sustaining philosophical concepts, never was. But Symonds was more conscious of his role as an intellectual; he tried deliberately to balance the extremes of the abstract and the passionate, even though he may have glossed over the crabbed and tortured way between them. Balance, as intuited through the senses, is central to his aesthetics and bestows upon his best criticism a certain quiet individuality, as it does also upon his more monumental works, including ***Renaissance, Michelangelo, Introduction to the Study of Dante*** (1872), and the ***Greek Poets,*** written for publishers at his and their suggesting. Experimentation of an "aesthetic" sort he reserved for his personal poetry and for some of the essays. To use one of his own favorite words, his mind was "speculative."

It is not surprising to find that Symonds' experience with painting and sculpture, like that with music, stemmed from childhood. His father had early encouraged his cultural interests, offering a library well supplied with engravings, photographs, and copies of Greek sculpture and Italian Renaissance painting. The autobiography is sprinkled with comments on the art he saw on trips to the continent; and letters from Switzerland to friends in England contained requests for reproductions of works by favorite English painters and sculptors.

One of his favorite painters was Tiepolo, and a stirring essay, **"On an Altar-Piece by Tiepolo,"** has much to say that is still incisive about a painter who has recently burst again into favor. One paragraph is of particular interest since it reveals so well the ordered, balanced, civilized qualities Symonds sought in Renaissance art. The contrast with medieval painting and with Caravaggio, Rubens, and Poussin is especially noteworthy, as is the concluding idea, pure Whistlerism, which assumes that the subject matter is far less important than the disposition of the work's visual properties. To some readers the remarks about "good breeding" may seem a little too genteel:

> . . . Tiepolo painted like a great gentleman. There is an unmistakable note of good breeding in all his work. I do not remember to have ever found him vulgar, brutal, or *bourgeois*. And here, where he skirted the very border of the abyss of physical torment, he avoids the clumsy symbolism of medieval painters—jocund women carrying their eyes or bleeding breasts on plates: he avoids the butcherly abominations of Italian or Flemish or French naturalists—Caravaggio's flayings, Rubens' flakes of spear-divided flesh with the blood and water gushing from a gaping wound, Poussin's bowels wound like ropes on capstans by brawny varlets. Tiepolo shows proper respect for the reality of his subject, together with noble breeding and a fine sense for the limits of art, by creating a thing of beauty, which, when examined *a la loupe*, betrays a tragic content, but does not force this in any painful way upon attention. Lovers of what is beautiful in art need not dwell upon the cruel details of the subject-matter. The picture itself suffices to give pleasure by its harmonies of wisely ordered lines and colours melting in a blaze of softened lustre.

While Symonds' knowledge of art was impressive for his time, his attempts to employ references to the several arts as a critical tool were not always successful. They share with so much late Victorian criticism (Swinburne's, George Moore's, and Andrew Lang's in particular) an easy regard for slippery allusions and a hyper-sophisticated tone. Max Beerbohm, in his imitation of George Moore, devastatingly parodied the mannerisms of this kind of aesthetic criticism ["Dickens," *A Christmas Garland*, 1912]. It is to Symonds' credit that such devices are rare in his more ambitious works, especially when we see in the letters and in the autobiography how easily he

could assume this particular pose. His treatment of Tennyson's "Lucretius" will display the method. After a precious explanation that he had done "full justice" to the work since he had read it in his gondola as he "glided by the Ducal Palace and beneath the bridges of St. Mark's," he reported that he found the poem "splendid" but wanting in dramatic force: "The whole is very pictorial, a symbol of our modern poetry, which has absorbed the spirit of the picturesque, and which is like a bit of Watts in words. It agreed singularly with the splendid sensualities of Veronese and Titian and Giorgione." The references here are almost too obvious. To Symonds, as to the Victorian aesthetes generally, the various worlds of art were familiar and their values constant—at least that is the illusion sustained, partly as one protest against the social power of an artistically-benighted bourgeoisie. But to move so gracefully among such parallels as these is a risky critical exercise, a lesson that Moore, Swinburne, Henley, and others did not always realize. The "attitude" supplants real insight. Symonds' ability to restrain these devices so well in the Renaissance studies indicates that when he did use them he did so consciously, and perhaps in direct imitation of the contemporary art criticism he was reading in the quarterlies and journals. [Peters adds in a footnote that Ruskin may have been Symonds' immediate source.]

In no one of his works did Symonds more thoroughly assume the overlapping of the arts than *In the Key of Blue* (1893). Holbrook Jackson has remarked [in his *The Eighteen Nineties*, 1950] that the work was "so typical . . . of the Nineties that it might well have been written by the younger generation." Symonds was fifty-three at the time. The title essay, a pallid experiment in prose-poetry, records Symonds' impressions of Augusto, his gondolier and retainer, dressed in various shades of blue and observed in varying degrees of light. A sample poem will indicate Symonds' attempt to create a "symphony" of sound and sight through the medium of words:

> A symphony of black and blue—
> Venice asleep, vast night, and you.
> The skies were blurred with vapours dank:
> The long canal stretched inky-blank,
> With lights on heaving water shed
> From lamps that trembled overhead.
> Pitch-dark! You were the one thing blue;
> Four tints of pure celestial hue:
> The larkspur blouse by tones degraded
> Through silken sash of sapphire faded,
> The faintly floating violet tie,
> The hose of lapis-lazuli. . . .

This poem is not one of Symonds' better efforts; the essay itself is actually one of the poorest in the book. **"On the Altar-Piece by Tiepolo," "Clifton and a Lad's Love,"** and **"Among the Euganean Hills"** have far more genuine charm and are less contrived. Symonds came to regret the book, perhaps because he suspected that English literature by the early nineties was moribund and that he had been taken in by one of its more affected motifs, perhaps because he realized that the sketchiness of the work, apart from its esoteric qualities, would hardly enhance his reputation. Interestingly enough, Brown, who shared Symonds' judgment of the work, in the *Biography* makes no reference to it at all. Nonetheless, *In The Key of Blue,* with its gold cover of hyacinths and laurels designed by Charles Ricketts, remains one of the more representative works of the nineties. The book also demonstrates Symonds' generally ambivalent attitude towards the more flamboyant varieties of Victorian aestheticism (as I have already pointed out, his own esoteric treatment of classic themes seems subdued by contrast). As his letters show, Symonds, stimulated by Shelley's and Whitman's concepts of the poet, wanted to be a leader and to attract disciples; yet he was sufficiently steeped in traditions of art other than the impressionistic (for example, he was fond of seeing himself as poet in the bardic role popularized by Morris and continued by Buchanan and Gosse) to permit himself more than an occasional dip in avant garde waters. His classicism, at least, had the sanction of tradition, and could hardly call down on his head the vituperations of the great Philistine beast, whom he believed, despite the generally poor sales of most of his books, he was trying to reach. He seemed unaware that his own experiments, as potentially moribund and restricted as any established by his fellow aesthetes in London, placed him securely in their company.

Symonds was responsive also to current trends in science. The range of his curiosity reminds one of Tennyson, who also had a renowned breadth of interest in such matters. Symonds was, however, of an even more mixed mind about the benefits of science, and his knowledge of one branch, formal psychology, surpassed Tennyson's.

Symonds was highly suspicious of the "science" which extolled "fact" to the exclusion of larger views of man, nature, and art. His fears were common, of course, among the Victorians; Swinburne, Whistler, and Wilde all attacked the intrusion of scientific method into art. In Symonds' mind, despite the fact that he admitted that in "such an age [as the Victorian] poetry must perforce be auxiliary to science," the pursuit of literal detail when employed as a method for art meant the decay of art. While he himself could create passages as ornate as any produced by a zealous pre-Raphaelite, he was on the whole suspicious of this kind of "realism." The true artist, he insisted, is not to reproduce nature's flaws and imperfections simply because they exist. Rather, he must transform and inform. "What one wants in Art is something other than the infinite particulars of life." He took comfort in a revealing quotation from Joubert, a quotation final in its escapism: " 'To escape from the mere frightful reality' is the function of the arts." When Science seduces the artist into assembling plethoric detail for its own sake, Symonds would deny Science. He objected also to the factualist's insistence that contemporary artists treat contemporary subjects. The critics who are "indignant with 'the idle singer of an empty day' . . . have forgotten the treasures of old-world speculation, the jewels of experience collected by our ancestors in times when life was simpler, the types of ever recurring tragedy and ever fresh emotion which lie embedded in primeval myths and allegories." The bulk of his own work is almost exclusively a reversion to the past.

There were three fields of science, however, which Symonds could easily endorse. 1). The conclusions of the evolutionists Darwin, Bruno, and Spencer supported his religious scepticism; his own personal "religion," of which he wrote a good deal in his letters, was developed out of the "freedom" he found in the revelations of the new scientists. 2). Findings of medical researchers offered hope for curing his own respiratory disease. 3). Contemporary psychology provided him with material for his writing and avenues for the alleviation of the painful psychological problems which had plagued him from childhood and which led to a serious nervous collapse in 1871 [in a footnote Peters adds that Symonds' biographer, Phyllis Grosskusth, "goes so far as to rank the problem of homosexuality ahead of literature as 'the overwhelming interest of his life . . .' "]. He had read widely in Krafft-Ebbing, Uhlrichs, and their followers.

It is in a vague alliance with Symonds' homosexual interests and his idealism—these two supported by classicism—that modern science and ancient art coalesce into a kind of emotional-intellectual "combine" joining the "real" ("Science" and sex) and the "ideal." The unpublished portions of the autobiography give a surprisingly frank, at times almost clinical account, of his struggles to subdue powerful homosexual impulses. Many of his unpublished letters, most of them hitherto suppressed or unknown, written to Edward Carpenter, Havelock Ellis (with whom Symonds worked on the first versions of *The Psychology of Sex*). Walt Whitman, T. S. Perry, Edmund Gosse, Horace Traubel, and Charles Kains-Jackson, reveal the depth of his problem and the extent of his absorption in contemporary psychology. There is some proof that he taught Havelock Ellis more about these matters than has been recognized. His two "Problems" pamphlets [*A Problem in Greek Ethics* and *A Problem in Modern Ethics*], published anonymously and circulated among his friends, were pioneering attempts to treat the problem historically and frankly. Some of his discussions interestingly anticipate Freud. (H. F. Brown suggested in a letter to Symonds' daughter Madge that Symonds would have followed Freud, if he had known him when he became a fashion.) These preoccupations seem to have aroused his deepest feelings as an artist, and when the letters, the complete autobiography, and the unpublished poems appear, Symonds will seem a more original and profound writer than he has up to this time.

Not surprisingly, Symonds found support for his ideas in the imaginative literature he admired. Partial always to works with a homosexual bent—Plato, Marlowe, Shakespeare, etc.—his discovery of Whitman in 1869 came as a revelation. Here was a writer who, himself inspired by a "scientific" attentiveness to the facts of life, had achieved the impossible, transmuting the crude ore of male passion into a golden idealism of comradeship and democracy! Symonds' long correspondence with Whitman (1871-1892), which resulted in the famous letter about the illegitimate sons, need not detain us except as it indicates the depth of Symonds' regard for the "Master." At the time of his death Symonds was negotiating for the proper volumes in order to produce an authoritative edition of Whitman's complete poems. His wish for accuracy as much as his desire to elicit a confession of comradeship led to the queries on "Calamus" and homosexual themes. It is these elements in Whitman which occupied most of Symonds' attention, not the socio-political meaning of the poems, which scarcely moved him. Believing that Whitman's cosmology was largely a camouflage for his sexual drives, Symonds wrote his fine **"Love and Death: A Symphony"** in praise of Whitman's ideals of sensuous comradeship.

Symonds remarks in his autobiography that he was born with "a Greek spirit." His point was that his tastes were not acquired at Harrow and at Balliol, the schools he attended; nor had he submitted to the standards of either the mercantile or the scientific worlds. His studies and his friendships—particularly with Benjamin Jowett, Graham Dakyns, Henry Sidgwick, and Norman Moor—simply intensified and deepened his childhood promptings and made him more than ever the citizen of "Athens" rather than of "Troy." A photograph of the Praxitelean cupid in his father's art collection had taught him early, he said, "to feel the secret of Greek sculpture." For hours he pored over "the divine loveliness" while his father read poetry to the family. Dr. Symonds, said the son, "did not quite approve," and often pointedly asked why Johnny "would not choose some other statue, a nymph of Hebe" for contemplation. Symonds' dreams were a tissue of images blent from art and from life: the Praxitelean face, Apollo sentenced to serve Admetus, and nude Bristol sailors. His comment on the Apollo indicates how interwoven were the fleshly and the mystical in his thoughts. The dream, he said, "shows how early and instinctively I apprehended the truth, by the light of which I still live, that a disguised god, communing with mortals, loving mortals and beloved by them, is more beautiful, more desirable, more enviable, than the same god uplifted on the snow-wreaths of Olympus, or the twin peaks of muse-haunted Parnassus." Symonds regarded these early fantasies as preparations for his later receptions through literature and art of Hermes, the Apoxyomenos, Plato's youths, Marlowe's Leander, Shakespeare's Adonis, and, as he said, "much more besides." When he moved his family (he had three daughters at the time) to Clifton Hill House, Bristol, in 1871, above the doors to his parlor he enshrined plaster casts of sections of the Elgin marbles showing Greek youths in procession. Later, in his Davos study, he displayed several models of Cellini's "Perseus."

In addition to satisfying his personal needs, classicism provided an antidote to the ugly fragmented world of the present, a Troy dominated by science and politics. Despite his verbal approval of science as "democratic," Symonds lamented that the "turbid" present lacked the "emergent" creeds to replace decayed ones; its "social conditions" were "shifting like the quicksands"; it "dispersed" the "nervous fluids of our brains through a thousand channels": "What is left for us modern men? We cannot be Greek now. The ages and the seasons of humanity do not repeat themselves. The cypress of knowledge springs and withers when it comes in sight of Troy; the cypress of pleasure likewise, if it has not died already at the root of cankering Calvinism; the cypress of religion is tottering, the axe is laid close to its venerable stem." What remains is the opiate of withdrawal into an Athens of one's imagining, an Athens so exclusive that it provides—and this is the base of Symonds' aesthetic-ethical totality absent from

the contemporary world. There are similarities, of course, between this view and the "beautiful soul" (schöne Seele) of German Romanticism. By "living the past again in reveries or learned studies, by illusions of the fancy and a life of self-indulgent dreaming" one dulls "the pangs of the present." The list of illusions he provided was representative and not meant to record his own recurring ones, excepting Athens, of course: "Behold, there is the Athens of Plato in your narcotic visions; Buddha and his anchorites appear; the raptures of St. Francis, and the fire-oblations of St. Dominic, the phantasms of mythologies, the birth-throes of religions, the neuroticism of chivalry, the passion of past poems; all pass before you in your Maya-world of hasheesh. . . ." Other artists, Rossetti, Swinburne, Burne-Jones, and William Morris among them, had sought their "hasheesh" in the middle ages. Symonds' territory, like that of Wincklemann, whom he somewhat resembles, was the antique world. Greece, he rhapsodized during a visit to Athens in 1873, is "the most purely beautiful place that exists. It is pure light, serenity, harmony, balance, definition, nothing too large, too crushing, but all human and beautiful. . . ." His concern, however, was hardly with an Homeric sweep of time, but rather with an esoteric and highly feverish adaptation of a few select themes: the death of handsome youths, the love of boys, comradeship in battle, the rapport of male minds exploring aesthetic questions, the longing of bloodless women for full-blooded males. There is little sense of sociology in his Hellenism; his inspiration was private and lyrical, not public and epical.

To model his aestheticism along Greek lines was not a completely easy task for Symonds. His fleshly cravings proved unsettling; his entire early career, up to the nervous crisis in Cannes (1871) after which he no longer deprived himself of homosexual consummations, had been spent in trying to sublimate his desires. The flagrant homosexual practices he had witnessed at Harrow offended his Puritanic sense, and, according to his own report, made sublimation more imperative. In the love poems, even after 1871 and his new freedom, the most passionate of his attachments were, at least on his part, love affairs of the spirit as much as of the flesh. In his poems he shows males smitten with one another through a vibrant clashing of souls, followed by physical desire and eventual consummation. Both parties absorb something of each other's idealism and virility. At these moments Symonds' diction can be as sensuous and as self-consciously religious as Rossetti's and Swinburne's celebrating heterosexual love.

The magic of homosexual love, when love is drossed of its excessive sensuality, occurs primarily through relationships between youths. This idea appears in the central portion of the manuscript version of **"Love and Death: A Symphony,"** the long poem originally addressed to Whitman:

> Noble, valiant, fair,
> Of equal youth and honour, for the pride
> Of Hellas they arose, a stately pair.
> Vast was the love between them—deep and wide
> As heaven up breaking through a myriad sphere:
> Sevenfold had it been proved and purified
> By yearnings, and by achings, and by tears—

Symonds in Venice.

By fierce abstentions, and by fierce recoils
Into the furnace-fire through throbbing years.
Now nobly tempered, from the transient toils
Of sense set free for luminous emprize,
This love, elate, arrayed in radiant spoils,
Shone like a beacon light from ardent eyes.

The transformation to the ideal plane is difficult, and it is not surprising that Symonds' most successful passages, most of which are unpublished, describe either the physical attributes of lovers or actual physical contacts. When he moves on to the higher plane, the tone is often forced; the passages sound as if the author wished more to prove a point than to allow the culminating emotion of the poem to speak for itself. One lyric in which he does avoid these pitfalls is **"Il Ponte del Paradiso."** The work describes the mystic power felt by the poet as he recalls a now dead lover whose remembered gaze will some day speed him along the bridge to Paradise, to a new and permanent union with the departed:

Soul cries to soul, as star to sundered star
    Calls through the void of intermediate night;
    And as each tiniest spark of stellar light
    Includes a world where moving myriads are,
Thus every glance seen once and felt afar

Symbols an universe: the spirit's might
Leaps through the gazing eyes, with infinite
Pulsations that no lapse of years can mar.
He therefore dwells within me still; and I
    Within him dwell; though neither clasp of hand
    Nor interchange of converse made us one:
And it shall surely be that when we die,
    In God shall both see clear and understand
    What soul to soul spake, sun to brother sun.

Symonds' specialized interest in Whitman, his absorption in Greek and Renaissance literature and art, and his dedication generally to sexual-aesthetic fusions in all art reflect a serious narrowing of artistic view, a refinement of taste and an exclusiveness of interest which we might term "aesthetic." And all of this despite the fact that he gave lip-service to science and democracy as vague social ideals. He conveniently overlooked nearly all of the religious implications of Greek art and some of the complex social values of Renaissance humanism, just as he had overlooked the sociological implications in Whitman. The prism through which he viewed both life and art was, though brilliant in its tone, quite single in its hue. His commitment to ethical idealism was prompted, at least in part, by his desire to publish some of the love poems in disguise. He could thus avoid public suspicion of his homosexual tendencies, while at the same time time through very carefully placed clues communicate clearly with friends. One example is his manuscript lyric, **"Kew Gardens,"** written to recapture the affair of an afternoon with a male friend. When the poem was finally published, Symonds had changed the title to **"L'Abbandonata":**

We sat together on the bank;
No human thing was near:
The sun above us rose and sank,
The sky was sunny clear.

. . . . .

I would that I had died that day
With his head on my knee,
For year by year the merry May
Brings less of love to me.

Another example is a poem **"Young Achilles,"** inspired by a virile Swiss peasant who posed for Symonds. Symonds reported to Kains-Jackson that an admiring friend suggested he could make the work publishable "by altering *young Achilles* into Amaryllis."

It should be remembered that in interpreting Hellenic culture this way, Symonds was not alone and that some of his models in this as in other areas, were to an extent responsible for his own attitudes. Much of Wilde's poetry is steeped in an eclectic classicism, with more than a few of the overtones Symonds desired. Burne-Jones', William Etty's, F. Poynter's, and Evelyn de Morgan's nudes frequently display a thinly concealed sensualism under the guise of Greek inspiration and Renaissance color. Even Pater's rather severe hedonism—a refreshing return to ancient roots in many ways—makes some bizarre departures. These are the main examples. They should indicate that Symonds' place in this particular absorption was not unique. In a revealing letter (1 Feb 1889) to Jowett, Symonds discussed at length his master's unwillingness to accept fully the influence of Plato's homosexual themes on British youth required to read the Greek writer in public schools and universities. So important was this letter that Symonds copied it complete into the central portion of the autobiography.

It is of course easy to be severe with Symonds for his evasions and for his harsh modifications of Greek art and life. Poets today are able to speak more openly of matters which he had to conceal. And if we consider withdrawal as one of the important features of late nineteenth century aestheticism, some of Symonds' reactions as well as his preciosity are inherent in the aesthetic climate itself. Possibly, if he had been more responsive to the vigorous art of the nineteenth century French poets, particularly to Baudelaire, Rimbaud, and Verlaine, he might have produced more exciting and original creative work. The monumental achievements of the **Renaissance,** the **Greek Poets,** and the **Michelangelo** still stand. But the artificiality at the root of so much of his personal writing makes the Athens he desired seem, from our vantage point, little more appealing than the Troy he despised. If he had had the courage to transform his intense inner perturbations into images of sin, struggle, renunciation, and, eventually, into beauty, as Baudelaire was able to do, he might have created a truly magnificent Athens to supplement his historical-biographical gifts. But the weaknesses, as I have suggested, are serious, and, if I may repeat, are as much due to the models he chose to follow and the atmosphere he absorbed as to the limitations of his own creative powers; the faults lay as much in British aestheticism as in his own mind. (pp. 14-24)

> *Robert L. Peters, "Athens and Troy: Notes on John Addington Symonds' Aestheticism," in* English Fiction in Transition, *Vol. 5, No. 5, 1962, pp. 14-26.*

Alan P. Johnson   (essay date 1969)

[In the following excerpt, Johnson focuses on Symonds's humanistic approach to the Renaissance, noting that his history balances praise and censure in describing this period.]

The attitude toward the Italian Renaissance expressed in the work of various Victorians has often been recognized as a useful indication of a general shift from the so-called religious pietism of the mid-nineteenth century to a humanism characteristic in the later part of the century. With regard to the Victorians' attitude toward the Italian Renaissance, the shift is usually charted as a movement from Ruskin's denunciations of Renaissance infidelity, pride, sensuality, and rationalism in *The Stones of Venice* (1851-1853) to John Addington Symonds' praise of the Renaissance's "discovery of the world and man" in his five-volume history, **The Renaissance in Italy** (1875-1886) and to Walter Pater's selective and impressionistic appreciations of art and literature in his famous volume of Renaissance studies, which appeared in 1873. Often, George Eliot's *Romola* (1862-1863) is taken as a transitional work, and Vernon Lee's works such as *Euphorion* (1884)

are regarded as derivative from Pater and perhaps from Symonds.

In general, the formula of a shift from Ruskin to Symonds and Pater is accurate and useful. The current understanding of the late Victorian attitude toward the Italian Renaissance may be inadequate in two ways, however. First, it may be oversimple in its view of figures of whom Symonds is the leading example. Second, it may be incomplete because of its neglect of two works by Oscar Wilde that are set in the Italian Renaissance. Although the works by Wilde are not of major importance in themselves, they represent the logic of the humanistic appreciation of the Renaissance carried to the extreme of admiration for satanic egoism.

In the past twenty years in two important studies of the history of the idea of an Italian Renaissance [J. R. Hale's *England and the Italian Renaissance,* 1954, and Wallace K. Ferguson's *The Renaissance in Historical Thought,* 1948], Symonds' interest in the period has been characterized as predominantly an admiration for what he supposedly took to be its outburst of intellectual, moral, and political freedom and its cultivation of sensuous pleasure. Despite clearly stated and perceptive qualifications in both studies, their reader may easily conclude that Symonds is the chief spokesman of an attitude that is simply antithetical to Ruskin's denunciation. Symonds himself appears in both studies as a man who turned to the Renaissance to find "the whole lives, the vivid contrasts, the self-reliant individuals he admired" because of a frustrated sense of his own intellectual inferiority, sexual ambiguity, and physical illness. Such a picture captures little more than half of the author of **The Renaissance in Italy.** Symonds, and other late Victorians whose views of the Italian Renaissance resemble his, clearly reveal minds divided between humanistic appreciation of the Renaissance and conventional, even Ruskinian, moral discomfort with its excesses.

Symonds' view of the Italian Renaissance somewhat resembles the view that Arnold adumbrates in *Culture and Anarchy.* Like Arnold, Symonds might be described as a skeptic in religion, antimystical and yet hopeful that by the use of reason man progresses along a "parabola" of human, evolutionary development toward "truth" and the "Divine Mind." And like Arnold, Symonds praises the Renaissance as a time of the reawakening of human capacities for self-development. Symonds also stresses, however, that the period was one of moral corruption and political tyranny. The balance of Symonds' praise and censure is apparent in many of his various descriptions of the Renaissance from his Oxford prize essay in 1863 to such late works as his study of Boccaccio in 1895. The most notable expression of his attitude is the five-volume **Renaissance in Italy.**

The well-known essay with which Symonds introduces his history is a deceptive indication of his attitude because the essay focuses upon "the spirit of the Renaissance" and not upon the broad historical period itself. Symonds limits himself to what he calls the "culture" of the period and of course accords it only praise. In the essay, he gives, for example, the often quoted definition of the word "Renaissance" that begins, "What the term Renaissance really means is new birth to liberty. . . ." It is in this essay, too, that he echoes Michelet in describing the "great achievements of the Renaissance" as "the discovery of the world and the discovery of man."

Although Symonds' praise of the Renaissance is lavish in the introductory essay, the five volumes of *The Renaissance in Italy* repeatedly note that the cost of Renaissance culture was immorality and tyranny that Symonds does not condone. In the first volume, *The Age of Despots,* for example, he rejects the too bright picture of the Italian despots painted in Macaulay's essay on Machiavelli and cites examples of bloody tyrants such as the Visconti, Galeazzo Sforza, and Sigismondo Malatesta. Malatesta, Symonds says, "might be selected as a true type of the princes who united a romantic zeal for culture with the vices of barbarians." Symonds begins his discussion of the popes of the period by affirming the truth of Lorenzo de' Medici's description of Rome as " 'a sink of all vices.' " Of Renaissance Italy generally, Symonds declares that "with reference to carnal vice, it cannot be denied that the corruption of Italy was shameful."

The balance of Symonds' praise and censure is similar in the other volumes. In *The Revival of Learning* the achievements of Petrarch and Lorenzo Valla are praised, while the corrupt wit of Poliziano and Beccadelli is censured. In *The Fine Arts,* Signorelli, Michelangelo, and Raphael are recognized as the culminators of a developing discovery of the world and man in art, while their successors are attacked as practitioners of "a new religious sentiment, emasculated and ecstatic," and a "crude naturalism and cruel sensualism" in painting. In sculpture, Symonds says, "what the Visconti and Borgias practised in their secret chambers, [sixteenth-century] sculptors exposed in marble." In *Italian Literature,* he praises the division of Petrarch's mind between Christian asceticism and classical sensuousness and describes Boccaccio as a beneficial sensualist who "freed the natural instincts from ascetic interdictions," but he indicts later literary men because "they overleaped [Petrarch's] conflict, and satisfied themselves with empty realizations of sensual desire." In Symonds' final volume, his tone generally is critical because his attention has shifted from the Renaissance proper to what he calls the "Catholic reaction" against it. (pp. 23-4)

> *Alan P. Johnson, "The Italian Renaissance and Some Late Victorians," in* The Victorian Newsletter, *No. 36, Fall, 1969, pp. 23-6.*

Richard Titlebaum   (essay date 1975)

[*In the following excerpt, Titlebaum examines Symonds's* Renaissance in Italy, *discussing its author's method of historical analysis and comparing it with that of other Victorian historians.*]

Of Symonds's project to write a history of the Italian Renaissance, Jowett said [in his *Letters of Benjamin Jowett,* 1899], "No Englishman probably has ever been so well qualified to undertake it by previous study". The Chancellor's Prize Essay of 1863 [entitled "**The Renaissance**"] which reflects the influence of Sismondi and Michelet, ig-

nited Symonds's professional interest in the period. Three years later in 1866, while on a trip to the Riviera and Mentone, he began to study Italian and read Italian literature in the original. Within two years his knowledge of the language was sufficient for him to read without trouble *Orlando Furioso.* In 1871, his research in Elizabethan drama led him to contemplate the composition of a large serious history of the Renaissance. Jowett's words were accurate: Symonds's knowledge was immense. But the undertaking that began merely as an idea took him eleven years to complete. What motivated Symonds throughout all the years of toil between 1875 and 1886 was not only the hope of literary fame and the desire to carve out a lineage for Victorian liberalism but a genuine love of Italy. "Italy", he once wrote, "has formed the dreamland of the English fancy". "As poets in the truest sense of the word, we English live and breathe through sympathy with the Italians. The magnetic touch which is required to inflame the imagination of the North is derived from Italy."

Symonds's practice as an historian epitomizes superbly what Herbert Butterfield has called "the Whig Interpretation of History". To see the past in terms of a formula, whether it be the rise of liberalism or the march of progress; to take advantage of the historian's principle of exclusion by reducing human complexities to the elucidation of one's own pet sympathies; to select from the past those personages or events which seem most relevant to one's own time; to perceive in each generation the conflict of the future against the past or the battle between progress and reaction or between Protestantism and Catholicism; to fall into the unexamined habit of mind whereby history becomes a mere trick of organization—This according to Herbert Butterfield, is the essence of the Whig Interpretation of History. Professor Butterfield's net takes in many fish. But his generalization, however much it says about Symonds's *Renaissance in Italy,* is at best only schematic. That Symonds's conception of the Renaissance mirrors the ideals of his class is obvious. Yet what is objectionable about *Renaissance in Italy,* as Professor Butterfield would insist, is not its bias. Bias lies, in fact, behind the work of many truly great historians. Macaulay's infatuation with progress, Burckhardt's patrician love of culture, Michelet's devotion to the Revolutionary Spirit, Toynbee's "prophetic powers"—these are only a few of the armatures of bias around which great historians have filled in their mere clay of fact. Symonds's bias was his liberalism. *Renaissance in Italy* elucidates the constituent elements of Victorian liberalism as applied to history.

In the nineteenth century there were, of course, many attitudes towards history: Froude and Carlyle and Marx and Renan had little in common except for their devotion to history itself. But in the midst of a multitude of conflicting opinions and antagonistic dogmas about history, one important attitude towards the study of the past stands out. It was the ideal of Leopold von Ranke to see history as it really was; *sehen es wie eigentlich gewesen ist*—an idea echoed in Pater's injunction "to see the object as it really is" and in Arnold's championship of "seeing things as they really are". Historians of today have come to acknowledge how impossible Ranke's ideal of total scientific detachment invariably is in the composition of any history. But writers such as Ranke or Mommsen or Maitland, repelled by the frequent imposition of arbitrary schemes and personal prejudices on the writing of history, sought diligently to remove all idiosyncratic biases from their books, to concentrate only on collecting and presenting the facts, and by an heroic effort of detachment, to write history not as it should have been, or may have been, but as it genuinely happened. Despite all of Symonds's claims to scientific rigour, there is nothing in *Renaissance in Italy* to warrant his inclusion in Ranke's school. A *litterateur,* Symonds possessed neither the training nor the library to be anything but confused about the implications of scientific historiography. He never got lost in the cross-fires of debate about historicism because he knew nothing about the controversies that were to plague Dilthey and Buckle. Naïvely he thought that scientific history was a collection of facts and the application to them of the theory of evolution. The true influences upon his mind were Taine and Macaulay. He took to heart Taine's claim that the duty of the historian was to "make the past present", as well as Macaulay's belief that "Facts are the mere dross of history". Symonds's strength lay not in scientific historiography but in his ability to apply ideas to history. *Renaissance in Italy* displays none of Carlyle's uncanny ability to magnetize the brain by means of cacophonous word-pictures or of Macaulay's introduction of chiaroscuro into history by means of a "but". Symonds's technique was more subtle. He wrote history not as a novelist but as a critic does. His classical and rhetorical prose marshals all the available facts about the Renaissance into consummate order by means of topics, such as the Revival of Learning or the Fine Arts. *Renaissance in Italy* contains no dramatic scenes, only the dramatization of ideas.

The resemblance that some critics have noticed between the histories of Symonds and Burckhardt was acknowledged by Symonds himself, but Symonds made clear that Burckhardt's *Civilization of the Renaissance in Italy* had come to his notice only after his first volume was nearly completed. It would be difficult, he admitted, "for me to exaggerate the profit I have derived from the comparison of my own opinions with those of a writer so thorough in learning and so delicate in perception as Jakob Burckhardt". Symonds could have learned much from Burckhardt who, rebelling against his teacher Ranke, defined history as "the most anti-scientific of all the sciences, though it transmits much that is worth knowing" [quoted in Benedetto Croce, *History: Its Theory and Practice,* 1961]. Using manuscripts, coins, inscriptions, monuments, and gossip, Burckhardt, in his attempt to delineate the *Geist* of the Renaissance, brought the genre of historical impressionism to its highest form of artistry. Whereas both Symonds and Burckhardt saw in the Renaissance an ideal subject for *Kulturgeschichte,* Burckhardt's history shows superbly how *aperçus,* aphorisms, and anecdotes centred around specific topics can be taken as the superior model. Burckhardt's method examines a particular aspect of the Renaissance from various points of view, each revealing distinctive qualities about the era. A typical paragraph in the history has the character of an impressionistic vignette because Burckhardt's ultimate aim was to tell a good story. On every page of his history Burckhardt left the evidence of his intuitive powers. Indeed, if R. G. Col-

lingwood was correct in his assertion that history is the re-enactment in the mind of the historian of "the experience of the people whose actions he is narrating", then one reason for Burckhardt's superiority over Symonds lay in his intuitive grasp of the *Geist* of the Renaissance. Burckhardt may have written from a position of tired blood and apocalyptic worry, but his great intelligence enabled him to see that Ranke's conception of scientific historiography was fatuous and that history is much more than a mere collection of dry-as-dust facts.

This Symonds did not see. His belief that history is a science, however absurd this belief may seem to us today, was of course, not idiosyncratic. Historians of the most profound erudition beguiled themselves with the illusion that they could imitate the complex mathematical manipulations of causal relations which is the scientific method, that the type of explanation commonly used to analyse external events in nature could be appropriated to describe the vicissitudes of man, and that scientific laws, themselves mere probabilities, could be elicited from the documents and monuments of history. If Burckhardt was too clever to give credence to this all-pervasive fallacy of the past century, Symonds because of his positivistic background deluded himself that he was a full-fledged scientist. "I sit down daily to my desk as an anatomist to the dissecting table", he confided in a letter while putting together the last volume of *Renaissance in Italy.* "The scientific historian must present his findings in an appropriate style. He must prune away irrelevant material, concerning himself always with hard, tangible fact, wrought into precise uncompromising argument, expressed in unmistakably plain language." That Symonds was a master of facts is self-evident to any reader of *Renaissance in Italy;* but, as he himself realized, to be a genuine scientist one had to have theories as well. And to Symonds, the good liberal who perceived in the spectacle of the Renaissance the origins of modern progress, no theory was a greater revelation than Darwinian evolution.

He himself in a late essay described the intellectual atmosphere that made Darwin's impact upon his mind into so stunning an event. "When I was a young man, in the sixties", he tells us, "I remember that we students of European culture had to choose between connoisseurs and metaphysicians as our guides. Between these opposed teachers . . . Goethe emerged like a steady guiding star. His felicitous summary of criticism, 'Im Ganzen, Guten, Schönen, resolut zu leben! . . .' came like a deliverance". The remark Symonds then makes reveals perhaps more about his mind than he himself could have imagined: "Instinctively we felt that the central point for us, if we could erect criticism into a science, was not caprice, not personal proclivity, not particular taste, but a steady comprehension of the whole." There exists a class of minds which driven by the compulsion to understand life, art, or history under the guise of one organizing principle, grasps at times in a fit of desperation, at some convenient or popular theory. Such was Symonds. "How to grasp the whole, how to reach a point of view from which all manifestations of the human mind should appear as correlated, should fall into their proper places as parts of a complex organism." This is what he was in search of. More than any other of

Symonds's contemporaries, Taine, famous for his application of physiological principles to culture and his theories of climatic and environmental influences, appealed to Symonds; but in Taine's scheme, he decided, there remained a rigidity of thought that did not make sufficient allowances for the resistance that man offers to his *milieu*. Taine, despite all the attractiveness of his ideas, was eclipsed by Darwin and his theory of evolution.

Symonds thought that to be a great critic and historian it is necessary to master the categories of one's age. There was no doubt in his mind that Darwinian evolution supplied a new and useful category. Without Darwin's influence **Renaissance in Italy** would have been only a pedantic collection of facts. Darwinian evolution provided Symonds with a coherent theory by which to understand both the past and the present. It provided him also with the intellectual support for a firm belief in progress. It provided him with a vision as well. "To trace the connection", he announced, "between such stages of evolution as the Renaissance, the Reformation, and the Revolution, and to recognize that the forces which produced them are still at work, is the true philosophy of history". Evolution meant essentially three things to Symonds: the ideas of process, development, and progress, all of which he used to formulate his conception of the Renaissance. Of course, the fallacy that lies in applying ideas relating to nature to the verbal construct that is history never occurred to Symonds. He thought erroneously that the biological process in nature called evolution, which theoretically does away with static and immutable archetypes, could be used to describe the development of Italy and Europe. His aim was grandiose: "To trace the continuity of civilization through the labyrinth of chance and error and suspended energy, apparent to a superficial glance or partial knowledge, but on closer observation and a wider sweep of vision found to disappear, is the highest aim of the historian". He saw history as a process and its main theme as culture, but the theory he used to explain history was nothing more than an organizing principle to hold together his facts. **Renaissance in Italy** is thus as much about the *quattrocento* as it is about its schematic development. Symonds not only subordinated particular aspects of Italian culture to one of several stages or periods of development, but he also, much against his professed aim, broke up the fabric of history arbitrarily into three stages of literary development or four periods of humanism or three eras of painting. The pervasiveness of the evolutionary viewpoint in his thinking is clear throughout **Renaissance in Italy.**

"Theory", remarked Croce [in his *History: Its Theory and Practice*], "is not the photograph of reality, but the criterion of the interpretation of reality". And, indeed, Symonds's conception of the Renaissance, by virtue of the fact that it supplied the criterion of choice as to what is included and excluded from **Renaissance in Italy,** plays the role in the history that theory does in scientific method. History is to a large extent the function of methodology; what the historian selects or doesn't select becomes *a priori* the fabric of history. Symonds's definition of the Renaissance as nothing but the liberation of humanity from a dungeon possesses in the history the function of an Archimedean point enabling him to discipline the tyranny of

facts. The dungeon mentioned is the Middle Ages—"that age of somnambulism" whose "ten centuries of ignorance" incarcerated Europe in "a sepulchre". Throughout his life Symonds displayed a marked hostility towards the Middle Ages. On a visit to Canossa he wrote that the Middle Ages had little to offer when one has been dazzled by the ever-living glories of Greece and the Renaissance. If in his occasional *aperçus* about the Middle Ages Symonds only parroted the prejudices of Voltaire and Hume, in his concept of the Renaissance he articulated the prejudices of Victorian liberalism. "The word Renaissance", he wrote, carrying on the tradition of Michelet, "means the recovery of the beauty of the outer world and of the body by art, the liberation of the reason by science and criticism, the emancipation of the conscience in religion, the restoration of culture to the intellect, the establishment of freedom for the individual". Such a concept, however, did not emerge out of the facts of the Renaissance. It is a concept that Symonds applied extrinsically to the Renaissance. The Renaissance became the rebirth of that historical progression which continued through the French Revolution to the England of Gladstone. "It is the history of the return to life of the whole Spirit of Humanity." It was an outburst of mental and moral independence, leading to the "reassertion of the individual in his rights to think and feel, to shape his conduct according to the dictates of his reason".

"Verily", Symonds sighed in a letter, "I shall end up with being what the French call a *polygraphe feconde*—a jack of all trades, aesthetical and a humbug who has gorged and disgorged Hegel". Despite his lamentations, Symonds found in Hegel, as he had in Darwin, support for his view that the animating force in history is progress. But whereas, it must be insisted, Symonds merely confused the process of evolution with the idea of progress, Hegel's philosophy of history enabled Symonds to use the vocabulary of a cosmic system in order to support his belief in progress and liberty, which to him were almost synonymous. When Hegel wrote [in his *Philosophy of History*] that "the history of the world is the discipline of the uncontrolled natural will, bringing it into obedience to a Universal Principle and conferring subjective freedom", he provided Symonds with a conception of history which has all the grand drama of religion with none of its mythical trappings. In Hegel's philosophy history possesses the character of a play in which vast spiritual forces are at work. Metaphysical entities analogous to those which Empedocles or Anaxagoras had assigned to the universe replaced the Christian mythos. What Comte himself said of history, that at various times religion succumbs to metaphysics, took place in Hegel's philosophy. Symonds, an ex-Christian, his mind nurtured from birth on the idea of an ultimate cosmic historical drama, was able to use Hegel's vocabulary because Hegel's triadic historical dialectic only replaced the familiar preoccupation of the European Christian intellectual with the theological subtleties of the Trinity. The actual process of history, which, for example, according to Bossuet in his *Discours sur l'histoire universelle,* emanates from the Trinity, was seen by Hegel to be the product of thesis, antithesis, and synthesis, which is the arcane mechanism the Spirit employs on its devious path towards self-consciousness or freedom. Historical causality, redefined by Hegel as a metaphysical dialectical process, enters the flux of events, above all, in the guise of World Historical Figures, who give character to the Spirit of the Age. All of these ideas—diluted, distorted, and re-worked—are part of the scaffolding of **Renaissance in Italy.**

"The 'Spirit of the Age' ", wrote John Stuart Mill in 1831, "is in some measure a novel expression . . . The idea of comparing one's own age with former ages . . . had occurred to philosophers; but it never before was itself the dominant idea of any age" [*Mill's Essays on Literature and Society,* 1965]. In the initial chapter of **The Age of Despots,** the first of the seven volumes that comprise **Renaissance in Italy,** Symonds reveals to what extent he viewed the Renaissance spirit as akin to the spirit of his own age. The topics of the chapter are virtually identical with those of his Chancellor's Prize Essay. Such explanations for the phenomenon of the Renaissance as language, a favourable climate, political freedom, and commercial prosperity indicate only an increase of speculation on Symonds's part not one of perception. Despite the passage of twelve years, the points of reference are all the same as in the undergraduate essay: the problem of precursors, the question of causality, the relation of feudalism to Renaissance politics—Symonds's approach to the Renaissance had not changed. His aim in writing the chapter may have been similar to Burckhardt's in *The Civilization of the Renaissance in Italy*—"to understand the spirit of the age in all its vigorous individuality"—but by spirit Symonds meant neither a hovering *Geist* animating all facets of Renaissance culture nor a merely convenient verbal abstraction, but that aspect of the period which gave birth to the ideals of modern liberalism. "The history of the Renaissance", he argued, "is not the history of arts, or of sciences, or of literature, or even of nations. It is the history of the attainment of self-conscious freedom by the human spirit manifested in the European races." And, he added, its political history was but "the prelude to that drama of liberty of which the Renaissance was the first act, the Reformation the second, the Revolution the third, and which we nations of the present are still evolving in the establishment of the democratic idea".

Walter Pater in his review of **The Age of Despots,** after praising Symonds for his dramatic effects, suggested that the book was flawed by the absence of one characteristic, "the quality of reserve". In many ways, perhaps because Symonds was uncertain of his powers as an historian, **The Age of Despots** is the most interesting of the seven volumes. Lacking the consistency of prose style that marks the later volumes, especially **The Catholic Reaction, The Age of Despots,** indeed marred by the absence of "the quality of reserve", is at times an expression of inflated rhetoric. Traditionally, the art of rhetoric, at least as it was formulated by Aristotle, centred on three concepts: the ideas of *logos, pathos,* and *ethos;* and of the three ideas it is *ethos*—the role that the writer or, in this instance, the historian, adopts towards his audience—which is central in **The Age of Despots.**

Often the supremely great historian, who takes for his theme a whole civilization, has been the spokesman for a set of dominant ideals. With Gibbon, for example, the ideal behind *The Decline and Fall of the Roman Empire* was the humanism of a Julian or a Cicero. Gibbon's *ethos* of lofty ironical condescension was very much a function of his belief that the achievements of classical humanism had been destroyed by the triumph of barbarism and religion. Macaulay's ideal expresses the aspirations of the bourgeois world. "The history of England", he affirmed, "is emphatically the history of progress." In **The Age of Despots,** Symonds articulated an ideal of a similar nature, but this ideal, or what Herbert Butterfield would call Symonds's "Whiggism", though it animates much of the content of **Renaissance in Italy,** conflicted with the realities of the Renaissance itself. The Age of Despots, Symonds believed, gave birth to the spirit of liberty, which is the hallmark of the modern world; but the social realities of the Renaissance—its unscrupulous and impious popes; its blood-thirsty tyrants and *condottieri;* its spectacle of Giovanni Vignate imprisoned by Filippo Maria Visconti in a wooden cage at Pavia and beating his brains out against its bars; its atrocities such as that of Dattari who was bound naked to a plank and killed piecemeal by the people, who sold and ate his flesh—were in conflict not only with the culture of the period but with the high moral sentiments of the Victorian Age. How to deal with the paradoxes of the Renaissance—with a barbarian such as Sigismondo Pandolfo Malatesta who made his mark as the Maecenas of Rimini—was Symonds's greatest problem. He shared the conviction of J. A. Froude who said in a speech delivered in 1864: "The address of history is less to the understanding than to the higher emotions. We learn in it to sympathize with what is great and good; we learn to hate what is base" [*The Science of History,* 1864]. He agreed with Lord Acton [who stated in his *Historical Essays and Studies*] that "the marrow of civilized history is ethical, not metaphysical, and the deep underlying cause of action passes through the shape of right and wrong". Thus he felt compelled not merely to describe the Renaissance but to judge it. The ethos of **The Age of Despots** is that of the ermined judge.

Symonds's *ethos* as an arbiter of morality is especially noticeable in the rhetoric of his historical characterization. Macaulay's ambition to give to history "those attractions which have been usurped by fiction" was beyond Symonds's powers, for he patently lacked the ability to emphathize with most of the figures of the past. If none of the character sketches in **The Age of Despots** rises to literary eminence, it is perhaps because Symonds, like Gibbon (though with little of Gibbon's genius), very often described historical personages according to a formula. In *The Decline and Fall of the Roman Empire,* the memorable portraits, and even the superficial sketches, follow a strict principle by which details are arranged and evaluated according to the morals and sanity of the subject. In hundreds of portraits, Gibbon painted an effect of overwhelming human depravity by incessantly emphasizing man's tendency to deviate from the golden mean. The reckless pursuit of pleasure is constantly set off against the norm of public and social duty, and the sophistries of the imagination are compared to the sobriety of common sense. Gibbon's terrifying images of depraved emperors and fanatical Christians are calculated to overpower the

Symonds in Davos Platz, Switzerland, where he settled permanently in 1880.

reader. The vast gallery of imperial debauchees produces the impression of incorrigible decadence. However dissimilar Gibbon's monsters may be, whether they indulged in murder like Constantine or in lechery like Gordius, their vices are incorporated in a rhetorical language of uniform moral condemnation. A very similar mechanism exists in the language of *The Age of Despots.* But whereas Gibbon's portraits both of the saints of the Church and of the sinners of the Palatine Hill are evaluated according to the golden mean and by an appeal to the neo-classical principle of the uniformity of human nature, Symonds's vignettes of the Renaissance despots are delineated in a rhetoric based upon the ideals of enlightened humanity and of a liberalism akin to that of John Stuart Mill. On the pages of *The Age of Despots* dozens of grotesque ghouls pass before the eyes of the reader. Sixtus IV is only one of them:

> Most singular is the attitude of a Sixtus, indulging his lust and pride in the Vatican, adorning the chapel called after his name with masterpieces, rending Italy with broils for the aggrandizement of favorites, haggling over the prices to be paid for bishoprics, extorting money from starved provinces, plotting murder against his enemies, hounding the semi-barbarous Swiss mountaineers on Milan by indulgences, refusing

aid to Venice in her championship of Christendom against the Turks—yet meanwhile thinking to please God by holocausts of Moors, by myriads of famished Jews, conferring on a faithless and avaricious Ferdinand the title of Catholic, endeavoring to wipe out his sins by the blood of others, to burn his own vices in the *auto da fe* of Seville, and by the foundation of that diabolical engine the Inquisition to secure the fabric his own infamy was undermining. This is not the language of a Protestant denouncing the Pope. With all respect for the Roman Church, that Alma Mater of the Middle Ages, that august and venerable monument of immemorial antiquity, we cannot close our eyes to the contradictions between practice and pretension upon which the History of the Italian Renaissance throws a light so lurid.

The great flaw in moralistic rhetoric such as this lies in the fact that the passage, though it reveals the sentiments of its author, really says very little about Sixtus. Where the irony of Gibbon, in Byron's words, saps "a solemn creed with solemn sneer", the rhetoric of Symonds is empty of content. Not rhetoric, but minute facts artfully arranged—those facts which Burckhardt was able to construct convincingly into a mosaic-like picture of the Renaissance—represent the real stuff and essence of history.

Gibbon's posthumous *Memoir* reveals that he was at heart an epicurean; that his ruling passions were rationality and self-cultivation; that in his lifetime he combined almost miraculously the retirement of a Lucretius with the duties of a parliamentarian. Identifying the London of George III with the Rome of Augustus, Gibbon eyed most of his historical personages with the incredulity and bemused disdain of a Roman praetor. His rhetoric has none of the inconsistency or hypocrisy of Symonds's. For Symonds, though he was a liberal in politics, assumed the guise in *The Age of Despots* of a conservative in morals. In his historical characterization he at times condemns in others the activities he himself practised. Thus he says of Filippo Strossi: "His private morals were infamous. He encouraged by precept and example the worst vices of his age and nation, consorting with young men, whom he instructed in the arts of dissolute living, and to whom he communicated his own selfish Epicureanism." In *The Age of Despots,* Symonds's *ethos* may be that of high moral seriousness, and the history of the Renaissance may appear at times to be merely a catalogue of sensational vices; but familiarity with the pattern of Symonds's life makes one aware of the discrepancy between his public pretensions and his private morality. In part this discrepancy was due to his role as a crusader for liberal sentiments, as well as to his fear of public exposure. The rhetoric of *The Decline and Fall of the Roman Empire,* on the contrary, is that of a philosopher, not of a crusader. Its aim is the delectation of the cultivated reader. Gibbon's history does not fight religion with shouts of *écrasez l'infâme.* It employs the more subtle sting of irony. It appeals to the reader's sense of dignity and respect for reason. If it is less effective in the market place, it is more long-lasting as literature.

The incorporation of moral judgements into an historical narrative has come under attack from several parties in this century. "Above all it is necessary", writes Herbert Butterfield, "to resist those who claim for the historian the solemn role of moral arbiter, and particularly those who transfer this ethical preoccupation into the reconstruction of the whole course of ages." [*The Philosophy of History in Our Time,* 1959, edited by Hans Meyerhoff]. In a scintillating essay, *Historical Inevitability,* Isaiah Berlin, a spokesman for the antagonistic viewpoint, has argued that moral judgements are inherent in language itself and that to try to eliminate them from historical writing would be comparable to altering the habits of human discourse. Whether one adheres to the first position or to the second, what is indisputable is that the moral judgements in *The Age of Despots* are of a nature to substantiate Burckhardt's argument that they are the "deadly enemies of true historical thought". Symonds, despite his scientific pretensions, could not resist moralizing. Moral judgements are part and parcel of the structure of *The Age of Despots,* and Symonds's rhetoric elucidates not ideas and facts but emotions and obsessions that haunted his mind such as his dislike of the popes who displayed, he asserts, "a pride so regal, a cynicism so unblushing, so selfish a cupidity, and a policy so suicidal as to favour the belief that they had been placed there in the providence of God to warn the

world against Babylon". At other times, Symonds's rhetorical imagination achieves a certain concreteness: "Yet the Pope is still a holy being. His foot is kissed by thousands. His curse and blessing carry death and life. He rises from the bed of harlots to unlock or bolt the gates of heaven and purgatory". Often individuals, such as Lucrezia Borgia, receive a verbal rapping: "Instead of viewing her with dread as a potent and malignant witch, we have to regard her with contempt as a feeble woman, soiled with sensual foulness from the cradle". Sometimes Symonds treats his subjects as if he were a lawyer in court as when he says of Alexander VI: "Whatever crimes may be condoned in Alexander, it is difficult to extenuate this traffic with the Turks . . . he stands arraigned for high treason against Christendom, of which he professed to be the chief, against civilization . . . against Christ."

Renaissance in Italy as a whole illustrates the type of history R. G. Collingwood attacked in his epochal work *The Idea of History.* With magisterial sarcasm Collingwood, coining the concept of 'scissors-and-paste' history, assigned to the rubbish heap of the mind, works whose methodology centred on the arrangement of sources. "Scissors and paste", he writes, "was the only historical method known to the later Greco-Roman world or the Middle Ages . . . An historian collected testimony, spoken or written, using his own judgement as to its trustworthiness, and put it together for publication; the work which he did on it being partly literary . . . and partly rhetorical." Such a form of history, pre-scientific in method, dominated the nineteenth century and prompted in people of intelligence, like Hegel and Marx, an attempt to transcend 'scissors-and-paste' by seeing in facts recurrent patterns or scientific laws. But the systems of Hegel and Marx were only the extensions of the archaic methodology; and repeating Lord Acton's injunction to "study problems, not civilization", Collingwood cast his ridicule upon those who practise what he considers an antiquated pursuit. The composition and structure of *The Age of Despots* illustrate to what extent Collingwood's criticism has validity. The fundamental thesis of the history, namely that the Renaissance gave birth to the spirit of liberty, is never proven, nor is there even an attempt to supply evidence for the legitimacy of this assumption. It is a more dogmatic statement thrown into the interstices of the narrative. And the narrative itself, despite its readability, is very much a pastiche of subjects, whose data Symonds assembled from a myriad of sources. The volume has a panoramic sweep. Symonds, like a traveller returning home from an antique land, paints a glowing picture of high culture, immoral rulers, a love of the world, a rediscovery of the body and the senses. But Symonds's history, viewed critically in terms of the highest ideals of historiography, lacks the sophistication of the mature historian. What it lacks in methodology it makes up for by being a landmark of Victorian liberalism. (pp. 88-98)

Richard Titlebaum, "John Addington Symonds as a Liberal Historian," in English Studies in Africa, *Vol. 18, No. 2, September, 1975, pp. 85-98.*

Kenneth Churchill   (essay date 1980)

[*In the following excerpt, Churchill evaluates Symonds's writings in the context of nineteenth-century English attitudes toward Italy.*]

John Addington Symonds devoted his adult life, from his Oxford Prize Essay on *The Renaissance* in 1863 until his death in Rome thirty years later, to literary work built around a central concern with the Renaissance in Italy. His seven volume work on the subject, *The Renaissance in Italy* (1876-86), though lacking the intellectual calibre and seminal importance of Burckhardt's study, which was one of his sources, was a significant literary achievement, clearly marking a stage in the development of English attitudes to Italy.

The obvious comparison, sketched out by a contemporary reviewer [F. Hueffer in *The Times,* 7 April 1882], is with Gibbon. He . . . was one of the last major figures in that humanist tradition whose awakening had been one of the features of Renaissance Italy. His book ends with Poggio's meditations on the ruins of Rome, meditations which helped arouse that desire to emulate in modern Europe the greatest achievements of ancient civilisation, which lasted as a major cultural force until the eruptions of the late eighteenth century left the world in fragments. From his works, and particularly his letters, it is clear that Symonds was familiar with [the major nineteenth-century English literary treatments of Italian material] and was aware of his own relation to them. Between his own day and that of Gibbon was a chasm; the humanist tradition was broken and the Romantic trauma and the increasing collapse of every kind of faith seemed to have plunged Europe into a new dark age requiring a new Renaissance to re-establish sound values and a purposeful sense of direction. An obvious approach was to analyse the experience of the earlier Renaissance. The Romantic treatment of the subject was vitiated by its sensationalism: the sufferings of Tasso and the violence of the Cenci had to be treated historically, not dramatically. Ruskin, though an invaluable stimulus, was limited by his rejection of the spirit of paganism: from the very beginning of his study of the subject the young Symonds observed that 'it is not necessary, with Mr Ruskin, to stigmatise the Renaissance as a monstrous growth of pride and infidelity', and tended rather towards the ethos represented by Browning in his portrait of Andrea del Sarto.

For to Symonds it was precisely the stress on individualism and the pagan enjoyment of life which was attractive and vital in the Renaissance and which was the major theme running through all his work. Lacking Ruskin's earnestness, Symonds believed that the object of life is 'to live as much as possible; & if it may be at the close of life to feel that every year has passed almost unheeded from its fullness of occupation!' There was nowhere better to look for guidance in pursuing this object than that age when 'How to make the best of human life, is substituted for the question how to ensure salvation in the world beyond the grave', the age whose motto had been 'Man made master of the world and of himself by spiritual freedom.'

Such was the spirit in which Symonds took up the study of the Renaissance, attempting to connect the post-Romantic world with the sources of vitality which had sustained the greatest ages of the past. The main single result of this study, the seven volumes of *The Renaissance in Italy,* is open to attack on several fronts. It overemphasises personalities, giving little attention to economic history. The personalities themselves are arbitrarily selected on the basis of Symonds' feelings of affinity, so that Giordano Bruno receives far more attention than Galileo, and Michelangelo than Leonardo, and they come mostly from the sixteenth century, at the expense of earlier periods of the Renaissance. There is a strong literary bias, the sections on music, painting, sculpture and architecture being markedly weaker than those on books and manuscripts. Even the best volumes, on literature, though based on first-hand knowledge of the subject, are unoriginal and rely heavily on previous historians; and the style is often tedious and repetitive.

On the other hand, the style is equally often irreproachable; and Symonds' is still the only comprehensive study of the period originally written in English, and demands respect for having brought a broad picture of that age before a wide audience. It can still stimulate serious thought on the Renaissance, and provides incomparably attractive introductions to those aspects of the subject which do enjoy Symonds' sympathy. Though the third volume, on the fine arts, is inadequate, the first is still fascinating and illuminating in its wealth of documentation on *The Age of Despots,* the second, despite its awkward and dated theory of intellectual evolution, is contagious with the excitement of *The Revival of Learning,* and the fourth and fifth remain unchallenged in English as a general non-technical account of Italian Renaissance literature.

Throughout the volumes runs Symonds' concern with seizing the vital creative spirit which could reconnect his own time with the great ages of the past. The identifiable manifestations of civilisation, which had been the source of the tradition culminating in Gibbon, were less important than the intangible play of free and joyous vitality which could be detected behind them. A crucial and brilliant passage is Symonds' discussion of Tasso's frequent use of the phrase 'un non so che.' Its vagueness, says Symonds, is something new in poetry, quite unlike the concrete, sculptural images of classical literature, the precise, mathematical art of Dante, or the painterly clarity of Petrarch, Boccaccio and Ariosto; a feeling for the ineffable and incomprehensible was the new dominant characteristic of art, and it was no accident, he argues, that the age of Tasso should have seen the creation of modern music, whose strength is precisely in its ability to render those feelings which cannot be put into words or stone or paint. The passage is the equivalent in Symonds to Pater's more famous 'All art constantly aspires towards the condition of music' in the *School of Giorgione* essay; both men sought less to analyse the great art of the past than to establish a tremulous relationship with the creative impulse which had made that art great, a relationship which had something of the intangibility of music.

In Symonds this effort produced both more prolific writing and a broader response to the experience of Italy than Pater did. But his works on the Italian Renaissance are unfortunately repetitive and show strikingly little intellectual development. The volumes which precede *The Renaissance in Italy* are an introduction to it, while those that follow are effectively appendices. (The relevant books, between 1863 and 1895, are listed in the bibliography.) Symonds' other works, on the English poets, Whitman, and Greek literature, and his poems, are all linked to this central interest in the spirit of the Renaissance; one sees clearly the connection in his writing about contemporary Italy.

From his first enthralment with Venice during the long vacation of 1862 until his death in Rome in 1893, Symonds visited Italy, first from England and after 1877 from his home in Davos, as often as his precarious health permitted. He was intimately familiar with the country, as well as with its history and literature. One of the features of *The Renaissance in Italy* is its frequent references to the small towns of Italy, especially Tuscany; and one of the most attractive offshoots of work on the book was his three collections of *Sketches in Italy and Greece* (1874), *Sketches and Studies in Italy* (1879) and *Italian Byways* (1883). These travel sketches, most of which appeared originally as magazine articles, are a major contribution to the genre. Ranging throughout Italy, both geographically and historically, Symonds' subjects vary from contemporary Venice through Medicean Florence to the Capri of Tiberius and Antinous. Everywhere he seeks to evoke the spirit of the place, to reveal those magical dimensions in which all the most vivid feelings which men have felt there in the past seem to flood back into a place and to pulse inspiritingly through the imagination of the attuned observer. With Symonds, who makes explicit in prose what had permeated Browning's Italian poems, the Italian past becomes life-enhancing; it is no longer a question of meditating over decay, or of comparing the state of modern England with that of ancient Rome or medieval Italy; rather, the traveller must seek to charge his spiritual batteries by making contact with the plenitude of the finest qualities of life which wells up from the great creative spots of Italy. At Taormina, for example,

> Every spot on which the eye can rest is rife with reminiscences. It was there, we say, looking northward to the Straits, that Ulysses tossed between Scylla and Charybdis; there, turning towards the flank of Etna, that he met with Polyphemus and defied the giant from his galley. From yonder snow-capped eyrie, Α'ιτγαδ σκοπια, the rocks were hurled on Acis. And all along that shore, after Persephone was lost, went Demeter, torch in hand, wailing for the daughter she could no more find among Sicilian villages.

All over Italy the sensitive traveller could find places which would stock his mind with images of this kind of resonance of association. Symonds is explicit about the value, the necessity, of such experience. Writing of the debt of English to Italian literature, he comments,

> As poets in the truest sense of the word, we English live and breathe through sympathy with the Italians. The magnetic touch which is required to inflame the imagination of the North,

is derived from Italy. The nightingales of English song who make our oak and beech copses resonant in spring with purest melody, are migratory birds, who have charged their souls in the South with the spirit of beauty, and who return to warble native woodnotes in a tongue which is their own.

He is talking, of course, of purely literary debt, as well as of the fruits of actual experience of the south. What is significant is the extremely high importance that Symonds assigns to the debt to Italy, a debt which is not to its civilisation, nor to the moral qualities of its early Christian art, but simply to the amorally inspiring effect of its atmosphere. In making this kind of stress, Symonds is creating the new, decadent attitude to Italy. His lines on Capri are characteristic:

> Capri, the perfect island—boys and girls
>　　Free as spring-flowers, straight, fair, and musical
> Of movement; in whose eyes and clustering curls
>　　The youth of Greece still lingers; whose feet fall
>　　Like kisses on green turf by cypress tall
> And pine-tree shadowed; who, unknowing care,
> Draw love and laughter from the innocent air.

It is, of course, well known that what really attracted Symonds to the feeling of the 'youth of Greece' in Italy was the beauty of Italian boys and young men, and he introduces to writing about Italy that atmosphere of homosexuality which then pervades the literary treatment of Italians, at least until Lawrence (and in more recent novels, like Donald Windham's *Two People* (1966) and Francis King's *A Domestic Animal* (1969)). In passages like the following, one is struck by the new note, and perhaps particularly by the contrast with the vigour with which Byron had celebrated the eyes of Italian peasant girls; Symonds, however, becomes ecstatic about the men:

> O the beautiful eyes of the contadini!
> O the ring of their voices on the hill-sides!
> O their gravity, grace of antique movement—
> Driving furrows athwart the autumnal cornland,
> Poised like statues above the laden axles
> Drawn by tardy majestic oxen homewards!
> What large melody fills you, ye divine youths,
> Meet companions of old Homeric heroes?

Some positive advances resulted from the introduction of the homosexual theme. In a particular case, his own propensities allowed Symonds to be fairly explicit, in his biography, about Michelangelo's homosexuality, a subject about which earlier biographers had been either ignorant or silent. It was also a considerable force in drawing sympathetic attention to the common life of Italy: lines like those above are obviously utterly unlike the eighteenth century's blanket contempt for all living Italians, while an essay in *Italian Byways* on **"The Gondolier's Wedding"** celebrates the happiness and amusement of an event in the domestic life of the ordinary people of Venice in a way which clearly owes something to George Sand.

But against these positive aspects of the work, one must weigh a sense of a certain thinness in the achievement. In

Symonds' Venice one feels painfully the lack of a Byronic toughness and openness to experience. Paradoxically, Byron, who stressed the melancholy and decay of the city, conveys far more vitality in his pictures of Venice than does Symonds, who ostensibly sets out to ignore the decay and extract the lasting genius of the city; there is always the danger that in seeking the aethereal one will become vapid; or that, Clough-like, one will find oneself tormented by the strength of the unbeautiful in the world, as is the case of the hero of Symonds' Venetian sonnet sequence, *Vagabunduli Libellus* (1884), which echoes, though adds nothing to, Clough's treatment of Venice. (Symonds wrote articles on Clough in 1866 and in 1868 helped his widow with her edition of the poems.) And in his account of the Renaissance, though his sympathies are much wider than Ruskin's, the effect of his work is much narrower, since he lacks the intensity and intellectual rigour with which Ruskin raises fundamental questions and stimulates the reader to thought far beyond the immediate significance of the particular work of art or architecture that happens to be under discussion.

However, the place of Symonds' work in the history of English attitudes to Italy is considerable. . . . [Browning originated] the typical modern attitudes to Italy; Symonds we may regard as filling out and popularising these attitudes, providing his readers with the example and the information which would give them a feeling of the frisson of the past whenever they went to Italy. Gibbon's volumes on Rome had marked the end of an epoch; when Symonds' seven volumes on the Renaissance took their place on the bookshelves of the upper middle classes they marked the opening of a new age of touristic values. Put beside any of the major [Victorian] works on Italy . . ., Symonds' books, despite their bulk, seem rather lightweight and superficial; but doubtless these very qualities contributed to his popularity and importance. (pp. 116-22)

> Kenneth Churchill, "The Victorians and the Renaissance," in his Italy and English Literature: 1764-1930, Barnes & Noble Books, 1980, pp. 116-28.

Peter Allan Dale   (essay date 1988)

[*In the following excerpt, Dale elucidates the influence of nineteenth-century philosophical thought and scientific speculation on Symonds's histories. He further discusses the effects of the author's homosexuality on the character of his work, pointing out that for Symonds, "true freedom lies not in the abstract progress of humanity towards a rational civilization, but in the release of humanity from . . . the endless antagonism of pagan and Christian, body and soul."*]

All historical discourse, says Hayden White [in his *Tropics of Discourse: Essays in Cultural Criticism*, 1978], is "tropological," a form of "emplotment" analogous to that engaged in by literary artists. "What the historian must bring to his consideration of the record are general notions of the *kinds of stories* that might be found there. . . . In other words, the historian must draw upon a fund of culturally provided *mythoi* in order to constitute the facts as figuring a story of a particular kind . . ." So common-

place has this post-modernist revision of orthodox historiography become that one is embarrassed to mention it. Still, mentioning it serves to prepare the point that in Symonds, self-consciously scientific historian though he is, we are no less likely than with his Romantic predecessors to find the past read in terms of contemporary *mythoi*. Ironically, John Addington Symonds himself makes the point in the very process of defending himself against criticism that he has had didactic designs on his reader. Of course it is true, he writes in the "Conclusion" of volume five of *The Renaissance of Italy*, one must write history objectively "without didactic objects." "We cannot extract from the Renaissance a body of ethical teaching . . . applicable to the altered . . . condition of the nineteenth century." But fewer than three pages later he allows himself the use of metaphors that suggest his critics may have had a point. What is so wonderful about the fifteenth- and sixteenth-century Italians, he concludes, is that at "a certain moment of . . . evolution" they nobly sacrificed their own interests for the advance of the human race. "This lends the interest of romance or drama" to the "tale" of the Renaissance. Clearly in his less guarded rhetorical moment, Symonds reveals that he does think of what he is doing as telling a particular kind of story, a story of human progress ("evolution"), a "romance" with "dramatic" conflict, and so on. What his metahistorical story is, what its source is, and how it differs from the stories told of this pivotal era by other Victorians is the subject of what follows.

Some sense of that difference and how significantly implicated it is in contemporary, that is, nineteenth-century, *mythoi*, is suggested by the review to which Symonds was probably responding in the remarks just cited. Writing for the *Quarterly* in 1877, W. J. Courthope complained of what he took to be an attempt on Symonds' part, as on the part of several recent admirers of the Renaissance, to purvey, under the guise of history, a "religion of culture," a religion which seeks "to revive Paganism as did the Humanists of medieval Italy, and with the same results." Like Ruskin, Courthope obviously worried over the threat to Christianity raised by this new, Renaissance-inspired humanism. But while he certainly was reading other admirers of the period and their objective correctly, he had strangely missed the point of Symonds' story. Had he read more attentively he would have seen that it was not humanism but another sort of gospel altogether Symonds was inscribing, namely, as the latter later put it [in his *Walt Whitman: A Study*, 1893], "that larger religion to which the modern world is being led . . . [by the] scientific view of the universe."

Courthope's is an instructive misreading. Just as a desire to understand the mentality of the Renaissance was almost automatically associated in his time with the "religion of culture" (humanism), so it is in ours. Only with us that new faith tends to be called not humanism, but hermeneutics, and its antagonist is not the old religion of Christianity but the still newer one of science (positivism). We may see this position developed in Husserl, Cassirer, Gadamer, Habermas, and a host of modern voices. From such a perspective, Symonds' reading of the Renaissance is remarkable, finding, as it were, in the very womb of modern humanism the seed of the enemy to come. So what we are exploring is not simply a particular—and largely forgotten—reading of a historical period, but a larger conflict of nineteenth-century ideologies (or *mythoi*), for which the meaning of the Renaissance became a crucial battleground. (pp. 109-10)

In the writing of his seven volumes on the Renaissance (1876-86), Symonds drew on all the major sources, traditional and modern—Vasari, Muratori, Roscoe, Sismondi, Ruskin, Rio, Michelet, Burckhardt, Crowe and Cavalcaselle, de Sanctis, to name only the more prominent. But the fundamental pattern of universal history according to which the Renaissance becomes a pivotal epoch in the progress of mankind almost certainly came to him from Hegel whom he, like many other bright Oxford undergraduates in the 1860s, was learning to think of as the premier metaphysician of the century. Hegel does not, in fact, write much about the Renaissance itself (he does not even use the word), but as he approaches the final section of the *Vorlesungen über die Philosophie der Geschichte,* (delivered 1830-31), that devoted to the triumphant arrival of *Geist* at its "modern" phase, he briefly evokes the "Revival of Learning" and "flourishing of the Fine Arts" in fifteenth- and sixteenth-century Italy as the first hopeful sign of man's emergence from the darkness of Medieval Catholicism into the light of the "Human Spirit"; it is "that blush of dawn, which after long storms first betokens the return of a bright and glorious day." (p. 111)

[Hegel's] concept of the Renaissance as the emergence of "Human Spirit," in dialectical opposition to an outmoded theism, had a profound effect on the historical vision of later nineteenth-century thinkers in search of an alternative to Christianity. Among these I would include Michelet, Burckhardt, George Eliot, Renan, Matthew Arnold, Dilthey, de Sanctis, and Pater. For all these writers, whether professional historians, critics, or artists, the Renaissance marks the signal movement of history towards a synthesis of pagan and medieval worldviews into a transcendant "gospel of culture." Burckhardt's closing paean to the age is characteristic. "Here the stream of medieval mysticism flows in the same current with Platonic doctrine, and with a characteristically modern spirit. Perhaps one of the most precious fruits of the discovery of the world and of man comes to maturity here, on whose account alone the Italian Renaissance must be called the mother of our modern age" [Burckhardt, *The Civilization of the Renaissance in Italy*]. In short, following Hegel the Renaissance becomes a trope at once for the self-generated, dialectical movement of history and its ultimate goal of human emancipation. Hence its appeal to the later, decreasingly Christian half of the century.

The influence of Hegel on Symonds is apparent from the outset of his career. He was reading in the German philosopher's work as early as 1860, probably under the guidance of T. H. Green, his future brother-in-law and a famous purveyor of Hegelianism among Oxonians. In his first published work, the 1863 prize essay on the Renaissance, Hegel enters almost immediately. "What," asks Symonds, "was the Renaissance?" and offers two opposing interpretations, one, in effect, Ruskin's, that it was a "de-

plorable" period of religious "decadence," the other, Hegel's, which we can identify as Hegel's by the young scholar's virtual quotation of the key passage from the *Vorlesungen . . .*: "others hail it as the dawning of a brief but glorious day." It is, of course, the second, positive reading of the period that Symonds is promoting as he echoes Hegel's point that with the Renaissance began the decisively "modern" spirit. More than a decade later when he is about to embark on his *magnum opus,* the Hegelian motif comes out unmistakably in the "Conclusion" to *Greek Poets,* second series (1876), which, in effect, provides the theoretical framework of the work to come.

> . . . [H]owever human progress is ruled by thesis and antithesis, by antagonism and repulsion in its several moments, still nothing can be lost that has been clearly gained. Each synthesis though itself destined to apparent contradiction, combines the indestructible, the natural and truly human, elements of the momenta which preceded it. . . . Thus the Greek conception of life was posed; the Christian conception was counterposed; the synthesis, crudely attempted in the age of the Renaissance, awaits mature accomplishment in the immediate future.

Here we also note that what Hegel meant by the modern spirit is apparently what Symonds means by it. "The history of the Renaissance is . . . the history of the attainment of self-conscious freedom by the human spirit manifested in the European races . . . The force then generated still continues, vital and expansive, in the spirit of the modern world." The central problem, not only of history but of philosophy in general, is, for Symonds no less than for Hegel, defining the exact nature of this consummate modern synthesis of human freedom.

But as we pursue Symonds' efforts to comprehend the modern spirit, we find merging with and ultimately overshadowing the German's influence, that of the first great elaborator of the latter's sparse remarks on the meaning of the Renaissance, the French historian, Jules Michelet. Michelet, the seventh volume of whose monumental *History of France* effectively founded Renaissance studies, follows Hegel, only to diverge from him on precisely this critical question of the meaning of freedom. Symonds, who used Michelet as well as Hegel for his undergraduate essay, read the French writer with increasing attention and became, in the end, his true continuator in contrast to the other great contemporary interpreters of the Renaissance who, while they may have learned from Michelet, adhered finally not to his, but to Hegel's understanding of the period's philosophical significance. (pp. 111-13)

Some departure from Hegel is implicit in the decision to concentrate on the Renaissance as the moment of human emancipation most in need of historical elaboration. For Hegel, again, had merely mentioned the period in passing, so eager was he to get on to the historical moment that mattered most to him, the German Reformation, a continuation, as he saw it, of what the Italians had started, but of far greater consequence. Our best key to the difference focus on the Renaissance makes lies by way of Michelet's famous formula [in his *Histoire de france*] for the period: "la découverte du monde, la découverte de l'homme." The "world" here is specifically the natural world, and the Renaissance's discovery of man and world, for Michelet, is finally the discovery of the conjunction of the two in man's derivation from the natural, the *terra mater*. Thus it is Leonardo, rather than Pico or Raphael or Michelangelo, who seems to Michelet to be the period's representative man. In the face of his art, "you are fascinated and troubled, a boundlessness affects you by a strange magnetism. . . . This canvas draws me, calls me, invades me. . . . This astonishing magician, Italian brother of Faust . . . stands alone as a prophet of the sciences . . ." (my translation). For the Renaissance, Michelet concludes, "the sovereign is Nature. And he will be triumphant on whom she bestows her smile, her pledge of eternal youth. Younger and older than all, mother and nurse of the gods, as of men, she lulls them back to ancient days and will smile over their tombs 'Follow Nature, this is the greeting the Renaissance addresses to us, its first word. And it is the last word of Reason' " (my translation). Michelet's last sentence, aimed as it almost certainly is at Hegel, serves to underline the critical difference in his understanding of the "modern."

For Hegel, the progress of spirit is nothing if not a departure from nature. To identify human emancipation with the Reformation, Protestantism, Germany, and the state rather than with the Renaissance, Catholicism, Italy, and art, is to insist on this point, to insist that the only proper human freedom is the realization of a rational order that transmutes or represses (depending on how one reads Hegel) the natural, the merely sensuous, instinctual, and primitive in man. "[T]he very essence of superstition [is] the fettering of the mind to a sensuous object, a mere Thing . . . for Spirit, having renounced its proper nature in its most essential quality . . . has lost its Freedom, and is held in adamantine bondage to what is alien to itself. . . . By Nature man is not what he ought to be; only through a transforming process does he arrive at the truth. . . . [The] individual is evil only when the Natural manifests itself in mere sensual desire . . ." With the Reformation, spirit at last discovers its "proper nature." "Thought is the grade to which Spirit has now advanced. It involves the Harmony of Being in the purest essence . . ." [*The Philosophy of History*]. For Michelet, to privilege the Renaissance over the Reformation is profoundly to question this over-hasty move of Hegel's to reason as man's proper nature. It is to draw on what were, traditionally, the two salient features of the period, its revival of paganism and its triumphs in the sensuous realms of painting and sculpture, to make the metahistorical point that man's proper nature might not, after all, be as rational as Hegel would wish. All the late nineteenth-century interpreters of the Renaissance—Burckhardt, Arnold, Renan, George Eliot, et al.—were bound by their very interest in the period to give the natural a more sympathetic hearing than Hegel had done, but, in the end, all saw the direction of history initiated by the Renaissance as proceeding away from nature toward reasoned culture. Only Symonds follows Michelet in what we may regard as the latter's concerted effort to free himself from the Hegelian metaphysic of reason.

With Michelet, Symonds insists that the human emancipation that begins in the Renaissance involves a return to, not a flight from, nature. For him still more explicitly than for Michelet, nature is mother earth in a sensuous, specifically sexual sense: The Renaissance brings the "resurrection of the human body"; it attests "to the delightfulness of physical existence, to the inalienable rights of natural desire, and to the participation of mankind in pleasures held in common by us with the powers of earth and sea and air." The principal cultural implications of this reorientation of Hegel are subsequently developed by Symonds in ways anticipated by Michelet. Both writers, for example, find in the Renaissance a healthy rejection of Christian asceticism. Symonds is almost obsessed with orthodox religion's constraint of human nature, and his language toward it reflects a desire not simply to usher it gently off the historical stage (in the manner, say, of Renan or Arnold) but to see the curtain brought mercilessly down. "The Renaissance shattered and destroyed [the "ascetic rules" of the Church], rending the thick veil which they had drawn between the mind of man and the outer world, and flashing the light of reality upon the darkened places of his own nature." Far more than Michelet he is preoccupied with the impending "ruin" that hangs over the dawn of the modern in the form of the Catholic revival of the Counter Reformation, which "gives the aspect of tragedy to much of my work." Again, on the political side, the return to nature involves for both writers a recognition of each individual's organic oneness with the mass of humanity despite his/her class origins. This, Michelet maintains, is the "prophecy" of Michelangelo's Sistine frescoes: "an heroic people born of justice who will establish justice in the world" (my translation). From the French historian, Symonds takes the notion of the Renaissance as the "first act" in a "drama of liberty" that culminates in the "French Revolution" with the achievement of total democracy as history's finest goal. What "the word Renaissance really means is new birth to liberty—the spirit of mankind recovering consciousness and the power of self-determination . . . [establishing] the principle of political freedom." Like his much-admired Whitman, though along independent and considerably more restrained lines, Symonds joins with Michelet (and anticipates Marcuse) in believing the emancipation of the natural self must issue in political equality. Hegel, one recalls, had little use either for the French Revolution or the voice of the people: "it is a dangerous and false prejudice, that the People *alone* have reason and insight, and know what justice is . . ."—as dangerous and false, no doubt, as reducing spirit to "mere physical desire" [Hegel, *Philosophy of Right,* 1952].

But the implication of Michelet's revision of Hegel that had the greatest intellectual impact on Symonds is what we may broadly call epistemological. By the time he wrote *The Renaissance,* Michelet had come to assume that a particular kind of knowledge must underlie or authorize all our discourse on humanity, namely scientific knowledge. (pp. 113-16)

The "renaissance" of the human spirit in fifteenth-century Italy Michelet imaginatively associated with his own individual "renovation." Returning to his book on the period, we see clearly that its account of the age's return to nature is intimately connected with his belief that it is also the age that marks the rise of modern science; it is the "age of science and of childishness at the same time." Science is the Renaissance's "evangile eternel" [*Oeuvres Complètes*]. Symonds, as we have intimated, was no less moved than Michelet by the evangel of modern science. We shall have occasion later to consider the difference between Symond's science and Michelet's; for the moment we need to see how the former elaborates upon the latter in his reading of the Renaissance.

> Interpretation belongs to the essential unity of understanding. One must take up into himself what is said to him in such fashion that it speaks and finds an answer in words of his own language.
>
> Gadamer

Wallace Ferguson [in *The Renaissance in Historical Thought,* 1948] has called Symonds the first British practitioner of *Kulturgeschichte,* a notoriously difficult term to define but, broadly speaking, a history that seeks to reconstruct the cultural identity of a period, its characteristic mental outlook, by examining several different structures of thought current at the time, religious, political, aesthetic, ethical, and so on. As its most renowned nineteenth-century practitioner Jacob Burckhardt put it [in his *Civilization of the Renaissance in Italy*], "Not politics but culture. . . . Not according to nations or chronology but according to the pervasive spiritual currents. . . . Not princes and their dynasties but people and their development in a common spirit." Put another way, *Kulturgeschichte* seeks to replace the rather easy metaphysical totalities of a previous generation of historians with a painstaking analysis of the multiplicity of "currents" which make up an age's distinctive character, the complex interrelationship of these currents, and, above all, their entirely human provenance in a particular historical situation.

The problem is that the more conscientiously the historian pursues the multiplicity underlying the supposed whole, the greater the risk he runs of losing sight of, even ceasing to believe in, that whole. This "ironic" possibility, as Hayden White has labeled it, lies just beyond the horizon of Symonds' many-volumed effort to identify the essential "type" of Renaissance mind. This type is always more in danger of eluding him, than it is, say, Burckhardt. "Over this vertiginous abyss of history," he cries Carlyle-like in the opening pages of his study, "how shall we guide our course?" In the end, he resolves the problem of multiplicity, of impending meaninglessness, in very much the way Hans Gadamer in the passage quoted above suggests all historians resolve it. The trouble, in Symonds' case, is that his own language is so strikingly discontinuous with that of the period he is interpreting. His principle of unity does not seem plausibly to dwell in the Renaissance at all. It is a distinctly paradoxical unifier, all too obviously applied retrospectively from the standpoint of the present, and, still more, from the standpoint of a discourse that is not really historical, as Hegel and his followers (such as Gadamer) have taught us to understand that word, for Symonds' unity is not finally a cultural but a biological concept. The common preoccupation with evoking and over-

coming multiplicity notwithstanding, Burckhardt and Symonds are writing in two entirely different metahistorical languages, and *Kulturgeschichte* may be an egregiously inappropriate term, after all, for that of Symonds.

Still, Symonds' **Renaissance** has drawn heavily on Burckhardt, to whom he acknowledges "especial obligations" in his opening volume. He divides his task into three general phases, the political/ethical, the philosophical/educational, and the aesthetic. Volume one, **The Age of Despots** (1876), begins as political history but merges into moral and religious concerns; volume two, **The Revival of Learning** (1877), covers the development of Renaissance philosophy and education, or "humanism"; volumes three through five, **The Fine Arts** (1877) and **Italian Literature** (two volumes, 1881), trace the period's aesthetic history. These five volumes, in effect, go over the same period, roughly 1400-1550, from several different perspectives, much in the manner of the more concentrated "parts" of Burckhardt's single-volume study, "The State As A Work of Art," "The Development of the Individual," "The Revival of Antiquity," etc. Symonds' final two volumes, **The Catholic Reaction** (1886), are a sequel, covering roughly 1550-1650 and rehearsing the "tragic," albeit temporary, defeat of the modern spirit.

In addition to seeing Symonds' first five volumes as treatments of the separate cultural "strands" (his term) that make up the same whole, we find in them a progressive movement toward articulating exactly what that whole is, or rather what it is that allows one to think of it as a whole. If we look closely at the first volume, we find that, while the apparent subject is political history, the overriding theme is disunity, a problem which Symonds not only sees as characteristic of fifteenth- and sixteenth-century Italian society but feels as a threat to his own historical discourse: ". . . we everywhere discern the want of a co-ordinating principle, The old religion had died; but there is no new faith." There is an abstract confidence that things must come right at last: "Art, Learning, Literature, Statecraft, Philosophy, Science build a sacred and inviolable city of the soul amid the tumult of seven thousand revolutions . . ." But what exactly is that "city of the soul"? We are not told in **The Age of Despots,** largely, one suspects, because Symonds himself is not yet sure what he means by it beyond a "spontaneous outburst of intelligence." In the absence of a more definitive answer, disunity remains the message, totality a goal that the discourse only looks forward to.

In the succeeding volume Symonds moves from an evocation of the absence of order to what amounts to the construction of a pseudo-order. He considers the proposition that the "spirit of intelligence" that formed the motive force of the Renaissance manifested itself most importantly in the return to classical learning or humanism, and gives an extensive account, the most extensive in English to date, of the several stages through which Renaissance humanism developed. Reviewing the first three volumes of **The Renaissance** in 1877, Edmund Gosse saw in this second volume Symonds' most original contribution to a growing scholarly industry. Gosse almost certainly had not read Burckhardt, for volume two is precisely where

"Am Hof," Symonds's home in Davos Platz.

Symonds comes closest to his Swiss predecessor, for whom the revival of classical antiquity is the intellectual center of the period and Pico della Mirandola, its pre-eminent spokesman. This point is taken up by Symonds, for whom Pico's "Oration on the Dignity of Man" is the "Epiphany of the modern spirit, contraposing God and man in a relation inconceivable to the ancients, unapprehended . . . by the Middle Ages." But the further one reads in the volume—and here Gosse . . . misses the point—the more it appears that, far from embracing Burckhardt's thesis, his unifying principle, Symonds is testing and ultimately rejecting it. The "revival of learning," he agrees, was an important beginning of the emancipation of the men's thought, but it could not become an adequate basis for a new belief. The humanists were "too ready to make culture all in all, and lost thereby the opportunity of grounding a rational philosophy of life upon a solid basis for the modern world." Humanism's "essential weakness" lies in a refinement without strength, a commitment to "no law beyond taste" and a tendency to decline into mere "eloquence" and "play of words." When Symonds goes on to suggest that this is a disability inherited by the modern products of Oxbridge, we see that his discussion of humanism, whatever it says about the Renaissance, also has a distinctly contemporary target in view. We have only to recall Arnold's contemporary prophecy of culture with its paean to Oxford and the *litterae humaniores,* "unravaged by the fierce intellectual life of our century," to get a fair idea of what this might be. The originality of Symonds' second volume lies finally not in its focus on humanism but in its deliberate divergence from Burckhardt's, Arnold's, Pater's, and others' efforts to derive from Renaissance humanism a "solid [philosophical] basis for the modern world," efforts which, as we have seen, continue into our own century.

Moving to the topic of fine art in his third volume, Symonds is now ready to offer a tentative—and not unexpected—solution to the problem of unity. In the aesthetic "mode of thinking," especially as it is expressed in painting, lies the "coordinating principle" that justifies us in thinking the Renaissance a distinct entity or epoch. "Art supplies the spiritual oxygen, without which the life of the Renaissance must have been atrophied. . . . [He] who would comprehend the Italians of the Renaissance must study their art, and cling fast to that Ariadne-thread throughout the labyrinthine windings of national character." Not Catholicism or despotism, or humanism, but aestheticism is the key to the Renaissance spirit, the first and noblest expression of the "freedom of the modern mind." Here the problem of originality becomes acute, as Gosse notes, for Symonds' quest for a unifying structure of consciousness seems at last to have led him to what everyone had assumed was the salient contribution of the Italian Renaissance to European civilization, and what all too many, even as early as 1877 had written about—

Stendhal, Rio, Ruskin, Jameson, Burckhardt, Crowe and Calvalcaselle, and, most recently and probably, for Symonds, most threateningly, Walter Pater. Still he does manage to achieve a new perspective, one which involves a significant revision not only of the meaning of Renaissance art but of the relation of aesthetic consciousness in general to the development of human thought.

In his interpretation of Renaissance painting, Symonds takes up a standard position but insists upon it to a degree that distinguishes him from his predecessors. The "frank" expression of "sensuality" is the characteristic note of Renaissance art; it celebrates, above all, in Symonds' bold phrase . . . , "physical existence and the inalienable right of natural desire." This is not only Ruskin utterly reversed, but, more interestingly, Pater extended to an extreme of "naturalism" (Symonds' term) that would have made that worshipper of Greek "Heiterkeit" quite uncomfortable. Pater, for all his emphasis on the sensuous embodiment of the idea, still clings to that idea with a tenacity that Symonds cannot accept. Art for Pater, as for many good Victorians before him, must have those "intellectual and spiritual ideas," lest it "fever the conscience" [Pater, *The Renaissance: Studies in Art and Poetry*]. At heart, Pater is in his own phrase (applied to Marius), *anima naturaliter Christiana,* an aesthete but also very much an ascetic. For Symonds the glory of Renaissance art is precisely its capacity for unsettling the conscience. This comes out nowhere more strikingly than in his account of the "pain" of "awakening to life" experienced by Michelangelo as his instinctual devotion to the human body carries him beyond the Christianity he is supposed to be illustrating. Symonds may not be as subtle a critic as Pater, but his response to Renaissance painting represents a more revolutionary gesture—the most revolutionary of any contemporary commentator on that painting—toward the validation, rather than sublimation, of the sensuous and the instinctual.

But it is less as a critic here than as an intellectual historian that Symonds is interesting. From this standpoint the originality of his treatment of Renaissance art lies in his argument that the artistic "mode of thinking," which became dominant in fifteenth-century Italy, is less important for the masterpieces it produced than as an intellectual force for liberation which, in retrospect, one sees, worked powerfully to subvert the hegemony of the Church and its restraints on human self-realization. Art, in other words, was offering itself at this historical moment as an alternative "spiritual empire" to the Church's, and, from Symonds' point of view, a far more progressive one than humanism. Yet when we consider closely this imperial aspect of art, or rather the artistic "mode of thinking," we find, says Symonds, a defect in it. . . . There is, Symonds maintains, a "doublemindedness" about the new "naturalism", a lingering spiritual resistance that will eventually surface with a vengeance in the Counter-Reformation. The contrast with Pater, again, needs bringing out. Though he claims to be writing only art history in his *Renaissance,* Pater clearly has a larger end in view, namely, the affirmation of a distinctly *aesthetic* humanism not only as the basis of Renaissance totality but also as the basis of a desired modern totality. Accordingly, he emphasizes not

the doublemindedness but the completeness or repose (*Heiterkeit*) of the period's mentality. It is the completeness to which we must look back in order to go forward. Symonds, as [René] Wellek long ago observed, is no aesthete. For him the case for aesthetic totality, while it may be historically more appropriate for the Renaissance and philosophically more forward-looking than that for Burckhardt's humanistic totality, masks a deeper structure of which it is only a sign or, better, an immature expression. What this is becomes apparent in his closing volumes.

We pass over the discussion of literature in volumes four and five, which adds little of theoretical consequence to what has already been said, and proceed directly to the "Conclusion" to the fifth volume, the last one of the study of the Renaissance proper. Here Symonds tells us that, difficult as the "journey" has been, he has at last achieved the "vantage-ground of contemplation, whence the conclusions [of each separate stage] can be surveyed in their relation to each other" and an idea of the whole presented. The whole, it turns out, can be grasped only from the position of the present, and the guiding intellectual principle of the present is physical science.

> To trace the continuity of civilization through the labyrinths of chance and error and suspended energy, apparent to a superficial glance or partial knowledge, but on closer observation and a wider sweep of vision found to disappear, is the highest aim of the historian. The germ of the new motive of man's life upon our planet was contained in the cardinal intuition of the Renaissance. . . . It [later] assumed the dignity of organized speculation in German philosophies of history, and in the positive philosophy of Auguste Comte. It has received its most powerful corroboration from recent physical discoveries, and has acquired firmer consistency in the Darwinian speculation.

With this *terminus ad quem* firmly before us, we can, in fact, return to all that has gone before and discern what at first reading is not so obvious, namely, how each successive volume in its own way and with increasing purposiveness adumbrates the promised end. Thus the lament in **The Age of Despots** over the want of a common basis of belief in the Renaissance—"the old religion has died; but there is no new faith"—is followed by an adumbration of one to come—"science has not been born." Again, **The Revival of Learning,** the humanist movement initiated by Petrarch fails to provide that desired basis for social order. What the world awaits, rather, is the new humanism of a Goethe, who can claim "superiority of humanism above Petrarch . . . by right of his participation in the scientific spirit." In **The Fine Arts,** an antithesis, initially established between the Renaissance's aesthetic mode of thinking and the modern scientific one, ultimately becomes a continuity, a point Symonds, like Michelet, finds it easiest to make with the example of da Vinci. "Lionardo . . . felt the primal sympathies that bind men to earth, their mother, and to living things, their brethren. . . . [The] borderland between humanity and nature allured him with a spell half aesthetic and half scientific. . . . The time was not yet come for accurate physiological investigation, or for the true birth of the scientific spirit. . . . "

We may quickly round out the story Symonds tells of the Renaissance and the modern spirit. The ensuing two volumes of *The Counter Reformation* rehearse the fall of the nascent modern spirit before the revitalized forces of Christianity: "the Church awoke to a sense of her peril . . . [and carried on] a war of extermination against the two-fold Liberalism of Renaissance and Reformation." Fortunately, the "extermination" was not complete. The modern spirit survived, most notably in the figure of the sixteenth-century philosopher and martyr, Giordano Bruno, a heroic counterpoint for Symonds to the false religious prophet Savonarola, and the precursor of Goethe and of Darwin.

> . . . [Bruno] appears before us as the man who most vitally and comprehensively grasped the leading tendencies of his age in their intellectual essence. He left behind him the medieval conception of an extra-mundane God, creating a finite world of which this globe is the centre, and the principal episode in the history of which is a series of events from the Fall, through the Incarnation and Crucifixion, to the Last Judgment. He substituted the conception of an ever-living, ever-acting, ever self-effectuating God, immanent in an infinite universe, to the contemplation of whose attributes the mind of man ascends by the study of Nature and interrogation of his conscience.

So, "tragic" as the intervention of the Counter-Reformation may have been, the overall shape of history is actually comedic. The modern spirit, born in the Renaissance but, as it were, disguised in aesthetic naturalism, finds itself temporarily blocked by the old religion, yet it survives to be reborn, "metamorphosed" into its "true" form, the religion of nineteenth-century science. We need now to look more closely at Symonds' version of this new gospel. (pp. 116-23)

. . . . .

How, asks Walter Pater, are we moderns to achieve that consummate (singleminded) reconciliation of paganism and Christianity that characterizes Renaissance art? The Hegelian antithesis at the heart of Pater's question underlies later nineteenth-century efforts to define a gospel of culture. How does one reconcile the great opposing interpretations of humanity? Are we earth-grown or heaven-sent? Pater's answer:

> A modern scholar occupied by this problem might observe that all religions . . . arise spontaneously out of the human mind . . . that every intellectual product must be judged from the point of view of the age . . . in which it was produced. He might go so far as to observe that each has contributed something to the development of the religious sense. . . . The basis of the reconciliation of the religious of the world would thus be the inexhaustible activity and creativeness of the human mind itself, in which all religions alike have their root, and in which all alike

are reconciled [*The Renaissance: Studies in Art and Poetry*].

Whatever its ontological origin, the constitutive mind is what now distinguishes us, and in its spontaneous, ongoing need to create a mental world in which it will be at home lies the solution to all contrarieties and our hope for the future. (pp. 123-24)

It is likely that Symonds had Pater's discussion of the reconciliation of pagan and Christian sentiment in mind when he approached the same "riddle" early in **The Fine Arts.** Raphael's painting, he writes, accomplished a more vital harmony between pagan and Christian than any other artist of the period. But this still falls short of an adequate "modern synthesis." Such a synthesis is beyond the power of art, for, "Nothing but the scientific method can . . . enable us to reach that further point, outside both Christianity and Paganism, at which the classical ideal of a temperate and joyous natural life shall be restored to the conscience educated by the Gospel." An ensuing reference to Joachim de Floris as a twelfth-century prophet of science is taken directly from Michelet and serves to remind us how closely Symonds follows the French historian in his understanding of where the "further point" is to be found.

For Michelet the greatest of modern scientific thinkers was Goethe and after him Lamarck and Geoffroy de Saint Hilaire. Darwin he did not read until 1862, and the word "evolution" he studiously avoided, preferring "transformationism" or the Goethean "metamorphosis." His focus was biological and his understanding of the mind's relation to nature of a piece with the "romantic" or idealist biology we associate with Goethe and Geoffroy and, still more, Schelling and Oken. The story of this early movement in biological science has been told elsewhere and needs no rehearsing here. Its guiding principle is the unity of all life in an ongoing process of development or "metamorphosis" from an original un-structure.

Symonds likewise looks back to Goethe as the great initiator of modern science, but for him the German has more recent and wider ranging heirs. Chief among these is Darwin, and to Darwin we may add two pioneers of thermodynamics, Helmholtz (offered with Darwin in 1886 as one of the two "types" of modern science) and John Tyndall (implicitly offered in 1887 [Symonds, **"The Progress of Thought in Our Time,"** *Fortnightly Review* 47] as the latest in a "progress of thought" that runs from Bruno through Goethe to Comte, and Darwin). Finally, Herbert Spencer's synthetic philosophy, with its application of evolutionism to all forms of human behavior, probably did more than anything else to convince Symonds that evolution must be the key to modern thought. Following these mentors, Symonds extends Michelet's essentially terrestrial, biological continuum into what he is fond of calling a "cosmic" continuum, and shifts the conceptualization of unity from the metaphor of structure or form to that of force or energy. Both developments signal a distinctly new phase in the scientific revolution or, rather, in man's effort to accommodate himself to that revolution.

In concluding the second series of his *Greek Poets* (1876), Symonds gives us a thumbnail sketch of modern scientific thought, a sketch in which evolutionism is everywhere implicit but appears explicitly not in a biological but a physical context. "The establishment of the law of the conservation of force has demonstrated the unity of all *cosmical* operations from the most gigantic to the most minute . . . ." We must now understand God "as the name of a hitherto unapprehended energy, the symbol of that which is the life and motion of the universe whereof we are a part. . . . To obey God in the moral order is to act in accordance with the [physical laws of energy] that have carried the races [as they have carried the cosmos] onwards. . . . " Symonds cites Helmholtz as a principal source for this new cosmic perspective on man's moral nature, but a more important source is almost certainly Tyndall, whose work Symonds had been reading since at least 1863 and whose controversial "Belfast Lecture" had come out just two years before. In that lecture, Tyndall contended that the "doctrine of the Conservation of Energy" was continuous with that of biological evolution, but "of still wider grasp and more radical significance," "bringing vital as well as physical phenomena under the dominion of that law of causal connection which . . . asserts itself everywhere in nature." "All we see around us, and all we feel within us— the phenomena of physical nature as well as those of the human mind—have their unsearchable roots in the cosmical life. . . . The impregnable position of science may be described in a few words. We claim, and we shall wrest, from theology the entire domain of cosmological theory" [Tyndall, *Fragments of Science,* 1897]. Three years later the brilliant Cambridge mathematician and scientific philosopher W. K. Clifford took up Tyndall's point—and a phrase from Symonds' close friend Henry Sidgwick—to describe what he took to be the coming modern religious sentiment: "cosmic emotion."

> We consider [our cosmos] . . . not a statical thing but a vast series of events. We want to contemplate . . . the history of its changes . . . The great use [of the nebular hypothesis] is to show that the life upon the earth must have been evolved from inorganic matter. . . . We arrive . . . at a common principle . . . which has created the . . . world, so far as it is living. This principle is . . . then, a fit object for cosmic emotion. . . . In this principle . . . we must recognize the mother of life, and especially human life . . . biding her time in the whole expanse of heaven, to make the highest cosmos out of inorganic chaos . . . [Clifford, *Lectures and Essays,* 1886].

Such efforts as these to impart a religious significance to modern science abound in the later-nineteenth, early-twentieth century. From Herbert Spencer's *First Principles* (1861) to Henri Bergson's *Creative Evolution* (1907), they form a distinct intellectual movement, whose attraction—apparent in the quotations from Tyndall and Clifford—was that it transmuted the profoundly disorienting implications of three closely related developments— Darwinism, physiological psychology, and the discovery of the conservation/dissipation of energy—into a comfortably optimistic philosophy. As J. H. Randall has observed, "cosmic evolutionary philosophy" became "the greatest and most seductive of the Romantic faiths" [Randall,

"The Changing Impact of Darwin on Philosophy," *Journal of the History of Ideas* 22 (1961)].

Applied to the understanding of history, Symonds' cosmic evolutionism produces an image of society, widely disseminated by Comte and Spencer, as an organism, in his own words, "evolving" by a "natural process" according to an "unwritten . . . law that governs human progress." The motive or "vital" force behind this progress is "human energy," which is the particular concern of the historian, as opposed, say, to chemical or electrical energy, but all energy is part of a continuous whole. More particularly, as a historian of the modern rather than ancient or medieval world, Symonds is concerned, at least initially, with "intellectual energy" or the energy of human "reason." Still more particularly, as Renaissance historian, he is concerned with the "outburst of intelligence" that gradually "metamorphoses" itself into a new "type of consciousness." This precocious modern type eventually disintegrates; the energy that generated it is temporarily "checked" by the Counter-Reformation. But it "flows" again towards a new flowering in the nineteenth century, and although Symonds expresses himself ignorant of the origins of the force and the exact mechanism by which social/cultural metamorphoses are produced, he has little doubt about its goal or final "type." Inherently unstable or "doubleminded," the Renaissance was a "phase through which . . . Europe was obliged to pass" before reaching its true synthesis: "this new gospel [of science] enables us to live daily and hourly in what Blake called 'eternity's sunrise,' the dawn of ever-broadening light and ever soaring expectation."

These words and the invocation of Blake well illustrate Randall's point about the "greatest Romantic faith." Although Symonds writes his history as if inspired by Darwin, he has carefully read out of Darwin (or perhaps never read in him) the rejection of teleology and with it the long-standing providential view of history as an inevitable progress toward human perfection. It was the denial of design, not the connection of men with apes, spirit with matter, that made real Darwinism so intolerable to theists, humanists, and positivists alike, and caused so many believers in science to rewrite evolution in more congenial terms. Providence, though never so named, in fact everywhere governs Symonds' concept of historical process in the form of natural law that "inevitably" leads mankind to the light of unending hope. It is easy, from the distance of over a century, to condescend to this sort of bowdlerizing of Darwin. But what we need to bear more in mind than the obvious failure (or refusal) to grasp the revolutionary implications of natural selection is that element of Darwinism and of the organic interpretation of human behavior in general that the cosmic evolutionists did retain.

In one crucial sense Randall's epithet of "romantic" is a misnomer for the sort of religious seduction offered by cosmic evolution. In the context of nineteenth-century theories of history, the most significant corollary of Symonds' evolutionism is the decidedly anti-Romantic subordination of the individual will to an ineluctable natural law. For Symonds' principal competitors, Burckhardt and Pater, the emergence of human individuality from the collective consciousness of medieval Catholics is a distinctive note of the Renaissance and the foundation of its claim to being the beginning of the modern spirit. As Pater quotes Blake [in Pater, *The Renaissance: Studies in Art and Poetry*], "the ages are all equal but genius is always above its age." Symonds' own symbolic use of Blake significantly transposes the motive force of history to the sun, a metonym, for Symonds, as for Tyndall, et al., for the physical, rather than mental, energy that drives the cosmos and with it, the microcosm of human culture. "After shifting the centre of gravity from men as personalities to men as exponents of their race and age, we gain a new interest in [history], a new sense of the spiritual vitality and solidarity of human thought. . . ." The theme of human "automatism" is thoroughly embedded in positivist philosophy of history. We find it as well as in the dialectical materialism of another great admirer (and misreader) of Darwin, Karl Marx: "It is not the consciousness of men that determines their being, but, on the contrary, their social being determines their consciousness" [Melvin Rader, *Marx's Interpretation of History*]. Marx's historical "holism" is no doubt far more sociologically sophisticated than what we find among the positivists, but its roots lie in the same scientific critique of Romantic individualism.

Here then we may mark the critical distinction between Michelet's scientific historicism and Symonds'. For Michelet, evolution, or rather "transformism," is still very much a Romantic religion. It affirms the unity of man and nature but leaves man triumphantly poised at the end of revolution, ready for what Michelet considered in archetypically Romantic fashion his Promethean mission of transforming the world. For a later generation of evolutionists, man's position shifted from an all-comprehending, all-commanding presence at the forefront of history, to a vanishing point against the background of a vast cosmic process. What Symonds and others, in fact, are grasping after is not the Romantic revision of Christianity, which M. H. Abrams has so thoroughly explored, but a much older, more primitive religious sentiment. Confronted with the absurdity of man's pretensions to individual significance, one throws oneself back on the mercy of an impersonal cosmic plan. Meaning no longer lies within the self but without. Our preeminent duty is not the Romantic-cum-Christian spiritual reordering of nature, but the wise subordination of spirit to the order of nature, a position Werner Jaeger locates among the preSocratics and identifies as the first emergence of genuinely religious thought among mankind. When Anaximander declares that the boundless cosmos encompasses and governs all things, he is expressing a demand "which religious thought has required of divinity from time immemorial" [Jaeger, *The Theology of the Early Greek Philosophers: The Gifford Lectures, 1936*]. Lucretius is the great Roman continuator of the preSocratic spirit—

> For it is not true, as I think, that the generations of mankind were let down from high heaven by some golden chair upon the fields, nor were they sprung from sea or waves beating upon the rocks, but the same earth generated them which feeds them now from herself [Lucretius, *De Rerum Natura,* trans. by W. H. D. Rouse].

—and Lucretius, says Symonds, stands "at the same point . . . as we, after the labors of Darwin and of Spencer, of Helmholz and of Huxley . . ." [Symonds, "Lucretius," *Fortnightly Review* 23 (1875)].

One of the Roman poet's most surprising arguments is that the acceptance of the mind's involvement in the web of natural causation is a form of freedom, and so we return to this question, the question at the heart of both humanist and positivist readings of the meaning of history. Symonds, we have seen, insists with Michelet, not to mention Hegel, Pater, and Burckhardt, that the Renaissance represents the first dawning of human freedom. But in what sense can Symonds be using the word if the spirit born in the Renaissance leads directly to the determinism of modern science? Certainly, in no Hegelian sense. To resolve this issue we need to move to a deeper level of Symonds' historical discourse. (pp. 124-29)

. . . . .

The Victorians, far more than ourselves, saw the ultimate object of science as the objectification of morality. For the most part this morality was simply the Christian one *redivivus,* a Victorian continuation of an earlier generation's preoccupation with natural theology. Still there developed, especially after the *Origin,* an important movement of ethical thought that sought to discover a genuinely scientific code of behavior, a code based on the growing evidence that the origin of mind is physical, the origin of human behavior, animal impulse. Such a morality, it became increasingly apparent, was not compatible with Christianity. On the contrary, it was a revolutionary morality with consequences far more unsettling to man's concept of himself than the threatened demise of God which figures so prominently in our standard accounts of the rise of scientific materialism. By Mill, Spencer, Lewes, Stephen, and many others, Victorians were told that what science means for human conduct is the necessity of acting according to the laws of the physical nature that is the source of our being. As W. K. Clifford put it, "human conduct is a subject for reverence only insofar as it is consonant to the demiurgic law, in harmony with the teaching of divine Nature. This . . . belongs to the essence of philosophic life . . . [and of] the scientific view of things." This is straightforward enough. Where the problem arises, however, is in one's definition of what exactly the "demiurgic" natural law is. For Spencer it is the spontaneous pursuit of self-interest. For Lewes and Stephen, on the contrary, it tends to be self-sacrificing concern for others. Mill is somewhere in between.

Far less adequately documented but more relevant to our present subject is an almost *subrosa* offshoot of this discussion, namely, the later nineteenth-century use of science to vindicate sexual desire as "in harmony" with nature—however out of harmony it may be with the precepts of both theistic and metaphysical morality (e.g., Hegel's). The pivotal document here is Darwin's *The Descent of Man and Selection in Relation to Sex,* the first widely distributed study in English to treat human sexuality as a scientific problem. The book, says Peter Gay [in his *Bourgeois Experience: Victoria to Freud,* 1984-86], "brought sexuality into the domain of the discussable." It did more than this. It treated sex as as natural to human behavior as it is to animal, and thus opened the way to a series of "scientific" discussions, which had in view nothing short of a moral revolution. The climactic, world-changing instance of these was the work of Sigmund Freud. Science, in short, was turned to the purpose of liberating repressed desire by naming it natural.

This agenda had been implicit in many arguments for a scientific morality that seemed to be working towards quite unexceptional ends, such as the vindication of altruism (Lewes) or the assertion of cosmic unity (Clifford). But by the 1880s it began to come out in its own distinctive voice in the work primarily of Carl Ulrichs, Richard von Kraft-Ebing, and Albert Moll in Germany, and, in England, Edward Carpenter and Havelock Ellis. Writing in a collection of essays entitled *The New Spirit* (1890), the last named defined that spirit, first generally as the scientific spirit—"wherever science goes the purifying breath of spring has passed and all things are recreated"—and then, specifically, as the scientifically authorized release from the "disease of the soul" into the full enjoyment of "physical love." For the scientific mind, "there is nothing in the loved one's body impure or unclean." Symonds was well read in Ulrichs, Kraft-Ebing, Moll, and Carpenter and became the friend and collaborator of Ellis. Insofar as he, like Michelet before him, formally pursued a scientific "alibi" apart from history, it was to write on human sexuality, portions of which work Ellis later incorporated into his monumental *Studies in the Psychology of Sex.* One may go further and opine that the principal object of Symonds' scientific enthusiasm was the problem of sex; that the cosmic force as it expressed itself in humanity he considered, finally, a form of sexual, not, as he was inclined to call it in the early volumes of *The Renaissance in Italy,* intellectual energy.

Of course, Symonds' primary concern was with a particular kind of sexual energy, that is, homosexual or, as he preferred to call it, "inverted" sexual energy. Phyllis Grosskurth has recently added to her excellent biographical scholarship on Symonds an edition of his *Memoirs,* which for late-twentieth-century readers may well become the one book by Symonds that is most worth reading. These memoirs give us one of the most explicit accounts of repressed—and not so repressed—sexual desire that we now have from the Victorians. As Grosskurth observes, it is "unique in the history of the genre," that genre being the nineteenth-century "confession" but mixed, in Symonds' case, with a strong element of the scientific treatise, as we see from this key statement of purpose.

> It was my primary object when I began these autobiographical notes to describe as accurately and candidly as I was able a type of character, which I do not at all believe to be exceptional, but which for various intelligible reasons has never been properly analysed. I wanted to supply material for the ethical psychologist and the student of mental pathology, by portraying a man of no mean talents, of no abnormal depravity, whose life has been perplexed from first to last by passion—natural, instinctive, healthy in his own particular case—but morbid and abominable from the point of view of the society in

which he lives—persistent passion for the male sex.

Symonds' homosexuality was scarcely a secret in his own lifetime. His father and wife knew of it early on and an increasingly large circle of friends and readers as, towards the end of his life, he expressed himself more and more openly on the subject. What becomes apparent, as we read the late works and correspondence, is that he wanted not simply to come out but to justify his "type of character" and make it acceptable to the public at large. As we see from the above passage and still more from *A Problem in Modern Ethics* (1891), science was his means of justification. Above all, he turned to Ulrichs, who in a dozen books from 1862 to 1875 insisted, against religious strictures and the contemporary penal code, that homosexuality examined scientifically proved to be a congenital misdirection or "inversion" of sexual energy, and therefore not morally and certainly not criminally wrong. As Symonds writes, paraphrasing Ulrichs, you cannot "expell nature with a fork."

In the extensive debate over homosexuality in the last quarter of the century (the period, argues Gay, "invented homosexuality"), the term "sexual inversion" (Ulrich's *Konträre Sexualempfindung*), became code for the naturalness, and therefore innocence, of homosexuality. What is striking about Symonds' own discussion is the desire seen (in the passage from *Memoirs* above) to carry the point further and insist (as Ellis carefully does not) on the full rights of that word "natural." Not only is inversion something that cannot be helped, it is "abnormal" only in the "view of . . . society." Symonds' hope, clearly, is that science will change society's view with factual knowledge and free yet another area of human experience from the religious stigma of "abnormal," not to say "abominable." It would take little to make much the same point about Symonds' mentor Michelet though the latter's concerns are not as explicitly homosexual as Symonds'. As Roland Barthes has argued, for Michelet the studies of history and science are progressively absorbed into the pursuit of the "ultrasex," the attempt, that is, to resolve the fundamental sexual antithesis of human experience, the source, for Michelet, of all human division. The last science for Michelet is the science of eros, and so it seems to be for Symonds.

The connection of this more intimate reading of Symonds' gospel of science to his interpretation of the Renaissance is not far to seek. Rehearsing the history of sexual inversion in *Studies in the Psychology of Sex,* Ellis predictably notices its currency among the Greeks, but goes on to observe that "in modern Europe we find the strongest evidence of . . . true sexual inversion when we investigate the men of the Renaissance." His authority for this historical judgment, he says, is J. A. Symonds, and he points particularly to Symonds' last booklength work on the period, the 1892 biography of Michelangelo. There Symonds offers Michelangelo as the preeminent type of the Renaissance, as, indeed, he had done some fifteen years earlier in *The Fine Arts,* only now the emphasis is overwhelmingly on the need to recognize Michelangelo's sexuality not only in itself but as the sign of a distinctive social situation. "The frank and hearty feeling for a youth [Tommaso Cavalieri] of singular distinction which is expressed in

[Michelangelo's] sonnets, gave no offense to society during the period of the . . . Renaissance; but after the [Counter Reformation] local feeling altered upon this and similar topics." It is as if, under the guise of biography, Symonds is not only writing autobiography, which is plain enough, but rewriting his earlier history, making explicit a theme which one may, with care, trace throughout that work, everywhere shadowing the more obvious unifying theme of the birth of modern science, as, for example, in this striking observation: "The rise of sculpture and painting indicated the quickening to life of new faculties . . . for comprehension of these arts implies . . . a new freedom of the mind produced by the regeneration of society through love." When Symonds writes in **The Fine Arts** that the modern age has progressed beyond the aesthetic mode of thinking to the scientific he does not mean, with Hegel who makes a similar point in the *Aesthetics,* that reason has separated itself once and for all from the natural man. He means, rather, that modern science has exchanged the *actual* recognition of the natural man for art's symbolic representations. In a properly scientific age, so Symonds hopes, there will be no need to "imply" (the key word in the passage just quoted) a "new freedom of mind" because freedom will be openly expressed and enjoyed. In his last essay on the Renaissance ["The New Spirit: An Analysis of the Emancipation of the Intellect in the Fourteenth, Fifteenth and Sixteenth Centuries," *Fortnightly Review* 93 (1893)], published weeks before his death, Symonds exchanges his long-employed Hegelian phrase, "the modern spirit," for Ellis' "new spirit" with its clear connotation of sexual liberation. Hegel, he says here, failed entirely to grasp the import of the "revolution" we call the Renaissance. Its "essential ingredient" was not reason, but "naturalism," which "freed the mind from prejudices regarding the uncleanliness or repulsiveness of anything which could be found in nature."

This, then, is Symonds' resolution of the paradox of human freedom through subordination to nature. He tells us in the **Memoirs** he initially came to the study of the Renaissance as a way of sublimating unacceptable sexual desires. "[In] the labyrinth of a young soul, lost, and seeking light . . . I had recourse to this one thing which has sustained me through the troubles of this life. I went to Malvern . . . and wrote an essay on the Renaissance. . . ." What he gradually learned from that first essay and the many versions of it which followed is that sublimation itself is the problem. We may make the point more incisively: for Symonds the real meaning of the Italian Renaissance came to be, not the triumph of "civilization" (*Kultur*) that Burckhardt immortalizes in his title and so many have continued to celebrate, but the discontent with it that Freud announces in his—*Des Unbehagen in der Kultur.* True freedom lies not in the abstract progress of humanity towards a rational civilization, but in the release of humanity from civilization's "doublemindedness," the endless antagonism of pagan and Christian, body and soul. The "new spirit" strikes at the factitious structures man over the centuries has erected to separate himself from the cosmos. As Freud says [in his *Civilization and Its Discontents,* trans. by James Strachey], the "cultural super-ego . . . does not trouble itself . . . about . . . the . . . constitution of human beings." Here we come to

the final awkwardness of Symonds' metahistory. If, as [Wilhelm] Dilthey was contemporaneously arguing and modern *umanisti* continue to believe, history is nothing if not the ongoing elaboration of these cultural structures, then Symonds has, in some sense, written his history against history. (pp. 129-34)

Peter Allan Dale, "Beyond Humanism: J. A. Symonds and the Replotting of the Renaissance," in CLIO, *Vol. 17, No. 2, Winter, 1988, pp. 109-37.*

FURTHER READING

Brooks, Van Wyck. *John Addington Symonds: A Biographical Study.* 1914. Reprint. New York: B. W. Huebsch, 1924, 234 p.

Important early biographical and critical study of Symonds.

Croft-Cooke, Rupert. "John Addington Symonds and the Greek Ideal." In his *Feasting with Panthers: A New Consideration of Some Late Victorian Writers,* pp. 93-159. London: W. H. Allen, 1967.

Examines Symonds's life as it affected his work, focusing on his struggles to rationalize and efforts to fulfill his homosexual desires.

Ferguson, Wallace K. "The Burckhardtian Tradition in the Interpretation of the Italian Renaissance." In his *The Renaissance in Historical Thought: Five Centuries of Interpretation,* pp. 195-252. Cambridge, Mass: Houghton Mifflin Company, 1948.

Compares *The Renaissance in Italy* with Jacob Burckhardt's *Civilization of the Renaissance in Italy,* concluding that Symonds's work "is the Burckhardtian Renaissance exaggerated, vaguely distorted, and, above all, dramatized."

Going, William T. "John Addington Symonds and the Victorian Sonnet Sequence." *Victorian Poetry* VIII (1970): 25-38.

Examines Symonds's sonnet sequences *Animi Figura* and *Vagabunduli Libellus,* noting his contributions to this genre both as poet and critic.

Grosskurth, Phyllis. "The Genesis of Symonds's Elizabethan Criticism." *Modern Language Review* LIX, No. 2 (April 1964): 183-93.

Assesses the limitations of Symonds's scientific, historical approach to literary criticism, focusing especially on his *Shakspere's Predecessors.*

———. *John Addington Symonds: A Biography.* London: Longmans, Green and Co., 1964, 370 p.

Standard biography that draws on Symonds's yet-unpublished memoirs to highlight the effects of his homosexuality on his life and work.

Harrison, Frederic. "John Addington Symonds." *The Nineteenth Century* XXXIX, No. 232 (June 1896): 979-92.

Appreciative overview of Symonds's writings that refers to him as "one who of all the men of our generation best knew, loved, and understood the Italian genius in literature."

Hyde, H. Montgomery. "Some Victorian Homosexuals." In his *The Love That Dared Not Speak Its Name,* pp. 90-133. Boston: Little, Brown and Company, 1970.

Discusses Symonds's homosexuality, describing briefly his two privately printed works on the subject, *A Problem in Modern Ethics* and *A Problem in Greek Ethics.*

Markgraf, Carl. "John Addington Symonds: An Annotated Bibliography of Writings About Him." *English Literature in Transition, 1880-1920* 18, No. 2 (1975): 79-138.

Comprehensive, alphabetical listing of secondary sources on Symonds.

————. "John Addington Symonds: Update of a Bibliography of Writings About Him." *English Literature in Transition, 1880-1920* 28, No. 1 (1985): 59-78.

Includes numerous additions to Markgraf's earlier compilation (above).

Munro, John M. Review of *John Addington Symonds: A Biography,* by Phyllis Grosskurth. *Victorian Studies* IX, No. 1 (September 1965): 66-8.

Discusses the effect of Symonds's homosexuality on his writings and choice of subjects.

Orsini, G. N. G. "Symonds and De Sanctis: a Study in the Historiography of the Renaissance." *Studies in the Renaissance* XI (1964): 151-87.

Examines Symonds's histories, noting the influence of Italian critic and literary historian Francesco De Sanctis on *The Renaissance in Italy.* Orsini maintains that Symonds was "more at home in dramatic presentation than conceptual synthesis."

Payne, William Morton. "John Addington Symonds." In his *Little Leaders,* pp. 229-36. Chicago: Way & Williams, 1895.

Asserts that Symonds's ill-health and self-imposed exile to Switzerland detracted from the quality of his later works. Payne adds that it was as author of *The Renaissance in Italy,* "distinctly the best and most attractive" history of the subject in English literature, that Symonds will be remembered.

Poston, Lawrence, III. " 'Born Dipsychic': The Symonds Letters Completed." *Prairie Schooner* XLIV, No. 3 (Fall 1970): 268-70.

Comments on the author's thought, temperament, and literary achievement as reflected in his letters.

Rousseau, G. S. "To a Grecian Urn." *Partisan Review* 36, No. 2 (Spring 1969): 316-21.

Reviews Symonds's *Letters,* asserting that "Symonds's self-deception—his intense yearning to lose himself in myriads of words—is in fact the marvelous thing about his letters." He comments briefly on the contents of the letters as they reflect the author's thought and temperament, and maintains that *The Renaissance in Italy* is Symonds's only enduring achievement.

Stanford, Derek. "John Addington Symonds." In his *Critics of the Nineties,* pp. 88-93. London: John Baker, 1970.

Surveys Symonds's critical studies.

Sutton, Denys. "A Bohemian Aesthete." *Apollo Magazine* XCIX, No. 146 (April 1974): 218-27.

Overview of Symonds's life and works. The critic characterizes Symonds as "an aesthete grappling with the problem of history and giving his views about works of art."

Symonds, John Addington. *The Memoirs of John Addington Symonds.* Edited by Phyllis Grosskurth. London: Hutchinson & Co., 1984, 319 p.

Includes an introduction by Grosskurth, numerous illustrations, and appendices featuring samples of Symonds's private correspondence and an extract from *Sexual Inversion.*

Symonds, Margaret. *Out of the Past.* New York: Charles Scribner's Sons, 1925, 318 p.

Sentimental account of Symonds's life, written by his daughter.

Symons, Arthur. "John Addington Symonds." In his *Studies in Two Literatures,* pp. 248-56. 1897. Reprint. New York: Garland Publishing, 1977.

Discusses various passages from Symonds's unpublished memoirs, offering a sketch of the author's temperament.

Thompson, Francis. "Mr. Symonds's Essays." In *The Real Robert Louis Stevenson, and Other Critical Essays,* edited by Rev. Terence L. Connolly, pp. 164-68. New York: University Publishers Incorporated, 1959.

Reviews *In the Key of Blue,* praising the essays on literary subjects while largely dismissing the other essays that comprise the volume. Thompson discusses at some length an essay in which Symonds asserted that culture is crippling to genius.

Fyodor Tyutchev

1803-1873

(Also transliterated as Tiutchev and Tjutcev) Russian poet and essayist.

Tyutchev is considered one of the most important Russian poets of the nineteenth century. His work is commonly divided into two categories, lyrical and political. The first category comprises both metaphysical nature poems—wherein Tyutchev used the mutability of the natural landscape to suggest the chaos underlying the ostensible order of the universe—and romantic poems, in which he emphasized eroticism and despair. Tyutchev's political poetry and essays advocate a conservative, nationalistic solution to the disorder then prevailing in Europe, maintaining that Russia should spearhead an international monarchial restoration and spiritual regeneration, under the aegis of its autocracy and its Orthodox church. Tyutchev's political writing is considered inferior to his lyrics, which are praised for their intimate tone, philosophical subtlety, and technical innovations.

Born on his family's country estate in the Orel province, Tyutchev was the younger of two sons of Ekaterina Lvovna and Ivan Nikolaevich Tyutchev. His parents were untitled nobles who enjoyed the slow-paced, comfortable, and secure lifestyle common among landed gentry not highly placed enough to serve in the government. When Tyutchev was nine, they engaged Semyon Raich, a well-known Classical scholar and poet, to tutor him. Raich supervised Tyutchev's education at home for five years and, after his charge entered Moscow University's humanities program, attended classes with him. Tyutchev performed inconsistently at the University, but achieved an "outstanding" performance on his final examinations. He graduated in 1821.

While still a student, Tyutchev had published translations of French and Latin poetry and had produced a small body of discursive odes on Classical subjects. However, he did not begin writing poetry in earnest until 1822, when he entered the Russian foreign service. He was made a subordinate diplomat in Bavaria, where the arts were thriving under the combined stimuli of the German Romantic movement and the cultural revival initiated by King Ludwig. The university Ludwig founded in the Bavarian capital of Munich drew many intellectuals and artists whom Tyutchev befriended, including Friedrich Schelling, the most notable philosopher of the German Romantic movement. In Munich, Tyutchev also met his first wife, a German countess named Eleanor Peterson. His undemanding diplomatic duties left Tyutchev with abundant leisure to translate a good deal of predominantly Romantic German poetry. He also wrote original poetry which he published in the small literary journals run by Raich and other friends in Russia. Between 1836 and 1840, thirty-nine of Tyutchev's poems appeared in the era's preeminent Russian literary journal, *Sovremennik*

(The Contemporary), published by Alexander Pushkin. In 1838, after Tyutchev had been transferred to Turin, his wife died. When he deserted his new post the following year to marry Ernestine Dornberg, a German baroness and his longtime mistress, the Foreign Service punitively dismissed him. He returned to Munich but remained unemployed and did not produce poetry as he had during his earlier period there. Tyutchev's output during the five years of his second Munich residency was limited to a few political poems, letters, and essays, but the fervently conservative patriotism he voiced in these restored him to his government's favor, and, in 1844, he returned to Russia.

Settling in St. Petersburg, Tyutchev was reinstated in the Foreign Service, and he eventually rose to become its Senior Censor. A volume of his poems was published in 1854 by the novelist Ivan Turgenev, who was an admirer of his work (Tyutchev was indifferent to the publication of his poems and, during his lifetime, they were published only at the insistence of friends). He lived in St. Petersburg for the remainder of his life, a sought-after conversationalist who frequented society functions and wrote increasingly conservative poems, essays, and letters. The vicissitudes of his final, adulterous liaison with a Russian woman named

Elena Denisieva were documented in an acclaimed cycle of love lyrics. Tyutchev died in 1873.

The poetry Tyutchev wrote during his twenty-two years in Bavaria exhibits the formal and thematic influence of the burgeoning Romantic movement. Adopting the lyrical free verse style common among Romantic poets, Tyutchev abbreviated line lengths and subtly manipulated conventional meter to produce a highly impressionistic style which critics consider well suited to his metaphysical landscape descriptions. These renderings of the natural world reflect Schelling's philosophy of nature: humanity springs from, remains spiritually part of, and returns to the universe's primeval chaos. Tyutchev's poetry frequently represents Schelling's dialectic between order and chaos as a contrast between day and night. However, Tyutchev disputed Schelling's conception of the artist, believing that the poet is not a transcendent teacher but a passive observer who surrenders the appealing fiction of discrete identity to merge with and transcribe chaos. His love lyrics are similar to the nature lyrics in their brevity and pessimism. In these, Tyutchev evokes the immoral sensuality and capricious impermanence of love. The poems inspired by his numerous extramarital affairs are especially notable for Tyutchev's powerful, skillfully wrought representations of desire, constraint, guilt, and anguish.

Although the few political poems Tyutchev wrote during his youth demonstrate some liberal sympathies, both the quantity and the conservatism of his political work increased as he aged. Between 1844 and 1850 he published three influential political essays, "Russia and Germany," "Russia and Revolution," and "The Papacy and the Roman Question," and political poetry constituted an increasingly large percentage of his output after he returned to Russia. These pieces, progressively more reactionary and nationalistic, articulate Tyutchev's support for the Panslav movement, which initially sought to unify all Slavic peoples under Russian political and religious leadership but later advocated imperial expansion ranging far beyond Eastern Europe. As an aristocrat, a conservative, and a Slavophil, Tyutchev believed that autocracies such as the Czarist government were best suited to rule not only Russia but all nations. Western Europe, Tyutchev argued, was collapsing beneath a flood tide of revolution and spiritual decay resulting from the Protestant Reformation and papal corruption. Unlike its European confreres, Russia's monarchy had remained allied with the undiminished purity and puissance of the Orthodox Church. This undefiled, unfragmented strength, he maintained, made Russia the power best equipped to restore political order and spiritual strength within Europe and, ultimately, around the world.

As a poet, Tyutchev was little known during his lifetime. He had prominent admirers among the Russian literati—Pushkin, Turgenev, Nikolay Nekrasov, and Leo Tolstoy—who prevailed upon him to release his poems for publication. Although he consented, Tyutchev's refusal to involve himself in the publication process resulted in the significant alteration of his published verse when early editors such as Turgenev eliminated the very deviations from standard line length, meter, and rhythm critics now consider Tyutchev's most significant formal innovations. In editions of his works published around the turn of the century, the Russian Symbolists, who regarded him as a precursor, restored the stylistic "discrepancies" which previous editors had standardized. The Symbolists also appreciated his thematic preoccupations with existential despair, sensuality, and romantic suffering and his often intensely personal poetic persona. During the twentieth century, critics have concurred in their dismissal of Tyutchev's political writing as formulaic conservatism, but they continue to esteem his lyrics, placing Tyutchev alongside Pushkin as one of the preeminent poets of nineteenth-century Russia.

PRINCIPAL WORKS

Stikhotvorenii (poetry) 1854
Polnoe sobranie sochinenii (poetry, essays, and letters) 1913
Versions from Fyodor Tyutchev (poetry) 1960
Lirika. 2 vols. (poetry) 1965
Poems and Political Letters of F. I. Tyutchev (poetry and letters) 1973
Poems of Day and Night (poetry) 1974

Edmund Wilson   (essay date 1944)

[*Wilson, considered America's foremost man of letters in the twentieth century, wrote widely on cultural, historical, and literary matters. He is often credited with bringing an international perspective to American letters through his widely read discussions of European literature. Wilson was allied with no critical school; however, several dominant concerns serve as guiding motifs throughout his work. He invariably examined the social and historical implications of a work of literature, particularly literature's significance as "an attempt to give meaning to our experience" and its value for the improvement of humanity. Although he was not a moralist, his criticism displays a deep concern with moral values. Another constant was his discussion of a work of literature as a revelation of its author's personality. Related to this is Wilson's theory that artistic ability is a compensation for a psychological wound; thus, a literary work can be fully understood only if one undertakes an emotional profile of its author. Wilson utilized this approach in many essays, and it is the element of his thought that is most often attacked. However, he rarely examined the historical and psychological elements of a work of literature at the expense of discussing its literary qualities. Perhaps Wilson's greatest contributions to American literature were his tireless promotions of writers of the 1920s, 1930s, and 1940s, and his essays introducing the best of modern literature to the general reader. In the following excerpt, Wilson compares Tyutchev with poets better known among Western readers to explain his stature within Russian poetry, his metrical developments, and his propensity for delicate treatments of ethereal subjects.*]

The literary career and reputation of the poet F. I. Tyutchev have certain points of resemblance to those, respectively and both together, of A. E. Housman and Gerard Manley Hopkins.

Tyutchev was four years older than Pushkin and eleven years older than Lermontov, and he is usually ranked by the Russians as one of the three great poets of his period; but, since he wrote no plays or novels or narrative poems as Pushkin and Lermontov did, he has supplied no opera librettos and no translatable stories, and is therefore quite unknown in the West. He was not a professional writer and did not care to be a literary figure. He was a diplomat who lived out of Russia for the better part of twenty-two years and from time to time sent verses to Pushkin, who published them in the quarterly he was editing. It was not till the early fifties that Nekrasov brought Tyutchev's poetry to the attention of the public and that Tyutchev edited a book of his lyrics. The whole work of Tyutchev consists merely of about three hundred short pieces—lyrics and political verses—which, although they are known by Russians as well as we know *A Shropshire Lad,* have no way of getting through to other languages.

The comparisons with Housman and Hopkins may, however, serve not only to indicate the position of Tyutchev in Russian poetry, but also to give some idea of his form and of the kind of poet he is. We must banish first of all from our minds the idea that Russian literature is necessarily loose or disorderly. The tendency of Russian poetry is, if anything, in the opposite direction of being too uniformly well-turned. Certainly these three Russian poets of the early nineteenth century are a good deal more consistently satisfactory from the point of view of form than any of the English Romantic poets except Keats. There are lyrics of Lermontov's and Pushkin's so classical in achieving their effects by the mere displacement or change of a word in the pattern of a line or a quatrain that we can hardly find anything of the kind in English till we come to A. E. Housman. And Tyutchev is the great Russian master of the pregnant and pointed and poignant short poem.

But the landscapes and seasons that Tyutchev prefers—and he largely lives on landscapes and seasons—with the feelings that these inspire, are quite different from the clear autumn bitterness or the sharp summer irony of Housman. Tyutchev loves the indeterminate moments between fair and rainy weather, when a thunderstorm is looming or passing, or between the night and the dawn or the sunset and the dark, which reflect indeterminate and variable emotions. There is a fine little poem of E. A. Robinson's which has something in common with Tyutchev:

> Dark hills at evening in the west,
> Where sunset hovers like a sound
> Of golden horns that sang to rest
> Old bones of warriors under ground,
> Far now from all the bannered ways
> Where flash the legions of the sun,
> You fade—as if the last of days
> Were fading, and all wars were done.

Imagine something halfway between this and certain poems of Léonie Adams's, where the phrases strike out

more facets, and the whole thing has a livelier psychological interest. There is piece after piece in *High Falcon* that is amazingly close to Tyutchev ("The Moon and Spectator," "The Mysterious Thing," "Evening Sky," "Sundown," "Twilit Revelation," "Country Summer" and others).

> How now are we tossed about by a windy heaven,
> The eye that scans it madded to discern
> In a single quarter all the wild ravage of light,
> Amazing light to quiver and suddenly turn
> Before the stormy demon fall of night;
> And yet west spaces saved celestial
> With silver sprinklings of the anointed sun. . . .

For though the stanza of Tyutchev is epigrammatic—he was in conversation a famous wit—his language is delicious and exquisite. He had brought over from an earlier period certain qualities that were alien to the age of Pushkin. The eighteenth century in Russia was distinguished by literary characteristics—a touch of reckless Aeschylean grandiloquence—quite different from anything we mean when we say "eighteenth century" in English, and closer to our seventeenth century. Even the foreign reader is surprised to come upon such a phrase as "a loud crimson exclamation." But in Tyutchev this style has been infinitely refined: there are a liquidity and a shifting suggestiveness that anticipate symbolist poetry. The Russian poets of the end of the century claimed him as a precursor of their school, and were impatient with Turgenev for having ironed out, in editing Tyutchev's poems—rather as Rimsky-Korsakov conventionalized the score of *Boris Godunov*—the metrical innovations of the poet. In this role of rediscovered "ancestor" of an advanced phase of poetry that did not derive from him, Tyutchev occupies a position not unlike that of Hopkins.

The sensibility of Tyutchev lives between light and shadow among the feelings and impressions and reflections of a region so vibrating and rarefied that it makes most English romantic poetry seem relatively sensual and downright. One of the best of his poems is **"Italian Villa,"** which is certainly all Russian and all Tyutchev in this coincidence of physical with moral awareness. The poet and a woman companion arrive at an Italian villa which has for a long time been uninhabited. You have a charming and lulling description of the old house asleep in the sun, with only the babble of the fountain and the twittering of a swallow rippling the settled silence. But the visitors enter; and in the tranquil darkness where a cypress looks in at the window, they suddenly feel that a change has occurred: the fountain seems to stop; a convulsive shudder runs through the branches of the cypress; there is a queer indistinct whisper like something muttered through sleep. "What was it, friend? Was it that cruel life—the life, alas! then quickening in our veins—that ruthless life, with its rebellious fire, had to no purpose crossed the sacred threshold?" (pp. 28-31)

Yet, admirable though Tyutchev is, he is somehow to an Anglo-Saxon a little unsympathetic. He is a little too weepy for our taste. In his poetry is audible, as it is not in Pushkin, that incurable minor key of resignation to grievance and complaint, that may move us when we hear it in an old Russian song but with which we become impatient when we find how habitual and incessant it is in all kinds of connections in Russian life.

In Tyutchev's case, this key is associated with a humidity of emotional atmosphere that is also rather alien to us. There are moments when the English-speaking reader, in his exploration of Russian literature, seems to come upon something clammy that makes him instinctively withdraw his hand. He is put off by it in certain passages of Herzen's fascinating memoirs where Herzen and his wife and his friends get themselves into messy mixed-up situations so that everybody languishes and agonizes and nobody will make a decision to straighten the thing out. It is a kind of thing that people objected to in the novels of Dostoevsky when they were first being read in English, though these episodes in Dostoevsky are usually brought to an end by thunderclaps that clear the air; the kind of thing that used to puzzle and exasperate the first foreign audiences of Chekhov's plays, though Chekhov exploits these situations for pathos and humor both. It is something which can perhaps be shortly described as a tendency of Russians in emotional relationships to "stew in their own juice"— which is a Russian phrase as well as an English one: masticating and gulping and regurgitating their problems, biting upon their suffering and doting over their guilt, sweating and freezing for years in the *impasses* of personal involvements as if they were waiting in Soviet breadlines or the reception rooms of callous officials.

And something of this complaisance in incurable heartbreak, this inveterate helpless quaver, one does find in the poetry of Tyutchev, especially if one reads him in bulk (which perhaps it is unfair to do: Housman, too, is always sounding the same note, and, with him, too, we tend to protest if we read too much at once). Tyutchev is always sighing for Italian suns, and he even thinks nostalgically of the malaria of Rome, by the granite and gray skies of the Neva; he is forever grieving over stricken loves, and he never seems to write when they are flourishing. That lugubrious word *rokovoy,* which means *destined, fateful, fatal,* seems to toll on every other page, with its deep recognition of defeat, its certainty that all the affairs of the heart have come out and must always come out badly.

Tyutchev was twice married, both times to German women; and at fifty-one he fell in love with a teacher at a Russian school. Says D. S. Mirsky,

> Their love was passionate and profound and an infinite source of torture to both. The young woman's reputation was ruined, and Tyutchev's own gravely tainted, as well as his family happiness. When in 1865 Mlle Denisova died, gloom and despair took possession of Tyutchev. The wonderful tact and forbearance of his wife in the whole affair only increased his suffering by a profound feeling of guilt.

Though I am usually interested in the lives of writers, I have not yet been able to bring myself to look this story up. I feel that I have heard enough about it in reading Tyutchev's poems on the subject.

With all this, there are in Tyutchev's pessimism a bitter

pride and a noble consistency. But it is as far from A. E. Housman as it is from Alfred de Vigny.

> Be still, be still, my soul; it is but for a season:
> Let us endure an hour and see injustice
>   done. . . .

says Housman; and,

> Gémir, pleurer, prier est également lâche.
> Fais énergiquement ta longue et lourde tâche,
> Dans la voie où le Sort a voulu t'appeler.
> Puis après, comme moi, souffre et meurs sans
>   parler.

says Alfred de Vigny's wolf. But Tyutchev, after Mlle Denisova's death, begs God to dispel his dullness of soul in order that he may feel his pain more severely, and this somehow disconcerts the Western reader.

So does Tyutchev's conception of Nature. Nature, for Housman and Vigny, is indifferent to men, and so they defy her.

> Those are the tears of morning,
> That weeps, but not for thee . . .

says Housman; and Vigny:

> Vivez, froide Nature, et revivez sans cesse
> Sous nos pieds, sur nos fronts, puisque c'est
>   votre loi;
> Vivez, et dédaignez, si vous êtes déesse,
> L'Homme, humble passager, qui dut vous être
>   un Roi;
> Plus que tout votre règne et que ses splendeurs
>   vaines
> J'aime la majesté des souffrances humaines:
> Vous ne recevrez pas un cri d'amour de moi.

For Wordsworth, the natural world holds a kind of divine presence that stands always behind what we see and to feel oneself in touch with which is to be strengthened, instructed, exalted. But the attitude of Tyutchev is quite distinct. Nature, in a sense, is indifferent to man, but man does not need to fight her. She is neither opponent nor friend: she has a life and a soul of her own which are larger than the life of man and which will eventually absorb and obliterate him. Tyutchev gives final expression to his fundamental point of view in a poem written not long before his death. Do the oaks, he asks, that grow on ancient barrows, that spread their branches and grow grand and speak with their leaves—do they care into whose dust and memory they are plunging their long roots? "Nature knows nothing of the past: our lives to her are alien and phantoms; and, standing in her presence, we dimly apprehend that we ourselves are but part of her revery. Indiscriminately, one by one, when they are done with their futile exploit, she welcomes all her children into her fathomless depths that swallow and reconcile all." (pp. 31-5)

Tyutchev's Nature is Pushkin's Bronze Horseman: the power that creates and that crushes; and there is a drama of feeling in relation to it in Tyutchev as there is in Pushkin. But Tyutchev, who was a reactionary in politics under Nicholas I and Alexander II and even held a post in the Censorship, is rather on the masochistic side, the side that submits to being crushed. And one of the elements of the

Russian character to which it is most difficult for the Westerner to adjust himself is the passion for self-immolation. (p. 35)

Edmund Wilson, "Notes from the Forties: Tyutchev," in A Window on Russia: For the Use of Foreign Readers, *Farrar, Straus and Giroux*, 1972, pp. 28-37.

Richard Hare (essay date 1951)

[*Hare was an English educator and critic who wrote numerous studies of Russian history and literature. In the following excerpt, he asserts that Tyutchev's poetic sensibility engendered his political convictions and examines these in his poems, essays, and letters.*]

Fyodor Tyutchev is less familiar to students of social thought than he is to that dwindling international group which still prizes thoughtful and intelligible poets. His intense and militant Slavophil activity has long been eclipsed by his more lasting and sensitive evocation of 'magic thoughts that hide away from the noise and glare of day'. At first sight, especially for those who are determined to equate Slavophils with pan-Slav politicians, these twin aspirations of Tyutchev seem strangely discordant. But closer scrutiny reveals that his Slavophil ideal of human culture flows as a natural consequence from his poetic imagination, through a struggle to find for his vision a more coherent and immediate shape. At the same time his work is tinged with a haunting sense of failure to achieve this fusion. His poem **'The Spoken Thought Becomes a Lie'** is an ominous reflection on that conflict within him.

Tyutchev spent most of his early adult years in Europe, served his country as a diplomat in Munich and Turin, married two Bavarian wives in succession, and he both spoke and wrote most naturally in flawless French. Not till 1844 did he return to his native St. Petersburg, where he was appointed a Court Chamberlain and served at various posts in the Ministry of Foreign Affairs. There his intellectual eminence alone excused his eccentric behaviour. At court functions he is known to have disguised himself as a footman in order to observe more freely what was going on. On one occasion he became so absorbed in argument with a friend that he halted the procession of the Grand Duchess whose train he had to hold. Count Sologub found Tyutchev's principal charm in his vivid flow of conversation, in which all his remarks *coulaient de source*. Awkward and shy until he warmed up, he shone in his element at Petersburg evening receptions under the soft glitter of chandeliers, when the gay rustle of ladies' silk dresses mingled with rippling laughter and brilliant repartee.

Most people expected that twenty-two formative years of cosmopolitan life in European cities would have turned Tyutchev not only into a polished worldly European, cultured to the finger-tips, but thence into a Westernizer as thoroughgoing as Turgenev in his painful conviction of boorish Russian backwardness. In fact the reverse took place. The longer Tyutchev lived in Europe, the less he liked it, and the more incurably Russian he felt at heart.

Though he much preferred French to Germans, he called the French 'that charming and absurd people, who inspire you with every kind of sentiment except respect'. It is true he made scathing remarks about Russia as 'the realm of official ranks and the knout', and sometimes pined to escape from the tedious Petersburg society which later lionized him. Nor did peasant Russia offer him the ideal haven of refuge which some of this contemporaries found in it. The soothing but bare and poverty-stricken countryside depressed his spirits. Nevertheless some inscrutable awakening of mind impelled him to give voice in his native tongue to an intimate vision of his motherland, a vision first seen in focus when he contrasted it with his prolonged but bitterly disappointing experience of Europe.

> These poor villages, this niggardly nature,
> Land of long endurance, land of the Russian
>   people,
> The proud stranger fails to see or value
> What shines secretly and modestly through your
>   meek nakedness;
>
> You, my native land, the King of Heaven trod
> In the guise of a serf, bowed down by the weight
>   of his cross,
> And blessed you in passing.
>
>   (1855)

Even as Tyutchev's mature lyrics penetrate far beyond the fleeting personal moment, so do his political poems and essays transcend the topical political issues which first provoked them; they build up step by step an increasingly articulate and emphatic plan of human action pieced together out of his mystic intuitions and ingrained Slavophil beliefs. Major historical events, impinging on the growth of his personal experience, clearly decided the shaping of this plan. As early as 1830 the Russian Government's suppression of the Polish revolt impelled him to write:

> Even as Agamemnon sacrificed his own daugh-
>   ter to the gods,
> So we in unhappy Warsaw
> Struck our fateful blow,
> Redeeming at the cost of blood
> Russia's integrity and peace.
>
> Cast away that infamous wreath
> Woven by a slavish hand!
> Not for the Koran of Autocracy
> Did rivers of Russian blood flow;
>
> Another thought, another faith, fired Russian
>   hearts.
> By the threat of a saving example,
> To gather under a single Russian banner
> The scattered family of Slavs,
> And lead them, like an army with one mind,
> Forward to feats of human culture!

His poem **'The Alps'** (1831) pictured the Slav countries as a range of frozen mountains lit up by the dawn, but significantly the lesser peaks shone with a rosy light *reflected* from the highest one, the Russian mountain, and the first to catch the rays of the rising sun.

The astonishing poem **'Russian Geography'** (1829) indulges in a more sinister piece of distinctly spatial megalomania;

> Seven inland seas and seven mighty rivers,
> From the Nile to the Neva, from the Elbe to
>   China,
> From the Volga to the Euphrates, from the Gan-
>   ges to the Danube,
> That is the Russian Empire.

By bringing this dream-Empire one step nearer to waking life, there would arise a new Eastern Europe, welded into a solid phalanx of states inspired and led by Russia. For Russia was neither a part of Asia, nor a world of its own detached from Asia and Europe, but a legitimate sister of Western Europe engaged in a heroic reconstruction of the Christian Eastern Empire, more European in essence, in uncorrupted Christian civilization, than Western Europe had been since 1789. Tyutchev clearly envisaged that immense Eastern bloc as the only rightful counterbalance to a Western Europe dominated by the German race (at that time represented by the Austrian Empire and Prussia).

Moreover, he conceived the Slav struggle with Germany not merely as a fight for political and economic supremacy in Europe, but as an indispensable prelude to the next step of world-wide unification on an Orthodox religious basis.

> Will Eastern Europe, this genuine Eastern Em-
> pire, already three-quarters formed, for which
> the first Empire of the Byzantine Cesars, and the
> second of the Orthodox Tsars, were only a feeble
> preliminary sketch—will this Empire ripen nat-
> urally into its final completion, or will it be
> obliged to win its rights by force of arms, by sub-
> jecting the whole world to the direst miseries?
> (**'Russia and Germany'**, 1844.)

There exists only one secular power, leaning on the Universal Church, which is capable of reforming the Papacy without injuring religion. No such power ever existed or could exist in the West. Nor is this power in present-day Russia. It will be in the great Graeco-Russian Orthodox Empire into which Russia must expand. . . . If the Russian Empire does not develop, it will explode.

Tyutchev was obsessed, and rightly so, by thoughts and forebodings about the German race as the most formidable obstacle to Slav fulfilment. His essay **'Russia and Germany'** is objective enough to admit that there exist two conflicting Germanys—or rather two contradictory tendencies fighting for mastery there, 'On the one hand you have the sovereigns, the governments of Germany, with their reliable carefully considered policy; on the other stands that second master of our age, public opinion, which turns and twists wherever it is blown by winds and waves.' Germany owed to Russia her liberation from Napoleon. Her rulers recognized this debt, and never had relations between the German states and Russia been friendlier and more fruitful than in the last thirty years. But German public opinion, in the shape of the popular Press, was fanning the flames of a senseless hostile clamour against Russia. Its favourite slander was to say that Russian policy aimed at luring the smaller states into her orbit at the expense of 'the legitimate influence of the two great states of the Union' (Austria and Prussia). Others, with equal injustice, accused the Russian government of systematically opposing constitutional reform in Germany. This irresponsible campaign was influencing German rulers against their better judgement, and it encouraged throughout Europe the imbecile fashion of gaping with horror at Russia as 'the ogre of the nineteenth century'. Such was her bitter reward for all she had endured in raising her Western neighbours from their downfall, for her valiant efforts 'to replace Europe on her former pedestal'. 'There is no need for me to plead in defence of Russia', Tyutchev concluded in proud disdain; 'her most reliable defender is History itself. All the trials suffered by Russia in the last three centuries History has irrevocably decided in her favour!'

Tyutchev's impassioned argument successfully pricks the bubble of pan-German pretensions, without convincing us that his country is therefore predestined to rule Europe more beneficially than Germany could. Rather, it looked as if the Russian government, with its German dynasty, Germanized officialdom and Prussian administrative methods, would continue to incorporate within its system a multitude of German defects. His criticisms of the Austrian Empire, which he aptly called 'an Achilles with heels everywhere', have sometimes a harsh but unadmitted relevance to his own country.

> Through her and in her, the German race feels
> the power to crush, exploit to its own advantage,
> and, even more in a moral than in a political
> sense, to reduce to nullity the two other great
> European races, the Latins in Italy, and the
> Slavs wherever they may be found. It seems ab-
> surd and laughable that people who for a thou-
> sand years proved so conspicuously unsuccessful
> in organizing their own affairs should be so pos-
> sessed by the passion for dominating others.

Tyutchev felt sure that Western hatred and dread of Russia would sooner or later lead to 'a second Punic War of the West'. That war would finally decide whether the most numerous of the three main European races, after having lost in the struggle against the other two for so long, was destined or not to be crushed by them, to lose its historical autonomy and to cease to be anything except 'a huge corpse with a borrowed soul'.

Tyutchev's next major political essay, **'Russia and Revolution'** (1848), widened the scope of **'Russia and Germany,'** by dividing the whole world into the two rival camps which its title indicates. In its forecast of implacable hostility between two major groups of Powers, the essay is prophetic. Only more recently the rôles seem to have been reversed. Russia (in the eyes of her new leaders) stands for the borrowed principle of revolution, discarded by the leaders of the West, while Europe, or Western Union, appears to have taken up the anti-revolutionary banner of Tyutchev's aspiring Empire—but on the whole without its ambiguous Christian faith, its iron discipline or farreaching territorial ambitions. And what was for Tyutchev a spiritual duel, fought to the death for straightforward vital principles, has today cooled down and turned more visibly into a clash of power politics, of astute calculations in gaining economic advantage, thinly disguised by moral or economic slogans which fewer people take at their face value.

Tyutchev's words glow with the fire of conviction:

Already in Europe there exist only two powers, Russia and Revolution. . . . Between them no negotiations, no treaties are possible. The existence of one of them alone is equivalent to the death of the other. On the result of that struggle now opening between them depends for many centuries to come the political and religious future of mankind.

Russia is above all the Christian Empire. The Russian people are Christian not only in their Orthodox faith, but especially by virtue of a quality even more intimate than Faith—I mean that faculty of self-renunciation and sacrifice which is the very core of their moral nature.

The Revolution is above all anti-Christian . . . the human ego referring to itself alone, recognising and accepting no duty beyond its own personal pleasure, the ego, in a word, substituting itself for God—that is not a new thing in history, but what is new is the absolutism of the human ego erected into a political and social right. . . . That novelty in 1789 was called the French Revolution. Since then, through all its external transformations the Revolution has remained true to its essential nature, and perhaps it has never felt so intensely anti-Christian as at the present moment, when it has adopted the Christian motto of 'brotherhood'. . . . Instead of a brotherhood preached and accepted in God's name, it claims to establish a brotherhood imposed by terror of the 'sovereign people'. . . . There is not a single human desire or need in our contemporary society, however sincere or legitimate it may be, which the Revolution does not capture and convert into a lie. . . .

Is it surprising that the West hates Russia, is ready to start a crusade against her—a crusade which was always the cherished dream of revolution? . . . But the West is vanishing, everything will fall and perish in that widespread conflagration—the Europe of Charlemagne and the Europe of the 1815 Treaties, the Roman Papacy and all the Western Kingdoms, Catholics and Protestants, faith long ago exhausted and reason carried to a senseless extreme. Law and order will become unthinkable, freedom no longer possible, and over all these ruins prepared by her own actions, Western civilization will commit suicide. And when, over that vast shipwreck, we see that still vaster Empire floating like a sacred ark, then who will dare to doubt the Russian mission? Will we, her children, show ourselves poor in faith or paltry in spirit? (**'Russia and Revolution,'** 1848.)

The 1848 revolutions inspired this *cri de coeur*. At that time the Russian Empire towered like a giant in solitary strength, and like an impregnable cliff withstood alone the waves of revolution that swept through a Europe of toppling thrones. So Tyutchev pictured her in his triumphant poem **'The Sea and the Cliff'** (1848). But a few years later came the Crimean War. The granite cliff began to crumble. Only the blind could fail to see that governmental Russia had in fact lost all sense and feeling of her vaunted historic mission. Tyutchev ruefully admitted that his hopes were dashed. 'Will those dry bones come to life?'

Could God's breath revive them, 'the breath of a storm?', he asked in one of his most disconsolate poems.

Yet since the Holy Alliance, and the majestic solidarity of European culture which it claimed to stand for, had collapsed before his eyes, Tyutchev believed more firmly than before that Western Europe was disintegrating. His injured patriotic pride found relief in even stronger moral condemnation of a West, victorious in arms and incontestably superior to Russia in material progress. 'Every blasphemous brain, every atheistic nation, has risen from the depths of the kingdom of darkness in the name of light and freedom', he wrote about Russia's enemies in the Crimean War. Nor had he any illusions about the kindly intentions expressed by the liberal Western politicians: 'The more liberal they sound, the baser they are; civilization is their fetish, but they have lost the key to its idea.'

Where Tyutchev saw most clearly the writing on the wall was in the latest European perversions of religion. His remarkable essay, **'The Papacy and the Roman Question'** (*Revue des Deux Mondes,* 1850) pays equal attention to the decline of genuine religious faith and to the infectious popularity of its misleading substitutes. He indicated that the organized brute force of Rome, deprived of its original spiritual virtue, might conquer in the end.

> Meanwhile Protestantism with its numerous ramifications, after having functioned for barely three centuries, is dying of senile decrepitude in all the countries where it reigned till now—with the solitary exception of England, and there its few remaining signs of life aspire to rejoin Rome. . . .
>
> We know the fetishism of the West, which clings to all forms, formulae and political mechanisms. *This fetishism has become the last religion of the West.* But only those with eyes blindfolded against evidence can suppose that the liberal or semi-liberal institutions imposed on the Pope will, in the present state of affairs in Europe, Italy and Rome, remain for long in the hands of moderate, balanced, temperate opinion. . . .

Soon they would turn into a battering-ram, not only against the temporal power of the Pope, but against the very foundations of religion. Such a result was inevitable, because the human ego, delivered to itself, becomes passionately anti-Christian.

> What is the sovereignty of the people except the human ego multiplied by numbers, *i.e.* relying on violence? That is the great novelty which the French Revolution brought into the world. For the first time a political society accepted to rule over it a state divorced from any superhuman sanctions, a state which admitted it had no soul, or if it had, a non-religious one. . . . But we know very well their so-called neutrality in religious matters is not a sincere component of revolutionaries. . . . If that hypocritical neutrality were to acquire a sense, if it could grow into something better than a lie and a trap, the modern state would consent to relinquish all moral authority, and resign itself to being a simple police institution for enforcing the law, a mere material fact. . . . But the modern state

does not proscribe state religions only because it has produced its own, and that religion is revolution.

How can so-called liberal opinion, Tyutchev concludes, pride itself on being so eminently reasonable and be so blind? How can liberals fail to see that institutions, once they have been wilfully deprived of the soul which gave them life, turn into nothing more than a dead encumbrance?

Because he ridiculed attempts to make the Papacy 'constitutional', it would be wrong to infer that Tyutchev cherished any sympathy for the Catholic Church as a bulwark of religion in a chaotic world. On the contrary (and in this he forestalled Dostoevsky) he vehemently loathed Catholicism, and he seems to have sincerely believed that the ambition and crookedness of Rome were largely responsible for Europe's spiritual decline. Certainly the curbing of the Pope's temporal power and fiscal privileges since 1848 had done nothing to decrease his spiritual claims. The famous Encyclical of Pope Pius IX, condemning the free exercise of individual conscience as one of the several 'errors of the age' (November 1864), roused Tyutchev to a fury of denunciation:

> Still more terrible and merciless
> In our time—the day of God's judgement,
> Will punishment overtake the false Vicar of
>   Christ
> In apostate Rome.
> Throughout the centuries much was forgiven
>   him,
> Crooked reasoning, blackest crimes,
> But God's truth will not forgive
> His latest censure . . .
>
>   (December, 1864.)

His increasingly cynical view of Russian political relations with the West was the consequence, not the cause, of Tyutchev's profound moral opposition to a sworn enemy. 'The only natural Russian policy towards the Western Powers—is not an alliance with one or the other, but a deliberate disruption and division of them all; divided against each other, through impotence, they may cease to be our enemies, but through conviction they never will!' Even though a sullen neutrality might occasionally give place to a short-lived tactical alliance with one European country or another, he reminded people of Danilevsky's trenchant saying that *civil war in the West is Russia's best ally.*

In 1858 Tyutchev was appointed President of the Committee on Foreign Censorship, where he started to serve as a link between the Ministry of Foreign Affairs and his son-in-law, Ivan Aksakov, whose eloquent articles played such an important part in rousing Slavophil opinion and action throughout the sixties. He praised the veteran Foreign Minister, Prince Gorchakov, for bringing to bear on world affairs the spiritual power of Russia, for being the first statesman to turn this power into a potent factor in international politics. In 1870 he wrote an enthusiastic poem to celebrate Russia's unilateral repudiation of that clause in the Treaty of Paris (1856) which restricted the movements of Russian warships in the Black Sea.

In his **'Letter about Censorship in Russia'** (1857), deploring the baleful influence of Herzen's *Bell* on immature minds, he urged the formation of a new officially-sponsored Russian journal, which should counteract sedition by attempting to direct and guide public opinion—a duty of the state, 'which', he said, 'bears as much direct responsibility for human souls as the Church does'. In the same letter he rather inconsistently argued, 'all the efforts of the crew will be in vain, unless the rising tide of national life itself lifts up the vessel and sets it afloat'. And despite the constant activity of these later years, Tyutchev was haunted by pessimistic forebodings about his country's future. 'Our days are numbered, who can count what's lost? The living life is now left far behind;' he wrote, and with an extra touch of premonition, 'Mental debauchery, distortion of words, still spread, still threaten you'. Sometimes even the threatening outlook in the West seemed to him brighter than his gloomy native land.

> Shadow has darkened half the sky, only the
>   West is bright with moving rays.
> Linger, twilight day; prolong, prolong your en-
>   chanting spell.

While he clung to minor consolations, Tyutchev saw no civilized future in a Europe which had neither restored nor superseded the guiding insight of her religious-minded monarchs and aristocrats. For European monarchy, though it precariously survived, had been adulterated, vulgarized and spoiled. One by one he caustically summed up the motives of Europe's principal rulers: the Emperor Franz Joseph, that 'Austrian Judas', Louis Philippe, 'the shopkeeper king', the last Napoleon, ambiguous heir of mighty powers, who in 1871 paid the penalty of having been no better than 'a popular actor on the throne'. Towards the end his doubts began to tarnish even the sacred Imperial halo of Holy Russia. A year before his death he wrote an enigmatic letter, appearing to welcome the maximum chaos and destruction in the outside world, if nothing but these disasters could save the Russian Empire. Some Soviet critics have taken it to mean much more than that; they seem to think that Tyutchev, having recognized his error, thereby renounced his lifelong crusade against the anti-Christ of Revolution, and now looked forward to see revolution rage through Europe and destroy her, in order that a strong *republican* Russia might rush into the resultant vacuum and start to lead the world.

'In the present state of minds in Europe', he wrote,

> that government which takes the initiative in making a majortransformation, opening the republican era in the European world, would enjoy a great advantage over all its neighbours. Dynastic feeling, without which monarchy cannot survive, is waning everywhere, and even if sometimes an opposite movement takes place, that merely delays the huge flood.

This rounds off what he wrote in 1854.

> If the West were united, we should probably be destroyed. But there are two, the Red West and the one which is to be swallowed by the Red. For forty years we have held back the Red from his prey. But now that we stand ourselves on the

edge of an abyss, it is the turn of the Red West
to save us!

(pp. 130-40)

*Richard Hare, "Five Political Slavophils," in
his* Pioneers of Russian Social Thought, *Oxford University Press, London, 1951, pp. 130-
70.*

Renato Poggioli   (essay date 1960)

[*Poggioli was an Italian-born American critic and translator. Much of his critical writing is concerned with Russian literature, including* The Poets of Russia: 1890-
1930, *one of the most important examinations of this literary era. In the excerpt below, he reviews Tyutchev's critical reception, characterizes his natural and metaphysical philosophies, and describes his poetic legacy to the Symbolists.*]

Born in 1803, on his family estate near Brjansk, in the Tula province, Fedor Tjutchev was less than twenty years old when he entered the diplomatic service, to spend abroad twenty years of his life, mainly in Munich, then capital of the kingdom of Bavaria. On his return home, he resumed after a break his service in the Ministry of Foreign Affairs. Strongly impressed by the Revolution of 1848, which led him to write and publish in French three important political essays, he became with the passing of time more and more of a Slavophile, and even a Panslavist. Married twice (both his wives were German), he yielded in late middle life to a frenetic "last love," which ended only with the death of his younger partner, and which inspired some of the best among his later poems. In his last years he became a man of the world and a drawing-room wit, exhibiting a not-too-feigned indifference toward his literary work, which won him unsolicited, but restricted and intermittent, recognition in his lifetime. Tjutchev died in 1873, but his posthumous glory began at the end of the century with a famous article by Vladimir Solov'ev, which was to be followed by the universal acclaim of the modernists and the Symbolists.

Habent sua fata libelli; yet the destiny of the single book which contains the whole of Tjutchev's poetic heritage (including translations, a total of about 300 pieces, hardly averaging twenty lines in length) is almost unique. From the late twenties on he published scattered verse here and there, yet a score or more poems which appeared in 1838 in *The Contemporary* (they were entitled "Poems Sent from Germany," and signed only with the author's initials) passed largely unnoticed. In 1850 Nekrasov, then editor of the same journal, praised the poet highly, and four years later issued under *The Contemporary*'s imprint the first collection in book form of Tjutchev's lyrics. The book was edited by Ivan Turgenev, who deserves great praise for the pains he took in this matter, but who revised and reworked the text so considerably as to make any exhaustive reconstruction of Tjutchev's canon almost impossible. It is true that that volume included only one third of Tjutchev's poetry, but much of that third was written in the poet's most creative period, the decade from 1830 to 1840. All too much of what Tjutchev composed after that date is made up of occasional patriotic pieces, interesting only

as biographical documents or political pronouncements. Their literary significance, if any, may be seen in the fact that many of these poems deeply impressed Dostoevskij, who found in them confirmation of several of his ideas. Tjutchev was Dostoevskij's favorite poet, and the latter cited him frequently in his writings. The novelist's most usual quotation from Tjutchev's verse was the last stanza of a famous poem, with its closing vision of Christ passing through the poet's native countryside and blessing forever, under the weight of the cross, the bare squalor of Russia, of her nature, people, and way of life.

Despite its aspiration toward an objective and impersonal lyricism, Tjutchev's poetry may yet look closer to Lermontov's than to Pushkin's. This impression might also be due to Tjutchev's literary education, which was less classical and less French than that of Pushkin and which was, as in the case of Lermontov, primarily, if not exclusively, Romantic. Yet, while Lermontov found his real masters in England, Tjutchev went instead to the school of German thought and poetry. He was acquainted, and corresponded, with Schelling; he met Heine, whose works he translated along with those of Schiller and Goethe, and he wrote, upon the death of the latter, a poem as lovely as the one which Baratynskij composed on the same occasion and theme. Tjutchev replaced Lermontov's introspective visions and subjective intuitions with mystical and metaphysical insights, revealing a conception of nature very different from that which so many continental Romantics had inherited from Rousseau. He saw nature not as the idyllic and immanent mirror of the self, but as a transcendental power, annihilating any other force, overshadowing all reality. In German Romantic terms, one could say that Tjutchev is the poet of *die Nachtseite der Natur,* of "nature's nightly side." Yet this does not mean that he considers nature to be blind and brute instinct, or inarticulate and senseless matter. Vladimir Solov'ev was the first to claim that Tjutchev's poetry is an attempt to bare the chaotic and mystic roots of being. In Tjutchev's view nature is neither a mother nor a stepmother; we cannot blame her for ignoring creatures like ourselves, since, as the poet says, "man is merely nature's dream." Although incommensurably superior to any created thing, nature herself is a living and suffering organism, a complex being with not only a body, but also a mind, will, and soul of her own. "Nature is not what you fancy," said Tjutchev in a famous poem, "she is neither a copy nor a soulless face; in her there is spirit and freedom, passion and tongue." By spiritualizing nature, Tjutchev fails, however, to humanize her: he rather turns her into a universal oversoul, both divine and demonic in essence. Hence her immense distance from man, "a trivial dust," as the poet says, "not allowed to burn with godly fire."

Tjutchev views the universe as the stage of an enormous drama, a tragic conflict between the opposing forces of order and disorder, between the consoling illusion of life and the awful mystery of creation. The poet symbolizes this drama or conflict in a series of polarities or antitheses such as Chaos and Cosmos, Death and Sleep, Winter and Spring, Night and Day. The conflict is, however, more apparent than real: the drama is perhaps a mere play. Yet the struggle, if any, ends with the inexorable victory of what man deems to be the negative and destructive element, although it may well be the positive and constructive one. Creation is also annihilation: this is why Night is always bound to triumph over Day, which the poet describes as the veil which hides from man the secrets of being and not-being; ultimately Night will forever frown over the world "like a beast with a hundred eyes."

The poet's moral and psychological attitude toward the sublime objects of his mystical and metaphysical speculation is, however, complex, and even mixed; one could say that his sentiment accepts that vision less readily, and more doubtfully, than his imagination. It is the poet in him, or, in Tjutchev's words, his "prophetic soul," that feels in harmony with the universal symphony, while his more human faculties feel and fear that elemental discord of which man is but a passive witness and a powerless victim. Thus the poet is both ecstatically attracted and tragically awed by the wonders and terrors of the "sacred night." There is no better proof of this ambivalent attitude than his famous poem to the wind, an element in which Tjutchev saw, as Blok would see after him, the over-all symbol of all powers of destruction and metamorphosis. In his apostrophe to that element, Tjutchev implores the wind, with a negative imperative, "not to sing those awful chants of the native chaos."

The mind of Tjutchev was obviously unable to choose logically between the alternatives of a mystic pantheism and a cosmic nihilism. Yet he resolved the dualism of these two world views, irreconcilable in philosophical terms, by focusing his inspiration on the unbridgeable gulf between them. That gulf is but a reflection of the chasm which the poet constantly saw in the infinite space of the created universe; or perhaps it is a projection of the very abyss which Tjutchev, like Pascal, carried within himself. That abyss was never void, even though it became all too often a well of perplexity, or a source of that despair and doubt which inspired the poems of dejection and despondency of the second part of Tjutchev's life. Yet that abyss turns sometimes into a spring of life, bringing forth many poems of serene and detached contemplation, mostly in the form of seasonal landscapes, often seen against an autumnal background and made uncanny by the presence of a miraculous peace.

It was the poet's unique sense of spiritual privacy, his almost total surrender to the claims of inner life, that explain, more than Tjutchev's morbid sensitivity to any unfriendly criticism, his outright refusal to enter the literary arena and to peddle in public his poetic wares. It was also the unworldly aloofness of his poetry which inspired **"Silentium,"** an apostrophe addressed to himself, closing with the singing words: "Listen to the song of your thoughts and visions, and keep silent." Despite its most famous line ("an uttered thought is but a lie"), that poem is but a reaffirmation of the Romantic disdain for the vulgarity of the multitude, and should not be read, as it was by many Symbolists, as an intimation of their paradoxical belief in the ineffability of that mystical experience in which they saw the single source of all the creations of art. Tjutchev paved the way for Symbolistic poetry more through his practice than through his theory: first by the

utter simplicity and the august solemnity of his diction, which perfectly blends the colloquial and the literary element, often represented by Slavonicisms and archaisms; then by the melodic dissonance of his metrical counterpoint, by that interplay of rigidity and flexibility with which he treated his favorite lines, which were the iambic tetrameter and pentameter; and finally by the visionary power of his metaphors, by the mystical quality of his imagery. (pp. 33-7)

> *Renato Poggioli, "The Masters of the Past," in his* The Poets of Russia: 1890-1930, *Cambridge, Mass.: Harvard University Press, 1960, pp. 1-45.*

Richard A. Gregg   (essay date 1965)

[*Gregg is an American educator and critic who specializes in Russian language and literature. In the following excerpt, he examines the impact of Tyutchev's years in Bavaria upon his poetic form, themes, and tone, proposing a psychological explanation for the metamorphosis in tone.*]

When in June, 1822, Tiutchev arrived in Munich, he was a boy of eighteen; when he left the West in 1844, he was a man of forty-one, prematurely gray, twice-married, and father of five. Between these moments stretch the twenty-two years which Aksakov has called "the most important of Tiutchev's life—the period of his intellectual and spiritual formation." He might have added that this period witnessed the lifecycle of a remarkable poetic talent from its adolescence, early youth, and maturity, to its sudden and curious withering away (c. 1841). (p. 32)

Thirty-five years ago the Russian "formalist" critic Iurii Tynianov performed a brilliant and erudite dissection of Tiutchev's poetic style in terms of literary genealogy. After briefly discussing Tiutchev's debts to German romanticism and (in somewhat greater detail) to Raich's "Italian School," Tynianov went on to analyze the essential features of Tiutchev's poetic style. His conclusion was that it constitutes nothing less than a new poetic genre, the genre of the lyrical "fragment," broken off from the eighteenth-century "monumental" form and, for all its romantic overtones, owing its deepest stylistic debts to Derzhavin. Now the choice of the term "fragment" for a literary type of rare artistic *unity* may seem unfortunate to some. But though a trifle arbitrary in his use of terms, Tynianov scores his points brilliantly—so brilliantly, indeed, that they have received the ultimate scholarly tribute: they have become the critical commonplaces of succeeding generations.

Fortunately our own chronological bias, stressing as it does the interior evolution of Tiutchev's poetry, puts the nicer details of stylistic genealogy beyond our reach. "Fortunately," for the accretion of scholarly findings since Tynianov has added weight to his ideas without, however, changing them substantially. Any serious treatment of the subject would therefore largely consist of reviewing other scholars' corroborations of a theory the significant lines of which we already know. Relieved, moreover, of this chore, we are free to replace Tynianov's largely synchronic approach by our own chronological one. In so doing we shall discover a very different—though not necessarily contradictory—order of truth concerning Tiutchev and his eighteenth-century heritage. We shall find that the poet's early development records a systematic *shedding* of the eighteenth-century poetic tradition (a tradition of which Derzhavin's verse was an important, though not always characteristic, part), and that this escape was not accidental or temporary but the necessary condition for the realization of his own poetic gifts.

All Tiutchev scholars agree that the poet's earliest serious poems (**"Uraniia," "On the New Year, 1816,"** and the translation from Horace) are imitations of the neoclassical ode. They are lengthy exercises with fluid stanzaic patterns and long, irregular (four to six feet) lines, replete with archaisms, abstractions, and cosmic-sounding imagery. The first ten lines of **"Uraniia"** may be considered typical: . . .

> It has been discovered! Is it not a dream? A new world! A new power has invested my lofty spirit like a flame! Who has given me, a youth, the soaring flight of the eagle! Behold the priceless gift of the Muses! Behold these wingèd inspirations! I am swiftly soaring, and the earthly vale has vanished before my eyes; that world, wrapped in a thick and misty shroud of turbulence, has vanished! Like the golden ray of the sun, the heavenly ether has touched my lids and blown away the earthly dust.

And so on for a hundred and eighty odd lines. Young Tiutchev wrote only three such pieces, it is true, but quantitatively they constitute the bulk of his early poetic output (eleven pages in Chulkov's edition); and the style of the shorter, less ambitious pieces of the period is, *mutatis mutandis,* very similar.

Within a year of his arrival in Germany, however, the poet had begun to dump his neoclassical ballast. In the place of the lengthy odes and pompous little *vers de circonstances* of the Russian years emerges the lyric, a poem of about twenty lines or less, organized in regular tetrameter or pentameter quatrains (*abab* or *abba*) in which the extravagantly lofty tone and cosmic imagery have been dropped, the archaisms and mythological machinery curtailed, and a new concrete—even sensuous—quality introduced. The first four stanzas from **"Tears,"** written in the summer of 1823, give an idea of the changes which were afoot: . . .

> O friends, I love to feast my eyes on the purple hue of sparkling wines, or on the fragrant ruby of the fruit between the leaves. I love to look on creatures plunged, as it were, in spring; and the world, fallen asleep in fragrance, smiles in its slumber. I love it when a zephyr flames the face of a beauty with its kiss, and sometimes blows up the voluptuous curls of silk, sometimes delving into the dimples of her cheeks! But what are all the charms of the Paphian Empress, the sap of grape clusters, the smell of roses, before you, holy source of tears, dew of a divine daybreak!

That these lines retain their share of eighteenth-century mannerism—for example, the archaic *iskrometnyi,* the

self-consciously classical "Paphian Empress" (for Venus), and the loftily euphemistic "dew of a divine daybreak" (for tears)—cannot be denied. But even if the theme were not so obviously romantic, and the epigraph ("O lacrymarum fons") not taken from a romantic poet (Gray), we could find in the increased concentration, sensuousness, and simplicity of these lines the middle term of a progression, which culminated a few years later in verse like this: . . .

> The misty noon breathes lazily; the river rolls lazily; and in the fiery pure firmament the clouds melt lazily. And hot drowsiness envelops all nature like a fog; and great Pan himself now dozes peacefully in the cave of the Nymphs.

It is important to understand that these changes represent something more than the immersion of a hesitant and immature talent in the rising romantic tide. They mark a deliberate and necessary step toward artistic self-realization. In this connection it will be recalled that young Tiutchev was at one time so dissatisfied with his neoclassically inspired verse that he considered giving poetry up altogether. And a clue to the sources of his early dissatisfaction may be seen in a critical remark which the poet made a number of years later to his friend Gagarin. Speaking of a Russian literary work which he particularly admired, Tiutchev remarked:

> Le sentiment poétique ne s'est pas entamé par la déclamation. J'aime à faire honneur à la nature même de l'esprit Russe de cet éloignement pour la rhétorique, cette peste, ou plutôt ce péché originel français. C'est là qui met Pouchkine si fort audessus de tous les poètes français contemporains.

For Tiutchev, who more than any other poet of his period has been identified with the eighteenth-century rhetorical tradition, these are singular words. It is important, moreover, to understand that the "rhetoric" word here cannot simply denote the use of apostrophe or the hortatory form of address. Nearly all the Russian romantic poets indulged in these modes of speech, Pushkin no less than the rest, and Tiutchev himself rather more. What he is condemning is the neoclassical rhetorical tradition, that "sin" which had, indeed, originated in France, and which, he justly observes, continued to color the verse of the contemporary French romantics. In its Russianized form Tiutchev himself had practiced it. Later he abandoned it; now we find him attacking it. Why? Because, he insists, such rhetoric is alien "to the very nature of the Russian mind." As literary criticism this is not very illuminating; but as literary autobiography it is extremely helpful. For the "Russian mind" in question is obviously Tiutchev's own. And it rejected the neoclassical tradition of rhetoric for the best of reasons: it was "contrary to [his] very nature," that is, *it did not offer him poetic resources which he could use.*

This, then, is the crucial point; for it both defines Tiutchev's fundamental attitude toward neoclassical rhetoric and suggests how greatly his own poetry was to differ from it. In this connection it should be noted that the most popular genre of the Russian neoclassical period was the ode, a long, loosely constructed verse form, which the poet could manipulate with considerable formal freedom, expending words without stint in the hope of attaining the desired effect, which was usually *loftiness,* or—to use a favorite term of the period—the *sublime.* Such a poetic approach may fairly be called *extensive,* and the Russian poet who exploited it with the greatest success was Derzhavin, whose plangently baroque diction and sweeping rhetorical periods acquire an impressive weight and momentum in such celebrated poems as the odes to God and the lines on the death of Prince Mescherskii.

Now this form and the methods it implied were profoundly uncongenial to Tiutchev's genius. His mature lyrical poetry is marked by the cultivation of the *intensive* method, where in the space of a few lines oxymoron, symmetrical word order, assonance, alliteration, onomatopoeia, and subtle metrical innovations cooperate to present one or two audacious images; then the poem is over. Formal brevity reacted on his talent like a corset: bracing, shaping, and condensing. His most successful poems (as Nekrasov and Turgenev both observed) are nearly always his shortest. And whenever he relapsed into the longer discursive style (as, curiously enough, he often did in his patriotic verse) his effects are dissipated and significantly weakened. The difference between the early discursive and the later condensing styles has already been suggested by illustration. The following two poems, written at opposite ends of the decade but on similar themes, show an even more striking contrast. The first three stanzas of **"Spring,"** written in 1821, will suffice: . . .

> Spring, the love of the earth and the charm of the year, breathes fragrantly on us! . . . Nature gives a banquet to creation and a rendezvous banquet to its sons. . . . The spirit of life, of force, and of freedom raises us aloft and breathes around us! And like the echo of nature's triumph, like the lifegiving voice of God, Joy is poured into the soul! Where are you, sons of Harmony? Come hither! . . . and with bold fingers touch the sleeping string, heated by the bright rays of love, enthusiasm, and spring!

The second, entitled **"Spring Storm,"** was written some eight years later. . . .

> I love a storm in early May. How gaily the spring thunder rumbles down the azure sky from one edge to the other! From the mountain runs the nimble stream: in the forest the birds' chatter is never still; the talk of birds and the mountain spring—everything gaily echoes the peals of thunder! One would say that windy Hebe, feeding Zeus' eagle, laughing had poured upon the earth her thunder-bubbling goblet from the sky.

These radical stylistic changes should not lead us to deny the importance of Tynianov's original insight. Vestiges of the old rhetorical style in the form of occasional archaisms, abstractions, and the frequent use of apostrophe do survive in the mature Tiutchev lyric. But they do not constitute—as Tynianov implies—its necessary ingredients. They appear rather as diluted solutions drawn from an earlier and very different mixture. When present in force they lend a special color to the poetic texture; but this

should not blind us to the fact that in a great number of Tiutchev's lyrics they are, in fact, not present at all.

One final caveat. Tynianov, and Pumpianskii after him, have observed that certain peculiarities of Derzhavin's "monumental" style (the term is Tynianov's), such as the use of barbarisms, compounds, and a special predilection for colors, are common to Tiutchev as well. This is perfectly true; but again the value of the insight changes when we add the temporal dimension. For it is precisely in Tiutchev's adolescent verse, where the eighteenth-century heritage is peculiarly pronounced, that the use of colors, compounds, and barbarisms is comparatively *rare.* They appear in quantity only in the Munich period, that is, *after* Tiutchev had discovered the small form, and for reasons that must be obvious: it was precisely at this stage that Tiutchev was mobilizing all linguistic means available to cultivate the new "intensive" method. Devices like compounds, barbarisms, and the use of colors (none of these peculiar to Derzhavin, we may note, but common poetic property of Russian baroque verse) obviously served this aim and were adopted. Their origins are, then, less a matter of literary genealogy than of autonomous poetic evolution. And they arose not because Tiutchev was so close to the eighteenth-century tradition as we find it reflected in his own early verse but because he had begun to move away from this tradition.

Hand in hand with these changes in style came equally striking thematic innovations. Pomp and circumstance had been the twin keynotes of the early Russian years, as an incomplete run-down of titles and first lines indicates: "I am at once all-powerful and weak," **"To Two Friends"** ("On this day, this blessed day, one of you / Took both the virtues and the name of that Virgin . . . "), a congratulatory poem to his tutor Raich, beginning "Having vanquished the treacherous sea chasms / The swimmer has attained the longed-for shores," and so on. These are didactic and ceremonious exercises on subjects a precocious schoolboy might choose for declamation on classday. (Such, indeed, seem to have been the circumstances attending the previously cited **"Uraniia."**) And we look in vain among them for those themes which characterize Tiutchev in his mature years: feminine love is wholly absent, and the beauties of nature appear only once, in the vague and florid oratory of **"Spring."**

Significantly, Tiutchev's life during these same years shows no corresponding lacunae in these areas. The young poet was already very much alive to the charms of feminine beauty; and as for nature, the Ovstug landscape had surrounded him since childhood. Neither, however, had impinged upon his poetic imagination—a fact which may help explain the prophylactic quality of his adolescent verse, the nature of which Aksakov was the first to observe ("heavy," "forced," and even "shackles" are the terms he used to describe it).

As the impact of German romanticism made itself felt on the poet, these "shackles" began to dissolve. As a result, for the first time the themes of nature and love make their appearance in his verse, and along with them, a constellation of familiar romantic themes. The young poet now writes about the joy of tears (**"Tears"**), night as a moment of mystical revelation (**"The Gleam," "A Vision," "In Crowds of People, in the Hurly-burly of the Day," "Insomnia," "As the Ocean Embraces the Earthly Sphere," "Dream at Sea"**), the exalted role of the poet (**"You Saw Him in the Mundane Spheres"**), escape from earthly bonds (**"The Soul Would Like to Be a Star"**), and even Napoleon (**"Napoleon's Grave"**). Indeed, of the twenty-five or thirty original poems of the period some twenty embody easily identifiable romantic motifs.

As one might expect, the earliest of these poems are the most clearly derivative. Thus the previously cited **"Tears,"** written in 1823, clearly looks back to the cult of feeling at the turn of the eighteenth century. But if it idealizes tears on the one hand, it also introduces a sensual motif: "I love it when a zephyr flames / The face of a beauty with its kiss, / And sometimes blows up the voluptuous curls of silk," which has no counterpart in the poems by Gray and Byron which seem to have suggested it. This early conjunction of sensuality with suffering is worthy of note. For in time Tiutchev will go beyond the typically pre-romantic juxtaposition of the two; he will equate them.

Similarly, Tiutchev's first love poem, **"To N.,"** where the innocent and pure love of a maiden is contrasted with the base and uncomprehending crowd, sounds at times like a compendium of romantic commonplaces. (The first stanza reads: "Your dear gaze, filled with innocent passion— / The golden dawn of your celestial thoughts / Could not, alas, propitiate them [i.e., the crowd, "society"], / It serves as a tacit rebuke to them.") And the frolicsome **"Cache-cache"** escapes banality only by becoming confusingly coy. As for the third love poem, **"To N.N.,"** the early romantic idealism has given way to a fair measure of cynicism.

Tiutchev's most substantial thematic debt to the German romantics (Cizevski singles out Eichendorff, Brentano, and Novalis as the most prominent) may be seen, however, in his "holy night" group of poems, a phrase used here to denote those poems where night is given the power of revealing some sublime spiritual or metaphysical truth to the poet. The theme receives its earliest—and somewhat overwrought—treatment in **"The Gleam,"** where the notes of an Aeolian harp at midnight evoke a vision of celestial truth too beautiful to endure. Profounder and more original is **"A Vision,"** where vestiges of the eighteenth-century cosmic imagery have been compressed into the "new" form of short lyric. Noteworthy, too, in the poem are the vividly realized sense of apocalyptic revelation and the early appearance of the "chaos" image, destined to figure prominently in the poems of the next decade: . . .

> There is a certain hour of universal silence in the night; and at that hour of apparitions and miracles the live chariot of creation rolls openly through the holy house of the heavens. Then the night thickens like chaos on the waters; oblivion, like Atlas, oppresses the land—only the virgin soul of the Muse do the gods stir in prophetic dreams.

Further examples of the theme are **"The Gay Day Still Sounded"** and **"As the Ocean Embraces the Earthly**

Sphere." Finally, in **"You Saw Him in the Mundane Spheres"** and **"In Crowds of People, in the Hurly-burly of the Day"** the night motif merges with other romantic themes common to the period: the special calling of the poet and romantic love respectively. Both poems draw the familiar comparison of the individual with the moon which, pale or invisible by day, emerges radiantly at night to achieve full self-realization; but the metaphor which climaxes the transformation refines and heightens the commonplace in a way which has nothing to do with stereotypes, romantic or otherwise: . . .

> Look, how in the daytime the lustrous moon, mistily white, barely glimmers in the sky. But when Night comes, upon pure glass the fragrant amber oil will pour!

Against these six variations on a single theme stands one night poem, **"Insomnia,"** belonging to the same period but pointing in a very different direction. To this important poem we shall return.

Of all the romantic themes, that of nature evoked the most mature and distinctive response in young Tiutchev. One of his very earliest Munich poems is **"Evening"**: . . .

> How quietly over the valley blow the distant belfry notes, like the rustle of a flock of cranes, and in the soughing of the leaves they die away. Like a spring sea in full tide, brightening, the day is motionless; and then more hastily, more silently, the evening shadows spread themselves across the valley.

And here are two stanzas taken from **"Summer Evening,"** written several years later: . . .

> Already the earth has rolled the incandescent sphere of the sun from its head, and the sea wave has swallowed the calm fire of the evening. . . . And a sweet tremor, like a stream, has run through the veins of nature, as if spring waters had touched her burning feet.

This is original and distinguished poetry. But having said this, we cannot deny the obvious: that these poems depict German scenes; that their subject matter—dusk, a sunset, spring (twice), the beauties of the Alps (twice), and a rainbow—are clichés of the preromantic and romantic schools, as indeed are many of the particulars—the tolling bell at dusk, mountains swathed in clouds (**"Morning in the Mountains"**), snow-capped peaks (**"Snowy Mountains"**), vernal storms (**"Spring Storm," "Tranquilization"**), and freshets (**"Spring Waters"**).

Other relevant points come to mind: that Tiutchev wrote a great many translations from the German poets (Goethe, Herder, Heine, and Schiller) at this time; that Coates's and Tynianov's investigations have shown an interdependence between Tiutchev's original verse and his translations; while Cizevski has clearly established a set of thematic borrowings (among which the mystical significance of night, sleep, and dreams is the most prominent) from still another group of German romantic poets: Eichendorff, Brentano, and Novalis. Taken together do not these facts suggest that more than anything else these poems appear to be literary exercises? May we not, in fact, go one step further and agree with Tynianov, who—partial to the formalist notion that all literature is a great self-winding clock—argued that "to a great measure Tiutchev's poetry is poetry about poetry"? No doubt we would if it were not that the available facts suggest quite a different order of truths—that the great majority of Tiutchev's poems were provoked by specific events of a nonliterary nature, that they were, in fact, *Gelegenheitsgedichte* in the Goethean sense.

The problem before us, that of assessing the roles of literature and "life" in Tiutchev's creative performance, is not new; and our ultimate conclusion—that both factors figure importantly—may seem obvious from the outset. But the strong *biographical* bias of the present study and the equally strong importance traditionally given to the purely *literary* sources of Tiutchev's creativity (culminating in Tynianov's extreme—and heretofore unchallenged—statement quote above) make it imperative for us to define as closely as possible the nature and relationship of these two factors before we proceed.

The fact of the matter is that Tiutchev possessed to an unusual degree what might be called a *literary imagination,* that is, an eye which habitually saw life through the prism of literature. For this reason Blagoi's astute observation that Tiutchev's image of nature is that of a tourist is worth citing. For the tourist, however docilely his eye may follow his predecessor's from alpine height to crystal lake, is, nonetheless, experiencing these things firsthand. And his responses, though partially conditioned by literature, are not, as Tynianov would have us believe, occasioned by it. For Tiutchev, literary associations constituted an important part of his enjoyment of nature. Poetic evidence indicates that this was particularly true of the Munich period, but in a diminished degree it survives in later years, as a passage from a letter written from Vevey to his wife in the summer of 1850 testifies:

> Tout cela [the Vevey countryside] est idéalement charmant. . . . Quand on pense que cette année il y a juste cent ans que l'illustration poétique de ce coin de terre a commencé par Jean-Jacques Rousseau, son Héloise étant, si je ne me trompe, de 1754.
>
> Depuis lors, trois quatre générations se sont succedées: Mme de Staël, Lord Byron, Karamsine dans ses Lettres du Ruskii Puteshestvennik [in Cyrillic] puis la génération de Lamartine, Zhukovskii [in Cyrillic], qui a tant aimé ce coté du lac et qui en si bien parlé; puis notre génération à nous . . . et toutes ces imaginations dans leur jeunesse ont habité avec amour cette terre bénie et elles ont passé, elles se sont évanouies les unes après les autres.
>
> *Mais on dirait qu'il en reste quelque chose dans l'air, la lumière, les splendeurs de ce lac et de ces montagnes.*

Evidently the poet's acquaintance with the literature of the past could play an important role in his enjoyment of the natural beauties of the present. (pp. 34-45)

Sometime in the early 1830s the sight, or the memory, of a weeping willow drooping its branches over a stream gave birth to this "philosophical" lyric: . . .

> Willow, why do you bend the crown of your head over the waters? And with trembling leaves, as if with greedy lips, why do you catch at the running stream? Although each of your leaves wearies itself and trembles over the stream, yet still the stream runs and splashes, and, lolling in the sun, shines and laughs at you.

But stored in Tiutchev's memory were fragments from another poem in another language, the words and images of which floated to the surface of his mind as he composed. For in one of Horace's odes (Tiutchev was a fine Latinist, and had in his boyhood committed large parts of Horace to memory) the following lines may be found:

> quo pinus ingens algaque populus
> umbram hospitalem consociare amant
> ramis? quid obliquo laborat
> lympha fugax trepidare rivo?
>
> Why do the tall pine and the white poplar love
> to interlace their branches in inviting shade?
> why does the fleeting water strive to dash down
> the winding stream?

The differences between these passages are obvious and fundamental. Where Horace merely juxtaposes his trees and river, Tiutchev links them. And whereas Horace makes them minor and parallel illustrations of his ultimate moral—*carpe diem*—in Tiutchev they stand alone and opposed; and this conflict is the point of the poem.

The similarities are nonetheless too numerous and close to ignore. The Horace passage beginning with a "why?" construction is followed by the image of the trees, of the interlacing branches, and finally of the "fleeting" current which tries to dash off downstream. Tiutchev, too, opens with a "why?" sentence; he, too, introduces the image of the tree. Like Horace he follows up with the idea of interlacement, where *listami* ("by means of leaves") is the grammatical equivalent of *ramis* ("by means of branches"). Moreover, like Horace's *lympha* these leaves weary themselves (*laborat* and *tomitsia* are not synonymous, but they both connote the fatigue that follows exertion); and like his *lympha* they are agitated. Tiutchev here simply makes a phonetic translation, rendering *trepidare* by its Slavic cousin *trepeschet*. Finally, Tiutchev like Horace makes his current "fleeting"—*fugax* and *beglyi* being identical in meaning and actually derived from a common root.

Literature not only conditioned Tiutchev's poetic apprehension of reality; it could even impinge on what, for want of a better word, may be called his prose consciousness. In the summer of 1866 the poet, having visited the park at Tsarskoe Selo, composed a poem beginning: . . .

> Quietly in the lake there flow reflections of golden roofs. Many bygone glories gaze into the lake.

In 1869, after visiting the historic city of Kiev during an official visit by the Tsar, Tiutchev in a letter to the poet Maikov described the beauty of the scene, "with the illumination of all those *glorious* Kievan [unfinished word, perhaps "temples," perhaps "ancient places"] with their *golden-capped* shrines and their *reflections in the Dnieper.*" Three years and a thousand miles away from the park at Tsarskoe Selo, similar surroundings and the presence of the Emperor (the necessary catalyst, it would seem, for the reaction) make Tiutchev rehearse not only the same complex of physical and psychological detail—the golden-roofed buildings reflected in a reach of flowing water become linked with thoughts of Russia's glorious past—but even bits of the language itself, e.g., *zoloto—zolotykh, dostoslavnykh—dostoslavnostei, otblesk—otrazhenie.*

Tiutchev's poetry, then, presents an invisible welding of the actual with the literary. And while we must give the literary genealogist his due and recognize the crucial role that literature sometimes played in Tiutchev's creative process, it is impossible to agree that these poems are largely "poetry about poetry." With relatively few exceptions the landscapes, the thoughts, and the emotions of his poems are, for all their literary coloration, as demonstrably real and a part of the poet's experience as the lake which lay before him at Vevey or the reflections which he saw in the Dnieper.

Up to now we have considered the poetry of these early years from two standpoints: the stylistic and the thematic. Still remaining, however, is another problem which is of great importance, namely the question of poetic *tone*.

Because of its impreciseness one should approach all generalizations concerning poetic tone with caution. Still, no one would deny that Tiutchev's poetry *taken as a whole* does not reveal a disposition to either lighthearted *joie de vivre* or youthful enthusiasm. Passion, frustration, skepticism, and despair: these are the moods which color the great majority of his mature verse. It is, therefore, of some interest that the poetic tone of the period under discussion oscillates largely between these two atypical moods. As an example of Tiutchev's carefree hedonistic tone we may cite **"Spring Waters."** . . .

> The snow is still white in the fields, but freshets gurgle with the sound of spring. They run and wake the sleepy banks. They run and dazzle and proclaim on all sides: "Spring is coming, spring is coming! We are the harbingers of youthful spring. She has sent us in advance." Spring is coming, spring is coming! And the rosy, bright dancing ring of the quiet, warm May days is flocking gaily after her.

The following lines, on the other hand, illustrate the strain of lofty enthusiasm, often tinged with romantic mysticism.

> You saw him in the mundane spheres, now selfishly gay, now sullen, distraught, or wild, or filled with secret thoughts. Such is the poet—and you scorned the poet! Look at the moon: all day, like a wasted cloud, it has almost perished in the skies. Night comes, and like a radiant god it shines over the sleeping grove.

The examples speak for themselves, and it only remains to make the following statistical observations. Of the twenty-nine poems which Chulkov assigns to these years, nineteen may be identified with either the "enthusiastic" or the "hedonistic" vein; of these same twenty-nine only six are in a minor key; and of these only one, **"Insomnia,"** is deeply pessimistic.

The significance of these observations comes more clearly into focus when we compare them with a similar set of facts drawn from a later eight-year period. From 1850 to 1858 Tiutchev wrote some fifty-four original poems. Of these, thirty-one are indisputably dark in tone: bitter, hostile, or despairing. In other words, the pessimism which marks less than one quarter of Tiutchev's early poetry prevails (and generally in far more somber colors) in more than a half of the later poems. When, on the other hand, we look for poems in the enthusiastic or hedonistic vein, we discover only five which might conceivably fit the definition—in other words, a drop from over 60 percent in the twenties to under 10 percent in the fifties.

To sum up and conclude: In later years Tiutchev came to idealize the early Munich period, turning it into a kind of Golden Age where worldly pleasures and otherworldly innocence could live side by side; furthermore, Tiutchev's poetry during these early years is uncharacteristically optimistic in tone, an optimism composed of two strains, the cheerful-hedonistic and the lofty enthusiastic. Now when the two sets of values are compared, it becomes obvious that the virtues which the latter-day myth imputes and the qualities which the earlier poems record are very similar. It is also obvious that they are not identical. And what separates them is, quite simply, a sense of sin. For to the guilt-ridden poet of later years youthful enthusiasm would inevitably appear to be innocence, and his carefree hedonism—earthly bliss, the bliss, if you will, before the Fall. How was this Golden Age destroyed, leaving behind only a world of memories, an "Elysium of shades . . . ghosts of past, best days"? How, in short, was innocence lost?

It should first be noted that Tiutchev's release into the life of the West was bought at the price of an almost total amputation from his former Russian existence, and that the one was a logical and necessary complement of the other. In insisting strongly on this point we are, in a sense, turning back the clock. Some eighty years ago Aksakov committed several factual errors in expressing similar opinions on Tiutchev's prolonged isolation in the West. These judgments stood for thirty years until V. Ia. Briusov sought to relegate them to the limbo of "legend." But in rectifying some minor errors of fact, Briusov, the better informed scholar, committed a major error of emphasis. For to point out that during these years abroad Tiutchev visited Russia infrequently (only three times in the first twenty years), entertained visitors from home, and continued to show an intellectual interest in things Russian is to modify, but not substantially to change, Aksakov's main point: that the poet spent the first two decades of his adult life almost entirely cut off from his family, his country, and, after Khlopov's departure in 1826, his language; that the majority of his friends were German, and that neither of his wives nor his German-reared and French-speaking children knew any Russian; in short, that for twenty-one years the poet's social, domestic, and cultural surroundings were to an overwhelming degree those provided by western Europe.

It is interesting that this radical and voluntary disinheritance seems at the time to have been accomplished almost painlessly. Indeed the alacrity with which Tiutchev accepted the West is a measure of the cleanness of the amputation: had the taproots into his Russian past been many and deep, he doubtless would, in Pogodin's words, have "smelled of the [Bavarian] court" a little less strongly. Here the qualifying words "at the time" and "almost" are important. For even during the high-spirited Munich days the anesthesia of Western pleasures would at moments wear off, and the wound would throb. Through the musty rhetoric (still significantly neoclassical) of Tiutchev's very early **"To My Friends, on Sending Schiller's 'Ode to Joy',"** we can perhaps detect the notes of real emotion: . . .

> And can I sing this joyous song, far from the hearts which are dear to me, in sorrow which I cannot share, can I sing of Joy on a muted lyre?

Some three years later the following "Lines Written in an Album at Malta," addressed by Byron to a Mrs. Spencer Smith:

> As o'er the cold sepulchral stone
> Some name arrests the passer-by,
> Thus when thou view'st this page alone
> May mine attract thy pensive eye.
> And when by thee that name is read,
> Perchance in some succeeding year
> Reflect on me as on the dead,
> And think my heart is buried near.

were "translated" by Tiutchev as follows:

> As the attention of a traveler lingers upon the cold gravestones, so will the writing of a familiar hand attract the attention of my friends. After many years it will remind them of a former friend: "He is no longer one of our circle; but his heart is buried here."

Tiutchev's choice of translation material is often of psychological importance, and the changes he made here are especially interesting. The feminine singular implicit in Byron's lines has become Tiutchev's masculine plural; and the reasons are obvious. In Munich young Tiutchev did not suffer from any dearth of feminine company. On the other hand, his old comrades of the Moscow University days—Raich, Ozobnishin, Pogodin *et al.*—seemed far removed indeed; and the poet, who was "no longer one of [their] circle," felt the loss and altered Byron's sense accordingly. (Still another instance, if any were needed, of the way actual conditions could shape what prima facie appears to be a purely literary excercise.)

In time these early random references to separation became more frequent and more urgent, crystallizing finally into the motif of *annihilating absence,* which recurs in Tiutchev's letters and poems. In 1843 we find him writing his wife: "Je suis certainement l'homme le plus mal organisé pour supporter l'absence, car pour moi, c'est comme un néant qui avait conscience de lui-même." And eight years later: "La véritable raison, je crois, qui fait que l'absence pour moi est plus pénible que pour toute autre créature humaine, c'est que pour moi l'absence, c'est le néant." Sometimes this sense of separation takes a metaphysical turn: "Jamais, je crois, personne ne s'est senti

plus néant que moi en présence de ces deux oppresseurs et tyrans de l'humanité, le temps et l'espace." Sometimes, too, it meant a sense of being cut off from the past: "Hélas il vient un moment ou le passé est bien décidément mort."

It would be easy to multiply these instances drawn from Tiutchev's correspondence. More pertinent, however, are the expressions of this theme in his poetry, where absence or separation becomes the destroyer of the most sacred values of life. As a philosophical proposition we find it expressed in this French epigram:

> Que l'homme est peu réel, qu'aisément il
>   s'éfface! . . .
> Présent, si peu de chose, et rien quand il est loin.
> Sa présence, ce n'est qu'un point—
> Et son absence—tout l'espace.

It emerges more poignantly in the lyric provoked by his separation from Baroness Dörnberg in Genoa which begins: "Thus here it was fated for us / To say a last farewell, / Farewell to everything the heart lived by, / Which, having killed your life, reduced it to ashes." The same destructive power of separation appears some fifteen years later in a remarkably candid poem addressed [to his second wife, Ernestine]: . . .

> In separation there is a lofty meaning: however long you may love, whether a day or an age, love is a dream, and a dream is but a moment. And sooner or later an awakening will come, and we must at last wake up.

In a later poem, also addressed to his wife, it appears again, now as a destroyer of faith in the simplest probabilities of daily existence: . . .

> Alas, what is more helpless and sadder than our ignorance? Who dares utter "until we meet again" across the abyss of two or three days?

And in some lines addressed to his final love, E. K. Bogdanova, separation is seen to leave in its wake a mysterious occluding film which seems more hateful than the absence itself: . . .

> The time of separation has passed and from it only a covering has remained in our hands, half-transparent to the eye. And we know that beneath this gauze is all that the soul suffers from. And like some strange invisible thing it hides from us and is silent. . . . The time of separation has passed, and we do not dare soon to touch and tear away the veil so hateful to us.

These varied instances of the separation-absence theme are not, of course, merely disguised reminiscences of Tiutchev's early life abroad. Rather it is being suggested that Tiutchev's early uprooting from home, parents, and country wounded a weak and affection-craving nature in a way that later made him abnormally sensitive to *any* kind of enforced separation from persons dear to him. In its most obvious forms this sensitivity, which seems to have amounted to a kind of spiritual allergy, may be seen in the passages just considered. More often, however, it takes the form of a special image which repeatedly insinuates itself into Tiutchev's letters and poems: that of *an offspring or scion who has been violently or fatally amputated from the parent stock.*

When in 1840 Tiutchev wrote to his parents: "Man's fate is a strange thing. In my case it had to make use of the remaining arm of Osterman-Tolstoi to hurl me so far from you," he was, perhaps, merely making the small joke that his biographers are so fond of quoting. But there is reason to think that this juxtaposition of fate, amputation, and forceful removal from one's family in a single sentence has a psychological significance that goes beyond the exigencies of wit. In this connection we may note that two of the commonest epithets in Tiutchev's poetic vocabulary are *rokovoi* (fatal or fateful) and *rodnoi* (native) or its more emotional variant *rodimyi*. The former forty times in Tiutchev's mature verse, the latter two at least twice as often. The instinctive affinity which Tiutchev felt toward these concepts may be seen in his early poem on Goethe's death, where he admires the latter's good fortune because "No late windstorm, no blustering summer shower / Tore you from your native branch." Obviously the hostile elements here symbolize fate; and in insisting on Goethe's good fortune, Tiutchev is drawing an implied comparison with his own less happy lot.

Violence and enforced exile are again implicit in a poem inspired a few years later by Heine beginning: . . .

> From place to place, from city to city, fate, like a whirlwind, hurls people along; and whether you are happy or not, what is it to her? . . . Onward, onward!

And similar themes and images recur in **"Byron,"** an adaption from Zedlitz's "Todtenkränze": . . .

> Why did you flee your own roof? Why did you betray your paternal *lares?* Ah you, who have untimely passed away, whither did the whirlwind drive you which bore you! . . . He abandoned the dwelling place of his fathers, where their silent shades wander—where dear pledges have remained. And as, all day long, the sea bird, dweller of barren cliffs, ruffles the waves with his wings, so along life's road the gods have fated him to pass, nowhere finding a peaceful bright abode! . . . The bard rushes on, a fugitive from his native country, across the stormy element toward the sun.

More impressive, perhaps, because it is independent of literary stereotypes is the curious metaphor which the poet used in a letter to his wife after meeting an old friend of his Munich days. Of the Bavarian past which the two had shared he observed that it now seemed like an "amputated limb" of his body. And a similar juxtaposition of unnatural death and separation in connection with his German past appears in a poem of the same period where he contrasts his Munich years to the "little brother" of his Russian childhood, who has "died in his swaddling clothes." Extending itself into other situations of enforced separation, the image appears a few years later in a letter to Ernestine: "There is decidedly nothing more agonizing . . . than the chimera of separation," he wrote. "It is constant disillusionment, privation, vexation. *Every time it is as if you forced me to undergo an amputation.*"

The poet's favorite variation on this theme, however, is the image of the orphan or helpless child, which makes its first appearance in a translation of Lamartine's "L'Isolement," written while Tiutchev was still in Russia. Investigation has established that this poem was first made public in March, 1822, only a month after Tiutchev had left his family for St. Petersburg. And since this is the only external evidence available, Pigarev has conjectured that the poem was written sometime between 1820 and 1822. Actually, however, internal clues pointing to a more precise date are not wanting. If we bear in mind that Tiutchev's choice of poems for translation was often dictated by his personal sympathy for the attitudes they expressed, the similarity between the isolation motif and Tiutchev's familyless status is certainly suggestive. A closer look at the texts, moreover, confirms this suspicion. In line 35 of the Russian translation Tiutchev describes paradise as "that world where there are no orphans"; and in the final line he calls on the winds: "Bear, O bear away this orphan!" Despite Tiutchev's over-all fidelity to the text, no orphan appears in Lamartine. Twice, then, he has diverged from the original to introduce the same unusual image. When we consider Tiutchev's proven capacity to inject autobiographical elements into his translations it is hard not to see in these gratuitously invented orphans a reflection of the young man's own parentless condition. And if this assumption is correct, we now know when the poem was composed: in or around February, 1822, the month of Tiutchev's departure for St. Petersburg.

Later instances of this peculiar image are far too widespread to be the products of coincidence. In **"Insomnia,"** written in the late twenties, the poet sees the entire world as "orphaned." In the lyric **"There Is in the Light of Autumn Evenings,"** he depicts a "sadly orphaned earth" before winter's coming storms. In **"The Current Has Thickened and Grown Opaque,"** another poem of the second German decade, he compares a frozen stream with man's "orphaned bosom / Killed by the cold of existence." During the same years Tiutchev translated Béranger's "Le Vieux Vagabond," where the subject's miserable fate contrasts strikingly with the earlier optimism of "The Wanderer" previously quoted. Here the vagabond complains that he has been "fated for a century to an orphan's lot"; but, as in the case of the Lamartine poem, the orphan is an invention of the translator. Likewise, in the versified rendition of a passage from Heine's *Reisebilder,* the German poet's "einsame" is extended and intensified to "odinoko, siro" (lonely, orphan-like). In **"The Holy Night Has Risen into the Firmament,"** mankind is compared to a "homeless orphan," who stands "naked and helpless"; and later in the same poem we find that man's "mind is demolished, his thoughts are orphaned." Twenty years later in **"The Fires,"** man, confronted with the evil element of fire, "despondently stands / A helpless child." And as the poet lay on his deathbed he compared the lonely human heart to a "foundling" (*podkidysh*).

It will be recalled that during these years Tiutchev's domestic position seems to have been complicated by a series of extramarital attachments. And as such it may be seen as the tragic sequel to that boyhood existence at Ovstug, where a gifted and charming child had once run loose in a loving and indulgent family. But the childish liberties had grown into the licence of adultery; and the effect of this licence upon [his first wife] Nelly was suffering so intense that it seems to have precipitated an attempt at suicide.

The irony of this analogy is that the enveloping parental love which may have helped weaken Fedia was itself rooted in a spiritual soil profoundly alien to any breach of the moral code. His parents were the image of conjugal happiness, and had brought up Fedia in that "Russo-Byzantine world where," he later admiringly observed, "life and religion are but one." This perfect integration of the spiritual and the actual under the aegis of "Old Russia" was always to remain Tiutchev's ideal. But spiritually "orphaned" in the West, living, as he himself remarked, "without a fatherland," the poet no longer had access to this world; and "hurled back upon himself"—that is, upon his own moral resources—he found only a will which was "paralyzed" (the word is Nelly's) by lifelong indulgence and—one suspects—a fair measure of congenital weakness. With this dubious moral equipment he soon learned that the simplest way to escape temptation is to surrender to it. It was a lesson which he never forgot.

In consequence there emerges that feature so characteristic of the mature Tiutchev: an almost total discrepancy between the ideal and the real; between the lofty principle of Christian self-abnegation on one hand and the observable fact of continued self-indulgence on the other. For obvious reasons this discrepancy became prominent and painful only after Tiutchev became a husband. For what, before marriage, had been the widely sanctioned hedonism of a young man's sowing his wild oats had now become in terms of both convention (the world has always been more tolerant of a bachelor's "affairs" than of a husband's adultery) and personal experience (Nelly's unhappiness was, after all, there to see) something very different: it was suffering born of Sin.

This new realization did not, of course, suddenly appear on Tiutchev's mental horizon blotting out all others. Indeed it was not until the decade 1830-40 that the motif took strong hold of Tiutchev's poetry. But if the majority of poems from 1822 to 1829 reflect the buoyant hedonism and idealism which we have already noted, three of them written at the end of the twenties give oblique but unmistakable hints of the change to come.

The first poem, "To N. N.," written according to Chulkov sometime between 1828 and 1830, reads as follows: . . .

> Loving, you know how to dissemble; when, in a crowd of people, stealthily I touch your foot with mine, you give answer without blushing. Still the same distraught and lifeless aspect, the same movement of your bosom, the same glance and smile; and all the while that hated watchman of a husband dotes on your docile loveliness. Thanks be to people and to fate that you have understood the price of secret joys; you have understood the world: it would call all our joys infidelity. . . . Infidelity flatters you. The never-to-return blush of shame has fled your youthful cheeks as Aurora's ray has fled from tender roses, bearing away their pure and fra-

grant soul. So be it: in the burning summer heat it is more flattering to the feelings, more seductive for the glance, to see, in the shadow, in the cluster of grapes, blood shining through thick green.

Visually, though not lexically, the final image of crimson fruit shining through green foliage is identical to the image which opens the previously cited "Tears." Significantly, however, the fresh vernal setting of the early poem has yielded to scorching summer; and the youthful expression of lofty romantic sentiments has hardened into a mood that is both passionate and callous. This is a truly immoral poem, for the poet seems not so much to be committing adultery for the sake of love as indulging in love for the sake of adultery. He has crossed the threshold of innocence without having acquired a sense of sin, and has thereby become a cynic.

"To Two Sisters," a poem placed by Chulkov at the very end of the decade, implies a similar situation; but it is seen from a very different ethical angle: . . .

> I saw you both together, and all of you I saw in her. The quiet glance, the gentle voice, the pristine charm of a morning hour that once breathed from your head. And then as in a magic glass, everything took shape and meaning again . . . of bygone days the sorrow and the joy, your lost youth, my perished love!

For the latter-day student there is something rather heartening in the fact that for eighty years scholars have failed to see in this poem anything more than a graceful but minor lyric of Tiutchev's early years; for there is strong evidence to indicate that it is also an interesting fragment of autobiography.

A prose summary of the poem would run thus: The poet is considering two sisters, one of whom—evidently the elder—he once deeply loved. Now, discerning in the younger traits similar to those which had once delighted him in her sister, he is painfully reminded of the latter's vanished beauty and of his own lost love.

The following pertinent facts about Tiutchev's domestic life are known. At or shortly before the time the poem was written Nelly Tiutchev's younger sister Clothilde was living in the Tiutchev household. By then, Nelly, four years her husband's senior and mother of three (and perhaps four), was crowding thirty, whereas Clothilde, a full ten years younger than her sister, was a lovely girl in her late teens. As for Tiutchev, his conjugal ardor had already cooled enough to allow extramarital attachments. Under these circumstances it was only natural that Clothilde's "morning" beauty should remind the poet of his wife's fading charms (the epithets "quiet" and "gentle" tally closely with the image of Nelly as it appears in Aksakov and her own letters) and of his own fading love. There is, in short, the strongest circumstantial evidence to indicate that the two sisters of the poem are in fact Nelly and Clothilde, that the "lost youth" is Nelly's, and that the vanished love is the poet's own.

This poem is in a sense, then, the companion piece to "To N. N.," for it represents the domestic sequel to the adulterous pursuits described in the latter. In tone, however, the two poems are significantly different. Here Clothilde's beauty provokes no amorous advances or passionate avowals. The prevailing mood is, rather, elegiac and regretful. And from regret to remorse is only a step.

The last of the three poems to be considered is **"Insomnia"**: . . .

> The monotonous stroke of the clock; the night's wearying narrative; a tongue equally alien to all, and plain to everyman as his conscience. Who of us can hear without spleen the muffled moanings of time, that prophetic farewell voice amid the general silence! It seems to us the world is orphaned! Our ineluctable fate has struck, and we, struggling with all of nature, are hurled back upon ourselves. And our life stands before us like a ghost at the edge of the earth; and with our age and our friends it pales in the gloomy distance. And a new young tribe in the meanwhile has blossomed in the sun, and long ago has swept us, O friends, and our age into oblivion. Only from time to time, as it performs the sad rite at midnight, the funereal voice of metal mourns us.

The first thing which impresses one about this poem is the depth and quality of its pessimism. Not only does the poet's *Weltanschauung* border on despair at a period when his poetry is only infrequently and superficially melancholy, but this pessimism is of a very different order: it is the pessimism of *Angst,* that untranslatable word denoting a gnawing, intolerably oppressive anxiety which seems to have no fixed object, but is rooted in obscure and profound feelings of personal guilt.

The last two words of this definition are the most important. Whereas the early pessimism of **"The Gleam"** is derived from young Tiutchev's romantically colored cosmology (day is a tiring dream, night a moment of truth, etc.), and the melancholy of **"To My Friends, on Sending Schiller's 'Ode to Joy' "** and **"To Two Sisters"** stems from simple circumstance (the separation from friends and an aging wife, respectively), in **"Insomnia"** the poet's misfortune is framed in terms of a personal sentence: "ineluctable fate" has overtaken him and those like him; and, as if insisting on the speaker's own involvement, the first-person plural pronoun tolls throughout the poem like the clock itself: "us . . . us . . . we," etc.—ten times in all.

But if the poem seems to consist of a personal sentence, what kind of transgression is at stake? Evidently it has moral overtones, for the sound of the striking clock is "plain to everyman as his conscience." Moreover, as the poem proceeds, fate's sentence is found to be connected in some essential way with the theme of separation: the world is "orphaned," we are "hurled back upon ourselves," and we find ourselves at odds with nature itself. The recurrence of such images in Tiutchev has already been linked to the poet's own renunciation of and separation from his Russian past. Can the entire poem be seen as an expression of this apostasy and its results?

Certainly a thematic sequence which moves from the passage of time to man's conscience, and thence to cosmic im-

ages of separation, does in a general way suggest such an interpretation. But it is only in the fourth stanza that these generalities come into sharper focus. At this point some kind of splitting off seems to occur, for the poet's life, "our life," now becomes *divorced* from the speaker, and "stands before us / Like a ghost." The simile is of obvious interest, for with the word "conscience" still echoing in our minds, the ghostly apparition has an undeniably comminatory flavor. Furthermore, twice this ghostlike life evokes a recollection of Tiutchev's "friends," and during these years this reference had only one meaning: his old Russian friends. Finally, this life and these friends are located "at the edge of the earth" and in "gloomy distances"; and gloom and vast distance are precisely the qualities which Tiutchev most often associated with Russia.

The reading we propose must be obvious by now. The life and friends of the poem are the life and friends of Tiutchev's Russian past; broken off and standing at "the edge of the earth," they appear before the poet "like a ghost" to haunt his insomniac thoughts. And because he has participated in this schism which has put him in a struggle "with all of nature" (that is, the natural, unfragmented order of things), the poet feels that all of them are condemned to oblivion to be replaced by a new generation which will be strong, whole, and (presumably) proof against the forces of division.

It should not be necessary to state that such an autobiographical reading does not pretend to exhaust all the possible meaning of this remarkable poem. Indeed the cosmic imagery and the consistent use of the first-person *plural* make it clear that the sentence of fate applies not only to the poet but to all those who have denied some essential part of themselves, who have preferred division to unity, and are thereby at odds with nature. But the central experience of the poem—spiritual schism, condemnation, oblivion, and replacement—has for its author who abandoned his native country, repudiated (in fact if not in theory) the moral values absorbed in childhood, and was now beginning to understand the meaning of his apostasy, a specific and personal application which cannot be ignored. (pp. 46-62)

> *Richard A. Gregg, in his* Fedor Tiutchev: The Evolution of a Poet, *Columbia University Press, 1965, 257 p.*

T. J. Binyon   (essay date 1973)

[*Binyon is an English novelist and critic. In the following excerpt, he identifies those formal features of Tyutchev's poetry that were common in eighteenth-century poetry and discusses several of Tyutchev's thematic concerns.*]

Tyutchev has been called: 'a union of two opposites: romanticism and baroque', and it is true that, from a formal point of view, his verse often seems to have more in common with that of his eighteenth-century predecessors— and especially [Gavrila Romanovich] Derzhavin—than with that of his contemporaries of the nineteenth century. His poems are full of lexical archaisms, such as: *vvyspr'* [upwards], *tolikiy* [such], *dnes'* [today], *podnes'* [to this day], *ogn'* [fire], *bregi* [banks], *zrak* [vision], *dobliy* [brave], *dkhnoven'e* [breath]. Occasionally, as Tynyanov points out, he will make use of an archaism humorously, with comic intent, as in a poem on the opening of the Suez canal in 1869, where the festivities in Turkey are described in a parody of an eighteenth-century ode: . . .

> Thunder of cannon and music! / Here is a concourse of all Europe, / Here all the world powers / Are celebrating their carnival. ('**Contemporary**': '**Sovremennoe**,' 1869)

but in another context will employ a related form in a mood of high seriousness: . . .

> There is melody in the sea waves, / Harmony in the strife of elements, / And a graceful musical rustle / Flows through the swaying reeds. (**'There is melody in the sea waves'** . . . : **'Pevuchest' est' v morskikh volnakh** . . . ,' 1865)

And it is this latter use which is more typical of Tyutchev's verse: his archaisms are not an affectation, but come to him naturally and unforcedly. He often employs a sustained, rhetorical high style, as in the poem **'Day and Night' ('Den' i noch' ')** (1839): . . .

> Day is this shining cover / Day, the quickener of the earthborn, / The healer of the ailing soul, / The friend of men and gods.

One might note in this stanza the typically eighteenth-century use of metonymy (*zemnorodnykh ozhivlen'e*—quickener of the earth-born), a device Tyutchev uses with some frequency in his verse: *Pernatykh pesn' po roshche razdalasya* [The song of the feathered [birds] resounded in the grove]; *Vysokyy dub, perunami srazhennyy* [The tall oak, struck by gods of lightning]; *Metalla golos pogrebal'nyy* [The funereal voice of metal] (compare Derzhavin's *Glagol vremen! metalla zvon!*—Word of time! Sound of metal!—which also refers to a bell).

Tyutchev's word order, too, exhibits archaic traits: a noun is often placed between two dependent adjectives, as in *Prestupnyy lepet i shal'noy* [Criminal prattle and crazy]; *Vselenskiy den' i pravoslavnyy* [A universal day and orthodox]; *Zheleznyy mir i dyshashchiy / Veleniem odnim* [An iron world and breathing / With one command].

The extension of this device to the sentence, when a word or phrase is removed from its normal position and placed between grammatically connected elements, gives the poet's style a Latinate flavour and, occasionally, leads to obscurities of meaning as in: . . .

> There is a certain hour of universal silence in the night . . .

or: . . .

> And he rested, shaded by the banner of popular grief . . .

or: . . .

> Only the virginal soul of the Muse / Do the gods disturb with prophetic dreams!

Perhaps the most obvious characteristic of Tyutchev's style, however, and one which emphasizes his debt to eigh-

teenth-century verse, is his use of compound and composite adjectives.

He employs a number of archaic compound adjectives: *iskrometnyy* [spark-throwing], *gromokipyashchiy* [thunder-seething], *ognetsvetnyy* [fiery-coloured], *zhivotrepetnyy* [live-quivering], *zlatotkanyy* [gold-embroidered], *shirokokrylyy* [wide-winged], *pyshnostruynyy* [luxurious-streaming], *edinokrovnyy* [consanguineous] etc. His predilection for this form is well illustrated when he chooses to translate the lines from Schiller's poem 'Das Siegesfest':

> Pallas, die die Städte gründet
> Und zertrümmert, ruft er an,

as: . . .

> Pallas, who founds cities / And destroys them, he invokes. ('The Funeral Feast': 'Pominki,' 1851)

Tyutchev's use of composite adjectives is more individual. If one examines composite adjectives in the work of an eighteenth-century writer such as Derzhavin, an obvious influence on the later poet, it can be seen that the most frequent type is that in which two colour adjectives are combined, as in: *krasno-rozovyy* [red-pink], *srebrorozovyy* [silver-pink], *cherno-ognennyy* [black-fiery], *safiro-svetlyy* [sapphire-radiant], *sizo-yantarnyy* [gray-amber] etc. A much smaller group is formed by those composite adjectives which unite noncolour epithets. Examples of this type, again from Derzhavin's poems, are: *nezhno-strastnyy* [tender-passionate], *svyashchenno-vdokhnovennyy* [sacred-inspired], *zhelezno-kamennyy* [iron-stone].

In Tyutchev's work, however, the proportions are reversed: composite colour adjectives are far outnumbered by those of the second type, and, furthermore, Tyutchev's coinages, in both types, tend to differ radically from those of his predecessor.

Derzhavin, in combining two adjectives, almost always chooses them from the same semantic group: *krasno-rozovyy, nezhnostrastnyy*. His aim is to define a particular shade of colour, to specify an object or an emotion by detailing it more exactly. And although composite adjectives of this kind are met with in Tyutchev's work, those which are most characteristic of his style are of a very different kind.

He combines adjectives from different semantic groups, and describes by contrast, rather than similarity. His colour adjectives are far more impressionistic than those met with in Derzhavin's verse: Tyutchev strives to convey the effect of the colour on the poet, the emotion it arouses within him. Simple combinations of two colours are replaced by composite adjectives such as: *tusklo-rdyanyy* [dull-red], *pyshno-zolotoy* [luxurious-golden], *pasmurno-bagrovyy* [cloudy-purple], *tumanisto-belyy* [misty-white] etc.

In the other, and by far the larger, group of composite adjectives, Tyutchev, although he sometimes employs conventional combinations—*mladencheski-zhivoy* [childish-lively], *mladencheski-bespechnyy* [childish-carefree], *nezabvenno-dorogoy* [unforgettable-dear]—more often and more typically unites seemingly disparate adjectives to produce not only a striking and, at times, almost paradoxical effect, but also, as it were, a synthesis of the two concepts rather than a refinement of one of them. Some examples are: *pritvorno-bespechnyy* [feigned-carefree], *prorocheski-proshchal'nyy* [prophetic-valedictory], *prorocheski-slepoy* [prophetic-blind], *nezrimo-rokovoy* [unseen-fatal], *blazhenno-rokovoy* [blessed-fatal], [blessed-indifferent], *volshebno-nemoy* [magic-dumb], *plamenno-chudesnyy* [ardent-miraculous], *tselomudrenno-svobodnyy* [chaste-free], *udushlivozemnoy* [stifling-earthly], *usypitel'no-bezmolvnyy* [soporific-silent], *gordo-boyazlivyy* [proud-timid].

The mode of thought implicit in this stylistic device seems central to Tyutchev's work as a whole. In a number of poems he, as it were, expands the device over the complete work. An example is **'The Fountain' ('Fontan')** (1836): . . .

> Look, how—a living cloud— / The shining fountain swirls; / How flames and scatters / Its moist smoke in the sun. / Having risen like a ray to heaven, it / Has touched the sacred height— / And again in fiery-coloured dust / Is fated to fall back to earth.
>
> O fountain of mortal thought, / O inexhaustible fountain! / What incomprehensible law / Drives you, crushes you? / How thirstily you strive towards heaven! . . . / But an unseen fatal hand, / Refracting your stubborn ray, / Hurls it down in spray from the height.

Here once again two disparate concepts, each of which defines the other, have been linked together, but have been developed from adjectives into stanzas.

In addition, we find this same approach expressed not only as hitherto, formally, but also thematically in that series of contrasts, oppositions and dichotomies which give Tyutchev's thought its profoundly dualistic nature.

As many critics have pointed out, Tyutchev views life as split between, on the one hand, the dark primordial forces of chaos and disorder, and, on the other, the realm of light, harmony and order. These two worlds are often symbolized by the alternation of day and night, as in the poems **'Day and Night' ('Den' i noch' ')** (1839) and **'Holy night has risen into the sky'** . . . **('Svyataya noch' na nebosklon vzoshla'** . . .) (1850). Both poems make use of the same imagery: day is visualized as a woven cloth of gold which temporarily conceals the dark, mysterious and unknowable abysses of the night: . . .

> Over the mysterious world of spirits, / Over this nameless abyss / A gold-embroidered veil has been thrown / By the exalted will of the gods. **('Den' i noch' ')**

and: . . .

> Holy night has risen into the sky, / And comforting day, kind day / It has rolled up like a golden cloth, / A cloth, thrown over the abyss. / And, like an apparition, the outer world has departed . . . / And man, like a homeless orphan, / Now stands, powerless and naked, / Face to face with the dark abyss.

In opposition to the world of chaos stands the ordered cosmos: the harmony and beauty of nature. But its existence is a precarious one; the day is not necessarily sacrosanct; even here the dark and disruptive forces can break in, as in the poem **'Mal'aria'** (1830), in which the same image is employed again, in slightly different form. Here the beauty of Rome, the purity and clarity of nature are revealed to be but a screen masking the inevitable approach of death: . . .

> Who knows, perhaps there are sounds in nature, / Fragrances, colours and voices, / Heralds for us of the final hour / And sweeteners of our final torture. / And by means of them the fatal messenger of Fate, / When he summons the sons of Earth from life, / Covers his image as with a light veil, / In order to conceal from them his terrible arrival!

In **'The Italian Villa' ('Ital'yanskaya villa')** (1837) the beauty and tranquillity of the day are again shattered by the incursion of an alien force, but here the contagion, the *tainstvennoe Zlo* [mysterious Evil] of the other poem has been personified as the *zlaya zhizn'* [evil life] of the guilty lovers, whose arrival disturbs the peace of the abandoned villa, once constructed by man, but now taken over by nature and absorbed into its harmony: . . .

> And we entered . . . everything was so tranquil! / So peaceful and dark was everything from time! . . . / The fountain murmured . . . Immobile and graceful / The neighbouring cypress looked in at the window.
>
> Suddenly everything was agitated: a convulsive shudder / Ran along the cypress branches,— / The fountain fell silent—and some strange babble, / As if through sleep, whispered incoherently.
>
> What is it, friend? Could it be that not for nothing has the evil life, / That life,—alas!—which then flowed in us, / That evil life, with its turbulent heat, / Has crossed the sacred threshold?

For Tyutchev man, like the universe, is split between the forces of light and those of darkness; his spiritual strivings align him with the former; his passions, his sensuality with the latter: . . .

> Though my suffering breast / Is excited by fatal passions— / My soul is ready, like Mary, / To cleave forever to the feet of Christ. (**'O my prophetic soul!'** . . .: **'O veshchaya dusha moya!'** . . . , 1855)

he writes, and this rift in his personality is often symbolized by another contrast: that between the valley and the heights, as in the following poem written in 1861: . . .

> Although I too wove my nest in the valley, / Sometimes I also feel / How invigoratingly on the summit / Rushes the airy stream,— / How our breast strains to escape from this thick layer, / How it thirsts for the heights, / How all that is suffocatingly earthly / It would like to spurn! (**'Although I too wove my nest'** . . . ; **'Khot' ya i svil gnezdo'** . . .)

He experiences in agonizing fashion this conflict between the Dionysian and the Apollonian within himself, and envies those who have never known this lack of inner unity, writing, for example, in memory of the poet Zhukovsky: . . .

> In him there was no lie, no duality— / He reconciled and combined all within himself. (**'In Memory of V. A. Zhukovsky': 'Pamyati V. A. Zhukovskogo,'** 1852)

At times he feels the fatal attraction of the abyss, is drawn reluctantly towards night and chaos: . . .

> O, do not sing those terrible songs / About ancient, native chaos! / How avidly the world of the night soul / Listens to the loved story! / It longs to burst out of the mortal breast, / It thirsts to merge with the unbounded! . . . / O, do not awaken sleeping storms— / Under them chaos is stirring! (**'Of what do you wail, wind of the night?'** . . . : **'O chem ty voesh', vetr nochnoy?'** . . . , 1836)

More often, however, the poet turns in the other direction, towards the order and harmony of nature, the cosmos, which he views pantheistically, as a manifestation of the divine: . . .

> Nature is not what you think: / Not a mould, not a soulless image— / In her there is a soul, in her there is freedom, / In her there is love, in her there is a tongue . . . (**'Nature is not what you think'** . . . : **'Ne to, chto mnite vy, priroda'** . . . , 1836)

He longs to submerge himself in it, to heal the rift within himself by becoming part of a higher unity: . . .

> Plaything and victim of private life! / Come, throw off the deceit of feelings / And throw yourself, brisk and self-possessed, / Into this revivifying ocean! / Come, with its ethereal stream / Lave your suffering breast— / And with the divine-universal life / Commune, if only for a moment! (**'Spring': 'Vesna,'** 1838)

But the point of this quotation lies in the last line: the experience of unity, if at all possible, can only be momentary; the poet can never attain to full possession of this other existence, never become part of the *zhizn' bozhesko-vsemirnaya* [divine-universal life], as he recognizes elsewhere, when he writes: . . .

> . . . it is not given to the insignificant dust / To breathe the divine fire. (**'The Gleam': 'Problesk,'** 1825)

The limitation placed on man's aspirations is, in fact, a recurrent theme in Tyutchev's verse. It is the subject of **'The Fountain,'** quoted earlier, and of the poem **'A buzzard has risen from the glade'** . . . (**'S polyany korshun podnyalsya'** . . .) (1836), which can also be seen as an example of the same formal pattern: . . .

> A buzzard has risen from the glade, / High into the sky it has soared; / Ever higher and further it circles, / And has vanished beyond the horizon.
>
> Mother nature gave it / Two powerful, living wings— / But I lie here in sweat and dust, / I,

the emperor of the earth, am rooted to the earth! . . .

And here the contrast between earthbound man, ironically described as the *tsar' zemli* [emperor of the earth] and the soaring bird leads us on to another aspect of Tyutchev's view of the relationship between man and nature.

More often than not the poet is aware of himself, not as a part of the natural order, but rather as a discordant element within it, a view expressed most clearly in the poem **'There is melody in the sea waves'** . . . (**'Pevuchest' est' v morskikh volnakh'** . . .) (1865): . . .

> There is melody in the sea waves, / Harmony in the strife of elements, / And a graceful musical rustle / Flows through the swaying reeds.
>
> An imperturbable order in everything, / A full consonance in nature,— / Only in our phantom freedom / Are we conscious of discord with it.
>
> Whence, and how did this discord arise? / And why in the general chorus / Does the soul not sing as the sea does, / And why does the thinking reed complain?

The answer to the poet's despairing question is given in the last line of the poem by the Pascalian image of man as *un roseau pensant*. It is man's capability for thought, his consciousness, that very quality which enables him to perceive himself as a dissonant chord in the harmony of nature, which is the cause of his inability to become part of it. For nature herself is sublimely unconscious of her own existence, and in this lies the essential difference between her and man. This concept is a key one in Tyutchev's thought: he returns to it again and again, amplifying and developing it.

Since the poet, man, is aware of his own existence, he strives to preserve and maintain it against the pressure of external forces, the strongest of which is time. For man lives in time, as well as in space. Indeed, his life only has significance in the past or the future, in the achieved or the potential, in what he was, or what he will be: he can never know the present. Nature, on the other hand, simply is, in the present; past and future have no meaning for her. Tyutchev draws the contrast in **'Spring'** (**'Vesna'**) (1838): . . .

> Not of the past the roses sigh / Nor the nightingale sings in the night; / Fragrant tears / Aurora sheds not for the past,— / And the fear of the inevitable end / Does not blow a single leaf from the tree: / Their life, like the boundless ocean, / Is completely diffused in the present.

and, again, in two lines from the poem **'From the life, that once raged here'** . . . (**'Ot zhizni toy, chto bushevala zdes' '**) (1871): . . .

> Nature knows nothing of the past, / Our phantom years are alien to her . . .

The epithet *prizrachnyy* [phantom] in the second line introduces an image which often occurs in this context. The passing of time emphasizes the fragile, transient quality of man's life; it makes of it something insubstantial and wraithlike. We endeavour desperately to cling to our past: . . .

> The past, like the phantom of a friend, / We try to clasp to our bosom . . . (**'The Gleam': 'Problesk,'** 1825)

but the poet realizes how impossible of fulfilment this attempt is when he apostrophizes his former happiness in the lines: . . .

> O, poor phantom, powerless and dim, / Of forgotten, mysterious happiness! . . . (**'So again I see you'** . . . : 'Itak, opyat' uvidelsya ya s vami' . . . , 1849)

He knows that his physical existence must come to an end with death; but it is far more bitter to contemplate the thought that the very essence of his personality—his memories of the past—is doomed to oblivion and extinction: . . .

> However heavy the final hour may be— / That incomprehensible to us / Weariness of mortal suffering,— / For the soul it is yet more terrible / To trace, how in itself are dying out / All the best memories . . . (**'However heavy the final hour may be'** . . . : 'Kak ni tyazhel posledniy chas' . . . , 1867)

Only nature is eternal: man cannot hope to preserve his individuality in the face of time, and will, eventually, leave no trace behind: . . .

> Nothing leaves a trace—and not to have been is so simple! / With me or without me—what is the difference? / Everything will be the same—the blizzard will howl in the same way, / The same dark, the same steppe on every side. (**'Brother, who accompanied me for so many years'** . . . : 'Brat, stol'ko let soputstvovavshiy mne' . . . , 1870)

he writes, journeying back to St. Petersburg after the funeral, in Moscow, of his brother Nikolay, and he repeats this conclusion in **'Look, how on the river expanse'** . . . (**'Smotri, kak na rechnom prostore'** . . .) (1851): . . .

> Look, how on the river expanse, / Down the incline of the revived waters, / Into the all-embracing sea / Ice-floe follows ice-floe.
>
> Whether shining radiantly in the sun, / Or at night in the late darkness, / They all, inevitably melting, / Float towards one goal.
>
> All together—small, large, / Losing their previous form, / All—indifferent as the element,— / Will merge with the fatal abyss! . . .
>
> O delusion of our thought, / You, the human I, / Is not such your significance, / Is not such your fate?

And here, with the image of the all-engulfing *bezdna rokovaya* [fatal abyss], we return to the chaotic forces of the dark side of the universe.

For Tyutchev, however, time has a double significance. It is not only a force which obliterates the individual's consciousness of his past, and hence his own existence, but

also one which makes him aware of the fact that he is but a part of the eternal cycle of death and renewal: . . .

> How sad it is as a sleepy shadow, / With exhaustion in one's bones, / Towards the sun and movement / To wander following a new generation! . . . (**'Like a little bird at early dawn'** . . . : 'Kak ptichka, ranneyu zarey' . . . , 1836)

he writes, and brings the two concepts together in **'Insomnia'** (**'Bessonnitsa'**) (1829), in which the image of man's life as a wraith, *prizrak*, returns: . . .

> And our life stands before us, / Like a phantom, on the edge of the earth, / And with our age and friends / Pales in the dusky distance;
>
> And a new young generation / Has since blossomed in the sun, / And we, friends, and our times / Have long been covered by oblivion!

And in **'I sit thoughtful and alone'** . . . (**'Sizhu zadumchiv i odin'** . . .) (1836) he draws the parallel between man and his natural surroundings: generation follows generation, as crop follows crop: . . .

> Year after year, century after century . . . / Why does man rage, / This earthly crop! . . . / He quickly, quickly withers—so, / But with a new summer there is a new crop / And another leaf.

One can, digressively, note that the image of this stanza illustrates both Tyutchev's closeness to Derzhavin, who writes: . . .

> Scarcely have I glimpsed this world, / Yet death already grinds his teeth, / Flashes his scythe like lightning, / And mows my days like a crop. (**'On the Death of Prince Meshchersky'**: 'Na smert' knyazya Meshcherskogo,' 1779)

and at the same time, in the progress from simile to metaphor, the difference between the two poets.

Chto zh negoduet chelovek? [Why does man rage?] the poet asks. Why can he, realizing as he does the inevitability of his fate, not submit peacefully to it? The answer is, in essence, that given to the earlier question: . . .

> . . . why in the general chorus / Does the soul not sing as the sea does, / And why does the thinking reed complain?

The parallel with the natural world is only partially true; it conceals a deeper contrast: because man, unlike nature, exists only through his consciousness of himself, he cannot accept without a struggle that his life should vanish without trace and he himself be succeeded by a new generation. *O vremya, pogodi!* [O Time, wait!] he cries in **'So, there are moments in life'** . . . (**'Tak, v zhizni est' mgnoveniya'** . . .) (1855): time must stop, the fleeting moment of life, symbolized by the ephemeral rainbow, must be held fast: . . .

> It is given us for a moment, / Catch it—catch it quickly! / Look—it has already faded, / Another minute or two—and what is there? / It has

vanished, as all that will completely vanish, / By which you breathe and live.

he writes in **'How unexpectedly and brightly'** . . . (**'Kak neozhidanno i yarko'** . . .) (1865)—another poem with a structure similar to that of **'The Fountain'** and **'A buzzard has risen from the glade'** . . .

In this context the poet's longing to become one with nature, expressed in **'Spring'**: . . .

> . . . throw yourself, brisk and self-possessed, / Into this revivifying ocean!

takes on an additional meaning: his divided self will be healed in the higher unity of the divine, and at the same time he will conquer the tyranny of time by becoming part of that life which: . . .

> . . . like the boundless ocean, / Is completely diffused in the present.

Yet the attempt must always be in vain; his yearning for a higher existence is always checked, like the fountain's spray, by the *dlan' nezrimo-rokovaya* [unseen fatal hand].

Where the poet fails, however, the poem can succeed. The very cry of anguish in which he announces the impossibility of his attempt denies its own meaning through its existence as a work of art. And the form of many of Tyutchev's poems—brief, abrupt, almost interjectional, which begin *in medias res,* as though continuing an idea or train of thought: . . .

> And bidding farewell to the cares of life . . .

> Still I pine with yearnings of desire . . .

> So, again I see you . . .

as exclamations: . . .

> O my prophetic soul! . . .

> O, how as our years decline . . .

or as aphorisms: . . .

> There is a certain hour of universal silence in the night . . .

> There are two forces—two fatal forces . . .

gives them the quality of fragments of emotion or thought which have escaped the flux of time.

Poetry can achieve this paradoxical triumph of form over content because, like nature, it is unaware of its own existence. To the poet, however, his own life must always appear evanescent and insubstantial. It is only when he turns his attention away from himself, towards the world which surrounds him, that he can fulfil his boast that: . . .

> The poet is omnipotent, like an element . . .
> (**'Do not believe the poet, maiden'** . . . : **'Ne ver', ne ver' poetu, deva'** . . . , 1839)

and eternalize the present moment, as he does in his landscapes, those descriptions of the cold North, or hot, languid South, in which the earth's motion seems to be stopped, arrested by slumber: . . .

> Here, where the vault of heaven so inertly /

Gazes on the meagre land,— / Here, sunk in iron slumber, / Tired nature sleeps . . . (**'Here, where the vault of heaven so inertly'** . . . : **'Zdes', gde tak vyalo svod nebesnyy'** . . . , 1830)

Here life is frozen into immobility, while in **'Noon'** (**'Polden'**) (1827-30) the same effect is achieved, the instant prolonged to eternity, by the drowsy heat of the summer midday:

> Lazily breathes the misty noon; / Lazily flows the river; / And in the fiery and pure firmament / Lazily melt the clouds.

> And all nature, as if with a mist, / Is embraced in a warm drowsiness; / And now great Pan himself / Peacefully slumbers in the nymphs' cave.

The final triumph over time has been achieved: the god himself has been lulled to sleep by the poem. (pp. 185-204)

> *T. J. Binyon "Lermontov, Tyutchev and Fet," in* Nineteenth-Century Russian Literature: Studies of Ten Russian Writers, *edited by John Fennell, University of California Press, 1973, pp. 168-224.*

Janko Lavrin   (essay date 1973)

[*A Yugoslavian-born educator and critic, Lavrin is noted for his numerous studies of Russian literature. In the following excerpt, he commends Tyutchev's sparse but evocative nature lyrics and the sense of impending loss that permeates his love lyrics, concluding by pointing out that his Russian reputation is eminent despite the misguided political prose and verse that he also produced.*]

Among the leading figures in Russian literature, the poet Fyodor Tyutchev is still merely a name in Western Europe. This is not surprising, for even in Russia it took two or three generations before his work was appreciated at its true value. As his early poems coincided with the Pushkin period, he is often mentioned among the members of the Pushkin *pléiade*. Some of his best verses actually appeared in Pushkin's periodical *The Contemporary* in 1836, while Pushkin was still alive. Apart from this, however, Tyutchev had no close connection with the group. Besides, on leaving Moscow University at the age of nineteen, he was attached, almost at once, to the Russian Legation in Munich and later to that in Turin. His stay abroad lasted some twenty-two years. During that time his genius reached its maturity away from his native land and largely under foreign influences.

The city which for several reasons he liked and enjoyed most was Munich. King Ludwig I, himself a poet, had succeeded in turning the Bavarian capital into a meeting-ground for writers, artists and cultural workers in general. Tyutchev felt thoroughly at home in this atmosphere and made good use of it, maintaining many stimulating personal contacts. In 1828 he was in touch with Heinrich Heine, who in a letter refers to him as his 'best Munich friend'. At the same time he often saw Schelling, whose philosophy of nature, together with Goethe's pantheism, exercised a strong influence upon his own poetry. And when, in 1832, Goethe died, his Russian admirer dedicated to him a poem worthy of its subject.

Tyutchev was only moderately prolific. The total number of poems to his credit is somewhere between 450 and 500. Considering the fact that he reached the age of seventy, this is not an overwhelming amount. He felt somewhat indifferent about his literary career, and it is significant that on his return to Petersburg, in 1844, he soon became famous as a brilliant society wit and causeur, whereas his poems were known only to the initiated few. Refusing to curry favour either with the critics or the readers, he had to wait until 1850 for the first competent appreciation (by the poet Nekrasov) of his work. But even after that he showed so little interest in the promise of a belated literary fame that he took no part in the first printed collection of his poems in 1854: he left it entirely to the discretion of his friend, the novelist I. S. Turgenev. The truth is that he wrote only when he could not help it, under inner compulsion, and even then with apparent reluctance, for he realised the inadequacy of the spoken or written word and felt sceptical about it. In one of his finest poems, 'Silentium,' he explains the reason for his own meagre output in these lines, known to every lover of Russian poetry:

> Heart knows not to speak with heart.
> Song and speech can ne'er impart
> Faith by which we live and die.
> A thought once spoken is a lie.
> Unbroken, undefiled, unstirred
> Thy fountain: drink and say no word.

Fortunately, Tyutchev did not always adhere to this rule. There were moments when he could not abstain from singing, whether he wanted to or not. His intimate contact with Nature, in particular, was responsible for a number of those moments, as was his emotionalised thought, aroused by an intense and distressingly visionary cosmic feeling. The spell of a tragic love, which swayed him in his later years, was responsible for a last and final crop of poignant lyrics. And since he wrote only when he felt impelled to, he put into his verse all the artistic and human integrity of which he was capable. Turgenev once said that Tyutchev's poems are not redolent of anything laboured, but seem to have been written, as Goethe wrote, on the spur of certain moments: instead of having been made, they have grown of their own accord 'like the fruits on a tree'.

To the average poetry-reader in Russia Tyutchev is known mainly for his nature lyrics. These are less ethereal but more direct and incisive in their laconic impressionism than the lyrics of his younger contemporary, Afanasy Fet (1820-92). They are also imbued with frequent philosophic contemplation spontaneously arising out of his moods rather than imposed upon them. He may sing about plains and mountains, spring floods, sea-waves, seasons, mornings and evenings—the array of motifs used by thousands of poets before and after him; yet he does it in his own manner, and his voice is unmistakable. As a rule he selects a few details only, which he arranges in such a way as to suggest the whole picture in its striking aspects without any superfluous words. Even such an obvious nature poem as his '**Spring Storm,**', now known from textbooks to

every Russian schoolboy, can serve as an example. It begins with the simplest lines imaginable:

> I like a storm at May's beginning,
> When Spring's first thunder with wild cries
> As though in frolic gaily spinning
> Rumbles around the pale blue skies.

The elements of the storm are then compressed into eight lines which are sufficient to show it in its fullness, with the 'jargon of the forests, brawl of the mountains—all echoing the thunder's roar'. A mental picture with an appropriate simile is added as a final touch and conclusion:

> Hebe, you'd say, had seized a brimming
> Cup from Jove's eagle in wild mirth,
> And laughingly had dashed the swimming
> Nectar from heaven across the earth.

But Tyutchev's lyrics are not always as cheerful as in the poem above. His impressionism often assumes a disquieting meditative character, tinged with symbolic meaning. The symbolist and the impressionist methods generally converge in him, containing now and then a summing-up comment as they do at the end of these lines:

> The light of autumn evening seems a screen,
> Some mystery with tender glamour muffling
> The trees in motley, cloaked and eerie sheen,
> The scarlet leaves that languid airs are ruffling.
> The still and misty azure, vaguely far,
> Above the earth that waits her orphan sorrow,
> And bitter winds in gusty fragrance are
> Forerunners of a bleak, storm-driven morrow.
>
> The woods are waning; withered in the sun;
> Earth shows the smile of passing, meekly tender
> As the grave shyness of the suffering one,
> In noble reticence of sad surrender.

The last three lines stress the meaning of the picture. The symbolism of the following motif—a willow leaning over the running water—is, however, transparent enough to explain itself without any comment:

> Why, O willow, to the river
> Leans thy head so low, and why
> Dost thou with long leaves that tremble,
> And that thirsty lips resemble
> Catch the ripples dancing by?
> Though thy leaflets faint and quiver,
> Mirrored in the fleeting stream,
> Yet the current speeds and splashes,
> In caressing sunshine flashes,
> And but mocks thy empty dream.

In Pushkin's poetry the phenomena of Nature exist as a rule in their own right, objectively, and are described as such. Tyutchev, on the other hand, prefers to approach them either as vehicles of his own moods and thoughts, or else to look upon them as a cover for what is clandestinely working behind and beyond the surface. His original contributions to Russian literature are, above all, those verses in which Nature herself is interpreted as a veil hiding from man's eyes the deeper cosmic processes active at the root of being.

It was here that certain influences of German thought left their mark in Tyutchev's work. Under the impact of Goethe's pantheism and even more of Schelling's philosophy of the identity between Spirit and Universe, he came to consider Nature as a living organism—with a soul, a mind and language of its own. These are accessible, however, only when the clarity of the day is replaced by the irrational element of the night. During the day we see the surface of Nature in all her alluring and deceptive beauty. But when the day is gone, man's consciousness can be attuned to the darker mysteries coming from the depths of being. He is then able to partake of universal life, provided he surrenders to the point of forgetting or even obliterating his own *moi haïssable* (hateful self). Such pantheistic moods at the hour of approaching night are well rendered in Tyutchev's '**Twilight**':

> Dove-blue shades have met and mingled,
> Colours fade and sound is sleeping—
> Life and movement all dissolve in
> Trembling twilight, far-off weeping.
> Moths upon their unseen journeys
> Murmuring through the darkness fall . . .
> Moment this of wordless yearning!
> All within me, I in all. . . .
>
> Gentle twilight, sleepy twilight,
> Penetrate my inmost soul,
> Tranquil, languid, full of odours,
> All suffusing, lulling all
> In a mist of self-oblivion
> Every feeling softly fold!
> Let me taste annihilation,
> Merge me with the sleeping world.

Night and twilight, imbued with this mystical flavour, became Tyutchev's favourite motifs. Appealing to his cosmic sense even more than to his sense of Nature, they affected him accordingly. What during the day appeared as harmony and beauty, was bound to dissolve at night into a foreboding of chaos as the lurking primeval essence of the universe. If the beauty of Nature gave him moments of ecstasy, the magic of night, charged with the bigger mystery of the cosmos, filled him with *angoisse* and metaphysical horror. His pantheism thus assumed the dualistic aspect of Day and Night, the symbolic meaning of which he expresses in this key-poem:

> Across the spirits' secret world,
> Hiding the chaos and the void,
> The great gods, lest we be destroyed,
> A golden curtain have unfurled.
> This radiant veil we call the Day,
> The lustrous Day, whose golden weave
> Gleams nimbus-like on all who grieve,
> And jewels with his joys the gay.
>
> But Day wanes: Night shrouded in dusk,
> Stalks forward, and with gestures gruff
> Crumbles and rends the precious stuff,
> And casts it down like any husk.
> Then the abyss is bared to sight,
> Its terrors grim, its shadows vast;
> We shrink back, desperate, aghast.
> Hence men, beholding fear the night.

Around the hackneyed antithesis of day and night Tyutchev spun some of his boldest imagery, but always with emphasis on the night. The poetry of night was in vogue among the romantics, especially in Germany where it had

devotees such as Novalis, Tieck, Eichendorff and others. Among its votaries in Russia was the tender lyrical poet Vasily Zhukovsky. Yet it would be hard to find a poet who knew how to render this 'shrinking back aghast' with such vigour as Tyutchev. If one can speak of nocturnal metaphysics at all, we find it in his verses. Moreover, it was not terror alone but also the fascination of the Night that drew him irresistibly with its mystery and magic.

> As ocean's stream girdles the ball of earth,
> From circling seas of dreams man's life emerges
> And at night moves in silence up the firth,
> The secret tide around our mainland surges.
>
> The voice of urgent waters softly sounds;
> The magic skiff uplifts white wings of wonder
> The tide swells swiftly and the white sail rounds,
> Where the blind waves in shoreless darkness
>   thunder.
>
> And the wide heavens, starred and luminous,
> Out of the deep in mystery aspire.
> The strange abyss is burning under us;
> And we sail onwards, and our wake is fire.

Tyutchev's awe of the waves thundering in the 'shoreless darkness' instead of abating as time went on, only grew stronger. He felt lost and forlorn like an orphan in the face of it, and while singing of man's 'fateful heritage', often obliterated the dividing line between things visual and things visionary. His impressionism passed into strangely realistic symbols.

> The night was dark with indignation;
> With cloud the sky was shrouded deep;
> It was not threat nor meditation,
> But drugged uncomfortable sleep.
>
> Only the lightning's summer revels
> Flashed alternating, out and in,
> As if a horde of deaf-mute devils
> Were holding conference of sin.
>
> As if a sign agreed were given,
> Broad conflagration fired the sky,
> And momently from the dark heaven
> Woods and far forests met the eye.
>
> Then disappeared again the vision;
> In visible darkness all was pent
> As if some great and dire decision
> Were taken in the firmament.

'A horde of deaf-mute devils holding conference of sin' is one of those pregnant phrases (Tyutchev's poetry is full of them) which, once read, cannot be forgotten. As an emanation of his *angoisse* it points to certain realities within his own mind which haunted him. For he found there the same conflicting tendencies as in the cosmic life at large, only more personal, more painful—with the chaotic 'nocturnal' element on top of them all:

> Oh, thou, my wizard soul, oh, heart
> That whelming agony immerses,
> The threshold of two universes
> In cleaving thee, tears thee apart.

Self-division of this kind anticipated certain *fin de siècle* traits. The agony alluded to was rendered even more unbearable because of the threat of scepticism, to which he was no stranger. As far back as 1851, he described to perfection (in eight lines) the inner vacuum resulting from that disposition which was doomed to undermine the generation of the 'moderns'.

> No sickness of the flesh is ours to-day
> Whose time is spent in grieving and despairing;
> Who pray all night that night will pass away—
> Who greet the dawn rebelliously uncaring.
> Withered and parched by unbelief, the soul
> Impossible, unbearable things is bearing.
> We are lost men, and ruin is our goal,
> Athirst for faith, to beg for faith not daring.

Tyutchev, too, was in danger of being inwardly paralysed by such a state of mind, and he knew it. In fact, during the decade preceding the above verses he wrote surprisingly little. He might have become silent altogether, had not chance provided him with a new source of inspiration. What happened was that in 1850 he, a married middle-aged man holding a high post in the department of censorship, fell passionately in love with a certain Mlle Denisyeva—a niece of the headmistress of the exclusive Smol'ny Institute, where his daughters were educated. Far from being a short platonic affair, this love lasted some fourteen years (until Mlle Denisyeva's death in 1864) and had a profound effect on Tyutchev's life and work.

There have been many—too many—poets of first love, but Tyutchev is not one of them. He sings of his last love instead. And his mood is not one of joy but of the nostalgic sadness of a parting day, the very beauty of which is tragic, as we can gather from his poem, '**Last Love**':

> As our years sink away, how tender it grows,
> Our love, and how filled with fateful boding . . .
> Shine on us, shine, thou farewell glow
> Of love's last ray, of the twilight's brooding.
>
> Shades have reft half the sky away:
> Westward alone the light still lingers.
> Bide with us, charm of the dying day;
> Withdraw not, enchantment, thy magic fingers!
>
> Let the coursing blood grow thin as gall,
> If the heart but keep its tender burning . . .
> O last and latest love of all,
> Thou art bliss unending, and hopeless yearning.

Tragic also was the love of Mlle Denisyeva. The position of a young and pretty society woman, who gave birth to three illegitimate children while her lover's German wife was still alive, was by no means easy. The gossip, slander and social ostracism she had to endure can well be imagined. Nor was Tyutchev himself invariably tender; there were times when his temper became unbearable. Besides, neither of the two lovers seemed able to separate love from torment and subsequent self-torment. A lyric in which he gives a condensed history of his last passion begins with the frank exclamation, 'Oh, how killingly we love; how in the reckless blindness of passions we are sure to ruin all that is dear to our heart!' The 'immortal vulgarity of men,' having chosen Mlle Denisyeva for its target, did the rest. And the result? Two wrecked lives, and a series of poignant love-lyrics. These are written in a realistic vein, with frequent colloquial inflection. In some of them Tyutchev castigates himself by putting into the mouth of his beloved

grave accusations, as though the verses had been written not by him but by her—in order to reproach him.

> That, as before, he loves me, tell me never,
> Nor that he treasures me as in the days gone
>   by . . .
> Oh no! My life's thin thread, he, ruthless seeks
>   to sever,
> For all I see the blade his fingers ply.
>
> Now raging, now in tears, with grief and anger
>   seething,
> Swept madly on, my soul plucked bare and raw,
> I ache, nor am alive . . . in him alone know
>   breathing;
> And needle-sharp is every breath I draw.
>
> He measures me the air more grudgingly and
>   sparsely
> Than one would mete it out to one's most hated
>   foe.
> I still can breathe; though painfully and harshly,
> I still draw breath—but life no longer know.

The contrition after each fit of harshness may have increased the depth and the sincerity of his more tender feelings, but continuous ups and downs of this kind were costly for both—costly emotionally and physically. After some fourteen years of such love, it was the woman who had to pay the price. A further glimpse of her (and his) agony can be obtained from this poem:

> All day unconscious she was lying there,
> And evening shadows came and wrapt her
>   round;
> Warm summer rain fell soft upon the leaves
> In steady flow and made a cheerful sound.
>
> And slowly she returned into herself,
> And trained her sense the pleasant sound to
>   hear,
> And listened long, her mind absorbed in thought
> That carried her away, yet left her near.
>
> Then, as one speaking to herself, alone,
> Now conscious of the sound and all beside
> (I watched her, yet alive, though death was near)
> 'How dearly have I loved all this!' she sighed.
>
> Oh how thou loved'st it! And to love like thee
> Has to no other in the world been given!
> My God! and can I then thy death survive
> And my poor heart in fragments not be riven?

Her death was an irreparable blow to Tyutchev. 'Only in her presence was I a personality, only in her love, her boundless love for me, was I aware of myself,' he owned to one of his friends in October 1864. 'Now I am a meaningless, painfully living nonentity.' Before long his poetic gift, too, began to decline. But while his lyrical vein seemed to be in abeyance, there was a sudden increase in the output of his political and civic verse—the last group of his poetry still to be considered.

With very few exceptions, Tyutchev's political poems cannot be compared either in depth or in technique with his lyrics. They are primarily a register of the ideological attitudes typical of Tyutchev the Russian and the aristocrat. His earliest political poem—an answer to Pushkin's *Ode to Liberty*—was written as early as 1820. Tyutchev wrote

it in the liberal spirit prevalent among the advanced aristocratic youths of that generation. Later, however, he
changed his opinions and after the Paris rebellion of 1830,
definitely sided with reaction and the ideas of the Holy Alliance. He also became an ardent Russian patriot (while
still continuing to use in private conversation and correspondence French in preference to his native tongue). In
1841 he, moreover, paid a visit to Prague, whence he returned a convinced pan-Slavist of the Russian brand.

From now on he considered Russia to be the only guarantee for the old order, since the West seemed to be in a constant ferment which had reached its climax in the revolutions of 1848. As a scion of the old serf-owning nobility,
he was so frightened by the revolutionary trend in Europe
that he wrote four essays (in French) in order to 'enlight-
en' the world at large. The most important of these is '**La
Russie et la Révolution**' (1849). The gist of it was summed
up by him in one of his political poems. '**The Rock and the
Sea**', in which tsarist Russia is likened to a cliff surrounded by the waves of the revolution vainly dashing against
its 'gigantic heel'.

In spite of his one-time friendship with Heine, Tyutchev
now turned his back on everything men of Heine's stamp
were fighting for. Having identified Europe with the revolution, he prophesied in verse and prose the decline of the
West. He even propped up his imperialistic pan-Slavism
with a rather sophisticated philosophy of history. Russia
would, in his opinion, eventually become the leader of all
the Slavs, and the universal monarchy she was destined to
found would extend as far as the Nile and Ganges, with
Constantinople as its capital. A *pax russica* would then
stem for ever the fury of the revolution, fomented by the
godless masses of the West. In his poem, '**Sunrise**', he
gives allegorical utterance to the adage of *ex oriente lux*—
quite in the spirit of militant Slavophilism. Little did he
suspect that some seventy years later the irony of history
would make Russia a communist country, whereas the
West would desperately try to save what it could of the
old order. It was for patriotic, rather than religious, reasons that Tyutchev now stressed also his allegiance to the
Russian Orthodox Church. In one of his poems he mentions Christ wandering in a slave's garb all over Russia
and bestowing blessing upon her—a symbol of that religious Messianism which was so dear to the Slavophils.

The setbacks of the Russian army during the Crimean
Campaign had a sobering effect upon Tyutchev. The morass into which the corrupt Russian bureaucracy had
plunged the country was something of a revelation to him,
and after the Tsar's death (during the campaign) he frankly said in a poem what he thought of him. Tyutchev's patriotism was sincere but, as he viewed the destinies of his
country through his semi-feudal and imperialist spectacles, he was bound to see things in a wrong perspective.
One more proof that good poets are rarely good politicians.

Tyutchev's place among the great Russian poets is no longer contested. Dostoevsky once called him the first poet-
philosopher in Russian literature. Leo Tolstoy, who otherwise cared little for poetry, rated Tyutchev even higher
than Pushkin. Touching with one end of his development

the classical eighteenth century of Derzhavin, Tyutchev
anticipated with the other the Russian school of Symbolism. He was a 'modern' before his time, which may have
been one of the reasons why he had to wait so long for recognition. In spite of the high tribute paid to him by such
contemporaries as Nekrasov, Turgenev, Apollon Grig-
oryev, and even the ultra-radical critic Dobrolyubov,
Tyutchev's work came into its own only towards the end
of the last century.

The pioneering article by the philosopher and poet Vladimir Solovyov (in 1895) was followed by a crop of essays
in which some of the leading Russian symbolists proclaimed Tyutchev one of their predecessors. The height of
his popularity was reached, however, in 1913, when a
complete edition of his works, prefaced by Valery Bryu-
sov, was launched as a supplement to the widely read
monthly, *Níva* (*The Cornfield*). Nor did it suffer an eclipse
after the Revolution of 1917 and in spite of his political
views, his poetry is still acclaimed by Soviet readers.
Among the more recent editions of his works there is even
a large one for Soviet children—surely a sign of popularity
the poet could never have dreamt of in his lifetime. (pp.
99-108)

> *Janko Lavrin, "Fyodor Tyutchev," in his* A
> Panorama of Russian Literature, *Barnes &
> Noble Books, 1973, pp. 99-108.*

Sarah Pratt   (essay date 1984)

[*In the following excerpt, Pratt analyzes three important
poems to demonstrate Tyutchev's conception of the poet
and the creative process.*]

[Lidia] Ginzburg is right when she observes that "it would
be difficult to find an important lyric poet of the nineteenth
century who wrote as little as Tiutchev in his verse about
the poet, poetry, and inspiration." There are, in fact, only
three major poems in which Tiutchev uses the word *poet*:
"**You saw him in society circles**" ("**Ty zrel ego v krugu
bol'shogo sveta**", 1829), "**Don't, don't believe the poet,
maiden**" ("**Ne ver', ne ver' poetu, deva,**" 1839), and "**With
a lively sense of greeting**" ("**Zhivym sochuvstviem pri-
veta,**" 1840). And in all three, Tiutchev takes a fairly standard view of the poet as a man engrossed in his own world,
alien to the insensitive crowd, given over to wild passions,
and all-powerful in his creative potential. None conveys
a concept of art that coincides with the deeper concerns
of Tiutchev's metaphysical poetry.

Tiutchev does consider the lot of the poet and inspiration
in his metaphysical poems. But because he usually presupposes an image of the poet as a mystic merged or merging
with nature, his treatment of the theme is sometimes so
indirect as to be obscure. The creative process appears as
a force inherent in nature, independent of the genius or
talent of any individual human being. Once the involvement of the figurative poet is diminished, few clues remain
to distinguish one kind of creativity from another. Often
the peak experience portrayed can be interpreted in terms
of spiritual regeneration, mystic transport, or sexual ecstasy as well as artistic inspiration. This [essay] treats only
three such poems: "**A Vision**" ("**Videnie,**" 1829), "**As the

ocean embraces the earthly sphere" ("Kak okean ob'emlet shar zemnoi," 1830), and **"Dream at Sea"** ("Son na more," 1836). But the poems **"Spring,"** . . . **"How sweetly slumbers the dark green garden"** ("Kak sladko dremlet sad temnozelenyi," 1836), and **"Holy night has risen into the firmament"** ("Sviataia noch' na nebosklon vzoshla," 1850) . . . could also logically be included in a discussion of the creative or regenerative experience.

"A Vision" is one of Tiutchev's most direct portrayals of inspiration because it includes specific mention of the Muse: . . .

> There is a certain hour, in the night, of universal silence, and at that hour of apparitions and miracles the living chariot of the universe rolls openly into the sanctuary of the heavens.
>
> Then night thickens, like chaos on the waters; unconsciousness, like Atlas, presses the land— only the Muse's virgin soul do the gods rouse in prophetic dreams.

Although the Muse does appear, she does so only in the penultimate line of the poem, effectively leaving the experience portrayed in the opening three-fourths of the poem open to various interpretations. Even the title is ambiguous. The word *videnie* (vision) might denote the visionary dreams of the Muse, or it might refer to the vision of the mystic poet-persona, a vision taking the form of the poem itself—or, of course, both phenomena at once.

No matter who the beneficiary of the vision may be, Tiutchev makes it clear that the vision depends on the setting—the coincidence of certain natural phenomena— rather than on any form of individual artistic consciousness. The important opening position of the verb *est'* emphasizes the existential fact that *there is* a certain hour. The second word, *nekii*, makes the statement more emphatic by repeating the stressed *e* sound in *est'*. And the third word, *chas*, takes on additional force because of the recurrence of the *ch* sound in *nochi, molchan'ia*, the repetition of the word *chas* itself in the second line, and the presence of both *ch* and *s* sounds in the word *chudes*. The three distinctive features of this hour—its occurrence specifically at night (*v nochi*), its association with some specific form of sound or absence-of-sound imagery (*vsemirnogo molchan'ia*), and its association with the supernatural (*chas iavlenii i chudes*)—are all characteristics that appear in a significant number of Tiutchev's metaphysical poems, especially those in which the powerful image of chaos is either explicitly or implicitly present.

The concluding lines of the first stanza continue the same train of thought. The fact that the chariot of the universe rolls openly (*otkryto*) reaffirms the notion that the experience is not limited to specially gifted beings: it is there for anyone who may happen to be present during the certain hour. The universality of the experience completely negates the function of the uniquely endowed visionary poet who takes such a prominent place in poems like Venevitinov's "Love the Child of Inspiration" and "The Poet and His Friend."

The total absence of the first-person pronoun further confirms the relative insignificance of the poet's function. In this aspect **"A Vision"** contrasts sharply with poems like Pushkin's "The Muse" ("Muza," 1821), in which the poet refers to himself eight times within fourteen lines, or with more typical second-rate romantic poems like Tumanskii's "The Muses" ("Muzy," 1822), in which the poet refers to himself seventeen times in forty lines and closes the poem with a boast showing no mean estimate of his own role in the creative process: *Ia slavil pesniami vysokikh dev liubov', / I sladko trepetal moi genii* (I praised the love of exalted maidens with songs, and my genius sweetly stirred). Even the title **"Videnie,"** which might at first seem to imply the presence of the poet, refers most directly only to the dreams (visions) of the Muse. Thus the only sure proof that the poet exists is the existence of the poem itself.

The second stanza of **"A Vision"** reaffirms the setting with the word *togda* (then)—meaning the certain hour just described—and by repetition of the word *noch'* (night). It also introduces two more elements that figure prominently in Tiutchev's metaphysical poetry: the image of chaos and an assertion of the irrational nature of the basic functions of the universe. The word *bespamiatstvo* denotes something more than simple unconsciousness. It conveys the specific absence of consciousness of self, the obliteration of human feelings and human ratiocination associated with participation in the universal-godly life in **"Spring."** *Bespamiatstvo* also acts as a counterpart to chaos in the parallel similes that open the second stanza: *Togda gusteet noch', kak khaos na vodakh, / Bespamiatstvo, kak Atlas, davit sushu* (Then night thickens, like chaos on the waters; unconsciousness, like Atlas, presses the land). In this reversal of the usual concept of Atlas as the holder of the heavens, the weight of the heavens presses on Atlas' body, which in turn presses down on the earth like the weighty unconsciousness of deep sleep. Thus both unconsciousness and chaos represent night forces, one pressing on the waters, the other pressing on the land. Since land and water comprise the earthly sphere, unconsciousness and chaos together subjugate the whole world to irrational forces.

The irregular arrangement of various stylistic elements supports the irrational aspect of the poem and contributes to the blurry visionary quality often associated with romantic poetry. Line length, for instance, varies from nine to thirteen syllables, and no two lines in one stanza have the same number of syllables. In the second stanza, even the number of feet per line varies in a more or less irregular pattern, the fifth line of the poem having six feet, the sixth line five feet, the seventh line four feet, and the final line five feet. This irregularity gives the poem a certain metrical vagueness in keeping with the hazy quality of the vision itself.

In addition, in both stanzas the tempo of the verse changes as the persona expresses himself in verbal waves that gather momentum, break, and then fall back. The pattern in both stanzas is the same: first a series of short phrases set off by commas that reflect the halting pattern of the images building up in the persona's mind. The pause between the images gives each one a distinct and lasting presence:

[stanza 1]
Est' nekii chas, / v nochi, / vsemirnogo mol-chan'ia /
There is a certain hour, / in the night, / of universal silence, /

[stanza 2]
Togda gusteet noch', / kak khaos na vodakh, / Bespamiatstvo, / kak Atlas, / davit sushu; /
Then night thickens, / like chaos on the waters, /Unconsciousness, / like Atlas, / presses the land; /

At a certain point, these accumulated images combine into one main image that carries through the rest of the stanza, mimicking the flash of inspiration portrayed by the poem as a whole: the commas disappear and the words come rushing out without a break as, in the first stanza, the living chariot of the universe rolls across the sky, and in the second, the soul of the Muse is roused by the gods in prophetic dreams.

The contorted syntax of the poem's concluding clause again shows the disordered quality of the persona's means of expression. If the clause is organized in accordance with the norms of Russian syntax, it still denotes the same phenomenon, but its impact differs from that in the poem.

Standard word order:

> *Bogi trevozhat lish' devstvennuiu dushu Muzy v prorocheskikh snakh.*

In the poem:

> *Lish' Muzy devstvennuiu dushu / V prorocheskikh trevozhat*
> *bogi snakh.*

Such details of syntax are impossible to translate accurately, but it suffices to note that if standard word order is represented by consecutive numbers from 1 through 9, the word order in the poem reads 3-6-4-5-7-8-2-1-9.

In the standard version, the subject and verb of the sentence—the gods and their rousing action—receive more syntactic weight than the other elements. In the poem, the situation is reversed: the words *trevozhat* (rouse) and *bogi* (gods) are buried in the middle of the line and obscured by syntactic confusion, while the more important elements stand out at the beginnings and ends of lines—the Muse, her soul, her dreams, and the visionary quality of the dreams. In one sense, however, analytic comprehension of the syntax is almost irrelevant, because the essential aspects of the persona's message emerge from the text of their own accord regardless of syntactic norms.

The classical concepts of the chariot of the universe and the sanctuary of the heavens as well as the references to Atlas, the Muse, and chaos give the poem strong mythological overtones. One particular myth may well have provided much of the material from which Tiutchev constructed the poem: the myth of creation. Since Tiutchev had a thorough training in the Latin classics, he was almost certainly acquainted with the myth as it appears in Ovid's *Metamorphoses*. Both this version and Hesiod's version, which Tiutchev may have known in translation, are centered on the role of chaos as the source of the universe. Hesiod says: "Verily at first Chaos came to be, but next wide-bosomed Earth, the ever-sure foundation of all. . . . From Chaos came forth Erebus and black night." Ovid's version reads as follows:

> Before the sea was, and the lands, and the sky that hangs over all, the face of Nature showed alike in her whole round, which state have men called chaos. . . . All objects were at odds, for within one body cold things strove with hot, moist with dry, soft things with hard, things having weight with weightless things.
>
> God—or kindlier Nature—composed this strife. . . . He set them each in its own place and bound them fast in harmony.

The main ideas about creativity expressed in **"A Vision"** can readily be derived from the ancients' image of chaos. The opposition to general order suggested by the nighttime setting, the mentions of dreams, unconsciousness, and chaos in the poem appears as the extreme disorder of Ovid's chaos, juxtaposed as it is to the concept of "eternal order." All three authors view this disorder as a source of fertility: chaos gives rise to the creation of the universe in Hesiod and Ovid, and to artistic inspiration in Tiutchev. At the same time, all exclude any reference to a human contribution to the creative process. The universe simply comes to be: it evolves from chaos through the workings of a nature inhabited by supernatural forces as a matter of course. Likewise, Tiutchev's vision simply comes to be as a result of the natural presence of supernatural night forces, which significantly thicken "like chaos on the waters." Thus the image of chaos, which at first seems to play only a minor role as a part of a simile, contains virtually the whole conceptual framework on which the poem is based.

Tiutchev's poem **"As the ocean embraces the earthly sphere"** contains no direct reference to inspiration: no muse appears to signal the precise meaning of the creative experience portrayed, and the imagery could suggest a number of equally plausible interpretations. But the movement of the poem remains the same. At the outset, the persona functions merely as an observer of the supernatural workings of the universe; but then, urged on by the voice of the Element, he is "carried away," and in the end finds himself in the very midst of the creativity and power omnipresent in the supernatural universe. . . .

> As the ocean embraces the earthly sphere, earthly life is wholly embraced by dreams; night falls—and in sonorous waves the Element pulses against its shore.
>
> This is its voice: it compels and beseeches us . . .
> The magic bark has already come alive at the wharf; the tide grows and carries us swiftly away into the immeasurability of the dark waves.
>
> The heavenly vault, burning with starry glory, mysteriously glances from the depths—and we float, surrounded by the flaming abyss on all sides.

The theme of inspiration is most directly symbolized by star imagery combined with the notion of contact with the metaphysical depths of the universe, notably in the first two lines of the last stanza: *Nebesnyi svod, goriashchii slavoi zvezdnoi, / Tainstvenno gliadit iz glubiny* (The heavenly vault, burning with starry glory, mysteriously glances from the depths). Certain striking similarities to **"A Vision"** further support the idea of inspiration by association. The simile that opens the poem, for instance, recalls the similes in the second stanza of **"A Vision,"** with the same juxtaposition of water, land, and unconsciousness or dreams. Here, however, the connections between the various parts of the simile are stronger because of the repetition of the adjective *zemnoi* (earthly) and the overall chiastic structure of the two lines. . . . (pp. 104-11)

The rhyming of symbolically important words for water and dreams also occurs in both poems: *snakh-vodakh* in **"A Vision"** and *snami-volnami* here. Finally, here again night seems to be a necessary condition for the evocation of the forces of creativity. The usage of the perfective aspect of the verb in the phrase *nastanet noch'* indicates that the future action, repeated or not, will be completed, thus emphasizing the fact that night will have fallen, rather than the process of night's falling, as a prelude to the ensuing experience.

Another possible interpretation focuses on the poem as the portrayal of a sexual experience. Tiutchev had a number of intense and complex amorous involvements, and one can assume that sexual passion played a particularly strong role in his life. And despite the moral conventions of nineteenth-century society, Tiutchev wrote about this passion with varying degrees of directness in a number of poems, especially in the well-known cycle related to his relationship with Elena Aleksandrovna Denis'eva. The sexual motif in **"As the ocean embraces the earthly sphere"** is stated most obviously through the repeated imagery of embracing in the opening simile, and less obviously through the imagery of the pulsing Element, which (like sexual desire) "compels and beseeches us," and finally "carries us swiftly away" into the immeasurable depths of experience.

The writings of Hesiod and Ovid on the creation of the universe once again serve as possible sources, in this instance suggesting a combination of metaphysical and sexual creative power. Ovid combines the imagery of surrounding and embracing in a manner that parallels Tiutchev's usage. In his version, when nature evolved a cosmic order: "The fiery weightless element that forms heaven's vault leaped up and made a place for itself upon the topmost height. Next came the air. . . . The earth was far heavier than these and . . . sank to the bottom by its own weight. The encircling sea took the last place of all, and held the solid land in its embrace." As in the poem, an act of metaphysical creativity takes place with fiery heavens above and the ocean embracing the land below. In the cosmogony of Hesiod, "Earth . . . is a disk surrounded by the River Oceanus," just as earth is surrounded by the ocean in the poem. But Hesiod then makes the sexual potential in the imagery explicit, for the contact between Earth and Oceanus results in offspring.

No matter which interpretation seems most valid—and these interpretations are by no means mutually exclusive—the essential characteristics of the experience re-

main the same. The first of these essential characteristics is that the experience falls outside the realm of the rational world. The opening reference to dreams and the imagery of embracing immediately suggest that the controlling forces stem from the irrational side of man's existence, the subconscious part of his mind and his passions. The Element (*stikhiia*) comprises that part of the human psyche that has a voice (*glas*) and speaks out in dreams, which simultaneously compels and beseeches us (*nudit nas i prosit*), and finally carries us away into the dark, unfathomable depths of our own souls. It is this irrational aspect of man, his own internal chaos, that forms a part of the pantheistic universe founded on chaos. It brings him into communion with the supernatural force that mysteriously glances down from the heavens, surrounding him with starry glory and giving rise to a sublime experience.

Secondly, this universe exists totally independently of man's consciousness of it. The ocean embracing the land and the dreams embracing rational (earthly) life are there whether man perceives them or not. If man lives in the middle of a desert, he may not believe that the ocean exists, but it does, and in fact it surrounds the continent on which the desert is located. Likewise, a person may not know that he has dreams, but they exist and surround his waking life all the same. The fact that the entity that combines the ocean and dream imagery is called the Element (*stikhiia*) shows its power as an irresistible force of nature that denies any possibility of interference by human consciousness. Perhaps the most significant aspect of the poem is that the actual creative impulse, the height of the experience depicted, stems from a downward glance of the starry heavens, and not from the genius or upward striving of the persona. Creativity is a function of nature, not a function of the human presence.

The passive and unselfconscious stance of the persona reinforces the notion of nature's independence of man. Signified by the first-person plural pronoun, the persona is probably meant to be mankind in general. At any rate, the figures involved never show any consciousness of themselves as distinct individuals; their whole consciousness is focused on the workings of nature. They are totally passive and appear only as they are acted upon by the supernatural forces at work within the poem. In grammatical terms, mankind, as represented by the first-person plural pronoun (*nas*), is twice a direct object—*nudit nas i prosit . . . bystro nas unosit* (compels and beseeches us . . . swiftly carries us away). As such, it is acted upon by the subjects of the clauses, which are metaphysically symbolic forces of nature, the Element (*stikhiia*) and the tide (*priliv*). And when the first-person pronoun does occur as the subject of a sentence, *my plyvem* (we are floating), it is not the initiator of assertive action on nature but rather the subject of an intransitive verb suggesting something like a state of being. Even in this instance nature retains ultimate control, because as man floats he is surrounded on all sides by the flaming abyss of nature: the word *okruzheny* (surrounded) significantly closes the poem.

The third characteristic of the creative experience is that it is an internal event portrayed in terms of external phenomena. The external metaphor allows Tiutchev to maintain the sense of objectivity, the same virtual denial of man's subjective point of view that we saw earlier in **"A Vision."** The opening simile establishes the two aspects, with the ocean, in reality a force outside man, equated with dreams, the product of the inner workings of man's soul. Although the dream imagery disappears after the first few lines, water imagery continues to the end of the poem. But since the opening simile has established a certain identity between the two, the water imagery takes on symbolic value for the internal process corresponding to the external process actually depicted.

This poem differs from **"A Vision"** in its indirect method of handling the theme of inspiration and the possible addition of the sexual motif, but the same concept of creativity and the same poetic method underlies both poems. The notion of creativity combines a typically romantic insistence on the irrational origins of the creative process and an almost classicist portrayal of the creative forces of nature as objective phenomena totally independent of the subjective view of the poet. In accordance with these ideas, metaphors of the external world are used to portray an essentially internal experience.

Tiutchev's mystic persona remains Tiutchev's own creation, but the concept he represents and the method he embodies show a close relation to the fundamental precepts Schelling outlines in his *System of Transcendental Idealism:* "The first principle of this philosophy is that a world of things outside us and independent of us exists. But in addition, our perceptions of things correspond so accurately to these things that they exist as we perceive them." Tiutchev portrays the supernatural universe as a world of things outside human consciousness and independent of human consciousness. Yet at the same time, the consciousness of his almost invisible persona acts in such close conjunction with that universe that his poems show the universe "as it really is."

In addition, the poem might well be related to Schelling's theory of art. Although Tiutchev had little use for Schelling's early notion of the artist as an outstanding individual or genius, preferring instead his later views on the merging of self-will with the universal will, he was served well by Schelling's basic concept of art as the highest form of *Indifferenz,* the resolution of the contradiction between the real (material) and the ideal (spiritual), and "the realization of the infinite in the finite." The artistic significance of *Indifferenz* appears here as the possibility of inspiration linked to the idea of being "surrounded on all sides" by "starry glory" from the stars above and their reflection in the ocean below, or, in another description of the same phenomenon, being surrounded by "the flaming abyss."

The reflection fits Schelling's concepts in a number of ways. On one hand, one might claim that the stars are real and that their reflection in the water is only an image, hence associated with the ideal. The number of stars, therefore, is finite, while the number of reflections, which can repeat with an echo effect any number of times, is infinite. The artistic vision of the poem's personae, their dreamlike perception of the surrounding universe, thus encompasses and actually merges the real and the ideal, the finite and the infinite.

On the other hand, on the basis of literary tradition, one could reverse the interpretation, arguing that the stars are only a symbol of inspiration and therefore belong to the realm of the spiritual, while the water reflecting the stars belongs to the realm of the material. Further, the stars, which exist in number beyond any human comprehension, represent the infinite, while the water and other earthly phenomena represent the finite. But here again the conclusion is the same and it relates to Schelling's principles equally well: art is the reconciliation of the real and the ideal, the realization of the infinite in the finite.

The image of the poet as creator in Tiutchev's **"Dream at Sea"** (**"Son na more,"** 1836) acts as a foil for the mystic personae who lurk behind the scenes in the two poems just discussed. Nonetheless, the basic view of creativity expressed in the other poems eventually comes to the surface here also.

> Both the sea and the storm rocked our bark; I was sleepy and given over to every whim of the waves. Two infinities were within me, and they played with me at will. The cliffs resounded around me like cymbals, the winds replied and the waves sang. I lay deafened in the chaos of sounds, but above the chaos of sounds skimmed my dream. Painfully vivid, magically mute, it wafted lightly over the thundering darkness. In the rays of a fever it unfolded its world—the earth shone green, the ether brightened, labyrinthine gardens, palaces, columns, and myriads of silent crowds swarmed around. I came to know many supernatural characters, saw magical creatures and mysterious birds; I strode like God along the summits of creation, and under me the motionless world glowed. But through all the dreams I heard the roar of the ocean's abyss like a magician's howl, and into the silent realm of visions and dreams burst the foam of the roaring waves.

"Dream at Sea" portrays the struggle between two sets of elements: those associated with the sea or chaos of sounds, which dominate the opening and closing sections, and those associated with the dream or inspiration of the persona-creator, which dominate the middle section. The main strands of imagery fall clearly into two opposing categories:

dve bespredel'nosti (two infinities)	
son (dream)	*more* (sea)
sonnyi (drowsy)	*buria* (storm)
grezy (dreams)	*khaos zvukov* (chaos of sounds)
oglushen (deafened)	*zvuchali* (resounded)
tikhaia oblast' videnii i snov (silent realm of visions and dreams)	*oklikalisia* (replied)
	peli (sang)
	valy, volny (billows, waves)

volshebno-nemoi (magically mute)

volshebnika voi (magician's howl)

pena revushchikh valov (foam of the roaring waves)

The lefthand column, with its emphasis on silence and supernatural phenomena, echoes the imagery of **"A Vision"** and creates a sense that recalls Tiutchev's "blissful world" (*blazhennyi mir*). This is a poetic realm permeated by a feeling of drowsy bliss and often identified with the warm, peaceful days of spring or summer, or with a southern locale. The words in the right-hand column, on the other hand, clearly pertain to Tiutchev's "stormy world" (*burnyi mir*), a world of raging winds, billowing waves, and a deafening array of storm noises.

The persona's statement that two infinities (*dve bespredel'nosti*) are within him suggests that he has the ability to ally himself with either side. Within the context of this particular event, though, his main function is as the creator of the dream, and he sees himself as an integral part of the dream. His only mention of himself in connection with the sea casts him in the role of a victim, as a man in a boat, possibly seasick, and given over to the whims of the waves; or, at the end, as a poet whose divine vision is ruined by the roar of the sea.

The dream with which the poet allies himself is quite different from the dreams in the other poems discussed. First of all, the dream has specifically depicted content. The dreams of the Muse in **"A Vision"** and the dreams that embrace earthly life in **"As the ocean embraces the earthly sphere"** are symbolic at most. Even more likely, they simply exist as totally amorphous irrational phenomena of unknowable content.

Second, this dream represents the rational. Everything is clear and bright; things are identified, perhaps even classified to the extent that the verb *uznat'* carries implications of recognizing or getting to know something on the basis of its given characteristics. In addition, the content of the dream emphasizes form, with its labyrinthine gardens, palaces, and columns reminiscent of the rigidly geometric gardens at Versailles.

Third, the personae in the other poems take part in the dreams only insofar as they absorb the supernatural aura or intuit the indistinct significance of the dreams. Here the persona is the creator of the dream. He actually takes on the role of God within his dream—*po vysiam tvoren'ia kak Bog ia shagal* (I strode like God along the summits of creation)—and he never loses sight of that role as he refers to himself no fewer than eleven times in the twenty-two-line poem. His constant focus on himself contrasts sharply with the extreme infrequency of self-reference by the personae in the other poems. In effect, this persona tries to make nature into the dream of man. This opposes the principle suggested in the other metaphysical poems and expressed in a poem cited earlier, **"Of the life that raged here"**—that man exists only as a dream of nature.

With his godly pretensions and his ever recurrent references to himself, the persona commits the deadly sin of pride. Chaos and the sea, in keeping with their usual roles in Tiutchev's poetry as elements of a higher reality—not simply as symbols of the hustle and bustle of everyday life—quite literally serve the cause of poetic justice when they burst into the poet's vision and destroy it. Chaos acts as a threatening yet positive force, for in breaking through the egoism of the persona and destroying the false inspiration, it provides him with an opportunity for a rebirth akin to the regeneration depicted in **"Spring."** Once he is rid of the self-centered life represented by his dream, the poet will be free to merge with the sea of the universal-godly life and the fertile chaos below.

Two additional pieces of evidence support this analysis of the relationship between the persona and chaos. The first is a translation of "The Lunatic, the Lover, and the Poet" from Shakespeare's *A Midsummer-Night's Dream* made by Tiutchev at roughly the same time he wrote **"Dream at Sea."** The exclamation that opens the poem asserts that lovers, madmen, and poets are all cast from the same mold. This is a bad portent for the poet in **"Dream at Sea,"** but carries no direct link to him. A connection does become evident in the last four lines of the translation, which more or less parody both the diction and the content of lines 15-18 of **"Dream at Sea,"** stating that the poet's imagination creates unheard-of creatures (*sushchestv nevedomykh*) and that his staff gives airy shadows name and spatial form—thus emphasizing the utter folly of the poet's godlike pretensions.

It is certainly possible, even probable, that Tiutchev appropriated the term "two infinities" from Pascal, but the poem as a whole has far more to do with Schelling's philosophy than with Pascal's. The opening of Pascal's *Pensées* states that man can comprehend neither the infinitely large nor the infinitely small, and so must turn to God for his understanding of the universe; the persona in **"Dream at Sea"** deals neither with the infinitely large nor with the infinitely small, and he does not turn to God in the end. Rather, the situation in the poem embodies a number of basic precepts that Schelling expresses in his *Inquiries on the Essence of Human Freedom.*

Tiutchev's two infinities, for instance, could easily be seen as counterparts to the "two deepest metaphysical centers," the two extreme forms of the modes of existence available to man, described by Schelling in the following passage: "The manifestation of the two deepest metaphysical centers occurs in no visible creatures other than man. In man appear the whole power of the Dark Principle and the whole power of Light. In him are the deepest abyss and the highest heaven, or both metaphysical centers." The principle of darkness is then identified with surrender to self-will, whereas surrender to the principle of light leads to merging with the universal will. Tiutchev's persona succumbs to the extreme form of self-will by creating a dream world to suit his own designs, and the ultimate destruction of his dream indicates that he has overstepped the proper bounds of human activity in this metaphysical universe.

Schelling provides a more explicit statement of the same notion as he explains that, when evil is engendered by man's attempt to become the ruling will, another spirit comes to occupy the place where God should be. This is "the Tempter" himself, who entices man into false plea-sures and plants the ideas of things that do not exist in his imagination. In sum: "Sin begins when man . . . steps over the boundary from Light into Darkness, tries to be-come a creative principle of his own accord, and tries to rule all things with the power of the metaphysical centers he has within him." Here, not only does Schelling speak of the false dominance of self-will, but, like Tiutchev, he makes specific note of its attempt to replace God, the true ruling will of Creation, with itself. In addition, Schelling's emphasis on the unreality of the self as God and the decep-tion of imagination relates to both Tiutchev's translation of "The Lunatic, the Lover, and the Poet" and, here, to his use of the dream or delirium as an image of unreal ex-perience. The poet's dream, in which the ether brightens, silent crowds swarm, and supernatural characters, magi-cal creatures, and mysterious birds appear, could easily be the work of "the Tempter" described by Schelling, though for Tiutchev the poem's primary significance remains metaphysical rather than religious.

Schelling also likens the domination of self-will to sickness marked by a "burning fever" (*Fieber*), suggesting the "fever" (*ognevitsa*) suffered by Tiutchev's persona. But just as the poet hints that the self-satisfied poet-creator may be saved by a good dousing in the fertile waters of metaphysical chaos, the philosopher is also willing to give the sinner another chance. He explains that it is impossible for man to remain in an ambiguous position, balanced pre-cariously between the two centers he has within him; therefore, a movement toward evil may be seen as an act that ultimately makes man conscious of good.

In sum, Tiutchev's view of creativity, like that expressed in Schelling's late philosophy, requires a totally passive stance on the part of the human being involved. In **"A Vi-sion"** the mystic persona becomes a part of the whole mag-ical aura of the "certain hour in the night," and in **"As the ocean embraces the earthly sphere"** he is "carried away" by the complex of forces signified by dream and water im-agery. The image of the poet that underlies Tiutchev's metaphysical poetry—if it can be called an image at all—has nothing to do with the markedly active figure of the philosopher, prophet, or rebellious outcast. Tiutchev's poet is a quiet, contemplative mystic oblivious of every-thing but the larger metaphysical workings of the uni-verse.

Unlike many other writers of the romantic period who symbolize the active poet as a keen-eyed eagle that soars above the chaos of daily life to glimpse the secrets of the universe, Tiutchev rarely uses any symbol at all. In one case in which he does use a symbol (but a rather vague one at that), a poem entitled **"The Swan"** (**"Lebed',"** 1839), he rejects the image of the eagle and, by implication, the con-cept of the poet usually associated with it. The image of the swan here furnishes an alternative, representing a pas-sive approach to metaphysical reflection: . . .

> Let the eagle encounter the lightning's course
> beyond the clouds and drink in the sun's bright-
> ness with his fixed gaze.

> But there is no lot more enviable, O pure swan,

than yours—and the deity has clothed you in an element as pure as you yourself.

> She nurtures your all-seeing dream between the
> double abyss—you are surrounded on all sides
> by the star-filled glory of the world.

Like **"As the ocean embraces the earthly sphere,"** which was written during the same period, **"The Swan"** has a nighttime setting on water, dreams, the presence of a mys-terious force of nature called "the element," and a con-cluding image of an abyss of starry glory reflected on the water and completely surrounding the main figure. And once again it is passive acceptance and contemplation of nature, not active striving, that leads to an experience of the sublime.

Tiutchev's mystic poet lacks the consciousness of his own gifted condition that characterizes even the passive aspects of the images of the poet as philosopher and the poet as outcast. Indeed, the inevitable destruction of the poet-creator's vision in **"Dream at Sea"** shows the folly of artis-tic consciousness inflated at the expense of submission to nature's own creative powers. Nature, in Tiutchev's major metaphysical poems, is a totally self-sustaining, inherently creative force. It exists as an objective entity, seemingly uninfluenced by the subjective views of any human figure. Even when the form of creativity clearly has associations with man's internal life, Tiutchev presents it through met-aphors of the external world, thereby maintaining a façade of objectivity. (pp. 111-22)

> *Sarah Pratt, "The Poet and Poetry," in her*
> Russian Metaphysical Romanticism: The Po-
> etry of Tiutchev and Boratynskii, *Stanford*
> *University Press, 1984, pp. 95-145.*

Borys Bilokur   (essay date 1988)

[*In the following excerpt, Bilokur examines Tyutchev's use of such folkloric devices as animistic imagery, repeti-tion, unstressed syllables, epithets, and proverbs.*]

Even as late as 1891 A. M. Skabičevskij maintained that the "majority of Tjutčev's poems can be read only with great difficulty and appreciated only by the strictest and the most zealous of aesthetes." This erroneous notion was gradually abandoned by later generations of readers and critics as Tjutčev's works and especially their language came to be scrutinized with greater rigour. In recent years Skabičevskij's evaluation has been completely reversed. As part of this re-evaluation some Soviet literary critics have observed aspects of Tjutčev's language that impart to it qualities inherent in Russian folklore, although no studies exist to support their observation. The first critic to raise the subject was Tjutčev's grand-nephew K. V. Pi-garev:

> It would seem difficult to establish some connec-
> tion between folklore and Tjutčev's works. Nev-
> ertheless, the folklore spirit often bursts forth
> unexpectedly in his poetry, sometimes by a folk-
> song beginning like: "*Ty volna moja
> morskaja.* . . ." reminiscent of the folksong be-
> ginning "*Ty, reka li, moja rečen'ka.* . . ." and
> sometimes by the use of the folklore epithets—

"kamen' samocvetnyj," "zemlja syraja," "serdce retivoe."

A closer reading of Tjutčev's poetry reveals more than a hundred such epithets and other linguistic and stylistic peculiarities typical of Russian folklore. My intention here is to examine Tjutčev's poetic language in order to establish the extent of the poet's utilization of Russian folkloric devices in his works.

In 1827 Tjutčev published his translation of Heine's *"Ein Fichtenbaum steht einsam . . . "* in *The Northern Lyre* (*Severnaja Lira*). Although this poem had already been translated by Lermontov, Majkov, and Fet, it was Tjutčev's version which D. Dubenskij found comparable to the folksong "It's Been Raining Often Since the Evening" ("So večera doždik častexon'ko idet . . . "). Similarly, Tjutčev's **"Spring Calm"** (**"Vesennee uspokoenie"**) translated from Uhland's *Fruhlingsruhe Grüne Erde* becomes *zemlja syraja* (damp earth), a typical folkloric epithet which is followed by another Russian folkloric device, namely, repetition: *skrojte, zarojte menja* (hide me, bury me). Elsewhere, in his translation of Goethe's *Wilhelm Meister*, Tjutčev employs the same practice. He translates the original *Im Grabe sein* with the common Russian folkloric tautological expression, *v grobu, v zemle syroj* (*in the grave, in damp earth*).

Further examination of Tjutčev's lexicon reveals that most folkloric elements are to be found in translations from a foreign language, primarily German. Surely this shows an appreciation of folk culture which contradicts Skabičevskij's assessment. Furthermore, although Tjutčev wrote no original poems imitating folkloric style or language, his poetry nevertheless yields many examples of stylistic devices considered typical of Russian folklore by several leading philologists, such as Ju. M. Sokolov. Among the most frequent folklore devices designated by Sokolov as belonging primarily to the provenance of folklore are folk epithets, vernacular lexicon, lexical and psychological parallelism, typically Russian folk beginning (*začin*), as well as ending, and lexical repetition.

Sokolov considers the basic compositional device of Russian folklore to be psychological parallelism. This parallelism stems from man's animistic conception of the world, with the authors projecting aspects of their own life upon the surrounding nature, a view also shared by Tjutčev. A. N. Veselovskij asserted:

> The parallelism rests upon a juxtaposition of subject and object according to the category of movement, action, as an indication of voluntary self-activity. The inorganic, immovable world was involuntarily drawn into this chain of parallelism: it also lived.

The same conception of nature is expressed in Tjutčev's poetry, as, for example, in his **"Summer Evening"** (**"Letnij večer"**):

Už solnca raskalennyj šar
S glavy svoej zemlja skatila,
I mirnyj večera požar
Volna morskaja poglotila.

Už zvezdy svetlye vzošli,

I tjagotejuščij nad nami
Nebesnyj svod pripodnjali
Svoimi vlažnymi glavami.

Reka vozdušnaja polnej
Tečet mež nebom i zemleju,
Grud' dyšit legče i vol'nej,
Osvoboždennaja ot znoju.

I sladkij trepet, kak struja,
Po žilam probežal prirody,
Kak by gorjačix nog eja
Kosnulis' ključevye vody.

The earth has already rolled off its head the incandescent sphere of the sun, and the sea wave has swallowed the peaceful fire of the evening. The bright stars have already risen and raised with their damp heads the heavenly vault weighing above us. The river of air flows fuller between the earth and sky; the chest breathes freer and easier liberated from heat. And a sweet tremor, like a stream, ran through nature's veins, as if spring waters had touched her burning feet.

Here the intensity of personification increases with the progression of the action of the poem. The earth and the stars are endowed with a "head" (*glava, glavami*) in the first and second stanzas, while in the fourth Nature acquires "veins" and "legs" (*po žilam, nog*)

Instances of personification abound in Tjutčev's poetry. For example, the day "breathes lazily": *Lenivo dyšit polden' mglistyj,* the thunder "plays" like a youth: *grom, Kak by rezvjasja i igraja, / Groxočet v nebe golubom. / Gremjat raskaty molodye,* the sun's rays "doze": *Poludennyj luč zadremal napolu,* the shadows "roam": *Xodili teni po stenam,* the sky "laughs": *Lazur nebesnaja smeetsja,* "tired nature sleeps": *ustalaja priroda spit.*

Such personifications of almost every aspect of nature persist throughout Tjutčev's oeuvre, although they are present to a slightly lesser degree in the later lyrics. Compare, for example, the above examples and **"Summer Eve"** with the use of personification in the following poem from his later period (1852), where the wave is portrayed as a willful (*svoenravnaja*) and playful child, full of life and laughter:

Ty, volna moja morskaja,
Svoenravnaja volna,
Kak, pokojas' il' igraja
Cudnoj žizni ty polna!

Ty na solnce li smeeš'sja,
Otražaja neba svod,
Il' mjateš'sja ty i b'eš'sja
V odičaloj bezdne vod,—
Sladok mne tvoj tixij šepot,
Polnyj laski i ljubvi;
Vnjaten mne i bujnyj ropot,
Stony veščie tvoi . . .

You, my sea wave, a willful wave, how full of enchanting life are you when you are at play or asleep, whether laughing in the sun reflecting the heavenly vault or thrashing and beating in the raging watery abyss. Your quiet whisper, full of love and caress, is sweet to me; I comprehend the wild grumble and your prophetic groans . . .

The wave in this poem is endowed with many human attributes and emotions: it lives, laughs, whispers and sighs. Elsewhere in his poetry trees bathe, nature sleeps, the river Neman stands guard, the spring whispers, the mountains gaze into lakes, the stars drown, the sea celebrates a holiday, the stars converse. According to Sokolov, "From such parallelisms follow many forms of imagery in language and in poetry: metaphors, metonymies, similies, symbols, and so forth." This is the "inorganic, immovable world" that gets drawn into the chain of parallelism and "lives."

This feature of psychological, internal, and other parallelism is characteristic also of all poetry, not just Russian folk poetry, as Sokolov would have it, and not just Russian poetry or Tjutčev's in particular, although in Tjutčev it seems to be especially frequent. Parallelism, moreover, may be concealed, as in metaphors and other figurative expressions, or it can be expressed structurally in the compositional parallelism of syntactic features or those of sound.

Syntactic parallelism is founded primarily on the poet's use of synonyms and word repetitions at the base of which lies the parallelism of sentence components. In Tjutčev's oeuvre it can be illustrated by the following lines from **"The Song of Scandinavian Warriors"** (**"Pesn' skandinavskix voinov"**):

> Rannij petel
> Vstrepenulsja,—
> Družina, vosprjan'!
> Vstavajte, o drugi!
> Bodrej, bodrej
> Na pir mečej,
> Na bran'!

> The early rooster has already risen,—Company, arise! Get up, friends! Livelier, livelier, to the feast of swords, to battle!

In these lines Tjutčev employs parallelism of two components: *Družina vosprjan'* (Company, arise) and *vstavajte, o drugi!* (Get up, friends) along with *Na pir mečej* (To the feast of swords) and *Na bran'!* (to battle).

Elsewhere there are other variations, as for example in **"Iz Gete,"** (**"From Goethe"**):

> Radost' i gore v živom upoen'i,
> Dumy i serdce v večnom volnen'i,
> V nebe likuja, tomjas' na zemli, [sic!]
> Strastno likujuščej,
> Strastno toskujuščej,
> Žizni blaženstvo v odnoj liš' ljubvi . . .

> Happiness and grief are in intoxication of life. Thoughts and heart are in eternal turmoil, rejoicing in heavens, tormented on earth; for a passionately rejoicing and passionately yearning life, bliss exists only in love.

In this poem the parallelism in lines 1, 2, and 6 is due to the syntactic construction of two lines each containing two components, a subject and an adverbial phrase. In line 3 the parallelism is achieved through the use of two antithetic components in each hemistich, each consisting of a gerund and an adverbial phrase of place, but arranged symmetrically to form a chiasmus. Lines 4 and 5 are also syntactically parallel in the morphological identity of the components of the two hemistichs. The syntactic structure of this poem may be represented by the following scheme, where each letter represents the same part of speech:

> abc
> abc
> deed
> fe
> fe
> abc

Compare also his poem **"Sakontalá"**:

> Čto junyj god daet cvetam—
> Ix devstvennyj rumjanec;
> Čto zrelyj god daet plodam—
> Ix carstvennyj bagrjanec;
> Čto nežit vzor i veselit,
> Kak perl, v morjax cvetuščij;
> Čto greet dušu i živit,
> Kak nektar vsemoguščij:
> Ves' cvet sokroviščnic mečty,
> Ves' polnyj cvet tvoren'ja,
> I, slovom, nebo krasoty
> V lučax voobražen'ja,—
> Vse, vse Poèzija slila
> V tebe odnoj—*Sakontalá.*

> What does youth give the flowers—their virginal blush; what does maturity give the fruit—their regal crimson; what gladdens and caresses the eye, like a pearl, blooming in the deep sea; what warms and animates the soul, like a nectar all-powerful: the whole bloom of the storehouse of imagination, the entire bloom of the creation and, in a word, heaven full of beauty in the rays of imagination, everything, everything Poetry has *poured into you alone*—Sakontalá.

Closely related to syntactic parallelism in Russian folklore is the device of repeating individual words, noted in Tjutčev in the poems quoted above, where *strastno, cto, kak, ves',* and *cvet* are repeated identically and *družina: drugi* and *vosprjan': vstavajte* are repeated tautologically. Both types of word repetition are common in Tjutčev's oeuvre. Here is another variant of repetition:

> Net dnja, čtoby duša ne nyla,
> Ne iznyvala o bylom,
> Iskala slov, ne naxodila,
> I soxla, soxla s každym dnem . . .

> Not a day passes that the soul doesn't ache and pain about the past, looking for words, not finding them, and dying, dying day by day.

Such repetition of individual and tautological expressions and words is one of the most prominent features of Russian folklore. Another type of repetition, not restricted to Russian folklore alone, is the use of refrain. In Tjutčev such repetitions occur in the closing line of **"Silentium,"** for example, where the first stanza closes with *Ljubujsja imi—i molči* (Admire them and be silent), the second with *Pitajsja imi—i molči* (Drink of them and be silent), and the third with *Vnimaj ix pen'ju—i molči* (Listen to their singing and be silent). Similarly, **"Nakanune godovščiny 4 av-**

gusta 1864 g." (**"On the Eve of the First Anniversary of August 4, 1864"**) has the following closing lines: stanza one: *Drug moj milyj, vidiš' li menja?* (My dearest, do you see me?) stanza two: *Angel moj, ty vidiš' li menja?* (My angel, do you see me?) and stanza three: *Angel moj, ty vidiš' li menja?* repeated identically as in stanza two.

Also the opening lines may be repeated in different stanzas, as the first lines of the two-stanza poem beginning with *Duša moja—Elizium tenej,* (My soul—Elysium of shadows). The opening lines may be repeated with a variation as well, just like the closing lines, illustrated by the following poem, where stanza one begins with *Vostok belel. Lad'ja katilas'* . . . (The east was whitening, the boat was gliding) stanza two with *Vostok alel. Ona molilas'* . . . (The east was reddening, she was praying) and stanza three with *Vostok vspylal . . . Ona sklonilas'* (The east flared up, she bowed down). In this poem the same action is developed progressively and is expressed by different verbs, similar to the variation the lines closing with *Drug* and *Angel.* This type of repetition of the opening lines, known in Russian as *začin,* is one of the most typical features of Russian folksongs.

Repetition of opening or closing lines is not restricted to primary parts of speech alone either in Tjutčev or in Russian folklore. Adjacent lines may begin with a preposition or a conjunction. Štokmar terms this variety of repetition *anaphora.*

Both in Russian folklore and in Tjutčev's poetry, anaphora often manifests itself by frequently involving negative particles, interrogative particles, prepositions, interjections and other parts of speech. For example:

> Ne to, čto mnite vy priroda:
> Ne slepok, ne bezdušnyj lik—
> V nej est' duša, v nej est' svoboda,
> V nej est' ljubov', v nej est' jazyk . . .

> Nature is not what you suppose; it is not a mold or a lifeless form. It has a soul, it has free will, it possesses speech and it has love.

Repetition may also involve either identical or synonymous words, as in:

> Tak svjazan, s'edinen ot veka
> Sojuzom krovnogo rodstva . . .

> Thus bound, united from age immemorial by a union of blood relationship . . .

or:

> O, ne kladite menja,
> V zemlju syruju—
> Skrojte, zarojte menja
> V travu gustuju . . .

> Oh, do not put me into damp earth—hide me, bury me in thick grass . . .

or:

> Ax, razve liš v grobu
> Ot nix ukryt'sja mne—
> V grobu, v zemle syroj . . .

> Is it in the grave that I should hide—in the grave, in damp earth . . .

In the last examples words are repeated in the succeeding line. This typical Russian folklore device, called *podxvatyvanie* is widely practiced by Tjutčev, sometimes repeated in several succeeding lines, as in "In my martyred stagnation . . . " (*"Est' i v moem stradal'českom zastoe"*):

> O Gospodi, daj žgucego stradan'ja
> I mertvennost' duši moej rassej:
> Ty vzjal ee, no muku vspominan'ja,
> Živuju muku mne ostav' po nej—

> Po nej, po nej, svoj podvig soveršivšej
> Ves' do konca v otčajannoj bor'be,
> Tak plamenno, tak gorjačo ljubivšej
> Naperekor i ljudjam i sud'be,—

> Po nej, po nej, sud'by ne odolevšej,
> No i sebja ne davšej pobedit',
> Po nej, po nej, tak do konca umevšej
> Stradat', molit'sja, verit' i ljubit'.

> O Lord, grant me burning agony and dissolve the numbness of my soul: You took her, but the torture of her memory, the living torture of her, leave me. Of her, of her, who accomplished her feat to the end in a desperate struggle, who loved so ardently, so dearly, in spite all people and fate; of her, of her, who could not vanquish her fate, but did not let herself be conquered; of her, of her, who knew till the end how to suffer, pray, believe and love.

In addition to the devices mentioned above, Tjutčev's poetry contains many proclitics and enclitics also typical of Russian folklore, such as those found in his **"To Ju. F. Abaza"** (**"Ju. F. Abaze"**):

> Po vsemoguščemu prizyvu
> Svet otdeljaetsja ot t'my,
> I my ne zvuki—dušu živu,
> V nix vašu dušu slyšim my.

> On almighty command the light separates from darkness and we hear not sounds—a living soul, your soul we hear.

Both Štokmar and Sokolov find the loss of stress in constant epithets very common in Russian folklore. According to Sokolov, the shift of stress occurs because of the mutual attraction of the consonants involved, such as liquids r or l as in Tjutčev's *zemlja syraja* above, or spirants *š* and *ž* in *dušu živu* in the example above.

Tjutčev's work, primarily his lyric poetry, also contains constant epithets such as *more glubokoe* (deep sea), *lokot' belyj* (white elbow), *noč' temnaja* (dark night) and others. The following poem illustrates most of the mentioned devices:

> Slezy ljudskie, o slezy ljudskie,
> L'etes' vy rannej i pozdnej poroj . . .
> L'etes' bezvestnye, l'etes' nezrimye,
> Neistoščimye, neisčislimye,—
> L'etes', kak l'jutsja strui doždevye
> V osen' gluxuju, poroju nočnoj.

> Tears of people, tears of people, you fall in the

morning and in the evening . . . You fall late at night, You pour unknown, you pour unseen, limitless and countless, you flow like torrents of rain in deep autumn at night.

In it we find the folklore simile *slezy—kak strui doždevye* (tears—like torrents of rain), the constant epithet *osen' gluxaja,* a typical folkloric inversion of the word order between the noun and its attribute, *poroju nočnoj,* as well as repetitions, dactylic lines, prominent caesura, and alliteration of "o," "ju," and "u." Alliteration is ubiquitous in Tjutčev's poetry, as was also observed by N. K. Gudzij, who found Tjutčev's poetry to be especially rich in alliterations and assonances.

Tjutčev's use of proverbs and proverbial phrases may also suggest some folklore influence. Proverbs appeared in Russian literature only after the second half of the last century. Before Puškin they were almost unknown in literature because of the traditional adherence to the accepted style, with the exception of their use by Krylov in his *Fables* (*Basni*). Puškin's admixture of vernacular to the literary language erased the boundaries of style and "genre."

As a form, proverbs are a part of folklore and originate among the " . . . less cultured classes of society." Vladimir Dal', the Russian lexicographer and collector of Russian folklore, formulates the reason for their absence from the literary language in the following way:

> No one can deny that one must go among the common people (*narod*) for proverbs and sayings. In the educated and enlightened society there are no proverbs; one comes across their weak and crippled echo, translated and debased by unnatural Russian to suit our mannerisms, or bad translations from a foreign language. High society does not accept ready-made proverbs because they portray a way of life foreign to it, and the language is not the same. . . .

According to Dal', or Thrall and Hibbard, proverbs must be assigned to at least non-literary, if not sub-literary forms. For this reason the presence of proverbial expressions in a literary work suggests in many cases a folklore tendency, i.e., a conscious attempt by the author to use the vernacular, to go beyond the limits of literary language as defined by the normative grammars:

> The ban imposed upon the current forms of speech varies. Some forms are permitted in a leisurely conversation, although they are rejected by school grammars; some are forbidden and are considered a sign of illiterate, uncultured and uneducated speech.

Ever since Puškin, poets and prose writers alike have frequently combined the cultured speech of the educated with the Russian vernacular, avoiding neither colloquialisms nor bookish expressions. In some works the vernacular element became the very essence of the creation, as in Krylov's *Fables.* Other works became the source of new vernacular expressions, even proverbs, as Griboedov's *Woe from Wit* or Puškin's *Eugene Onegin* or Krylov's *Fables.* In some cases, this folklorism became a literary affectation that plagued the nineteenth century. Therefore it is not surprising to find folklore elements, such as proverbs,

constant epithets or other linguistic, structural and stylistic devices in Tjutčev's poetry.

Since Tjutčev had to fit proverbs into the confines of a literary work, namely a poem, they seldom remained exact replicas of the proverbs registered in Dal's collection, *Russian Folk Proverbs* (*Poslovicy russkogo naroda*). This is not unusual, for the proverbs are " . . . a turn of phrase which the user changes according to his goals." Among the proverbs registered by Dal', we find the following in Tjutčev: *Delo v šljape* (It's in the hat); *sel kak rak na meli* (moored like a crawfish on the shallows); *Ne po xorošu mil, a po milu xoroš* (dear not because of beauty, but beautiful because he's dear); *Zloj konec načalu zlomu* (Evil beginning begets an evil end); *Zloe zloj konec priemlet* (Evil begets an evil end); *Vzjat' s boju* (win in a battle); *Legkoveren ženskij nrav,/I izmenčiv i poročen* (women's nature is gullible, fickle and wanton).

In addition to actual proverbs, there are numerous expressions which might be called proverbial expressions and stock phrases which were not located in Dal'. Some of these simply escaped Dal's registration, while others may be of purely literary origin, possibly not even Russian. Still others may have been coined by Tjutčev himself, such as: *bespomoščnoe ditja* (helpless child); *vražda slepaja* (blind animosity); *dux golubinyj* (spirit of a dove, i.e., meek like a dove); *zdravyj smysl* (common sense); *zmeinaja mudrost'* (wisdom of a serpent); *legkovernoe ditja* (gullible child); *ljubovnik strastnyj* (passionate lover); *ljubov' sobač'ja* (dog's fidelity); *nevernyj blesk, pustoj* (deceiving, empty glitter); *nerazumnoe ditja* (foolish child); *nicem ne nasytimyj vremenščik* (avaricious money lender, i.e., greedy loan shark); *oslepitel'naja krasa* (blinding beauty); *ot/do grobovoj doski* (till death, i.e., till the coffin); *sirota bezdomnyj* (homeless orphan); *junost' veselaja* (gay or carefree youth), and certainly many others.

There are also proverbs where the motif, rather than the actual expression itself, forms the basis for a poem. Thus the proverb *Mnogo šumu, malo tolku* (much noise but little sense, i.e., much ado about nothing) is developed by Tjutčev in **"In the Village" ("V derevne').** This poem depicts a tranquil rural scene disturbed by a vicious dog who has just broken loose from his chain (another proverb not registered by Dal': *Kak s cepi sorvalsja* [as if released from a chain]) and is pursuing a noisy flock of geese and ducks for "a higher purpose." In this poem we find four colloquial forms: *gvalt, gam, sorvanec, and razmykat'* (uproar, racket, brat, and shake up). But even in this poem of five stanzas, the first two, depicting the rural scene, contain three of the four colloquial forms used. In the second half of the poem, which interprets the occurrences, the vocabulary is of the classical middle and high-style type, with *genij, prednaznačen'e, vysšyj dolg,* and only one colloquial form, *sorvanec.*

A similar development of a proverbial motif can be found in the poet's translation of Heine's poem "With Which of the Two Shall I Fall in Love?" ("*In welche soll'ich mich verlieben . . .* "). Here the dilemma of a choice between two equally desirable objects has made its way into popular phraseology in the expression *lakomyj kusoček* (a tasty morsel), used in this way by Gogol' in Dead Souls (*Mert-*

vye duši), and rendered by Tjutčev as *Kotoryj lakomej iz dvux?* Another example of the development of a proverbial motif is found in **"Kogda drjaxlejuščie sily" ("When Our Deteriorating Strength")**, in which the poet develops the proverb *Ot staryx durakov molodym žyt'ja net* (Because of the old fools the youth has no life), registered in Dal's collection.

Almost all the proverbial expressions in Tjutčev's works can also be found in Puškin. Their use by the two poets seems to indicate the existence of two groups of Russian vocabulary: one common to both the educated society and the peasants, and the other—a vast storehouse of expressions pertaining specifically to the everyday life of the Russian peasant and not used in the language of the educated society. This deduction is corroborated by Gor'kij:

> The division of the language into literary and popular means only one thing: that we have, so to say, "the raw" language and the language polished by the masters. Puškin was the first to fully understand this and to show how one can use the linguistic material of the people . . .

Proverbs and proverbial expressions seem to be restricted to Tjutčev's lyric poetry almost entirely. They also tend to occur in the middle and last periods of his life (1840-73). There seems to be a connection here with Tjutčev's Slavophile affiliation during his later period, when he wrote epigrams in great numbers. Apparently the concise statement of the proverb was best suited to the terse form of the epigram, though not entirely restricted to it.

Another group of words absent from nineteenth century literature remains outside the so-called literary language even today. These words belong to the colloquial language (*Razgovornyj jazyk*) of informal conversation and letters, and are considered unsuited to formal speech or writing. Some of these words were admissible in the direct speech of literary characters or, occasionally, in the author's speech of nineteenth century works.

There are altogether thirty-eight words from this category in Tjutčev's poetry: *gam, gvalt, drjazgi, grubijan, lad, ljul'ka, ognevica, prok, sorvanec, tolk, čered, gorazd, goremyčnyj, ljutyj, xilyj, šal'noj, bajati, golosit', izdyxat', kinut'sja, merzit', nudit', oduret', posobit', razmykat', umajat', čujat', avos', vpot'max, dale, dole, dol', živo, kol', nynče, otkol', otsel', pušče* (possibly others). Such forms were used in literature only for characterization through speech. Tjutčev's use of this type of vocabulary is restricted to the words above, because poems with dialogue are rare. Of the poems containing dialogue, most are translations, and in these Tjutčev relies heavily on traditional language due to limitations inherent in translation. Such is the case in "Hector and Andromache" (*"Gektor i Andromaxa"*) from Schiller, as well as Goethe's "The Singer" (*"Pevec"*) or "From Goethe's 'Faust'" (*"Iz 'Fausta' Gete"*), all rendered in the traditional high style language. Such is also the case in the one poem that is almost entirely in dialogue form, **"The Storm Rages Ever More Violently" ("Vse bešennej burja")**, where only three instances are found.

From the evidence presented in the preceding pages one is forced to conclude that in spite of the trend among some Russian poets of his day, especially his friends and acquaintances in the Slavophile movement, Tjutčev does not follow the fashion of the day of imitating folklore. He does, however, use compositional devices peculiar to folklore, such as personification of nature, syntactical parallelism, word repetition, constant epithets, proverbs and colloquial forms. Neither does he imitate folklore language. In the instances where constant epithets or colloquial forms are found, they remain inconspicuous, unexaggerated and integrated with the rest of the language of the poem. (pp. 112-26)

> *Borys Bilokur, "Folkloric Devices in Tjutčev's Poetry," in* The Supernatural in Slavic and Baltic Literature: Essays in Honor of Victor Terras, *edited by Amy Mandelker and Roberta Reeder, Slavica Publishers, Inc., 1988, pp. 112-28.*

FURTHER READING

Bilokur, Borys. "On Tjutcev's Archaisms." *Slavic and East European Journal* 18, No. 4 (Winter 1974): 373-76.
  Qualifies twentieth-century Russian critic Jurij Tynjanov's contention that Tyutchev was an archaic poet, demonstrating that archaic stylistic features appear primarily in his juvenilia, his early lyrics, and his translations. Bilokur also asserts that the later poetry's less common archaisms are frequently ironic, conforming to a more general Russian literary trend, and concludes that poets often utilize language which has passed from the vernacular.

Byrns, Richard. "Temporal and Spatial Enclosures in the Poetry of Tjutcev." *Slavic and East European Journal* 21, No. 2 (Summer 1977): 180-90.
  Examines Tyutchev's propensity for creating safe enclosures in his poetry to control the frightening immensities of time and space.

Chopyk, D. B. "Schelling's Influence in F. I. Tyutchev's Poetry." *Russian Language Journal* XXVII, No. 96 (Winter 1973): 17-23.
  Demonstrates Schelling's influence on Tyutchev by examining several poems in which Tyutchev incorporated the German Romantic philosopher's concepts.

Gustafson, Richard F. "Tjutcev's Imagery and What It Tells Us." *Slavic and East European Journal* IV, No. XVIII (1960): 1-16.
  Examines dialectical images in Tyutchev's nature lyrics, asserting that such imagery expresses his idea of the ongoing conflict between the rational and the irrational and his conviction that this conflict operates in humanity as it does in nature. Gustafson concludes that this metaphysical dichotomy is superficial because irrational chaos invariably prevails over rational order in Tyutchev's poetry.

Lane, R. C. "Tyutchev's Place in the History of Russian Literature." *The Modern Language Review* 71, No. 2 (April 1976): 344-56.

> Assesses critical viewpoints on the movement with which Tyutchev is best identified and on the period during which he produced his strongest work, maintaining that his best poems are the early, Romantic lyrics.

————. "Pascalian and Christian-Existential Elements in Tyutchev's Letters and Poems." *Forum for Modern Language Studies* XVIII, No. 4 (October 1982): 317-34.

> Asserts that Tyutchev's letters and poetry demonstrate that he was influenced by Pascal's anxiety over ephemeral man's impotent smallness in the face of infinite time, immense space, and uncertain life. Tyutchev, however, could not assuage his existential fears as Pascal did, by completely submitting to God, and attempted to reinforce his own, less soothing faith by idealizing his past and by embracing Panslavism's fusion of Russian nationalism and Russian Orthodox devotion.

Weeks, Andrew. "Tiutchev, Schelling, and The Question of Influence." *Germano-Slavica* 111, No. 5 (spring 1981): 307-17.

> Reviews assessments of Schelling's influence on Tyutchev and, after summarizing Schelling's doctrine and examining Tyutchev's nature lyrics, offers his own: Schelling's *Naturphilosophie,* which proposed that nature possesses a living spirit whose interactive opposing qualities are akin to those contending within humanity, provided Tyutchev "with a flexible semantic system for expressing his own recurrent, intensely personal and deeply unsettling experience."

Nineteenth-Century Literature Criticism

Cumulative Indexes
Volumes 1-34

This Index Includes References to Entries in These Gale Series

Children's Literature Review includes excerpts from reviews, criticism, and commentary on works of authors and illustrators who create books for children.

Classical and Medieval Literature Criticism offers excerpts of criticism on the works of world authors from classical antiquity through the fourteenth century.

Contemporary Authors Series encompasses five related series. *Contemporary Authors* provides biographical and bibliographical information on more than 97,000 writers of fiction and nonfiction. *Contemporary Authors New Revision Series* provides completely updated information on authors covered in *CA*. *Contemporary Authors Permanent Series* consists of listings for deceased and inactive authors. *Contemporary Authors Autobiography Series* presents specially commissioned autobiographies by leading contemporary writers. *Contemporary Authors Bibliographical Series* contains primary and secondary bibliographies as well as analytical bibliographical essays by authorities on major modern authors.

Contemporary Literary Criticism presents excerpts of criticism on the works of novelists, poets, dramatists, short story writers, scriptwriters, and other creative writers who are now living or who have died since 1960.

Dictionary of Literary Biography encompasses four related series. *Dictionary of Literary Biography* furnishes illustrated overviews of authors' lives and works. *Dictionary of Literary Biography Documentary Series* illuminates the careers of major figures through a selection of literary documents, including letters, interviews, and photographs. *Dictionary of Literary Biography Yearbook* summarizes the past year's literary activity and includes updated entries on individual authors. *Concise Dictionary of American Literary Biography* a six-volume series, collects revised and updated sketches on major American authors that were originally presented in *Dictionary of Literary Biography*.

Drama Criticism provides excerpts of criticism on the works of playwrights of all nationalities and periods of literary history.

Literature Criticism from 1400 to 1800 compiles significant passages from the most noteworthy criticism on authors of the fifteenth through eighteenth centuries.

Nineteenth-Century Literature Criticism offers significant passages from criticism on authors who died between 1800 and 1899.

Poetry Criticism presents excerpts of criticism on the works of poets from all eras, movements, and nationalities.

Short Story Criticism compiles excerpts of criticism on short fiction written by authors of all eras and nationalities.

Something about the Author Series encompasses three related series. *Something about the Author* contains well-illustrated biographical sketches on juvenile and young adult authors and illustrators from all eras. *Something about the Author Autobiography Series* presents specially commissioned autobiographies by prominent authors and illustrators of books for children and young adults. *Authors & Artists for Young Adults* provides high school and junior high school students with profiles of their favorite creative artists.

Twentieth-Century Literary Criticism contains critical excerpts by the most significant commentators on poets, novelists, short story writers, dramatists, and philosophers who died between 1900 and 1960.

Yesterday's Authors of Books for Children contains heavily illustrated entries on children's writers who died before 1961. Complete in two volumes.

Literary Criticism Series
Cumulative Author Index

Author Index

This index lists all author entries in the Gale Literary Criticism Series and includes cross-references to other Gale sources. References in the index are identified as follows:

AAYA: *Authors & Artists for Young Adults,* Volumes 1-7
CA: *Contemporary Authors* (original series), Volumes 1-135
CAAS: *Contemporary Authors Autobiography Series,* Volumes 1-14
CABS: *Contemporary Authors Bibliographical Series,* Volumes 1-3
CANR: *Contemporary Authors New Revision Series,* Volumes 1-35
CAP: *Contemporary Authors Permanent Series,* Volumes 1-2
CA-R: *Contemporary Authors* (first revision), Volumes 1-44
CDALB: *Concise Dictionary of American Literary Biography,* Volumes 1-6
CLC: *Contemporary Literary Criticism,* Volumes 1-68
CLR: *Children's Literature Review,* Volumes 1-25
CMLC: *Classical and Medieval Literature Criticism,* Volumes 1-8
DC: *Drama Criticism,* Volume 1
DLB: *Dictionary of Literary Biography,* Volumes 1-112
DLB-DS: *Dictionary of Literary Biography Documentary Series,* Volumes 1-9
DLB-Y: *Dictionary of Literary Biography Yearbook,* Volumes 1980-1990
LC: *Literature Criticism from 1400 to 1800,* Volumes 1-18
NCLC: *Nineteenth-Century Literature Criticism,* Volumes 1-34
PC: *Poetry Criticism,* Volumes 1-3
SAAS: *Something about the Author Autobiography Series,* Volumes 1-13
SATA: *Something about the Author,* Volumes 1-66
SSC: *Short Story Criticism,* Volumes 1-8
TCLC: *Twentieth-Century Literary Criticism,* Volumes 1-43
YABC: *Yesterday's Authors of Books for Children,* Volumes 1-2

A. E. 1867-1935 . . . . TCLC **3, 10**
See also Russell, George William
See also DLB 19

Abbey, Edward 1927-1989 . . . . . . CLC **36, 59**
See also CANR 2; CA 45-48;
obituary CA 128

Abbott, Lee K., Jr. 19??- . . . . CLC **48**

Abe, Kobo 1924- . . . . CLC **8, 22, 53**
See also CANR 24; CA 65-68

Abell, Kjeld 1901-1961 . . . . CLC **15**
See also obituary CA 111

Abish, Walter 1931- . . . . CLC **22**
See also CA 101

Abrahams, Peter (Henry) 1919- . . . . . CLC **4**
See also CA 57-60

Abrams, M(eyer) H(oward) 1912-. . . CLC **24**
See also CANR 13; CA 57-60; DLB 67

Abse, Dannie 1923-. . . . . CLC **7, 29**
See also CAAS 1; CANR 4; CA 53-56;
DLB 27

Achebe, (Albert) Chinua(lumogu)
1930- . . . . CLC **1, 3, 5, 7, 11, 26, 51**
See also BLC 1; CLR 20; CANR 6, 26;
CA 1-4R; SATA 38, 40

Acker, Kathy 1948- . . . . CLC **45**
See also CA 117, 122

Ackroyd, Peter 1949-. . . . . CLC **34, 52**
See also CA 123, 127

Acorn, Milton 1923-. . . . . CLC **15**
See also CA 103; DLB 53

Adamov, Arthur 1908-1970 . . . . . CLC **4, 25**
See also CAP 2; CA 17-18;
obituary CA 25-28R

Adams, Alice (Boyd) 1926- . . . CLC **6, 13, 46**
See also CANR 26; CA 81-84; DLB-Y 86

Adams, Douglas (Noel) 1952- . . . CLC **27, 60**
See also CA 106; DLB-Y 83

Adams, Francis 1862-1893 . . . . . . NCLC **33**

Adams, Henry (Brooks)
1838-1918 . . . . TCLC **4**
See also CA 104; DLB 12, 47

Adams, Richard (George)
1920- . . . . CLC **4, 5, 18**
See also CLR 20; CANR 3; CA 49-52;
SATA 7

Adamson, Joy(-Friederike Victoria)
1910-1980 . . . . CLC **17**
See also CANR 22; CA 69-72;
obituary CA 93-96; SATA 11;
obituary SATA 22

Adcock, (Kareen) Fleur 1934-. . . . . CLC **41**
See also CANR 11; CA 25-28R; DLB 40

Addams, Charles (Samuel)
1912-1988 . . . . CLC **30**
See also CANR 12; CA 61-64;
obituary CA 126

Addison, Joseph 1672-1719 . . . . LC **18**
See also DLB 101

Adler, C(arole) S(chwerdtfeger)
1932- . . . . CLC **35**
See also CANR 19; CA 89-92; SATA 26

Adler, Renata 1938-. . . . . CLC **8, 31**
See also CANR 5, 22; CA 49-52

Ady, Endre 1877-1919 . . . . TCLC **11**
See also CA 107

Afton, Effie 1825-1911
See Harper, Francis Ellen Watkins

Agee, James 1909-1955 . . . . TCLC **1, 19**
See also CA 108; DLB 2, 26;
CDALB 1941-1968

Agnon, S(hmuel) Y(osef Halevi)
1888-1970 . . . . CLC **4, 8, 14**
See also CAP 2; CA 17-18;
obituary CA 25-28R

Ai 1947-. . . . . CLC **4, 14**
See also CA 85-88

Author Index

Author Index

Cade, Toni   1939-
See Bambara, Toni Cade

CAEdmon   fl. 658-680 . . . . **CMLC 7**

Cage, John (Milton, Jr.)   1912- . . . . . **CLC 41**
See also CANR 9; CA 13-16R

Cain, G.   1929-
See Cabrera Infante, G(uillermo)

Cain, James M(allahan)
1892-1977 . . . . **CLC 3, 11, 28**
See also CANR 8; CA 17-20R;
obituary CA 73-76

Caldwell, Erskine (Preston)
1903-1987 . . . . **CLC 1, 8, 14, 50, 60**
See also CAAS 1; CANR 2; CA 1-4R;
obituary CA 121; DLB 9, 86

Caldwell, (Janet Miriam) Taylor (Holland)
1900-1985 . . . . **CLC 2, 28, 39**
See also CANR 5; CA 5-8R;
obituary CA 116

Calhoun, John Caldwell
1782-1850 . . . . **NCLC 15**
See also DLB 3

Calisher, Hortense   1911- . . . . **CLC 2, 4, 8, 38**
See also CANR 1, 22; CA 1-4R; DLB 2

Callaghan, Morley (Edward)
1903-1990 . . . . **CLC 3, 14, 41, 65**
See also CANR 33; CA 9-12R;
obituary CA 132; DLB 68

Calvino, Italo
1923-1985 . . . . **CLC 5, 8, 11, 22, 33, 39;**
SSC 3
See also CANR 23; CA 85-88;
obituary CA 116

Cameron, Carey   1952- . . . . **CLC 59**

Cameron, Peter   1959- . . . . **CLC 44**
See also CA 125

Campana, Dino   1885-1932 . . . . **TCLC 20**
See also CA 117

Campbell, John W(ood), Jr.
1910-1971 . . . . **CLC 32**
See also CAP 2; CA 21-22;
obituary CA 29-32R; DLB 8

Campbell, (John) Ramsey   1946- . . . . **CLC 42**
See also CANR 7; CA 57-60

Campbell, (Ignatius) Roy (Dunnachie)
1901-1957 . . . . **TCLC 5**
See also CA 104; DLB 20

Campbell, Thomas   1777-1844 . . . . **NCLC 19**

Campbell, (William) Wilfred
1861-1918 . . . . **TCLC 9**
See also CA 106

Camus, Albert
1913-1960 . . . **CLC 1, 2, 4, 9, 11, 14, 32,**
63
See also CA 89-92; DLB 72

Canby, Vincent   1924- . . . . **CLC 13**
See also CA 81-84

Canetti, Elias   1905- . . . . **CLC 3, 14, 25**
See also CANR 23; CA 21-24R; DLB 85

Canin, Ethan   1960- . . . . **CLC 55**

Cape, Judith   1916-
See Page, P(atricia) K(athleen)

Capek, Karel
1890-1938 . . . . **TCLC 6, 37; DC 1**
See also CA 104

Capote, Truman
1924-1984 . . . . . **CLC 1, 3, 8, 13, 19, 34,**
38, 58; SSC 2
See also CANR 18; CA 5-8R;
obituary CA 113; DLB 2; DLB-Y 80, 84;
CDALB 1941-1968

Capra, Frank   1897- . . . . **CLC 16**
See also CA 61-64

Caputo, Philip   1941- . . . . **CLC 32**
See also CA 73-76

Card, Orson Scott   1951- . . . . **CLC 44, 47, 50**
See also CA 102

Cardenal, Ernesto   1925- . . . . **CLC 31**
See also CANR 2; CA 49-52

Carducci, Giosue   1835-1907 . . . . . . **TCLC 32**

Carew, Thomas   1595?-1640 . . . . **LC 13**

Carey, Ernestine Gilbreth   1908- . . . . **CLC 17**
See also CA 5-8R; SATA 2

Carey, Peter   1943- . . . . **CLC 40, 55**
See also CA 123, 127

Carleton, William   1794-1869 . . . . . . **NCLC 3**

Carlisle, Henry (Coffin)   1926- . . . . . . **CLC 33**
See also CANR 15; CA 13-16R

Carlson, Ron(ald F.)   1947- . . . . **CLC 54**
See also CA 105

Carlyle, Thomas   1795-1881 . . . . . . **NCLC 22**
See also DLB 55

Carman, (William) Bliss
1861-1929 . . . . **TCLC 7**
See also CA 104

Carpenter, Don(ald Richard)
1931- . . . . **CLC 41**
See also CANR 1; CA 45-48

Carpentier (y Valmont), Alejo
1904-1980 . . . . **CLC 8, 11, 38**
See also CANR 11; CA 65-68;
obituary CA 97-100

Carr, Emily   1871-1945 . . . . **TCLC 32**
See also DLB 68

Carr, John Dickson   1906-1977 . . . . . . **CLC 3**
See also CANR 3; CA 49-52;
obituary CA 69-72

Carr, Virginia Spencer   1929- . . . . **CLC 34**
See also CA 61-64

Carrier, Roch   1937- . . . . **CLC 13**
See also DLB 53

Carroll, James (P.)   1943- . . . . **CLC 38**
See also CA 81-84

Carroll, Jim   1951- . . . . **CLC 35**
See also CA 45-48

Carroll, Lewis   1832-1898 . . . . **NCLC 2**
See also Dodgson, Charles Lutwidge
See also CLR 2; DLB 18

Carroll, Paul Vincent   1900-1968 . . . . **CLC 10**
See also CA 9-12R; obituary CA 25-28R;
DLB 10

Carruth, Hayden   1921- . . . . **CLC 4, 7, 10, 18**
See also CANR 4; CA 9-12R; SATA 47;
DLB 5

Carter, Angela (Olive)   1940- . . . . . **CLC 5, 41**
See also CANR 12; CA 53-56; DLB 14

Carver, Raymond
1938-1988 . . . **CLC 22, 36, 53, 55; SSC 8**
See also CANR 17; CA 33-36R;
obituary CA 126; DLB-Y 84, 88

Cary, (Arthur) Joyce (Lunel)
1888-1957 . . . . **TCLC 1, 29**
See also CA 104; DLB 15

Casanova de Seingalt, Giovanni Jacopo
1725-1798 . . . . **LC 13**

Casares, Adolfo Bioy   1914-
See Bioy Casares, Adolfo

Casely-Hayford, J(oseph) E(phraim)
1866-1930 . . . . **TCLC 24**
See also BLC 1; CA 123

Casey, John   1880-1964
See O'Casey, Sean

Casey, John   1939- . . . . **CLC 59**
See also CANR 23; CA 69-72

Casey, Michael   1947- . . . . **CLC 2**
See also CA 65-68; DLB 5

Casey, Patrick   1902-1934
See Thurman, Wallace

Casey, Warren   1935- . . . . **CLC 12**
See also Jacobs, Jim and Casey, Warren
See also CA 101

Casona, Alejandro   1903-1965 . . . . . . **CLC 49**
See also Alvarez, Alejandro Rodriguez

Cassavetes, John   1929-1991 . . . . **CLC 20**
See also CA 85-88, 127

Cassill, R(onald) V(erlin)   1919- . . . **CLC 4, 23**
See also CAAS 1; CANR 7; CA 9-12R;
DLB 6

Cassity, (Allen) Turner   1929- . . . . **CLC 6, 42**
See also CANR 11; CA 17-20R

Castaneda, Carlos   1935?- . . . . **CLC 12**
See also CA 25-28R

Castedo, Elena   1937- . . . . **CLC 65**
See also CA 132

Castellanos, Rosario   1925-1974 . . . . . **CLC 66**
See also CA 131; obituary CA 53-56

Castelvetro, Lodovico   1505-1571 . . . . . **LC 12**

Castiglione, Baldassare   1478-1529 . . . **LC 12**

Castro, Rosalia de   1837-1885 . . . . . **NCLC 3**

Cather, Willa (Sibert)
1873-1947 . . . . . . **TCLC 1, 11, 31; SSC 2**
See also CA 104; SATA 30; DLB 9, 54;
DLB-DS 1; CDALB 1865-1917

Catton, (Charles) Bruce
1899-1978 . . . . **CLC 35**
See also CANR 7; CA 5-8R;
obituary CA 81-84; SATA 2;
obituary SATA 24; DLB 17

Cauldwell, Frank   1923-
See King, Francis (Henry)

Caunitz, William   1935- . . . . **CLC 34**

Causley, Charles (Stanley)   1917- . . . . . **CLC 7**
See also CANR 5; CA 9-12R; SATA 3;
DLB 27

Caute, (John) David   1936- . . . . **CLC 29**
See also CAAS 4; CANR 1; CA 1-4R;
DLB 14

Cavafy, C(onstantine) P(eter)
1863-1933 . . . . **TCLC 2, 7**
See also CA 104

Cavanna, Betty   1909-.............. CLC 12
See also CANR 6; CA 9-12R; SATA 1, 30

Caxton, William   1421?-1491? .... LC 17

Cayrol, Jean   1911-.............. CLC 11
See also CA 89-92; DLB 83

Cela, Camilo Jose   1916-...... CLC 4, 13, 59
See also CAAS 10; CANR 21; CA 21-24R

Celan, Paul   1920-1970 ...... CLC 10, 19, 53
See also Antschel, Paul
See also DLB 69

Celine, Louis-Ferdinand
1894-1961 ..... CLC 1, 3, 4, 7, 9, 15, 47
See also Destouches,
Louis-Ferdinand-Auguste
See also DLB 72

Cellini, Benvenuto   1500-1571 .... LC 7

Cendrars, Blaise   1887-1961........ CLC 18
See also Sauser-Hall, Frederic

Cernuda, Luis (y Bidon)
1902-1963 .... CLC 54
See also CA 89-92

Cervantes (Saavedra), Miguel de
1547-1616 .... LC 6

Cesaire, Aime (Fernand)   1913-.. CLC 19, 32
See also BLC 1; CANR 24; CA 65-68

Chabon, Michael   1965?-........... CLC 55

Chabrol, Claude   1930-............ CLC 16
See also CA 110

Challans, Mary   1905-1983
See Renault, Mary
See also CA 81-84; obituary CA 111;
SATA 23; obituary SATA 36

Chambers, Aidan   1934- .... CLC 35
See also CANR 12; CA 25-28R; SATA 1

Chambers, James   1948-
See Cliff, Jimmy

Chambers, Robert W.   1865-1933... TCLC 41

Chandler, Raymond   1888-1959 ... TCLC 1, 7
See also CA 104

Channing, William Ellery
1780-1842 .... NCLC 17
See also DLB 1, 59

Chaplin, Charles (Spencer)
1889-1977 .... CLC 16
See also CA 81-84; obituary CA 73-76;
DLB 44

Chapman, Graham   1941?- .... CLC 21
See also Monty Python
See also CA 116; obituary CA 169

Chapman, John Jay   1862-1933 ..... TCLC 7
See also CA 104

Chappell, Fred   1936- .... CLC 40
See also CAAS 4; CANR 8; CA 5-8R;
DLB 6

Char, Rene (Emile)
1907-1988 .... CLC 9, 11, 14, 55
See also CA 13-16R; obituary CA 124

Charles I   1600-1649 .... LC 13

Chartier, Emile-Auguste   1868-1951
See Alain

Charyn, Jerome   1937-........ CLC 5, 8, 18
See also CAAS 1; CANR 7; CA 5-8R;
DLB-Y 83

Chase, Mary (Coyle)   1907-1981 ...... DC 1
See also CA 77-80, 105; SATA 17, 29

Chase, Mary Ellen   1887-1973....... CLC 2
See also CAP 1; CA 15-16;
obituary CA 41-44R; SATA 10

Chateaubriand, Francois Rene de
1768-1848 .... NCLC 3

Chatier, Emile-Auguste   1868-1951
See Alain

Chatterji, Bankim Chandra
1838-1894 .... NCLC 19

Chatterji, Saratchandra
1876-1938 .... TCLC 13
See also CA 109

Chatterton, Thomas   1752-1770 .... LC 3

Chatwin, (Charles) Bruce
1940-1989 .... CLC 28, 57, 59
See also CA 85-88,; obituary CA 127

Chaucer, Geoffrey   c. 1340-1400 ..... LC 17

Chayefsky, Paddy   1923-1981....... CLC 23
See also CA 9-12R; obituary CA 104;
DLB 7, 44; DLB-Y 81

Chayefsky, Sidney   1923-1981
See Chayefsky, Paddy
See also CANR 18

Chedid, Andree   1920-............ CLC 47

Cheever, John
1912-1982 ..... CLC 3, 7, 8, 11, 15, 25,
64; SSC 1
See also CANR 5, 27; CA 5-8R;
obituary CA 106; CABS 1; DLB 2;
DLB-Y 80, 82; CDALB 1941-1968

Cheever, Susan   1943-.......... CLC 18, 48
See also CA 103; DLB-Y 82

Chekhov, Anton (Pavlovich)
1860-1904 ...... TCLC 3, 10, 31; SSC 2
See also CA 104, 124

Chernyshevsky, Nikolay Gavrilovich
1828-1889 .... NCLC 1

Cherry, Caroline Janice   1942-
See Cherryh, C. J.

Cherryh, C. J.   1942-.............. CLC 35
See also CANR 10; CA 65-68; DLB-Y 80

Chesnutt, Charles Waddell
1858-1932 .... TCLC 5, 39; SSC 7
See also BLC 1; CA 106, 125; DLB 12, 50,
78

Chester, Alfred   1929?-1971 .... CLC 49
See also obituary CA 33-36R

Chesterton, G(ilbert) K(eith)
1874-1936 .... TCLC 1, 6; SSC 1
See also CA 104; SATA 27; DLB 10, 19,
34, 70

Chiang Pin-Chin   1904-1986
See Ding Ling
See also obituary CA 118

Ch'ien Chung-shu   1910-........... CLC 22

Child, Lydia Maria   1802-1880 .... NCLC 6
See also DLB 1, 74

Child, Philip   1898-1978 .... CLC 19
See also CAP 1; CA 13-14; SATA 47

Childress, Alice   1920-......... CLC 12, 15
See also BLC 1; CLR 14; CANR 3, 27;
CA 45-48; SATA 7, 48; DLB 7, 38

Chislett, (Margaret) Anne   1943?- ... CLC 34

Chitty, (Sir) Thomas Willes   1926-.. CLC 11
See also Hinde, Thomas
See also CA 5-8R

Chomette, Rene   1898-1981
See Clair, Rene
See also obituary CA 103

Chopin, Kate (O'Flaherty)
1851-1904 .... TCLC 5, 14; SSC 8
See also CA 122; brief entry CA 104;
DLB 12, 78; CDALB 1865-1917

Christie, (Dame) Agatha (Mary Clarissa)
1890-1976 ...... CLC 1, 6, 8, 12, 39, 48
See also CANR 10; CA 17-20R;
obituary CA 61-64; SATA 36; DLB 13

Christie, (Ann) Philippa   1920-
See Pearce, (Ann) Philippa
See also CANR 4; CA 7-8

Christine de Pizan   1365?-1431?....... LC 9

Chulkov, Mikhail Dmitrievich
1743-1792 .... LC 2

Churchill, Caryl   1938-......... CLC 31, 55
See also CANR 22; CA 102; DLB 13

Churchill, Charles   1731?-1764....... LC 3

Chute, Carolyn   1947-............ CLC 39
See also CA 123

Ciardi, John (Anthony)
1916-1986 .... CLC 10, 40, 44
See also CAAS 2; CANR 5; CA 5-8R;
obituary CA 118; SATA 1, 46; DLB 5;
DLB-Y 86

Cicero, Marcus Tullius
106 B.C.-43 B.C.............. CMLC 3

Cimino, Michael   1943?-........... CLC 16
See also CA 105

Cioran, E. M.   1911-.............. CLC 64
See also CA 25-28R

Clair, Rene   1898-1981 .... CLC 20
See also Chomette, Rene

Clampitt, Amy   19??-.............. CLC 32
See also CA 110

Clancy, Tom   1947-................ CLC 45
See also CA 125

Clare, John   1793-1864 .... NCLC 9
See also DLB 55

Clark, Al C.   1937?-1974
See Goines, Donald

Clark, (Robert) Brian   1932-........ CLC 29
See also CA 41-44R

Clark, Eleanor   1913- .... CLC 5, 19
See also CA 9-12R; DLB 6

Clark, John Pepper   1935-......... CLC 38
See also BLC 1; CANR 16; CA 65-68

Clark, Mavis Thorpe   1912?- .... CLC 12
See also CANR 8; CA 57-60; SAAS 5;
SATA 8

Clark, Walter Van Tilburg
1909-1971 .... CLC 28
See also CA 9-12R; obituary CA 33-36R;
SATA 8; DLB 9

Clarke, Arthur C(harles)
1917- ...... CLC 1, 4, 13, 18, 35; SSC 3
See also CANR 2; CA 1-4R; SATA 13

Author Index

Corso, (Nunzio) Gregory 1930-... **CLC 1, 11**
See also CA 5-8R; DLB 5, 16

Cortazar, Julio
1914-1984 ..... **CLC 2, 3, 5, 10, 13, 15,
33, 34; SSC 7**
See also CANR 12; CA 21-24R

Corvo, Baron 1860-1913
See Rolfe, Frederick (William Serafino
Austin Lewis Mary)

Cosic, Dobrica 1921- .... **CLC 14**
See also CA 122

Costain, Thomas B(ertram)
1885-1965 .... **CLC 30**
See also CA 5-8R; obituary CA 25-28R;
DLB 9

Costantini, Humberto 1924?-1987... **CLC 49**
See also obituary CA 122

Costello, Elvis 1955-.............. **CLC 21**

Cotter, Joseph Seamon, Sr.
1861-1949 .... **TCLC 28**
See also BLC 1; CA 124; DLB 50

Couperus, Louis (Marie Anne)
1863-1923 .... **TCLC 15**
See also CA 115

Courtenay, Bryce 1933-........... **CLC 59**

Cousteau, Jacques-Yves 1910-..... **CLC 30**
See also CANR 15; CA 65-68; SATA 38

Coward, (Sir) Noel (Pierce)
1899-1973 .... **CLC 1, 9, 29, 51**
See also CAP 2; CA 17-18;
obituary CA 41-44R; DLB 10

Cowley, Malcolm 1898-1989 .... **CLC 39**
See also CANR 3; CA 5-6R;
obituary CA 128; DLB 4, 48; DLB-Y 81

Cowper, William 1731-1800...... **NCLC 8**

Cox, William Trevor 1928- ..... **CLC 9, 14**
See also Trevor, William
See also CANR 4; CA 9-12R

Cozzens, James Gould
1903-1978 .... **CLC 1, 4, 11**
See also CANR 19; CA 9-12R;
obituary CA 81-84; DLB 9; DLB-Y 84;
DLB-DS 2; CDALB 1941-1968

Crabbe, George 1754-1832....... **NCLC 26**

Crace, Douglas 1944-............. **CLC 58**

Crane, (Harold) Hart
1899-1932 .... **TCLC 2, 5; PC 3**
See also CA 127; brief entry CA 104;
DLB 4, 48; CDALB 1917-1929

Crane, R(onald) S(almon)
1886-1967 .... **CLC 27**
See also CA 85-88; DLB 63

Crane, Stephen
1871-1900 ..... **TCLC 11, 17, 32; SSC 7**
See also YABC 2; CA 109; DLB 12, 54, 78;
CDALB 1865-1917

Craven, Margaret 1901-1980....... **CLC 17**
See also CA 103

Crawford, F(rancis) Marion
1854-1909 .... **TCLC 10**
See also CA 107; DLB 71

Crawford, Isabella Valancy
1850-1887 .... **NCLC 12**
See also DLB 92

Crayencour, Marguerite de 1903-1987
See Yourcenar, Marguerite

Creasey, John 1908-1973.......... **CLC 11**
See also CANR 8; CA 5-8R;
obituary CA 41-44R; DLB 77

Crebillon, Claude Prosper Jolyot de (fils)
1707-1777 .... **LC 1**

Creeley, Robert (White)
1926- .... **CLC 1, 2, 4, 8, 11, 15, 36**
See also CANR 23; CA 1-4R; DLB 5, 16

Crews, Harry (Eugene)
1935- .... **CLC 6, 23, 49**
See also CANR 20; CA 25-28R; DLB 6

Crichton, (John) Michael
1942- .... **CLC 2, 6, 54**
See also CANR 13; CA 25-28R; SATA 9;
DLB-Y 81

Crispin, Edmund 1921-1978........ **CLC 22**
See also Montgomery, Robert Bruce
See also DLB 87

Cristofer, Michael 1946- .... **CLC 28**
See also CA 110; DLB 7

Croce, Benedetto 1866-1952 ...... **TCLC 37**
See also CA 120

Crockett, David (Davy)
1786-1836 .... **NCLC 8**
See also DLB 3, 11

Croker, John Wilson 1780-1857 .. **NCLC 10**

Cronin, A(rchibald) J(oseph)
1896-1981 .... **CLC 32**
See also CANR 5; CA 1-4R;
obituary CA 102; obituary SATA 25, 47

Cross, Amanda 1926-
See Heilbrun, Carolyn G(old)

Crothers, Rachel 1878-1953....... **TCLC 19**
See also CA 113; DLB 7

Crowley, Aleister 1875-1947 ...... **TCLC 7**
See also CA 104

Crowley, John 1942-
See also CA 61-64; DLB-Y 82

Crumb, Robert 1943- .... **CLC 17**
See also CA 106

Cryer, Gretchen 1936?- .... **CLC 21**
See also CA 114, 123

Csath, Geza 1887-1919........... **TCLC 13**
See also CA 111

Cudlip, David 1933-.............. **CLC 34**

Cullen, Countee 1903-1946 ..... **TCLC 4, 37**
See also BLC 1; CA 108, 124; SATA 18;
DLB 4, 48, 51; CDALB 1917-1929

Cummings, E(dward) E(stlin)
1894-1962 ...... **CLC 1, 3, 8, 12, 15, 68**
See also CANR 31; CA 73-76; DLB 4, 48;
CDALB 1929-1941

Cunha, Euclides (Rodrigues) da
1866-1909 .... **TCLC 24**
See also CA 123

Cunningham, J(ames) V(incent)
1911-1985 .... **CLC 3, 31**
See also CANR 1; CA 1-4R;
obituary CA 115; DLB 5

Cunningham, Julia (Woolfolk)
1916- .... **CLC 12**
See also CANR 4, 19; CA 9-12R; SAAS 2;
SATA 1, 26

Cunningham, Michael 1952- .... **CLC 34**

Currie, Ellen 19??- .... **CLC 44**

Dabrowska, Maria (Szumska)
1889-1965 .... **CLC 15**
See also CA 106

Dabydeen, David 1956?-.......... **CLC 34**
See also CA 106

Dacey, Philip 1939- .... **CLC 51**
See also CANR 14; CA 37-40R

Dagerman, Stig (Halvard)
1923-1954 .... **TCLC 17**
See also CA 117

Dahl, Roald 1916-............ **CLC 1, 6, 18**
See also CLR 1, 7; CANR 6; CA 1-4R;
SATA 1, 26

Dahlberg, Edward 1900-1977... **CLC 1, 7, 14**
See also CA 9-12R; obituary CA 69-72;
DLB 48

Daly, Elizabeth 1878-1967........ **CLC 52**
See also CAP 2; CA 23-24;
obituary CA 25-28R

Daly, Maureen 1921-............. **CLC 17**
See also McGivern, Maureen Daly
See also SAAS 1; SATA 2

Daniken, Erich von 1935-
See Von Daniken, Erich

Dannay, Frederic 1905-1982
See Queen, Ellery
See also CANR 1; CA 1-4R;
obituary CA 107

D'Annunzio, Gabriele
1863-1938 .... **TCLC 6, 40**
See also CA 104

Dante (Alighieri)
See Alighieri, Dante

Danziger, Paula 1944- .... **CLC 21**
See also CLR 20; CA 112, 115; SATA 30,
36

Dario, Ruben 1867-1916 .... **TCLC 4**
See also Sarmiento, Felix Ruben Garcia
See also CA 104

Darley, George 1795-1846........ **NCLC 2**

Daryush, Elizabeth 1887-1977.... **CLC 6, 19**
See also CANR 3; CA 49-52; DLB 20

Daudet, (Louis Marie) Alphonse
1840-1897 .... **NCLC 1**

Daumal, Rene 1908-1944........ **TCLC 14**
See also CA 114

Davenport, Guy (Mattison, Jr.)
1927- .... **CLC 6, 14, 38**
See also CANR 23; CA 33-36R

Davidson, Donald (Grady)
1893-1968 .... **CLC 2, 13, 19**
See also CANR 4; CA 5-8R;
obituary CA 25-28R; DLB 45

Davidson, John 1857-1909....... **TCLC 24**
See also CA 118; DLB 19

Davidson, Sara 1943-............. **CLC 9**
See also CA 81-84

Davie, Donald (Alfred)
    1922- .... CLC **5, 8, 10, 31**
    See also CAAS 3; CANR 1; CA 1-4R;
    DLB 27

Davies, Ray(mond Douglas) 1944- .. CLC **21**
    See also CA 116

Davies, Rhys 1903-1978.......... CLC **23**
    See also CANR 4; CA 9-12R;
    obituary CA 81-84

Davies, (William) Robertson
    1913- .... CLC **2, 7, 13, 25, 42**
    See also CANR 17; CA 33-36R; DLB 68

Davies, W(illiam) H(enry)
    1871-1940 .... TCLC **5**
    See also CA 104; DLB 19

Davis, Frank Marshall 1905-1987
    See also BLC 1; CA 123, 125; DLB 51

Davis, H(arold) L(enoir)
    1896-1960 .... CLC **49**
    See also obituary CA 89-92; DLB 9

Davis, Rebecca (Blaine) Harding
    1831-1910 .... TCLC **6**
    See also CA 104; DLB 74

Davis, Richard Harding
    1864-1916 .... TCLC **24**
    See also CA 114; DLB 12, 23, 78, 79

Davison, Frank Dalby 1893-1970 ... CLC **15**
    See also obituary CA 116

Davison, Peter 1928- .... CLC **28**
    See also CAAS 4; CANR 3; CA 9-12R;
    DLB 5

Davys, Mary 1674-1732............ LC **1**
    See also DLB 39

Dawson, Fielding 1930- .... CLC **6**
    See also CA 85-88

Day, Clarence (Shepard, Jr.)
    1874-1935 .... TCLC **25**
    See also CA 108; DLB 11

Day, Thomas 1748-1789............ LC **1**
    See also YABC 1; DLB 39

Day Lewis, C(ecil)
    1904-1972 .... CLC **1, 6, 10**
    See also CAP 1; CA 15-16;
    obituary CA 33-36R; DLB 15, 20

Dazai Osamu 1909-1948 .... TCLC **11**
    See also Tsushima Shuji

De Crayencour, Marguerite 1903-1987
    See Yourcenar, Marguerite

Deer, Sandra 1940-.............. CLC **45**

De Ferrari, Gabriella 19??- .... CLC **65**

Defoe, Daniel 1660?-1731 .... LC **1**
    See also SATA 22; DLB 39

De Hartog, Jan 1914-............. CLC **19**
    See also CANR 1; CA 1-4R

Deighton, Len 1929-....... CLC **4, 7, 22, 46**
    See also Deighton, Leonard Cyril
    See also DLB 87

Deighton, Leonard Cyril 1929-
    See Deighton, Len
    See also CANR 19; CA 9-12R

De la Mare, Walter (John)
    1873-1956 .... TCLC **4**
    See also CLR 23; CA 110; SATA 16;
    DLB 19

Delaney, Shelagh 1939-.......... CLC **29**
    See also CA 17-20R; DLB 13

Delany, Mary (Granville Pendarves)
    1700-1788 .... LC **12**

Delany, Samuel R(ay, Jr.)
    1942- .... CLC **8, 14, 38**
    See also BLC 1; CANR 27; CA 81-84;
    DLB 8, 33

de la Ramee, Marie Louise 1839-1908
    See Ouida
    See also SATA 20

De la Roche, Mazo 1885-1961 ..... CLC **14**
    See also CA 85-88; DLB 68

Delbanco, Nicholas (Franklin)
    1942-.................... CLC **6, 13**
    See also CAAS 2; CA 17-20R; DLB 6

del Castillo, Michel 1933- .... CLC **38**
    See also CA 109

Deledda, Grazia 1871-1936 .... TCLC **23**
    See also CA 123

Delibes (Setien), Miguel 1920- ... CLC **8, 18**
    See also CANR 1; CA 45-48

DeLillo, Don
    1936- .... CLC **8, 10, 13, 27, 39, 54**
    See also CANR 21; CA 81-84; DLB 6

De Lisser, H(erbert) G(eorge)
    1878-1944 .... TCLC **12**
    See also CA 109

Deloria, Vine (Victor), Jr. 1933-.... CLC **21**
    See also CANR 5, 20; CA 53-56; SATA 21

Del Vecchio, John M(ichael)
    1947- .... CLC **29**
    See also CA 110

de Man, Paul 1919-1983 .... CLC **55**
    See also obituary CA 111; DLB 67

De Marinis, Rick 1934-........... CLC **54**
    See also CANR 9, 25; CA 57-60

Demby, William 1922-............ CLC **53**
    See also BLC 1; CA 81-84; DLB 33

Denby, Edwin (Orr) 1903-1983 ..... CLC **48**
    See also obituary CA 110

Dennis, John 1657-1734........... LC **11**

Dennis, Nigel (Forbes) 1912-........ CLC **8**
    See also CA 25-28R; obituary CA 129;
    DLB 13, 15

De Palma, Brian 1940-............ CLC **20**
    See also CA 109

De Quincey, Thomas 1785-1859 ... NCLC **4**

Deren, Eleanora 1908-1961
    See Deren, Maya
    See also obituary CA 111

Deren, Maya 1908-1961.......... CLC **16**
    See also Deren, Eleanora

Derleth, August (William)
    1909-1971 .... CLC **31**
    See also CANR 4; CA 1-4R;
    obituary CA 29-32R; SATA 5; DLB 9

Derrida, Jacques 1930-........... CLC **24**
    See also CA 124, 127

Desai, Anita 1937- .... CLC **19, 37**
    See also CA 81-84

De Saint-Luc, Jean 1909-1981
    See Glassco, John

De Sica, Vittorio 1902-1974 .... CLC **20**
    See also obituary CA 117

Desnos, Robert 1900-1945........ TCLC **22**
    See also CA 121

Destouches, Louis-Ferdinand-Auguste
    1894-1961
    See Celine, Louis-Ferdinand
    See also CA 85-88

Deutsch, Babette 1895-1982 .... CLC **18**
    See also CANR 4; CA 1-4R;
    obituary CA 108; SATA 1;
    obituary SATA 33; DLB 45

Devenant, William 1606-1649 .... LC **13**

Devkota, Laxmiprasad
    1909-1959 .... TCLC **23**
    See also CA 123

DeVoto, Bernard (Augustine)
    1897-1955 .... TCLC **29**
    See also CA 113; DLB 9

De Vries, Peter
    1910- .... CLC **1, 2, 3, 7, 10, 28, 46**
    See also CA 17-20R; DLB 6; DLB-Y 82

Dexter, Pete 1943-............. CLC **34, 55**
    See also CA 127

Diamano, Silmang 1906-
    See Senghor, Leopold Sedar

Diamond, Neil (Leslie) 1941-....... CLC **30**
    See also CA 108

Dick, Philip K(indred)
    1928-1982 .... CLC **10, 30**
    See also CANR 2, 16; CA 49-52;
    obituary CA 106; DLB 8

Dickens, Charles
    1812-1870 .... NCLC **3, 8, 18, 26**
    See also SATA 15; DLB 21, 55, 70

Dickey, James (Lafayette)
    1923- .... CLC **1, 2, 4, 7, 10, 15, 47**
    See also CANR 10; CA 9-12R; CABS 2;
    DLB 5; DLB-Y 82; DLB-DS 7

Dickey, William 1928-.......... CLC **3, 28**
    See also CANR 24; CA 9-12R; DLB 5

Dickinson, Charles 1952-.......... CLC **49**

Dickinson, Emily (Elizabeth)
    1830-1886 .... NCLC **21**; PC **1**
    See also SATA 29; DLB 1;
    CDALB 1865-1917

Dickinson, Peter (Malcolm de Brissac)
    1927- .... CLC **12, 35**
    See also CA 41-44R; SATA 5; DLB 87

Didion, Joan 1934-..... CLC **1, 3, 8, 14, 32**
    See also CANR 14; CA 5-8R; DLB 2;
    DLB-Y 81, 86; CDALB 1968-1987

Dillard, Annie 1945-............ CLC **9, 60**
    See also CANR 3; CA 49-52; SATA 10;
    DLB-Y 80

Dillard, R(ichard) H(enry) W(ilde)
    1937- .... CLC **5**
    See also CAAS 7; CANR 10; CA 21-24R;
    DLB 5

Dillon, Eilis 1920-.............. CLC **17**
    See also CLR 26; CAAS 3; CANR 4;
    CA 9-12R; SATA 2

Durang, Christopher (Ferdinand)
1949- .... **CLC 27, 38**
See also CA 105

Duras, Marguerite
1914- ...... **CLC 3, 6, 11, 20, 34, 40, 68**
See also CA 25-28R; DLB 83

Durban, Pam 1947-............. **CLC 39**
See also CA 123

Durcan, Paul 1944-............. **CLC 43**

Durrell, Lawrence (George)
1912-1990 .... **CLC 1, 4, 6, 8, 13, 27, 41**
See also CA 9-12R; DLB 15, 27

Durrenmatt, Friedrich
1921- .... **CLC 1, 4, 8, 11, 15, 43**
See also Duerrenmatt, Friedrich
See also DLB 69

Dutt, Toru 1856-1877.......... **NCLC 29**

Dwight, Timothy 1752-1817...... **NCLC 13**
See also DLB 37

Dworkin, Andrea 1946- .... **CLC 43**
See also CANR 16; CA 77-80

Dylan, Bob 1941- .... **CLC 3, 4, 6, 12**
See also CA 41-44R; DLB 16

Eagleton, Terry 1943-............. **CLC 63**

East, Michael 1916-
See West, Morris L.

Eastlake, William (Derry) 1917-..... **CLC 8**
See also CAAS 1; CANR 5; CA 5-8R;
DLB 6

Eberhart, Richard 1904-... **CLC 3, 11, 19, 56**
See also CANR 2; CA 1-4R; DLB 48;
CDALB 1941-1968

Eberstadt, Fernanda 1960-........ **CLC 39**

Echegaray (y Eizaguirre), Jose (Maria Waldo)
1832-1916 .... **TCLC 4**
See also CA 104

Echeverria, (Jose) Esteban (Antonino)
1805-1851 .... **NCLC 18**

Eckert, Allan W. 1931- .... **CLC 17**
See also CANR 14; CA 13-16R; SATA 27,
29

Eco, Umberto 1932-.......... **CLC 28, 60**
See also CANR 12; CA 77-80

Eddison, E(ric) R(ucker)
1882-1945 .... **TCLC 15**
See also CA 109

Edel, Leon (Joseph) 1907-...... **CLC 29, 34**
See also CANR 1, 22; CA 1-4R

Eden, Emily 1797-1869 .... **NCLC 10**

Edgar, David 1948-............. **CLC 42**
See also CANR 12; CA 57-60; DLB 13

Edgerton, Clyde 1944- .... **CLC 39**
See also CA 118

Edgeworth, Maria 1767-1849...... **NCLC 1**
See also SATA 21

Edmonds, Helen (Woods) 1904-1968
See Kavan, Anna
See also CA 5-8R; obituary CA 25-28R

Edmonds, Walter D(umaux) 1903-.. **CLC 35**
See also CANR 2; CA 5-8R; SAAS 4;
SATA 1, 27; DLB 9

Edson, Russell 1905- .... **CLC 13**
See also CA 33-36R

Edwards, Eli 1889-1948
See McKay, Claude

Edwards, G(erald) B(asil)
1899-1976 .... **CLC 25**
See also obituary CA 110

Edwards, Gus 1939-............. **CLC 43**
See also CA 108

Edwards, Jonathan 1703-1758....... **LC 7**
See also DLB 24

Ehle, John (Marsden, Jr.) 1925-.... **CLC 27**
See also CA 9-12R

Ehrenburg, Ilya (Grigoryevich)
1891-1967 .... **CLC 18, 34, 62**
See also CA 102; obituary CA 25-28R

Eich, Guenter 1907-1971
See also CA 111; obituary CA 93-96

Eich, Gunter 1907-1971.......... **CLC 15**
See also Eich, Guenter
See also DLB 69

Eichendorff, Joseph Freiherr von
1788-1857 .... **NCLC 8**
See also DLB 90

Eigner, Larry 1927-............... **CLC 9**
See also Eigner, Laurence (Joel)
See also DLB 5

Eigner, Laurence (Joel) 1927-
See Eigner, Larry
See also CANR 6; CA 9-12R

Eiseley, Loren (Corey) 1907-1977.... **CLC 7**
See also CANR 6; CA 1-4R;
obituary CA 73-76

Eisenstadt, Jill 1963-............. **CLC 50**

Ekeloef, Gunnar (Bengt) 1907-1968
See Ekelof, Gunnar (Bengt)
See also obituary CA 25-28R

Ekelof, Gunnar (Bengt) 1907-1968.. **CLC 27**
See also Ekeloef, Gunnar (Bengt)

Ekwensi, Cyprian (Odiatu Duaka)
1921- .... **CLC 4**
See also BLC 1; CANR 18; CA 29-32R

Elder, Lonne, III 1931-
See also BLC 1; CANR 25; CA 81-84;
DLB 7, 38, 44

Eliade, Mircea 1907-1986 .... **CLC 19**
See also CA 65-68; obituary CA 119

Eliot, George 1819-1880.... **NCLC 4, 13, 23**
See also DLB 21, 35, 55

Eliot, John 1604-1690 .... **LC 5**
See also DLB 24

Eliot, T(homas) S(tearns)
1888-1965 .... **CLC 1, 2, 3, 6, 9, 10, 13,
15, 24, 34, 41, 55, 57**
See also CA 5-8R; obituary CA 25-28R;
DLB 7, 10, 45, 63; DLB-Y 88

Elizabeth 1866-1941............. **TCLC 41**
See also Russell, Mary Annette Beauchamp

Elkin, Stanley (Lawrence)
1930- .... **CLC 4, 6, 9, 14, 27, 51**
See also CANR 8; CA 9-12R; DLB 2, 28;
DLB-Y 80

Elledge, Scott 19??- .... **CLC 34**

Elliott, George P(aul) 1918-1980..... **CLC 2**
See also CANR 2; CA 1-4R;
obituary CA 97-100

Elliott, Janice 1931-............. **CLC 47**
See also CANR 8; CA 13-16R; DLB 14

Elliott, Sumner Locke 1917-....... **CLC 38**
See also CANR 2, 21; CA 5-8R

Ellis, A. E. 19??-................. **CLC 7**

Ellis, Alice Thomas 19??-......... **CLC 40**

Ellis, Bret Easton 1964-.......... **CLC 39**
See also CA 118, 123

Ellis, (Henry) Havelock
1859-1939 .... **TCLC 14**
See also CA 109

Ellis, Trey 1964-................. **CLC 55**

Ellison, Harlan (Jay) 1934-... **CLC 1, 13, 42**
See also CANR 5; CA 5-8R; DLB 8

Ellison, Ralph (Waldo)
1914- .... **CLC 1, 3, 11, 54**
See also BLC 1; CANR 24; CA 9-12R;
DLB 2, 76; CDALB 1941-1968

Ellmann, Lucy 1956- .... **CLC 61**
See also CA 128

Ellmann, Richard (David)
1918-1987 .... **CLC 50**
See also CANR 2; CA 1-4R;
obituary CA 122; DLB-Y 87

Elman, Richard 1934-............. **CLC 19**
See also CAAS 3; CA 17-20R

El-Shabazz, El-Hajj Malik 1925-1965
See Malcolm X

Eluard, Paul 1895-1952........ **TCLC 7, 41**
See also Grindel, Eugene

Elyot, Sir Thomas 1490?-1546....... **LC 11**

Elytis, Odysseus 1911-......... **CLC 15, 49**
See also CA 102

Emecheta, (Florence Onye) Buchi
1944- .... **CLC 14, 48**
See also BLC 2; CANR 27; CA 81-84

Emerson, Ralph Waldo
1803-1882 .... **NCLC 1**
See also DLB 1, 59, 73; CDALB 1640-1865

Eminescu, Mihail 1850-1889..... **NCLC 33**

Empson, William
1906-1984 .... **CLC 3, 8, 19, 33, 34**
See also CA 17-20R; obituary CA 112;
DLB 20

Enchi, Fumiko (Veda) 1905-1986... **CLC 31**
See also obituary CA 121

Ende, Michael 1930-............. **CLC 31**
See also CLR 14; CA 118, 124; SATA 42;
DLB 75

Endo, Shusaku 1923-..... **CLC 7, 14, 19, 54**
See also CANR 21; CA 29-32R

Engel, Marian 1933-1985......... **CLC 36**
See also CANR 12; CA 25-28R; DLB 53

Engelhardt, Frederick 1911-1986
See Hubbard, L(afayette) Ron(ald)

Enright, D(ennis) J(oseph)
1920- .... **CLC 4, 8, 31**
See also CANR 1; CA 1-4R; SATA 25;
DLB 27

Enzensberger, Hans Magnus
1929- .... **CLC 43**
See also CA 116, 119

Hillis, Richard Lyle 1956-
See Hillis, Rick

Hillis, Rick 1956-.............. **CLC 66**
See also Hillis, Richard Lyle

Hilton, James 1900-1954........ **TCLC 21**
See also CA 108; SATA 34; DLB 34, 77

Himes, Chester (Bomar)
1909-1984 .... **CLC 2, 4, 7, 18, 58**
See also BLC 2; CANR 22; CA 25-28R;
obituary CA 114; DLB 2, 76

Hinde, Thomas 1926-.......... **CLC 6, 11**
See also Chitty, (Sir) Thomas Willes

Hine, (William) Daryl 1936-....... **CLC 15**
See also CANR 1, 20; CA 1-4R; DLB 60

Hinton, S(usan) E(loise) 1950- ..... **CLC 30**
See also CLR 3, 23; CA 81-84; SATA 19,
58; AAYA 2

Hippius (Merezhkovsky), Zinaida
(Nikolayevna) 1869-1945..... **TCLC 9**
See also Gippius, Zinaida (Nikolayevna)

Hiraoka, Kimitake 1925-1970
See Mishima, Yukio
See also CA 97-100; obituary CA 29-32R

Hirsch, Edward (Mark) 1950-... **CLC 31, 50**
See also CANR 20; CA 104

Hitchcock, (Sir) Alfred (Joseph)
1899-1980 .... **CLC 16**
See also obituary CA 97-100; SATA 27;
obituary SATA 24

Hoagland, Edward 1932-.......... **CLC 28**
See also CANR 2; CA 1-4R; SATA 51;
DLB 6

Hoban, Russell C(onwell) 1925- .. **CLC 7, 25**
See also CLR 3; CANR 23; CA 5-8R;
SATA 1, 40; DLB 52

Hobson, Laura Z(ametkin)
1900-1986 .... **CLC 7, 25**
See also CA 17-20R; obituary CA 118;
SATA 52; DLB 28

Hochhuth, Rolf 1931-........ **CLC 4, 11, 18**
See also CA 5-8R

Hochman, Sandra 1936-......... **CLC 3, 8**
See also CA 5-8R; DLB 5

Hochwalder, Fritz 1911-1986 ...... **CLC 36**
See also CA 29-32R; obituary CA 120

Hocking, Mary (Eunice) 1921-..... **CLC 13**
See also CANR 18; CA 101

Hodgins, Jack 1938-............. **CLC 23**
See also CA 93-96; DLB 60

Hodgson, William Hope
1877-1918 .... **TCLC 13**
See also CA 111; DLB 70

Hoffman, Alice 1952-............. **CLC 51**
See also CA 77-80

Hoffman, Daniel (Gerard)
1923- .... **CLC 6, 13, 23**
See also CANR 4; CA 1-4R; DLB 5

Hoffman, Stanley 1944-........... **CLC 5**
See also CA 77-80

Hoffman, William M(oses) 1939- ... **CLC 40**
See also CANR 11; CA 57-60

Hoffmann, E(rnst) T(heodor) A(madeus)
1776-1822 .... **NCLC 2**
See also SATA 27; DLB 90

Hoffmann, Gert 1932-............ **CLC 54**

Hofmannsthal, Hugo (Laurenz August
Hofmann Edler) von
1874-1929 .... **TCLC 11**
See also CA 106; DLB 81

Hogg, James 1770-1835.......... **NCLC 4**

Holbach, Paul Henri Thiry, Baron d'
1723-1789 .... **LC 14**

Holberg, Ludvig 1684-1754 .... **LC 6**

Holden, Ursula 1921-............. **CLC 18**
See also CAAS 8; CANR 22; CA 101

Holderlin, (Johann Christian) Friedrich
1770-1843 .... **NCLC 16**

Holdstock, Robert (P.) 1948-....... **CLC 39**

Holland, Isabelle 1920- .... **CLC 21**
See also CANR 10, 25; CA 21-24R;
SATA 8

Holland, Marcus 1900-1985
See Caldwell, (Janet Miriam) Taylor
(Holland)

Hollander, John 1929-...... **CLC 2, 5, 8, 14**
See also CANR 1; CA 1-4R; SATA 13;
DLB 5

Holleran, Andrew 1943?-.......... **CLC 38**

Hollinghurst, Alan 1954-.......... **CLC 55**
See also CA 114

Hollis, Jim 1916-
See Summers, Hollis (Spurgeon, Jr.)

Holmes, John Clellon 1926-1988.... **CLC 56**
See also CANR 4; CA 9-10R;
obituary CA 125; DLB 16

Holmes, Oliver Wendell
1809-1894 .... **NCLC 14**
See also SATA 34; DLB 1;
CDALB 1640-1865

Holt, Victoria 1906-
See Hibbert, Eleanor (Burford)

Holub, Miroslav 1923-............. **CLC 4**
See also CANR 10; CA 21-24R

Homer c. 8th century B.C.-....... **CMLC 1**

Honig, Edwin 1919-............. **CLC 33**
See also CAAS 8; CANR 4; CA 5-8R;
DLB 5

Hood, Hugh (John Blagdon)
1928- .... **CLC 15, 28**
See also CANR 1; CA 49-52; DLB 53

Hood, Thomas 1799-1845........ **NCLC 16**

Hooker, (Peter) Jeremy 1941-...... **CLC 43**
See also CANR 22; CA 77-80; DLB 40

Hope, A(lec) D(erwent) 1907- .... **CLC 3, 51**
See also CA 21-24R

Hope, Christopher (David Tully)
1944- .... **CLC 52**
See also CA 106

Hopkins, Gerard Manley
1844-1889 .... **NCLC 17**
See also DLB 35, 57

Hopkins, John (Richard) 1931-...... **CLC 4**
See also CA 85-88

Hopkins, Pauline Elizabeth
1859-1930 .... **TCLC 28**
See also BLC 2; DLB 50

Horgan, Paul 1903-............ **CLC 9, 53**
See also CANR 9; CA 13-16R; SATA 13;
DLB-Y 85

Horovitz, Israel 1939-........... **CLC 56**
See also CA 33-36R; DLB 7

Horwitz, Julius 1920-1986........ **CLC 14**
See also CANR 12; CA 9-12R;
obituary CA 119

Hospital, Janette Turner 1942-..... **CLC 42**
See also CA 108

Hostos (y Bonilla), Eugenio Maria de
1893-1903 .... **TCLC 24**
See also CA 123

Hougan, Carolyn 19??-............ **CLC 34**

Household, Geoffrey (Edward West)
1900-1988 .... **CLC 11**
See also CA 77-80; obituary CA 126;
SATA 14, 59; DLB 87

Housman, A(lfred) E(dward)
1859-1936 .... **TCLC 1, 10; PC 2**
See also CA 104, 125; DLB 19

Housman, Laurence 1865-1959..... **TCLC 7**
See also CA 106; SATA 25; DLB 10

Howard, Elizabeth Jane 1923-... **CLC 7, 29**
See also CANR 8; CA 5-8R

Howard, Maureen 1930- ..... **CLC 5, 14, 46**
See also CA 53-56; DLB-Y 83

Howard, Richard 1929-...... **CLC 7, 10, 47**
See also CANR 25; CA 85-88; DLB 5

Howard, Robert E(rvin)
1906-1936 .... **TCLC 8**
See also CA 105

Howe, Fanny 1940-............. **CLC 47**
See also CA 117; SATA 52

Howe, Julia Ward 1819-1910 ..... **TCLC 21**
See also CA 117; DLB 1

Howe, Tina 1937-.............. **CLC 48**
See also CA 109

Howell, James 1594?-1666........ **LC 13**

Howells, William Dean
1837-1920 .... **TCLC 7, 17, 41**
See also brief entry CA 104; DLB 12, 64,
74, 79; CDALB 1865-1917

Howes, Barbara 1914-............ **CLC 15**
See also CAAS 3; CA 9-12R; SATA 5

Hrabal, Bohumil 1914-........ **CLC 13, 67**
See also CAAS 12; CA 106

Hubbard, L(afayette) Ron(ald)
1911-1986 .... **CLC 43**
See also CANR 22; CA 77-80;
obituary CA 118

Huch, Ricarda (Octavia)
1864-1947 .... **TCLC 13**
See also CA 111; DLB 66

Huddle, David 1942-............ **CLC 49**
See also CA 57-60

Hudson, W(illiam) H(enry)
1841-1922 .... **TCLC 29**
See also CA 115; SATA 35

Hueffer, Ford Madox 1873-1939
See Ford, Ford Madox

Hughart, Barry 1934-............ **CLC 39**

Hughes, David (John) 1930- .... **CLC 48**
See also CA 116, 129; DLB 14

Jami, Nur al-Din 'Abd al-Rahman
1414-1492 .... LC 9

Jandl, Ernst 1925- .... CLC 34

Janowitz, Tama 1957- .... CLC 43
See also CA 106

Jarrell, Randall
1914-1965 .... CLC 1, 2, 6, 9, 13, 49
See also CLR 6; CANR 6; CA 5-8R;
obituary CA 25-28R; CABS 2; SATA 7;
DLB 48, 52; CDALB 1941-1968

Jarry, Alfred 1873-1907 .... TCLC 2, 14
See also CA 104

Jeake, Samuel, Jr. 1889-1973
See Aiken, Conrad

Jean Paul 1763-1825 .... NCLC 7

Jeffers, (John) Robinson
1887-1962 .... CLC 2, 3, 11, 15, 54
See also CA 85-88; DLB 45;
CDALB 1917-1929

Jefferson, Thomas 1743-1826 .... NCLC 11
See also DLB 31; CDALB 1640-1865

Jeffrey, Francis 1773-1850 ...... NCLC 33

Jellicoe, (Patricia) Ann 1927- ...... CLC 27
See also CA 85-88; DLB 13

Jenkins, (John) Robin 1912- .... CLC 52
See also CANR 1; CA 4R; DLB 14

Jennings, Elizabeth (Joan)
1926- .... CLC 5, 14
See also CAAS 5; CANR 8; CA 61-64;
DLB 27

Jennings, Waylon 1937- .... CLC 21

Jensen, Johannes V. 1873-1950 .... TCLC 41

Jensen, Laura (Linnea) 1948- ...... CLC 37
See also CA 103

Jerome, Jerome K. 1859-1927 ..... TCLC 23
See also CA 119; DLB 10, 34

Jerrold, Douglas William
1803-1857 .... NCLC 2

Jewett, (Theodora) Sarah Orne
1849-1909 .... TCLC 1, 22; SSC 6
See also CA 108, 127; SATA 15; DLB 12, 74

Jewsbury, Geraldine (Endsor)
1812-1880 .... NCLC 22
See also DLB 21

Jhabvala, Ruth Prawer
1927- .... CLC 4, 8, 29
See also CANR 2, 29; CA 1-4R

Jiles, Paulette 1943- .... CLC 13, 58
See also CA 101

Jimenez (Mantecon), Juan Ramon
1881-1958 .... TCLC 4
See also CA 104

Joel, Billy 1949- .... CLC 26
See also Joel, William Martin

Joel, William Martin 1949-
See Joel, Billy
See also CA 108

John of the Cross, St. 1542-1591 .... LC 18

Johnson, B(ryan) S(tanley William)
1933-1973 .... CLC 6, 9
See also CANR 9; CA 9-12R;
obituary CA 53-56; DLB 14, 40

Johnson, Charles (Richard)
1948- .... CLC 7, 51, 65
See also BLC 2; CA 116; DLB 33

Johnson, Denis 1949- .... CLC 52
See also CA 117, 121

Johnson, Diane 1934- .... CLC 5, 13, 48
See also CANR 17; CA 41-44R; DLB-Y 80

Johnson, Eyvind (Olof Verner)
1900-1976 .... CLC 14
See also CA 73-76; obituary CA 69-72

Johnson, Fenton 1888-1958
See also BLC 2; CA 124;
brief entry CA 118; DLB 45, 50

Johnson, James Weldon
1871-1938 .... TCLC 3, 19
See also Johnson, James William
See also BLC 2; CA 125;
brief entry CA 104; SATA 31; DLB 51;
CDALB 1917-1929

Johnson, James William 1871-1938
See Johnson, James Weldon
See also SATA 31

Johnson, Joyce 1935- .... CLC 58
See also CA 125, 129

Johnson, Lionel (Pigot)
1867-1902 .... TCLC 19
See also CA 117; DLB 19

Johnson, Marguerita 1928-
See Angelou, Maya

Johnson, Pamela Hansford
1912-1981 .... CLC 1, 7, 27
See also CANR 2, 28; CA 1-4R;
obituary CA 104; DLB 15

Johnson, Samuel 1709-1784 .... LC 15
See also DLB 39, 95

Johnson, Uwe
1934-1984 .... CLC 5, 10, 15, 40
See also CANR 1; CA 1-4R;
obituary CA 112; DLB 75

Johnston, George (Benson) 1913- ... CLC 51
See also CANR 5, 20; CA 1-4R; DLB 88

Johnston, Jennifer 1930- .... CLC 7
See also CA 85-88; DLB 14

Jolley, Elizabeth 1923- .... CLC 46
See also CA 127

Jones, D(ouglas) G(ordon) 1929-.... CLC 10
See also CANR 13; CA 29-32R, 113;
DLB 53

Jones, David
1895-1974 .... CLC 2, 4, 7, 13, 42
See also CANR 28; CA 9-12R;
obituary CA 53-56; DLB 20

Jones, David Robert 1947-
See Bowie, David
See also CA 103

Jones, Diana Wynne 1934- .... CLC 26
See also CLR 23; CANR 4, 26; CA 49-52;
SAAS 7; SATA 9

Jones, Gayl 1949- .... CLC 6, 9
See also BLC 2; CANR 27; CA 77-80;
DLB 33

Jones, James 1921-1977 .... CLC 1, 3, 10, 39
See also CANR 6; CA 1-4R;
obituary CA 69-72; DLB 2

Jones, (Everett) LeRoi
1934- ...... CLC 1, 2, 3, 5, 10, 14, 33
See also Baraka, Amiri; Baraka, Imamu
Amiri
See also CA 21-24R

Jones, Louis B. 19??- .... CLC 65

Jones, Madison (Percy, Jr.) 1925- ... CLC 4
See also CAAS 11; CANR 7; CA 13-16R

Jones, Mervyn 1922- .... CLC 10, 52
See also CAAS 5; CANR 1; CA 45-48

Jones, Mick 1956?- .... CLC 30
See also The Clash

Jones, Nettie 19??- .... CLC 34

Jones, Preston 1936-1979 .... CLC 10
See also CA 73-76; obituary CA 89-92;
DLB 7

Jones, Robert F(rancis) 1934- .... CLC 7
See also CANR 2; CA 49-52

Jones, Rod 1953- .... CLC 50
See also CA 128

Jones, Terry 1942?- .... CLC 21
See also Monty Python
See also CA 112, 116; SATA 51

Jong, Erica 1942- .... CLC 4, 6, 8, 18
See also CANR 26; CA 73-76; DLB 2, 5, 28

Jonson, Ben(jamin) 1572(?)-1637 ..... LC 6
See also DLB 62

Jordan, June 1936- .... CLC 5, 11, 23
See also CLR 10; CANR 25; CA 33-36R;
SATA 4; DLB 38; AAYA 2

Jordan, Pat(rick M.) 1941- .... CLC 37
See also CANR 25; CA 33-36R

Josipovici, Gabriel (David)
1940- .... CLC 6, 43
See also CAAS 8; CA 37-40R; DLB 14

Joubert, Joseph 1754-1824 .... NCLC 9

Jouve, Pierre Jean 1887-1976 ...... CLC 47
See also obituary CA 65-68

Joyce, James (Augustine Aloysius)
1882-1941 ...... TCLC 3, 8, 16, 26, 35;
SSC 3
See also CA 104, 126; DLB 10, 19, 36

Jozsef, Attila 1905-1937 .... TCLC 22
See also CA 116

Juana Ines de la Cruz 1651?-1695 .... LC 5

Julian of Norwich 1342?-1416? .... LC 6

Just, Ward S(wift) 1935- .... CLC 4, 27
See also CA 25-28R

Justice, Donald (Rodney) 1925- .. CLC 6, 19
See also CANR 26; CA 5-8R; DLB-Y 83

Juvenal c. 55-c. 127 .... CMLC 8

Kacew, Romain 1914-1980
See Gary, Romain
See also CA 108; obituary CA 102

Kacewgary, Romain 1914-1980
See Gary, Romain

Kadare, Ismail 1936- .... CLC 52

Kadohata, Cynthia 19??- .... CLC 59

Kafka, Franz
1883-1924 .... TCLC 2, 6, 13, 29; SSC 5
See also CA 105, 126; DLB 81

Kahn, Roger 1927- .... CLC 30
See also CA 25-28R; SATA 37

Author Index

McKay, Claude   1889-1948
See McKay, Festus Claudius

McKay, Festus Claudius   1889-1948
See also BLC 2; CA 124; brief entry CA 104

McKuen, Rod   1933-............ CLC 1, 3
See also CA 41-44R

McLuhan, (Herbert) Marshall
1911-1980 .... CLC 37
See also CANR 12; CA 9-12R;
obituary CA 102; DLB 88

McManus, Declan Patrick   1955-
See Costello, Elvis

McMillan, Terry   1951- .... CLC 50, 61

McMurtry, Larry (Jeff)
1936- .... CLC 2, 3, 7, 11, 27, 44
See also CANR 19; CA 5-8R; DLB 2;
DLB-Y 80, 87; CDALB 1968-1987

McNally, Terrence   1939-..... CLC 4, 7, 41
See also CANR 2; CA 45-48; DLB 7

McPhee, John   1931-.............. CLC 36
See also CANR 20; CA 65-68

McPherson, James Alan   1943- .... CLC 19
See also CANR 24; CA 25-28R; DLB 38

McPherson, William   1939- .... CLC 34
See also CA 57-60

McSweeney, Kerry   19??-.......... CLC 34

Mead, Margaret   1901-1978....... CLC 37
See also CANR 4; CA 1-4R;
obituary CA 81-84; SATA 20

Meaker, M. J.   1927-
See Kerr, M. E.; Meaker, Marijane

Meaker, Marijane   1927-
See Kerr, M. E.
See also CA 107; SATA 20

Medoff, Mark (Howard)   1940- ... CLC 6, 23
See also CANR 5; CA 53-56; DLB 7

Megged, Aharon   1920-............. CLC 9
See also CANR 1; CA 49-52

Mehta, Ved (Parkash)   1934- .... CLC 37
See also CANR 2, 23; CA 1-4R

Mellor, John   1953?-
See The Clash

Meltzer, Milton   1915-............. CLC 26
See also CLR 13; CA 13-16R; SAAS 1;
SATA 1, 50; DLB 61

Melville, Herman
1819-1891 ...... NCLC 3, 12, 29; SSC 1
See also SATA 59; DLB 3, 74;
CDALB 1640-1865

Membreno, Alejandro   1972- .... CLC 59

Mencken, H(enry) L(ouis)
1880-1956 .... TCLC 13
See also CA 105, 125; DLB 11, 29, 63;
CDALB 1917-1929

Mercer, David   1928-1980.......... CLC 5
See also CANR 23; CA 9-12R;
obituary CA 102; DLB 13

Meredith, George   1828-1909...... TCLC 17
See also CA 117; DLB 18, 35, 57

Meredith, George   1858-1924..... TCLC 43

Meredith, William (Morris)
1919- .... CLC 4, 13, 22, 55
See also CANR 6; CA 9-12R; DLB 5

Merezhkovsky, Dmitri
1865-1941 .... TCLC 29

Merimee, Prosper
1803-1870 .... NCLC 6; SSC 7

Merkin, Daphne   1954-............ CLC 44
See also CANR 123

Merrill, James (Ingram)
1926- .... CLC 2, 3, 6, 8, 13, 18, 34
See also CANR 10; CA 13-16R; DLB 5;
DLB-Y 85

Merton, Thomas (James)
1915-1968 .... CLC 1, 3, 11, 34
See also CANR 22; CA 5-8R;
obituary CA 25-28R; DLB 48; DLB-Y 81

Merwin, W(illiam) S(tanley)
1927- ..... CLC 1, 2, 3, 5, 8, 13, 18, 45
See also CANR 15; CA 13-16R; DLB 5

Metcalf, John   1938-.............. CLC 37
See also CA 113; DLB 60

Mew, Charlotte (Mary)
1870-1928 .... TCLC 8
See also CA 105; DLB 19

Mewshaw, Michael   1943-.......... CLC 9
See also CANR 7; CA 53-56; DLB-Y 80

Meyer-Meyrink, Gustav   1868-1932
See Meyrink, Gustav
See also CA 117

Meyers, Jeffrey   1939- .... CLC 39
See also CA 73-76

Meynell, Alice (Christiana Gertrude
Thompson)   1847-1922 .... TCLC 6
See also CA 104; DLB 19

Meyrink, Gustav   1868-1932...... TCLC 21
See also Meyer-Meyrink, Gustav

Michaels, Leonard   1933-........ CLC 6, 25
See also CANR 21; CA 61-64

Michaux, Henri   1899-1984 ...... CLC 8, 19
See also CA 85-88; obituary CA 114

Michelangelo   1475-1564........... LC 12

Michelet, Jules   1798-1874 ...... NCLC 31

Michener, James A(lbert)
1907- .... CLC 1, 5, 11, 29, 60
See also CANR 21; CA 5-8R; DLB 6

Mickiewicz, Adam   1798-1855 ..... NCLC 3

Middleton, Christopher   1926- ...... CLC 13
See also CANR 29; CA 13-16R; DLB 40

Middleton, Stanley   1919-........ CLC 7, 38
See also CANR 21; CA 25-28R; DLB 14

Migueis, Jose Rodrigues   1901- ..... CLC 10

Mikszath, Kalman   1847-1910 ..... TCLC 31

Miles, Josephine (Louise)
1911-1985 .... CLC 1, 2, 14, 34, 39
See also CANR 2; CA 1-4R;
obituary CA 116; DLB 48

Mill, John Stuart   1806-1873..... NCLC 11
See also DLB 55

Millar, Kenneth   1915-1983 .... CLC 14
See also Macdonald, Ross
See also CANR 16; CA 9-12R;
obituary CA 110; DLB 2; DLB-Y 83;
DLB-DS 6

Millay, Edna St. Vincent
1892-1950 .... TCLC 4
See also CA 103; DLB 45;
CDALB 1917-1929

Miller, Arthur
1915- ...... CLC 1, 2, 6, 10, 15, 26, 47;
DC 1
See also CANR 2, 30; CA 1-4R; CABS 3;
DLB 7; CDALB 1941-1968

Miller, Henry (Valentine)
1891-1980 .... CLC 1, 2, 4, 9, 14, 43
See also CA 9-12R; obituary CA 97-100;
DLB 4, 9; DLB-Y 80; CDALB 1929-1941

Miller, Jason   1939?-............... CLC 2
See also CA 73-76; DLB 7

Miller, Sue   19??-................. CLC 44

Miller, Walter M(ichael), Jr.
1923-......................... CLC 4, 30
See also CA 85-88; DLB 8

Millett, Kate   1934-............... CLC 67
See also CANR 32; CA 73-76

Millhauser, Steven   1943-........ CLC 21, 54
See also CA 108, 110, 111; DLB 2

Millin, Sarah Gertrude   1889-1968 .. CLC 49
See also CA 102; obituary CA 93-96

Milne, A(lan) A(lexander)
1882-1956 .... TCLC 6
See also CLR 1, 26; YABC 1; CA 104, 133;
DLB 10, 77, 100

Milner, Ron(ald)   1938-............ CLC 56
See also BLC 3; CANR 24; CA 73-76;
DLB 38

Milosz Czeslaw
1911- .... CLC 5, 11, 22, 31, 56
See also CANR 23; CA 81-84

Milton, John   1608-1674............. LC 9

Miner, Valerie (Jane)   1947-........ CLC 40
See also CA 97-100

Minot, Susan   1956- .... CLC 44

Minus, Ed   1938-................. CLC 39

Miro (Ferrer), Gabriel (Francisco Victor)
1879-1930 .... TCLC 5
See also CA 104

Mishima, Yukio
1925-1970 .... CLC 2, 4, 6, 9, 27; DC 1;
SSC 4
See also Hiraoka, Kimitake

Mistral, Gabriela   1889-1957 .... TCLC 2
See also CA 104

Mitchell, James Leslie   1901-1935
See Gibbon, Lewis Grassic
See also CA 104; DLB 15

Mitchell, Joni   1943-.............. CLC 12
See also CA 112

Mitchell (Marsh), Margaret (Munnerlyn)
1900-1949 .... TCLC 11
See also CA 109, 125; DLB 9

Mitchell, S. Weir   1829-1914...... TCLC 36

Mitchell, W(illiam) O(rmond)
1914- .... CLC 25
See also CANR 15; CA 77-80; DLB 88

Mitford, Mary Russell   1787-1855.. NCLC 4

Mitford, Nancy   1904-1973........ CLC 44
See also CA 9-12R

Miyamoto Yuriko 1899-1951 ..... TCLC 37

Mo, Timothy 1950- .... CLC 46
See also CA 117

Modarressi, Taghi 1931- .... CLC 44
See also CA 121

Modiano, Patrick (Jean) 1945- ..... CLC 18
See also CANR 17; CA 85-88; DLB 83

Mofolo, Thomas (Mokopu)
1876-1948 .... TCLC 22
See also BLC 3; brief entry CA 121

Mohr, Nicholasa 1935- .... CLC 12
See also CLR 22; CANR 1; CA 49-52;
SAAS 8; SATA 8

Mojtabai, A(nn) G(race)
1938- .... CLC 5, 9, 15, 29
See also CA 85-88

Moliere 1622-1673 .... LC 10

Molnar, Ferenc 1878-1952 .... TCLC 20
See also CA 109

Momaday, N(avarre) Scott
1934- .... CLC 2, 19
See also CANR 14; CA 25-28R; SATA 30,
48

Monroe, Harriet 1860-1936 .... TCLC 12
See also CA 109; DLB 54, 91

Montagu, Elizabeth 1720-1800 .... NCLC 7

Montagu, Lady Mary (Pierrepont) Wortley
1689-1762 .... LC 9

Montague, John (Patrick)
1929- .... CLC 13, 46
See also CANR 9; CA 9-12R; DLB 40

Montaigne, Michel (Eyquem) de
1533-1592 .... LC 8

Montale, Eugenio 1896-1981 ... CLC 7, 9, 18
See also CANR 30; CA 17-20R;
obituary CA 104

Montesquieu, Charles-Louis de Secondat
1689-1755 .... LC 7

Montgomery, Marion (H., Jr.)
1925- .... CLC 7
See also CANR 3; CA 1-4R; DLB 6

Montgomery, Robert Bruce 1921-1978
See Crispin, Edmund
See also CA 104

Montherlant, Henri (Milon) de
1896-1972 .... CLC 8, 19
See also CA 85-88; obituary CA 37-40R;
DLB 72

Monty Python .... CLC 21

Moodie, Susanna (Strickland)
1803-1885 .... NCLC 14

Mooney, Ted 1951- .... CLC 25

Moorcock, Michael (John)
1939- .... CLC 5, 27, 58
See also CAAS 5; CANR 2, 17; CA 45-48;
DLB 14

Moore, Brian
1921- .... CLC 1, 3, 5, 7, 8, 19, 32
See also CANR 1, 25; CA 1-4R

Moore, George (Augustus)
1852-1933 .... TCLC 7
See also CA 104; DLB 10, 18, 57

Moore, Lorrie 1957- .... CLC 39, 45, 68
See also Moore, Marie Lorena

Moore, Marianne (Craig)
1887-1972 ... CLC 1, 2, 4, 8, 10, 13, 19,
47
See also CANR 3; CA 1-4R;
obituary CA 33-36R; SATA 20; DLB 45;
CDALB 1929-1941

Moore, Marie Lorena 1957-
See Moore, Lorrie
See also CA 116

Moore, Thomas 1779-1852 .... NCLC 6

Morand, Paul 1888-1976 .... CLC 41
See also obituary CA 69-72; DLB 65

Morante, Elsa 1918-1985 .... CLC 8, 47
See also CA 85-88; obituary CA 117

Moravia, Alberto
1907- .... CLC 2, 7, 11, 18, 27, 46
See also Pincherle, Alberto

More, Hannah 1745-1833 .... NCLC 27

More, Henry 1614-1687 .... LC 9

More, Sir Thomas 1478-1535 .... LC 10

Moreas, Jean 1856-1910 .... TCLC 18

Morgan, Berry 1919- .... CLC 6
See also CA 49-52; DLB 6

Morgan, Edwin (George) 1920- ..... CLC 31
See also CANR 3; CA 7-8R; DLB 27

Morgan, (George) Frederick
1922- .... CLC 23
See also CANR 21; CA 17-20R

Morgan, Janet 1945- .... CLC 39
See also CA 65-68

Morgan, Lady 1776?-1859 .... NCLC 29

Morgan, Robin 1941- .... CLC 2
See also CA 69-72

Morgan, Seth 1949-1990 .... CLC 65
See also CA 132

Morgenstern, Christian (Otto Josef Wolfgang)
1871-1914 .... TCLC 8
See also CA 105

Moricz, Zsigmond 1879-1942 ..... TCLC 33

Morike, Eduard (Friedrich)
1804-1875 .... NCLC 10

Mori Ogai 1862-1922 .... TCLC 14
See also Mori Rintaro

Mori Rintaro 1862-1922
See Mori Ogai
See also CA 110

Moritz, Karl Philipp 1756-1793 ...... LC 2

Morris, Julian 1916-
See West, Morris L.

Morris, Steveland Judkins 1950-
See Wonder, Stevie
See also CA 111

Morris, William 1834-1896 .... NCLC 4
See also DLB 18, 35, 57

Morris, Wright (Marion)
1910- .... CLC 1, 3, 7, 18, 37
See also CANR 21; CA 9-12R; DLB 2;
DLB-Y 81

Morrison, James Douglas 1943-1971
See Morrison, Jim
See also CA 73-76

Morrison, Jim 1943-1971 .... CLC 17
See also Morrison, James Douglas

Morrison, Toni 1931- ..... CLC 4, 10, 22, 55
See also BLC 3; CANR 27; CA 29-32R;
SATA 57; DLB 6, 33; DLB-Y 81;
CDALB 1968-1987; AAYA 1

Morrison, Van 1945- .... CLC 21
See also CA 116

Mortimer, John (Clifford)
1923- .... CLC 28, 43
See also CANR 21; CA 13-16R; DLB 13

Mortimer, Penelope (Ruth) 1918- .... CLC 5
See also CA 57-60

Mosher, Howard Frank 19??- ...... CLC 62

Mosley, Nicholas 1923- .... CLC 43
See also CA 69-72; DLB 14

Moss, Howard
1922-1987 .... CLC 7, 14, 45, 50
See also CANR 1; CA 1-4R;
obituary CA 123; DLB 5

Motion, Andrew (Peter) 1952- ...... CLC 47
See also DLB 40

Motley, Willard (Francis)
1912-1965 .... CLC 18
See also CA 117; obituary CA 106; DLB 76

Mott, Michael (Charles Alston)
1930- .... CLC 15, 34
See also CAAS 7; CANR 7, 29; CA 5-8R

Mowat, Farley (McGill) 1921- ..... CLC 26
See also CLR 20; CANR 4, 24; CA 1-4R;
SATA 3, 55; DLB 68; AAYA 1

Mphahlele, Es'kia 1919-
See Mphahlele, Ezekiel

Mphahlele, Ezekiel 1919- .... CLC 25
See also BLC 3; CANR 26; CA 81-84

Mqhayi, S(amuel) E(dward) K(rune Loliwe)
1875-1945 .... TCLC 25
See also BLC 3

Mrozek, Slawomir 1930- .... CLC 3, 13
See also CAAS 10; CANR 29; CA 13-16R

Mtwa, Percy 19??- .... CLC 47

Mueller, Lisel 1924- .... CLC 13, 51
See also CA 93-96

Muir, Edwin 1887-1959 .... TCLC 2
See also CA 104; DLB 20

Muir, John 1838-1914 .... TCLC 28

Mujica Lainez, Manuel
1910-1984 .... CLC 31
See also CA 81-84; obituary CA 112

Mukherjee, Bharati 1940- .... CLC 53
See also CA 107; DLB 60

Muldoon, Paul 1951- .... CLC 32
See also CA 113, 129; DLB 40

Mulisch, Harry (Kurt Victor)
1927- .... CLC 42
See also CANR 6, 26; CA 9-12R

Mull, Martin 1943- .... CLC 17
See also CA 105

Munford, Robert 1737?-1783 .... LC 5
See also DLB 31

Munro, Alice (Laidlaw)
1931- .... CLC 6, 10, 19, 50; SSC 3
See also CA 33-36R; SATA 29; DLB 53

Munro, H(ector) H(ugh) 1870-1916
See Saki
See also CA 104; DLB 34

Owl, Sebastian 1939-
See Thompson, Hunter S(tockton)

Oz, Amos 1939- ... **CLC 5, 8, 11, 27, 33, 54**
See also CANR 27; CA 53-56

Ozick, Cynthia 1928-...... **CLC 3, 7, 28, 62**
See also CANR 23; CA 17-20R; DLB 28;
DLB-Y 82

Ozu, Yasujiro 1903-1963 .... **CLC 16**
See also CA 112

Pa Chin 1904-............................ **CLC 18**
See also Li Fei-kan

Pack, Robert 1929-...................... **CLC 13**
See also CANR 3; CA 1-4R; DLB 5

Padgett, Lewis 1915-1958
See Kuttner, Henry

Padilla, Heberto 1932-............... **CLC 38**
See also CA 123

Page, Jimmy 1944-...................... **CLC 12**

Page, Louise 1955-...................... **CLC 40**

Page, P(atricia) K(athleen)
1916-......................... **CLC 7, 18**
See also CANR 4, 22; CA 53-56; DLB 68

Paget, Violet 1856-1935
See Lee, Vernon
See also CA 104

Paglia, Camille 1947-.................. **CLC 68**

Palamas, Kostes 1859-1943 .... **TCLC 5**
See also CA 105

Palazzeschi, Aldo 1885-1974...... **CLC 11**
See also CA 89-92; obituary CA 53-56

Paley, Grace 1922-.... **CLC 4, 6, 37; SSC 8**
See also CANR 13; CA 25-28R; DLB 28

Palin, Michael 1943- .... **CLC 21**
See also Monty Python
See also CA 107

Palliser, Charles 1948?-............. **CLC 65**

Palma, Ricardo 1833-1919........ **TCLC 29**
See also CANR 123

Pancake, Breece Dexter 1952-1979
See Pancake, Breece D'J

Pancake, Breece D'J 1952-1979 .... **CLC 29**
See also obituary CA 109

Papadiamantis, Alexandros
1851-1911 .... **TCLC 29**

Papini, Giovanni 1881-1956....... **TCLC 22**
See also CA 121

Paracelsus 1493-1541.............. **LC 14**

Parini, Jay (Lee) 1948- .... **CLC 54**
See also CA 97-100

Parker, Dorothy (Rothschild)
1893-1967 .... **CLC 15, 68; SSC 2**
See also CAP 2; CA 19-20;
obituary CA 25-28R; DLB 11, 45. 86

Parker, Robert B(rown) 1932-..... **CLC 27**
See also CANR 1, 26; CA 49-52

Parkin, Frank 1940-.................. **CLC 43**

Parkman, Francis 1823-1893..... **NCLC 12**
See also DLB 1, 30

Parks, Gordon (Alexander Buchanan)
1912-........................... **CLC 1, 16**
See also BLC 3; CANR 26; CA 41-44R;
SATA 8; DLB 33

Parnell, Thomas 1679-1718.......... **LC 3**

Parra, Nicanor 1914-.............. **CLC 2**
See also CA 85-88

Pasolini, Pier Paolo
1922-1975 .... **CLC 20, 37**
See also CA 93-96; obituary CA 61-64

Pastan, Linda (Olenik) 1932-...... **CLC 27**
See also CANR 18; CA 61-64; DLB 5

Pasternak, Boris
1890-1960 .... **CLC 7, 10, 18, 63**
See also CA 127; obituary CA 116

Patchen, Kenneth 1911-1972... **CLC 1, 2, 18**
See also CANR 3; CA 1-4R;
obituary CA 33-36R; DLB 16, 48

Pater, Walter (Horatio)
1839-1894 .... **NCLC 7**
See also DLB 57

Paterson, Andrew Barton
1864-1941 .... **TCLC 32**

Paterson, Katherine (Womeldorf)
1932- .... **CLC 12, 30**
See also CLR 7; CANR 28; CA 21-24R;
SATA 13, 53; DLB 52; AAYA 1

Patmore, Coventry Kersey Dighton
1823-1896 .... **NCLC 9**
See also DLB 35

Paton, Alan (Stewart)
1903-1988 .... **CLC 4, 10, 25, 55**
See also CANR 22; CAP 1; CA 15-16;
obituary CA 125; SATA 11

Paulding, James Kirke 1778-1860.. **NCLC 2**
See also DLB 3, 59, 74

Paulin, Tom 1949- .... **CLC 37**
See also CA 123; DLB 40

Paustovsky, Konstantin (Georgievich)
1892-1968 .... **CLC 40**
See also CA 93-96; obituary CA 25-28R

Paustowsky, Konstantin (Georgievich)
1892-1968
See Paustovsky, Konstantin (Georgievich)

Pavese, Cesare 1908-1950 .... **TCLC 3**
See also CA 104

Pavic, Milorad 1929-............. **CLC 60**

Payne, Alan 1932-
See Jakes, John (William)

Paz, Octavio
1914- ...... **CLC 3, 4, 6, 10, 19, 51, 65;**
PC 1
See also CANR 32; CA 73-76

p'Bitek, Okot 1931-1982
See also BLC 3; CA 124; obituary CA 107

Peacock, Molly 1947-............. **CLC 60**
See also CA 103

Peacock, Thomas Love
1785-1886 .... **NCLC 22**

Peake, Mervyn 1911-1968....... **CLC 7, 54**
See also CANR 3; CA 5-8R;
obituary CA 25-28R; SATA 23; DLB 15

Pearce, (Ann) Philippa 1920-...... **CLC 21**
See also Christie, (Ann) Philippa
See also CLR 9; CA 5-8R; SATA 1

Pearl, Eric 1934-
See Elman, Richard

Pearson, T(homas) R(eid) 1956- .... **CLC 39**
See also CA 120, 130

Peck, John 1941-.................. **CLC 3**
See also CANR 3; CA 49-52

Peck, Richard 1934-.............. **CLC 21**
See also CLR 15; CANR 19; CA 85-88;
SAAS 2; SATA 18; AAYA 1

Peck, Robert Newton 1928-........ **CLC 17**
See also CA 81-84; SAAS 1; SATA 21;
AAYA 3

Peckinpah, (David) Sam(uel)
1925-1984 .... **CLC 20**
See also CA 109; obituary CA 114

Pedersen, Knut 1859-1952
See Hamsun, Knut
See also CA 104, 109, 119

Peguy, Charles (Pierre)
1873-1914 .... **TCLC 10**
See also CA 107

Pepys, Samuel 1633-1703.......... **LC 11**

Percy, Walker
1916-1990 ... **CLC 2, 3, 6, 8, 14, 18, 47,**
65
See also CANR 1, 23; CA 1-4R;
obituary CA 131; DLB 2; DLB-Y 80

Perec, Georges 1936-1982 .... **CLC 56**
See also DLB 83

Pereda, Jose Maria de
1833-1906................. **TCLC 16**

Perelman, S(idney) J(oseph)
1904-1979 ... **CLC 3, 5, 9, 15, 23, 44, 49**
See also CANR 18; CA 73-76;
obituary CA 89-92; DLB 11, 44

Peret, Benjamin 1899-1959 .... **TCLC 20**
See also CA 117

Peretz, Isaac Leib 1852?-1915..... **TCLC 16**
See also CA 109

Perez, Galdos Benito 1853-1920... **TCLC 27**
See also CA 125

Perrault, Charles 1628-1703 .... **LC 2**
See also SATA 25

Perse, St.-John 1887-1975.... **CLC 4, 11, 46**
See also Leger, (Marie-Rene) Alexis
Saint-Leger

Pesetsky, Bette 1932-................ **CLC 28**

Peshkov, Alexei Maximovich 1868-1936
See Gorky, Maxim
See also CA 105

Pessoa, Fernando (Antonio Nogueira)
1888-1935 .... **TCLC 27**
See also CA 125

Peterkin, Julia (Mood) 1880-1961... **CLC 31**
See also CA 102; DLB 9

Peters, Joan K. 1945-............. **CLC 39**

Peters, Robert L(ouis) 1924-........ **CLC 7**
See also CAAS 8; CA 13-16R

Petofi, Sandor 1823-1849........ **NCLC 21**

Petrakis, Harry Mark 1923-......... **CLC 3**
See also CANR 4, 30; CA 9-12R

Petrov, Evgeny 1902-1942........ **TCLC 21**

Petry, Ann (Lane) 1908- ...... **CLC 1, 7, 18**
See also CLR 12; CAAS 6; CANR 4;
CA 5-8R; SATA 5; DLB 76

Reid, Christopher 1949-.......... CLC 33
See also DLB 40

Reid Banks, Lynne 1929-
See Banks, Lynne Reid
See also CANR 6, 22; CA 1-4R; SATA 22

Reiner, Max 1900-
See Caldwell, (Janet Miriam) Taylor
(Holland)

Reizenstein, Elmer Leopold 1892-1967
See Rice, Elmer

Remark, Erich Paul 1898-1970
See Remarque, Erich Maria

Remarque, Erich Maria
1898-1970 .... CLC 21
See also CA 77-80; obituary CA 29-32R;
DLB 56

Remizov, Alexey (Mikhailovich)
1877-1957 .... TCLC 27
See also CA 125

Renan, Joseph Ernest
1823-1892 .... NCLC 26

Renard, Jules 1864-1910 .... TCLC 17
See also CA 117

Renault, Mary 1905-1983 .... CLC 3, 11, 17
See also Challans, Mary
See also DLB-Y 83

Rendell, Ruth 1930-.......... CLC 28, 48
See also Vine, Barbara
See also CA 109; DLB 87

Renoir, Jean 1894-1979 .... CLC 20
See also CA 129; obituary CA 85-88

Resnais, Alain 1922-............. CLC 16

Reverdy, Pierre 1899-1960 .... CLC 53
See also CA 97-100; obituary CA 89-92

Rexroth, Kenneth
1905-1982 ...... CLC 1, 2, 6, 11, 22, 49
See also CANR 14; CA 5-8R;
obituary CA 107; DLB 16, 48; DLB-Y 82;
CDALB 1941-1968

Reyes, Alfonso 1889-1959 .... TCLC 33

Reyes y Basoalto, Ricardo Eliecer Neftali
1904-1973
See Neruda, Pablo

Reymont, Wladyslaw Stanislaw
1867-1925 .... TCLC 5
See also CA 104

Reynolds, Jonathan 1942?- ...... CLC 6, 38
See also CANR 28; CA 65-68

Reynolds, Michael (Shane) 1937-... CLC 44
See also CANR 9; CA 65-68

Reynolds, Sir Joshua 1723-1792..... LC 15

Reznikoff, Charles 1894-1976 .... CLC 9
See also CAP 2; CA 33-36;
obituary CA 61-64; DLB 28, 45

Rezzori, Gregor von 1914-........ CLC 25
See also CA 122

Rhys, Jean
1890-1979 ..... CLC 2, 4, 6, 14, 19, 51
See also CA 25-28R; obituary CA 85-88;
DLB 36

Ribeiro, Darcy 1922- .... CLC 34
See also CA 33-36R

Ribeiro, Joao Ubaldo (Osorio Pimentel)
1941- .... CLC 10, 67
See also CA 81-84

Ribman, Ronald (Burt) 1932- .... CLC 7
See also CA 21-24R

Rice, Anne 1941- .... CLC 41
See also CANR 12; CA 65-68

Rice, Elmer 1892-1967.......... CLC 7, 49
See also CAP 2; CA 21-22;
obituary CA 25-28R; DLB 4, 7

Rice, Tim 1944- .... CLC 21
See also CA 103

Rich, Adrienne (Cecile)
1929- .... CLC 3, 6, 7, 11, 18, 36
See also CANR 20; CA 9-12R; DLB 5, 67

Richard, Keith 1943-............. CLC 17
See also CA 107

Richards, David Adam 1950-...... CLC 59
See also CA 93-96; DLB 53

Richards, I(vor) A(rmstrong)
1893-1979 .... CLC 14, 24
See also CA 41-44R; obituary CA 89-92;
DLB 27

Richards, Keith 1943-
See Richard, Keith
See also CA 107

Richardson, Dorothy (Miller)
1873-1957 .... TCLC 3
See also CA 104; DLB 36

Richardson, Ethel 1870-1946
See Richardson, Henry Handel
See also CA 105

Richardson, Henry Handel
1870-1946 .... TCLC 4
See also Richardson, Ethel

Richardson, Samuel 1689-1761....... LC 1
See also DLB 39

Richler, Mordecai
1931- .... CLC 3, 5, 9, 13, 18, 46
See also CLR 17; CA 65-68; SATA 27, 44;
DLB 53

Richter, Conrad (Michael)
1890-1968 .... CLC 30
See also CANR 23; CA 5-8R;
obituary CA 25-28R; SATA 3; DLB 9

Richter, Johann Paul Friedrich 1763-1825
See Jean Paul

Riddell, Mrs. J. H. 1832-1906..... TCLC 40

Riding, Laura 1901-............. CLC 3, 7
See also Jackson, Laura (Riding)

Riefenstahl, Berta Helene Amalia
1902- .... CLC 16
See also Riefenstahl, Leni
See also CA 108

Riefenstahl, Leni 1902- .... CLC 16
See also Riefenstahl, Berta Helene Amalia
See also CA 108

Rilke, Rainer Maria
1875-1926 .... TCLC 1, 6, 19; PC 2
See also CA 104, 132; DLB 81

Rimbaud, (Jean Nicolas) Arthur
1854-1891 .... NCLC 4; PC 3

Ringwood, Gwen(dolyn Margaret) Pharis
1910-1984 .... CLC 48
See also obituary CA 112

Rio, Michel 19??-................ CLC 43

Ritsos, Yannis 1909-......... CLC 6, 13, 31
See also CA 77-80

Ritter, Erika 1948?-.............. CLC 52

Rivera, Jose Eustasio 1889-1928... TCLC 35

Rivers, Conrad Kent 1933-1968..... CLC 1
See also CA 85-88; DLB 41

Rizal, Jose 1861-1896........... NCLC 27

Roa Bastos, Augusto 1917-........ CLC 45

Robbe-Grillet, Alain
1922- ...... CLC 1, 2, 4, 6, 8, 10, 14, 43
See also CA 9-12R; DLB 83

Robbins, Harold 1916-............ CLC 5
See also CANR 26; CA 73-76

Robbins, Thomas Eugene 1936-
See Robbins, Tom
See also CA 81-84

Robbins, Tom 1936-......... CLC 9, 32, 64
See also Robbins, Thomas Eugene
See also CANR 29; CA 81-84; DLB-Y 80

Robbins, Trina 1938-............. CLC 21

Roberts, (Sir) Charles G(eorge) D(ouglas)
1860-1943 .... TCLC 8
See also CA 105; SATA 29; DLB 92

Roberts, Kate 1891-1985 .... CLC 15
See also CA 107; obituary CA 116

Roberts, Keith (John Kingston)
1935- .... CLC 14
See also CA 25-28R

Roberts, Kenneth 1885-1957 ...... TCLC 23
See also CA 109; DLB 9

Roberts, Michele (B.) 1949-........ CLC 48
See also CA 115

Robinson, Edwin Arlington
1869-1935 .... TCLC 5; PC 1
See also CA 104; DLB 54;
CDALB 1865-1917

Robinson, Henry Crabb
1775-1867 .... NCLC 15

Robinson, Jill 1936-.............. CLC 10
See also CA 102

Robinson, Kim Stanley 19??-....... CLC 34
See also CA 126

Robinson, Marilynne 1944- .... CLC 25
See also CA 116

Robinson, Smokey 1940- .... CLC 21

Robinson, William 1940-
See Robinson, Smokey
See also CA 116

Robison, Mary 1949-............. CLC 42
See also CA 113, 116

Roddenberry, Gene 1921-......... CLC 17
See also CANR 110; SATA 45

Rodgers, Mary 1931-............. CLC 12
See also CLR 20; CANR 8; CA 49-52;
SATA 8

Rodgers, W(illiam) R(obert)
1909-1969 .... CLC 7
See also CA 85-88; DLB 20

Rodman, Howard 19??- .... CLC 65

Rodriguez, Claudio 1934-......... CLC 10

Steffens, (Joseph) Lincoln
    1866-1936 . . . . TCLC 20
    See also CA 117; SAAS 1

Stegner, Wallace (Earle) 1909- . . . CLC 9, 49
    See also CANR 1, 21; CA 1-4R; DLB 9

Stein, Gertrude 1874-1946 . . . TCLC 1, 6, 28
    See also CA 104; DLB 4, 54, 86;
    CDALB 1917-1929

Steinbeck, John (Ernst)
    1902-1968 . . . . . CLC 1, 5, 9, 13, 21, 34,
                                            45, 59
    See also CANR 1; CA 1-4R;
    obituary CA 25-28R; SATA 9; DLB 7, 9;
    DLB-DS 2; CDALB 1929-1941

Steinem, Gloria 1934- . . . . CLC 63
    See also CANR 28; CA 53-56

Steiner, George 1929- . . . . CLC 24
    See also CA 73-76; DLB 67

Steiner, Rudolf(us Josephus Laurentius)
    1861-1925 . . . . TCLC 13
    See also CA 107

Stendhal 1783-1842 . . . . NCLC 23

Stephen, Leslie 1832-1904 . . . . TCLC 23
    See also CANR 9; CA 21-24R, 123;
    DLB 57

Stephens, James 1882?-1950 . . . . TCLC 4
    See also CA 104; DLB 19

Stephens, Reed
    See Donaldson, Stephen R.

Steptoe, Lydia 1892-1982
    See Barnes, Djuna

Sterchi, Beat 1949- . . . . CLC 65

Sterling, George 1869-1926 . . . . TCLC 20
    See also CA 117; DLB 54

Stern, Gerald 1925- . . . . CLC 40
    See also CA 81-84

Stern, Richard G(ustave) 1928- . . . CLC 4, 39
    See also CANR 1, 25; CA 1-4R; DLB 87

Sternberg, Jonas 1894-1969
    See Sternberg, Josef von

Sternberg, Josef von 1894-1969 . . . . . CLC 20
    See also CA 81-84

Sterne, Laurence 1713-1768 . . . . LC 2
    See also DLB 39

Sternheim, (William Adolf) Carl
    1878-1942 . . . . TCLC 8
    See also CA 105

Stevens, Mark 19??- . . . . CLC 34

Stevens, Wallace 1879-1955 . . . . . TCLC 3, 12
    See also CA 104, 124; DLB 54

Stevenson, Anne (Katharine)
    1933- . . . . CLC 7, 33
    See also Elvin, Anne Katharine Stevenson
    See also CANR 9; CA 17-18R; DLB 40

Stevenson, Robert Louis
    1850-1894 . . . . NCLC 5, 14
    See also CLR 10, 11; YABC 2; DLB 18, 57

Stewart, J(ohn) I(nnes) M(ackintosh)
    1906- . . . . CLC 7, 14, 32
    See also CAAS 3; CA 85-88

Stewart, Mary (Florence Elinor)
    1916- . . . . CLC 7, 35
    See also CANR 1; CA 1-4R; SATA 12

Stewart, Will 1908-
    See Williamson, Jack
    See also CANR 23; CA 17-18R

Still, James 1906- . . . . CLC 49
    See also CANR 10, 26; CA 65-68;
    SATA 29; DLB 9

Sting 1951-
    See The Police

Stitt, Milan 1941- . . . . CLC 29
    See also CA 69-72

Stoker, Abraham
    See Stoker, Bram
    See also CA 105; SATA 29

Stoker, Bram 1847-1912 . . . . TCLC 8
    See also Stoker, Abraham
    See also SATA 29; DLB 36, 70

Stolz, Mary (Slattery) 1920- . . . . CLC 12
    See also CANR 13; CA 5-8R; SAAS 3;
    SATA 10

Stone, Irving 1903-1989 . . . . CLC 7
    See also CAAS 3; CANR 1; CA 1-4R, 129;
    SATA 3

Stone, Robert (Anthony)
    1937?- . . . . CLC 5, 23, 42
    See also CANR 23; CA 85-88

Stoppard, Tom
    1937- . . . CLC 1, 3, 4, 5, 8, 15, 29, 34, 63
    See also CA 81-84; DLB 13; DLB-Y 85

Storey, David (Malcolm)
    1933- . . . . CLC 2, 4, 5, 8
    See also CA 81-84; DLB 13, 14

Storm, Hyemeyohsts 1935- . . . . CLC 3
    See also CA 81-84

Storm, (Hans) Theodor (Woldsen)
    1817-1888 . . . . NCLC 1

Storni, Alfonsina 1892-1938 . . . . TCLC 5
    See also CA 104

Stout, Rex (Todhunter) 1886-1975 . . . CLC 3
    See also CA 61-64

Stow, (Julian) Randolph 1935- . . CLC 23, 48
    See also CA 13-16R

Stowe, Harriet (Elizabeth) Beecher
    1811-1896 . . . . NCLC 3
    See also YABC 1; DLB 1, 12, 42, 74;
    CDALB 1865-1917

Strachey, (Giles) Lytton
    1880-1932 . . . . TCLC 12
    See also CA 110

Strand, Mark 1934- . . . . CLC 6, 18, 41
    See also CA 21-24R; SATA 41; DLB 5

Straub, Peter (Francis) 1943- . . . . . . CLC 28
    See also CA 85-88; DLB-Y 84

Strauss, Botho 1944- . . . . CLC 22

Straussler, Tomas 1937-
    See Stoppard, Tom

Streatfeild, (Mary) Noel 1897- . . . . . CLC 21
    See also CA 81-84; obituary CA 120;
    SATA 20, 48

Stribling, T(homas) S(igismund)
    1881-1965 . . . . CLC 23
    See also obituary CA 107; DLB 9

Strindberg, (Johan) August
    1849-1912 . . . . TCLC 1, 8, 21
    See also CA 104

Stringer, Arthur 1874-1950 . . . . . . TCLC 37
    See also DLB 92

Strugatskii, Arkadii (Natanovich)
    1925- . . . . CLC 27
    See also CA 106

Strugatskii, Boris (Natanovich)
    1933- . . . . CLC 27
    See also CA 106

Strummer, Joe 1953?-
    See The Clash

Stuart, (Hilton) Jesse
    1906-1984 . . . . CLC 1, 8, 11, 14, 34
    See also CA 5-8R; obituary CA 112;
    SATA 2; obituary SATA 36; DLB 9, 48;
    DLB-Y 84

Sturgeon, Theodore (Hamilton)
    1918-1985 . . . . CLC 22, 39
    See also CA 81-84; obituary CA 116;
    DLB 8; DLB-Y 85

Styron, William
    1925- . . . . CLC 1, 3, 5, 11, 15, 60
    See also CANR 6; CA 5-8R; DLB 2;
    DLB-Y 80; CDALB 1968-1987

Sudermann, Hermann 1857-1928 . . TCLC 15
    See also CA 107

Sue, Eugene 1804-1857 . . . . NCLC 1

Sukenick, Ronald 1932- . . . . . CLC 3, 4, 6, 48
    See also CAAS 8; CA 25-28R; DLB-Y 81

Suknaski, Andrew 1942- . . . . CLC 19
    See also CA 101; DLB 53

Sully Prudhomme 1839-1907 . . . . . TCLC 31

Su Man-shu 1884-1918 . . . . TCLC 24
    See also CA 123

Summers, Andrew James 1942-
    See The Police

Summers, Andy 1942-
    See The Police

Summers, Hollis (Spurgeon, Jr.)
    1916- . . . . CLC 10
    See also CANR 3; CA 5-8R; DLB 6

Summers, (Alphonsus Joseph-Mary Augustus)
    Montague 1880-1948 . . . . TCLC 16
    See also CA 118

Sumner, Gordon Matthew 1951-
    See The Police

Surtees, Robert Smith
    1805-1864 . . . . NCLC 14
    See also DLB 21

Susann, Jacqueline 1921-1974 . . . . CLC 3
    See also CA 65-68; obituary CA 53-56

Suskind, Patrick 1949- . . . . CLC 44

Sutcliff, Rosemary 1920- . . . . CLC 26
    See also CLR 1; CA 5-8R; SATA 6, 44

Sutro, Alfred 1863-1933 . . . . TCLC 6
    See also CA 105; DLB 10

Sutton, Henry 1935-
    See Slavitt, David (R.)

Svevo, Italo 1861-1928 . . . . TCLC 2, 35
    See also Schmitz, Ettore

Swados, Elizabeth 1951- . . . . CLC 12
    See also CA 97-100

Swados, Harvey 1920-1972 . . . . CLC 5
    See also CANR 6; CA 5-8R;
    obituary CA 37-40R; DLB 2

Urdang, Constance (Henriette)
    1922- . . . . **CLC 47**
    See also CANR 9, 24; CA 21-24R

Uris, Leon (Marcus) 1924- . . . . . . **CLC 7, 32**
    See also CANR 1; CA 1-4R; SATA 49

Ustinov, Peter (Alexander) 1921- . . . . **CLC 1**
    See also CANR 25; CA 13-16R; DLB 13

Vaculik, Ludvik 1926- . . . . **CLC 7**
    See also CA 53-56

Valenzuela, Luisa 1938- . . . . **CLC 31**
    See also CA 101

Valera (y Acala-Galiano), Juan
    1824-1905 . . . . **TCLC 10**
    See also CA 106

Valery, Paul (Ambroise Toussaint Jules)
    1871-1945 . . . . **TCLC 4, 15**
    See also CA 104, 122

Valle-Inclan (y Montenegro), Ramon (Maria)
    del 1866-1936 . . . . **TCLC 5**
    See also CA 106

Vallejo, Cesar (Abraham)
    1892-1938 . . . . **TCLC 3**
    See also CA 105

Van Ash, Cay 1918- . . . . **CLC 34**

Vance, Jack 1916?- . . . . **CLC 35**
    See also DLB 8

Vance, John Holbrook 1916?-
    See Vance, Jack
    See also CANR 17; CA 29-32R

Van Den Bogarde, Derek (Jules Gaspard
    Ulric) Niven 1921-
    See Bogarde, Dirk
    See also CA 77-80

Vandenburgh, Jane 19??- . . . . **CLC 59**

Vanderhaeghe, Guy 1951- . . . . **CLC 41**
    See also CA 113

Van der Post, Laurens (Jan) 1906- . . . **CLC 5**
    See also CA 5-8R

Van de Wetering, Janwillem
    1931- . . . . **CLC 47**
    See also CANR 4; CA 49-52

Van Dine, S. S. 1888-1939 . . . . **TCLC 23**

Van Doren, Carl (Clinton)
    1885-1950 . . . . **TCLC 18**
    See also CA 111

Van Doren, Mark 1894-1972 . . . . . **CLC 6, 10**
    See also CANR 3; CA 1-4R;
    obituary CA 37-40R; DLB 45

Van Druten, John (William)
    1901-1957 . . . . **TCLC 2**
    See also CA 104; DLB 10

Van Duyn, Mona 1921- . . . . **CLC 3, 7, 63**
    See also CANR 7; CA 9-12R; DLB 5

Van Itallie, Jean-Claude 1936- . . . . . . **CLC 3**
    See also CAAS 2; CANR 1; CA 45-48;
    DLB 7

Van Ostaijen, Paul 1896-1928 . . . . . **TCLC 33**

Van Peebles, Melvin 1932- . . . . . . **CLC 2, 20**
    See also CA 85-88

Vansittart, Peter 1920- . . . . **CLC 42**
    See also CANR 3; CA 1-4R

Van Vechten, Carl 1880-1964 . . . . . . **CLC 33**
    See also obituary CA 89-92; DLB 4, 9, 51

Van Vogt, A(lfred) E(lton) 1912- . . . . . **CLC 1**
    See also CANR 28; CA 21-24R; SATA 14;
    DLB 8

Varda, Agnes 1928- . . . . **CLC 16**
    See also CA 116, 122

Vargas Llosa, (Jorge) Mario (Pedro)
    1936- . . . . **CLC 3, 6, 9, 10, 15, 31, 42**
    See also CANR 18; CA 73-76

Vassa, Gustavus 1745?-1797
    See Equiano, Olaudah

Vassilikos, Vassilis 1933- . . . . **CLC 4, 8**
    See also CA 81-84

Vaughn, Stephanie 19??- . . . . **CLC 62**

Vazov, Ivan 1850-1921 . . . . **TCLC 25**
    See also CA 121

Veblen, Thorstein Bunde
    1857-1929 . . . . **TCLC 31**
    See also CA 115

Verga, Giovanni 1840-1922 . . . . **TCLC 3**
    See also CA 104, 123

Verhaeren, Emile (Adolphe Gustave)
    1855-1916 . . . . **TCLC 12**
    See also CA 109

Verlaine, Paul (Marie)
    1844-1896 . . . . **NCLC 2; PC 2**

Verne, Jules (Gabriel) 1828-1905 . . . **TCLC 6**
    See also CA 110; SATA 21

Very, Jones 1813-1880 . . . . **NCLC 9**
    See also DLB 1

Vesaas, Tarjei 1897-1970 . . . . **CLC 48**
    See also obituary CA 29-32R

Vian, Boris 1920-1959 . . . . **TCLC 9**
    See also CA 106; DLB 72

Viaud, (Louis Marie) Julien 1850-1923
    See Loti, Pierre
    See also CA 107

Vicker, Angus 1916-
    See Felsen, Henry Gregor

Vidal, Eugene Luther, Jr. 1925-
    See Vidal, Gore

Vidal, Gore
    1925- . . . . **CLC 2, 4, 6, 8, 10, 22, 33**
    See also CANR 13; CA 5-8R; DLB 6

Viereck, Peter (Robert Edwin)
    1916- . . . . **CLC 4**
    See also CANR 1; CA 1-4R; DLB 5

Vigny, Alfred (Victor) de
    1797-1863 . . . . **NCLC 7**

Vilakazi, Benedict Wallet
    1905-1947 . . . . **TCLC 37**

Villiers de l'Isle Adam, Jean Marie Mathias
    Philippe Auguste, Comte de
    1838-1889 . . . . **NCLC 3**

Vinci, Leonardo da 1452-1519 . . . . . . **LC 12**

Vine, Barbara 1930- . . . . **CLC 50**
    See also Rendell, Ruth

Vinge, Joan (Carol) D(ennison)
    1948- . . . . **CLC 30**
    See also CA 93-96; SATA 36

Visconti, Luchino 1906-1976 . . . . **CLC 16**
    See also CA 81-84; obituary CA 65-68

Vittorini, Elio 1908-1966 . . . . . **CLC 6, 9, 14**
    See also obituary CA 25-28R

Vizinczey, Stephen 1933- . . . . **CLC 40**

Vliet, R(ussell) G(ordon)
    1929-1984 . . . . **CLC 22**
    See also CANR 18; CA 37-40R;
    obituary CA 112

Voight, Ellen Bryant 1943- . . . . **CLC 54**
    See also CANR 11; CA 69-72

Voigt, Cynthia 1942- . . . . **CLC 30**
    See also CANR 18; CA 106; SATA 33, 48;
    AAYA 3

Voinovich, Vladimir (Nikolaevich)
    1932- . . . . **CLC 10, 49**
    See also CA 81-84

Voltaire 1694-1778 . . . . **LC 14**

Von Daeniken, Erich 1935-
    See Von Daniken, Erich
    See also CANR 17; CA 37-40R

Von Daniken, Erich 1935- . . . . **CLC 30**
    See also Von Daeniken, Erich

Vonnegut, Kurt, Jr.
    1922- . . . . . . **CLC 1, 2, 3, 4, 5, 8, 12, 22,
                                    40, 60; SSC 8**
    See also CANR 1, 25; CA 1-4R; DLB 2, 8;
    DLB-Y 80; DLB-DS 3;
    CDALB 1968-1988; AAYA 6

Vorster, Gordon 1924- . . . . **CLC 34**

Voznesensky, Andrei 1933- . . . **CLC 1, 15, 57**
    See also CA 89-92

Waddington, Miriam 1917- . . . . **CLC 28**
    See also CANR 12, 30; CA 21-24R;
    DLB 68

Wagman, Fredrica 1937- . . . . **CLC 7**
    See also CA 97-100

Wagner, Richard 1813-1883 . . . . **NCLC 9**

Wagner-Martin, Linda 1936- . . . . **CLC 50**

Wagoner, David (Russell)
    1926- . . . . **CLC 3, 5, 15**
    See also CAAS 3; CANR 2; CA 1-4R;
    SATA 14; DLB 5

Wah, Fred(erick James) 1939- . . . . . . **CLC 44**
    See also CA 107; DLB 60

Wahloo, Per 1926-1975 . . . . **CLC 7**
    See also CA 61-64

Wahloo, Peter 1926-1975
    See Wahloo, Per

Wain, John (Barrington)
    1925- . . . . **CLC 2, 11, 15, 46**
    See also CAAS 4; CANR 23; CA 5-8R;
    DLB 15, 27

Wajda, Andrzej 1926- . . . . **CLC 16**
    See also CA 102

Wakefield, Dan 1932- . . . . **CLC 7**
    See also CAAS 7; CA 21-24R

Wakoski, Diane
    1937- . . . . **CLC 2, 4, 7, 9, 11, 40**
    See also CAAS 1; CANR 9; CA 13-16R;
    DLB 5

Walcott, Derek (Alton)
    1930- . . . . **CLC 2, 4, 9, 14, 25, 42, 67**
    See also BLC 3; CANR 26; CA 89-92;
    DLB-Y 81

Waldman, Anne 1945- . . . . **CLC 7**
    See also CA 37-40R; DLB 16

Wertmuller, Lina 1928- .... CLC 16
    See also CA 97-100

Wescott, Glenway 1901-1987....... CLC 13
    See also CANR 23; CA 13-16R;
    obituary CA 121; DLB 4, 9

Wesker, Arnold 1932- .... CLC 3, 5, 42
    See also CAAS 7; CANR 1; CA 1-4R;
    DLB 13

Wesley, Richard (Errol) 1945-....... CLC 7
    See also CA 57-60; DLB 38

Wessel, Johan Herman 1742-1785 .... LC 7

West, Anthony (Panther)
    1914-1987 .... CLC 50
    See also CANR 3, 19; CA 45-48; DLB 15

West, Jessamyn 1907-1984 ...... CLC 7, 17
    See also CA 9-12R; obituary CA 112;
    obituary SATA 37; DLB 6; DLB-Y 84

West, Morris L(anglo) 1916-..... CLC 6, 33
    See also CA 5-8R; obituary CA 124

West, Nathanael 1903?-1940 .... TCLC 1, 14
    See also Weinstein, Nathan Wallenstein
    See also CA 125, 140; DLB 4, 9, 28

West, Paul 1930- .... CLC 7, 14
    See also CAAS 7; CANR 22; CA 13-16R;
    DLB 14

West, Rebecca 1892-1983 .. CLC 7, 9, 31, 50
    See also CANR 19; CA 5-8R;
    obituary CA 109; DLB 36; DLB-Y 83

Westall, Robert (Atkinson) 1929-... CLC 17
    See also CLR 13; CANR 18; CA 69-72;
    SAAS 2; SATA 23

Westlake, Donald E(dwin)
    1933- .... CLC 7, 33
    See also CANR 16; CA 17-20R

Westmacott, Mary 1890-1976
    See Christie, (Dame) Agatha (Mary
    Clarissa)

Whalen, Philip 1923- .... CLC 6, 29
    See also CANR 5; CA 9-12R; DLB 16

Wharton, Edith (Newbold Jones)
    1862-1937 ...... TCLC 3, 9, 27; SSC 6
    See also CA 104; DLB 4, 9, 12, 78;
    CDALB 1865-1917

Wharton, William 1925-....... CLC 18, 37
    See also CA 93-96; DLB-Y 80

Wheatley (Peters), Phillis
    1753?-1784................. LC 3; PC 3
    See also BLC 3; DLB 31, 50;
    CDALB 1640-1865

Wheelock, John Hall 1886-1978.... CLC 14
    See also CANR 14; CA 13-16R;
    obituary CA 77-80; DLB 45

Whelan, John 1900-
    See O'Faolain, Sean

Whitaker, Rodney 1925-
    See Trevanian

White, E(lwyn) B(rooks)
    1899-1985 .... CLC 10, 34, 39
    See also CLR 1; CANR 16; CA 13-16R;
    obituary CA 116; SATA 2, 29, 44;
    obituary SATA 44; DLB 11, 22

White, Edmund III 1940-......... CLC 27
    See also CANR 3, 19; CA 45-48

White, Patrick (Victor Martindale)
    1912-1990 ..... CLC 3, 4, 5, 7, 9, 18, 65
    See also CA 81-84; obituary CA 132

White, T(erence) H(anbury)
    1906-1964 .... CLC 30
    See also CA 73-76; SATA 12

White, Terence de Vere 1912-...... CLC 49
    See also CANR 3; CA 49-52

White, Walter (Francis)
    1893-1955 .... TCLC 15
    See also BLC 3; CA 115, 124; DLB 51

White, William Hale 1831-1913
    See Rutherford, Mark
    See also CA 121

Whitehead, E(dward) A(nthony)
    1933-...................... CLC 5
    See also CA 65-68

Whitemore, Hugh 1936-.......... CLC 37

Whitman, Sarah Helen
    1803-1878 .... NCLC 19
    See also DLB 1

Whitman, Walt
    1819-1892 .... NCLC 4, 31; PC 3
    See also SATA 20; DLB 3, 64;
    CDALB 1640-1865

Whitney, Phyllis A(yame) 1903-.... CLC 42
    See also CANR 3, 25; CA 1-4R; SATA 1,
    30

Whittemore, (Edward) Reed (Jr.)
    1919-....................... CLC 4
    See also CAAS 8; CANR 4; CA 9-12R;
    DLB 5

Whittier, John Greenleaf
    1807-1892 .... NCLC 8
    See also DLB 1; CDALB 1640-1865

Wicker, Thomas Grey 1926-
    See Wicker, Tom
    See also CANR 21; CA 65-68

Wicker, Tom 1926-................ CLC 7
    See also Wicker, Thomas Grey

Wideman, John Edgar
    1941- .... CLC 5, 34, 36, 67
    See also BLC 3; CANR 14; CA 85-88;
    DLB 33

Wiebe, Rudy (H.) 1934-...... CLC 6, 11, 14
    See also CA 37-40R; DLB 60

Wieland, Christoph Martin
    1733-1813 .... NCLC 17

Wieners, John 1934-.............. CLC 7
    See also CA 13-16R; DLB 16

Wiesel, Elie(zer) 1928-..... CLC 3, 5, 11, 37
    See also CAAS 4; CANR 8; CA 5-8R;
    SATA 56; DLB 83; DLB-Y 87

Wiggins, Marianne 1948-......... CLC 57

Wight, James Alfred 1916-
    See Herriot, James
    See also CA 77-80; SATA 44

Wilbur, Richard (Purdy)
    1921- .... CLC 3, 6, 9, 14, 53
    See also CANR 2; CA 1-4R; CABS 2;
    SATA 9; DLB 5

Wild, Peter 1940-................ CLC 14
    See also CA 37-40R; DLB 5

Wilde, Oscar (Fingal O'Flahertie Wills)
    1854-1900 .... TCLC 1, 8, 23, 41
    See also CA 119; brief entry CA 104;
    SATA 24; DLB 10, 19, 34, 57

Wilder, Billy 1906-............... CLC 20
    See also Wilder, Samuel
    See also DLB 26

Wilder, Samuel 1906-
    See Wilder, Billy
    See also CA 89-92

Wilder, Thornton (Niven)
    1897-1975 ..... CLC 1, 5, 6, 10, 15, 35;
                                        DC 1
    See also CA 13-16R; obituary CA 61-64;
    DLB 4, 7, 9

Wiley, Richard 1944-............. CLC 44
    See also CA 121, 129

Wilhelm, Kate 1928-.............. CLC 7
    See also CAAS 5; CANR 17; CA 37-40R;
    DLB 8

Willard, Nancy 1936-.......... CLC 7, 37
    See also CLR 5; CANR 10; CA 89-92;
    SATA 30, 37; DLB 5, 52

Williams, C(harles) K(enneth)
    1936-.................... CLC 33, 56
    See also CA 37-40R; DLB 5

Williams, Charles (Walter Stansby)
    1886-1945 .... TCLC 1, 11
    See also CA 104

Williams, Ella Gwendolen Rees 1890-1979
    See Rhys, Jean

Williams, (George) Emlyn
    1905-1987 .... CLC 15
    See also CA 104, 123; DLB 10, 77

Williams, Hugo 1942-............. CLC 42
    See also CA 17-20R; DLB 40

Williams, John A(lfred) 1925-.... CLC 5, 13
    See also BLC 3; CAAS 3; CANR 6, 26;
    CA 53-56; DLB 2, 33

Williams, Jonathan (Chamberlain)
    1929-..................... CLC 13
    See also CANR 8; CA 9-12R; DLB 5

Williams, Joy 1944-.............. CLC 31
    See also CANR 22; CA 41-44R

Williams, Norman 1952- .... CLC 39
    See also CA 118

Williams, Paulette 1948-
    See Shange, Ntozake

Williams, Sherley Anne 1944-
    See also BLC 3; CANR 25; CA 73-76;
    DLB 41

Williams, Shirley 1944-
    See Williams, Sherley Anne

Williams, Tennessee
    1911-1983 .... CLC 1, 2, 5, 7, 8, 11, 15,
                              19, 30, 39, 45
    See also CA 5-8R; obituary CA 108; DLB 7;
    DLB-Y 83; DLB-DS 4;
    CDALB 1941-1968

Williams, Thomas (Alonzo) 1926-... CLC 14
    See also CANR 2; CA 1-4R

Williams, Thomas Lanier 1911-1983
    See Williams, Tennessee

Author Index

Literary Criticism Series
Cumulative Topic Index

This index lists all topic entries in the Gale Literary Criticism Series *Contemporary Literary Criticism, Literature Criticism from 1400 to 1800, Nineteenth-Century Literature Criticism,* and *Twentieth-Century Literary Criticism.*

Topic Index

NCLC Cumulative Nationality Index

Nationality Index

Title Index to Volume 34

Title Index

Title Index

ISBN 0-8103-5834-4

9 780810 358348

90000>